Koren Talmud Bavli
THE NOÉ EDITION

NEDARIM

Steinsaltz Center
KOREN

תלמוד בבלי

KOREN TALMUD BAVLI

THE NOÉ EDITION

נדרים

NEDARIM

Daf 32b through Daf 60a

COMMENTARY BY

Rabbi Adin Even-Israel Steinsaltz

EDITOR-IN-CHIEF

Rabbi Dr Tzvi Hersh Weinreb

SENIOR CONTENT EDITOR

Rabbi Dr Shalom Z Berger

EXECUTIVE EDITOR

Rabbi Joshua Schreier

•

STEINSALTZ CENTER

KOREN PUBLISHERS JERUSALEM

Supported by the Matanel Foundation

Koren Talmud Bavli, The Noe Edition
Vol. 16b: Tractate Nedarim, Daf 32b through Daf 60a
Paperback, ISBN, 978-965-7765-78-4

First Hebrew/English paperback edition, 2021

Koren Publishers Jerusalem Ltd.
PO Box 4044, Jerusalem 91040, ISRAEL
PO Box 8531, New Milford, CT 06776, USA
www.korenpub.com

Steinsaltz Center

Steinsaltz Center is the parent organization of institutions established by Rabbi Adin Even-Israel Steinsaltz

PO Box 45187, Jerusalem 91450 ISRAEL
Telephone: +972 2 646 0900, Fax +972 2 624 9454
www.steinsaltz-center.org

הִנֵּה יָמִים בָּאִים, נְאֻם אֲדֹנָי יֱהוִֹה, וְהִשְׁלַחְתִּי רָעָב בָּאָרֶץ,
לֹא־רָעָב לַלֶּחֶם וְלֹא־צָמָא לַמַּיִם, כִּי אִם־לִשְׁמֹעַ אֵת דִּבְרֵי יהוה.

Behold, days are coming – says the Lord God – I will send a hunger to the land, not a hunger for bread nor a thirst for water, but to hear the words of the Lord. (AMOS 8:11)

The Noé edition of the Koren Talmud Bavli
with the commentary of Rabbi Adin Even-Israel Steinsaltz
is dedicated to all those who open its covers
to quench their thirst for Jewish Knowledge,
in our generation of Torah renaissance.

This beautiful edition is for the young, the aged,
the novice and the savant alike,
as it unites the depth of Torah knowledge
with the best of academic scholarship.

Within its exquisite and vibrant pages,
words become worlds.

It will claim its place in the library of classics,
in the bookcases of the Beit Midrash,
the classrooms of our schools,
and in the offices of professionals and business people
who carve out precious time to grapple with its timeless wisdom.

For the Student and the Scholar

DEDICATED BY LEO AND SUE NOÉ

Steinsaltz Center

Executive Director, Steinsaltz Center

Rabbi Meni Even-Israel

Managing Editor

Rabbi Jason Rappoport

Senior Content Editor

Rabbi Dr. Shalom Z. Berger

Editors

Rabbi Dr. Joshua Amaru, *Coordinating Editor*
Rabbi Avishai Magence, *Content Curator*
Menucha Chwat
Rabbi Yehoshua Duker
Betzalel Philip Edwards
Rabbi Yonatan Shai Freedman
Catriel Lev
Elisha Loewenstern
Adina Luber
Yedidya Naveh
Rabbi Eli Ozarowski
Noam Shapiro
Rabbi Michael Siev
Rabbi David Strauss
Rabbi Binyamin Zimmerman

Copy Editors

Aliza Israel, *Coordinator*
Bracha Hermon
Ita Olesker
Debbie Ismailoff
Shira Finson
Ilana Sobel
Deena Nataf
Eliana Kurlantzick Yorav
Erica Hirsch Edvi
Nava Wieder

Language Consultants

Dr. Stephanie E. Binder, *Greek & Latin*
Rabbi Yaakov Hoffman, *Arabic*
Dr. Shai Secunda, *Persian*
Shira Shmidman, *Aramaic*

KOREN

Design & Typesetting

Dena Landowne Bailey, *Typesetting*
Tani Bayer, *Jacket Design*
Raphaël Freeman, *Design & Typography*

Images

Eliahu Misgav, *Illustration & Image Acquisition*
Daniel Gdalevich, *Illustration & Image Acquisition*

Introduction by the Publisher

The Talmud has sustained and inspired Jews for thousands of years. Throughout Jewish history, an elite cadre of scholars has absorbed its learning and passed it on to succeeding generations. The Talmud has been the fundamental text of our people.

Beginning in the 1960s, Rabbi Adin Even-Israel Steinsaltz שליט״א created a revolution in the history of Talmud study. His translation of the Talmud, first into modern Hebrew and then into other languages, as well the practical learning aids he added to the text, have enabled millions of people around the world to access and master the complexity and context of the world of Talmud.

It is thus a privilege to present the *Koren Talmud Bavli*, an English translation of the talmudic text with the brilliant elucidation of Rabbi Steinsaltz. The depth and breadth of his knowledge are unique in our time. His rootedness in the tradition and his reach into the world beyond it are inspirational.

Working with Rabbi Steinsaltz on this remarkable project has been not only an honor, but a great pleasure. Never shy to express an opinion, with wisdom and humor, Rabbi Steinsaltz sparkles in conversation, demonstrating his knowledge (both sacred and worldly), sharing his wide-ranging interests, and, above all, radiating his passion. I am grateful for the unique opportunity to work closely with him, and I wish him many more years of writing and teaching.

Our intentions in publishing this new edition of the Talmud are threefold. First, we seek to fully clarify the talmudic page to the reader – textually, intellectually, and graphically. Second, we seek to utilize today's most sophisticated technologies, both in print and electronic formats, to provide the reader with a comprehensive set of study tools. And third, we seek to help readers advance in their process of Talmud study.

To achieve these goals, the *Koren Talmud Bavli* is unique in a number of ways:

- The classic *tzurat hadaf* of Vilna, used by scholars since the 1800s, has been reset for great clarity, and opens from the Hebrew "front" of the book. Full *nikkud* has been added to both the talmudic text and Rashi's commentary, allowing for a more fluent reading with the correct pronunciation; the commentaries of *Tosafot* have been punctuated. Upon the advice of many English-speaking teachers of Talmud, we have separated these core pages from the translation, thereby enabling the advanced student to approach the text without the distraction of the translation. This also reduces the number of volumes in the set. At the bottom of each *daf*, there is a reference to the corresponding English pages. In addition, the Vilna edition was read against other manuscripts and older print editions, so that texts which had been removed by non-Jewish censors have been restored to their rightful place.
- The English translation, which starts on the English "front" of the book, reproduces the *menukad* Talmud text alongside the English translation (in bold) and commentary and explanation (in a lighter font). The Hebrew and Aramaic text is presented in logical paragraphs. This allows for a fluent reading of the text for the non-Hebrew or non-Aramaic reader. It also allows for the Hebrew reader to refer easily to the text alongside. Where the original text features dialogue or poetry, the English text is laid out in a manner appropriate to the genre. Each page refers to the relevant *daf*.

- Critical contextual tools surround the text and translation: personality notes, providing short biographies of the Sages; language notes, explaining foreign terms borrowed from Greek, Latin, Persian, or Arabic; and background notes, giving information essential to the understanding of the text, including history, geography, botany, archaeology, zoology, astronomy, and aspects of daily life in the talmudic era.
- Halakhic summaries provide references to the authoritative legal decisions made over the centuries by the rabbis. They explain the reasons behind each halakhic decision as well as the ruling's close connection to the Talmud and its various interpreters.
- Photographs, drawings, and other illustrations have been added throughout the text – in full color in the Standard and Electronic editions, and in black and white in the Daf Yomi edition – to visually elucidate the text.

This is not an exhaustive list of features of this edition, it merely presents an overview for the English-speaking reader who may not be familiar with the "total approach" to Talmud pioneered by Rabbi Steinsaltz.

Several professionals have helped bring this vast collaborative project to fruition. My many colleagues are noted on the Acknowledgments page, and the leadership of this project has been exceptional.

RABBI MENACHEM EVEN-ISRAEL, DIRECTOR OF THE STEINSALTZ CENTER, was the driving force behind this enterprise. With enthusiasm and energy, he formed the happy alliance with Koren and established close relationships among all involved in the work.

RABBI DR. TZVI HERSH WEINREB שליט״א, EDITOR-IN-CHIEF, brought to this project his profound knowledge of Torah, intellectual literacy of Talmud, and erudition of Western literature. It is to him that the text owes its very high standard, both in form and content, and the logical manner in which the beauty of the Talmud is presented.

RABBI JOSHUA SCHREIER, EXECUTIVE EDITOR, assembled an outstanding group of scholars, translators, editors, and proofreaders, whose standards and discipline enabled this project to proceed in a timely and highly professional manner.

RABBI MEIR HANEGBI, EDITOR OF THE HEBREW EDITION OF THE STEINSALTZ TALMUD, lent his invaluable assistance throughout the work process, supervising the reproduction of the Vilna pages.

RAPHAËL FREEMAN, EXECUTIVE EDITOR OF KOREN, created this Talmud's unique typographic design which, true to the Koren approach, is both elegant and user friendly.

It has been an enriching experience for all of us at Koren Publishers Jerusalem to work with the Steinsaltz Center to develop and produce the *Koren Talmud Bavli*. We pray that this publication will be a source of great learning and, ultimately, greater *avodat Hashem* for all Jews.

Matthew Miller, Publisher
Koren Publishers Jerusalem
Jerusalem 5772

Contents

For the vocalized Vilna Shas layout, please open as a Hebrew book.

Introduction to **Perek IV**

Many vows are reactions to interpersonal disputes or results of these interactions. The one who vows seeks to chastise the other person or to modify his conduct, and consequently prohibits that person from deriving benefit from him. This vow can assume one of two forms: That benefit from his food is forbidden to the other, and that all benefit from him is forbidden to the other. This chapter addresses those vows and raises several questions, particularly with regard to the latter type of vow.

The first issue is defining the difference between these two vows. Since benefit from one's food is not limited to food alone but includes any monetary gain that could facilitate the purchase of food, when one vows that benefit from his food is forbidden, he prohibits the other from deriving any benefit with monetary value. Therefore, the difference between those two vows must be delineated.

An additional series of issues stems from an analysis of the relationship between the one who vowed and the one subject to the prohibition in the vow. Typically, relations between people with close familial or collegial ties are precisely those that tend to deteriorate into quarrels that lead to vows. Therefore, situations could arise where one of the parties seeks to assist the other in times of need, but is prevented from doing so by the vow. Therefore, the Gemara first explains those actions that are not considered benefit and that the one who vowed may consequently perform for the one for whom benefit is forbidden. In addition, in circumstances where the one for whom benefit is forbidden is in dire straits and the other seeks to help him, the question is whether there are ways to circumvent the prohibition and assist him despite the vow. The Gemara in this chapter will address these and other related questions.

מתני׳ אֵין בֵּין הַמּוּדָּר הֲנָאָה מֵחֲבֵירוֹ לְמוּדָּר הֵימֶנּוּ מַאֲכָל אֶלָּא דְּרִיסַת הָרֶגֶל, וְכֵלִים שֶׁאֵין עוֹשִׂין בָּהֶם אוֹכֶל נֶפֶשׁ.

MISHNA **The difference between one for whom benefit from another is forbidden by vow** [***hamuddar hana'a meḥaveiro***][HN] **and one for whom** benefit **from his food is forbidden by vow** concerns **only setting foot** on the other person's property **and** borrowing from that person **utensils that one does not use** in **preparation of food** but for other purposes. Those two benefits are forbidden to the former but permitted to the latter.

הַמּוּדָּר מַאֲכָל מֵחֲבֵירוֹ – לֹא יַשְׁאִילֶנּוּ נָפָה וּכְבָרָה וְרֵיחַיִם וְתַנּוּר, אֲבָל מַשְׁאִיל לוֹ חָלוּק וְטַבַּעַת וְטַלִּית וּנְזָמִים.

Therefore, with regard to **one for whom** benefit **from another's food is forbidden by vow,** that person **may not lend him** utensils used in the preparation of food, e.g., **a sieve, or a strainer, or a millstone, or an oven. However, he may lend him a garment, or a finger ring, or a cloak, or nose rings,** as these are not used in the preparation of food. However, he may not lend them to one for whom benefit from him is forbidden by vow.

גמ׳ מַאן תַּנָּא? אָמַר רַב אַדָּא בַּר אַהֲבָה: רַבִּי אֱלִיעֶזֶר הִיא. דְּתַנְיָא, רַבִּי אֱלִיעֶזֶר אוֹמֵר: אֲפִילּוּ וִיתּוּר אָסוּר בְּמוּדָּר הֲנָאָה.

GEMARA **Who is the** ***tanna*** who taught this mishna? **Rav Adda bar Ahava said: It is Rabbi Eliezer, as it is taught** in a *baraita* that **Rabbi Eliezer said: Even overlooking** [***vittur***][LN] a matter for which one is typically indifferent to the actions of others, e.g., people setting foot on one's property, **is prohibited in** the case of **one prohibited by vow from deriving benefit** from another.

״הַמּוּדָּר מַאֲכָל מֵחֲבֵירוֹ לֹא יַשְׁאִילֶנּוּ״ וכו׳.

§ We learned in the mishna: With regard to **one for whom** benefit **from another's food is forbidden by vow,** that person **may not lend him** utensils used in the preparation of food.

HALAKHA

The difference between one for whom benefit from another is forbidden by vow – אֵין בֵּין הַמּוּדָּר הֲנָאָה מֵחֲבֵירוֹ: With regard to one for whom benefit from another is forbidden by vow, he may not set foot on his property and he may not borrow utensils, even if they are not used in the preparation of food. This is the ruling even in a place where it is customary to lend those utensils without charge. That is because even items that people generally overlook are forbidden to one for whom benefit is forbidden by vow (Rambam *Sefer Hafla'a, Hilkhot Nedarim* 6:3; *Shulḥan Arukh, Yoreh De'a* 221:1).

LANGUAGE

Overlooking [*vittur*] **– וִיתּוּר:** From the Hebrew root *yod, tav, reish,* whose primary meaning is addition to the original price or measure. People who are not careful about their money routinely overlook that additional cost. The more common meaning refers to relinquishing an item that one owns or to which he is entitled. That is extended to refer to one who overlooks the compromise of some of his rights and does not insist on the letter of the law.

NOTES

One for whom benefit from another is forbidden by vow [*hamuddar hana'a meḥaveiro*] **– הַמּוּדָּר הֲנָאָה מֵחֲבֵירוֹ:** This phrase is vague, as this situation could result from various scenarios. If Reuven says to Shimon: I vow that benefit from me is forbidden to you, Reuven is the one who vowed [*medir*], and Shimon is the one for whom benefit from Reuven is forbidden by vow [*muddar*]. The result is that it is prohibited for Shimon to benefit from Reuven's property. There is a dispute among the early commentaries with regard to which of them is liable for violating the vow if Shimon derives benefit from Reuven's property.

Another scenario is where Reuven says to Shimon that he vows that benefit from Shimon's property is forbidden to him. In that case, Reuven is the one who vowed [*noder*] and also the one for whom benefit is forbidden by vow [*muddar*]. The ambiguity of the term *muddar* is at the basis of discussions later in the Gemara (33b), where it is not clear in every case to which *muddar* the *halakha* applies. This lack of clarity can lead to complex cases, as one can vow that benefit from another's property is forbidden and at the same time render his property forbidden to another. Or, two people can each vow that benefit from them is forbidden to the other, or that benefit from the other is forbidden to each of them.

Even overlooking [*vittur*] **– אֲפִילּוּ וִיתּוּר:** The commentaries explain the term *vittur* in the sense of *yittur*, addition. These are items that a merchant would add without charge beyond the precise size or weight that was purchased. Although that is standard practice in sales, it is prohibited to do so for one for whom benefit from the seller is forbidden. The Rid writes that it is the opinion of the Sages that any matter that one typically overlooks for others and for which the other person would not be beholden to him is permitted. Rabbi Eliezer holds that it is forbidden.

BACKGROUND

Chew wheat kernels – יִלְעוֹס חִיטִּין: The chewed wheat creates a sort of bandage whose outer surface hardens and prevents infection of the wound. Apparently, some of the natural ingredients in wheat, when combined with saliva, facilitate healing and prevent infection, e.g., vitamin E.

Basket – צַנָּא: This is referring to a plain, wide basket typically woven from palm branches. However, there may have been utensils of this type fashioned from sturdier material. Some were even sealed so that they may be used to hold liquids, e.g., honey.

NOTES

A horse upon which to ride – סוּס לִרְכּוֹב עָלָיו: Most commentaries explain that the horse in question transports the rider to a feast. However, Rabbeinu Tam, in *Sefer HaYashar*, says that the Gemara is referring to a case where the horse is used to transport produce. One wants use of it either to arrive at his destination faster or because he wants to appear important, so that he will be given priority over others. The Rid holds that in all these cases the benefit need not be directly tied to food, as even if it results in some ancillary profit, it indirectly leads to food and is forbidden.

וְהָא מִן מַאֲכָל נָדַר! אָמַר רַבִּי שִׁמְעוֹן בֶּן לָקִישׁ: בְּאוֹמֵר ״הֲנָאַת מַאֲכָלְךָ עָלַי״.

The Gemara asks: **But didn't he vow** that he is prohibited **from** partaking of **food,** and those items are not food items? **Rabbi Shimon ben Lakish said:** The mishna is referring to a case **where he says: Benefit from your food is forbidden to me,** which includes any benefit associated with food.

אֵימָא שֶׁלֹּא יִלְעוֹס חִיטִּין וְיִתֵּן עַל מַכָּתוֹ! אָמַר רָבָא: בְּאוֹמֵר ״הֲנָאָה הַמְּבִיאָה לִידֵי מַאֲכָלְךָ עָלַי״.

The Gemara asks: **Say that** the result of a vow formulated in that manner is that **he may not chew wheat** kernels[BH] belonging to the one from whose food benefit is forbidden **and place** them **on his wound,** as that is a benefit that results from food. However, that vow does not render items used in the preparation of food forbidden. **Rava said** that the mishna is referring to a case **where he says: Benefit that leads to** preparation of **your food is forbidden to me.**

אָמַר רַב פַּפָּא: שַׂק לְהָבִיא פֵּירוֹת, וַחֲמוֹר לְהָבִיא עָלָיו פֵּירוֹת, וַאֲפִילּוּ צַנָּא בְּעָלְמָא – הֲנָאָה הַמְּבִיאָה לִידֵי מַאֲכָל הוּא. בָּעֵי רַב פַּפָּא: סוּס לִרְכּוֹב עָלָיו, וְטַבַּעַת לֵירָאוֹת בָּהּ, מַהוּ? מִיפְסַק וּמֵיזַל בְּאַרְעֵיהּ מַאי?

Rav Pappa said: Borrowing from him **a sack** in which **to bring produce,**[H] **or a donkey upon which to bring produce, or even merely a basket,**[B] each renders **benefit that leads to food,** and this benefit is forbidden. **Rav Pappa raised a dilemma:** If he seeks to borrow **a horse upon which to ride**[NH] **or a ring with which to be seen** when attending a feast, to create the impression that he is wealthy, **what is** the ruling? Is it prohibited to borrow these items, since having them in one's possession may indirectly result in his being served before others or being served higher-quality food; and therefore, borrowing those items provides benefit that leads to food? With regard to **traversing and walking on his land** that facilitates one's quick return home, enabling him to eat sooner, **what** is the *halakha*?

תָּא שְׁמַע: אֲבָל מַשְׁאִיל לוֹ חָלוּק וְטַלִּית נְזָמִים וְטַבָּעוֹת. הֵיכִי דָּמֵי? אִילֵימָא שֶׁלֹּא לֵירָאוֹת בָּהֶן – צְרִיכָא לְמֵימַר? אֶלָּא לָאו אֲפִילּוּ לֵירָאוֹת בָּהֶן, וְקָתָנֵי ״מַשְׁאִילוֹ״!

The Gemara proposes: **Come** and **hear** a proof from the mishna: **However, he may lend him a garment, and a cloak, and nose rings, and finger rings.** The Gemara asks: **What are the circumstances** of that situation? **If we say** it is a case **where** it is **not** the borrower's intent **to be seen with them,** and therefore there is no benefit that leads to food, does this **need to be said?** The vow rendered only food forbidden. **Rather, isn't** this *halakha* stated **even** in a case where he borrowed those items **to be seen with them, and it is taught** in the mishna that **he may lend** it to **him?**

לָא, לְעוֹלָם שֶׁלֹּא לֵירָאוֹת, וְאַיְּידֵי דְּקָתָנֵי רֵישָׁא ״לֹא יַשְׁאִילֶנּוּ״ – תְּנָא סֵיפָא ״מַשְׁאִילוֹ״.

The Gemara refutes this. **No, actually** the mishna is referring to a case where he borrowed those items with the intention **not to be seen** with them. In response to the question: Is it necessary to say so, the Gemara answers that it is not necessary to teach this *halakha*. However, **since it is taught in the first clause: He may not lend him,** when listing the matters that may not be loaned, the *tanna* **taught the latter clause** of the mishna with a parallel formulation: **He may lend him.** Rav Pappa's dilemma remains unresolved.

HALAKHA

That he may not chew wheat kernels – שֶׁלֹּא יִלְעוֹס חִיטִּין: If one says to another: Benefit from your food is forbidden to me, it is prohibited for him to eat food belonging to that person or to chew his wheat to place upon a wound. It is permitted for him to borrow utensils from that person, even utensils used for food (*Shulḥan Arukh, Yoreh De'a* 221:1).

A sack in which to bring produce – שַׂק לְהָבִיא פֵּירוֹת: If one says to another: Benefit that leads to preparation of your food is forbidden to me, it is prohibited for him to take not only food items from him, but it is also prohibited for him to take utensils used in the preparation of food. The Rema wrote in the name of Rabbeinu Yeruḥam that even an ax used to cut wood is forbidden, but not an ax used for other labor. Similarly, it is prohibited for him to borrow a sack in which to bring produce or a donkey upon which to bring produce. However, it is permitted for him to chew wheat kernels belonging to the other person and place them on a wound, in accordance with the opinions of Rava and Rav Pappa (Rambam *Sefer Hafla'a, Hilkhot Nedarim* 6:1; *Shulḥan Arukh, Yoreh De'a* 221:1).

A horse upon which to ride – סוּס לִרְכּוֹב עָלָיו: If one vows: Benefit that leads to preparation of your food is forbidden to me, he is prohibited from borrowing a horse upon which to ride or a ring with which to be seen, and he is prohibited from walking on the other's land if doing so benefits him. As Rav Pappa's dilemma was not resolved, the ruling is stringent due to that uncertainty. However, if one violates the vow he does not receive lashes (Rambam *Sefer Hafla'a, Hilkhot Nedarim* 6:2; *Shulḥan Arukh, Yoreh De'a* 221:1).

מתני׳ וְכָל דָּבָר שֶׁאֵין עוֹשִׂין בּוֹ אוֹכֶל נֶפֶשׁ, מָקוֹם שֶׁמַּשְׂכִּירִין כַּיּוֹצֵא בָּהֶן – אָסוּר.

MISHNA And with regard to **any item that one does not use in the preparation of food,** in a place **where one rents** items **of that kind,**[HN] that item is **forbidden.** Meaning, one for whom benefit from another is forbidden by vow is prohibited from borrowing this type of item from the one who vowed and imposed the prohibition. This is because one can use the money saved by borrowing the item rather than renting it to purchase food.

גמ׳ מִכְּלָל דְּרֵישָׁא אַף עַל פִּי שֶׁאֵין מַשְׂכִּירִין. מַאן תַּנָּא? אָמַר רַב אַדָּא בַּר אַהֲבָה: רַבִּי אֱלִיעֶזֶר הִיא.

GEMARA The Gemara states: **By inference,** one may conclude **that the first clause** of the mishna, which states that the one for whom benefit from another is forbidden by vow is prohibited from deriving benefit from utensils used in the preparation of food, e.g., a sieve or a strainer, applies **even if** they are a place **where one does not rent** items of that kind but typically lends them at no cost. The Gemara asks: **Who is the** ***tanna*** who **taught**[N] this mishna? **Rav Adda bar Ahava said: It is Rabbi Eliezer,** who maintains that overlooking is prohibited in the case of one for whom benefit from another is forbidden by vow.

מתני׳ הַמּוּדָּר הֲנָאָה מֵחֲבֵירוֹ – שׁוֹקֵל לוֹ אֶת שִׁקְלוֹ, וּפוֹרֵעַ אֶת חוֹבוֹ, וּמַחֲזִיר לוֹ אֶת אֲבֵידָתוֹ. מָקוֹם שֶׁנּוֹטְלִין עָלֶיהָ שָׂכָר – תִּפּוֹל הֲנָאָה לַהֶקְדֵּשׁ.

MISHNA With regard to **one prohibited by vow from deriving benefit from another,** if that other person chooses, **he may contribute the half-shekel** to the Temple **on his** behalf,[HB] **and repay his debt, and return his lost item to him,**[N] and the one prohibited from benefiting is not considered to have benefited from him. In **a place where one takes payment**[N] for returning a lost item, that **benefit should fall into** the category of **consecrated** Temple property.[N]

גמ׳ אַלְמָא אַבְרוּחֵי אֲרִי בְּעָלְמָא הוּא, וְשָׁרֵי.

GEMARA The mishna allowed one who vowed and imposed the prohibition to pay the financial obligations of the one who is prohibited by vow to derive benefit from him. Based on this, the Gemara concludes: **Apparently,** repaying his debts is tantamount to **merely driving away a lion**[N] from him, **and it is permitted.** He is not actually giving him anything. Rather, he is preventing potential future harm. That is not considered a benefit.

מַאן תַּנָּא? אָמַר רַב הוֹשַׁעְיָא: זוֹ

The Gemara asks: **Who is the** ***tanna*** who **taught** that in performing the actions listed in the mishna one is merely preventing harm? **Rav Hoshaya said: This**

HALAKHA

A place where one rents items of that kind – מָקוֹם שֶׁמַּשְׂכִּירִין כַּיּוֹצֵא בָּהֶן: In a place where one rents utensils for payment, if one vows: Benefit that leads to preparation of your food is forbidden to me, it is prohibited for him to borrow utensils from the other person, even if they are not used in the preparation of food (Rambam *Sefer Hafla'a, Hilkhot Nedarim* 6:2; *Shulḥan Arukh, Yoreh De'a* 221:1).

He may contribute the half-shekel to the Temple on his behalf – שׁוֹקֵל לוֹ אֶת שִׁקְלוֹ: One who vowed that benefit from him is forbidden to another may contribute a half-shekel to the Temple on the other person's behalf. He may also pay his debts. Many later halakhic authorities hold that he may repay only an undocumented loan but not a loan for which a promissory note was drafted and signed, or for which collateral was taken (*Baḥ*; *Shakh*, citing Rabbeinu Ḥananel; Rabbeinu Tam; Rosh). Some say that even according to this opinion, it is permitted for him to repay debt that the debtor could avoid paying, even if it is accompanied by a promissory note (Rambam *Sefer Hafla'a, Hilkhot Nedarim* 6:4; *Shulḥan Arukh, Yoreh De'a* 221:2, *Ḥoshen Mishpat* 128:1).

BACKGROUND

He may contribute the half-shekel to the Temple on his behalf – שׁוֹקֵל לוֹ אֶת שִׁקְלוֹ: All male Jews over the age of twenty were required to contribute a half-shekel to the Temple annually, before the first day of the month of Nisan, which was the beginning of the new Temple year in terms of the sacrifice of public offerings from the new half-shekels. This money was used to cover the expenses of the Temple, including purchasing communal sacrifices and paying for repairs to the structure of the Temple. It was also used to maintain and repair the walls of Jerusalem. From the beginning of the month of Adar, notice was served to the public that the half-shekel contributions would soon be due.

Today, during the afternoon prayer at the conclusion of the Fast of Esther on the thirteenth of Adar, before the beginning of Purim, it is customary to make a charitable donation in commemoration of the half-shekel contribution. The *halakhot* of the half-shekel contributions made to the Temple are discussed in tractate *Shekalim*.

NOTES

A place where one rents items of that kind – מָקוֹם שֶׁמַּשְׂכִּירִין כַּיּוֹצֵא בָּהֶן: Early commentaries discuss the following question: In a place where items of a certain kind are rented, is it permitted for the one for whom benefit is forbidden to pay the full rental fee to the one from whom it is forbidden? In that case, there is no obvious benefit derived. The Meiri cites two possibilities. Some rule that it is permitted if he pays the standard rental fee. Others rule that a rental agreement benefits both parties; therefore, it is prohibited even if he pays rent (see Rid on 35b).

Who is the *tanna* who taught – מַאן תַּנָּא: Although it was proven that the mishna is in accordance with the opinion of Rabbi Eliezer, *Tosafot* explain that the mishna can be interpreted in accordance with the opinion of the Rabbis as well, if it is explained as referring to setting foot in his courtyard or in a place where he does not overlook trespass. Therefore, that proof is not conclusive. In contrast, proof cited from a precise analysis of the mishna is conclusive (*Tosafot*).

And return his lost item to him – וּמַחֲזִיר לוֹ אֶת אֲבֵידָתוֹ: Later in the Gemara (33b) it is explained that one who returns a lost item to another person gives him nothing of his own. He merely returns an item that originally belonged to the other. The mishna specifically writes that he returns the lost item to him, meaning that if by happenstance he finds the lost item, he returns it. However, he may not expressly search for the item in order to return it to him (*Shita*).

In a place where one takes payment – מָקוֹם שֶׁנּוֹטְלִין עָלֶיהָ שָׂכָר: Ostensibly, returning a lost item is a mitzva; what payment is there? Some commentaries explain that if, in the course of returning the lost item, one is idle from labor and therefore loses payment that he could have otherwise received, he is entitled to compensation for that time. This is the payment that is referred to here. However, the Rambam, in his Commentary on the Mishna, writes that this payment is not a legal obligation. Rather, there is a local custom that the owner of the lost item gives the one who returns it a reward of his own volition. In a place where that is the custom, failure to accept the compensation would provide forbidden benefit to the owner of the lost item.

Benefit should fall into the category of consecrated Temple property – תִּפּוֹל הֲנָאָה לַהֶקְדֵּשׁ: Some commentaries explain that the reference here is not specifically to consecration. Rather, the mishna means that he may not use the item, and the same would be true if he destroys it in another manner. However, the consensus among the commentaries is that since vows, particularly those articulated with the term *konam*, contain an element of sanctity, as one rendered benefit to him forbidden as though it were consecrated, he should donate the money to the Temple treasury (Rosh; Re'em). The Gemara establishes that this is the ruling even in a case where the property of the owner of the lost item is forbidden to the one returning the lost item. Therefore, the reward is benefit that cannot be used. According to the opinion that the payment here is compensation for lost wages, not all the benefit is consecrated. Only that payment that he received beyond his lost wages is forbidden benefit that is consecrated. The Meiri explains that it does not mean that it is prohibited for the one who returns the item to receive compensation. Rather, if he chooses not to accept payment for any reason, whether it is compensation for lost wages or a reward for returning the item, the owner cannot keep the money because he would thereby benefit from him. Therefore, the owner must consecrate the money.

Is tantamount to merely driving away a lion – אַבְרוּחֵי אֲרִי בְּעָלְמָא הוּא: The question arises: The one for whom benefit is forbidden is benefiting from the fact that he need not repay his debt; how can the Gemara say that he does not benefit? Rabbeinu Tam, in *Sefer HaYashar*, holds that the reference in the Gemara is not to all debts. Rather, the reference is to a specific debt, similar to the debt one has to his wife to provide for her sustenance, which is mentioned in the Gemara (33b). Since with regard to one who provides sustenance for his wife in his absence, it is not clear whether the husband is obligated to reimburse him, that person does not actually benefit the husband. He does nothing more than drive away a lion, i.e., distance a potential threat. Most commentaries disagree and hold that the reference is to all debts, and they base their opinions on the conclusion of the Jerusalem Talmud: The main reason that he may pay the debt is that there is no direct benefit from the one who vowed to the one for whom benefit is forbidden. The benefit is indirect and therefore it is not at all forbidden (see Ritva).

דִּבְרֵי חָנָן הִיא.

is the statement of Ḥanan[N] in a dispute pertaining to one who pays the debt of another. Ḥanan holds that he cannot demand to be reimbursed for that payment, since he merely prevented potential damage.

רָבָא אָמַר: אֲפִילּוּ תֵּימָא דִּבְרֵי הַכֹּל, גַּבֵּי מוּדַּר הֲנָאָה דְּיָהֵיב עַל מְנָת שֶׁלֹּא לִפְרוֹעַ.

Rava said: Even if you say that **everyone agrees** that this is the *halakha*, it was stated **with regard to one prohibited by vow from deriving benefit from another** who borrowed money, and the creditor stipulated **that** it was **on the condition that** if he so chooses **he** does **not** need **to repay**[N] the loan. In that case, by repaying the loan, one who vowed and imposed the prohibition did not actually repay his debt.

מַאי חָנָן? דִּתְנַן: מִי שֶׁהָלַךְ לִמְדִינַת הַיָּם וְעָמַד אֶחָד וּפִירְנֵס אֶת אִשְׁתּוֹ, חָנָן אָמַר: אִיבֵּד אֶת מְעוֹתָיו.

The Gemara asks: **What** is the opinion of **Ḥanan** to which the Gemara referred? The Gemara answers that it is **as we learned** in a mishna: In the case of a husband **who went to a country overseas, and one** other man **arose and supported his wife** on his own initiative and then demanded to be reimbursed for that support when the husband returned, **Ḥanan said:** The one who took the initiative to support the wife **lost his money,** since the husband neither asked him to do so nor committed to compensate him.

נֶחְלְקוּ עָלָיו בְּנֵי כֹהֲנִים גְּדוֹלִים, וְאָמְרוּ: יִשָּׁבַע כַּמָּה הוֹצִיא וְיִטּוֹל. אָמַר רַבִּי דּוֹסָא בֶּן הָרְכִּינָס כְּדִבְרֵיהֶם. אָמַר רַבִּי יוֹחָנָן בֶּן זַכַּאי: יָפֶה אָמַר חָנָן, הִנִּיחַ מְעוֹתָיו עַל קֶרֶן הַצְּבִי.

The sons of High Priests[B] **disagreed with him and said:** The one who took the initiative to support his wife **will take an oath** as to **how much he spent and take** repayment from the husband. **Rabbi Dosa ben Harkinas said in accordance with the statement** of the sons of High Priests. **Rabbi Yoḥanan ben Zakkai said: Ḥanan spoke well,**[H] as in any case of this type **he placed his money on the antler of a deer,**[B] i.e., a risky venture with no guaranteed return.

רָבָא לָא אָמַר כְּרַב הוֹשַׁעְיָא – דְּקָא מוֹקֵים לַהּ לְמַתְנִיתִין כְּדִבְרֵי הַכֹּל, רַב הוֹשַׁעְיָא לָא אָמַר כְּרָבָא – גְּזֵירָה שֶׁלֹּא לִיפָּרַע מִשּׁוּם לִיפָּרַע.

The Gemara explains the dispute between Rava and Rav Hoshaya with regard to attribution of the mishna: **Rava did not say** that the mishna is in accordance with the opinion of Ḥanan, **as did Rav Hoshaya,** and he preferred a different explanation, **as he establishes the mishna in accordance with the statements** upon which **everyone** agrees, rather than attributing it to an individual *tanna*. **Rav Hoshaya did not say** that the mishna is in accordance with the opinion of all the *tanna'im* **as did Rava,** as there is basis to issue a rabbinic **decree** prohibiting repayment of a loan for one for whom benefit from another is forbidden by vow **on the condition that he** does **not** need **to repay** the loan, **due to** a standard loan that he is required **to repay.** Therefore, he prefers to establish the mishna in accordance with the opinion of Ḥanan.

BACKGROUND

The sons of High Priests – בְּנֵי כֹהֲנִים גְּדוֹלִים: At the end of the Second Temple period, the position of High Priest was no longer inherited. Rather, various members of priestly families were appointed, often by means of bribing the authorities. In any case, apparently during the reign of the royal house of Herod, High Priests were chosen from a limited number of families who divided the tasks in the Temple among themselves (see *Pesaḥim* 57a). Therefore, there was a group of sons of High Priests, who also engaged in matters of *halakha*, perhaps, in the framework of a priestly court (see *Ketubot* 12a).

The antler of a deer – קֶרֶן הַצְּבִי: Although the meaning of this term is clear: One who places his money purse on the antler of a deer will lose it when the deer flees, this term may be related to an experiment in which deer antlers were plated with silver and the deer were sent to a faraway place. Seven years later, the deer returned home. According to this, whenever anyone places an item in a situation where there is only faint hope of recovery, it is characterized as placing it on the antler of a deer.

HALAKHA

Ḥanan spoke well – יָפֶה אָמַר חָנָן: If a husband traveled overseas and another supported his wife, the other person lost his money, as the husband is not obligated to compensate him for his outlay, in accordance with the opinion of Ḥanan. However, if the wife borrowed money to support herself, her husband must reimburse the creditor for his expenditure (Rambam *Sefer Nashim*, *Hilkhot Ishut* 12:19; *Shulḥan Arukh*, *Oraḥ Ḥayyim* 70:8 and *Ḥoshen Mishpat* 128:1).

NOTES

This is the statement of Ḥanan – דִּבְרֵי חָנָן הִיא: From Ḥanan's statement, it is apparent that if one repays a debt on behalf of another, that other person owes him nothing and he cannot demand compensation, as he is merely driving a lion from his property.

Tosafot ask: Didn't we learn that if one's property was attacked by a lion, and another spent money to drive the lion away, he can collect compensation for his expenses? Apparently, one driving a lion away from another does render benefit to him. They explain that there is a distinction between a case where the danger is virtually inevitable and the one who drove away the lion is entitled to payment, and a case where the danger is not inevitable and one is not entitled to payment.

In the Jerusalem Talmud, this issue is addressed at length, and there it is stated that even in a case where the creditor is pressuring the debtor to repay the debt, he can claim that he could have evaded payment by placating him. Even if the creditor has collateral, the debtor can claim that he could persuade the creditor to return the collateral. It is only in a case involving certain governmental taxes, payment of which is absolutely unavoidable, that one who pays his debt may collect compensation.

On the condition that he does not need to repay – עַל מְנָת שֶׁלֹּא לִפְרוֹעַ: Although one may eventually repay the debt to avoid unpleasantness with the lender, since he could avoid payment, it is not considered a debt (Ran). Others explain that the reference is not to a case where the creditor stipulated at the outset that the debtor need not repay the loan, as in that case it is a gift rather than a loan. Rather, it is a case where the debtor thought from the outset that he would not repay the loan but would somehow placate the creditor (*Sheyarei Korban* on *Ketubot*, Jerusalem Talmud; see Rashba). According to this, an explanation must be found for the fact that one contributes the half-shekel for the other. Rashi explains that the reference is to a case where one does not benefit the other at all by contributing the half-shekel, e.g., where he already paid his half-shekel but it was lost on the way to Jerusalem. Although in that case it was customary to contribute a replacement half-shekel, there is no pressure to repay the debt, as the one who contributed the half-shekel on his behalf has no legal recourse to collect compensation.

"מחזיר לו את אבידתו". פליגי בה רבי אמי ורבי אסי, חד אמר: לא שנו אלא בשנכסי מחזיר אסורין על בעל אבידה, דכי מהדר ליה – מידעם דנפשיה קא מהדר ליה. אבל נכסי בעל אבידה אסורין על מחזיר – לא קא מהדר ליה, דקא מהני ליה פרוטה דרב יוסף.

§ We learned in the mishna: **He returns his lost item to him.**[H] **Rabbi Ami and Rabbi Asi disagree about this. One said: They taught** this **only** in a case **where the property of the one returning** the lost item **is forbidden to the owner of the lost item, as when he returns it to him he is returning** to him **something of his own** and is not giving him anything new. Consequently, returning a lost item in no way violates the vow. **However,** in a case **where the property of the owner of the lost item is forbidden to the one returning** the lost item, **he may not return it to him,** as in that case the owner indirectly **benefits** the one returning the lost item by enabling **him** to acquire the ***peruta* of Rav Yosef.**[N] Rav Yosef said that the legal status of one tending to the return of a lost item is like that of a paid bailee. Since one who is engaged in a mitzva is exempt from performing another mitzva, while he is tending to the lost item he is exempt from giving charity to a pauper. Since the one returning the lost item profits from engaging in the return of the lost item, it is prohibited for him to do so, as he is prohibited by vow from deriving benefit from the owner of the lost item.

וחד אמר: אפילו נכסי בעל אבידה אסורין על מחזיר – מהדר ליה, ומשום פרוטה דרב יוסף – לא שכיח.

And one said: Even in a case **where the property of the owner of the lost item is forbidden to the one returning** the lost item, **he returns** it to him. **And** with regard to the concern **due to the *peruta* of Rav Yosef,** it is not a concern because it is **uncommon** for a pauper to happen upon a person just when he is tending to the lost item. Therefore, it cannot be said that there is profit in the return of a lost item.

HALAKHA

He returns his lost item to him – מחזיר לו את אבידתו: One who vows that benefit from another is forbidden to him may return that person's lost item because doing so is a mitzva (Rambam *Sefer Hafla'a, Hilkhot Nedarim* 7:1; *Shulḥan Arukh, Yoreh De'a* 221:3).

NOTES

The owner indirectly benefits him by enabling him to acquire the *peruta* of Rav Yosef – דקא מהני ליה פרוטה דרב יוסף: *Tosafot* ask: As there is no direct benefit, why wouldn't the owner of the lost item be considered merely as one who drives a lion, i.e., the poor person, away from the one returning the item? They explain that the leniency applied to cases where one is driving away a lion pertains only to cases where there is no direct benefit to the one for whom benefit is forbidden. However, in this case it is as though he received compensation directly from the property of the owner of the lost item.

Perek **IV**
Daf **34** Amud **a**

תנן: מקום שנוטלין עליה שכר – תפול הנאה להקדש. בשלמא למאן דאמר אפילו בשנכסי בעל אבידה אסורים על מחזיר נמי מהדר – היינו דקתני: מקום שנוטלין עליה שכר תפול הנאה להקדש.

We learned in the mishna: In **a place where one takes payment** for returning a lost item, the **benefit** that he receives for returning the item **should fall into** the category of **consecrated** Temple property. The Gemara asks: **Granted, according to the one who says that even** in a case **where the property of the owner of the lost item is forbidden to the one returning** the lost item, **he returns** it to him. **This** explanation **is** consistent with **that which** the mishna **teaches:** In **a place where one takes payment** for returning a lost item, the **benefit** that he receives for returning the item **should fall into** the category of **consecrated** Temple property.

אלא למאן דאמר כשנכסי בעל אבידה אסורים על מחזיר לא מהדר, אמאי תפול הנאה להקדש?

However, according to the one who says that in a case **where the property of the owner of the lost item is forbidden to the one returning** the lost item, **he may not return** it to him, and the mishna is referring exclusively to a case where the property of the one returning the lost object is forbidden to the owner of the lost object, **why should the benefit fall into** the category of **consecrated** Temple property?[N] It is not prohibited for him to benefit from the property of the owner.

NOTES

Why should the benefit fall into the category of consecrated Temple property – אמאי תפול הנאה להקדש: Rashi's version of the Gemara is as it appears here, and the question is posed to the one who says that if the property of the owner of the lost item is forbidden to another, that other person does not return the item to him. However, according to that opinion, the *halakha* that one may not return an item when the property of the owner is forbidden to him is part of the mishna, in the sense of: The mishna is incomplete. The Gemara then asks: In that case, there is no benefit that falls into the category of consecrated Temple property. When the property of the owner is forbidden to another, he does not return the item and therefore receives no reward.

However, there is a variant reading cited by the Ran: According to the opinion of the one who says that in a case where the property of the one returning the item is forbidden to the owner of the lost item he returns it to him, then clearly, in a place where there is payment for returning the item and the one who returns the item refuses to accept it, the benefit is donated to the Temple, since benefit from the one returning the lost item is forbidden. And in a case where the property of the owner is forbidden to another, he may not return the lost item due to the *peruta* of Rav Yosef. However, according to the one who says that even in a case where the property of the owner is forbidden to another he returns a lost item to him, if the one who returned the item refuses to take payment, it is permitted for the owner to keep the payment himself, as the property of the one returning the item is not prohibited to him; why, then, should it be donated to the Temple? That is the opinion of the Rashba and the teachers of the Ran.

The Ran himself interprets the final question: Why should the benefit be donated to the Temple? Let the owner pay the one who returned the item, since according to the Ran he receives remuneration merely for lost wages, not benefit. Later commentaries noted that the basis of the dispute between Rashba and Ran is whether one for whom benefit from another is forbidden can receive wages for labor performed for that other person.

אַחֲדָא קָתָנֵי.

The Gemara answers: The *tanna* of the mishna **teaches about** only **one** of the cases: The property of the one returning the lost object is forbidden to the owner, and the one returning the lost object refuses to accept compensation. In that case, the owner of the lost item benefits from the one returning the lost object by allowing him to keep the compensation. Therefore, the benefit is donated to the Temple treasury.

אִיכָּא דְּמַתְנֵי לַהּ בְּהַאי לִישָּׁנָא; פְּלִיגִי בָּהּ רַבִּי אַמִּי וְרַבִּי אַסִּי; חַד אָמַר: לֹא שָׁנוּ אֶלָּא בְּשֶׁנִּכְסֵי בַּעַל אֲבֵידָה אֲסוּרִין עַל מַחֲזִיר, וּמִשּׁוּם פְּרוּטָה דְּרַב יוֹסֵף – לָא שְׁכִיחַ. אֲבָל נִכְסֵי מַחֲזִיר אֲסוּרִים עַל בַּעַל אֲבֵידָה – לָא מַהֲדַר לֵיהּ, מִשּׁוּם דְּקָא מְהַנֵּי לֵיהּ.

There are those **who teach** the dispute **in this formulation: Rabbi Ami and Rabbi Asi disagree about this. One said: They taught** this **only** in a case **where the property of the owner of the lost item is forbidden to** the **one returning** the lost item, **and** the concern **due to** the ***peruta* of Rav Yosef** is not a concern, because it is **not common. However,** in a case **where the property of** the **one returning** the lost item **is forbidden to** the **owner of the lost item, he may not return** it **to him, due to** the fact **that** in doing so **he benefits him.**

וְחַד אָמַר: אֲפִילּוּ נִכְסֵי מַחֲזִיר אֲסוּרִים עַל בַּעַל אֲבֵידָה – מוּתָּר, דְּכִי מַהֲדַר לֵיהּ – מִידֵּי דְּנַפְשֵׁיהּ קָמַהֲדַר לֵיהּ.

And one said: Even if the property of the **one returning** the lost item **is forbidden to** the **owner of the lost item,** it is **permitted** to return it to him, **as when he returns it, he is returning** to him **something of his own** and is not giving him anything new.

תְּנַן: מָקוֹם שֶׁנּוֹטְלִין עָלֶיהָ שָׂכָר תִּפּוֹל הֲנָאָה לַהֶקְדֵּשׁ. בִּשְׁלָמָא לְמַאן דְּאָמַר אֲפִילּוּ בְּשֶׁנִּכְסֵי מַחֲזִיר אֲסוּרִים עַל בַּעַל אֲבֵידָה מַהֲדַר – הַיְינוּ דְּמִתָּרֵץ מָקוֹם,

We learned in the mishna: In **a place where one takes payment**[H] for returning a lost item, the **benefit** that he receives for returning the item **should fall into** the category of **consecrated** Temple property. The Gemara asks: **Granted, according to the one who says that even if the property of** the **one returning** the lost item **is forbidden**[H] **to** the **owner of the lost item he returns** it to him, **this is** the reason **that** it is necessary to **resolve** the *halakha* in **a place** where one takes payment.

אֶלָּא לְמַאן דְּאָמַר בְּשֶׁנִּכְסֵי מַחֲזִיר אֲסוּרִין, וְלָא מַהֲדַר, הֵיכִי מִתָּרֵץ מָקוֹם? קַשְׁיָא.

However, according to the one who said that **in** a case **where the property of** the **one returning** the lost item **is forbidden** to the owner of the lost item **he may not return** it to him, **how does he explain** the *halakha* taught with regard to **a place** where one takes payment? Since the mishna is referring to a case where the property of the owner of the lost item is forbidden to the one returning the lost item, why is it prohibited for the owner of the lost item to keep the payment? It is not prohibited for him to benefit from the property of the one returning the lost item. The Gemara concludes: Indeed, it is **difficult.**

HALAKHA

In a place where one takes payment – מָקוֹם שֶׁנּוֹטְלִין עָלֶיהָ שָׂכָר: In a place where there is payment for return of a lost item, if the property of the owner of a lost item is forbidden to another, that other person may not take compensation for returning the item. Or, he may take the payment and consecrate it. If the property of a person is forbidden to the owner of a lost item, he may not return it without taking payment. If each are prohibited from benefiting from each other, the one who returns the lost item takes payment and consecrates it (Rambam *Sefer Hafla'a, Hilkhot Nedarim* 7:1; *Shulḥan Arukh, Yoreh De'a* 221:3).

The property of the one returning the lost item is forbidden – נִכְסֵי מַחֲזִיר אֲסוּרִים: Even if the owner of a lost item is prohibited to benefit from another, that other person may still return the item. This is because returning lost items is a mitzva, and by doing so one is merely giving him what is his. The ruling is in accordance with the opinion of the one who permits returning the item because the question on the opinion of the one who prohibits doing so remains difficult (Rambam *Sefer Hafla'a, Hilkhot Nedarim* 7:1 and *Kesef Mishne* there).

אָמַר רָבָא: הָיְתָה לְפָנָיו כִּכָּר שֶׁל הֶפְקֵר וְאָמַר ״כִּכָּר זוֹ הֶקְדֵּשׁ״, נְטָלָהּ לְאוֹכְלָהּ – מָעַל לְפִי כּוּלָּהּ, לְהוֹרִישָׁהּ לְבָנָיו – מָעַל לְפִי טוֹבַת הֲנָאָה שֶׁבָּהּ.

Rava said: In a case where **there was a loaf of ownerless** bread **before** a person,[N] **and he said: This loaf is consecrated,**[N] **if he took** the loaf **to eat it,**[HN] **he misused consecrated** property.[B] His repayment to the Temple for that misuse is **based on** the loaf's **entire value.** However, if his intent was not to take the loaf for himself but **to bequeath it to his sons, he misused the consecrated** property, and his repayment to the Temple is **based on the discretionary benefit that** he derived[N] from the fact that his children are indebted to him for the bequest, as he himself derived no direct benefit from the loaf.

בְּעָא מִינֵּיהּ רַב חִיָּיא בַּר אָבִין מֵרָבָא: ״כִּכָּרִי עָלֶיךָ״ וּנְתָנָהּ לוֹ בְּמַתָּנָה מַהוּ; ״כִּכָּרִי״ אָמַר לוֹ – כִּי אִיתֵיהּ בִּרְשׁוּתֵיהּ הוּא דְּאָסוּר, אוֹ דִּלְמָא ״עָלֶיךָ״ אֲמַר לֵיהּ – עִילָּוֵיהּ שְׁוִיתֵיהּ הֶקְדֵּשׁ?

Rav Ḥiyya bar Avin raised a dilemma before Rava. If one said to another: **My loaf is** *konam* **for you, and then he gave it to him as a gift,**[H] what is the *halakha*? Should one infer: **My loaf** is forbidden, i.e., **he said to him** that **when the loaf is in his possession, that is when it is forbidden,** but when he gives him a gift, it is no longer in his possession and it is no longer forbidden? **Or, perhaps** the inference is: Forbidden **to you,** i.e., **he said to him** that **he rendered** the loaf **for him like a consecrated item** that is forbidden even after the loaf is no longer in his possession.

אֲמַר לֵיהּ: פְּשִׁיטָא, דְּאַף עַל גַּב דִּיהֲבָהּ לֵיהּ בְּמַתָּנָה – אָסוּר. אֶלָּא ״כִּכָּרִי עָלֶיךָ״ לְאַפּוֹקֵי מַאי – לָאו לְאַפּוֹקֵי דְּאִי גְּנָבָהּ מִינֵּיהּ מִיגְנַב? אֲמַר לֵיהּ: לָא, לְאַפּוֹקֵי דְּאִי אַזְמְנֵיהּ עֲלָהּ.

Rava **said to him:** It **is obvious that although he gave it to** the other person **as a gift,** it is **forbidden.** Rav Ḥiyya bar Avin asked him: **But** if that is so, when he said: **My loaf** is forbidden **to you,** with emphasis on the word my, **what does it come to exclude? Does it not come to exclude** a case **where he stole it from him,** as in that case it is permitted?[N] The same would be true if he gave it to him as a gift. Rava **said to him: No, it** comes **to exclude** a case where **he invited him**[N] to eat from the loaf before he vowed. In that case, that part of the loaf that he invited him to eat is his, and the owner cannot render it forbidden. However, even if he invited the other person before he vowed, the entire loaf remains forbidden if he gave it to him as a gift.

HALAKHA

He took the loaf to eat it – נְטָלָהּ לְאוֹכְלָהּ: In a case where an ownerless loaf of bread was before a person and he said: This loaf is consecrated, if he took the loaf to eat it, he is liable for misuse of the entire value of the consecrated item. If he took the loaf in order to bequeath it to his sons, he is liable for misuse for the discretionary benefit that he derives from the consecrated item, in accordance with the opinion of Rava (Rambam *Sefer Avoda, Hilkhot Me'ila* 4:9).

My loaf is *konam* for you, and then gave it to him as a gift – כִּכָּרִי עָלֶיךָ וּנְתָנָהּ לוֹ בְּמַתָּנָה: If one says to another: My loaf is consecrated for you, and then he gives the loaf to the other as a gift or sells it to him, the loaf is forbidden to the other person. Therefore, if he receives the loaf and uses it, he is liable for misuse of consecrated property (Rambam *Sefer Avoda, Hilkhot Me'ila* 4:10; *Shulḥan Arukh, Yoreh De'a* 216:8).

BACKGROUND

Misuse of consecrated property – מְעִילָה: The *halakhot* of misuse of consecrated property are stated in the Torah (see Leviticus 5:14–16) and discussed at length in tractate *Me'ila*. The basic principle is that anyone who derives benefit from consecrated property unwittingly, i.e., without the knowledge that it is consecrated property, violates this prohibition. One who does so is obligated to bring a guilt-offering and pay to the Temple the value of the object from which he benefited. In addition, he pays an additional one-fifth of the value as a fine. After that item is misused, it loses its consecrated status, and the sanctity is transferred to the money that he pays to the Temple. The Torah does not discuss the case of one who derives benefit intentionally. Atonement for intentional misuse cannot be attained by sacrifice of a guilt-offering or by payment of a fine of one-fifth of the value of the misused item.

NOTES

In a case where there was a loaf of ownerless bread before a person – הָיְתָה לְפָנָיו כִּכָּר שֶׁל הֶפְקֵר: From the language of the Gemara, it is clear that this person did not hold the loaf in his hand. With regard to the question of how he took possession of the loaf in order to consecrate it, there are commentaries who explain that the loaf was within four cubits of him, and there is a principle that the legal status of one's proximate four cubits is like that of his courtyard in terms of acquiring an item (Rosh; Ran). Or, even if the object was not within four cubits of him, if the loaf was closer to him than it was to anyone else, he is able to consecrate it because he is able to take possession of it (*Tosafot*; Rosh, citing Ri). According to the Ran, if the loaf was within four cubits of him, his stipulation is effective; he does not acquire the loaf and it is consecrated. Some hold that he is able to consecrate the loaf based on the principle: The legal status of one's declaration to God is equal to that of his transfer to a common person (Rid).

This loaf is consecrated – כִּכָּר זוֹ הֶקְדֵּשׁ: *Tosafot* ask: Why is Rava's statement concerning consecration cited in this tractate? It seems more germane to a different tractate, e.g., *Arakhin*. They explain that Rava is not referring specifically to consecration. Rather, he is referring to a *konam*, in accordance with the opinion that one is liable for misuse of property forbidden by *konam*. They say that this is the reason that one is liable for misuse for the discretionary benefit, as one is liable only for misuse of consecrated property worth more than a *peruta*. However, one is liable for misuse of any item forbidden by *konam*, even if it is worth less than a *peruta*. The Rosh, though, holds that one is liable for misuse only if the discretionary benefit was worth more than a *peruta*. Apparently, most of the commentaries hold that the reference here is to actual consecration.

He took the loaf to eat it – נְטָלָהּ לְאוֹכְלָהּ: The Ran notes that his primary intent was that sanctity take effect on the loaf. Indeed, the sanctity takes effect at the moment that he takes possession of the loaf. When he then takes the loaf to eat it, even if he did not yet eat it, it is tantamount to removing it from consecrated to non-sacred status. By contrast, if he consecrated a loaf that originally belonged to him, he is liable for misuse only if he actually utilized the loaf for his own purposes. He is not liable if he merely took the loaf, because wherever the loaf is, it is in the domain of the Temple treasurer. By taking the loaf without using it, he is considered an agent of the treasurer who is guarding a sanctified object. *Tosafot* interpret this passage to mean that he took the loaf to eat after he acquired it in some other manner and consecrated it. The Rashba and the Rid agree. Others explain that it does not mean that he took the loaf to eat it. Rather, after he sanctified it, another person took the loaf, and that person is the one liable for misuse. It is clear why that person is liable for misuse in that case. It is because he took the loaf into another domain.

Based on the discretionary benefit that he derived – לְפִי טוֹבַת הֲנָאָה שֶׁבָּהּ: There is nothing beyond the discretionary benefit here, since he is not giving them the loaf now. Rather, he promises it to them in the future. His benefit is that they are grateful to him for his desire to give them a gift (Ran). The benefit is the value of the compensation that his sons will give him for bequeathing the item to one or all of them. That benefit has value. Some explain that the value is determined by how much a person would give to another in exchange for that other person giving a gift of that sort to his sons (Rid).

Does it not come to exclude a case where he stole it from him, as in that case it is permitted – לָאו לְאַפּוֹקֵי דְּאִי גְּנָבָהּ מִינֵּיהּ מִיגְנַב: There are variant readings of this passage that influence its meaning. Some hold that this passage is a continuation of Rava's statement, and it means: Of course the phrase: My loaf is forbidden to you, comes to render the loaf forbidden, even if it is given to the one for whom it is forbidden as a gift. Did the one who vowed consider the possibility that he would steal the loaf? As long as the loaf is in his possession, it belongs exclusively to him. He certainly did not intend to prohibit another from stealing the loaf (*Tosafot*; Ran). The Rosh explains this in a similar vein. However, he explains the question as follows: Certainly this is not referring to a case of theft, as even if it is stolen, it is forbidden as long as the owner did not despair. Others cite a variant reading and accordingly understand this passage as an explanation of the question of Rav Ḥiyya, who asks: Doesn't the phrase: My loaf is forbidden to you, come to exclude a case where it is no longer my loaf, e.g., if it is stolen, and it will then be permitted? If so, why would it be any different if he gives it as a gift (Rabbi Avraham min HaHar, citing Rashi)?

Where he invited him – דְּאִי אַזְמְנֵיהּ עֲלָהּ: Rashi explains that Rava's answer is that the statement: My loaf is forbidden to you, comes to exclude a case where, before the vow, the owner of the loaf invited the one for whom the loaf is forbidden by the vow to eat from the loaf. Due to that invitation, he owns part of the loaf, and therefore the owner of the loaf cannot render that loaf forbidden to him (*Tosefot Rabbeinu Peretz*).

Others explain to the contrary. This means that even if the owner of the loaf invites him, he may not give him to eat from that loaf, as that is why he said: Forbidden to you (*Tosafot*; Ran; Ritva). Rabbeinu Yona, cited by the Rosh, had a variant reading: Where he stole it from him. Or, alternatively: Where he invited him. He considers both as answers to the question: What does it come to exclude? Rava answers: It is obvious that although he gave it to the other person as a gift, it is forbidden. The phrase: My loaf is forbidden to you, comes to say that whether the one for whom the loaf is forbidden stole the loaf from him or whether the owner of the loaf invited him to partake of the loaf, it is forbidden. Rava is saying that not only is it prohibited to eat the loaf, but the very invitation to partake of the loaf is prohibited, because the owner of the loaf benefits the one for whom benefit is forbidden by the regard he shows him through that invitation.

HALAKHA

During the life of the one who vowed it is forbidden – בְּחַיָּיו אָסוּר: One who says to another: This loaf of mine is forbidden to you, it is forbidden to him, even if he gave it to him as a gift or sold it to him. However, if the one who vowed dies and it is inherited by the one to whom it is forbidden, or if the one who vowed gave it as a gift to another, who then gave it to the one to whom it is forbidden, then the loaf is permitted. This is because it was prohibited only as long as it belonged to the one who vowed, and it is no longer his (Rambam *Sefer Hafla'a, Hilkhot Nedarim* 5:4; *Shulḥan Arukh, Yoreh De'a* 216:8).

This loaf is *konam* for me like consecrated property – כִּכָּר זוֹ עָלַי לְהֶקְדֵּשׁ: If one says: This loaf is like an offering upon me or like a consecrated item, and he then eats the loaf, he is liable for misuse of consecrated items, although the loaf is not forbidden to others. Anyone to whom the loaf is forbidden by *konam* is also liable for misuse, in accordance with the opinion of Rabbi Meir. This loaf cannot be redeemed because it is sacred only for this particular person and not for everyone (Rambam *Sefer Avoda, Hilkhot Me'ila* 4:9).

NOTES

Both vows taken in this manner and vows taken in that manner – בֵּין כָּךְ וּבֵין כָּךְ: From the version of the text in the Gemara, it is clear that the Rabbis disagree with Rabbi Meir in both cases that he mentioned. They hold that in the case of both a general *konam* and an individual *konam* there is no liability for misuse. Others, especially those whose version of the Gemara is: This loaf is consecrated property, have a variant reading: Neither this one nor that one is liable for misuse. According to this reading, the Rabbis agree with Rabbi Meir in the case of a general *konam* and disagree in the case of a specific *konam* (see *Tosefot Yom Tov*).

אֵיתִיבֵיהּ: אָמַר לוֹ ״הַשְׁאִילֵנִי פָּרָתְךָ״, אָמַר לוֹ: ״קוֹנָם פָּרָה שֶׁאֲנִי קָנוּי לָךְ״, ״נְכָסַי עָלֶיךָ אִם יֵשׁ לִי פָּרָה אֶלָּא זוֹ״. ״הַשְׁאִילֵנִי קַרְדּוּמְךָ״, אָמַר לוֹ: ״קוֹנָם קַרְדּוֹם שֶׁיֵּשׁ לִי שֶׁאֲנִי קָנוּי״, ״נְכָסַי עָלַי אִם יֵשׁ לִי קַרְדּוֹם אֶלָּא זֶה״, וְנִמְצָא שֶׁיֵּשׁ לוֹ; בְּחַיָּיו – אָסוּר, מֵת אוֹ שֶׁנִּתְּנָה לוֹ בְּמַתָּנָה – הֲרֵי זֶה מוּתָּר.

The Gemara **raised an objection to** Rava. If another person **said to him: Lend me your cow,** and the owner answered and **said to him:** Every **cow that I purchased** other than this one, which I need, **is *konam* for you;** or if he said: **My property** is forbidden **to you if I have a cow other than this one,** and in fact, he owns other cows; or if another said to him: **Lend me your spade,** and the owner of the spade **said to him:** Every **spade that I have that I purchased is *konam* for you;** or if he said: **My property** is forbidden **to me if I have a spade other than this one, and it is discovered that he has** another spade and the *konam* takes effect, then **during the life** of the one who vowed, the cow or the spade is **forbidden**[H] to the subject of the vow. If the one who vowed **died or** if the cow or the spade **was given to** the subject of the vow **as a gift, it is permitted.** Apparently, the *konam* is in effect only as long as the property is in his possession.

אָמַר רַב אַחָא בְּרֵיהּ דְּרַב אִיקָא: שֶׁנִּיתְּנָה לוֹ עַל יְדֵי אַחֵר.

Rav Aḥa, son of Rav Ika, said: It is referring to a case where it **was given to** the subject of the vow **by another** person. The one who vowed did not give him the gift directly. He sold or transferred the item to a third party, who gave it to the subject of the vow as a present. Since the property left the possession of its owner before it was given to the subject of the vow, the prohibition does not take effect upon it.

אָמַר רַב אַשִׁי: דַּיְקָא נַמִי, דְּקָתָנֵי ״שֶׁנִּיתְּנָה לוֹ״, וְלָא קָתָנֵי שֶׁנְּתָנָהּ לוֹ.

The Gemara states that **Rav Ashi said:** The language **is also precise, as it teaches: That was given to him, and it is not taught: That he gave it to him.** This indicates that this *halakha* applies specifically to a gift that was given to him by a third party, but not by the one who vowed.

בְּעָא מִינֵּיהּ רָבָא מֵרַב נַחְמָן: יֵשׁ מְעִילָה בְּקוֹנָמוֹת אוֹ לָא?

§ **Rava raised a dilemma before Rav Naḥman: Is there** liability for **misuse of consecrated property** in cases of ***konamot*** **or not?** Since the legal status of an item that was rendered a *konam* is like that of consecrated property in that it is forbidden to the one who one vowed, is it like consecrated property in every sense, including liability for misuse of consecrated property?

אֲמַר לֵיהּ, תְּנֵיתוּהָ: מָקוֹם שֶׁנּוֹטְלִין עָלֶיהָ שָׂכָר – תִּיפּוֹל הֲנָאָה לַהֶקְדֵּשׁ. לְמֵימְרָא – כִּי הֶקְדֵּשׁ, מַה הֶקְדֵּשׁ יֵשׁ בּוֹ מְעִילָה – אַף קוֹנָמוֹת יֵשׁ בָּהֶן מְעִילָה.

Rav Naḥman **said to** him: **You learned** this *halakha* from a mishna (33a): In **a place where one takes payment** for returning a lost item, that **benefit** that he receives for returning the item **should fall into** the category of **consecrated** Temple property. That is **to say,** an item forbidden by a *konam* is like **consecrated property. Just as** with regard to **consecrated property there is** liability for **misuse, so too** with regard to ***konamot*** **there is** liability for **misuse.**

כְּתַנָּאֵי: ״קוֹנָם כִּכָּר זוֹ הֶקְדֵּשׁ״ וַאֲכָלָהּ, בֵּין הוּא וּבֵין חֲבֵירוֹ – מָעַל, לְפִיכָךְ יֵשׁ לָהּ פִּדְיוֹן. ״כִּכָּר זוֹ עָלַי לַהֶקְדֵּשׁ״ וַאֲכָלָהּ – הוּא מָעַל, חֲבֵירוֹ לֹא מָעַל, לְפִיכָךְ אֵין לָהּ פִּדְיוֹן, דִּבְרֵי רַבִּי מֵאִיר.

The Gemara comments on this. This dilemma is **like** a dispute between *tanna'im*. If one said: **This loaf is *konam*** to all like **consecrated property, and he ate it,** then, **whether he** ate it **or whether another** ate it, the one who ate it **misused consecrated property. Therefore,** since its status is that of consecrated property, **it has** the possibility of desanctification through **redemption.** If one said: **This loaf is *konam* for me** like **consecrated property**[H] **and he eats it, he misused consecrated property.** If **another** eats it, **he did not misuse consecrated property,** as he said: To me. **Therefore, it does not have** the possibility of desanctification through **redemption,** since its status is not that of full-fledged consecrated property. This is **the statement of Rabbi Meir.**

וַחֲכָמִים אוֹמְרִים: בֵּין כָּךְ וּבֵין כָּךְ לֹא מָעַל, לְפִי שֶׁאֵין מְעִילָה בְּקוֹנָמוֹת.

And the Rabbis say: In the case of **both** vows taken **in this manner and** vows taken **in that manner,**[N] **no one misused consecrated property because there is no** liability for **misuse** of consecrated objects **in** cases of ***konamot***. Rabbi Meir disagrees and holds that there is liability for misuse in *konamot*.

אָמַר לֵיהּ רַב אַחָא בְּרֵיהּ דְּרַב אָוְיָא לְרַב אָשֵׁי: ״כִּכָּרִי עָלֶיךָ״ וּנְתָנָהּ לוֹ בְּמַתָּנָה, מִי מָעַל? לִמְעוֹל נוֹתֵן – הָא לָא אֲסִירָא עֲלֵיהּ, לִמְעוֹל מְקַבֵּל – יָכוֹל דְּאָמַר: הֶיתֵּירָא בָּעֵיתִי, אִיסּוּרָא לָא בָּעֵיתִי. אָמַר לֵיהּ: מְקַבֵּל מָעַל לִכְשֶׁיּוֹצִיא, שֶׁכׇּל הַמּוֹצִיא מְעוֹת הֶקְדֵּשׁ לְחוּלִּין, כִּסְבוּר שֶׁל חוּלִּין הוּא – מוֹעֵל, אַף זֶה מוֹעֵל.

Rav Aḥa, son of Rav Avya, said to Rav Ashi: If one said to another: **My loaf is** *konam* **for you, and he** then **gave it to him as a gift, which** of them **misused consecrated property?** If you say: **Let the one who gives** the loaf be liable for **misuse,** why would he be liable; the loaf **is not forbidden to him?** If you say: **Let the one who receives** the loaf be liable for **misuse, he can say: I wanted** to receive **a permitted** item; **I did not want** to receive **a forbidden** item.[N] Since the loaf is forbidden, if I accepted it from you, it was not my intention to do so. Rav Ashi **said to him: The one who receives** the loaf is liable for **misuse when he utilizes** the loaf,[H] as the principle with regard to misuse is **that anyone who utilizes consecrated money for non-sacred** purposes,[H] **when he is under the impression that it is non-sacred, misuses consecrated property. This** person who received the loaf **also misuses consecrated property.**

NOTES

I did not want to receive a forbidden item – אִיסּוּרָא לָא בָּעֵיתִי: Although liability for misuse of consecrated property applies only to unwitting misuse, and therefore the fact that one does not want to acquire an item should not be a reason to exempt him, there is a distinction. Here the Gemara is saying that the one receiving the gift would be in violation of the prohibition from the moment that it was given to him, as that constitutes a change of location of the consecrated item, even though he did not perform a transaction to acquire the item. Therefore, the Gemara explains that the change of location, as opposed to eating, is not an actual action, and his intent determines whether or not he acquires the item. When it becomes clear that he has no interest in acquiring the item, there is no transaction at all. The result is that the item never left the domain of its previous owner (Ran; Rosh).

HALAKHA

The one who receives the loaf is liable for misuse when he utilizes the loaf – מְקַבֵּל מָעַל לִכְשֶׁיּוֹצִיא: If one says to another: My loaf is a consecrated item to you, and he then gives it to the other person, the one who receives the loaf is liable for misuse of consecrated property when he uses it, in accordance with the opinion of Rav Ashi (Rambam *Sefer Avoda, Hilkhot Me'ila* 4:10).

Anyone who utilizes consecrated money for non-sacred purposes – כׇּל הַמּוֹצִיא מְעוֹת הֶקְדֵּשׁ לְחוּלִּין: If one uses consecrated money for his own purposes because he thinks it is non-sacred, he is liable for misuse of consecrated property. That is the case not only if he uses it for non-sacred purposes but even if he uses it for sacred purposes. Since he benefits from it, he is liable for misuse (Rambam *Sefer Avoda, Hilkhot Me'ila* 6:11).

Perek **IV**
Daf **35** Amud **b**

מתני׳ וְתוֹרֵם אֶת תְּרוּמָתוֹ וּמַעַשְׂרוֹתָיו לְדַעְתּוֹ, וּמַקְרִיב עָלָיו קִינֵּי זָבִין, קִינֵּי זָבוֹת, קִינֵּי יוֹלְדוֹת, חַטָּאוֹת וַאֲשָׁמוֹת. וּמְלַמְּדוֹ מִדְרָשׁ, הֲלָכוֹת וְאַגָּדוֹת, אֲבָל לֹא יְלַמְּדֶנּוּ מִקְרָא. אֲבָל מְלַמֵּד הוּא אֶת בָּנָיו וְאֶת בְּנוֹתָיו מִקְרָא.

MISHNA The mishna proceeds to list other tasks that one may perform for someone who is prohibited by vow from benefiting from him. **And he separates his** *teruma*[H] **and his tithes,** provided that it is **with the knowledge** and consent of the owner of the produce. **And he sacrifices for him the bird nests,** i.e., pairs of birds, pigeons and turtledoves, **of** *zavin*[H] (see Leviticus 15:13–15); **the bird nests of** *zavot* (see Leviticus 15:28–30); **the bird nests of women after childbirth** (see Leviticus 12:6–8); **sin-offerings;** and **guilt-offerings. And he teaches him midrash,**[NH] ***halakhot,*** **and** ***aggadot,*** **but he may not teach him Bible. However, he may teach his sons and daughters Bible.**

NOTES

Midrash – מִדְרָשׁ: Midrash includes those *halakhot* derived from verses, e.g., halakhic midrash and the like (Rambam's Commentary on the Mishna).

HALAKHA

And he separates his ***teruma*****, etc. – וְתוֹרֵם אֶת תְּרוּמָתוֹ וכו׳:** In a case where benefit from another is forbidden due to a vow, that other person may separate *teruma* and tithes on behalf of the one bound by the vow. The Gemara explains how this can be done with the knowledge of the one for whom benefit is forbidden without it being considered as benefiting him (Rambam *Sefer Hafla'a, Hilkhot Nedarim* 6:6).

And he sacrifices for him bird nests of ***zavin*****, etc. – וּמַקְרִיב עָלָיו קִינֵּי זָבִין וכו׳:** If one vowed that benefit from a specific priest is forbidden to him, that priest may still sacrifice offerings on his behalf (Rambam *Sefer Hafla'a, Hilkhot Nedarim* 6:5).

And he teaches him midrash, etc. – וּמְלַמְּדוֹ מִדְרָשׁ וכו׳: One may teach Oral Torah to one for whom benefit from him is forbidden by vow because it is prohibited to take payment for doing so. However, he may not teach him Written Torah in places where it is customary to take payment for that. In any case, it is permitted for him to teach the son of the one for whom benefit from him is forbidden.

In the *Shulḥan Arukh*, the ruling is that even in cases where it is permitted to teach one for whom benefit from him is forbidden, this is permitted only if the teacher does so on his own initiative, but not if he was asked to teach by the one bound by the vow. Others disagree and rule that it is permitted in that case as well (Rema, citing Rosh and *Tur*). The ruling of the *Shulḥan Arukh* is that today, when it is customary to take payment for teaching Oral Torah, one may not teach even Oral Torah to the one bound by the vow (Rambam *Sefer Hafla'a, Hilkhot Nedarim* 6:7; *Shulḥan Arukh, Yoreh De'a* 221:2).

גמ׳ איבעיא להו: הני כהני, שלוחי דידן הוו או שלוחי דשמיא? למאי נפקא מינה – למודר הנאה. אי אמרת דשלוחי דידן הוו – הא מהני ליה, ואסור. ואי אמרת שלוחי דשמיא – שרי. מאי?

GEMARA **A dilemma was raised before the Sages: Are these priests our agents**[N] **or agents of Heaven** when they perform the Temple service? The Gemara elaborates: **What is the practical difference** whether they are our agents or God's agents? The Gemara answers: The difference is with regard **to one prohibited by vow from deriving benefit** from another. **If you say that** the priests **are our agents, don't** the priests provide **benefit** for the one[N] for whom benefit is forbidden by vow, **and** therefore, sacrificing that person's offering is **prohibited? And if you say that they are agents of Heaven,** it is **permitted.**[NH] **What is** the status of priests?

תא שמע, דתנן: מקריב עליו קיני זבין כו׳. אי אמרת שלוחי דידן – קא מהני ליה!

Come and **hear** proof to resolve the dilemma, **as we learned** in the mishna: **And he sacrifices for him the bird nests of *zavin*, etc.** The Gemara infers: **If you say** that the priests are **our agents,** the priests would thereby provide **benefit** to one for whom benefit from them is forbidden. Based on the ruling in the mishna, apparently, priests are agents of Heaven.

וליטעמיך, ליתני: מקריב עליו קרבנות! אלא, מחוסרי כפרה שאני. דאמר רבי יוחנן: הכל צריכין דעת, חוץ ממחוסרי כפרה, שהרי אדם מביא קרבן על בניו ועל בנותיו הקטנים, שנאמר "זאת תורת הזב" – בין גדול בין קטן.

The Gemara rejects the proof: **And according to your reasoning,** that the mishna holds that priests are agents of Heaven, **let** the mishna **teach** in general: **He sacrifices for him offerings.** Why did the mishna list these particular offerings? **Rather,** perforce, offerings brought by **those lacking atonement**[N] **are different** from other offerings, **as Rabbi Yoḥanan said: Everyone** who brings an offering **requires knowledge**[H] and intent in order to bring the offering, **except for those lacking atonement,** who bring the offering in order to complete their purification. This can be proven from the fact **that a person brings** a purification **offering for his minor sons and daughters,** although they lack halakhic intelligence, **as it is stated: "This is the law of the *zav*"** (Leviticus 15:32). This apparently superfluous verse comes to teach that the *halakhot* of the *zav* apply to **both an adult and a minor.**

אלא מעתה לרבי יוחנן "זאת תורת הילדת" וגו׳ – בין קטנה ובין גדולה, קטנה בת לידה היא?! והא תני רב ביבי קמיה דרב נחמן: שלש נשים משמשות במוך: קטנה, ומעוברת, ומניקה. קטנה – שמא תתעבר ותמות!

The Gemara asks: **However, if that is so** according **to Rabbi Yoḥanan,** with regard to that which is written: **"This is the law of a woman after childbirth"** (Leviticus 12:7), would he interpret that the *halakhot* of a woman after childbirth apply to **both an adult and a minor? Is a minor capable of** giving **birth? But didn't Rav Beivai teach** a *baraita* **before Rav Naḥman:** It is permitted for **three women** to **engage in intercourse with a contraceptive resorbent:**[NB] **A minor, and a pregnant** woman, **and a nursing** woman; **a minor** may do so **lest she conceive and die.** Apparently, a minor is incapable of giving birth, as she would die first.

ההיא "זאת תורת הילדת" – בין פקחת בין שוטה, שכן אדם מביא קרבן על אשתו שוטה,

The Gemara explains: **That** verse: **"This is the law of a woman after childbirth,"** does not come to include a minor. Rather, it comes to teach that the *halakhot* of a woman after childbirth apply to **both a halakhically competent woman and a woman** who is **an imbecile, as a man brings an offering for his wife who is an imbecile.**[H]

NOTES

Are these priests our agents, etc. – הני כהני שלוחי דידן הוו וכו׳: The early commentaries note that this dilemma, which remains unresolved here, was resolved by Rav Huna, son of Rav Yehoshua, in tractate *Kiddushin* (23b). There he proved that priests are agents of Heaven. They cannot be our agents, as it is permitted for priests to perform actions that it is prohibited for their dispatchers to perform. The Ran and the Rashba wrote that the Gemara here seeks to resolve the dilemma from a mishna or *baraita*, not from the opinion of an *amora*.

The Rashba, on tractate *Kiddushin*, wrote that the Gemara here is discussing a case where the one for whom benefit is forbidden is himself a priest, in which case the priest who sacrifices the offering is performing an action permitted to his dispatcher. The Ritva writes there that the question here pertains to those sacrificial rites that even an Israelite may perform, e.g., slaughtering. *Tosafot* on *Kiddushin* write that even if there is proof that priests are agents of Heaven, the dilemma here is whether they are the agents of the people as well.

Don't the priests benefit one – הא מהני ליה: Although a priest is performing a mitzva, and mitzvot were not given for one to benefit from them, still, through the mere performance of an action on behalf of another, he benefits that other person. Therefore, it is prohibited for one to sacrifice an offering on behalf of one for whom benefit from him is prohibited, as explained later with regard to separating *teruma* (*Tosafot*).

And if you say that they are agents of Heaven, it is permitted – ואי אמרת שלוחי דשמיא שרי: Although the priest indirectly benefits the person on whose behalf he sacrificed the offering by enabling him to eat consecrated food, since the priest does not benefit the person bringing the offering directly, it is not forbidden. The Gemara, in rejecting the proofs cited previously, stated that indirect benefit is permitted (Ran).

Those lacking atonement – מחוסרי כפרה: Those lacking atonement are those listed in the mishna here. Their offerings, even the sin-offerings and guilt-offerings, are not brought as atonement for a sin but are designed to complete the purification process. Although without those offerings the person in question is considered pure with regard to certain matters, e.g., partaking of *teruma*, he is still prohibited from partaking of consecrated food until those offerings are brought.

Engage in intercourse with a contraceptive resorbent – משמשות במוך: Most commentaries explain that the Gemara means they are required to use a resorbent due to the potential danger to the mother or the fetus. However, others understand that the emphasis of the Gemara is that these women may use a resorbent, and in doing so they do not violate the prohibition against destroying the husband's seed (Re'em).

BACKGROUND

Engage in intercourse with a contraceptive resorbent – משמשות במוך: The problem of women using a contraceptive resorbent is discussed at length in *halakha*. Here, the reference is to barrier methods of contraception, which prevent penetration of the sperm into the womb and are effective only during intercourse and not thereafter. This method of contraception is permitted only in life-threatening situations. In tractate *Yevamot* (12a) it is explained that this is the opinion of Rabbi Meir; however, the Rabbis disagree and rule that its use is prohibited in all cases. Apparently, the basis of the dispute between Rabbi Meir and the Rabbis is to what degree need one be concerned with these risks.

HALAKHA

And if you say that they are agents of Heaven, it is permitted – ואי אמרת שלוחי דשמיא שרי: Priests are considered agents of Heaven and not agents of those bringing the offerings. Therefore, a priest can sacrifice all offerings on behalf of one from whom benefit is forbidden by vow. Although the dilemma with regard to the priests is not resolved here, the Gemara in tractates *Yoma* and *Kiddushin* concludes that priests are agents of Heaven (Radbaz; Rambam *Sefer Hafla'a, Hilkhot Nedarim* 6:5).

Everyone who brings an offering requires knowledge – הכל צריכין דעת: Generally, offerings may be brought on behalf of those obligated to do so only with their knowledge and intent. The exceptions are offerings on behalf of those lacking atonement, which do not require knowledge. Consequently, one may bring offerings for his minor sons and daughters who lack atonement, thereby enabling them to eat the meat of the offerings (Rambam *Sefer Korbanot, Hilkhot Meḥusrei Kappara* 1:5).

A man brings an offering for his wife who is an imbecile – אדם מביא קרבן על אשתו שוטה: Anyone can become impure with the emissions of a *zav*, even a one-day-old baby, a deaf person, an imbecile, or a slave. The Rambam notes that apparently, according to the Gemara here, it is permitted to bring an atonement offering for a deaf person, an imbecile, and a minor, in order to enable them to eat consecrated foods, and their sin-offering may be eaten (Rambam *Sefer Korbanot, Hilkhot Meḥusrei Kappara* 3:6).

כְּדִבְרֵי רַבִּי יְהוּדָה. דְּתַנְיָא, רַבִּי יְהוּדָה אוֹמֵר: אָדָם מֵבִיא קׇרְבַּן עָשִׁיר עַל אִשְׁתּוֹ, וְכׇל קׇרְבָּנוֹת שֶׁחַיֶּיבֶת.

This *halakha* is **in accordance with the statement of Rabbi Yehuda, as it is taught** in a *baraita* that **Rabbi Yehuda says: A man brings the offering of a wealthy person for his wife,**[H] **as well as all offerings that she is obligated** to bring. A wealthy woman after childbirth brings a lamb as a burnt-offering and a dove or turtledove as a sin-offering. A poor woman brings two turtledoves or two pigeons, one as a burnt-offering and one as a sin-offering. Even if the woman is poor, and based on her usufruct property, she would bring the offering of the poor; if her husband is wealthy, he brings the offering of a wealthy person on her behalf. And he must bring on her behalf all the offerings **for which she is obligated.**

שֶׁכָּךְ כּוֹתֵב לָהּ: וְאַחֲרָיוּת דְּאִית לֵיךְ עָלַי מִן קַדְמַת דְּנָא.

The fact that he is obligated to bring a wealthy person's offering on her behalf is due to the fact **that this** is what **he writes** in **her** marriage contract:[N] **And responsibility** to pay any financial obligations **that you have** incurred **before this** moment **is** incumbent **upon me.** Offerings that she is obligated to bring are included in those obligations, irrespective of her degree of halakhic competence. The offering of a woman after childbirth is one of the offerings brought by those lacking atonement. Therefore, even if priests are our agents, they may sacrifice the offering on behalf of the woman; since they may do so without her knowledge and intent, no agency is required. Therefore, there is no proof from the mishna that priests are agents of Heaven.

HALAKHA

Brings the offering of a wealthy person for his wife – מֵבִיא קׇרְבַּן עָשִׁיר עַל אִשְׁתּוֹ: One may bring all of the offerings that his wife is obligated to bring on her behalf. If he is a poor person, he brings a poor person's offering, and if he is wealthy, he brings a rich man's offering. The type of offering that one brings is completely dependent on his own status, and the status of his wife is irrelevant (Rambam *Sefer Korbanot, Hilkhot Shegagot* 10:6).

NOTES

This is what he writes in her marriage contract – שֶׁכָּךְ כּוֹתֵב לָהּ: There is no direct proof from here for the *halakha* that a man brings an offering for his wife who is an imbecile. However, since there is proof from here that once a man marries, he is responsible for his wife's offerings, he is obligated to bring atonement offerings for her as well. These do not require knowledge and intent, and his imbecilic wife is included in this obligation (see Re'em).

Perek **IV**
Daf **36** Amud **a**

מְתִיב רַב שִׁימִי בַּר אַבָּא: אִם הָיָה כֹּהֵן – יִזְרוֹק עָלָיו דַּם חַטָּאתוֹ וְדַם אֲשָׁמוֹ!

Rav Shimi bar Abba raised an objection from the *Tosefta* (2:7): **If** the one who vowed to prohibit another from benefiting from him **was a priest, he may sprinkle the blood of his sin-offering and the blood of his guilt-offering on** the other's behalf.[N] Apparently, the priest may perform all sacrificial rites for one prohibited from benefiting from him, even those that require knowledge of the one for whom the offering atones.

דַּם חַטָּאתוֹ שֶׁל מְצוֹרָע, וְדַם אֲשָׁמוֹ שֶׁל מְצוֹרָע, דִּכְתִיב ״זֹאת תִּהְיֶה תּוֹרַת הַמְּצֹרָע״ – בֵּין גָּדוֹל וּבֵין קָטָן.

The Gemara answers. The reference is to **blood of the sin-offering of a leper and blood of the guilt-offering of a leper.** These are offerings brought by a leper who is lacking atonement, in order to complete his purification process, **as it is written: "This is the law of the leper"** (Leviticus 14:2). And the verse comes to teach that the *halakhot* of a leper apply to **both an adult and a minor.**[H] This offering, too, does not require the knowledge of the one for whom the offering atones.

תְּנַן: הַכֹּהֲנִים שֶׁפִּיגְּלוּ בַּמִּקְדָּשׁ, מְזִידִין – חַיָּיבִין. הָא שׁוֹגְגִין – פְּטוּרִין, אֶלָּא שֶׁפִּיגּוּלָן פִּיגּוּל.

The Gemara cites another proof to resolve the dilemma with regard to the nature of the agency of a priest. **We learned** in a mishna: In the case of **priests who rendered** an offering ***piggul* in the Temple,**[H] i.e., they sacrificed an offering intending to consume it after its appointed time, if **they did** so **intentionally,** i.e., with full awareness of the period during which the offering may be consumed, **they are obligated** to pay. The Gemara infers: If **they did** so **unwittingly, they are exempt** from payment. **However,** in any event, when **they** rendered the offering ***piggul,*** it acquired the status of ***piggul*** and is disqualified.

אִי אָמְרַתְּ בִּשְׁלָמָא שְׁלוּחֵי דִשְׁמַיָּא הָווּ – הַיְינוּ שֶׁפִּיגּוּלָן פִּיגּוּל. אֶלָּא אִי אָמְרַתְּ שְׁלוּחֵי דִידַן הָווּ – אַמַּאי פִּיגּוּלָן פִּיגּוּל? לֵימָא לֵיהּ: שְׁלִיחָא שַׁוִּיתִיךְ לְתַקּוֹנֵי וְלָא לְעַוּוֹתֵי!

The Gemara asks: **Granted, if you say** that the priests **are agents of Heaven, this is** why when **their** actions cause ***piggul*** it is ***piggul***; their actions are independent of the one bringing the offering. **However, if you say** that the priests **are our agents, why** when **their** actions cause ***piggul*** is it ***piggul*? Let the one bringing the offering say to the priest: I designated you an agent to perform** the task **properly but not to perform** the task **improperly.**

NOTES

He may sprinkle the blood of his sin-offering and the blood of his guilt-offering on his behalf – יִזְרוֹק עָלָיו דַּם חַטָּאתוֹ וְדַם אֲשָׁמוֹ: The early commentaries wondered: Why didn't the Gemara raise an objection from the mishna where sin-offerings and guilt-offerings are listed? *Tosafot* explain that the question could have been raised from the mishna; however, others explain that in the version of the mishna available to Rav Simi bar Abba, sin-offerings and guilt-offerings were not listed (Ran). Others explain that in the list in the mishna, sin-offerings and guilt-offerings appear adjacent to bird nests of *zavin* and *zavot*, indicating that the reference is to sin-offerings and guilt-offerings of those lacking atonement. That is not the case in the *baraita*, in which there is no mention of those lacking atonement. It is formulated in a more general manner, indicating that it is referring to all sin-offerings (Rosh; Rashba; Ran).

HALAKHA

This is the law of the leper to both an adult and a minor – זֹאת תִּהְיֶה תּוֹרַת הַמְּצֹרָע בֵּין גָּדוֹל וּבֵין קָטָן: Anyone apart from a resident alien and a gentile can be rendered impure by leprosy, even a child who is one day old and slaves (Rambam *Sefer Tahara, Hilkhot Tumat Tzara'at* 9:1).

Priests who rendered an offering *piggul* in the Temple – הַכֹּהֲנִים שֶׁפִּיגְּלוּ בַּמִּקְדָּשׁ: If while a priest is performing the sacrificial rites for an offering he thinks that it will be eaten beyond its designated time, he renders the offering *piggul*. If he has that thought intentionally, he must pay compensation to the owner of the offering. If he does so unwittingly, he is exempt from payment. The Ra'avad and the Ramban disagree and hold that even if he does so intentionally he is exempt under the laws of man, and cannot be compelled to pay by the court, because damage that is not evident is not considered damage. In the *Maggid Mishne* it is explained that the Rambam rules in accordance with the unattributed mishna and holds that if one did so intentionally, he is obligated to pay compensation (Rambam *Sefer Nezikim, Hilkhot Ḥovel UMazik* 7:4).

NOTES

Sin-offering for forbidden fat – חַטַּאת חֵלֶב: The reference here is to any sin-offering brought by one who unwittingly violates a prohibition whose intentional violation is punishable by *karet*. The sin-offering for unwittingly eating forbidden fat is the exemplar chosen by the Sages, because it is common for one to eat forbidden fat unwittingly, based on the mistaken assumption that it is permitted fat (Rabbi Yitzḥak Tzarfati).

HALAKHA

A sin-offering on behalf of another – חַטַּאת חֵלֶב עַל חֲבֵירוֹ: One may bring a sin-offering on behalf of another only with the knowledge and intent of that other person (Rambam *Sefer Avoda*, *Hilkhot Pesulei HaMukdashin* 15:7).

One ate forbidden fat…and became an imbecile – אָכַל חֵלֶב...וְנִשְׁתַּטָּה: If one sinned inadvertently, set aside a sin-offering, became demented, and then regained his competence, then although the offering was disqualified when he was demented, its fitness is restored when he became normal again. The Rambam rules in accordance with the opinion of Rav, who holds that animals that were disqualified remain disqualified only as long as the cause of the disqualification continues to exist (Rambam *Sefer Korbanot*, *Hilkhot Shegagot* 3:8 and *Kesef Mishne* there).

One who separated a Paschal lamb on behalf of another – הִפְרִישׁ פֶּסַח עַל חֲבֵירוֹ: One cannot slaughter the Paschal lamb on behalf of another without his knowledge. That is true even for one's wife and adult children. However, one may slaughter the Paschal lamb for his minor sons and daughters even without their knowledge (Rambam *Sefer Korbanot*, *Hilkhot Korban Pesaḥ* 2:8).

אָמְרִי: שָׁאנֵי גַּבֵּי פִּיגּוּל, דְּאָמַר קְרָא ״לֹא יֵחָשֵׁב לוֹ״ – מִכׇּל מָקוֹם.

The Sages **say** in response: It **is different with regard to** *piggul*, as in its regard **the verse states** and emphasizes: "He who offered it, **it will not be imputed to him**" (Leviticus 7:18). This implies that it is *piggul* **in any case**, e.g., even if one's actions cause the offering to be *piggul* without the consent of the owner. Therefore, there is no proof with regard to the nature of the agency of the priest.

גּוּפָא, אָמַר רַבִּי יוֹחָנָן: הַכֹּל צְרִיכִין דַּעַת, חוּץ מִמְּחוּסַּר כַּפָּרָה, שֶׁהֲרֵי אָדָם מֵבִיא קׇרְבָּן עַל בָּנָיו וְעַל בְּנוֹתָיו הַקְּטַנִּים. אֶלָּא מֵעַתָּה יָבִיא אָדָם חַטַּאת חֵלֶב עַל חֲבֵירוֹ, שֶׁכֵּן אָדָם מֵבִיא עַל אִשְׁתּוֹ שׁוֹטָה כְּרַבִּי יְהוּדָה. אַלְמָה אָמַר רַבִּי אֶלְעָזָר: הִפְרִישׁ חַטַּאת חֵלֶב עַל חֲבֵירוֹ – לֹא עָשָׂה כְּלוּם!

§ With regard to **the matter itself, Rabbi Yoḥanan said: Everyone** who brings an offering **requires knowledge, except for** those offerings brought by **those lacking atonement;** this can be proven from the fact **that a person brings** a purification **offering for his minor sons and daughters.** The Gemara asks: **However, if that is so, let a person bring a sin-offering on** behalf of **another** who unwittingly ate forbidden **fat**[N] without his knowledge, **just as a man brings** an offering **for his wife who is an imbecile, in accordance with** the opinion of **Rabbi Yehuda. Why** then **did Rabbi Elazar say:** One who **separated a sin-offering on** behalf of **another**[H] who unwittingly ate forbidden **fat has done nothing?**

אִשְׁתּוֹ שׁוֹטָה הֵיכִי דָּמֵי? אִי דְּאָכְלָה כְּשֶׁהִיא שׁוֹטָה – לָאו בַּת קׇרְבָּן הִיא,

The Gemara refutes the analogy between the cases. **What are the circumstances of** the case of **his wife who is an imbecile? If she ate** the forbidden **fat when she was an imbecile, she is not subject** to liability to bring **an offering,** as one lacking halakhic competence is exempt from punishment and needs no atonement.

וְאִי דְּאָכְלָה כְּשֶׁהִיא פִּקַּחַת וְנִשְׁתַּטֵּית – הָא אָמַר רַבִּי יִרְמְיָה אָמַר רַבִּי אַבָּהוּ אָמַר רַבִּי יוֹחָנָן: אָכַל חֵלֶב וְהִפְרִישׁ קׇרְבָּן וְנִשְׁתַּטָּה וְחָזַר וְנִשְׁתַּפָּה – פָּסוּל, הוֹאִיל וְנִדְחָה – יִדָּחֶה.

And if she ate the forbidden fat **when she was** halakhically **competent and** then **became an imbecile, didn't Rabbi Yirmeya say** that **Rabbi Abbahu said** that **Rabbi Yoḥanan said:** If one **ate** forbidden **fat** unwittingly, **and separated an offering, and became an imbecile,**[H] **and became competent again, the offering is disqualified. Since it was disqualified** when he was demented, **it will be disqualified** forever. It is clear, therefore, that the sin-offering that one brings for his wife who is an imbecile is not a sin-offering for eating forbidden fat, as that would require halakhic intelligence. It is merely for completion of the purification process, e.g., a woman after childbirth, for which halakhic competence is not required. Therefore, no proof may be cited from the case of one's wife who is an imbecile to the case of bringing a sin-offering on behalf of another who ate fat.

אֶלָּא מֵעַתָּה יָבִיא אָדָם פֶּסַח עַל חֲבֵירוֹ, שֶׁכֵּן אָדָם מֵבִיא עַל בָּנָיו וְעַל בְּנוֹתָיו הַקְּטַנִּים. אַלְמָה אָמַר רַבִּי אֶלְעָזָר: הִפְרִישׁ פֶּסַח עַל חֲבֵירוֹ – לֹא עָשָׂה כְּלוּם!

The Gemara asks: **However, if that is so, let a person bring a Paschal lamb on** behalf of **another** without his knowledge, **just as a person brings** a Paschal lamb **for his minor sons and daughters. Why** then **did Rabbi Elazar say:** One who **separated a Paschal lamb on** behalf of **another**[H] **has done nothing?**

אָמַר רַבִּי זֵירָא: ״שֶׂה לְבֵית אָבֹת״ לָאו דְּאוֹרָיְיתָא.

Rabbi Zeira said: The verse states: **"A lamb for each father's house,** a lamb for the household" (Exodus 12:3). From here it is derived that all members of a household, including minor sons and daughters, are registered to the group eating a Paschal lamb. However, this is a custom; it **is not by Torah law.**

וּמִמַּאי – מִדִּתְנַן: הָאוֹמֵר לְבָנָיו ״הֲרֵינִי שׁוֹחֵט אֶת הַפֶּסַח עַל מִי שֶׁיַּעֲלֶה מִכֶּם רִאשׁוֹן לִירוּשָׁלַיִם״ כֵּיוָן שֶׁהִכְנִיס רִאשׁוֹן רֹאשׁוֹ וְרוּבּוֹ – זָכָה בְּחֶלְקוֹ, וּמְזַכֶּה אֶת אַחָיו עִמּוֹ. וְאִי אָמְרַתְּ ״שֶׂה לְבַיִת״ דְּאוֹרָיְיתָא – עַל בִּישְׂרָא קָאֵי וּמְזַכֵּי לְהוּ?!

And from where is this *halakha* learned? It **is from that which we learned** in a mishna (*Pesaḥim* 89a): With regard to **one who says to his** minor **sons: I am hereby slaughtering the Paschal lamb on** behalf of **the one of you who will ascend to Jerusalem first,** and he will be privileged to eat from that lamb, then **once the first** of his children **introduces his head and most of** his body into Jerusalem, **he acquires his portion and acquires** portions on **behalf of his brothers with him. And if you say** that the *halakha* derived from the phrase **"a lamb for the household" is by Torah law,** and the minors are obligated to register for the Paschal lamb, although the son who reached Jerusalem first acquired his portion based on the stipulation of his father, how can **he stand over the meat** of the Paschal lamb after it was slaughtered **and acquire it on behalf of** his brothers? Apparently, minors are not required by Torah law to register as members of the group eating the Paschal lamb.

אֶלָּא לָמָּה לְהוּ דַּאֲמַר לְהוֹן אֲבוּהוֹן – כְּדֵי לְזָרְזָן בְּמִצְוֹת. תַּנְיָא נַמִי הָכִי: מַעֲשֶׂה הָיָה וְקָדְמוּ בָּנוֹת לַבָּנִים, וְנִמְצְאוּ בָּנוֹת זְרִיזוֹת וּבָנִים שְׁפָלִים.

The Gemara asks: **However, why do they** require **that their father say to them:** The one of you who will ascend to Jerusalem first will be privileged to eat from that lamb, when no actual acquisition takes place? It is **in order to motivate them in** the performance of **mitzvot. This is also taught** in a *baraita*: **There was an incident** that transpired where a father said to his sons and daughters that they should compete to see who reaches the sacrifice of the Paschal lamb first, **and the daughters preceded the sons, and the daughters were found** to be **motivated and the sons** to be **lazy** [*shefalim*].[L] Since the *baraita* did not say that the result was that daughters acquired their portion, apparently the father's statement was merely motivational.

וְתוֹרֵם אֶת תְּרוּמָתוֹ כו׳.

§ We learned in the mishna that among the tasks that one may perform for someone who is prohibited by vow from benefiting from him is: **And he separates his *teruma*.**

LANGUAGE

Lazy [*shefalim*] – שְׁפָלִים: The primary meaning of the term *shefel* is low or bottom. The usage here is related to that meaning, as the daughters were superior to the sons. The word is also used to mean lethargic, indolent, or lazy. This is the primary meaning here. The sons were lazy relative to the daughters, who were motivated.

Perek IV
Daf **36** Amud **b**

אִיבַּעְיָא לְהוּ: הַתּוֹרֵם מִשֶּׁלּוֹ עַל שֶׁל חֲבֵירוֹ צָרִיךְ דַּעְתּוֹ אוֹ לֹא? כִּי אָמְרִינַן: כֵּיוָן דִּזְכוּת הוּא לוֹ – לֹא צָרִיךְ דַּעַת, אוֹ דִּלְמָא מִצְוָה דִּילֵיהּ הִיא, וְנִיחָא לֵיהּ לְמִיעַבְדֵיהּ?

A dilemma was raised before the Sages: In the case of **one who separates *teruma* from his own** produce **on** behalf of the produce **of another,** does he **require the knowledge** and consent of the owner of the produce **or not? Do we say: Since it is a benefit for** the other to have his produce tithed, **it does not require his knowledge,** as one may act in a person's interest in his absence? **Or, perhaps it is his mitzva,** and it is **preferable for him to perform** the mitzva himself, and therefore, it does not benefit him to have the produce tithed on his behalf.

תָּא שְׁמַע: תּוֹרֵם אֶת תְּרוּמוֹתָיו וְאֶת מַעַשְׂרוֹתָיו לְדַעְתּוֹ. בְּמַאי עָסְקִינַן? אִילֵימָא מִן בַּעַל הַכְּרִי עַל שֶׁל בַּעַל הַכְּרִי, וּלְדַעְתּוֹ דְּמַאן? אִילֵימָא לְדַעְתּוֹ דִּילֵיהּ – מַאן שַׁוְּיֵהּ שָׁלִיחַ?

Come and **hear** a proof from the mishna: For one for whom benefit from him is forbidden by vow, **he separates his *teruma* and his tithes,** provided that it is **with his knowledge** and consent. The Gemara analyzes this statement: **With what are we dealing? If we say** that he separates *teruma* from the produce of the **owner of the pile for** the produce **of the** same **owner of the pile,** the question is: **And with the knowledge** and consent **of whom** may he do so? **If we say** it is **with the knowledge** of the one tithing the produce, **who designated him an agent** to do so? One cannot tithe another's produce unless he is designated as an agent.

אֶלָּא לְדַעְתּוֹ דְּבַעַל הַכְּרִי – הָא קְמְהַנֵּי לֵיהּ, דְּקָעָבֵיד שְׁלִיחוּתֵיהּ! אֶלָּא מִשֶּׁלּוֹ עַל שֶׁל הַכְּרִי. וּלְדַעְתּוֹ דְּמַאן? אִילֵימָא לְדַעְתּוֹ דְּבַעַל הַכְּרִי – הָא קְמְהַנֵּי לֵיהּ! אֶלָּא לָאו – לְדַעְתֵּיהּ דְּנַפְשֵׁיהּ, וּמִשֶּׁלּוֹ תּוֹרֵם עַל שֶׁל חֲבֵירוֹ. וְאִי אָמְרַתְּ צָרִיךְ דַּעַת – הָא קְמְהַנֵּי לֵיהּ! אֶלָּא לָאו – אֵין צָרִיךְ דַּעַת.

Rather, it must be that he is tithing **with the knowledge of the owner of the pile.** However, in that case, by tithing the produce **isn't he benefiting** the owner, as **he is performing** the action in fulfillment of the **agency** of the owner?[N] **Rather,** it must be that he separates *teruma* **from his own** produce **on** behalf of the produce of the owner of **the pile.** The Gemara asks: **And with the knowledge** and consent **of whom** is he doing so? **If we say** it is **with the knowledge of the owner of the pile, isn't he benefiting** the owner? He is performing the action in fulfillment of the agency of the owner. **Rather, is it not** that he is tithing **on** the basis of **his own knowledge,**[N] **and he is separating from his own** produce **on** behalf of **the produce of another? And if you say that** in order to tithe from one's produce on behalf of the produce of the owner, it **requires** the owner's **knowledge** and consent, **isn't he benefiting** the owner? **Rather, is it not** that one may conclude from here that in order to tithe from one's produce on behalf of the produce of another, one **does not require** the **knowledge** and consent of the owner of the pile?

NOTES

Isn't he benefiting the owner as he is performing the action in fulfillment of the agency of the owner – הָא קְמְהַנֵּי לֵיהּ דְּקָעָבֵיד שְׁלִיחוּתֵיהּ: Throughout the discussion in the Gemara, the assumption is that when a person from whom benefit is forbidden for him performs an action on his behalf, it is characterized as benefit. Some maintain, on this basis, that even in the case of services that the one for whom benefit is forbidden may receive, e.g., being taught Torah, the service is forbidden if he specifically requests it. This is because fulfilling a request is considered a benefit in and of itself.

The question arises: Doesn't one benefit from the fact that more of his produce remains available to him, as he need not designate any of it as *teruma*? The commentaries answer: By Torah law, one fulfills his obligation by separating one kernel of wheat for the entire pile, and therefore the benefit that the one separating the *teruma* provides the owner of the produce is minuscule. Any *teruma* that he separates beyond that kernel is on his own initiative, and he does not thereby benefit the owner of the produce (Rabbi Yitzḥak Tzarfati).

On the basis of his own knowledge – לְדַעְתֵּיהּ דְּנַפְשֵׁיהּ: Although he gave of his own property to render the produce of one who is prohibited from benefiting from him exempt, this is not considered benefit, because he did not actually give him anything. This is in accordance with the opinion of Ḥanan (33b), that as long as the benefit is not directly transferred to the one who is prohibited from benefiting, it is not forbidden (Rashba; Meiri). The Ran holds that this *halakha* is even in accordance with the opinion of the sons of High Priests, as the one who separates the *teruma* from his own produce derives benefit from doing so, i.e., the discretionary benefit and fulfillment of a mitzva. Therefore, when separating the *teruma* from his own produce he indirectly causes benefit for the one for whom benefit is forbidden.

לְעוֹלָם מִשֶּׁל בַּעַל הַכְּרִי עַל בַּעַל הַכְּרִי. כִּדְאָמַר רָבָא: בְּאוֹמֵר ״כׇּל הָרוֹצֶה לִתְרוֹם יָבֹא וְיִתְרוֹם״, הָכָא נַמִי בְּאוֹמֵר וכו׳.

The Gemara rejects that conclusion. **Actually,** it is a case where he separates *teruma* **from** the produce of the **owner of the pile for** the produce **of the same owner of the pile.** However, the circumstances here are parallel to those addressed by Rava in another context, **as Rava said** that there is a case **where one says: Anyone who wishes to come and separate *teruma*[H] may come and separate *teruma*.[H] Here too,** this is a case **where one says:** Anyone who wishes to come and separate *teruma* may come and separate *teruma*. In that case, one may tithe another's produce without being designated as his agent.

בְּעָא מִינֵּיהּ רַבִּי יִרְמְיָה מֵרַבִּי זֵירָא: הַתּוֹרֵם מִשֶּׁלּוֹ עַל שֶׁל חֲבֵירוֹ, טוֹבַת הֲנָאָה שֶׁל מִי? מִי אָמְרִינַן: אִי לָאו פֵּירֵי דְּהָאֵיךְ – מִי מִתַּקְנָא כַּרְיָא דְּהַהוּא, אוֹ דִּלְמָא אִי לָאו כַּרְיָא דְּהַהוּא – לָא הָוְיָין פֵּירֵי דְּהָדֵין תְּרוּמָה?

Rabbi Yirmeya raised a dilemma before Rabbi Zeira: In a case where **one separates *teruma* from his own** produce **for** the produce **of another, who** is entitled to **the discretionary benefit,**[N] i.e., the right to give the *teruma* to the priest of his choosing? **Do we say: If not for the produce of this** one separating the *teruma*, **would the pile of that** owner of the produce **be properly tithed,** and therefore the one separating the *teruma* is entitled to the discretionary benefit? **Or, perhaps** we say: **If not for the pile of that** owner of the pile, **the produce of this** one separating the *teruma* **would not be *teruma*,** and therefore the owner is entitled to the discretionary benefit.

אֲמַר לֵיהּ: אָמַר קְרָא ״אֵת כׇּל תְּבוּאַת זַרְעֶךָ...וְנָתַתָּ״.

Rabbi Zeira **said to him** that as **the verse states:** "You shall tithe **all the produce of your seed... and you shall give**" (Deuteronomy 14:22, 26), this indicates that the discretion to give the *teruma* to the priest of his choosing is the prerogative of the one to whom the pile of the produce belongs.

אֵיתִיבֵיהּ: תּוֹרֵם אֶת תְּרוּמוֹתָיו וְאֶת מַעַשְׂרוֹתָיו לְדַעְתּוֹ. וְאִי אָמְרַתְּ טוֹבַת הֲנָאָה דְּבַעַל הַכְּרִי – הָא קָא מְהַנֵּי לֵיהּ! אֶלָּא שְׁמַע מִינַּהּ – טוֹבַת הֲנָאָה דִּילֵיהּ. אָמְרִי: לָא, מִשֶּׁל בַּעַל הַכְּרִי עַל שֶׁל בַּעַל הַכְּרִי. וּלְדַעְתּוֹ דְּבַעַל הַכְּרִי, בְּאוֹמֵר ״כׇּל הָרוֹצֶה לִתְרוֹם יָבֹא וְיִתְרוֹם״.

Rabbi Yirmeya **raised an objection to** Rabbi Zeira from the mishna: For someone who is prohibited by vow from benefiting from him, **he separates his *teruma* and his tithes,** provided that it is **with the knowledge** and consent of the owner of the produce. **And if you say** that the right to **the discretionary benefit** belongs **to the owner of the pile,** by separating *teruma* for his produce, **isn't he benefiting** the owner? **Rather, conclude from** the mishna that the right to **the discretionary benefit** belongs **to** the one separating the *teruma*. The Sages **say: No,** actually this could even be a case where one separates *teruma* **from** the produce **of the owner of the pile for** the produce **of the owner of the pile, and** he does so with the **knowledge of the owner of the pile, where he says: Anyone who wishes to come and separate *teruma* may come and separate *teruma*.**

תָּא שְׁמַע, דְּאָמַר רַבִּי אַבָּהוּ אָמַר רַבִּי יוֹחָנָן: הַמַּקְדִּישׁ מוֹסִיף חוֹמֶשׁ, וּמִתְכַּפֵּר עוֹשֶׂה תְּמוּרָה, וְהַתּוֹרֵם מִשֶּׁלּוֹ עַל שֶׁאֵינוֹ שֶׁלּוֹ – טוֹבַת הֲנָאָה שֶׁלּוֹ.

Come and **hear** a resolution of Rabbi Yirmeya's dilemma, **as Rabbi Abbahu said** that **Rabbi Yoḥanan said:** In a case where one consecrates an animal as an offering for another and it becomes blemished, only **the one who consecrates** the animal **adds one-fifth**[NH] to the cost of redeeming the animal, and the one seeking atonement through this offering does not. **And** since the body of the animal belongs to **the one seeking atonement** through the offering, only he **renders** a non-sacred animal exchanged for the sacred animal, consecrated as **a substitute.**[NH] **And** in the case of **one who separates *teruma* from his own** produce **for** produce **that is not his, the discretionary benefit is his.**[H]

NOTES

The discretionary benefit – **טוֹבַת הֲנָאָה**: In general, discretionary benefit is not the result of direct payment. Rather, it is profit that stems from one's very ability to perform a certain action. Here too, although it is prohibited for a priest to pay a Jew in exchange for receiving *teruma*, the priest is still aware of who is giving him *teruma*, and he may be inclined to privilege the one who donated *teruma* to him in some way. Therefore, being able to decide to which priest one gives his *teruma* provides one with benefit.

As the commentaries have noted, this discretionary benefit can be manifest in financial gain, as it is permitted for one to give a gift to a Jew so that he will give his *teruma* to a specific priest. The question of the discretionary benefit received from separating *teruma* from one's own produce on behalf of another is also discussed in the Jerusalem Talmud, where there is a dispute among *amora'im*. Some say that the recipient of the discretionary benefit is the owner of the pile, and others hold that it is the one separating the *teruma*.

The one who consecrates the animal adds one-fifth – **הַמַּקְדִּישׁ מוֹסִיף חוֹמֶשׁ**: The *halakha* with regard to owners who redeem their own consecrated property is that they add one-fourth of the value of the consecrated item, which is one-fifth of the total payment. *Tosafot* write that the verse directly ties the payment of one-fifth to the one who consecrated the item, as it is written: "And if he that sanctified it will redeem his house, then he shall add the fifth part of the money of your valuation unto it, and it shall be his" (Leviticus 27:15).

And the one seeking atonement through the offering, only he renders it a substitute – **וּמִתְכַּפֵּר עוֹשֶׂה תְּמוּרָה**: The law of substitution appears in the Torah (see Leviticus 27:33) and is addressed in detail in tractate *Temura*. If one had a consecrated animal and exchanged it for another animal of the same species or a different species, blemished or unblemished, he receives lashes, because he violated an explicit Torah prohibition. The original animal remains consecrated and the substitute animal becomes consecrated. The *halakha* that only the one seeking atonement with that animal can render the substituted animal consecrated is discussed at length in tractate *Temura* (10a), and the *amora'im* derive the *halakha* based on logical reasoning.

HALAKHA

Anyone who wishes to come and separate *teruma* – **כׇּל הָרוֹצֶה לִתְרוֹם**: In the case of one who announced: Anyone who wishes to separate *teruma* may come and separate it, and he did not name a specific individual, even one from whom benefit is forbidden may separate the *teruma*. This ruling is in accordance with the opinion of Rava (Rambam *Sefer Hafla'a*, *Hilkhot Nedarim* 6:6).

Anyone who wishes to come and separate *teruma* may come and separate *teruma* – **כׇּל הָרוֹצֶה לִתְרוֹם יָבֹא וְיִתְרוֹם**: If one separates *teruma* from his own produce on behalf of the produce of another, it is *teruma* and the other person's produce is no longer untithed produce. The Rambam holds that the resolution of the next dilemma in the Gemara, which concerns the discretionary benefit, resolves this dilemma as well, as there one separates the *teruma* without the knowledge of the owner of the produce (Rambam *Sefer Zera'im*, *Hilkhot Terumot* 4:2 and *Kesef Mishne* there).

The one who consecrates the animal adds one-fifth – **הַמַּקְדִּישׁ מוֹסִיף חוֹמֶשׁ**: If an animal consecrated for sacrifice on the altar develops a blemish, the one who consecrated it adds one-fifth when he redeems it. However, if it is redeemed by another person, even if the offering was designated to atone for him, he need not add one-fifth (Rambam *Sefer Hafla'a*, *Hilkhot Arakhin VaḤaramim* 7:4).

And the one seeking atonement through the offering, only he renders it a substitute – **וּמִתְכַּפֵּר עוֹשֶׂה תְּמוּרָה**: If one consecrates an offering, e.g., a nazirite offering, on behalf of another, only the nazirite is capable of substituting another animal for that one, i.e., he is flogged and both animals are sacred. The one who consecrated the offering is unable to do so, as it is no longer his (Rambam *Sefer Korbanot*, *Hilkhot Temura* 1:4).

The discretionary benefit is his – **טוֹבַת הֲנָאָה שֶׁלּוֹ**: If one separates *teruma* from his own produce on behalf of another, the discretionary benefit belongs to the one who separated the *teruma*, and he can give the *teruma* to any priest that he chooses (Rambam *Sefer Zera'im*, *Hilkhot Terumot* 4:2).

"מְלַמְּדוֹ מִדְרָשׁ הֲלָכוֹת וְאַגָּדוֹת. אֲבָל לֹא יְלַמְּדֶנּוּ מִקְרָא". מִקְרָא מַאי טַעֲמָא לֹא יְלַמְּדֶנּוּ – מִשּׁוּם דְּקָמְהַנֵּי לֵיהּ, מִדְרָשׁ נַמִּי קָמְהַנֵּי לֵיהּ! אָמַר שְׁמוּאֵל: בְּמָקוֹם שֶׁנּוֹטְלִין שָׂכָר עַל הַמִּקְרָא וְאֵין נוֹטְלִין שָׂכָר עַל הַמִּדְרָשׁ. מַאי פָּסְקָא?

§ We learned in the mishna that one **teaches** someone who is prohibited by vow from benefiting from him **midrash, *halakhot*, and *aggadot*, but he may not teach him Bible.** The Gemara asks: **What is the reason** that **he may not teach him Bible?** Is it **due to** the fact **that** the teacher **benefits** the one for whom benefit from him is forbidden by teaching him Bible? When he teaches him **midrash he also benefits him. Shmuel said:** The mishna is referring **to a place where one takes payment for** teaching **Bible**[N] **and one does not take payment for** teaching **midrash.** By teaching him Bible, the one for whom benefit is forbidden, benefits from the fact that he does not pay. The Gemara asks: **Why was the *halakha*** stated **without qualification?** There is no apparent fundamental difference between Bible and midrash. Why did the mishna refer specifically to a case where payment is taken for teaching Bible?

NOTES

Where one takes payment for teaching Bible – שֶׁנּוֹטְלִין שָׂכָר עַל הַמִּקְרָא: According to the Rid, in a place where one takes payment for teaching Bible, it is prohibited to teach it to one for whom benefit is forbidden from him, even if the other pays him for teaching him, because he provides benefit to him by teaching him. The Rid consistently holds that one may not provide benefit to someone who may not benefit from him, even if he pays him for that benefit. Rabbi Avraham min HaHar holds that if he pays for the benefit, it is not considered benefit and it is permitted.

Perek **IV**
Daf **37** Amud **a**

הָא קָא מַשְׁמַע לָן, דַּאֲפִילּוּ בְּמָקוֹם שֶׁנּוֹטְלִין שָׂכָר, עַל הַמִּקְרָא – שָׁרֵי לְמִשְׁקַל, עַל הַמִּדְרָשׁ – לָא שָׁרֵי לְמִשְׁקַל.

The Gemara answers: **This teaches us that even in a place where one takes payment** for teaching, **for** teaching **Bible** it is **permitted to take** payment,[H] but **for** teaching **midrash** it is **not permitted to take** payment.

מַאי שְׁנָא מִדְרָשׁ דְּלָא – דִּכְתִיב "וְאֹתִי צִוָּה ה׳ בָּעֵת הַהִיא לְלַמֵּד אֶתְכֶם" וּכְתִיב "רְאֵה לִמַּדְתִּי אֶתְכֶם חֻקִּים וּמִשְׁפָּטִים כַּאֲשֶׁר צִוַּנִי ה׳" מָה אֲנִי בְּחִנָּם – אַף אַתֶּם נַמִּי בְּחִנָּם. מִקְרָא נַמִּי בְּחִנָּם!

The Gemara asks: In **what** way **is midrash different** from Bible, **that** one may **not** take payment for teaching it? Based on that **which is written,** which Moses said to the people: **"And the Lord commanded me at that time to teach you** statutes and laws" (Deuteronomy 4:14), **and** also that which **is written: "Behold, I have taught you statutes and laws, as the Lord** my God **commanded me,** that you should do so in the midst of the land where you go in to possess it" (Deuteronomy 4:5), God said: **Just as I** teach you **for free,**[N] without payment, **so too you also** shall teach **for free.** There should be no difference between Bible and midrash, and **Bible too,** like midrash, should be taught **for free.**

רַב אָמַר: שְׂכַר שִׁימּוּר, וְרַבִּי יוֹחָנָן אָמַר: שְׂכַר פִּיסּוּק טְעָמִים.

Rav said: As Bible is typically taught to children, one who teaches Bible takes **payment** for **watching** the children. **And Rabbi Yoḥanan said:** He takes **payment** for teaching **punctuation** of the text with **cantillation notes.**[N]

תְּנַן: לֹא יְלַמְּדֶנּוּ מִקְרָא. בִּשְׁלָמָא לְמַאן דְּאָמַר שְׂכַר פִּיסּוּק טְעָמִים – הַיְינוּ דְּלֹא יְלַמְּדֶנּוּ, אֶלָּא לְמַאן דְּאָמַר שְׂכַר שִׁימּוּר – גָּדוֹל בַּר שִׁימּוּר הוּא? בְּקָטָן קָתָנֵי.

We learned in the mishna that one for whom benefit from another is forbidden by a vow, that other person **may not teach him Bible. Granted, according to the one who says** that the **payment** is for teaching **punctuation** of the text with **cantillation notes, this is** the reason **that he shall not teach him Bible,** as teaching punctuation is a component of teaching the biblical text. **However, according to the one who says** it is **payment** for **watching** the students, **is an adult one who requires watching,** and would payment be taken for doing so? Since the teacher typically does not receive payment for teaching adults, there is no benefit when he teaches for free the one for whom benefit is forbidden; why, then, is it prohibited? The Gemara answers: The mishna **is teaching** about the case **of a minor** who requires watching and who is prohibited by a vow from deriving benefit from the teacher.

אִי בְּקָטָן – אֵימָא סֵיפָא: אֲבָל מְלַמֵּד אֶת בָּנָיו מִקְרָא, קָטָן בַּר בָּנִים הוּא?! חַסּוּרֵי מִחַסְּרָא וְהָכִי קָתָנֵי: לֹא יְלַמְּדֶנּוּ מִקְרָא – בְּקָטָן. אִם הָיָה גָּדוֹל – מְלַמְּדוֹ לוֹ וּלְבָנָיו מִקְרָא.

The Gemara asks: **If** it is the case **of a minor, say the latter clause** of the mishna: **However, he may teach his sons Bible. Is a minor one** who is **capable of** bearing **sons?** The Gemara answers: **The mishna is incomplete, and this** is what **it is teaching: He may not teach him Bible, in** the case of **a minor. If** the student **is an adult, he may teach him and his sons Bible.** He may teach him because he does not require watching, and he may teach his son because the payment is for watching his son.

HALAKHA

For teaching Bible, it is permitted to take payment – עַל הַמִּקְרָא שָׁרֵי לְמִשְׁקַל: In a place where it is customary to take payment for teaching Bible, it is permitted to do so. However, it is prohibited to take payment for teaching Oral Torah. Later authorities rule that today it is permitted to take payment for teaching Oral Torah under certain conditions (*Beit Yosef*; Rambam *Sefer HaMadda, Hilkhot Talmud Torah* 1:7; *Shulḥan Arukh, Yoreh De'a* 245:6, and in the comment of Rema).

NOTES

Just as I teach you for free – מָה אֲנִי בְּחִנָּם: Most commentaries understood this as follows: Just as I teach you for free, so too you also shall teach your students for free. *Tosafot* write that the fact that Moses taught for free is a logical conclusion, as he was wealthy and did not need payment. The Rosh and the Rambam understood this derivation: Just as I learned from God for free, so too you shall learn for free throughout the generations.

Payment for teaching punctuation with cantillation notes – שְׂכַר פִּיסּוּק טְעָמִים: Some have explained that the reference is not to the cantillation notes themselves, as they were received as a tradition from Sinai. Similarly, the reference is not to the punctuation that facilitates the interpretation of the verses, as that is integral to the study of those verses. Rather, the reference here is to the oral rendition of those notes, which is a manner of reading based on custom and not integral to the learning process (*Keren Ora*; *Birkat Avraham*).

HALAKHA

Children may not read a passage in the Bible for the first time – **תִּינוֹקוֹת לֹא קוֹרִין בַּתְּחִילָּה**: On Shabbat, it is prohibited to teach small children material that they did not learn previously, due to the exertion involved. However, it is permitted for them to review material that they were taught once before (Rambam *Sefer HaMadda, Hilkhot Talmud Torah* 2:2; *Shulḥan Arukh, Yoreh De'a* 245:14).

Does not give him payment for Shabbat – **אֵין נוֹתְנִין לוֹ שְׂכַר שַׁבָּת**: If one hires a laborer to safeguard an item for him, that laborer cannot receive direct payment for doing so on Shabbat. Therefore, if the item is stolen or lost on Shabbat, the laborer is not responsible to compensate the owner. However, if he was hired for a longer period of time, e.g., a week, the owner may incorporate payment for Shabbat within the general payment. In this case, the laborer is responsible to compensate the owner if the item is stolen on Shabbat. The laborer must not explicitly demand payment for Shabbat but should request payment for the entire period (Rambam *Sefer Zemanim, Hilkhot Shabbat* 6:25; *Shulḥan Arukh, Oraḥ Ḥayyim* 306:4).

BACKGROUND

Read for the first time – **קוֹרִין בַּתְּחִילָּה**: The educational method in those days involved the teacher teaching the children a verse until they were able to read it themselves. He would provide an age-appropriate explanation. After learning the verse and its meaning, they would review it several times until the children learned it by heart. They would then continue to the next verse. Clearly, the first time they learned the verse was the most difficult, and it became easier with each subsequent review.

מֵיתִיבֵי: תִּינוֹקוֹת לֹא קוֹרִין בַּתְּחִילָּה בְּשַׁבָּת, אֶלָּא שׁוֹנִין בְּרִאשׁוֹן. בִּשְׁלָמָא לְמַאן דְּאָמַר שְׂכַר פִּיסּוּק טְעָמִים – הַיְינוּ דְּאֵין קוֹרִין בַּתְּחִילָּה בְּשַׁבָּת. אֶלָּא לְמַאן דְּאָמַר שְׂכַר שִׁימּוּר – אַמַּאי אֵין קוֹרִין בַּתְּחִילָּה בְּשַׁבָּת וְאַמַּאי שׁוֹנִין בְּרִאשׁוֹן? הָא אִיכָּא שְׂכַר שִׁימּוּר דְּשַׁבָּת!

The Gemara **raises an objection** from a *baraita*: **Children may not read** a passage in the Bible **for the first time**[HB] **on Shabbat; however, they may review** a passage that they already learned **once. Granted, according to the one who says** that **payment** for teaching Bible is for teaching **punctuation** of the text with **cantillation notes, this is** the reason that **children may not read** a passage in the Bible **for the first** time **on Shabbat,** as it would be necessary to pay the teacher. **However, according to the one who says** it is **payment** for **watching** the children, **why may** children **not read** a passage in the Bible **for the first** time **on Shabbat? And why may** children **review** a passage that they already learned **once? Isn't there payment** for **watching** the children **on Shabbat** in both cases?

וְלִיטַעֲמִיךְ, שְׂכַר פִּיסּוּק בְּשַׁבָּת מִי אָסוּר? הַבְלָעָה הִיא, וְהַבְלָעָה מִישְׁרָא שְׁרֵי. דְּתַנְיָא: הַשּׂוֹכֵר אֶת הַפּוֹעֵל לִשְׁמוֹר אֶת הַתִּינוֹק, לִשְׁמוֹר אֶת הַפָּרָה, לִשְׁמוֹר אֶת הַזְּרָעִים – אֵין נוֹתְנִין לוֹ שְׂכַר שַׁבָּת. לְפִיכָךְ

The Gemara responds: **And according to your reasoning, is** receiving **payment** for teaching **punctuation prohibited on Shabbat? It is** a case of **incorporation** of the payment for teaching on Shabbat into the teacher's weekly salary, **and incorporation is permitted, as it is taught** in a *baraita*: **One who hires** a day **laborer to watch a child, to watch a cow,** or **to guard seeds does not give him payment for Shabbat.**[HN] **Therefore,**

NOTES

Payment for Shabbat – **שְׂכַר שַׁבָּת**: Payment for work performed on Shabbat is not prohibited due to the labor, as the Gemara is referring to actions permitted on Shabbat. It is prohibited because gives the appearance of a business transaction, which is prohibited by rabbinic decree on Shabbat. When payment for work done on Shabbat is incorporated within a general payment it is inconspicuous and therefore permitted (Meiri).

Perek **IV**
Daf **37** Amud **b**

NOTES

At leisure, etc. – **דִּיפְנוּ וכו׳**: Rashi explains that teaching new material to children on Shabbat involves the expenditure of significant time and effort, leaving the parents unable to fulfill the mitzva [*lemitzvata*] of delighting in Shabbat. *Tosafot* write that if the parents exert themselves to teach their children new material they will not have time to eat the Shabbat meal in a relaxed manner. The Ran writes that if parents teach their children new material, the parents will not want to interrupt their studies and will not have the opportunity to enjoy their company on Shabbat. There is a variant reading of the text: To listen to them [*lemitzta*], meaning that children may not read a passage in the Bible for the first time, so that the parents can devote the time to listening to the children review their lessons (Rabbi Yitzḥak Tzarfati). On a similar note, there is another variant reading of the text: To study together [*lemetzavta*] with the children, which they are able to do when the material being studied was already learned by the child (*Shita Mekubbetzet*).

אִם אָבְדוּ – אֵינוֹ חַיָּיב בְּאַחֲרָיוּתָן. וְאִם הָיָה שְׂכִיר שַׁבָּת, שְׂכִיר חֹדֶשׁ, שְׂכִיר שָׁנָה, שְׂכִיר שָׁבוּעַ – נוֹתֵן לוֹ שְׂכַר שַׁבָּת. לְפִיכָךְ, אִם אָבְדוּ – חַיָּיב בְּאַחֲרָיוּתָן.

if the items that the laborer was entrusted to watch **were lost** on Shabbat, **he does not bear** financial **responsibility** to compensate the owners **for them,** since he is not a paid bailee on that day. **And if** he is a laborer **hired for a week, hired for a month, hired for a year,** or **hired for seven years,** the one who hired him **gives him payment** for labor performed on **Shabbat** as well. **Therefore, if** the items **were lost** on Shabbat, **he bears** financial **responsibility** to compensate the owners **for them.** If payment for Shabbat is incorporated within payment for a longer period, it is not prohibited to accept payment for permitted actions performed on Shabbat.

אֶלָּא גַּבֵּי שַׁבָּת הַיְינוּ טַעְמָא דְּאֵין קוֹרְאִין בַּתְּחִילָּה – מִשּׁוּם דִּיפְנוּ אֲבָהָתְהוֹן דְּיָנוֹקֵי לְמִצְוָתָא דְּשַׁבְּתָא. וְאִיבָּעֵית אֵימָא: מִשּׁוּם דְּבְשַׁבְּתָא אָכְלִין וְשָׁתִין, וְיַקִּיר עֲלֵיהוֹן עָלְמָא. כִּדְאָמַר שְׁמוּאֵל: שִׁינּוּי וֶסֶת תְּחִילַּת חוֹלִי מֵעַיִם.

Rather, with regard to Shabbat, this is the reason that children **may not read** a passage in the Bible **for the first** time on Shabbat, **so that the fathers of the children will be at leisure**[N] **to fulfill the mitzva of delighting in Shabbat.** Teaching new material to their children would occupy more of their fathers' time, limiting their opportunity to fulfill that mitzva. **And if you wish, say** instead: **Due to** the fact **that on Shabbat** children **eat and drink** more than they are accustomed to eating, **their world is heavy upon them,** i.e., their head and their limbs are sluggish, and they are incapable of concentrating and studying well, **as Shmuel said: A change in routine** [*veset*] in eating and the like causes **the onset of an intestinal ailment.**[B]

BACKGROUND

The onset of an intestinal ailment – **תְּחִילַּת חוֹלִי מֵעַיִם**: A radical change in eating habits, a change in the type of food consumed, or a substantial increase in the amount of food consumed, causes parallel changes in the digestive system. Although such drastic changes do not usually cause actual illness, they can create an uncomfortable sensation and even pain

וּלְמַאן דְּאָמַר שְׂכַר פִּיסּוּק טְעָמִים, מַאי טַעְמָא לָא אָמַר שְׂכַר שִׁימּוּר? קָסָבַר: בָּנוֹת מִי קָא בָּעְיָין שִׁימּוּר?

And according to the one who says that the payment for teaching Bible is **payment** for teaching **punctuation** of the text with **cantillation notes,**[B] and therefore in the case of one for whom benefit from another is forbidden by vow, that other person may not teach his sons and daughters Bible, **what is the reason** that he **did not say** that it is **payment** for **watching** the children? The Gemara answers: **He holds: Do girls need watching?** They stay home and are not accustomed to going out.

וּלְמַאן דְּאָמַר שְׂכַר שִׁימּוּר, מַאי טַעְמָא לָא אָמַר שְׂכַר פִּיסּוּק טְעָמִים? קָסָבַר: (שְׂכַר) פִּיסּוּק טְעָמִים דְּאוֹרָיְיתָא הוּא.

The Gemara asks: **And according to the one who says** that the payment for teaching Bible is **payment** for **watching** the children, **what is the reason** that he **did not say** that it is **payment** for teaching **punctuation** of the text with **cantillation notes?** The Gemara answers: **He holds** that **the punctuation** of the text with **cantillation notes is by Torah law;** therefore, it is included in the prohibition against taking payment for teaching Torah.

דְּאָמַר רַב אִיקָא בַּר אָבִין אָמַר רַב חֲנַנְאֵל אָמַר רַב: מַאי דִּכְתִיב "וַיִּקְרְאוּ בַסֵּפֶר בְּתוֹרַת הָאֱלֹהִים מְפֹרָשׁ וְשׂוֹם שֶׂכֶל וַיָּבִינוּ בַּמִּקְרָא". "וַיִּקְרְאוּ בַסֵּפֶר בְּתוֹרַת הָאֱלֹהִים" – זֶה מִקְרָא: "מְפֹרָשׁ" זֶה תַּרְגּוּם: "וְשׂוֹם שֶׂכֶל" – אֵלּוּ הַפְּסוּקִים: "וַיָּבִינוּ בַּמִּקְרָא" – זֶה פִּיסּוּק טְעָמִים, וְאָמְרִי לַהּ: אֵלּוּ הַמָּסוֹרוֹת.

This is **as Rabbi Ika bar Avin said** that **Rav Ḥananel said** that **Rav said: What is** the meaning of that **which is written: "And they read in the book, in the Torah of God, distinctly; and they gave the sense, and caused them to understand the reading"** (Nehemiah 8:8)? The Gemara explains: **"They read in the book, in the Torah of God"; that is the Bible. "Distinctly"; that is** the Aramaic **translation. "And they gave the sense"; these are the** division into **verses. "And caused them to understand the reading"; this is punctuation** of the text with **cantillation notes,** which facilitate the understanding of the verses. **And some say: These are the traditions**[N] that determine the proper vocalization of the Bible. Rav holds that the cantillation notes are an integral part of Torah study.

אָמַר רַבִּי יִצְחָק: מִקְרָא סוֹפְרִים, וְעִיטּוּר סוֹפְרִים, וְקִרְיָין וְלָא כְּתִיבָן, וּכְתִיבָן וְלָא קִרְיָין – הֲלָכָה לְמֹשֶׁה מִסִּינַי.

On a related note, **Rabbi Yitzḥak said: The vocalization of the scribes,**[N] **and the ornamentation of the scribes, and** the verses with words that are **read but not written, and** those that are **written but not read** are all ***halakha*** transmitted **to Moses from Sinai.**

מִקְרָא סוֹפְרִים – "אָרֶץ", "שָׁמַיִם" "מִצְרַיִם".

The Gemara elaborates: **The vocalization of the scribes** is referring to words that when they appear at the end of phrases, clauses, or verses, their vocalization changes, e.g., *eretz* with a *segol* under the letter *alef* to **aretz** with a *kamatz* under the letter *alef*; *shamayim* with a *pataḥ* under the letter *mem*, to **shamayim** with a *kamatz* under the letter *mem*; and *mitzrayim* with a *pataḥ* under the letter *reish*, to **mitzrayim** with a *kamatz* under the letter *reish*.

NOTES

And some say these are the traditions – וְאָמְרִי לַהּ אֵלּוּ הַמָּסוֹרוֹת: These are the principles of tradition that dictate the manner in which the text of the Bible is to be read. There are many instances where a word is read differently than it is written. The list that follows in the Gemara is incomplete, as it includes only entire words, while most instance involve the addition or subtraction of letters in a word. There are additional instances where the manner in which words are read and punctuated is based on tradition. The commentaries write that the opinion of Rabbi Yoḥanan, who permits accepting payment for teaching punctuation of the text with cantillation notes, is based on this opinion that the cantillation notes are not an integral part of the Oral Torah; it is the traditions that are integral to the Oral Torah.

The vocalization of the scribes – מִקְרָא סוֹפְרִים: Rashi explains that this is referring to traditions concerning vocalization, as the proper pronunciation of words whose vocalization is not dictated by their spelling is learned only from tradition. For example, the word *eretz* is pronounced that way although it is not written *alef, yod, reish, yod, tzadi* and *aretz* is not written *alef, alef, reish, yod, tzadi* to indicate their vocalization. Others interpret this in a more limited manner, corresponding to the written examples, that it is only through tradition that it is known when to read *aretz* and when to read *eretz*. With regard to other words, it is through tradition that it is known to use the plural form used for pairs, e.g., *mitzrayim* and *shamayim*, and not the simple plural, *mitzrim* and *shamim* (Rosh; Ran). *Tosafot* explain that the reference is to the instances where the vocalization is changed from *segol* to *kamatz*, or from *pataḥ* to *kamatz* when the word appears at one of the stops in the verse.

BACKGROUND

Punctuation of the text with cantillation notes – פִּיסּוּק טְעָמִים: There are neither spaces nor punctuation indicating the beginnings and ends of verses in a Torah scroll. Yet clearly, the first step in properly understanding a verse is reading it properly. There was a dispute between Rav and Rabbi Yoḥanan whether the cantillation notes are considered an integral part of the Bible, as Oral Torah accompanying the Written Torah, or whether they are merely an aid to Torah study that are not an integral part of that study.

It is also possible that the reference is to the punctuation based on the tune of the cantillation notes of ancient origin, and the question is: Are the tunes integral to the understanding of the Bible or merely a supplement to the punctuation of the Bible?

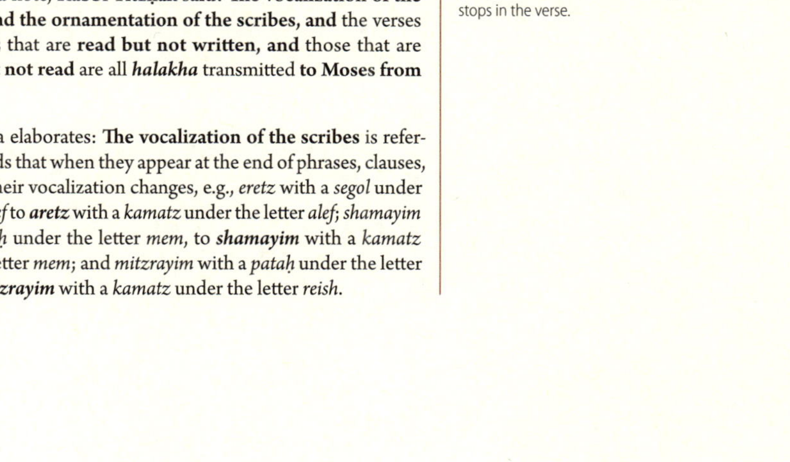

Identical Torah texts with cantillation notes (right) as often appears in print, and without cantillation notes (left) as the text appears in a Torah scroll

עִיטּוּר סוֹפְרִים – ״אַחַר תַּעֲבֹרוּ״, ״אַחַר תֵּלֵךְ״, ״אַחַר תֵּאָסֵף״, ״קִדְּמוּ שָׁרִים אַחַר נֹגְנִים״, ״צִדְקָתְךָ כְּהַרְרֵי אֵל״.

The ornamentation of the scribes[N] are expressions that the scribes understood in a manner that differs slightly from its plain understanding. For example: **"Then [*aḥar*] go on"** (Genesis 18:5); **"then [*aḥar*] she will go"** (Genesis 24:55); **"afterward [*aḥar*] you will be gathered"** (Numbers 31:2); **"the singers go before, the minstrels follow after [*aḥar*]"** (Psalms 68:26); **"Your righteousness is like the mighty mountains"** (Psalms 36:7).[N]

קַרְיָין וְלָא כְּתִיבָן – ״פְּרָת״ דִּ״בְלֶכְתּוֹ״, ״אִישׁ״ דְּ״כַאֲשֶׁר יִשְׁאַל אִישׁ בִּדְבַר הָאֱלֹהִים״, ״בָּאִים״ דְּ״נִבְנְתָה״, ״לָהּ״ דִּ״פְלֵיטָה״, ״אֶת״ דְּ״הֻגֵּד הֻגַּד״, ״אֵלַי״ דְּ״הַגֹּרֶן,״ ״אֵלַי״ דְּ״הַשְּׂעֹרִים״ – הָלֵין קַרְיָין וְלָא כְּתַבָן.

Words that are **read but not written** are included in the *halakha* transmitted to Moses from Sinai. For example, the word **"Euphrates" that** is in the phrase **"as he went** to establish his control over the river Euphrates" (II Samuel 8:3) is not written in the text of the Bible. The same is true for the word **"man" that** is in the verse "now the counsel of Ahithophel, which he counseled in those days, **was as if a man inquired of the word of God"** (II Samuel 16:23); and for the word **"come" that** is in the verse "behold, the days come, says the Lord, that the city **shall be built** to the Lord from the tower of Hananel unto the gate of the corner" (Jeremiah 31:37); and for **"her" that** is in the phrase "let her not have **escape"** (Jeremiah 50:29); **unto that** is in the verse "it has **been told me,** all that you have done unto your mother-in-law" (Ruth 2:11); and for **"to me" that** is found in the passage "and she said unto her: All that you say to me I will do. And she went down to **the threshing floor"** (Ruth 3:4–5); and for **"to me" that** is in the verse "he gave me these six measures of **barley;** for he said to me" (Ruth 3:17). **These** words **are read but not written.**

וּכְתַבָן וְלָא קַרְיָין – ״נָא״ דְּ״יִסְלַח״.

And there are words that are **written but not read.** For example, the word **"may" that** is in the verse "may God **forgive** your servant" (II Kings 5:18) appears in the Bible text but is not vocalized.

NOTES

The ornamentation [*ittur*] of the scribes – עִיטּוּר סוֹפְרִים: There are different explanations of the term ornamentation and the meaning of this entire phrase. Some explain that the term *ittur* is from the term *atara*, meaning crown, or in this context, ornament (see *Berakhot* 4a). Rashi explains that ornamentation of the scribes refers to instances where the words in the verse are not ordered according to the optimal manner to convey its meaning. Rather, the order is changed for aesthetic purposes, e.g., *aḥar ta'avoru*, "then go on," instead of *ta'avoru aḥar*, "go on then." The Rid explains in a similar fashion that ornamentation of the scribes refers to the proper manner in which the scribes understood the verse, which did not always correspond to the meaning of the text based on how it is written.

The Meiri cites an explanation that *ittur* means encirclement or revolution, referring in this context to the fact that words are situated adjacent to one another, not in the conventional order. The Meiri himself and the Ran, citing his teacher, explain *ittur* in the sense of beauty. The cantillation notes for these words are not for the purpose of punctuation. Rather, their purpose is that the verse read more aesthetically. The Ran explains that the word *aḥar* in each of these verses is superfluous, as the verses are comprehensible without it. The word is added so that the verse will read with a flourish.

The *ge'onim*, the *Arukh*, *Tosafot*, and the Rosh in their wake interpret *ittur* as elimination and prove this from the verse: "But the public altars were not eliminated [*lo saru*]" (I Kings 15:14), which is translated in *Targum Yonatan* as *la atra*. The verse: "Then go on [*aḥar ta'avoru*]" (Genesis 18:5) is commonly read as it should have been written: And then go on [*ve'aḥar ta'avoru*]. The scribes who were more meticulous in their reading would eliminate the conjunctive prefix, i.e., the *vav*, and read the verse properly. Rav Hai Gaon comments that in his days uneducated people would add the conjunctive prefix to words when it seemed to them appropriate in context.

Your righteousness is like the mighty mountains – צִדְקָתְךָ כְּהַרְרֵי אֵל: This verse is unlike the others cited, and the commentaries explain why it is here. Rashi explains that it should have been written in a different order: Like the mighty mountains is Your righteousness. The Ran explains that, based on the context, the verse should have been written: Your righteousness is the mighty mountains. In the name of his teacher, the Ran explains that there is a stop after the word mountains, and the meaning of the verse is: Your righteousness is like the mountains, God. However, the Rosh holds that this is another example of *ittur* as elimination because, based on context, the continuation of the verse should have been: And Your judgments [*umishpatekha*] are like the great deep, but the scribes read it properly, without the conjunctive prefix: And.

״זֹאת״ דְּ״הַמִּצְוָה״, ״יִדְרֹךְ״ דְּ״הַדֹּרֵךְ״, ״חֲמֵשׁ״ דִּ״פְאַת נֶגֶב״, ״אִם״ דְּ״כִי גֹאֵל״ – הָלֵין כְּתַבָן וְלָא קַרְיָין.

The same is true for “**this**” **that** is in the verse “and this is **the mitzva**” (Deuteronomy 6:1);[N] and for “**bend**” **that** is in the verse “let **the archer** bend his bow” (Jeremiah 51:3); and for “**five**” **that** is in the verse “and **the south side** four thousand and five hundred” (Ezekiel 48:16); and for “**if**” **that** is in the verse “**that** if I am a **near kinsman**” (Ruth 3:12). All **these are written but not read.**

אֲמַר רַב אַחָא בַּר אַדָּא: בְּמַעַרְבָא פָּסְקִין לְהָדֵין פְּסוּקָא לִתְלָתָא פְּסוּקִין ״וַיֹּאמֶר ה׳ אֶל מֹשֶׁה הִנֵּה אָנֹכִי בָּא אֵלֶיךָ בְּעַב הֶעָנָן״.

Rav Aḥa bar Adda said: In the West, Eretz Yisrael, they **divide this verse**[N] **into three verses: “And the Lord said to Moses, behold I come to you in a thick cloud,** that the people may hear as I speak with you, and may also believe in you forever; and Moses told the words of the people unto the Lord” (Exodus 19:9).

אָמַר רַבִּי חָמָא בְּרַבִּי חֲנִינָא: לֹא הֶעֱשִׁיר מֹשֶׁה אֶלָּא מִפְּסוֹלְתָּן שֶׁל לוּחוֹת, שֶׁנֶּאֱמַר ״פְּסָל לְךָ שְׁנֵי לֻחֹת אֲבָנִים כָּרִאשֹׁנִים״ – פְּסוֹלְתָּן שֶׁלְּךָ יְהֵא.

§ **Rabbi Ḥama, son of Rabbi Ḥanina, said: Moses became wealthy only from the waste** remaining **from** hewing **the Tablets**[N] of the Covenant, **as it is stated: “Hew for you two tablets of stone like the first”** (Exodus 34:1). “Hew for you” means that **their waste shall be yours.** As the tablets were crafted from valuable gems, their remnants were similarly valuable.

אָמַר רַבִּי יוֹסֵי בְּרַבִּי חֲנִינָא: לֹא נִיתְּנָה תּוֹרָה אֶלָּא לְמֹשֶׁה וּלְזַרְעוֹ, שֶׁנֶּאֱמַר ״כְּתָב לְךָ״ ״פְּסָל לְךָ״, מַה פְּסוֹלְתָּן שֶׁלְּךָ – אַף כְּתָבָן שֶׁלְּךָ. מֹשֶׁה נָהַג בָּהּ טוֹבַת עַיִן וּנְתָנָהּ לְיִשְׂרָאֵל, וְעָלָיו הַכָּתוּב אוֹמֵר ״טוֹב עַיִן הוּא יְבֹרָךְ״ וגו׳.

Rabbi Yosei, son of Rabbi Ḥanina, said: The Torah was given initially **only to Moses**[N] **and his descendants, as it is stated: “Write for you”** (Exodus 34:27), and it is also stated: **“Hew for you”** (Exodus 34:1), meaning: **Just as their waste is yours, so too their writing is yours.** However, **Moses treated** the Torah **with generosity and gave it to the Jewish people. And about him, the verse says: “He that has a bountiful eye shall be blessed,** as he gives of his bread to the poor” (Proverbs 22:9).

NOTES

This, that is in the verse: And this is the mitzva [*zot dehamitzva*] – זֹאת דְּהַמִּצְוָה: Early commentaries note that in the traditional standard text of the Bible, there is no word in this verse that is written and not read (*Tosafot*; Ran). There is a variant reading of the Gemara: *Et dehamitzva* instead of *zot dehamitzva*, and the reference is to the verse: “So I took the deed of the purchase, both that which was sealed, the mitzva [*et heḥatum hamitzva*] and the statutes, and that which was open” (Jeremiah 32:11). There are different traditions in Babylonia and in Eretz Yisrael. One tradition is: That which was sealed and the mitzva, and another tradition is: That which was sealed, the mitzva.

In the West they divide this verse, etc. – בְּמַעַרְבָא פָּסְקִין וכו׳: This is cited here in the context of traditions and verses, and Rav Aḥa bar Adda said that even in later generations there are differences with regard to the division of the text into verses.

From the waste remaining from hewing the tablets – מִפְּסוֹלְתָּן שֶׁל לוּחוֹת: The Maharal interprets this as an allusion, meaning that wealth is ancillary, i.e., waste, relative to the transcendent Torah, as it is stated: “Length of days is in her right hand; in her left hand are riches and honor” (Proverbs 3:16).

The Torah was given initially only to Moses, etc. – לֹא נִיתְּנָה תּוֹרָה אֶלָּא לְמֹשֶׁה וכו׳: This statement is difficult, as several verses in the Torah indicate that the Torah was given to the entire Jewish people. Some commentaries explain that when Moses received the first tablets the Torah was given to the entire Jewish people, but here the Gemara is referring to the second tablets (*Iyyun Ya’akov*). Others explain that Rabbi Yosei, son of Rabbi Ḥanina, was referring to those matters mentioned at the conclusion of the Gemara: The Torah, all its mitzvot, and the rules governing their performance were certainly given to the entire Jewish people; however, the profound analysis of the Torah, its allusions, and its esoterica were initially given only to Moses, as they are beyond the comprehension of laymen. Moses generously gave all of it to the Jewish people (Rabbi Yitzḥak Tzarfati).

HALAKHA

The Holy One, Blessed be He, rests His Divine Presence only upon one who is mighty, and wealthy, and wise, and humble – **אין הקדוש ברוך הוא משרה שכינתו אלא על גבור ועשיר וחכם ועניו**: The Rambam wrote that prophecy is bestowed only upon one who is endowed with great wisdom, outstanding character, comprehensive knowledge, and an understanding heart. Some commentaries note that the Rambam interpreted the mishna as a parable (Rambam *Sefer HaMadda*, *Hilkhot Yesodei HaTorah* 7:1).

BACKGROUND

Tablets of the Covenant – **לוחות הברית**: According to the dimensions cited in the Gemara here, even if the material of the tablets was the weight of common solid stone, the weight of the two tablets together would be approximately 250 kg.

מתיב רב חסדא: "ואותי צוה ה׳ בעת ההיא ללמד אתכם"! ואותי צוה, ואני לכם. "ראה למדתי אתכם חקים ומשפטים כאשר צוני ה׳ אלהי"! אותי צוה, ואני לכם.

Rav Ḥisda raised an objection from the verse that states: **"And the Lord commanded me at that time to teach you** statutes and laws" (Deuteronomy 4:14). This indicates that Moses was commanded to teach Torah to the Jewish people from the outset. The Gemara answers: The verse means: **And the Lord commanded** the Torah to **me**, Moses, **and I,** on my own initiative, decided **to** teach **you** its statutes and laws. The Gemara cites an additional verse proving that God commanded to teach the Jewish people from the outset: **"Behold, I have taught you statutes and laws, as the Lord my God commanded me"** (Deuteronomy 4:5). The Gemara answers: **The Lord commanded** the Torah to **me,** Moses, **and I** decided **to** teach **you** statutes and laws.

"ועתה כתבו לכם את השירה הזאת"! השירה לחודה. "למען תהיה לי השירה הזאת לעד בבני ישראל"! אלא פילפולא בעלמא.

The Gemara cites an additional verse: **"Now therefore write this song for you,** and teach it the children of Israel" (Deuteronomy 31:19). Apparently, Moses was commanded to teach the Torah to the Jewish people. The Gemara answers: The verse is referring to **the song** of *Ha'azinu* (Deuteronomy 31) **alone** and not to the rest of the Torah. The Gemara asks: But the continuation of that cited verse: **"That this song may be a witness for Me among the children of Israel"** (Deuteronomy 31:19), indicates that the reference is to the entire Torah, in which the mitzvot are written. Rather, the Torah was given from the outset to all of the Jewish people, and when Rabbi Yosei, son of Rabbi Ḥanina, said that the Torah was given exclusively to Moses, he was referring **merely** to the **profound analysis** of the Torah. Moses opted to teach it to the people on his own initiative.

אמר רבי יוחנן: אין הקדוש ברוך הוא משרה שכינתו אלא על גבור ועשיר וחכם ועניו, וכולן ממשה. גבור – דכתיב "ויפרש את האהל על המשכן" ואמר מר: משה רבינו פרסו, וכתיב "עשר אמות ארך הקרש" וגו׳. אימא דאריך וקטין?

Rabbi Yoḥanan said: The Holy One, Blessed be He, rests His Divine Presence only upon one who is **mighty, and wealthy, and wise, and humble.**[H] **And all of these** qualities are derived **from Moses.** He was **mighty, as it is written: "And he spread the tent over the Tabernacle"** (Exodus 40:19), **and the Master said: Moses, our teacher, spread it** himself. **And it is written: "Ten cubits shall be the length of a board,** and a cubit and a half the breadth of each board" (Exodus 26:16). Moses was tall and strong enough to spread the tent over the boards alone. The Gemara asks: **Say that he was tall and thin,**[N] and the fact that he was mighty cannot be derived.

אלא מן הדין קרא, דכתיב "ואתפש בשני הלחת ואשלכם מעל שתי ידי ואשברם", ותניא: הלוחות ארכן ששה ורחבן ששה ועביין שלשה.

Rather, the fact that Moses was mighty is derived **from this verse, as it is written: "And I took hold of the two tablets, and cast them out of my two hands, and broke them** before your eyes" (Deuteronomy 9:17), **and it is taught** in a *baraita*: **The tablets, their length was six** handbreadths, **and their width was six** handbreadths, **and their thickness was three** handbreadths. If Moses was capable of lifting and casting a burden that heavy, apparently he was mighty.

עשיר – "פסל לך" – פסולתן שלך יהא. חכם – רב ושמואל דאמרי תרוייהו: חמשים שערי בינה נבראו בעולם, וכולם נתנו למשה חסר אחת, שנאמר "ותחסרהו מעט מאלהים". עניו – דכתיב "והאיש משה ענו מאד".

Moses was **wealthy,** as it is written: **"Hew for you"** (Exodus 34:1), from which it was derived: The **waste** of the Tablets of the Covenant[B] **shall be yours,** and that waste consisted of precious stones. That Moses **was wise** is derived from the statement of **Rav and Shmuel, who both say: Fifty measures of understanding were created in the world,**[N] **and all were given to Moses except one, as it is stated: "Yet you have deprived him of little, of God"** (Psalms 8:6). He lacked only complete knowledge of God. Moses was **humble, as it is written: "Now the man Moses was very humble"** (Numbers 12:3).

NOTES

Tall and thin – **אריך וקטין**: Most commentaries explain that this phrase means tall and frail. Rabbi Ya'akov Emden explains that it means tall and thin. In both cases, the indication is that Moses was weak.

Fifty measures of understanding were created in the world – **חמשים שערי בינה נבראו בעולם**: There are several different explanations for this expression, primarily based on the esoteric. The Ran explains this in a manner closer to the plain meaning of the phrase: Moses attained all the transcendent perceptions save the fiftieth measure, the perception of the essence of the Creator, as that is beyond the capacity of human perception.

אמר רבי יוחנן: כל הנביאים עשירים היו, מנלן – ממשה ומשמואל מעמוס ומיונה.

§ **Rabbi Yoḥanan said: All the prophets were wealthy.**[N] **From** where do we derive this? It is derived **from Moses, and from Samuel,** and **from Amos, and from Jonah,** who were all wealthy.

משה – דכתיב "לא חמור אחד מהם נשאתי", אי בלא אגרא – לאפוקי מאן דשקל בלא אגרא?! אלא דאפילו באגרא. דילמא משום דעני הוה. אלא מן "פסל לך" – פסולתן יהא שלך.

Moses was wealthy, **as it is written: "I have not taken one donkey from them"** (Numbers 16:15). The Gemara analyzes the statement of Moses. **If** he said that he did not take a donkey **without payment,** was his intent **to exclude** himself from the category of **one who takes** items that belong to others **without paying?** That is obvious, as one who does so is a thief. **Rather,** he said **that even with payment** he did not take a donkey. Apparently, he was wealthy and did not need to purchase anything. The Gemara rejects this proof. **Perhaps,** on the contrary, he did not purchase a donkey **because he was poor** and could not afford it. **Rather,** it is derived from the verse written with regard to the Tablets of the Covenant: **"Hew for you"** (Exodus 34:1), which indicates that **their waste shall be yours.**

שמואל – דכתיב "הנני ענו בי נגד ה' ונגד משיחו את שור מי לקחתי וחמור מי לקחתי", אי בחנם – לאפוקי מאן דשקל בחנם?! אלא דאפילו בשכר. דלמא דעני הוה. אלא מהכא "ותשבתו הרמתה כי שם ביתו" ואמר רבא: כל מקום שהלך – ביתו עמו.

Samuel was wealthy, **as it is written: "Here I am; witness against me before the Lord, and before His anointed: Whose ox have I taken, or whose donkey have I taken?"** (I Samuel 12:3). **If** he is saying that he did not take an ox or a donkey **for free,** was his intent **to exclude** himself from the category of **one who takes** items that belong to others **for free? Rather,** he is saying **that even with payment** he did not take a donkey or an ox. Apparently, he was wealthy. The Gemara rejects this proof. **Perhaps,** on the contrary, the reason he did not purchase the donkeys is due to the fact **that he was poor. Rather,** the fact that Samuel was wealthy is derived **from here,** as it is written: **"And his return was to Ramah, for there was his house"** (I Samuel 7:17). **And Rava said: Everywhere he went, his home was with him.** He was so wealthy that he could afford to hire servants and pack animals to take all his belongings from place to place.

אמר רבא: גדול מה שנאמר בשמואל יותר משנאמר במשה, דאילו במשה רבינו כתיב "לא חמור אחד מהם נשאתי" – דאפילו בשכר, ואילו גבי שמואל – אפילו ברצון לא שכרו, דכתיב "ויאמרו לא עשקתנו ולא רצותנו" וגו'.

Rava said: That which is stated with regard to Samuel is greater than that which is stated with regard to Moses, as with regard to Moses our teacher it is written: "I have not taken one donkey from them" (Numbers 16:15), meaning that he did not take an item from another against his will **even with payment. Whereas with regard to Samuel, even with** the **consent**[N] of the owner, **he would not rent** an item from him, **as it is written: "And they said: You have not defrauded us, nor oppressed us** [*ratzotanu*], neither have you taken anything from any man's hand" (I Samuel 12:4), even with his consent [*ratzon*].

עמוס – דכתיב "ויען עמוס ויאמר אל אמציה לא נביא אנכי ולא בן נביא אנכי כי בוקר אנכי ובולס שקמים" כדמתרגם רב יוסף: ארי מרי גיתי אנא, ושקמין לי בשפלתא וגו'.

Amos was wealthy, **as it is written: "Then answered Amos, and said to Amaziah: I was no prophet, neither was I a prophet's son; but I was a herdsman, and a dresser of sycamore-trees"** (Amos 7:14). Amos is saying, **as Rav Yosef translates: Because I am the owner of flocks and I have sycamores in the lowland,** and I do not come to prophesy for financial gain. Apparently, Amos was wealthy.

יונה – דכתיב "ויתן שכרה וירד בה" ואמר רבי יוחנן: שנתן שכרה של ספינה כולה. אמר רבי רומנוס: שכרה של ספינה הויא ארבע אלפים דינרי דהבא.

Jonah was wealthy, **as it is written:** "And he went down to Jaffa, and found a ship going to Tarshish, **so he paid its cost and went down into it"** (Jonah 1:3), **and Rabbi Yoḥanan said: He paid the cost of the entire ship.**[N] **Rabbi Romanus said: The cost for the** entire **ship was four thousand gold dinars.**

NOTES

All the prophets were wealthy – כל הנביאים עשירים היו: This is because people tend to respect, and therefore heed, wealthy people. Beyond that, prophets are wealthy for the same reason that the Sages said it is appropriate for a Torah scholar to be wealthy: One who is dependent on the support of others will be unable to castigate the people when necessary. The wealth of prophets empowered them and enabled them to be independent and unconcerned about public opinion.

NOTES

Even with consent – אפילו ברצון: His concern was that they consented to rent him the item only because they were embarrassed to refuse (*Tosafot*).

The cost of the entire ship – שכרה של ספינה כולה: Some explain that this is inferred from the phrase "he paid its cost," literally: He paid her cost. The verse uses the feminine pronoun, referring to the ship, rather than the masculine pronoun, referring to the cost of Jonah's passage (Re'em). The Maharsha explains that since Jonah was in a hurry to flee, he did not wait for the ship to be filled to capacity. He paid the fare that would have been paid had the ship been filled to capacity, so that the captain would embark immediately.

וְאָמַר רַבִּי יוֹחָנָן: בַּתְּחִלָּה הָיָה מֹשֶׁה לָמֵד תּוֹרָה וּמְשַׁכְּחָהּ, עַד שֶׁנִּיתְּנָה לוֹ בְּמַתָּנָה, שֶׁנֶּאֱמַר ״וַיִּתֵּן אֶל מֹשֶׁה כְּכַלֹּתוֹ לְדַבֵּר אִתּוֹ״.

And Rabbi Yoḥanan said: Initially, Moses would study Torah and forget it, until it was given to him as a gift, as it is stated: "And He gave it to Moses when he concluded speaking with him" (Exodus 31:18). Once the Torah was given him as a gift, it became his and he was able to remember it.

מתני׳ וְזָן אֶת אִשְׁתּוֹ וְאֶת בָּנָיו אַף עַל פִּי שֶׁהוּא חַיָּיב בִּמְזוֹנוֹתָן. וְלֹא יָזוּן אֶת בְּהֶמְתּוֹ, בֵּין טְמֵאָה בֵּין טְהוֹרָה. רַבִּי אֱלִיעֶזֶר אוֹמֵר: זָן אֶת הַטְּמֵאָה, וְאֵינוֹ זָן אֶת הַטְּהוֹרָה. אָמְרוּ לוֹ: מַה בֵּין טְמֵאָה לִטְהוֹרָה? אָמַר לְהוּ: שֶׁהַטְּהוֹרָה נַפְשָׁהּ לַשָּׁמַיִם וְגוּפָהּ שֶׁלּוֹ, וּטְמֵאָה

MISHNA **And** with regard to one for whom benefit from another is forbidden by vow, that other person **may feed** his **wife and children,**[NH] **although** the one who is bound by the vow **is obligated in their support** and benefits when another supports them. **And he may not feed his animal, whether** it is a **kosher** animal or **whether** it is a **non-kosher** animal. **Rabbi Eliezer says: He may feed the non-kosher** animal, **and he may not feed the kosher** animal. The Rabbis **said to him: What is the** difference **between kosher and non-kosher** animals in this respect? Rabbi Eliezer **said to them: The kosher** animal's **being** belongs **to Heaven, and** the animal's **body is** the property of its owner, as he can eat it. Therefore, the owner benefits directly when another feeds his animal. **And a non-kosher** animal,

NOTES

And that other person may feed his wife and children – וְזָן אֶת אִשְׁתּוֹ וְאֶת בָּנָיו: Early commentaries discussed at length whether this *halakha* is in accordance with the opinion of Ḥanan or even in accordance with the opinion of the Rabbis. Most commentaries explain that the Rabbis agree with this *halakha*, as they disagree with Ḥanan only where one supports the wife when the husband is away. However, support of a wife when the husband is present is certainly a gift to her and not a benefit for her husband (Rid). The Ran wrote that the one who gives support provides benefit directly to the wife and children, but the husband benefits only indirectly from the fact that he need not support them, and this is not considered actual benefit. Others explain that this refers to a case where he does not provide them with food that they need for subsistence but with food beyond those needs. In that case, the benefit the husband derives is negligible (Rashi; *Talmidei Rabbeinu Peretz*; Re'em, citing Ri).

HALAKHA

And that other person may feed his wife and children – וְזָן אֶת אִשְׁתּוֹ וְאֶת בָּנָיו: One whose benefit is forbidden by vow to another may feed the other person's wife and children; however, he may not feed his kosher and non-kosher animals, in accordance with the unattributed mishna (Rambam *Sefer Hafla'a*, *Hilkhot Nedarim* 6:4; *Shulḥan Arukh*, *Yoreh De'a* 221:2).

נַפְשָׁהּ וְגוּפָהּ לַשָּׁמַיִם. אָמְרוּ לוֹ: אַף הַטְּמֵאָה נַפְשָׁהּ לַשָּׁמַיִם וְגוּפָהּ שֶׁלּוֹ, שֶׁאִם יִרְצֶה – הֲרֵי הוּא מוֹכְרָהּ לְגוֹיִם, אוֹ מַאֲכִילָהּ לִכְלָבִים.

both **its being and its body** belong **to Heaven,**[N] as it is prohibited for its owner to eat its meat. The Rabbis **said to him: The non-kosher** animal **too, its being** belongs **to Heaven, and its body** is the property of its owner, because **if** the owner **chooses, he sells it**[N] **to gentiles or feeds it to dogs.**

גמ׳ אָמַר רַב יִצְחָק בַּר חֲנַנְיָה אָמַר רַב הוּנָא: הַמּוּדָּר הֲנָאָה מֵחֲבֵירוֹ – מוּתָּר לְהַשִּׂיא לוֹ בִּתּוֹ. הָוֵי בָּהּ רַבִּי זֵירָא: בְּמַאי עָסְקִינַן? אִילֵימָא בְּשֶׁנִּכְסֵי אֲבִי כַלָּה אֲסוּרִין עַל הֶחָתָן – הֲרֵי מוֹסֵר לוֹ שִׁפְחָה לְשַׁמְּשׁוֹ!

GEMARA **Rav Yitzḥak bar Ḥananya said** that **Rav Huna said:** In the case of **one for whom benefit from another is forbidden by vow, he is permitted to marry his daughter to him. Rabbi Zeira discussed it: With what** case **are we dealing? If we say** that it is a case where **the property of the father of the bride is forbidden to the groom,** this cannot be, as when one marries his daughter to the groom, **he provides him a maidservant to serve him** and thereby benefits him.

אֶלָּא בְּנִכְסֵי חָתָן אֲסוּרִין עַל אֲבִי כַלָּה – גְּדוֹלָה מִזּוֹ אָמְרוּ: זָן אֶת אִשְׁתּוֹ וְאֶת בָּנָיו, וְאַף עַל פִּי שֶׁהוּא חַיָּיב בִּמְזוֹנוֹתָן. וְאַתְּ אָמְרַתְּ מוּתָּר לְהַשִּׂיא לוֹ בִּתּוֹ?!

Rather, it is a case where **the property of the groom is forbidden to the father of the bride,** and although the groom supports the bride, her father is not considered to have benefited from the property of the groom. However, it cannot be this case either, as the Sages **stated** a *halakha* with a **greater** novel element **than that** in the mishna itself: And with regard to one for whom benefit from another is forbidden by vow, that other person **may feed** his **wife and children, although** the one who is bound by the vow **is obligated in their support. And you say that it is permitted to marry his daughter to him?** Isn't that obvious?

לְעוֹלָם בְּשֶׁנִּכְסֵי אֲבִי כַלָּה אֲסוּרִין עַל הֶחָתָן, וּבְבִתּוֹ בּוֹגֶרֶת, וּמִדַּעְתָּהּ.

The Gemara answers: **Actually,** it is a case **where the property of the father of the bride is forbidden to the groom, and where his daughter is a grown woman, and** where her father may marry her to another only **with her consent.** Therefore, it is not from her father that the groom is deriving benefit.

NOTES

Its being…belong to Heaven – נַפְשָׁהּ...לַשָּׁמַיִם: Most commentaries explain the phrase: Its being belongs to Heaven, to mean that its life is essentially not its own. The Meiri explains that it means that one may consecrate the non-kosher animal for maintenance of the Temple.

He sells it – הֲרֵי הוּא מוֹכְרָהּ: Some explain the reason for the opinion of Rabbi Eliezer as follows: It is generally not beneficial for one to fatten a beast of burden, as that will impair its work capacity. While with regard to a kosher animal whose meat is typically eaten, it may be worthwhile to fatten the animal, it is not worthwhile in the case of a non-kosher animal, which is typically used for work (Ran; see *Naḥalat Moshe*).

תַּנְיָא נַמִי הָכִי: הַמּוּדָּר הֲנָאָה מֵחֲבֵירוֹ אָסוּר לְהַשִּׂיא לוֹ בִּתּוֹ, אֲבָל מַשִּׂיאוֹ בִּתּוֹ בּוֹגֶרֶת, וּמִדַּעְתָּהּ.

The Gemara comments: **That is also taught** in a *baraita*. In the case of one for whom benefit from another is forbidden by vow, it is **prohibited** for that other person **to marry his daughter to him.**[H] **However, he may marry off his daughter,** who is **a grown woman,** to that other person **with her consent.**

אָמַר רַבִּי יַעֲקֹב: הַמַּדִּיר בְּנוֹ לְתַלְמוּד תּוֹרָה – מוּתָּר לְמַלְאוֹת לוֹ חָבִית שֶׁל מַיִם, וּלְהַדְלִיק לוֹ אֶת הַנֵּר. רַבִּי יִצְחָק אָמַר: לִצְלוֹת לוֹ דָּג קָטָן. אָמַר רַבִּי יִרְמְיָה אָמַר רַבִּי יוֹחָנָן: הַמּוּדָּר הֲנָאָה מֵחֲבֵירוֹ – מוּתָּר לְהַשְׁקוֹתוֹ כּוֹס שֶׁל שָׁלוֹם. מַאי נִיהוּ? הָכָא תַּרְגִּימוּ: כּוֹס שֶׁל בֵּית הָאָבֵל, בְּמַעַרְבָא אָמְרִי: כּוֹס שֶׁל בֵּית הַמֶּרְחָץ.

Similarly, **Rabbi Ya'akov said:** If **one vows** that benefit **from** him is forbidden to **his son,** in order to induce him to engage in **Torah study,**[HN] the one who took the vow may nevertheless perform actions that provide his son with minor benefit. It is **permitted** for him **to fill a barrel of water for** his son[N] **and to kindle a lamp for him. Rabbi Yitzḥak said:** It is **permitted** for him **to roast a small fish for him. Rabbi Yirmeya said** that **Rabbi Yoḥanan said:** In the case of **one for whom benefit from another is forbidden by vow it is permitted** for the other **to give him a cup of peace to drink.**[H] The Gemara asks: **What is this** cup of peace? **Here,** in Babylonia, the Sages **interpreted** this term as referring to **a cup of** wine given to mourners to drink at the meal of comfort in **the house of mourning.**[N] **In the West,** Eretz Yisrael, the Sages **said** that it is the **cup of** wine that one drinks upon leaving **the bathhouse.**[N]

HALAKHA

It is prohibited to marry his daughter to him – אָסוּר לְהַשִּׂיא לוֹ בִּתּוֹ: One may not marry off his minor daughter to a man who is prohibited from benefiting from him. However, if she is a grown woman, her father may do so with her consent (Rambam *Sefer Hafla'a, Hilkhot Nedarim* 6:5; *Shulḥan Arukh, Yoreh De'a* 221:3).

If one vows that benefit from him is forbidden to his son in order to induce him to engage in Torah study – הַמַּדִּיר בְּנוֹ לְתַלְמוּד תּוֹרָה: If one vows that his son is prohibited from benefiting from him because his son is not studying Torah, he may fill a bucket of water, light a candle, and roast a fish for his son, because he did not intend to render inconsequential benefit forbidden to him (Rambam). If the father vowed that benefit from his son is forbidden for him so that his son will be able to study Torah undistracted, the son may perform those tasks for his father, as they will not distract him from the study of Torah (Ra'avad; Ramban; Rambam *Sefer Hafla'a, Hilkhot Nedarim* 6:17; *Shulḥan Arukh, Yoreh De'a* 223:1).

To give him a cup of peace to drink – לְהַשְׁקוֹתוֹ כּוֹס שֶׁל שָׁלוֹם: If one vowed that benefit from another is forbidden for him, it is permitted for him to receive a cup of comfort and a cup of the bathhouse from that other person, provided that the wine belongs to the one for whom benefit is forbidden (*Kesef Mishne*), as in that case there is no benefit involved (Rambam *Sefer Hafla'a, Hilkhot Nedarim* 6:10; *Shulḥan Arukh, Yoreh De'a* 221:2).

NOTES

If one vows that benefit from him is forbidden to his son in order to induce him to engage in Torah study – הַמַּדִּיר בְּנוֹ לְתַלְמוּד תּוֹרָה: There are two primary opinions with regard to this issue. One possibility is that this is a case where the son does not wish to study Torah, and therefore the father vows to prohibit his son from benefiting from him (Rashi; Rambam; Ritz; *Tosefot Rabbeinu Peretz*). The other possibility is that the father wants his son to study Torah and therefore vows that benefit from his son is forbidden to him, so that the son will not be distracted from his studies by performing tasks for him (Ra'avad; Ramban; Ritva; Rid; Ran). Some commentaries cite both opinions (Rosh; Rashba; Meiri), but most agree with the second opinion, as the language here as well as in the *Tosefta* and the Jerusalem Talmud support that opinion. Many commentaries that cite both opinions hold that the *halakha* of Rabbi Ya'akov applies in both cases, whether benefit from the son is forbidden to the father or whether benefit from the father is forbidden to the son and that the dispute is with regard to the explanation of the statement of Rabbi Ya'akov.

To fill a barrel of water for his son – לְמַלְאוֹת לוֹ חָבִית שֶׁל מַיִם: According to Rashi and the Ritz, there is no difference between a case where benefit from one's son is forbidden and a case where benefit from another is forbidden. The principle is: In any case where the benefit is insignificant, that is not what the one who vowed had in mind. Others explain that the father vowed that benefit from him is forbidden to his son, in order to encourage the son to study Torah. By performing these tasks for his son, he facilitates his Torah study. Those who maintain that it is the father who is prohibited from benefiting from his son hold that these are insignificant tasks and their performance would not impede the son's Torah study (Ritva). Others explain that these tasks do not require significant exertion, and a son is required by Torah law to perform them for his father (Rabbi Avraham min HaHar).

A cup of the house of mourning – כּוֹס שֶׁל בֵּית הָאָבֵל: The Sages instituted that those comforting mourners should give them wine in the framework of the meal of comfort, and everyone present drinks with him. In the talmudic period, it was customary to drink ten cups of wine after the Grace after Meals in the home of the mourner. The Rambam and the Ran explain that the one from whom benefit is forbidden gives the one prohibited from receiving benefit wine that belongs to the latter. Therefore, he provides the mourner merely with the benefit of service. Others explain that even if the wine belongs to the one from whom benefit is forbidden, performing this act is permitted, because he merely brings the wine to the house of mourning. Since there are many people drinking the wine, it is not considered as though he provided the wine directly to the one for whom benefit is forbidden (Rosh; *Talmidei Rabbeinu Peretz*). Others explain that since his intent is not to benefit him, as the mourner drinks the wine only for comfort, it is not considered forbidden benefit (Rabbi Avraham min HaHar).

Cup of the bathhouse – כּוֹס שֶׁל בֵּית הַמֶּרְחָץ: People would typically drink hot water after bathing in hot water, and then a cold drink to cool down. Here too, the Rambam writes that this is a case where the one from whom benefit is forbidden gives the one for whom benefit is forbidden wine that belongs to the latter, and this does not constitute actual benefit. The Ra'avad, who may have had a different version of the *halakha* in the Rambam (see *Kesef Mishne*), disagrees, and he holds that this is permitted because it is crucial to restoring one's health. The Rashba questions both opinions and explains that it is permitted because the benefit is slight; it is permitted for the sake of the mitzva of performing an act of lovingkindness. Others explain that it is permitted because his intent is to cure him, not to benefit him (Rabbi Avraham min HaHar). Some explain that since providing one with a drink after bathing is common practice and failure to do so is contemptible, he certainly did not intend to render that benefit forbidden (Rid). The Ran likewise writes that it is permitted due to the importance of maintaining peace. Failure to give him a cup would lead to antagonism.

״וְלֹא יָזוּן אֶת בְּהֶמְתּוֹ בֵּין״ כו׳. תַּנְיָא, יְהוֹשֻׁעַ אִישׁ עוּזָּא אוֹמֵר: זָן עֲבָדָיו וְשִׁפְחוֹתָיו הַכְּנַעֲנִים, וְלֹא יָזוּן אֶת בְּהֶמְתּוֹ, בֵּין טְמֵאָה בֵּין טְהוֹרָה. מַאי טַעְמָא? עֲבָדָיו וְשִׁפְחוֹתָיו הַכְּנַעֲנִים – לְמַנְחֲרוּתָא עֲבִידָן, בְּהֵמָה – לְפִטּוּמָא עֲבִידָא.

§ We learned in the mishna: **And he may not feed the animal** of one for whom benefit from him is forbidden, **whether it** is a kosher animal or whether it is a non-kosher animal. **It is taught** in a *baraita* that **Yehoshua of Uzza says:** One who vows that benefit from him is forbidden to another **may feed** the other person's **Canaanite slaves and maidservants;**[NH] **however, he may not feed his animal, whether** it is **a non-kosher** animal or **whether** it is **a kosher** animal. The Gemara asks: **What is the reason** for the distinction? The Gemara explains: **His Canaanite slaves and maidservants**[B] **are designated for labor,** whereas **an animal is designated for fattening.** The one bound by the vow derives benefit from the other person feeding the kosher animal when he eats it and derives benefit from the other person feeding the non-kosher animal when he sells it to a gentile.

מתני׳ הַמּוּדָּר הֲנָאָה מֵחֲבֵירוֹ וְנִכְנָס לְבַקְּרוֹ – עוֹמֵד אֲבָל לֹא יוֹשֵׁב, וּמְרַפְּאוֹ רְפוּאַת נֶפֶשׁ אֲבָל לֹא רְפוּאַת מָמוֹן.

MISHNA In the case of **one for whom benefit from another is forbidden by vow and he enters** his house **to visit him, he stands** there[H] **but does not sit. And** that other person **heals him** with **a cure** of the *nefesh* **but not a cure of** *mamon*.

NOTES

May feed his Canaanite slaves and maidservants – זָן עֲבָדָיו וְשִׁפְחוֹתָיו הַכְּנַעֲנִים: The Ran explains that the reference is not to food that they need for subsistence, but to food provided beyond those needs. Others explain that since the master of the slaves is not required to feed them, doing so is not considered a benefit.

HALAKHA

May feed his Canaanite slaves and maidservants, etc. – זָן עֲבָדָיו וְשִׁפְחוֹתָיו הַכְּנַעֲנִים וכו׳: In the case of one from whom benefit for another is forbidden by vow, he may feed the Canaanite slaves and maidservants belonging to that other person (Rambam *Sefer Hafla'a, Hilkhot Nedarim* 6:4; *Shulḥan Arukh, Yoreh De'a* 221:2).

He enters to visit him, he stands there – נִכְנָס לְבַקְּרוֹ עוֹמֵד: If Reuven vowed that benefit from him is forbidden to Shimon, and Shimon fell ill, it is permitted for Reuven to visit him. In places where one who sits with an ill person is paid, he may not sit with him but he may stand with him. It is permitted for him to cure him, even actively. In places where doctors are paid, it is prohibited for him to treat the one for whom benefit is forbidden for free (Rambam *Sefer Hafla'a, Hilkhot Nedarim* 6:8; *Shulḥan Arukh, Yoreh De'a* 221:4).

BACKGROUND

Canaanite slaves and maidservants – עֲבָדָיו וְשִׁפְחוֹתָיו הַכְּנַעֲנִים: Any gentile slave purchased by a Jew is characterized as a Canaanite slave (Leviticus 25:44–46). A gentile purchased by a Jew must be immersed in a ritual bath, and, if male, circumcised. These acts effect a change in the slave's status. Though not yet a Jew in all respects, a Canaanite slave must observe all the Torah's prohibitions and fulfill all positive mitzvot that are not time bound. Furthermore, a Canaanite slave owned by a priest may partake of *teruma*.

In many respects, Canaanite slaves are their masters' property and may be sold and purchased like other possessions. Generally, the *halakhot* governing slaves resemble those of landed property. For example, they are acquired by means of the same legal transactions as landed property, and their legal status with regard to the *halakhot* of fraud is the same. A Canaanite slave serves his master for life and is inherited by his master's heirs. His master can free him by giving him a bill of manumission, whose legal status is like that of a bill of divorce. However, there is a positive mitzva not to free a Canaanite slave without compelling reasons. An exception to this principle is that a master must free his slave if the master blinds him, knocks out his tooth, or damages any one of his fingers or toes. This *halakha* applies whether or not the master caused the damage intentionally (Exodus 21:26–27). If a master severely beats his slave to the extent that the slave dies within twenty-four hours of the beating, the master is executed as a murderer (Exodus 21:20–21). If a master living in Eretz Yisrael sells his Canaanite slave to a gentile, or if an adult Canaanite slave flees to Eretz Yisrael, the court compels his master to give him a bill of manumission.

גמ׳ בְּמַאי עָסְקִינַן? אִי בְּשֶׁנִּכְסֵי מְבַקֵּר אֲסוּרִין עַל חוֹלֶה – אֲפִילּוּ יוֹשֵׁב נַמִי, אִי בְּשֶׁנִּכְסֵי חוֹלֶה אֲסוּרִין עַל הַמְבַקֵּר – אֲפִילּוּ עוֹמֵד נַמִי לָא! אָמַר שְׁמוּאֵל: לְעוֹלָם בְּשֶׁנִּכְסֵי מְבַקֵּר אֲסוּרִין עַל הַחוֹלֶה, וּבְמָקוֹם שֶׁנּוֹטְלִין שָׂכָר עַל הַיְשִׁיבָה, וְאֵין נוֹטְלִין שָׂכָר עַל הָעֲמִידָה.

GEMARA **With what are we dealing? If** it is a case **where the property of the visitor is forbidden to the ill person, even** if he is **sitting,** this should **also** be permitted. **If** it is a case **where the property of the ill person is forbidden to the visitor,**[H] **even** if he is **standing,** it should **also not** be permitted,[N] as one derives benefit from entering the house. **Shmuel said: Actually,** it is a case **where the property of the visitor is forbidden to the ill person,**[H] **and** it is **in a place where one takes payment for** visiting and **sitting** with an ill person **and one does not take payment for** visiting and **standing** with an ill person. Therefore, by sitting with the ill person the visitor provides him forbidden benefit by sparing him the expense of hiring another person to sit with him.

מַאי פָּסְקָא? הָא קָא מַשְׁמַע לָן: דְּאַף בְּמָקוֹם שֶׁנּוֹטְלִין שָׂכָר, עַל הַיְשִׁיבָה – בָּעֵי לְמִשְׁקַל, עַל הָעֲמִידָה – לָא בָּעֵי לְמִשְׁקַל. וְאִיבָּעֵית אֵימָא כִּדְרַבִּי שִׁמְעוֹן בֶּן אֶלְיָקִים: גְּזֵירָה שֶׁמָּא יִשְׁהֶא בַּעֲמִידָה, הָכָא נַמִי: גְּזֵירָה שֶׁמָּא יִשְׁהֶא בִּישִׁיבָה.

Why was this distinction stated **without qualification?** There is no apparent fundamental difference between sitting and standing when visiting the ill. The Gemara answers: It **teaches us this: Even in a place where one takes payment** for visiting the ill, **for sitting, one ought to take** payment, but **for standing, one ought not to take** payment.[N] **And if you wish, say** instead that the distinction can be explained **in accordance with** the statement that **Rabbi Shimon ben Elyakim** said elsewhere (42a), that one who is prohibited to derive benefit from another due to a rabbinic **decree** may not enter a field that is owned by the latter, **lest he remain standing** there longer than permitted. **Here too,** sitting is prohibited due to a rabbinic **decree, lest he remain sitting** there longer than is necessary to perform the mitzva of visiting the ill.

עוּלָּא אָמַר: לְעוֹלָם בְּשֶׁנִּכְסֵי חוֹלֶה אֲסוּרִין עַל הַמְבַקֵּר, וּכְגוֹן דְּלָא אַדְרֵיהּ מִן חַיּוּתֵיהּ. אִי הָכִי אֲפִילּוּ יוֹשֵׁב נַמִי! הָא אֶפְשָׁר בַּעֲמִידָה.

Ulla said: Actually, it is a case **where the property of the ill person is forbidden to the visitor, and where** the ill person **did not vow** that his property would be forbidden in cases where its use enables the visitor to meet needs pertaining to **his** continued **existence.** The Gemara asks: **If so,** then **even sitting** should be permitted **as well,** since the vow did not prohibit use pertaining to his existential needs. The Gemara answers: **Isn't it possible** to meet those needs and visit the ill **while standing?** Therefore, sitting is not an existential need.

מֵיתִיבֵי: חָלָה הוּא – נִכְנָס לְבַקְּרוֹ, חָלָה בְּנוֹ – שׁוֹאֲלוֹ בַּשּׁוּק. בִּשְׁלָמָא לְעוּלָּא, דְּאָמַר בְּשֶׁנִּכְסֵי חוֹלֶה אֲסוּרִין עַל הַמְבַקֵּר, וּכְגוֹן דְּלָא אַדְרֵיהּ מִן חַיּוּתֵיהּ – שַׁפִּיר.

The Gemara **raises an objection** from a *baraita*: **If he became ill, he enters to visit him; if his son became ill, he inquires** about **his** son's health **in the marketplace** but may not enter the house to visit him. **Granted, according to Ulla, who said:** It is a case **where the property of the ill person is forbidden to the visitor and where** the ill person **did not vow** that the property be forbidden in cases pertaining to his continued **existence,** this works out **well,** as he excluded his own existential needs from the vow, not his son's existential needs.

HALAKHA

A case where the property of the ill person is forbidden to the visitor – בְּשֶׁנִּכְסֵי חוֹלֶה אֲסוּרִין עַל הַמְבַקֵּר: If one vows that benefit from him is forbidden to another, the latter may visit him when he is ill; he may stand but not sit. If the son of the one who vowed falls ill, that other person may not enter his house to visit the son but may inquire about his health outside in the marketplace (Rambam *Sefer Hafla'a, Hilkhot Nedarim* 6:8; *Shulḥan Arukh, Yoreh De'a* 221:4).

Actually, it is a case where the property of the visitor is forbidden to the ill person – בְּשֶׁנִּכְסֵי מְבַקֵּר אֲסוּרִין עַל הַחוֹלֶה: If one vows that benefit from him is forbidden to another, that other person may visit him when he is ill; he may stand but not sit. If the son of the one who vowed falls ill, the one for whom benefit is forbidden may not enter his house to visit the son but may inquire about his health outside in the marketplace (*Shulḥan Arukh, Yoreh De'a* 221:4).

NOTES

Even standing should also not be permitted – אֲפִילּוּ עוֹמֵד נַמִי לָא: The commentaries explain that it is prohibited for the visitor to stand in the house of the ill person, because the visitor benefits from stepping into the house (*Tosafot*; Ran). They explained that although there is a tannaitic dispute whether it is prohibited to set foot into the courtyard belonging to one from whom benefit is forbidden by vow, that is specifically with regard to a courtyard, as one could claim that there is no actual benefit derived by merely being there. However, there is benefit in setting foot into a house, where one is protected from heat and rain.

For standing, one ought not to take payment – עַל הָעֲמִידָה לָא בָּעֵי לְמִשְׁקַל: There are several explanations for this. Some explain that since the essential mitzva of visiting the ill can be performed standing, no payment should be taken. However, since sitting is not integral to the mitzva it is permitted to take payment (Ran). Rashi explains that a visit to the ill while standing is of limited duration, and therefore it is inappropriate to take payment for it. Since sitting is typically for a longer duration, he should at least be paid for his time. The Rosh and Rabbi Avraham min HaHar explain that when someone visits the ill while standing, he is not providing him with companionship. Therefore, there is no payment. However, sitting with an ill person provides him with companionship, and it is customary to take payment for doing so.

אֶלָּא לִשְׁמוּאֵל, דְּאָמַר בְּשֶׁנִּכְסֵי מְבַקֵּר אֲסוּרִין עַל הַחוֹלֶה, מַאי שְׁנָא הוּא וּמַאי שְׁנָא בְּנוֹ? אָמַר לָךְ: מַתְנִיתִין בְּשֶׁנִּכְסֵי מְבַקֵּר אֲסוּרִין עַל הַחוֹלֶה, בָּרַיְיתָא – בְּשֶׁנִּכְסֵי חוֹלֶה אֲסוּרִין עַל הַמְבַקֵּר.

However, according to Shmuel, who said: It is a case **where the property of the visitor is forbidden to the ill person, what is different** about **him and what is different** about **his son?** Why is it prohibited for him to visit when the son is ill? The Gemara answers: **Shmuel** could have **said to you: The mishna** is referring to a case **where the property of the visitor is forbidden to the ill person;** the *baraita* is referring to a case **where the property of the ill person is forbidden to the visitor.**

מַאי פָּסְקָא? אֲמַר רָבָא (אֲמַר): שְׁמוּאֵל

The Gemara asks: **Why** was this distinction between the mishna and the *baraita* stated **without qualification? Rava said:** With regard to **Shmuel,**

Perek **IV**
Daf **39** Amud **b**

מַתְנִיתִין קְשִׁיתֵיהּ; מַאי אִירְיָא דְּתָנֵי עוֹמֵד אֲבָל לֹא יוֹשֵׁב – שְׁמַע מִינָּהּ דְּנִכְסֵי מְבַקֵּר אֲסוּרִין עַל הַחוֹלֶה.

the mishna was difficult for him:[N] **Why does the** *tanna* **specifically teach:** He **stands** in his house but **may not sit? Conclude from it that the property of the visitor is forbidden to the ill person.**

אָמַר רֵישׁ לָקִישׁ: רֶמֶז לְבִיקּוּר חוֹלִין מִן הַתּוֹרָה מִנַּיִן – שֶׁנֶּאֱמַר ״אִם כְּמוֹת כָּל הָאָדָם יְמֻתוּן אֵלֶּה וּפְקֻדַּת כָּל הָאָדָם״ וגו׳. מַאי מַשְׁמַע? אָמַר רָבָא: אִם כְּמוֹת כָּל הָאָדָם יְמוּתוּן אֵלֶּה – שֶׁהֵן חוֹלִים וּמוּטָּלִים בַּעֲרִיסָתָן, וּבְנֵי אָדָם מְבַקְּרִים אוֹתָן, מַה הַבְּרִיּוֹת אוֹמְרִים – לֹא ה׳ שְׁלָחַנִי לָזֶה.

§ Apropos the *halakhot* of visiting the ill, the Gemara cites related statements. **Reish Lakish said: From where** is there **an allusion from the Torah to visiting the ill?** It is **as it is stated: "If these men die the common death of all men, and** be visited after **the visitation of all men,** then the Lord has not sent me" (Numbers 16:29). The Gemara asks: **From where** in this verse **may** visiting the ill **be inferred? Rava said** that this is what Moses is saying: **If these men,** the congregation of Korah, **die the common death of all men, who become ill, and are confined to their beds, and people come to visit them;** if that happens to them, **what do the people say?** They say: **The Lord has not sent me for this** task.

דָּרַשׁ רָבָא: ״אִם בְּרִיאָה יִבְרָא ה׳״ אִם בְּרִיאָה גֵּיהִנָּם – מוּטָּב תִּהְיֶה, אִם לָאו – יִבְרָא ה׳.

Apropos Korah and his congregation, **Rava interpreted** the repetitive formulation in this verse **homiletically: "But if the Lord will create a creation** [*beria yivra*], and the ground opens its mouth, and swallows them, and all that is theirs, and they will descend alive into the pit, then you shall understand that these men have despised God" (Numbers 16:30). Here, Moses is saying: **If Gehenna** is already **a creation** [*beria*] and exists, **that is optimal; if not, God should create** [*yivra*] it now.

אִינִי? וְהָא תַּנְיָא: שִׁבְעָה דְּבָרִים נִבְרְאוּ קוֹדֶם שֶׁנִּבְרָא הָעוֹלָם, אֵלּוּ הֵן: תּוֹרָה, וּתְשׁוּבָה, גַּן עֵדֶן, וְגֵיהִנָּם, כִּסֵּא הַכָּבוֹד, וּבֵית הַמִּקְדָּשׁ, וּשְׁמוֹ שֶׁל מָשִׁיחַ.

The Gemara asks: **Is that so?** Was there uncertainty at that point as to whether Gehenna had already been created? **But isn't it taught** in a *baraita*: **Seven phenomena were created before the world was created,**[N] **and they are: Torah, and repentance, the Garden of Eden, and Gehenna, the Throne of Glory, and the Temple, and the name of the Messiah.**

תּוֹרָה – דִּכְתִיב ״ה׳ קָנָנִי רֵאשִׁית דַּרְכּוֹ״ וגו׳.

The Gemara provides sources for each of these phenomena. **Torah** was created before the world was created, **as it is written: "The Lord made me as the beginning of His way,** the first of His works of old" (Proverbs 8:22). Based on the subsequent verses, this is referring to the Torah.

תְּשׁוּבָה – דִּכְתִיב ״בְּטֶרֶם הָרִים יֻלָּדוּ וַתְּחוֹלֵל וגו׳ תָּשֵׁב אֱנוֹשׁ עַד דַּכָּא״ וגו׳.

Repentance was created before the world was created, **as it is written: "Before the mountains were brought forth,** or ever You had formed the earth and the world, even from everlasting to everlasting, You are God" (Psalms 90:2), **and it is written** immediately afterward: **"You return man to contrition;** and You say: Repent, children of man" (Psalms 90:3).

גַּן עֵדֶן – דִּכְתִיב ״וַיִּטַּע ה׳ אֱלֹהִים גַּן בְּעֵדֶן מִקֶּדֶם״ וגו׳.

The Garden of Eden was created before the world was created, **as it is written: "And the Lord God planted a garden in Eden eastward** [*mikedem*]" (Genesis 2:8). "Eastward [*mikedem*]" is interpreted in the sense of before [*mikodem*], i.e., before the world was created.

NOTES

The mishna was difficult for him – מַתְנִיתִין קְשִׁיתֵיהּ: The distinction between standing and sitting in the mishna is reasonable once it is understood that benefit from the visitor is forbidden for the ill person, as he must minimize benefit to whatever degree possible. Although the mishna can also be reconciled according to the opinion of Ulla, that the ill person's vow did not pertain to situations involving his existential needs, Shmuel holds that this explanation is difficult (Rashi).

Seven phenomena were created before the world was created – שִׁבְעָה דְּבָרִים נִבְרְאוּ קוֹדֶם שֶׁנִּבְרָא הָעוֹלָם: The simple meaning here is that these phenomena were created before the Creation of the world, and they existed in a spiritual state before they were actualized at the appropriate time in concrete form (see Maharsha). The Ran explains that it entered the mind of the Creator to create each of these items; however, they were actually created later. Some commentaries cite a variant reading that says so explicitly.

The Rashba explains that the seven items listed here form the basis of the meaningful existence of the world. The Torah is the manner in which the world is conducted; repentance is the manner in which one can rectify his behavior; the Garden of Eden and Gehenna are the principal forms of reward and punishment; the Throne of Glory symbolizes God's dominion over the world; the Temple is the focal point of life; and the name of the Messiah is the symbol of the purpose and objective of the world. All these constitute the infrastructure without which the world cannot exist.

גֵּיהִנָּם – דִּכְתִיב ״כִּי עָרוּךְ מֵאֶתְמוּל תָּפְתֶּה״.

Gehenna was created before the world was created, **as it is written: "For its hearth is ordained of old"** (Isaiah 30:33). The hearth, i.e., Gehenna, was created before the world was created.

כִּסֵּא כָּבוֹד – דִּכְתִיב ״נָכוֹן כִּסְאֲךָ מֵאָז״.

The Throne of Glory was created before the world was created, **as it is written: "Your throne is established of old,** You are from everlasting" (Psalms 93:2).

בֵּית הַמִּקְדָּשׁ – דִּכְתִיב ״כִּסֵּא כָבוֹד מָרוֹם מֵרִאשׁוֹן״.

The Temple was created before the world was created, **as it is written: "Your Throne of Glory on high from the beginning,** in the place of our Temple" (Jeremiah 17:12).

שְׁמוֹ שֶׁל מָשִׁיחַ – דִּכְתִיב ״יְהִי שְׁמוֹ לְעוֹלָם״ וגו׳!

The name of the Messiah was created before the world was created, **as it is written** about him: **"May his name endure forever;** his name existed before the sun" (Psalms 72:17). The name of the Messiah predated the creation of the sun and the rest of the world. Apparently, Rava's explanation that Moses was uncertain whether Gehenna had been created yet is contradicted by this *baraita*.

אֶלָּא הָכִי קָאָמַר: אִי אִיבְרִי לֵיהּ פּוּמָּא – מוּטָב, וְאִם לָאו – יִבְרָא ה׳. וְהָכְתִיב: ״אֵין כָּל חָדָשׁ תַּחַת הַשָּׁמֶשׁ״! הָכִי קָאָמַר: אִי הָכָא לָא מְקָרַב פּוּמָּא – לְהָכָא לִיקָּרַב.

Rather, the interpretation of the repetitive formulation of the verse is that **this is what** Moses **is saying: If the opening was created for** Gehenna, that is **optimal, and if not, the Lord should create** it now. The Gemara asks: **But isn't it written:** "And **there is nothing new under the sun"** (Ecclesiastes 1:9)? How, then, could Moses request that God create the mouth of Gehenna now? The Gemara answers: **This is what** Moses **said: If the mouth** of Gehenna **is not close to here, let** God **bring it closer.**

דָּרַשׁ רָבָא, וְאָמְרִי לָהּ אָמַר רַבִּי יִצְחָק: מַאי דִּכְתִיב ״שֶׁמֶשׁ יָרֵחַ עָמַד זְבֻלָה״, שֶׁמֶשׁ וְיָרֵחַ בִּזְבוּל מַאי בָּעְיָין? וְהָא בָּרָקִיעַ קְבִיעִי! מְלַמֵּד שֶׁעָלוּ שֶׁמֶשׁ וְיָרֵחַ מֵרָקִיעַ לִזְבוּל, וְאָמְרוּ לְפָנָיו: רִבּוֹנוֹ שֶׁל עוֹלָם! אִם אַתָּה עוֹשֶׂה דִּין לְבֶן עַמְרָם – אָנוּ מְאִירִים, וְאִם לָאו – אֵין אָנוּ מְאִירִין.

Apropos the conflict between Moses and Korah, the Gemara cites an additional verse that **Rava interpreted homiletically, and some say that** it was **Rabbi Yitzḥak** who **said: What is the** meaning of that **which is written: "The sun and moon stood still in their habitation** [*zevula*],[N] at the light of Your arrows as they go, at the shining of Your glittering spear" (Habakkuk 3:11)? **What do the sun and moon seek in** *zevul*, which is the fourth heaven; **aren't they fixed in** *rakia*, the second heaven? Rather, this **teaches that the sun and moon ascended from** *rakia* **to** *zevul* **and said before Him: Master of the Universe! If You do justice for the son of Amram,** i.e., Moses, in his dispute with Korah, **we will** continue to **illuminate** the world, **and if not, we will not illuminate** the world.

בְּאוֹתָהּ שָׁעָה יָרָה בָּהֶן חִיצִּים וַחֲנִיתוֹת, אָמַר לָהֶם: בְּכָל יוֹם וָיוֹם מִשְׁתַּחֲוִים לָכֶם וְאַתֶּם מְאִירִים, בִּכְבוֹדִי לֹא מְחִיתֶם – בִּכְבוֹד בָּשָׂר וָדָם מְחִיתֶם! וּבְכָל יוֹם וָיוֹם יוֹרִין בָּהֶן חִיצִּין וַחֲנִיתוֹת וּמְאִירִים, שֶׁנֶּאֱמַר ״לְאוֹר חִצֶּיךָ יְהַלֵּכוּ״ וגו׳.

At that moment, the Holy One, Blessed be He, **shot arrows, and** threw **spears at them,** and **said to them: Each and every day** idolaters **bow to you and you** continue to **illuminate** the world and do not protest. **In My honor, you did not protest, but in honor of flesh and blood, you protested? And** ever since, **each and every day** the heavenly hosts **shoot arrows and** throw **spears** at the sun and the moon,[N] and only then do they emerge and **illuminate** the world, **as it is stated: "At the light of Your arrows as they go, at the shining of Your glittering spear"** (Habakkuk 3:11).

תַּנְיָא: בִּיקּוּר חוֹלִים אֵין לָהּ שִׁיעוּר. מַאי אֵין לָהּ שִׁיעוּר? סָבַר רַב יוֹסֵף לְמֵימַר: אֵין שִׁיעוּר לְמַתַּן שְׂכָרָהּ. אֲמַר לֵיהּ אַבָּיֵי: וְכָל מִצְוֹת מִי יֵשׁ שִׁיעוּר לְמַתַּן שְׂכָרָן? וְהָא תְּנַן: הֱוֵי זָהִיר בְּמִצְוָה קַלָּה כְּבַחֲמוּרָה, שֶׁאֵין אַתָּה יוֹדֵעַ מַתַּן שְׂכָרָן שֶׁל מִצְוֹת! אֶלָּא אָמַר אַבָּיֵי: אֲפִילּוּ גָּדוֹל אֵצֶל קָטָן. רָבָא אָמַר: אֲפִילּוּ מֵאָה פְּעָמִים בַּיּוֹם.

§ Returning to the topic of visiting the ill, the Gemara states: It **is taught** in a *baraita*: The mitzva of **visiting the ill has no** fixed **measure.** The Gemara asks: **What is the** meaning of: **Has no** fixed **measure? Rav Yosef thought to say: There is no** fixed **measure for the granting of its reward. Abaye said to him: And do all** other **mitzvot have** a fixed **measure for the granting of their reward? But didn't we learn** in a mishna (*Avot* 2:1): **Be as meticulous in** the observance of **a minor mitzva as a major one, as you do not know the granting of reward for mitzvot. Rather, Abaye said:** There is no fixed measure for the disparity between the ill person and his visitor, as **even a prominent** person pays a visit **to a lowly** person[NH] and should not say that doing so is beneath a person of his standing. **Rava said:** There is no fixed measure for the number of times that one should visit the ill, as **even one hundred times a day** is appropriate.

NOTES

The sun and moon stood still in their habitation – שֶׁמֶשׁ יָרֵחַ עָמַד זְבֻלָה: The Ran writes that later in that chapter, it appears that the prophet is referring to the exodus from Egypt and what followed: The splitting of the Red Sea, the Revelation at Sinai, and the earth swallowing Korah and his congregation (see Riaf). Almost all commentaries hold that the reference is to Korah and his congregation. However, Rabbeinu Tam (*Sefer HaYashar*) explains that the reference here is to the war of Sihon and Og, as Moses requested that they fall into his hands, and in the midrash it is stated that the sun and moon stood still during that war, as was the case in the days of Joshua.

And each and every day the heavenly hosts shoot arrows and throw spears at the sun and the moon – וּבְכָל יוֹם וָיוֹם יוֹרִין בָּהֶן חִיצִּין וַחֲנִיתוֹת: Rashi explains, based on parallel discussions elsewhere (*Sanhedrin* 110a), that since that day the sun and moon do not shine willingly, in protest against the idolaters, who undermine the honor of the Holy One, Blessed be He.

Even a prominent person pays a visit to a lowly person – אֲפִילּוּ גָּדוֹל אֵצֶל קָטָן: The novel element here is that with regard to other mitzvot that obligate one to act on behalf of another, e.g., returning a lost item, if one is older, it is not in keeping with his dignity and he is exempt from the obligation. Therefore, the Gemara underscores that with regard to visiting the ill, even a great person visits a lesser person who is ill, and that is in no way beneath him (*Shita*).

HALAKHA

Even a prominent person pays a visit to a lowly person – אֲפִילּוּ גָּדוֹל אֵצֶל קָטָן: Visiting the ill is a mitzva incumbent upon all, and even a great person visits a lesser person. The more often one visits, the better, even several times a day, provided that he does not thereby disturb the ill person, and each person who visits eases the illness somewhat. The Rema writes that although one is obligated visit even an enemy who is ill, it is inappropriate to do so, as it could upset the ill person (Rambam *Sefer Shofetim, Hilkhot Evel* 14:4; *Shulḥan Arukh, Yoreh De'a* 335:2).

אָמַר רַבִּי אַחָא בַּר חֲנִינָא: כׇּל הַמְבַקֵּר חוֹלֶה נוֹטֵל אֶחָד מִשִּׁשִּׁים בְּצַעֲרוֹ. אָמְרִי לֵיהּ: אִם כֵּן לִיעֲלוּן שִׁיתִּין וְלוֹקְמוּהּ! אֲמַר לֵיהּ: כְּעִישּׂוּרַיְיתָא דְּבֵי רַבִּי, וּבְבֶן גִּילוֹ.

Rav Aḥa bar Ḥanina said: Anyone who visits an ill person takes from him **one-sixtieth of his suffering.** The Sages **said to him: If so, let sixty** people **enter** to visit him, **and stand him up,** and restore him to health. Rav Aḥa bar Ḥanina **said to them:** It is **like the tenths of the school of Rabbi** Yehuda HaNasi, who said that each of one's daughters inherits one-tenth of his possessions. His intent was that each daughter would receive one-tenth of the remainder after the previous daughter took her portion. Here too, each visitor takes from the ill person one-sixtieth of the suffering that remains, and consequently a degree of suffering will always remain with the ill person. **Furthermore,** visiting is effective in easing the suffering of the ill person only when the visitor is **one** born under the **same constellation**[N] as the ill person.

דְּתַנְיָא, רַבִּי אוֹמֵר: בַּת הַנִּיזּוֹנֵית מִנִּכְסֵי אַחִין – נוֹטֶלֶת עִישּׂוּר נְכָסִים. אָמְרוּ לוֹ לְרַבִּי: לִדְבָרֶיךָ, מִי שֶׁיֵּשׁ לוֹ עֶשֶׂר בָּנוֹת וּבֵן, אֵין לוֹ לַבֵּן בִּמְקוֹם בָּנוֹת כְּלוּם! אָמַר לָהֶן: רִאשׁוֹנָה נוֹטֶלֶת עִישּׂוּר נְכָסִים, שְׁנִיָּה בְּמַה שֶּׁשִּׁיְּירָה, שְׁלִישִׁית בְּמַה שֶּׁשִּׁיְּירָה, וְחוֹזְרוֹת וְחוֹלְקוֹת בְּשָׁוֶה.

The Gemara elaborates on the tenths of the school of Rabbi Yehuda HaNasi, **as it is taught** in a *baraita* that **Rabbi** Yehuda HaNasi **says: A daughter who is supported from the property of** her **brothers** after the death of their father **receives one-tenth** of the **estate** as her dowry. The Sages **said to Rabbi** Yehuda HaNasi: **According to your statement,** in the case of **one who has ten daughters and a son, no** property **at all** remains **for the son in a place** where there are **daughters,** as they receive the entire inheritance. Rabbi Yehuda HaNasi **said to them: The first** daughter **takes one-tenth of the estate,**[H] **the second** takes one-tenth **of** that **which** the first **left** of the inheritance, **the third** takes one-tenth **of** that **which** the second **left** of the inheritance, and so on. After each succeeding daughter takes her share, they pool their resources and **then divide** the property **equally.** Therefore, the son is left with a share of the inheritance.

רַב חֶלְבּוֹ חֲלַשׁ, נְפַק אַכְרֵיז רַב כָּהֲנָא:

The Gemara relates: **Rav Ḥelbo**[P] **fell ill. Rav Kahana went out and announced:**

NOTES

One born under the same constellation – בְּבֶן גִּילוֹ: Rashi, and perhaps Rabbi Avraham min HaHar as well, explain that it means one close in age, i.e., the young visiting the young and the elderly visiting the elderly. In the *Arukh*, a similar explanation is cited: A member of the same generation. The Ran and another opinion cited in the *Arukh* explain that it means one born under the same constellation. In a variant reading of the Gemara cited in *Vayikra Rabba*, the term is a soul mate, meaning, as the Meiri explained: One whom the ill person is glad to see and whose visits he enjoys. Others interpreted that the explanations of Rashi and the Ran have the same meaning, one close in age or born under the same constellation, who is a kindred spirit and whose visit is agreeable to the ill person.

HALAKHA

The first daughter takes one-tenth of the estate – רִאשׁוֹנָה נוֹטֶלֶת עִישּׂוּר נְכָסִים: If one dies leaving several daughters, the first to marry receives one-tenth of his possessions as a dowry, the second takes one-tenth of what remains, and so forth. After they all marry, they divide the total inheritance, and each takes an equal part. The brothers inherit the remainder. The Rema cites the *Maggid Mishne* and writes that although the one-tenth of the possessions is not claimed until the daughter marries, one estimates each daughter's share based on the estate left by the father when he died (Rambam *Sefer Nashim*, *Hilkhot Ishut* 20:4; *Shulḥan Arukh*, *Even HaEzer* 113:4).

PERSONALITIES

Rav Ḥelbo – רַב חֶלְבּוֹ: Rav Ḥelbo, also known as Rabbi Ḥelbo, was a third-generation Babylonian *amora* who ascended to Eretz Yisrael. He was the primary student of Rav Huna and learned most of his Torah knowledge from him. Apparently, Rabbi Ḥelbo ascended to Eretz Yisrael toward the end of Rav Huna's life and was already in Eretz Yisrael when Rav Huna's body was taken there for burial. In Eretz Yisrael, Rabbi Ḥelbo was a colleague-disciple of the more prominent students of Rabbi Yoḥanan and became one of the leaders and halakhic authorities of his generation. In the field of *aggada*, he was a disciple of Rabbi Shmuel bar Naḥmani, and he cites aggadic traditions in his name. Rabbi Ḥelbo resided in Tiberias, where he had ties with Rabbi Yehuda Nesia II. The Talmud relates that he was not survived by any children.

רב חלבו באיש. לא איכא דקא אתי. אמר להו: לא כך היה מעשה בתלמיד אחד מתלמידי רבי עקיבא שחלה. לא נכנסו חכמים לבקרו, ונכנס רבי עקיבא לבקרו, ובשביל שכיבדו וריבצו לפניו חיה. אמר לו: רבי, החייתני. יצא רבי עקיבא ודרש: כל מי שאין מבקר חולים – כאילו שופך דמים.

Rav Ḥelbo fell ill. There was no one who came to visit him. Rav Kahana **said to** the Sages: **Didn't the incident involving one of the students of Rabbi Akiva who became sick** transpire **in that manner?** In that case, **the Sages did not enter to visit him, and Rabbi Akiva entered to visit him** and instructed his students to care for him. **And since they swept and sprinkled water on the** dirt **floor before** the sick student,[B] **he recovered.** The student **said to** Rabbi Akiva: **My teacher, you revived me. Rabbi Akiva went out and taught:** With regard to **anyone who does not visit the ill, it is as though he is spilling blood,** as it could be that the sick person has no one to care for him. If there are no visitors, no one will know his situation and therefore no one will come to his aid.

כי אתא רב דימי אמר: כל המבקר את החולה – גורם לו שיחיה, וכל שאינו מבקר את החולה – גורם לו שימות. מאי גרמא? אילימא כל המבקר את החולה מבקש עליו רחמים שיחיה, וכל שאין מבקר את החולה מבקש עליו רחמים שימות – שימות סלקא דעתך?! אלא: כל שאין מבקר חולה – אין מבקש עליו רחמים לא שיחיה ולא שימות.

When Rav Dimi came from Eretz Yisrael to Babylonia **he said: Anyone who visits the ill causes that he will live, and anyone who does not visit the ill**[H] **causes that he will die.** The Gemara asks: In **what** way are his actions **the cause** of that result?[N] **If we say** that **anyone who visits the ill pleads for mercy** from God **that he will live, and anyone who does not visit the ill pleads for mercy that he will die, does it enter your mind** that he would pray **that** the sick person **will die? Rather, anyone who does not visit the ill does not plead for mercy for him, neither that he will live nor that he will die.**[N] Since he might have saved the sick person with prayers had he visited, his failure to visit is tantamount to causing his death.

רבא, יומא קדמאה דחליש אמר להון: לא תיגלו לאיניש, דלא לתרע מזליה. מכאן ואילך אמר להון: פוקו ואכריזו בשוקא. דכל דסני לי ליחדי לי, וכתיב "בנפל אויבך אל תשמח" וגו׳, ודרחים לי ליבעי עלי רחמי.

The Gemara relates with regard to **Rava:** On **the first day that he was ill, he** would **say to** his family: **Do not reveal to any person**[N] that I am ill, so **that his luck not suffer.**[N] **From this point forward,** when his situation deteriorated **he** would **say to them: Go and proclaim in the marketplace** that I am ill, as thereby **let all who hate me rejoice over my** distress, **and it is written: "Rejoice not when your enemy falls, and let not your heart be glad when he stumbles; lest the Lord see it, and it displease Him, and He turn away His wrath from him"** (Proverbs 24:17–18). **And let** all **who love me pray** that God have **mercy upon me.**

BACKGROUND

And since they swept and sprinkled water on the dirt floor before the sick student – ובשביל שכיבדו וריבצו לפניו: It is understood from the narrative that the sick student was in a small and airless bedroom. Dust gathers in a place like this and the air becomes stifling. The dust was cleared and the room was ventilated when they swept and sprinkled water on the floor. Removal of other polluting factors that had certainly exacerbated the condition of the ill student also contributed to his recovery.

HALAKHA

And anyone who does not visit the ill – וכל שאינו מבקר את החולה: One who fails to visit the ill is like one who spills blood (Rambam *Sefer Shofetim*, *Hilkhot Evel* 14:4).

NOTES

In what way are his actions the cause of that result – מאי גרמא: This question is difficult, as it is clear from the incident involving Rabbi Akiva that visiting the ill causes the sick person to live; it follows that one who fails to visit him facilitates his death. Rav Dimi may have sought to introduce an additional aspect of visiting the ill beyond what was stated previously: Rabbi Akiva spoke of the benefit provided by the visitor by his tending to the sick person and Rav Dimi spoke of the benefit provided by the visitor by his praying for the sick person.

Neither that he will live nor that he will die – לא שיחיה ולא שימות: The Rosh explains that one who fails to visit the ill does not pray for him to live or to die, and this leads to others failing to pray for him to live. The Maharsha supports that interpretation. The Ran explains that in some situations the suffering of the sick person is so great that it is appropriate to pray for his death. By failing to visit him and pray for him, he neither causes him to recover nor does he cause him to die.

Do not reveal to any person – לא תיגלו לאיניש: Self-reliance is one of the most valuable and significant qualities of the human psyche. For many people, dependence upon others or an inability to fend for oneself is a source of embarrassment and an indication of personal failure. Even when suffering from an illness that saps one's strength, it is psychologically deleterious to turn to others for help in resolving the issue before attempting to cope alone. Therefore, the Gemara recommends waiting a day before publicizing one's distress. This important quality, however, should be tempered by a realistic assessment of one's capabilities. Society exists to enable people to rely on one other. Once it becomes clear that outside assistance is required, accepting help from others forges societal bonds and leads to close relationships between people that facilitate formation of a community (Rabbi Avraham Yitzḥak Kook, *Ein Aya*).

So that his luck not suffer – דלא לתרע מזליה: Some commentaries explain that this means that as long as others are unaware of his illness and it is not discussed explicitly, he can recover immediately. However, once his illness is discussed, its mere mention opens the door for Satan, based on the principle: A covenant exists with the lips (Maharsha). Others explain that when one's illness becomes public knowledge, some people speak derogatorily about the sick person. This can lead to his public condemnation, which could lead in turn to his condemnation in the heavenly court as well (*Shita Mekubbetzet*).

HALAKHA

Let one not visit a sick person, neither during the first three hours of the day – לָא לִיסְעוֹד אִינִישׁ קְצִירָא לָא בִּתְלָת שָׁעֵי קַדְמָיְיתָא: One should not visit the ill during the first three or last three hours of the day; rather, he should visit only between those hours, as that is the time to pray for the sick person. The Rema, citing the Ramban, writes that anyone who visits a sick person and fails to pray for him does not fulfill the mitzva of visiting the ill (Rambam *Sefer Shofetim*, *Hilkhot Evel* 14:5; *Shulḥan Arukh*, *Yoreh De'a* 335:4).

אָמַר רַב: כׇּל הַמְבַקֵּר אֶת הַחוֹלֶה נִיצּוֹל מִדִּינָהּ שֶׁל גֵּיהִנָּם, שֶׁנֶּאֱמַר ״אַשְׁרֵי מַשְׂכִּיל אֶל דָּל בְּיוֹם רָעָה יְמַלְּטֵהוּ ה׳״, אֵין דַּל אֶלָּא חוֹלֶה, שֶׁנֶּאֱמַר ״מִדַּלָּה יְבַצְּעֵנִי״, אִי נָמֵי מִן הָדֵין קְרָא – ״מַדּוּעַ אַתָּה כָּכָה דַּל בֶּן הַמֶּלֶךְ בַּבֹּקֶר בַּבֹּקֶר״ וגו׳. אֵין רָעָה אֶלָּא גֵּיהִנָּם, שֶׁנֶּאֱמַר ״כֹּל פָּעַל ה׳ לַמַּעֲנֵהוּ וְגַם רָשָׁע לְיוֹם רָעָה״.

Rav said: Anyone who visits the ill is spared from the judgment of Gehenna, as it is stated: "Happy is he that considers the poor; the Lord will deliver him in the day of evil" (Psalms 41:2). In this verse, the term **poor** [*dal*] means **nothing other** than **ill, as it is stated** in the prayer of Hezekiah when he was ill: **"He will cut me off from the illness** [*middalla*]**"** (Isaiah 38:12). **Alternatively,** it may be derived **from this verse** in which Jonadab asked his sick friend Amnon, son of King David: **"Why, son of the king, are you so sick** [*dal*] **from morning to morning?"** (II Samuel 13:4). **And** the term **evil means nothing other** than **Gehenna, as it is stated: "The Lord made everything for His own purpose, and even the wicked for the day of evil"** (Proverbs 16:4), and the ultimate punishment of the evildoer is Gehenna.

וְאִם בִּיקֵּר מָה שְׂכָרוֹ? מָה שְׂכָרוֹ?! כִּדְאָמַר: נִיצּוֹל מִדִּינָהּ שֶׁל גֵּיהִנָּם! אֶלָּא מָה שְׂכָרוֹ בָּעוֹלָם הַזֶּה?

And if one visited the ill, **what is his reward?** The Gemara wonders at that question: **What is his reward?** It is **as** Rav **said:** He **is spared from the judgment of Gehenna. Rather,** the question is: **What is his reward in this world?**

״ה׳ יִשְׁמְרֵהוּ וִיחַיֵּהוּ וְאֻשַּׁר בָּאָרֶץ וְאַל תִּתְּנֵהוּ בְּנֶפֶשׁ אֹיְבָיו״. ״ה׳ יִשְׁמְרֵהוּ״ – מִיֵּצֶר הָרָע; ״וִיחַיֵּהוּ״ – מִן הַיִּסּוּרִין; ״וְאֻשַּׁר בָּאָרֶץ״ – שֶׁיְּהוּ הַכֹּל מִתְכַּבְּדִין בּוֹ; ״וְאַל תִּתְּנֵהוּ בְּנֶפֶשׁ אֹיְבָיו״ – שֶׁיִּזְדַּמְּנוּ לוֹ רֵיעִים כְּנַעֲמָן שֶׁרִיפּוּ אֶת צָרַעְתּוֹ, וְאַל יִזְדַּמְּנוּ לוֹ רֵיעִים כִּרְחַבְעָם שֶׁחִילְּקוּ אֶת מַלְכוּתוֹ.

Rav continues: His reward is as it is written: **"The Lord will preserve him, and keep him alive, let him be called happy in the land; and deliver not You him unto the greed of his enemies"** (Psalms 41:3). He elaborates: **"The Lord will preserve him"** from **the evil inclination; "and keep him alive"** and spare him **from suffering; "let him be called happy in the land"** means that **everyone will be honored** from their association **with him; "and deliver not You him unto the greed of his enemies,"** so **that companions like** those who counseled **Naaman** to seek **a cure for his leprosy** from Elisha (II Kings 5:3) **will happen to** associate with **him,** and **companions like** those who counseled **Rehoboam** with advice that resulted in **the schism in his kingdom** (I Kings 12:6–19) **will not happen to** associate with **him.**

תַּנְיָא, רַבִּי שִׁמְעוֹן בֶּן אֶלְעָזָר אוֹמֵר: אִם יֹאמְרוּ לְךָ יְלָדִים ״בְּנֵה״ וּזְקֵנִים ״סְתוֹר״ – שְׁמַע לִזְקֵנִים, וְאַל תִּשְׁמַע לִילָדִים. שֶׁבִּנְיַן יְלָדִים סְתִירָה, וּסְתִירַת זְקֵנִים בִּנְיָן. וְסִימָן לַדָּבָר רְחַבְעָם בֶּן שְׁלֹמֹה.

On a similar note, **it is taught** in a *baraita* that **Rabbi Shimon ben Elazar says: If youths would say to you: Construct, and Elders would say to you: Demolish, heed the Elders and do not heed the youths, as the construction of youths is demolition, and the demolition of Elders is construction. And a mnemonic** device **for this matter is "Rehoboam, son of Solomon"** (I Kings 12:21). Had he heeded the advice of the Elders and yielded at that time, there would have been no schism.

אָמַר רַב שִׁישָׁא בְּרֵיהּ דְּרַב אִידִי: לָא לִיסְעוֹד אִינִישׁ קְצִירָא לָא בִּתְלָת שָׁעֵי קַדְמָיְיתָא וְלָא בִּתְלָת שָׁעֵי בָּתְרָיְיתָא דְּיוֹמָא, כִּי הֵיכִי דְּלָא לֵיסַח דַּעְתֵּיהּ מִן רַחֲמֵי. תְּלָת שָׁעֵי קַדְמָיְיתָא – רַוְוחָא דַּעְתֵּיהּ, בָּתְרָיְיתָא – תָּקֵיף חוּלְשֵׁיהּ.

Rav Sheisha, son of Rav Idi, said: Let one not visit a sick person, neither during the first three hours of the day,[HB] **nor in the last three hours of the day, so that he will not be diverted from** praying for **mercy.** Rav Sheisha elaborates: During **the first three hours** the sick person **is relieved,** as after a night's sleep his suffering is somewhat alleviated and the visitor will conclude that there is no need for prayer. In **the last** three hours of the day **his weakness is exacerbated,** and the visitor will despair of ameliorating his suffering and will conclude that prayer is futile.

אָמַר רָבִין אָמַר רַב: מִנַּיִין שֶׁהַקָּדוֹשׁ בָּרוּךְ הוּא זָן אֶת הַחוֹלֶה – שֶׁנֶּאֱמַר ״ה׳ יִסְעָדֶנּוּ עַל עֶרֶשׂ דְּוָי״ וגו׳. וְאָמַר רָבִין אָמַר רַב: מִנַּיִין שֶׁהַשְּׁכִינָה שְׁרוּיָה לְמַעְלָה מִמִּטָּתוֹ שֶׁל הַחוֹלֶה – שֶׁנֶּאֱמַר ״ה׳ יִסְעָדֶנּוּ עַל עֶרֶשׂ דְּוָי״.

§ **Ravin said** that **Rav said: From where** is it derived **that the Holy One, Blessed be He** Himself **sustains the sick person?** It is **as it is stated: "The Lord will support him upon the bed of suffering"** (Psalms 41:4). Support in this context is understood to mean that He will feed him. **And Ravin said** that **Rav said: From where** is it derived **that the Divine Presence is resting above the bed of the sick person?** It is also **as it is stated: "The Lord will support him upon the bed of suffering,"** which indicates that God is actually over his bed.

BACKGROUND

The first three hours of the day – תְּלָת שָׁעֵי קַדְמָיְיתָא: Body temperature fluctuates throughout the course of the day, and is usually lower in the morning and higher toward evening. These fluctuations are often more acute during illness, particularly when there is an infectious disease, and fever sometimes spikes in the evening. Fluctuation in body temperature is often related to fluctuation in the severity of the illness. After a good night's sleep, the patient's condition is often better in the morning and gradually deteriorates throughout the day. Ultimately, during the first three hours of the day, his general condition is good; in the evening hours, his situation is dire.

תניא נמי הכי: הנכנס לבקר את החולה לא ישב לא על גבי מטה, ולא על גבי ספסל, ולא על גבי כסא, אלא מתעטף ויושב על גבי קרקע, מפני שהשכינה שרויה למעלה ממטתו של חולה, שנאמר "ה׳ יסעדנו על ערש דוי".

The Gemara notes that **this is also taught** in a *baraita*: **One who enters to visit a sick person may neither sit on the bed nor** sit **on a bench or on a chair**[H] that is higher than the bed upon which the sick person is lying. **Rather, he** deferentially **wraps himself** in his garment **and sits on the ground,**[N] **because the Divine Presence is resting above the bed of the sick person, as it is stated: "The Lord will support him upon the bed of suffering,"** and it is inappropriate for one to sit above the place where the Divine Presence rests.

ואמר רבין אמר רב: מטרא במערבא – סהדא רבה פרת. ופליגא דשמואל, דאמר שמואל: נהרא מכיפיה מתבריך. ופליגא דשמואל אדשמואל, דאמר שמואל: אין המים מטהרין בזוחלין

And apropos statements of Rav cited by Ravin, the Gemara cites an additional statement that **Ravin said** that **Rav said: When** there is **rain in the West,** Eretz Yisrael,[B] **a great witness to** that rainfall **is the Euphrates River,** as ultimately that rainwater increases the water flow in the Euphrates River. **And** this statement of Rav **disagrees** with a statement **of Shmuel, as Shmuel said: A river is blessed from its banks,**[NB] i.e., the increase in its water flow is attributable to its tributaries and not to rain. The Gemara comments: **And** this statement **of Shmuel disagrees with** another statement **of Shmuel, as Shmuel said: The water purifies when flowing**[N]

NOTES

Rather, he wraps himself and sits on the ground – אלא מתעטף ויושב על גבי קרקע: The Meiri writes that if the visitor sits comfortably and above the sick person, the latter will become despondent and will fail even to pray for himself. However, if the visitor sits below him in a serious and reverent manner, the sick person is strengthened to pray.

Is blessed from its banks [*mikeifei*] – מכיפיה מתבריך: The commentaries write that this means that even when one sees that the water originates elsewhere, e.g., from rain or melting snow, a rise in the river should not be attributed to those sources but rather to its tributaries. Some say the term *keifei* means its rocks, referring to the rocks located at the river's source (Ran; Rosh). However, the *ge'onim*, based on *Targum Yonatan*, explain *keifei* as the river's banks.

The water purifies when flowing – המים מטהרין בזוחלין: The Torah mentions purification through immersion in two water sources, a spring and a cistern. Halakhically, there are several differences between spring water and water pooled in a cistern. Spring water purifies both when it is pooled in one place and when it is flowing, whereas the legal status of immersion in a cistern is that of a ritual bath and one is purified only when the water is pooled. The halakhic issue here is how much water from rain and snow can be added to spring water and have it maintain its capacity to purify when flowing.

BACKGROUND

Rain in the West, Eretz Yisrael – מטרא במערבא: Recent research has shown that there is a correlation between the amount of rainfall in Eretz Yisrael and the precipitation in the drainage basin of the Euphrates River. Therefore, there is a correlation between that rainfall and the water flow in the river.

A river is blessed from its banks – נהרא מכיפיה מתבריך: Water levels in rivers rise markedly during the rainy season. However, it is clear that not all the additional water is from the drainage of rainwater into the rivers. The water in springs that flow into the rivers also increases due to rainwater that seeps through the ground and eventually flows through the springs. Therefore, it is impossible to accurately estimate the amount of additional water that flows from the springs and the amount that comes directly from rainwater.

HALAKHA

On a chair – על גבי כסא: One who visits a sick person should not sit on a bed, chair, or bench, and not behind his head. He should wrap himself and sit before his head. The Ramah, citing the Ran, writes that this *halakha* is referring to a case where the sick person is lying on the floor, as the visitor is prohibited from sitting above him. However, if he is lying in bed, it is permitted for the visitor to sit on a chair, and that is the custom (Rambam *Sefer Shofetim, Hilkhot Evel* 14:6; *Shulḥan Arukh, Yoreh De'a* 335:3).

אֶלָּא פְּרָת בְּיוֹמֵי תִשְׁרֵי בִּלְבַד.

in the Euphrates River **only during the days of Tishrei**[B] **alone,** as after the summer, when no rain falls, it is clear that the water in the river flows from the source of the river. During the rest of the year, rain and snow are mingled with the river water, and water from rain and snow purify one who immerses in them only when the water is standing.

אֲבוּהּ דִּשְׁמוּאֵל עֲבַד לְהוּן מִקְוָואוֹת לִבְנָתֵיהּ בְּיוֹמֵי נִיסָן, וּמַפְצֵי בְּיוֹמֵי תִשְׁרֵי.

The Gemara relates: **Shmuel's father**[P] **fashioned ritual baths for his daughters during the days of Nisan**[H] **and** placed **mats**[HB] in the Euphrates River **during the days of Tishrei.**[N] He fashioned ritual baths during Nisan due to the concern that the rainwater and snow water that accumulated in the river exceeded the amount of water that originated in the river's sources. Since immersion in the flowing water would be ineffective, he fashioned ritual baths of standing water elsewhere for them. He placed mats during the days of Tishrei, when they immersed in the river itself, to prevent the mud on the riverbed from acting as an interposition that would invalidate the immersion.

אָמַר רַבִּי אַמִי אָמַר רַב: מַאי דִּכְתִיב "וְאַתָּה בֶן אָדָם עֲשֵׂה לְךָ כְּלֵי גוֹלָה" – זוֹ נֵר וּקְעָרָה

Rabbi Ami said that **Rav said: What is** the meaning of that **which is written: "And you, son of man, make for yourself implements of exile"** (Ezekiel 12:3)? **That is** referring to **a lamp, and a bowl,**

NOTES

And placed mats during the days of Tishrei – וּמַפְצֵי בְּיוֹמֵי תִשְׁרֵי: Some say that he placed mats for his daughters to stand upon, to prevent the mud in the river from seeping between their toes and acting as an interposition that would invalidate their immersion (Rashi). Others write that the mats were placed on the banks of the river so that they would not enter the river with muddy feet (Rabbi Avraham min HaHar). Another interpretation is that he erected mats around the place where they immersed for purposes of modesty, as others would be present at the river (Rosh; Ran; Ritva). The Rambam explains that Shmuel's father had concerns even after the summer in Tishrei that the rainwater exceeded the river water and in that case, the water does not purify while flowing. Therefore, he erected mats to pool the water so that immersion would be effective (Rabbi Avraham min HaHar).

PERSONALITIES

Shmuel's father – אֲבוּהּ דִּשְׁמוּאֵל: This is the prominent Sage Abba bar Abba, to whom the Gemara generally refers as the father of Shmuel, the great *amora*, who was his son. Abba bar Abba, who traveled extensively as a silk merchant, spent some time in Eretz Yisrael and developed close ties with Rabbi Yehuda HaNasi and his sons.

HALAKHA

Ritual baths for his daughters during the days of Nisan – מִקְוָואוֹת לִבְנָתֵיהּ בְּיוֹמֵי נִיסָן: If the amount of rainwater in a river or spring exceeds that of river or springwater, the water purifies only when pooled, not while flowing. Therefore, it was necessary to use mats to construct an enclosure in which the water would pool and be rendered suitable for immersion. That is how the Rambam and the Rosh understand the actions of Shmuel's father, and they based their halakhic ruling on that understanding. The Rema, citing the Maharik, writes that one must rule stringently *ab initio*. However, others hold that immersion in a river is effective even if the amount of rain and melting snow exceeds that of the river water, provided that there is water in the river other than the rainwater (*Tur*, citing Rabbeinu Ḥananel; *Beit Yosef*, citing Rashi; *Sefer HaTeruma*; *Smag*). This is the custom in places where there is no ritual bath, and those who act according to the lenient opinion should not be reprimanded (Maharik and Mahari Weil; Rambam *Sefer Tahara, Hilkhot Mikvaot* 9:13; *Shulḥan Arukh, Yoreh De'a* 201:2).

Mats – מַפְצֵי: A woman should not immerse in a port. The concern is that due to the embarrassment involved in immersion in the presence of the passersby, she will not immerse properly. However, if an enclosure of mats is constructed to ensure her privacy, it is permitted (Rambam). This *halakha* is based on one interpretation of the incident involving mats. A woman should not immerse in a place with mud on its floor *ab initio*, unless branches or mats that are not susceptible to ritual impurity are placed there, as otherwise the mud will act as an interposition. Some say that not only is it prohibited to immerse in a place with a muddy floor, but the immersion is invalid even after the fact (Ra'avad). However, most commentaries rule that it is effective after the fact. This *halakha* is based on another interpretation of the incident involving mats (Rambam *Sefer Tahara, Hilkhot Mikvaot* 1:11; *Shulḥan Arukh, Yoreh De'a* 198:33–34).

BACKGROUND

The Euphrates River…during the days of Tishrei – פְּרָת בְּיוֹמֵי תִשְׁרֵי: The primary sources of the Euphrates River are in Turkey, near Mount Ararat, but there are several other tributaries as well. There are very marked differences between periods when the current flows powerfully, during the winter due to the rain and during the spring because of the melting snow, and periods when the water in the river lessens and is limited to the water that flows from the river's sources, in the summer and autumn.

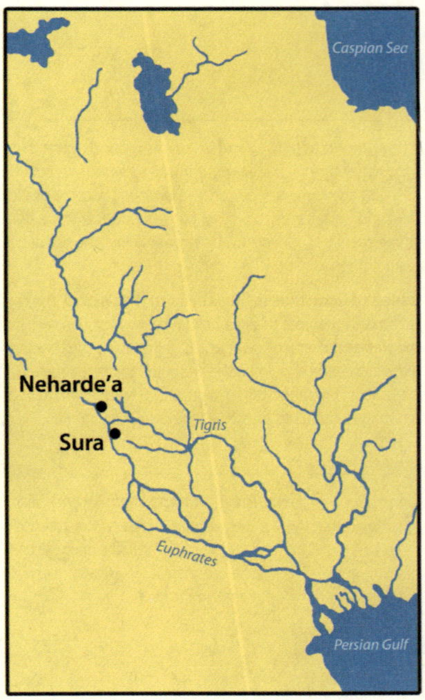

Above: Section of the Euphrates in Turkey during the summer

Right: Euphrates river

Mats [*mapetzei*] – מַפְצֵי: These mats were made of a weave of reeds and the like. A standard mat, *maḥtzelet*, was woven from whole reeds, while the *mapatz*, which was much softer, was woven from parts of reeds, perhaps the soft interior part.

וְשָׁטִיחַ. ״בְּחֹסֶר כֹּל״ – אָמַר רַבִּי אַמִי אָמַר רַב: בְּלֹא נֵר וּבְלֹא שֻׁלְחָן, רַב חִסְדָּא אָמַר: בְּלֹא אִשָּׁה, רַב שֵׁשֶׁת אָמַר: בְּלֹא שַׁמָּשׁ, רַב נַחְמָן אָמַר: בְּלֹא דֵּעָה. תָּנָא: בְּלֹא מֶלַח וּבְלֹא רְבָב.

and a rug, as an exile needs those items and they are portable. The Sages interpreted the following verse describing the exile experience: "Therefore shall you serve your enemy whom the Lord shall send against you, in hunger, and in thirst, and in nakedness, and **in want of all things;**[N] and he shall put a yoke of iron upon your neck, until he has destroyed you" (Deuteronomy 28:48). **Rabbi Ami said** that **Rav said:** "In want of all things" means **without a lamp and without a table** to eat upon. **Rav Ḥisda said: Without a wife. Rav Sheshet said: Without an attendant** to aid him. **Rav Naḥman said: Without intelligence.** One of the Sages **teaches** in a *baraita*: **Without salt and without fat** [*revav*][L] in which to dip his bread.

אָמַר אַבַּיֵי: נָקְטִינַן, אֵין עָנִי אֶלָּא בְּדֵעָה. בְּמַעְרְבָא אָמְרִי: דְּדָא בֵּיהּ – כּוּלָּא בֵּיהּ, דְּלָא דָא בֵּיהּ – מַה בֵּיהּ, דָּא קְנֵי – מַה חֲסַר, דָּא לָא קְנֵי – מַה קְנֵי.

Abaye said that **we have a tradition: A poor person is only** one lacking **in intelligence,** in agreement with the opinion of Rav Naḥman. **In the West,** Eretz Yisrael, **they say:** One who has **this** attribute, intelligence, **in him** has **everything in him.** One **who does not** have **this** attribute **in him, what is in him? If he acquired this, what** else **is lacking? If he has not acquired this, what has he acquired?**[N]

אָמַר רַבִּי אֲלֶכְּסַנְדְּרִי אָמַר רַבִּי חִיָּיא בַּר אַבָּא: אֵין הַחוֹלֶה עוֹמֵד מֵחׇלְיוֹ עַד שֶׁמּוֹחֲלִין לוֹ עַל כׇּל עֲוֹנוֹתָיו, שֶׁנֶּאֱמַר ״הַסֹּלֵחַ לְכׇל עֲוֹנֵכִי הָרֹפֵא לְכׇל תַּחֲלוּאָיְכִי״. רַב הַמְנוּנָא אָמַר: חוֹזֵר לִימֵי עֲלוּמָיו, שֶׁנֶּאֱמַר ״רֻטֲפַשׁ בְּשָׂרוֹ מִנֹּעַר יָשׁוּב לִימֵי עֲלוּמָיו״. ״כׇּל מִשְׁכָּבוֹ הָפַכְתָּ בְחׇלְיוֹ״ – אָמַר רַב יוֹסֵף: לוֹמַר דְּמִשְׁתַּכַּח תַּלְמוּדוֹ.

§ **Rabbi Alexandri said** that **Rabbi Ḥiyya bar Abba said: The sick person recovers from his illness only when** the heavenly court **forgives him for all his sins,**[N] **as it is stated: "Who forgives all your iniquity; Who heals all your diseases"** (Psalms 103:3). **Rav Hamnuna said:** When he recovers, **he returns to the days of his youth,**[N] **as it is stated** in a verse with regard to one recovering from illness: **"His flesh is tenderer than a child's; he returns to the days of his youth"** (Job 33:25). Interpreting the verse: "The Lord will support him upon the bed of suffering; **You overturned all his lying down in his illness"** (Psalms 41:4), **Rav Yosef said:** That **is to say that** the sick person **forgets his studies,**[NB] as everything that is organized is overturned.

רַב יוֹסֵף חֲלַשׁ, אִיעֲקַר לֵיהּ תַּלְמוּדֵיהּ, אַהַדְרֵיהּ אַבַּיֵי קַמֵּיהּ. הַיְינוּ דְּבְכׇל דּוּכְתָּא אָמְרִינַן: אֲמַר רַב יוֹסֵף: לָא שְׁמִיעַ לִי הָדָא שְׁמַעְתָּא, אֲמַר לֵיהּ אַבַּיֵי: אַתְּ אֲמַרְתְּ נִיהֲלַן, וּמֵהָא מַתְנִיתָא אֲמַרְתָּהּ נִיהֲלַן.

The Gemara relates: **Rav Yosef**[P] himself **fell ill and his studies were forgotten. Abaye**[P] **restored** his studies by reviewing what he had learned from Rav Yosef **before him. This is** the background for that **which we say everywhere** throughout the Talmud, that **Rav Yosef said: I did not learn this *halakha*,** and **Abaye said to him** in response: **You said this to us and it was from this *baraita* that you said it to us.**

PERSONALITIES

Rav Yosef – רַב יוֹסֵף: Rav Yosef bar Ḥiyya was one of the most prominent third-generation Babylonian *amora'im*. Rav Yosef was termed Sinai, while his colleague, Rabba, was characterized as one who uproots mountains. Sinai refers to one who received the Torah itself, i.e., one who is exceedingly knowledgeable in matters of *halakha* and whose opinions are based on the most authoritative sources. Because of this knowledge, he was recommended as the replacement for Rav Yehuda as the head of the yeshiva in Pumbedita. However, he deferred to Rabba and took the position only after Rabba's death. He served in that position for two years, until his own passing in the year 323 CE.

Abaye – אַבַּיֵי: One of the outstanding Sages of the Talmud, Abaye was a fourth-generation Babylonian *amora*. It is possible that his real name was Naḥmani or Kilil and that Abaye was just a nickname.

Abaye was orphaned at an early age and was raised by his paternal uncle, Rabba. Abaye's foster mother, who was the nursemaid that assisted his uncle in raising him, impressed upon him many life lessons that he quotes in her name. The Gemara relates several stories that illustrate his intelligence even as a child, including several where Rabba tests him with questions.

Abaye was the primary student of his uncle and of Rav Yosef, and after Rav Yosef's death, Abaye succeeded him as the head of the yeshiva in Pumbedita. In addition to his prominence as a Torah scholar, he was known for his righteousness and acts of kindness. He celebrated the study of Torah and would announce a celebration for the Sages whenever one of them completed a tractate. Although his uncle was a priest and the head of the yeshiva, he lived in poverty, as did Abaye, and therefore, he was aware of the difficulties of the Sages who lacked financial means. The Gemara in tractate *Berakhot* (35b) relates that Abaye observed that many were successful following the path of Rabbi Yishmael, who instructed his students to plow, plant, and harvest at the appropriate time, and that only a few were successful following the path of Rabbi Shimon bar Yoḥai, who taught that one should devote himself entirely to Torah and ignore worldly pursuits.

Abaye's exchanges and halakhic disputes with Rabba and, even more so, with Rav Yosef, are found throughout the Talmud. However, his disputes with his colleague Rava are especially significant. Their disputes, known as the discussions of Abaye and Rava, are examples of profound and edifying disputes and are among the foundations of the Babylonian Talmud. In these disputes, with six exceptions, the *halakha* is ruled in accordance with the opinion of Rava.

NOTES

In want of all things – בְּחֹסֶר כֹּל: Apparently, each of these Sages explained the verse based on his life experience. Rav, who previously stated that the implements of exile are a lamp, a bowl, and a table, holds that people require those items and considers their lack to be the "want of all things." Rav Ḥisda said (*Kiddushin* 29b) that the reason he is superior to his colleagues is due to the fact that he married at a young age; therefore, his definition of one who is "in want of all things" is one without a wife. Rav Sheshet, who was blind and needed an attendant, stated that one without an attendant is "in want of all things" (*Iyyun Ya'akov*).

If he has not acquired this, what has he acquired – דָּא לָא קְנֵי מַה קְנֵי: This means that if one lacks intelligence, he does not know how to utilize his possessions properly and it is as though he has nothing (Ran). The Maharsha explains possessions to be referring to both material and spiritual possessions. This explains why genuine poverty is lack of intelligence, as the property of one lacking intelligence has no value.

Only when the heavenly court forgives him for all his sins – עַד שֶׁמּוֹחֲלִין לוֹ עַל כׇּל עֲוֹנוֹתָיו: Anyone ill is considered to be in a situation of danger, at which point one is judged for his actions, and there is concern that he might die as a result. If he recovers, clearly he was judged to be innocent. Furthermore, his suffering atones for his sins. Therefore, when he is cured, his sins are forgiven (Rabbi Yitzḥak Tzarfati).

He returns to the days of his youth – חוֹזֵר לִימֵי עֲלוּמָיו: *Tosafot* explain according to the plain meaning of the expression, that one is healthier after recovery than he was before the illness. See Rava's statement beginning at the end of 41a. However, Rashi explains that the meaning is that he returns to his youth in the sense that his sins are expiated, so he is like a child without sin.

That is to say that he forgets his studies – לוֹמַר דְּמִשְׁתַּכַּח תַּלְמוּדוֹ: The Rosh and the Ran derive this from the verse "he returns to the days of his youth [*alumav*]." The term *alumav* is from *alum*, meaning concealed, indicating that he returns to a time when he knew nothing. Others explain likewise, that he is restored to his childhood, when he had not yet learned anything (Riaf). These explanations are apparently based on a variant reading of the Gemara, as, in the version printed here, the fact that one forgets his studies is derived from the verse "You overturned all his lying down [*mishkavo*] in his illness." However, the relationship between this verse and that which is derived from it is unclear. Some explain that *mishkavo* is an abbreviation for *meshekh bo* meaning that in which he was engaged, i.e., his studies. Alternatively, the reference is to the basic material that he learned by heart, e.g., *mishnayot* and *baraitot*, that lie there in his mind (*Shita Mekubbetzet*).

LANGUAGE

Fat [*revav*] – רְבָב: This refers to oily materials like fat and the like. Once it also meant stain, originally a stain from fat.

BACKGROUND

Forgets his studies – מִשְׁתַּכַּח תַּלְמוּדוֹ: There are various afflictions that attack the brain first, e.g., internal hemorrhaging and meningitis, which can severely curtail brain function and lead to coma. Some infectious diseases do not directly afflict the brain, e.g., measles and whooping cough, but complications resulting from those diseases can lead to brain damage. These afflictions can damage various sensory centers as well as consciousness and cognition. Therefore, they can cause full or partial memory loss.

כי הוה גמיר רבי תלת עשרי אפי הילכתא – אגמריה לרבי חייא שבעה מנהון. לסוף חלש רבי, אהדר רבי חייא קמיה הנהו שבעה אפי דאגמריה. שיתא אזדו. הוה ההוא קצרא, הוה שמיע ליה לרבי כדהוה גריס להו, אזל רבי חייא וגמר יתהון קמי קצרא, ואתא ואהדר יתהון קמי רבי. כד הוה חזי ליה רבי להוא קצרא אמר ליה רבי: אתה עשית אותי ואת חייא. איכא דאמרי הכי קאמר ליה: אתה עשית את חייא, וחייא עשה אותי.

The Gemara relates: **When Rabbi** Yehuda HaNasi[P] **would learn thirteen aspects of a** ***halakha*** on a certain issue, **he taught Rabbi Ḥiyya**[P] **seven of them. Ultimately, Rabbi** Yehuda HaNasi **fell ill** and forgot all thirteen aspects. **Rabbi Ḥiyya restored those seven aspects that** Rabbi Yehuda HaNasi **taught him** by reviewing them before Rabbi Yehuda HaNasi. However, **six were gone** and forgotten, as Rabbi Yehuda HaNasi had not taught them to anyone. There **was a certain launderer** who **would hear Rabbi** Yehuda HaNasi **when he was studying** those *halakhot*. **Rabbi Ḥiyya went and learned** those *halakhot* **from the launderer and he came and restored them** by reviewing them **before Rabbi** Yehuda HaNasi. **When Rabbi** Yehuda HaNasi **saw that launderer, Rabbi** Yehuda HaNasi **said to him: You made me and Ḥiyya,** as we were able to learn these *halakhot* that otherwise would have been forgotten. **Some say** that **this is what he said to** the launderer: **You made Ḥiyya, and Ḥiyya made me.**

ואמר רבי אלכסנדרי אמר רבי חייא בר אבא: גדול נס שנעשה לחולה יותר מן הנס שנעשה לחנניה מישאל ועזריה. של חנניה מישאל ועזריה – אש של הדיוט, והכל יכולים לכבותה. וזו של חולה – של שמים היא, ומי יכול לכבותה?

And Rabbi Alexandri said that **Rabbi Ḥiyya bar Abba said: Greater is the miracle performed for the sick person than the miracle that was performed for Hananiah, Mishael, and Azariah,** who were rescued from the fiery furnace (see Daniel, chapter 3), as in the miracle of **Hananiah, Mishael, and Azariah,** they were rescued from **the fire of a layman, and anyone is capable of extinguishing it. And that** fire afflicting **a sick person** with a fever is the fire **of Heaven, and who can extinguish it?**

ואמר רבי אלכסנדרי אמר רבי חייא בר אבא, ואמרי לה אמר רבי יהושע בן לוי: כיון שהגיע קיצו של אדם – הכל מושלים בו, שנאמר "והיה כל מצאי יהרגני". רב אמר: מן הדין קרא – "למשפטיך עמדו היום כי הכל עבדיך".

And Rabbi Alexandri said that **Rabbi Ḥiyya bar Abba said, and some say Rabbi Yehoshua ben Levi said: Once the end** of the time allotted for the life **of a person arrived, everything has dominion over him, as it is stated** that Cain said: **"Whosoever finds me will slay me"** (Genesis 4:14). Cain feared that since God sentenced him to death he would be susceptible to all threats and vulnerable to anyone seeking to murder him. **Rav said** that it is derived **from this verse: "They stand this day according to Your judgments; for all are Your servants"** (Psalms 119:91). When the decree emerges from Heaven that the time has arrived for a person to die, everyone is a servant of God, an agent to kill him.

רבה בר שילא אמרו ליה: שכיב גברא. גבוה הוה רכיב גירדונא זוטרא, מטא תיתורא איסתויט, שדייה וקא שכיב. קרי על נפשיה: "למשפטיך עמדו היום".

The Gemara relates that people **said to Rabba bar Sheila: A man died.** This person **was tall** and was **riding on a small mule** [*giredona*].[L] **When he reached a bridge** [*tittora*],[L] the mule **was frightened** [*istavveit*][L] and **cast off** the rider, **and** although the rider was tall and the mule was short and the rider did not fall far, **he died.** Rabba bar Sheila **read** the verse and applied it **to** the rider: **"They stand this day according to Your judgments."**

שמואל חזייה להוא קרוקיתא דעקרבא יתיבא על אקרוקתא ועברה נהרא, טרקא גברא ומיית. קרי עליה "למשפטיך עמדו היום".

Shmuel saw a certain frog [*kerokita*],[L] and also noticed **that a scorpion was sitting upon the frog and the frog crossed the river.** The scorpion **stung a man** on the other side of the river **and** the man **died.** Shmuel **read** and applied the verse **to** the dead man: **"They stand this day according to Your judgments."** Even the frog and scorpion are servants and agents of God. The only way the scorpion could reach the man and kill him was by means of the frog taking it across the river.

אמר שמואל: אין מבקרין את החולה אלא למי שחלצתו חמה. לאפוקי מאי? לאפוקי הא דתניא, רבי יוסי בן פרטא אומר משום רבי אליעזר: אין מבקרין לא חולי מעיים, ולא חולי העין, ולא מחושי הראש. בשלמא חולי מעיים – משום כיסופא, אלא חולי העין, ומחושי הראש מאי טעמא?

§ **Shmuel said: One visits a sick person only if** that person is **one whom fever overcame.** The Gemara asks: **What** illnesses **does** this statement come to **exclude?** The Gemara answers: It comes **to exclude that which is taught** in a *baraita*: **Rabbi Yosei ben Perata says in the name of Rabbi Eliezer: One visits neither those with intestinal illness, nor those with eye illness, nor** those suffering from **headaches.**[H] The Gemara asks: **Granted,** one does not visit **those with intestinal sickness, due to** the sick person's **embarrassment,** as he would need to frequently relieve himself and it would be awkward for him in the presence of the visitor. **However, what is the reason** that one does not visit **those with eye illnesses and headaches?**

PERSONALITIES

Rabbi Yehuda HaNasi – רבי: The period of the *tanna'im* concluded with Rabbi Yehuda HaNasi's redaction of the Mishna. The son of Rabbi Shimon ben Gamliel II, Rabbi Yehuda HaNasi lived from 135–220 CE. When he was thirty years old he was appointed as *Nasi*, and his great scholarship led him to be referred to in the Talmud simply as: Rabbi. Rabbi Yehuda HaNasi spoke Greek, which was the language spoken by the elite in Eretz Yisrael, and he was friendly with the Roman emperor Antoninus. His knowledge of Hebrew was legendary, to the extent that the Sages learned the meaning of difficult words from servants employed in his household.

Rabbi Ḥiyya – רבי חייא: Rabbi Ḥiyya ben Abba, from the city of Kafri in Babylonia, was among the last *tanna'im*. He was descended from a family of distinguished lineage that traced its ancestry back to King David and produced many Sages. While he was still in Babylonia, Rabbi Ḥiyya was considered a Torah luminary, and when he ascended to Eretz Yisrael with his family, some, speaking in hyperbole, said that the Torah was on the verge of being forgotten until he came from Babylonia and reestablished it.

When Rabbi Ḥiyya came to Eretz Yisrael, he became a disciple and a colleague of Rabbi Yehuda HaNasi, developing a very close relationship with him. He was especially close to Rabbi Yehuda HaNasi's son, Shimon, who was also his business partner. Rabbi Ḥiyya was among the prominent Torah scholars in his generation and was a close advisor of his nephew, Rav, who, although known as the rabbi of all Israel, received certain traditions from Rabbi Ḥiyya. In addition to his prominence as a Torah scholar, Rabbi Ḥiyya was exemplary in his piety, as reflected in anecdotes related throughout the Talmud.

LANGUAGE

Mule [*giredona*] – גירדונא: Apparently, it should be read *giderona*, from the Greek γάιδαρος, *gaidaron*, meaning small donkey

Bridge [*tittora*] – תיתורא: This means bridge; an item that connects two parts.

Frightened [*istavveit*] – איסתויט: This is the reflexive form of the root *samekh, yod, tav*, which appears in the noun form as *siuta*, meaning nightmare or sudden fear. Therefore this means one stricken with sudden panic. Some hold that this is a variation of the Aramaic *ziata*. Others consider it an independent root with this unique meaning.

Frog [*kerokita*] – קרוקיתא: This word seems to be onomatopoetic, as it approximates the croaking of a frog.

HALAKHA

One visits neither those with intestinal illness, nor those with eye illness, nor those suffering from headaches – אין מבקרין לא חולי מעיים, ולא חולי העין, ולא מחושי הראש: One should not visit one suffering from a stomach illness, eye illness, or headaches, and in general, one should not visit anyone for whom speaking causes discomfort. One should not directly visit a person in that condition. However, he enters an outer room, inquires whether he can be of any assistance, and prays for the well-being of the patient (Rambam *Sefer Shofetim*, *Hilkhot Evel* 14:5; *Shulḥan Arukh*, *Yoreh De'a* 335:8).

מִשּׁוּם דְּרַב יְהוּדָה. דְּאָמַר רַב יְהוּדָה: דִּיבּוּרָא קַשְׁיָא לְעֵינָא וּמַעֲלֵי לְאִישְׁתָּא. אֲמַר רָבָא: הַאי אִישְׁתָּא, אִי לָאו דְּפַרְוַונְקָא דְּמַלְאֲכָא דְמוֹתָא – מַעֲלֵי

The Gemara answers: **It is due to** that which **Rav Yehuda said,** as **Rav Yehuda said: Speech is injurious for the eye**[B] and **beneficial for** curing **a fever.**[B] Therefore, if one suffers from pain in his eye or his head it is better for him not to talk. If he has visitors, he will need to speak to them, which will cause him harm. **Rava said:** With regard to **this fever** [*ishta*],[L] **were it not the agent** [*parvanka*][L] **of the Angel of Death,** i.e., the cause of serious, potentially deadly illnesses, it could be deemed **beneficial,**

BACKGROUND

Speech is injurious for the eye – דִּיבּוּרָא קַשְׁיָא לְעֵינָא: This may be because one typically looks into the eyes of whoever speaks to him. Keeping one's eyes open and straining the muscles of the eye are particularly difficult for one suffering from an eye illness. Also, pain in the eyes is typically accompanied by a headache that is exacerbated by noise.

Beneficial for curing a fever – מַעֲלֵי לְאִישְׁתָּא: It may be that the benefit of the easing of fever is primarily psychological, by taking the sick person's mind off the fever and the chill that accompanies it.

LANGUAGE

Fever [*ishta*] – אִישְׁתָּא: Literally meaning fire, this word is used as a term for fever and particularly for various forms of malaria.

Agent [*parvanka*] – פַּרְוַונְקָא: From the Middle Iranian term, parwānak, meaning a guide or messenger.

Perek **IV**
Daf **41** Amud **b**

כְּחִיזְרָא לְדִיקְלֵי, חַד לִתְלָתִין יוֹמִין, וְכִי תִּירְיָיקֵי לְגוּפָא. רַב נַחְמָן בַּר יִצְחָק אָמַר: לָא הִיא וְלָא תִּירְיָיקָהּ.

like thorns **for palm trees,** as the thorns prevent people and animals from touching and ruining the dates. The fever is advantageous if its incidence is **once in thirty days, and it is like an antidote** [*tiraiki*][L] **for** poison in **the body. Rav Naḥman bar Yitzḥak said:** It is preferable for one to have **neither** fever **nor** the benefits of **its** capacity to serve as an **antidote.**[B]

אָמַר רַבָּה בַּר יוֹנָתָן אָמַר רַב יְחִיאֵל: עַרְסָן יָפֶה לְחוֹלֶה לִרְפוּאָתוֹ. מַאי עַרְסָן? אָמַר רַבִּי יוֹנָתָן: חוּשְׁלָא דְּשַׂעֲרֵי עַתִּיקָתָא דְּרֵישׁ נָפְיָא. אָמַר אַבָּיֵי: בָּעֲיָין בִּישּׁוּלָא כְּעֵין בִּישְׂרָא דְּתוֹרָא. רַב יוֹסֵף אָמַר: סְמִידֵי דְּשַׂעֲרֵי עַתִּיקָתָא דְּרֵישׁ נָפְיָא. אָמַר אַבָּיֵי: בָּעֲיָין בִּישּׁוּלָא כְּבִשְׂרָא דְּתוֹרָא.

Rabba bar Yonatan said that Rav Yeḥiel said: *Arsan* **is beneficial for the sick person for his cure.** The Gemara asks: **What is** *arsan*? **Rabbi Yonatan said:** It is **old hulled barley from the beginning of** the sifting process.[N] **Abaye said:** And that barley **requires** extensive **cooking like the meat of a bull.**[B] **Rav Yosef said:** *Arsan* **is fine flour** [*semida*][L] ground **from old barley from the beginning of** the **sifting** process. **Abaye said:** And that flour **requires** extensive **cooking like the meat of a bull.**

אָמַר רַבִּי יוֹחָנָן: בּוֹרְדָּם אֵין מְבַקְּרִים, וְאֵין מַזְכִּירִין שְׁמוֹ. מַאי טַעְמָא? אָמַר רַבִּי אֶלְעָזָר: מִפְּנֵי שֶׁהוּא כְּמַעְיָין הַנּוֹבֵעַ. וְאָמַר רַבִּי אֶלְעָזָר: לָמָּה נִקְרָא שְׁמוֹ בּוֹרְדָּם – שֶׁהוּא כְּמַעְיָין הַנּוֹבֵעַ.

Rabbi Yoḥanan said: One does not visit a person suffering from *buredam*,[NL] an intestinal illness, **nor is the name** of that illness **mentioned,**[N] because it is embarrassing for the one suffering from the illness. The Gemara asks: **What is the reason** that one does not visit him? **Rabbi Elazar said:** It is due to the fact **that he is like a flowing spring,** as the symptom of the illness is severe diarrhea. **And Rabbi Elazar said: Why is** the illness **called** *buredam*? It is due to the fact **that** the one suffering from the illness **is like a flowing spring,** a bottomless pit [*bor*] of blood [*dam*].

LANGUAGE

Antidote [*tiraiki*] – תִּירְיָיקֵי: From the Greek θηριακή, *thēriakē*, a purported antidote for snake venom. It was highly valued during the Middle Ages and was prepared from a large number of ingredients. It was believed to be a wonder drug effective against all kinds of poison and venom.

Fine flour [*semida*] – סְמִידָא: Related to the Greek σεμίδαλις, *semidalis*, meaning fine wheat flour.

***Buredam* – בּוֹרְדָּם:** Possibly from the Greek βροτός, *brotos*, meaning filled with blood, which describes a characteristic symptom of this sickness. From the description in the Gemara and the interpretation of the commentaries, it appears to be dysentery. This is a sickness with many causes, e.g., bacteria and amoebas, and is characterized by severe diarrhea containing blood and mucus. Due to the frequent diarrhea, which is unpleasant and causes significant pain, it is difficult for people suffering from this illness to receive visitors. Furthermore, dysentery is contagious and can be carried by tasting or handling food touched by the sick person

NOTES

From the beginning of the sifting process – דְּרֵישׁ נָפְיָא: Some explain that this refers to the kernels that remain stuck on the sieve due to their size (Rashi). Others claim that the reference is to the kernels that emerge at the beginning of the sifting process (Ran). Still others say that the reference is to fine flour ground from the kernels (*Tosafot*).

***Buredam* – בּוֹרְדָּם:** Some commentaries explain that this is persistent diarrhea (*Arukh*; Rashi) or a wound with pus (Rashi). However, most explain that it is dysentery.

Nor is the name of that illness mentioned – וְאֵין מַזְכִּירִין שְׁמוֹ: Some explain that the reason is that the sick person is embarrassed when others are told he is suffering from this illness (*Tosafot*; Rosh). Others assert that it is inappropriate language (Ran). See Rashi, who says that the mere mention of the illness is an evil harbinger.

BACKGROUND

Neither fever nor the benefits of its capacity to serve as an antidote – לָא הִיא וְלָא תִּירְיָיקָהּ: A rise in body temperature of five or six degrees Fahrenheit is potentially dangerous and can even cause death, which is why it is characterized as an agent of the Angel of Death. On the other hand, certain bacteria and viruses are sensitive to heat, and when the body temperature rises it kills the bacteria and viruses and the person recovers from the illness, as is the case with malaria. There were periods when doctors would attempt to induce fever in order to overcome a more serious condition. However, the effectiveness of that cure is unproven and the danger posed by a high fever is great.

Requires extensive cooking like the meat of a bull – בָּעֲיָין בִּישּׁוּלָא כְּעֵין בִּישְׂרָא דְּתוֹרָא: Although various types of meal and fine flour may be nutritious and beneficial for the ill, the sick person may encounter difficulty digesting them due to his weakness. Therefore, Abaye said that they should be cooked for several hours, like the meat of a bull, in order to soften them and facilitate digestion.

״וּמְרַפְּאֵהוּ רְפוּאַת הַנֶּפֶשׁ״ כּו׳. הֵיכִי קָתָנֵי? אִילֵימָא דִּרְפוּאַת נֶפֶשׁ – בְּחִנָּם, רְפוּאַת מָמוֹן – בְּשָׂכָר, לִיתְנֵי הָכִי: מְרַפְּאֵהוּ בְּחִנָּם אֲבָל לֹא בְּשָׂכָר! אֶלָּא: רְפוּאַת נֶפֶשׁ – גּוּפוֹ, וּרְפוּאַת מָמוֹן – בְּהֶמְתּוֹ. אָמַר רַבִּי זוּטְרָא בַּר טוֹבִיָּה אָמַר רַב: אֲבָל אוֹמֵר לוֹ ״סַם פְּלוֹנִי יָפֶה לָהּ, סַם פְּלוֹנִי רַע לָהּ״.

§ We learned in the mishna that if one is prohibited by a vow from deriving benefit from another, that other person **heals him** with **a cure of the *nefesh***[N] but not a cure of property [*mamon*]. The Gemara asks: **How is the mishna taught? If we say that cure of the *nefesh*** means that he cures him **for free and cure of *mamon*** means that he cures him **for a fee,** then **let** the mishna **teach this: He cures him for free but not for a fee. Rather, cure of the *nefesh*** means that he cures **his body, and cure of *mamon***[H] means that he cures **his animal. Rabbi Zutra bar Toviya said** that **Rav said:** It is prohibited to cure the animal. **However, he says to him: Such and such medicine is beneficial** for the animal, **and such and such medicine is harmful** for the animal. Advice, as opposed to treatment, is not considered benefit.

מתני׳ וְרוֹחֵץ עִמּוֹ בְּאַמְבָּטִי גְּדוֹלָה, אֲבָל לֹא בִּקְטַנָּה, וְיָשֵׁן עִמּוֹ בְּמִטָּה.

MISHNA And with regard to another person who is prohibited from deriving benefit from him, **one may bathe with him in a large bath** [*ambati*],[LH] in which his presence does not affect the other person. **However,** he may **not** bathe with him **in a small** bath,[N] as his presence moderates the temperature of water if it is too hot or too cold, thereby benefiting the other person. **And he may sleep with him in** one **bed.**[H]

רַבִּי יְהוּדָה אוֹמֵר: בִּימוֹת הַחַמָּה, אֲבָל לֹא בִּימוֹת הַגְּשָׁמִים, מִפְּנֵי שֶׁהוּא מְהַנֵּהוּ. וּמֵיסֵב עִמּוֹ עַל הַמִּטָּה, וְאוֹכֵל עִמּוֹ עַל הַשּׁוּלְחָן, אֲבָל לֹא מִן הַתַּמְחוּי. אֲבָל אוֹכֵל הוּא עִמּוֹ מִן הַתַּמְחוּי הַחוֹזֵר.

Rabbi Yehuda says: That is permitted **during the days of summer, but** he may **not** sleep with him in one bed **during the rainy season,** i.e., the winter, **because he benefits him** by warming the bed. **And he may recline with him on a divan** even during the rainy season, as no benefit is involved. **And he may eat with him** at the same **table, but not from** a common **platter**[B] from which several people eat, as if one leaves food on the platter, the other derives benefit from him. **However, he may eat with him from a platter that returns** to the host, as everyone takes a small portion and leaves food on the platter. No benefit is derived. Since there is enough food for everyone, none of the diners receives part of another's portion.

NOTES

Cure of the *nefesh* – רְפוּאַת הַנֶּפֶשׁ: Some explain (Ran; Rabbi Avraham min HaHar) that in the first interpretation, that cure of the *nefesh* means cure for free, the term *nefesh* is apparently related to will, as in the verse "if it is your will [*nafshekhem*]" (Genesis 23:8). However, according to the conclusion of the Gemara, *nefesh* means body, as is its meaning in several places in the Bible (*Gilyon Maharsha*).

However, not in a small bath – אֲבָל לֹא בִּקְטַנָּה: Many commentaries explain that the reason is that when one enters a small bath the water rises and covers the other person's body. Others say that by entering a small tub, he raises the temperature of the water (Rashi). There are also those who write that the concern is that more water will be added on his behalf, which would also benefit the other person (*Tosefot Rabbeinu Peretz*).

HALAKHA

Cure of *mamon* – רְפוּאַת מָמוֹן: One who vowed that benefit from him is forbidden to another may not cure the other person's animal; however, he may recommend medicines that are beneficial for the animal. If the one for whom benefit is forbidden is unable to cure his own animal and it might die, it is permitted for the one who vowed that benefit from him is forbidden to heal the animal, because it is tantamount to returning a lost item (Rambam *Sefer Hafla'a*, *Hilkhot Nedarim* 6:9; *Shulḥan Arukh*, *Yoreh De'a* 221:4).

One may bathe with him in a…bath – רוֹחֵץ עִמּוֹ בְּאַמְבָּטִי: One who vowed that benefit from him is forbidden to another may bathe together with him in a large bath but not in a small one, because by entering the small bath he raises the water level (Rambam *Sefer Hafla'a*, *Hilkhot Nedarim* 6:9; *Shulḥan Arukh*, *Yoreh De'a* 221:5).

And he may sleep with him in one bed – וְיָשֵׁן עִמּוֹ בְּמִטָּה: It is permitted for one who vowed that benefit from him is forbidden to another to sleep with him in the same bed during the summer. He may not do so during the rainy season, because he thereby benefits him. In a large bed it is permitted in every season (Rambam *Sefer Hafla'a*, *Hilkhot Nedarim* 6:9; *Shulḥan Arukh*, *Yoreh De'a* 221:5).

LANGUAGE

Bath [*ambati*] – אַמְבָּטִי: From the Greek ἐμβατή, *embatē*, meaning tub or other vessel used for bathing.

Small bathtub in Pylos, Greece, dating from 1300 BCE

BACKGROUND

A common platter – הַתַּמְחוּי: From descriptions in the sources it appears that this was an outsized vessel, like a large, deep platter used to serve several people. Most were apparently made of earthenware, although some were made of metals like copper and silver, and others of wood or glass. There were also very large platters divided into compartments so that various types of food could be placed on it separately.

גמ׳ תַּנְיָא: לֹא יִרְחַץ עִמּוֹ בְּאַמְבָּטִי, וְלֹא יִשַּׁן עִמּוֹ בְּמִטָּה, בֵּין גְּדוֹלָה בֵּין קְטַנָּה, דִּבְרֵי רַבִּי מֵאִיר. רַבִּי יְהוּדָה אוֹמֵר: גְּדוֹלָה בִּימוֹת הַגְּשָׁמִים, וּקְטַנָּה בִּימוֹת הַחַמָּה – מוּתָּר. רוֹחֵץ עִמּוֹ בְּאַמְבָּטִי גְּדוֹלָה, וּמֵזִיעַ עִמּוֹ בִּקְטַנָּה. אֲבָל מֵיסֵב עִמּוֹ עַל הַמִּטָּה, וְאוֹכֵל עִמּוֹ עַל הַשּׁוּלְחָן, אֲבָל לֹא מִן הַתַּמְחוּי. אֲבָל אוֹכֵל הוּא מִן הַתַּמְחוּי הַחוֹזֵר. אָמַר רַבִּי יוֹסֵי בַּר חֲנִינָא: מִן הַתַּמְחוּי הַחוֹזֵר לְבַעַל הַבַּיִת.

GEMARA **It is taught** in a *baraita*: **One may neither bathe with him in a bath nor sleep with him in a bed,**[N] and there is no difference **whether** it is **a large** bed or **whether** it is **a small** bed; this is **the statement of Rabbi Meir. Rabbi Yehuda says:** It is **permitted** for him to sleep with him in a **large** bed **during the rainy season and a small** bed **during the days of summer,** as no benefit is derived. **He may bathe with him in a large bath and sweat with him in a small one,**[H] as his presence provides no benefit for the other. However, **he may recline with him on a divan, and he may eat with him** at the same **table but not from a** common **platter.**[HN] **However, he may eat with him from a platter that returns.**[N] **Rabbi Yosei bar Ḥanina said:** That means **a platter that returns to the host.**

מתני׳ לֹא יֹאכַל עִמּוֹ מִן הָאֵבוּס שֶׁלִּפְנֵי הַפּוֹעֲלִים, וְלֹא יַעֲשֶׂה עִמּוֹ בְּאוּמָן, דִּבְרֵי רַבִּי מֵאִיר. וַחֲכָמִים אוֹמְרִים: עוֹשֶׂה וְהוּא בְּרָחוֹק מִמֶּנּוּ.

MISHNA **One may neither eat with him from the large vessel** of food placed **before the laborers, nor may he work with him in** the same **row in a vineyard;**[HN] this is **the statement of Rabbi Meir. And the Rabbis say: He may work** in the same row with him provided that **he is at a distance from him.** If he is close, the other would derive forbidden benefit from him.

גמ׳ בְּקָרוֹב – לָא פְּלִיגִי דַּאֲסִיר, כִּי פְּלִיגִי – בְּרָחוֹק; רַבִּי מֵאִיר סָבַר: גָּזְרִינַן רָחוֹק מִשּׁוּם קָרוֹב, דְּקָא מְרַפֵּי לָהּ לְאַרְעָא קַמֵּיהּ. וְרַבָּנַן סָבְרִי: לָא גָּזְרִינַן.

GEMARA In a case **where** one is **proximate** to the other, the *tanna'im* **do not disagree that it is prohibited** for them to work together. **When they disagree,** it is in a case **where** one is **distant** from the other. **Rabbi Meir holds: We issue a decree** prohibiting their working together when one is **distant** from the other, **due to** the prohibition against their working together when one is **proximate** to the other, **as he loosens for him the earth before him. And the Rabbis hold: We do not issue a decree.**

HALAKHA

And sweat with him in a small one – וּמֵזִיעַ עִמּוֹ בִּקְטַנָּה: It is permitted for one who vowed that benefit from him is forbidden to another to sweat together with the other person in a small bath (*Shulḥan Arukh, Yoreh De'a* 221:5).

He may eat with him at the same table but not from a common platter – אוֹכֵל עִמּוֹ עַל הַשּׁוּלְחָן אֲבָל לֹא מִן הַתַּמְחוּי: One who vows that benefit from another is forbidden to him may eat with that other person at the same table but not from the same platter, lest he come to eat from the other person's portion. However, it is permitted if the host refills the platter after the food is eaten from it. It is also permitted if there is enough food on the platter for them to eat and return the remaining food to the host (Rema, citing Ra'avad; Rambam *Sefer Hafla'a, Hilkhot Nedarim* 6:9; *Shulḥan Arukh, Yoreh De'a* 221:5).

Nor may he work with him in the same row in a vineyard – וְלֹא יַעֲשֶׂה עִמּוֹ בְּאוּמָן: For one for whom benefit from another is forbidden by vow, it is prohibited to dig in the same furrow in a vineyard with that other person, because he benefits from the other's digging, which softens the ground. If there is a distance between them it is permitted, in accordance with the opinion of the Rabbis (Rambam *Sefer Hafla'a, Hilkhot Nedarim* 6:17; *Shulḥan Arukh, Yoreh De'a* 221:5).

NOTES

Nor sleep with him in a bed – וְלֹא יִשַּׁן עִמּוֹ בְּמִטָּה: Some hold that the mishna is the opinion of Rabbi Yehuda and he does not dispute the beginning of the mishna, but merely explains it (Rashba; Ran). Others hold that there are three separate opinions here. Rabbi Meir does not distinguish between a large and a small bath, or between a large and a small bed, or between the summer and the rainy season, and he rules that bathing or sleeping with the other person is prohibited in all cases. The first *tanna* rules that sleeping with him is permitted in any kind of bed, and Rabbi Yehuda rules that it is prohibited only in a small bed during the rainy season (Rid; Ritz).

But not from a common platter – אֲבָל לֹא מִן הַתַּמְחוּי: Some interpret this to mean that the concern is that one might eat less, thereby benefiting the one to whom benefit is forbidden (Ran). Others explain that the concern is that the homeowner might provide better food because of the one who vowed that benefit from him is forbidden, thereby benefiting the one to whom benefit is forbidden (Rashi; Meiri; Rid). Another possibility is that the concern is that the one who vowed that benefit from him is forbidden will offer the vessel with the food to the one for whom benefit is forbidden or offer him a larger portion, as an act of courtesy (Rambam).

From a platter that returns – מִן הַתַּמְחוּי הַחוֹזֵר: One explanation brought by Rashi and others (Jerusalem Talmud; Rosh; Ran) is that the reference is to a platter so large that the remainder returns to the host and no one benefits from the fact that others ate less. Others explain that after each person takes a portion, the host sends the platter around again so everyone can take additional portions. No one benefits from the food left by others (*Arukh*; Ritva). Alternatively, the reference is to a case where after each person takes his portion, the host takes the bowl and places it before the next person (Rambam). Others explain that guests typically divide the food remaining on the platter and take it home. Therefore, if one eats less, others benefit. However, if it is a platter that returns to the host, no one benefits from the fact that others eat less (Rashi). In the Jerusalem Talmud another explanation is cited, that the reference is to portions cut on a platter, where the host sends the platter around and each person takes one of the portions.

Nor may he work with him in the same row in a vineyard – וְלֹא יַעֲשֶׂה עִמּוֹ בְּאוּמָן: The Gemara is apparently speaking of digging in adjacent furrows. The Rambam in his Commentary on the Mishna and Rabbi Ovadya Bartenura explain that the reference is to harvesting produce from the furrows, as cutting the produce in one furrow facilitates work in the adjacent furrow. The Rambam rules in the *Mishne Torah* that it is prohibited by decree, lest one come to assist the other, from whom benefit is forbidden, in his own harvest (see *Kesef Mishne*).

MITNEI' הַמּוּדָּר הֲנָאָה מֵחֲבֵירוֹ, לִפְנֵי שְׁבִיעִית – אֵינוֹ יוֹרֵד לְתוֹךְ שָׂדֵהוּ, וְאֵינוֹ אוֹכֵל מִן הַנּוֹטוֹת. וּבַשְּׁבִיעִית – אֵינוֹ יוֹרֵד לְתוֹךְ שָׂדֵהוּ, אֲבָל אוֹכֵל הוּא מִן הַנְּטִיעוֹת הַנּוֹטוֹת. נָדַר הֵימֶנּוּ מַאֲכָל לִפְנֵי שְׁבִיעִית – יוֹרֵד לְתוֹךְ שָׂדֵהוּ וְאֵינוֹ אוֹכֵל מִן הַפֵּירוֹת, וּבַשְּׁבִיעִית – יוֹרֵד וְאוֹכֵל.

MISHNA In the case of **one for whom benefit from another is forbidden, before,** i.e., a year other than **the Sabbatical Year,**[B] **he may neither enter**[H] **the field** of that other person, **nor eat from** the produce that leans out of the field, even if he does not enter the field. **And during the Sabbatical Year,** when the produce of the trees is ownerless, **he may not enter his field;**[N] **however, he may eat from the growths that lean** out of the field, as the produce does not belong to the other person. If **one vowed before the Sabbatical Year** that benefit **from** another's **food** is forbidden[H] for him, **he may enter his field; however, he may not eat of the produce. And during the Sabbatical Year, he may enter** the field **and may eat** the produce.

GEM' רַב וּשְׁמוּאֵל דְּאָמְרִי תַּרְוַיְיהוּ: "נְכָסִים אֵלּוּ עָלֶיךָ" לִפְנֵי שְׁבִיעִית – אֵין יוֹרֵד לְתוֹךְ שָׂדֵהוּ, וְאֵינוֹ אוֹכֵל מִן הַנּוֹטוֹת, אַף עַל פִּי שֶׁהִגִּיעַ שְׁבִיעִית. וְאִם בַּשְּׁבִיעִית נָדַר – אֵין יוֹרֵד לְתוֹךְ שָׂדֵהוּ, אֲבָל אוֹכֵל מִן הַנּוֹטוֹת.

GEMARA It is **Rav and Shmuel who both say** that if one vowed **before the Sabbatical Year:** Benefit from **this property** is forbidden **to you,** the other **may neither enter his field, nor eat from** the produce **that leans** out of the field, **even though the Sabbatical Year arrived** in the interim, because the prohibition of the produce took effect before the Sabbatical Year and remained in effect after the Sabbatical Year began. **And if he vowed during the Sabbatical Year, he may not enter a field** that is included in that property; **however, he may eat from** the produce that leans out of the field, because the produce was ownerless when he vowed.

וְרַבִּי יוֹחָנָן וְרֵישׁ לָקִישׁ דְּאָמְרִי תַּרְוַיְיהוּ: "נְכָסַי עָלֶיךָ" לִפְנֵי שְׁבִיעִית – אֵין יוֹרֵד לְתוֹךְ שָׂדֵהוּ וְאֵין אוֹכֵל מִן הַנּוֹטוֹת, הִגִּיעַ שְׁבִיעִית – אֵינוֹ יוֹרֵד לְתוֹךְ שָׂדֵהוּ, אֲבָל אוֹכֵל הוּא אֶת הַנּוֹטוֹת.

And it is **Rabbi Yoḥanan and Reish Lakish**[N] **who both say** that if one vowed **before the Sabbatical Year:** Benefit from **my property** is forbidden **to you,** the other **may neither enter his field nor eat from** the produce that leans out of the field. When **the Sabbatical Year arrives, he may not enter his field; however, he may eat from** the produce that leans out of the field, because the produce is ownerless.

לֵימָא בְּהָא קָמִיפַּלְגִי, דְּרַב וּשְׁמוּאֵל סָבְרִי: אָדָם אוֹסֵר דָּבָר שֶׁבִּרְשׁוּתוֹ אֲפִילּוּ לִכְשֶׁיֵּצֵא מֵרְשׁוּתוֹ, וְרַבִּי יוֹחָנָן וְרֵישׁ לָקִישׁ סָבְרִי: אֵין אָדָם אוֹסֵר דָּבָר שֶׁבִּרְשׁוּתוֹ לִכְשֶׁיֵּצֵא מֵרְשׁוּתוֹ?

The Gemara suggests: **Let us say that they disagree about this, that Rav and Shmuel hold: A person** can **render an item in his possession forbidden,**[N] and the prohibition remains in effect **even when it leaves his possession.** Since he rendered the produce forbidden before the Sabbatical Year, the prohibition remains in effect after the produce becomes ownerless during the Sabbatical Year. **And Rabbi Yoḥanan and Reish Lakish hold: A person cannot render an item in his possession forbidden** and have the prohibition remain in effect **when it leaves his possession.** Therefore, it is permitted to eat the produce during the Sabbatical Year.

וְתִסְבְּרָא? מִי אִיכָּא לְמַאן דְּאָמַר אֵין אָדָם אוֹסֵר דָּבָר שֶׁבִּרְשׁוּתוֹ לִכְשֶׁיֵּצֵא מֵרְשׁוּתוֹ? אִם כֵּן נִיפְלְגִי בְּ"נְכָסִים אֵלּוּ", וְכׇל שֶׁכֵּן בְּ"נְכָסַי"!

The Gemara asks: **And** how can **you understand** it in that manner? **Is there anyone who says that a person cannot render an item in his possession forbidden** and have the prohibition remain in effect **when it leaves his possession? If so,** if Rabbi Yoḥanan and Reish Lakish hold that one cannot do so, **let them disagree in** the case of one who said: Benefit from **this property** is forbidden to you, **and** that would be true **all the more so** if he said: Benefit from **my property** is forbidden to you. In the latter case, it is clear that the prohibition remains in effect only as long as the item remains in his possession.

HALAKHA

Before the Sabbatical Year, he may neither enter, etc. – **לִפְנֵי שְׁבִיעִית אֵינוֹ יוֹרֵד וכו׳**: If one vows prior to the Sabbatical Year that benefit from the property of another is forbidden to him, employing the language: This property, it is prohibited for him to enter the other person's field and eat his produce, even during the Sabbatical Year. If he vows during the Sabbatical Year, it is prohibited for him to enter the field; however, he may eat produce that leans outside the field (Rambam *Sefer Hafla'a*, *Hilkhot Nedarim* 6:13).

If one vowed before the Sabbatical Year that benefit from another's food is forbidden – **נָדַר הֵימֶנּוּ מַאֲכָל לִפְנֵי שְׁבִיעִית**: If one vows prior to the Sabbatical Year that another's food is forbidden to him, he may enter the other person's field but may not eat its produce. If he vows during the Sabbatical Year, he may also eat the produce, as it is ownerless (Rambam *Sefer Hafla'a*, *Hilkhot Nedarim* 6:15).

NOTES

He may not enter his field – **אֵינוֹ יוֹרֵד לְתוֹךְ שָׂדֵהוּ**: This is because he benefits from stepping into his field. The consensus is that the Gemara is referring to the summer, when owners of fields are particular about people stepping in their fields (*Shita*).

And it is Rabbi Yoḥanan and Reish Lakish – **וְרַבִּי יוֹחָנָן וְרֵישׁ לָקִישׁ**: This dispute between Rav and Shmuel on the one hand and Rabbi Yoḥanan and Reish Lakish on the other hand is also cited in the Jerusalem Talmud; however, there it is a dispute between Rabbi Yoḥanan and Reish Lakish. Rabbi Yoḥanan's opinion there corresponds to his opinion here, and Reish Lakish's opinion corresponds to the opinion of Rav and Shmuel here. According to the understanding of the Gemara here, at this stage it is a dispute with regard to the interpretation of the mishna: Rav and Shmuel understand the mishna as distinguishing between one who vowed prior to the Sabbatical Year and one who vowed during the Sabbatical Year. However, Rabbi Yoḥanan and Reish Lakish understand the mishna to be discussing only a vow made prior to the Sabbatical Year, and the distinction is between entering the field and eating the produce before the Sabbatical Year and during the Sabbatical Year. That is how the dispute is explained in the Jerusalem Talmud, and it is in accordance with the interpretation of *Tosafot*, the Rashba, and the Ran.

A person can render an item…forbidden – **אָדָם אוֹסֵר דָּבָר**: The basis of this dispute is the question of whether the legal status of an item that is *konam* is the same as that of consecrated property. Consecrated property remains consecrated even after it is no longer in the possession of the one who consecrated it. There are those who rule that an object forbidden as *konam* is permitted once it leaves the possession of the one who vowed. This is because the object is consecrated only for certain individuals and only as long as the object remains in the possession of the one who vowed. Therefore, the prohibition remains in effect only as long as the item is in his possession and it is no longer in effect once the item leaves his possession (*Shita*).

BACKGROUND

Sabbatical Year – **שְׁבִיעִית**: The Sabbatical Year is the last year in the seven-year Sabbatical cycle. The first cycle began after the conquest and subsequent settlement of Eretz Yisrael under the leadership of Joshua. The *halakhot* of the Sabbatical Year are based on Torah law (Leviticus 25:1–7), but most authorities maintain that the conditions for the applicability of the mitzva by Torah law do not currently exist, and therefore its present-day observance is based on rabbinic ordinance.

The Hebrew term for the Sabbatical Year, *shemitta*, means abandonment or relinquishment. During the Sabbatical Year, all agricultural land must lie fallow, and it is prohibited to work the land, except for those tasks necessary to sustain existing crops. All produce that grows is ownerless and must be left unguarded in the fields, accessible to any person, animal, or bird. As long as produce remains in the fields, the produce of that type may continue to be eaten, although it may not be bought and sold in the typical manner or used for purposes other than food. After the last remnants of the crop are removed from the field, that crop may no longer be eaten and must be removed from the house. There is a dispute among the authorities as to whether elimination entails physical destruction of the produce or declaring it ownerless.

וְתוּ: הָא תְּנַן דְּאָדָם אוֹסֵר דָּבָר שֶׁבִּרְשׁוּתוֹ לִכְשֶׁיֵּצֵא מֵרְשׁוּתוֹ. דִּתְנַן: הָאוֹמֵר לִבְנוֹ "קוֹנָם שֶׁאַתָּה נֶהֱנֶה לִי", מֵת – יִירָשֶׁנּוּ: "בְּחַיָּיו וּבְמוֹתוֹ",

And furthermore, didn't we learn in a mishna (*Bava Kamma* 108b) **that a person** can **render an item in his possession forbidden** and the prohibition remains in effect **when it leaves his possession?** This is **as we learned** in a mishna, that with regard to **one who says to his son: Benefit from my** property is *konam*[H] **for you,** if the father **dies,** the son **will inherit him.** He is not deriving benefit from his father's property, as after death it is no longer his. If the father vowed to render benefit from his property forbidden to his son **during his lifetime and upon his death,**

HALAKHA

One who says to his son, benefit from my property is *konam* – הָאוֹמֵר לִבְנוֹ קוֹנָם: If one vows that benefit from him is forbidden to his son, then if the father dies his son inherits from him. But if the father stipulated that the prohibition will remain in effect during his lifetime and after his death, his son does not inherit from him (Rambam *Sefer Hafla'a, Hilkhot Nedarim* 5:6; *Shulḥan Arukh, Yoreh De'a* 216:7; 223:2).

Perek **IV**
Daf **42** Amud **b**

אִם מֵת – לֹא יִירָשֶׁנּוּ! שָׁאנֵי הָכָא, דְּקָא אָמַר לֵיהּ "בְּחַיָּיו וּבְמוֹתוֹ".

then **if** the father **dies,** his son **does not inherit** from **him.**[N] Apparently, one can render his property forbidden and have it remain forbidden after it is no longer in his possession. The Gemara rejects that proof: It **is different here, as he said to him** explicitly: **During his lifetime and upon his death.** There is no proof that in a case where he did not explicitly extend the prohibition to the period after it leaves his possession, the prohibition would not remain in effect.

מִכׇּל מָקוֹם קַשְׁיָא! אֶלָּא בְּ"נְכָסִים אֵלּוּ" – כּוּלֵּי עָלְמָא לָא פְּלִיגִי. כִּי פְּלִיגִי בְּ"נְכָסַי";

The second question was answered, but **in any case** the first question remains **difficult:**[N] Why didn't Rabbi Yoḥanan and Reish Lakish disagree in a case where he said: This property, as well? **Rather,** this is the explanation of their dispute: **In** the case of one who said: Benefit from **this property** is forbidden to you, **everyone agrees** that the prohibition remains in effect even after the item is no longer in his possession. **When they disagree,** it is **in** the case of one who said: Benefit from **my property**[H] is forbidden to you.

רַב וּשְׁמוּאֵל סָבְרִי: לָא שְׁנָא "נְכָסִים אֵלּוּ" לָא שְׁנָא "נְכָסַי" – אָדָם אוֹסֵר, וְרַבִּי יוֹחָנָן וְרֵישׁ לָקִישׁ סָבְרִי: "נְכָסִים" – אָדָם אוֹסֵר: "נְכָסַי" – אֵין אָדָם אוֹסֵר.

Rav and Shmuel hold: It **is no different** if he said: **This property,** and it **is no different** if he said: **My property;** in both cases, a **person renders** an item **forbidden** and the prohibition remains in effect even after the item is no longer in his possession. **And Rabbi Yoḥanan and Reish Lakish hold:** If one said: **Property, a person renders** an item **forbidden** and the prohibition remains in effect. However, if he said: **My property, a person does not render** an item **forbidden** for the period after it is no longer in his possession, as the phrase my property means property in my possession.

וּמִי אִיכָּא לְמַאן דְּאָמַר לָא שְׁנָא "נְכָסִים אֵלּוּ" וְלָא שְׁנָא "נְכָסַי"? וְהָא תְּנַן: הָאוֹמֵר לַחֲבֵירוֹ "קוֹנָם לְתוֹךְ בֵּיתְךָ שֶׁאֲנִי נִכְנָס", "שָׂדְךָ שֶׁאֲנִי לוֹקֵחַ", מֵת אוֹ שֶׁמְּכָרוֹ לְאַחֵר – מוּתָּר. "לְבַיִת זֶה שֶׁאֲנִי נִכְנָס", "שָׂדֶה זוֹ שֶׁאֲנִי לוֹקֵחַ" מֵת אוֹ שֶׁמְּכָרוֹ לְאַחֵר – אָסוּר!

The Gemara asks: **And is there anyone who says** that it **is no different** if he said: **This property, and** it **is no different** if he said: **My property,** and that the prohibition remains in effect even after the item is no longer in his possession? **But didn't we learn** in a mishna (46a): **If one says to another: Entering into your house is *konam* for me,** or: **Buying your field is *konam* for me,** then if the owner **died or sold** the property **to another,** it is **permitted** for the one who vowed to enter the house or buy the field, as the prohibition is in effect only as long as it belongs to that person. However, if he said: **Entering this house** is *konam* **for me,** or: **Buying this field** is *konam* **for me,** then if the owner **died or sold** the property **to another,** it remains **forbidden.** Apparently, there is a difference between a case where he simply renders an item forbidden and a case where he renders an item belonging to a particular individual forbidden.

NOTES

If the father dies, his son does not inherit from him – אִם מֵת לֹא יִירָשֶׁנּוּ: The Ran writes that this does not mean that the son is completely disinherited, as it is explained later that the heir has certain rights in that property. Rather, it means that he may not benefit from the property directly, due to the prohibition (see 47a).

In any case, the first question remains difficult – מִכׇּל מָקוֹם קַשְׁיָא: Most commentaries explain that the reference here is to the first question: Why did Rabbi Yoḥanan and Reish Lakish state their opinion in a case where the one who vowed stated: My property? If the dispute is with regard to the principle, they should have formulated their disagreement in a case where the one who vowed stated: This property. The Rid interprets that the fundamental question of whether one can establish a prohibition that will remain in effect after the object leaves his possession is resolved in the mishna, where it is taught that if he stipulates that the vow will be in effect during his lifetime and after his death, his son does not inherit from him. Although the language that is effective in extending the prohibition is subject to dispute, it is clear that one can extend the prohibition to a time after the object leaves his possession.

HALAKHA

This property…my property – נְכָסִים אֵלּוּ...נְכָסַי: If one vows that benefit from another's property is forbidden, or if another person vowed that benefit from his own property is forbidden to another, benefit is forbidden when it is not the Sabbatical Year. However, during the Sabbatical Year he may eat the produce, because he vowed to render the produce that belongs to him forbidden and during the Sabbatical Year it is ownerless. However, he may not enter the field. By contrast, if one vowed prior to the Sabbatical Year that: This property is forbidden, it is forbidden even during the Sabbatical Year. If he vowed during the Sabbatical Year, it is permitted for him to eat the produce, but he may not enter the field (Rambam *Sefer Hafla'a, Hilkhot Nedarim* 6:13–14).

אֶלָּא, כִּי אָמְרִי רַבִּי יוֹחָנָן וְרֵישׁ לָקִישׁ – בִּ״נְכָסַי״, וְרַב וּשְׁמוּאֵל – בִּ״נְכָסִים אֵלּוּ״, וְלָא פְּלִיגִי.

Rather, this is the explanation of the statements of the *amora'im*: **When Rabbi Yoḥanan and Reish Lakish said**[N] that the prohibition is no longer in effect after the item is no longer in his possession, it was **in** a case where he said: **My property. And** when **Rav and Shmuel** said that the prohibition remains in effect after the item is no longer in his possession, it was **in** a case where he said: **This property. And they do not disagree,** as each pair of *amora'im* addressed a different situation.

״וּבַשְּׁבִיעִית אֵין יוֹרֵד לְתוֹךְ שָׂדֵהוּ״ כו׳. מַאי שְׁנָא דְּאוֹכֵל מִן הַנּוֹטוֹת – דְּפֵירֵי דְּהֶפְקֵירָא אִינּוּן, אַרְעָא נַמִּי אַפְקְרָהּ!

We learned in the mishna: **And during the Sabbatical Year he may not enter his field;** however, he eats from the produce that leans out of the field. The Gemara asks: **What is different** about the Sabbatical Year **that he** is permitted to **eat of** the produce that leans out of the field? It is **due to** the fact **that the produce is ownerless.** With regard to **land as well,** the Torah **rendered it ownerless,** as during the Sabbatical Year, it is permitted for everyone to enter the field and eat the produce.

אָמַר עוּלָּא: בְּעוֹמְדִין אִילָנוֹת עַל הַגְּבוּלִים. רַבִּי שִׁמְעוֹן בֶּן אֶלְיָקִים אָמַר: גְּזֵירָה שֶׁמָּא יִשְׁהֶא בַּעֲמִידָה.

Ulla said: The mishna is referring to a case **where the fruit trees are standing on the borders** of the field.[N] Since it is possible to eat the produce without entering the field, it is not permitted for him to enter it. **Rabbi Shimon ben Elyakim said:** Even in a case where the fruit trees are standing in the middle of the field, it is also prohibited for him to enter the field, due to a rabbinic **decree lest he remain standing**[HN] there longer than necessary for purposes of eating, which is prohibited even during the Sabbatical Year.

מתני׳ הַמּוּדָּר הֲנָאָה מֵחֲבֵירוֹ – לֹא יַשְׁאִילֶנּוּ וְלֹא יִשְׁאַל מִמֶּנּוּ, לֹא יַלְוֶנּוּ וְלֹא יִלְוֶה מִמֶּנּוּ, וְלֹא יִמְכּוֹר לוֹ וְלֹא יִקַּח מִמֶּנּוּ.

MISHNA In the case of **one for whom benefit from another is forbidden by vow,** that other person **may neither lend** an item **to him**[H] **nor borrow** an item **from him.** Similarly, **he may neither lend** money **to him nor borrow** money **from him. And he may neither sell** an item **to him**[N] **nor purchase** an item **from him.**

HALAKHA

A decree lest he remain standing – גְּזֵירָה שֶׁמָּא יִשְׁהֶא בַּעֲמִידָה: If one who vowed that benefit from another is forbidden, vowed in a manner that during the Sabbatical Year the other person's produce is permitted for him, it is prohibited for him to enter the field lest he remain standing there longer than necessary for purposes of eating, as the Torah did not render the field ownerless for any purpose other than taking Sabbatical Year produce. (Rambam *Sefer Hafla'a*, *Hilkhot Nedarim* 6:13).

That other person may neither lend an item to him – לֹא יַשְׁאִילֶנּוּ: One for whom benefit from another is forbidden by a vow may borrow neither items nor money from him. By rabbinic law, he may lend neither items nor money to him lest he come to benefit from him (Rambam *Sefer Hafla'a*, *Hilkhot Nedarim* 6:16; *Shulḥan Arukh*, *Yoreh De'a* 221:5).

NOTES

When Rabbi Yoḥanan and Reish Lakish said – כִּי אָמְרִי רַבִּי יוֹחָנָן וְרֵישׁ לָקִישׁ: Some explain that according to the Gemara's conclusion, Rav and Shmuel and Rabbi Yoḥanan and Reish Lakish do not relate to the mishna at all. Rather, they discuss general *halakha* with no direct connection to the mishna (see *Meromei Sadeh*). However, the Rosh holds that the dispute is not with regard to the general *halakha*, but with regard to the interpretation of the mishna. Rav and Shmuel who hold that the mishna is referring to a case where the one who vowed said: This property, interpret that when the mishna said: During the Sabbatical Year, it means that he vowed during the Sabbatical Year. However, Rabbi Yoḥanan and Reish Lakish, who hold that the mishna is referring to a case where the one who vowed said: My property, interpret that when the mishna said: During the Sabbatical Year, it means when the Sabbatical Year arrives. The Ran explains that Rav and Shmuel explain the mishna and Rabbi Yoḥanan and Reish Lakish do not dispute that interpretation. They merely cite an additional *halakha*.

Where the fruit trees are standing on the borders of the field – בְּעוֹמְדִין אִילָנוֹת עַל הַגְּבוּלִים: As explained by Rashi and others, the land is considered ownerless only for purposes of eating. Therefore, it is not permitted for others to enter the field and use it for purposes other than eating.

Lest he remain standing – שֶׁמָּא יִשְׁהֶא בַּעֲמִידָה: According to this, there is a halakhic difference between the opinions of Ulla and Rabbi Shimon ben Elyakim. Ulla says that this land in ownerless only in terms of facilitating eating the produce, and he may not enter the field for any other purpose. Therefore, it is permitted for him to enter the field to eat produce even in the middle of the field, as the Torah rendered the property ownerless for this purpose. However, according to Rabbi Shimon ben Elyakim, one for whom benefit from the owner of the field is forbidden may eat only the produce that leans out of the field while he remains outside the field; he may not enter the field due to the prohibition (Rashi; Ran).

He may neither sell an item to him – לֹא יִמְכּוֹר לוֹ: *Tosafot* explain that the reference here is to an equitable sale where both parties benefit; therefore, the one for whom benefit is forbidden may neither buy nor sell. However, if only one of the parties benefits, e.g., the seller overcharges or the buyer underpays, it is permitted if the one for whom benefit is forbidden is the one who does not benefit. Rabbi Ovadya Bartenura explains that the reference here is to a case where one undercharges for an item that he sells; this is prohibited by rabbinic decree, lest the one for whom benefit is forbidden come to underpay when purchasing an item from the one from whom benefit is forbidden. However, if it is an equitable sale, neither party benefits (see *Tosefot Yom Tov*).

גמ׳ בִּשְׁלָמָא לֹא יַלְוֶנּוּ – דְּקָא מְהַנֵּי לֵיהּ. אֶלָּא לֹא יִלְוֶה הֵימֶנּוּ, מַאי קָא מְהַנֵּי לֵיהּ? וּבִשְׁלָמָא לֹא יִלְוֶה הֵימֶנּוּ וְלֹא יִקַּח הֵימֶנּוּ – דְּקָמִיתְהֲנֵי מִינֵּיהּ. אֶלָּא לֹא יִשְׁאַל הֵימֶנּוּ, מַאי קָא מִיתְהֲנֵי מִינֵּיהּ?

GEMARA **Granted** that the person from whom benefit is forbidden **may not lend** money **to** the person for whom benefit is forbidden,[N] **as he** thereby **benefits him. However,** with regard to the fact that the former **may not borrow** money **from** the latter, in **what** way **does he benefit him** by borrowing his money? **And** it could even be said, **granted** that **he may neither borrow** money **from him nor purchase** an item **from him, as one benefits** in lending money by preserving the value of that money in case the coins deteriorate, and in selling by ridding oneself an item that is difficult to sell. **However,** with regard to the fact that the person from whom benefit is forbidden **may not borrow** an item **from** the person for whom benefit is forbidden, in **what** way **does** the lender **benefit from him?** The borrower returns the same item to the lender.

אָמַר רַבִּי יוֹסֵי בְּרַבִּי חֲנִינָא: כְּגוֹן שֶׁנָּדְרוּ הֲנָאָה זֶה מִזֶּה. אַבַּיֵּי אָמַר: גְּזֵירָה לִשְׁאוֹל מִשּׁוּם לְהַשְׁאִיל, וְכֵן בְּכוּלְּהוּ גְּזֵירָה.

Rabbi Yosei, son of Rabbi Ḥanina, said: The mishna is referring to a case **where they** both **vowed** that **benefit from each other** is forbidden. Clearly, then, neither of them may lend to the other or borrow from him. **Abaye said:** It is possible to explain the mishna as it is written, as referring to a case where only one vowed that benefit from the other is forbidden. However, the Sages issued **a decree** that it is also prohibited for one **to borrow**[H] from a person for whom benefit from him is forbidden, **due to** the concern that he might come **to lend** to him, as reciprocity is common in these matters. **And likewise,** that is the explanation **in all** the cases in the mishna; it is prohibited to borrow money, borrow items, and to purchase items from him due to a rabbinic **decree,** lest he come to benefit him.

מתני׳ אָמַר לוֹ: הַשְׁאִילֵנִי פָּרָתְךָ. אָמַר לוֹ: אֵינָהּ פְּנוּיָה. אָמַר: ״קוֹנָם שָׂדִי שֶׁאֲנִי חוֹרֵשׁ בָּהּ לְעוֹלָם״. אִם הָיָה דַּרְכּוֹ לַחֲרוֹשׁ – הוּא אָסוּר וְכָל אָדָם מוּתָּרִים, וְאִם אֵין דַּרְכּוֹ לַחֲרוֹשׁ – הוּא וְכָל אָדָם אֲסוּרִין.

MISHNA **One said to** another: **Lend me your cow.** The other person **said to him:** My cow **is not available.** The one seeking to borrow the cow responded angrily: **Plowing my field with** this cow **is *konam* forever.**[NH] **If it was his** typical **manner to plow** the field himself, then it is **prohibited** for **him** to plow his field with that cow **but** it is **permitted** for **every** other **person. If it is not his** typical **manner to plow** the field himself, and he has others plow for him, it is **prohibited** for **him and** for **every** other **person** to plow his field with that cow, because his intent was to render benefit from plowing with this cow forbidden.

הַמּוּדָּר הֲנָאָה מֵחֲבֵירוֹ וְאֵין לוֹ מַה יֹּאכַל, הוֹלֵךְ אֵצֶל הַחֶנְוָנִי וְאוֹמֵר: אִישׁ פְּלוֹנִי נוֹדֵר מִמֶּנִּי הֲנָאָה, וְאֵינִי יוֹדֵעַ מָה אֶעֱשֶׂה. וְהוּא נוֹתֵן לוֹ, וּבָא וְנוֹטֵל מִזֶּה.

In the case of **one for whom benefit from another is forbidden by vow and who does not have anything to eat,** the one from whom benefit is forbidden **goes to the shopkeeper and says**[H] to him: **So-and-so vowed that benefit from me is forbidden** for him **and I do not know what I will do.** After grasping his intent, the shopkeeper **gives** food **to** the one for whom benefit is forbidden, **and** then the shopkeeper **comes and takes** payment for the food **from that** one who spoke to him.[N]

NOTES

Granted that he may not lend money to him, etc. – בִּשְׁלָמָא לֹא יַלְוֶנּוּ וכו׳: The commentaries explain why the prohibition is more understandable with regard to the loan of money and sale of an item than it is with regard to lending items. In the case of a loan of money, the lender might benefit by receiving higher-quality coins in repayment of the loan than the coins he lent. In the case of a purchase, the seller may benefit if it is low-quality merchandise and he is relieved to find someone to buy it. However, if one lends an item, he receives that very item in return. Furthermore, it could lose value through use or with the passage of time.

The Rashash adds that one who lends money to another who vowed that benefit from him is forbidden derives benefit from the satisfaction that a person who hates him was forced to turn to him for help in his time of need.

Plowing my field with this cow is *konam* forever – קוֹנָם שָׂדִי שֶׁאֲנִי חוֹרֵשׁ בָּהּ לְעוֹלָם: Some explain that the one who sought to borrow the cow and was rebuffed was angry. Therefore he vowed never to plow with that cow (Rashi; *Tosafot*; Ran). Alternatively, perhaps he thought that the reason the owner refused to lend him his cow was that he assumed that he wanted it for plowing. Therefore he vowed, so that the owner would lend it to him for other purposes (*Shita Mekubbetzet*; Rabbi Avraham min HaHar, citing Rashi; Meiri).

Some commentaries explain differently, that the owner of the cow vowed to reinforce his refusal and support his assertion that the cow is not available for plowing (Ritva; Re'em Horowitz).

He comes and takes payment from that one who spoke to him – וּבָא וְנוֹטֵל מִזֶּה: The one who approached the shopkeeper pays if he chooses. However, he is not legally required to do so. If the one who approached the shopkeeper was required to repay the debt, the shopkeeper would be the agent of the one from whom benefit is forbidden. That is the explanation in the Jerusalem Talmud, and the commentaries explained accordingly.

HALAKHA

A decree that it is prohibited to borrow – גְּזֵירָה לִשְׁאוֹל: One for whom benefit from another is forbidden by vow may neither borrow money or items from that other person nor lend money or items to him. The latter is due to a decree issued by the Sages lest it lead to deriving benefit from him, in accordance with the opinion of Abaye (Rambam *Sefer Hafla'a*, *Hilkhot Nedarim* 6:16; *Shulḥan Arukh*, *Yoreh De'a* 221:5).

Plowing my field with this cow is *konam* forever – קוֹנָם שָׂדִי שֶׁאֲנִי חוֹרֵשׁ בָּהּ לְעוֹלָם: With regard to one who asks another to lend him his cow, and after being refused vows that plowing his field with that cow is forbidden forever, if he typically plows the field himself, it is prohibited for him to plow his field with that cow; however, others may do so for him. If others typically plowed the field for him, it is prohibited both for him and for others to plow the field with that cow (Rambam *Sefer Hafla'a*, *Hilkhot Nedarim* 8:12; *Shulḥan Arukh*, *Yoreh De'a* 218:5).

He goes to the shopkeeper and says – הוֹלֵךְ אֵצֶל הַחֶנְוָנִי וְאוֹמֵר: With regard to one for whom benefit from another is forbidden by a vow who has nothing to eat, the one who vowed to render benefit from him forbidden may go to a shopkeeper and say: It is prohibited by vow for this person to benefit from me, and I do not know what I will do. The shopkeeper then gives food to the one for whom benefit is forbidden, and then the shopkeeper goes to the one who vowed, to seek compensation, although the one who vowed is not legally obligated to reimburse him. Similarly, if one for whom benefit from another is forbidden by a vow needs work done, the one who vowed to render benefit from him forbidden may approach laborers and say: It is prohibited by a vow for this person to benefit from me. The laborers may perform the task and seek compensation from the one who vowed (Rambam *Sefer Hafla'a*, *Hilkhot Nedarim* 7:12–13; *Shulḥan Arukh*, *Yoreh De'a* 221:8).

NOTES

He gives food to one other person as a gift – **נוֹתֵן לְאֶחָד לְשׁוּם מַתָּנָה**: *Tosafot* and the Rosh write that the Sages permitted doing so only in exigent circumstances, when one is on the road and has nothing to eat. This is because the Gemara later distinguishes between this type of gift, which is permitted, and the gift of Beit Ḥoron, which is prohibited.

הָיָה בֵּיתוֹ לִבְנוֹת, גְּדֵרוֹ לִגְדּוֹר, שָׂדֵהוּ לִקְצוֹר – הוֹלֵךְ אֵצֶל הַפּוֹעֲלִים, וְאוֹמֵר: אִישׁ פְּלוֹנִי מוּדָּר מִמֶּנִּי הֲנָאָה וְאֵינִי יוֹדֵעַ מָה אֶעֱשֶׂה. וְהֵן עוֹשִׂין עִמּוֹ, וּבָאִין וְנוֹטְלִין שָׂכָר מִזֶּה.

Similarly, if the **house** of one for whom benefit is forbidden by a vow **was to be built, his fence to be erected,** or **his field to be harvested,** and laborers were required but he had no money to hire them, the one from whom benefit is forbidden **goes to the laborers and says** to them: **Benefit from me is forbidden by vow to so-and-so and I do not know what I will do. And** the laborers **perform** those tasks **with him, and come and take payment** for their labor **from that** person who approached them.

הָיוּ מְהַלְּכִין בַּדֶּרֶךְ וְאֵין לוֹ מַה יֹּאכַל – נוֹתֵן לְאֶחָד לְשׁוּם מַתָּנָה, וְהַלָּה מוּתָּר בָּהּ. אִם אֵין עִמָּהֶם אַחֵר – מַנִּיחַ עַל הַסֶּלַע אוֹ עַל הַגָּדֵר, וְאוֹמֵר: הֲרֵי הֵן מוּפְקָרִים לְכָל מִי שֶׁיַּחְפּוֹץ, וְהַלָּה נוֹטֵל וְאוֹכֵל. וְרַבִּי יוֹסֵי אוֹסֵר.

If the one who vowed to render benefit from him forbidden and the one for whom benefit is forbidden **were traveling** together **along the road**[H] **and** the one for whom benefit is forbidden **does not have anything to eat,** the one who from whom benefit is forbidden **gives** food **to one** other person **as a gift,**[N] **and** it is **permitted** for **that** person for whom benefit is forbidden to eat the food because it no longer belongs to the one from whom benefit is forbidden. **If there is no other** person **with them,** the one who vowed **places** the food **on the** nearest **rock or on the** nearest **fence and says: These** food items **are hereby rendered ownerless** and are available **to anyone who wants** them. Then **that** person for whom benefit is forbidden **takes and eats** the food. **Rabbi Yosei prohibits** doing so.

גמ׳ אֲמַר רַבִּי יוֹחָנָן: מַאי טַעְמָא דְּרַבִּי יוֹסֵי – קָסָבַר: הֶפְקֵר כְּמַתָּנָה, מַה מַּתָּנָה – עַד דְּאָתְיָא מֵרְשׁוּת נוֹתֵן לִרְשׁוּת מְקַבֵּל, אַף הֶפְקֵר – עַד דְּאָתְיָא לִרְשׁוּת זוֹכֶה.

GEMARA With regard to the dispute between the Rabbis and Rabbi Yosei whether one from whom benefit is forbidden to another can give the other person food by declaring the food ownerless, **Rabbi Yoḥanan said: What is the reason** for the opinion **of Rabbi Yosei? He holds** that the legal status of the process of rendering property **ownerless is like** that of the acquisition of **a gift. Just as** acquisition of **a gift** is not complete **until** the item **comes from the possession of** the **one** who **gives** the gift **into the possession of** the **one** who **receives** the gift, **so too,** the process of rendering property **ownerless** is not complete **until** the item **comes into the possession of** the **one** who **acquires** it. According to Rabbi Yosei, it is prohibited for the one for whom benefit is forbidden to take the food that was declared ownerless. Since it still belongs to the one from whom benefit is forbidden, by taking the food he derives forbidden benefit from him.

מְתִיב רַבִּי אַבָּא: וְהַלָּה נוֹטֵל וְאוֹכֵל, וְרַבִּי יוֹסֵי אוֹסֵר. אָמַר רַבִּי יוֹסֵי: אֵימָתַי – בִּזְמַן שֶׁנִּדְרוֹ קוֹדֵם לְהֶפְקֵירוֹ.

Rabbi Abba raises an objection from a *baraita*: **And** then **that** person **takes and eats** the food; **and Rabbi Yosei prohibits** doing so. **Rabbi Yosei said: When** is it prohibited to do so? **When his vow predates his** declaration that the food is **ownerless.** In that case, the vow took effect on all his possessions, including those that he later declared ownerless.

HALAKHA

They were traveling along the road – **הָיוּ מְהַלְּכִין בַּדֶּרֶךְ**: If one for whom benefit from another is forbidden by a vow and that other person travel together, and the former has nothing to eat, the other person may give food to a third person as a gift, and that person may then give it to the one for whom benefit is forbidden. If there is no one accompanying them, the one from whom benefit is forbidden may place the food down and declare: These food items are hereby rendered ownerless and are available to anyone who wants them, and the one for whom benefit is forbidden may take the food and eat it. However, if the one from whom benefit is forbidden gives the food to a third person and stipulates that he is giving it so the one from whom benefit is forbidden can eat it, or even if it is obvious from his actions that his intent is that the second person can eat it and he does not give it as a full-fledged gift, that is a gift of Beit Ḥoron and he may not eat the food (Rambam *Sefer Hafla'a, Hilkhot Nedarim* 14:15; *Shulḥan Arukh, Yoreh De'a* 221:9).

אֲבָל אִם הָיָה הֶפְקֵירוֹ קוֹדֵם לְנִדְרוֹ – הֲרֵי זֶה מוּתָּר. וְאִי אָמְרַתְּ עַד דְּאָתֵי לִרְשׁוּת זוֹכֶה – מַה לִּי נִדְרוֹ קוֹדֵם לְהֶפְקֵירוֹ, מַה לִּי הֶפְקֵירוֹ קוֹדֵם לְנִדְרוֹ?

However, if his declaration that the food is **ownerless predates his vow,** it is **permitted** for the other person to eat the food. **And if you say** that the reason for the opinion of Rabbi Yosei is because the food remains in the possession of the owner **until it comes into the possession of the one** who **acquires** it, **what is** different **for me** if **his vow predates his declaration** that the food is **ownerless,** and **what is** different **for me** if **his declaration** that the food is **ownerless predates his vow?** In any event, the item remains in the possession of its owner and the one for whom benefit is forbidden benefits from it.

הוּא מוֹתִיב לַהּ וְהוּא מְשַׁנֵּי לַהּ: כׇּל הַנּוֹדֵר – אֵין דַּעְתּוֹ עַל מַה שֶּׁהִפְקִיר.

The Gemara answers: Rabbi Abba **raised the objection and he answered** that objection. The difference between the cases does not relate to the *halakhot* of ownerless property; rather, it relates to the nature of vows. **The intent of anyone who vows is** that the vow **not** apply **to** an item **that he rendered ownerless.** Therefore, when he declares the food ownerless and then vows, he does not intend to include the ownerless food in his vow, and the prohibition does not take effect upon it.

מְתִיב רָבָא: ״מִקְצָתָן לָרִאשׁוֹן וְכוּלָּן לַשֵּׁנִי״ – רִאשׁוֹן קָנָה,

Rava raised an objection: With regard to a person on his deathbed who ordered his executor to distribute all his property, if he recovers, he may retract the gift. However, if he ordered him to distribute only a portion of his property and kept the rest, he cannot retract the gift. If he ordered him to distribute his property to two people and said: **A portion of** the property is given **to the first** person **and all of** the remaining property is given **to the second** person, then if he recovered, the **first** person **acquired** the property that was given him, as it was a partial gift.

שֵׁנִי לֹא קָנָה!

And the **second** person **did not acquire** the property[N] that was given him, as it was a gift of all his remaining property, which can be retracted. Although the first person did not yet acquire the property, as the person on his deathbed did not die, the property is no longer considered to be in the possession of the one who owned it. This is clear from the fact that if it were still in his possession, the gift to the second person would not be a gift of all his remaining property. This contradicts the opinion of Rabbi Yoḥanan, who said in explanation of the opinion of Rabbi Yosei: Acquisition of a gift is not complete until the item comes from the possession of the one who gives the gift into the possession of the one who receives the gift.

NOTES

The first person acquired the property, and the second person did not acquire the property – רִאשׁוֹן קָנָה, שֵׁנִי לֹא קָנָה: According to this version, the *baraita* is referring to a person on his deathbed who gave a portion of his possessions to one person, and all of his remaining possessions to another person. Since his gift to the first person included only a portion of his property, its legal status is like that of any other gift, and it is irrevocable.

Rashi explains that Rava's objection is based on the fact that the gift to the second person is considered a gift of all his property, even though the first person did not yet receive the portion given to him. If, as Rabbi Yoḥanan said in explanation of the opinion of Rabbi Yosei, acquisition of a gift is not complete until the item comes from the possession of the one who gives the gift into the possession of the one who receives the gift, both gifts should have been irrevocable, as the person on his deathbed gives each recipient only a portion of his property. According to this, the question is on Rabbi Yoḥanan's explanation of Rabbi Yosei's opinion. The Ra'avad, cited in the Meiri, agrees.

Rabbeinu Tam (cited by *Tosafot*) explains that it is clear that the *baraita* is referring to a case where the person on his deathbed reconsidered his gift to the first person and gave all his property to the second person. The objection raised by Rava is based on the fact that apparently, even after he gave the gift to the first person, he continued to consider the property his, contrary to the opinion of Rabbi Abba. The Rosh, in his first explanation, agrees.

Many of the early commentaries cite a variant reading: If the owner distributes a portion to the first person and all of it to the second person, the first is enslaved to the second. This is from the *Tosefta* in tractate *Bava Batra* (9:11), which is referring to a case where one on his deathbed gave his possessions to his slaves. If he gave a portion of his property to the first slave, that slave is not freed, because perhaps the slave is included in that portion that remained in the possession of the owner. If the owner gave all his remaining property to the second slave, the second slave acquired not only the property and title to himself, but also title to the first slave. Here too, the objection raised by Rava is based on the fact that apparently, even after he gave the gift to the first slave, he continued to consider the property his, contrary to the opinion of Rabbi Abba (Rashba; Ran; *Tosafot*; Rosh). The Rid also cites that variant reading but interprets it as referring not to slaves, but to one who gives away his property. He interprets the phrase: The first is enslaved to the second, not in the sense of actual slavery, but in the sense that the second person has a right to the property of the first and may repossess it from him.

HALAKHA

One who declares his field ownerless – הַמַּפְקִיר אֶת שָׂדֵהוּ: If one declares his field ownerless and no one takes possession of it, for the first three days thereafter he can retract his declaration and it is as though he never declared it ownerless at all. However, once three days pass, he cannot retract his declaration. His only recourse is to take possession of the field, and his legal status is that of one who acquired an ownerless field (Rambam *Sefer Hafla'a, Hilkhot Nedarim* 2:17; *Shulḥan Arukh, Ḥoshen Mishpat* 273:9).

אֶלָּא אֲמַר רָבָא, הַיְינוּ טַעְמָא דְּרַבִּי יוֹסֵי: גְּזֵירָה מִשּׁוּם מַתְּנַת בֵּית חוֹרוֹן.

Rather, Rava said[N] that **this is the reason** for the opinion **of Rabbi Yosei:** It is prohibited by rabbinic **decree** for the one for whom benefit is forbidden to take food that was declared ownerless, **due to the gift of Beit Ḥoron.**[N] An incident occurred in Beit Ḥoron involving a person who employed artifice and gave a gift to another to circumvent a vow. The Sages ruled that artifice of that sort is forbidden. Here too, when he renounced ownership he merely employed artifice to circumvent the vow.

תַּנְיָא: הַמַּפְקִיר אֶת שָׂדֵהוּ, כָּל שְׁלֹשָׁה יָמִים – יָכוֹל לַחֲזוֹר בּוֹ, מִכָּאן וְאֵילָךְ – אֵין יָכוֹל לַחֲזוֹר בּוֹ.

It is taught in a *baraita*: In the case of **one who declares his field ownerless,**[H] for the **entire three days** after that declaration **he is able to retract it.**[N] **From this point forward, he is unable to retract** the declaration.

NOTES

Rather Rava said, etc. – אֶלָּא אֲמַר רָבָא וכו׳: Rashi cites two explanations of this passage. According to the first, Rabbi Yosei, contrary to the explanation of Rabbi Yoḥanan, holds that ownerless status takes effect immediately, unrelated to the acquisition of that item by another. However, here Rabbi Yosei issued a decree to prohibit ownerless status of that sort due to the gift of Beit Ḥoron. Since it appears that the owner declared the item ownerless merely to enable the one for whom the item is forbidden to acquire it, it is prohibited for the latter to do so.

According to the second interpretation, Rava agrees with Rabbi Yoḥanan's explanation of Rabbi Yosei's opinion that a declaration of ownerlessness is effective only when that item is acquired by another; however, due to the swindlers, the Sages instituted in general that the declaration is effective immediately. However, in this case, due to the concern for the gift of Beit Ḥoron, the food remains forbidden. Its status is according to Torah law, and it is not ownerless.

The gift of Beit Ḥoron – מַתְּנַת בֵּית חוֹרוֹן: This is described in detail in several places throughout the Talmud (e.g., 48a). There was an incident involving a man whose father was prohibited by a vow from deriving benefit from him. The man made a wedding feast to which he wished to invite his father. Therefore, he transferred ownership of his courtyard and the food to a resident of Beit Ḥoron to enable his father to participate without deriving forbidden benefit from him. However, the one to whom ownership was transferred was concerned that it was prohibited to make this arrangement, and he consecrated everything that he received. The person who transferred ownership to him protested, as he had no intention to give him an actual gift. Therefore, the Sages instituted that any gift that cannot be consecrated by its recipient is not considered a gift. In the case in the Gemara here, where it is clear from the actions or words of the one giving the gift that he is doing so only to circumvent the vow, the gift is not a valid gift.

For the entire three days he is able to retract it – כָּל שְׁלֹשָׁה יָמִים יָכוֹל לַחֲזוֹר בּוֹ: This *halakha* relates to the *halakhot* of tithes. The obligation to tithe the produce is abrogated when the produce is rendered ownerless. Therefore, there is concern that one will declare his field ownerless to abrogate his obligation to tithe and then retake possession of the field with no obligation to tithe. Therefore, the Sages instituted that for three days after declaring the produce ownerless one can retract the declaration and thereby maintain ownership. If he retracts the declaration, based on the rabbinic ordinance, the field was never ownerless and he is obligated to tithe the produce. If he leaves the field ownerless for more than three days, the chance that another will acquire it is great. Therefore, one would be less likely to risk losing his field in order to avoid tithing his produce. Everything mentioned in this context ostensibly contradicts the mishna, as the mishna is referring to a case where one declares an item ownerless and the one for whom benefit was forbidden acquires it immediately.

Tosafot answer (45a) that the rabbinic ordinance that divestment of ownership takes effect only three days after the declaration applies only for fields and the like, due to the concern that the objective is to exempt oneself from the obligation to tithe; however, the ordinance does not apply to movable property. Another explanation in *Tosafot* and the Rosh, citing Rabbi Eliezer of Metz, is that the rabbinic ordinance that the declaration does not take effect for three days applies only to a case where he seeks to avoid tithing. The prohibition of untithed produce is known to all but his declaration divesting ownership of the field is not so widely known. The rabbinic ordinance seeks to prevent onlookers from getting the impression that the owner of the field did not tithe his produce and he is eating untithed produce. In this case, since both the prohibition created by the vow and the declaration of ownerlessness are not well known, no false impression will be created and the ordinance is not necessary.

אָמַר ״תְּהֵא שָׂדֶה זוֹ מוּפְקֶרֶת לְיוֹם אֶחָד, לְשַׁבָּת אַחַת, לְחֹדֶשׁ אֶחָד, לְשָׁנָה אַחַת, לְשָׁבוּעַ אַחַת״ עַד שֶׁלֹּא זָכָה בָּהּ, בֵּין הוּא בֵּין אַחֵר – יָכוֹל לַחֲזוֹר בּוֹ. כְּשֶׁזָּכָה בָּהּ, בֵּין הוּא בֵּין אַחֵר – אֵין יָכוֹל לַחֲזוֹר בּוֹ. רֵישָׁא רַבָּנַן, סֵיפָא רַבִּי יוֹסֵי!

If one said: **This field will be ownerless for one day,**[H] **for one week, for one month, for one year,** or **for one** seven-year Sabbatical cycle, **as long as no one took possession of** the field, **neither** the one who declared it ownerless **nor another** person, **he is able to retract** his declaration. **Once one took possession** of the field, **whether** it is **he** or **whether** it is **another** person, **he is unable to retract** his declaration.[N] This *baraita* is difficult, as **the first clause** is apparently in accordance with the opinion of **the Rabbis,** who hold that rendering property ownerless is unilateral and not contingent upon whether one took possession of it, and **the latter clause** is in accordance with the opinion of **Rabbi Yosei,** who holds that rendering property ownerless is complete only when one takes possession of that property.

אֲמַר עוּלָּא: סֵיפָא נַמִי רַבָּנַן הִיא. אִי הָכִי, אַמַּאי עַד שֶׁלֹּא זָכָה בָּהּ בֵּין הוּא בֵּין אַחֵר, יָכוֹל לַחֲזוֹר בּוֹ? שָׁאנֵי שָׁנָה וְשָׁבוּעַ דְּלָא שְׁכִיחִי.

Ulla said: The latter clause is also in accordance with the opinion of **the Rabbis.** The Gemara asks: **If so, why** is the ruling in the *baraita*: **As long as one did not take possession of** the field, **neither** the one who declared it ownerless **nor another** person, **he is able to retract** his declaration; according to the Rabbis, once he declared the property ownerless, although he can take possession of it, he is unable to retract the declaration. The Gemara answers: It **is different** when one declares an item ownerless for **a year or a seven-year** period, **as** doing so is **uncommon.** Since from the outset he limited the duration of ownerless status, clearly he reserved for himself certain rights; therefore, he can retract his declaration.

רֵישׁ לָקִישׁ אָמַר: מִדְּסֵיפָא רַבִּי יוֹסֵי – רֵישָׁא נַמִי רַבִּי יוֹסֵי, וְרֵישָׁא הַיְינוּ טַעְמָא – דְּלָא לִישְׁתַּכַּח תּוֹרַת הֶפְקֵר.

Reish Lakish said: From the fact **that the latter clause** is in accordance with the opinion of **Rabbi Yosei, the first clause is also** in accordance with the opinion of **Rabbi Yosei. And** in **the first clause, this is the reason** that one cannot retract his declaration once three days have passed: It is an ordinance instituted by the Sages to ensure **that the** halakhic **status of ownerlessness** would **not be forgotten.** If one could retract his declaration of ownerless status after three days, people would not distinguish between a case where another took possession, where, according to Rabbi Yosei, one is unable to retract the declaration, and a case where another did not take possession, where, according to Rabbi Yosei, one is able to retract the declaration. The result would be that people would mistakenly conclude that ownerless status can always be reversed, even after it was claimed by another. Therefore, the Sages instituted a limit of three days, after which one may not retract his declaration.

אִי הָכִי אֲפִילּוּ מִיּוֹם הָרִאשׁוֹן נַמִי לֶיהֱוֵי הֶפְקֵר! אֲמַר רַבָּה: מִפְּנֵי הָרַמָּאִין, דְּמַפְקִירִין וְהָדְרִין בְּהוֹן.

The Gemara asks: **If so,** then **let** the Sages institute that the item **is** considered **ownerless even from the first day as well**[N] and that he cannot retract his declaration at all. **Rabba said:** The reason that the Sages did not render the item ownerless from the first day **is due to the swindlers,**[N] **who declare** the field **ownerless** in order to render the produce of the field exempt from the requirement of tithing, **and** then **retract** that declaration and immediately reclaim the field. Therefore, the Sages instituted that ownerless status takes effect only after three days.

אֲבָל דְּאוֹרַיְיתָא לָא הָוֵי הֶפְקֵר?

The Gemara asks: The Sages instituted that one cannot retract his declaration of ownerless status once three days have passed. **However, by Torah law, isn't** the item **ownerless** according to Rabbi Yosei, regardless of when he retracted his declaration as long as no other person acquired it?

HALAKHA

This field will be ownerless for one day, etc. – תְּהֵא שָׂדֶה זוֹ מוּפְקֶרֶת לְיוֹם אֶחָד וכו׳: If one declares: This field will be ownerless for one day, for one week, for one month, for one year he can subsequently retract that declaration, provided that no one has yet taken possession of the field. This is due to the fact that it is atypical for one to declare a field ownerless for a fixed period, and the Sages do not institute ordinances and issue decrees in unusual circumstances, in accordance with the statement of Ulla, which is the principal statement on the matter (Rambam *Sefer Hafla'a, Hilkhot Nedarim* 2:18 and *Kesef Mishne* there, citing Ran; *Shulḥan Arukh, Ḥoshen Mishpat*, 273:10).

NOTES

Once one took possession, whether it is he or whether it is another person, he is unable to retract his declaration – מִשֶּׁזָּכָה בָּהּ, בֵּין הוּא בֵּין אַחֵר אֵין יָכוֹל לַחֲזוֹר בּוֹ: Early commentaries ask: According to Rabbi Yosei, since another person did not take possession of the item, it was not ownerless; therefore, why would his taking possession of the item be effective in exempting him from tithing? He is merely taking possession of produce that is already his. Due to this question, the Rid holds that the text should be emended to read only: When another person takes possession he is unable to retract his declaration. One may infer that if the owner of the field reacquires the field, the status of the field remains unchanged.

Other early commentaries cite the version of the text that appears in the Gemara and therefore must address the difficulty. The Rashba explains that fundamentally, if the one who declared it ownerless claims the produce, its legal status should be like produce that was never declared ownerless; however, because the Sages did not want to distinguish between the cases, they ruled that even if he takes possession of the ownerless property, its status is like that of ownerless property that he acquired. The Ran explains in a slightly different manner: Since the field was declared ownerless, and anyone can take possession of it, he too can do so, and its status is like that of ownerless property that he acquired and not like that of property whose declaration of ownerless status was retracted.

If so, let the Sages institute that the item is considered ownerless even from the first day as well – אִי הָכִי אֲפִילּוּ מִיּוֹם הָרִאשׁוֹן נַמִי לֶיהֱוֵי הֶפְקֵר: From Rashi's explanation, apparently this question is addressed to Rabbi Yosei; since an ordinance was instituted so that the halakhic status of being ownerless would not be forgotten, let the Sages institute that it takes effect on the first day. After Rabba's response to that question, the Gemara raises an objection: According to Rabbi Yosei, by Torah law it is not ownerless.

The Rid explains that the Gemara raises the question only according to the opinion of the Rabbis: Why is it not deemed ownerless immediately, as in their opinion that this is the fundamental *halakha*? Rabba answers that it is a decree issued due to the swindlers. Then the Gemara raises an objection according to the variant reading of the Rid: However, by Torah law it is ownerless.

Others hold that the question is posed to the opinions of both the Rabbis and Rabbi Yosei (*Tosafot*; Rabbi Avraham min HaHar). The understanding of the continuation of the Gemara depends on the different versions: The question is posed to the opinion of Rabbi Yosei according to the reading as it appears here, and is posed to the opinion of the Rabbis according to the variant reading of the Rid: However, by Torah law it is ownerless. However, the Rosh explains that the phrase in the version here: However, by Torah law, the item is not ownerless, is not a question; rather, it is the conclusion of the declarative statement of Reish Lakish that the item is ownerless by rabbinic ordinance, not by Torah law.

Due to the swindlers – מִפְּנֵי הָרַמָּאִין: The Rosh asks: Since Rabbi Yosei holds that it is not ownerless by Torah law even after three days have passed, how would rendering their produce ownerless provide any benefit for the swindlers? He answers that once the Sages instituted that it will be ownerless, it is ownerless produce in every sense and it is the full-fledged property of anyone who takes possession of it. Therefore, the Gemara says that the produce will be exempt from the obligation to tithe, as its status is that of property declared ownerless by the court, whose status is ownerless in every sense.

וְדִלְמָא אָתֵי לְעַשּׂוּרֵי מִן הַחִיּוּב עַל הַפָּטוּר, וּמִן הַפָּטוּר עַל הַחִיּוּב!

And that ordinance could lead to a problem, as **perhaps he will come to tithe**[N] **from** produce that **requires** tithing by Torah law **for** produce **exempt** from tithing by Torah law[N] **and from** produce **exempt** from tithing by Torah law **for** produce that **requires** tithing by Torah law. By Torah law, the produce is not ownerless and requires tithing. However, due to the ordinance, people might relate to it as ownerless produce and assume that one is exempt from tithing it. Alternatively, they will erroneously conclude that the obligation to tithe from that produce is by rabbinic law and will tithe produce from it that one is exempt from tithing by Torah law, or they will tithe that produce from produce that one is exempt from tithing by Torah law. The result will be produce that is not properly tithed, as one may tithe produce that one is obligated to tithe by Torah law only from other produce that one is obligated to tithe by Torah law.

דְּאָמְרִינַן לֵיהּ: כִּי מְעַשְּׂרַתְּ – עַשַּׂר מִינֵּיהּ וּבֵיהּ.

The Gemara answers: That problem will not arise, **because** if the declaration of ownerless status is retracted after three days, **we say to** the person who ultimately takes possession of the produce: **When you tithe, tithe from** that produce **itself.** In that way, the above problem does not arise.

מֵיתִיבֵי: הַמַּפְקִיר אֶת כַּרְמוֹ, וְלַשַּׁחַר עָמַד וּבְצָרוֹ – חַיָּיב בְּפֶרֶט וּבְעוֹלְלוֹת וּבְשִׁכְחָה וּבְפֵאָה, וּפָטוּר מִן הַמַּעֲשֵׂר.

The Gemara **raises an objection** from a *baraita*: **One who declares his vineyard ownerless,**[H] **and at dawn he arose and picked grapes** from the vineyard, **is obligated in** the mitzva of leaving **individual fallen** grapes left for the poor [*peret*], **and in** the mitzva of leaving **incompletely formed clusters** of grapes for the poor [*olelot*], **and in** the mitzva of leaving **forgotten** sheaves, **and in** the mitzva of *pe'a*,[N] produce from the corner of the field or vineyard, as the obligation to separate those gifts from the poor is incumbent upon the one who harvests the field (see Leviticus 19:9–10). **And he is exempt from** the obligation to separate **the tithe** from the grapes. Because the vineyard is ownerless, there is no obligation to tithe the produce.

HALAKHA

One who declares his vineyard ownerless – הַמַּפְקִיר אֶת כַּרְמוֹ: If one declared his vineyard ownerless and then arose in the morning and reacquired it, he is obligated to leave single grapes, incompletely formed clusters of grapes, forgotten sheaves, and *pe'a*. This is because it is written with regard to all these: "Your field," or: "Your vineyard" (see Leviticus 19:10) and that vineyard was his and remains his. However, if he acquired a field that had been declared ownerless by another, he is exempt from the obligation to separate the gifts to the poor. In both cases, he is exempt from the obligation to tithe the produce (Rambam *Sefer Zera'im, Hilkhot Mattenot Aniyyim* 5:27).

NOTES

And perhaps he will come to tithe, etc. – וְדִלְמָא אָתֵי לְעַשּׂוּרֵי וכו׳: This question has been explained differently by the commentaries according to various opinions. Rashi proposes two interpretations. According to the first, this question is difficult according to the opinion of Rabbi Yosei, who says that if the owner retracts the declaration within three days, the produce is not considered ownerless at all and his obligation to tithe is by Torah law. The concern is that when he takes possession of the produce he will think that it is in fact ownerless by Torah law, and it is actually the Sages who instituted the requirement to tithe. That will result in his utilizing that produce to tithe other produce, produce that he is obligated to tithe by rabbinic law. According to Rashi's second explanation, the question relates to the other aspect of this *halakha*, the fact that after three days have passed, even if he retracts his declaration the produce remains ownerless, although by Torah law it is not ownerless until it enters the possession of another. The owner of the produce who retracted his declaration will mistakenly think that the produce is ownerless by Torah law and that the obligation to tithe it is by rabbinic law.

Rabbeinu Yitzḥak, cited by *Tosafot*, and the Rosh explain that the question and answer are according to the opinions of both Rabbi Yosei and the Rabbis. The Rid and Rabbeinu Tam, cited by *Tosafot*, explain that since he is told that he is required to tithe the produce he will mistakenly think that he is obligated to do so by Torah law and will come to use it to tithe produce that one is obligated to tithe by Torah law. In their opinion, the question is posed only to the opinion of the Rabbis, as according to Rabbi Yosei it is not ownerless by Torah law, and one is obligated by Torah law to tithe the produce. Therefore, there is no concern, as he can actually utilize it to tithe produce by Torah law.

From produce that requires tithing for produce exempt from tithing by Torah law – מִן הַחִיּוּב עַל הַפָּטוּר: The prohibition against tithing from produce that one is obligated to tithe for produce that one is exempt from tithing also applies to produce that one is totally exempt from tithing, e.g., non-sacred produce from which *terumot* and tithes were taken; however, that is an uncommon circumstance. The concern relates to the more common circumstance where one tithes from produce that one is required to tithe by Torah law for produce that one is required to tithe by rabbinic law, e.g., produce that grew in an unperforated flowerpot, which is exempt from tithing by Torah law because it does not grow in the ground, but which requires tithing by rabbinic law, or produce that grew in the countries bordering on Eretz Yisrael, in which the Sages instituted that one is obligated to tithe.

Rashi cites two reasons for the prohibition against tithing from produce that one is obligated to tithe for produce that one is exempt from tithing, and vice versa. The first reason is that if one tithes from produce that he is exempt from tithing for produce that one is obligated to tithe, it appears that he is redeeming the *teruma* and tithes of the latter produce with money, or its equivalent, and there is no concept of redemption with regard to *teruma* and tithes. The other reason is that if one tithes from produce that one is obligated to tithe for produce that one is exempt from tithing, then even if he gives the *teruma* and the *teruma* of the tithe to a priest, it is problematic. The priest who receives it will think that it is actual *teruma*, and since one is exempt from separating *ḥalla* from dough made from *teruma*, the concern is that the priest will not separate *ḥalla* from dough made from that produce, even though it is not actual *teruma*.

Is obligated in the mitzva of leaving individual fallen grapes, and in the mitzva of leaving incompletely formed clusters, and in the mitzva of leaving forgotten sheaves, and in the mitzva of *pe'a* – חַיָּיב בְּפֶרֶט וּבְעוֹלְלוֹת וּבְשִׁכְחָה וּבְפֵאָה: Produce that is ownerless in every sense is exempt from all the gifts typically separated from produce, i.e., *teruma* and tithes, as well as gifts to the poor, e.g., single grapes or incomplete clusters. However, here the reference is to a case where the ownerless status is partial. Therefore, there is a distinction between gifts to the poor, which one is obligated to separate, and *teruma* and tithes, from which one is exempt.

Most commentaries explain that the reason for the distinction between these *halakhot* is based on the Gemara in tractate *Bava Kamma* (94a). With regard to gifts to the poor, the term "you shall leave" is written twice (Leviticus 19:10, 23:22), from which it is derived that the obligation is in effect even in cases of uncertainty. The Rambam explains that only with regard to gifts to the poor is the term "your field" written, indicating that even if he declared it ownerless and reacquired it, it remains his field and he retains the obligation to give these gifts. However, with regard to *teruma* and tithes, where those terms are not employed, one is exempt even in cases where the ownerless status is less than full-fledged.

בִּשְׁלָמָא לְעוּלָּא – דְּרַבָּנַן קָתָנֵי לַהּ, וּדְאוֹרָיְיתָא קָתָנֵי לַהּ. אֶלָּא לְרֵישׁ לָקִישׁ, אַמַּאי פָּטוּר מִן הַמַּעֲשֵׂר?

The Gemara asks: **Granted,** this is so **according to Ulla,** who explained **that the Rabbis taught** the previous *baraita*[N] and explains that although the Sages instituted that the ownerless status does not take effect completely until three days have passed, by Torah law it takes effect immediately, **and that** this *baraita* is **taught in accordance with Torah law.** That is the reason that one is exempt from tithing the grapes. **However, according to Reish Lakish, why is he exempt from** separating **the tithe?** Until three days after the declaration, neither by Torah law nor by rabbinic law does ownerless status take effect.

אָמַר לָךְ: כִּי אָמְרִי אֲנָא – לְרַבִּי יוֹסֵי, הָא – רַבָּנַן הִיא.

The Gemara answers that Reish Lakish could have **said to you:** Although **when** I explained the first clause and the latter clause of that *baraita* **I said** that both are **in accordance with** the opinion of **Rabbi Yosei,** who said that an ownerless item leaves the possession of the owner only when it enters the possession of another, **this** *baraita* is in accordance with the opinion of **the Rabbis,** who hold that it leaves the possession of the owner immediately upon the declaration of ownerless status.

NOTES

Granted according to Ulla, who explained that the Rabbis taught the previous *baraita* – בִּשְׁלָמָא לְעוּלָּא דְּרַבָּנַן קָתָנֵי לַהּ: According to Ulla, who holds that the first *baraita* cited previously with regard to ownerless status is in accordance with the opinion of the Rabbis, the very declaration of the field as ownerless renders it ownerless according to the Rabbis. Therefore, once the field is declared ownerless there is no obligation by Torah law to tithe the produce. That is the reason it says in the *baraita*: And he is exempt from the obligation to separate the tithe. Although the Sages instituted that one is required to tithe the produce, he is exempt by Torah law. There is an obligation by Torah law only to leave the gifts for the poor, i.e., single grapes, incompletely formed clusters of grapes, forgotten sheaves, and *pe'a*. However, according to the opinion that the *baraita* is in accordance with the opinion of Rabbi Yosei, who holds that by Torah law the field is not rendered ownerless by means of the declaration until another takes possession of it, why would he be exempt from separating the tithe? According to Reish Lakish, even Rabbi Yosei agrees that for the first three days following his declaration he is not exempt from separating the tithe, even by rabbinic law (see Rabbi Avraham min HaHar).

Perek **IV**
Daf **45** Amud **a**

אִיבָּעֵית אֵימָא: הָא – דְּאַפְקְרֵיהּ בְּאַנְפֵּי תְּרֵין, וְהָא – דְּאַפְקְרֵיהּ בְּאַפֵּי תְּלָתָא. דְּאָמַר רַבִּי יוֹחָנָן מִשּׁוּם רַבִּי שִׁמְעוֹן בֶּן יְהוֹצָדָק: כׇּל הַמַּפְקִיר בִּפְנֵי שְׁלֹשָׁה – הָוֵי הֶפְקֵר, בִּפְנֵי שְׁנַיִם – לָא הָוֵי הֶפְקֵר.

If you wish, say instead: **That** *baraita,* in which it is taught that the item does not leave the possession of the owner until it enters the possession of another, is referring to a case **where** one declared it ownerless **before two** people; **and this** *baraita,* in which it is taught that the item is ownerless when it is declared ownerless, is referring to a case **where** one declared it ownerless **before three** people. **As Rabbi Yoḥanan said in the name of Rabbi Shimon ben Yehotzadak:** With regard to **anyone who declares** an item **ownerless before three** people, that item **is ownerless;** if he does so **before two** people, **it is not ownerless.**[N]

NOTES

Before two people, it is not ownerless – בִּפְנֵי שְׁנַיִם לָא הָוֵי הֶפְקֵר: The Ran cites two explanations. According to the first, this means that there were two people there, one of whom declared the item ownerless; before three means that there are two others in addition to the one declaring the item ownerless. According to the second explanation, before two means that there are two others in addition to the one declaring the item ownerless, and before three means there are three in addition to him.

The difference between the explanations is somewhat dependent upon the understanding of Rabbi Yosei's opinion. It could be understood that if there is only one person other than the owner, it would not be considered a declaration of ownerless status; it would be considered a gift to that person. Alternatively, it could be explained that only when the declaration is before three people does it become public, and the item immediately becomes ownerless. However, when the declaration is before fewer than three it does not become public, and the status of the item is like that of a gift. *Tosafot* explain that in the case of a declaration before two, since it does not become public, there is concern that he might be employing artifice to avoid tithing; therefore, it is not considered ownerless. Another possibility is that the concern is that it is a gift like the gift of Beit Ḥoron (Ritva).

The Rabbis also disagreed with regard to the meaning of the phrase: It is not ownerless. Some interpret that it means that a field does not become ownerless immediately but only after three days, due to the concern that he is employing artifice to exempt himself from tithing. It does not have full-fledged ownerless status, in the sense that he can retract his declaration; however, if another took possession of it, he acquires it outright (Rosh). It could also be said that if the declaration was before two people, it is not considered ownerless at all (Rosh; *Talmidei Rabbeinu Peretz*). The Rosh comments that one could explain that there are three opinions: According to Rabbi Yoḥanan himself, not in the name of his teacher, until someone takes possession of the item, the item is not ownerless at all. In the name of his teacher, Rabbi Yoḥanan holds that there is a distinction between a declaration before two people and a declaration before three people. And Rabbi Yehoshua ben Levi holds that the item is ownerless by Torah law whether he declared it ownerless before two or he declared it ownerless before three.

וְרַבִּי יְהוֹשֻׁעַ בֶּן לֵוִי אָמַר: דְּבַר תּוֹרָה – אֲפִילּוּ בְּאֶחָד הָוֵי הֶפְקֵר, וּמַה טַּעַם אָמְרוּ בִּשְׁלֹשָׁה – כְּדֵי שֶׁיְּהֵא אֶחָד זוֹכֶה וּשְׁנַיִם מְעִידִין.

הדרן עלך אין בין המודר

And Rabbi Yehoshua ben Levi said:[N] **By Torah law, even with one** person,[H] the item **is ownerless, and what** is the **reason** that the Sages **said** that ownerless status must be declared **with three** people?[N] It is **so that one will take possession** of the item **and two** will **testify** that the item was declared ownerless and that it was acquired by that person. It is not a requirement fundamental to the declaration of ownerless status.

NOTES

And Rabbi Yehoshua ben Levi said, etc. – **וְרַבִּי יְהוֹשֻׁעַ בֶּן לֵוִי אָמַר וכו׳**: According to most commentaries (Rashi; Rabbeinu Tam, *Sefer HaYashar*; *Tosafot*; *Tosefot Rabbeinu Peretz*), the dispute between Rabbi Yoḥanan and Rabbi Yehoshua ben Levi parallels the dispute between Rabbi Yosei and the Rabbis. Rabbi Yoḥanan holds in accordance with the opinion of Rabbi Yosei that there are restrictions on ownerless status by Torah law, and full-fledged ownerless status can be achieved only before three people. However, Rabbi Yehoshua ben Levi holds in accordance with the opinion of the Rabbis that by Torah law the declaration of ownerless status renders the item ownerless. The requirement to declare ownerless status before three was instituted by the Sages only in specific cases.

Others question that parallel, as if that were the dispute between Rabbi Yoḥanan and Rabbi Yehoshua ben Levi they should have stated their dispute in terms of whether the *halakha* is in accordance with the opinion of Rabbi Yosei or the opinion of the Rabbis (*Shita*). Therefore, they raise the possibility that even Rabbi Yehoshua son of Levi stated his opinion in accordance with the opinion of Rabbi Yosei. In his opinion, a declaration before one is effective by Torah law; however, by rabbinic law, due to concern for artifice or the gift of Beit Ḥoron, the declaration must be before three.

And what is the reason that the Sages said with three people – **וּמַה טַּעַם אָמְרוּ בִּשְׁלֹשָׁה**: According to this, even according to Rabbi Yehoshua ben Levi, by rabbinic law the declaration must be before three people. If so, how did the Rabbis in the mishna permit one to declare his food ownerless for the benefit of one for whom benefit is forbidden, before fewer than three people? Furthermore, there are several *halakhot* concerning Shabbat where one can privately declare an item ownerless to avoid violating a Shabbat prohibition. Some commentaries hold that these questions are without basis, as even Rabbi Yehoshua ben Levi holds that three are required by rabbinic law only according to Rabbi Yosei, and the *halakha* is not ruled in accordance with his opinion. However, according to the Rabbis, a private declaration is also effective (Meiri).

Tosafot explain that a declaration before three is necessary only in cases involving land, due to the concern that one is employing artifice to avoid tithing; however, there is no such requirement for moveable property. Alternatively, the requirement of a declaration before three people was instituted only with regard to tithing; however, with regard to other *halakhot*, e.g., Shabbat and one for whom benefit is forbidden, it was not instituted. Others explain that when the objective is to circumvent a prohibition, a declaration before one is sufficient; however, to enable others to take possession of it, the declaration must be before three.

The Ritva holds that in exigent circumstances, e.g., where the one for whom benefit is forbidden has nothing to eat, the Sages did not enforce their ordinance, and therefore declaration before one person is sufficient, in keeping with Torah law. Re'em Horowitz explains that there is no proof from the *halakhot* of Shabbat, as the ordinance according to Beit Shammai that one can declare his pot ownerless on Shabbat to avoid violating a prohibition is something that is commonly done, and everyone is familiar with the procedure. Therefore, it is tantamount to a public declaration and there is no need for three people (see *Tosafot* on *Shabbat* 18b).

HALAKHA

By Torah law, even with one person – **דְּבַר תּוֹרָה אֲפִילּוּ בְּאֶחָד**: By Torah law, if one declares his property ownerless before even one person, he thereby renders the property ownerless. However, by rabbinic law, it is ownerless only if he declared it ownerless before three people, so that one acquires the property if he wishes and the other two serve as witnesses. Others hold that even if he declared ownerlessness while alone it is effective (*Tur*, citing Rosh; Rambam *Sefer Hafla'a, Hilkhot Nedarim*, 2:16; *Shulḥan Arukh, Ḥoshen Mishpat* 273:7).

Summary of **Perek IV**

The difference between benefit from another's food being forbidden by vow and all benefit from another being forbidden by vow is a minor one, as in the former case, any benefit that can be translated into food, i.e., all monetary benefit, is forbidden. For one for whom all benefit from another is forbidden it is prohibited even to borrow utensils unrelated to food. Actions that provide no monetary benefit are also forbidden. Furthermore, it is prohibited for him to work for or serve the one who vowed. The prohibition of benefit includes seemingly insignificant benefits. The principle is that for one for whom all benefit from another is forbidden, that other person may not perform even actions that people typically overlook.

On the other hand, there are actions that are halakhically not considered benefit, primary among them performance of mitzvot. It is permitted for one to perform a mitzva on behalf of a person for whom benefit from him is forbidden, based on the principle: Mitzvot were not given to benefit from them. Furthermore, it is permitted even if by performing the mitzva for him he provides him with indirect monetary benefit.

The Sages said that if one for whom benefit from another is forbidden is in dire straits, that other person may intimate to a third party to perform certain actions or to provide sustenance for the first, provided that he does not undertake any halakhic commitment to reimburse him. In such a case any indirect giving by means of a third party, or even by means of declaring property ownerless, is permitted. In the course of the discussion of these issues, several matters relating to the general *halakhot* of ownerless status were raised.

The chapter discussed the fact that it is permitted to teach Torah to one for whom benefit from him is forbidden. Matters relating to whether it is permitted to take payment for the study of Torah, to the punctuation of the Torah text with cantillation notes, and to rabbinic traditions with regard to the Bible were also discussed. In addition, the Gemara discussed the praiseworthiness and significance of the mitzva of visiting the ill as part of the question of whether one may visit a sick person from whom benefit is forbidden for him.

Introduction to **Perek V**

As explained in the previous chapter, if one is prohibited by a vow from deriving benefit from another, even the most minimal benefit is forbidden. Therefore, the one who takes the vow will be enjoined not only from deriving benefit from the other's property, but also from deriving benefit from shared property, lest he benefit from the other's share.

This chapter deals primarily with issues of deriving benefit from property shared by multiple owners. This occurs primarily through partnerships or from benefit gained through communal or public property, although shared ownership can result from a number of other situations. In the case of public property, one must determine each party's degree of ownership, since their share may be so small as to be negligible, thereby rendering the property ownerless.

The chapter also discusses effective and ineffective ways of circumventing vows in order to indirectly benefit the prohibited individual. While some methods may be considered legitimate means of offering indirect benefit, loopholes that are solely legal fictions are rendered invalid.

Finally, this chapter explores the possibility of rendering entities forbidden to oneself or to another that have not yet come into or have already left one's possession.

Perek **V**
Daf **45** Amud **b**

מתני׳ הַשּׁוּתָּפִין שֶׁנָּדְרוּ הֲנָאָה זֶה מִזֶּה – אֲסוּרִין לִיכָּנֵס לֶחָצֵר. רַבִּי אֱלִיעֶזֶר בֶּן יַעֲקֹב אוֹמֵר: זֶה נִכְנָס לְתוֹךְ שֶׁלּוֹ, וְזֶה נִכְנָס לְתוֹךְ שֶׁלּוֹ.

MISHNA **Partners**[H] **who vowed** not to derive **benefit from one another are prohibited from entering into a courtyard** that they jointly own, since each one has a portion in it and benefits from the share owned by the other, thereby leading to a violation of the vow. **Rabbi Eliezer ben Ya'akov says:** It is permitted for both to use the courtyard, as it can be said that since each has a portion in the courtyard; **this one enters**[N] **into his own** portion **and that one enters into his own** portion.[N]

HALAKHA

Partners, etc. – הַשּׁוּתָּפִין וכו׳: If there are two partners in a courtyard, each of whom vows not to derive benefit from the other, and the courtyard is not large enough to be divided into four square cubits for each partner, it is permitted for them to enter the courtyard. This is in accordance with the opinion of Rabbi Eliezer ben Ya'akov and the subsequent explanation in the Gemara (Rambam *Sefer Hafla'a, Hilkhot Nedarim* 7:4; *Shulḥan Arukh, Yoreh De'a* 226:1).

NOTES

This one enters – זֶה נִכְנָס: *Tosafot* write that Rabbi Eliezer ben Ya'akov permits entering only as much of the courtyard as can be said to be his own portion. However, he cannot make use of a majority of the courtyard at one time, since that would certainly entail using his partner's portion as well.

That one enters into his own portion – וְזֶה נִכְנָס לְתוֹךְ שֶׁלּוֹ: The reasoning of Rabbi Eliezer ben Ya'akov is apparently predicated upon a halakhic principle known as *bereira* (see *Bava Kamma* 51b). *Bereira*, retroactive clarification or designation, means that a later decision can be applied retroactively and thereby viewed as if it had been decided from the outset. Rabbi Eliezer ben Ya'akov appears to hold that due to retroactive clarification, one may consider every step that he takes in the courtyard as if it were taken in his own territory. Since there are several instances in this tractate where the Gemara rules in accordance with the opinion of Rabbi Eliezer ben Ya'akov, the Ri understands the principle of *bereira* as the accepted *halakha*. Elsewhere, however (*Beitza* 38a), the Talmud rejects *bereira* with regard to matters of Torah law. Rabbeinu Tam explains that the Gemara rules in accordance with Rabbi Eliezer ben Ya'akov in this instance for a different reason: Rights which are ordinarily waived, such as exclusive passage in a courtyard, are not forbidden by prohibitory vows.

Perek **V**
Daf **46** Amud **a**

וּשְׁנֵיהֶם אֲסוּרִים לְהַעֲמִיד רֵיחַיִם וְתַנּוּר וּלְגַדֵּל תַּרְנְגוֹלִים.

And all agree that **they are both prohibited**[NH] **from setting up a mill**[B] **or an oven** in the jointly owned courtyard, **or to raise chickens** in it.

NOTES

And they are both prohibited – וּשְׁנֵיהֶם אֲסוּרִים: *Tosafot* and the Ran explain that although partners generally do not mind one another performing these types of activities in their shared courtyard, each has a theoretical right to prohibit the other from doing so, thereby rendering these activities a tangible benefit and consequently, forbidden. *Tosafot* provide another reason for the prohibition. Since mills are normally set up for commercial purposes, they may lead to heavy foot traffic of clients who will end up on the partner's property as well. Rabbi Eliezer of Metz adds that chickens raised in the courtyard might eat food that belongs to the other partner. Other commentaries explain that the activities mentioned are forbidden because they create the appearance of establishing the courtyard as one's own, which is prohibited (*Tosefot Rabbeinu Peretz*; Rabbi Avraham min HaHar; see Rid).

HALAKHA

And they are both prohibited – וּשְׁנֵיהֶם אֲסוּרִים: When two partners in a courtyard prohibit each other from deriving benefit from their portions by means of a vow, they are both prohibited from setting up an oven or a millstone and from raising chickens in the courtyard. If only one of them was forbidden by means of a vow, then it is prohibited only for him to derive benefit from the other's portion. The *Shakh* notes that this holds true even with regard to a courtyard which is too small to be divided (Rambam *Sefer Hafla'a, Hilkhot Nedarim* 7:4–5; *Shulḥan Arukh, Yoreh De'a* 226:2).

BACKGROUND

Mill – רֵיחַיִם:

Roman bas relief of a donkey and mill dating back to the first century

הָיָה אֶחָד מֵהֶם מוּדָּר הֲנָאָה מֵחֲבֵירוֹ – לֹא יִכָּנֵס לֶחָצֵר. רַבִּי אֱלִיעֶזֶר בֶּן יַעֲקֹב אוֹמֵר: יָכוֹל הוּא לוֹמַר לוֹ: לְתוֹךְ שֶׁלִּי אֲנִי נִכְנָס, וְאֵינִי נִכְנָס לְתוֹךְ שֶׁלְּךָ. וְכוֹפִין אֶת הַנּוֹדֵר לִמְכּוֹר אֶת חֶלְקוֹ.

If only **one of the** partners **was prohibited by a vow**[H] **from deriving benefit from the other, he may not enter the courtyard. Rabbi Eliezer ben Ya'akov says: He can say to** the partner: **I am entering into my own** portion **and I am not entering into your** portion. **And** the court **forces the one who took** such **a vow**[NH] **to sell his portion**[N] so that he does not cause the other to transgress.

הָיָה אֶחָד מִן הַשּׁוּק מוּדָּר בְּאֶחָד מֵהֶם הֲנָאָה – לֹא יִכָּנֵס לֶחָצֵר. רַבִּי אֱלִיעֶזֶר בֶּן יַעֲקֹב אוֹמֵר: יָכוֹל לוֹמַר לוֹ: לְתוֹךְ שֶׁל חֲבֵירְךָ אֲנִי נִכְנָס, וְאֵינִי נִכְנָס לְתוֹךְ שֶׁלְּךָ.

If someone from the marketplace[N] **is prohibited by a vow from deriving benefit from one of the** partners, **he may not enter a courtyard** of the partners, since it belongs partly to the one from whom he may not benefit. **Rabbi Eliezer ben Ya'akov says: He can say to him: I am entering into the** portion **of another** resident of the courtyard[NH] **and I am not entering your** own portion since it does not belong entirely to you.

הַמּוּדָּר הֲנָאָה מֵחֲבֵירוֹ וְיֵשׁ לוֹ מֶרְחָץ וּבֵית הַבַּד מוּשְׂכָּרִין בָּעִיר, אִם יֵשׁ לוֹ בָּהֶן תְּפִיסַת יָד – אָסוּר, אֵין לוֹ בָּהֶן תְּפִיסַת יָד – מוּתָּר.

With regard to **one prohibited by a vow from deriving benefit from another and he has a bathhouse**[H] **or an olive press in the city that is leased out** and available for public use, **if** the one who took the vow **has a right** to profits from **usage in the** property, i.e., he retains some rights in the property and has not leased them out completely, it is **forbidden** for the one who took the vow to use it. If **he has no right of usage in the** property, it is **permitted.**

הָאוֹמֵר לַחֲבֵירוֹ: ״קוֹנָם לְבֵיתְךָ שֶׁאֲנִי נִכְנָס וְשָׂדְךָ שֶׁאֲנִי לוֹקֵחַ״, מֵת אוֹ שֶׁמְּכָרוֹ לְאַחֵר – מוּתָּר. ״קוֹנָם בַּיִת זֶה שֶׁאֲנִי נִכְנָס, שָׂדֶה זוֹ שֶׁאֲנִי לוֹקֵחַ״, מֵת אוֹ שֶׁמְּכָרוֹ לְאַחֵר – אָסוּר.

With regard to one **who says to another: Entering your house is** ***konam*** **for me,**[H] or: **Purchasing your field is** ***konam*** **for me,** then if **he,** i.e., the owner of the house or field, **dies or sells** the house **to another,** it is **permitted** for the one who took the vow to enter the house or purchase the field, as it is no longer in the possession of the prior owner. But if he said: **Entering this house is** ***konam*** **for me,**[H] or: **Purchasing this field** is ***konam*** **for me,** then even if the owner **dies or sells it to another,** it is **forbidden.**

גמ׳ אִיבַּעְיָא לְהוּ: בְּנָדְרוּ פְּלִיגִי, הִדִּירוּ זֶה אֶת זֶה מַאי? מִי אָמְרִינַן: בְּנָדְרוּ הוּא דִּפְלִיגִי, אֲבָל בְּהִדִּירוּ זֶה אֶת זֶה – מוֹדוּ לֵיהּ רַבָּנַן לְרַבִּי אֱלִיעֶזֶר בֶּן יַעֲקֹב, דְּכִי אֲנוּסִין דָּמוּ. אוֹ דִּילְמָא: אֲפִילּוּ בְּהִדִּירוּ זֶה אֶת זֶה פְּלִיגִי רַבָּנַן?

GEMARA **A dilemma was raised before** the Sages: In the mishna, the Rabbis and Rabbi Eliezer ben Ya'akov **disagree** with regard to the permissibility of entering a jointly owned courtyard **where** the partners **vowed** not to derive benefit from one another. However, if they instead **vowed to prohibit one another** from deriving benefit from them and their property, **what** is the *halakha*? **Do we say that they disagree where** the partners **each vowed** not to benefit from the other, **but where they** each **vowed to prohibit one another** from deriving benefit from them, **the Rabbis concede**[N] **to Rabbi Eliezer ben Ya'akov, as they are** each **considered to be** forbidden **due to circumstances beyond their control? Or perhaps the Rabbis disagree even in a** case where **each vowed to prohibit one another** from deriving benefit?

NOTES

And the court forces the one who took such a vow, etc. – כּוֹפִין אֶת הַנּוֹדֵר וכו׳: Several commentaries explain that this statement is the opinion of the Rabbis, who prohibit entering the jointly owned field (Rashi; Rabbi Avraham min HaHar). Others explain that even Rabbi Eliezer ben Ya'akov agrees that there are some limitations on the prohibited partner's use of the courtyard, and therefore there is still a legitimate fear that he will violate the vow if he does not sell his portion (Rashba; *Tosefot Rabbeinu Peretz*; Ran).

The Ran explains that the one who vowed is forced to sell his share only if he alone prohibited his partner with a vow, but he is not forced to sell if both took vows prohibiting the other from using the courtyard. In a case where only one partner is limited in his rights of usage, he may become jealous of his partner's use of the courtyard and be tempted to transgress the vow (see Rashba).

The straightforward understanding of the Gemara's conclusion, accepted by the majority of the commentaries, is that the one who took the vow is forced to sell his share, since he has a responsibility to ensure that the vow is not transgressed. However, other commentaries (Ra'avad; Ramban) hold that the forbidden party must sell his share, since only he is in danger of transgressing the vow.

To sell his portion – לִמְכּוֹר אֶת חֶלְקוֹ: Some commentaries explain that when both partners are prohibited from deriving benefit from each other, they cannot purchase from nor sell to one another either. When only one partner is prohibited from benefiting from the other, he may sell his share to his partner to avoid transgressing the vow. However, he must sell for slightly less than the market value so as not to benefit from the sale.

If someone from the marketplace – הָיָה אֶחָד מִן הַשּׁוּק: *Tosafot* explain that according to the Rabbis there is no novelty in this statement. Rather, it is merely mentioned in the mishna to illustrate that Rabbi Eliezer ben Ya'akov permits this case as well. The novelty with regard to his opinion is that even an outsider who owns no portion of the field can rely on retroactive clarification to claim that he is not benefiting from the forbidden partner, despite having no rights to usage of the property. The Ran, however, understands that even according to the Rabbis this statement presents a novelty.

I am entering into the portion of another resident of the courtyard – לְתוֹךְ שֶׁל חֲבֵירְךָ אֲנִי נִכְנָס: According to the Ra'ah, this individual may enter the jointly owned courtyard for any reason. The Rashba, however, limits the license to situations where his activity in the courtyard benefits the permitted partner (see Ritva).

Where they each vowed…the Rabbis concede – בְּהִדִּירוּ זֶה אֶת זֶה, מוֹדוּ...רַבָּנַן: If this is the case, the dispute between the Rabbis and Rabbi Eliezer ben Ya'akov cannot be based on the principle of retroactive clarification. If there really is no retroactive clarification according to the Rabbis, the fact that the partner is not in control of his prohibition is irrelevant. Rather, all agree that there is retroactive clarification but disagree as to whether one who vowed not to benefit from his partner should be punished by limiting his access to the courtyard. In cases where the prohibition is beyond the partner's control, there is no reason to punish him even according to the opinion of the Rabbis (Ritva; Ran).

HALAKHA

Was prohibited by a vow – מוּדָּר: If someone was prohibited by a vow from deriving benefit from his partner, he is permitted to enter his partner's house and a jointly owned courtyard, but he cannot make any use of them. This ruling is in accordance with the opinion of Rabbi Eliezer ben Ya'akov (Rambam *Sefer Hafla'a, Hilkhot Nedarim* 7:5; *Shulḥan Arukh, Yoreh De'a* 226:1).

And the court forces the one who took such a vow – וְכוֹפִין אֶת הַנּוֹדֵר: If one partner in a courtyard vows that the other partner may not derive benefit from him, he is forced to sell his portion of the field (Rambam). The Ra'avad and the Ramban explain that the Rambam's ruling is in accordance with the understanding presented in the Jerusalem Talmud. It is stated in the Babylonian Talmud, however, that the one forbidden by the vow must sell his portion (Rambam *Sefer Hafla'a, Hilkhot Nedarim* 7:5 and Radbaz and *Kesef Mishne* there; *Shulḥan Arukh, Yoreh De'a* 226:2).

I am entering into the portion of another resident of the courtyard – לְתוֹךְ שֶׁל חֲבֵירְךָ אֲנִי נִכְנָס: If a third party was prohibited by a vow from deriving benefit from one of the partners, he is still permitted to enter the jointly owned courtyard solely for the purpose of engaging with the permitted partner. This ruling is also in accordance with the opinion of Rabbi Eliezer ben Ya'akov (Rambam *Sefer Hafla'a, Hilkhot Nedarim* 7:6; *Shulḥan Arukh, Yoreh De'a* 226:1).

And he has a bathhouse, etc. – וְיֵשׁ לוֹ מֶרְחָץ וכו׳: If one is prohibited by a vow from deriving benefit from another, and the other has a bathhouse or olive press which he leases to others, the forbidden party may use the bathhouse or olive press only if the owner has forfeited his right of usage and has not explicitly prohibited him from entering (Rambam *Sefer Hafla'a, Hilkhot Nedarim* 6:12; *Shulḥan Arukh, Yoreh De'a* 221:6).

Entering your house is *konam* for me – קוֹנָם לְבֵיתְךָ שֶׁאֲנִי נִכְנָס: If one takes a vow prohibiting himself from benefiting from the house or possessions of another, and the other dies or sells his possessions, it is permitted for the one who took the vow to use them (Rambam *Sefer Hafla'a, Hilkhot Nedarim* 5:5, 8:11; *Shulḥan Arukh, Yoreh De'a* 216:4).

Entering this house is *konam* for me – קוֹנָם בַּיִת זֶה שֶׁאֲנִי נִכְנָס: If one takes a vow prohibiting himself from deriving benefit from a specific item by mentioning it explicitly, he is prohibited from using it even if it changes ownership (Rambam *Sefer Hafla'a, Hilkhot Nedarim* 5:5, 8:11; *Shulḥan Arukh, Yoreh De'a* 216:5).

תָּא שְׁמַע: הָיָה אֶחָד מֵהֶן מוּדָּר הֲנָאָה מֵחֲבֵירוֹ, וּפְלִיגִי רַבָּנַן. תְּנֵי: נָדַר מֵחֲבֵירוֹ הֲנָאָה.

Come and hear a proof from the mishna: If only **one of the** partners **was prohibited by a vow from deriving benefit from the other,** he may not enter the shared courtyard. Here, the prohibitive vow was stated by the other party, **and** still **the Rabbis disagree** and forbid the use of the courtyard. Evidently, the dispute in the mishna applies equally to cases beyond the control of the one forbidden by the vow. The Gemara responds: **Teach** an emended version of the mishna: If one **had vowed to prohibit himself** from deriving **benefit from another.** According to this emended version, the mishna may be addressing only the one who brought the prohibition upon himself.

הָכִי נַמִי מִסְתַּבְּרָא, דְּקָתָנֵי סֵיפָא: וְכוֹפִין אֶת הַנּוֹדֵר לִמְכּוֹר אֶת חֶלְקוֹ. אִי אָמְרַתְּ בִּשְׁלָמָא דְּנָדַר הוּא – הַיְינוּ דְּקָתָנֵי כּוֹפִין, אֶלָּא אִי אָמְרַתְּ דְּאַדְּרֵיהּ – אַמַּאי כּוֹפִין אוֹתוֹ? הָא מֵינַס אֲנִיס!

So too, it is reasonable to assume that the mishna is referring to one who imposes the prohibition upon himself, **as it was taught in the latter clause** with regard to the same case: **And** the court **forces the one who took** such **a vow to sell his portion. Granted, if you say** that the mishna is speaking of a case where **he** himself **vowed** not to benefit from the other, **this is** consistent with **that which teaches** that the court **forces** him to sell his portion; since he created the problem, he is forced to resolve it. **But if you say that** it is referring to a case **where the other prohibited him with a vow, why does** the court **force him** to sell his property? **He is put in a situation beyond his control.** This clause offers no proof, and the Rabbis may still concede in a case where one is forbidden due to another's vow.

אָמַר רַבָּה אָמַר זְעֵירִי:

Rabba said that **Ze'eiri said:**

Perek **V**
Daf **46** Amud **b**

מַחְלוֹקֶת שֶׁיֵּשׁ בָּהּ כְּדֵי חֲלוּקָה, אֲבָל אֵין בָּהּ כְּדֵי חֲלוּקָה – דִּבְרֵי הַכֹּל מוּתָּר.

The **dispute** between Rabbi Eliezer ben Ya'akov and the Rabbis is with regard to a courtyard **where there is sufficient** area **in the** courtyard[N] for it to be **divided**[N] into four square cubits for each partner, so each can be said to have a real portion that can be forbidden to the other. **But** if **there is not sufficient** area **in it** to be **divided,**[H] **everyone agrees** that it is **permitted** to benefit from it, since the entire courtyard is viewed as belonging to both of them and each one can say that he is entering his own portion.

אָמַר לֵיהּ רַב יוֹסֵף: הֲרֵי בֵּית הַכְּנֶסֶת, דִּכְמִי שֶׁאֵין בּוֹ כְּדֵי חֲלוּקָה דָּמֵי, וּתְנַן: שְׁנֵיהֶן אֲסוּרִין בְּדָבָר שֶׁל אוֹתָהּ הָעִיר!

Rav Yosef said to Rabba: **A synagogue**[N] belongs to the entire public and is therefore **considered like** a courtyard in which **there is not sufficient** area **in it** to be **divided, and we learned in** a mishna later in the chapter (48a) that with regard to two people who vow not to derive benefit from each other, **both are prohibited** from deriving benefit **from an entity belonging to that city** such as a synagogue. Evidently, the Rabbis prohibit deriving benefit even from such entities.

HALAKHA

There is not sufficient area in it to be divided – אֵין בָּהּ כְּדֵי חֲלוּקָה: Even though Rabbi Eliezer ben Ya'akov permits the prohibited partner to use a portion of a jointly owned courtyard, this applies only when the courtyard cannot be divided. If the courtyard is of sufficient area to be divided, he concedes that the partners should divide the property between themselves and neither should use the portion of his partner, in accordance with the ruling of Rav Yosef (Rambam *Sefer Hafla'a, Hilkhot Nedarim* 7:4; *Shulḥan Arukh, Yoreh De'a* 226:1).

NOTES

The dispute is where there is sufficient area in the courtyard – מַחְלוֹקֶת שֶׁיֵּשׁ בָּהּ: According to the Ran, the Rabbis disagree with Rabbi Eliezer ben Ya'akov with regard to a field that can be divided, since they reject the principle of retroactive clarification. However, other commentaries explain that even the Rabbis accept this principle and dispute only its scope. In a field that is large enough to be divided one cannot claim retroactive clarification, as either partner could have stipulated that the courtyard be divided at the outset (Rosh; *Tosefot Rabbeinu Peretz*). According to this understanding, when the courtyard cannot be divided, all agree that it is permitted for each partner to benefit from the courtyard, since neither has the right to demand a division of the property (Rashi).

Sufficient area in it to be divided – כְּדֵי חֲלוּקָה: In tractate *Bava Batra* (11a), the Sages explain that a courtyard is considered sufficiently large to be divided provided it contains four square cubits for each partner. In such a case, one may force his partner to divide the courtyard.

A synagogue, etc. – בֵּית הַכְּנֶסֶת וכו׳: The Ran explains that this mishna cannot be reconciled with the opinion of Rabbi Eliezer ben Ya'akov, as he maintains that it is permissible to derive benefit from a shared courtyard that cannot be divided. Since the opinion of Rabbi Eliezer ben Ya'akov is accepted as *halakha*, it seems that this mishna is not accepted as such. The Rambam, however, rules in accordance with the mishna. Various explanations have been provided to defend the Rambam's ruling. Rabbi Avraham min HaHar, for example, explains that a courtyard provides only the right of passage, and is therefore treated more leniently. A synagogue, however, is used more frequently, and is therefore forbidden.

אֶלָּא אָמַר רַב יוֹסֵף אָמַר זְעֵירִי: מַחֲלוֹקֶת שֶׁאֵין בָּהּ כְּדֵי חֲלוּקָה, אֲבָל יֵשׁ בָּהּ כְּדֵי חֲלוּקָה – דִּבְרֵי הַכֹּל אָסוּר.

Rather, Rav Yosef said: Ze'eiri must have **said: The dispute** holds **where there is not sufficient** area **in** the courtyard **for it to be divided, but if there is sufficient** area **in it for it to be divided, everyone agrees that it is forbidden,**[N] since if either enters it he may be entering the other's portion.

אָמַר רַב הוּנָא: הֲלָכָה כְּרַבִּי אֱלִיעֶזֶר בֶּן יַעֲקֹב, וְכֵן אָמַר רַבִּי אֶלְעָזָר: הֲלָכָה כְּרַבִּי אֱלִיעֶזֶר בֶּן יַעֲקֹב.

Rav Huna said: The *halakha* is in accordance with the opinion of **Rabbi Eliezer ben Ya'akov. And so too, Rabbi Elazar said: The *halakha* is in accordance with** the opinion of **Rabbi Eliezer ben Ya'akov.**

״הַמּוּדָּר הֲנָאָה מֵחֲבֵירוֹ וְיֵשׁ לוֹ שָׁם מֶרְחָץ״ וכו׳. וְכַמָּה תְּפִיסַת יָד? אָמַר רַב נַחְמָן: לְמֶחֱצָה לִשְׁלִישׁ וְלִרְבִיעַ, אֲבָל בִּבְצִיר – לָא. אַבַּיֵי אָמַר: אֲפִילּוּ בִּבְצִיר – אָסוּר. הֵיכִי דָּמֵי דְּשָׁרֵי – דִּמְקַבֵּל בְּטַסְקָא.

§ The mishna teaches: With regard to **one prohibited by a vow from deriving benefit from another and he has a bathhouse** or an olive press in the city that is leased out and available for public use, the forbidden party may use it only if the owner has forfeited his own right to profits from usage. The Gemara asks: **And how much** is this **right** to profits from **usage** that prohibits the subject of the vow from entering the bathhouse? **Rav Naḥman said:** In cases where he receives **one half, one-third,**[N] **or one-quarter** of the profits of the bathhouse. **But in** a case where he receives **less,** it is **not** forbidden.[N] **Abaye said: Even in** a case where he receives **less,** it is **forbidden.**[H] If so, **what are the circumstances in which** it is **permitted** and he is not considered to have a right to profits from usage? **Where he** completely forfeits all profits and **receives** only **an annual rental fee** [***taska***][LN] from a tenant.

HALAKHA

Even in a case where he receives less it is forbidden – אֲפִילּוּ בִּבְצִיר אָסוּר: If one is prohibited from deriving benefit from another, he may use the other's bathhouse as long as it is rented out to a third party and the owner retains no rights to profits from its usage, in accordance with the concluding statement of Abaye (Rambam *Sefer Hafla'a, Hilkhot Nedarim* 6:12; *Shulḥan Arukh, Yoreh De'a* 221:6).

LANGUAGE

Annual rental fee [*taska*] – טַסְקָא: Similar to the Arabic, طسق, *ṭasq*, this word usually denotes a land tax in the Talmud. Here it refers to a fixed rental payment which, like the *taska* tax, is not tied to the amount of profit the property generates.

NOTES

But if there is sufficient area in it for it to be divided, everyone agrees that it is forbidden – אֲבָל יֵשׁ בָּהּ כְּדֵי חֲלוּקָה דִּבְרֵי הַכֹּל אָסוּר: According to the Rashba, this prohibition remains in effect even after the division is made. The Rambam, however, maintains that the prohibition is in effect only prior to the division of the property. In the Jerusalem Talmud it appears that the dispute between Rabbi Eliezer ben Ya'akov and the Rabbis concerns a courtyard that has not been divided, but all agree that once the property is divided with a fence, each partner has exclusive rights to his respective portion.

One half, one-third, etc. – לְמֶחֱצָה לִשְׁלִישׁ וכו׳: This explanation is found also in the Jerusalem Talmud. The reasoning seems to be that less than one-quarter of the profits is considered insignificant, and therefore does not qualify as a right to profits from usage of the property.

But in a case where he receives less [*bivetzir*] it is not forbidden – אֲבָל בִּבְצִיר לָא: Most of the commentaries had an alternate version of the Gemara text that read *beveitzim*, meaning eggs, rather than *bivetzir*. According to this version, if one's rights in the bathhouse extend only to eggs, then one is viewed as not having a right to profits from usage of the property. The commentaries explain this clause in several ways. The Ran explains that if the owner of the property retains rights only to profits generated from the concession stands of eggs that were customarily sold outside of a bathhouse, then he is not considered to have a right to profits from usage of the property.

Others explain that the Gemara is referring to eggs of the potter, spheres of clay from which vessels are made and were left to dry in bathhouses. If the owner of the property retains only the minor right of placing his potter's eggs there (*Arukh*; Rashi), or in a small area therein (Meiri; *Shita Mekubbetzet*), he is not considered to have a true right of usage in the property.

The Rid explains that eggs were used as a common form of payment for the right to use a bathhouse, and therefore if the owner of the property sold the entire usage of the bathhouse for the day for a specified sum of eggs, then he is considered to have sold his right to profits from usage of the bathhouse for that day. Abaye, however, reasons that since the rental is only for one day, the property owner retains a general right to profits from usage of the property.

Annual rental fee [*taska*] – טַסְקָא: The commentaries discuss the nature of the *taska* payment. Most understand it as referring to an annual fee paid by the tenant regardless of the profits. Since there is no connection between the owner and the bathhouse itself other than the fixed annual payment, he is considered to no longer have his right to profits from usage of the property. The Rosh has a similar understanding but offers another explanation, found in Rabbeinu Tam's *Sefer HaYashar*: The *taska* is the property tax due to the government from the owner of the property. If the tenant pays this in addition to his rental fee, the owner is considered to be removed from the property and to have forfeited his right to profits from the usage of the property. Based on the statements of the Ran further on, it seems that others explain that the rent for the property is considered to be like a *taska*, or royal property tax, in the sense that the renter is the primary owner and simply assumes an obligation to pay a fixed sum each year.

"הָאוֹמֵר לַחֲבֵירוֹ" וכו׳. בָּעֵי אֲבִימִי: "קוֹנָם לְבֵית זֶה שֶׁאַתָּה נִכְנָס", מֵת אוֹ שֶׁמְּכָרוֹ לְאַחֵר, מַהוּ? אָדָם אוֹסֵר דָּבָר שֶׁבִּרְשׁוּתוֹ לִכְשֶׁיֵּצֵא מֵרְשׁוּתוֹ אוֹ לֹא?

§ The mishna teaches: With regard to one **who says to another:** Entering your house is *konam* for me, and the owner dies or sells the house, the prohibition is lifted. But if he said: Entering this house is *konam* for me, he remains prohibited from entering the house even after the owner dies or sells the house. **Avimi raises a dilemma:** If the owner of a house said: **Entering this house is *konam* for you,**[N] and then **he died or sold it to another, what is the *halakha*?** Do we say that **a person** can **render an item in his possession forbidden** even for a time **after it will leave his possession, or not?**

אָמַר רָבָא, תָּא שְׁמַע: הָאוֹמֵר לִבְנוֹ "קוֹנָם שֶׁאִי אַתָּה נֶהֱנֶה לִי" וּמֵת – יִירָשֶׁנּוּ. "בְּחַיָּיו וּבְמוֹתוֹ" וּמֵת – לֹא יִירָשֶׁנּוּ. שְׁמַע מִינַּהּ: אָדָם אוֹסֵר דָּבָר שֶׁבִּרְשׁוּתוֹ לִכְשֶׁיֵּצֵא מֵרְשׁוּתוֹ, שְׁמַע מִינַּהּ.

Rava said:[N] **Come and hear** a proof from a mishna (*Bava Kamma* 108b–109a): **If one says to his son: Benefiting from me is *konam* for you, and dies,** the son still **inherits from him.** If, however, the father explicitly states that benefit is forbidden both **in his lifetime and after his death,**[N] **and dies,** the son **does not inherit from him.**[N] Rava suggests: **Conclude from** the mishna that a **person** can **render an item in his possession forbidden**[H] even for a time **after it will leave his possession.** The Gemara notes: **Conclude from** the mishna that this is so.

תְּנַן הָתָם: "קוֹנָם פֵּירוֹת הָאֵלּוּ עָלַי, קוֹנָם הֵן עַל פִּי, קוֹנָם הֵן לְפִי" – אָסוּר בְּחִילּוּפֵיהֶן וּבְגִידּוּלֵיהֶן.

§ **We learned** in a mishna **there** (57a): If one says: **This produce is *konam* upon me,**[H] or: **It is *konam* upon my mouth,** or: **It is *konam* for my mouth,** he is **prohibited** from eating even **its replacements,** should they be traded or exchanged, **and** anything that **grows from it** if it is replanted.

בָּעֵי רָמִי בַּר חָמָא: אָמַר "קוֹנָם פֵּירוֹת הָאֵלּוּ עַל פְּלוֹנִי" מַהוּ בְּחִילּוּפֵיהֶן? מִי אָמְרִינַן: גַּבֵּי דִּילֵיהּ, הוֹאִיל וְאָדָם אוֹסֵר פֵּירוֹת חֲבֵירוֹ עַל עַצְמוֹ – אָדָם אוֹסֵר דָּבָר שֶׁלֹּא בָּא לָעוֹלָם עַל עַצְמוֹ, גַּבֵּי חֲבֵירוֹ, הוֹאִיל וְאֵין אָדָם אוֹסֵר פֵּירוֹת חֲבֵירוֹ עַל חֲבֵירוֹ – אֵין אָדָם אוֹסֵר דָּבָר שֶׁלֹּא בָּא לָעוֹלָם עַל חֲבֵירוֹ.

Rami bar Ḥama raises a dilemma:[N] If one said: **This produce is *konam* for so-and-so,**[H] **what is the *halakha* with regard to their replacements?**[N] **Do we say: With regard to himself, since a person can render another's produce forbidden for himself,** though it is not presently in his possession, so too, **a person can render an entity that has not yet come into the world forbidden to himself?** Is this why the replacement produce and anything that grows from it is forbidden to him, even if it did not yet exist when he took the vow? If so, **with regard to another, since a person cannot render another's produce forbidden to another,** i.e., to that owner himself, similarly **one cannot render an entity that has not yet come into the world forbidden to another.** The produce's replacements would therefore be permitted to him.

HALAKHA

A person can render an item in his possession forbidden, etc. – אָדָם אוֹסֵר דָּבָר שֶׁבִּרְשׁוּתוֹ וכו׳: One can render an item that is in his possession forbidden even for after it will leave his possession. For example, if one prohibits another from deriving benefit from a house by stating in a vow: This house, then even if he dies or sells the house that individual may not benefit from it (Rambam *Sefer Hafla'a, Hilkhot Nedarim* 5:5; *Shulḥan Arukh, Yoreh De'a* 216:7).

This produce is *konam* upon me, etc. – קוֹנָם פֵּירוֹת הָאֵלּוּ עָלַי וכו׳: If one says: This produce is *konam* upon me, he is prohibited from deriving benefit not only from the produce itself but also from its replacements and from that which grows from it. Liquids that emerge or that are squeezed from it are forbidden to him as well. He is also prohibited from deriving benefit from second-generation growths of plants such as garlic and onions, which remain intact even when new plants grow from them. Second-generation growths of plants, such as wheat, whose seeds disintegrate after sprouting, are permitted. It is also permitted to derive benefit from replacements of the replacements.

The Rosh holds that even if the item is generally forbidden, only the one who replaced it is prohibited from benefiting from the replacements, and it is permitted for others to benefit from the replacements. Similarly, if one exchanged an item forbidden only to someone else, the forbidden party is permitted to derive benefit from the object. The Ran, however, prohibits deriving benefit in all cases (Rambam *Sefer Hafla'a, Hilkhot Nedarim* 5:13–15; *Shulḥan Arukh, Yoreh De'a* 216:1).

This produce is *konam* for so-and-so – קוֹנָם פֵּירוֹת הָאֵלּוּ עַל פְּלוֹנִי: If one takes an oath or vow prohibiting another from benefiting from his produce, their replacements and that which grows from them are also forbidden *ab initio*. However, since this query is not resolved in the Gemara, if one violates the vow or oath and derives benefit from the replacements or growths, he is not flogged. The Ra'avad holds that growths are certainly forbidden, and therefore one is flogged if he derived benefit from them (Rambam *Sefer Hafla'a, Hilkhot Nedarim* 5:16 and Radbaz, *Kesef Mishne* there; *Shulḥan Arukh, Yoreh De'a* 216:2).

NOTES

Entering this house is *konam* for you – קוֹנָם לְבֵית זֶה שֶׁאַתָּה נִכְנָס: The Rosh distinguishes between Avimi's formulation and the case in the mishna. In the mishna, the individual vows to prohibit himself from benefiting from his own house. Even when the house leaves his possession it remains forbidden to him, since he had the capability to prohibit himself from benefiting from his neighbor's house. Here, however, one prohibits his friend from benefiting from his house. One cannot prohibit another individual from benefiting from the property of a third party, and therefore Avimi questions whether the vow remains in effect when the house is transferred to someone else.

Rava said, etc. – אָמַר רָבָא וכו׳: The early commentaries question why the Gemara offers this proof here, having already refuted Rava's claim it in the previous chapter (42a). Some commentaries explain that the refutation of Rava's statement in the previous chapter is not conclusive, since there as well the Gemara ultimately concludes that one can forbid an item in his possession even after it leaves his possession (Rashba; Ran). The Rosh writes that the Gemara there refuted only the notion that one can assume a person's intent to forbid an item in his possession even after it leaves his possession, even if he did not say so explicitly. Here, however, the issue is the ability to expressly forbid an item in one's possession even after it leaves his possession. This is what can be learned from Rava's statement.

In his lifetime and after his death – בְּחַיָּיו וּבְמוֹתוֹ: It is stated in the Jerusalem Talmud that the only way for one to prohibit his child from inheriting his possessions is by stating these exact words. If he said only that the prohibition holds for the duration of his lifetime, the son inherits his possessions after his death. If he said only that the prohibition takes effect after his death, his son still inherits him because after he dies he no longer owns his possessions and the prohibition cannot take effect. Only when he says both that the prohibition holds in his lifetime and after his death does he prohibit the son from inheriting, as the prohibition takes effect while he is still alive and maintains control over his possessions, and it is not annulled upon his death (*Yefe Einayim*; see commentaries on Jerusalem Talmud).

Does not inherit from him – לֹא יִירָשֶׁנּוּ: The Ran explains that this statement does not mean that he has no right to his portion of the inheritance and that it is given to other heirs. Rather, the inheritance belongs to him but he cannot derive any benefit from it. Therefore, in certain cases, his creditors can claim their debts from the inheritance.

Rami bar Ḥama raises a dilemma – בָּעֵי רָמִי בַּר חָמָא: This query seems out of place and is better suited to the subsequent discussion (57a) concerning the mishna that deals with prohibitions on replacements and growths from prohibited items. Nevertheless, it is discussed here since it is similar to the previous question with regard to the effectiveness of a vow even after the forbidden item changes hands (see *Nidrei Zerizin*).

What is the *halakha* with regard to their replacements – מַהוּ בְּחִילּוּפֵיהֶן: *Tosafot* and the Ran note that it is prohibited to replace or exchange an item from which one is prohibited from deriving benefit *ab initio*, as this in itself constitutes deriving benefit. The Gemara is therefore not questioning whether an act of replacement is permitted, but rather, if the forbidden item was unlawfully replaced, is the replacement forbidden after the fact by rabbinic law. A possible rationale for a rabbinic prohibition is that allowing one to use the replacement items may lead people to use the prohibited items as well (see Rosh, *Kiddushin* 2:31).

אוֹ דִּילְמָא מִשּׁוּם דְּחִילּוּפִין כְּגִידּוּלִין דָּמֵי, לָא שְׁנָא הוּא וְלָא שְׁנָא חֲבֵרוֹ?

Or perhaps the prohibition on replacement produce in the mishna is **due to** the fact **that replacements** of the produce are viewed as being **like that which grows**[N] from them? They are both forbidden because they derive from the forbidden produce. If this is the case, it **is no different** for **him and** it **is no different** for **another.** Neither may derive benefit from the replacements.

אֲמַר רַב אַחָא בַּר מִנְיוּמִי, תָּא שְׁמַע: הָאוֹמֵר לְאִשְׁתּוֹ ״קוֹנָם שֶׁאֲנִי נֶהֱנֶה לֵיךְ״ – לוֹוָה, וּבַעֲלֵי חוֹבִין בָּאִין וְנִפְרָעִין. מַאי טַעְמָא בַּעֲלֵי חוֹבִין נִפְרָעִין – לָאו מִשּׁוּם דְּחִילּוּפִין לָאו כְּגִידּוּלִין דָּמֵי?

Rav Aḥa bar Minyumi said: Come and hear a proof from a *baraita*: With regard to **one who says to his wife: Benefiting from me is** ***konam*** **for you,**[N] **she may** nevertheless **borrow** money to sustain herself, **and the creditors can come and collect**[N] her debts from her husband. **What is the reason** that **the creditors can collect** from the husband? **Is it not because** she benefits only indirectly, and it must be **that replacements,** i.e., the creditors' money, **are not like that which grows** from the original item?

אֲמַר רָבָא: דִּילְמָא לְכַתְּחִילָּה הוּא דְּלָא, וְאִי עֲבַד – עֲבַד.

Rava said: This is not proof: **Perhaps it is** the case **that** one should **not** benefit from replacements ***ab initio,***[N] **but if** one **did** it, it is **done** after the fact. Since the wife lacks any other means to support herself, the case is considered to be after the fact, and it is permitted for her to benefit indirectly. Still, replacements of an item are considered to be like that which grows from it *ab initio.*

NOTES

That replacements of the produce are viewed as being like that which grows – דְּחִילּוּפִין כְּגִידּוּלִין דָּמֵי: Just as it is prohibited to derive benefit from that which grows from a forbidden item, it is also prohibited to benefit from its replacements (Rashi). The Rashba reasons that replacements should be more obviously forbidden than growths, citing the case of *hekdesh*, Temple property, wherein replacements are forbidden but growths are permitted. Why shouldn't the same hold true for objects which are *konam* and therefore forbidden? The Rashba answers that even Rabbi Meir, who explicitly compares the concept of *konam* to *hekdesh*, only does so with regard to an item which is *konam* for everyone. If the item is *konam* for only one individual, then it is not comparable to *hekdesh*, but rather to prohibitions such as *teruma*, whose growths are forbidden and replacements are permitted.

Benefiting from me is *konam* for you – קוֹנָם שֶׁאֲנִי נֶהֱנֶה לֵיךְ: Most commentaries understand this case as referring to a husband who takes a vow prohibiting his wife from deriving any benefit from him. The commentaries take issue with the language of the Gemara, which, by employing the reflexive term *neheneh*, seems to indicate that the husband is prohibiting himself from benefiting from his wife. Due to this difficulty, a number of commentaries preferred alternate versions of the text, or otherwise suggested interpreting the text in a different manner. Other commentaries contend that the case in the Gemara should be understood to mean that it is prohibited for the husband to derive benefit from property his wife brought into the marriage. If he must derive benefit, he may then borrow money and allow the creditors to collect from that property. This understanding of the Gemara provides a more literal understanding of the text, and resolves difficulties inherent to the first explanation.

One such difficulty is whether the husband can impose a prohibitive vow upon his wife. Every husband at the time of marriage accepts upon himself the obligation to sustain his wife, and a prohibitive vow would constitute abrogation of his marital obligations. *Tosafot* explain that the Gemara is dealing with a case where the husband pronounced the vow during the period of betrothal, before the actual marriage took place. Alternatively, they explain that the husband can formulate the vow in specific ways to ensure it is effective.

The creditors can come and collect – בַּעֲלֵי חוֹבִין בָּאִין וְנִפְרָעִין: The creditors are able to collect the wife's debt from the husband because her loan places a lien on his possessions. The creditors do not transgress any prohibition by lending her money, nor is it prohibited for them to accept payment from the husband, as they have no connection to the vow. Since the wife may borrow the money and the husband may repay the debts, the loan represents a replacement for the husband's assets. Therefore, this case would seem to indicate that replacements of forbidden loans are permitted (Ran).

Perhaps it is that one should not benefit *ab initio* – דִּילְמָא לְכַתְּחִילָּה הוּא דְּלָא: According to this response, there is a prohibition against replacing items which are *konam* and therefore forbidden *ab initio*, but once one does so it is permitted for him to derive benefit from the replacement. As such, it appears that Rava understands the Gemara as referring to a woman who happened to borrow money, not that she was permitted to do so (Rosh; Rid). The Rashba understands the *baraita* as advising the wife to borrow from others *ab initio* if necessary, since the wife benefits from the loan before it becomes a replacement for the husband's property. Alternatively, one might understand the Gemara to mean that since the woman is already entitled to sustenance from her husband's possessions due to marital obligations, the entire case is no longer considered *ab initio*.

אֶלָּא, תָּא שְׁמַע: הַמְקַדֵּשׁ בְּעָרְלָה – אֵינָהּ מְקוּדֶּשֶׁת, מְכָרָן וְקִידֵּשׁ בִּדְמֵיהֶן – הֲרֵי זוֹ מְקוּדֶּשֶׁת. הָכָא נַמִּי, לְכַתְּחִילָּה הוּא דְּלָא, וְאִי עָבֵד – עָבֵד.

Rather, come and **hear** a proof from another mishna (*Kiddushin* 56b): With regard to **one who betroths** a woman **with** fruit of ***orla***,[HB] i.e., fruit of the first three years of a tree's growth, from which it is forbidden to benefit, **she is not betrothed** because the fruits have no value. Betrothal can be performed only with an object worth at least one *peruta*. But if **he sold them and betrothed her with the money** he received, **she is betrothed.**[N] Evidently, replacements of a forbidden item are permitted. The Gemara responds: **Here also, one should not** benefit from the replacement items given in exchange for the *orla* ***ab initio*****, but if one did** it, it is **done** after the fact. Replacements of an item may still be considered to be like that which grows from it *ab initio*.

מתני׳ ״הֲרֵינִי עָלֶיךָ חֵרֶם״ – הַמּוּדָּר אָסוּר. ״הֲרֵי אַתְּ עָלַי חֵרֶם״ – הַנּוֹדֵר אָסוּר. ״הֲרֵינִי עָלֶיךָ וְאַתְּ עָלַי״ – שְׁנֵיהֶם אֲסוּרִין, וּשְׁנֵיהֶם מוּתָּרִין בְּדָבָר שֶׁל עוֹלֵי בָבֶל,

MISHNA If someone says to another: **I am hereby** forbidden **to you** like an item **dedicated** to the Temple,[HN] then **the one prohibited by the vow is prohibited** from benefiting from the possessions of the one who took the vow. If someone says: **You are hereby** forbidden **to me** like an item **dedicated** to the Temple, then **the one who took the vow is prohibited** from benefiting from the possessions of the other. If he says: **I am hereby** forbidden **to you and you are** hereby forbidden **to me** like an item dedicated to the Temple, **both are prohibited** from benefiting from the possessions of the other. **But it is permitted for both of them** to benefit **from the objects belonging to those who ascended from Babylonia,**[N] i.e., common property of the nation as a whole, which is not considered to be the property of any individual.

HALAKHA

One who betroths with fruit of *orla*, etc. – הַמְקַדֵּשׁ בְּעָרְלָה וכו׳: If one betroths a woman with an item from which it is prohibited to derive benefit by rabbinic law, with no basis in the Torah for the prohibition, the betrothal takes effect. If the prohibition is due to a rabbinic expansion of Torah law, it is uncertain whether she is betrothed. She must therefore be betrothed again in order to marry the man in question, but if she wishes to marry someone else she requires a bill of divorce. If the item is itself forbidden by Torah law, the betrothal does not take effect. If the man transgressed and sold the forbidden item, then used the money received to betroth a woman, she is betrothed. If he initially sold the forbidden item to a Jew who was unaware that he was purchasing a forbidden item, then it is uncertain whether she is betrothed. If the forbidden item is an object of idol worship, even a betrothal with money received from its sale does not take effect (Rambam *Sefer Nashim*, *Hilkhot Ishut* 5:1; *Shulḥan Arukh*, *Even HaEzer* 28:21–22).

I am hereby forbidden to you like an item dedicated to the Temple – הֲרֵינִי עָלֶיךָ חֵרֶם: If one says to another: I am hereby forbidden to you, or uses any other language to prohibit the other from benefiting from him, the other may not derive benefit from him. However, the one who took the vow may benefit from the other. If the latter violates the vow by benefiting from him, he is not flogged, as he himself did not state the vow and therefore cannot be considered fully responsible for the transgression. If one says: I am hereby forbidden to you and you are hereby forbidden to me, they are both prohibited from benefiting from one another (Rambam *Sefer Hafla'a*, *Hilkhot Nedarim* 5:1–2; *Shulḥan Arukh*, *Yoreh De'a* 224:1).

BACKGROUND

***Orla* – עָרְלָה:** It is prohibited to eat or derive benefit from fruit that grows during the first three years after a tree has been planted (Leviticus 19:23). This prohibition applies only to the fruit and its protective coverings; it is permitted to derive benefit from the tree itself, as well as from its leaves, roots, etc. This prohibition applies only to the produce of trees grown expressly for their fruit and does not apply to trees planted as a property boundary or a wind buffer.

NOTES

She is betrothed – הֲרֵי זוֹ מְקוּדֶּשֶׁת: Several commentaries explain that the betrothal is valid and the Sages do not require a new act of betrothal. This implies that replacement articles are permitted after an exchange, even by rabbinic law (Ran; Meiri). Seemingly, one can derive from this that replacements of the replacements are also permitted, since the betrothal takes place in exchange for money and he is permitted to marry the woman. According to *Tosafot* however, secondary replacements are forbidden. Here, specifically with regard to betrothal, there is no rabbinic prohibition against deriving benefit from the secondary replacements, i.e., the woman, since the betrothal was in accordance with Torah law and the Sages did not want to annul a mitzva. However, in other cases secondary replacements are forbidden by rabbinic law.

According to the Rid, the Gemara entertains the possibility that it is permitted not only to use the replacement of a forbidden object *ab initio*, but it is also permitted to replace forbidden objects by selling them to a gentile *ab initio*. This reasoning assumes that it is prohibited to derive direct benefit from the objects themselves only by using them; a sale, however, does not constitute direct benefit.

I am hereby forbidden to you like an item dedicated to the Temple – הֲרֵינִי עָלֶיךָ חֵרֶם: The commentaries note that the term *ḥerem* may denote objects dedicated to the Temple rather than refer to a prohibitive vow. The Ran explains that this case is referring to one who took a vow while in the Galilee, as the people of the Galilee are ignorant of the *halakhot* pertaining to Temple dedications, and therefore it must presumed that the vow was intended to render benefit completely forbidden (see 18b). The Vilna Gaon writes that the expression: I am hereby forbidden to you, would be meaningless in the context of dedication to the Temple, and therefore it must always be assumed that it refers to rendering benefit completely forbidden.

Rabbi Natan bar Yosef writes that this mishna includes another novelty. Although the one taking the vow said: I am hereby forbidden to you, seemingly indicating that the vow renders forbidden only his benefit to the individual, the mishna teaches that he presumably renders the individual's benefit from his possessions forbidden as well.

The objects belonging to those who ascended from Babylonia – בְּדָבָר שֶׁל עוֹלֵי בָבֶל: Most commentaries understand that these objects are permitted because those who came from Babylonia declared all communal property ownerless and therefore permitted for use by all Jews (Ran). *Tosafot* add that by declaring their possessions ownerless, they ensured that there would be no issue of shared ownership of the property. In this way, no member of the community could render the property forbidden to a fellow Jew. The Rambam, in his Commentary on the Mishna, and the Meiri explain that the objects are viewed as belonging to all of the Jewish people in partnership, and are not ownerless. Nevertheless, one cannot take a vow rendering them forbidden to another, as each partner's relative portion is so small as to be negligible.

וַאֲסוּרִים בְּדָבָר שֶׁל אוֹתָהּ הָעִיר. וְאֵיזֶהוּ דָּבָר שֶׁל עוֹלֵי בָבֶל – כְּגוֹן הַר הַבַּיִת, וְהָעֲזָרוֹת, וְהַבּוֹר שֶׁבְּאֶמְצַע הַדֶּרֶךְ. וְאֵיזֶהוּ דָּבָר שֶׁל אוֹתָהּ הָעִיר – כְּגוֹן הָרְחָבָה, וְהַמֶּרְחָץ, וּבֵית הַכְּנֶסֶת, וְהַתֵּיבָה, וְהַסְּפָרִים. וְהַכּוֹתֵב חֶלְקוֹ לַנָּשִׂיא.

But it is prohibited for them to benefit **from objects of that city,**[H] which are considered to be jointly owned by all its residents. **And what** are examples of **objects belonging to those who ascended from Babylonia?**[H] **For example, the Temple Mount,**[N] **and the** Temple **Courtyards, and the water cistern in the middle of the road. And what are objects of that city? For example, the** city **square,**[N] **and the bathhouse,**[N] **and the synagogue, and the ark**[N] which houses the Torah scrolls, **and the** Torah **scrolls.**[N] **And one who writes,** i.e., signs, **his portion** of the shared objects of that city over **to the *Nasi*.**[HB]

רַבִּי יְהוּדָה אוֹמֵר: אֶחָד כּוֹתֵב לַנָּשִׂיא וְאֶחָד כּוֹתֵב לְהֶדְיוֹט. מַה בֵּין כּוֹתֵב לַנָּשִׂיא לְכוֹתֵב לְהֶדְיוֹט? שֶׁהַכּוֹתֵב לַנָּשִׂיא – אֵין צָרִיךְ לְזַכּוֹת, לְהֶדְיוֹט – צָרִיךְ לְזַכּוֹת. וַחֲכָמִים אוֹמְרִים: אֶחָד זֶה וְאֶחָד זֶה צְרִיכִין לְזַכּוֹת, לֹא דִּבְּרוּ בְּנָשִׂיא אֶלָּא בַּהוֹוֶה. רַבִּי יְהוּדָה אוֹמֵר: אֵין אַנְשֵׁי גָלִיל צְרִיכִין לִכְתּוֹב, שֶׁכְּבָר כָּתְבוּ אֲבוֹתֵיהֶן עַל יְדֵיהֶן.

Rabbi Yehuda says: This is the *halakha* with regard to **both** one who **writes** his portion over **to the *Nasi***[N] **and one** who **writes** it over **to a common person.** Rabbi Yehuda adds: **What** is the difference **between** one who **writes** it over **to the *Nasi*** and one who **writes** it over **to a common person? That one who writes it to the *Nasi* need not** formally **confer possession** of the item, whereas one who writes it over **to a common person must confer possession** to him. **And the Rabbis say:**[N] **Both this** one **and that** one **must confer possession,** and they specifically **mentioned the *Nasi* only** so as to speak **in the present,** addressing situations that were prevalent. **Rabbi Yehuda says: The people of Galilee do not have to write** their portion over to the *Nasi* **because their fathers already wrote it for them,** declaring that all the public property belongs to him.

HALAKHA

But it is prohibited for them to benefit from objects of that city – וַאֲסוּרִים בְּדָבָר שֶׁל אוֹתָהּ הָעִיר: If two individuals vowed to prohibit one another from deriving benefiting from each other, it is permitted for them to benefit from objects that belong to all the Jewish people. However, it is prohibited for them to benefit from items or establishments which are jointly owned by residents of their city (Rambam *Sefer Hafla'a*, *Hilkhot Nedarim* 7:2; *Shulḥan Arukh*, *Yoreh De'a* 224:1).

Objects belonging to those who ascended from Babylonia – דָּבָר שֶׁל עוֹלֵי בָבֶל: The following are examples of objects that belong to all the Jewish people: The Temple Mount, the Temple courtyards and chambers, and the wells on the roadways. Objects that belong to the city include the city square, the public bathhouse, the synagogue, the ark, and Torah scrolls (Rambam *Sefer Hafla'a*, *Hilkhot Nedarim* 7:2; *Shulḥan Arukh*, *Yoreh De'a* 224:1).

One who writes his portion over to the *Nasi* – הַכּוֹתֵב חֶלְקוֹ לַנָּשִׂיא: If two people are prohibited by a vow from deriving benefit from one another, they may write over their respective portions of city property to the *Nasi*. A third party must perform an act of acquisition on behalf of the *Nasi*, in accordance with the opinion of the Rabbis. The *Shakh* notes that some hold it is permitted for the individuals to benefit from any item or property that cannot be divided, such as a synagogue. Nevertheless, the early Sages instituted that one cannot prohibit others from using his portion in a synagogue or Torah scrolls; if he attempts to do so, the prohibition has no effect (Rambam *Sefer Hafla'a*, *Hilkhot Nedarim* 7:3; *Shulḥan Arukh*, *Yoreh De'a* 224:1 and *Oraḥ Ḥayyim* 153:16).

BACKGROUND

One who writes his portion over to the *Nasi* – הַכּוֹתֵב חֶלְקוֹ לַנָּשִׂיא: Traditionally, the *Nasi* of the Sanhedrin was a descendant of Hillel, tracing his ancestry back to the house of David. He was accorded the status of a prince in a number of matters, held in high esteem by the gentile authorities, and represented the Jews in Eretz Yisrael with regard to diplomatic issues. Therefore, writing over one's portion in communal property to the *Nasi* was a form of showing respect. Moreover, the house of the *Nasi* had large land holdings, some of which were given to the house of the *Nasi* by the local ruling authorities. These holdings were essentially national property, used to finance the various costs incurred by the house of the *Nasi* on behalf of the community. It was therefore an accepted practice that people who wished to contribute their share in communal possessions for the benefit of the community would do so by writing their shares over to the *Nasi*.

NOTES

The Temple Mount, etc. – הַר הַבַּיִת וכו׳: It is permitted to benefit from the entire Temple area, and it appears that it is also permitted to benefit from any other property that belongs to all of the Jewish people, such as the walls of Jerusalem. The reason that these places are specified while other permitted areas are not is because they are used by everyone, unlike those parts of the Temple that are accessible only to the priests (*Tosefot Yom Tov*).

The city square – הָרְחָבָה: It says in the Jerusalem Talmud that a square through which a public thoroughfare passes is not considered to be the property of the residents of the city, but rather that of the general public.

The square and the bathhouse, etc. – הָרְחָבָה וְהַמֶּרְחָץ וכו׳: These sites are built by the residents of the city, who are therefore accorded the status of shareholders in their ownership. As noted in tractate *Megilla* (25a), the residents of the city also have the right to collectively sell such properties to others (Ritva).

The ark – הַתֵּיבָה: *Tosafot* explain that this is the ark that houses the Torah scrolls. Others say it is the table upon which the Torah scrolls are placed for reading (Ritva; Ran).

The scrolls [*sefarim*] – הַסְּפָרִים: Whenever the word *sefarim* is used in an unspecified form it refers to Torah scrolls, as they are the scrolls that are used by everyone (Rashi). Some commentaries explain that here *sefarim* refers to all the books in the synagogue bought by the community or donated specifically so the residents can study them (*Tosafot*). A number of commentaries note that Torah study is a mitzva, and the performance of mitzvot is not considered an act from which one derives benefit. As such, use of the *sefarim* would not constitute deriving benefit from communal property.

Rabbi Avraham min HaHar explains that while the performance of a mitzva is generally not viewed as an act from which one derives benefit, Torah study is different. The mitzva of Torah study was given for the benefit and delight of the one who studies. This idea is echoed in a number of other sources, which stress that the enjoyment of Torah study is an intrinsic part of the mitzva (see introduction to *Eglei Tal*). Furthermore, since one can fulfill the mitzva of learning Torah by reciting the daily *Shema*, any additional study is not strictly mandatory, and therefore it may be considered as benefit.

One who writes…to the *Nasi* – כּוֹתֵב לַנָּשִׂיא: One who signs over his portion of the communal property to the *Nasi* immediately relinquishes his rights to the property. The Sages determined that out of deference to the *Nasi*, no further act is required on behalf of the *Nasi* in order to validate the acquisition (see *Tosafot* and Rosh). According to the *Tosefot Yom Tov*, the Sages enacted this mechanism to protect one who is prohibited by a vow from needing to leave the city, which would cause him extreme hardship. The Rashash, however, explains that this mechanism was not instituted by the Sages, since in any event one may transfer property to someone who is accorded special honor without any further act of acquisition on his part. According to the Meiri, all public possessions are considered to be property of the *Nasi*, and one who relinquishes his rights to public property automatically transfers them to the *Nasi* without further need for an act of acquisition.

And the Rabbis say – וַחֲכָמִים אוֹמְרִים: The *Tosefot Yom Tov* explains that the opinion of the Rabbis is identical to the initial statement in the mishna with regard to signing over one's portion to the *Nasi*. The Rashash, however, explains that Rabbi Yehuda and the Rabbis disputed the meaning of this initial statement. According to Rabbi Yehuda, one may write his portion over to the *Nasi* without an act of acquisition, but writing one's portion over to a common person requires an additional act of acquisition. The Rabbis hold that there is no difference between the two, and the mishna mentioned the *Nasi* simply to reflect the common practice.

גמ׳ אַמַּאי מִיתְסַר? אָמַר רַב שֵׁשֶׁת: הָכִי קָתָנֵי: וּמַה תַּקָּנָתָן – יִכְתְּבוּ חֶלְקָן לַנָּשִׂיא.

GEMARA The mishna appears to teach that one who is prohibited by a vow from benefiting from another may not benefit from property written over to the *Nasi*. The Gemara asks: **Why is it forbidden? Rav Sheshet said: This is what** the mishna **is teaching: And what is their remedy,**[N] i.e., what can be done to enable the forbidden individuals to benefit from communal property? **They should write their portion** over **to the *Nasi*,** thereby relinquishing their shares in the communal property.

רַבִּי יְהוּדָה אוֹמֵר: אֶחָד כּוֹתֵב לַנָּשִׂיא וְאֶחָד כּוֹתֵב לְהֶדְיוֹט. וּמַה בֵּין כּוֹתֵב לַנָּשִׂיא לְכוֹתֵב לְהֶדְיוֹט? הַכּוֹתֵב לַנָּשִׂיא – אֵין צָרִיךְ לְזַכּוֹת, וְהַכּוֹתֵב לְהֶדְיוֹט – צָרִיךְ לְזַכּוֹת. וַחֲכָמִים אוֹמְרִים: אֶחָד זֶה וְאֶחָד זֶה צְרִיכִים לְזַכּוֹת, לֹא דִּבְּרוּ בְּנָשִׂיא אֶלָּא בַּהוֹוֶה.

The Gemara continues its quotation from the mishna: This is the *halakha* with regard to **both** one who **writes** his portion over **to the *Nasi* and one** who **writes** it over **to a common person.** Rabbi Yehuda adds: **What** is the difference **between** one who **writes** it over **to the *Nasi* and** one who **writes** it over **to a common person? That one who writes it to the *Nasi* need not** formally **confer possession** of the item, whereas one who writes it over **to a common person must confer possession** to him. **And the Rabbis say: Both this** one **and that** one **must confer possession,** and **they** specifically **mentioned the *Nasi* only** so as to speak **in the present.**[N]

"רַבִּי יְהוּדָה אוֹמֵר: אֵין אַנְשֵׁי גָלִיל צְרִיכִין לְזַכּוֹת, שֶׁכְּבָר כָּתְבוּ אֲבוֹתֵיהֶן עַל יְדֵיהֶן". תַּנְיָא, רַבִּי יְהוּדָה אוֹמֵר: אַנְשֵׁי גָלִיל קַנְטְרָנִין הָיוּ, וְהָיוּ נוֹדְרִין הֲנָאָה זֶה מִזֶּה, עָמְדוּ אֲבוֹתֵיהֶם וְכָתְבוּ חֶלְקֵיהֶן לַנָּשִׂיא.

§ The mishna teaches: **Rabbi Yehuda says: The people of Galilee do not have to confer possession** of their portion to the *Nasi* **because their forefathers already wrote it for them. It is taught** in a *baraita* that **Rabbi Yehuda says: The people of Galilee were quarrelsome** [*kanteranin*][L] **and would** often **take vows prohibiting benefit from one another.** So **their forefathers arose**[N] **and wrote their portions** of the public property over **to the *Nasi*** so that they would be able to use communal property.

מתני׳ הַמּוּדָּר הֲנָאָה מֵחֲבֵירוֹ וְאֵין לוֹ מַה יֹּאכַל – נוֹתְנוֹ לְאַחֵר לְשׁוּם מַתָּנָה, וְהַלָּה מוּתָּר בָּהּ. מַעֲשֶׂה בְּאֶחָד בְּבֵית חוֹרוֹן שֶׁהָיָה אָבִיו נוֹדֵר הֵימֶנּוּ הֲנָאָה, וְהָיָה מַשִּׂיא אֶת בְּנוֹ, וְאָמַר לַחֲבֵרוֹ: חָצֵר וּסְעוּדָה נְתוּנִים הֵינָן לְפָנֶיךָ, אֶלָּא כְּדֵי שֶׁיָּבֹא אַבָּא וְיֹאכַל עִמָּנוּ בַּסְּעוּדָה.

MISHNA With regard to **one who is prohibited by a vow from deriving benefit from another and he does not have anything to eat,**[H] the other **may give** the food **to someone else as a gift and he is** then **permitted** to eat **it.** The mishna recounts: **An incident** occurred **involving someone** in the city of **Beit Ḥoron**[B] **whose father had vowed not to derive benefit from him, and** the son **was marrying off** his own **son** and wanted his father to be able to participate in the wedding meal. **And** he therefore **said to another: The courtyard** where the wedding will take place **and the** wedding **meal are given before you** as a gift, but **only so that my father will come and eat with us at the meal.**

אָמַר: אִם שֶׁלִּי הֵם – הֲרֵי הֵם מוּקְדָּשִׁין לַשָּׁמַיִם. אָמַר לוֹ: נָתַתִּי לְךָ אֶת שֶׁלִּי שֶׁתַּקְדִּישֵׁם לַשָּׁמַיִם?! אָמַר לוֹ: נָתַתָּ לִי אֶת שֶׁלְּךָ – אֶלָּא שֶׁתְּהֵא אַתָּה וְאָבִיךָ אוֹכְלִין וְשׁוֹתִין וּמִתְרַצִּין זֶה לָזֶה, וִיהֵא עָוֹן תָּלוּי בְּרֹאשׁוֹ. אָמְרוּ חֲכָמִים: כָּל מַתָּנָה שֶׁאֵינָהּ שֶׁאִם הִקְדִּישָׁהּ תְּהֵא מְקוּדֶּשֶׁת – אֵינָהּ מַתָּנָה.

The recipient **said: If they are mine, they are** all **hereby consecrated to Heaven,** i.e., the Temple, and are forbidden to everyone. The son **said to him** in anger: And **did I give you my** property **so that you should consecrate it to Heaven? He,** the recipient, **said to him: You gave me your** property **only** so **that you and your father would eat and drink and** thereby **appease each other, and the sin** of transgressing the vow **would be hung on his,** i.e., my, **head,** as I enabled the transgression. **The Sages** therefore **said: Any gift**[H] **that is not** so absolute so **that if** the recipient **were to consecrate** the gift **it would be consecrated,**[N] **is not a gift.** In other words, in order for it to be a gift, the recipient must have the ability to consecrate it.

NOTES

And what is their remedy – וּמַה תַּקָּנָתָן: The reason that this solution is not used in the case of two partners in a shared courtyard is because the courtyard is owned only by the two partners. If they were to sign it over to the *Nasi* they would relinquish their right to use the property. By contrast, communal property belonging to a city is shared equally by all residents, and therefore no one loses his right to usage by assigning his portion to the *Nasi* (*Tosafot*).

In the present – בַּהוֹוֶה: Property was commonly written over to the *Nasi* because there was no concern that the *Nasi* would subsequently vow to render the property forbidden to a resident of the city. This is not necessarily true with regard to a private individual, who is a resident of the city and may vow to render the property forbidden to another in the future (Ran).

Their forefathers arose, etc. – עָמְדוּ אֲבוֹתֵיהֶם וכו׳: Some commentaries explain that the leadership in the Galilee foresaw a situation in which residents would constantly render communal property forbidden to one another. Therefore, they compelled all the members of their community to give their portions over to the *Nasi*. Others explain that the language of the Gemara is meant to indicate that even in earlier generations, the forefathers wrote their portions over to the *Nasi* (*Shita Mekubbetzet*).

That if he were to consecrate it, it would be consecrated – שֶׁאִם הִקְדִּישָׁהּ תְּהֵא מְקוּדֶּשֶׁת: The Ran asks: When one gives a gift and stipulates that it must be returned, the gift is valid for the allotted period, despite the fact that the recipient cannot consecrate it. What is the distinction between that *halakha* and the concept discussed in the Gemara here, which states that any gift that cannot be consecrated is not considered a gift? He answers that although a gift given based on the condition that it be returned is valid, the gift described here is invalid since it is given only for a limited purpose.

It is explained in the Jerusalem Talmud that the Sages did not render any gift invalid if the giver cannot consecrate it, as one may stipulate that the gift he gives not be consecrated. This principle applies only in cases where there is legitimate concern that the gift is a legal fiction.

LANGUAGE

Quarrelsome [*kanteranin*] – קַנְטְרָנִין: Derived from the Greek κεντρόω, *kentroo*, meaning to sting or pierce.

BACKGROUND

Beit Ḥoron – בֵּית חוֹרוֹן: Beit Ḥoron was a city located near the northern border of the land allocated to the tribe of Judah, and was divided into two neighboring towns, Upper Beit Ḥoron and Lower Beit Ḥoron. These cities are mentioned in the Bible, and due to their strategic location on the main road to Jerusalem they were the site of many famous battles, including the victory of Judah Maccabee and a victory over the Romans during the Great Revolt. Ancient settlements such as these, which were resettled upon the return from the Babylonian exile, were often host to a tradition of Torah learning. The incident recounted here illustrates the sensitivity of the local residents and their commitment to observing the mitzvot with great care.

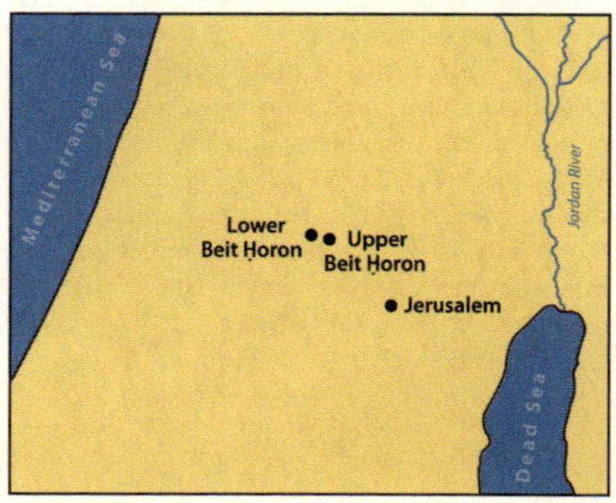

Location of Beit Ḥoron

HALAKHA

And he does not have anything to eat – וְאֵין לוֹ מַה יֹּאכַל: If one takes a vow prohibiting another from deriving benefit from him, and that person does not have anything to eat, the one who vowed may give items to a third party in the form of a gift, and that individual can in turn give it to the one prohibited by the vow. If, upon giving the gift, he specifies that it is only for the purpose of benefiting the other, or if it is otherwise obvious from his behavior that the gift is a legal fiction, then the one prohibited by the vow may not derive benefit from it (Rambam *Sefer Hafla'a, Hilkhot Nedarim* 7:15; *Shulḥan Arukh, Yoreh De'a* 221:9).

Any gift, etc. – כָּל מַתָּנָה וכו׳: Any gift that one gives while stipulating that the recipient cannot consecrate it is invalid (Rambam *Sefer Hafla'a, Hilkhot Nedarim* 7:16).

גמ׳ מַעֲשֶׂה לִסְתּוֹר! חַסּוּרֵי מִיחַסְּרָא וְהָכִי קָתָנֵי: וְאִם הוֹכִיחַ סוֹפוֹ עַל תְּחִילָּתוֹ – אָסוּר. וּמַעֲשֶׂה נַמִי בְּבֵית חוֹרוֹן בְּאֶחָד דַּהֲוָה סוֹפוֹ מוֹכִיחַ עַל תְּחִילָּתוֹ.

GEMARA The Gemara asks: Was **an incident** cited **to contradict**[N] that which was initially stated in the mishna? The mishna explicitly stated that one may give a gift to another in order to bypass the prohibition of a vow. The Gemara answers: The mishna **is incomplete and is teaching like this:**[B] **And if his ultimate** actions **prove** the nature of **his initial** intent, i.e., if the prior owner protests that he gave the gift only as a technicality in order to bypass the vow, it is **forbidden. And** to illustrate this point, **there was also an incident in Beit Ḥoron concerning someone whose ultimate** protest **proved** that **his initial** intent was not to give a true gift.

אֲמַר רָבָא: לֹא שָׁנוּ אֶלָּא דַּאֲמַר לֵיהּ ״וְהִינָּן לְפָנֶיךָ אֶלָּא כְּדֵי שֶׁיָּבֹא אַבָּא״. אֲבָל אֲמַר לֵיהּ ״שֶׁיְּהוּ לְפָנֶיךָ, שֶׁיָּבֹא אַבָּא״ – מִדַּעְתְּךָ הוּא דַּאֲמַר לֵיהּ.

Rava said: They taught this prohibition **only** in a case **where he said to him: And** the gifts **are** given **before you only so that** my **father should come,** as he explicitly mentioned that he did not intend to give an absolute gift. **But if he said to him** less explicitly: **That they should be before you that** my **father should come,** there is no prohibition, **since he is** essentially **saying to him:** It is **up to your judgment** whether or not to invite him.

לִישָּׁנָא אַחֲרִינָא אָמְרִין לָהּ, אֲמַר רָבָא: לָא תֵּימָא טַעְמָא דַּאֲמַר לֵיהּ ״וְהִינָּן לְפָנֶיךָ״ הוּא דְּאָסוּר, אֲבָל אֲמַר לֵיהּ ״הֵן לְפָנֶיךָ, שֶׁיָּבֹא אַבָּא וְיֹאכַל״ – מוּתָּר. אֶלָּא אֲפִילּוּ אֲמַר לֵיהּ ״הֵן לְפָנֶיךָ, יָבֹא אַבָּא וְיֹאכַל״ – אָסוּר. מַאי טַעְמָא – סְעוּדָתוֹ מוֹכַחַת עָלָיו.

Some say another version of this statement. **Rava said: Do not say** that **the reason** for the prohibition **is because he said to him: And** the gifts **are** given **before you** only so that my father will come, and **that** is why **it is forbidden; but if he said to him: They are before you so my father should come and eat,** it would be **permitted.** This is not so. **Rather, even if he said to him: They are before you,** my **father should come and eat,** it is **forbidden. What is the reason** for this? **His wedding meal proves about him**[N] that his sole intention was to bypass the vow.

NOTES

An incident cited to contradict – מַעֲשֶׂה לִסְתּוֹר: The Ran writes that this incident does not truly contradict the aforementioned *halakha*, but it does limit its application. The *halakha* seems to indicate that the prohibition may be circumvented by any gift to a third party, while the incident recorded seems to indicate that only gifts that can be consecrated by the recipient suffice.

His wedding meal proves about him – סְעוּדָתוֹ מוֹכַחַת עָלָיו: Certainly, such a large feast was not prepared for the benefit of the recipient of the gift. The giver clearly sought only to circumvent the prohibition of the vow and enable his father to attend his son's wedding. The Rambam writes that this type of gift is forbidden even if the giver did not make the stipulation at the outset and mentioned this only later on. The Rashba, however, holds that the gift is invalid only if the stipulation was stated explicitly at the time the gift was given. Some explain that this issue revolves around the two versions of the statement made by Rava, as recorded in the Gemara (see *Kesef Mishne*).

BACKGROUND

The mishna is incomplete and is teaching like this – חַסּוּרֵי מִיחַסְּרָא וְהָכִי קָתָנֵי: This method of explanation is often found in the Gemara as a means of understanding passages in the mishna that seem to be incomplete. Generally, after raising difficulties with regard to the text of the mishna that render the mishna in its original form incoherent or inconsistent with another authoritative source, the Gemara introduces an addition to the mishna that provides the necessary clarification.

Perek **V**
Daf **48** Amud **b**

הַהוּא גַּבְרָא דַּהֲוָה לֵיהּ בְּרָא דַּהֲוָה שָׁמֵיט כֵּיפֵי דְּכִיתָנָא, אַסְרִינְהוּ לְנִכְסֵיהּ עֲלֵיהּ. אָמְרוּ לֵיהּ: וְאִי הָוֵאי בַּר בְּרָךְ צוּרְבָא מֵרַבָּנַן מַאי? אֲמַר לְהוֹן: לִיקְנֵי הָדֵין, וְאִי הָוֵאי בַּר בְּרִי צוּרְבָא מֵרַבָּנַן – לִקְנְיֵיהּ. מַאי?

There was **a certain man who had a son who seized** in theft **sheaves** [*keifei*] **of flax,**[LN] and the father took a vow **prohibiting** his son **from** deriving any benefit **from his possessions. They said to** the father: **And if the son of your son**[HN] **would become a Torah scholar,** and you would want him to be able to inherit your possessions, **what** would you do? **He said to them: Let this** son of mine **acquire** the possessions,[N] **and** only **if the son of my son becomes a Torah scholar** then **let him,** my grandson, **acquire them** from my son. They asked: **What is** the ruling?

LANGUAGE

Sheaves [*keifei*] – כֵּיפֵי: This word, which appears in both Hebrew and Aramaic, has several meanings, some of which are interrelated. One meaning of *keifei* is rocks, sometimes referring specifically to precious stones and jewelry. It can also mean piles of grain. At other times it refers to bundles of plants, palm leaves, or other vegetation. Due to these multiple meanings, there are often disputes among the commentaries concerning how to understand the word in a given context, thereby leading to variant interpretations of this Gemara.

HALAKHA

And if the son of your son, etc. – וְאִי הָוֵאי בַּר בְּרָךְ וכו׳: If one prohibits his son from deriving benefit from him, but stipulates that if his grandson becomes a Torah scholar the son will acquire his possessions in order to transfer them to the grandson, it remains forbidden for the son to benefit from his father's possessions. However, it is permitted for the grandson to benefit from them, in accordance with the opinion of Rav Naḥman. This is the ruling of the Rambam as cited in the *Shulḥan Arukh*.

The Ra'avad understands the ruling of the Rambam to mean that the grandson is permitted to benefit from the possessions only if he is a Torah scholar. However, the *Kesef Mishne*, the *Perisha*, the Ra'avad, and the *Tur* understand that the grandson can use the property regardless. The Rosh and the Ran rule that the grandson acquires nothing in this manner, in accordance with the opinion of Rav Ashi (Rambam *Sefer Hafla'a*, *Hilkhot Nedarim* 5:7; *Shulḥan Arukh*, *Yoreh De'a* 223:3).

NOTES

Seized sheaves of flax – שָׁמֵיט כֵּיפֵי דְּכִיתָנָא: Most commentaries explain that the son stole bundles of flax from their owners. According to Rav Hai Gaon's version of the text, the son would steal bundles of flax from his father. Others explain that he would steal women's caps that were made of flax (Rosh), or that he stole cloaks or sheaves from the field (Meiri). According to another explanation found in the Commentary on *Nedarim*, the son spent his time purchasing bundles of flax, keeping some for himself and selling the remainder for a profit, instead of engaging in Torah study (*Arukh*; Rabbeinu Yitzḥak).

If the son of your son, etc. – אִי הָוֵאי בַּר בְּרָךְ וכו׳: The Ran maintains that a father cannot prevent his son from inheriting his property by means of a vow, but he can formulate a vow which prevents his son from deriving benefit from the inheritance. Since the son actually inherits the property and is merely prohibited from using it, the inheritance will pass on to the grandson anyway. It is therefore difficult to understand the father's need to add such a proviso. The Ran explains that the father had another son, to whom he wished to leave the entire inheritance in the event that the grandson was not a Torah scholar, and therefore the stipulation that the inheritance would go to the first son is contingent only upon the grandson's actions. The Rosh and the Rashba explain similarly. The Meiri maintains that the need for this acquisition was to enable the grandson to benefit from the inheritance even when his father was alive, since otherwise he may not have anything to eat.

Let this son acquire the possessions, etc. – לִיקְנֵי הָדֵין וכו׳: The straightforward understanding of this case is that the grandfather allows his son to perform an act of acquisition on behalf of the grandson. Some explain that the reason the son must acquire it on behalf of the grandson is because the child has not yet been born, and therefore the grandfather cannot confer possession to him directly (Rashi; *Talmidei Rabbeinu Peretz*).

The Meiri notes that even if the grandson is already born, he has not yet become a Torah scholar, and as such cannot acquire the possessions directly at the time of the stipulation. The Rashba, however, interprets the statement of the grandfather as referring to a third party who would acquire the property on the condition that he transfer it to the grandson in the event that he becomes a Torah scholar. According to the *Ḥatam Sofer*, the grandfather also intended that this gift would indirectly benefit his own son, who may use the possessions to cover his own expenditures on behalf of the grandson.

אָמְרִי פּוּמְבְּדִיתָאֵי: ״קְנֵי עַל מְנָת לְהַקְנוֹת״ הוּא, וְכׇל ״קְנֵי עַל מְנָת לְהַקְנוֹת״ – לָא קָנֵי.

The Sages of **Pumbedita say:** This is just as if he stated: **Acquire** the property **on the condition that you transfer**[N] it to your son. In such a case he has not given anything to the recipient, but has merely made him a conduit to transfer the item to someone else. **And** in **any** case where one says: **Acquire** this item **on the condition that you transfer** ownership, the recipient **does not acquire** the item, and the statement has no effect.

וְרַב נַחְמָן אֲמַר: קָנֵי, דְּהָא כּוּדָרָא קְנֵי עַל מְנָת לְהַקְנוֹת הוּא.

But Rav Naḥman said: He does acquire, as an acquisition by means of a **cloth**[B] **is** a case of an act of **acquisition** performed only **in order to transfer** ownership. In such a case, one gives another a cloth in order to confer ownership of some other item, but the cloth itself does not assume new ownership. Still, this is an effective means of acquisition. So too, the property of the grandfather may be effectively conferred upon the grandson through the son, without the son acquiring it himself.

אֲמַר רַב אַשִׁי: וּמַאן לֵימָא לָן דְּסוּדָרָא, אִי תָּפֵיס לֵיהּ לָא מִיתְפִּיס? וְעוֹד: סוּדָרָא – ״קְנֵי עַל מְנָת לְהַקְנוֹת וּקְנֵי מִן הַשְׁתָּא״, הָלֵין נִיכְסִין דְּהָדֵין, לְאֵימָתַי קָנֵי – לְכִי הָוֵי בַּר בְּרֵיהּ צוּרְבָּא מֵרַבָּנַן, לְכִי הָוֵה – הֲדַר סוּדָרָא לְמָרֵיהּ!

Rav Ashi said: And who will say to us concerning the cloth that if the recipient of the cloth would **seize it** with the intention of keeping it that it would **not** be an effective **seizure?** While the cloth is technically transferred, the recipient does not usually exercise his right to it. **And furthermore,** an acquisition by means **of a cloth**[H] is a case where the giver is saying: **Acquire** only **in order to transfer** ownership, **but acquire from now.**[N] However, with regard to **these possessions of this** one who took the vow, **when does** the son **acquire?** Only **when his son's son becomes a Torah scholar. And when he becomes** a Torah scholar, **the cloth has** already been **returned to its owner,**[N] i.e., the act of acquisition had taken place long before the grandson became a Torah scholar. The initial transfer therefore has no effect.

אֲמַר לֵיהּ רָבָא לְרַב נַחְמָן: וְהָא מַתְּנַת בֵּית חוֹרוֹן, דִּקְנֵי עַל מְנָת לְהַקְנוֹת הוּא, וְלָא קָא קָנֵי!

Rava said to Rav Naḥman: But the gift of Beit Ḥoron[N] discussed in the mishna **is** an example of an **acquisition** performed only **in order to transfer** ownership, **and there he did not acquire** it at all.

BACKGROUND

Cloth – סוּדָרָא: Transferring ownership by means of a cloth is a means of acquisition rooted in the principle of property exchange. When two articles are exchanged for one another, the formal acquisition of one of the articles automatically transfers ownership of the second. While exchanging articles is generally performed when they are of equal value, there is no formal requirement that this be so. Therefore, the practice of formalizing acquisitions using a cloth can be understood as an extension of the principle of exchange. In this form of acquisition, the symbolic transfer of a handkerchief or some other small article from one party to another formalizes an agreement made between them, as it is indicative of their willingness to proceed with the acquisition.

The source for the validity of this form of acquisition is in the book of Ruth, where Boaz purchases land and property by means of exchanging a shoe with his kinsman (Ruth 4:7). Normally, with regard to the transfer of ownership by means of a cloth, the seller takes the buyer's cloth in his hand and then returns the cloth to the buyer, having symbolically formalized the sale.

HALAKHA

Cloth, etc. – סוּדָרָא וכו׳: Some commentaries rule that an acquisition by means of a cloth is ineffective unless the transfer of property occurs immediately. However, if one expressly stipulates: Acquire immediately and after thirty days, the acquisition takes effect. The Rema, citing the *Terumat HaDeshen*, rules that even without an express stipulation it is assumed that the intention was to state: Acquire now and after thirty days, since one presumably does not perform an act of acquisition with the intention of its having no effect (*Shulḥan Arukh, Ḥoshen Mishpat* 195:5).

NOTES

Acquire on the condition that you transfer – קְנֵי עַל מְנָת לְהַקְנוֹת: The *halakha* generally allows one to confer property upon an absentee recipient by permitting a third party to perform an act of acquisition on the recipient's behalf. *Tosafot*, however, explain that the situation here is different. Typically, the third party acts only as an agent for the recipient, and he himself does not acquire ownership of the property. Here, however, the son is receiving ownership of the gift on the condition that he will later transfer it to someone else. His ability to convey the gift to the grandson is therefore contingent upon his ability to acquire it himself.

Similarly, the Ran explains that this case is different from a gift given on the condition that it later be returned to the giver, which is generally valid. In such a case, although the recipient does not acquire the item permanently, he may benefit from it during the period of his ownership. Here, however, it is prohibited for the son to derive benefit from that which was given to him.

But acquire from now – וּקְנֵי מִן הַשְׁתָּא: The Rashba discusses whether Rav Naḥman also holds that immediate acquisition is necessary in order to render an acquisition by means of a cloth as acceptable. The Ran writes that Rav Naḥman might respond to Rav Ashi by saying that the father implicitly intends for the transfer of ownership to his son to take effect immediately, just as an acquisition by means of a cloth takes effect immediately.

The cloth has already been returned to its owner – הֲדַר סוּדָרָא לְמָרֵיהּ: This implies that the desired transfer of ownership can occur only at the moment of the symbolic act of acquisition. The Rashba, however, explains that this principle applies only to acquisition by means of a cloth or similar formal acts of acquisition. If the grandfather had instead signed the item over to his grandson, the document would remain in effect even after it had been written, and the transfer of ownership could occur at a later date, once the grandson had proven himself. According to *Tosafot* and the Ran, no method of acquisition can go into effect at a later date alone, unless the intermediate recipient gains some right to the acquired item in the meantime.

But the gift of Beit Ḥoron, etc. – וְהָא מַתְּנַת בֵּית חוֹרוֹן וכו׳: Rava understands that the gift of Beit Ḥoron was invalid from the outset, since the recipient did not acquire true rights to the courtyard or the meal. His acquisition of the meal was limited to only one day and did not entitle him to any greater benefit than the other guests (see Meiri).

זִימְנִין אֲמַר לֵיהּ: מִשּׁוּם דִּסְעוּדָתוֹ מוֹכַחַת עָלָיו, וְזִימְנִין אֲמַר לֵיהּ: רַבִּי אֱלִיעֶזֶר הִיא, דְּאָמַר: אֲפִילּוּ וִיתּוּר אָסוּר בְּמוּדַּר הֲנָאָה.

The Gemara recounts: **Sometimes** when Rav Naḥman was asked this question **he said to him:** That is **because his** wedding **meal proves about him**[N] that he did not truly intend to give the items to the recipient, and not because such an acquisition is invalid per se. **And sometimes he said to him**[N] that in **that** case they followed the stringent opinion of **Rabbi Eliezer, who said: Even** negligible benefits ordinarily **waived** are **forbidden**[N] **to one prohibited by a vow from deriving benefit** from another. So too, Rabbi Eliezer holds that one cannot rely on an act of acquisition performed merely in order to transfer ownership to a third party.

תְּנַן: אָמְרוּ חֲכָמִים, כָּל מַתָּנָה שֶׁאֵינָהּ שֶׁאִם הִקְדִּישָׁהּ תְּהֵא מְקוּדֶּשֶׁת – אֵינָהּ מַתָּנָה. "כָּל" לְאֵיתוֹיֵי מַאי, לָאו לְאֵתוֹיֵי הָא מִילְּתָא דְּשַׁדְיָא בְּכֵיפֵי? לָא, לְאֵתוֹיֵי לִישָּׁנָא בַּתְרָאָה דִּשְׁמַעְתֵּיהּ דְּרָבָא.

§ **We learned** in the mishna (48a): **The Sages** therefore **said: Any gift that is not** so absolute so **that, if** the recipient **were to consecrate** the gift **it would be consecrated, is not a gift.** The Gemara asks: **What is added** by the word: **Any? Is it not adding this matter of** one who **seized sheaves** of flax, and to say that the gift of the father has no effect? The Gemara responds: **No,** the intent is **to add the latter version of the** aforementioned **statement of Rava,** that a gift given as a means of circumventing a vow has no effect, even when the giver mentions the nature of the gift only casually and does not stipulate it as a formal condition.

הדרן עלך השותפין

NOTES

His meal proves about him – דִּסְעוּדָתוֹ מוֹכַחַת עָלָיו: Some explain that the festive wedding meal proves he did not intend to give anything to the recipient, as the elaborate meal was clearly prepared for the wedding celebration and not for him alone. The gift is rendered invalid only because it is a legal fiction, and not because the giver wanted the recipient to acquire it on behalf of someone else. According to the Ran, the meal illustrates the son's desire to directly benefit the forbidden party, his father. Here, by contrast, the grandfather wants only to benefit his grandson, which is permitted; however, he must do so indirectly, using his son as a conduit.

And sometimes he said to him, etc. – וְזִימְנִין אֲמַר לֵיהּ וכו׳: Some explain that Rav Naḥman did not find his first answer to be sufficient, so he later provided a revised, more thorough answer (Rabbi Eliyahu Mizraḥi).

Even benefits ordinarily waived are forbidden – אֲפִילּוּ וִיתּוּר אָסוּר: Most commentaries hold that there is no substantive connection between these two rulings. Rav Naḥman means that just as Rabbi Eliezer is stringent with regard to benefits which are ordinarily waived, so too, he is stringent with regard to gifts which are given in order to bypass vows. According to this understanding, any acquisition undertaken on the condition that the property be transferred to a third party remains in effect, but if the acquisition is used as a means to circumvent a vow it is rendered invalid (*Tosafot*; Ran; see Meiri). The *Ḥatam Sofer* explains that Rabbi Eliezer deems the gift of Beit Ḥoron forbidden due to the giver's explicit statement that he is giving the items only to circumvent the vow.

Summary of **Perek V**

With regard to property owned in partnership, the Gemara rules leniently that one partner does not have the ability to prevent the other from entering the property or deriving benefit from his share. The reason for this is that one can prohibit another from benefiting from his own property only by means of a vow, and the Gemara rules that the principle of retroactive clarification makes it possible for each partner to benefit exclusively from his share. In principle, however, even partial ownership of something gives one the power to ban by means of a vow another who is not also a partner from deriving benefit from that property. Accordingly, when one prohibits another from deriving benefit from him, all property belonging to the community of the person who took the vow becomes prohibited to the object of the vow. The only way that person can then benefit from community property is if the person who took the vow transfers his share to a third party. This is the case with regard to property that belongs to a particular community. However, property that belongs to the whole community of Israel is not considered to be held in partnership and one does not have the power to prohibit another from benefiting from it.

The Gemara rules that vows that take effect on objects one owns remain in effect even after the objects are sold or given away. However, it is inconclusive with regard to whether vows can take effect on objects that do not yet exist.

It is possible to circumvent a prohibitory vow by giving a gift to a third party with the understanding that he will then give it to the object of the vow. However, the gift must be unconditional, and the third party is not legally bound to pass the gift along. The event that took place in Beit Ḥoron (48a–b) serves as an example of such a conditional gift and of how important it is to take one's vows seriously without using legal fictions to circumvent them.

Introduction to **Perek VI**

This chapter resumes discussion of the exact meaning of terms and expressions used in vows. As in Chapter Three, the discussion here pertains to a specific vocabulary, namely foods and the manners in which they are processed and prepared for consumption.

Also discussed in this chapter is the distinction between expressions such as: That which is cooked, cooked food, food cooked in a dish, and: That which enters a dish. Additionally, there are distinctions between one who prohibits himself from eating a certain food and one who vows not to taste it. There is also a distinction between a vow not to eat a particular food item and a vow not to eat a type of food. A practical question that pertains to the latter two distinctions is whether one who vows that a particular food item is forbidden to him is prohibited from eating another food into which it was mixed.

The Gemara also discusses whether one is allowed to eat the liquid that emerges from a food that he has deemed forbidden to himself. It distinguishes between produce that is eaten in and of itself and produce that is used only for its juice, and it also distinguishes between a derivative of the food that carries the name of its source and a derivative that has its own name. Furthermore, this chapter explores how the definition of a word or phrase is established.

מתני׳ הַנּוֹדֵר מִן הַמְבוּשָּׁל – מוּתָּר בְּצָלִי וּבְשָׁלוּק. אָמַר ״קוֹנָם תַּבְשִׁיל שֶׁאֵינִי טוֹעֵם״ – אָסוּר בְּמַעֲשֵׂה קְדֵרָה רַךְ, וּמוּתָּר בְּעָבֶה, וּמוּתָּר בְּבֵיצָה טוּרְמוּטָא וּבִדְלַעַת הָרְמוּצָה. הַנּוֹדֵר מִמַּעֲשֵׂה קְדֵרָה – אֵין אָסוּר אֶלָּא מִמַּעֲשֵׂה רְתַחְתָּה. אָמַר ״קוֹנָם הַיּוֹרֵד לַקְּדֵרָה שֶׁאֵינִי טוֹעֵם״ – אָסוּר בְּכׇל הַמִּתְבַּשְּׁלִין בַּקְּדֵרָה.

MISHNA In the case of **one who vows** that **cooked foods** are forbidden to him,[H] he is **permitted** to eat **roasted and boiled**[N] foods, as they are not defined as cooked. If one **said: Cooked** food **is** ***konam*** for me, and for **that** reason **I will not taste** it, he is **prohibited from** tasting **a loose cooked** food **but is permitted to** taste **a thick** one, which people do not generally refer to as a cooked food. **And** he is likewise **permitted to** eat **a** ***turemuta*** **egg and the** ***remutza*** **gourd,** as they are not considered cooked foods either. In the case of **one who vows** that food **cooked in a dish** is forbidden to him,[H] he is **prohibited** from deriving benefit **only from** food that is **cooked by boiling**[N] it in a dish. However, if **one said: That which enters into a dish is** ***konam*** for me, and for **that** reason **I will not taste** it, he is **prohibited** from tasting **anything cooked in a dish.**

גמ׳ תַּנְיָא: רַבִּי יֹאשִׁיָּה אוֹסֵר. וְאַף עַל פִּי שֶׁאֵין רְאָיָה לַדָּבָר – זֵכֶר לַדָּבָר, שֶׁנֶּאֱמַר ״וַיְבַשְּׁלוּ אֶת הַפֶּסַח בָּאֵשׁ כַּמִּשְׁפָּט״.

GEMARA **It is taught** in a *baraita*: In the case of one who vowed that cooked foods are forbidden to him, **Rabbi Yoshiya** maintains that he is **prohibited** from eating roasted foods. **And although there is no** biblical **proof of the matter, there is an allusion to the matter, as it is stated: "And they cooked the Paschal offering with fire according to the ordinance"** (II Chronicles 35:13). Since the Paschal offering must be roasted, it is evident that roasting can also be referred to as cooking.

לֵימָא בְּהָא קָמִיפַּלְגִי; דְּרַבִּי יֹאשִׁיָּה סָבַר: הַלֵּךְ אַחַר לְשׁוֹן תּוֹרָה, וְתַנָּא דִּידַן סָבַר: בִּנְדָרִים הַלֵּךְ אַחַר לְשׁוֹן בְּנֵי אָדָם?

The Gemara suggests: **Let us say that they disagree with regard to this** following principle, **that Rabbi Yoshiya holds** that one should **follow the language of** the **Torah, and our** ***tanna*** **holds** that **with regard to vows** one should **follow the language of people.**[H]

לָא, דְּכוּלֵּי עָלְמָא בִּנְדָרִים הַלֵּךְ אַחַר לְשׁוֹן בְּנֵי אָדָם, מָר כִּי אַתְרֵיהּ וּמָר כִּי אַתְרֵיהּ; בְּאַתְרָא דְּתַנָּא דִּידַן – לְצָלִי קָרוּ לֵיהּ צָלִי, וְלִמְבוּשָּׁל קָרוּ לֵיהּ מְבוּשָּׁל. בְּאַתְרָא דְּרַבִּי יֹאשִׁיָּה – אֲפִילּוּ צָלִי קָרוּ מְבוּשָּׁל.

The Gemara refutes this suggestion: **No,** it is possible **that everyone** agrees that **with regard to vows** one should **follow the language of people.** Rather, this **Sage** stated his opinion **in accordance** with the language of **his locale,** and this **Sage** stated his opinion **in accordance with** the language of **his locale. In the locale of our** ***tanna*****, roasted food is called roasted and cooked food is called cooked, and in the locale of Rabbi Yoshiya even roasted food is called cooked.**

וְהָא קְרָא נָסֵיב לַהּ! אַסְמַכְתָּא בְּעָלְמָא.

The Gemara raises a difficulty: **But doesn't** Rabbi Yoshiya **cite a verse** as proof for his opinion, which shows that his opinion is not based on the vernacular? The Gemara answers: The verse is cited as **a mere support** for his opinion, as implied by his statement that the verse is only an allusion, not a full proof.

״קוֹנָם תַּבְשִׁיל״ כו׳. וְהָא מִתַּבְשִׁיל נָדַר!

It is stated in the mishna that one who said: **A cooked** food **is** ***konam*** for me and for that reason I will not taste it, he is prohibited from tasting a loose cooked food but is permitted to taste a thick one. The Gemara asks: Why is he permitted to eat it? **But didn't he vow** that **a cooked** food, which includes one that is thick, is forbidden **to him?**[N]

אָמַר אַבָּיֵי: הַאי תַּנָּא, כׇּל מִידֵּי דְּמִתְאֲכֵל בֵּיהּ רִיפְתָּא – תַּבְשִׁיל קָרוּ לֵיהּ. וְהַתַּנְיָא: הַנּוֹדֵר מִן הַתַּבְשִׁיל – אָסוּר בְּכׇל מִינֵי תַבְשִׁיל, וְאָסוּר בְּצָלִי וּבְשָׁלוּק וּבִמְבוּשָּׁל, וְאָסוּר בְּהִיטְרִיּוֹת רַכּוֹת שֶׁהַחוֹלִין אוֹכְלִין בָּהֶן פִּיתָּן.

Abaye said: This ***tanna*** maintains that **anything with which bread is eaten is called a cooked** food, whereas a thick dish is eaten without bread. **And it is taught** likewise **in a** ***baraita*****: One who vows** that **a cooked** food is forbidden **to him is prohibited from** eating **all types of cooked** foods, **and** he is therefore **prohibited from** eating **roasted, boiled, and cooked** foods. **And he** is also **prohibited from** eating **soft gourds** [*hiteriyyot*],[L] **with which the sick eat their bread.** This indicates that a cooked food is one eaten with bread.

HALAKHA

One who vows that cooked foods are forbidden to him – הַנּוֹדֵר מִן הַמְבוּשָּׁל: With regard to one who vows that cooked foods are forbidden to him, if the local people generally refer to roasted or boiled foods as cooked, then roasted or boiled foods are forbidden to him. If they use the expression: Cooked, only in reference to cooked or spiced meat, he is prohibited only from eating those foods (Rambam *Sefer Hafla'a, Hilkhot Nedarim* 9:1; *Shulḥan Arukh, Yoreh De'a* 217:1).

One who vows that food cooked in a dish is forbidden to him – הַנּוֹדֵר מִמַּעֲשֵׂה קְדֵרָה: One who vows that food cooked in a pot is forbidden to him is prohibited from eating foods boiled in a dish. However, if one says: Anything that entered a dish is forbidden to me, he is prohibited from eating anything cooked in a dish (Rambam *Sefer Hafla'a, Hilkhot Nedarim* 9:7; *Shulḥan Arukh, Yoreh De'a* 217:2).

Follow the language of people – הַלֵּךְ אַחַר לְשׁוֹן בְּנֵי אָדָם: The language of the people in a particular time and in a particular place should be used to decipher the intent of one who took a vow in that time and place (Rambam *Sefer Hafla'a, Hilkhot Nedarim* 9:1; *Shulḥan Arukh, Yoreh De'a* 217:1).

NOTES

Boiled foods [*shaluk*] – שָׁלוּק: According to some commentaries, these are overcooked foods (Commentary on *Nedarim*; Rosh; Rabbi Avraham min HaHar). Others maintain that although this phrase is sometimes used in reference to overcooked foods, here it refers to undercooked foods, as the phrase carries both meanings (Ran; *Tosefot Rabbeinu Peretz*; Rashba; Rabbi Eliezer of Metz). A slightly different interpretation is offered by the Rambam and the Rid. In their opinion, cooked foods are foods cooked with spices, whereas boiled foods are cooked in water without spices.

Cooked by boiling [*retaḥta*] – רְתַחְתָּה: In the Commentary on *Nedarim*, it is explained that this refers to food that is cooked in a dish and does not require any further preparation in a stewpot. Another interpretation of this expression is that it is anything that melts while it is being cooked (Meiri, citing Rashi). Other commentaries maintain that it refers to a dish made from cooked cereals (Rabbi Natan bar Yosef, cited in *Shita Mekubbetzet*). A fourth interpretation is that it is a dish prepared by boiling wheat or by placing soft bread in boiling water (Rambam).

But didn't he vow that a cooked food is forbidden to him – וְהָא מִתַּבְשִׁיל נָדַר: Some commentaries explain that the Gemara is asking why a thick dish is permitted to him, as it too is cooked (Commentary on *Nedarim*; Ritva). Others explain that the question is why a soft dish is prohibited, as it is too watery to be referred to as a cooked dish (*Tosafot*; Rosh; *Tosefot Rabbeinu Peretz*). Rabbi Avraham min HaHar claims that the question is twofold, in accordance with both explanations.

LANGUAGE

Gourds [*hiteriyyot*] – הִיטְרִיּוֹת: Probably a Hebrew-Aramaic form of the Greek ἴτριον, *itrion*, a kind of cake. In Syrian the word bears the same meaning as in Modern Hebrew: Noodle or spaghetti. Based on the context of the Gemara here, and in accordance with the commentaries, it presumably refers to a cake made from a mixture of cooked gourds and squash wrapped in dough.

אִינִי?! וְהָא רַבִּי יִרְמְיָה חֲלַשׁ, עָל לְגַבֵּיהּ הַהוּא אָסְיָא לְאַסְוֹתֵיהּ. חֲזָא קָרָא דְּמָחַת בְּבֵיתֵיהּ – שַׁבְקֵיהּ וּנְפַק, אֲמַר: מַלְאַךְ מוֹתָא אִית לֵיהּ לְדֵין בְּבֵיתֵיהּ, וַאֲנָא אֵיעוֹל לְאַסָּאָה יָתֵיהּ?!

The Gemara asks: **Is that so,** that the sick eat gourds? **But Rabbi Yirmeya fell ill, and a certain doctor came to him to heal him. He saw a gourd**[B] **that was placed in his house, and he left** Rabbi Yirmeya **and exited** the house **and said: This** person **has an angel of death,** a gourd, **in his house, and I will enter to heal him?** This incident teaches that gourds are detrimental for the sick.

לָא קַשְׁיָא; הָא – בְּרַכִּיכֵי, הָא – בְּאַשּׁוּנֵי. רָבָא בַּר עוּלָּא אֲמַר: הָא – בְּקָרָא גּוּפֵיהּ, וְהָא – בְּגַוֵּיהּ דְּקָרָא. דְּאָמַר רַב יְהוּדָה: לוּלִיבָא דְּקָרָא בְּסִילְקָא, לוּלִיבָא דְּכִיתָּנָא בְּכוּתְחָא. וְדָבָר זֶה אָסוּר לְאוֹמְרוֹ בִּפְנֵי עַם הָאָרֶץ.

The Gemara responds: This is **not difficult. This** *baraita* is referring **to soft** gourds, which are beneficial to the sick, and **this** incident is referring **to hard** ones, which are detrimental. **Rava bar Ulla said** a different answer: **This** incident is referring **to the gourd itself,** which is detrimental, **and this** *baraita* is referring **to the innards [*luliva*]**[L] **of the gourd, as Rav Yehuda said: The innards of the gourd** are best eaten **with chard;**[B] **the innards of flax** seeds are best eaten **with *kuteḥa*,**[B] a dip made from bread crumbs and sour milk. **And one may not say**[N] **this matter in the presence of an ignoramus,** so that ignoramuses do not uproot flax for consumption of its seeds.

רָבָא אֲמַר: מַאן חוֹלִין – רַבָּנַן. רָבָא לְטַעְמֵיהּ, דְּאָמַר רָבָא:

Rava said a different response: **Who are** the **sick** mentioned in the *baraita*, for whom a gourd is beneficial? They are **the Sages,** who are weakened by their toil in the study of Torah and their abstention from worldly pleasures, although they are not actually sick. Therefore, there is no contradiction. Gourds are harmful for people who are actually sick. The Gemara comments: **Rava** conforms **to his** standard line of **reasoning, as Rava said:**

LANGUAGE

Innards [*luliva*] – לוּלִיבָא: This word usually refers to the soft, blossoming parts of various plants. The soft tips of the branches of plants such as the caper bush, grapevines, and palms were eaten as a delicacy.

According to a different interpretation of the word, based on its use with regard to a gourd, it comes from the Aramaic *liba*, heart, and refers to the soft hearts, or innards, of various plants.

According to both explanations, it refers to a small, soft part of the plant that is eaten, while the rest is discarded or fed to animals.

Blossoms of a caper bush

BACKGROUND

Gourd [*kara*] – קָרָא: This refers to the bottle gourd, or *Lagenaria vulgaris*, a leafy summer crop of the gourd family. It is usually grown scattered across the ground; however, it is sometimes cultivated on tree trellises. The greenish-white gourd produced by the plant is rather large, 40–50 cm long and 25–30 cm wide. It is shaped like a vase or bottle. While still young, it is typically eaten cooked and its seeds are often served as a dessert.

Certain species of gourds have a high nutritional value, but the fruits tend to harden. For this reason, and also due to the many fibers they contain, gourds can be difficult to digest, especially for ill people who require easily digestible food.

Bottle gourd

Chard – סִילְקָא: The *Beta vulgaris*, also known as Swiss chard, is an annual garden beet plant from the Chenopodiaceae family. Chard leaves are eaten cooked and taste like spinach. The plant continues to grow after its leaves are pruned. Nowadays, its leaves are also used as birdfeed.

Swiss chard

Kuteḥa – כּוּתְחָא: *Kuteḥa*, or *kutaḥ*, is a typical Babylonian dip made from whey, salt, and bread that fermented to the point of moldiness. This dip was so sharp that it could be eaten only by the Babylonians, who were accustomed to eating it. In the Mishna, it is referred to as Babylonian *kutaḥ*.

NOTES

May not say, etc. – אָסוּר לְאוֹמְרוֹ וכו׳: The Commentary on *Nedarim* explains that one may not inform an ignoramus of the healing qualities of flax seeds, so that he not benefit from them. *Tosafot* reject this suggestion. The Ran explains that this advice should not be given to an ignoramus so that he will not eat the innards of small plants such as flax seeds, thereby wasting them. *Tosafot* and the Rosh suggest that this information may not be disseminated lest people mock the Sages for occupying themselves with such matters, especially as these facts were common knowledge. A different interpretation is offered by the *Ḥatam Sofer*. He maintains that one should not praise soft gourds before an ignoramus in case he inadvertently eats hard ones instead, which are harmful, especially to the sick. Scholars should avoid telling ignoramuses anything that might cause them adverse effects.

כְּמַאן מְצַלֵּינַן עַל קְצִירֵי וְעַל מְרֵיעֵי [כְּמַאן – כְּרַבִּי יוֹסֵי]. מִדְּאָמַר קְצִירֵי וּבְרִיעֵי, שְׁמַע מִינַּהּ: קְצִירֵי – קְצִירֵי מַמָּשׁ, מְרֵיעֵי – רַבָּנַן.

In accordance with whose opinion **do we pray** every day **for the sick and for the suffering? In accordance with whose** opinion? **In accordance with** the opinion of **Rabbi Yosei,**[N] who holds that one is judged every day, not only on Rosh HaShana, and therefore it is appropriate to pray for people every day. **From** the fact **that he said: The sick and the suffering,** one can **learn from** his statement that the term: **The sick,** is referring to **actual sick** people, while the term: **The suffering,** is referring to **the Sages,** who typically are physically frail.

״וּמוּתָּר בְּעָבֶה״. מַתְנִיתִין דְּלָא כְּבַבְלָאֵי. דְּאָמַר רַבִּי זֵירָא: בַּבְלָאֵי טִפְּשָׁאֵי, דְּאָכְלִי לַחְמָא בְּלַחְמָא.

§ It is stated in the mishna that one who vowed that loose cooked food is forbidden to him is **permitted to** taste **a thick** cooked food. The Gemara comments: **The mishna is not in accordance with the** custom of the **Babylonians, as Rabbi Zeira**[P] **said: Babylonians are foolish, as they eat bread with bread.** They eat thick porridge with their bread, which is essentially eating one kind of bread with another. According to their custom, one who vows that cooked foods are forbidden to him is prohibited from eating even a thick cooked food.

אֲמַר רַב חִסְדָּא: דְּמִשְׁאִיל לְהוֹן לְהָלֵין נַקְדָּנֵי דְּהוּצַל: הָדֵין דַּיְיסָא הֵיכִין מַעֲלֵי לְמֵיכְלֵהּ? דְּחִיטֵּי – בְּלַחְמָא דְּחִיטֵּי, וּדְשַׂעֲרֵי – בְּלַחְמָא דְּשַׂעֲרֵי, אוֹ דִּלְמָא דְּחִיטֵּי – בִּדְשַׂעֲרֵי, וּדְשַׂעֲרֵי – בִּדְחִיטֵּי?

In that context, **Rav Ḥisda said that those fastidious residents of Huzal,**[B] Babylonia **were asked: How is it best to eat this porridge?** Should **wheat** porridge be eaten **with wheat bread and barley** porridge **with barley bread, or perhaps wheat** porridge should be eaten **with barley** bread **and barley** porridge **with wheat** bread?

רָבָא אָכְלֵיהּ בְּחַסִּיסֵי. רַבָּה בַּר רַב הוּנָא אַשְׁכְּחֵיהּ לְרַב הוּנָא דְּקָאָכֵיל דַּיְיסָא בְּאֶצְבְּעָתֵיהּ. אֲמַר לֵיהּ: אַמַּאי קָאָכֵיל מָר בִּידֵיהּ? אֲמַר לֵיהּ: הָכִי אֲמַר רַב: דַּיְיסָא בְּאֶצְבְּעָתָא בְּסִים, וְכׇל דְּכֵן בְּתַרְתֵּין, וְכׇל דְּכֵן בִּתְלָת.

The Gemara relates: **Rava would eat** his bread **with** ***ḥasisei,***[NL] a porridge made of toasted barley grains. **Rabba, son of Rav Huna, found Rav Huna eating porridge with his fingers. He said to him: Why is the Master eating with his hands?** Rav Huna **said to him: This is what Rav said: Porridge** eaten **with a finger is tasty, and all the more so** if it is eaten **with two** fingers, **and all the more so with three.** It is more enjoyable to eat porridge with your hands.

אֲמַר לֵיהּ רַב לְחִיָּיא בְּרֵיהּ, וְכֵן אֲמַר לֵיהּ רַב הוּנָא לְרַבָּה בְּרֵיהּ: מְזַמְּנִים לָךְ לְמֵיכַל דַּיְיסָא – עַד פַּרְסָה, לְמֵיכַל בִּישְׂרָא דְּתוֹרָא – עַד תְּלָתָא פַּרְסִין. אֲמַר לֵיהּ רַב לְחִיָּיא בְּרֵיהּ, וְכֵן אֲמַר לֵיהּ רַב הוּנָא לְרַבָּה בְּרֵיהּ: כׇּל מִידַּעַם לָא תִּפְלוֹט קַמֵּיהּ רַבָּךְ, לְבַר מִן קָרָא וְדַיְיסָא, שֶׁהֵן דּוֹמִין לִפְתִילְתָּא שֶׁל אֲבָר, וַאֲפִילּוּ קַמֵּי שָׁבוּר מַלְכָּא פְּלוֹט.

Rav said to his son Ḥiyya, and Rav Huna similarly said to his son Rabba: If you are invited to eat porridge, for such a meal you should travel **up to** the distance of **a parasang** [*parsa*].[NL] If you are invited **to eat ox meat,** you should travel **up to three parasangs. Rav said to his son Ḥiyya, and Rav Huna similarly said to his son Rabba: You should not spit out anything before your teacher,** as this is disrespectful, **apart from gourd and porridge, as they are like** a burning **lead wick**[B] in the intestines when they cannot be digested, **and** therefore **spit** them **out even before King Shapur,** due to the danger involved.

NOTES

In accordance with the opinion of Rabbi Yosei – כְּרַבִּי יוֹסֵי: The Meiri stresses that even according to the opinion of the Rabbis who disagree with Rabbi Yosei, one may pray at every time of peril. The verdict on Rosh HaShana does not obviate the need to pray over any distressful situation. According to the Meiri, the opinion that daily prayer is ineffective refers only to general prayers recited for people in general, not to a prayer one recites on his own behalf or on the behalf of another individual.

Ḥasisei – חַסִּיסֵי: Some commentaries explain that this is flour made from toasted barley grains (Commentary on *Nedarim*; Ran). *Tosafot* accept Rabbeinu Ḥananel's opinion that it refers to lentil flour.

To eat porridge you should go up to a parasang, etc. – דַּיְיסָא עַד פַּרְסָה וכו׳: In the Commentary on *Nedarim* two interpretations of this statement are offered. The first explanation is that it is worthwhile to travel up to a parasang for porridge and up to three parasangs for ox meat. According to the second interpretation, porridge provides sufficient nourishment for one to walk a parasang, while ox meat provides enough nourishment for a journey of three parasangs. In the *Shita Mekubbetzet* the opposite interpretation is suggested: If one is invited to eat porridge he should refuse for the amount of time it takes to walk a parasang, as it is unhealthy, and ox meat is even more harmful.

BACKGROUND

Those fastidious residents of Huzal – נַקְדָּנֵי דְּהוּצַל: The Babylonian city of Huzal was one of the first places to be settled by the exiles of Judah, as it was settled in the days of King Jehoiachin. Since it was an ancient settlement founded by exiled nobility, it earned a reputation as a city of refined eating habits. Therefore, the fastidious residents of Huzal were looked upon as authorities on dining.

Lead wick – פְּתִילְתָּא שֶׁל אֲבָר: Those sentenced to death by burning would be executed by burning their intestines, as is expounded upon in tractate *Sanhedrin* (52a). This was done by means of a piece of lead shaped like a wick, which was melted and poured into the mouth of the sentenced person.

LANGUAGE

Ḥasisei – חַסִּיסֵי: The source of this word is unclear. Some commentaries define it as a dish made from the flour of roasted grains (Commentary on *Nedarim*; *Arukh*). When unripe wheat grains are roasted, part of the starch turns to sugar, and it can then be ground into a somewhat sweet kind of flour. Others maintain that *ḥasisei* is lentil flour, similar to the Hebrew *ashishim*, which is a dish made of lentils.

Parasang [*parsa*] – פַּרְסָה: This word appears relatively early on in Iranian languages, and it was borrowed into Greek as *παρασάγγης*, *parasangēs*. It is probably from Greek that it entered the Hebrew language. One parasang is somewhat less than three miles.

PERSONALITIES

Rabbi Zeira – רַבִּי זֵירָא: Born in Babylonia, Rabbi Zeira, was one of the great third-generation *amora'im* in Eretz Yisrael. His father was a Persian government tax collector who was lauded as one of the few who performed that function honestly. When Rabbi Zeira ascended to Eretz Yisrael he decided to devote himself exclusively to the Torah of Eretz Yisrael. The Gemara relates that he undertook one hundred fast days to forget the Torah he studied in Babylonia.

Rabbi Zeira was renowned for his sharp intellect and authored many incisive *halakhot*. He was also known as an extremely God-fearing man, as attested by several stories. Due to his modesty, he did not even want to be ordained with the title Rabbi. He relented only after being told that ordination atones for one's sins.

The Gemara relates that he undertook one hundred additional fasts so that the fire of Gehenna would not harm him, and he would periodically check whether the fasts worked by entering a fiery furnace.

On one occasion his legs were scorched, and from then on he was called: The little man with the scorched legs. Rabbi Zeira was a contemporary of Rav Ḥisda, Rav Sheshet, and Rabba in Babylonia, and one of the disciples of Rabbi Yoḥanan in Eretz Yisrael, and he engaged in extensive halakhic discourse with them. Apparently, he worked in Eretz Yisrael as a flax merchant, and it is likely that for business reasons he returned to Babylonia several times.

The text of the beginning of Rabbi Zeira's eulogy is preserved in the Talmud: The land of Shinar, i.e., Babylonia, conceived and gave birth; the land of splendor, i.e., Eretz Yisrael, raised her delight. Woe to me, said Reket, i.e., Tiberias, as she has lost her beloved instrument.

רַבִּי יוֹסֵי וְרַבִּי יְהוּדָה, חַד אָכֵיל דַּיְיסָא בְּאֶצְבְּעָתֵיהּ וְחַד אָכֵיל בְּהוּצָא. אֲמַר לֵיהּ דְּאָכֵיל בְּהוּצָא לְדְאָכֵיל בְּאֶצְבְּעָתֵיהּ: עַד מָתַי אַתָּה מַאֲכִילֵנִי צוֹאָתְךָ! אֲמַר לֵיהּ דְּאָכֵיל בְּאֶצְבְּעָתֵיהּ לְדְאָכֵיל בְּהוּצָא: עַד מָתַי אַתָּה מַאֲכִילֵנִי רוּקְךָ!

The Gemara relates more incidents: **Rabbi Yosei and Rabbi Yehuda** dined together. **One of them ate porridge with his fingers, and the** other **one ate with a fork** [*hutza*].[N] The one **who was eating with a fork said to** the one **who was eating with his fingers: For how long will you** keep **feeding me your filth?** Must I keep eating off of your dirty fingernails? The one **who was eating with his fingers said to** the one **who was eating with a fork: For how long will you** keep **feeding me your spittle,**[N] as you eat with a fork which you then put back in the common bowl.

רַבִּי יְהוּדָה וְרַבִּי שִׁמְעוֹן אַיְיתוּ לְקַמַּיְיהוּ בְּלוֹסְפַּיִין, רַבִּי יְהוּדָה אֲכַל, רַבִּי שִׁמְעוֹן לָא אֲכַל. אֲמַר לֵיהּ רַבִּי יְהוּדָה: מַאי טַעְמָא לָא אָכֵיל מָר? אֲמַר לֵיהּ רַבִּי שִׁמְעוֹן: אֵלּוּ אֵין יוֹצְאִין מִבְּנֵי מֵעַיִם כָּל עִיקָּר. אֲמַר לֵיהּ רַבִּי יְהוּדָה: כׇּל שֶׁכֵּן שֶׁנִּסְמוֹךְ עֲלֵיהֶן לְמָחָר.

Belospayin,[L] a type of figs, **were brought before Rabbi Yehuda and Rabbi Shimon. Rabbi Yehuda ate** them, **but Rabbi Shimon did not eat** them. **Rabbi Yehuda said to him: What is the reason** that the **Master is not eating? Rabbi Shimon said to him: These do not leave the intestines at all.** They remain undigested. **Rabbi Yehuda said to him:** If so, **all the more that one can rely on them** to feel full **tomorrow.**

רַבִּי יְהוּדָה הֲוָה יָתֵיב קַמֵּיהּ דְּרַבִּי טַרְפוֹן. אֲמַר לֵיהּ רַבִּי טַרְפוֹן: הַיּוֹם פָּנֶיךָ צְהוּבִּין. אֲמַר לֵיהּ: אֶמֶשׁ יָצְאוּ עֲבָדֶיךָ לַשָּׂדֶה, וְהֵבִיאוּ לָנוּ תְּרָדִין, וַאֲכַלְנוּם בְּלֹא מֶלַח. וְאִם אֲכַלְנוּם בְּמֶלַח – כׇּל שֶׁכֵּן שֶׁהָיוּ פָּנֵינוּ צְהוּבִּין.

Rabbi Yehuda was sitting before Rabbi Tarfon. Rabbi Tarfon said to him: Your face today is ruddy, i.e., a rosy, healthy color. Rabbi Yehuda **said to him: Last night your servants,** i.e., we students, **went out to the field, and beets were brought to us, and we ate them without salt.** This is the reason for our healthy complexion. **And had we eaten them with salt, all the more so would our faces have been ruddy.**

אָמְרָה הַהִיא מַטְרוֹנִיתָא לְרַבִּי יְהוּדָה: מוֹרֶה וְרָוֵי?! אֲמַר לָהּ: הֵימָנוּתָא בִּידָא דְּהַהִיא אִיתְּתָא, אִי טָעֵימְנָא אֶלָּא קִידּוּשָׁא וְאַבְדַּלְתָּא וְאַרְבָּעָה כָּסֵי דְּפִסְחָא, וְחוֹגְרַנִי צִידְעַי מִן הַפֶּסַח עַד הָעֲצֶרֶת. אֶלָּא: ״חׇכְמַת אָדָם תָּאִיר פָּנָיו״.

The Gemara cites related incidents: **A certain** gentile **lady** [*matronita*][L] **said to Rabbi Yehuda,** whose face was ruddy: How can one **teach** the Jews **and** be **a drunk** at the same time? **He said to her:** I place my **integrity in the hands of this woman** and should no longer be deemed credible **if I** ever **taste** any wine **except** for that of ***kiddush, havdala,* and the four cups of Passover. And** after I drink those four cups **I tie my temples**[N] **from Passover to** ***Shavuot***, as wine gives me a headache. **Rather,** my complexion is explained by the verse **"A man's wisdom makes his face to shine"** (Ecclesiastes 8:1).

אֲמַר לֵיהּ הַהוּא מִינָא לְרַבִּי יְהוּדָה: פָּנֶיךָ דּוֹמִין אִי כְּמַלְוֵי רִבִּית אִי כִּמְגַדְּלֵי חֲזִירִין. אֲמַר לֵיהּ: בִּיהוּדָאֵי תַּרְוַיְיהוּ אֲסִירָן, אֶלָּא עֶשְׂרִים וְאַרְבָּעָה בֵּית הַכִּסֵּא אִית לִי מִן בֵּיתָא עַד בֵּי מִדְרָשָׁא, וְכׇל שָׁעָה וְשָׁעָה אֲנִי נִכְנָס לְכׇל אֶחָד וְאֶחָד.

A certain heretic said to Rabbi Yehuda: Your face is similar either to usurers or to pig breeders. These people would earn a good living without expending much energy, which gave them plump, healthy complexions. Rabbi Yehuda **said to him: Both** of these occupations **are prohibited to Jews. Rather,** my face is ruddy because **I have twenty-four bathrooms**[B] on the way **from my home to the study hall, and all the time I enter each and every one** of them. He did not suffer from constipation, which had a beneficial effect on his complexion.

רַבִּי יְהוּדָה כַּד אָזֵיל לְבֵי מִדְרָשָׁא שָׁקֵיל גּוּלְפָּא עַל כַּתְפֵיהּ, אֲמַר: גְּדוֹלָה מְלָאכָה שֶׁמְּכַבֶּדֶת אֶת בְּעָלֶיהָ. רַבִּי שִׁמְעוֹן שָׁקֵיל צַנָּא עַל כַּתְפֵיהּ, אֲמַר: גְּדוֹלָה מְלָאכָה שֶׁמְּכַבֶּדֶת אֶת בְּעָלֶיהָ.

§ The Gemara relates: **When Rabbi Yehuda would go to the study hall he would carry a pitcher** [*gulefa*][L] **on his shoulder** to sit on, **saying: Labor is great, as it brings honor to the laborer** who performs **it.** It brought him honor by enabling him to avoid sitting on the floor of the study hall. Similarly, **Rabbi Shimon would carry a basket on his shoulder, saying: Labor is great, as it brings honor to the laborer** who performs **it.**

דְּבֵיתְהוּ דְּרַבִּי יְהוּדָה נָפְקַת נָקְטַת עַמְרָא, עָבְדָה גְּלִימָא דְּהוּטְבֵי. כַּד נָפְקַת לְשׁוּקָא מִיכַּסְיָא בֵּיהּ, וְכַד נָפֵיק רַבִּי יְהוּדָה לְצַלּוּיֵי הֲוָה מְכַסֵּי וּמְצַלֵּי. וְכַד מִיכַּסֵּי בֵּיהּ הֲוָה מְבָרֵךְ ״בָּרוּךְ שֶׁעֲטָנִי מְעִיל״.

The Gemara further relates: **Rabbi Yehuda's wife went out** to the market, **collected wool,** and **made a thick** [*hutevei*][L] **cloak. When she would go out to the market she would cover herself with it, and when Rabbi Yehuda would go out to pray he would cover himself** with the cloak **and pray. And when he** would **cover himself with it he would recite the blessing: Blessed is He who wrapped me in a coat,** as he took much pleasure in it.

זִימְנָא חֲדָא גְּזַר רַבָּן שִׁמְעוֹן בֶּן גַּמְלִיאֵל תַּעֲנִיתָא, רַבִּי יְהוּדָה לָא אֲתָא לְבֵי תַּעֲנִיתָא. אָמְרִין לֵיהּ: לָא אִית לֵיהּ כְּסוּיָא. שְׁדַר לֵיהּ גְּלִימָא וְלָא קַבֵּיל.

On **one occasion Rabban Shimon ben Gamliel,** the *Nasi*, **decreed a fast. Rabbi Yehuda did not come to the house of the fast,** where everyone gathered. The people **said to** Rabban Shimon ben Gamliel: Rabbi Yehuda **does not have** a dignified garment to **cover** himself with, and therefore he shies away from public events. Rabban Shimon ben Gamliel **sent him a cloak** of his own, **but** Rabbi Yehuda **did not accept** this gift.

NOTES

Fork [*hutza*] – הוּצָא: *Hutza* literally refers to one of the hard, thorny leaves of a palm tree. However, it was apparently also used in reference to certain wooden utensils, e.g., wooden spoons and forks.

Feeding me your spittle – מַאֲכִילֵנִי רוּקְךָ: The Maharsha cites the Rosh's explanation: As opposed to one who eats with a fork, one who eats with his finger cleans it every so often.

And I tie my temples – וְחוֹגְרַנִי צִידְעַי: Most commentaries explain that he had such a headache after drinking the four cups that he would wrap a bandage around his head until *Shavuot*. The interpretation in the *Arukh* is that the wine gave him such a headache that he felt as though a belt were tied around his head.

LANGUAGE

***Belospayin* – בְּלוֹסְפַּיִין:** The many different versions of this word make its identification difficult. Some scholars assert that it is an adaptation of the Greek φιβάλεως, *fibaleos*, which is a type of fig that does not fully ripen. It may have been named after its place of origin. This fits the explanation of most commentaries, namely that it is a low-quality fig. In Greek, the word also refers to a dry, dull person. Others claim that it is a variation of the Greek βολβός, *bolbos*, meaning plants that grow from bulbs.

Lady [*matronita*] – מַטְרוֹנִיתָא: An Aramaic form of the Latin matrona, which means an important or wealthy woman.

Pitcher [*gulefa*] – גּוּלְפָּא: Some scholars claim that the origin of this word is the Greek κάλπη, *kalpē*, meaning a pitcher or vessel for holding water.

Thick [*hutevei*] – הוּטְבֵי: The meaning of this word is uncertain. Some claim that it refers to a thick, coarse garment. Others say it means felt. According to the latter interpretation, the significance of Rabbi Yehuda's cloak is that the wool collected by Rabbi Yehuda's wife was not enough for weaving, so she made a felt garment out of it. A third opinion is that *hutevei* refers to something fine and unique, similar to one meaning of the word *ḥatav*.

BACKGROUND

Twenty-four bathrooms – עֶשְׂרִים וְאַרְבָּעָה בֵּית הַכִּסֵּא: Rabbi Yehuda's answer is based on the premise that constipation and digestion problems not only cause physical discomfort but also have a negative effect on one's facial appearance and health. The Rambam recommends that one eat foods that can cause diarrhea in order to avoid the health problems associated with constipation.

דְּלִי צִיפְּתָא, וַאֲמַר לֵיהּ לִשְׁלוּחָא: חֲזִי מַאי אִיכָּא. מִיהוּ, לָא נִיחָא לִי דְּאִיתְהֲנֵי בְּהָדֵין עָלְמָא.

He lifted the mat [*tzifeta*][L] upon which he was sitting **and said to the messenger: See what there is** here. The place was miraculously filled with gold dinars. This demonstrated that Rabbi Yehuda could have had plenty of money if he had so desired. He explained: **However, it is not amenable to me to derive benefit in this world.**

רַבִּי עֲקִיבָא אִיתְקַדְּשַׁתְּ לֵיהּ בְּרָתֵיהּ (דְּבַר) דְּכַלְבָּא שָׂבוּעַ, שָׁמַע (בַּר) כַּלְבָּא שָׂבוּעַ אַדְּרַהּ הֲנָאָה מִכׇּל נְכָסֵיהּ. אָזְלָא וְאִיתְנְסִיבָא לֵיהּ.

§ In connection to the above incident concerning the poverty of scholars and their potential to become wealthy through remarkable circumstances, the Gemara relates an incident: **Rabbi Akiva became betrothed to the daughter of bar Kalba Savua.**[B] When **bar Kalba Savua heard** about their betrothal, he took a vow **prohibiting her from** deriving benefit from **all of his property.** Despite this, **she went** ahead **and married** Rabbi Akiva.

בְּסִיתְוָא הֲוָה גָּנוּ בֵּי תִּיבְנָא, הֲוָה קָא מְנַקֵּיט לֵיהּ תִּיבְנָא מִן מַזְיַהּ. אֲמַר לַהּ: אִי הֲוַאי לִי – רָמֵינָא לִיךְ יְרוּשָׁלַיִם דְּדַהֲבָא. אֲתָא אֵלִיָּהוּ אִידַּמֵּי לְהוֹן כֶּאֱנָשָׁא, וְקָא קָרֵי אַבָּבָא, אֲמַר לְהוּ: הֲבוּ לִי פּוּרְתָּא דְּתִיבְנָא, דִּילְדַת אִתְּתִי וְלֵית לִי מִידַּעַם לְאַגּוֹנַהּ. אֲמַר לַהּ רַבִּי עֲקִיבָא לְאִנְתְּתֵיהּ: חֲזִי גַּבְרָא דַּאֲפִילּוּ תִּיבְנָא לָא אִית לֵיהּ.

In the winter they would sleep in a storehouse of straw, and Rabbi Akiva **would gather** strands of **straw from her hair. He said to her: If I** had the means **I would place on your** head **a Jerusalem of Gold,**[B] a type of crown. **Elijah** the prophet **came and appeared to them as a** regular **person and started calling** and knocking **on the door. He said to them: Give me a bit of straw, as my wife gave birth and I do not have anything on which to lay her. Rabbi Akiva said to his wife: See this man, who does not even have straw.** We should be happy with our lot, as we at least have straw to sleep on.

אָמְרָה לֵיהּ: זִיל הֲוֵי בֵּי רַב. אֲזַל תַּרְתֵּי סְרֵי שְׁנִין קַמֵּי דְּרַבִּי אֱלִיעֶזֶר וְרַבִּי יְהוֹשֻׁעַ. לְמִישְׁלַם תַּרְתֵּי סְרֵי שְׁנִין, קָא אֲתָא לְבֵיתֵיהּ, שָׁמַע מִן אֲחוֹרֵי בֵּיתֵיהּ דְּקָאָמַר לַהּ חַד רָשָׁע לִדְבֵיתְהוּ: שַׁפִּיר עָבֵיד לִיךְ אֲבוּךְ; חֲדָא – דְּלָא דָּמֵי לִיךְ, וְעוֹד – [שְׁבַקָךְ] אַרְמְלוּת חַיּוּת כּוּלְּהוֹן שְׁנִין. אָמְרָה לֵיהּ: אִי צָאֵית לְדִילִי – לֶיהֱוֵי תַּרְתֵּי סְרֵי שְׁנִין אַחֲרַנְיָיתָא. אֲמַר: הוֹאִיל וִיהַבְתְּ לִי רְשׁוּתָא – אִיהֲדַר לַאֲחוֹרַי. הֲדַר אֲזַל הֲוָה תַּרְתֵּי סְרֵי שְׁנֵי אַחֲרַנְיָיתָא.

She said to him: Go and **be a student** of Torah. **He went** and studied Torah for **twelve years before Rabbi Eliezer and Rabbi Yehoshua. At the completion of** the **twelve years, he was coming home** when **he heard from behind his house that one wicked person was saying to his wife: Your father behaved well toward you.** He was right to disinherit you. **One** reason is **that** your husband **is not similar to you,**[N] i.e., he is not suitable for you. **And furthermore, he has left you in widowhood in his lifetime all these years. She said to him: If he listens to me, he should be** there for **another twelve years.** Rabbi Akiva **said: Since she has given me permission** through this statement, **I will go back** and study more. **He turned back** and **went** to the study hall, and he **was** there for **another twelve years.**

אֲתָא בְּעֶשְׂרִין וְאַרְבְּעָה אַלְפִין זוּגֵי תַּלְמִידֵי. נְפוּק כּוּלֵּי עָלְמָא לְאַפֵּיהּ, וְאַף הִיא קָמַת לְמִיפַּק לְאַפֵּיהּ. אֲמַר לַהּ הַהוּא רָשִׁיעָא: וְאַתְּ לְהֵיכָא? אָמְרָה לֵיהּ: ״יוֹדֵעַ צַדִּיק נֶפֶשׁ בְּהֶמְתּוֹ״. אָתַת לְאִיתְחַזּוֹיֵי לֵיהּ, קָא מַדְחָן לַהּ רַבָּנַן. אֲמַר לְהוֹן: הַנִּיחוּ לָהּ, שֶׁלִּי וְשֶׁלָּכֶם שֶׁלָּהּ הוּא. שָׁמַע (בַּר) כַּלְבָּא שָׂבוּעַ, אֲתָא וְאִיתְשִׁיל עַל נִידְרֵיהּ וְאִשְׁתְּרֵי וְאִשְׁתְּרֵי.

Eventually **he came** back accompanied **by 24,000 pairs of students. Everyone went out to greet him,** as he was by then a renowned teacher, **and she too arose to go out to** greet **him. That wicked person said to her: And to where are you** going? As she was excessively poor, she was not dressed in a grand manner, as fit for the wife of one so esteemed. **She said to him: "A righteous man regards the life of his beast"**[N] (Proverbs 12:10); he knows that I am in this state as a result of my dedication to him. **She came to present herself before** Rabbi Akiva, but **the Sages** tried to **fend her off,** as they were unaware of her identity. **He said to them: Leave her.** Both **my** Torah knowledge **and yours are hers.** When **bar Kalba Savua heard** that the famous man was his son-in-law, **he came** before halakhic authorities **and requested the dissolution of his vow, and it was dissolved.**

LANGUAGE

Mat [*tzifeta*] – **צִיפְּתָא**: Similar to the Arabic صفة, *ṣuffah*, a mat or some other kind of mattress.

BACKGROUND

Bar Kalba Savua – בַּר כַּלְבָּא שָׂבוּעַ: Kalba Savua was the name, or perhaps the epithet, of a prominent family from Judea, and bar Kalba Savua was from this family. This family was renowned for its great wealth, and was listed as one of the three wealthiest families in Jerusalem during the time of the destruction of the Second Temple. The family was also known for its philanthropy and hospitality. The standard explanation for their name is that anyone who came to them hungry as a dog [*kalba*] would leave satisfied [*savua*]. However, that was probably a homiletic interpretation of their name. Its more likely meaning is that the family descended from Caleb ben Jephunneh, as related in the Jerusalem Talmud.

Jerusalem of Gold – יְרוּשָׁלַיִם דְּדַהֲבָא: According to descriptions throughout rabbinic literature, a city of gold was apparently a mural crown representing the shape of a city and its walls. Accordingly, a Jerusalem of Gold was a gold mural crown with Jerusalem and its walls emblazoned upon it. Jewelry of this kind was quite expensive. Only the wealthiest of women would don it.

The Jerusalem of Gold that Rabbi Akiva promised his wife is mentioned several times throughout the Talmud. In the Jerusalem Talmud, it is told that the wife of the *Nasi*, Rabban Shimon ben Gamliel, complained to him that she did not have so luxurious an ornament. He asked her: Would you have done for me what Rabbi Akiva's wife did for him? Rabbi Akiva's wife sold the braids of her hair so that he could study Torah; she deserved that ornament.

Coin of Jerusalem from the time of Antoninus Pius, depicting Tyche with a mural crown

NOTES

That he is not similar to you – דְּלָא דָּמֵי לִיךְ: The Commentary on *Nedarim* explains that this man meant that Rabbi Akiva was not suitable for her. The Maharsha explains that this person was referring to Rabbi Akiva's inferior lineage, as he was a descendant of converts, whereas the daughter of bar Kalba Savua came from one of the most illustrious families of Judea.

A righteous man regards the life of his beast – יוֹדֵעַ צַדִּיק נֶפֶשׁ בְּהֶמְתּוֹ: Some commentaries explain that she already knew the identity of the great scholar who came to town, and that is why she was confident about going out to greet him. Others claim she was unaware that it was her husband. Rather, she had simply heard of the arrival of a famous Sage and was sure that a great Torah scholar would not humiliate a poor woman.

מן שית מילי איעתר רבי עקיבא: מן כלבא שבוע, מן אילא דספינתא – דכל ספינתא עבדין ליה מין עינא, זימנא חדא אנשיוה על כיף ימא, אתא הוא אשכחיה.

The Gemara adds: **Rabbi Akiva became wealthy from six things.** First, **from** the money he received from **Kalba Savua** after his vow was dissolved. Second, he gained money **from the ram of a ship** [*eila disfineta*],[L] as craftsmen would **fashion** a sculpture of **a type of sheep for every ship,** which would be placed on its bow, and which would be used to conceal money. On **one occasion,** the sailors **forgot** this ram **on the seashore,** and Rabbi Akiva **came** and **found it** with the money stored inside.

ומן גוזא – דזימנא חדא יהיב ארבעה זוזי לספונאי, אמר להו: אייתי לי מדעם, ולא אשכחו אלא גוזא על כיף ימא. אתיוה ליה, אמרו ליה: עביד מרנא עליה. אישתכח דהוה מלי דינרי, דזימנא חדא טבעת ספינתא וכולי עיסקא הוה מחית בההוא גוזא, ואישתכח בההוא זימנא.

And third, he became wealthy **from a log** [*gavza*][L] of wood,[N] **as** on **one occasion he gave four dinars to sailors** and **said to them: Bring me something** worthwhile. **And they found only a log** of wood **on the seashore. They brought it to him** and **said to him: May our master wait with this** until we bring a more worthy item. **He found that** the log **was full of dinars, as** on **one** occasion **a ship sunk and all the merchandise,** i.e., the money, owned by the people on the ship **was placed in that log, and it was found on that occasion** by the sailors.

דמן דסרוקיתא, ומן מטרוניתא,

Rabbi Akiva became wealthy **from** a convoy of **Ishmaelites** [***Serukita***].[NL] **And** he became wealthy **from** a certain **lady.** Rabbi Akiva borrowed money from a lady and said that God would be his guarantor. When it came time to return the loan, the king's daughter became insane and threw a purse of jewelry into the sea, which was found by that lady. She told Rabbi Akiva that his guarantor had paid his debt and she allowed him to keep the loan.

NOTES

A log [*gavza*] of wood – גוזא: Some commentaries explain the word *gavza* according to its usual meaning, a log of wood or a beam (*Arukh*; Rosh). Others claim that it means a box (Commentary on *Nedarim*; Ran).

From Ishmaelites – דמן דסרוקיתא: The *Baḥ* claims that this phrase should appear earlier in the text, that the ship with the ram sculpture had belonged to Ishmaelites. The Maharsha concurs, reasoning that without this modification, the Gemara lists seven sources for Rabbi Akiva's wealth, not six.

LANGUAGE

Ram of a ship [*eila disfineta*] – אילא דספינתא: Some assert that the word comes from the Greek εἰλεός, *eileos*, a hiding place. It apparently refers to a sculpture attached to the bow of a ship in the form of a man or a beast, e.g., a ram. Warships would affix statues of rams with iron horns in order to gore enemy ships, whereas ships used for peaceful transport would attach them as decoration.

Fragment of a Roman tombstone dating back to the third century, depicting a boat with decorative statues

Log [*gavza*] – גוזא: Probably from Iranian languages, where it can refer to a goad or prod, as in the Parthian word gawāz. In Babylonian Jewish Aramaic it can simply mean sticks, cut branches, or logs.

Ishmaelite [*Serukita*] – סרוקיתא: Possibly derived from the Latin Saraceni, meaning Arabs.

Perek **VI**
Daf **50** Amud **b**

ומן אשתו של טורנוסרופוס, ומן קטיעא בר שלום.

And Rabbi Akiva also grew wealthy **from the wife of Turnus Rufus,**[P] who converted and gave him her money, **and from Ketia bar Shalom,**[P] a Roman minister who bequeathed his fortune to him.

רב גמדא יהיב ארבעה זוזי לספונאי לאתויי בהון מידעם, לא אשכחו. אתיוה ליה בהון קופא. אישתמיט, על לחרתא, חפרו בתריה, אשכחוה דרביע על מרגלייתא, אייתינון ליה כולהון.

§ The Gemara relates a similar incident: **Rav Gamda gave four dinars to sailors to bring** him **something** from overseas in exchange **for them.** However, they **did not find** anything of worth, so **they** bought him **a monkey with** the coins and **brought it to him.** The monkey **escaped** and **entered a hole.** When **they dug after it** to retrieve it, **they found it crouching over pearls,** and **they brought all of** the pearls to Rav Gamda.

אמרה ליה בת קיסר לרבי יהושע בן חנניה: תורה מפוארה בכלי מכוער! אמר לה: למדי מבית אבוך, במה מניחין יין? אמרה ליה: במאני דפחרא. אמר לה: כולי עלמא בפחרא ואתון במאני דפחרא?! אתון אחיתון במאני דכספא ודהבא!

The daughter of the emperor said to Rabbi Yehoshua ben Ḥananya: You are the epitome of **magnificent Torah,** but it is stored **in an ugly vessel,** as Rabbi Yehoshua ben Ḥananya was an unattractive man. **He said to her: You may learn** the answer to your statement **from your father's house. In what** container **do you place wine? She said to him: In earthenware vessels. He said to her:** Is it conceivable that **everyone** stores their wine **in earthenware** vessels, **and you** also store it **in earthenware vessels?** Is there no distinction between the emperor and ordinary people? **You** should **place** your wine **in vessels of silver and gold.**

PERSONALITIES

Turnus Rufus – טורנוסרופוס: This is the appellation given to the Roman governor Quintus Tineius Rufus, ruler of Judea during the bar Kokheva revolt. He was given this nickname because he suppressed the revolt with the utmost cruelty. It comes from the Greek τύραννος, *turannos*, which means ruthless tyrant.

The Talmud records several of his discussions with Rabbi Akiva. It was he who sentenced Rabbi Akiva to a torturous death. The Gemara also relates that he ordered the plowing of the Temple Mount following the destruction of the Temple, as a symbol of its complete obliteration.

Ketia bar Shalom – קטיעא בר שלום: Ketia bar Shalom is the name, or perhaps the nickname, of a prominent Roman who defended the Jews against the emperor's intention to order their annihilation. Despite his success in preventing this decree, he provoked the emperor's wrath and was himself put to death. Just before his execution, he bequeathed his fortune to Rabbi Akiva and his colleagues, and Rabbi Akiva received half.

אָזְלַת וּרְמַת חַמְרָא בְּמָאנֵי דְכַסְפָּא וְדַהֲבָא, וּסְרִי. אֲמַר לַהּ: אַף אוֹרַיְיתָא כֵּן. וְהָאִיכָּא שַׁפִּירִין וּגְמִירִין! אֲמַר לַהּ: אִי הֲווּ סְנוּ – הֲווּ גְּמִירִין טְפֵי.

She went and placed the wine in vessels of silver and gold,[B] **and it spoiled.** Rabbi Yehoshua **said to her: The same is** also true of **the Torah.** It spoils if it is contained in a handsome person. She asked him: **But are there not** people who are both **good** looking **and learned** in Torah? **He said to her: If they were ugly**[N] **they would be** even **more learned.**

הַהִיא דַּאֲתָיָא לְקַמֵּיהּ דְּרַב יְהוּדָה מִנְּהַרְדְּעָא לְדִינָא, וְאִיתְחַיְּיבַת מִן דִּינָא. אָמְרָה לֵיהּ: שְׁמוּאֵל רַבָּךְ הָכִי דָּן?! אֲמַר לַהּ: יָדְעַתְּ לֵיהּ? אָמְרָה לֵיהּ: אִין, גּוּצָא, וְרַבָּה כְּרֵיסֵיהּ, אוּכָּם וְרַבָּה שִׁינֵּיהּ. אֲמַר לַהּ: לְבַזּוֹיֵיהּ קָאָתֵית? תֶּיהֱוֵי הַהִיא אִתְּתָא בְּשַׁמְתָּא! פָּקְעָה וּמֵתָה.

A certain woman came before Rav Yehuda of the city of **Neharde'a for judgment, and she was found guilty in the judgment** of her case. **She said to him: Would Shmuel your teacher have judged** me in this manner? **He said to her: Did you know him? She said to him: Yes.** He was **short and potbellied.** He was **dark and his teeth were large. He said to her: Did you come** here **to disparage him** by describing him in this manner? **Let that woman be** in a state of **excommunication.** After he excommunicated her, her belly **split** open **and she died,** as a punishment for having disparaged a Torah scholar.

״וּמוּתָּר בְּבֵיצָה טוּרְמִיטָא״. מַאי בֵּיצָה טוּרְמִיטָא? אָמַר שְׁמוּאֵל: עַבְדָּא דְּעָבֵיד לַהּ שָׁוֵי אַלְפָּא דִּינָרֵי, וּמְעַיֵּיל לַהּ אַלְפָּא זִימְנֵי בְּמַיָּא חַמִּימֵי, וְאַלְפָּא זִימְנֵי בְּמַיָּא קְרִירֵי, עַד דְּמִתְזוּטְרָא כִּי הֵיכִי דְּבַלְעִיתַהּ וְאִם אִית כִּיבָא – סָרֵיךְ עֲלַהּ, וְכַד נָפְקָא וְאָתְיָא – יָדַע אָסְיָא מַאי סַמָּא מִתְבָּעֵי לֵיהּ וּבְמַאי מִתַּסֵּי.

§ The mishna teaches that if one said: Cooked food is *konam* for me, and for that reason I will not taste it, he is prohibited from tasting a loose cooked food but is permitted to taste a thick one, **and** he is likewise **permitted to** eat **a *turemita* egg.** The Gemara asks: **What is a *turemita* egg?**[L] **Shmuel said: A slave who** knows how to **prepare it is worth a thousand dinars.** And this is how one prepares it: **He insets it into hot water a thousand times and in cold water a thousand times, until it shrinks**[B] enough **so that it can be swallowed** whole. **And if there is a lesion**[B] in one's intestines, part of the lesion **adheres** to the egg, **and when** the egg **emerges the doctor knows what medicine** the patient **requires and with what** he **can be healed.** It is therefore an important dish for medicinal purposes.

שְׁמוּאֵל הֲוָה בָּדֵיק נַפְשֵׁיהּ בְּקוּלְחָא עַד דְּמִסְתַּתְרִין אֱינָשֵׁי בֵּיתֵיהּ עֲלֵיהּ שַׂעֲרֵיהוֹן.

The Gemara relates: **Shmuel would examine himself with a stalk**[N] that he would swallow for this purpose. This would weaken his body and cause him to look faint **to such an extent that the members of his household would tear their hairs out for him** in grief, as they would think he was dying.

תְּנַן הָתָם: הָיָה עוֹשֶׂה בִּכְלוּפְסִין – לֹא יֹאכַל בִּבְנוֹת שֶׁבַע, בִּבְנוֹת שֶׁבַע – לֹא יֹאכַל בִּכְלוּפְסִין. מַאי כְּלוּפְסִין? מִינָא דִּתְאֵינֵי דְּעָבְדִין מִנְּהוֹן לִפְדֵי.

Besides vows, there are other areas of *halakha* where there is a distinction between different varieties of the same food. **We learned** in a mishna **there** (*Ma'asrot* 2:8): A hired worker who **was working with *keloppasin*,**[NHL] a type of fig, **may not partake of *benot sheva*,** a different species of fig, during his work. A worker may partake only of the fruit that he is handling at the time (see Deuteronomy 23:25–26). Similarly, if he was working **with *benot sheva* he may not partake of *keloppasin*.** The Gemara asks: **What are *keloppasin*?** The Gemara answers: **A type of fig from which compote [*lifdei*]**[L] **is made.**

הַהוּא גַּבְרָא דִּיהַב עַבְדָּא לְחַבְרֵיהּ לְאַגְמוּרֵיהּ אַלְפָּא מִינֵי לִפְדֵי, אַגְמְרֵיהּ תְּמָנֵי מְאָה. אַזְמְנֵיהּ לְדִינָא לְקַמֵּיהּ דְּרַבִּי. אָמַר רַבִּי: אֲבוֹתֵינוּ אָמְרוּ ״נָשִׁינוּ טוֹבָה״, אָנוּ אֲפִילּוּ בְּעֵינֵינוּ לֹא רָאִינוּ.

The Gemara relates: There was **a certain man who gave a slave to his friend so that** the friend would **teach him** how to prepare **a thousand varieties of compote** from figs. However, **he taught him** only **eight hundred. He** therefore **brought** his friend **for judgment before Rabbi** Yehuda HaNasi. **Rabbi** Yehuda HaNasi **said: Our forefathers said: We have forgotten prosperity** (see Lamentations 3:17). They forgot the opulence they enjoyed in better times, but they at least experienced it. By contrast, **we have not even seen** it **with our eyes.** Rabbi Yehuda HaNasi had not imagined that so many types of compote could be prepared from figs.

BACKGROUND

Wine in vessels of silver and gold – חַמְרָא בְּמָאנֵי דְכַסְפָּא וְדַהֲבָא: Wine was not stored in metal vessels because wine and vinegar dissolve most metals, including copper and even silver. Furthermore, many of the compounds of these metals are poisonous, which not only impaired the taste of the wine but even caused a serious health risk.

Until it shrinks – עַד דְּמִתְזוּטְרָא: Like other proteins, eggs that are cooked for a long time will shrivel in size. In tractate *Shabbat* (38a), the Talmud mentions eggs that shriveled to the size of hawthorns, smaller than a common grape.

And if there is a lesion – וְאִם אִית כִּיבָא: This practice of examining the stomach and the intestines was based on the capacity of an egg to absorb other materials. Accordingly, a lesion should leave a mark on the egg. A well-cooked egg is small enough to be swallowed whole and hard enough not to be digested, allowing it to exit the intestines whole. It thereby served as an instrument for this examination.

NOTES

If they were ugly, etc. – אִי הֲווּ סְנוּ וכו׳: According to *Tosafot* (*Ta'anit* 7a), cited by the Maharsha, this means: Had they hated beauty. He explains that there is no essential relationship between one's appearance and his wisdom. Just as an ugly person can be a great scholar, so can a handsome man. Rather, Rabbi Yehoshua meant that one who knows he is handsome is likely to spend too much time cultivating his looks and his impression on others, which will have a detrimental effect on his studies. He therefore asserted that if those handsome scholars had hated their good looks and paid no attention to them, they would have been more learned.

With a stalk [*kuleḥa*] – בְּקוּלְחָא: Some commentaries maintain that *kuleḥa* is merely another name for a *turemita* egg (*Tosafot*; Rosh). Others explain that it is a highly diarrheic drink, which Shmuel would take for examination of his intestines (Rabbi Yitzḥak Tzarfati). In the *Arukh*, the term is interpreted as a cabbage stalk. Shmuel swallowed it whole in order to check his intestines, as is done with a *turemita* egg, which was not available to Shmuel. The size of the stalk would cause Shmuel to suffer and swoon while swallowing it.

Who was working with *keloppasin* – הָיָה עוֹשֶׂה בִּכְלוּפְסִין: A worker is generally permitted to partake of the fruit he is handling (see Deuteronomy 23:25–26). However, this principle is subject to several limitations. One limitation is that he may partake only of the particular type of fruit he is working with at the time. This mishna therefore teaches that although *keloppasin* and *benot sheva* are both figs, they are not considered the same species with regard to this *halakha* (*Tosafot*; Rosh).

HALAKHA

Working with *keloppasin*, etc. – הָיָה עוֹשֶׂה בִּכְלוּפְסִין וכו׳: A worker working with one type of tree is not permitted to partake of the fruit of a different species, even if he plans on working with that type of tree later (Rambam *Sefer Mishpatim*, *Hilkhot Sekhirut* 12:10; *Shulḥan Arukh*, *Ḥoshen Mishpat* 337:9).

LANGUAGE

A *turemita* egg – בֵּיצָה טוּרְמִיטָא: According to the Gemara, this is an egg that was cooked to such an extent that it had thoroughly shriveled. The Rambam, however, interprets the term as related to the Greek τρομητός, *tromētos*, which are slightly cooked eggs.

***Keloppasin* – כְּלוּפְסִין:** Apparently a variant of the word *belospayin* mentioned above (49b). Both words mean a type of fig.

Compote [*lifdei*] – לִפְדֵי: Apparently from Greek, some claim that it stems from the word λοπαδεύω, *lopadeuo*, which means to prepare a dish.

PERSONALITIES

Rabbi Shimon, son of Rabbi Yehuda HaNasi – רַבִּי שִׁמְעוֹן בְּרַבִּי: Rabbi Shimon was the youngest son of Rabbi Yehuda HaNasi and a close student of his. He was a member of the circle of the great students of Rabbi Yehuda HaNasi and discussed various halakhic issues with them. He was especially close to Rabbi Ḥiyya, who was also his partner in the silk business.

It is evident from several stories that Rabbi Shimon was meticulous about his honor, which he considered related to the honor of the *Nasi*. In particular, he was careful to ensure that nothing he did would imply offense to his great father.

At least one of Rabbi Shimon's statements is found in the Mishna, although he lived in the transitional generation between *tanna'im* and *amora'im*. His teachings are often introduced by the phrase: It was said, which is used for *amora'im*.

Rabbi Yehuda HaNasi considered Rabbi Shimon to be a great scholar. Before Rabbi Yehuda HaNasi's death, he appointed him to be the *Ḥakham*, the third highest position in the Sanhedrin after the *Nasi* and the president of the court. Rabban Gamliel, Rabbi Shimon's older brother, was appointed by Rabbi Yehuda HaNasi to take his place as *Nasi*.

רַבִּי עֲבַד לֵיהּ הִלּוּלָא לְרַבִּי שִׁמְעוֹן בְּרַבִּי. כְּתַב עַל בֵּית גְּנָנָא: עֶשְׂרִין וְאַרְבָּעָה אַלְפִּין רִיבּוֹאִין דִּינָרִין נְפַקוּ עַל בֵּית גְּנָנָא דֵּין, וְלָא אַזְמְנֵיהּ לְבַר קַפָּרָא. אֲמַר לֵיהּ: אִם לְעוֹבְרֵי רְצוֹנוֹ כָּךְ – לְעוֹשֵׂי רְצוֹנוֹ עַל אַחַת כַּמָּה וְכַמָּה. אַזְמְנֵיהּ, אֲמַר: לְעוֹשֵׂי רְצוֹנוֹ בָּעוֹלָם הַזֶּה כָּךְ – לָעוֹלָם הַבָּא עַל אַחַת כַּמָּה וְכַמָּה.

§ The Gemara relates: **Rabbi** Yehuda HaNasi **made a wedding for Rabbi Shimon, son of Rabbi** Yehuda HaNasi.[P] Someone **wrote on the canopy:**[N] **24,000 myriad dinars were expended on this canopy, and** nevertheless Rabbi Yehuda HaNasi **did not invite bar Kappara** to the wedding. The insulted bar Kappara **said to** Rabbi Yehuda HaNasi: **If to those who transgress** God's **will,** i.e., you who act improperly, their reward is **such,** as Rabbi Yehuda HaNasi was very wealthy, **all the more so those who perform His will** are to be rewarded. Upon hearing his reaction, Rabbi Yehuda HaNasi **invited him.** Bar Kappara then **said:** If **to those who perform His will** their reward is **such in this world, all the more so** will they be rewarded **in the World-to-Come.**

יוֹמָא דִּמְחַיֵּיךְ בֵּיהּ רַבִּי, אָתְיָא פּוּרְעֲנוּתָא לְעָלְמָא. אֲמַר לֵיהּ לְבַר קַפָּרָא: לָא תְּבַדִּיחָן, וִיהֵיבְנָא לָךְ אַרְבְּעִין גְּרִיוֵי חִיטֵּי. אֲמַר לֵיהּ: לֶיחֱזֵי מָר

The Gemara relates additional incidents that occurred between the two scholars. **On a day when Rabbi** Yehuda HaNasi **would laugh,**[N] **calamity would befall the world,** as Rabbi Yehuda HaNasi's sufferings would atone for the sins of the Jewish people. He therefore **said to bar Kappara: Do not cause me to laugh, and I will give you forty *se'a* of wheat** in return. Bar Kappara **said to him:** The **Master will see**

NOTES

Someone wrote on the canopy – כְּתַב עַל בֵּית גְּנָנָא: The Maharsha writes that this was written by bar Kappara himself.

On a day when Rabbi Yehuda HaNasi would laugh – יוֹמָא דִּמְחַיֵּיךְ בֵּיהּ רַבִּי: Rabbi Yehuda HaNasi was renowned for his holy ways. In fact, he was referred to as Our Holy Teacher even in his lifetime. He was careful to maintain a solemn state of mind, shunning all forms of joy and lightheartedness (*Iyyun Ya'akov*). Bar Kappara felt that it was nevertheless a great mitzva to gladden others, especially those who generally withdraw from laughter. He therefore went to great lengths to give joy to Rabbi Yehuda HaNasi (Maharsha).

Perek **VI**
Daf **51** Amud **a**

NOTES

Singing [*kirekanei*] – קִירְקָנֵי: The Ran maintains that the word stems from *kirkur*, with the letter *kuf*, which means to crow. Accordingly, bar Kappara meant that Rabbi Yehuda HaNasi's wife should sing. *Tosafot* and the Rosh hold that the term refers to dancing, like the word *kirkur* with the letter *kaf*. In The Commentary on *Nedarim* and the *Arukh*, the word is defined as pouring, as evident later in the story, where bar Kappara asks for Rabbi Yehuda HaNasi's wife to pour him wine.

LANGUAGE

Singing [*kirekanei*] – קִירְקָנֵי: There are various opinions with regard to the source and meaning of this word. Some assert that it comes from the Hebrew root *kuf, reish, kuf, reish*, which means to sound. In Syrian it means to sing. Others claim that it comes from the Greek χορικός, *khorikos*, which refers to dance accompanied by music. According to this interpretation, bar Kappara requested that Rabbi Yehuda HaNasi's wife dance before him like her husband.

דְּכָל גְּרִיוָא דְּבָעֵינָא שָׁקֵילְנָא. שְׁקַל דִּיקוּלָא רַבָּה, חַפְיֵיהּ כּוּפְרָא וּסְחָפֵיהּ עַל רֵישֵׁיהּ, וַאֲזַל וַאֲמַר לֵיהּ: לֵיכִיל לִי מָר אַרְבְּעִין גְּרִיוֵי חִיטֵּי דְּרָשֵׁינָא בָּךְ. אֲחוּךְ רַבִּי. אֲמַר לֵיהּ: לָאו אַזְהַרְתָּךְ דְּלָא תְּבַדְּחָן! אֲמַר לֵיהּ: חִיטֵּי דְּרָשֵׁינָא קָא נָסֵיבְנָא.

that any *se'a* **I wish I will take. He took a large palm basket, smeared it with tar, and overturned it upon his head, and went, and said to** Rabbi Yehuda HaNasi: **Let the Master measure for me the forty *se'a* of wheat that I am owed by you. Rabbi** Yehuda HaNasi **laughed** at this **and said to him: Did I not warn you not to make me laugh? He said to him:** What I am taking from you is simply **the wheat that I am owed by you.**

אֲמַר לָהּ בַּר קַפָּרָא לִבְרַתֵּיהּ דְּרַבִּי: לְמָחָר שָׁתֵינָא חַמְרָא בְּרִיקוּדָא דַּאֲבוּךְ וּבְקִירְקָנֵי דְּאִמָּךְ. בֶּן אֶלְעָשָׂה חֲתָנֵיהּ דְּרַבִּי הֲוָה, וְעָשִׁיר גָּדוֹל הֲוָה, אַזְמְנֵיהּ לְבֵי הִילּוּלָא דְּרַבִּי שִׁמְעוֹן בְּרַבִּי.

The Gemara relates another story. **Bar Kappara**[P] **said to the daughter of Rabbi** Yehuda HaNasi, whose husband's name was ben Elasa: **Tomorrow I will drink wine at your father's dancing and your mother's singing [*kirekanei*].**[NL] **Ben Elasa was the son-in-law of Rabbi** Yehuda HaNasi **and was a very wealthy man. Rabbi** Yehuda HaNasi **invited him to the wedding of Rabbi Shimon, son of Rabbi** Yehuda HaNasi.

PERSONALITIES

Bar Kappara – בַּר קַפָּרָא: Bar Kappara lived in Eretz Yisrael during the transitional generation between the *tanna'im* and the *amora'im*. His first name is unknown, although some claim it was Shimon. His family relationship, if he had one, to Rabbi Elazar HaKappar is also unclear.

Bar Kappara was one of the most important disciples of Rabbi Yehuda HaNasi. He composed an anthology of *baraitot* quoted in the Talmud as bar Kappara's Teachings. His rulings are found in many places in the Talmud. He was also renowned as one of the most prominent homilists of his generation, and several of his homiletic teachings appear in the Babylonian and Jerusalem Talmud. Bar Kappara was famous for his brilliance and sharpness as well. Many of his sayings on different subjects are cited in the Talmud. Apparently, he was also considered an expert in Bible in his day, as even Rabbi Yehuda HaNasi would consult with him with regard to the meaning of verses in the Bible. His tendency to utter sharp retorts and his jocularity embarrassed Rabbi Yehuda HaNasi's family on several occasions, yet Rabbi Yehuda HaNasi still held him in great esteem. He too lauded Rabbi Yehuda HaNasi and was the first to eulogize him at his funeral.

Almost all of the first generation *amora'im* of Eretz Yisrael were students of his, including Rabbi Yehuda ben Padda, his nephew. They often cited *halakhot* in his name.

Bar Kappara lived in the Galilee, at least toward the end of his life, and was buried in the city of Parod, southeast of Safed.

אֲמַר לֵיהּ בַּר קַפָּרָא לְרַבִּי: מַאי ״תּוֹעֵבָה״? כָּל דְּאָמַר לֵיהּ רַבִּי דְּהָכֵין הוּא ״תּוֹעֵבָה״ פָּרְכָהּ בַּר קַפָּרָא. אֲמַר לֵיהּ: פָּרְשֵׁיהּ אַתְּ! אֲמַר לֵיהּ: תֵּיתֵי דְּבֵיתְהִי תִּירְמֵי לִי נַטְלָא. אָתַת רַמְיָא לֵיהּ. אֲמַר לֵיהּ לְרַבִּי: קוּם וְקוּד לִי, דְּאֵימַר לָךְ. הָכִי אָמַר רַחֲמָנָא: ״תּוֹעֵבָה״ – תּוֹעֶה אַתָּה בָּהּ.

Bar Kappara said to Rabbi Yehuda HaNasi at the wedding: **What** is the meaning of the word ***to'eva***, abomination, used by the Torah to describe homosexual intercourse (see Leviticus 18:22)? **Whatever** it was **that Rabbi** Yehuda HaNasi **said to** bar Kappara in explanation, claiming **that this is** the meaning of ***to'eva*, bar Kappara refuted it** by proving otherwise. Rabbi Yehuda HaNasi **said to him: You explain it.** Bar Kappara **said to him: Let your wife come and pour me a goblet** of wine. **She came** and **poured him** wine. Bar Kappara then **said to Rabbi** Yehuda HaNasi: **Arise** and **dance for me, so that I will tell you** the meaning of the word: **This is what the Merciful One is saying** in the Torah in the word ***to'eva*: You are straying after it** [***to'e ata bah***], i.e., after an atypical mate.

לְכָסָא אַחֲרִינָא אֲמַר לֵיהּ: מַאי ״תֶּבֶל״? אֲמַר לֵיהּ כִּי עִנְיָינָא קַדְמָאָה. אֲמַר לֵיהּ: עֲבִיד לִי דְּאוֹמַר לָךְ. עֲבַד. אֲמַר לֵיהּ: ״תֶּבֶל הוּא״ – תְּבָלִין יֵשׁ בָּהּ? מִי שָׁנְיָא הָדָא בִּיאָה מִן כּוּלְּהוֹן בִּיאוֹת?

When they came **to** drink **another cup,** bar Kappara **said to him: What** is the meaning of the word *tevel*, perversion, as in the verse: "Neither shall any woman stand before a beast, to lie down thereto; it is perversion [*tevel*]" (Leviticus 18:23)? Rabbi Yehuda HaNasi **said** various explanations **to him, as** he did **the previous** time, which were all refuted again by bar Kappara. Bar Kappara then **said to him: Perform for me** as you did before, so **that I will tell you.** Rabbi Yehuda HaNasi **did** so. Bar Kappara then **said to him** that the phrase: **"It is *tevel*"** means: Does **it have** any spice [***tevalin yesh bah***]**? Is this act of sexual intercourse** with an animal **different than all other acts of sexual intercourse,** which would cause one to engage in such a repulsive action?

אֲמַר לֵיהּ: וּמַאי ״זִימָּה״. אֲמַר לֵיהּ: עֲבִיד כִּי עִנְיָינָא קַדְמָאָה. עֲבַד, וַאֲמַר לֵיהּ: זוֹ מָה הִיא. לָא יָכֵיל בֶּן אֶלְעָשָׂה לְמִיסְבַּל, קָם וּנְפַק הוּא וְאִינְתְּתֵיהּ מִתַּמָּן.

Rabbi Yehuda HaNasi **said to** bar Kappara: **And what** is the meaning of the word *zimma*,[N] lewdness, as in the verse: "They are near kinswomen; it is lewdness [*zimma*]" (Leviticus 18:17), stated with regard to a man who engages in sexual intercourse with a woman and her daughter? **He said to him: Perform for me as** you did **the previous** time. Rabbi Yehuda HaNasi **did** so, **and** bar Kappara **said to him** that *zimma* means: **What is she** [***zo ma hi***]? This man would be confused about how to refer to his wives; his wife is also his other wife's mother or daughter. **Ben Elasa could not tolerate** Rabbi Yehuda HaNasi's humiliation, so **he and his wife arose and left** the wedding.

מַאי בֶּן אֶלְעָשָׂה? דְּתַנְיָא: לֹא לְחִנָּם פִּיזֵּר בֶּן אֶלְעָשָׂה אֶת מָעוֹתָיו, אֶלָּא לְהַרְאוֹת בָּהֶן תִּסְפּוֹרֶת שֶׁל כֹּהֵן גָּדוֹל,

In **what** other context is **ben Elasa** mentioned? He is mentioned in a *baraita*, **as it is taught: Ben Elasa did not dispense his money** on his special haircut **for naught. Rather,** he spent it **to show** others what **the haircut of a High Priest** looked like.

דִּכְתִיב ״כָּסוֹם יִכְסְמוּ אֶת רָאשֵׁיהֶם״. תָּנָא: כְּעֵין לוּלְיָנִית. מַאי לוּלְיָנִית? אֲמַר רַב יְהוּדָה: תִּסְפָּרְתָּא יְחִידָתָא. הֵיכִי דָּמֵי? אֲמַר רָבָא: רֹאשׁוֹ שֶׁל זֶה בְּצַד עִיקָּרוֹ שֶׁל זֶה, וְהַיְינוּ תִּסְפּוֹרֶת שֶׁל כֹּהֵן גָּדוֹל.

As it is written with regard to the priests: **"They shall poll their heads"** (Ezekiel 44:20), and it is **taught** in a *baraita*: This haircut is **like a *luleyanit*.**[L] The Gemara asks: **What is a *luleyanit*? Rav Yehuda said:** It is **a unique haircut.** The Gemara asks: **What is** this haircut **like? Rava said: The edge of this** hank of hair[H] **is by the roots of that** hank of hair.[N] The hair is cut in the form of hanks that do not overlap. **And this is the haircut of a High Priest,** for which ben Elasa paid a large sum.

״וּבִדְלַעַת הָרְמוּצָה״. מַאי דְּלַעַת הָרְמוּצָה? אֲמַר שְׁמוּאֵל: קָרָא קַרְקוּזַאי. רַב אַשִׁי אָמַר: דְּלַעַת הַטְּמוּנָה בְּרֶמֶץ.

§ It is stated in the mishna that one who said: Cooked food is *konam* for me, and for that reason I will not taste it, is **permitted** to taste a *turemita* egg **and the *remutza* gourd.** The Gemara asks: **What is the *remutza* gourd?**[B] **Shmuel said:** A type of **gourd** that grows in **Karkuza** [***kara karkuzai***],[L] which does not cook well. **Rav Ashi said: A gourd that is insulated in embers** [***remetz***].

NOTES

What is the meaning of the word *zimma* – מַאי זִימָּה: Several commentaries explain that Rabbi Yehuda HaNasi was referring to the verse "And the land will become full of lewdness [*zimma*]" (Leviticus 19:29). Bar Kappara's answer, that the word means: What is she, refers accordingly to the statement in *Yevamot* (37b) that a man should not marry several wives in different locations, as this will cause people not to know who their relatives are, which might lead to forbidden relations. What is she, means, accordingly: Is she my relative? A different opinion is that the question refers to the verse "It is lewdness" (Leviticus 18:17), which speaks of a man who engages in sexual intercourse with a woman and her daughter. According to this opinion, the question: What is she, relates to the man's confusion as to what he should call his wives (*Ben Yehoyada*).

The edge of this is by the roots of that – רֹאשׁוֹ שֶׁל זֶה בְּצַד עִיקָּרוֹ שֶׁל זֶה: According to the Rambam, this refers to every individual hair. In other words, the hair is all cut very short, so that none of the hairs overlap. The Ra'avad, on the other hand, interprets that the hair is fashioned into rows, between which the head is shaven entirely. The hairs in each row are just long enough to reach to roots of the adjacent rows (see *Kesef Mishne*).

HALAKHA

The edge of this hank of hair, etc. – רֹאשׁוֹ שֶׁל זֶה וכו׳: The High Priest cuts his hair in such a manner that the edge of one hair reaches the root of the adjacent hair (Rambam *Sefer Avoda*, *Hilkhot Kelei HaMikdash* 5:6 and *Kesef Mishne* there; see Ra'avad).

BACKGROUND

The *remutza* gourd – דְּלַעַת הָרְמוּצָה: In the Jerusalem Talmud, this is defined as a kind of gourd that is naturally so bitter that it is inedible raw. However, when cooked in hot ash, it sweetens and is rendered fit for human consumption. This explains the difference of opinion between Shmuel and Rav Ashi.

LANGUAGE

***Luleyanit* – לוּלְיָנִית:** The name of this haircut apparently stems from the Roman name Julianus. The haircut was named after a particular Roman emperor or some other notable figure of this name who had this kind of haircut.

Gourd that grows in Karkuza [*kara karkuzai*] – קָרָא קַרְקוּזַאי: The meaning is unclear. Several possible explanations and sources have been suggested. While Karkuza refers to a specific location, perhaps the region and city of Circasia, the *kara karkuzai* is apparently a type of gourd that was found in that region.

אֵיתִיבֵיהּ רָבִינָא לְרַב אַשִׁי: רַבִּי נְחֶמְיָה אוֹמֵר: דְּלַעַת אֲרָמִית הִיא דְּלַעַת הַמִּצְרִית, כִּלְאַיִם עִם הַיְּוָנִית, כִּלְאַיִם עִם הָרְמוּצָה! תְּיוּבְתָּא.

Ravina raised an objection to the definition given by **Rav Ashi** from a *baraita*: The halakha is that one who plants different types of vegetables in close proximity to each other violates, by rabbinic law, the transgression of diverse kinds (see *Kilayim*). Concerning which types of gourd are considered to be different types, **Rabbi Neḥemya says** that **an Aramean gourd is** identical to **the Egyptian gourd,** and one is permitted to plant them together. However, there is a prohibition of **diverse kinds** when it is planted **with the Greek** gourd, and there is a prohibition of **diverse kinds** when it is planted **with the** ***remutza*** gourd. This indicates that the *remutza* gourd is a type of gourd rather than a gourd prepared in a certain manner. This is **a conclusive refutation** of Rav Ashi's opinion.

מתני׳ הַנּוֹדֵר מִמַּעֲשֵׂה קְדֵרָה – אֵין אָסוּר אֶלָּא מִמַּעֲשֵׂה רְתַחְתָּא. אָמַר ״קוֹנָם הַיּוֹרֵד לַקְּדֵרָה שֶׁאֲנִי טוֹעֵם״ – אָסוּר בְּכָל הַנַּעֲשֶׂה בִּקְדֵרָה.

MISHNA In the case of **one who vows** that food **cooked in a dish** is forbidden to him,[H] he **is prohibited from** eating **only** food that is **cooked by boiling** it in a dish, i.e., its main preparation is in a dish. However, if **one said: That which enters into a dish is** ***konam*** for me, and for **that** reason **I** will not **taste** it, he is **prohibited** from tasting **anything cooked in a dish,** even if the final stage of the food's preparation is not in a dish.

גמ׳ תַּנְיָא: הַנּוֹדֵר מִן הַיּוֹרֵד לַקְּדֵרָה אָסוּר בַּיּוֹרֵד לָאִלְפָּס, שֶׁכְּבָר יָרַד לַקְּדֵרָה קוֹדֶם שֶׁיּוֹרֵד לָאִלְפָּס. מִן הַיּוֹרֵד לָאִלְפָּס – מוּתָּר בַּיּוֹרֵד לַקְּדֵרָה. מִן הַנַּעֲשֶׂה בִּקְדֵרָה – מוּתָּר בַּנַּעֲשֶׂה בָּאִלְפָּס, מִן הַנַּעֲשֶׂה בָּאִלְפָּס – מוּתָּר בַּנַּעֲשֶׂה בִּקְדֵרָה.

GEMARA **It is taught** in a *baraita*: **One who vows** that **that which enters into a dish** is forbidden **to** him is also **prohibited from** eating **that which enters a stewpot,**[B] **as it has already entered into a dish before it enters into the stewpot.** Food would be cooked in a dish and then it would be cooked some more in a stewpot. However, if one **vowed that that which enters into the stewpot** is forbidden to him,[N] he is **permitted to** eat from **that which enters into a dish,** i.e., food that is cooked only in a regular dish. If one **vows** that **that which is cooked in a dish** is forbidden to him, he is **permitted to** eat **that which is cooked in a stewpot,** as he referred only to foods whose main preparation is in a dish. Similarly, if one **vows** that **that which is cooked in a stewpot** is forbidden to him, he is **permitted to** eat **that which is cooked in a dish.**

הַנּוֹדֵר מִן הַיּוֹרֵד לַתַּנּוּר – אֵין אָסוּר אֶלָּא בְּפַת. וְאִם אָמַר ״כָּל מַעֲשֵׂה תַּנּוּר עָלַי״ – אָסוּר בְּכָל הַנַּעֲשִׂים בְּתַנּוּר.

One who vows that **that which enters into an oven** is forbidden **to** him[H] is **prohibited only from** eating **bread,** as that is the main food that is baked in an oven. **But if** one **said: Anything made in an oven is** forbidden **to me,**[N] he is **prohibited from** eating **anything made in an oven.**

HALAKHA

One who vows that food cooked in a dish is forbidden to him – הַנּוֹדֵר מִמַּעֲשֵׂה קְדֵרָה: One who vows that food cooked in a dish is forbidden to him is prohibited from eating foods cooked exclusively in a dish. However, if one said: That which enters into a dish is *konam* for me, and for that reason I will not taste it, he is prohibited from tasting anything cooked in a dish (Rambam *Sefer Hafla'a*, *Hilkhot Nedarim* 9:7; *Shulḥan Arukh*, *Yoreh De'a* 217:2).

That which enters into an oven – מִן הַיּוֹרֵד לַתַּנּוּר: One who vows that that which enters into an oven is forbidden to him is prohibited from eating only bread. If he said: Anything made in an oven is forbidden to me, he is prohibited from eating anything made in an oven (*Shulḥan Arukh*, *Yoreh De'a* 217:2).

BACKGROUND

Stewpot [*ilpas*] – אִלְפָּס: The *ilpas*, derived from the Greek λοπάς, *lopas*, was a clay pot with a wide base, generally with straight sides and a large opening. The sides of the *ilpas* were thinner than other pots. An *ilpas* also differed from other pots in that it had a lid with sharp edges. The lid sometimes would have a hole. The *ilpas* was used for regular cooking but was used particularly for foods that cook swiftly and for reheating food that was already cooked.

Greek *lopas*

NOTES

That which enters into the stewpot is forbidden to him, etc. – מִן הַיּוֹרֵד לָאִלְפָּס וכו׳: The Rosh cites an opinion that the expression: That which enters into a stewpot, refers exclusively to food that was cooked in a stewpot before it was cooked in a dish. Therefore, food that was first cooked in a dish is permitted. In *Tosefot Rabbeinu Peretz*, however, the ruling is that only food that was not cooked in a stewpot at all is permitted. Accordingly, the novel element of the mishna's statement is that even if the food is meant to be cooked in a stewpot after it was cooked in a dish, as long as it hasn't been cooked in a stewpot yet it is permitted.

Anything made in an oven is forbidden to me – עָלַי כָּל מַעֲשֵׂה תַּנּוּר: *Tosafot* point out that the word anything, is misleading, as it indicates that the stringency here vis-à-vis the previous case is due to this inclusive wording, while in fact it is due to the difference between the expressions: That which enters into the oven, and: That which is made in the oven. The Ritva raises another difficulty with this passage. The expression: That which enters into the oven, seems more general than the phrase: That which is made in an oven. The latter phrase apparently refers to food whose main preparation is in an oven, as evident from the previous statements of the *baraita* concerning the dish and the stewpot. Nevertheless, the mishna states that specifically in the latter case, anything made in the oven is forbidden, even if that is not the main stage in its preparation. The Ritva therefore accepts an alternative version of the *baraita*, which states the opposite ruling: One who vows that that which enters into an oven is forbidden to him is prohibited from eating anything made in an oven. But if one vows that that which is made in an oven is forbidden to him, he is prohibited from eating only bread.

מתני׳ ״מִן הַכָּבוּשׁ״ – אֵין אָסוּר אֶלָּא מִן הַכָּבוּשׁ שֶׁל יָרָק: ״כָּבוּשׁ שֶׁאֲנִי טוֹעֵם״ – אָסוּר בְּכָל הַכְּבוּשִׁים. ״מִן הַשָּׁלוּק״ – אֵינוֹ אָסוּר אֶלָּא מִן הַשָּׁלוּק שֶׁל בָּשָׂר: ״שָׁלוּק שֶׁאֲנִי טוֹעֵם״ – אָסוּר בְּכָל הַשְּׁלוּקִים.

MISHNA One who vows that **pickled** food is forbidden **to him**[HN] **is prohibited from** eating **only pickled vegetables,** as that is what people usually mean when referring to pickled food. However, if he says: **Pickled food** is *konam* for me, and for **that** reason **I will not taste** it, **he is prohibited** from tasting **all pickled** foods. Similarly, one who vows that **boiled food** is forbidden **to him is prohibited from** eating **only boiled meat,** as that is the common meaning of the expression boiled food. On the other hand, if he says: **Boiled food** is *konam* for me, and for **that** reason **I will not taste it, he is prohibited from** eating **all boiled foods.**

גמ׳ אֲמַר לֵיהּ רַב אַחָא בְּרֵיהּ דְּרַב אַוְיָא לְרַב אַשִׁי: אֲמַר ״דִּכְבִישׁ״ מַאי: ״דִּשְׁלִיק״ מַאי: ״דִּצְלִי״ מַאי: ״דִּמְלִיחַ״ מַאי, הֵיכִין מַשְׁמַע? תִּיבָּעֵי.

GEMARA Rav Aḥa, son of Rav Avya, said to Rav Ashi: If one **said:** That **which is pickled** is forbidden to me, **what** is the *halakha*?[N] If one said: That **which is boiled** is forbidden to me, **what** is the *halakha*? If one said: That **which is roasted** is forbidden to me, **what** is the *halakha*? If one said: That **which is salted** is forbidden to me, **what** is the *halakha*? **What** do these expressions **indicate?** Do they refer to specific foods or to all foods prepared in these ways? **The dilemma remains** unresolved.

מתני׳ ״מִן הַצָּלִי״ – אֵין אָסוּר אֶלָּא מִן הַצָּלִי שֶׁל בָּשָׂר, דִּבְרֵי רַבִּי יְהוּדָה. ״צָלִי שֶׁאֲנִי טוֹעֵם״ – אָסוּר בְּכָל הַצְּלוּיִים. ״מִן הַמָּלִיחַ״ – אֵין אָסוּר אֶלָּא מִן הַמָּלִיחַ שֶׁל דָּג. ״מָלִיחַ שֶׁאֲנִי טוֹעֵם״ – אָסוּר בְּכָל הַמְּלוּחִים.

MISHNA One who vows that **roasted food** is forbidden **to him is prohibited from** eating **only roasted meat;** this is **the statement of Rabbi Yehuda.** However, if one says: **Roasted food** is *konam* for me, and for **that** reason **I will not taste** it, **he is prohibited from** eating **all roasted foods.** One who vows that **salted food** is forbidden **to him is prohibited from** eating **only salted fish,** as that is the common meaning of the expression salted food. If, on the other hand, he says: **Salted food** is *konam* for me, and for **that** reason **I will not taste** it, **he is prohibited from** eating **all salted foods.**

״דָּג דָּגִים שֶׁאֲנִי טוֹעֵם״ – אָסוּר בָּהֶן בֵּין גְּדוֹלִים בֵּין קְטַנִּים, בֵּין מְלוּחִים בֵּין תְּפֵלִים, בֵּין חַיִּים בֵּין מְבוּשָּׁלִים, וּמוּתָּר בְּטָרִית טְרוּפָה וּבְצִיר. הַנּוֹדֵר מִן הַצַּחֲנָה – אָסוּר בְּטָרִית טְרוּפָה וּמוּתָּר בְּצִיר וּבְמוּרַיְיס, הַנּוֹדֵר מִטָּרִית טְרוּפָה – אָסוּר בְּצִיר וּבְמוּרַיְיס.

If one says: **Fish or fishes**[N] are *konam* for me, and for **that** reason **I will not taste**[H] them, **he is prohibited from** eating all of **them, whether large** fish **or small, whether salted or unsalted, whether raw or cooked. But he is permitted** to taste **minced sardines**[B] and to taste **fish brine,** as these are not included in the common meaning of the word fish. **One who vows** that ***tzaḥana*,**[LN] a concoction of whole and chopped fish, is forbidden **to him is prohibited from** eating **minced sardines** as well, **but he is permitted** to eat **fish brine and fish gravy** [***morays***].[L] **One who vows** that **minced sardines** are forbidden **to him is prohibited from** eating **fish brine and from** eating **fish gravy.**

HALAKHA

One who vows that pickled food is forbidden to him – מִן הַכָּבוּשׁ: If one vows that pickled food is forbidden to him, if all pickled foods are referred to this way in the vernacular, he is prohibited from eating all of them. If only pickled vegetables are referred to as pickled food, he is prohibited from eating only pickled vegetables (Rambam *Sefer Hafla'a, Hilkhot Nedarim* 9:3; *Shulḥan Arukh, Yoreh De'a* 217:3).

Fish or fishes that I will not taste – דָּג דָּגִים שֶׁאֲנִי טוֹעֵם: One who vows that fish are forbidden to him is permitted to eat fish brine and fish gravy (Rambam *Sefer Hafla'a, Hilkhot Nedarim* 9:8; *Shulḥan Arukh, Yoreh De'a* 217:12).

BACKGROUND

Minced sardines – טָרִית טְרוּפָה: Sardines, *Sardinella aurita* or round sardinella, which are plentiful in the Mediterranean, were eaten salted. They were abundant off the shores of Eretz Yisrael and were considered a delicacy in the region.

Due to their diminutive size, large quantities of sardines were placed in large barrels, which would cause them to get crushed into small pieces over time. For this reason, they were called minced sardines.

Round sardinella

LANGUAGE

Tzaḥana – צַחֲנָה: From the Aramaic root *tzadi*, *ḥet*, *nun*, meaning parched, as well as the Arabic صحناة, *ṣiḥnā'ah*, which means small, salty fish.

Fish gravy [*morays*] – מוּרַיְיס: From the Latin muria, meaning brine from salty fish.

NOTES

One who vows that pickled food is forbidden to him – מִן הַכָּבוּשׁ וכו׳: Various explanations have been suggested for the difference between a vow using the phrase: Pickled food is forbidden, and a vow using the phrase: Pickled food is *konam* for me, and for that reason I will not taste it. One opinion is that the addition of the phrase: That I will not taste it, serves to include in the prohibition any food that is pickled (Meiri, citing Rashi; *Tosafot*; Ran's second interpretation; Rosh). An alternative explanation is that the vow using the phrase: Pickled food is forbidden, refers to a specific food called pickled food, whereas the vow using the phrase: That I will not taste it, refers in general terms to food that is pickled (Ra'avad; Rid; Rabbi Natan bar Yosef, cited in *Shita Mekubbetzet*).

If one said: That which is pickled [*dekavish*] is forbidden to me, what is the *halakha*, etc. – אֲמַר דִּכְבִישׁ מַאי וכו׳: The question in this case is whether or not the Aramaic word *dekavish* refers to a particular pickled food. The Ran adds that it is unclear whether the prefix *de* serves here as a definite article. The Rid maintains that the correct version is *dekevesh*, and the question is whether this word carries the same meaning as the Hebrew *hakevesh*.

Fish or fishes, etc. – דָּג דָּגִים וכו׳: Some commentaries explain that the mishna is referring to a vow that uses either the word fish or the word fishes, as both wordings result in the same outcome (*Tosafot*; Rid; Meiri). The mishna's ruling is therefore in conflict with the opinion of Rabbi Shimon ben Elazar cited in the Gemara. The Ritva disagrees, maintaining that the word fish refers to large fish, as they are sold individually, whereas the word fishes refers to small fish, which are sold together. He therefore interprets that only the expression: Fish or fishes, includes both large and small ones. The Rambam claims that the expression the mishna is referring to is: Fish of fishes, which is a Hebrew form of speech that stresses greatness, e.g., the Song of Songs. Accordingly, the phrase fish of fishes refers to the entire species.

Tzaḥana – צַחֲנָה: *Tosafot* explain that this means minced fish. The Ran maintains that these are small fish sold together. Naturally, parts of fish are included as well, which is why minced fish are included in the vow of one who vows that *tzaḥana* is forbidden to him. The name *tzaḥana*, literally stench, stems from the fish's strong-smelling brine. The Rambam defines *tzaḥana* as fish that was left out until it became almost rotten, thereby emitting a stench. This fish is also known to crumble into small pieces.

NOTES

Tziḥin – ציחין: According to the commentaries, *tziḥin* is similar to *tzaḥana*. However, it might be considered a more specific term, thereby excluding minced sardines (*Tosafot*; Commentary on *Nedarim*), or a more general term, thereby including fish brine and gravy as well (Ran; Rosh).

Whey [*kum*] – קום: Most commentaries define this as milk serum. The Ra'avad, however, maintains that *kum* is the milk itself, which is hardened before being made into cheese.

HALAKHA

Milk is forbidden to him – מִן הֶחָלָב: One who vows that milk is forbidden to him is permitted to partake of whey, and one who vows that whey is forbidden to him is permitted to partake of milk (Rambam *Sefer Hafla'a*, *Hilkhot Nedarim* 9:8; *Shulḥan Arukh*, *Yoreh De'a* 217:11).

Cheese is forbidden to him – מִן הַגְּבִינָה: One who vows that cheese is forbidden to him is prohibited from eating all types of cheese, whether salted, unsalted, moist, or dry (Rambam *Sefer Hafla'a*, *Hilkhot Nedarim* 9:8; *Shulḥan Arukh*, *Yoreh De'a* 217:11).

LANGUAGE

Whey [*kum*] – קום: From the root *kuf*, *vav*, *mem*, which means to stand. It was expanded to denote freezing, congealing, and souring. The part of the milk that congeals becomes cheese, and what remains from the standing milk is whey, a liquid that was mixed into drinks or dough.

גמ׳ תַּנְיָא, רַבִּי שִׁמְעוֹן בֶּן אֶלְעָזָר אוֹמֵר: ״דָּג שֶׁאֲנִי טוֹעֵם״ – אָסוּר בִּגְדוֹלִים וּמוּתָּר בִּקְטַנִּים. ״דָּגָה שֶׁאֲנִי טוֹעֵם״ – אָסוּר בִּקְטַנִּים וּמוּתָּר בִּגְדוֹלִים. ״דָּג דָּגָה שֶׁאֲנִי טוֹעֵם״ – אָסוּר בֵּין בִּגְדוֹלִים בֵּין בִּקְטַנִּים.

GEMARA It is taught in a *baraita* that **Rabbi Shimon ben Elazar says:** If one says: **Fish** [*dag*] is *konam* for me, and for **that** reason **I will not taste** it, **he is prohibited from** eating **large** fish **and permitted to** eat **small** fish. If one says: **Fish** [*daga*] is *konam* for me, and for **that** reason **I will not taste** it, he is prohibited **from** eating **small fish and permitted to eat large ones,** as this term is commonly used with regard to small fish. If one says: **Fish** [*dag*] or **fish** [*daga*] are *konam* for me, and for **that** reason **I will not taste** them, **he is prohibited from** eating **both large and small** fish.

אֲמַר לֵיהּ רַב פָּפָּא לְאַבָּיֵי: מִמַּאי דְּ״דָּג שֶׁאֲנִי טוֹעֵם״ גָּדוֹל הוּא – דִּכְתִיב ״וַיְמַן ה׳ דָּג גָּדוֹל לִבְלוֹעַ אֶת יוֹנָה״. וְהָכְתִיב ״וַיִּתְפַּלֵּל יוֹנָה אֶל ה׳ אֱלֹהָיו מִמְּעֵי הַדָּגָה״!

Rav Pappa said to Abaye: From where is it derived **that** the phrase: **Fish** [*dag*] is *konam* for me, and for **that** reason **I will not taste** it, a reference to **a large** fish? **As it is written: "And the Lord prepared a great fish** [*dag*] **to swallow up Jonah"** (Jonah 2:1). The Gemara asks: **But isn't it written** in the following verse: **"Then Jonah prayed to the Lord his God out of the belly of the fish** [*daga*]**"** (Jonah 2:2)? This indicates that a large fish can be referred to as a *daga* as well.

הָא לָא קַשְׁיָא; דִּלְמָא פְּלָטֵיהּ דָּג גָּדוֹל וּבְלָעֵיהּ דָּג קָטָן. אֶלָּא ״וְהַדָּגָה אֲשֶׁר בַּיְאוֹר מֵתָה״ – קְטַנִּים מֵתוּ גְּדוֹלִים לֹא מֵתוּ?! אֶלָּא: דָּגָה מַשְׁמַע גְּדוֹלִים וּמַשְׁמַע קְטַנִּים, וּבִנְדָרִים הַלֵּךְ אַחַר לְשׁוֹן בְּנֵי אָדָם.

The Gemara answers: **This is not difficult,** as **perhaps a large fish spat him out and a small fish** then **swallowed him. Rather,** the *baraita* is difficult according to the following verse: **"And the fish** [*daga*] **that were in the river died"** (Exodus 7:21). Is it possible that the **small** fish **died** but the **large ones did not die?** The Gemara answers: **Rather,** the biblical word ***daga*** evidently **indicates large** fish **and** also **indicates small** fish. **However, with regard to vows** one should **follow the language of people,** and the word *daga* is used only in reference to small fish.

״הַנּוֹדֵר מִן הַצַּחֲנָה״ כו׳. אֲמַר לֵיהּ רָבִינָא לְרַב אָשֵׁי: אֲמַר ״הֲרֵי עָלַי צִיחִין״ מַאי? תִּיבְּעֵי.

The mishna teaches that **one who vows** that *tzaḥana* is forbidden **to** him is prohibited from eating minced sardines as well, but he is permitted to eat fish brine and to eat fish gravy. **Ravina said to Rav Ashi:** If one **said:** ***Tziḥin***[N] **are hereby** forbidden **to me, what** is the *halakha*? Is this the same as *tzaḥana* or not? **The dilemma remains** unresolved.

מתני׳ הַנּוֹדֵר מִן הֶחָלָב מוּתָּר בְּקוֹם, וְרַבִּי יוֹסֵי אוֹסֵר. מִן הַקּוֹם – מוּתָּר בֶּחָלָב. אַבָּא שָׁאוּל אוֹמֵר: הַנּוֹדֵר מִן הַגְּבִינָה – אָסוּר בָּהּ בֵּין מְלוּחָה וּטְפֵלָה. הַנּוֹדֵר מִן הַבָּשָׂר

MISHNA **One who vows** that **milk** is forbidden **to** him[H] **is permitted to** partake of **whey** [*kum*],[NL] the liquid that separates from milk when it is made into cheese. **But Rabbi Yosei prohibits** him from partaking of whey. If one vows that **whey** is forbidden **to** him, **he is permitted to** partake of **milk. Abba Shaul says: One who vows** that **cheese** is forbidden **to** him[H] **is prohibited** from eating **it whether** it is **salted or unsalted. One who vows** that **meat** is forbidden **to** him

Perek **VI**
Daf **52** Amud **a**

NOTES

Sediments of boiled meat [*kifa*] – קִיפָה: Most commentaries explain that these are the leftover bits of meat, gravy, or stew that stick to the sides of the pot and harden. The Rambam, on the other hand, defines *kifa* as spices.

HALAKHA

When he says: This meat is forbidden to me – בִּזְמַן שֶׁיֹּאמַר בָּשָׂר זֶה עָלַי: If one vows the following: This meat is hereby forbidden to me, he is prohibited from eating all foods to which that particular piece of meat gave flavor, including its gravy and spices (Rambam *Sefer Hafla'a*, *Hilkhot Nedarim* 5:11; *Shulḥan Arukh*, *Yoreh De'a* 216:9).

מוּתָּר בְּרוֹטֶב וּבְקִיפָה, וְרַבִּי יְהוּדָה אוֹסֵר.

is permitted to eat **gravy and sediments of** boiled meat [*kifa*].[N] **But Rabbi Yehuda** maintains that he is **prohibited** from eating them.

אָמַר רַבִּי יְהוּדָה: מַעֲשֶׂה וְאָסַר עָלֵינוּ רַבִּי טַרְפוֹן בְּבֵיצִים שֶׁנִּתְבַּשְּׁלוּ עִמּוֹ. אָמְרוּ לוֹ: כֵּן הַדָּבָר, אֵימָתַי – בִּזְמַן שֶׁיֹּאמַר ״בָּשָׂר זֶה עָלַי״, שֶׁהַנּוֹדֵר מִן הַדָּבָר וְנִתְעָרֵב בְּאַחֵר, אִם יֵשׁ בּוֹ בְּנוֹתֵן טַעַם – אָסוּר.

Rabbi Yehuda said: There was **an incident** where one took such a vow **and Rabbi Tarfon prohibited us from** even **eggs that were cooked with** meat. The Rabbis **said to him: Indeed so,** but **when** is this the *halakha*? **When he says: This meat is** forbidden **to me,**[H] referring to a specific piece of meat. This is **because** in the case of **one who vows** that **an item** is forbidden **to him, and it becomes mixed into another** item, **if** the latter **contains** an amount of the forbidden food **that gives** it **flavor,** i.e., the forbidden food can be tasted in the permitted food, the mixture **is forbidden.** However, if one vows that meat in general is forbidden to him, without specifying a particular piece, only the meat itself is forbidden, not the gravy, sediments, or eggs cooked with that meat.

הַנּוֹדֵר מִן הַיַּיִן – מוּתָּר בְּתַבְשִׁיל שֶׁיֵּשׁ בּוֹ טַעַם יַיִן. אָמַר ״קוֹנָם יַיִן זֶה שֶׁאֲנִי טוֹעֵם״ וְנָפַל לְתַבְשִׁיל, אִם יֵשׁ בּוֹ בְּנוֹתֵן טַעַם – הֲרֵי זֶה אָסוּר.

Likewise, one who vows that **wine** is forbidden **to him is permitted to eat a cooked dish that has the flavor of wine.**[N] However, if **he said: Wine is** ***konam*** for me, and for **that** reason **I will not taste it, and** the wine **fell into a cooked dish, if** the dish **contains** an amount of the wine **that gives** it **flavor, it is forbidden.**

NOTES

Permitted to eat a cooked dish that has the flavor of wine – מוּתָּר בְּתַבְשִׁיל שֶׁיֵּשׁ בּוֹ טַעַם יַיִן: It is permitted because the vow mentions wine, not the taste of wine. In the next case of the mishna, where he says: This wine, the vow refers to specific wine, and therefore, even a taste of it violates the vow. This explanation is according to the standard version of the Talmud. However, according to the version of the text before the Ran, the vow in the next case does not refer to specific wine. He explains that in that case the mixture is forbidden because the vow refers to tasting wine, not drinking it.

גמ׳ וּרְמִינְהוּ: ״מִן הָעֲדָשִׁים״ – אָסוּר בָּאֲשִׁישִׁים, וְרַבִּי יוֹסֵי מַתִּיר!

GEMARA The mishna cited a dispute between Rabbi Yosei and the Rabbis, in which Rabbi Yosei ruled that one who vows that milk is forbidden to him is prohibited from eating whey as well. **And** the Gemara **raises a contradiction** between this ruling and Rabbi Yosei's opinion in a later mishna (53b): One who vows that **lentils are** forbidden **to him is prohibited from** eating ***ashishim***,[NL] a dish made from lentils. **But Rabbi Yosei permits** it. Apparently, Rabbi Yosei holds that if the forbidden food changes in form, it is permitted, contrary to his opinion with regard to whey.

לָא קַשְׁיָא; מָר כִּי אַתְרֵיהּ וּמָר כִּי אַתְרֵיהּ. בְּאַתְרָא דְּרַבָּנַן קָרוּ לְחַלְבָא חַלְבָא וּלְקוּמָא קוּמָא, בְּאַתְרֵיהּ דְּרַבִּי יוֹסֵי לְקוּמָא נַמִי קָרוּ לֵיהּ ״קוּמָא דַּחֲלָבָא״.

The Gemara answers: This is **not difficult.** The opinion of this **Sage** is **in accordance with** the custom of **his locale, and** the opinion of that **Sage in accordance with** the custom of **his locale. In the Rabbis' locale**[NH] **they call milk, milk and whey, whey,** whereas **in Rabbi Yosei's locale they also call whey, milk whey.** In the latter location, the word milk is used in reference to whey, and therefore one who vows there that milk is forbidden to him is prohibited from eating whey as well.

תַּנְיָא: הַנּוֹדֵר מִן הֶחָלָב – מוּתָּר בְּקוּם, מִן הַקּוּם – מוּתָּר בְּחָלָב. מִן הֶחָלָב – מוּתָּר בִּגְבִינָה, מִן הַגְּבִינָה – מוּתָּר בְּחָלָב. מִן הָרוֹטֶב – מוּתָּר בְּקִיפָה, מִן הַקִּיפָה – מוּתָּר בְּרוֹטֶב. אִם אָמַר ״בָּשָׂר זֶה עָלַי״ – אָסוּר בּוֹ וּבְרוֹטְבוֹ וּבְקִיפוֹ.

It is taught in a *baraita*: **One who vows** that **milk** is forbidden **to** him **is permitted to** partake of **whey.** One who vows that **whey** is forbidden **to** him **is permitted to** partake of **milk.** One who vows that **milk** is forbidden **to him is permitted to eat cheese.** One who vows that **cheese** is forbidden **to** him **is permitted to** partake of **milk.** One who vows that **gravy** is forbidden **to** him **is permitted to eat sediments of boiled meat.** One who vows that **sediments of boiled meat** are forbidden to him **is permitted to eat gravy. If** one **said: This** piece of **meat is** hereby forbidden **to me,** he **is prohibited** from eating **it, and from its gravy, and from its sediments.**

הַנּוֹדֵר מִן הַיַּיִן – מוּתָּר בְּתַבְשִׁיל שֶׁיֵּשׁ בּוֹ טַעַם יַיִן. אָמַר ״קוֹנָם יַיִן זֶה שֶׁאֵינִי טוֹעֵם״ וְנָפַל לְתוֹךְ הַתַּבְשִׁיל, אִם יֵשׁ בּוֹ טַעַם יַיִן – הֲרֵי זֶה אָסוּר.

One who vows: Wine is forbidden **to** me, **is permitted to** eat **a cooked dish that has the flavor of wine.** However, if he **said: This wine is** ***konam*** for me, and for **that** reason **I will not taste** it, **and** the wine **fell into a cooked dish, if** the dish **contains** an amount of the wine **that gives** it **flavor, it is forbidden.**

LANGUAGE

Ashishim – **אֲשִׁישִׁים:** The source of this word is obscure. Although it appears in the Bible (see Hosea 3:1), most Bible commentaries interpret that it means goblets or cups, perhaps similar to the word *ashashit*, lantern. This interpretation does not fit the context of the Gemara. Other biblical commentaries, however, explain that it means cakes (Rashi on Song of Songs 2:5), which fits the context here according to the Jerusalem Talmud.

HALAKHA

In the Rabbis' locale, etc. – בְּאַתְרָא דְּרַבָּנַן וכו׳: The Rema cites the Ran, that in a place where whey is called milk whey, one who vows that milk is forbidden to him is prohibited from eating whey as well (*Shulḥan Arukh*, *Yoreh De'a* 217:11).

NOTES

Ashishim – **אֲשִׁישִׁים:** The Rambam defines *ashishim* as a dish made from lentils and flour. In the Commentary on *Nedarim*, *ashishim* is defined as bread into which lentil flour was mixed. The Ran cites the Jerusalem Talmud, in which it is stated that *ashishim* consists of fried lentils flavored with honey. According to *Tosafot* and the Meiri, *ashishim* is the waste product of lentils.

In the Rabbis' locale, etc. – בְּאַתְרָא דְּרַבָּנַן וכו׳: According to the Commentary on *Nedarim*, the Gemara's answer is that there is no fundamental dispute between Rabbi Yosei and the Rabbis. Rather, the ruling depends on the vernacular. In Rabbi Yosei's locale, whey was referred to as milk whey, and therefore a prohibition on milk would include whey, whereas in the Rabbis' locale whey was simply called whey. Accordingly, the proposition must logically continue that in the case of *ashishim* the opposite was true. Where the Rabbis lived it was referred to as lentil *ashishim*, and in Rabbi Yosei's town it was merely called *ashishim*. Therefore, a prohibition on lentils includes *ashishim* only in the location of the Rabbis.

The Ran, however, contends that there is a fundamental disagreement between Rabbi Yosei and the Rabbis. Rabbi Yosei maintains that the criteria for being included as the object of a vow is being identified by name. Therefore, *ashishim* is not included in a prohibition on lentils, although it is a lentil dish. Whey, however, is referred to as milk whey in the vernacular, and it is therefore included in a prohibition on milk. Conversely, the Rabbis maintain that anything that has been substantially transformed from its previous state is no longer included in the vow. Consequently, whey is permitted while *ashishim* is forbidden.

מתני׳ הַנּוֹדֵר מִן הָעֲנָבִים – מוּתָּר בְּיַיִן, מִן הַזֵּיתִים – מוּתָּר בְּשֶׁמֶן. אָמַר ״קוֹנָם זֵיתִים וַעֲנָבִים אֵלּוּ שֶׁאֵינִי טוֹעֵם״ – אָסוּר בָּהֶן וּבַיּוֹצֵא מֵהֶן.

MISHNA **One who vows that grapes are forbidden to him**[H] is **permitted to** partake **of wine. One** who vows that **olives** are forbidden **to him is permitted to** partake of **oil.** However, if one **said: Olives and grapes are** *konam* for me, and for **that** reason **I will not taste these** items, he is **prohibited** from tasting **them and** the wine and oil **that emerge from them.**

גמ׳ בָּעֵי רָמִי בַּר חָמָא: ״אֵלּוּ״ דַּוְקָא, אוֹ ״שֶׁאֵינִי טוֹעֵם״ דַּוְקָא?

GEMARA With regard to the last ruling in the mishna, that one who vows: Olives and grapes are *konam* for me, and for that reason I will not taste these items, he is prohibited from tasting them and the wine and oil that emerge from them, **Rami bar Ḥama raises a dilemma:** Is it **specifically** because he said **these,**[N] i.e., he referred to specific olives or grapes, **or** is it **specifically** because he said: For **that** reason **I will not taste,**[H] i.e., he referred not to eating but to tasting?

אִי סָלְקָא דַּעְתָּךְ ״אֵלּוּ״ דַּוְקָא: ״שֶׁאֵינִי טוֹעֵם״ לָמָּה לִי? הָא קָא מַשְׁמַע לָן: דְּאַף עַל גַּב דְּאָמַר ״שֶׁאֵינִי טוֹעֵם״ אִי דְּאָמַר ״אֵלּוּ״ – מִיתְּסַר, וְאִי לָא – לָא.

The Gemara asks: **If it enters your mind** that it is **specifically** because he said **these, why do I** need the phrase: **That I will not taste?** The Gemara answers: **This teaches us that even if he said: That I will not taste,** only **if he said** the word **these is he prohibited** from tasting oil or wine, **but if** he did **not** say the word these, he is **not** prohibited from doing so. The dilemma therefore cannot be resolved by inference from the phrasing of the vow in the mishna.

אֲמַר רָבָא, תָּא שְׁמַע: ״קוֹנָם פֵּירוֹת הָאֵלּוּ עָלַי״ ״קוֹנָם הֵן לְפִי״ – אָסוּר בְּחִילּוּפֵיהֶן וּבְגִידּוּלֵיהֶן. הָא בַּיּוֹצֵא מֵהֶן – מוּתָּר!

Rava said: Come and **hear** a resolution to this dilemma from the mishna below (57a): If one says: **This produce is *konam* upon me,** or: **It is *konam* to my mouth, he is prohibited from** eating **their replacements and** anything that **grows from them.** It may be inferred that liquids **that emerge from them are permitted.** Evidently, referring to specific produce is not sufficient to render their juice forbidden. Rather, the prohibition in the mishna is apparently due to the phrase: And for that reason I will not taste.

הוּא הַדִּין דַּאֲפִילּוּ בַּיּוֹצֵא מֵהֶן אָסוּר, וְהָא עֲדִיפָא לֵיהּ לְאַשְׁמוּעִינַן, דְּחִילּוּפֵיהֶן כְּגִידּוּלֵיהֶן דָּמֵי.

The Gemara refutes this proof: **The same** ruling as in the mishna above **is true** with regard to liquids **that emerge from** the produce; they **too are forbidden. And** the reason this ruling isn't mentioned there is that **it is preferable for** that mishna **to teach us that their replacements are** forbidden just **like what grows from them** is forbidden, although they contain no substance of the forbidden item.

תָּא שְׁמַע: ״שֶׁאֵינִי אוֹכֵל״ וְ״שֶׁאֵינִי טוֹעֵם״ – מוּתָּר בְּחִילּוּפֵיהֶן וּבְגִידּוּלֵיהֶן. הָא הַיּוֹצֵא מֵהֶן – אָסוּר. אַיְּידֵי דְּלָא נָסֵיב בְּרֵישָׁא יוֹצֵא מֵהֶן, לָא נָסֵיב נַמִי בְּסֵיפָא יוֹצֵא מֵהֶן.

Come and **hear** a resolution from the continuation of that same mishna: If one says: This produce is *konam* upon me, and for **that** reason **I will not eat** them, or: This produce is *konam* upon me, and for **that** reason **I will not taste** them, he **is permitted to** eat **their replacements and** anything that **grows from them.** It may be inferred that liquids **that emerge from them are forbidden.** The Gemara rejects this argument: **Since** that mishna **did not cite** liquids **that emerge from them in the first clause, it did not cite** liquids **that emerge from them in the latter clause either.** Therefore, it cannot be inferred that liquids that come from the produce are forbidden.

תָּא שְׁמַע, אָמַר רַבִּי יְהוּדָה: מַעֲשֶׂה וְאָסַר רַבִּי טַרְפוֹן עָלַי בֵּיצִים שֶׁנִּתְבַּשְּׁלוּ עִמּוֹ. אָמְרוּ לוֹ: אֵימָתַי – בִּזְמַן שֶׁאָמַר ״בָּשָׂר זֶה עָלַי״, שֶׁהַנּוֹדֵר מִן הַדָּבָר וְנִתְעָרֵב בְּאַחֵר, וְיֵשׁ בּוֹ בְּנוֹתֵן טַעַם – הֲרֵי זֶה אָסוּר.

Come and **hear** a resolution from the previous mishna (52a): **Rabbi Yehuda said:** There was **an incident where Rabbi Tarfon prohibited me from** eating even **eggs that were cooked with** meat. The **Rabbis said to him: Indeed so,** but **when** is this the *halakha*? **When** the one who took the vow **said: This meat is** forbidden **to me,** referring to a specific piece of meat. This is **because** in the case of **one who vows** that **something** is forbidden **to him and it gets mixed into another** food, **and** the latter food **contains** an amount of the forbidden food **that gives** it **flavor,** i.e., the prohibited food can be tasted in the permitted food, the mixture **is forbidden.** Evidently, referring to a specific food causes what emerges from it to be forbidden as well.

בְּ״אֵלּוּ״ לָא קָא מִיבַּעְיָא לָן דְּדַוְקָא הוּא. כִּי מִיבַּעְיָא לָן בְּ״שֶׁאֵינִי טוֹעֵם״, דַּוְקָא אוֹ לָאו דַּוְקָא?

The Gemara reinterprets the dilemma: **We do not raise the dilemma with regard to** the word **these, as** using **specifically this** word is certainly sufficient to render the liquids that come from the produce forbidden. **When we raise a dilemma, it is with regard to** the phrase: **That I will not taste** it. Is this phrase mentioned by the mishna **specifically** to teach that using it in a vow is sufficient to render the juice forbidden, **or** is it **not** mentioned **specifically** for that purpose?

HALAKHA

Grapes are forbidden to him, etc. – מִן הָעֲנָבִים וכו׳: One who vows that grapes are forbidden to him is permitted to partake of wine, even if it is freshly squeezed. Similarly, one who vows that olives are forbidden to him is permitted to consume olive oil (Rambam *Sefer Hafla'a, Hilkhot Nedarim* 5:13; 9:14; *Shulḥan Arukh, Yoreh De'a* 216:12).

Is it specifically because he said: That I will not taste them – שֶׁאֵינִי טוֹעֵם דַּוְקָא: One who vows that these grapes are forbidden to him is prohibited from eating the grapes, their juice, and anything to which they give flavor. Likewise, if one says: Grapes are *konam* for me, and for that reason I will not taste them, he is prohibited from tasting them, their juice, and anything to which they give flavor. The reason is that Rami bar Ḥama's dilemma was left unresolved, and where there is an uncertainty with regard to a Torah prohibition, one must act stringently (Rambam *Sefer Hafla'a, Hilkhot Nedarim* 5:13; *Shulḥan Arukh, Yoreh De'a* 216:12).

NOTES

Is it specifically because he said these, etc. – אֵלּוּ דַּוְקָא וכו׳: This dilemma is explained in several ways. The Rid maintains that Rami bar Ḥama's dilemma is whether oil and wine are forbidden only if one said both the word these and the phrase: I will not taste, or is either element of the vow sufficient. The Rashba disagrees, claiming that reference to tasting is certainly not sufficient. Rather, the dilemma is whether reference to a specific type of produce is enough to render its juice forbidden, or whether reference to tasting must be included as well. The Ran explains that it is obvious to Rami bar Ḥama that one of these two elements is sufficient and the other is not. He is uncertain as to which element is the sufficient one.

תָּא שְׁמַע: ״דָּג דָּגִים שֶׁאֵינִי טוֹעֵם״ – אָסוּר בָּהֶן, בֵּין גְּדוֹלִים בֵּין קְטַנִּים, בֵּין חַיִּים בֵּין מְבוּשָּׁלִים, וּמוּתָּר בְּטָרִית טְרוּפָה וּבְצִיר.

Come and hear a resolution from the mishna above (51b): If one vows: **Fish or fishes** are *konam* for me, and for **that** reason **I will not taste** them, **he is prohibited with regard to** all of **them, whether large** fish **or small,** and **whether raw or cooked. But he is permitted** to taste **minced sardines and** to taste **fish brine.** The phrase: I will not taste, clearly does not render fish brine forbidden, although it contains that which emerged from fish.

אָמַר רָבָא: וּכְבָר יָצָא מֵהֶן.

Rava said: But there is no evidence from here, as the fish brine that is permitted by the mishna may be referring to brine that **already emerged from them** before the vow was taken, and was therefore not included in the fish that were rendered forbidden by the vow. The dilemma therefore remains unresolved.

Perek **VI**
Daf **53** Amud **a**

מתני׳ הַנּוֹדֵר מִן הַתְּמָרִים – מוּתָּר בִּדְבַשׁ תְּמָרִים, מִסִּתְוָנִיּוֹת – מוּתָּר בְּחוֹמֶץ סִתְוָנִיּוֹת. רַבִּי יְהוּדָה בֶּן בְּתֵירָא אוֹמֵר: כׇּל שֶׁשֵּׁם תּוֹלַדְתּוֹ קְרוּיָה עָלָיו, וְנוֹדֵר הֵימֶנּוּ – אָסוּר בַּיּוֹצֵא הֵימֶנּוּ, וַחֲכָמִים מַתִּירִים.

MISHNA **One who vows** that **dates** are forbidden **to him**[H] **is permitted** to eat **date honey.**[N] One who vows that **late grapes**[N] are forbidden **to him is permitted** to eat **vinegar of late grapes. Rabbi Yehuda ben Beteira says:** In the case of **any** food **that the name of its derivative is called after its** name, i.e., the liquid that emerges from it bears its name, e.g., date honey or vinegar of late grapes, **and one vows** that the item itself, e.g., the grape, is forbidden to him, he is also **prohibited from** consuming the liquid **that emerges from it. But the Rabbis permit** this.

גמ׳ [חֲכָמִים] הַיְינוּ תַּנָּא קַמָּא!

GEMARA The statement of **the Rabbis is** identical to the statement of **the first** ***tanna*** of the mishna, who rules that one who vows that dates are forbidden to him is permitted to eat date honey. What is the difference between them?

אִיכָּא בֵּינַיְיהוּ הָדָא דְּתַנְיָא: כְּלָל זֶה אָמַר רַבִּי שִׁמְעוֹן בֶּן אֶלְעָזָר: כׇּל שֶׁדַּרְכּוֹ לֶאֱכוֹל, וְדֶרֶךְ הַיּוֹצֵא מִמֶּנּוּ לֶאֱכוֹל, כְּגוֹן תְּמָרִים וּדְבַשׁ תְּמָרִים, נָדַר בּוֹ – אָסוּר בַּיּוֹצֵא מִמֶּנּוּ, נוֹדֵר מִיּוֹצֵא מִמֶּנּוּ – אָסוּר בּוֹ.

The Gemara answers: **There is** a difference **between them** with regard to **that which is taught**[N] in a *baraita*: **Rabbi Shimon ben Elazar said this principle:** With regard to **anything that is commonly eaten** in its existing form, **and it is** also **common to eat** the liquid **that emerges from it, for example, dates and date honey,** if one **vowed** that **it is forbidden to him,** he is also **prohibited** from consuming the liquid **that emerges from it.** Similarly, if **one vows** that the liquid **that emerges from it** is forbidden to him, he is also **prohibited from** partaking **of it.**

HALAKHA

Dates are forbidden to him, etc. – מִן הַתְּמָרִים וכו׳: One who vows that dates are forbidden to him is permitted to eat date honey, and one who vows that late grapes are forbidden to him is permitted to eat their vinegar, in accordance with the ruling of the first *tanna* in the mishna (Rambam *Sefer Hafla'a, Hilkhot Nedarim* 9:14; *Shulḥan Arukh, Yoreh De'a* 217:13).

NOTES

Permitted to eat date honey – מוּתָּר בִּדְבַשׁ תְּמָרִים: The commentaries raise a difficulty: There is a dispute in the mishna between Rabbi Yosei and the Rabbis whether one who vows not to partake of milk may eat whey (51b). The Gemara explains that both sides concede that it depends on the vernacular (52b). In a place where whey is called milk whey, it is forbidden, as the word milk is included in its name, and where it is merely referred to as whey, it is permitted. Accordingly, this mishna seems to contradict both sides of the dispute, as the phrase date honey includes the word date, and nevertheless it is permitted to one who vows that dates are forbidden to him. This problem exists with regard to vinegar of late grapes as well.

The Rashba answers that the two *mishnayot* are not comparable, as whey is not substantially transformed from its milk state, whereas date honey and vinegar of late grapes have changed from fruit to an entirely different substance. Therefore, the ruling for the latter foods is more lenient. The Ran explains that whey is called milk whey after the milk from which it was extracted, whereas date honey is referred to as such only to differentiate between it and other types of honey. Therefore, according to the first *tanna* of the mishna, it is permitted.

Late grapes [*sitvaniyot*] – סִתְוָנִיּוֹת: Most commentaries explain that *sitvaniyot* are grapes that do not ripen fully in the summer and remain on the vine until winter [*stav*]. These grapes never reach a fully ripened state and are barely edible, which is why they are used in the production of vinegar. The Rosh cites an alternate version of the text, which reads: *Sefoniyot*, which he takes to mean grapes from the end [*sof*] of the season. Others explain, probably in accordance with the version of the text cited by the Rosh, that it refers to poor-quality grapes from the ends of the vineyard (*Tosefot Rabbeinu Peretz*).

There is a difference between them with regard to that which is taught, etc. – אִיכָּא בֵּינַיְיהוּ הָדָא דְּתַנְיָא: What difference is derived from Rabbi Shimon ben Elazar's opinion? Several commentaries explain that the Rabbis follow Rabbi Shimon ben Elazar's opinion that if the produce mentioned in the vow is not commonly eaten, the produce is permitted and its derivative is forbidden. This is contrary to the opinion of the first *tanna* that the produce is always forbidden and its derivative is permitted (Commentary on *Nedarim*; Ran). Another explanation, cited in *Tosafot*, is that the Rabbis agree with Rabbi Shimon ben Elazar's opinion only insofar as to prohibit the derivative of a type of produce that is not commonly eaten. Otherwise, they agree with the first *tanna*. A third opinion, also cited in *Tosafot*, is that the first *tanna* concedes that if the produce is inedible, its derivative is forbidden. The dispute is with regard to the produce itself: The first *tanna* holds that it is prohibited, whereas the Rabbis follow Rabbi Shimon ben Elazar's opinion that it is forbidden. This explanation posits that late grapes are in fact commonly eaten.

כָּל שֶׁאֵין דַּרְכּוֹ לֶאֱכוֹל, וְדֶרֶךְ הַיּוֹצֵא מִמֶּנּוּ לֶאֱכוֹל, נוֹדֵר בּוֹ – אֵין אָסוּר אֶלָּא בַּיּוֹצֵא מִמֶּנּוּ, שֶׁלֹּא נִתְכַּוֵּון זֶה אֶלָּא לַיּוֹצֵא מִמֶּנּוּ.

The *baraita* continues: Conversely, with regard to **anything that is not commonly eaten** as it is, **and it is common to eat the liquid that emerges from it,** if one **vowed** that he will not eat **from it,** he is **prohibited from** consuming **only** the liquid **that emerges from it, as this** person **intended to** prohibit himself from eating **only** from the liquid **that emerges from it.** The first *tanna* does not distinguish between dates, which are commonly eaten in their original state, and late grapes, which are not. In both cases, he rules that the produce itself is forbidden and the derivative is permitted. By contrast, the Rabbis agree with Rabbi Shimon ben Elazar's ruling with regard to produce that is not commonly eaten in its original state. They permit the produce itself and prohibit that which has emerged from it. Therefore, in the last case of the mishna, they permit eating the late grapes and prohibit eating their vinegar, whereas in the first case they prohibit both dates and date honey.

מתני׳ הַנּוֹדֵר מִן הַיַּיִן – מוּתָּר בְּיֵין תַּפּוּחִים, מִן הַשֶּׁמֶן – מוּתָּר בְּשֶׁמֶן שׁוּמְשְׁמִין, מִן הַדְּבַשׁ – מוּתָּר בִּדְבַשׁ תְּמָרִים,

MISHNA **One who vows** that **wine** is forbidden **to him**[H] **is permitted** to partake of **apple wine,** i.e., cider, as the unspecified term wine refers only to grape wine. One who vows that **oil is** forbidden **to** him is **permitted** to partake of **sesame oil,** as the unspecified term oil refers only to olive oil. One who vows that **honey** is forbidden to him is **permitted** to eat **date honey,** as the unspecified term honey refers only to bee honey.

מִן הַחוֹמֶץ – מוּתָּר בְּחוֹמֶץ סִתְוָנִיּוֹת, מִן הַכְּרֵישִׁין – מוּתָּר בְּקַפְלוֹטוֹת, מִן הַיָּרָק – מוּתָּר בְּיַרְקוֹת הַשָּׂדֶה, שֶׁהוּא שֵׁם לְוַוי.

One who vows that **vinegar** is forbidden to him is **permitted** to partake of **vinegar of late grapes,** as vinegar is typically made from wine. One who vows that **leeks**[B] are forbidden to him is **permitted** to eat ***kaflutot***,[NL] a type of leek. One who vows that **vegetables** are forbidden to him is **permitted** to eat wild **field vegetables, as this** type of vegetable has **a modifier**[B] and is not referred to by the unspecified term vegetable.

גמ׳ תַּנְיָא: הַנּוֹדֵר מִן הַשֶּׁמֶן, בְּאֶרֶץ יִשְׂרָאֵל – מוּתָּר בְּשֶׁמֶן שׁוּמְשְׁמִין וְאָסוּר בְּשֶׁמֶן זַיִת, וּבְבָבֶל – אָסוּר בְּשֶׁמֶן שׁוּמְשְׁמִין וּמוּתָּר בְּשֶׁמֶן זַיִת, מְקוֹם שֶׁמִּסְתַּפְּקִין מִזֶּה וּמִזֶּה – אָסוּר בָּזֶה וּבָזֶה.

GEMARA **It is taught** in a *baraita*: With regard to **one who vows** that **oil** is forbidden **to him,**[H] if he is **in Eretz Yisrael** he is **permitted to** eat **sesame oil and** is **prohibited from** eating **olive oil,** as in Eretz Yisrael the unspecified term oil refers to olive oil. **And** if he took the vow **in Babylonia, sesame oil** is **forbidden** to him, as oil in Babylonia was generally made from sesame seeds, **and** it is **permitted** for him **to** eat **olive oil,** which was rarely used there. If he takes the vow in **a locale where** people **use** both **this** type of oil **and that** type, **he is prohibited from** eating both **this** type **and that.**

HALAKHA

Wine is forbidden to him – מִן הַיַּיִן: One who vows that wine is forbidden to him is permitted to partake of apple wine. Similarly, one who vows that oil is forbidden to him is permitted to eat sesame oil. One who vows that honey is forbidden to him is permitted to eat date honey. One who vows that vinegar is forbidden to him is permitted to eat the vinegar of late grapes. One who vows that vegetables are forbidden to him is permitted to eat field vegetables. This is because the names of all these foods have modifiers, and the one who took the vow mentioned only the unspecified term (Rambam *Sefer Hafla'a, Hilkhot Nedarim* 9:14; *Shulḥan Arukh, Yoreh De'a* 217:14–15).

Oil is forbidden to him – מִן הַשֶּׁמֶן: With regard to one who vows that oil is forbidden to him, if he is in a locale where olive oil is used, e.g., Eretz Yisrael, he is permitted to partake of other types of oil. If sesame oil is the oil that is used in his locale, he may not eat that type of oil but is permitted to partake of other kinds. If both olive and sesame oil are used where he lives, he is prohibited from eating both, even if the majority of the people use only one of them. However, the Rambam rules that one is not liable to receive lashes for eating the type of oil that is used only by a minority of the residents (Rambam *Sefer Hafla'a, Hilkhot Nedarim* 9:5; *Shulḥan Arukh, Yoreh De'a* 217:17).

NOTES

***Kaflutot* – קַפְלוֹטוֹת:** All commentaries agree that *kaflutot* are a type of leek. However, they describe them differently. Some claim that they are larger than regular leeks (*Arukh*; Commentary on *Nedarim*, as cited by *Baḥ*). The Rambam writes that they are a type of leek native to Eretz Yisrael. Rabbi Avraham min HaHar describes them as leeks that grow in the desert.

LANGUAGE

***Kaflutot* – קַפְלוֹטוֹת:** From the Greek κεφαλωτός, *kephalotos*, meaning head or small head. In this context it refers to the thick heads of leeks.

BACKGROUND

Leeks – כְּרֵישִׁין: *Allium porrum*, known as *kerishin* or *karti* in the Talmud, is an edible vegetable botanically related to onion and garlic. Its long, flat leaves, ranging from 5–30 cm in length, form the equivalent of a stalk. Nowadays these leaves are primarily eaten cooked, as seasoning in soup or with meat. In the Far East, however, leeks are still eaten raw. Some commentaries note that the *ḥatzir* mentioned among the foods desired by those who left Egypt (see Numbers 11:5) refers to leeks, which were commonly grown in vegetable gardens in ancient Egypt.

Leeks

Modifier – שֵׁם לְוַוי: A modifier is a special appellation added to the name of an item so as to distinguish the item from the normal meaning of the word. For example, typical vinegar in talmudic times was made from sour grape juice, so the unspecified word vinegar would refer to that type of vinegar. Adding the modifier: Of late grapes, as in the mishna, indicates that one is referring to a different type of vinegar. The unspecified word wine refers to wine made from grapes. Its unmodified form does not include wine or cider made from other fruits. The unspecified word vegetables refers to vegetables cultivated in a garden, as opposed to the modified term: Field vegetables. It is implied in the *baraita* that the general meaning of a word depends on the local custom. In a place where people use mainly sesame oil, that oil is considered regular oil, and olive oil is referred to as olive oil. This definition can also depend on the time of reference. During the Sabbatical Year, the unspecified term vegetables refers to field vegetables as opposed to garden-grown ones.

פְּשִׁיטָא! לָא צְרִיכָא, דְּרוּבָּא מִן חַד מִסְתַּפְּקִין. מַהוּ דְּתֵימָא: אֵיזִיל בָּתַר רוּבָּא, קָא מַשְׁמַע לָן: סְפֵק אִיסּוּרָא לְחוּמְרָא.

The Gemara asks with regard to the last statement: **Isn't** it **obvious** that he is prohibited from eating both types of oil? The statement seems superfluous. The Gemara answers: **No,** it is not superfluous. It is **necessary** only to teach that this is the *halakha* even **where most** people **use** only **one** type of oil. **Lest you say: I should follow the majority** and permit the other kind of oil, the *baraita* **teaches us** that **an uncertain** Torah **prohibition** is treated **stringently.** Therefore, the other type is forbidden as well, as it is possibly included in the meaning of the vow, although it is used only by a minority of the residents.

הַנּוֹדֵר מִן הַיָּרָק בִּשְׁאָר שְׁנֵי שָׁבוּעַ – אָסוּר בְּיַרְקוֹת הַגִּינָּה וּמוּתָּר בְּיַרְקוֹת הַשָּׂדֶה, וּבַשְּׁבִיעִית אָסוּר בְּיַרְקוֹת הַשָּׂדֶה וּמוּתָּר בְּיַרְקוֹת הַגִּינָּה. אָמַר רַבִּי אַבָּהוּ מִשּׁוּם רַבִּי חֲנִינָא בֶּן גַּמְלִיאֵל:

The *baraita* continues: With regard to **one who vows** that **vegetables** are forbidden **to** him, if he takes the vow **during the** first six **years of the seven-year** Sabbatical **cycle,** he is **prohibited from** eating **garden vegetables and permitted to** eat **field vegetables. But** if he takes the vow **during the Sabbatical Year,** he is **prohibited from** eating **field vegetables,** which are commonly eaten in the Sabbatical Year, **and** he is **permitted to** eat **garden vegetables,** which are rarely consumed during that period, as it is prohibited to work the land. **Rabbi Abbahu said in the name of Rabbi Ḥanina ben Gamliel:**

Perek **VI**
Daf **53** Amud **b**

לֹא שָׁנוּ אֶלָּא בְּמָקוֹם שֶׁאֵין מְבִיאִין יָרָק מִחוּצָה לָאָרֶץ לָאָרֶץ, אֲבָל בְּמָקוֹם שֶׁמְּבִיאִין יָרָק מִחוּצָה לָאָרֶץ לָאָרֶץ – אָסוּר.

They taught that if he takes the vow in the Sabbatical Year he is permitted to eat garden vegetables **only** if he is **in a place where** people **do not bring vegetables from outside** of **Eretz** Yisrael **to Eretz** Yisrael. **However, in a place where** people **bring vegetables from outside** of **Eretz** Yisrael, where the *halakhot* of the Sabbatical Year do not apply, **to Eretz** Yisrael, he is **prohibited** from eating garden vegetables as well, as they are widely available, and therefore included in the unspecified word vegetable.

כְּתַנָּאֵי: אֵין מְבִיאִין יָרָק מִן חוּצָה לָאָרֶץ לָאָרֶץ. רַבִּי חֲנַנְיָה בֶּן גַּמְלִיאֵל אוֹמֵר: מְבִיאִין יָרָק מִחוּצָה לָאָרֶץ לָאָרֶץ. מַאי טַעְמֵיהּ דְּמַאן דְּאָמַר אֵין מְבִיאִין? אָמַר רַבִּי יִרְמְיָה: מִשּׁוּם גּוּשׁ.

The Gemara comments that this distinction is **like** a dispute between *tanna'im* cited in a *baraita*: **One may not bring vegetables from outside** of **Eretz** Yisrael **to Eretz** Yisrael. **Rabbi Ḥananya ben Gamliel says: One may bring vegetables from outside** of **Eretz** Yisrael **to Eretz** Yisrael. The Gemara asks: **What is the reason of the one who said** that **one may not bring** vegetables from outside of Eretz Yisrael? **Rabbi Yirmeya said:** It is **because a clod** of earth might be brought with the vegetables to Eretz Yisrael. Earth from outside of Eretz Yisrael is ritually impure, and bringing it to Eretz Yisrael would spread ritual impurity in the land.

מתני׳ מִן הַכְּרוּב – אָסוּר בְּאִיסְפַּרְגּוֹס, מִן הָאִיסְפַּרְגּוֹס – מוּתָּר בִּכְרוּב.

MISHNA One who vows that **cabbage** is forbidden **to him**[H] **is prohibited from** eating ***ispargus***,[NLB] as that is a type of cabbage. However, one who vows that ***ispargus*** is forbidden **to** him is **permitted to eat cabbage.** One who vows that **pounded beans** are forbidden **to** him **is prohibited from** eating pounded bean **stew** [***mikpa***].[L] **However, Rabbi Yosei** rules that he is **permitted** to eat it.

HALAKHA

Cabbage is forbidden to him, etc. – מִן הַכְּרוּב: One who vows that cabbage is forbidden to him is prohibited from eating *ispargus*. However, one who vows that *ispargus* is forbidden to him is permitted to eat cabbage. Likewise, one who vows that pounded beans are forbidden to him is prohibited from eating pounded bean stew, whereas one who vows that stew is forbidden to him is permitted to eat pounded beans. One who vows that stew is forbidden to him is prohibited from eating garlic, but one who vows that garlic is forbidden to him is permitted to eat stew (Rambam *Sefer Hafla'a, Hilkhot Nedarim* 9:10; *Shulḥan Arukh, Yoreh De'a* 217:10).

NOTES

Ispargus – אִיסְפַּרְגּוֹס: Several commentaries maintain that this is a kind of cabbage (Commentary on *Nedarim*; Rosh). Rav Hai Gaon is cited in the *Arukh* as explaining that it is a drink made from cabbage soaked in wine. The Rambam states that *ispargus* is water in which cabbage was pickled. It is forbidden because the water in which a food was pickled shares its name. The Rid agrees with the Rambam's definition. However, he claims that only with regard to a vegetable that is not commonly eaten raw, are the vegetable and its pickled water considered one and the same with regard to vows. In talmudic times this was true of cabbage.

LANGUAGE

Ispargus – אִיסְפַּרְגּוֹס: From the Greek ἀσπάραγος, *asparagos*, this word refers to a species of cabbage that was ground up, soaked in wine, and used as an energy drink. The term may be connected to the Greek σπάραγμα, *sparagma*, which means something crushed or ground.

Stew [*mikpa*] – מִקְפָּה: Apparently a thick cooked dish that was composed mainly of ground grits. Garlic was added to give it flavor.

BACKGROUND

Ispargus – אִיסְפַּרְגּוֹס: Some identify *ispargus* as a type of cabbage. Others are of the opinion that this is a reference to the stalk of kale, a vegetable similar to wild cabbage.

Kale bundle

מִן הַגְּרִיסִין – אָסוּר בְּמִקְפָּה, וְרַבִּי יוֹסֵי מַתִּיר. מִן הַמִּקְפָּה – מוּתָּר בִּגְרִיסִין, מִן הַמִּקְפָּה – אָסוּר בְּשׁוּם, וְרַבִּי יוֹסֵי מַתִּיר. מִן הַשּׁוּם – מוּתָּר בְּמִקְפָּה.

One who vows that **pounded beans** are forbidden **to** him is **prohibited from** eating pounded bean **stew. However, Rabbi Yosei** rules that he is **permitted** to eat it. One who vows that pounded bean **stew** is forbidden **to** him **is permitted to** eat **pounded beans**[N] according to all opinions. One who vows that **stew** is forbidden **to** him **is prohibited from** eating the **garlic**[N] of the stew. **However, Rabbi Yosei** rules that he is **permitted** to eat the garlic. One who vows that **garlic** is forbidden **to** him **is permitted to** eat **stew.**[N]

מִן הָעֲדָשִׁים – אָסוּר בַּאֲשִׁישִׁים, רַבִּי יוֹסֵי מַתִּיר. מִן הָאֲשִׁישִׁים – מוּתָּר בַּעֲדָשִׁים.

One who vows that **lentils** are forbidden **to** him **is prohibited from** eating *ashishim*, a dish made from lentils. However, **Rabbi Yosei permits** it. It is agreed by all opinions that one who vows that *ashishim* is forbidden **to** him **is permitted to** eat **lentils.**

״חִטָּה חִטִּין שֶׁאֲנִי טוֹעֵם״ – אָסוּר בָּהֶן, בֵּין קֶמַח בֵּין הַפַּת. ״גְּרִיס גְּרִיסִין שֶׁאֲנִי טוֹעֵם״ – אָסוּר בָּהֶן, בֵּין חַיִּין בֵּין מְבוּשָּׁלִין. רַבִּי יְהוּדָה אוֹמֵר: ״קוֹנָם גְּרִיס אוֹ חִטָּה שֶׁאֲנִי טוֹעֵם״ – מוּתָּר לָכוּס חַיִּים.

If one says: *Ḥitta*, wheat in singular form, or *ḥittim*,[N] wheat in plural form, are *konam* for me, and for **that** reason **I will not taste** them, he is **prohibited from** eating wheat, **whether** as **flour or bread.** If one says: **Pounded bean** or **pounded beans** are *konam* for me, and for **that** reason **I will not taste** them, he is **prohibited from** eating **them, whether raw or cooked. Rabbi Yehuda says**[N] that if one says: **Pounded bean or *ḥitta* is *konam*** for me, and for **that** reason I will not **taste** them, he is **permitted to chew** them **raw,** as that is not the normal way to eat them, and therefore was not included in the intention of the vow.

גמ׳ תַּנְיָא, רַבִּי שִׁמְעוֹן בֶּן גַּמְלִיאֵל אוֹמֵר: ״חִטָּה שֶׁאֲנִי טוֹעֵם״ – אָסוּר לֶאֱפוֹת וּמוּתָּר לָכוּס: ״חִטִּים שֶׁאֲנִי טוֹעֵם״ – אָסוּר לָכוּס וּמוּתָּר לֶאֱפוֹת: ״חִטָּה חִטִּין שֶׁאֲנִי טוֹעֵם״ – אָסוּר בֵּין לָכוּס בֵּין לֶאֱפוֹת.

GEMARA **It is taught** in a *baraita* that **Rabbi Shimon ben Gamliel says** that if one vows: *Ḥitta* is *konam* for me, and for **that** reason **I will not taste**[N] it, he is **prohibited from** eating **baked** wheat, i.e., baked wheat bread, **but** he is **permitted to chew** wheat grains. If one says: *Ḥittim* are *konam* for me, and for **that** reason **I will not taste** them, he is **prohibited from chewing** wheat grains **but** is **permitted to bake** them, as this term is referring to grains of wheat. If one says: *Ḥitta* or *ḥittin* are *konam* for me, and for **that** reason **I will not taste**[H] them, he is **prohibited both from chewing** wheat grains and **from baking** wheat bread.

״גְּרִיס שֶׁאֲנִי טוֹעֵם״ – אָסוּר לְבַשֵּׁל וּמוּתָּר לָכוּס: ״גְּרִיסִין שֶׁאֲנִי טוֹעֵם״ – אָסוּר לָכוּס וּמוּתָּר לְבַשֵּׁל: ״גְּרִיס גְּרִיסִין שֶׁאֲנִי טוֹעֵם״ – אָסוּר בֵּין לְבַשֵּׁל בֵּין לָכוּס.

Similarly, if one says: **Pounded bean** is *konam* for me, and for **that** reason **I will not taste**[H] it, he is **prohibited from cooking** pounded bean, i.e., from eating a dish of cooked pounded beans, as that is what the word pounded bean commonly means, **but** he is **permitted to chew** raw pounded beans. If one says: **Pounded beans** are *konam* for me, and for **that** reason **I** will not **taste** them, he is **prohibited from chewing** pounded beans **but** is **permitted to cook** them. If one says: **Pounded bean** or **pounded beans** are *konam* for me, and for **that** reason **I** will not **taste** them, he is **prohibited from both cooking and chewing** pounded beans.

הדרן עליך הנודר מן המבושל

NOTES

One who vows that stew is forbidden to him is permitted to eat pounded beans – מִן הַמִּקְפָּה מוּתָּר בִּגְרִיסִין: First, this is because not all stews are made from pounded beans. Furthermore, stew is only one particular dish made from pounded beans.

One who vows that stew is forbidden to him is prohibited from eating the garlic – מִן הַמִּקְפָּה אָסוּר בְּשׁוּם: Some commentaries maintain that this refers to the garlic in the stew (Rabbi Natan bar Yosef, cited in *Shita Mekubbetzet*). Others claim that it refers to garlic in general. Although he is permitted to eat pounded beans, garlic is forbidden, as garlic was the main flavor in stew, and no stew was made without it, as opposed to pounded beans, which were not an essential ingredient (Rosh).

One who vows that garlic is forbidden to him is permitted to eat stew – מִן הַשּׁוּם מוּתָּר בְּמִקְפָּה: Some commentaries explain that the one who took the vow assumedly meant only raw garlic (*Shita Mekubbetzet*). Others claim that he is prohibited from eating the heads of garlic found in stew. The rest of the stew is permitted, even if it is flavored with garlic (Ritva).

Ḥitta or *ḥittin* – חִטָּה חִטִּין: One explanation is that the singular form of wheat indicates bread, whereas the plural refers to raw wheat, as elaborated in the *baraita* below. Therefore, the one who took the vow is prohibited from tasting both. Another opinion is that using both terms indicates inclusion of all forms of wheat (Rosh). The Rambam claims that the expression referred to in the mishna is wheat of wheat, which is a Hebrew form of speech that stresses greatness, e.g., the Song of Songs. This follows the Rambam's opinion mentioned with regard to fish (51b).

Rabbi Yehuda says, etc. – רַבִּי יְהוּדָה אוֹמֵר וכו׳: The wording of this statement seems to indicate a dispute between Rabbi Yehuda and the unspecified *tanna* of the mishna. This understanding is indicated by the Rambam as well (see *Tosafot* and Rid). However, the Commentary on *Nedarim* and the Rosh maintain that there is no disagreement. Rabbi Yehuda simply adds to the mishna's statement.

Ḥitta that I will not taste, etc. – חִטָּה שֶׁאֲנִי טוֹעֵם וכו׳: Why does the singular *ḥitta* refer to bread, whereas the plural *ḥittim* connotes wheat grains? In the Jerusalem Talmud, it is explained that that is simply the way people speak. The Ran explains that bread is eaten as a singular item, as opposed to grains of wheat, which are separated from each other when eaten raw.

HALAKHA

Ḥitta or *ḥittin* that I will not taste – חִטָּה חִטִּין שֶׁאֲנִי טוֹעֵם: One who vows that wheat is forbidden to him is prohibited from eating raw or cooked wheat grains. One who vows: *Ḥitta* or *ḥittin* are *konam* for me, and for that reason I will not taste them, he may not taste any wheat products, including flour and bread. One who vows: *Ḥitta* is *konam* for me, and for that reason I will not taste it, he may not taste bread. However, he is permitted to taste wheat grains. One who vows: *Ḥittim* are *konam* for me, and for that reason I will not taste them, he is permitted to taste bread but is prohibited from tasting raw grains of wheat, in accordance with the opinion of Rabban Shimon ben Gamliel (Rambam *Sefer Hafla'a*, *Hilkhot Nedarim* 9:9; *Shulḥan Arukh*, *Yoreh De'a* 217:20).

Pounded bean that I will not taste – גְּרִיס שֶׁאֲנִי טוֹעֵם: One who vows: Pounded bean is *konam* for me, and for that reason I will not taste it, is prohibited from tasting cooked pounded beans. However, he is permitted to chew raw ones. One who vows: Pounded beans are *konam* for me, and for that reason I will not taste them, is prohibited from tasting raw pounded beans and permitted to taste cooked ones. One who vows: Pounded bean or pounded beans are *konam* for me, and for that reason I will not taste them, may not taste either raw or cooked pounded beans (*Shulḥan Arukh*, *Yoreh De'a* 217:21).

Summary of **Perek VI**

This chapter discussed the meaning of terms and names of various types of food, including those which have a wide literal meaning but a narrower meaning in the vernacular. For example, the expression: Roasted food, was used only in reference to roasted meat. It was established that the vernacular is followed with regard to the interpretation of vows. Accordingly, the interpretation of a term or expression may change from place to place and from generation to generation.

A type of food that has a modifier in its name is not included in the vow if the modifier was not mentioned. Therefore, wild vegetables are not included in a vow that refers to vegetables.

If one has vowed that a particular food is forbidden to him, a derivative of that food is permitted to him unless the vow referred to a particular food item. In that case, if the forbidden food got mixed into another food, the mixture is prohibited, provided that the flavor of the forbidden food is noticeable in the mixture.

Stories about how some Sages studied Torah in poverty and others became very wealthy were related tangentially.

Introduction to **Perek VII**

This chapter is a continuation of the previous chapter in terms of the issues addressed by the Gemara, and it deals with the precise definitions of various terms and the delineation of the parameters relevant to those terms.

Unlike the previous chapter, this chapter addresses several different topics, beginning with the definition of terms relating to food and proceeding to garments, houses, beds, and places. In all these areas, the Gemara seeks to cite proofs from language usage, some from the Bible, and some from the vernacular employed in everyday conversation and the practical understanding of the scope of those terms.

Another question discussed in this chapter is: Does a prohibition generated by a vow with regard to a specific item take effect exclusively on that item, or does the prohibition remain in effect for every item that comes into being due to that item, e.g., growths from produce that was forbidden by vow, or an item exchanged for an item forbidden by vow? This question exists with regard to various Torah prohibitions as well: To what extent does the prohibition take effect upon items that grow from or are exchanged with forbidden items? To what Torah prohibition is the prohibition of vows comparable? Does the extension of the prohibition to growths apply with regard to all produce or are there differences between different kinds of produce?

At the end of the chapter, issues related to conditional vows are discussed, specifically concerning cases where the condition relates to an action that will take place in the future, while the vow is in the present.

These, among others, are the topics that will be addressed in this chapter.

מתני׳ הַנּוֹדֵר מִן הַיָּרָק – מוּתָּר בִּדְלוּעִין, וְרַבִּי עֲקִיבָא אוֹסֵר. אָמְרוּ לוֹ לְרַבִּי עֲקִיבָא: וַהֲלֹא אוֹמֵר אָדָם לִשְׁלוּחוֹ ״קַח לִי יָרָק״, וְהוּא אוֹמֵר ״לֹא מָצָאתִי אֶלָּא דְּלוּעִין״?

MISHNA For **one who vows** that **vegetables** are forbidden **to him,**[H] it **is permitted** for him **to eat gourds,**[N] as people typically do not include gourds in the category of vegetables; **and Rabbi Akiva prohibits** him from eating gourds. The Rabbis **said to Rabbi Akiva: But doesn't a person say to his agent: Purchase vegetables for me, and** the agent, after failing to find vegetables, returns with gourds and **says: I found only gourds?** This indicates that gourds are not considered vegetables.

אָמַר לָהֶם: כֵּן הַדָּבָר, אוֹ שֶׁמָּא אוֹמֵר הוּא ״לֹא מָצָאתִי אֶלָּא קִיטְנִית״? אֶלָּא שֶׁהַדְּלוּעִין בִּכְלַל יָרָק, וְקִיטְנִית אֵינוֹ בִּכְלַל יָרָק. וְאָסוּר בְּפוֹל הַמִּצְרִי לַח, וּמוּתָּר בְּיָבֵשׁ.

Rabbi Akiva **said to them: The matter is so,** and that proves my opinion; **or perhaps,** does the agent return and **say: I found only legumes? Rather,** it is apparent **that gourds are included in** the category of **vegetables,** although they differ from other vegetables, and therefore, the agent purchases gourds and explains that he found only gourds. **And legumes are not included in** the category of **vegetables,** and that is why the agent dispatched to purchase vegetables would not purchase legumes at all. **And** for one who vows that vegetables are forbidden to him, it **is prohibited to** eat **the fresh cowpea,**[B] which is considered a vegetable, **and it is permitted to** eat **dry** cowpea,[N] which is not a vegetable.

BACKGROUND

Cowpea [*pol hamitzri*] – **פּוֹל הַמִּצְרִי**: According to the Jerusalem Talmud, it appears that this plant, *pol hamitzri*, an Aramaic term literally meaning Egyptian bean, is *Vigna unguiculata* of the Fabaceae, or pea family. The stems of the cowpea climb or spread out a considerable distance. The pods are 7–13 cm long, and the beans are small. The cowpea is edible fresh or dry. Today it is grown primarily as animal fodder, but it is still consumed by humans in some parts of the world.

Cowpea beans

Flower of cowpea plant

HALAKHA

One who vows that vegetables are forbidden to him – הַנּוֹדֵר מִן הַיָּרָק: For one who vows that vegetables are forbidden to him, without elaboration, only vegetables that are eaten raw are forbidden. If he vows that vegetables of a pot are forbidden to him, both cooked and pickled vegetables are forbidden. If he vows that vegetables that are cooked in a pot are forbidden to him, pickled vegetables are permitted and cooked vegetables are forbidden. Gourds are included in this prohibition, in accordance with the ruling of Rabbi Akiva, as the Gemara deliberates with regard to his opinion, and in accordance with the conclusion of the Gemara (Rambam *Sefer Hafla'a*, *Hilkhot Nedarim* 9:10; *Shulḥan Arukh*, *Yoreh De'a* 217:4).

NOTES

For one who vows that vegetables are forbidden to him, it is permitted to eat gourds – הַנּוֹדֵר מִן הַיָּרָק מוּתָּר בִּדְלוּעִין: The Ran cites two explanations for the fact that gourds are not considered vegetables. One approach is that the term vegetables in this context refers to leaves or other edible parts of a plant, and not its fruit; gourds are fruits. Later commentaries discuss whether edible roots and bulbs are in the category of vegetables. A second explanation is that vegetables are eaten raw, while gourds are eaten only cooked. There are certain difficulties with each of these explanations, and some commentaries combine the two approaches into a single definition. The Rid explains that in common parlance, the term vegetables refers to both edible leaves, whether eaten raw, e.g., lettuce, or cooked, e.g., spinach, and to fruits of plants that grow in the ground and are eaten uncooked. Gourds are fruits that are eaten exclusively after cooking and therefore are not in that category. In the Jerusalem Talmud, it is stated that this applies only to the Egyptian gourd, which is not eaten raw at all. However, even the Rabbis concede that the Greek gourd, which is softer and eaten raw, is included in the category of vegetables.

And it is permitted to eat dry cowpea – וּמוּתָּר בְּיָבֵשׁ: The commentaries explain that the cowpea, or Egyptian bean, is a type of grain, consistent with Rabbi Meir's opinion in the next mishna. In the Jerusalem Talmud, it is stated that this distinction between fresh produce, which are vegetables, and dry ones, which are not, applies only to crops similar to the Egyptian cowpea, which are placed in a pile when dry. Other legumes, however, that are eaten raw when they are fresh, are considered vegetables even when dry.

GEMARA

גמ׳ ״הַנּוֹדֵר מִן הַיָּרָק״ כו׳. וְהָא מִן יָרָק נָדַר! אָמַר עוּלָּא: בְּאוֹמֵר ״יַרְקֵי קְדֵרָה עָלַי״. וְדִילְמָא יָרָק הַנֶּאֱכָל בִּקְדֵרָה קָאָמַר? בְּאוֹמֵר ״יָרָק הַמִּתְבַּשֵּׁל בִּקְדֵרָה עָלַי״.

GEMARA We learned in the mishna: For **one who vows** that **vegetables** are forbidden **to** him, it is permitted to eat gourds, and Rabbi Akiva prohibits him from eating gourds. The Gemara questions Rabbi Akiva's ruling: **But** how can his vow include gourds, which are fruits and not vegetables; **didn't he vow** to refrain **from** eating **vegetables?**[N] **Ulla said:** The mishna is referring **to one who said: Vegetables** cooked **in a pot** are forbidden **to me.** Gourds are included in the category of vegetables cooked in a pot. The Gemara asks: **And** if that is what he said, **perhaps he is saying: A vegetable that is eaten in a pot,** i.e., a vegetable that is added to flavor the food cooked in the pot, is forbidden to me?[N] The Gemara answers: The mishna is referring **to one who said: A vegetable that is cooked in a pot**[N] is forbidden **to me,** a statement that can include gourds.

בְּמַאי קָא מִיפַּלְגִי? רַבָּנַן סָבְרִי: כָּל מִילְּתָא דִּצְרִיךְ שְׁלִיחָא לְאִמְלוֹכֵי עֲלַהּ – לָאו מִינֵּיהּ הוּא, וְרַבִּי עֲקִיבָא סָבַר: כָּל מִילְּתָא דְּמִימְלִיךְ שְׁלִיחָא עֲלַהּ – מִינֵּיהּ הוּא. אָמַר אַבַּיֵי: מוֹדֶה רַבִּי עֲקִיבָא לְעִנְיַן מַלְקוֹת, שֶׁאֵינוֹ לוֹקֶה.

The Gemara asks: **With regard to what** principle **do** Rabbi Akiva and the Rabbis **disagree?** The Gemara explains that **the Rabbis maintain: Any item with regard to which an agent must consult** the person who dispatched him before purchasing it, **is not** considered the same **type.** Since the agent must ask whether he can purchase gourds, apparently they are not a vegetable. **And Rabbi Akiva maintains: Any item with regard to which an agent** must **consult**[HN] **is** considered the same **type.** With regard to food of a different type, he does not consult. **Abaye said: Rabbi Akiva concedes with regard to lashes that** the one who vowed **is not flogged**[N] if he ate gourds, as the issue of whether or not he violated his vow is not entirely clear.

תְּנַן הָתָם: הַשָּׁלִיחַ שֶׁעָשָׂה שְׁלִיחוּתוֹ – בַּעַל הַבַּיִת מָעַל, לֹא עָשָׂה שְׁלִיחוּתוֹ – שָׁלִיחַ מָעַל.

We learned in a mishna **there** (*Me'ila* 20a): With regard to **an agent who performed his mission**[H] properly,[N] if he was tasked to use a particular item, and the one who dispatched him forgot that it was a consecrated item, **the employer,** who dispatched him, **misused** the consecrated item and is liable, as the agent acted on his behalf. However, if the agent **did not perform his mission** properly, and the **agent misused** the consecrated item, he is liable, as once the agent deviates from his mission, he ceases to be an agent and his actions are attributable to him.

HALAKHA

Any item with regard to which an agent must consult – כָּל מִלְּתָא דְּמִימְלִיךְ שְׁלִיחָא עֲלַהּ: With regard to any item concerning which an agent consults his employer about whether it is included in the category of items that he was sent to bring, the item is included in that vow (Rambam *Sefer Hafla'a, Hilkhot Nedarim* 9:6; *Shulḥan Arukh, Yoreh De'a* 217:4).

An agent who performed his mission – הַשָּׁלִיחַ שֶׁעָשָׂה שְׁלִיחוּתוֹ: With regard to one who unwittingly gave his agent consecrated coins to purchase an item, if the agent fulfills his mission as instructed, the employer is liable for misuse of consecrated property and is liable to bring a guilt-offering. If the agent deviated from his mission, e.g., the employer instructed the agent to serve meat to his guests and he served them liver, or vice versa, the agent is liable (Rambam *Sefer Avoda, Hilkhot Me'ila* 7:1).

NOTES

But didn't he vow to refrain from eating vegetables – וְהָא מִן יָרָק נָדַר: Almost all commentaries maintain that this poses a difficulty with regard to Rabbi Akiva's opinion: How can he say that gourds are included in the category of vegetables, when, as the Ran says in his first explanation, they are certainly a fruit, or, as the Ran states in his second explanation and as the Rosh likewise explains, a vegetable is eaten raw and gourds are cooked? Rabbi Akiva explains that gourds are considered vegetables because agents return to the one who dispatched them to purchase vegetables and say that they found only gourds. According to the understanding of the commentaries, the Rabbis consider this an unsatisfactory explanation, and they wonder how a plant that is not a vegetable can be included in the vow. Others claim that this is not the primary reason for Rabbi Akiva's opinion. The Meiri states that the difficulty is in the example cited by Rabbi Akiva, as the Gemara maintains that the agent does not consider gourds in the category of vegetables at all, and an agent would not consult the one who dispatched him in that case. See Rabbi Yitzḥak Tzarfati, who contends that this poses a difficulty with regard to the opinions of both the Rabbis and Rabbi Akiva.

And perhaps he is saying: A vegetable that is eaten in a pot is forbidden to me – וְדִילְמָא יָרָק הַנֶּאֱכָל בִּקְדֵרָה קָאָמַר: Many authorities state that this suggestion is the *halakha*. It is not merely a refutation of the previous suggestion, but actually the connotation of: Vegetables in a pot. With regard to the phrase: A vegetable that is eaten in a pot, some explain that it is referring to cooked vegetables, e.g., onions and garlic, whose primary use is to flavor food cooking in a pot, rather than as foods in and of themselves (Rashi; *Tosafot*; see Ran). Others maintain that: A vegetable that is eaten in a pot, is referring to vegetables that are eaten both raw and after being cooked in a pot (Ritva; Ran). The Rosh explains that the reference is to vegetables typically pickled in a pot. Yet others state that it refers to vegetables cooked in a pot in their natural state, unlike gourds, which must first be peeled and chopped. Others explain that a vegetable that is eaten in a pot is cooked alone, as opposed to gourds, which require additional ingredients to enhance their taste.

A vegetable that is cooked in a pot – יָרָק הַמִּתְבַּשֵּׁל בִּקְדֵרָה: This is referring only to vegetables that must be cooked in a pot (Rashi), or that are generally and extensively cooked in a pot and are not eaten raw (Ran). The Rid writes that the Rabbis nevertheless maintain that the expression: Vegetables cooked in a pot, includes only vegetables that are cooked; gourds, however, are not categorized as vegetables at all.

Any item with regard to which an agent must consult, etc. – כָּל מִילְּתָא דְּמִימְלִיךְ שְׁלִיחָא וכו׳: The Meiri claims that this applies only to an agent who was given a general directive, in a case where it can be said that his inquiry refers to an item that could be included in that category. If, however, he was instructed to acquire a specific item, e.g., cabbage, then even if the agent asks about a similar item, it is not included in the vow. Several early commentaries maintain that Rabbi Akiva stated this only with regard to the specific case of vegetables and gourds, but not other vows (Rashba; Ran). However, the Meiri and several opinions cited in the *Shita Mekubbetzet* contend that according to Rabbi Akiva this applies in all cases.

That the one who vowed is not flogged – שֶׁאֵינוֹ לוֹקֶה: Various explanations were suggested for this ruling. Some commentaries maintain that even according to Rabbi Akiva, there is uncertainty whether the vow includes gourds. Although that uncertainty is sufficient to render the gourds forbidden, it is an uncertainty with regard to a Torah prohibition: He shall not profane his word" (Numbers 30:3), and he is not flogged for an uncertain transgression (*Tosafot*). Others maintain that Rabbi Akiva ruled stringently only due to the severity of the prohibition against violating vows, but he too agrees that the fact that an agent asks about something does not mean that it is definitely classified as such (Rabbeinu Tam, *Sefer HaYashar*; Rosh). Rabbi Yitzḥak Tzarfati states that the reason he is not liable to receive lashes is that the one who vowed can excuse himself by saying he did not have that food in mind, and since there is no way of proving his intention he cannot be warned with regard to lashes.

An agent who performed his mission properly – הַשָּׁלִיחַ שֶׁעָשָׂה שְׁלִיחוּתוֹ: Misuse of consecrated items is an exception to the principle: There is no agent for transgression. In most cases, the one who performs the action is liable even if he acted on behalf of another. However, it is derived from biblical verses that an agent who misuses consecrated items renders the one who dispatched him liable, just as one can acquire objects on his behalf in monetary cases and other areas of *halakha*.

מַאן תַּנָּא? אָמַר רַב חִסְדָּא: מַתְנִיתִין דְּלָא כְּרַבִּי עֲקִיבָא. דִּתְנַן כֵּיצַד? אָמַר לוֹ ״תֵּן בָּשָׂר לָאוֹרְחִים״ וְנָתַן לָהֶם כָּבֵד: ״תֵּן כָּבֵד״ וְנָתַן לָהֶם בָּשָׂר – הַשָּׁלִיחַ מָעַל. וְאִי רַבִּי עֲקִיבָא – הָא אָמַר רַבִּי עֲקִיבָא: כָּל מִילְּתָא דְּמִימְּלִיךְ עֲלָהּ שָׁלִיחַ – מִינֵּיהּ הוּא, לִמְעוֹל בַּעַל הַבַּיִת וְלָא לִמְעוֹל שָׁלִיחַ!

The Gemara asks: **Who is the** ***tanna*** who **taught** this *halakha* in the mishna? **Rav Ḥisda said: The mishna is not in accordance with** the opinion of **Rabbi Akiva as we learned** in the mishna: **How so?** If the employer **said to** the agent: **Give meat to the guests, and he gave them liver;** or if he said: **Give them** **liver, and he gave them meat, the agent has misused** the consecrated item, as he deviated from his mission. **And if** this were in accordance with the opinion of **Rabbi Akiva, didn't Rabbi Akiva say: Any matter with regard to which an agent must consult is** considered the same **type?** Since based on that criterion, liver is certainly considered meat, **let the employer** be liable **for misuse** of consecrated property[N] **and let the agent not** be liable **for misuse** of consecrated property, as he fulfilled his mission.

אָמַר אַבָּיֵי: אֲפִילּוּ תֵּימָא רַבִּי עֲקִיבָא,

Abaye said: Even if you say that the mishna is in accordance with the opinion of **Rabbi Akiva,**

NOTES

Let the employer be liable for misuse of consecrated property – לִמְעוֹל בַּעַל הַבַּיִת: The early commentaries ask: In light of the ruling that Rabbi Akiva concedes that he is not flogged, why is the employer liable for misuse, which is a prohibition for which he is liable to bring a guilt-offering, and will result in the slaughter of a non-sacred animal in the Temple courtyard? *Tosafot* answer that this does not mean that the employer is actually guilty of misuse of a consecrated item. Rather, the emphasis is on the claim that the agent is not liable for misuse. Others explain that the ruling that he is not flogged refers only to the case of gourds and vegetables, as it is clear that gourds are not a type of vegetable. Liver, however, is a kind of meat, and included in the employer's instructions (*Tosafot*; Ran). The Rid explains that Rav Ḥisda disagrees with Abaye and holds that according to Rabbi Akiva he is liable to be flogged by Torah law in the case of gourds and vegetables.

מִי לָא מוֹדֶה רַבִּי עֲקִיבָא דְּצָרִיךְ אִימְּלוּכֵי? אִיתְּמַר שְׁמַעְתָּא קַמֵּיהּ דְּרָבָא. אֲמַר לְהוֹן: שַׁפִּיר אֲמַר נַחְמָנִי.

doesn't Rabbi Akiva concede[N] **that** the agent **must consult** his employer? Because he failed to do so and acted on his own, he is not considered to have performed his mission. This *halakha* **was stated before Rava. He said to** those who stated the *halakha* before him: **Naḥmani,**[N] i.e., Abaye, **spoke well.**

מַאן תַּנָּא דִּפְלִיג עֲלֵיהּ דְּרַבִּי עֲקִיבָא – רַבָּן שִׁמְעוֹן בֶּן גַּמְלִיאֵל הִיא. דְּתַנְיָא: הַנּוֹדֵר מִן הַבָּשָׂר – אָסוּר בְּכָל מִינֵי בָּשָׂר, וְאָסוּר בָּרֹאשׁ וּבָרַגְלַיִם וּבַקָּנֶה וּבַכָּבֵד וּבַלֵּב וּבְעוֹפוֹת, וּמוּתָּר בִּבְשַׂר דָּגִים וַחֲגָבִים.

§ The Gemara asks: **Who is the** ***tanna*** **who disagrees with** the opinion **of Rabbi Akiva**[N] in the mishna here? The Gemara answers: **It is Rabban Shimon ben Gamliel, as it is taught** in a dispute in the *baraita*: For **one who vows** that **meat** is forbidden **to him,**[H] **it is prohibited** to eat **all types of meat, and it is prohibited** for him to eat meat **of the head, and of the feet, and of the windpipe, and of the liver, and of the heart,** although people do not typically eat meat from those parts of the body. **And** it is prohibited for him to eat meat **of birds,** as it too is popularly called meat. **However, it is permitted** for him to eat **of the meat of fish and grasshoppers,** as their flesh is not called meat.

HALAKHA

One who vows that meat is forbidden to him – הַנּוֹדֵר מִן הַבָּשָׂר: For one who vows that meat is forbidden to him, and therefore he will refrain from eating meat, he is prohibited from eating bird meat and the innards of an animal. If he resided in a place where an agent instructed to purchase meat would consult his employer about whether he should purchase fish, the meat of a fish is also prohibited by the vow, unless it is evident that when he vowed he meant to include only the meat of animals and birds. The *halakha* is in accordance with the opinion of Rabbi Akiva, the unattributed *baraita*, and the statement of Abaye (Rambam *Sefer Hafla'a*, *Hilkhot Nedarim* 9:6; *Shulḥan Arukh*, *Yoreh De'a* 217:8).

NOTES

Doesn't Rabbi Akiva concede – מִי לָא מוֹדֶה רַבִּי עֲקִיבָא: According to this, the halakhic distinction between vows and misuse of consecrated property by means of an agent is clear. Any item with regard to which an agent would consult his employer is in the category of foods forbidden by that vow. However, with regard to the *halakhot* of misuse, since the agent failed to consult his employer, he is considered to have acted on his own, and therefore, he alone is liable (Rashi; Ran).

Naḥmani – נַחְמָנִי: The tradition of the *ge'onim* is that Abaye's real name was Naḥmani, but since he was raised by his uncle, Rabba bar Naḥmani, he was called Abaye, which is a variation of the word *avi*, my father. He was called this either affectionately or because Rabba did not wish to call him by his father's name. The Ran, however, maintains that Naḥmani was not his real name. It was a name he received because he was raised in the house of Rabba bar Naḥmani.

Who is the ***tanna*** **who disagrees with the opinion of Rabbi Akiva – מַאן תַּנָּא דִּפְלִיג עֲלֵיהּ דְּרַבִּי עֲקִיבָא:** According to most commentaries, the question is: Who is the first *tanna* in the mishna, who disagrees with Rabbi Akiva with regard to vows? However, with regard to misuse of consecrated property, everyone agrees that even items with regard to which an agent consults his employer are not considered the same type. Rabbi Yitzḥak Tzarfati agrees that the question is: Who is the first *tanna* who disagrees with Rabbi Akiva with regard to vows? However, he holds that he is the same *tanna* that taught the unattributed mishna in tractate *Me'ila*. That *tanna* maintains that even items with regard to which an agent consults his employer are not considered the same type. Rabbi Akiva disagrees. The Rashash writes that there are three opinions with regard to these *halakhot*. According to the first *tanna*, gourds are not considered vegetables, but liver is in the category of meat. Rabbi Akiva maintains that gourds are in the category of vegetables. Rabban Shimon ben Gamliel holds that liver is not in the category of meat, and all the more so, gourds are not in the category of vegetables.

BACKGROUND

Innards – **קְרָבַיִים**: Not only in the talmudic period, but even until recent generations the internal organs of an animal were deemed insignificant relative to the main parts of the animal, i.e., the muscle and even the fat. Therefore, not only the trachea, and to a certain extent the gullet, but also the liver, spleen, heart, lungs, and other organs were eaten by the poor, who could not afford actual meat. The ethnic Jewish dishes prepared from these organs were originally eaten exclusively by the poor, or underwent special preparation for specific uses, e.g., as remedies.

רַבָּן שִׁמְעוֹן בֶּן גַּמְלִיאֵל אוֹמֵר: הַנּוֹדֵר מִן הַבָּשָׂר – אָסוּר בְּכׇל מִינֵי בָשָׂר, וּמוּתָּר בָּרֹאשׁ וּבָרַגְלַיִם וּבַקָּנֶה וּבַכָּבֵד וּבַלֵּב וּבְעוֹפוֹת, וְאֵין צָרִיךְ לוֹמַר בְּשַׂר דָּגִים וַחֲגָבִים. וְכֵן הָיָה רַבָּן שִׁמְעוֹן בֶּן גַּמְלִיאֵל אוֹמֵר: קְרָבַיִים לָאו בָּשָׂר, וְאוֹכְלֵיהֶן לָאו בַּר אֱינָשׁ. אוֹכְלֵיהֶן – כְּבָשָׂר, לְעִנְיַן זְבִינֵי – לָאו בַּר אֱינָשׁ.

Rabban Shimon ben Gamliel says: One who vows that meat is forbidden **to him, is forbidden in all types of meat, and is permitted** to eat meat **of the head, and of the feet, and of the windpipe, and of the liver, and of the heart and of birds, and needless to say** he may also partake of **fish and grasshoppers. And Rabban Shimon ben Gamliel would likewise say: Innards**[B] **are not** considered **meat, and one who eats them is not a person,** meaning that the innards are not fit for human consumption. The Gemara elaborates: With regard to **one who eats them,** in terms of the *halakhot* related to their consumption, e.g., vows, they are considered **as meat.** However, **with regard to purchase,**[N] one who purchases them **is not a person.** In any case, apparently, Rabban Shimon ben Gamliel disagrees with Rabbi Akiva, as he maintains that although if an agent fails to find meat he is required to consult his employer before replacing it with liver, it is not considered meat with regard to vows.

מַאי שְׁנָא בְּשַׂר עוֹף לְתַנָּא קַמָּא דַּאֲסִיר – דַּעֲבֵיד שְׁלִיחָא דְּמִימְלִיךְ עֲלֵיהּ. בְּשַׂר דָּגִים נַמִי עֲבִיד שְׁלִיחָא דְּאִי לָא מַשְׁכַּח בִּישְׂרָא מִימְלִיךְ עֲלֵיהּ, דְּאָמַר: אִי לָא מַשְׁכַּחְנָא בִּישְׂרָא – אַיְיתֵי דָּגִים? וְלִיתַּסְרוּ!

The Gemara asks: **What is different** about **the meat of a bird according to the first** ***tanna*****, that he prohibits it** since it is considered meat, due to the fact **that** when **the agent** fails to find meat, **he tends to consult** his employer **about it?** The same should be true of the **meat of fish too.**[N] **If the agent does not find meat, he tends to consult** his employer **about it, as he says: If I do not find**[N] **meat, should I bring fish? And** therefore, **let** fish also **be forbidden** according to the first *tanna*.

NOTES

With regard to one who eats them they are considered as meat; with regard to purchase, etc. – **אוֹכְלֵיהֶן כְּבָשָׂר לְעִנְיַן זְבִינֵי וכו׳**: This is a difficult passage and is omitted in variant readings cited by many commentaries. Rashi explains that innards are considered meat with regard to vows, as they are fattier than other interior organs. Even Rabban Shimon ben Gamliel agrees that they are in the category of meat (see Rashba). With regard to purchase, however, one who buys innards at the price of meat is not considered levelheaded. Rabbi Avraham min HaHar questions Rashi's difficult explanation. He explains that the term innards refers to the previously listed internal organs, the windpipe, liver, heart, etc. All these are not in the category of meat with regard to vows, and likewise one who purchases them is not a person. A similar explanation appears in the *Berit Ya'akov*, citing the *ge'onim*. The Meiri adds that innards are not in the category of meat, in the sense that one who stipulated to give meat to another may not give him innards. Likewise they differ from meat in the sense that they do not strengthen the heart at all. The author of the *Berit Ya'akov* adds that for that reason one should not eat innards after bloodletting.

Meat of fish too – **בְּשַׂר דָּגִים נַמִי**: The Rambam rules in accordance with the opinion of Rabbi Akiva that any item with regard to which the agent consults his employer is considered the same type with regard to vows. However, in the case of meat he distinguishes between the meat of birds, which is certainly in the category of meat, and the meat of fish and grasshoppers, whose status depends on whether an agent would consult his employer about them. The early commentaries question the ruling of the Rambam, as it is clear from the Gemara that only in rare cases, e.g., that it is not to be eaten after bloodletting, fish does not fall under the category of meat. Some authorities rejected the Rambam's ruling in accordance with the opinion of Rabbi Akiva (see *Shita Mekubbetzet*); others rejected his opinion with regard to fish (Rashba). According to other commentaries, the Rambam's ruling is based on an unattributed mishna in *Ḥullin* (104a), where it is stated that for one who vows that meat is forbidden to him, it is permitted for him to eat fish and grasshoppers. They contend that the contrary opinion in the Gemara here is merely a refutation of the previous statement, and not a normative halakhic ruling (Rabbi Avraham min HaHar). See the Meiri, whose opinion differs slightly from that of the Rambam.

As he says: If I do not find – **דְּאָמַר אִי לָא מַשְׁכַּחְנָא**: The Maharik in his responsa explains that the employer says to himself that if his agent fails to find meat he should buy fish. Therefore, the agent who senses his employer's wishes consults him in that regard.

אֲמַר אַבַּיֵי: כְּגוֹן שֶׁהִקִּיז דָּם, דְּלָא אָכֵיל דָּגִים. אִי הָכִי אֲפִילּוּ עוֹפוֹת נַמִי לָא אָכֵיל, דְּאָמַר שְׁמוּאֵל: דְּמִסּוֹכַר וְאָכֵיל בִּישְׂרָא דְּצִפְּרָא – פָּרַח לִבֵּיהּ כְּצִפְּרָא. וְתַנְיָא: אֵין מַקִּיזִין לֹא עַל דָּגִים וְלֹא עַל עוֹפוֹת וְלֹא עַל בָּשָׂר מָלִיחַ. וְתַנְיָא: הִקִּיז דָּם – לֹא יֹאכַל לֹא חָלָב, וְלֹא גְּבִינָה, וְלֹא בֵּיצִים, וְלֹא שַׁחֲלַיִים, וְלֹא עוֹפוֹת, וְלֹא בָּשָׂר מָלִיחַ! שָׁאנֵי עוֹפוֹת דְּאֶפְשָׁר עַל יְדֵי שְׁלִיקָה.

Abaye said: This is referring to a case **where he let** his **blood**[B] when he vowed, as a person in that condition **does not eat fish.** It was common knowledge then that eating fish after bloodletting is harmful. The Gemara asks: **If so, he would not eat birds either, as Shmuel said:** With regard to one **who lets blood and eats the meat of a bird,**[N] **his heart** rate accelerates and **flies like a bird.**[B] Clearly, bird meat too is deleterious for his health. **And it is taught** in a *baraita*: **One neither lets blood before** eating **fish, nor before** eating **birds, nor before** eating **salted meat.**[N] **And it is taught** in another *baraita*: If one **let blood, he may eat neither milk, nor cheese, nor eggs, nor cress,**[B] **nor birds, nor salted meat.** The Gemara answers: Meat of **birds is different, as it is possible** to eat it safely after bloodletting **by means of** thoroughly **boiling** it.

אַבַּיֵי אֲמַר: כְּגוֹן דְּכָיְיבִין לֵיהּ עֵינֵיהּ, דְּדָגִים קָשִׁין לָעֵינַיִם. אִי הָכִי אָכֵיל דָּגִים, דְּהָא אֲמַר שְׁמוּאֵל: נו״ן סמ״ך עי״ן – נוּנָא סַמָּא לָעֵינַיִם! הַהוּא סוֹף אוּכְלָא.

Abaye said: This is referring to a case **where his eyes hurt him, as fish are harmful for eyes.** Therefore, meat of birds is permitted, but not fish. The Gemara asks: **If so,** and he is suffering from eye pain, he should **eat fish, as Shmuel said** an acronym: ***Nun, samekh, ayin,*** which stands for: ***Nuna samma la'einayim,*** which means: Fish is a medicine for eyes. The Gemara answers: **That** statement of Shmuel is referring to the **latter** stages **of the** eye **infection.**[N]

NOTES

And eats the meat of the bird – וְאָכֵיל בִּישְׂרָא דְּצִפְּרָא: Rabbi Yitzḥak Tzarfati states that this is referring only to the meat of small birds, which does not satiate the one who eats it. The meat of large birds certainly falls under the category of meat in this regard (see Rabbi Eliezer of Metz, cited in *Shita Mekubbetzet*). As for the expression: His heart flies like a bird, Rabbi Eliezer of Metz explains that his pulse will begin racing like the pulse of a bird.

Nor before eating salted meat – וְלֹא עַל בָּשָׂר מָלִיחַ: The Ran explains that despite this ruling, salted meat is included in the prohibition of the vow. The criterion for inclusion in the vow of the agent consulting his employer applies only to those items that are not obviously included in the original vow. However, when the vow is stated in general terms, everything subsumed under that general category is included unless he specifies otherwise.

The latter stages of the eye infection [*ukhla*] – סוֹף אוּכְלָא: The commentary attributed to Rashi explains that fish is an effective remedy at the latter stages of an infection, but not at the outset. In tractate *Me'ila*, however, Rashi explains that the opposite is true. This is just one of myriad proofs that the Commentary on *Nedarim* attributed to Rashi was written not by Rashi but by his student. The *Arukh* explains, similar to the commentary attributed to Rashi here, that the phrase: The latter stages of the infection, refers to the stage when the infection is healed but there is residual pain in the eyes. Rabbi Yitzḥak Tzarfati explains the term differently. In his opinion, *ukhla* does not mean infection. Rather, it means: The end of his meal. Fish eaten at the end of a meal have a salutary effect on the eyes.

BACKGROUND

Let blood – הִקִּיז דָּם: Throughout history, bloodletting was considered effective in maintaining one's health, and many people would let their blood on occasion. Performed in some places by means of leeches, bloodletting was also considered an effective cure for various illnesses. Because the loss of a significant amount of blood causes fatigue, after undergoing bloodletting, one would eat foods that were believed to restore the lost blood to the body. As a rule, the advice was to eat foods with nutritional value, as well as foods that were easily digested and high in sugar content, to provide an immediate burst of energy. The foods listed as deleterious after bloodletting are foods that were believed to take a while to digest slowly and are low in calories.

Bloodletting depicted on an ancient Greek urn

Heart rate accelerates and flies like a bird – פָּרַח לִבֵּיהּ כְּצִפְּרָא: The flying of the heart, cited in several places in the Talmud, is the sensation felt by a person on the verge of losing consciousness, a phenomenon that is liable to follow significant blood loss, accompanied by an accelerated heartbeat and unusual feeling of lightheadedness or flying. Eating bird meat, considering that birds then were significantly smaller than modern-day chickens, was insufficient to facilitate recovery, especially if the meat was cooked in a way that was not digested quickly. Therefore, the Gemara distinguished between roasted or fried bird meat and chicken boiled extensively, which is quickly digested.

Cress – שַׁחֲלַיִים: This plant, known today as garden cress, *Lepidium sativum* L., is an annual plant with green-blue leaves that reaches a height of approximately 60 cm. It is cultivated primarily for its branches, which are prepared as a spice or added to salads. For that purpose the plant is cut to a height of approximately 10 cm above the ground. It then grows again and is cut once more.

The crushed fruit of the cress can be used for medicinal purposes. That was its typical use in the talmudic period, when the fruit was mixed with wine or vinegar.

Cress

MISHNA For one who vows that grain [*dagan*] is forbidden **to him,**[H] it **is prohibited to** eat **the dry cowpea,** because, like grain, its final stage of production involves being placed in a pile; this is **the statement of Rabbi Meir. And the Rabbis say:** It **is prohibited** for him to partake **of only the five species** of grain: Wheat, barley, oats, spelt, and rye, as that is the connotation of the term *dagan* in the Torah. **Rabbi Meir says:** For **one who vows** that grain is forbidden to him, and therefore he will refrain **from** eating **grain** [*tevua*], **it is prohibited** for him to eat **from** only **the five species** of grain. **However,** for **one who vows** that grain is forbidden to him, and therefore he will refrain **from** eating **grain** [*dagan*], **it is prohibited to** eat **all** produce whose final stage of production involves being placed in a pile, e.g., dry cowpea, **and** it **is permitted** for him **to** eat **fruits of the tree and vegetables.**

מתני׳ הַנּוֹדֵר מִן הַדָּגָן אָסוּר בְּפוֹל הַמִּצְרִי יָבֵשׁ, דִּבְרֵי רַבִּי מֵאִיר. וַחֲכָמִים אוֹמְרִים: אֵינוֹ אָסוּר אֶלָּא בַּחֲמֵשֶׁת הַמִּינִין. רַבִּי מֵאִיר אוֹמֵר: הַנּוֹדֵר מִן הַתְּבוּאָה – אֵינוֹ אָסוּר אֶלָּא מֵחֲמֵשֶׁת הַמִּינִין, אֲבָל הַנּוֹדֵר מִן הַדָּגָן – אָסוּר בַּכֹּל, וּמוּתָּר בְּפֵירוֹת הָאִילָן וּבְיָרָק.

GEMARA The Gemara asks: **Is this to say that** according to Rabbi Meir, the term ***dagan*** **means** any produce **that is** harvested at one time and **placed in a pile** [***midgan***]?[N] **Rav Yosef raised an objection:** After King Hezekiah called upon the people to give *teruma* and tithes properly, the verse states: **"And as soon as the matter was publicized, the children of Israel gave in abundance the first fruits of *dagan*, wine, and oil,** and honey, **and of all the *tevua* of the field;** and the tithe of all that they brought **in abundance"** (II Chronicles 31:5). **And if you say** that ***dagan*** **means** any produce **that is placed in a pile, what is** the meaning of the words **"As soon as the matter was publicized,** the children of Israel **gave in abundance**[N] the first fruits of *dagan*… and of all the *tevua* of the field"? There is no need to list both *dagan* and all *tevua* of the field. **Abaye said:** *Tevua* comes **to include fruits of the tree and vegetables,** which they tithed although they are not included in *dagan*, as they are not harvested at one time and placed in a pile.

גמ׳ לְמֵימְרָא דְּדָגָן כָּל דְּמִידְּגַן מַשְׁמַע. מְתִיב רַב יוֹסֵף: ״וְכִפְרֹץ הַדָּבָר הִרְבּוּ בְנֵי יִשְׂרָאֵל [רֵאשִׁית] דָּגָן תִּירוֹשׁ וְיִצְהָר וְכָל תְּבוּאַת שָׂדֶה לָרֹב״ וגו׳, וְאִי אָמְרַתְּ דָּגָן כָּל דְּמִידְּגַן מַשְׁמַע – מַאי ״כִּפְרֹץ הַדָּבָר הִרְבּוּ״? אֲמַר אַבַּיֵי: לְאַתּוּיֵי פֵּירוֹת הָאִילָן וְיָרָק.

§ We learned in the mishna that **Rabbi Meir says:** For **one who** vows that **grain** [*tevua*] is forbidden **to** him, it is prohibited for him to eat from only the five species of grain. **Rabbi Yoḥanan said: Everyone concedes with regard to one who vows**[N] that *tevua* is forbidden **to him that** it **is prohibited** for him to eat **from only the five species** of grain. The Rabbis do not disagree with Rabbi Meir in that regard. **That is also taught** in a *baraita*: **And they agree with regard to one who vows** that *tevua* is forbidden **to him that it is prohibited** for him to eat **from only the five species** of grain. The Gemara asks: **Isn't** that **obvious,** as it is only those species that are called *tevua*. The Gemara answers: It is necessary; **lest you say** that ***tevua* means all items** that grow from the ground, therefore, the *tanna* **teaches us that** this expression **does not mean all items** that grow from the ground.

״רַבִּי מֵאִיר אוֹמֵר: הַנּוֹדֵר מִן הַתְּבוּאָה״ וכו׳. אָמַר רַבִּי יוֹחָנָן: הַכֹּל מוֹדִים בְּנוֹדֵר מִן הַתְּבוּאָה שֶׁאֵין אָסוּר אֶלָּא מֵחֲמֵשֶׁת הַמִּינִין. תַּנְיָא נַמִּי הָכִי: שָׁוִין בְּנוֹדֵר מִן הַתְּבוּאָה שֶׁאֵין אָסוּר אֶלָּא מֵחֲמֵשֶׁת הַמִּינִין. פְּשִׁיטָא! מַהוּ דְּתֵימָא: תְּבוּאָה – כָּל מִילֵּי מַשְׁמַע, קָמַשְׁמַע לָן דְּלָא מַשְׁמַע כָּל מִילֵּי.

Rav Yosef raised an objection: With regard to the verse **"And as soon as the matter was publicized, the children of Israel** gave in **abundance…** and of all the *tevua* of the field," the phrase "and of all the *tevua* of the field" comes to include all crops that grow in the field. **Rava said:** ***Tevua*** **is discrete** and refers to only the five species of grain, **and *tevua* of the field is discrete** and refers to all crops that grow in the field.

מְתִיב רַב יוֹסֵף: ״וְכִפְרֹץ הַדָּבָר הִרְבּוּ בְנֵי יִשְׂרָאֵל״ כו׳! אֲמַר רָבָא: תְּבוּאָה לְחוּד, תְּבוּאַת שָׂדֶה לְחוּד.

HALAKHA

For one who vows that grain [*dagan*] is forbidden to him – הַנּוֹדֵר מִן הַדָּגָן: For one who vows with regard to eating *dagan* or *tevua*, it is prohibited to eat only the five species of grain (Rambam *Sefer Hafla'a*, *Hilkhot Nedarim* 9:9; *Shulḥan Arukh*, *Yoreh De'a* 217:18).

NOTES

Any produce that is placed in a pile – כָּל דְּמִידְּגַן מַשְׁמַע: Based on the conclusion of the Gemara, the dispute is whether the term *dagan* when used in a vow is to be interpreted as grain, which is its biblical meaning, or whether common parlance is different, and any produce harvested at one time and placed in a pile is included in that term (Rabbi Natan bar Yosef).

What is the meaning of the words: As soon as the matter was publicized, the children of Israel gave in abundance – מַאי כִּפְרֹץ הַדָּבָר הִרְבּוּ: Rashi explains this question based on the version of the text cited in the Gemara: If *dagan* includes all produce placed in a pile, in what sense did the children of Israel give in abundance beyond that which they were required to tithe according to *halakha*? One is obligated to tithe all the other types of produce listed as well. The *She'iltot* cites a variant reading of the question: What is the meaning of the phrase "and all the produce of the field in abundance"? According to this reading, the question is: If *dagan* in this verse means any produce placed in a pile, all the produce of the field is included. Why the redundancy? Although the Rosh adopts the version of the text that appears in the Gemara, he too maintains that the difficulty arises from the phrase "and of all the *tevua* of the field." He claims that when the Gemara cited the phrase: And as soon as the matter was publicized, the children of Israel gave in abundance, it was merely citing the beginning of the verse. Some early commentaries explain that although everyone, even Rabbi Meir, agrees that the term *dagan* in the Torah refers only to the five species of grain, the language in the book of Chronicles corresponds to the common parlance (*Tosafot*; Rashba).

NOTES

Everyone concedes with regard to one who vows – הַכֹּל מוֹדִים בְּנוֹדֵר: Although this is cited in the mishna as an individual opinion, it is in fact a consensus opinion (Ran). The Rosh writes that one could assume that the two *tanna'im* have conflicting understandings of the terms in question, as Rabbi Meir holds that *dagan* is a general term and *tevua* refers specifically to the five species of grain, and the Rabbis, who restrict the meaning of *dagan* to the five species of grain, hold that *tevua* has a broader meaning, including all produce that grows. That is the Gemara's question: Isn't it obvious that one who vowed to refrain from eating *tevua* would not eat from the five grains? The answer that follows is based on the understanding that *tevua* has a broader connotation (Rashba).

בַּר מָר שְׁמוּאֵל פְּקִיד דְּלִיתְנוּן הְלֵיסַר אַלְפֵי זוּזֵי לְרָבָא מִן עֲלַלְתָּא דִּנְהַר פַּנְיָא. שַׁלְחָהּ רָבָא לְקַמֵּיהּ דְּרַב יוֹסֵף: עֲלַלְתָּא הֵיכִי מִיקַּרְיָא? אֲמַר רַב יוֹסֵף, מַתְנִיתִין הִיא: וְשָׁוִין בְּנוֹדֵר מִן הַתְּבוּאָה שֶׁאֵין אָסוּר אֶלָּא מֵחֲמֶשֶׁת הַמִּינִין. אֲמַר לֵיהּ אַבַּיֵי: מִי דָּמֵי? תְּבוּאָה לָא מַשְׁמַע אֶלָּא מֵחֲמֶשֶׁת הַמִּינִין, עֲלַלְתָּא – כָּל מִילֵּי מַשְׁמַע.

§ The Gemara relates: **The son of Master Shmuel commanded** his workers **that they give thirteen thousand dinars to Rava from the crop** [*alalta*] produced in his fields on the banks **of the Panya River.**[NB] **Rava sent** this question **before Rav Yosef: What is called** *alalta*;[N] what crops are included in the category of *alalta*? **Rav Yosef said: It is** as it is taught in the *baraita* cited above: **And they agree with regard to one who vows that** *tevua* is forbidden to him **that it is prohibited** for him to eat **from only the five species** of grain; just as *tevua* includes only the five species, so too *alalta* includes only the five species. **Abaye said to** him: Are the two cases **comparable?** Although *tevua* **means** grain and includes **only the five species,** *alalta* **means** crop and includes **all items** that grow.

אַהַדְרוּהוּ לְקַמֵּיהּ דְּרָבָא. אֲמַר: הָא לָא קָא מִיבַּעְיָא לִי דַּעֲלַלְתָּא כָּל מִילֵּי מַשְׁמַע. הָדָא הוּא דְּאִיבַּעְיָא לִי: שְׂכַר בָּתִּים וּשְׂכַר סְפִינוֹת מַאי? מִי אָמְרִינַן: כֵּיוָן דְּפָחֲתָן – לָאו עֲלַלְתָּא הִיא, אוֹ דִּילְמָא כֵּיוָן דְּלָא יְדִיעַ פַּחְתַיְיהוּ – עֲלַלְתָּא הִיא. אֲמָרוּהָ רַבָּנַן קַמֵּיהּ דְּרַב יוֹסֵף. אֲמַר: וְכִי מֵאַחַר דְּלָא צְרִיךְ לָן אַמַּאי שָׁלַח לָן? אִיקְפַּד רַב יוֹסֵף.

The messengers **returned** with the answer to his question and came **before Rava. He said: That was not a dilemma for me,** i.e., the fact **that** *alalta* **means all items** that grow. **This is** the matter **that is a dilemma for me: What is** the legal status of profits from the **rent of houses and the rent of boats? Do we say: Since they depreciate,**[N] their legal status is **not** comparable to **that** of **a crop?** Only items that are consistently profitable are similar to crops. House boats deteriorate with use, and their depreciation diminishes the profits. **Or perhaps, since their depreciation is not conspicuous,** their legal status **is** comparable to that of **a crop. The Rabbis stated**[N] Rava's reaction **before Rav Yosef.** Rav Yosef **said: And since he does not need us,** and he believes that he knows the answer himself, **why did he send us** the question? **Rav Yosef became angry** with Rava.

שָׁמַע רָבָא וַאֲתָא לְקַמֵּיהּ בְּמַעֲלֵי יוֹמָא דְּכִפּוּרֵי. אַשְׁכַּחֵיהּ לְשַׁמָּעֵיהּ דַּהֲוָה קָא מָזֵיג קַמֵּיהּ כָּסָא דְּחַמְרָא. אֲמַר לֵיהּ: הַב לִי דְּאִמְזִיג לֵיהּ אֲנָא. יְהַב לֵיהּ וְקָא מָזֵיג אִידוּ כָּסָא דְּחַמְרָא. כִּי קָא שָׁתֵי, אֲמַר: הָדֵין מִיזְגָא דָּמֵי לְמִיזְגָא דְּרָבָא בְּרֵיהּ דְּרַב יוֹסֵף בַּר חָמָא. אֲמַר לֵיהּ: הוּא נִיהוּ.

Rava heard that Rav Yosef was angry **and came before him on Yom Kippur eve**[N] to appease him. **He found the attendant of** Rav Yosef, **who was diluting a cup of wine** with water **before him.** Rava **said to** the attendant: **Give me** the cup so **that I will dilute** the wine **for him.** The attendant **gave it to him and** Rava **diluted the cup of wine. While** Rav Yosef, who was blind, **was drinking** the wine, **he said: This dilution is similar to the dilution of Rava, son of Rav Yosef bar Ḥama,** who would dilute wine with more than the standard amount of water. Rava **said to him:** Correct, **it is he.**

אֲמַר לֵיהּ: לָא תֵּיתִיב אַכַּרְעָךְ עַד דְּאָמְרַתְּ לִי פֵּירוּשָׁא דְּהָדֵין מִילְּתָא: מַאי דִּכְתִיב "וּמִמִּדְבָּר מַתָּנָה וּמִמַּתָּנָה נַחֲלִיאֵל וּמִנַּחֲלִיאֵל בָּמוֹת"?

Rav Yosef said to Rava: **Do not sit on your feet**[N] **until you tell me the explanation of this matter: What is** the meaning of that **which is written: "And from the wilderness**[N] **Mattana and from Mattana Nahaliel, and from Nahaliel Bamot"** (Numbers 21:18–19)?

אֲמַר לֵיהּ: כֵּיוָן שֶׁעוֹשֶׂה אָדָם אֶת עַצְמוֹ כְּמִדְבָּר, שֶׁהוּא מוּפְקָר לַכֹּל – תּוֹרָה נִיתְּנָה לוֹ בְּמַתָּנָה, שֶׁנֶּאֱמַר "וּמִמִּדְבָּר מַתָּנָה". וְכֵיוָן שֶׁנִּיתְּנָה לוֹ בְּמַתָּנָה – נְחָלוֹ אֵל, שֶׁנֶּאֱמַר "וּמִמַּתָּנָה נַחֲלִיאֵל". וְכֵיוָן שֶׁנְּחָלוֹ אֵל – עוֹלֶה לִגְדוּלָּה, שֶׁנֶּאֱמַר "וּמִנַּחֲלִיאֵל בָּמוֹת". וְאִם הִגְבִּיהַּ עַצְמוֹ – הַקָּדוֹשׁ בָּרוּךְ הוּא מַשְׁפִּילוֹ, שֶׁנֶּאֱמַר "וּמִבָּמוֹת הַגַּיְא", וְלֹא עוֹד אֶלָּא שֶׁשּׁוֹקְעִין אוֹתוֹ בַּקַּרְקַע, שֶׁנֶּאֱמַר "וְנִשְׁקָפָה עַל פְּנֵי הַיְשִׁימוֹן". וְאִם חוֹזֵר בּוֹ – הַקָּדוֹשׁ בָּרוּךְ הוּא מַגְבִּיהוֹ,

Rava **said to him** that it means: **Once a person renders himself like a wilderness, deserted before all,**[N] **the Torah is given to him as a gift** [*mattana*], **as it is stated: "And from the wilderness Mattana."** And **once it is given to him as a gift, God bequeaths** [*naḥalo*] it **to him,**[N] **as it is stated: "And from Mattana Nahaliel." And once God bequeaths it to him, he rises to greatness, as it is stated: And from Nahaliel, Bamot,** which are elevated places. **And if he elevates himself** and is arrogant about his Torah, **the Holy One, Blessed be He, degrades him, as it is stated: "And from Bamot the valley"** (Numbers 21:20). **And not only** is he degraded, **but one lowers him**[N] **into the ground, as it is stated: "And looking over** [*nishkafa*] **the face of the wasteland"** (Numbers 21:20), like a threshold [*iskopa*] that is sunken into the ground. **And if he reverses** his arrogance and becomes humble, **the Holy One, Blessed be He, elevates him,**

NOTES

God bequeaths it to him – נְחָלוֹ אֵל: Rabbi Yitzḥak Tzarfati explains that he inherits both worlds. According to the *Ḥatam Sofer*, his reward is that the Torah is given to him as a full-fledged gift, like an inheritance that is never taken from him. Others state that it means God will forgive his sins (*Iyyun Ya'akov*).

One lowers [*shoke'in*] **him** – שׁוֹקְעִין אוֹתוֹ: There is a variant reading cited in the early commentaries, *shokefin*, meaning that he is lowered and sunk into the ground, which more closely bears a resemblance to the term *nishkafa* in the verse. It means that not only will he be degraded by Heaven, and from Bamot the valley, but if he is arrogant, people will degrade him as well (Meiri).

BACKGROUND

Panya River – נְהַר פַּנְיָא: Some hold that the reference here is not to a river but to a city named Hurpanya, which people assumed was a contraction of *Nehar Panya*, Panya River. Others maintain that the reference is to the city Nehar Ban, located on the east bank of the Tigris River.

NOTES

From the crop on the banks of the Panya River – מִן עֲלַלְתָּא דִּנְהַר פַּנְיָא: On the one hand, this stipulation for repayment of the debt is favorable for Rava, as it grants him monetary rights over the property on the banks of the river until the debt is repaid. On the other hand, it is unfavorable, as it restricts his ability to collect the debt to the crops that grow there (Rabbi Natan bar Yosef). Apparently, those crops were insufficient to repay the debt. That is why Rava asked if he had rights to other profits from Master Shmuel's property.

What is called *alalta* – עֲלַלְתָּא הֵיכִי מִיקַּרְיָא: The early commentaries state that Rav Yosef based his opinion on Onkelos's translation of *tevua* as *alalta*, indicating that the two terms are synonymous (Ran). Although Abaye and Rava maintain that the connotation of *alalta* is broader than that of the biblical *tevua*, many early commentaries (see *Piskei HaRosh*) rule in accordance with the opinion of Rav Yosef that at least when the term is written in a document, it is understood in its most limited sense, as the burden of proof rests upon the claimant who seeks to collect his debt with the document.

Since they depreciate – כֵּיוָן דְּפָחֲתָן: According to most commentaries, the question is: Does the fact that the profits from houses and boats involve depreciation of the property itself mean that these should not be considered profits at all? They understand that the term *alalta* is a variation of the term *ilui*, meaning increase. The Rosh explains that because the rent of houses and animals fluctuates wildly, perhaps it does not fall within the category of *tevua* (*Shita Mekubbetzet*).

The Rabbis stated, etc. – אֲמָרוּהָ רַבָּנַן וכו׳: Apparently, they did not report Rava's comments in their entirety. They told Rav Yosef that Rava said: That was not a dilemma for me. They did not tell Rav Yosef Rava's explanation why that was not his dilemma. That is why Rav Yosef took umbrage (Ḥaver ben Ḥayyim).

On Yom Kippur eve – בְּמַעֲלֵי יוֹמָא דְּכִפּוּרֵי: Based on the *halakha* that Yom Kippur does not atone for interpersonal transgression until the sinner appeases the injured party, he went to appease him on Yom Kippur eve (Rabbi Eliezer of Metz).

Do not sit on your feet – לָא תֵּיתִיב אַכַּרְעָךְ: Apparently Rav Yosef was well aware of the homiletic interpretation of the verse, and that Rava was aware of that interpretation as well (*Shita Mekubbetzet*). He asked Rava to repeat it to him as an allusion that he should conduct himself with greater humility (Rashi; Ran). Other commentaries explain to the contrary, that he sought to honor him by having him recite the homiletic interpretation in his presence, after seeing that he humbled himself and deferred to him (*Shita Mekubbetzet*).

What is the meaning of that which is written: And from the wilderness, etc. – מַאי דִּכְתִיב וּמִמִּדְבָּר וכו׳: This cannot be read as a simple list of the travels of the children of Israel, as its style is different from the standard record of their journeys, e.g., the preposition "to" is lacking (Riaf). Furthermore, these places are not among those enumerated in the list of the encampments of the children of Israel (see Numbers, chapter 33; *Torah Temima*).

Deserted before all – שֶׁהוּא מוּפְקָר לַכֹּל: The commentaries explain that he teaches Torah to all, and does not believe that the Torah is his and he will teach it only when and to whom he chooses.

שֶׁנֶּאֱמַר "כׇּל גֶּיא יִנָּשֵׂא".

as it is stated: "Every valley shall be lifted" (Isaiah 40:4).[N] When Rav Yosef heard that interpretation, he understood that Rava was aware of the error of his ways in acting arrogantly toward his teacher, and was pacified by Rava's display of humility.

תַּנְיָא הַנּוֹדֵר מִן הַדָּגָן – אָסוּר אַף בְּפוֹל הַמִּצְרִי יָבֵשׁ, וּמוּתָּר בְּלַח. וּמוּתָּר בְּאוֹרֶז, בְּחִילְקָא, בְּטַרְגִּיס וּבְטִיסְנֵי. הַנּוֹדֵר מִן פֵּירוֹת הַשָּׁנָה – אָסוּר בְּכׇל פֵּירוֹת הַשָּׁנָה, וּמוּתָּר בִּגְדָיִים וּבִטְלָאִים וּבְחָלָב וּבְבֵיצִים וּבְגוֹזָלוֹת, וְאִם אָמַר "גִּידּוּלֵי שָׁנָה עָלַי" – אָסוּר בְּכוּלָּן.

§ **It is taught** in a *baraita*: For **one who vows that grain** [*dagan*] is forbidden **to him,** it is **prohibited to** partake **of the dry cowpea, and** it **is permitted** for him to partake **of fresh** cowpea. **And it is permitted** for him to partake **of rice,**[N] as well as **of wheat kernels split into two parts** [*ḥilka*],[LN] **of wheat kernels crushed into three parts** [*targeis*],[L] **and wheat kernels crushed into four parts** [*tisnei*].[L] For **one who vows that produce of the year**[N] is forbidden **to him,**[H] it is **prohibited to** partake **of all produce of the year** that grew from the ground or on trees, **and** it **is permitted** for him to partake **of goats, and of lambs, and of milk, and of eggs, and of chicks** born that year, as they are not included in the category of produce. **And if he said: Growths of the year**[N] are forbidden **to me, it is prohibited for him** to eat **all of them.**

הַנּוֹדֵר מִן פֵּירוֹת הָאָרֶץ – אָסוּר בְּכׇל פֵּירוֹת הָאָרֶץ, וּמוּתָּר בִּכְמֵהִין וּפִטְרִיּוֹת. וְאִם אָמַר "גִּידּוּלֵי קַרְקַע עָלַי" – אָסוּר בְּכוּלָּן.

For **one who vows that produce of the land** is forbidden **to him,**[H] **it is prohibited** for him **to** partake **of all produce** that grow from **the land, and it is permitted** for him to partake **of truffles and mushrooms**[N] that are not in the category of produce of the land. **But if he said: The growths of the ground are forbidden to me, it is prohibited for him** to eat **all of them.**

LANGUAGE

Wheat kernels split into two parts [*ḥilka*] – חִילְקָא: Some claim that this is from the Latin alica, meaning grits. According to this opinion, the explanations for this word cited here are attempts to find an allusion in a foreign language for a foreign word, a common phenomenon in the Talmud.

Wheat kernels crushed into three parts [*targeis*] – טַרְגִּיס: From the Greek τράγος, *tragos*, meaning, among other things, wheat grits.

Wheat kernels crushed into four parts [*tisnei*] – טִיסְנֵי: From the Greek πτισάνη, *ptisanē*, meaning grits, particularly barley grits.

HALAKHA

One who vows that produce of the year is forbidden to him – הַנּוֹדֵר מִן פֵּרוֹת הַשָּׁנָה: For one who vows that produce of the year is forbidden to him, it is prohibited to eat fruits and vegetables, but not animals born that year, nor milk, nor eggs. However, for one who said: The growths of this year are forbidden to me, it is prohibited to eat all of those foods (Rambam *Sefer Hafla'a, Hilkhot Nedarim* 9:12; *Shulḥan Arukh, Yoreh De'a* 217:22).

One who vows that produce of the land is forbidden to him – הַנּוֹדֵר מִן פֵּרוֹת הָאָרֶץ: For one who vows that produce of the land is forbidden to him, it is prohibited to eat produce of the ground and fruits of trees, but it is permitted to eat truffles and mushrooms. For one who said: The growth of the land is forbidden to me, it is prohibited to eat all those foods (Rambam *Sefer Hafla'a, Hilkhot Nedarim* 9:11; *Shulḥan Arukh, Yoreh De'a* 217:23).

NOTES

Every valley shall be lifted – כׇּל גֶּיא יִנָּשֵׂא: Although this is a verse from the Prophets and is not adjacent to the Torah verse that is being interpreted, once it was taught that an arrogant person is degraded like a valley, the phrase "every valley shall be lifted" can be interpreted as his remedy (Ran).

And it is permitted for him to partake of rice – וּמוּתָּר בְּאוֹרֶז: This is because rice is not placed into a pile (Rosh). Even according to the opinion of Rabbi Meir, which is the opinion cited in this *baraita*, the case of one who vows that *dagan* is forbidden to him does not come to exclude all produce from the vow. Rather, it comes to exclude produce similar to grain or that originates from grain. The reason that rice is mentioned in particular is to exclude the opinion of the *tanna* who holds that rice is a species of grain with regard to leavened bread on Passover (Rabbi Eliezer of Metz).

Of wheat kernels split into two parts, etc. – בְּחִילְקָא וכו׳: These wheat kernels broken into halves, thirds, or quarters are excluded from the vow, as, due to their change in form, they are not called grain in the common parlance (Rashi). The Rosh suggests two possible explanations. One is that the grains were split before he vowed, and therefore he never considered including them in his vow. Alternatively, when he vowed, they were in the form of whole kernels. Once their form is altered, the prohibition no longer applies.

Produce of the year – פֵּירוֹת הַשָּׁנָה: The early and later commentaries write that with regard to both produce and the growths of the land, the term has different meanings in different contexts. In certain contexts, animals are in the category of produce, and with regard to second-tithe money in Jerusalem, one may purchase animals as growths of the ground. Here, however, the decisive factor is common parlance, and animals do not fall into the category of produce.

Growths of the year – גִּידּוּלֵי שָׁנָה: The Ran states that this applies only to one who vows that growths of the year are forbidden for a limited period. If, however, he vows for an extended period, or forever, it is impossible to fulfill that vow, and therefore, it is considered a vow taken in vain.

And it is permitted for him to partake of truffles and mushrooms – וּמוּתָּר בִּכְמֵהִין וּפִטְרִיּוֹת: Rashi explains that these are not considered produce of the land because they can grow on trees and other surfaces. In any case, the main reason is as stated, that there is a difference between items that grow and receive their sustenance from the ground, and truffles and mushrooms that grow from the ground but are not sustained by it.

וּרְמִינְהִי: עַל דָּבָר שֶׁאֵין גִּידּוּלוֹ מִן הָאָרֶץ אוֹמֵר ״שֶׁהַכֹּל נִהְיָה בִּדְבָרוֹ״. וְתַנְיָא: עַל הַמֶּלַח וְעַל הַזְּמִית וְעַל כְּמֵהִין וּפִטְרִיּוֹת אוֹמֵר ״שֶׁהַכֹּל נִהְיָה בִּדְבָרוֹ״! אָמַר אַבַּיֵי: מִירְבָא רָבוּ מֵאַרְעָא, מֵינַק – מֵאֲוִירָא יָנְקִי, וְלָא מֵאַרְעָא. וְהָא קָתָנֵי ״עַל דָּבָר שֶׁאֵין גִּידּוּלוֹ מִן הָאָרֶץ״! תְּנִי: עַל דָּבָר שֶׁאֵין יוֹנֵק מִן הָאָרֶץ.

And the Gemara **raises a contradiction** from a mishna (*Berakhot* 40b): And over a food **item whose growth is not from the ground,**[H] **one recites: By Whose word all things came to be. And it is taught** in a *baraita*: **Over salt and over brine** [*zamit*],[LN] **and over truffles and mushrooms, one recites: By Whose word all things came to be.** Apparently, truffles and mushrooms are not in the category of growths of the ground. **Abaye said: They grow from the earth,** but with regard **to sustenance, they draw sustenance from the air and not from the earth.** The Gemara asks: Why is that distinction significant? **Isn't it taught: Over** a food **item whose growth is not from the ground** one recites the blessing: By whose word all things came to be? Even according to Abaye, mushrooms grow from the ground. The Gemara answers: **Emend** the mishna to read: **Over** a food **item that does not draw sustenance from the ground,** one recites: By Whose word all things came to be.

מַתְנִי׳ הַנּוֹדֵר מִן הַכְּסוּת – מוּתָּר בְּשַׂק וּבִירִיעָה וּבַחֲמִילָה. אָמַר ״קוֹנָם צֶמֶר עוֹלֶה עָלַי״ – מוּתָּר לְהִתְכַּסּוֹת בְּגִיזֵּי צֶמֶר. ״הַפִּשְׁתָּן עוֹלֶה עָלַי״ – מוּתָּר לְהִתְכַּסּוֹת בְּאָנִיצֵי פִשְׁתָּן.

MISHNA For **one who vows** that a **garment** is forbidden **to him,**[HN] **it is permitted to wear sackcloth, and to wear a sheet, and to wear a coarse curtain** [*ḥamila*],[LN] as these are not in the category of garments. For one who **said: Wool is *konam*** for me[H] and I will therefore not **place it upon myself,** it **is permitted** for him **to cover himself with wool fleece,** which is not considered a garment, and it is prohibited for him to wear only a woolen fabric. For one who said: **Flax is *konam*** for me and I will therefore not **place it upon myself, it is permitted** for him **to cover himself with** uncombed **flax in bundles,** and it is prohibited for him to wear only a flaxen fabric.

רַבִּי יְהוּדָה אוֹמֵר: הַכֹּל לְפִי הַנּוֹדֵר; טָעַן וְהִזִּיעַ וְהָיָה רֵיחוֹ קָשֶׁה, אָמַר ״קוֹנָם צֶמֶר וּפִשְׁתִּים עוֹלִים עָלַי״ – מוּתָּר לְהִתְכַּסּוֹת, וְאָסוּר לְהַפְשִׁיל לַאֲחוֹרָיו.

Rabbi Yehuda says: Everything is determined **according to the one who vows.**[N] **If one was bearing** a burden of wool and linen, **and was sweating, and its smell was unpleasant** for him, and in reaction, **he said: Wool and linen are *konam*** for me and I will therefore not **place them upon myself,** it **is permitted** for him **to cover himself** with wool and linen garments, **but** it **is prohibited** for him **to sling** them over his shoulder **behind him** as a burden. The circumstances of his vow make it clear that he intends to forswear carrying wool and linen as a burden rather than the wearing of them as a garment.

HALAKHA

And over a food item whose growth is not from the ground – עַל דָּבָר שֶׁאֵין גִּידּוּלוֹ מִן הָאָרֶץ: Before partaking of food or drink that does not grow from the ground, one recites the blessing: By Whose word all things came to be (Rambam *Sefer Ahava, Hilkhot Berakhot* 8:1; *Shulḥan Arukh, Oraḥ Ḥayyim* 204:1).

One who vows that a garment is forbidden to him – הַנּוֹדֵר מִן הַכְּסוּת: For one who vows that a garment is forbidden to him, and therefore he will refrain from wearing one, it is permitted to wear sacks, sheets, and coarse curtains (Rambam *Sefer Hafla'a, Hilkhot Nedarim* 9:15; *Shulḥan Arukh, Yoreh De'a* 217:27).

For one who said: Wool is *konam* for me, etc. – אָמַר קוֹנָם צֶמֶר וכו׳: For one who was carrying a burden of wool or linen and was sweating and suffering from the odor he produced, and he vowed that it is forbidden for wool or linen to be placed upon him, it is permitted to wear wool or linen clothes and cover himself with them; it is prohibited only to carry them. For one who was wearing a woolen garment that was causing him discomfort, and his vow rendered it forbidden for wool or linen to be placed upon him, it is prohibited to wear woolen garments and it is permitted to carry woolen clothes and cover himself with wool fleece, as his intent was to prohibit wearing garments. The *halakha* is in accordance with the opinion of Rabbi Yehuda in the mishna and the *baraita* (Rambam *Sefer Hafla'a, Hilkhot Nedarim* 8:8; *Shulḥan Arukh, Yoreh De'a* 218:1).

LANGUAGE

Brine [*zamit*] – זְמִית: A Hebrew form of the Greek ζωμός, *zomos*, meaning soup or sauce. The Sages used it to refer to gravy, salty soup, or brine.

Coarse curtain [*ḥamila*] – חֲמִילָה: Similar to the Aramaic *ḥamalta*, meaning a very thick curtain.

NOTES

Brine – זְמִית: Various interpretations were suggested for this term. Some say it is a type of soup (Rabbeinu Ḥananel) or brine (Rashi). Others maintain that it is the foam that forms in a pot (Rav Hai Gaon). Yet others claim that it is congealed soup (Rav Hai Gaon, cited in *Shita Mekubbetzet*). *Ba'al Halakhot Gedolot* cites an opinion that it is the liquid strained from *kutaḥ*, a Babylonian dip made from sour milk and breadcrumbs, and others say it refers to the *kutaḥ* itself.

One who vows that a garment is forbidden to him – הַנּוֹדֵר מִן הַכְּסוּת: In the Jerusalem Talmud there is a distinction between one who vows with regard to a garment using the term *kesut*, in which case he may not cover himself with any fabric with which people cover themselves, and one who vows with regard to a garment using the term *malbush*, in which case he is prohibited only from wearing garments typically worn.

Coarse curtain – חֲמִילָה: Rashi explains that this means a kind of curtain. Others claim that it is a thick head-covering (Rambam's Commentary on the Mishna; Meiri), or a fabric used by merchants to cover their goods (*Talmidei Rabbeinu Peretz*, cited by Meiri).

Everything is determined according to the one who vows – הַכֹּל לְפִי הַנּוֹדֵר: Even if one spoke in general terms, the vow is interpreted based on his intent when he vowed. At times, his intent limits the meaning of the statement, or invests it with particular meaning. Some commentaries maintain that Rabbi Yehuda does not disagree with the Rabbis but merely explains their statement: They referred only to a non-specific vow. However, if it is clear from the circumstances that he had a particular meaning in mind, his vow is interpreted accordingly. Others explain that Rabbi Yehuda disagreed with the Rabbis, as the latter consider intent evident only from his actual words. Either way, the *halakha* is in accordance with the opinion of Rabbi Yehuda, as there is an unattributed mishna (63b) according to his opinion, as explained in the Jerusalem Talmud (Rashba).

LANGUAGE

Money belt [*punda*] – פונדא: From the Latin funda, or the Greek φοῦνδα, *funda*, meaning belt or purse. Sometimes it appears in the Talmud as *apunda*. It is a hollow belt containing a compartment for coins, and was used both as a belt and as a money belt.

Sash [*pesakiyya*] – פסקיא: From the Greek φασκία, *faskiya*, or the Latin fascia, meaning a wide belt or sash.

Sekurtiyya – סקורטיא: From the Latin scortea, an upper leather garment.

Leather spread [*katavliyya*] – קטבליא: From the Greek καταβολή, *katabolē*, meaning mat or foundation.

Leather sock [*anpilya*] – אנפליא: From the Greek ἐμπίλια, *empiliya*, meaning felt shoes.

Leather apron [*pelinya*] – פליניא: There are many versions of this word. Most scholars maintain that the proper reading is pamalanya, from the Latin, or from the Greek by way of Latin, feminalia, meaning a type of trousers that cover the area from the waist to the shins.

Coarse woolen blanket [*sagos*] – סגוס: Probably from the Greek σάγος, *sagos*, meaning a coarse cloak, perhaps a cloak with a hood. This garment was occasionally used as bedding, and even as a blanket for horses. Others claim that it is from the Greek σάκκος, *sakkos*, which originated in the Hebrew term for sackcloth.

HALAKHA

Shepherds may go out on Shabbat covered in sackcloth – הרועים יוצאין בשקים: It is permitted to go out into the public domain on Shabbat in a sack, a sheet, a coarse curtain, and the like as protection against the rain. That is because they are considered a form of garment. One may not, however, carry a box, container, or a mat to protect himself from the rain, as they are not classified as garments at all (Rambam *Sefer Zemanim*, *Hilkhot Shabbat* 19:17; *Shulḥan Arukh*, *Oraḥ Ḥayyim* 301:21).

גמ׳ תניא: הנודר מן הכסות – מותר בשק וביריעה ובחמילה, ואסור בפונדא ובפסקיא ובסקורטיא ובקטבליא ואנפליא ופליניא ומכנסים וכובע. מאי איסקורטי? אמר רבה בר חנה: כיתונא דצלא.

GEMARA It is taught in a *baraita*: For **one who vows** that a **garment** is forbidden **to** him, it **is permitted** to wear **sackcloth, and** to wear **a sheet and** to wear **a coarse curtain, and it is prohibited** for him **to** wear **a money belt** [*punda*],[L] **or** to wear **a sash** [*pesakiyya*],[L] **or** to wear **a *sekurtiyya*,**[L] **or** to wear **a leather spread** [*katavliyya*],[L] **or** to wear **a leather sock** [*anpilya*][L] **or** to wear **a leather apron** [*pelinya*],[L] **and trousers, and a hat.** The Gemara asks: **What is the meaning of *iskurtei*,** mentioned in the *baraita* as *sekurtiyya*? **Rabba bar Ḥana said:** It means **a tanner's apron.**[N]

תניא: יוצאין בשק עבה ובסגוס עבה וביריעה ובחמילה מפני הגשמים, אבל לא בתיבה ולא בקופה ולא במחצלת מפני הגשמים. הרועים יוצאין בשקים. ולא רועים בלבד אמרו אלא כל אדם, אלא שדברו חכמים בהווה.

It is taught in a *baraita*: **One may go out** into the public domain on Shabbat covered **in thick sackcloth**[N] **or in a coarse** woolen **blanket** [*sagos*],[L] **or in a sheet or in a coarse curtain** as protection **from the rain.** They are considered garments, not burdens. **However,** he may **neither** go out covered **in a box, nor in a basket, nor in a mat** as protection **from the rain,** as they are considered burdens, not garments. **Shepherds may go out** on Shabbat covered **in sackcloth,**[H] as they typically go out in sackcloth garments. **And** the Sages **did not say** this **only** with regard to **shepherds; rather,** they said that **all people** may go out wearing sackcloth; **however, the Sages spoke in the present,** addressing situations that were prevalent.

״רבי יהודה אומר הכל לפי הנודר״ כו׳. תניא, כיצד אמר רבי יהודה הכל לפי הנודר? היה לבוש צמר, והיצר, ואמר ״קונם צמר עולה עלי״ – אסור ללבוש ומותר לטעון. היה טעון פשתן, והזיע, ואמר ״קונם פשתן עולה עלי״ – מותר ללבוש ואסור לטעון.

§ We learned in the mishna that **Rabbi Yehuda says: Everything** is determined **according to the one who vows. It is taught** in a *baraita*: **How,**[N] i.e., in what circumstances, did **Rabbi Yehuda say: Everything is according to the one who vows? If one was wearing a woolen** garment **and it caused him discomfort, and** in reaction **he said: Wool is *konam*** for me, and I will therefore not **place it upon myself,** it **is prohibited** for him **to wear** woolen garments, **but** it **is permitted to place** a burden of woolen garments upon him. **If one was burdened with flax and was sweating, and said: Flax is *konam*** for me, and I will therefore not **place it upon myself,** it **is permitted** for him **to wear** flaxen garments **and it is prohibited** for him **to place** a burden of flaxen garments upon him.

NOTES

A tanner's apron – כיתונא דצלא: There is a variant reading cited by the Meiri: *Kituna detzila*, meaning a robe made of coarse flax that is so thick that it does not cling to the skin of the one wearing it.

May go out in thick sackcloth – יוצאין בשק עבה: These *baraitot* refer to the *halakhot* of Shabbat, not the *halakhot* of vows. These *halakhot* are cited here to give examples of materials with which one occasionally covers himself that are not full-fledged garments, but with regard to Shabbat they are considered to be garments, not burdens. However, materials that are not considered garments at all, e.g., boxes or baskets, are considered burdens on Shabbat, and all the more so with regard to vows, despite the fact that people use them as protection against the rain.

It is taught in a *baraita*: How, etc. – תניא, כיצד וכו׳: The Ran maintains that the opinion in this *baraita* is not identical to the opinion of Rabbi Yehuda in the mishna. The mishna indicates that for one who vows with regard to wool and linen in general, it is prohibited to wear them unless the circumstances make it clear that his intent was otherwise. In contrast, the *baraita* rules that everything depends on the circumstances of the vow. However, the Rambam and the Rosh both contend that there is no difference between the sources, as Rabbi Yehuda agrees that absent evidence to the contrary, his vow prohibits wearing wool and linen garments.

מתני׳ הַנּוֹדֵר מִן הַבַּיִת – מוּתָּר בַּעֲלִיָּיה, דִּבְרֵי רַבִּי מֵאִיר. וַחֲכָמִים אוֹמְרִים: עֲלִיָּיה בִּכְלַל הַבַּיִת. הַנּוֹדֵר מִן עֲלִיָּיה – מוּתָּר בַּבַּיִת.

MISHNA For **one who vows that a house** is forbidden **to him,**[H] entry **is permitted** for him **in the upper story**[N] of the house; this is **the statement of Rabbi Meir. And the Rabbis say: An upper story is included in the house,** and therefore, entry is prohibited there as well. However, for **one who vows** that **an upper story** is forbidden **to him,** entry **is permitted in the house,** as the ground floor is not included in the upper story.

גמ׳ מַאן תַּנָּא: ״בַּבָּיִת״ – לְרַבּוֹת אֶת הַיָּצִיעַ: ״בַּבָּיִת״ – לְרַבּוֹת אֶת הָעֲלִיָּיה? אָמַר רַב חִסְדָּא: רַבִּי מֵאִיר הִיא. דְּאִי רַבָּנַן – הָאָמְרִי רַבָּנַן עֲלִיָּיה בִּכְלַל הַבַּיִת, לָמָּה לִי קְרָא ״בַּבָּיִת״ לְרִיבּוּיָא?

GEMARA The Gemara asks: **Who is the** *tanna* who **taught** with regard to the *halakhot* of leprosy that in the verse "it appears to me as it were a plague in the house" (Leviticus 14:35), the term **"in the house"** comes **to include the gallery,**[N] a half story above the ground floor, and **"in the house"** comes **to include the upper story? Rav Ḥisda said:** The *tanna* is **Rabbi Meir, as,** if the *tanna* was **the Rabbis, didn't the Rabbis say** that **a second story is included in the house? Why** then **do I need the verse**[N] containing the phrase **"in the house" to include** the second story?

אַבַּיֵי אָמַר: אֲפִילּוּ תֵּימָא רַבָּנַן, בָּעֲיָא קְרָא, דְּסָלְקָא דַּעְתָּךְ אָמִינָא: ״בְּבֵית אֶרֶץ אֲחֻזַּתְכֶם״ כְּתִיב, דִּמְחַבַּר בְּאַרְעָא – שְׁמֵיהּ בַּיִת, עֲלִיָּיה – הָא לָא מְחַבַּר בְּאַרְעָא.

Abaye said: Even if you would say that the *tanna* is **the Rabbis,** they too **require a verse** to include the second story in this case, **as it might enter your mind to say** that since **it is written: "In a house of the land of your possession"** (Leviticus 14:34), only that **which is attached to the ground**[N] has the **status of a house** but with regard to **a second story, that is not attached to the ground.** Even according to the Rabbis, the verse is necessary to prevent the conclusion that the legal status of a second story is not that of a house with regard to leprosy.

כְּמַאן אָזְלָא הָא דְּאָמַר רַב הוּנָא בַּר חִיָּיא מִשְּׁמֵיהּ דְּעוּלָּא: ״בַּיִת בְּבֵיתִי אֲנִי מוֹכֵר לְךָ״ – מַרְאֵהוּ עֲלִיָּיה. טַעְמָא דְּאָמַר לֵיהּ ״בַּיִת שֶׁבְּבֵיתִי אֲנִי מוֹכֵר לְךָ״, אֲבָל ״בַּיִת״ סְתָם – אֵינוֹ מַרְאֵהוּ עֲלִיָּיה, לֵימָא רַבִּי מֵאִיר הִיא? אֲפִילּוּ תֵּימָא רַבָּנַן, מַאי עֲלִיָּיה – מְעוּלָּה שֶׁבַּבָּתִּים.

The Gemara asks: **In accordance with whose** opinion **is that which Rav Huna bar Ḥiyya said in the name of Ulla?** If the seller says to the buyer: **A house in my house**[NH] **I am selling to you, he may show** the buyer that he purchased the **second story** [*aliyya*]. The Gemara infers: **The reason is that** the seller **said to him: A house in my house I am selling to you. However, if** he sold him **a house, unspecified, he may not show him a second story. Let us say** that **this** is the opinion of **Rabbi Meir,** who states that the second story is not included in the house. The Gemara rejects this claim: **Even if you would say** that it is in accordance with the opinion of **the Rabbis, what is** the meaning of the term *aliyya* in this context? It does not mean second story; it means **the most outstanding of the houses.**[N] Rav Huna bar Ḥiyya said in the name of Ulla that when one says a house in my house, he must show him the most outstanding part of his house. However, if he sold him a house without specification, he may show him a second story.

HALAKHA

For one who vows that a house is forbidden to him – הַנּוֹדֵר מִן הַבַּיִת: For one who vows that a house is forbidden to him, it is prohibited to enter its upper story, as that is considered part of the house, in accordance with the opinion of the Rabbis. However, for one who vows that the upper story is forbidden to him, it is permitted to enter the house (Rambam *Sefer Hafla'a, Hilkhot Nedarim* 9:15; *Shulḥan Arukh, Yoreh De'a* 217:28).

A house in my house – בַּיִת בְּבֵיתִי: For one who writes in a document that he is selling a house in his house to another, it is permitted to give the buyer any house in his possession, even the smallest, as the rights of the owner of the document are inferior. He may not, however, give him an upper story. Only if he stated that he is selling him merely a house, may he give the buyer an upper story. This is in accordance with the opinion of the Rabbis that an upper story is included in the house (Rambam *Sefer Kinyan, Hilkhot Mekhira* 21:19; *Shulḥan Arukh, Ḥoshen Mishpat* 214:12, in the note).

NOTES

Entry is permitted in the upper story – מוּתָּר בַּעֲלִיָּיה: The commentaries note that in tractate *Bava Batra* (61a) it states that one who sells a house sells its upper story as well, indicating that it is included in the house. They explain that in a transaction or as a gift, an upper story is certainly considered part of the house and it is sold along with it. Here, however, the discussion is whether the upper story is defined as a house (*Keren Ora*). In the Jerusalem Talmud, it is stated that Rabbi Meir's opinion is more reasonable in the case of a city dweller, because in cities it is common to use the upper story separately, and therefore it not included in the house (*Korban HaEda*). Others explain that in the common parlance in cities, the word house does not include the upper story (*Penei Moshe*).

To include the gallery – לְרַבּוֹת אֶת הַיָּצִיעַ: One explanation is that gallery refers to the story above the balcony of the upper story. Others maintain that it is a half story inside the house itself, used for storage and the like (Rabbi Yitzḥak Tzarfati). Most early commentaries are of the opinion that the text here is corrupted, as it is clear from other sources that the walls of the gallery are not considered part of the house in the *halakhot* of leprosy. Therefore, they adopt the variant reading cited in the halakhic midrash of *Torat Kohanim*: To include the painted walls of the house. The novel element in this *halakha* is that although dyed garments are not susceptible to leprosy of garments, painted houses are susceptible to leprosy of houses.

Why then do I need the verse – לָמָּה לִי קְרָא: One could say that common parlance differs from the language of the Torah, and in vows the discussion is with regard to common parlance, and perhaps in the language of the Torah the upper story is not included in the house. However, the reliance on common parlance applies only where it is clear that the common parlance differs from the language of the Torah. In this case it is not clear, as there is a dispute between Rabbi Meir and the Rabbis with regard to precisely that matter. Therefore, the thinking was that in this case one can determine the *halakha* based on the language of the Torah (Rabbi Eliezer of Metz).

Which is attached to the ground – דִּמְחַבַּר בְּאַרְעָא: Although with regard to other types of impurity, the upper story is considered attached to the ground, it is possible that with regard to leprosy, the *halakha* applies only to structures directly attached to the ground and not to structures connected to structures attached to the ground (Rabbi Eliezer of Metz).

A house in my house – בַּיִת בְּבֵיתִי: The early commentaries note that the parallel discussion in tractate *Menaḥot* (108b) differs from the discussion here, especially in terms of its conclusions. The Gemara here initially raised the possibility that a house in my house is referring to any part of his house that is within his house and not in another building. However, from the passage in *Menaḥot* it is clear that the phrase is referring to his highest-quality house. The Gemara there concludes that the decisive factor is not the precise definition of the term, but rather the principle: The rights of the owner of the document are inferior, meaning that the person seeking to claim the house on the basis of the document is entitled only to that which is included in the narrowest interpretation. Therefore, he is entitled to the upper story, despite the fact that it is not the highest-quality house.

What is *aliyya*? It means the most outstanding of the houses – מַאי עֲלִיָּיה מְעוּלָּה שֶׁבַּבָּתִּים: *Aliyya*, therefore, does not refer to the second story of the house, but it means the highest-quality section of the house, or of any item in question. This usage is common in rabbinic literature. Clearly then, the upper story is not the highest-quality section of a house, as climbing up and down the stairs demands exertion.

מתני׳ הַנּוֹדֵר מִן הַמִּטָּה – מוּתָּר בְּדַרְגָּשׁ, דִּבְרֵי רַבִּי מֵאִיר. וַחֲכָמִים אוֹמְרִים: דַּרְגָּשׁ בִּכְלַל מִטָּה. הַנּוֹדֵר מִן הַדַּרְגָּשׁ – מוּתָּר בְּמִטָּה.

MISHNA For **one who vows** that **a bed** is forbidden **to him,**[H] **it is permitted** to lie **in a *dargash*,**[LN] which is not commonly called a bed; this is **the statement of Rabbi Meir. And the Rabbis say: A *dargash* is included** in the category **of a bed.** Everyone agrees that for **one who vows** that **a *dargash*** is forbidden **to him,** it **is permitted** to lie **in a bed.**

גמ׳ מַאי דַּרְגָּשׁ? אֲמַר עוּלָּא: עַרְסָא דְּגַדָּא. אֲמַרוּ לֵיהּ רַבָּנַן לְעוּלָּא: הָא דִּתְנַן: כְּשֶׁהֵן מַבְרִין אוֹתוֹ, כָּל הָעָם מְסוּבִּין עַל הָאָרֶץ וְהוּא מֵיסֵב עַל הַדַּרְגָּשׁ. כּוּלָּהּ שַׁתָּא לָא יָתֵיב עֲלָהּ, הַהוּא יוֹמָא יָתֵיב עֲלָהּ? מַתְקִיף לָהּ רָבִינָא: מִידֵּי דַּהֲוָה אַבָּשָׂר וְיַיִן, דְּכוּלָּהּ שַׁתָּא אִי בָּעֵי – אָכֵיל, וְאִי בָּעֵי – לָא אָכֵיל, הַהוּא יוֹמָא – אֲנַן יָהֲבִינַן לֵיהּ!

GEMARA The Gemara asks: **What is a *dargash*? Ulla said:** It is **a bed of** good **fortune,**[N] placed in the house as a fortuitous omen, and not designated for sleeping. **The Rabbis said to Ulla: That which we learned** in a mishna: **When** the people **serve** the king **the meal of comfort**[H] after he buries a relative, **all the people recline on the ground and** the king **reclines on a *dargash*** during the meal. According to your explanation, during **the entire year he does not sit on** the bed; on **that day** of the funeral **he sits on it? Ravina objects to** the question of the Rabbis: This anomaly is **just as it is** with regard **to meat**[N] **and wine,** as throughout **the entire year if he wishes he eats** them, **and if he wishes he does not eat** them; on **that day** of the funeral, **we give him** meat and wine in the meal of comfort.

אֶלָּא הָא קַשְׁיָא; דְּתַנְיָא: דַּרְגָּשׁ לֹא הָיָה כּוֹפֵהוּ אֶלָּא זוֹקְפוֹ. וְאִי אָמְרַתְּ עַרְסָא דְּגַדָּא הוּא, וְהָתַנְיָא: הַכּוֹפֶה אֶת מִטָּתוֹ – לֹא מִטָּתוֹ בִּלְבַד הוּא כּוֹפֶה, אֶלָּא כָּל מִטּוֹת שֶׁיֵּשׁ לוֹ בְּתוֹךְ הַבַּיִת הוּא כּוֹפֶה! הָא לָא קַשְׁיָא,

Rather, this is difficult, as it is taught in a *baraita* with regard to the custom of overturning the beds in the house of a mourner: With regard to **a *dargash*** in his house, the mourner **would not overturn it, but** he merely **stands it**[N] on its side. **And if you say** that a *dargash* **is a bed of fortune, isn't it taught** in a *baraita*: A mourner **who** is required to **overturn his bed**[H] is required to **overturn not only his own bed, but** to **overturn all of the beds that he has inside his house,** even those not used for sleeping. Why, then, is he not required to overturn the *dargash*? The Gemara rejects this contention: **This is not difficult;**

LANGUAGE

Dargash – דַּרְגָּשׁ: Based on the discussion here, it is clear that even the Sages were uncertain of the precise meaning of *dargash*. The source of the word is also unclear. Some deem it parallel to the Armenian *darguc*, meaning a stretcher or bed used for carrying a person. However, it remains unclear whether it originated in Persian or another language.

HALAKHA

One who vows that a bed is forbidden to him – הַנּוֹדֵר מִן הַמִּטָּה: For one who vows that lying on a bed is forbidden to him, it is prohibited to lie on a *dargash* as well, in accordance with the opinion of the Rabbis. For one who vows that lying on a *dargash* is forbidden to him, it is permitted to lie on a bed (Rambam *Sefer Hafla'a, Hilkhot Nedarim* 9:15).

When the people serve the king the meal of comfort – כְּשֶׁהֵן מַבְרִין אוֹתוֹ: If a king is a mourner and the people come to console him, the people sit on the ground and he sits on a *dargash* (Rambam *Sefer Shofetim, Hilkhot Evel* 7:8; *Sefer Shofetim, Hilkhot Melakhim* 2:4).

Who is required to overturn his bed – הַכּוֹפֶה אֶת מִטָּתוֹ: A mourner is required to overturn his bed during the seven days of mourning. He must overturn all the beds in his house. Nowadays the custom of overturning the beds is no longer observed (Rambam *Sefer Shofetim, Hilkhot Evel* 5:18; *Shulḥan Arukh, Yoreh De'a* 387:1–2).

NOTES

Dargash – דַּרְגָּשׁ: Many commentaries explain that a *dargash* is a small bed used as a ladder to climb onto a larger, higher bed (Rambam's Commentary on the Mishna; Meiri; Rabbi Ovadya Bartenura). This interpretation fits the conclusion of the Gemara.

Bed of fortune [*gadda*] – עַרְסָא דְּגַדָּא: Some commentaries explain that this is a bed that is placed exclusively for decoration and good fortune (Rashi; *Tosafot*). The *ge'onim* explain that it is a magnificent, high-quality bed. A slightly different explanation is that it is a bed prepared in honor of the guardian angel of the house. In that case, *gadda* would mean demon or minister (*Arukh*; Ran; Rosh). Others explain that based on the adage that there is nothing below on earth that does not have a corresponding angel above, the bed is placed in deference to the emissary of God. That is why it, like the chair designated for Elijah the Prophet during the circumcision ceremony, does not constitute idolatry (*Shita Mekubbetzet*).

Just as it is with regard to meat – מִידֵּי דַּהֲוָה אַבָּשָׂר: There is a common reason for both of these practices. They are each part of the attempt to alleviate the mourner's pain and to comfort him. Just as one provides him with meat and wine for this purpose, perhaps one arranges a particularly fine bed for him to raise his spirits (*Shita Mekubbetzet*).

Stands it – זוֹקְפוֹ: One need not overturn the bed entirely, with the surface facing down, as he does with other beds; he merely stands it on its side (Rashi). According to the Rosh, the term stand it means that he may leave the bed in place and need not overturn it at all. Others state that even if it was overturned he may restore it to an upright position (*Shita Mekubbetzet*).

מִידֵּי דַּהֲוָה אַמִּטָּה הַמְיוּחֶדֶת לְכֵלִים, דְּתַנְיָא: אִם הָיְתָה מִטָּה הַמְיוּחֶדֶת לְכֵלִים – אֵין צָרִיךְ לְכְפוֹתָהּ.

this is just as it is with regard **to** the case **of a bed designated** exclusively **for vessels,**[H] **as it is taught** in a *baraita*: **If** the bed in a mourner's house **was a bed designated for vessels** and not for sleeping, **one need not overturn it.** The same is true with regard to the bed of fortune. Since it is not for sleeping, one need not overturn it.

אֶלָּא אִי קַשְׁיָא – הָא קַשְׁיָא, דְּתַנְיָא: רַבָּן שִׁמְעוֹן בֶּן גַּמְלִיאֵל אוֹמֵר: דַּרְגָּשׁ מַתִּיר קַרְבִּיטָיו וְהוּא נוֹפֵל מֵאֵלָיו. וְאִי דַּרְגָּשׁ עַרְסָא דְּגַדָּא הוּא – קַרְבִּיטִין מִי אִית לֵיהּ? כִּי אֲתָא רָבִין אֲמַר: שְׁאִילְתֵּיהּ לְהַהוּא מֵרַבָּנַן, וְרַב תַּחֲלִיפָא בַּר מַעַרְבָא שְׁמֵיהּ, דַּהֲוָה שְׁכִיחַ בְּשׁוּקָא דְּצַלָּעֵי, וַאֲמַר לִי: מַאי דַּרְגָּשׁ – עַרְסָא דְּצַלָּא.

Rather, if defining a *dargash* as a bed of fortune **is difficult, this is difficult, as it is taught** in a *baraita* that **Rabban Shimon ben Gamliel says:** A mourner need not overturn **a** ***dargash***; rather, he **loosens** the **loops**[H] that connect the straps that support the bedding to the bedframe, **and it collapses on its own. And if a** ***dargash*** **is a bed of fortune, does it have loops** [*karvitin*]**?**[LN] **When Ravin came** from Eretz Yisrael to Babylonia, **he said: I asked one of the Sages** about the meaning of *dargash*, **and Rav Taḥalifa, from the West, was his name, who frequented the tanners' market. And he said to me: What is a** ***dargash***? It is **a leather bed.**[N]

אִיתְּמַר, אֵיזֶהוּ מִטָּה וְאֵיזֶהוּ דַּרְגָּשׁ? אָמַר רַבִּי יִרְמְיָה: מִטָּה – מְסָרְגִין אוֹתָהּ עַל גַּבָּהּ, דַּרְגָּשׁ – מְסָרְגִין אוֹתוֹ מִגּוּפוֹ. מֵיתִיבֵי: כְּלֵי עֵץ מֵאֵימָתַי מְקַבְּלִין טוּמְאָה? הַמִּטָּה וְהָעֲרִיסָה – מִשֶּׁיְּשׁוּפֵם בְּעוֹר הַדָּג. וְאִי מִטָּה מִסְתָּרֶגֶת עַל גַּבָּהּ – לָמָּה לִי שִׁיפַת עוֹר הַדָּג?

It was stated: Which is a bed and which is a ***dargash***? **Rabbi Yirmeya said:** In **a bed, one fastens** the supporting **straps over** the bedframe;[B] in **a** ***dargash***, **one fastens the straps through** holes in the bedframe **itself.**[NB] The Gemara **raises an objection** from a mishna in tractate *Kelim* (16:1): With regard to **wooden vessels, from when** are they considered finished vessels and **susceptible to ritual impurity? A bed and a crib** are susceptible **from when he smooths them**[H] **with the skin of a fish.**[B] And the objection is: **If** in **a bed the straps are fastened over** the bedframe, **why do I need smoothing with the skin of a fish?** The wood of the bedframe is obscured from view.

HALAKHA

A bed designated exclusively for vessels – **מִטָּה הַמְיוּחֶדֶת לְכֵלִים:** A mourner who is required to overturn the beds in his house need not overturn a bed designated exclusively for vessels or coins (Rambam *Sefer Shofetim*, *Hilkhot Evel* 5:18).

A ***dargash***, **he loosens the loops** – **דַּרְגָּשׁ מַתִּיר קַרְבִּיטָיו:** When the mourner overturns the beds, he need not overturn a *dargash*. He merely loosens its loops and the bedding falls away on its own, in accordance with the opinion of Rabban Shimon ben Gamliel (Rambam *Sefer Shofetim*, *Hilkhot Evel* 5:18).

A bed and a crib from when he smooths them – **הַמִּטָּה וְהָעֲרִיסָה מִשֶּׁיְּשׁוּפֵם:** Wooden beds and cribs are considered finished only after their surfaces are smoothed with fish skin (Rambam *Sefer Tahara*, *Hilkhot Kelim* 5:1).

LANGUAGE

Loops [*karvitin*] – **קַרְבִּיטִין:** From the Greek κράββατος, *krabbatos*, meaning mattress, bed, or intersecting straps that support a mattress.

BACKGROUND

The skin of a fish – **עוֹר הַדָּג:** In the past, the skin of certain kinds of fish was used for smoothing wood and other materials, which is accomplished today with sandpaper. One such fish is the cowtail stingray. This fish, from the Dasyatidae family, has a broad pectoral fin as well as a long, whip-like tail equipped with an extended poisonous barb.

Cowtail stingray

NOTES

Does it have loops – **קַרְבִּיטִין מִי אִית לֵיהּ:** Rashi explains that the *dargash* had no loops because it was not intended to be moved; rather, it remained fixed in one spot. Therefore, the supporting straps were fixed in place. Others explain that despite its decorative function, it had no loops, like other beds.

A leather bed – **עַרְסָא דְּצַלָּא:** Rashi states that this type of bed was not significant and therefore did not require overturning. *Tosafot* state that it was low to the ground and therefore overturning would not be noticeable (*Tosafot*). That is why Rabban Shimon ben Gamliel instructed to loosen the loops, as that engenders a conspicuous change in the bed. Others maintain that overturning leather bedding could ruin it. Therefore, the Sages exempted the *dargash* from this custom (Rosh; Ran).

In a ***dargash*** **one fastens the straps through holes in the bedframe itself** – **דַּרְגָּשׁ מְסָרְגִין אוֹתוֹ מִגּוּפוֹ:** According to most commentaries, the difference between a bed and a *dargash* is in the manner in which the straps are fastened, i.e., over the bedframe or through the bedframe. *Tosafot*, however, explain that in contrast to a regular bed, a *dargash* is crafted in a manner in which the straps are fastened below the bedframe. The result is that a *dargash* is lower than a standard bed, even if its legs are the same height.

BACKGROUND

One fastens the supporting straps over the bedframe – **מְסָרְגִין אוֹתָהּ עַל גַּבָּהּ:**

Detail of bedframe in which the straps supporting the mattress are tied over the bedframe

One fastens the supporting straps through holes in the bedframe itself – **מְסָרְגִין אוֹתוֹ מִגּוּפוֹ:**

Detail of bedframe in which the straps supporting the mattress are tied through the bedframe

אֶלָּא, הָא וְהָא מִגּוּפָן; מִטָּה – אַעוּלֵי וְאַפּוּקֵי בִּבְזִינֵי, דַּרְגָּשׁ – אַעוּלֵי וְאַפּוּקֵי בְּאִבְקָתָא.

Rather, with regard to both **this,** a bed, **and that,** a *dargash*, one fastens the straps **through** holes in the bedframes **themselves,** and the difference between them is: In **a bed,** the straps **are inserted and extracted through holes** in the bedframe; in **a *dargash*,** the straps **are inserted and extracted through loops** attached to the bedframe, as Rabban Shimon ben Gamliel said that one loosens the loops and the bedding falls on its own.

אָמַר רַבִּי יַעֲקֹב בַּר אַחָא אָמַר רַבִּי: מִטָּה שֶׁנַּקְלִיטֶיהָ יוֹצְאִין – זוֹקְפָהּ, וְדַיּוֹ. אָמַר רַבִּי יַעֲקֹב בַּר אִידִי אָמַר רַבִּי יְהוֹשֻׁעַ בֶּן לֵוִי: הֲלָכָה כְּרַבָּן שִׁמְעוֹן בֶּן גַּמְלִיאֵל.

Rabbi Ya'akov bar Aḥa said that **Rabbi** Yehuda HaNasi **said:** With regard to **a bed whose two posts** [*nakliteha*][L] **protrude,**[HB] rendering its overturning impossible, **he stands it** on its side, **and** that **is sufficient for him.**[N] **Rabbi Ya'akov bar Idi said** that **Rabbi Yehoshua ben Levi said: The *halakha* is in accordance with** the opinion **of Rabban Shimon ben Gamliel** with regard to the overturning of a *dargash*.

מתני׳ הַנּוֹדֵר מִן הָעִיר – מוּתָּר לִיכָּנֵס לִתְחוּמָהּ שֶׁל עִיר, וְאָסוּר לִיכָּנֵס לְעִיבּוּרָהּ. אֲבָל הַנּוֹדֵר מִן הַבַּיִת – אָסוּר מִן הָאֲגַף וְלִפְנִים.

MISHNA For **one who vows** that **the city** is forbidden **to him,**[H] **it is permitted to enter the** Shabbat **boundary of** that **city,** the two-thousand-cubit area surrounding the city, **and** it **is prohibited to enter its outskirts,**[N] the seventy-cubit area adjacent to the city. **However,** for **one who vows** that **a house** is forbidden **to him,**[H] **it is prohibited** to enter only **from the doorstop and inward.**[N]

גמ׳ מְנָלַן דְּעִיבּוּרָא דְּמָתָא כְּמָתָא דָּמֵי? אָמַר רַבִּי יוֹחָנָן: דְּאָמַר קְרָא ״וַיְהִי בִּהְיוֹת יְהוֹשֻׁעַ בִּירִיחוֹ״ וגו׳. מַאי ״בִּירִיחוֹ״? אִילֵימָא בִּירִיחוֹ מַמָּשׁ – וְהָכְתִיב ״וִירִיחוֹ סֹגֶרֶת וּמְסֻגֶּרֶת״! אֶלָּא שְׁמַע מִינָּהּ – בְּעִיבּוּרָהּ.

GEMARA The Gemara asks: **From where do we** derive **that the** legal status of **the outskirts of a city are like that of the city** itself? **Rabbi Yoḥanan said** that it is **as the verse states: "And it came to pass when Joshua was in Jericho,** that he lifted up his eyes and looked" (Joshua 5:13). **What** is the meaning of **"in Jericho"? If we say** that it means **in Jericho proper, isn't it written: "And Jericho was completely shut"** (Joshua 6:1)? **Rather, learn from here** that Joshua was **in the outskirts** of the city. And although he was in the outskirts, the verse states that he was in Jericho.

LANGUAGE

Two posts [*naklitin*] – נַקְלִיטִין: From the Greek ἀνάκλιτα, *anaklita*, meaning armrests or headrests of a bed or a chair.

HALAKHA

A bed whose two posts protrude – מִטָּה שֶׁנַּקְלִיטֶיהָ יוֹצְאִין: A bed whose two posts protrude need not be overturned during the period of mourning. It is sufficient to stand it on its side (Rambam *Sefer Shofetim*, *Hilkhot Evel* 5:18).

One who vows that the city is forbidden to him – הַנּוֹדֵר מִן הָעִיר: For one who vows that a town is forbidden to him it is permitted to enter its two-thousand-cubit Shabbat boundary. However, he may not enter its approximately 70.71-cubit outskirts (Rambam *Sefer Hafla'a*, *Hilkhot Nedarim* 9:16; *Shulḥan Arukh*, *Yoreh De'a* 217:29).

One who vows that a house is forbidden to him – הַנּוֹדֵר מִן הַבַּיִת: For one who vows that a house is forbidden to him it is prohibited to enter the house, including the entire area from the door inward. He may, however, enter into the area beyond the door that is beneath the lintel and above the threshold (Rambam *Sefer Hafla'a*, *Hilkhot Nedarim* 9:16; *Shulḥan Arukh*, *Yoreh De'a* 217:30).

BACKGROUND

A bed whose two posts protrude – מִטָּה שֶׁנַּקְלִיטֶיהָ יוֹצְאִין: The parts of this bed that support the head and the feet protrude from the bed. It is difficult to overturn it and if it is overturned, it is not conspicuous.

Bed with protruding posts found in Eretria, dating back to 300 BCE

NOTES

He stands it on its side, and that is sufficient for him – זוֹקְפָהּ וְדַיּוֹ: Most commentaries explain that this means to stand it on its side, as overturning it is impossible (Rosh; Meiri). Others, however, maintain that the bed remains upright. He merely places a covering over the posts, rendering it impossible to sit or lie upon it (*Tosafot*; Rabbi Avraham min HaHar, citing Rashi).

Its outskirts – לְעִיבּוּרָהּ: All commentaries agree that outskirts is referring to the area closest to a city that is considered part of the city itself with regard to the *halakhot* of Shabbat boundaries (see *Eiruvin*, chapter 5). There are, however, differences of opinion concerning the practical application of this definition. Rashi and *Talmidei Rabbeinu Peretz* maintain that it refers to recessed inward and recessed outward, meaning that the outermost houses of the city are not in a straight line. Most commentaries, however, maintain that the term outskirts of a city has a precise halakhic definition: The area that lies within a bit more than seventy cubits, roughly 70.71 cubits, of a city. That corresponds to the length of the side of a square with an area of five thousand cubits (Rosh; Ran).

It is prohibited to enter only from the doorstop and inward – אָסוּר מִן הָאֲגַף וְלִפְנִים: The novel element in this *halakha* is not the prohibition, but the leniency that anywhere beyond the doorstop is not considered part of the house, even if it is within the entrance beneath the lintel. This is the explanation of the term: However, in the phrase: However, for one who vows that a house is forbidden to him, as, for one who vows that a city is forbidden to him, it is prohibited to enter even places adjacent to the city, while for one who vows that a house is forbidden to him, it is prohibited to enter only beyond the door. In certain areas of *halakha*, e.g., areas concerning the sanctity of the Temple and Jerusalem, the area beneath the lintel of the doors and frames of the windows are considered to be on the inside, while in other areas of *halakha* that space is considered to be on the outside.

אימא אפילו בתחומה! הא כתיב בתחומה "ומדתם מחוץ לעיר".

The Gemara asks: **Say** that the legal status of one located **even in** the Shabbat **boundary** of a city is like that of one inside the town itself, and perhaps although Joshua was merely within the Shabbat boundary, the verse characterizes him as being in Jericho. The Gemara rejects this: **Isn't it written with regard to the boundary** of a city: **"And you shall measure outside the city…** two thousand cubits" (Numbers 35:5)? This indicates that the boundary of a city is considered outside the town and not part of the city itself.

"הנודר מן הבית אינו אסור אלא מן האגף ולפנים". אבל מן האגף ולחוץ – לא. מתיב רב מרי: "ויצא הכהן מן הבית" יכול ילך לביתו ויסגיר – תלמוד לומר "אל פתח הבית". אי אל פתח הבית, יכול יעמוד תחת המשקוף ויסגיר – תלמוד לומר "מן הבית", עד שיצא מן הבית כולו.

§ We learned in the mishna: For **one who vows** that **a house** is forbidden **to** him, it **is prohibited** to enter **only from the doorstop and inward.** The Gemara infers: **However, from the doorstop outward,**[B] **no,** it is permitted to enter. **Rav Mari raised an objection** based on a verse written with regard to leprosy: **"And the priest shall go out from the house** to the entrance of the house, and he shall quarantine the house" (Leviticus 14:38). And the question was raised in the halakhic midrash: One **might** have thought that the priest **may go to his house and quarantine**[N] the leprous house that he examined from there. Therefore, **the verse states: "To the entrance of the house"** (Leviticus 14:38). **If** he may go only **to the entrance of the house,** one **might** have thought that **he may stand beneath the lintel**[N] **and quarantine** the house from there. Therefore, **the verse states:** "And the priest shall go out **from the house,"** indicating that he may not quarantine the house **until he goes out from the entire house.**

הא כיצד – עומד בצד המשקוף ויסגיר. ומנין שאם הלך לביתו והסגיר, או שעמד תחת השקוף והסגיר, שהסגירו מוסגר – תלמוד לומר "והסגיר את הבית", מכל מקום! שאני גבי בית דכתיב "מן הבית" – עד שיצא מן הבית כולו.

How so? *Ab initio*, the priest **stands** outside, **alongside the door jamb, and quarantines** the house.[H] **And from where** is it derived **that if he went to his house and quarantined** the house, **or stood beneath the lintel and quarantined** the house, **that his quarantine** is an effective **quarantine** after the fact? **The verse states: "And he shall quarantine the house"** (Leviticus 14:38), which means **in any case.** Apparently, the legal status of the area beneath the lintel is identical to the status inside the house, even if it is beyond the doorstop. The Gemara answers: It **is different with regard to** a leprous **house, as it is written:** "And the priest shall go out **from the house,"**[N] indicating that he cannot quarantine the house **until he goes out from the entire house.**

BACKGROUND

From the doorstop outward – מן האגף ולחוץ: When the thickness of a doorway is significant, as is the case in a house with thick walls, and the doorstop is located on the side of the entrance closer to the house, there is a space in the doorway beneath the lintel and beyond the doorstop. This area is not considered part of the house. Clearly, if the door is located on the side of the entrance farther from the house, the legal status of the area beneath the lintel is like that of the house.

Doorway in thick wall

HALAKHA

He stands outside alongside the door jamb and quarantines the house – עומד בצד המשקוף ויסגיר: After the priest has determined that the house is afflicted with leprosy, he leaves the house, stands at its entrance alongside the doorpost, and quarantines the house. If he stood beneath the lintel, or went to his own house and quarantined the house from there, the house is quarantined, although he did not perform his role in the prescribed manner (Rambam *Sefer Tahara, Hilkhot Tumat Tzara'at* 14:5).

NOTES

One might have thought that the priest may go to his house and quarantine – יכול ילך לביתו ויסגיר: Most commentaries explain that this refers to physically sealing the house and declaring it a leprous house. In resolving the practical question as to how a priest can physically seal a house from a distance, they explain that he does so through an agent or by means of a long rope (*Tosafot*; Rosh; Ran; Rabbi Avraham min HaHar). The *Mishne LaMelekh* notes that based on numerous sources throughout the Talmud, the Rambam maintains that he need not physically seal the house. Rather, he quarantines the house by declaring it leprous.

Beneath the lintel [*mashkof*] – תחת המשקוף: Rashi distinguishes between the term *mashkof*, which refers to the lintel above the door, and *shakuf*, which refers to the threshold, called *askupa* or *askupa taḥtona* in the language of the Sages. Whether the reference is to beneath the lintel or above the threshold, the meaning is the same, and the space beyond the threshold is not considered part of the house.

As it is written: And the priest shall go out from the house – דכתיב מן הבית: These words are superfluous in the verse, as the verse then states: "To the entrance of the house," indicating that the priest cannot quarantine the house until he exits the house. Therefore, this phrase comes to emphasize that he must exit the house completely (Ran).

מתני׳ ״קוֹנָם פֵּירוֹת הָאֵלּוּ עָלַי״, ״קוֹנָם הֵן עַל פִּי״, ״קוֹנָם הֵן לְפִי״ – אָסוּר בְּחִילּוּפֵיהֶן וּבְגִידּוּלֵיהֶן. ״שֶׁאֲנִי אוֹכֵל״ וְ״שֶׁאֲנִי טוֹעֵם״ – מוּתָּר בְּחִילּוּפֵיהֶן וּבְגִידּוּלֵיהֶן בְּדָבָר שֶׁזַּרְעוֹ כָּלֶה, אֲבָל בְּדָבָר שֶׁאֵין זַרְעוֹ כָּלֶה – אֲפִילּוּ גִּידּוּלֵי גִידּוּלִין אֲסוּרִין.

MISHNA For one who says: **This produce is *konam* upon me, or it is *konam* upon my mouth,**[N] or **it is *konam* to my mouth, it is prohibited** to partake of the produce, or of **its replacements,**[HN] or of anything that **grows from it.** If he says: This produce is *konam* for me, and for **that** reason **I will not eat it,**[N] **or** for **that** reason **I will not taste it,**[H] **it is permitted** for him to partake of **its replacements or** of anything that **grows from it.** This applies only **with regard to an item whose seeds cease** after it is sown.[N] **However, with regard to an item whose seeds do not cease** after it is sown,[N] e.g., bulbs, which flower and enter into a foliage period and repeat the process, it **is prohibited** for him to partake even of the **growths of** its **growths,**[N] as the original, prohibited item remains intact.

הָאוֹמֵר לְאִשְׁתּוֹ ״קוֹנָם מַעֲשֵׂה יָדַיִךְ עָלַי״, ״קוֹנָם הֵן עַל פִּי״, ״קוֹנָם הֵן לְפִי״ – אָסוּר בְּחִילּוּפֵיהֶן וּבְגִידּוּלֵיהֶן. ״שֶׁאֲנִי אוֹכֵל״, ״שֶׁאֲנִי טוֹעֵם״ – מוּתָּר בְּחִילּוּפֵיהֶן וּבְגִידּוּלֵיהֶן בְּדָבָר שֶׁזַּרְעוֹ כָּלֶה, אֲבָל דָּבָר שֶׁאֵין זַרְעוֹ כָּלֶה – אֲפִילּוּ גִּידּוּלֵי גִידּוּלִין אֲסוּרִין.

For **one who says to his wife: Your handicraft is *konam* upon me,**[HN] or **it is *konam* upon my mouth,** or **it is *konam* to my mouth,** it **is prohibited** to benefit from her handicraft, and from **their replacements and** anything that **grows from them.** However, if he said to his wife: Your handicraft is *konam* for me only in the sense **that I will not eat**[N] from your handicraft, **or that I will not taste** from your handicraft, it **is permitted** for him to benefit from **their replacements and** anything that **grows from them.** This applies only **with regard to an item whose seeds cease** after it is sown. **However, with regard to an item whose seeds do not cease** after it is sown, it **is prohibited** for him to benefit even from the **growths of their growths.**

HALAKHA

It is prohibited to partake of the produce or its replacements – אָסוּר בְּחִילּוּפֵיהֶן: With regard to one who says: This produce is forbidden to me, or: It is *konam* to my mouth, or any similar expression, he is prohibited from partaking not only of the produce itself but of its replacements and growth as well, and all the more so of its juice. He is likewise prohibited from partaking of the growths of its growth, if their seeds do not perish, but he is permitted to partake of the replacements of its replacements (Rambam *Sefer Hafla'a, Hilkhot Nedarim* 5:13; *Shulḥan Arukh, Yoreh De'a* 216:1).

For that reason I will not eat it, or for that reason I will not taste it – שֶׁאֲנִי אוֹכֵל וְשֶׁאֲנִי טוֹעֵם: For one who said: This produce is *konam* for me, and for that reason I will not eat it, or for that reason I will not taste it, if it was an item whose seeds cease, it is permitted for him to partake of food for which it is exchanged and of its growths. If its seeds do not cease, even the growths of its growths are forbidden. Liquids that emerge from the produce are forbidden due to uncertainty with regard to their status (Rambam *Sefer Hafla'a, Hilkhot Nedarim* 5:14; *Shulḥan Arukh, Yoreh De'a* 216:2).

For one who says to his wife: Your handicraft is *konam* upon me – הָאוֹמֵר לְאִשְׁתּוֹ קוֹנָם מַעֲשֵׂה יָדַיִךְ עָלַי: With regard to one who says to his wife: Your handicraft is *konam* upon me or it is *konam* upon my mouth, or a similar formulation, items for which they are exchanged and their growths are forbidden. If he said: Your handicraft is *konam* for me only in the sense that I will not eat from it or that I will not taste from it, if it is an item whose seeds cease, it is permitted for him to partake of items for which it is exchanged and their growths. If its seeds do not cease, even the growths of their growths are forbidden (Rambam *Sefer Hafla'a, Hilkhot Nedarim* 5:15; *Shulḥan Arukh, Yoreh De'a* 216:3).

NOTES

Upon me, or it is *konam* upon my mouth, etc. – עָלַי, קוֹנָם הֵן עַל פִּי וכו׳: In the *Tiferet Yisrael* it is explained that in each succeeding formulation: *Konam* upon me, *konam* upon my mouth, *konam* to my mouth, there is an additional novel element. In all of them, he renders it forbidden to eat and derive benefit from the produce and from items exchanged for the produce. This is true not only in the case where he says that the produce is *konam* upon me; even if he says *konam* upon my mouth, he renders it forbidden to eat and derive benefit. The same is true even with regard to the phrase *konam* to my mouth, although it appears to refer only to eating. The Ritva explains that to my mouth means to myself and renders any kind of benefit forbidden.

It is prohibited to partake of the produce or of its replacements – אָסוּר בְּחִילּוּפֵיהֶן: There are various explanations why the items for which they were exchanged and their growths are also forbidden to him. *Tosafot* and the Rosh explain that the main reason is that he stated *konam* without specifying what he is rendering forbidden. Therefore, all forms of benefit are forbidden. The Meiri, adopting the approach of *Tosafot*, explains that it is the phrase: Upon me, that renders benefit forbidden. The Rosh writes that according to this opinion the novel element is that even though he vowed that certain produce was forbidden to him, since he said this produce, their growths are forbidden as well. Obviously, had he vowed without specification, all produce would be forbidden, both those before him and those not before him at the time. Others explain that benefit is forbidden because when he said this produce, he rendered benefit from them forbidden. Therefore, all benefit is forbidden, including benefit from items exchanged for the produce or its growth (Rashba; Ran; Meiri). According to the Ritva, the expression: *Konam* upon me, by definition means that benefit is forbidden.

This produce is *konam* for me, and for that reason I will not eat it – שֶׁאֲנִי אוֹכֵל: Although this prohibition appears to be more specific and therefore more strict, since he mentioned eating or tasting, only that specific produce is forbidden, as produce for which it is exchanged and its growths do not have flavor identical to that of the original produce (Ran). Rabbi Natan bar Yosef explains that this applies only to one who said: This produce; however, if he failed to say: This, all produce of that species is forbidden.

With regard to an item whose seeds cease after it is sown, etc. – בְּדָבָר שֶׁזַּרְעוֹ כָּלֶה וכו׳: Some commentaries maintain that this *halakha* is referring to both the first clause and the latter clause. In other words, the *halakha* that their growths but not the growths of their growths are forbidden applies only to an item whose seeds cease; however, for an item whose seeds do not cease, even the growths of their growths are forbidden. Others claim that it refers only to the latter clause: The growths of the produce are permitted for an item whose seeds cease; however, for an item whose seeds do not cease, its growths are forbidden. With regard to the first clause there is no need to state this *halakha*, as it is clear that in that case, the growths of growth are also forbidden (Ran; Rabbi Avraham min HaHar).

Whose seeds do not cease after it is sown – שֶׁאֵין זַרְעוֹ כָּלֶה: The simplest explanation is that this refers to plants with bulbs that remain intact as the plant grows, e.g., onions and garlic. Some commentaries, however, maintain that the reference is to plants that develop new bulbs in addition to the preexisting ones, e.g., shallots.

Even of the growths of its growths – אֲפִילּוּ גִּידּוּלֵי גִידּוּלִין: In the Jerusalem Talmud, it is stated that this prohibition lasts up to only three harvests, growths of growths of growths. Beginning with the fourth harvest, the growths are permitted.

Your handicraft is *konam* upon me – קוֹנָם מַעֲשֵׂה יָדַיִךְ עָלַי: It is unclear why this vow should take effect; as its object lacks substance since her handicraft has not yet come into existence, therefore it cannot be forbidden by a vow. Consequently, some commentaries maintain that the formulation must be emended into an effective vow, which will take effect if one says: Your hands are *konam* for their craft. The vow takes effect, as her hands exist (Ran). Rabbi Natan bar Yosef, however, claims that the formula is effective as it appears in the Gemara, as even though it does not take effect by Torah law, it takes effect by rabbinic law. The Ran, citing Rabbeinu Yona and the Ritva, adds that the prohibition does not always apply to the entire product of her handicraft, e.g., if she baked bread for him using his flour, the value of the entire loaf is not forbidden; only the value added by means of her handicraft is forbidden.

Your handicraft is *konam* for me only in the sense that I will not eat, etc. – שֶׁאֲנִי אוֹכֵל וכו׳: The Ran, consistent with his overall approach with regard to these *halakhot*, states that the novel element in this passage, relative to the earlier cases, is that although he rendered a particular item, i.e., her handicraft, and not an entire category, forbidden, the addition of the words: That I will not eat, indicates that his intent was not to prohibit benefit but was limited to the objects themselves.

"שאת עושה איני אוכל עד הפסח", "שאת עושה איני מתכסה עד הפסח", עשתה לפני הפסח – מותר לאכול ולהתכסות אחר הפסח. "שאת עושה עד הפסח איני אוכל" ו"שאת עושה עד הפסח איני מתכסה", עשתה לפני הפסח – אסור לאכול ולהתכסות אחר הפסח. "שאת נהנית לי עד הפסח אם הולכת את לבית אביך עד החג", הלכה לפני הפסח – אסורה בהנאתו עד הפסח,

If the husband said: From that **which you prepare, I will not eat until Passover,**[NH] or, with that **which you prepare, I will not cover myself until Passover,** then, if she **prepared** it **before Passover,** it is **permitted** for him **to eat or to cover himself** with them **after Passover.** If, however, he said: From that **which you prepare until Passover, I will not eat,** or from that **which you prepare until Passover, I will not cover myself,** then, if she **prepared** it **before Passover,** it **is prohibited** for him **to eat or cover himself** with it **after Passover.** If he said to her: **Benefit from me until Passover**[H] **if you go to your father's house** from now **until the festival** of *Sukkot* is forbidden for you, and **she went** to his house **before Passover,** it **is prohibited** for her to derive **benefit** from **him until Passover.**

NOTES

From that which you prepare I will not eat until Passover – שאת עושה איני אוכל עד הפסח: It says in the Rambam's Commentary on the Mishna that although it is obvious that the vow takes effect, the novel element is the inference from his statement that his intent is that the prohibition extends only until Passover, rather than that his intent was that anything she prepares before Passover is forbidden to him forever (Ran).

HALAKHA

From that which you prepare I will not eat until Passover – שאת עושה איני אוכל עד הפסח: If a husband said to his wife: From that which you prepare I will not eat until Passover, anything that she prepares is forbidden to him until Passover, but afterward it is permitted. However, if he said: From that which you prepare until Passover I will not eat, anything that she prepares until Passover is forbidden to him forever (*Shulḥan Arukh, Yoreh De'a* 220:21).

Benefit from me until Passover – שאת נהנית לי עד הפסח: One who said to his wife: That you benefit from me until Passover if you go to your father's house until the festival of *Sukkot* is *konam* for me, and she went there before Passover, benefit from him is forbidden for her until Passover. If she went there after Passover after having derived benefit from him before Passover, she violates the prohibition: He shall not profane his word. The Rambam maintains that the man is flogged, as he uttered the vow, while the Ran and others hold that his wife is flogged (Rambam *Sefer Hafla'a, Hilkhot Nedarim* 10:12; *Shulḥan Arukh, Yoreh De'a* 220:22).

Perek **VII**
Daf **57** Amud **b**

לאחר הפסח – ב"בל יחל". "שאת נהנית לי עד החג אם הולכת את לבית אביך עד הפסח", הלכה לפני הפסח – אסורה בהנאתו עד החג, ומותרת לילך אחר הפסח.

If she derived benefit from him before Passover and went to visit her father **after Passover,** she is liable **for** violating the prohibition of: **He shall not profane**[N] his word (Numbers 30:3), as the condition was fulfilled and she violated the vow retroactively. If the husband vowed: **Benefit from me is** *konam* **for you until the Festival**[H] **if you go to your father's house** from now **until Passover,** then if **she went** to his house **before Passover, it is prohibited** for her to **derive benefit from him until the Festival, and** it **is permitted** for her **to go**[N] to her father's house **after Passover,** as that time period is not included in his stipulation.

NOTES

After Passover she is liable for violating the prohibition of: He shall not profane – לאחר הפסח בבל יחל: The Rambam rules that in any case, it is prohibited for her to go to her father's house after Passover *ab initio*, as through his vow he prohibited her from doing so until the festival of *Sukkot*. Although she does not receive lashes for doing so in a case where she derived no benefit from him, she may not treat his vow with contempt. The Ra'avad disagrees and maintains that if she derived no benefit before Passover, it is not at all prohibited for her to visit her father's house after Passover. Rabbi Yitzḥak Tzarfati cites proof for the Rambam's opinion from the fact that the mishna does not state: It is permitted for her to go after Passover, indicating that although she does not receive lashes, it is prohibited for her to do so (*Shita Mekubbetzet*).

And it is permitted for her to go – ומותרת לילך: The Ran writes earlier in the tractate (15b) that the novel element in this statement is that even if she went before Passover, thereby rendering benefit from her husband forbidden to her, it is permitted for her to visit her father after Passover. *Tosafot* there claim that there is nothing novel in this statement, and it is stated only to contrast it with the previous *halakha* (see *Tosefot Yom Tov*).

HALAKHA

Benefit from me is *konam* for you until the Festival – שאת נהנית לי עד החג וכו׳: If one says to his wife: Benefit from me is *konam* for you until the Festival if you go to your father's house before Passover, and she went and visited her father before Passover, it is prohibited for her to derive benefit from him until the Festival. If she does so he is liable by Torah law to receive lashes. After Passover, though, it is permitted for her to visit her father's house (Rambam *Sefer Hafla'a, Hilkhot Nedarim* 10:13; *Shulḥan Arukh, Yoreh De'a* 220:23).

גמ׳ הָאוֹמֵר לְאִשְׁתּוֹ ״קוֹנָם מַעֲשֵׂה יָדַיִךְ עָלַי״, ״קוֹנָם הֵן עַל פִּי״, ״קוֹנָם הֵן לְפִי״ וכו׳. יִשְׁמָעֵאל אִישׁ כְּפַר יַמָּא, וְאָמְרִי לָהּ אִישׁ כְּפַר דִּימָא, הֶעֱלָה בְּיָדוֹ: בָּצָל שֶׁעֲקָרוֹ בַּשְּׁבִיעִית וּנְטָעוֹ בַּשְּׁמִינִית, וְרַבּוּ גִּידּוּלָיו עַל עִיקָּרוֹ. וְהָכִי קָא מִיבַּעְיָא לֵיהּ: גִּידּוּלָיו הֶיתֵּר וְעִיקָּרוֹ אָסוּר, כֵּיוָן דְּרַבּוּ גִּידּוּלָיו מֵעִיקָּרוֹ – אוֹתָן גִּידּוּלֵי הֶיתֵּר מַעֲלִין אֶת הָאִיסּוּר, אוֹ לֹא? אֲתָא לְקַמֵּיהּ דְּרַבִּי אַמִּי – לָא הֲוָה בִּידֵיהּ.

GEMARA We learned in the mishna: For **one who says to his wife: Your handicraft is *konam* upon me,** or it is ***konam* upon my mouth,** or it is ***konam*** to my **mouth,** it is prohibited to benefit from her handicraft. **Yishmael, a man of Kefar Yamma,**[B] **and some say, a man of Kefar Dima, raised** a dilemma with regard to **an onion**[N] **that one uprooted during** the **Sabbatical Year,**[HN] which was therefore sanctified with the sanctity of the Sabbatical Year, **and** he then **planted it during the eighth** year, **and its growths** that developed in the eighth year **exceeded its principal**[N] original Sabbatical-Year onion. **And this is the dilemma that he raised: Its** eighth-year **growth is permitted, and its** Sabbatical-Year **principal is prohibited. Since its growth exceeded its principal,** do **those permitted growths neutralize**[N] **the prohibition** of the onion, **or** do they **not?** Yishmael **came** and raised the dilemma **before Rabbi Ami, and he did not have** an answer readily **available.**

BACKGROUND

Kefar Yamma – כְּפַר יַמָּא: Kefar Yamma is a village near Tiberias on the south side of the Sea of Galilee, adjacent to the modern Yavne'el.

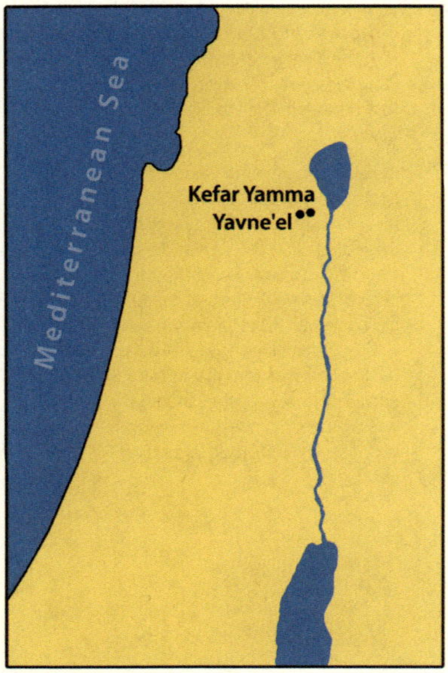

Location of Kefar Yamma

HALAKHA

An onion that one uprooted during the Sabbatical Year – בָּצָל שֶׁעֲקָרוֹ בַּשְּׁבִיעִית: If an onion was uprooted in the seventh year and replanted in the eighth year, and its subsequent growths exceeded those of the original plant, the entire plant is permitted because the permitted growth neutralizes the prohibition of Sabbatical-Year produce after the date of removal, as per the opinion of Rabbi Yitzḥak Nappaḥa. The Ra'avad holds that the conclusion of the Jerusalem Talmud is that this *halakha* applies only to an onion whose leaves are bent (see 58a). However, the *Kesef Mishne* and the Radbaz contend that this was stated in the Jerusalem Talmud as a refutation, not as a ruling (Rambam *Sefer Zera'im*, *Hilkhot Shemitta VeYovel* 4:21).

NOTES

Raised a dilemma with regard to an onion – הֶעֱלָה בְּיָדוֹ בָּצָל: Most commentaries explain that this phrase simply means that he raised a dilemma before the Sages. The Ran cites proof for this interpretation from the Aramaic translation of Isaiah 6:6. Rabbi Avraham min HaHar explains that he brought an actual onion of that kind in his hand, to raise a dilemma with regard to its status.

That one uprooted [*she'akaro*] during the Sabbatical Year – שֶׁעֲקָרוֹ בַּשְּׁבִיעִית: The case is where the onion began to grow during the Sabbatical Year. One uprooted it during that year and failed to remove it from his possession when the period of removal arrived. He then replanted it during the eighth year. Rashi, perhaps, bases his comment on a variant reading. Instead of: That one uprooted [*she'akaro*], it means: That the onion's primary part [*she'ikaro*] grew during the Sabbatical Year. Rashi explains that most of the plant grew during the Sabbatical Year, but it remained in the ground into the eighth year.

And its growths exceeded its principal – וְרַבּוּ גִּידּוּלָיו עַל עִיקָּרוֹ: The meaning here, as in the other cases cited previously, is that its growths were sufficient to neutralize the prohibition with a majority of, depending on the case, sixty times the prohibition for most prohibited items, one hundred times the prohibition for *teruma*, or two hundred times the prohibition for *orla* (see Ran).

Do those permitted growths neutralize, etc. – גִּידּוּלֵי הֶיתֵּר מַעֲלִין וכו׳: There are numerous explanations of this dilemma, which relate to several fundamental halakhic issues with regard to the neutralization of prohibitions. There is a dispute between the early commentaries with regard to the part of the plant that grew during the eighth year, as some authorities maintain that the dilemma relates not only to the neutralization of the prohibition by the permitted growth, but it also concerns whether or not the growths themselves are permitted. According to those who say that the growths neutralize the prohibition, clearly the growths are permitted. According to those who rule that the growths do not neutralize the prohibition, some hold that the growths themselves are forbidden, as they grew from the forbidden onion (Ran; Rid). Rabbi Eliezer of Metz, cited in *Tosafot*, asks: Why not say here that the growths are caused by both this, the forbidden onion, and that, the permitted ground, and the accepted *halakha* is that in a case where there are both permitted and forbidden causes, the result is permitted. He answers that the Sage in the Gemara who raised the dilemma holds that in a case where there are permitted and forbidden causes the result is forbidden. Others explain that the ground is not considered a cause in this regard, as it is not of the species of the prohibited plant (Rabbeinu Meir in *Tosafot*). Most commentaries, however, contend that everyone agrees that growths that grew in the eighth year are permitted, as the Sages issued a decree to prohibit only the growths of *teruma*, not the growths of any other forbidden growths. The dilemma is whether or not the growths neutralize the prohibition of the original onion (*Tosafot*; Rashba; Rosh; Rabbi Avraham min HaHar).

Some explain that the dilemma is whether the majority neutralizes the prohibition, or whether the original onion is significant and therefore not subject to neutralization (*Tosafot*; Rashba). The Ran maintains that the dilemma is whether the status of the growths is that of a different object and therefore they can neutralize the prohibition, or whether because they grew from the original forbidden plant, they are considered part of the original plant and therefore cannot neutralize the prohibition. Others explain that one might have thought that just as the primary part of the plant does not neutralize the prohibition of the growths, because it is significant as it continues to grow, by the same token, the growths should not neutralize the prohibition of the plant. Alternatively, the plant is not neutralized because it remains intact and is never completely intermingled with the growth (Rosh). The Rid explains that one might say that the prohibition of the original plant is neutralized by the ground, and therefore it is all permitted even if the forbidden part is more than one-sixtieth of the entire plant; or perhaps, since the growth receives sustenance from the original part of the plant, the entire plant is forbidden.

Additional problems were raised in this context. Among them, why not say that since the growths increase incrementally, perhaps as it grows, each increment is negated by the original plant, and therefore, the original plant and growths should remain forbidden? The answer is that the principle: Each and every increment is neutralized as it enters the mixture, does not apply to items that naturally grow all the time. Furthermore, the growths are considered discrete entities that are separate from the original plant and therefore their prohibition cannot be neutralized by the original plant (Rabbi Eliezer of Metz). The *Keren Ora* asks why the growth should not be forbidden like the original plant, as it grew from the original plant. He answers that the growth is considered a new entity, as its growth results primarily from the ground and the air.

אֲתָא לְקַמֵּיהּ דְּרַבִּי יִצְחָק נַפָּחָא – פְּשַׁט לֵיהּ מִן הָדָא דְּאָמַר רַבִּי חֲנִינָא תְּרִיתָאָה אָמַר רַבִּי יַנַּאי: בָּצָל שֶׁל תְּרוּמָה שֶׁנְּטָעוֹ, וְרַבּוּ גִּידּוּלָיו עַל עִיקָּרוֹ – מוּתָּר. אֲמַר לֵיהּ רַבִּי יִרְמְיָה, וְאִיתֵּימָא רַבִּי זְרִיקָא: שָׁבֵיק מָר תְּרֵין וְעָבֵיד כְּחַד?!

Yishmael **came** and raised the dilemma **before Rabbi Yitzḥak Nappaḥa,** who **resolved it for him from that which Rabbi Ḥanina Terita'a**[L] **said that Rabbi Yannai said:** With regard to **an onion of** *teruma*[H] **that one planted, if its growths exceeded its principal,** it **is permitted.**[N] Here too, the eighth-year growth should neutralize the prohibition of the Sabbatical-Year onion. **Rabbi Yirmeya said, and some say** it was **Rabbi Zerika** who said to Rabbi Yitzḥak Nappaḥa: **Did the Master abandon** the opinion of **two** Sages **and conduct** himself **in accordance with** the opinion of **one** Sage?

מַאן נִינְהוּ תְּרֵין – דְּאָמַר רַבִּי אַבָּהוּ אָמַר רַבִּי יוֹחָנָן: יַלְדָּה שֶׁסִּיבְּכָהּ בִּזְקֵינָה וּבָהּ פֵּירוֹת, אַף עַל פִּי שֶׁהוֹסִיפָה מָאתַיִם – אָסוּר.

The Gemara asks: **Who are they,** the **two** Sages who disagree with his opinion? The Gemara answers: It is **as Rabbi Abbahu said** that **Rabbi Yoḥanan said:** With regard to **a young** vine within three years of its planting, whose fruits are *orla* and forbidden, **that one grafted**[B] **onto an old,** permitted vine,[HN] **and there were fruits on** the younger vine, **even though** the younger vine **added two hundred** times the number of fruits that were there when it was grafted, and those additional fruits are permitted because they draw their nourishment from the older vine, the fruit that was on the younger vine before it was grafted is **forbidden.** Although, in principle, when the permitted part of the mixture is two hundred times the forbidden *orla*, the prohibition is neutralized, in this case, the prohibition is not neutralized, as the forbidden fruit was there from the outset.

LANGUAGE

Terita'a – תְּרִיתָאָה: The name of this Sage appears in many different forms in manuscripts and other sources. Therefore, it is difficult to ascertain the meaning of this appellation. According to the version here, and especially according to the variant reading Torta'a, the name is apparently connected to the Aramaic *tor*, meaning bull, and it implies that the Sage in question was an animal merchant. According to the version Terita'a written with the letter *tet*, from the Greek τρι, τρεῖς [*tri, treis*], meaning three, perhaps it means the third. Yet another version, Kartina'a, refers to the place where he lived, Carthage.

BACKGROUND

Grafted – סִיבְּכָה: Grafting, a procedure employed for improving the quality of fruit or creating different varieties of fruit, can be performed in a variety of ways. One of the standard methods involves inserting the branch of one tree into the branch of another. Another method involves attaching branches from two trees whose bark was peeled. Typically, the branch is severed from the first tree and grafted onto the second. However, it may also be accomplished by grafting a branch still attached to the original tree, and that branch is severed from the original tree only after the branch has grown and become part of the second tree. The Talmud's use of the term that usually means entangled [*sibkha*], rather than the term meaning grafted [*hirkiv*], indicates that the reference is to the latter type of grafting, with the two entangled trees growing together.

Branch from a young olive tree grafted onto an old olive tree

HALAKHA

An onion of *teruma* – בָּצָל שֶׁל תְּרוּמָה וכו׳: If an onion of *teruma* was planted and its growths exceeded those of the original plant, by Torah law its status is no longer that of *teruma*; rather, its status is that of untithed produce. The Sages, however, decreed that, like *teruma*, it is forbidden to non-priests. The commentaries on the Rambam state that the reference is to growths of growth, or to items whose seeds cease, not onions (see Mahari Kurkus; Radbaz; Rambam *Sefer Zera'im*, *Hilkhot Terumot* 11:21–22 and *Kesef Mishne* there).

A young vine that that one grafted onto an old, permitted vine – יַלְדָּה שֶׁסִּיבְּכָה בִּזְקֵינָה: If the branch of a sapling within three years of planting, whose fruit is *orla*, was grafted onto an older tree, and the fruit of the younger plant grew, even if that branch subsequently grew fruit in an amount more than two hundred times the original *orla*, the fruit that grew on the younger vine before it was grafted remains forbidden, as the permitted growth does not neutralize the prohibition of the original fruit (Rambam *Sefer Zera'im*, *Hilkhot Ma'aser Sheni* 10:16; *Shulḥan Arukh*, *Yoreh De'a* 294:22).

NOTES

An onion of *teruma* that one planted, if its growths exceeded its principal it is permitted – בָּצָל שֶׁל תְּרוּמָה שֶׁנְּטָעוֹ וְרַבּוּ גִּידּוּלָיו עַל עִיקָּרוֹ מוּתָּר: The growths are permitted in terms of the prohibition of *teruma*, as it does not have the status of *teruma*. However, eating it in its current state is forbidden, as its legal status remains that of untithed produce.

A young vine that one grafted onto an old, permitted vine – יַלְדָּה שֶׁסִּיבְּכָה בִּזְקֵינָה: Most commentaries explain that he cut a branch from the young vine and grafted it onto the old one. The Rashba contends that the fruits that grew prior to the grafting are forbidden only because the branch already bore fruit. Otherwise, the prohibition would be entirely neutralized and any fruit that grew would be permitted. According to the Rid, we are dealing with intertwining, a temporary form of grafting intended to accelerate the ripening of the fruit of the young branch. However, standard grafting, whose purpose is to restore an aging tree, would render the entire tree or vine forbidden as *orla*.

HALAKHA

An onion that one planted in a vineyard – בְּצַל שֶׁנְּטָעוֹ בְּכֶרֶם: An onion that was planted in a vineyard is forbidden as a forbidden mixture of food crops in a vineyard. Even if the vineyard was later uprooted, and the onions that sprouted from the original plant were two hundred times those of the original plant, the original onion remains forbidden, as the permitted growth does not neutralize the prohibition (Rambam *Sefer Zera'im*, *Hilkhot Kilayim* 5:24; *Shulḥan Arukh*, *Yoreh De'a* 296:18).

A *litra* of onions that one tithed – לִיטְרָא בְּצָלִים שֶׁתִּיקְּנָהּ: If *terumot* and tithes were properly separated from a *litra* of onions, and one sowed the entire *litra* and they sprouted, he must tithe the original onions along with the additional growths, as the growths neutralize the prohibition of the original onions (Rambam *Sefer Zera'im*, *Hilkhot Ma'asrot* 6:4 and *Kesef Mishne* there).

LANGUAGE

Litra – לִיטְרָא: From the Greek λίτρα, *litra*, which has several meanings, among them measures of volume or weight, as well as the name of a coin. The volume of a *litra* is less than 100 cc, which would constitute a very small quantity of onions. The weight of a *litra* is 327 grams. Consequently, a *litra* of silver is worth a large sum.

וְאָמַר רַבִּי שְׁמוּאֵל בַּר רַבִּי נַחְמָנִי אָמַר רַבִּי יוֹנָתָן: בְּצַל שֶׁנְּטָעוֹ בְּכֶרֶם, וְנֶעֱקַר הַכֶּרֶם – אָסוּר.

And Rabbi Shmuel bar Rabbi Naḥmani said that **Rabbi Yonatan said:** With regard to **an onion that one planted in a vineyard,**[H] creating a forbidden mixture of food crops in a vineyard, **and then the vineyard was uprooted,** and most of the onion grew in a permitted manner, it is **forbidden.** Apparently, both Rabbi Yoḥanan and Rabbi Yonatan disagree with the opinion of Rabbi Yannai, and therefore, there is no clear resolution to the dilemma.

הֲדַר אֲתָא לְקַמֵּיהּ דְּרַבִּי אַמִי, וּפְשַׁט לֵיהּ מִן הָדָא דְּאָמַר רַבִּי יִצְחָק אָמַר רַבִּי יוֹחָנָן: לִיטְרָא בְּצָלִים שֶׁתִּיקְּנָהּ וּזְרָעָהּ – מִתְעַשֶּׂרֶת לְפִי כּוּלָּהּ. אַלְמָא: אוֹתָן גִּידּוּלִין מְבַטְּלִין עִיקָּר.

Yishmael **then came** and raised the dilemma **before Rabbi Ami, who resolved it for him from that which Rabbi Yitzḥak said** that **Rabbi Yoḥanan said:** With regard to **a** ***litra***[L] **of onions that one tithed,**[H] **and** then he **sowed** a field with the entire *litra* of onions, when the field yields the crop, **it is tithed according to the entire** crop. Although some of the onions that he sowed were already tithed, he is obligated to tithe them because the volume of the growths exceeds the volume of the original onions and the entire crop has untithed status. **Apparently, those growths neutralize the** prohibition of the **primary,** original, tithed onions.

דִּלְמָא לְחוּמְרָא שָׁאנֵי!

The Gemara rejects that resolution: There is no proof from the ruling in the case of the *litra* of onions, as **perhaps it is different** when the ruling **is a stringency.**[N] Perhaps, due to the concern that the growths neutralize the prohibition of the original, the ruling is that he must tithe the entire crop. However, there is no proof that the same would be true in cases where the ruling is a leniency, e.g., to neutralize the prohibition of the Sabbatical Year or *teruma*.

אֶלָּא מִן הָדָא: דְּתַנְיָא, רַבִּי שִׁמְעוֹן אוֹמֵר.

Rather, proof may be cited from **this** source; **as it is taught** in a *baraita* that **Rabbi Shimon says:**

NOTES

Perhaps it is different when the ruling is a stringency – לְחוּמְרָא שָׁאנֵי: The early commentaries ask: Doesn't this stringency lead to various pitfalls? Based on the principle that if one tithes from produce that one is obligated to tithe for produce that one is not obligated to tithe, the produce that he tithed remains untithed produce, then, if the prohibition of the main part of the plant is not neutralized and remains forbidden, some of the tithe that one tithes from other produce for this entire plant will be tithed unnecessarily, and it will remain untithed produce. Moreover, if he tithes from the original plant for the growths, he would be tithing from produce that one is not obligated to tithe for produce that one is obligated to tithe and that is not considered tithed at all. Most early commentaries, however, maintain that he may not tithe that mixture from itself; rather, he tithes for that produce from other produce. With regard to the first concern, the Rosh writes that he can tithe this *litra* from produce that one is obligated to tithe by rabbinic law, relying on the principle that by Torah law, a simple majority is sufficient to neutralize a prohibition. The Rashba claims that there is no concern that the tithe will be rendered untithed produce, as the very obligation to tithe onions is by rabbinic law. Rabbi Eliezer of Metz also maintains that he does not tithe the *litra* from its own produce; rather, he does so from other produce. He adds that the tithe will indeed be untithed produce, as fundamentally, not all of it is actual tithe. The Ran explains otherwise. He contends that even the growths are actually non-sacred produce, as they grew from non-sacred produce. Therefore, he can tithe from the *litra* itself, as there is no mixture here between produce that one is obligated to tithe and produce that one is not obligated to tithe.

כל דבר שיש לו מתירין, כגון טבל, ומעשר שני, והקדש, וחדש – לא נתנו בהן חכמים שיעור. וכל דבר שאין לו מתירין, כגון תרומה, ותרומת מעשר, וחלה, וערלה, וכלאי הכרם – נתנו בהם חכמים שיעור.

For **any item that can become permitted,**[H] i.e., a forbidden object whose prohibition can or will lapse, **for example, untithed produce**[N] that can be permitted through tithing, **and second tithe** that is permitted through redemption or bringing it to Jerusalem (Deuteronomy 14:24–26), **and consecrated items** that are also permitted through redemption, **and** produce of the **new** crop that is permitted after the sacrifice of the *omer* offering (Leviticus 23:14), **the Sages did not determine a measure for their** neutralization,[N] and no mixture with any quantity of permitted items neutralizes their prohibition. **And** for **any item that cannot become permitted,**[H] **for example,** ***teruma*****, and** ***teruma*** **of the tithe, and** ***ḥalla*** (Numbers 15:20–21); **fruit of a tree during the first three years after its planting [*****orla*****]; and forbidden food crops in a vineyard** (Deuteronomy 22:9), **the Sages determined a measure for their** neutralization.

אמרו לו: והלא שביעית אין לה מתירין, ולא נתנו בה חכמים שיעור. דתנן: השביעית אוסרת כל שהוא במינה! אמר להן: אף אני לא אמרתי אלא לביעור,

The Rabbis **said to** Rabbi Shimon: **But isn't Sabbatical-Year** produce **an item that cannot become permitted, and** nevertheless, **the Sages did not determine a measure for its** neutralization, **as we learned** in a mishna (*Shevi'it* 7:7): **The Sabbatical-Year** produce **prohibits** permitted produce **of its own species** with which it is mixed **in any amount.**[NH] Rabbi Shimon **said to them: I too said** that Sabbatical-Year produce prohibits permitted produce in a mixture and permitted growths that develop from it **only** with regard **to the removal**[N] of the produce. Sabbatical-Year produce may be eaten only as long as produce of that species remains in the field, after which it must be removed from one's possession. Since it is permitted to eat the produce before that time, its legal status during this period is that of an item that can become permitted.

HALAKHA

Any item that can become permitted – כל דבר שיש לו מתירין: Any forbidden object whose prohibition can become permitted by means of action or with the passage of time, which enters into a mixture with permitted substances, cannot be neutralized, and even a minimal amount of the forbidden object renders the entire mixture forbidden (Rambam *Sefer Kedusha, Hilkhot Ma'akhalot Assurot* 15:9–10 and *Sefer Zemanim, Hilkhot Yom Tov* 1:20; *Shulḥan Arukh, Yoreh De'a* 102:1, *Oraḥ Ḥayyim* 513:1).

Any item that cannot become permitted – דבר שאין לו מתירין: The Sages determined the measure for the neutralization of forbidden substances that cannot become permitted. If the forbidden substances entered into a mixture with permitted substances, neutralization varies based on the prohibition in question, on a scale of a majority of sixty, one hundred, or two hundred times the prohibition (Rambam *Sefer Kedusha, Hilkhot Ma'akhalot Assurot* 15:13).

The Sabbatical-Year produce prohibits permitted produce of its own species with which it is mixed in any amount – השביעית אוסרת כל שהוא: If Sabbatical-Year produce was mixed with permitted produce of the same type, even a minimal amount of the forbidden produce renders the entire mixture forbidden. If it was mixed with a different type, the forbidden produce renders the mixture forbidden if it imparts flavor to the mixture. Some say that even a minimal amount of Sabbatical-Year produce renders its own type forbidden in a mixture only after the time of removal (Rabbi Shimshon of Saens; Rambam *Sefer Kedusha, Hilkhot Ma'akhalot Assurot* 15:8 and *Sefer Zera'im, Hilkhot Shemitta VeYovel* 7:22; *Pe'at HaShulḥan* 27:22).

NOTES

For example, untithed produce – כגון טבל: The Gemara in tractate *Avoda Zara* (73b) states another reason why any amount of untithed produce renders the entire mixture forbidden: Its prohibition is parallel to its permission. Just as a single grain separated as *teruma* renders the untithed produce permitted, so too, any amount, even a single grain, of untithed produce renders a mixture forbidden. *Tosafot* ask why the Gemara there fails to cite the reason cited here: That it is an item that can become permitted. They answer that the Gemara there is dealing with untithed produce whose owner traveled overseas, rendering it impossible for another to tithe his produce. Some later commentaries add that the reason cited in tractate *Avoda Zara* applies only to untithed *teruma*, as standard untithed produce requires not only the separation of *teruma* but the separation of tithes and the *teruma* of tithes as well. Since there is a fixed measure for tithes and *teruma* of tithes, the reason that any amount of standard untithed produce renders the entire mixture forbidden is as stated in our Gemara: Because it is an item that can become permitted.

The Sages did not determine a measure for their neutralization – לא נתנו בהן חכמים שיעור: Most commentaries and authorities hold in accordance with the ruling of the Jerusalem Talmud that this applies only to a prohibited item that was mixed with items of the same type. However, if it was mixed with items of a different type, the prohibition is neutralized in the manner that other prohibitions are neutralized, when the permitted amount obscures the flavor of the prohibited item (see *Tosafot*, Rosh, and Ran).

The Sabbatical-Year produce prohibits permitted produce of its species with which it is mixed in any amount – השביעית אוסרת כל שהוא במינה: The early commentaries question the relevance of this *halakha* to the discussion in the Gemara, as ostensibly, it is not at all related to the topic of permitted growth neutralizing a prohibition. Some explain that the manner in which to understand the case of a mixture of Sabbatical-Year produce with other produce with regard to the obligation of removal is in terms of growths from Sabbatical-Year produce, e.g., a sixth-year onion that continued to grow in the Sabbatical Year. In that case, the forbidden Sabbatical-Year growths neutralize the prohibition of the permitted original plant. It is apparent that growths from a plant neutralize the prohibition of the original plant, and the same should be true with regard to the dilemma of Yishmael of Kefar Yamma; the permitted eighth-year growths should neutralize the prohibition of the original Sabbatical-Year plant (Rosh).

The Rashba rejects this proof, as the *halakha* here applies even to minimal growth of forbidden produce. Therefore, it is not that the forbidden produce neutralizes the permitted original plant; rather, it is that the permitted original plant is unable to neutralize the forbidden growths. Therefore, he explains that from the fact that the prohibition of the growths are not neutralized by the original plant, it is apparent that the growths are not considered part of the original plant. One can therefore conclude that if the original plant was forbidden, all the more so is its prohibition not neutralized by permitted growth. According to the Rid, although the *halakha* refers only to a mixture; one can learn from it the *halakha* with regard to growths as well. Rabbi Avraham min HaHar states that from the fact that the Gemara made no distinction between mixtures and growths, apparently one can derive one from the other.

With regard to removal – לביעור: The *halakha* of removal is that one may store Sabbatical-Year produce only as long as produce of that type remains on the trees available to the animals in the field. When produce is no longer available to the animals in the field, one must remove that type of produce from his house, and only then may he benefit from it. According to the Ramban's Commentary on the Torah, removal entails declaring all produce gathered in one's house ownerless and making it available to be eaten by all. Therefore, the status of food that is to undergo removal is that of an item that will become permitted; as one may reclaim it and continue to eat it after it was declared ownerless. According to the Rambam's opinion that removal entails burning and destroying the produce, it must be explained according to the Ran that it can become permitted in the sense that it may be eaten before removal.

HALAKHA

Onions upon which rain fell – בְּצָלִים שֶׁיָּרְדוּ עֲלֵיהֶם גְּשָׁמִים: In a case where rain fell during the Sabbatical Year upon sixth-year onions and they sprouted leaves, if the leaves are light green they are permitted. However, if they are dark green they are prohibited as Sabbatical-Year plants that grew on their own. In both cases, the original onions are permitted (Rambam *Sefer Zera'im, Hilkhot Shemitta VeYovel* 4:20).

LANGUAGE

Black [*sheḥorin*] – שְׁחוֹרִין: In the Bible, and all the more so in the parlance of the Sages, black does not always mean black. Rather, just as white is often used to refer to a bright-colored item, black often refers to anything dark, whether it is black, red, or green.

Here too, the black leaves are the darker ones, an indication that they sprouted and draw their sustenance from the ground. In contrast, lighter leaves could indicate that the leaves sprouted from the bulb.

Turned green [*horiku*] – הוֹרִיקוּ: This means that the color is no longer dark green; it is paler and closer to yellow. The Sages often employ the word green to describe what is commonly called yellow.

Crushed [*medukhanin*] – מְדוּכָנִין: The commentaries explain this as a variation of the term mortar, in which items are crushed. There are both linguistic and substantive problems with that interpretation. From the context, apparently the reference is to a horticultural treatment to prevent growth of plants, as was explained according to the variant reading *merukhanin*.

אֲבָל לַאֲכִילָה – בְּנוֹתֵן טַעַם. וְדִלְמָא הָא נַמִּי לְחוּמְרָא שָׁאנֵי!

However, with regard **to** the permissibility of **eating** Sabbatical-Year produce after the time of removal has passed, when eating that produce is prohibited, the Sages determined a measure for their neutralization. The mixture is forbidden only if the measure of that produce is enough **to impart flavor** to the mixture. Apparently, permitted growths can neutralize the prohibition of the original item. The Gemara rejects the proof: **And perhaps here too, it is different** when the ruling **is a stringency.**[N] In this case, the stringency is that the original item is sacred with the sanctity of the Sabbatical Year. However, here too, there is no proof that the same would be true in cases where the result is a leniency.

אֶלָּא מִן הָדָא פְּשַׁטָהּ, דִּתְנַן: בְּצָלִים שֶׁיָּרְדוּ עֲלֵיהֶם גְּשָׁמִים וְצָמְחוּ, אִם הָיוּ עָלִין שֶׁלָּהֶן שְׁחוֹרִין – אֲסוּרִין, הוֹרִיקוּ – מוּתָּרִין.

Rather, Yishmael of Kefar Yamma **resolved** his dilemma **from this** source, **as we learned** in a mishna (*Shevi'it* 6:3): With regard to sixth-year **onions upon which rain fell**[HN] during the Sabbatical Year, **and they sprouted, if their leaves were black [*sheḥorin*],**[NL] i.e., dark green, an indication of fresh, recent growth, the onions are **forbidden** as Sabbatical-Year growth. If their leaves **turned green [*horiku*],**[L] i.e., lighter and yellower, and appeared withered, the onions are **permitted,** as they are considered a product of the sixth year.

רַבִּי חֲנַנְיָא בֶּן אַנְטִיגְנוֹס אוֹמֵר: אִם יְכוֹלִין לִיתָּלֵשׁ בֶּעָלִין שֶׁלָּהֶן – אֲסוּרִין. וּכְנֶגְדָּן לְמוֹצָאֵי שְׁבִיעִית מוּתָּרִין. לְמֵימְרָא דְּגִידּוּלֵי הֶיתֵּר מַעֲלִין אֶת הָאִיסּוּר. וְדִלְמָא בִּמְדוּכָנִין!

Rabbi Ḥanina ben Antigonus says: There is a different indicator; **if** the plants **can be uprooted**[N] **by their leaves,** clearly the leaves are fresh and recent, and they are **forbidden. And in the parallel** situation, if that indicator was discovered in a Sabbatical-Year onion that sprouted **at the conclusion of the Sabbatical Year,**[N] i.e., during the eighth year, the onions are **permitted.** The Gemara asks: **Is this to say that** one may conclude from here that **permitted growth neutralizes the prohibition** of the original plant? The Gemara rejects this conclusion: **And perhaps** the *halakha* **is with regard to crushed [*medukhanin*],**[L] pounded onions,[N] and the reason that the prohibition of the original plant is neutralized is not that the permitted growth neutralizes the prohibition, but that it is no longer fit for consumption.

אֶלָּא מִן הָדָא, דְּתַנְיָא.

Rather, the dilemma can be resolved **from this** source; **as it is taught** in a *baraita*:

NOTES

And perhaps here too, it is different when the ruling is a stringency – וְדִלְמָא הָא נַמִּי לְחוּמְרָא שָׁאנֵי: Didn't the Gemara reject the previous proof in a similar manner? Why, then, cite another proof that can be rejected in the same manner? The Ran answers that in this case, one might have thought that this *halakha* is not a stringency, as there are two stringencies in this *halakha*: First, the stringency that the status of food that is to undergo removal is that of an item that will become permitted, and therefore, the prohibition is not neutralized; and second, the stringency that even minimal growths render the original plant forbidden. Therefore, one might conclude that if the Sages sought merely to be stringent, they would not have instituted two stringencies; one might at least question whether the *halakha* that even minimal growths render the original plant forbidden is a stringency, and contend, rather, that it is part of the fundamental *halakha*.

Onions upon which rain fell – בְּצָלִים שֶׁיָּרְדוּ עֲלֵיהֶם גְּשָׁמִים: The simple understanding of the Gemara is that it is referring to ripe onions left on the ground for storage purposes. *Tosafot*, however, question that understanding, as there is no precedent for minimal growth rendering the entire plant forbidden. Therefore, they explain, and the Rashba elaborates, that the reference is to a sixth-year onion that one uprooted and replanted during the Sabbatical Year. Since planting it then is prohibited, the Sages penalized him and decreed that even minimal growth renders the entire plant forbidden.

Black – שְׁחוֹרִין: Most commentaries understand that black in this context is referring to a dark color. If the leaves are dark green, that is an indication that they are healthy and receive their nourishment from the ground, and that they are not growths from the onion itself (Rashi; Ran). The Rosh explains that when onions grow, their leaves blacken and spread. Rabbi Yitzḥak Tzarfati suggests that the reference is to the thin peel covering a large onion, which begins red and gradually darkens as the onion ripens.

If the plants can be uprooted – אִם יְכוֹלִין לִיתָּלֵשׁ: Most commentaries understand the ruling of Rabbi Ḥanina ben Antigonus as a stringency, as in his opinion it is not necessary that the leaves turn black in order for it to be considered that the plant grew during the Sabbatical year; rather, it is sufficient if the onion can be uprooted by grasping the leaves, proving that there is a strong connection to the onion itself, and the leaves are not merely a withered growth loosely attached to the plant. Others maintain that Rabbi Ḥanina does not disagree with the previous indicator. It is merely an additional indicator of the same status.

And in the parallel situation, at the conclusion of the Sabbatical Year – וּכְנֶגְדָּן לְמוֹצָאֵי שְׁבִיעִית: This is the relevant proof for the issue at hand, as it indicates that the permitted eighth-year growth neutralizes the prohibition of the original Sabbatical-Year plant. The question though, arises: If it was established that minimal forbidden growths prohibit the original permitted plant, it cannot be said that permitted growths will neutralize the prohibition of the forbidden plant only if their volume exceeds the volume of the prohibition. The Rosh concedes that this is not a full-fledged analogy and it means that even minimal forbidden growths render the plant forbidden, while permitted growths neutralize the prohibition only if if their volume exceeds the volume of the prohibition. The Ran explains that earlier in the Gemara it means that the permitted growth neutralizes the prohibition of the minuscule forbidden element intermingled with it. According to the Ran, the prohibition of the original plant is not neutralized; it is only the growths themselves that are rendered permitted. Rabbi Shimshon of Saens in his commentary on the Mishna explains that the reference is to the sixth-year onion mentioned earlier that underwent minimal growth during the Sabbatical Year, which was subsequently uprooted and replanted in the eighth year, and continued to grow. In that case, the permitted growths combine with the permitted original plant to neutralize the prohibited Sabbatical-Year growths (see Rabbi Avraham min HaHar).

With regard to crushed [*medukhanin*] onions – בִּמְדוּכָנִין: There are different opinions about the meaning of this term. Some explain that he crushed and pounded the original plant, which grew nevertheless. Since the original plant is no longer intact, the growths can neutralize its prohibition (Rashi). The Ran adds that once the plant was crushed the growths are no longer attributable to it. The Rosh explains differently. He maintains that both the original plant and the growths are crushed. Since there is no way to distinguish between them, their legal status is like any other prohibition in a mixture that is neutralized by the permitted majority. Rabbi Avraham min HaHar explains similarly. The Meiri, apparently based on the Jerusalem Talmud, cites a variant reading: *Merukhanin*, bent, instead of *medukhanin*, crushed, meaning that he bent the tops of the onions, thereby indicating that he does not want them to grow.

הַמְנַכֵּשׁ עִם הַכּוּתִי בַּחֲסָיוֹת – אוֹכֵל מֵהֶן אֲכִילַת עֲרַאי, וּמְעַשְּׂרָן וַדַּאי.

One who weeds ***ḥasayot***[NL] **with a Samaritan**[N] **may eat a casual meal from them**[N] without tithing, as any untithed produce may be eaten in the framework of a casual meal. **And** when he completes the labor on the *ḥasayot*, places them into a pile, and they require tithing, **he tithes them** as produce that is **definitely** obligated in tithing, not as doubtfully tithed produce, as the assumption is that the Samaritan did not tithe the *ḥasayot*.

רַבִּי שִׁמְעוֹן בֶּן אֶלְעָזָר אוֹמֵר: אִם יִשְׂרָאֵל חָשׁוּד עַל הַשְּׁבִיעִית – לְמוֹצָאֵי שְׁבִיעִית מוּתָּר. לְמֵימְרָא דְּגִידּוּלֵי הֶיתֵּר מַעֲלִין אֶת הָאִיסּוּר. וְדִלְמָא בְּדָבָר שֶׁזַּרְעוֹ כָּלֶה! הָא תַּנְיָא: אֵלּוּ הֵן חֲסָיוֹת – כְּגוֹן הַלּוּף הַשּׁוּם וְהַבְּצָלִים.

Rabbi Shimon ben Elazar says: If the *ḥasayot* belong to **a Jew** who is **suspect** about observance of **the Sabbatical Year,**[N] **at the conclusion of the Sabbatical Year** it **is permitted**[N] to weed with him, as there is no concern that there might be Sabbatical-Year sanctity. The Gemara asks: **Is this to say that the permitted growths** of the eighth year **neutralize the prohibition,** and that is why there is no concern about Sabbatical-Year sanctity? The Gemara rejects that inference: **And perhaps** the *tanna* is speaking **with regard to an item whose seeds cease**[B] after it is sown, whose growths neutralize the original prohibition? The Gemara rejects that possibility: **Isn't it taught** in a *baraita*: **These are *ḥasayot*, for example, arum,**[B] **garlic, and onions,** whose seeds do not cease?

LANGUAGE

Ḥasayot – חֲסָיוֹת: This is a general term for plants whose bulbs are eaten, e.g., onions, from the Hebrew root *ḥasa*, meaning concealed. These plants are cultivated primarily for the parts buried in the ground, not those visible above ground.

BACKGROUND

An item whose seeds cease – דָּבָר שֶׁזַּרְעוֹ כָּלֶה: Many species of plants, e.g., grains and legumes, most vegetables, and even trees, grow from seeds. In addition to the germ, the seed contains starches and sugars with which the germ is sustained. When the germ begins to sprout, it draws sustenance from its own reserves until it grows roots and draws sustenance from the ground. At that point, the seed withers until it completely decays in the ground. These plants are described as those whose seeds cease. However, there are other species of plants, usually grown from bulbs, e.g., arum and taro in the talmudic era or potatoes, garlic, and onions today, that are also sown in the ground. Although parts of these bulbs decay in the ground after they grow roots and stalks, most of the bulbs remain intact and grow over time, by accumulating additional layers or by developing new bulbs. These plants are described as those whose seeds do not cease. There are other plants that are bulbs where the bulb decays completely before new bulbs sprout.

Development of a bean sprout, whose seed ceases and decays in the ground

Arum – לוּף: This plant is commonly identified as the Palestine arum, *Arum palaestinum*, from the Araceae family. The plant has a bulb in the ground from which large leaves sprout. The arum's inflorescence has a unique structure and is covered with a special type of leaf called a spathe. All parts of the plant contain calcium oxalate, $Ca(COO)_2$, which is poisonous and causes severe irritation to the skin on contact. Therefore, people refrain from consuming arum in its raw state, and only rarely do animals draw sustenance from it. The bulb and leaves are cooked or roasted to render them edible. The plant grows in the wild in all regions of Eretz Yisrael.

NOTES

Ḥasayot – חֲסָיוֹת: The Gemara explains that *ḥasayot* are plants with bulbs, or onions. The Meiri explains that *ḥasayot* are small onions.

One who weeds…with a Samaritan – הַמְנַכֵּשׁ עִם הַכּוּתִי: The Ran explains that the precise definition of weeding in this context involves removing unnecessary leaves from the vegetables, and others maintain that it refers to the removal of extraneous plants from the flowerbed. This difference in interpretation is related to certain differences in the discussion in the Gemara. Later the Gemara learns a practical *halakha* from the fact that it is a case involving weeding. *Tosafot* explain that the *baraita* discusses the case of one weeding with a Samaritan because it was rare for Jews and Samaritans to fraternize; therefore, the case of one eating a casual meal from produce belonging to a Samaritan is feasible when the Jew is working for the Samaritan. Several commentaries explain that it is permitted for the one weeding to eat from the crops that he is weeding, as the *halakha* is that a worker may partake of his employer's produce in the course of performing his task. The Rashash rejects that explanation, as it is permitted to eat the produce while working only when performing tasks that constitute the final stages of processing that produce. Other early commentaries explain that the worker is partaking of the produce not based on the fact that this is permitted for a worker; rather, it is the manner in which the owner of the field chose to pay him (Rabbi Avraham min HaHar; Meiri).

May eat a casual meal from them – אוֹכֵל מֵהֶן אֲכִילַת עֲרַאי: As a rule, it is permitted for one to eat a casual meal from the produce in the field, provided that the produce was not placed in a pile and brought into the house, which are the final stages of its processing and at which point one is required to tithe the produce. The novel element here is that there is no concern that the Samaritan sowed untithed produce that is already obligated in tithes, even though Samaritans were of the opinion that grain sowed in the ground does not require tithing. Since the Sages ruled that the status of growths of untithed produce parallels that of untithed produce itself, there should be concern that perhaps he is eating untithed produce. There are various explanations why that is not a concern. The Ran explains that it is not a concern since the entire obligation to tithe *ḥasayot* is by rabbinic law. According to the Rid, the decree that the status of growths of untithed produce parallels that of untithed produce itself applies only to growths of produce that is certainly untithed; in this case there is uncertainty, as the Samaritan might have bought and sown tithed produce.

Some early commentaries cite a variant reading: Gentile, instead of Samaritan. Rabbi Eliezer of Metz explains: The obligation to tithe is established by placing the produce in a pile, and there is no obligation to tithe produce placed in a pile by a gentile. Although the Sages issued a decree that one must tithe the produce of a gentile, they did not apply the decree to casual meals.

Suspect about observance of the Sabbatical Year – חָשׁוּד עַל הַשְּׁבִיעִית: This does not mean that the concern is only that perhaps he will sow the seeds during the Sabbatical Year. Rather, this is the *halakha* even if there is certainty that he did so (Rosh). The term suspect, therefore, is a form of euphemism, and it refers to one who violated this prohibition.

At the conclusion of the Sabbatical Year it is permitted – לְמוֹצָאֵי שְׁבִיעִית מוּתָּר: According to the explanation of the Ran that weeding refers to the removal of extraneous leaves, clearly the volume of the permitted eighth-year leaves exceeds the volume of the forbidden ones, and therefore it is permitted to eat them. In contrast, the Rid explains according to his opinion that the permitted growth neutralizes the prohibition of the original, as, even in a case of uncertainty it would not be permitted, as it is uncertainty involving Torah law. That is not the case with regard to tithes, as the obligation to tithe *ḥasayot* is by rabbinic law.

וְדִלְמָא בִּמְדוּכָנִין? חָשׁוּד עַל הַשְּׁבִיעִית קָתָנֵי. וְדִלְמָא בְּתַעֲרוֹבֶת? הַמְנַכֵּשׁ קָתָנֵי.

The Gemara asks: **And perhaps** the *tanna* is speaking **with regard to** plants that were **crushed**[N] before they sprouted growths? The Gemara answers: It is the case of one who is **suspect about** observance of **the Sabbatical Year,** that **is taught** in the *baraita*, and one who is suspect would not bother to eliminate the prohibition by crushing it. The Gemara asks: **And perhaps** the *tanna* is speaking **with regard to a mixture** of forbidden *ḥasayot* and permitted ones, and the reason that it is permitted is that the prohibition was neutralized by the majority of permitted *ḥasayot*? The Gemara answers: **One who weeds, is taught**[N] in the *baraita*, indicating that he is eating the leaves as he weeds them, leaving no opportunity for the *ḥasayot* to be mixed with others.

לֵימָא תֶּיהֱוֵי תְּיוּבְתֵּיהּ דְּרַבִּי יוֹחָנָן וּדְרַבִּי יוֹנָתָן? אָמַר רַבִּי יִצְחָק: שָׁנְיָא שְׁבִיעִית, הוֹאִיל וְאִיסּוּרָהּ עַל יְדֵי קַרְקַע – בְּטֵילָתָהּ נַמִי עַל יְדֵי קַרְקַע.

The Gemara suggests: **Let us say that this is a conclusive refutation** of the opinions **of Rabbi Yoḥanan and Rabbi Yonatan,** who stated regarding *orla* and food crops in a vineyard that their permitted growth does not neutralize the prohibition of the original fruit or food crops respectively. **Rabbi Yitzḥak said:** The **Sabbatical-Year** produce **is different. Since its prohibition** is engendered **by means of the ground,**[HN] **its nullification** is effected **by means of the ground as well.** The prohibition can be neutralized by means of the growth that results from replanting the forbidden plant in a permitted manner.

הֲרֵי מַעֲשֵׂר, דְּאִיסּוּרוֹ עַל יְדֵי קַרְקַע וְאֵין בְּטֵילָתוֹ עַל יְדֵי קַרְקַע. דְּתַנְיָא: לִיטְרָא מַעֲשֵׂר טֶבֶל שֶׁזְּרָעָהּ בְּקַרְקַע וְהִשְׁבִּיחָה, וַהֲרֵי הִיא כְּעֶשֶׂר לִיטְרִין – חַיֶּיבֶת בְּמַעֲשֵׂר וּבַשְּׁבִיעִית, וְאוֹתָהּ לִיטְרָא מְעַשֵּׂר עָלֶיהָ מִמָּקוֹם אַחֵר לְפִי חֶשְׁבּוֹן!

The Gemara asks: Isn't there the case of **tithe, whose prohibition is** engendered **by means of the ground,**[N] **but its nullification is not** effected **by means of the ground? As it is taught** in a *baraita*: With regard to **a *litra* of untithed** first **tithe**[H] from which the *teruma* of the tithe was not taken, **which one sowed in the ground, and it grew and it is** now **approximately ten *litra*,** that additional growth **is obligated** to have **tithe** taken[N] **and** is subject to the *halakhot* of **Sabbatical-Year** produce.[N] **And** with regard to **that** original ***litra*** of untithed first tithe that he sowed, one **tithes for it from** produce in **a different place,**[N] and not from the *litra* itself, **based on a calculation** of how much *teruma* of the tithe needed to be taken from that litra. Apparently, the growth that results from sowing the first tithe in the ground does not neutralize its prohibition.

HALAKHA

The Sabbatical-Year produce is different, since its prohibition is engendered by means of the ground – שָׁנְיָא שְׁבִיעִית הוֹאִיל וְאִיסּוּרָהּ עַל יְדֵי קַרְקַע: If the growth of a Sabbatical-Year onion during the eighth year exceeds its previous size, the entire plant is permitted. Since the prohibition of the Sabbatical Year is engendered by means of the ground, its neutralization is effected by means of the ground as well (Rambam *Sefer Zera'im, Hilkhot Shemitta VeYovel* 4:7; 24).

A *litra* of untithed first tithe – לִיטְרָא מַעֲשֵׂר טֶבֶל: If a *litra* of tithe from which *teruma* of the tithe was not separated was sown in the ground, and it sprouted until it reached ten *litra*, one is obligated to tithe it like regular produce. One separates *teruma* of the tithe for the tithed *litra* from some produce in a different place. The Ra'avad states that this *halakha* applies only to items whose seeds do not cease, and the *Kesef Mishne* maintains that this is the ruling of the Rambam as well. The Radbaz, however, maintains that the Rambam disagrees and that this *halakha* applies to all plants (Rambam *Sefer Zera'im, Hilkhot Ma'aser* 6:4).

NOTES

And perhaps the *tanna* is speaking with regard to plants that were crushed [*medukhanin*] – וְדִלְמָא בִּמְדוּכָנִין: Most commentaries explain the term *medukhanin* here as it was explained previously: The part of the plant that grew during the Sabbatical Year was crushed. The Gemara responds: Since he is suspect about observance of the Sabbatical Year, he would not take the trouble to mitigate the prohibition. Although there is a principle that one would not forsake permitted food to partake of forbidden food, that applies only where partaking of the permitted food does not require exertion (*Tosafot*; Ran). Rabbi Avraham min HaHar interprets this differently. He maintains that *medukhanin* is from the term *dekhei*, meaning pure. The Gemara explains that this produce is pure in the sense that there is no concern about the Sabbatical Year. The Gemara answers that since the person himself is suspect about observance of the Sabbatical Year, it is unlikely that the seeds are beyond suspicion.

One who weeds is taught – הַמְנַכֵּשׁ קָתָנֵי: This indicates that he is eating the produce that he is weeding, and there is no mixture, as he uproots and eats the *ḥasayot* that began to grow during the Sabbatical Year. The Rashba questions the Gemara's answer, as it could still be explained that there is a mixture of Sabbatical-Year plants and permitted ones. He answers that since he is suspect about observance of the Sabbatical Year, it is likely that the entire plant is Sabbatical-Year produce.

Its prohibition is engendered by means of the ground – וְאִיסּוּרָהּ עַל יְדֵי קַרְקַע: One explanation is that it is the ground that renders Sabbatical-Year produce forbidden, as opposed to *orla*, whose prohibition is engendered by time, or food crops in a vineyard, whose prohibition is engendered by the mixture. Therefore, the neutralization of the prohibition of Sabbatical-Year produce is effected by the ground as well (Rashi; Ran). The Rid explains differently: During the Sabbatical Year there is a prohibition against working the ground itself, while with regard to *orla* and food crops in a vineyard, the fruit is prohibited. Other early commentaries maintain that the difference between the cases discussed by Rabbi Yoḥanan and Rabbi Yonatan and this one is that in order to permit *orla* or food crops in a vineyard one must perform an action, e.g., grafting a young vine onto an old one, or uprooting the vineyard, respectively. Otherwise, the prohibition remains intact. It is prohibited to neutralize a prohibition *ab initio*. However, with regard to Sabbatical-Year produce, even if one were to take no action, the permitted eighth-year growths would neutralize the prohibition (*Tosafot*; Rosh; Meiri; see Rashba).

Tithe, whose prohibition is by means of the ground – מַעֲשֵׂר, דְּאִיסּוּרוֹ עַל יְדֵי קַרְקַע: The Rid explains that the obligation to tithe is not dependent upon what one sows, as even if he were to sow tithed produce, the moment that it sprouts from the ground there is a renewed obligation to tithe it. Rabbi Yitzḥak Tzarfati explains that this refers to the *halakha* that one is not obligated by Torah law to tithe plants that grew in a non-perforated pot; one is obligated to tithe only those plants that grow in the ground, or in a perforated pot.

Obligated to have tithe taken – חַיֶּיבֶת בְּמַעֲשֵׂר: Some commentaries maintain that one is obligated to tithe the original *litra* and its growths. It is a stricture by rabbinic law. On the other hand, he is also obligated to separate *teruma* of the tithe from the *litra* that he sowed, as its seeds do not cease (Rashi; Rosh). Others say that one is obligated to tithe only the growths; one tithes the nine *litra*, and separates only *teruma* of the tithe from the tenth (*Tosefot Rabbeinu Peretz*).

Is obligated to have tithe taken and is subject to the *halakhot* of Sabbatical-Year produce – חַיֶּיבֶת בְּמַעֲשֵׂר וּבַשְּׁבִיעִית: According to some commentaries, this is referring to two separate *halakhot* that do not take effect simultaneously. It means that during years other than the Sabbatical Year one is obligated to tithe, and during the Sabbatical Year, the *halakhot* of the Sabbatical Year apply (Rosh; *Tosefot Rabbeinu Peretz*). Others maintain that both prohibitions take effect during the Sabbatical Year. For example, if one sowed the plant during the sixth year and it grew during the Sabbatical Year, the ruling is stringent with regard to both *halakhot*; the growths neutralize the prohibition of the original plant in terms of the *halakhot* of the Sabbatical Year, but do not do so in terms of the *halakhot* of tithes (Meiri). The Rashba asks: Since one is obligated with regard to this produce in the *halakhot* of both tithes and the Sabbatical Year, there is no proof that the prohibition of the growths are neutralized, as in the other case the growths neutralize the prohibition of the original plant. Therefore, the Rashba explains that this is not a difficulty, but merely a point of clarification: How is the *baraita* to be understood, as it appears to be self-contradictory with regard to the status of growths?

One tithes for it from produce in a different place – מְעַשֵּׂר עָלֶיהָ מִמָּקוֹם אַחֵר: Most commentaries explain that he cannot tithe from the *litra* itself because there is a mixture of the growths and the original plant. The result would be that he is tithing from exempt produce for produce that is obligated (Ran). The Rashba adds that not only may he not separate tithes from this *litra* itself, but he may not do so from the growths either, due to the same concern. Other commentaries maintain that the phrase: From produce in a different place, is imprecise. Since it is prohibited to tithe from the produce of one year for the produce of another year, he must tithe from produce that was obligated in tithes the previous year, as the obligation to separate *teruma* of the tithe from the first *litra* was incurred the previous year (Rashi; Rid).

אָמְרִי: מַעֲשֵׂר – דִּיגּוּן הוּא דְּקָא גָּרֵים לֵיהּ.

The Sages of the Gemara **say:** With regard to **tithe,** the ground does not engender the obligation; **placement** of the produce **in a pile engenders** the obligation,[N] as it is only at that point that one is obligated to tithe his produce. Therefore neutralization of the prohibition is not effected by planting it in the ground.

מְתִיב רָמִי בַּר חָמָא: ״קוֹנָם פֵּירוֹת הָאֵלּוּ עָלַי״, ״קוֹנָם הֵן עַל פִּי״, ״קוֹנָם הֵן לְפִי״ – אָסוּר בְּחִילּוּפֵיהֶן וּבְגִידּוּלֵיהֶן. ״שֶׁאֲנִי אוֹכֵל״ וְ״שֶׁאֲנִי טוֹעֵם״ – מוּתָּר בְּחִילּוּפֵיהֶן וּבְגִידּוּלֵיהֶן בְּדָבָר שֶׁזַּרְעוֹ כָּלֶה, אֲבָל בְּדָבָר שֶׁאֵין זַרְעוֹ כָּלֶה – אֲפִילּוּ גִּידּוּלֵי גִידּוּלִין אֲסוּרִין!

Rami bar Ḥama raised an objection to the opinion of Rabbi Yannai based on the mishna (57a): For one who says: **This produce is *konam*[N] upon me,** or **it is *konam* upon my mouth,** or **it is *konam* to my mouth, it is prohibited** to partake of the produce, or **of its replacements, or** of anything that **grows from it.** If he says: This produce is *konam* for me, and for **that** reason **I will not eat** it, **or** for **that** reason **I will not taste** it, **it is permitted** for him to partake **of its replacements or** of anything that **grows from it.** This applies only **with regard to an item whose seeds cease** after it is sown. **However, with regard to an item whose seeds do not cease** after it is sown, it **is prohibited** for him to partake even of the **growths of** its **growths.** Apparently, permitted growths do not neutralize the prohibition.

אָמַר רַבִּי אַבָּא: שָׁאנֵי קוֹנָמוֹת, הוֹאִיל וְאִי בָּעֵי מִתְשִׁיל עֲלַייהוּ – הָווּ לְהוּ כְּדָבָר שֶׁיֵּשׁ לוֹ מַתִּירִין, וְאֵין בָּטֵיל בְּרוֹב.

Rabbi Abba said: *Konamot* **are different; since if he wishes** to do so he can **request** that a halakhic authority dissolve the vows and render the objects of the vows permitted, **their** legal status **is like** that of **an item that can become permitted,**[N] **and** its prohibition **is not nullified by a majority** of permitted items.

NOTES

Placement of the produce in a pile engenders the obligation – דִּיגּוּן הוּא דְּקָא גָּרֵים: The Ran explains that the ground does not engender the obligation to tithe produce; rather, it is engendered by placement in a pile. The Rosh adds that it is not the sowing and growth of the produce that creates untithed produce; it is the actions of the person who harvests it and places it into a pile. Rashi states, consistent with his earlier explanation, that one's obligation to tithe this *litra* of onions was effected by its placement in a pile during the previous year, prior to its resowing.

This produce is *konam* – קוֹנָם פֵּירוֹת: The commentaries (see *Shita Mekubbetzet*) note that the difficulty is not posed from the first *halakha*, as it could be explained that through the *konam* he renders forbidden to him not only benefit from the produce itself, but also any benefit that derives from it. The proof is from the second *halakha*: This produce is *Konam* for me, and for that reason I will not eat, or I will not taste it. In those cases, if the seeds do not cease, its growths are forbidden, proving that although he vowed that the produce itself is forbidden to him, since it does not cease entirely, its growths do not neutralize the prohibition of the original plant.

The early commentaries say: According to the principle: An item whose prohibition is engendered by means of the ground, its neutralization is effected by means of the ground as well, since the prohibition of *konamot* is not engendered by means of the ground, but by his vow, there is no reason to presume that their neutralization would be effected by means of the ground. The Rid explains that the Gemara could have answered in that manner, but opted for the answer that an item forbidden by a *konam* is an item that can become permitted. Rabbi Avraham min HaHar cites an explanation in the name of Rashi that is even more radical: The Gemara at this stage of the discussion does not accept the principle: An item whose prohibition is engendered by means of the ground, etc. Others maintain that the Gemara continues to accept that principle. However, one might have thought that the growths of an item forbidden by a *konam* are similar to those of Sabbatical-Year produce; just as their prohibition results from the fact that they grew from a forbidden item, the neutralization of their prohibition is due to the fact that they grew in the ground (*Tosafot*). According to the Rosh, the growths of an item forbidden by a *konam* are different from those of tithes, as the prohibition of tithes is effected by the actions of a person after the produce was already detached from the ground, whereas in the case of *konam* the mixture of prohibited and permitted parts of the plant takes place while it remains connected to the ground.

Their legal status is like that of an item that can become permitted – הָווּ לְהוּ כְּדָבָר שֶׁיֵּשׁ: The Gemara does not say that it is an item that can become permitted, because a *konam* does not become permitted on its own like other prohibitions; one must find an extenuation for the vow to be dissolved. Although there is no certainty that he will be able to find an extenuation, its legal status is like that of an item that can become permitted, as nevertheless, the chance is good that he will find a way to have the vow dissolved (*Meromei Sadeh*; *Teshuva MeAhava*).

וַהֲרֵי תְּרוּמָה, דְּאִי בָּעֵי מִיתְשִׁיל עֲלַהּ, וּבָטְלִי בְּרוֹב. דִּתְנַן: סְאָה תְּרוּמָה טְמֵאָה שֶׁנָּפְלָה לְפָחוֹת מִמֵּאָה חוּלִּין – תֵּרָקֵב, הָא לְמֵאָה – תַּעֲלֶה! אָמְרִי: בִּתְרוּמָה בְּיַד כֹּהֵן עָסְקִינַן, דְּלָא מָצֵי מִיתְשִׁיל עֲלַהּ.

The Gemara asks: **And** isn't there the case of ***teruma*****,** in **which if** he **wishes** he can **request** that a halakhic authority dissolve the designation of the produce as *teruma*[HN] **and** yet it is **nullified by a majority**[N] of permitted items? **As we learned** in a mishna (*Terumot* 5:1): **A *se'a* of ritually impure *teruma***[H] **that fell into less than one hundred *se'a*** of **non-sacred produce** must be left **to decay.**[N] The impure *teruma*, which is forbidden to all, renders the entire mixture forbidden. The Gemara infers: If it fell **into one hundred *se'a*** of non-sacred produce, its prohibition **is neutralized.**[N] The Sages of the Gemara **say** in response: **We are dealing with *teruma*** that is **in the possession of a priest,**[N] for which the owner **can no** longer **request** that a halakhic authority dissolve the designation. However, as long as the *teruma* is in the owner's possession he can request that its designation be dissolved, and therefore its prohibition cannot be neutralized.

אִי הָכִי אֵימָא סֵיפָא: אִם הָיְתָה טְהוֹרָה – תִּמָּכֵר לְכֹהֵן! אֶלָּא בְּיִשְׂרָאֵל שֶׁנָּפְלוּ לוֹ מִבֵּית אֲבִי אִמּוֹ כֹּהֵן עָסְקִינַן.

The Gemara asks: **If so, say the latter clause** of that mishna: **If** the *teruma* mixed with the non-sacred produce **was ritually pure,** it may **be sold to a priest,** who treats all the produce as though it were *teruma*. This indicates that the mishna is dealing with *teruma* in its owner's possession that was not yet given to a priest. **Rather, we are dealing with** the case of **an Israelite who inherited** the produce **from** a member of **the house of his mother's father,** who is **a priest.** The heir owns the *teruma*; however, since he was not the one who designated it as *teruma*, he may not request that the designation be dissolved.

[וְהָא] קָתָנֵי סֵיפָא: תִּימָּכֵר לְכֹהֵן חוּץ מִדְּמֵי אוֹתָהּ סְאָה!

The Gemara asks: **But isn't it taught in** that **latter clause** of that mishna: It must **be sold to a priest**; however, the price must reflect the value of the entire mixture **except for the value of that *se'a*** of *teruma* that fell into the non-sacred produce, as the *teruma* belongs to the priest. If the mishna is referring to the case of an heir who owns the *teruma*, why can he not collect the value of that *se'a* as well, as it is his property?

HALAKHA

Which if he wishes he can request that a halakhic authority dissolve the designation of the produce as *teruma* – דְּאִי בָּעֵי מִיתְשִׁיל עֲלַהּ: One who separated *teruma* and tithes and regretted doing so may request that a halakhic authority dissolve their designation, just as he would for a vow. The produce would then revert to its previous state (Rambam *Sefer Zera'im*, *Hilkhot Terumot* 4:17; *Shulḥan Arukh*, *Yoreh De'a* 331:48).

A *se'a* of ritually impure *teruma* – סְאָה תְּרוּמָה טְמֵאָה: If a *se'a* of impure *teruma* fell into less than one hundred *se'a* of other non-sacred produce, first tithe, second tithe, or consecrated produce, it becomes a mixture that contains *teruma*, and the status of the entire mixture is that of ritually impure *teruma*. Its consumption is forbidden, and it must be left to decay (Rambam *Sefer Zera'im*, *Hilkhot Terumot* 14:11).

NOTES

In which if he wishes he can request that a halakhic authority dissolve the designation of the produce as *teruma* – דְּאִי בָּעֵי מִיתְשִׁיל עֲלַהּ: Some commentaries ask: Since Rabbi Yannai states this *halakha* with regard to an onion of *teruma*, doesn't this constitute a direct contradiction of his ruling? The Ran answers that Rabbi Yannai was referring to *teruma* whose designation cannot be dissolved, e.g., *teruma* that is in the possession of a priest or that he received as an inheritance from his maternal grandfather.

And yet it is nullified by a majority – וּבָטְלִי בְּרוֹב: This is difficult, as *teruma* is never neutralized by a simple majority; it requires one hundred permitted parts to neutralize one part of *teruma*. Although that is a stringency by rabbinic law, the *halakha* that an item that can become permitted is not neutralized is also by rabbinic law; therefore the discussion is not about the *halakha* by Torah law but rather about rabbinical ordinances and decrees. Therefore, the Vilna Gaon deletes the word majority. Others explain that majority in this context means most of its growth, which includes not only a simple majority but even a majority of one hundred to one (Rashi; Rabbi Avraham min HaHar; *Shita Mekubbetzet*).

Left to decay – תֵּרָקֵב: There is no remedy for this produce, as it is forbidden to an Israelite since it is *teruma*, and to a priest as it is impure. A priest may not even use it to kindle a fire, despite the fact that in general he may use impure *teruma* for that purpose. The Sages prohibited doing so in this case lest he keep the mixture in his possession for an extended period and inadvertently eat it (Ran).

If it fell into one hundred *se'a* of non-sacred produce, its prohibition is neutralized – הָא לְמֵאָה תַּעֲלֶה: The result is that the impure *teruma* is completely neutralized, and there is no obligation to give any part of that mixture to a priest. There is no concern that he will thereby be stealing from the tribe of priests, as that *se'a* of *teruma* is not given to any priest because the *teruma* is impure and fit only for kindling (Rabbi Avraham min HaHar).

***Teruma* that is in the possession of a priest – תְּרוּמָה בְּיַד כֹּהֵן:** Many commentaries question why one cannot request dissolution of the designation of *teruma* once the *teruma* is in the possession of the priest. Rashi and the Ran explain simply that once another person has acquired it, the original owner does not have the right to dissolve its designation (see *Beit HaLevi*). The Rosh cites the opinion of Rabbi Eliezer of Metz, who explains that the priest cannot dissolve its designation as *teruma* because he was not the one who separated it. The Rosh adds that according to that approach, the Israelite who separated the *teruma* can request to have its designation dissolved.

However, that is an unlikely scenario, as the only reason that he might do so is because there is nothing else to eat. By the time that he gives the *teruma* to the priest, all the produce from which he separated the *teruma* and tithes is available to him. Because that is unlikely, the *teruma* is not considered an item that can become permitted. The *Shakh* (*Hoshen Mishpat* 255:6) explains that giving the *teruma* to the priest is accomplished through action and dissolving its designation is accomplished through speech; the principle is that speech cannot negate an action.

אֶלָּא אֵימָא: בִּשְׁלָמָא קוֹנָמוֹת – מִצְוָה לְאִיתְשׁוֹלֵי עֲלֵיהֶן, מִשּׁוּם דְּרַבִּי נָתָן. דְּאָמַר רַבִּי נָתָן: כָּל הַנּוֹדֵר – כְּאִילּוּ בָּנָה בָּמָה, וְהַמְקַיְּימוֹ – כְּאִילּוּ מַקְטִיר עָלֶיהָ. תְּרוּמָה מַאי מִצְוָה לְאִיתְשׁוֹלֵי עֲלַהּ?

Rather, say that there is another distinction between *konamot* and other cases where one may request dissolution by a halakhic authority. **Granted,** in the case of ***konamot,*** there is **a mitzva to request** that a halakhic authority dissolve **them,**[N] **due to** the statement **of Rabbi Natan, as Rabbi Natan said: Anyone who vows, it is as if he built a** personal **altar** outside the Temple, **and one who fulfills** that vow, it is **as though he burns** an offering **upon it.** However, in the case of ***teruma,*** **what mitzva** is there **to request** that a halakhic authority dissolve **its** designation?[N] Therefore, items forbidden by *konamot* are considered items that can become permitted, and *teruma* is not.

גּוּפָא, אָמַר רַבִּי יוֹחָנָן: לִיטְרָא בְּצָלִים שֶׁתִּיקְּנָהּ וּזְרָעָהּ – מִתְעַשֶּׂרֶת לְפִי כּוּלָּהּ. יָתֵיב רַבָּה וְקָאָמַר לְהָא שְׁמַעְתָּא. אֲמַר לֵיהּ רַב חִסְדָּא: מַאן צָאֵית לָךְ וּלְרַבִּי יוֹחָנָן רַבָּךְ! הֶיתֵּר שֶׁבָּהֶן לְהֵיכָן הָלַךְ? אֲמַר לֵיהּ: מִי לָא תְּנַן דִּכְוָותָהּ: בְּצָלִים שֶׁיָּרְדוּ עֲלֵיהֶם גְּשָׁמִים וְצִימְּחוּ,

§ With regard to **the matter itself, Rabbi Yoḥanan said:** With regard to **a *litra* of onions that one tithed, and then sowed, it is tithed according to the entire** crop. **Rabba sat and stated this *halakha.* Rav Ḥisda said to him: Who listens to you and Rabbi Yoḥanan, your teacher?**[P] **The permitted part of** the ***litra,* to where did it go?**[N] The original *litra* that he sowed was permitted by virtue of the fact that he tithed it, but why is he obligated to tithe the entire crop? The original *litra* should be subtracted from the crop that must be tithed. **Rabba said to Rav Ḥisda: Didn't we learn a corresponding *halakha*** in a mishna (*Shevi'it* 6:3): With regard to sixth-year **onions upon which rain fell** during the Sabbatical Year, **and they sprouted,**

NOTES

There is a mitzva to request that a halakhic authority dissolve them – מִצְוָה לְאִיתְשׁוֹלֵי עֲלֵיהֶן: Therefore, even though he did not yet request to dissolve the vow, because there is a mitzva to do so, it is as though he already did so, and therefore it is an item that can become permitted (Rashi; Ran). The Rosh explains that an object that is forbidden by a *konam* is considered an item that can become permitted because presumably he will request the dissolution of the vow.

What mitzva is there to request that a halakhic authority dissolve its designation – מַאי מִצְוָה לְאִיתְשׁוֹלֵי עֲלַהּ: Since there is no mitzva to do so, presumably, he will not request dissolution of the designation (Rashi). The Ran explains that since the prohibition surrounding the item will not lapse on its own, and although in theory he can request dissolution of its designation he has no reason to do so, it is considered an item that cannot become permitted.

The permitted part of the *litra*, to where did it go – הֶיתֵּר שֶׁבָּהֶן לְהֵיכָן הָלַךְ: The Rosh explains that this question is based on the assumption that the prohibited growths cannot neutralize the prohibition of the permitted original plant. Therefore, Rav Ḥisda asks: The permitted part of the *litra*, to where did it go? The Ran disagrees and holds that the question is raised according to all opinions: Since the *baraita* said that one tithes the *litra* based on a calculation of how much *teruma* of the tithe needed to be taken, the question arises: Why is the produce tithed according to the entire crop; the permitted part of the *litra*, to where did it go? The neutralization of the prohibition of the original plant by its growths is irrelevant here.

PERSONALITIES

Rabbi Yoḥanan, your teacher – רַבִּי יוֹחָנָן רַבָּךְ: In the Talmud, there is no record of Rabba ascending to Eretz Yisrael; however, it is related that his brothers, who immigrated to Eretz Yisrael, implored him to follow them to Eretz Yisrael and study Torah under the tutelage of Rabbi Yoḥanan. That could be the impetus that led him to go to Eretz Yisrael for a brief period, study Torah with Rabbi Yoḥanan, and occasionally cite *halakhot* in his name. It could not have been any more than a brief period, as the Gemara relates that Rabba died at the age of forty. However, it is also possible that Rabba considered himself a student of Rabbi Yoḥanan from a distance and was exposed to Rabbi Yoḥanan's Torah through his brothers.

Perek **VII**
Daf **59** Amud **b**

אִם הָיוּ עָלִין שֶׁלָּהֶן שְׁחוֹרִין – אֲסוּרִין, הוֹרִיקוּ – מוּתָּרִין. וְכִי שְׁחוֹרִין אַמַּאי אֲסוּרִין? לֵימָא: הֶיתֵּר שֶׁבָּהֶן לְהֵיכָן הָלַךְ? אֲמַר לֵיהּ: מִי סָבְרַתְּ עַל עִיקָּר קָתָנֵי? אַתּוֹסֶפֶת קָתָנֵי אֲסוּרִין. אִי הָכִי מַאי אֲתָא רַבָּן שִׁמְעוֹן בֶּן גַּמְלִיאֵל לְמֵימַר? דְּתַנְיָא, רַבָּן שִׁמְעוֹן בֶּן גַּמְלִיאֵל אוֹמֵר: הַגָּדֵל בְּחִיּוּב – חַיָּיב, הַגָּדֵל בִּפְטוּר – פָּטוּר. תַּנָּא קַמָּא נַמִי הָכִי אָמַר!

if their leaves were black,[N] the onions are **forbidden.** If their leaves **turned green,** the onions are **permitted. And if** the leaves **are black, why** are the onions **forbidden? Let us say** in this case too: **The permitted part,** the original onion, **to where did it go?** **Rav Ḥisda said to** Rabba: **Do you maintain** that this ***halakha*** **is taught about the primary,** original onion, that it is prohibited? **It is taught with regard to the additional** growth[N] that sprouted, and it is those leaves that **are forbidden.** The Gemara asks: **If so, what is Rabban Shimon ben Gamliel,** who apparently disagrees with the *tanna* of the mishna, **coming to say? As it is taught** in a *baraita* that **Rabban Shimon ben Gamliel says: That which grew during** a period of **liability is liable**[N] and is considered Sabbatical-Year produce, and that **which grew during** a period of **exemption is exempt.** According to Rav Ḥisda's explanation, **the first *tanna*,** cited in the mishna, **also said that.**

NOTES

If their leaves were black – אִם הָיוּ עָלִין שֶׁלָּהֶן שְׁחוֹרִין: Some commentaries, consistent with their overall approach, maintain that there is no dispute here with regard to the original plant, as it certainly retains its status; the dispute concerns only the leaves. Therefore, they explain that the problem is with regard to leaves that grew in the sixth year (*Tosafot*), or to that portion that sprouts from the original plant (Ran), and the question is: Are they forbidden as Sabbatical-Year produce?

It is taught with regard to the additional growth – אַתּוֹסֶפֶת קָתָנֵי: Only the additional Sabbatical-Year growths are prohibited, and were it possible to distinguish between the portion that grew before the Sabbatical Year and the portion that grew during that year, the former would be permitted. The practical implication of this distinction is that if these growths are mixed with permitted produce, that produce must be sufficient to neutralize only the prohibited portion of that growth (Rashba; Rosh). The Rashba maintains that Rav Ḥisda is explaining that although the onions are completely forbidden, it is not because the forbidden growth exceeds the volume of the original plant; rather, it is because of the prohibition that imbues the entire plant.

That which grew during a period of liability is liable – הַגָּדֵל בְּחִיּוּב חַיָּיב: Most commentaries explain that this *baraita* originally addressed this mishna, and the opposing opinion of Rabban Shimon ben Gamliel is cited as a continuation of the mishna. The Rosh disagrees and explains that the *baraita* addresses an entirely different issue: Concerning a tree that grew on the borders of Eretz Yisrael, that part of the tree that grew in Eretz Yisrael is liable and that part of the tree that grew outside Eretz Yisrael is exempt. Although this *halakha* does not completely parallel the discussion here, it is clear that only Rabban Shimon ben Gamliel maintains that there can be a plant part of which is forbidden and part of it is permitted, and neither part neutralizes the prohibition of the other. According to this approach, the Gemara's answer should be understood: Anywhere this opinion is found in a mishna or *baraita*, Rabban Shimon ben Gamliel taught it. The *Keren Ora* raised several difficulties with regard to the explanation of the Rosh and rejects it even though he fails to resolve the difficulties raised by the Rosh, e.g., the use of the terms liable and exempt, which are not appropriate in the case of the onion.

כּוּלָּהּ מַתְנִיתִין רַבָּן שִׁמְעוֹן בֶּן גַּמְלִיאֵל קָתָנֵי לָהּ. וְעַד כָּאן לָא שָׁמְעַתְּ לֵיהּ לְרַבָּן שִׁמְעוֹן בֶּן גַּמְלִיאֵל – דְּלָא קָא טָרַח, אֲבָל הֵיכָא דְּקָא טָרַח – בָּטֵיל בְּרוּבָּא.

The Gemara explains: This is not difficult, as this **entire mishna, Rabban Shimon ben Gamliel taught it.** In the *baraita* Rabban Shimon ben Gamliel is not disagreeing with the opinion of the first *tanna* of the mishna; he is merely restating it. **And** nevertheless, the mishna and the *baraita* pose no difficulty with regard to the opinion of Rabba, as **you heard that Rabban Shimon ben Gamliel** said that the prohibition of the primary, original part is not neutralized **only**[N] in a case where **he did not exert** himself, and the leaves sprouted on their own. **However,** in the case **where he exerted** himself,[N] e.g., by sowing or planting, the prohibition of the original onions is **neutralized by the majority.**

וְכָל הֵיכָא דְּקָא טָרַח בָּטֵיל בְּרוּבָּא? וַהֲרֵי לִיטְרָא מַעֲשֵׂר טֶבֶל, דְּקָטָרַח, וְקָתָנֵי: וְאוֹתָהּ לִיטְרָא מְעַשֵּׂר עָלָיו מִמָּקוֹם אַחֵר לְפִי חֶשְׁבּוֹן! שָׁאנֵי גַּבֵּי מַעֲשֵׂר דְּאָמַר קְרָא ״עַשֵּׂר תְּעַשֵּׂר״ וְגוֹ׳, וְהֶיתֵּירָא – זָרְעִי אֱינָשֵׁי, אִיסּוּרָא – לָא זָרְעִי אֱינָשֵׁי.

The Gemara asks: **And anywhere that one exerts** himself, **is the** original part **nullified by the majority?** The Gemara asks: **And** isn't there the case of one who sowed **a** ***litra*** **of untithed tithe,** where **he exerts** himself to sow it, **and it is taught: And that** original *litra* of untithed first tithe that he sowed, one **proportionally tithes for it from** produce in **a different place,** and its prohibition is not neutralized by the growth. The Gemara answers: It **is different with regard to tithe, as the verse states: "You shall tithe**[N] all the produce of your seed that is brought forth in the field" (Deuteronomy 14:22), indicating that all permitted seeds that are sown must be tithed, since **permitted** seeds that were tithed, **people** typically **sow. Forbidden** seeds that were not tithed, **people do not** typically **sow,** but the Sages penalized one who sowed untithed seeds and required him to tithe that which he was originally obligated to tithe and decreed that it is not neutralized by the majority.

גּוּפָא, אָמַר רַבִּי חֲנִינָא תִּירְתָּאָה אָמַר רַבִּי יַנַּאי: בָּצָל שֶׁל תְּרוּמָה שֶׁנְּטָעוֹ, וְרַבּוּ גִּידּוּלָיו עַל עִיקָּרוֹ – מוּתָּר. לְמֵימְרָא דְּגִידּוּלֵי

§ With regard to **the** matter **itself, Rabbi Ḥanina Tirta'a said** that **Rabbi Yannai said:** With regard to **an onion of** ***teruma*** **that one planted,** if **its growths exceeded its principal,** it **is permitted.** The Gemara asks: **Is this to say that growths** that are

NOTES

And you heard that Rabban Shimon ben Gamliel said only – וְעַד כָּאן לָא שָׁמְעַתְּ לֵיהּ: According to Rashi, this is the Gemara's answer: There is no proof from the ruling of Rabban Shimon ben Gamliel that he holds that growths never neutralize the prohibition of the original plant, as perhaps that is his opinion only in a particular case, where one did not exert himself at all as the onions were planted, and the rain caused them to sprout. The Ran explains it slightly differently: The Gemara is saying that although no proof can be cited from here that growths neutralize the prohibition of the original plant, this *baraita* poses no difficulty to the *halakha* of a *litra* of onions, as that is a case where one exerted himself. Others maintain that this is Rabba's answer to Rav Ḥisda: Rabban Shimon ben Gamliel addresses only a situation where one exerted himself (*Tosafot*; Rabbi Avraham min HaHar; Meiri). The Rosh, consistent with his general approach, explains that this is an additional answer to the Gemara's question. Rabban Shimon ben Gamliel's opinion is not an individual opinion, as the *tanna* who taught the *halakha* of sixth-year onions agrees with him in a case that does not involve exertion. However, he concedes that in a case that involves exertion, e.g., where he sowed the plants, the growths neutralize the prohibition of the original plant.

However, in the case where he exerted himself – אֲבָל הֵיכָא דְּקָא טָרַח: There are various explanations for the difference between a case that involves exertion and one that does not. Rashi explains simply that since he performed an action the prohibition of the plant is neutralized. The Ran explains that the difference is between the case where one exerted himself to neutralize the prohibition of the original plant and the case where one did not exert himself to do so. *Tosafot* explain that if he did not exert himself to facilitate the growths but they grew on their own, they are not significant to him, and therefore, they do not neutralize the prohibition of the original plant. Conversely, if he exerted himself he demonstrates that the growths are significant to him, and therefore, they neutralize the prohibition of the original plant. Rabbeinu Meir's opinion, cited in *Tosafot*, is that this must be understood in light of the Gemara in *Menaḥot* (70a), which distinguishes between conventional sowing, in which case the growths neutralize the prohibition of the original plant, and conduct that is not considered sowing at all, which the Gemara characterizes as a case where he did not exert himself.

As the verse states: You shall tithe – דְּאָמַר קְרָא עַשֵּׂר תְּעַשֵּׂר: The proof from this verse is explained as follows: Although he sowed seeds that are completely permitted, the prohibition of the original plant is neutralized and all the produce that grows from it is untithed produce. That is true only with regard to sowing permitted seeds. However, the Torah did not address the unusual case of one who sowed forbidden seeds, and therefore, the Torah did not determine that the prohibition of the original plant would be neutralized in that case (Rosh; Rid). The Ran explains in a similar manner that the Torah decree is that when permitted seeds are sown, they grow into untithed produce. However, the Ran asks: Since the verse is referring only to that produce that one is obligated to tithe by Torah law, and there is no grain whose seeds do not cease, what relevance does this verse have for the matter under discussion in the Gemara? Therefore, he explains that the verse is a mere support, not an actual derivation, and the primary proof is from the general *halakha* that in a mixture between permitted and forbidden items, the prohibition can be neutralized; however, if it is a mixture between forbidden items, there can be no neutralization. Therefore, in any case where the seeds themselves are forbidden as untithed Sabbatical-Year produce, no other forbidden item can be neutralized by it.

Some commentaries note that the Gemara could have resolved this difficulty in several alternative manners. For example, the Gemara could have said that the *halakha* of untithed produce is different, as it is an item that can become permitted. Alternatively, the Gemara could have answered that this is in accordance with the opinion of the *tanna* with regard to onions, who holds that growths do not neutralize the prohibition of the original plant, but the Gemara preferred a response based on a verse in the Torah.

הֶיתֵּר מַעֲלִין אֶת הָאִיסּוּר? וְהָתְנַן: גִּידּוּלֵי תְּרוּמָה – תְּרוּמָה! בְּגִידּוּלֵי גִידּוּלִין קָאָמְרִינַן. הָא נַמִי תָּנֵינָא: גִּידּוּלֵי גִידּוּלִין – חוּלִּין! הָא קָא מַשְׁמַע לָן: אֲפִילּוּ בְּדָבָר שֶׁאֵין זַרְעוֹ כָּלֶה.

permitted neutralize the prohibition?[N] But didn't we learn in a mishna: **The growths of *teruma* are *teruma*,**[NH] indicating that they do not neutralize the prohibition of the original part of the plant? The Gemara answers: **We are speaking of the growths of growths.** Rabbi Yannai permits the *teruma*, not due to the majority of direct growths of *teruma*; he permitted it due to the majority of growths that sprouted from its growths. The Gemara asks: **We** already **learned that too:**[N] **The** status of **growths of growths** of *teruma* is that of **non-sacred** produce.[H] The Gemara answers: **This teaches us** that the growths of growths are permitted **even in items whose seeds do not cease,** e.g., onions.

וְהָתְנַן: הַטֶּבֶל – גִּידּוּלָיו מוּתָּרִין, בְּדָבָר שֶׁזַּרְעוֹ כָּלֶה. אֲבָל דָּבָר שֶׁאֵין זַרְעוֹ כָּלֶה – גִּידּוּלֵי גִידּוּלִין אֲסוּרִין! רִבּוּיָא דְּרַבּוּ גִּידּוּלִין עַל עִיקָּרוֹ מוּתָּר קָא מַשְׁמַע לָן.

The Gemara asks: **But didn't we learn** in a mishna: With regard to **untithed produce, its growths are permitted**[NH] **in items whose seeds cease; however,** concerning **items whose seeds do not cease, the growths of growths are forbidden.** The Gemara answers: **It teaches us that** if **the increase of the growths of** growths **exceeded**[N] **its primary,** original part, that original part is **permitted.**

הדרן עלך הנודר מן הירק

HALAKHA

The growths of *teruma* are *teruma* – גִּידּוּלֵי תְּרוּמָה תְּרוּמָה: By Torah law, the status of growths of *teruma* is like that of non-sacred produce in every sense; however, the Sages issued a decree to consider them like *teruma* in that they are permitted exclusively to priests. Therefore, in contrast to *teruma*, these growths may be eaten by a priest who immersed that day, and with impure hands (Rambam *Sefer Zera'im*, *Hilkhot Terumot* 11:21).

The status of growths of growths of *teruma* is that of non-sacred produce – גִּידּוּלֵי גִידּוּלִין חוּלִּין: The status of growths of growths of *teruma* is like that of non-sacred produce in every sense, even if it was *teruma* from an item whose seeds do not cease. If the growths of growths exceed the growths, the prohibition of the growths are neutralized and permitted to non-priests. The Ra'avad claims that this *halakha* applies only to items whose seeds cease, and not to items whose seeds do not cease. The Radbaz maintains that undoubtedly that was what the Rambam meant as well (Rambam *Sefer Zera'im*, *Hilkhot Terumot* 11:22, and see *Kesef Mishne* there).

Untithed produce, its growths are permitted – הַטֶּבֶל גִּידּוּלָיו מוּתָּרִין: With regard to one who sows untithed produce, if he is able to gather it before it takes root in the ground, the Sages penalized him and required him to do so. If growths grew from untithed produce, and it was a plant whose seeds cease, the growths are permitted like non-sacred produce. If it was a plant whose seeds do not cease, its growths are forbidden, as are the growths of its growths. Only the quaternary growths are permitted (Rambam *Sefer Zera'im*, *Hilkhot Ma'aser* 6:6).

NOTES

Growths that are permitted neutralize the prohibition – גִּידּוּלֵי הֶיתֵּר מַעֲלִין אֶת הָאִיסּוּר: The Rashba questions the Gemara's formulation here, as this question refers to neutralization of the prohibition of the original plant by the permitted growths, while the difficulty here is a more fundamental one: Isn't it a fact that these growths are not permitted at all, as their legal status is like that of *teruma* itself, and neutralization is not at all relevant? The Ran eases the difficulty somewhat, although he does not completely resolve the problem, as he notes that from the mishna's statement: The growths of *teruma* are *teruma*, one learns that the status of growths is like that of the original plant, from which one can conclude that the growths certainly do not neutralize the prohibition of the original plant.

The growths of *teruma* are *teruma* – גִּידּוּלֵי תְּרוּמָה תְּרוּמָה: According to the Gemara in *Shabbat* (17b), this is one of the eighteen decrees issued by the Sages on a single day. The reason for the decree is that if the status of the growths was like that of non-sacred produce, which is its status by Torah law, the concern is that the priest would keep impure *teruma* in his possession in order to sow it, and he might inadvertently eat it.

We already learned that too – הָא נַמִי תָּנֵינָא: Here too, the Rashba asks: It is explicit that the reference there is to onions, whose seeds do not cease, and the growths of growths of those plants are forbidden. The Rashba and the Ran answer that it is possible that this *baraita* is cited only to explicate the matter, as one might have thought that the statement of Rabbi Ḥanina Terita'a mentioned onions only as an example, and his ruling applies to all plants, even those whose seeds cease.

Untithed produce, its growths are permitted – הַטֶּבֶל גִּידּוּלָיו מוּתָּרִין: The prohibition of growths of untithed produce whose seeds do not cease is more stringent than standard untithed produce. Until the processing of standard untithed produce is completed with its placement into a pile, it is permitted to eat it in a casual meal. However, one may not eat the growths of untithed produce even in the framework of a casual meal. The status of *teruma* is derived from that of untithed produce through an *a fortiori* inference: If for untithed produce, whose growths are permitted in items whose seeds cease, growths of its growths are forbidden in items whose seeds do not cease; all the more so for *teruma*, whose growths are forbidden even in items whose seeds cease, are the growths of its growths forbidden in items whose seeds do not cease (Rosh). Rabbi Avraham min HaHar explains simply that in the Jerusalem Talmud it is stated that the reason the growths of untithed produce are forbidden is that they contain *teruma*, as untithed produce is forbidden only due to the *teruma* it contains; clearly, the *teruma* itself is prohibited.

If the increase of the growths of growths exceeded – רִבּוּיָא דְּרַבּוּ: Rashi and other commentaries explain, based on an inference from the text of the Gemara, that although the growths of growths are forbidden, additional growths beyond that are permitted. *Tosafot* and the Rosh explain, and *Tosafot* cite a variant reading, that even the growths of growths are forbidden only if the volume of all the growths together do not exceed the volume of the original plant; however, if they exceed the volume of the original plant, not only the growths of growths, but the growths themselves are permitted. The Rashba maintains that even growths of the growths of untithed produce are forbidden specifically in terms of the seeds that emerge from the growths, but not in terms of the growths themselves.

Summary of **Perek VII**

A significant portion of this chapter addressed the definition of various terms: What is considered a vegetable? What is considered grain? What is considered a garment? What is considered a bed? What is considered a house? What is considered a city? Although each category is discussed individually, the Gemara concludes that when a person employs a general term, any item with regard to which an agent would ask the sender whether it is included in the general term, is included in that term with regard to vows. The Gemara also stated that with regard to one who vows that a general category is forbidden to him, all items in that category are rendered forbidden. However, with regard to one who vows that a particular item is forbidden to him, only that specific item is forbidden and it is not viewed as a representative example of an entire category.

Just as the item that one prohibits by vow is forbidden to him, growths from and exchanges for that item are also forbidden to him. This principle applies only in a case where he vowed that a certain item is forbidden to him; however, if he vowed that eating that item is forbidden, its growths are forbidden only when the original item that he sowed or planted remains intact, e.g., a tree. If it does not remain intact, its growths are permitted in that case. On a related note, the Gemara discusses additional halakhic dilemmas in cases where prohibitions take effect on plants, e.g., if and when subsequent growths neutralize the original prohibition.

In vows taken on condition that the vow will take effect only if a condition is fulfilled, it was determined that if the vow was to take effect before the condition in question is fulfilled, one must be careful to refrain from violating the vow until the condition is fulfilled, due to the concern that the condition will be fulfilled and the vow will take effect. Once the condition is fulfilled, the vow takes effect and one who violates it is liable to receive lashes.

Image **Credits**

p164 left image © Evgeny Genkin; **p168** © Dan Diffendale; **p185** © Chris 73; **p202** top left image © David Eickhoff; **p202** right image © mercedesfromtheeighties; **p205** © Courtesy of Dr. David and Jemima Jeselsohn, Zurich; **p206** © Stefan Kühn; **p210** © Dan Diffendale; **p211** © NOAA Photo Library; **p216** © Biso; **p217** © Evan-Amos; **p223** 1st image © The International Institute of Tropical Agriculture in Nigeria (IITA); **p223** 2nd image © Bambo; **p227** left image © Marie-Lan Nguyen (2011); **p227** right image © Ma[illegible]te; **p235** right image © Julien Willem; **p236** © Marie-Lan Nguyen; **p241** © FCG, www.shutterstock.com; **p245** © Bogdan Wankowicz, www.shutterstock.com.

My Notes

My Notes

My Notes

My Notes

My Notes

My Notes

My Notes

תלמוד בבלי

— מהדורת נאה —

נדרים חלק ב

Steinsaltz Center

KOREN

Please note that the number ranges that appear at the bottom of each daf of the Vilna pages indicate the corresponding pages of the Koren Talmud Bavli translation and commentary.

תלמוד בבלי

הוצאת קורן ירושלים

— מהדורת נאה —

מסכת נדרים
דף לב: עד דף ס.

COMMENTARY BY

Rabbi Adin Even-Israel Steinsaltz

EDITOR-IN-CHIEF

Rabbi Dr Tzvi Hersh Weinreb

EXECUTIVE EDITOR

Rabbi Joshua Schreier

•

STEINSALTZ CENTER

KOREN PUBLISHERS JERUSALEM

א א ב מיי' פרק ו מהל' נדרים הלכה ג סמג לאוין רמב טוש"ע י"ד סימן רכא סעיף א:

השטן בחושבנא תלת מאה ושיתין וארבע הוו. ויומות החמה שס"ה, א"כ איכא חד יומא דלית ליה רשותא לשטן, דהיינו יוה"כ. שתי עינים ושתי אזנים. שבתחלה המליכו הקב"ה על אבריו שהם ברשותו ליזהר מעבירה, אבל עיניו ואזניו של אדם אינם ברשותו, שהרי על כרחו יראה בעיניו ובאזניו ישמע. ולבסוף כשנמול המליכו הקב"ה אפי' על אלו, שלא יסתכל ולא ישמע כי אם דבר מצוה. ראש הגוייה. שנמול. מעשרה שליטים. שולטים באדם, שרוב מעשי האדם נעשין על ידיהם. ומלכי צדק. הוא שם בן נח. לפיכך הוציאה מאברהם. ואע"פ שאברהם מזרעו של שם — לא זכה בכהונה מחמת שם, אלא מחמת עצמו. והיינו דאמרינן הוא כהן ואין זרעו כהן, כלומר שלא זכה זרעו בכהונה מחמתו — מש"ה נטלה מכל שאר זרעו של שם ונתנה לאברהם. נאם ה' לאדני. דוד הוא דקאמר ד"נאם ה' היה לאדני" דהיינו אברהם, "שב לימיני" — שהבטיחו במלחמת ארבעה מלכים שישב לימין השם, כלומר שיהא בעזרו לשית אויביו הדום רגליו, וכתיב בההוא מזמור "אתה כהן לעולם".

[נ"ל רבי אמי וכ"ה בע"י]

[נ"ל רבי אמי וכ"ה בע"י]

הדרן עלך ארבעה נדרים

אין בין המודר הנאה וכו' אלא דריסת הרגל. שהמודר הנאה אסור לעבור דרך חצרו, ומודר ממנו מאכל שרי. **וכלים שאין עושין בהן אוכל נפש.** דשרו במודר מאכל כל שאין משכירין כיוצא בהם, כדמפרש ואזיל. ובמודר הנאה אסור. **לא ישאילנו נפה וכברה רחים ותנור.** איצטריך למיתני הני, כי היכי דלא תיסק אדעתין דכי אמר דכלים שעושין בהם אוכל נפש אסירי נמי במודר מאכל — ה"מ קדרה שמבשלין בה, א"נ שפוד שצולין בו בשר. אבל הני — גורם דגורם ניניהו, וליסרו במודר מאכל, קמ"ל. **אבל משאילו חלוק וטלית נזמים וטבעות.** בגמ' שקלי וטרי אי אשמועינן רבותא בהני או לא, אלא דתנינהו אגב רישא. **גמ' מאן תנא.** דמודר הנאה אסור בדריסת הרגל. **אפי' ויתור.** מה שדרכן של מוכרים לוותר ללוקחין, שמוסיפין להם כשלוקחין פירות אחד או שנים, אפילו אותו ויתור אסור במודר הנאה, ואע"ג דהוי זבינא דרמי על אפיה. הלכך, דריסת הרגל אסור אע"ג דלא קפדי בה שנתעסק

תורה אור

"הַשָּׂטָן" בְּחוּשְׁבְּנֵיהּ תְּלָת מְאָה וְשִׁיתִּין וְאַרְבְּעָה. וְאָמַר *רָמִי בַּר אַבָּא: כְּתִיב "אַבְרָם" וּכְתִיב "אַבְרָהָם", בַּתְּחִלָּה הִמְלִיכוֹ הקב"ה עַל מָאתַיִם וְאַרְבָּעִים וּשְׁלֹשָׁה אֵבָרִים, וּלְבַסּוֹף הִמְלִיכוֹ עַל מָאתַיִם וְאַרְבָּעִים וּשְׁמוֹנָה אֵבָרִים, אֵלּוּ הֵן: שְׁתֵּי עֵינַיִם, וּשְׁתֵּי אָזְנַיִם, וְרֹאשׁ הַגְּוִיָּה. וְאָמַר *רָמִי בַּר אַבָּא: מַאי דִּכְתִיב "עִיר קְטַנָּה וַאֲנָשִׁים" קהלת ט וגו'. "עִיר קְטַנָּה" — זֶה הַגּוּף, "וַאֲנָשִׁים בָּהּ מְעָט" — אֵלּוּ אֵבָרִים, "וּבָא אֵלֶיהָ מֶלֶךְ גָּדוֹל וְסָבַב אֹתָהּ" — זֶה יֵצֶר הָרַע, "וּבָנָה עָלֶיהָ מְצוֹדִים וַחֲרָמִים" — אֵלּוּ עֲוֹנוֹת, "וּמָצָא בָהּ אִישׁ מִסְכֵּן וְחָכָם" — זֶה יֵצֶר טוֹב, "וּמִלַּט הוּא אֶת הָעִיר בְּחָכְמָתוֹ" — זוֹ תְּשׁוּבָה וּמַעֲשִׂים טוֹבִים, "וְאָדָם לֹא זָכַר אֶת הָאִישׁ הַמִּסְכֵּן הַהוּא" — דְּבִשְׁעַת יֵצֶר הָרַע לֵית דְּמִדְכַּר לֵיהּ לִיצ"ט. "הַחָכְמָה תָּעֹז לֶחָכָם שם ז מֵעֲשָׂרָה שַׁלִּיטִים". "הַחָכְמָה תָּעֹז לֶחָכָם" — זוֹ תְּשׁוּבָה וּמַעֲשִׂים טוֹבִים, "מֵעֲשָׂרָה שַׁלִּיטִים" (א) שְׁתֵּי עֵינַיִם, וּשְׁתֵּי אָזְנַיִם, וּשְׁתֵּי יָדַיִם, וּשְׁתֵּי רַגְלַיִם, וְרֹאשׁ הַגְּוִיָּה, וּפֶה. אָמַר רַבִּי זְכַרְיָה מִשּׁוּם רַבִּי יִשְׁמָעֵאל: בִּיקֵּשׁ הקב"ה לְהוֹצִיא כְּהוּנָּה מִשֵּׁם, שֶׁנֶּאֱמַר "וְהוּא כֹהֵן לְאֵל עֶלְיוֹן". בראשית יד כֵּיוָן שֶׁהִקְדִּים בִּרְכַּת אַבְרָהָם לְבִרְכַּת הַמָּקוֹם — הוֹצִיאָהּ מֵאַבְרָהָם. שֶׁנֶּאֱמַר "וַיְבָרְכֵהוּ וַיֹּאמַר שם בָּרוּךְ אַבְרָם לְאֵל עֶלְיוֹן קֹנֵה שָׁמַיִם וָאָרֶץ וּבָרוּךְ אֵל עֶלְיוֹן" — אָמַר לוֹ אַבְרָהָם: וְכִי מַקְדִּימִין בִּרְכַּת עֶבֶד לְבִרְכַּת *קוֹנוֹ? מִיָּד נְתָנָהּ לְאַבְרָהָם, שֶׁנֶּאֱמַר "נְאֻם ה' לַאדֹנִי שֵׁב לִימִינִי עַד אָשִׁית אֹיְבֶיךָ הֲדֹם לְרַגְלֶיךָ" וּבָתְרֵיהּ כְּתִיב "נִשְׁבַּע ה' וְלֹא יִנָּחֵם אַתָּה כֹהֵן לְעוֹלָם עַל דִּבְרָתִי מַלְכִּי צֶדֶק" עַל דִּיבּוּרוֹ שֶׁל מַלְכִּי צֶדֶק, וְהַיְינוּ דִּכְתִיב "וְהוּא כֹּהֵן לְאֵל עֶלְיוֹן" — הוּא כֹּהֵן, וְאֵין זַרְעוֹ כֹּהֵן.§

[כע"י הגי' לברכת רבו לפיכך הוציאה מאברהם וכו']

שס"ד יָמִים אִית לֵיהּ(ב) וכו'. וִימֵי הַשָּׁנָה שס"ה יָמִים. הִמְלִיכוֹ. הִשְׁלִיטוֹ. אֵלּוּ הֵן שְׁתֵּי עֵינַיִם. דִּלְאַחַר שֶׁמָּל הָיָה שָׁלֵם בְּכָל אֵבָרָיו. רֹאשׁ הַגְּוִיָּה. הוּא אֵבֶר. מֵעֲשָׂרָה שַׁלִּיטִים. שֶׁהֵן מוֹעִילִין לַגּוּף יוֹתֵר מֵעֲשָׂרָה שַׁלִּיטִים, וְאֵלּוּ הֵן כו'. הוֹצִיאָהּ. לַכְּהוּנָּה. עַל דִּיבּוּרוֹ שֶׁל מַלְכִּי צֶדֶק. נִיטְּלָה מִמֶּנּוּ הַכְּהוּנָּה.

הדרן עלך ארבעה נדרים

אֵין בֵּין הַמּוּדָּר הֲנָאָה מֵחֲבֵירוֹ. שֶׁחֲבֵירוֹ הִדִּירוֹ שֶׁלֹּא יֵהָנֶה מִמֶּנּוּ בְּשׁוּם עִנְיָן. לְמוּדָּר מִמֶּנּוּ מַאֲכָל. שֶׁלֹּא הִדִּירוֹ אֶלָּא הֲנָאַת מַאֲכָל. **אֶלָּא** דְּרִיסַת הָרֶגֶל. לַעֲבוֹר בַּחֲצֵרוֹ וּלְקַצֵּר דַּרְכּוֹ. וְכֵלִים.(ג) וּלְהִשְׁתַּמֵּשׁ בְּכֵלִים שֶׁל מַדִּיר שֶׁאֵין עוֹשִׂין בָּהֶם מַאֲכָל, דְּמוּדָּר הֲנָאָה אָסוּר בִּדְרִיסַת הָרֶגֶל — דְּהַיְינוּ הֲנָאָה, שֶׁמְּקַצֵּר דַּרְכּוֹ, וּלְהִשְׁתַּמֵּשׁ בְּכֵלָיו. אֲבָל מוּדָּר מִמֶּנּוּ מַאֲכָל — מוּתָּר בִּשְׁתֵּיהֶן, לְפִי שֶׁזֶּה לֹא הִדִּיר מִמֶּנּוּ אֶלָּא מַאֲכָל. **גמ'** מַאן תַּנָּא. דְּמוּדָּר הֲנָאָה אָסוּר בִּדְרִיסַת הָרֶגֶל וּבְכֵלִים וכו', אע"ג דְּלָא מִיחֲזֵי הֲנָאָה. רַבִּי אֱלִיעֶזֶר הִיא דְּאָמַר **אֲפִילּוּ** וִיתּוּר כו'. וִיתּוּר זֶהוּ כְּגוֹן שֶׁלָּקַח מִדָּה שֶׁל תַּפּוּחִים בִּפְרוּטָה, וּלְאַחַר שֶׁמָּדַד לוֹ הַמִּדָּה מוֹסִיף לוֹ שְׁתַּיִם אוֹ שְׁלֹשָׁה. וְזֶהוּ דֶּרֶךְ שֶׁל חֶנְוָונִין לְהוֹסִיף עַל הַמִּדּוֹת מִשֶּׁלָּהֶן, הוֹאִיל וּבְלֹא תְּנַאי נוֹתֵן לוֹ — לָא מִיחֲזֵי כְּמִקָּח אֶלָּא כְּמַתָּנָה. וְאַלִּיבָּא דְּרַבִּי אֱלִיעֶזֶר אָסוּר הַמּוּדָּר בְּאוֹתוֹ הַוִּיתּוּר שֶׁל מְדַדֵּת פֵּירוֹת. הָכָא נַמִי, אַף עַל גַּב דִּדְרִיסַת הָרֶגֶל לָא הָוְיָא הֲנָאָה גְּמוּרָה — אָסוּר. וְהָא

הדרן עלך ארבעה נדרים

אֵין *בֵּין [א]הַמּוּדָּר הֲנָאָה מֵחֲבֵירוֹ לְמוּדָּר הֵימֶנּוּ מַאֲכָל אֶלָּא דְּרִיסַת הָרֶגֶל, וְכֵלִים שֶׁאֵין עוֹשִׂין בָּהֶם אוֹכֶל נֶפֶשׁ. הַמּוּדָּר מַאֲכָל מֵחֲבֵירוֹ לֹא יַשְׁאִילֶנּוּ נָפָה וּכְבָרָה וְרֵיחַיִם וְתַנּוּר, אֲבָל מַשְׁאִיל לוֹ חָלוּק וְטַבַּעַת וְטַלִּית וּנְזָמִים.§ מגילה ח.

גמ' מַאן תַּנָּא? אָמַר רַב אַדָּא בַּר אַהֲבָה: רַבִּי אֱלִיעֶזֶר הִיא. דְּתַנְיָא, *ר' אֱלִיעֶזֶר אוֹמֵר: [ב]אֲפִי' וִיתּוּר אָסוּר בְּמוּדָּר הֲנָאָה.§ "הַמּוּדָּר מַאֲכָל מֵחֲבֵירוֹ לֹא יַשְׁאִילֶנּוּ" כו'.§ וְהָא [מגילה שם ב"ב לג. מח:]

הגהות הב"ח

(א) גמ' מעשרה שליטים אלו הן שתי עינים: (ב) רש"י ד"ה שס"ד ימים אית ליה רשות לקטרג וימי השנה שס"ה ימים וביוה"כ לית ליה רשות הש"ד: (ג) רש"י ד"ה וכלים שאין עושין בהן אוכל נפש ולהשתמש בכלים:

תוספות

שתי עינים וב' אזנים וראש הגוייה. ראש האבר שנימול ושמע וראה ושלט בעיניו ואזניו שהמלות מפקיחות את העינים והאזנים כדכתיב (דברים כט) ולא נתן ה' לכם לב לדעת ועינים לראות ואזנים לשמוע עד היום הזה אבל הכא לא קחשיב לב דהא כתיב (נחמיה ט) ומצאת את לבבו נאמן לפניך וכרות עמו הברית וגו' על המילה אלמא קודם המילה היה כבר לבו שלם לשמים: **להוציא** כהונה משם. תימה דאברהם נמי היה מזרעו של שם וי"ל דמכל בניו של שם קאמר ולבסוף ניטל משאר בניו וניתנה לאברהם לבדו א"נ י"ל לפי שלא היה בכור בכל בניו ולא היה לו לירש הכהונה מן הדין אלא דוקא הבכור: הדרן עלך ארבעה נדרים

אין בין המודר הנאה וכו' אלא דריסת הרגל. במקום דלא קפדי אינשי כגון בקעה בימות החמה: **ולא** ישאילנו נפה וכברה. אבל לא נקט מחבת ופיטפוט שלא ישאילנו דהא פשיטא שלא ישאיל דהנאה המביאה לידי מאכל הוא אלא אפי' נפה וכברה שאינו יכול לאכול אחר תיקון זה בכלי זה אלא צריך תיקון אחר אפייה ובישול אפ"ה אסור לשאול לו נפה: **מקום** שמשכירים אסור. דחשיב הנאת מאכל ממה שנהנה השוכר וראוי לקנות מן המעות מאכל: **מני** ר"א היא. ומיירי בבקעה בימות החמה דלא קפדי כדפרישית וא"ת ולוקמה הכא בחצר דקפדי וכ"ע וי"ל דא"כ הוה ליה מקום שמשכירין והיה אסור במודר מאכל: **אפי'** ויתור. שמוותר לו כדרך המוכרין ומתני' דלעיל דמוכר בפחות ולוקח ביותר מסתברא דאתי כר"א:

אבל הני גורם דגורם מיקרו קמ"ל דה"ה (ריחים) [רחיים] ותנור: **אבל משאיל לו חלוק וכו'.** מילתא דפסיקא נקט: שדרך אדם לוותר משלו ואינו מקפיד עליו כגון התנוני אחר שנתן המנין או המדה שרגילין ליתן בפונדיון הוא שוה בשוה מותר דהיינו זבינא דרמי על אפיה וכיון דמחמיר כולי האי הכא אימא

פי' הרא"ש

השטן בגימטריא שס"ד הוי. וימות החמה שס"ה רמז שכל השנה יש לו רשות לקטרג חוץ מיום אחד והיינו יוה"כ: **שתי עינים ושתי אזנים וראש הגוייה.** והם אברים המתפרסים בעבירה ואינן מסורין ביד האדם ומרוב נלקתו מסרם בידו (ע"א ב) רגלי חסידיו ישמור כשאדם מתגבר על יצרו סוף שהקב"ה מוסרו בידו: **זה יצר הרע.** כדכתיב מלך זקן וכסיל: **איש מסכן וחכם זה יצה"ט.** כדכתיב טוב ילד מסכן וחכם וזהו יצ"ט שהוא ילד בשנים כנגד יצה"ר שהוא פחות ממנו י"ג שנה וחכמתו בזויה שאין האברים נשמעין לו: **נאם ה' לאדני.** אדוני הוא אברהם אבינו שקראו [ראשון] להקב"ה אדון כדאיתא בברכות (דף ז:) למען אדני למען אברהם שקראו אדון: הדרן עלך ארבעה נדרים

אין בין המודר הנאה וכו' אלא דריסת הרגל. לעבור דרך ארצו או להשאיל כלים שאין עושין בהן אוכל נפש שמותרין במודר הימנו מאכל ואסור במודר הימנו הנאה: **נפה וכברה רחים ותנור.** שמתקנין בהן אוכל נפש ואיצטריך לאשמועינן כלים הללו דלא תימא דוקא קדרה ושפוד שהאוכל עומד בתוכו כאכילה: **גמ' מאן תנא.** דמחמיר במודר הנאה לאסור אף דריסת הרגל: **אפי' ויתור אסור במודר הנאה** מה שדרך אדם לוותר משלו ואינו מקפיד עליו כגון התנוני אחר שנתן המנין או המדה שרגילין ליתן בפונדיון הוא רגיל להוסיף משלו כדי להרגילו לבא אצלו אותו ויתור אסור למודר הנאה כיון שהוא מוותר שלו אבל כולי האי הלכך אפי' דריסת הרגל שאין דרך להקפיד עליו אסור במודר:

והא

וְהָא מִן מַאֲכָל נָדַר! אָמַר רשב"ל: בְּאוֹמֵר "הֲנָאַת מַאֲכָלְךָ עָלַי". [א]אֵימָא שֶׁלֹּא יִלְעוֹס חִיטִּין וְיִתֵּן עַל מַכָּתוֹ! אָמַר רָבָא: [ב]בְּאוֹמֵר "הֲנָאָה הַמְּבִיאָה לִידֵי מַאֲכָלְךָ עָלַי". אָמַר רַב פַּפָּא: [ג]שַׂק לְהָבִיא פֵּירוֹת, וַחֲמוֹר לְהָבִיא עָלָיו פֵּירוֹת, וַאֲפִי' צַנָּא בְּעָלְמָא – הֲנָאָה הַמְּבִיאָה לִידֵי מַאֲכָל הוּא. [ד]בָּעֵי רַב פַּפָּא: סוּס לִרְכּוֹב עָלָיו, וְטַבַּעַת לֵירָאוֹת בָּהּ, מַהוּ? מִפְסַק וּמֵיזַל בְּאַרְעֵיהּ מַאי? תָּא שְׁמַע: אֲבָל מַשְׁאִיל לוֹ חָלוּק וְטַלִּית נְזָמִים וְטַבָּעוֹת. הֵיכִי דָּמֵי? אִילֵימָא שֶׁלֹּא לֵירָאוֹת בָּהֶן – צְרִיכָא לְמֵימַר? אֶלָּא לָאו אֲפִילּוּ לֵירָאוֹת בָּהֶן, וְקָתָנֵי "מַשְׁאִילוֹ"! לָא, לְעוֹלָם שֶׁלֹּא לֵירָאוֹת, וְאַיְּידֵי דְּקָתָנֵי רֵישָׁא "לֹא יַשְׁאִילֶנּוּ" – תְּנָא סֵיפָא "מַשְׁאִילוֹ".§ **מתני'** [ה]וְכָל דָּבָר שֶׁאֵין עוֹשִׂין בּוֹ אוֹכֶל נֶפֶשׁ, מָקוֹם שֶׁמַּשְׂכִּירִין כַּיּוֹצֵא בָּהֶן – אָסוּר.§ **גמ'** מִכְּלָל דְּרֵישָׁא אַף עַל פִּי שֶׁאֵין מַשְׂכִּירִין. מַאן תַּנָּא? *אָמַר רַב אַדָּא בַּר אַהֲבָה: ר' אֱלִיעֶזֶר הִיא.§ **מתני'** *[ו]הַמּוּדָּר הֲנָאָה מֵחֲבֵירוֹ – שׁוֹקֵל לוֹ אֶת שִׁקְלוֹ, וּפוֹרֵעַ אֶת חוֹבוֹ, וּמַחֲזִיר לוֹ אֶת אֲבֵידָתוֹ. מָקוֹם שֶׁנּוֹטְלִין עָלֶיהָ שָׂכָר – תִּפּוֹל הֲנָאָה לְהֶקְדֵּשׁ.§ **גמ'** אַלְמָא *אַבְרוּחֵי אֲרִי בְּעָלְמָא הוּא, וְשָׁרֵי. מַאן תַּנָּא? *[ז]אָמַר רַב הוֹשַׁעְיָא: זוֹ דִּבְרֵי

רש"י

וְהָא מִן מַאֲכָל עַצְמוֹ נָדַר. וְאַמַּאי אָסוּר לְהַשְׁאִילוֹ נָפָה? וְהָנֵי לָאו מַאֲכָל נִינְהוּ! הֲנָאַת מַאֲכָלְךָ עָלַי. יְהֵא אָסוּר. וְאֵימָא. מַאי "הֲנָאַת מַאֲכָלְךָ" – שֶׁלֹּא יִלְעוֹס חִיטִּין שֶׁלּוֹ וְיִתֵּן עַל גַּבֵּי מַכָּתוֹ, וְהַיְינוּ נַמִּי הֲנָאַת מַאֲכָלְךָ, וְהָכָא אַמַּאי לֹא יַשְׁאִילֶנּוּ נָפָה וּכְבָרָה? הַמְּבִיאָה לִידֵי מַאֲכָלְךָ עָלַי. וְנָפָה וּכְבָרָה מְבִיאָה מַאֲכָלוֹ לְמַאֲכָל, וּלְהָכִי לֹא יַשְׁאִילֶנּוּ לוֹ. אֲפִי' שַׂק וְכוּ' וַאֲפִי' צַנָּא בְּעָלְמָא. שֶׁל מַדִּיר, אָסוּר לַמּוּדָּר לִיתֵּן בָּהּ פֵּירוֹת, דַּהֲנָאָה הַמְּבִיאָה לִידֵי מַאֲכָל הוּא, וְאָסוּר. סוּס לִרְכּוֹב עָלָיו. לֵילֵךְ לְבֵית הַמִּשְׁתֶּה. אוֹ טַבַּעַת לֵירָאוֹת בָּהּ. בְּבֵית הַמִּשְׁתֶּה, כְּדֵי שֶׁיִּנְהֲגוּ בּוֹ כָּבוֹד, וְהַיְינוּ הֲנָאָה. מִיפְסַק וּמֵיזַל בְּאַרְעֵיהּ. שֶׁהוֹלֵךְ דֶּרֶךְ קַרְקָעוֹ לְבֵית הַמִּשְׁתֶּה, וּמְקַצֵּר דַּרְכּוֹ. מַהוּ. מִי הָוֵי הֲנָאָה הַמְּבִיאָה לִידֵי מַאֲכָל בְּכָל הָנֵי, אוֹ לָא? צְרִיכָא לְמֵימַר. דְּשָׁרֵי? הָא לֵיכָּא הֲנָאָה כְּלָל! וְקָתָנֵי מַשְׁאִילוֹ. וּשְׁמַע מִינַּהּ דְּשָׁרֵי. לָא לְעוֹלָם. אֲפִי' שֶׁלֹּא לֵירָאוֹת בָּהּ. וּבְדִין הוּא דְּלָא הָיָה צָרִיךְ לְמִיתְנֵי "מַשְׁאִילוֹ". אֶלָּא אַיְּידֵי וְכוּ'. וּמֵהָא לֵיכָּא לְמִשְׁמַע מִינָּהּ. **מתני'** מָקוֹם שֶׁמַּשְׂכִּירִין. שֶׁנּוֹהֲגִין לְהַשְׁאִיל כָּל אֵלּוּ הַדְּבָרִים עַל יְדֵי שְׂכִירוּת – אָסוּר לַמַּדִּיר לְהַשְׁאִילוֹ. דְּכֵיוָן שֶׁנּוֹהֲגִים לְהַשְׂכִּיר – מֶיחֱזֵי כַּהֲנָאָה הַמְּבִיאָה לִידֵי מַאֲכָל, וְאָסוּר. **גמ'** מִכְּלָל דְּרֵישָׁא. דְּקָתָנֵי: לֹא יַשְׁאִילֶנּוּ נָפָה וּכְבָרָה – הָוֵי אַף עַל פִּי שֶׁאֵין מַשְׂכִּירִין, כְּלוֹמַר שֶׁאֵין נוֹהֲגִין לְהַשְׁאִיל בִּשְׂכִירוּת. אַף עַל גַּב דְּלָא הָוֵי הֲנָאָה גְּמוּרָה, דְּכֵיוָן שֶׁאֵין מַשְׂכִּירִין מַאי קָא מְהַנֵּי לֵיהּ? אִם זֶה לֹא יַשְׁאִילֶנּוּ – שְׁכֵנוֹ אַחֵר מַשְׁאִילוֹ בְּחִנָּם, שֶׁהֲרֵי מָקוֹם שֶׁאֵין מַשְׂכִּירִין הוּא. מַאן תַּנָּא. דַּאֲפִילּוּ הָכִי אָסוּר. ר' אֱלִיעֶזֶר הִיא. אֲבָל סֵיפָא דְּקָתָנֵי: מָקוֹם שֶׁמַּשְׂכִּירִין אָסוּר – דִּבְרֵי הַכֹּל הִיא, דַּהֲנָאָה גְּמוּרָה הִיא. **מתני'** שׁוֹקֵל לוֹ אֶת שִׁקְלוֹ. הַמַּדִּיר יָכוֹל לִיתֵּן בִּשְׁבִילוֹ מַחֲצִית הַשֶּׁקֶל שֶׁנּוֹתְנִין לִתְרוּמַת הַלִּשְׁכָּה, וְיָכוֹל לִפְרוֹעַ חוֹבוֹ, וְאֵין מְהַנֶּה לוֹ כְּלוּם. (א) מִדְּקָתָנֵי "פּוֹרֵעַ חוֹבוֹ" – אַלְמָא לָא מְהַנֵּי לֵיהּ מִנְּכָסָיו, דְּהָא לָא יָהֵיב לֵיהּ בְּיָדַיִם מַמָּשׁ: **גמ'** אַלְמָא אַבְרוּחֵי אֲרִי בְּעָלְמָא הוּא. שֶׁמַּבְרִיחַ חוֹבוֹ מֵעָלָיו, וְשָׁרֵי. מַאן תַּנָּא. דְּאַבְרוּחֵי שָׁרֵי. דִּבְרֵי

[לעיל לב: ושם נסמן] כתובות קז. [ב"ק נח. ב"ב נג.] [כתובות קח. ע"ש]

ר"ן

אינשי אסור במודר הנאה, אבל רבנן דפליגי עליה סברי דכל היכא דלא אסר עליו אלא הנאתו – כה"ג לא מקרי הנאה, דכיון דמידי דלא קפדי בה אינשי הוא – אין זה קרוי נהנה מחבירו. ואם תאמר: דהכא משמע דבדריסת הרגל לא קפדי אינשי, ומש"ה שרו רבנן, ואילו בפ' "חזקת הבתים" (ב"ב דף נז:) אמרינן גבי אלו דברים שאין להם חזקה, ואמרינן: הכא בחצר של שותפות עסקינן, דאהעמדה כדי לא קפדי. אלמא דוקא שותפין הוא דלא קפדי, הא אינשי דעלמא קפדי, וכיון שכן ליתסר אפילו לרבנן! תירץ הרמב"ן ז"ל: דהעמדה דאמר התם היינו להתעכב ולישב בחצר, דומיא דהעמדת בהמה, דתנן התם במתני'. ובכי האי גוונא הוא דאמר דדוקא שותפין לא קפדי, הא אינשי דעלמא – קפדי. אבל הכא בדריסת הרגל בעלמא עסקינן, דהיינו לעבור דרך חצרו ולא להתעכב שם, ובכה"ג אפי' אינשי דעלמא דלא שותפין לא קפדי, ומש"ה שרו רבנן. ולענין הלכה. פסק הרמב"ן ז"ל כר' אליעזר דאמר ויתור אסור, כיון דסתם לן תנא הכא כוותיה. ועוד, דסוגיין דפ' "השותפין שנדרו" (לקמן מח) כוותיה אזלא. אבל ר"ח ז"ל כתב בפרק "חזקת הבתים" [גבי] אלו דברים שאין להם חזקה דלית הלכתא כרבי אליעזר, וכן דעת ר"ת ז"ל. **והא מן מאכל נדר.** וכיון שכן למה יאסר? **דאמר הנאת מאכלך עלי.** דכיון שהוסיף ואמר הנאת המאכל – הרי אסר על עצמו כל מה שגורם אותו, וקרי ליה "מאכלך" משום דבגרמת הנאה שלו הוא מתוקן. והוה סלקא דעתך הכי, דאי לא – מאי מיקרי הנאת מאכל? **ואימא שלא ילעום חיטים ויתן על גבי מכתו.** דהנאת מאכל לא משמע אלא שלא יהנה מגוף המאכל עצמו, ולאסור אפי' הנאת המאכל אמר "הנאת מאכלך", ואכתי ליסתרי. **אמר רבא באומר הנאה המביאה לידי מאכל עלי.** איכא מאן דאמר דבכה"ג אסור בין בלעיסת חטים על גבי מכתו, בין בנפה בין בכברה. ואין נוח לי, דבכלל הנאה המביאה לידי מאכל לא משמע נתינת חטים לעוסין ע"ג מכתו. אלא הכי הוי פסקא דמילתא: דאי נדר ממאכל – אינו אסור אלא באכילה בלבד, ומותר בכל דבר אחר. אמר "הנאת מאכלך עלי" – אסור באכילה, ואסור ללעום חטים על גבי מכתו, אבל לשאול ממנו נפה וכברה שרי. אמר הנאה המביאה לידי מאכל עלי אסור באכילה ואסור לשאול נפה וכברה מיהו ללעום חיטין וליתן על גבי מכתו שרי כך נראה בעיני. **שק להביא עליו פירות וכו' הנאה המביאה לידי מאכל הוא.** דלא תימא לא מקריא הנאה המביאה לידי מאכל אלא לתקן המאכל כנפה וכברה, אבל להביא אליו המאכל בלבד בשק וחמור שרי, קמ"ל רב פפא. **צנא.** סל. **סוס לרכוב עליו וטבעת ליראות בה מיפסק ומיזל בארעיה מאי.** דמי אמרינן: נהי דהקרבת המאכל אליו מקרי הנאה המביאה לידי מאכל, אפי' הכי להקריב עצמו למאכל כמפסק ומיזל בארעיה כדי שיהיה שם מהרה – לאו הנאה המביאה לידי מאכל היא, דשאני התם שעשה במאכל עצמו. וכן נמי סוס לרכוב עליו *ליראות בה, כדי שיראה כאדם חשוב כשירכוב על סוס, ותהא טבעת על ידו ובשביל זה יתנו לו מנה יפה – כי האי גוונא גרמא בעלמא הוא. [נ"ל וטבעת ליראות] **אילימא שלא ליראות בהן צריכא למימר.** דשרי במודר מאכל כיון דאין משכירין בהן כיוצא בהן – פשיטא! אלא לאו אפילו ליראות בהן, וקתני משאילו, אלמא גרמא דמאכל שרי. וכל הני דבעי רב פפא גרמא בעלמא נינהו. **איידי דקתני רישא לא ישאילנו.** לאשמועינן דנפה וכברה כלים שעושין בהם אוכל נפש הן, וכמו שפירשתי במשנתנו – תנא סיפא משאילו. ולענין הלכה. בעיא דרב פפא לא איפשיטא. הלכך נקטינן בה לחומרא. **מתני'** מקום שמשכירין כיוצא בהן **אסור.** אפי' במודר מאכל. דהאי מודר מאכל דמתני' הא מוקמת ליה בגמרא באומר "הנאה המביאה לידי מאכל עלי", והני כיון דרגילין להשכירן, וזה משאילו בלא שכר – הנאה המביאה לידי מאכל היא, שהרי בדמי השכירות שמחל לו יקח מאכל. **גמ'** מכלל דרישא. דהיינו לא ישאילנו נפה וכברה, אף על פי שאין משכירין. דמאי דשרי בחלוק וטלית נזמים וטבעות – אסרינן בנפה וכברה. **מתני'** שוקל לו **את** שקלו. המדיר למודר, וכן פורע לו חובו. ובגמרא מפרש טעמא. ומחזיר לו **אבידתו.** דלא מידי יהיב ליה, אלא מידעם דנפשיה קמהדר ליה. מקום שנוטלים עליה שכר. דהיינו אם היה מחזיר בטל מן הסלע, דבכי האי גוונא מחייב בעל אבידה ליתן לו שכר, כדאיתא ב"אלו מציאות" (ב"מ דף ל:). **תפול הנאה להקדש.** אם אין מחזיר רוצה לקבל השכר – יתננו מודר להקדש, שאילו היה מוחל לו מדיר – נמצא מהנהו. **גמ'** **אלמא אברוחי ארי בעלמא הוא ושרי.** אשוקל לו שקלו ופורע לו חובו קאי. דלהכי שרי, משום דלאו מידי יהיב ליה, אלא שמסלק המלוה מעליו. ומש"ה נמי שוקל לו שקלו, דהא לא מהני, דבלאו הכי יש לו חלק בקרבנות צבור, כדתנן (כתובות קח. ב"מ נח.): תורמין על האבוד ועל הגבוי ועל העתיד לגבות. מאי אמרת – הא קא מהני ליה דפרע חובו – אברוחי ארי הוא, ושרי. **אמר ר' אושעיא הא מני חנן היא.** דס"ל שהמפרנס אשת חבירו שפורע לו חוב מזונותיו – הניח מעותיו על קרן הצבי, משום דלא חשיב מהני, אלא מבריח ארי בעלמא.

אפילו

עין משפט נר מצוה

ב א ב ג ד ה מיי' פ"ו מהל' נדרים הל' ב סמג לאוין רמב טוש"ע י"ד סי' רכא סעיף א:
ג ו ז מיי' פ"ו שם הל"ד ופ"ז הל' א סמג שם טור ש"ע שם סעי' בג:

תוספות

אימא שלא ילעוס חיטין. משום הנאת מאכל לעיסתך ואפי' מחטין של מדיר עצמו: **וטבעת** להראות בו. כאדם עשיר בבית המשתה וע"י כך יתנו לו מנה יפה: **מאן** תנא אמר רבא ר"א היא. וא"ת תנן חדא זימנא ברישא ר"א וי"ל דמכח הך דהכא מדקדק לעיל דאתי כר"א דאי לאו האי הוה מוקמינן ליה בחצר ודכ"ע ולכך מדקדק הכא מסיפא:

הגהות הב"ח

(א) רש"י ד"ה שוקל וכו' כלום הס"ד ואח"כ נ"ל פיסקא גמ' ואח"כ מ"ה מדקתני וכו' בידים ממש אלמא כצ"ל והד"א:

פי' הרא"ש

והא מן מאכל נדר. דמשמע דוקא אוכל נפש: **אימא שלא ילעום חיטין על מכתו.** דרפואה למכה היא כדתנן בפרק [שני דפסחים] (ד' לט:) לא ילעום אדם חטים ויתן על גבי מכתו מפני שהם מחמיצות דהנאת מאכלך משמע שהוא הנאה מגוף המאכל בלא אכילה: **הנאה המביאה לידי מאכל עלי.** היינו תקון או דבר שיכול לקנות בו מאכל: **שק להביא בו פירות כו'.** דלא תימא דוקא תקון מאכל קמ"ל דהך נמי מקרי הנאה המביאה לידי מאכל: **סוס לרכוב עליו.** לבית המשתה: **וטבעת ליראות בה.** כדי שיכבדוהו להוסיף לו מנות: **מיפסק ומיזל בארעיה.** לקצר דרכו לילך לבית המשתה: **ואיידי דתנא רישא לא ישאילנו.** דלא תימא דוקא שפוד וקדרה: **מתני' מקום שמשכירין כיוצא בכן אסור.** דכיון דדרך להשכיר כיוצא בזה והוא מוחל לו השכירות באותן הדמים הוא יכול לקנות אוכל נפש והוא הדירו מהנאה המביאה לידי מאכל: **גמ' מכלל דרישא אע"פ שאין משכירין.** כלים שעושין בהם אוכל נפש למודר ממנו [מאכל]: **מתני' שוקל לו שקלו.** מחצית השקל חייב כל אחד מישראל בכל שנה לצורך קרבנות ציבור *)והמודר יכול לשקלו בשבילו דמצוה בעלמא הוא דעבד ואין דינו כפורע שאר חובותיו: **ופורע חובו.** בגמרא מפרש לה: **ומחזיר לו אבידתו.** בגמרא מפרש לה: **תפול הנאה להקדש.** שאין יכול לעכבו שאז היה נהנה ממנו וצריך ליתנו להקדש לפי שאסר עליו הנאתו כהקדש הלכך כל הנאה הבאה לידו ממנו הקדש הוא ולא מצי להוליכה לים המלח דלאו כל כמיניה להפסיד להקדש והיינו דדייק מהכא בגמרא דיש מעילה בקונמות: **גמ' אלמא אברוחי ארי בעלמא הוא.** הפורע חובו של חבירו חשוב כמבריח ארי מעדר חבירו שאינו חייב ליתן לו על זה שכר כדאיתא בפרק הכונס צאן לדיר (ב"ק נח.) פורע חובו נמי אינו חייב לשלם ומחיל לו דאי לא נמצא מהנהו:

*) נ"ל והמדיר

חנן

דִּבְרֵי חָנָן הִיא. רָבָא אָמַר: אֲפִי' תֵּימָא דִּבְרֵי הַכֹּל, גַּבֵּי מוּדָּר הֲנָאָה דְּיָהֵיב (א) עַל מְנָת שֶׁלֹּא לִפְרוֹעַ. מַאי חָנָן? דִּתְנַן: *מִי שֶׁהָלַךְ לִמְדִינַת הַיָּם וְעָמַד אֶחָד וּפִירְנֵס אֶת אִשְׁתּוֹ, חָנָן אָמַר: אִיבֵּד אֶת מָעוֹתָיו. נֶחְלְקוּ עָלָיו בְּנֵי כֹהֲנִים גְּדוֹלִים, וְאָמְרוּ: יִשָּׁבַע כַּמָּה הוֹצִיא וְיִטּוֹל. א"ר דּוֹסָא בֶּן הָרְכִּינָס כְּדִבְרֵיהֶם. אָמַר ר' יוֹחָנָן בֶּן זַכַּאי: אִיָּפֶה אָמַר חָנָן, הִנִּיחַ מָעוֹתָיו עַל קֶרֶן הַצְּבִי. רָבָא לָא אֲמַר כְּרַב הוֹשַׁעְיָא — דְּקָא מוֹקִים לָהּ לְמַתְנִיתִין כד"ה רַב הוֹשַׁעְיָא לָא אֲמַר כְּרָבָא גְּזֵירָה שֶׁלֹּא לִיפָּרַע מִשּׁוּם לִיפָּרַע.§ "מַחֲזִיר לוֹ אֶת אֲבֵידָתוֹ".§ פְּלִיגִי בָּהּ ר' אַמִּי וְר' אַסִּי, חַד אֲמַר: לֹא שָׁנוּ אֶלָּא בְּשֶׁנִּכְסֵי מַחֲזִיר אֲסוּרִין עַל בַּעַל אֲבֵידָה, דְּכִי מַהֲדַר לֵיהּ מִידַּעַם דְּנַפְשֵׁיהּ קָא מַהֲדַר לֵיהּ. אֲבָל נִכְסֵי בַּעַל אֲבֵידָה אֲסוּרִין עַל מַחֲזִיר — לָא קָא מַהֲדַר לֵיהּ, דְּקָא (ב) מְהַנֵּי לֵיהּ פְּרוּטָה *דְּרַב יוֹסֵף. וְחַד אֲמַר: בְּאֲפִי' נִכְסֵי בַּעַל אֲבֵידָה אֲסוּרִין עַל מַחֲזִיר — מַהֲדַר לֵיהּ, וּמִשּׁוּם פְּרוּטָה דְּרַב יוֹסֵף — לָא שְׁכִיחַ.

תְּנַן

ר"נ

אפי' תימא דברי הכל. דאפי' לרבנן דאמרי שחייב לוה להחזיר לזה דמי החוב שפרע בשבילו, גבי מודר הנאה דהיינו מתני' — דיהיב על מנת שלא לפרוע עסקינן. כלומר, דכשהלוהו התנה עמו שלא יהא כח בחבירו לכופו, אלא כשירצה הלוה יפרענו מדעתו. הלכך, כי פרע ליה מדיר לאותו חוב, דאע"ג דאפשר דמודר משום כסופא פרע ליה, אפ"ה כיון דאי בעי לא פרע ליה — לאו מידי יהיב ליה למודר. וכ"ת: תינח פורע לו חובו, אלא שוקל לו את שקלו היכי שרי אליבא דרבנן? איכא למימר דמתניתין לדידהו משכחת לה כגון שלא את שקלו ונגנב או אבד משנתרמה תרומה, דכי ה"ג פטור מלשלם. כדתניא ב"הזהב" (ב"מ נז:): בני העיר ששקלו את שקליהם ונגנבו או אבדו, אם משנתרמה תרומה — נשבעין לגזברים. הלכך, כי שוקל מדיר את שקלו — מידי דלא מחייב בה מודר קיהיב. וקמ"ל שאע"פ שהיה דרכן לפרוע אותו — שרי, כיון שאין הגזברים יכולין לכופו. **גזירה שלא לפרוע אטו לפרע.** כלומר, דאי אמרי' דמדיר פורע לו חובו של מודר כשלוה ע"מ שלא לפרוע — איכא למיגזר דלמא פרע ליה אע"פ שלוה אותו המודר ע"מ שיכפנו המלוה לפרוע. הלכך אי מתני' רבנן — ליכא גוונא דשרי. אלא ודאי חנן היא, ומותר בכל ענין. ובפרק "שני דייני גזירות" (כתובות קח.) מסקינן בגוונא אחרינא, דאמר התם: נהי דהנאה לית ליה — כסופא מי לית ליה? והאי עמד א' ופירנס את אשתו, דאמר דלחנן הניח מעותיו על קרן הצבי, כתב הרשב"א ז"ל: דדוקא במפרש שמחמת מזונות שחייב לה בעלה הוא נותן לה, דבכה"ג אמר חנן דפטור אבל פרנס סתם — חוזר וגובה, לפי שכל המפרנס סתם אינו מפרנס בתורת מתנה אלא בתורת הלואה, ונמצא שהיא חייבת לו, ומי שפרנס אותה גובה ממנה, והיא גובה מבעלה. וכמו שפרש"י ז"ל בפרק "שני דייני גזירות" גבי לוותה ואכלה, מאי דאמר דאכלה והיא נפרעת מבעלה ובעל חוב גובה ממנה. והביא ראיה דהמפרנס סתם לא אמרי' במתנה קיהיב אלא לשם הלוואה, מיורד לתוך שדה חבירו ונטעה שלא ברשות (כתובות פ. ב"מ קא.) דחייב בעל השדה לשלם, ולא כל הימנו שיאמר "במתנה נתת לי". ועוד ראיה, מדגרס בירושלמי בפרק "איזהו נשך": חד בר נש אישאל לחבריה דינרין, אשריתיה גו ביתיה, אמר ליה: הב לי דינרי אמר ליה הב לי אגר ביתי. אתא עובדא קמיה דר' אבא בר זבינא ומריקו ליה מאי דהוה חמי למשרייה. והכא ודאי בשהעמידו סתם בתוך ביתו מיירי, ולא בשהעמידו בפירוש בשכר — דא"כ לא הוה אמר ליה אידך "הב לי כל דינרי" דהוה פרע ליה מה שהתנה עמו לתת לו בשכירותו. וכן נמי ליכא למימר דמשום רבית קאמר, דא"כ הוה ליה למימר "נכה לי אגר ביתי". אלמא המשרה חבירו בתוך ביתו סתם — לא למתנה איכוון, אלא לשכירות. וכיון שכן, המפרנס אשת חבירו סתם — חוזר וגובה ממנו. אלו דבריו ז"ל. ואינם מחוורים לדעתי, דנהי דהני מוכחי דהמהנה את חבירו סתם לאו לשם מתנה קא מכוון, אפילו הכי המפרנס את אשת חבירו סתם — לחנן הניח מעותיו על קרן הצבי, מיהו סתמא זו אדעתא דבעל נחית ולאו אדעתא דידה. שכבר הוא יודע שאין לאשה זו נכסים שיהא נפרע מהן, אלא מבעלה, ולא מסיק אדעתיה לומר שתתחייב היא בהן כדי שתוכל לגבות מבעלה ולהגבותו, דלאו כולהו אינשי דינא גמירי, אלא סתמא אדעתא דבעל נחית. ומש"ה, נהי דלאו בתורת מתנה קעביד, כדמוכחי הנך ראיות דאייתי הרשב"א ז"ל — אפילו הכי לחנן הניח מעותיו על קרן הצבי, דמסתמא אדעתא דבעל קעביד. ולענין הלכה. קיי"ל כחנן, הלכך פורע חובו של חבירו — הניח מעותיו על קרן הצבי, ואפילו בבעל חוב דוחק נמי, דליכא למימר דטעמא דחנן משום דמצי אמר ליה "מפייס הוינא ליה והוה מחיל לי", דהא מתני' דשוקל לו את שקלו אתיא לן שפיר כחנן, אף על גב דלא מצי אמר שימחלו לו הגזברים. ומסתברא לי דבמלוה שיש עליה משכון נמי אבד מעותיו. דהא אמרינן הכי בירושלמי אליבא דבני כהנים גדולים, דאמר התם דאפילו לבני כהנים גדולים דאמרי במפרנס את אשתו דישבע כמה הוציא ויטול — התם היינו טעמא משום דלא עלה על דעתו שתמות אשתו ברעב. אבל בפורע חובו — מודו לחנן דפטור, דמצי אמר "מפייס הוינא ליה והוה מחיל לי". ואמרינן התם: הגע עצמך שהיה בידו משכון? מפייס הוינא ליה ומהדר לי משכוני. ונהי דבגמרא דילן לא סבירא לן הכי אליבא דבני כהנים גדולים, דא"כ לא הוה מצטריך לאוקמא למתניתין בשלוה על מנת שלא לפרוע, אפילו הכי נקטינן מהא דירושלמי, דחנן אפילו מלוה שיש עליה משכון אמר. דכיון דבירושלמי אמר בפשיטות דמודו ליה רבנן[א] דחנן בהכי — אלמא שמיע להו דחנן אמר הכי. ונהי דלפום גמרא דילן בני כהנים גדולים לא מודו, אפילו הכי גמרינן מירושלמי דחנן אמר אפילו במלוה שיש עליה משכון, ובהא לא אשכחן איפכא בגמרא דילן. כן נראה לי. מידעם דנפשיה **קא** מהדר ליה. ולא מהני ליה מידי, אלא שמבריח נזק אבידתו מעליו. דקא מהני ליה פרוטה דרב יוסף. דכי מהדר ליה אבידתו מיפטר מלמיתב ליה פרוטה לעני, שהעוסק במצוה פטור מן המצוה. ותלי לה בדרב יוסף משום דפליגי רבה ורב יוסף פ' "הכונס צאן לדיר" (ב"ק נו:) בשומר אבידה, אי הוי כשומר שכר, וסבירא ליה לרב יוסף דכיון דמיפטר מלמיתב פרוטה לעני — שומר שכר הוי. **פרוטה** דרב יוסף **לא** שכיח. שיבא עני לישאל ממנו באותה שעה, דנימא לא מהדר משום דמתהני מידי. דכי האי גוונא, כיון דלא שכיח לא הוי בכלל איסור הנאה. ומיהו, כיון דאפשר דאתי ומתהני מינה — שומר שכר הוא עליה, וחייב בגניבה ואבידה.

א) [נ"ל לחנן]

רש"י

דִּבְרֵי חָנָן הִיא. דְּאָמַר אִיבֵּד מָעוֹתָיו, שֶׁאֵין לַמַּלְוֶה עַל בַּעְלָהּ שֶׁל זוֹ כְּלוּם, הוֹאִיל וְלֹא נָתַן בְּיָדוֹ אֶלָּא הִבְרִיחַ אֲרִי מֵעָלָיו, שֶׁפִּירְנֵס אֶת אִשְׁתּוֹ שֶׁהוּא חַיָּיב לְזוּנָהּ. ה"נ, כִּי פָּרַע חוֹבוֹ — אַבְרוּחֵי אֲרִי הוּא, שֶׁאֵין לוֹ לִפְרוֹעַ(ג) עַל הַחוֹב כְּלוּם — וּלְהָכִי שָׁרֵי. דְּאִי כֹּהֲנִים גְּדוֹלִים דִּפְלִיגִי עֲלֵיהּ דְּחָנָן הִיא, כֵּיוָן דְּאָמְרִי: יִשָּׁבַע כַּמָּה הוֹצִיא וְיִטּוֹל מִן הַבַּעַל — הָכָא נַמִי סְבִירָא לְהוּ כִּי פָּרַע חוֹבוֹ יָכוֹל הַפּוֹרֵעַ לִגְבּוֹת מִן הַלֹּוֶה, וּלְהָכִי הָוֵי הֲנָאָה גְּמוּרָה אִם אֵין הַפּוֹרֵעַ חוֹזֵר וְגוֹבֶה מִמֶּנּוּ, וְאָסוּר. דְּיָהֵיב לֵיהּ ע"מ שֶׁלֹּא לִפְרוֹעַ. מִזֶּה. דְּהַשְׁתָּא כִּי פּוֹרְעוֹ זֶה לָא הָוֵי הֲנָאָה, הוֹאִיל וְאִי בָּעֵי — לָא מָצֵי לְמִיגְבָּא מִינֵּיהּ כְּלוּם. "וְשׁוֹקֵל לוֹ אֶת שִׁקְלוֹ" נַמִי מוֹקְמִינַן לֵיהּ לְדִבְרֵי הַכֹּל כה"ג שֶׁאֵינוֹ מְהַנֶּה לוֹ כְּלוּם, כְּגוֹן שֶׁהוּא עַצְמוֹ שָׁקַל אֶת שִׁקְלוֹ וְשִׁגְּרוֹ לִירוּשָׁלַיִם, וְנִגְנַב אוֹ אָבַד לְאַחַר שֶׁנִּתְרְמָה הַלִּשְׁכָּה. וְהַאי לֹא נִתְחַיֵּיב בְּאַחֲרָיוּתוֹ, וְלֹא הָיָה לוֹ לְפוֹרְעוֹ, דְּהָכִי קיי"ל (ב"מ נז:): בְּנֵי הָעִיר שֶׁשִּׁיגְּרוּ אֶת שִׁקְלֵיהֶן וְנִגְנְבוּ אוֹ שֶׁאָבְדוּ, אִם נִתְרְמָה הַתְּרוּמָה — נִשְׁבָּעִין הַשְּׁלוּחִין לַגִּזְבָּרִים שֶׁאָבְדוּ, וּבְעָלִים פְּטוּרִים, דְּתוֹרְמִין עַל הָאָבוּד. וְאִם קוֹדֶם שֶׁנִּתְרְמָה הַלִּשְׁכָּה — נִשְׁבָּעִין לִבְנֵי הָעִיר. לְפִיכָךְ כִּי חָזַר הַנּוֹדֵר וּפָרַע שִׁקְלוֹ — מוּתָּר, דְּלָא מְהַנֶּה לֵיהּ כְּלָל. מִשּׁוּם לִפְרוֹעַ. דְּהָתָם, אִי הֲוָה פָּרַע חוֹבוֹ — הֲוָה מַהֲנֵי לֵיהּ. תִּפּוֹל הֲנָאָה לְהֶקְדֵּשׁ. מְפָ' בַּגְּמָרָא:

לֹא שָׁנוּ. דְּמַחֲזִיר לוֹ אֲבֵידָתוֹ אֶלָּא כְּשֶׁנִּכְסֵי מַחֲזִיר אֲסוּרִין עַל בַּעַל אֲבֵידָה שֶׁהַמַּחֲזִיר הַדִּירוֹ מִנְּכָסָיו. דְּכִי מַהֲדַר לֵיהּ מִידַּעַם דְּנַפְשֵׁיהּ קָמַהֲדַר לֵיהּ. וְלֵיכָּא הֲנָאָה שֶׁאֵינוֹ מְהַנֵּהוּ מִנְּכָסָיו כְּלוּם. אֲבָל נִכְסֵי בַּעַל אֲבֵידָה אֲסוּרִין עַל מַחֲזִיר. דְּמַחֲזִיר מוּדָּר מִבַּעַל אֲבֵידָה לָא מָצֵי מַהֲדַר לֵיהּ אֲבֵידָתוֹ מִשּׁוּם דְּאִי מַהֲדַר לֵיהּ הָוֵה מִתְהַנֵּי מִבַּעַל אֲבֵידָה. פְּרוּטָה דְּרַב יוֹסֵף. דְּאָמַר רַב יוֹסֵף הָעוֹסֵק בְּמִצְוָה פָּטוּר מִן הַמִּצְוָה וְלָא בָּעֵי לְמֵיתַב לֵיהּ פְּרוּטָה לְעַנְיָא בִּשְׁבִיל אוֹתָהּ מִצְוָה שֶׁמְּקַיֵּים הִלְכָּךְ אֵין מַחֲזִיר לוֹ אֲבֵידָתוֹ. פְּרוּטָה דְּרַב יוֹסֵף לָא שְׁכִיחַ. דְּלָא שְׁכִיחַ כה"ג דְּלֶהֱוֵי שָׁבִיק וְלָא יָהֵיב פְּרוּטָה לְעַנְיָא בִּשְׁבִיל אוֹתָהּ מִצְוָה וְלָא מִתְהַנֵּי מִינֵּיהּ כְּלָל לְפִיכָךְ מַחֲזִיר לוֹ אֲבֵידָתוֹ.

מָקוֹם

עין משפט נר מצוה

ד א מיי' פי"ב מהל' אישות הל' יט ופכ"ז מהל' מלוה הל"ו סמג עשין מח ולאוין פח טוש"ע אה"ע סימן ע סעיף ח וטוש"ע ח"מ סימן קכח סעיף א:

ה ב מיי' פ"ז מהלכות נדרים ה"א סמג לאוין רמב טוש"ע י"ד סימן רכא סעיף ג:

הגהות הב"ח

(א) גמ' דיהיב ליה על מנת: (ב) שם דקא מתהני פרוטה דרב יוסף: (ג) רש"י ד"ה דברי חנן וכו' לפרוע החוב כלוס וכו' דאי בני כהנים כצ"ל ותיבת על נמחק:

תוספות

חנן אומר איבד מעותיו. משום דהוי מבריח ארי בעלמא ואע"ג דחייב במזונות אשתו מ"מ יכול לומר שהיתה מספקת ממעשה ידיה וא"ת והא פרק השוכר [את] הפועלים (ב"מ צג:) דרועה שהקדים ברועים ובמקלות חוזרין ונוטלין שכרם מבעל הבית ואמאי מבריח ארי בעלמא וי"ל דלאו מבריח הוא כיון דברי היזיקא שאם לא הקדים הארי היה אוכל הבהמות והיכא דלא ברי היזיקא שהארי אינו ממש עומד ומזומן ואינו מצילו כי אם מפחד הארי לא הוי ברי היזיקא וא"ת בפורע חובו מבריח מינייה והלא ידוע לכל שיש לו לפרוע חובו וא"כ מהנהו וי"ל דפורע חובו היינו זן אשתו ובניו דאיפשר שיתפרנסו ממעשה ידיהם ולא ברי היזיקא אבל לא נראה דמדקאמר אחרי כן וזן את בניו ואת בנותיו אלמא משמע דמה שאמר זן בניו לאו פורע חובו וי"ל דרישא מיירי שזן אשתו ואת בניו שלא בפניו וסיפא מיירי בפניו וזהו חידוש ואף על גב שמפרנסם בפניו ואין מוחהו אפ"ה חשבינן להו מבריח עי"ל דפורע חובו היינו פורע ממש וא"ת א"כ ודאי [לאו] מבריח ארי י"ל דיכול לומר בע"ח לפורע חובו מפייסינן ליה דמחיל לי ואפילו במשכון מפייסנא ליה והדר לי משכוני הלכך לאו ברי היזיקא ולכך הוי מבריח ארי: **דמהני** ליה פרוטה דרב יוסף. פי' בשעה שעסק במצות אבידה וא"ת ישיב לו אכילת הנאה להקדש אותה פרוטה במקום שנוטלין עליה שכר וי"ל דלא מצי לדיין לדעת כמה פעמים פטור הוא על ידה ממיתב ריפתא לענייא וא"ת והא אברוחי ארי בעלמא הוא שמבריח מעליו העני דאפי' גבי פורע חוב חשבינן ליה מ[בריח] ליה מבריח ארי משום דמצי למימר מפייסי' ליה לפיכך לא ברי היזיקא כ"ש הכא גבי פרוטה שאינה מצויה כ"כ והא לא חשיב הנאה וי"ל דפורע חובו היינו אותו שפורע חובו עבורו מבריח ארי מעליו הלכך לאו ברי היזיקא ולכך הוי כמבריח ארי אבל הכא המחזיר עצמו כמבריח הארי מעל עצמו ע"י שמתעסק באבידת חבירו והרי הוא כאילו נוטל מכיסו של בעל אבידה ונותנה לעני ה"נ גבי פורע חובו אם הבעל חוב נוטל מעות מזה לפטור חובו כמו כן היה אסור:

בשלמא

פי' הרא"ש

חנן היא. דאמר איבד את מעותיו ואינו יכול לומר את חובך פרעתי שלם לי וה"ה ה"נ לכל חוב שעליו ועמד זה ופרעו וזה לא אמר לו הלויה אינו חייב לו כלום וכיון דאילו פרעיה לשם הלואה לאו הלואה כי פרעיה נמי בשם מחילה לאו מידי קיהיב ליה: **ע"מ שלא לפרוע.** עד שירצה לפרוע מעצמו אבל לא יכול ללוחצו הלכך לא מהני ליה מידי. כך פרש"י ז"ל בפ' בתרא דכתובות: **מידעם דנפשיה קמהדר ליה.** מלוה בעלמא קעביד ולא מהני ליה מידי: **מהני ליה פרוטה דרב יוסף.** דאמר בפרק המפקיד (ב"מ כט.) דשומר אבידה כש"ש בההוא הנאה דלא קבעי למיתב ריפתא לעני אם יזדמן לו עני בשעה שהוא עסוק בשמירת האבידה כגון לשטחה דהעוסק במצוה פטור מן המצוה וכן נמי הכא בשעה שהוא מוליך האבידה לביתו פטור מן הצדקה: **פרוטה דרב יוסף לא שכיח.** שיזדמן לו עני באותה שעה: *) **בשלמא למאן דאמר אף בנכסי בעל אבידה אסורין על המחזיר.** פירוש כשנכסיהם מודרין זה מזה היינו דקתני תפול הנאה בהקדש **בנכסי מחזיר אסורין** שהמחזיר אינו יכול לקבל ממנו שכר ובעל אבידה אסור לעכבו: **אלא למאן דאמר בנכ[סי]** **אחדא.** על דרך אחר כגון על בעל אבידה דוקא בהכי איירי מתניתין אמאי תפול הנאה להקדש: אם אין המחזיר רוצה לקבל שכר ובעל אבידה אינו יכול לעכבו הלכך תפול הנאה להקדש יקבל המחזיר שכרו משום דכולה מתניתין איירי במחזיר בחנם דהא קתני בריש[א] מחזיר לו אבידתו היינו בחנם דאי בשכר פשיטא דהא נכסי בעל אבידה מותרים למחזיר הלכך בסיפא נמי איירי במחזיר בחנם ולהכי תנא תפול הנאה להקדש:

*) שייך לדף שא"ח וכספרים

מסורת הש"ס

כתובות קח.

ב"ק נו: ב"מ כט. פב. שבועות מד:

תְּנַן: מָקוֹם שֶׁנּוֹטְלִין עָלֶיהָ שָׂכָר — תִּפּוֹל הֲנָאָה לַהֶקְדֵּשׁ. בִּשְׁלָמָא לְמ"ד אֲפִילּוּ בְּשֶׁנִּכְסֵי בַּעַל אֲבֵידָה אֲסוּרִים עַל מַחֲזִיר נַמִּי מַהֲדַר — הַיְינוּ דְּקָתָנֵי: מָקוֹם שֶׁנּוֹטְלִין עָלֶיהָ שָׂכָר תִּפּוֹל הֲנָאָה לַהֶקְדֵּשׁ. אֶלָּא לְמ"ד כְּשֶׁנִּכְסֵי בַּעַל אֲבֵידָה אֲסוּרִים עַל מַחֲזִיר לָא מַהֲדַר, אַמַּאי תִּפּוֹל הֲנָאָה לַהֶקְדֵּשׁ? אַחֲדָא קָתָנֵי. אִיכָּא דְּמַתְנֵי לָהּ בְּהַאי לִישָּׁנָא; פְּלִיגֵי בָּהּ ר' אַמִּי ור' אַסִּי; חַד אָמַר: לֹא שָׁנוּ אֶלָּא בְּשֶׁנִּכְסֵי בַּעַל אֲבֵידָה אֲסוּרִין עַל מַחֲזִיר, וּמִשּׁוּם פְּרוּטָה דְּרַב יוֹסֵף — לָא שְׁכִיחַ. אֲבָל נִכְסֵי מַחֲזִיר אֲסוּרִים עַל בַּעַל אֲבֵדָה — לָא מַהֲדַר לֵיהּ, מִשּׁוּם דְּקָא מְהַנֵּי לֵיהּ. וְחַד אָמַר: [א]אפי' נִכְסֵי מַחֲזִיר אֲסוּרִים עַל בַּעַל אֲבֵידָה (א) מוּתָּר, דְּכִי מַהֲדַר לֵיהּ — מִידֵּי דְּנַפְשֵׁיהּ קָמַהֲדַר לֵיהּ. תְּנַן: מָקוֹם שֶׁנּוֹטְלִין עָלֶיהָ שָׂכָר תִּפּוֹל הֲנָאָה לַהֶקְדֵּשׁ. בִּשְׁלָמָא לְמ"ד אֲפִילּוּ בְּשֶׁנִּכְסֵי מַחֲזִיר אֲסוּרִים עַל בַּעַל אֲבֵידָה מַהֲדַר (ב) הַיְינוּ דְּמִתָּרֵץ מָקוֹם, אֶלָּא לְמ"ד בְּשֶׁנִּכְסֵי מַחֲזִיר אֲסוּרִין, וְלָא מַהֲדַר, הֵיכִי מְתָרֵץ מָקוֹם? קַשְׁיָא.

אָמַר

רש"י

מקום שנוטלין עליה שכר. (ג) חזרת אבידה שכר. תפול הנאה להקדש. דכיון דמודר מימנו הנאה – לא מצי האי למיתב ליה שכר. **בשלמא** למ"ד. אפי' בשנכסי בעל אבידה אסורין על מחזיר נמי מהדר ליה אבידתו היינו דקתני מקום שנוטלין עליה שכר תפול הנאה [להקדש] כיון דמחזיר לא מצי למשקל מיניה השכר, לפי שזה בעל אבידה הדירו מנכסיו, אינו יכול להשתייר השכר בידו, דמקום שנוטלים עליה שכר הוא (ד) – לא מצי בעל אבידה למימר: הואיל ואינו יכול ליטול השכר יהא שלי, לפיכך תפול הנאה להקדש. ואי נכסי מחזיר אסורי' על בעל אבידה, והאי מחזיר אדם עשיר הוא ואינו רוצה לקבל שכרו, דזילותא הוא לקבל השכר – מכל מקום האי בעל אבידה לא מצי תפיס לשכרו, משום דמודר הוא מנכסי מחזיר, ושכרו איתיה גביה, דמקום שנוטלין עליה שכר הוא, לפיכך תפול הנאה להקדש. **אלא** למ"ד. כשנכסי מחזיר אסורין על בעל אבידה מהדר, והתם איכא למימר תפול הנאה להקדש. אבל נכסי בעל אבידה אסורים על מחזיר לא מהדר. הואיל ולא מהדר ליה – לא יהיב ליה אגרא, אם כן מאי "תפול הנאה להקדש" איכא למימר הכא? הואיל ולאו בר אגרא הוא. תריץ **אחדא** קתני. אחד לחוד מיירי "תפול הנאה להקדש" – בשנכסי מחזיר אסורין על בעל אבידה. דבעל אבידה לא מצי תפיס אגריה דמחזיר, דלא מצי למיתהני מיניה. ומחזיר נמי לא בעי ליטול שכר, דעשיר הוא, להכי תפול הנאה להקדש. **לא שכיחא.** וליכא הנאה כלל. משום **דקא** מהני ליה. דאע"ג דמידעם דנפשיה מהדר ליה, אפ"ה מהני ליה, דדמי כמאן דמהני ליה מנכסיו. מהדר ליה. משום דמידעם דנפשיה מהדר ליה, ולא מהני ליה כלום: בשלמא למ"ד אף בשנכסי מחזיר אסורין על בעל אבידה מהדר. היינו דמתרץ מקום. כלומר, דמשכחת ליה מקום שנוטלים עליה שכר תפול הנאה להקדש. דכיון דנכסי מחזיר אסורין על בעל אבידה – לא מצי בעל אבידה לשייר השכר לעצמו, דהא נכסי מחזיר הן, ואסורין עליו, וצריך לו ליתן השכר. והמחזיר, אי אדם עשיר (ה) ואינו רוצה לקבל השכר – להכי תפול הנאה להקדש. **אלא** למאן דאמר בשנכסי מחזיר אסורין על בעל אבידה לא מהדר היכי מתרץ מקום. שנוטלין עליה שכר? הא ליכא (ו) שכרו כלל, דלא מהדר! והכא ליכא לתרוצי "אחדא קתני". דהתם דכיון דקאמר בשנכסי מחזיר אסורין על בעל אבידה קא מוקי ביה תפול הנאה להקדש, דכופין לבעל אבידה שיתן השכר להקדש, ואין יכול להחזיק בו, דנכסי מחזיר אסורין הן עליו. אבל הכא ליכא לתרוצי "אחדא קתני" אנכסי בעל אבידה אסורין עליה. דכיון דנכסי מחזיר אין אסורין על בעל אבידה – מצי האי בעל אבידה למיתפס השכר לנפשיה, ולא נפיל להקדש, והיכי מתרץ מקום? קשיא.

כבר

ר"ן

תנן מקום שנוטלין עליה שכר תפול הנאה להקדש **בשלמא** למאן דאמר בשנכסי מחזיר אסורין על בעל **אבידה אבל** דבעל **אבידה** אסורין על מחזיר **לא** מהדר היינו דקתני מקום שנוטלין עליה שכר תפול הנאה להקדש **אלא** למאן דאמר אפילו נכסי בעל **אבידה אסורים** על מחזיר נמי מהדר **אמאי** תפול הנאה להקדש. כך היא עיקר הגירסא. וה"פ: בשלמא למ"ד דמתני' בשנכסי מחזיר אסורין על בעל אבידה – דוקא היא, דאילו נכסי בעל אבידה אסורין על מחזיר לא מהדר משום פרוטה דרב יוסף, מש"ה קתני סיפא דמקום שנוטלין עליה שכר, אם זה המחזיר גברא יקירא ואינו רוצה לקבל שכרו – לא ישהנו בעל אבידה לאותו שכר אצלו, דהא מתהני מיניה, אלא תפול הנאה להקדש. אלא למ"ד דאפילו נכסי בעל אבידה אסורין על המחזיר מהדר, אם כן רישא דקתני "ומחזיר לו אבידתו" – אפי' בשנכסי בעל אבידה אסורין על מחזיר נמי היא, וסיפא דקתני "תפול הנאה להקדש" אכולא מילתא קאי. ובשלמא בנכסי מחזיר אסורין – אתי שפיר אי מחזיר גברא יקירא הוא, כדפרישית. אבל בשנכסי בעל אבידה אסורין על מחזיר – למה לי דתפול הנאה להקדש? ישהנו בעל האבידה לעצמו, שהרי לא נאסרו נכסי מחזיר וליכא למימר דהכא כשבעל אבידה גברא יקירא ורוצה ליתן שכר, ומקבל לא מצי שקיל – דהא נכסי בעל אבידה אסורין עליו, ומשום הכי תפול הנאה להקדש – דבכהאי גוונא לא שייך יקירא לקבל אבידתו בחנם, כך פירשו רבותי. ולי נראה דהכי קאמר: אמאי תפול הנאה להקדש? יתן שכרו בעל אבידה למחזיר. דנהי דנכסי בעל אבידה אסורין על המחזיר – אפילו הכי מותר ליקח ממנו שכרו, דהא *)התלמוד זבינא דרמי על אפיה אמר לעיל דהנאת מוכר הוא ולא לוקח, ונפקא מינה דאי לוקח מודר ממוכר – מותר ליקח ממנו זבינא דרמי על אפיה, מאי טעמא? דהא מכל מקום מודר מיתהני מההוא מידי דמוכר! אלא ודאי היינו טעמא, דכיון דזבינא דרמי על אפי' – הא משכח מינה לוקח טובא, וכל כה"ג, אע"ג דאתי לידיה ממדיר – לא מקריא הנאה. הכא נמי, במקום שנותנין עליה שכר, דהיינו בבטל מן הסלע, אע"ג דיהיב ליה כי ההוא אגרא בעל אבידה למחזיר – לא מיתהני מחזיר מיניה דבעל אבידה כלל, שאותו שכר כבר היה מגוי בידו. וכיון שכן – אמאי תפול הנאה להקדש? הא מצי בעל אבידה למתביה למחזיר! כנ"ל ונכון הוא. ומשני אחדא קתני. כלומר, רישא דמחזיר אבידתו – בין בנכסי מחזיר אסורין על בעל אבידה בין בנכסי בעל אבידה אסורין על מחזיר. אבל סיפא, במקום שנותנין עליה שכר תפול הנאה להקדש – אחדא בלחוד קאי, דהיינו אנכסי מחזיר אסורין על בעל אבידה. **איכא** דמתני לה בהדין **לישנא** וכו' **לא** שנו **אלא** בנכסי בעל **אבידה אסורין** על **מחזיר**. ומתני' לנדדין קתני: שוקל לו את שקלו ופורע לו את חובו – מדיר למודר, ומחזיר לו אבידתו*) – מדיר למודר, ותורם לו את תרומותיו – מדיר למודר. ומשום דבעי תנא למיתני כולהו גווני דשרי בין מדיר למודר תנא הכי. כך נראה בעיני. אבל בנכסי מחזיר אסורין על בעל אבידה – לא מהדר ליה, משום דקא מהני ליה. ועדיף טפי מפורע לו חובו דהא קא ממטי ליה בידיה, ואי לא דקא מהדר ליה – אפשר דפסדא מיניה לגמרי. בשלמא למ"ד אף בשנכסי מחזיר אסורין מהדר. כלומר דמודר מחזיר למדיר, ומדיר למודר – היינו דמתרץ "מקום", דאיכא לתרוצי דאחדא קתני, כלומר היכא דמהדר מדיר למודר. אלא למ"ד בשנכסי מחזיר אסורין על בעל אבידה לא מהדר, וא"כ מתני' דמחזיר לו אבידתו בשנכסי בעל אבידה אסורין על מחזיר בלחוד היא, וא"כ היכי מתרץ "מקום"? דבכה"ג ליכא למימר תפול הנאה להקדש וכמו שכתבתי למעלה. ולענין הלכה קיי"ל דבין בשנכסי מחזיר אסורין על בעל אבידה בין בשנכסי בעל אבידה אסורין על המחזיר – מהדר, דהא מ"ד דבנכסי מחזיר אסורין על בעל אבידה לא מהדר אתותב. ואע"ג דמ"ד בלישנא קמא דנכסי בעל אבידה אסורין על מחזיר לא מהדר לא אתותב, דאדרבה אתיא לדידיה מתניתין טפי שפיר – אפ"ה כיון דהאי לישנא בתרא הוא, והך סברא דבין בנכסי מחזיר אסורין בין בנכסי בעל אבידה אסורין מהדר, איתמרא בתרתי לישני – כוותיה נקטינן. וכן פסק הרמב"ם ז"ל.

אמר

*) נ"ל מודר למדיר

*) נ"ל הספא זבינא. יעב"ץ

פי' הרא"ש

ובספרים נמצא נ"א בשלמא למ"ד בשנכסי מחזיר אסורין על בעל אבידה אבל דבעל אבידה אסורין על מחזיר לא מהדר היינו דקתני מקום שנוטלין עליה שכר תפול הנאה להקדש אם אין המחזיר רוצה לקבל שכר אלא למ"ד אף נכסי בעל אבידה אסורין על מחזיר נמי מהדר ומתני איירי נמי בכל ענין בין בשנכסי בעל אבידה אסורין על המחזיר אבל נכסי המחזיר מותרין לבעל האבידה ובין בשנכסי מחזיר אסורין על בעל אבידה אבל נכסי בעל אבידה מותרין למחזיר אמאי תפול הנאה להקדש היכא דנכסי מחזיר מותרין: **אחדא קתני.** האי תפול הנאה להקדש לא קאי אדנכסי מחזיר מותרין לבעל אבידה אלא אדנכסי בעל אבידה מותרין למחזיר והמחזיר אינו רוצה לקבל שכר וליכא למימר נמי דקאי אהיכא דנכסי בעל אבידה אסורין למחזיר ותפול הנאה להקדש אם אין בעל אבידה רוצה לעכב השכר דהא לא איצטריך למיתני דכיון דאין המחזיר יכול ליטול שכר הרי הוא של בעל האבידה ואם ירצה יתן כל ממונו להקדש אבל כשאינו יכול לעכב השכר הוצרך לפרש מה יעשה בו: **משום דקא מהני ליה.** ולית ליה הך סברא מדעם דנפשיה קא מהדר ליה: **אף בשנכסי מחזיר אסורין על בעל אבידה היינו דמתרץ מקום.** דכיון דשניהם מודרין זה מזה מחזיר אינו יכול ליטול ובעל אבידה אינו יכול לעכב: **בשנכסי מחזיר אסורין לא מהדר.** ולא איירי מתניתין אלא בשנכסי בעל אבידה אסורין על המחזיר אבל נכסי מחזיר מותרין לבעל אבידה היכי מתרץ מקום אמאי לא מעכב השכר לעצמו:

היתה

עין משפט נר מצוה

ו א מיי' פ"ז מהלכות נדרים הלכה א סמג לאוין רמב טוש"ע י"ד סימן רכא סעיף ג:

תוספות

בשלמא למאן דאמר בשנכסי כו'. פירוש שניהם מודרי' זה מזה לכך תפול הנאה להקדש אלא מ"ד וכו' אמאי תפול הנאה להקדש יתן שכרו למחזיר שהרי אינו מודר מבעל אבדה: **ה"ג** אחדא. פי' לגבי חדא מינייהו קתני תפול (עלי) הנאה להקדש לגבי בעל אבידה שאם המחזיר אינו רוצה לקבל השכר א"כ נהנה מן המחזיר והוא מודר הנאה ממנו אשמעי' במתני' שצריך שיתן הבעל אבידה שכר ויפול הנאה להקדש וא"ת איכפל תנא לאשמועינן שאם היכא שאין המחזיר רוצה לקבל וי"ל דאורחא דמילתא הוא שאינו חושש לקבל שכר הואיל דמצוה הוא אע"פ שאינו מחוייב לעשות כיון שהוא בטל ממלאכתו: **היכי** מתרץ מקום קשיא. וא"ת ולישני כדלעיל דחדא קתני ורישא מיירי שאין בעל אבידה רוצה לעכב השכר לעצמו ואז צריך שתפול הנאה להקדש שאין המחזיר רשאי לאוכלו שמודר הנאה ממנו יש לומר דלא דמי בשלמא לעיל רגילות הוא שאין המחזיר רוצה ליטול שכר על השבת אבידה משום מצוה דגנאי הוא אבל הכא לאו אורחא דמלתא שהרי אין גנאי מלעכבו לעצמו:

הגהות הב"ח

(א) גמ' על בעל אבידה מהדר ליה דכי מהדר ליה מידי דנפשיה: (ב) שם מהדר ליה היינו דמתרץ וכו' אסורים לא מהדר היכי מתרץ: (ג) רש"י ד"ה מקום שנוטלין עליה שכר נוטלין על חזרת אבידה שכר הס"ד: (ד) ד"ה בשלמא וכו' ולא מצי בעל: (ה) ד"ה היינו וכו' עשיר הוא ואינו: (ו) ד"ה אלא למ"ד וכו' הא ליכא שכר כלל כיון דלא מהדר והכא ליכא לתרוצי אחדא קתני כדלעיל דהתם ניחא דקאמר כשנכסי מחזיר וכו' אסורין עליה דמחזיר דכיון דנכסי:

ז א מיי' פ"ד מהלכות מעילה הלכה ט:
ח ב מיי' שם הלכה י ופ"ה מהלכות נדרים הלכה ד סמג לאוין רמב טוש"ע י"ד סימן רטז סעיף ח:

אָמַר רָבָא: אהָיְתָה לְפָנָיו כִּכָּר שֶׁל הֶפְקֵר וְאָמַר "כִּכָּר זוֹ הֶקְדֵּשׁ", נְטָלָהּ לְאוֹכְלָהּ — מָעַל לְפִי כּוּלָּהּ, לְהוֹרִישָׁהּ לְבָנָיו — מָעַל לְפִי טוֹבַת הֲנָאָה שֶׁבָּהּ. בְּעָא מִינֵּיהּ רַב חִיָּיא בַּר אָבִין מֵרָבָא: "כִּכָּרִי עָלֶיךָ" וּנְתָנָהּ לוֹ בְּמַתָּנָה מַהוּ; "כִּכָּרִי" אָמַר לוֹ כִּי אִיתֵיהּ בִּרְשׁוּתֵיהּ הוּא דְּאָסוּר, אוֹ דִּלְמָא "עָלֶיךָ" אֲמַר לֵיהּ — עִילָּוֵיהּ שַׁוְּיתֵיהּ הֶקְדֵּשׁ? א"ל: בפְּשִׁיטָא, דאע"ג דִּיהֲבָהּ לֵיהּ בְּמַתָּנָה — אָסוּר. אֶלָּא "כִּכָּרִי עָלֶיךָ" לְאַפּוּקֵי מַאי — לָאו לְאַפּוּקֵי דְּאִי גָּנְבָה מִינֵּיהּ מִיגְנַב? א"ל: לָא, לְאַפּוּקֵי דְּאִי אַזְמְנֵיהּ עֲלָהּ.
אֵיתִיבֵיהּ

ר"ן

אמר רבא היתה לפניו ככר של הפקר **ואמר** ככר זו הקדש נטלה לאכלה מעל לפי כולה. האי דנקיט לה בככר של הפקר ולא נקט ליה בככר שלו שהיתה עומדת בחצרו והקדישה, משום דבכי האי גוונא נטלה לאכלה לא מעל. דכיון דמקמי הקדש שלו היתה, ולאחר הקדש ג"כ ברשותו עומדת – ה"ל כגזבר של הקדש, דאמרי' בסוף פ"ק דחגיגה (דף יא.) שאם נטל דבר של הקדש לזכות בו – לא מעל, משום דמעיקרא נמי ברשותיה קאי והשתא נמי ברשותיה, ואין מעילה בהקדש אלא במוציא מרשות הקדש לרשות אחר, ומה לי בחצרו מה לי בידו, הכא והכא לא נפיק מרשותיה. להכי נקיט ליה בככר של הפקר, שהיתה עומדת תוך ד' אמותיו שקונות לו בכל מקום. ומש"ה, כי אמר "ככר זו הקדש" – חייל, ומקדיש זה לא זכה בו מעולם. דאע"ג דאמר בפ"ק דב"מ (דף י.) דד' אמות של אדם קונות לו אפי' כי לא אמר "אקנה" – הכא שאני, משום דכיון דאמר "ככר זו הקדש" – גלי אדעתיה דלהקדש ניחא ליה דליקני, לדידיה לא ניחא. וגילויי דעתא כי האי מהני, כדמוכח סוגיא דהתם, ומאי למעבד הכי, דה"ל כמגביה מציאה לחבירו, דקנה חבירו ולא הוא. הכא נמי – הקדש קני, ואיהו מעולם לא קנה. זה נ"ל. ומש"ה נטלה לאכלה מעל לפי כולה, שכיון שלא זכה בו מעולם – אינו כגזבר עליה, ולפיכך כשנטלה – הוציאה מרשות הקדש, ומשום הכי מעל. להורישה לבניו מעל לפי טובת הנאה שבה. דכיון דלא הגביהה אלא להורישה לבניו, ולא שיקנו אותה עכשיו – לא נפקא לחולין. אבל מ"מ מעל לפי טובת הנאה, לפי שמעכשיו יחזיקו לו בניו טובה, כיון שהוא מחזר להורישם. ובניו מועלין כשיוציאו. והא דאייתי הכא הך מימריה דרבא – משום דדמיא ליה להך בעיא דבעא מיניה רב חייא בר אבין, דכי היכי דהכא הקדיש הככר ואח"כ נטלה לאכלה, בדרב חייא בר אבין נמי אסר הככר ואח"כ נתנה לו. **בעא מיניה רב חייא בר אבין מרבא ככרי** עליך ונתנה לו במתנה מהו ככרי **א"ל כי איתיה ברשותיה אסור**. ד"ככרי" בעוד שהככר שלו משמע, אבל לאחר שנתנה, כיון דלא הוי שלו – מותר בה. או דלמא "עליך" א"ל, ועילויה שויה הקדש. דה"ק ליה: זו שהיא עכשיו ככרי – אסורה עליך לעולם. ובודאי פשיטא ליה לרב חייא דהיכא שנתן מדיר ככר זה לאדם אחר – מותר המודר בו, וכדתנן לקמן בפרק "השותפין" (דף מו.): "ביתך שאני נכנס" "שדך שאני לוקח" – מת, או שמכרן לאחר – מותר. אלמא, כל היכא דאפסקיה אחר – שרי. אלא היינו טעמא דמבעיא הכא משום דלא אפסקיה אחר, דממדיר למודר קאתי. וכ"ת: תפשוט מההיא דפ' "השותפין" לאיסורא, מדקתני: מכרן לאחר – מותר, משמע הא מכרן למודר – אסור, ליתא, דאיכא למימר דמשום דבעי למתנא סיפא "ביתך זה שאני נכנס", "שדך זה שאני לוקח" – מת או שמכרן לאחר אסור, דהתם נקט אחר לרבותא, מש"ה איכא למימר דנקט רישא נמי לאחר, ולאו דוקא, דה"ה לו. והקשה רשב"ס ז"ל: מאי קמבעיא לרב חייא בר אבין? מתני' היא, דתנן בפירקין (לקמן דף מג.): המודר הנאה מחבירו ואין לו מה יאכל – הולך אצל חנווני הרגיל אצלו, ואומר לו: פלוני מודר הנאה ממני ואיני יודע מה אעשה לו. הרי זה נותן לו, ובא ונוטל מזה. היה מהלך במדבר – נותן לאחר וכו' אם אין עמהם אחר – מניח על הסלע וכו'. והתם ודאי לא באומר "נכסים אלו עליך", דבכה"ג אפילו אפסקיה אחר נמי אסור, אלא ודאי באומר "נכסי עליך", ואפ"ה, טעמא – דאיכא אחר, הא מידו של מדיר למודר – אסור! וי"ל: דהתם במדירו מהנאתו, וכיון שכן, אם נותן מתנה – בשעת מתנה הרי הוא נהנה ממנו. אבל הכא דאמר "ככרי" איכא למימר דשרי, משום דבשעה שנהנה מן הככר אינו של מדיר. **אמר ליה פשיטא דאף** על גב דיהבה נהליה במתנה **אסור דאי לא עליך לאפוקי מאי לאפוקי דאי גנבה מיגנב**. בתמיה. כלומר, ודאי דאף על גב דיהבה ניהליה במתנה אסר עליו ככרו, דאי לא – לאיזה ענין אסרה עליו ומאי נפקא ליה מן איסורו? הרי בעוד שהככר שלו וברשותו אין צריך לאסרו עליו, שהרי אסור ועומד הוא לו. וליכא למימר דמש"ה אסרו עליו – משום דאי מגנבא מיניה תתסר עליה. דליכא דמסיק אדעתיה הכי. אלא ודאי להכי אסרה – כדי שלא יפליר בו שיתנה לו. וכיון שכן על כרחיך אפילו לאחר מתנה אסרה עליה. **אמר ליה לאפוקי דאי אזמניה עלה**. כלומר, לעולם אימא לך דאי יהיב ליה במתנה שריא ליה וכי קאמר ליה "עליך" – לאפוקי דאי אזמניה עלה תתסר ליה, דההיא שעתא נמי ככרו היא.
איתיביה

רש"י

כִּכָּר שֶׁל הֶפְקֵר. וְכ"ש אִי דְּנַפְשֵׁיהּ. אֶלָּא רְבוּתָא קמ"ל, דְּמָצֵי זָכֵי בְּהֶפְקֵר לְחָלֵיהּ קְדוּשָּׁה עִילָּוֵיהּ. נְטָלָהּ עַל מְנָת לְאוֹכְלָהּ. דְּכֵיוָן שֶׁהֶחֱזִיק (א) בּוֹ קְנָאָהּ, וְאִם אֲכָלָהּ – מָעַל לְפִי כּוּלָּהּ, וּמְשַׁלֵּם לַהֶקְדֵּשׁ לְפִי כּוּלָּהּ וְחוֹמֶשׁ, שֶׁהֲרֵי הוֹצִיאָהּ לְחוּלִּין. אֲבָל נְטָלָהּ עַל מְנָת לְהוֹרִישָׁהּ לְבָנָיו. וְאַחַר כָּךְ הִקְדִּישָׁהּ עָסְקִינַן, דְּקוֹדֶם לָכֵן לֹא יָכוֹל לְהַקְדִּישָׁהּ. לֹא מָעַל אֶלָּא לְפִי טוֹבַת הֲנָאָה שֶׁבָּהּ. שֶׁאֵינוֹ מְשַׁלֵּם לַהֶקְדֵּשׁ אֶלָּא כְּפִי חֲזָקַת טוֹבָה שֶׁנּוֹתֵן לְאָבִיו אֶחָד מִן הַבָּנִים בִּשְׁבִיל שֶׁמּוֹרִישָׁהּ לוֹ, וְהַיְינוּ טוֹבַת הֲנָאָה: כִּכָּרִי יְהֵא אָסוּר עָלֶיךָ וְחָזַר וּנְתָנוֹ לַמּוּדָּר בְּמַתָּנָה מַהוּ. כִּי אִיתֵיהּ בִּרְשׁוּתֵיהּ. כְּלוֹמַר, כָּל זְמַן שֶׁהוּא שֶׁל מַדִּיר הוּא דְּאָסוּר, דְּהָכִי מַשְׁמַע "כִּכָּרִי" – כָּל זְמַן שֶׁהוּא שֶׁלִּי. אוֹ דִּלְמָא עָלֶיךָ א"ל. וְעִלָּוֵיהּ שַׁוְיֵיהּ לְאוֹתוֹ כִּכָּר הֶקְדֵּשׁ, וְאע"פ שֶׁנְּתָנוֹ לוֹ בְּמַתָּנָה – אָסוּר. אֶלָּא. הָא קָמִבַּעְיָא (ב) לֵיהּ: הַאי דְּאָמַר "כִּכָּרִי עָלֶיךָ", אִי אָמְרִי' דְּכָל זְמַן שֶׁהוּא בִּרְשׁוּתֵיהּ, דְּאִי אָתֵי לִידֵיהּ מִינֵּיהּ דִּילֵיהּ קָאָמַר לֵיהּ. וּלְאַפּוּקֵי דְּאִי גְּנָבָהּ מִיגְנַב. לְאוֹתוֹ כִּכָּר, וּנְתָנָהּ לוֹ הַגַּנָּב בְּמַתָּנָה – שֶׁאֵינוֹ אָסוּר בָּהּ, הוֹאִיל וְהוּא עַצְמוֹ לֹא נְתָנָהּ לוֹ. אוֹ דִּלְמָא אע"ג דְּאִי גְּנָבָהּ לֵיהּ מִיגְנַב – אֲסִירָה לֵיהּ. לֹא לְאַפּוּקֵי דְּאִי אַזְמְנֵיהּ עֲלֶיהָ. לְמֵיכַל מֵהַהוּא כִּכָּר מֵעִיקָּרָא, וַהֲדַר א"ל: כִּכָּרִי עָלֶיךָ. דְּהָתָם, כֵּיוָן דְּאַזְמְנֵיהּ עָלֶיהָ – קָנָה חֶלְקוֹ כַּמָּה שֶׁהוּא יָכוֹל לֶאֱכוֹל הֵימֶנָּה, וְאֵינוֹ יָכוֹל לְאוֹסְרָהּ עָלָיו, דְּלָאו כּוּלֵּיהּ דְּנוֹתֵן הוּא, אֶלָּא גַּם דִּמְזוּמָּן.
ה"ג

תוספות

היתה לפניו ככר של הקדש וכו'. תימה אי איירי בהקדש מאי שייכא כאן מלתא דרבא גבי מתני' דמיירי בקונמות ונראה דרבא מיירי בקונמות והקדש דנקט לאו דוקא אלא כהקדש קאמר וא"ת אמאי נקט מלתא בקונמות כיון דבהקדש מצי למינקט וי"ל דבהקדש לא אמרי' מעל לפי טובת הנאה שבה אם אין בו שוה פרוטה דאין מועל בהקדש בפחות משוה פרוטה אבל בקונמות בכל דהו איכא איסור הנאה: **ואמר** ככר זו הקדש. בלשון זה אמר אע"פ שלא אמר לכשאזכה בה אפ"ה כי זכה בה הוי הקדש והואיל ודעתו לזכות בה וא"ת והא אין אדם מקדיש דשלב"ל ולא דמי לאומר הרי פסח קדושה לאחר שלשים דהויא קדושה התם בידו להקדיש מיד אבל הכא לאו בידו להקדיש מיד לכ"נ שנטלה וזכה בה ולאח"כ הקדישה ובא אדם אחר ונטלה ואכלה או הוא עצמו מתחילתו שזכה בה נטלה לאוכלה זכה בכולה והלכך הקדש נמי חל על כולה ולכך מעל לפי כולה ואם מתחלת נטילתה לזכות בה בכולה להוריש לבניו לחלוק להם או ליתנה למי שירצה ואין לו בה אלא טובת הנאה אבל גוף הדבר אינו שלו והקדש כמו כן שהרי אין אדם מקריב אלא מה שיש לו בה ולכך מעל לפי טובת הנאה שבה ול"נ דלישנא דרבא לא משמע הכי דקאמר ככר זה הקדש ואחר מכאן נטלה לאוכלה משמע דהאי אחר שהקדיש שלא זכה בה עני אחר מכיון שהקדישה לכ"נ דלעולם לא זכה בה עדיין בשעת הקדש וכי תימא אין אדם מקדיש דבר שלא בא לעולם ועדיין לא זכה בה מיירי שהוא בתוך ארבע אמותיו וארבע אמות שלו קנו לו אי נמי כיון שבידו לזכות בה שהוא קרוב ממנה יותר משום אדם הוי חשיב שפיר דבר (שלא) בא לעולם כדאמר פרק האומר בקידושין (דף סב.) כל שבידו לאו כמחוסר מעשה דמי נטלה לאכלה כלומר אחר שזכה בה והקדישה כדפרישית שהיתה תוך ארבע אמותיו והקדישה אחר מכאן: **נטלה** לאוכלה מעל לפי כולה. לפי שנתכוון לשנות כולה מרשות הקדש ולכך מעל לפי כולה נטלה ע"מ להורישה לבניו א"כ לא נתכוון לשנות בכולה ולכך לא מעל אלא לפי טובת הנאה ומידי דהוה אמשאיל קרדום של הקדש ובקע בו לא מעל אלא לפי טובת הנאה שבה: **או** דלמא עליך אמר ליה ועילויה דידיה שוויה הקדש. לפי גירסא זו דייק מלשון עליך וקשה דא"כ מאי פריך בסמוך מפרה שאני נהנה לך הא לא אמר ליה עליך הא ליכא למימר דבסמוך פריך מנכסי עליך וכו' דהא מדגרסינן בסיפא או שניתנה לו במתנה ולא קתני שנתנה לו משמע דאפרה קאי ולא אנכסים לכ"נ דגרס הכא או דלמא עילוייה שווי' הקדש בלא עליך: אמר ליה פשיטא דאע"ג*) דמהני במתנה אסור: **אלא** לאפוקי מאי לאפוקי דאי גנבה מיגנב אמר ליה לאפוקי דאי אזמניה עליה. הכי גריס ר"ת וה"פ פשיטא דאסור כי יהבה ליה במתנה אלא לאפוקי מאי כלומר ומה שאסר לענין מה אסרה עליו וכי תעלה על דעתך לומר שאסרה עליו לענין דאי גנבה מיגנב זהו תימה דלא אסרה עליו אלא כשבא לידו דאין זו סברא לומר דאסיק אדעתיה דמיגנבא וכן נ"ל ע"כ דאי ס"ד דבמתנה מותרת הא ודאי כל זמן שבידו לא הוצרך לאוסרה דבע"כ לא יקחנה ונ"ל דלענין גניבה אסרה עליו וזהו תימה כדפי' ומשני דאי אזמניה עליה זה בא לאוסרה עליו דמזה אסיק אדעתיה שפיר ולעולם אימא לך דבמתנה מותרת ואע"ג שדחה סברא פשיטותא מ"מ רבא במילתיה דאמר רבא לאסור על ידי מתנה ולהכי פריך ליה:

*) נ"ל דיהביה

קונס

פי' הרא"ש

היתה לפניו ככר של הפקר. בתוך ד' אמותיו ואמר ככר זו הקדש וכיון שהוא בתוך ארבע אמותיו חל עליו הקדש כדאמרינן בפ"ק דב"מ (דף י.) דארבע אמות של אדם קונות לו בכל מקום: **נטלה לאכלה מעל לפי כולה.** דכיון שכוון לזכות בה הוציאה לחולין ומעל דמעילה היינו שינוי רשות שמתכוין לשנותה מרשות גבוה לרשות הדיוט ובלבד שיהא שוגג ומשלם אותה ואת חומשה: **להורישה לבניו מעל לפי טובת הנאה שבה.** אבל לפי כולה לא מעל לפי שלא זכה בה אדם ולא יצתה מרשות הקדש דהא לא נתכוין לזכות בה אלא לצורך בניו נטלה ובניו נמי לא זכו בה למ"ד המגביה מציאה לחבירו לא קנה חבירו ולמ"ד מי קנה הכא לא קנה משום דאיסורא לא ניחא לה דליקני וה"ה נמי אם נטלה לזכות בה לאחר או לזכות בה מיד לבניו אלא אורחא דמילתא נקט דכל עמל האדם לבניו והקשה ה"ר אליעזר ממיי"ן אמאי נקט ככר של הפקר ניחא היתה לפניו ככר של הקדש ופי' בשם ה"ר יצחק שהככר של *) הקדש היתה רחוקה ממנו הרבה ואין אדם סמוך לה שיוכל לזכות אלא הוא ואמר לכשאזכה בככר זה תהיה הקדש וקמ"ל דחל עליה הקדש דכיון דבידו לזכות בו כדאמר בפרק אע"פ שדה זו שמשכנתי לך לכשאפדנה תקדש דקדשה הואיל ובידו לפדות: **נטלה לאכלה.** ובעי למהדר ביה מעל דאמירתו לגבוה כמסירתו להדיוט: **מעל לפי טובת הנאה שבה.** אם יש בה שוה פרוטה במה שבניו מחזיקין לו טובה שרצה לזכות בה לצרכם משלם פרוטה וחומשה להקדש: **ככרי עליך ונתנה לו במתנה מהו.** אי אמר ככר זה אפילו אי יהבה לאחר אסורה לו כדתנן לקמן בפרק השותפין (דף מו.) לבית זה שאני נכנס מת או שמכרו לאחר אסור וכיון דלא אמר זה אם נתנו לאחר פשיטא שמותר כדתנן לקמן לביתך שאני נכנס מת או שמכרו לאחר מותר ומיבעיא ליה אם נתנו למודר עצמו אי הוי כאחר דכיון דאמר ככרי ולא אמר זה דוקא כי איתיה ברשותיה אסור: **או עליך א"ל ושוייה עליה כהקדש.** לעולם אפילו לאחר שנתנה לו: **א"ל פשיטא אע"ג דיהביה ליה במתנה אסור.** דעליך לעולם משמע: **אלא ככרי לאפוקי מאי כיון דאפילו נתנה במתנה אסור.** לשון ככרי דמשמע כל זמן שהוא שלי דוקא: **לאפוקי דאי גנבה מגנב.** בתמיה שאם גנבה ממנו שמותרת לו לפי שיצתה מרשותו ולא נתנה לו במתנה ומ"ש מההוא טעמא דשרית נגנבה אית לך למשרי נמי נתנה לו במתנה כך פירש ה"ר אליעזר ממיי"ץ ולא נראה דאי לא נתייאש ממנו אכתי לא נפיק מרשותיה ואסורה לו ואי נתייאש ממנו הוי כמו נתנה לאחר אלא הכי קאמר ע"כ לאפוקי דאגנבה מגנב שיהיה מותר בתמיה הא לא נפק מרשותיה כל זמן שלא נתייאש ממנה אלא ע"כ למעוטי נתנה לו במתנה והוה מצי לשנויי למעוטי אם נתנה לאחר: **אמר ליה לאפוקי דאזמניה עילויה.** שאם הזמינו לאכול עמו והיה ככר מונח לפניהם על השלחן ואמר ככרי עליך ואם אמר ככר הוה משמע כל הככרות שבבית אהני הא דאמר ככרי דדרא ככר שלפניהם אסר עליו ויש ספרים גורסים אי נמי דאזמניה עילויה ולאפוקי דאגנבה מגנב שיטויא הוא וכגון שנתייאש הימנה אי נמי לאפוקי דאזמינה וקשה לי אמאי נקט דאזמניה ליכא כגון שהיה ככר מונח לפניהם ואמר ככרי לאפוקי שאר ככרות ועוד מה שהשיב לו פשיטא דאי יהביה במתנה אסור היינו דוקא כשהככר מונח לפניהם דליכא למימר דככרי אתי לאפוקי שאר ככרות ונראה כפירוש הרב רבי יונה ז"ל וכגירסתו פשיטא דאי יהביה במתנה אסור דאי לא ככרי עליך לאפוקי מאי דאי שרית ליה אם נתנה לו במתנה היכי משכחת לה שאסרו עליו דסתם ככר אין בו כי אם הנאת אכילה ומסתמא המודר לא יאכלנה אלא כן יתננה לו המדיר ומשני דאי גנבה מגנב שאם גנב לו הככר אסור המודר להנות ממנו אי נמי דאזמניה עילויה לענין זה חל עליו האיסור שאסור להזמינו עליו שמיד כשהזמינו עליו הוא נהנה במה שהוא מכבדו ורוצה להאכילו אף על פי שעדיין לא אכיל:

*) נ"ל הפקר

קונס

הגהות הב"ח (א) רש"י ד"ה נטלה וכו' שהחזיק בה קנאה ואח"כ הקדישה עסקינן דקודם לכן לא יכול להקדישה ואם אכלה מעל וכו' ע"מ להורישה לבניו לא מעל אלא לפי כצ"ל והד"א: (ב) ד"ה אלא הא קמיבעיא ליה וכו' מי אמרינן כו' קאמר ליה ולאפוקי כצ"ל והד"א:

איתִיבֵיהּ: אָמַר לוֹ "הַשְׁאִילֵנִי פָּרָתְךָ", אָמַר לוֹ: "קוֹנָם פָּרָה שֶׁאֲנִי קָנוּי לָךְ" "נְכָסַי עָלֶיךָ אִם יֵשׁ לִי פָּרָה אֶלָּא זוֹ". "הַשְׁאִילֵנִי קַרְדּוּמְךָ", אָמַר לוֹ: "קוֹנָם קַרְדּוֹם (א) שֶׁיֵּשׁ לִי שֶׁאֲנִי קָנוּי" "נְכָסַי עָלַי אִם יֵשׁ לִי קַרְדּוֹם אֶלָּא זֶה", וְנִמְצָא שֶׁיֵּשׁ לוֹ; [א]בְּחַיָּיו – אָסוּר, מֵת אוֹ שֶׁנְּתָנָהּ לוֹ בְּמַתָּנָה – הֲרֵי זֶה מוּתָּר! א"ר אַחָא בְּרֵיהּ דְּרַב אִיקָא: [ב]שֶׁנִּיתְּנָה לוֹ עַל יְדֵי אַחֵר. א"ר אַשִׁי: דַּיְקָא נַמִי, דְּקָתָנֵי "שֶׁנִּיתְּנָה לוֹ", וְלָא קָתָנֵי שֶׁנְּתָנָהּ לוֹ. בְּעָא מִינֵּיהּ רָבָא מֵרַב נַחְמָן: יֵשׁ מְעִילָה בְּקוֹנָמוֹת אוֹ לָא? אֲמַר לֵיהּ, תְּנֵיתוּהָ: מָקוֹם שֶׁנּוֹטְלִין עָלֶיהָ שָׂכָר – תִּיפּוֹל הֲנָאָה לַהֶקְדֵּשׁ. לְמֵימְרָא – כִּי הֶקְדֵּשׁ, מַה הֶקְדֵּשׁ יֵשׁ בּוֹ מְעִילָה אַף קוֹנָמוֹת יֵשׁ בָּהֶן מְעִילָה. כְּתַנָּאֵי, *[ג]"קוֹנָם כִּכָּר זוֹ הֶקְדֵּשׁ" וַאֲכָלָהּ, בֵּין הוּא וּבֵין חֲבֵירוֹ – מָעַל, לְפִיכָךְ יֵשׁ לָהּ פִּדְיוֹן. "כִּכָּר זוֹ עָלַי (ב) לַהֶקְדֵּשׁ" וַאֲכָלָהּ – הוּא מָעַל, חֲבֵירוֹ לֹא מָעַל, לְפִיכָךְ אֵין לָהּ פִּדְיוֹן, דִּבְרֵי ר' מֵאִיר. וחכ"א: בֵּין כָּךְ וּבֵין כָּךְ לֹא מָעַל, לְפִי שֶׁאֵין מְעִילָה בְּקוֹנָמוֹת. א"ל רַב אַחָא בְּרֵיהּ דְּרַב אָוְיָא לְרַב אַשִׁי: "כִּכָּרִי עָלֶיךָ" וּנְתָנָהּ לוֹ בְּמַתָּנָה, מִי מָעַל? לִמְעוֹל נוֹתֵן – הָא לָא אֲסִירָא עֲלֵיהּ, לִמְעוֹל מְקַבֵּל יָכוֹל דְּאָמַר: הֶיתֵּירָא בָּעֵיתִי, אִיסּוּרָא לָא בָּעֵיתִי. אֲמַר לֵיהּ: [ד]מְקַבֵּל מָעַל לִכְשֶׁיּוֹצִיא, [ה]שֶׁכָּל הַמּוֹצִיא מְעוֹת הֶקְדֵּשׁ לְחוּלִּין, כִּסְבוּר שֶׁל חוּלִּין הוּא – מוֹעֵל, אַף זֶה מוֹעֵל.§

מתני'

רש"י

ה"ג קוֹנָם פָּרָה שֶׁאֲנִי הֲנָאָה לָךְ. וְהָכִי מַשְׁמַע: קוֹנָם יְהוּ עָלֶיךָ שְׁאָר פֵּרוֹת שֶׁיֵּשׁ לִי שֶׁאֲנִי מְהַנֶּה לָךְ. כְּלוֹמַר, שֶׁאֵין לִי פָּרָה אַחֶרֶת, וְזוֹ שֶׁיֵּשׁ לִי אֵינִי מַשְׁאִילָךְ. שֶׁזּוֹ לֹא רָצָה לְהַשְׁאִילוֹ, וְהָאֲחֵרוֹת אֲסוּרוֹת עָלָיו בְּנֶדֶר. אוֹ שֶׁאָמַר לוֹ: נְכָסַי אֲסוּרִין עָלֶיךָ אִם יֵשׁ לִי פָּרָה אַחֶרֶת אֶלָּא זוֹ, וְנִמְצָא שֶׁיֵּשׁ לוֹ פָּרָה אַחֶרֶת – אָסוּר לִישָּׁאֵל (ג) לֵיהָנוֹת. קוֹנָם קוֹרְדּוֹם שֶׁיֵּשׁ לִי שֶׁאֵינִי קָנוּי. כְּלוֹמַר, שֶׁלֹּא קָנִיתִי קוֹרְדּוֹם אַחֵר, וְזֶה אֵינִי מַשְׁאִילָךְ שֶׁאֲנִי צָרִיךְ לוֹ. אוֹ שֶׁאָמַר לוֹ: קוֹנָם נְכָסַי יְהוּ אֲסוּרִים עָלַי אִם יֵשׁ לִי קוֹרְדּוֹם אַחֵר אֶלָּא זֶה, וְנִמְצָא שֶׁיֵּשׁ לוֹ קוֹרְדּוֹם אַחֵר. בְּחַיָּיו אָסוּר. בַּעַל הַקּוֹרְדּוֹם אָסוּר לֵיהָנוֹת מִנְּכָסָיו כָּל יְמֵי חַיָּיו. אִי נַמִי, בְּחַיָּיו דְּמַדִּיר אֲסוּרִין נְכָסָיו עַל הַמּוּדָּר. מֵת. הַמַּשְׁאִיל. אוֹ שֶׁנְּתָנָהּ לוֹ בְּמַתָּנָה. לַמּוּדָּר. קָמַר לָן הַמּוֹרֶה: הַאי דְּקָתָנֵי מֵת – לָא קָאֵי אַסֵּיפָא כְּלָל, דְּהֵיכִי מָצֵי קָתָנֵי אַסֵּיפָא? [דְּהָא] קָתָנֵי "נְכָסַי עָלַי", מֵת אוֹ שֶׁנְּתָנָהּ לוֹ בְּמַתָּנָה – הֲרֵי זֶה מוּתָּר. מִי מוּתָּר? הֲרֵי אַנַּפְשֵׁיהּ קָאָמַר. אֶלָּא אַרֵישָׁא קָתָנֵי, אַ"הַשְׁאִילֵנִי פָּרָתְךָ", שֶׁאִם מֵת הַמַּדִּיר – מוּתָּר בַּפָּרָה אוֹ בַּנְּכָסִים שֶׁל מַדִּיר, דְּהָא אָמַר "נְכָסַי" (ד) וּמֵאַחַר שֶׁמֵּת – לָאו נִכְסֵיהּ דִּידֵיהּ אִינּוּן, וְהָכָא נַמִי אִם נִיתְּנוּ לוֹ בְּמַתָּנָה. וְאָמַר לָן הַמּוֹרֶה, דְּהכה"ג "שֶׁאֲנִי הֲנָאָה שֶׁאֵינוֹ קָנוּי" – כִּינּוּי לְשׁוֹן בְּנֵי אָדָם [הֵן] (שָׁרֵי), דְּהָכִי הָיוּ נוֹדְרִים בִּירוּשָׁלַיִם, וּבִנְדָרִים הַלֵּךְ אַחַר לְשׁוֹן בְּנֵי אָדָם. קָתָנֵי שֶׁנִּיתְּנוּ לוֹ בְּמַתָּנָה הֲרֵי זֶה מוּתָּר, וְקַשְׁיָא לְרָבָא, דְּאָמַר: אע"ג דִּיהֵיב לֵיהּ בְּמַתָּנָה – אָסוּר. אָמַר לָךְ רָבָא הָכָא בְּמַאי עָסְקִינַן כְּגוֹן שֶׁנִּיתְּנָה לוֹ עַל יְדֵי אַחֵר. שֶׁבַּעַל הַפָּרָה נְתָנוֹ לְאַחֵר, וְאוֹתוֹ אַחֵר נְתָנוֹ לַשּׁוֹאֵל. וְלָהָכִי מוּתָּר, שֶׁכְּבָר הוֹצִיאָהּ מַשְׁאִיל מֵרְשׁוּתוֹ כְּשֶׁנְּתָנָהּ לְאַחֵר. אֲבָל הֵיכָא דְּאָמַר לֵיהּ "כִּכָּרִי עָלֶיךָ" וְלֹא נְתָנָהּ לוֹ עַל יְדֵי אַחֵר, הוֹאִיל וְלֹא יָצָאת מֵרְשׁוּתוֹ קוֹדֶם לָכֵן – אָסוּר. וְלָא דָּמֵי לְהֵיכָא דְּאִיגְּנְבָה מִינֵּיהּ, מִשּׁוּם דְּהֵיכָא דְּאִיגְּנְבָה מִינֵּיהּ, הוֹאִיל וְשֶׁלֹּא מִדַּעְתּוֹ דְּבַעַל הַכִּכָּר יָצָאת מֵרְשׁוּתוֹ – כְּעוֹדָהּ בְּיָדוֹ דָּמֵי, וְאָסוּר. אֲבָל הֵיכָא שֶׁנְּתָנָהּ לוֹ בְּמַתָּנָה עַל יְדֵי אַחֵר – יָצָאת מֵרְשׁוּתוֹ מִדַּעְתּוֹ. וְלָא קָתָנֵי שֶׁנְּתָנָהּ לוֹ. דְּמַשְׁמַע שֶׁהוּא עַצְמוֹ נְתָנוֹ לוֹ. יֵשׁ מְעִילָה בְּקוֹנָמוֹת. הֵיכָא דְּאָמַר "קוֹנָם כִּכָּר זֶה" וַאֲכָלוֹ, מִי הָוֵי כְּהֶקְדֵּשׁ מְעַלְיָא דְּיֵשׁ בּוֹ מְעִילָה, וּמָעַל, אוֹ לָא? [תְּנֵיתוּהָ מָקוֹם] שֶׁנּוֹטְלִין עָלֶיהָ שָׂכָר. וּמוּדָּר הַיְינוּ דְּאָמַר "קוֹנָם", וּמְדַמֵּי לֵיהּ לְהֶקְדֵּשׁ. קוֹנָם כִּכָּר זֶה הֶקְדֵּשׁ. שֶׁאָמַר בִּלְשׁוֹן הַקֹּדֶשׁ וּבִלְשׁוֹן קוֹנָם. וְהוּא הַדִּין נַמִי לֹא אֲמָרָהּ אֶלָּא בִּלְשׁוֹן קוֹנָם. בֵּין הוּא בֵּין חֲבֵירוֹ מָעַל. שֶׁהֲרֵי הִקְדִּישָׁהּ סְתָם אַכּוּלֵּי עָלְמָא. לְפִיכָךְ. הוֹאִיל וְיֵשׁ בָּהּ מְעִילָה – יֵשׁ בָּהּ פִּדְיוֹן וְיָצְאָה לְחוּלִּין, דְּהָוֵי כִּשְׁאָר הֶקְדֵּשׁ. אָמַר זוֹ עָלַי הֶקְדֵּשׁ. כֵּיוָן דְּאָמַר "עָלַי" – עֲלֵיהּ דִּידֵיהּ שַׁוְיֵהּ הֶקְדֵּשׁ, וְהוּא מָעַל, אִם אָכַל חַיָּיב לְשַׁלּוּמֵי. חֲבֵירוֹ לֹא מָעַל. דְּלֹא אֲסָרָהּ אֶלָּא עַל עַצְמוֹ, וְגַבֵּי חֲבֵירוֹ הָוֵי כְּחוּלִּין. לְפִיכָךְ אֵין לָהּ פִּדְיוֹן. שֶׁהוּא עַצְמוֹ אֵין יָכוֹל לִפְדּוֹתָהּ לְעוֹלָם, שֶׁהֲרֵי אָמַר "עָלַי" וְלֹא עַל אַחֵר, וְאַחֵר אֵין יָכוֹל לִמְעוֹל בָּהּ. בֵּין כָּךְ וּבֵין כָּךְ. בֵּין אָמַר סְתָם בֵּין אָמַר "עָלַי" – לֹא מָעַל בֵּין הוּא וּבֵין חֲבֵירוֹ, אַף עַל פִּי שֶׁאָמַר הֶקְדֵּשׁ, כֵּיוָן דְּאָמַר נַמִי קוֹנָם – שֶׁאֵין מְעִילָה בְּקוֹנָמוֹת. מִי מָעַל. אַלִּיבָּא דְּמַאן דְּאָמַר יֵשׁ מְעִילָה בְּקוֹנָמוֹת קָבָעֵי. הָא לָא אֲסִירָא עֲלֵיהּ. דְּנוֹתֵן. הֶתֵּירָא נִיחָא לִי דְּתֵיתִיב לִי אִיסּוּרָא לָא בָּעֵיתִי. כְּלוֹמַר, דִּבְתוֹרַת הֶיתֵּר קִבַּלְתִּיהָ מִמְּךָ, וְלֹא בְּתוֹרַת אִיסּוּר. וּכְסָבוּר שֶׁל חוּלִּין הֵן (ה) מָעַל. אעפ"כ, הָכִי נַמִי אַף זֶה הַמְקַבֵּל אע"פ שֶׁסָּבוּר זֶה הַמְקַבֵּל שֶׁהֶיתֵּר הוּא, כִּי אֲכָלָהּ – מָעַל.

מתני'

ר"ן

איתיביה וכו' השאילני פרתך הקנויה. פרה המונחת בפניהם. קונם פרה שאני קנוי עליך. קונם עליך פרתי זו אם אני קניתי אלא פרה זו, או שאוסר עליו כל נכסיו אם יש לו פרה אלא זו. בחייו אסור. אם נמצא שיש לו פרה אחרת, או קורדום אחר. מת או שנתנה לו במתנה הרי זה מותר. משום דכי מת או שנתנה לו במתנה – לא פרתו ולא קרדומו ולא נכסיו הן. וקס"ד שהמדיר נתן למודר, ואפ"ה שרי, ◉וקשיא לרבא דאסר. שנתנה לו על ידי אחר. שנתנו מדיר לאיניש דעלמא, ואח"כ נתנו זה למודר. דיקא נמי דקתני שניתנו לו. כלומר, שכך היתה קבלה בידם לקרות נתנו בחירק, אף על פי ◉שאין בכתיבה שום הפרש. ולענין הלכה קיימא לן אע"ג דיהביה ניהליה במתנה – אסור. דהכי פשט ליה רבא, ואסיקנא דיקא נמי דקתני כו'. וכתב הרשב"א ז"ל דכי היכי דיהבה במתנה אסור, ה"ה אם לקחו מודר ממנו, דחד טעמא הוא. יש מעילה בקונמות. האוסר דבר עליו בקונס ונהנה ממנו, מי מחייב מעילה או לא? מי אמרינן דעשאו כקרבן וחייב עליו אשם מעילה, כנהנה מן הקדשים. תפול הנאה להקדש למימרא כהקדש. דאי לא דמי קונמות להקדש הוה ליה למימר: יוליך הנאה לים המלח, כדקתני בכל דוכתא. אלא משום דבקונמות יש בהן מעילה כהקדש, כיון דבהקדש עסיק – תנא: תפול הנאה להקדש. קונם ככר זו הקדש. שאסרה בקונם לכל כהקדש שהוא אסור לכל אדם. אבלה בין הוא בין חברו מעל. דיש מעילה בקונמות. לפיכך יש לה פדיון. דכיון דמתסר אכולי עלמא כהקדש – תפיס פדיונו. ככר זו עלי הקדש אבלה הוא מעל. דנהי דלא מיתסרה אלא עליה, כי מתהני איהו מינה – מעל. חבירו לא מעל לפיכך אין לה פדיון. דכיון דחבירו לא מעל – לא אלים כהקדש למתפס פדיונה. וחכ"א בין כך ובין כך לא מעל לפי שאין מעילה בקונמות. בין בקונס כללי שאסר לכל, בין בקונס פרטי. ולענין הלכה קי"ל כר"מ, דיש מעילה בקונמות. דהא רב נחמן פשיט ליה לרבא ממתניתין שיש מעילה, ובפ' "שבועות שתים בתרא" (דף כב:) נמי מפכינן דר"מ לרבנן. הלכך קי"ל דיש מעילה, וקי"ל נמי דקונס כללי יש לו פדיון. ומסתפקא לי מאן דמעל בקונמות אי מישתרי ההוא קונס לבתר דמעיל, כהקדש שיוצא לחולין ע"י מעילה. ככרי עליך ונתנה לו במתנה מי מעל. כלומר, מי מעל בנתינה זו? דכיון דיש מעילה, כי היכי דאמר בהקדש *דנטל אבן או קורה של הקדש מעל, אע"פ שלא הוציאה – הכא נמי, מכיון שזכה בה שייכא מעילה, שיצאה מרשות אוסר ונכנסה לרשות מקבל. למעול נותן הא לא אסרה עליה. ומכאן תשובה להרמב"ם ז"ל שכתב (בפרק): המדיר את חבירו והאכילו – לוקה משום "לא יחל דברו", כמו שכתבתי למעלה בפ' "ואלו מותרים"*. למעול מקבל יכול דאמר התירא בעינא איסורא לא בעינא. שאילו היה יודע שהוא של איסור – לא היה רוצה לזכות בה. ונמצא זכיה בטעות, ואינה זכיה. ואע"ג דבמוציא מרשות הקדש אפשר דאפי' בטעות מעל – שאני הכא שהוא לא הוציאה, אלא חבירו הוציאה וזה לא עשה אלא שקבלה. אמר ליה מקבל מעל לכשיוציא. כלומר, מהשתא אין אחד מהם מועל מהנך טעמי דאמרת. אלא מיהו, לכשיוציא – מעל. נהי דגבי זכיה אמרינן דזכיה בטעות היא, לכשיוציא לא אמרינן הכי, מידי דהוה אכל מוציא מעות הקדש לחולין. ירושלמי נדר מן הככר מהו לחמם בו את ידיו? ולא איפשיטא.

מתני'

פי' הרא"ש

קונם פרה שאני קנוי. כקונם יהא עליך אם יש לי פרה אלא זו ולזו אני צריך ויש לו פרות אחרות ונאסרו נכסיו על המודר. **או שנתנה לו במתנה הרי זה מותר.** ותיובתא דרבא: **שנתנה לו על ידי אחר.** שנתנה לאחר והוא נתנה למודר: **דיקא נמי דקתני שניתנה ולא קתני שנתנה לו.** בעל פה היתה הגירסא שגורה בפיהם: **למימרא כהקדש.** כדפרישנא במתני' מדקתני דדוקא להקדש צריך ליתן השכר ואינו יכול להשליכו לאבוד אלמא כל הנאה הבאה לו ממנה הרי הוא הקדש ויש לו בה מעילה: **ככר זה הקדש.** פירוש הקדש גמור ומילתא דפשיטא היא ולא איצטריך להך בבא כלל אלא אגב סיפא נקט: **הוא מעל.** דקסבר יש מעילה בקונמות: **אין לה פדיון.** דאין בו מעילה לכל כמו הקדש דלא אליס למתפס פדיוניה: **וחכ"א אחד זה ואחד זה לא מעל.** בין הוא בין חבירו לא מעל דאין מעילה בקונמות: **מי מעל.** למאן דאמר יש מעילה בקונמות: **למעול נותן.** כמו הנותן הקדש בשוגג לחבירו דמעל: **הא לא אסרה עילויה.** ולא מצינו מעילה בדבר המותר לו לאדם: **איסורא לא בעי דליקני.** דכל מעילה בשוגג הוא ואילו הייתי יודע שהיא אסורה לא הייתי מקבלה אבל המוציא מעות של הקדש בשוגג מעל אע"פ שאילו היה יודע שהיה של הקדש לא היה רוצה לזכות בהם כיון שהוא עצמו לקחם כדי לזכות בהם אבל מה שנותן לו על ידי אחר מצי למימר איסורא לא בעינא למקני: **מקבל מעל לכשיוציא.** דכל דבר של הקדש א) אינו יוצא עד שימעול בו והכי אמרינן במעילה האומר לשלוחו תן דינר לחנוני ונזכר בעל הבית קודם שנתנו לחנווני חנווני מעל לכשיוציא:

א) נ"ל אינו מועל בו עד שיוציא.

תוספות

קונם פרה שיש לי שאני הנאה לך נכסי עליך אם יש לי פרה אלא זו. שני נדרים הוו ואי קאמר שאומר לו קונם פרה שיש לי שאוכל ליהנות לך ממנה כלו' שאין לי פרה אחרת ואם יש לי תהא קונם עליך או שאמר בלשון הזה נכסי עליך קונם אם יש לי פרה אלא זו שאני עושה בה מלאכתי ונמצא שיש לו פרה אחרת ועתה נאסרה הפרה והנכסים עליו וגבי קונם נמי ה"פ כדפירשתי: **מת** או שנתנה לו במתנה מותרת. מת דתו לא מיקרו פרה וקרדום שלו וכן שנתנה לו במתנה מותרת וקס"ד שנתנה המדיר למודר ומשני שניתנה לו על ידי אחר לפירוש שני דלעיל ניחא דפריך מנתנה לו במתנה דאפרה ואקרדום קאי ואע"ג דלא אמר עליך אבל לפי' ראשון דלעיל דדייק מעליך קשה מאי פריך מנתנה לו פרה וקרדום הא לא אמר עליך וי"ל דלפי פירוש ראשון גרס שניתנו לשון רבים וקאי נמי אנכסים ודוחק הוא שבכל הספרים גרסי' שניתן לשון יחיד דמשמע דקאי דוקא אפרה ואקרדום לכ"נ כפירוש שני וא"ת אכתי היא גופה תקשה לך אמאי לא תנא שניתנו משום נכסים הלא מיירי משנה גם מנכסים וי"ל מ"מ לא נחת לאשמועינן לאשריותא דפרה וקרדום שהיה רוצה לישאל ממנו היה עיקר הנדר וגם בכלל נכסים הם דמיתסר נמי בנדר כנכסים: **הוא** מעל וחבירו לא מעל לפיכך אין לו פדיון וחכ"א בין כך ובין כך לא מעל. פירוש וחכמים לא קאי לרישא אלא קאי לסיפא דבעי למימר בין הוא בין חבירו לא מעל וקשה דלישנא דבין כך ובין כך משמע דקאי לכולה מלתא דר"מ ועוד משמע דאפילו לר"מ דיש בו מעילה מכל מקום אין לו פדיון וקשה בפרק האשה רבה (יבמות דף פח.) משמע האי יש בו מעילה משום דבידו לפדותו אלמא משמע דיש בו פדיה בקונמות וע"ק ברישא קאמר ככר זה הקדש מעל מאי קמשמע לן פשיטא דהקדש גמור יש בו פדיון ומעילה לכ"נ לפרש דרישא לא מיירי בהקדש ממש אלא בקונם בלשון הקדש שאסר הככר לכל כמו הקדש ולכך יש בו מעילה כיון שנאסר לכל כהקדש גמור ככר זה עלי הקדש דמיירי בקונם שאינו אסור לכ"ע אלא לדידיה לכך אין לו פדיון דהא דאמרינן בשיש בו מעילה משום שבידו לפדותו היינו קונם שאסור לכל כמו הקדש. וחכמים אומרים בין כך ובין כך כו' קאי אפילו לרישא משום דאין מעילה בשום קונמות וכיון שאמר הקדש בלשון קונמות אין מועלין:

מסורת הש"ס

שבועות כב. [ע"ש ובתוס' דשם ותוס' יבמות פח. ד"ה אי קסבר]

[חגיגה י: וש"נ]

[דף טו. ד"ה הלכה]

עין משפט נר מצוה

ט א ב מיי' פ"ה מהל' נדרים הלכה ד סמג לאוין רמב טוש"ע י"ד סימן רטז סעיף ה:

י ג מיי' פ"ד מהלכות מעילה הלכה ט:

יא ד מיי' שם הלכה י:

יב ה מיי' שם פ"ו הלכה יא:

הגהות הב"ח

(א) גמ' קונם קרדום לי כצ"ל ותיבת שיש נמחק: (ב) שם ככר זו עלי הקדש כצ"ל ואות ל' נמחק: (ג) רש"י ד"ה ה"ג וכו' וליהנות: (ד) ד"ה או שנתנה לו וכו' נכסי עליך ומאחר שמת וכו' והכי נמי אם: (ה) ד"ה וכסבור של חולין הן אעפ"כ מעל הכא נמי:

גליון הש"ס

בהר"ן ד"ה מת וכו' וק' לרבא דאסר ק"ל הא רבא פשט רק מכח הוכחה דאילו ככרי עליך לאפוקי מאי וכדפי' הר"ן לעיל וזהו שייך בככר דסתם הנאת ככר רק לאכילה וכמ"ש הרא"ש אבל הכא בפרה ובקורדום ל"ש הוכחה זו. דבא לאפוקי בעוד שהפרה שלו אסור להשאילו ליהנות ממנה אם כן י"ל דרבא מודה בזה למותר בנותן במתנה וצ"ע: **בהר"ן** ד"ה דיקא נמי וכו' שאין בכתיבה שום וכו'. וכיוצא בזה כתובות ג ע"ב:

מקריב

עין משפט נר מצוה

יג א מיי' פ"ו מהלכות נדרים הלכה ו סמג לאוין רמב טור י"ד סימן רכא:
יד ב מיי' שם הלכה ה:
[ויומא דף יט.]
טו ג מיי' שם הלכה ז וסמג שם טוש"ע יו"ד סימן רכא סעיף ב:
טז ד מיי' שם הל' ה:
יז ה מיי' פ"א מהלכות מחוסרי כפרה הל' ה:
יח ו מיי' שם פ"ג הלכה ו
יט ז מיי' פ"י מהלכות שגגות הלכה ו סמג עשין ריז:

תורה אור

מתני' [א]וְתוֹרֵם אֶת תְּרוּמָתוֹ וּמַעַשְׂרוֹתָיו לְדַעְתּוֹ, [ב]וּמַקְרִיב עָלָיו קִינֵּי זָבִין קִינֵּי זָבוֹת קִינֵּי יוֹלְדוֹת חַטָּאוֹת וַאֲשָׁמוֹת. [ג]וּמְלַמְּדוֹ מִדְרָשׁ הֲלָכוֹת וְאַגָּדוֹת, אֲבָל לֹא יְלַמְּדֶנּוּ מִקְרָא. אֲבָל מְלַמֵּד הוּא אֶת בָּנָיו וְאֶת בְּנוֹתָיו מִקְרָא.§ **גמ'** אִיבַּעְיָא לְהוּ: *הָנֵי כָּהֲנֵי, שְׁלוּחֵי דִידַן הָווּ אוֹ שְׁלוּחֵי דִשְׁמַיָּא? לְמַאי נָפְקָא מִינָּהּ – לְמוּדָּר הֲנָאָה. אִי אָמְרַתְּ דִּשְׁלוּחֵי דִידַן הָווּ – הָא מְהַנֵּי לֵיהּ, וְאָסוּר. וְאִי אָמְרַתְּ שְׁלוּחֵי דִשְׁמַיָּא – [ד]שָׁרֵי. מַאי? ת"ש, דִּתְנַן: (א) מַקְרִיב עָלָיו קִינֵּי זָבִין כו'. אִי אָמְרַתְּ שְׁלוּחֵי דִידַן – קָא מְהַנֵּי לֵיהּ! וְלִיטַעְמִיךְ, לִיתְנֵי: מַקְרִיב עָלָיו קָרְבָּנוֹת! אֶלָּא, מְחוּסְּרֵי כַּפָּרָה שָׁאנֵי. דא"ר יוֹחָנָן: [ה]הַכֹּל צְרִיכִין דַּעַת, חוּץ מִמְּחוּסְּרֵי כַּפָּרָה, שֶׁהֲרֵי אָדָם מֵבִיא קָרְבָּן עַל בָּנָיו וְעַל בְּנוֹתָיו הַקְּטַנִּים, שֶׁנֶּאֱמַר °"זֹאת תּוֹרַת הַזָּב" (ויקרא טו) – בֵּין גָּדוֹל בֵּין קָטָן. אֶלָּא מֵעַתָּה לר' יוֹחָנָן °"זֹאת תּוֹרַת הַיֹּלֶדֶת" (שם יג) וגו' – בֵּין קְטַנָּה וּבֵין גְּדוֹלָה, *קְטַנָּה בַּת לֵידָה הִיא?! וְהָא *תָּנֵי רַב בֵּיבָי קַמֵּיהּ דְּרַב נַחְמָן: שָׁלֹשׁ נָשִׁים מְשַׁמְּשׁוֹת בְּמוֹךְ: קְטַנָּה, וּמְעוּבֶּרֶת, וּמֵינִיקָה. קְטַנָּה – שֶׁמָּא תִּתְעַבֵּר וְתָמוּת! הַהִיא "זֹאת תּוֹרַת הַיֹּלֶדֶת" – בֵּין פִּקַּחַת בֵּין שׁוֹטָה, שֶׁכֵּן אָדָם [ו]מֵבִיא קָרְבָּן עַל אִשְׁתּוֹ שׁוֹטָה, כְּדִבְרֵי רַבִּי יְהוּדָה. *דְּתַנְיָא, *)רַבִּי יְהוּדָה אוֹמֵר: [ז]אָדָם מֵבִיא קָרְבָּן עָשִׁיר עַל אִשְׁתּוֹ, וְכָל קָרְבָּנוֹת שֶׁחַיֶּיבֶת. שֶׁכָּךְ כּוֹתֵב לָהּ: וְאַחֲרָיוּת דְּאִית לִיךְ עֲלַי מִן קַדְמַת דְּנָא.

מתיב

ר"ן

מתני' ותורם את תרומתו ואת מעשרותיו לדעתו. מפרש בגמ' לדעתו דמאן. ומקריב עליו. אי האי מדיר כהן הוא. קיני זבין וקיני זבות וקיני יולדות. לפי שכל אלו מביאין שתי תורים קרבן. ומלמדו מדרש. דמלות לאו ליהנות ניתנו. ולא ילמדנו מקרא. בגמ' מפרש טעמא. **גמ'** איבעיא להו הני כהני שלוחי דידן הם. אע"ג דבפ"ק דקדושין (דף כג:*) אסיק רב הונא דשלוחי דרחמנא נינהו, דאי ס"ד שלוחי דידן נינהו מי איכא מידי דאנן לא מצינן למיעבד ואינהו עבדי? אפילו הכי בעי הכא למיפשטא ממתני' או מברייתא. **הא** קמהני ליה. וכיון דעביד שליחותיה – מהני ליה הוא. דבשלמא אי שלוחי דשמיא נינהו, אע"ג דשרי להו בהאי קרבן למיכל בקדשים – אין זה אלא גרמת הנאה בעלמא, ושרי. וליטעמיך. דבעית למיפשט ממתני', ליתני: מקריב עליו קרבנות. אלא מחוסר כפרה שאני. כלומר, ואדרבה, תפשוט לאידך גיסא. דכיון דתנא מחוסרי כפרה בלחוד, דאין צריכין דעת – משמע דוקא הני, משום דכיון דאין צריכין דעת – ודאי כהן לאו שליחותן קעביד. אבל בשאר קרבנות הצריכין דעת – שלוחי דידן נינהו. דאי לא – ליתני: מקריב עליו קרבנות, והוה רבותא טפי. ומיהו, לא מיפשטא בעיין לגמרי, דאיכא למימר דתנא מחוסרי כפרה לאשמועי' רבותא, דאע"פ שמתירו לאכול בקדשים שרי, וכל שכן בשאר קרבנות. ומדרבי יוחנן נמי, דאמר הכל צריכין דעת, לא מיפשטא בעיין לומר דשלוחי דידן נינהו. דאיכא למימר דרחמנא שוינהו לכהני שלוחין – כל היכא דאיכא דעת בעלים. חוץ ממחוסרי כפרה. זב וזבה ומצורע ומצורעת ויולדת, ובכולהו כתיב "תורת". וקרי להו מחוסרי כפרה – משום שאסורין ליכנס למקדש ולאכול בקדשים עד שיביאו כפרתן. והני, כיון דאין קרבן בא לכפרה – אין צריכין דעת. אבל כל שצריכין כפרה על חטא – צריכין דעת. שנאמר זאת תורת הזב בין גדול בין קטן. וכי היכי דאדם מביא קרבן על בנו קטן שאין לו דעת – הכי נמי שלא מדעתו על חבירו. **אלא** מעתה לרבי יוחנן. דס"ל ד"תורת" אתי לרבויי קטן, "זאת תורת היולדת" מאי איכא לרבויי? אילימא בין גדולה בין קטנה – והא תני רב ביבי וכו'! משמשות במוך. חייבות לשמש במוך משום סכנה, שמא תתעבר ותמות. אלמא לא משכחת לה יולדת שהיא קטנה. וכי תימא: מאי קושיא? הא אסיקנא בפ"ק דיבמות (דף יב:) דשמא תמות קאמר, ואפשר נמי דלא מייתא! איכא למימר: מאן דסבר הכי התם ס"ל דבנים הרי הן כסימנים, אי נמי עדיפי מסימנים, הלכך גדולה היא. ולא משכחת קטנה שתלד. ההיא זאת תורת היולדת בין פקחת בין שוטה שכן אדם **מביא** קרבן על **אשתו** כר' יהודה. כלומר, אי לא אשכחן דאדם מביא קרבן על אשתו – לא הוה מרבינן שוטה, דלמאן קא מזהר רחמנא? בשלמא בקטן – לאבוה קא מזהר, אלא שוטה למאן? אבל השתא דאמר רבי יהודה דאדם מביא קרבן על אשתו – איכא לאוקמי קרא ד"זאת תורת" ליולדת שוטה, שאין אנו צריכין דעתה אלא דעת הבעל, כיון שהוא מביא קרבנותיה. ה"ג: *)**דתניא אדם מביא קרבן עשיר על אשתו וכל קרבנות שהיא חייבת א"ר יהודה לפיכך אם פטרה אינו חייב באחריותן שכך כותבת לו אחריות דאית לי עליך מן קדמת דנא***). וה"פ: אדם מביא קרבן עשיר על אשתו. שאע"פ שכל אשה שיש לה בעל לא הויא עשירה, שהרי כל מה שקנתה אשה קנה בעלה, אפ"ה כיון שבעלה עשיר – מביא בשבילה קרבן עשיר בקרבנות שהיא בעולה ויורד, לפי שהבעל חייב בקרבנות אשתו. וכן כל קרבנות שהיא חייבת, למעוטי נדריה ונדבותיה. ר' יהודה אומר: לפיכך אם פטרה, כלומר שגרשה – אינו חייב באחריותן. שכך כותבת לו בשובר שהיא עושה לו בשעת גירושין מכתובתה, כותבת לו שהיא מוחלת כל אחריות שיש לה עליו מקודם לכן, ויש בכלל לשון זה אפילו קרבנות, דר' יהודה דריש לשון הדיוט. ומהכא ילפינן לה בפ' "המקבל" (ב"מ קד.). והא דאמר הכא: שכן מביא אדם קרבן על אשתו כר' יהודה – לאו דוקא כר' יהודה, דהא תני רישא סתמא אדם מביא קרבן עשיר על אשתו. אלא משום דלא ידעינן מאן ניהו ת"ק, ור' יהודה איירי בה – תלינן לה לדידיה.

מתיב

*) [עיין היטב ברש"י ב"מ קד. ד"ה אדם מביא וכו' וד"ה כל הקרבנות כו' וד"ה ה"ג לה בת"כ וכו' תמצא מכוון כגי' הר"ן דהכא ועי' גי' הר"ש במשנה י"ב פי"ד דנגעים ועי' נזיר כד. אמר ר"ח רבנן היא דאי ס"ד ר' יהודה היא וכו' דתניא ר"י אומר אדם מביא קרבן עשיר וכו' ע"ש כל הסוגיא וצ"ע]:

רש"י

מתני' וְתוֹרֵם אֶת תְּרוּמָתוֹ וכו'. מְפָרֵשׁ בַּגְּמָרָא. [וּמַקְרִיב עָלָיו]. אִם הָיָה כֹּהֵן אוֹתוֹ שֶׁנָּדַר שֶׁלֹּא יֵהָנֶה מִמֶּנּוּ – יָכוֹל לְהַקְרִיב עָלָיו קִינֵּי זָבִין וְקִינֵּי זָבוֹת וכו'. **גמ'** הָנֵי כָּהֲנֵי. שֶׁמַּקְרִיבִין קָרְבָּנוֹת. שְׁלוּחֵי דִידַן. דְּבַעֲלֵי קָרְבָּן. **הָא קָא** מְהַנֵּי לֵיהּ. שָׁלִיחַ לְכַפֵּר כַּפָּרָתוֹ, וְאִיהוּ הִדִּירוֹ שֶׁלֹּא יֵהָנֶה מִמֶּנּוּ. **אֶלָּא**. מִדְּקָתָנֵי: מַקְרִיב עָלָיו קִינֵּי זָבִין וכו' – ש"מ דִּשְׁלוּחֵי דִשְׁמַיָּא נִינְהוּ. [וְלִיטַעְמִיךְ]. אִם כֵּן דִּשְׁלוּחֵי דִשְׁמַיָּא נִינְהוּ – לִיתְנֵי סְתָם מַקְרִיב עָלָיו קָרְבָּנוֹת. אֶלָּא מִדְּלָא קָתָנֵי אֶלָּא קִינֵּי זָבִין וכו' – ש"מ דִּשְׁלוּחֵי דִידַן נִינְהוּ, וּדְקַשְׁיָא לָךְ: הָא קָמְהַנֵּי לֵיהּ – תְּרֵיץ: לָא קָמְהַנֵּי לֵיהּ, דְּבִמְחוּסְּרֵי כַּפָּרָה שָׁאנֵי, כִּי הָנֵי דְּמַתְנִי'. **דא"ר** יוֹחָנָן הַכֹּל צְרִיכִין דַּעַת. כָּל הַקָּרְבָּנוֹת צְרִיכִין שֶׁיְּהוּ מַקְרִיבִים בְּעָלִים, חוּץ מִמְּחוּסְּרֵי וכו'. עַל בָּנָיו וְעַל בְּנוֹתָיו הַקְּטַנִּים. כְּשֶׁהֵן מְחוּסְּרֵי כַּפָּרָה, דִּכְתִיב "זֹאת תּוֹרַת הַזָּב" וגו' וְנָשִׁים (ב) שֶׁמֵּבִיא קָרְבָּן עֲלֵיהֶן – אע"פ שֶׁאֵין לָהֶם דַּעַת הֵם. הָכִי נַמִי גְּדוֹלִים אֵין צְרִיכִין לְהָבִיא כַּפָּרָתָן לְדַעְתָּן. הִלְכָּךְ הוֹאִיל וּמַקְרִיב עָלָיו שֶׁלֹּא לְדַעְתּוֹ – לָא מְהַנֵּי לֵיהּ, דְּהָא לָא יָדַע, (ג) וּמוּתָּר. **אֶלָּא** מֵעַתָּה לְר' יוֹחָנָן. דְּמַפֵּיק מִ"זֹּאת תּוֹרַת הַזָּב" בֵּין גָּדוֹל בֵּין קָטָן, (ד) הָכָא נַמִי מָצֵי לְמֵימַר מֵהַאי קְרָא נַמִי. **שֶׁמָּא** תִּתְעַבֵּר וְתָמוּת. וַדַּאי. אַלְמָא לָאו בַּת לֵידָה הִיא. **אָמַר** לָךְ רַבִּי יוֹחָנָן. הַהוּא "זֹאת תּוֹרַת הַיּוֹלֶדֶת" לָא מְרַבֵּי לָהּ לִקְטַנָּה, אֶלָּא בִּגְדוֹלָה מַיְירֵי, וְקָא מְרַבֶּה אֲפִילּוּ יוֹלֶדֶת שׁוֹטָה. **שֶׁכֵּן** אָדָם מֵבִיא קָרְבָּן עָשִׁיר אֲפִילּוּ עַל אִשְׁתּוֹ שׁוֹטָה. **אָדָם** מֵבִיא קָרְבָּן עָשִׁיר עַל אִשְׁתּוֹ, בֵּין פִּקַּחַת בֵּין שׁוֹטָה, וְלָא אָמְרִינַן דְּאע"פ שֶׁנִּשֵּׂאת לְעָשִׁיר – עֲנִיָּה הִיא, דְּמַה שֶּׁקָּנְתָה אִשָּׁה קָנָה בַּעְלָהּ. אֶלָּא כָּל הַקָּרְבָּנוֹת שֶׁחַיֶּיבֶת מֵבִיא עָלֶיהָ. שֶׁכָּךְ כָּתַב לָהּ וְאַחֲרָיוּת כו'. דְּהָכִי מַשְׁמַע אַחֲרָיוּתָא עָלַי. וְכִי הֵיכִי דְּהַאי מֵבִיא קָרְבָּן עַל אִשְׁתּוֹ יוֹלֶדֶת אֲפִילּוּ שׁוֹטָה, כָּךְ כָּל מְחוּסְּרֵי כַּפָּרָה – אֵין צְרִיכִין דַּעַת, וּלְעוֹלָם שְׁלוּחֵי דִידַן נִינְהוּ.

אם

תוספות

מקריב עליו קינין וכו'. אם היה המדיר כהן מקריב לזה המודר: **לא** ילמדנו מקרא. מפרש בגמרא דבלימוד מקרא נוטל שכר אבל מלמדו מדרש כמו ת"כ והלכות דאין נוטלין עליה שכר ובגמ' מפרש טעמא דנוטלין שכר על המקרא ואין נוטלין שכר על המדרש: **אבל** מלמד בניו מקרא. מצוה קא עביד ולא הוי אלא גורם הנאה בעלמא ואפילו במקום נמי דנוטלין שכר עליה דמ"מ לא היה המודר נותן שכר למלמד לבניו: **איבעי'** להו הני כהני שלוחי דרחמנא נינהו וכו'. ואי אמרת שלוחי [דידן] נינהו הא מהני ליה דעבד שליחותא. דודאי גוף הקרבן מצוה קעביד מיהו כיון דהאי כהן שלוחו בזה אסור וה"נ אמרינן גבי תורם דאי אמרת צריך דעת הא קמהני ליה וה"נ אי שלוחי דידן נינהו אסור מיהו קשה אמאי לא פשיט ליה מההוא דפ' קמא דקידושין (דף כג.) אמר רב כהנא הני כהני שלוחי דרחמנא נינהו דאי ס"ד שלוחי דידן נינהו מי איכא מידי דאנן לא מצינן למיעבד ואינהו קא עבדי וי"ל דרוצה לפשוט ממשנה או מברייתא: **ת"ש** ומקריב עליו קיני זבים ואי אמרת שלוחי דידן הא קמהני ליה. ויש להקשות דלמא דאמר כל הרוצה להקריב יבוא ויקריב דכה"ג לא מהני ליה ושמא נראה לו דמיירי במודר הנאה בכל כהני דהאי ודאי לא מצינו למימר כי בכה"ג שאני דאז לא יצטרך דעת בעלים ואותן הוו שלוחי דידן: **כדרבי** יוחנן. דאמר הכל צריך דעת בעלים אם מחוייב אדם עולה ושלמים אינו יכול לפטור אותו חבירו שלא מדעתו: **שהרי** מקריב אדם על בניו ועל בנותיו. להתירן לאכול בקדשים דכתיב זאת תורת הזב בין גדול בין קטן וקטן לאו בר דעת הוא אלמא דאין צריך דעת בעלים להתירו לאכול בקדשים במחוסר כפרה: **אלא** מעתה לרבי יוחנן זאת תורת היולדת וכו'. קלא קשה דבלאו רבי יוחנן ברייתא היא בפ' בנות כותים (נדה דף לח:) דכתיב זאת תורת הזב בין גדול בין קטן: **ומשני** ההיא זאת תורת היולדת בין פקחת בין שוטה. שכך מצינו שאדם מביא קרבן על אשתו שוטה: **מביא** אדם קרבן עשיר על אשתו. אם היא חייבת קרבן לידה או מצורעת ואין יכול לומר עניה היא ואין לה שום דבר שכך כתב לה בכתובתה לאחריות דאית לך עלי מן קדמת דנא דמשמע ליה אפילו שוטה נ"ע מנא ליה הא דמשמע שהוא חייב כל מה שחייבת קודם מזה יש ללמוד דאדם חייב לפרוע חובות אשתו שהיא חייבת קודם שישאנה ולא נראה דבפרק יש נוחלין (ב"ב דף קלט.) איבעיא ליה אי בעל בנכסי אשתו לוקח הוי או יורש הוי דאי לוקח הוי לא יפרע לבעלי חובות של אשתו שלוותה קודם ואפילו מנכסי מלוג שלה ואם יורש הוי יפרע מנכסי מלוג שלה כמו יורש שפורע חובות אביו מקרקעי ואם כן לא מיבעי אלא מנכסי מלוג שלה אבל מנכסים שלו לא יפרע שום דבר. והך בעיא ללוקח הוי או יורש הוי פסק רבינו שמואל בן בתו של רש"י קבלה מרבינו חננאל דיורש הוי וצריך הבעל לפרוע מנכסי מלוג שהכניסה לו אשתו והכי הלכתא שאדם פורע חוב אשתו שהיא חייבת קודם לכן אם יש מטלטלין או חובות כעין שהכניסה לו אע"פ שיורש אינו פורע ממטלטלין מיהו לאחר תקנות גאונים שתיקנו להיות עתה מטלטלין כמקרקעי וגובה כתובתה ממטלטלין אע"ג דממנה אין לגבות כ"א ממקרקעי כמו כן גם החובות נמי יתפרעו מן המטלטלין דכל הדין הנוהג בקרקעות נוהג במטלטלין והא דאמר הכא כל קרבנות שהיא חייבת דוקא קרבנות אבל חוב לא יפרע אלא ממה שהכניסה לו דכיון דיורש הוי ומטלטלין כקרקעות עתה שיעבודם על אותן נכסים אין יכולת ביד הבעל להפקיען אבל יותר ממה שהכניסה לו [אינו פורע] וקרבנותיה נמי דוקא קרבנות חובה אבל לא נדרים ונדבות ואם לאחר ניסואין [נדרה קרבן] לא ישלם נדריה דאם לא כן יכולה להחריב בעלה. והכי משמע בירושלמי. גרסא אחרת אם פטרה אינו חייב וה"פ כל קרבנות שהיא חייבת כשהיא תחתיו חייב לפרוע ולפיכך אם פטרה שגירשה אינו חייב שכך כתבה בשובר של כתובה והתקבלתי כתובתי ואחריות דאית לי עלך מן קדמת דנא ולגירסא זו אינו חייב לשלם כלום מקודם ניסואין:

אם

מסורת הש"ס

יומא יט. קדושין כג:

[וע' תוס' סנהדרין סט. ד"ה בידוע]

*יבמות יב: ק[?] נדה מה. כתובות לט. [תוספתא נדה פ"ב]

[סיומא דמילתא שכך כותב לה כו' ליתא במשנה לכך שפיר גרסי' דתנא]

*) נגעים פי"ד [מ"ב] ב"מ קד. נזיר כד. תוספתא כתובות פ"ד]

גליון הש"ס

בהר"ן ד"ה ומלמדו מדרש למכלה וכו'. עיין ר"ה דף כר ע"א ובעורי אבן שם ד"ה ובשופר: **ד"ה** איבעיא להו וכו'. ממתני' או מברייתא. עיין לקמן דף ע"ב ע"א בר"ן ד"ה ולעבן: **ד"ה** משמשות במוך וכו' קטנה שתלד. עיין בסדרי טהרה בחי' למסכת נדה דף נב ע"ב ד"ה ודב למסקנין:

פי' הרא"ש

מתני' ומקריב עליו קיני זבין וקיני זבות. כהן שהדיר את ישראל הנאה ממנו יכול להקריב קרבנותיו זב וזבה מביאין שתי תורין או שני בני יונה ביום טהרתם וכן יולדת עניה: **ותורם תרומתו.** בגמ' מפרש לה: **גמ' דלא מחוסר כפרה שאני.** דלא בעינן דעת הלכך לאו שליחותיה קא עביד כיון דיכול להקריב בלא דעתו אבל שאר קרבנות דבעי דעת שלוחי דידן נינהו ואסור: **שכל צריכין דעת.** אם ראובן חייב קרבן אין שמעון יכול להפרישו ולהקריבו שיפטר בו ראובן **חוץ ממחוסר כפרה** דגלי ביה קרא שהאב מביא על בניו להתירם בקדשים והכהן מקריבו אע"פ שאינו יודע שהוא של קטן: **זאת תורת הזב בין גדול בין קטן.** לענין קרבן כתיב וקטן לאו בר דעת הוא להביא קרבן אלא אביו מביא על ידו: **קטנה בת לידה היא.** וכיון דביולדת לא מצי למידרשיה לרבות קטנה גבי זב נמי לא דרשינן ליה לרבות קטן: **שלש נשים משמשות במוך.** צריכות לשום מוך באותו מקום לקלוט את הזרע שלא תתעבר: **בין פקחת בין שוטה.** נהי דלא מצינן לרבויי קטנה מרבינן שוטה דגם היא לאו בת דעת היא ובעלה מביא עליה בלא דעתה להתירה בקדשים כדברי רבי יהודה דאמר הבעל חייב להביא קרבנות אשתו הלכך אפילו שוטה נמי מביא קרבן עשיר על אשתו ולא מצי למימר עניה היא אביא עליה קרבן עני אלא כיון שהוא מחוייב להביא קרבנותיה והוא עשיר צריך להביא קרבן עשיר וכן כל קרבנות שהיא חייבת כשהיא מחוסרת כפרה או אכלה חלב או אם חייבת אשם אבל לא אם נדרה קרבן דאם כן תדור בכל יום כדי להקניטו: **שכך כתבה לו כל אחריות דאית לי עלך מן קדמת דנא.** כשהבעל מגרשה היא כותבת לו שובר שהיא פוטרתו מכל אחריות שהיה לה עליו אלמא כל דבר שהיה עליה באחריות היה הבעל חייב קודם שגירשה: *) **לזרוק עליו מדם חטאתו ודם אשמו.** האי דלא פריך ליה מחטאות ואשמות דמתניתין משום דתני ליה גבי קיני זבין וזבות הוה ידע דמשני ליה דאיירי

*) [שייך לדף שאח"ז]

במחוסרי

הגהות הב"ח (א) גמ' דתנן ומקריב וכו' שלוחי דידן הוי הא קא מהני ליה: (ב) רש"י ד"ה על בניו וכו' ונשים נמי שמביא וכו' שאין להם דעת הוא הדין נמי נ"ב כלומר שלא לדעתן: (ג) בא"ד לא ידע המודר הס"ד: (ד) ד"ה אלא וכו' הכי נמי וכו' מהאי קרא הס"ד ותיבת נמי נמחק:

מתיב רב שימי בר אבא: אם היה כהן – יזרוק עליו דם חטאתו ודם אשמו! דם חטאתו של מצורע, ודם אשמו של מצורע, דכתיב °"זאת תהיה תורת המצורע" – [א]בין גדול ובין קטן. תנן: *[ב]הכהנים שפיגלו במקדש, מזידין – חייבין. [ג]הא שוגגין – פטורין, *אלא שפיגולן פיגול. אי אמרת בשלמא שלוחי דשמיא הוו – היינו שפיגולן פיגול. אלא אי אמרת שלוחי דידן הוו אמאי פיגולן פיגול? לימא ליה: שליחא שויתיך *לתקוני ולא לעוותי! אמרי: שאני גבי פיגול, דאמר קרא °"לא יחשב לו" – מכל מקום.§ גופא, א"ר יוחנן: הכל צריכין דעת, חוץ ממחוסר כפרה, שהרי אדם מביא קרבן על בניו ועל בנותיו הקטנים. אלא מעתה יביא אדם חטאת חלב על חבירו, •שכן אדם מביא על אשתו שוטה כר' יהודה. אלמה א"ר אלעזר: [ד]הפריש חטאת חלב על חבירו – לא עשה כלום! אשתו שוטה היכי דמי? אי דאכלה כשהיא שוטה – לאו בת קרבן היא, ואי דאכלה כשהיא פקחת ונשתטית – הא *א"ר ירמיה אמר ר' אבהו אמר רבי יוחנן: [ה]אכל חלב והפריש קרבן ונשתטה וחזר ונשתפה – פסול, הואיל ונדחה – ידחה. אלא מעתה יביא אדם פסח על חבירו, שכן אדם מביא על בניו ועל בנותיו הקטנים. אלמה אמר ר' אלעזר: [ו]הפריש פסח על חבירו – לא עשה כלום! אמר רבי זירא: °"שה לבית אבת" לאו דאורייתא. וממאי מדתנן: *האומר לבניו "הריני שוחט את הפסח על מי שיעלה מכם ראשון לירושלים" כיון שהכניס ראשו ורובו – זכה בחלקו, ומזכה את אחיו עמו. ואי אמרת "שה לבית" (א) דאורייתא – על בישרא קאי ומזכי להו?! אלא למה להו דאמר להון אבוהון – כדי לזרזן במצות. *תניא נמי הכי: מעשה היה וקדמו בנות לבנים, ונמצאו בנות זריזות ובנים שפלים.§ "ותורם את תרומותיו" כו'.§

איבעיא

תורה אור: ויקרא יד | שם ז | שמות יב

רש"י

אם היה כהן. המדיר. יזרוק עליו דם חטאתו ודם אשמו. קתני סתם, דמשמע כל חטאות ואשמות, ואע"ג דלא מחוסרי כפרה נינהו. לא לעולם שלוחי דידן נינהו ומאי דם חטאתו ודם אשמו דקתני חטאתו של מצורע כו'. דהיינו מחוסרי כפרה וכו', וה"ה לגדול. מזידין חייבין. לשלם קרבן לבעלים. לתקוני שויתיך. שליח, ולא לעוותי. אמרי. לעולם שלוחי דידן נינהו, ולהכי פיגולו פיגול. לא יחשב לו. פיגול יהיה מכל מקום. אלא מעתה. יביא אדם אפי' חטאת חלב על חבירו, שכן מביא קרבן על אשתו שוטה, דמשמע כל קרבנות שהיא חייבת, אפי' אם אכלה חלב. ומתרץ (ב) רבי יוחנן אשתו שוטה היכי דמי. שתהא מחוייבת קרבן, אי דאכלה כו'. פסול. הקרבן, דהואיל ונדחה כשנשתטית, דלאו בת קרבן היא – ידחה. התם נמי גבי אשה, הואיל ונדחית בשעת אכילה – נדחית מהכל, ואין אדם מביא קרבן חלב על אשתו שוטה, וליכא למירמא מהכא. וכי קאמינא דלר' יהודה הא דמביא קרבן על אשתו שוטה – כגון זבה או יולדת או מצורעת. וקפריך תו יביא אדם כו'. אלמה אמר ר' אלעזר: הפריש פסח על חבירו שלא מדעתו כו'. אמר רבי זירא שה לבית אבות. דמשמע אדם מביא פסח ושוחט על בניו ועל בנותיו הקטנים. לאו דאורייתא הוא. (ג) להכי, הפריש פסח על חבירו – לא עשה ולא כלום. וממאי. דלאו דאורייתא הוא – מדתנן וכו'. ואי אמרת שה לבית אבות. דאדם שוחט על בניו הקטנים דאורייתא. על בישרא קאי ומזכי להו. כלומר היאך יכול זה לזכות את אחיו מאחר שנשחט? והא תנן (פסחים פט.): נמנין ומושכין ידיהן עד שישחט. אלא אזמוני להו לאחר שחיטה – לאו דאורייתא, והך משנה משמע דבבניו קטנים מיירי. אלא. הואיל ולאו דאורייתא הוא למה ליה לאבוהון למימר: הריני שוחט את הפסח על מי שיעלה מכם לירושלים – כדי לזרזן במצות. תניא נמי הכי. כדי לזרזן קאמר, מדקאמר: בנים שפלים, ולא קאמר: ובנים לא יצאו ידי חובתן – מכלל דלא מחייבי מדאורייתא, אלא לזרזן קאמר.

כיון

גיטין נג. מנחות מט. | [נ"ל ותני עלה כך איתא במנחות מט.] | [קדושין מב: וש"נ] | זבחים יב: כריתות ז. סנהדרין מז. [הוריות יח.] | [פסחים פט. גיטין כה.] | פסחים פט. גיטין כה.

ר"ן

מתיב רב שימי בר אבא אם היה כהן זורק עליו דם חטאתו ואשמו. איכא מאן דאמר דמדאותיב רב שימי בר אבא מברייתא ולא אותיב ממתני' – ש"מ דלא גרס במתניתין חטאות ואשמות. ואי מהא לא איריא, דהאי דלא אותיב ליה ממתני' – משום דכיון דתנא להו בהדי קיני זבין, ממילא מוכח דחטאות ואשמות דמצורע קאמר. אבל מתניתא דתני סתמא זורק דם חטאתו ואשמו – משמע ליה דבכל חטאות קאמר. ואפי' הכי שני ליה דדם חטאתו ואשמו של מצורע קאמר. תנן הכהנים שפגלו במקדש וכו' **אא"ב שלוחי דשמיא** נינהו היינו שפגולן פגול. דרחמנא שוינהו שלוחי לכל מילי. **אלא א"א שלוחי דידן נינהו אמאי פגולן פגול.** שוגג הוא [דקשה] ליה. בשלמא במזיד, נהי דשלוחי דידן נינהו פיגולן פיגול, דכיון שמפגל במזיד – אינו עושה שליחותו, אלא אדעתא דנפשיה קעביד, וקי"ל בפ"ב דחולין (דף מ.) דאדם אוסר דבר שאינו שלו על ידי מעשה. אבל בשוגג, אי שלוחי דידן נינהו – אמאי פיגולן פיגול? דהא כיון דשוגג הוא – לאו אדעתא דנפשיה קעביד, שמתכוין הוא לעשות שליחותו, ולימא: שליח שויתיך לתקוני ולא לעוותי. ודחי': שאני גבי פגול דאמר קרא וכו'. הלכך בעיין הכא לא איפשיטא. ומיהו, נהי דהכא לא איפשיטא לה, מההיא דפ"ק דקידושין מוכח דשלוחי שמיא נינהו, וכמו שכתבתי למעלה. **גופא א"ר יוחנן הכל צריכין דעת** וכו'. הקשו בתוס': התנן, ומייתי לה בפרק "האיש מקדש" (קדושין נה.): בהמה שנמצאת מירושלים למגדל עדר – זכרים לעולות, כלומר ויקרבו. אלמא אין צריכין דעת. ותירצו: דהתם שאני, דכיון שנאבד – דעת בעלים הוא שכל כהן שירצה להקריב – יקריב. **אלא מעתה יביא אדם חטאת חלב על חבירו אלמה אמר רבי אלעזר** וכו' **לא עשה ולא כלום**. משום דאין דנין אפשר משאי אפשר. **אשתו שוטה היכי דמי**. כלומר, לעולם בכי הא דנין. אלא למאי דאמר לר' יהודה דאדם מביא על אשתו שוטה – לא חטאת חלב קאמר, אלא קרבן יולדת. דחטאת חלב אי אפשר, דהיכי דמי וכו' וכיון שהיא פטורה – אי אפשר שיביא בעלה עליה. **אלא מעתה יביא אדם פסח על חבירו**. לדידך, דדנית אפשר משאי אפשר. **לא עשה כלום**. שצריך שימנה עמהם מדעתו. **א"ר זירא שה לבית אבות לאו דאורייתא**. לעולם בכי האי דנין, ומיהו מפסח לא מצי למידק, דשה לבית אבות לאו דאורייתא. דמן התורה אין הקטנים צריכין להמנות בשה עם בני חבורה, אלא אוכלין ממנו אף על פי שלא נמנו עליו. דאף על גב דאין פסח נאכל אלא למנוייו – ה"מ בראויין להמנות, אבל קטנים דלאו בני הכי – לית לן בה. **הריני שוחט את הפסח על מי שיעלה מכם ראשון לירושלים**. אמר לבניו: הריני עולה לירושלים, ולאחר שאהיה שם אשחוט את הפסח על מי שיעלה מכם ראשון. **על בשרא קאי**. כשעלה זה כבר נשחט, ואם כן היאך נמנה עליו? והכתיב "מהיות משה" ודרשינן: מחיותא דשה (פסחים פט.). **ומזכי להון**. בתמיה, היאך האב מזכה לאחד מבניו אחר שחיטה? א"נ, האי "ומזכה להם" אההוא בן שעולה ראשון קאי, היאך מזכה לאחיו? דבשלמא איהו זכי דאיכא למימר כיון שעלה ראשון הוברר שכשנשחט הפסח – עליו נשחט, אבל היאך מזכה לאחיו? והכי מוכח סוגיין דפרק "כל הגט" (גיטין דף כה.). **כדי לזרזן**. שיהיו רגילין להזדרז במצות. **ונמצאו בנות זריזות**. ולא קתני "בנות זכו", אלמא לא נתכוין אלא לזרז בלבד.

איבעיא

עין משפט נר מצוה

כ א מיי' פ"ט מהלכות טומאת צרעת הלכ' ח:

כא ב ג מיי' פ"ז מהל' חובל ומזיק הלכ' ד:

כב ד מיי' פט"ו מהל' פסולי המוקדשין הלכ' ז (ופ"ג מהל' שגגות הלכה ג):

כג ה מיי' פ"ג מהל' שגגות הלכה ח [ופסק שחזר ונראה ע"ש בכ"מ]:

כד ו מיי' פ"ב מהל' קרבן פסח הלכה ח וע"ש

הגהות הב"ח

(א) גמ' שה לבית אבות דאורייתא על בישרא קאי ומזכי. נ"ב וע"ע דהרי בגיטין פ' כל הגט דף כ"ה מוקמינן ליה משום קושיא זו לאיירי שכבר אימנה עליהם מעיקרא ולאמת לעולם דאורייתא היא וצ"ע מנאתי קושיא זו בתוס' דפסחים דף פ"ט ד"ה אלא: (ב) רש"י ד"ה ומתרץ אשתו שוטה לר' יוחנן היכי דמי: (ג) ד"ה לאו דאורייתא ולהכי:

גליון הש"ס

גמ' שכן אדם מביא על אשתו שוטה כר"י. קשה לי הא מה דאמרינן לעיל גבי יולדת שכן מביא על אשתו כר"י היינו כיון דחיובי קרבן לאשה על בעלה מוקמי לקרא דזאת תורת היולדת לרבות אשתו שוטה וכמ"ש הר"ן שם אבל בחלב דלא כתיב תורת ליכא רבויא ובהא אין מביא על אשתו שוטה כיון דצריך דעת ודלע"ג:

תוספות

אם היה כהן. אותו המדיר ממנו זורק חטאתו ואשמו דמשמע ליה דמיירי בחטאת חלב ודם אלמא שלוחי דרחמנא נינהו וה"ה דמצי לאותובי ממתני' חטאות ואשמות: **אמאי** פיגולו פיגול לימא לתיקוני שדרתיך ולא לעוותי: **אלמה** אמר ר' אלעזר הפריש חטאת חלב וכו'. תימה מדרבי יוחנן גופיה תיקשי דהכל צריכין דעת וצ"ע וי"ל דמצינן למימר דר' יוחנן מיירי בכהן המקריב שצריך דעת בעלים: **שוטה** לאו בת קרבן היא. והא דאמר לעיל זאת תורת היולדת בין פיקחת בין שוטה מיהו איהו לא מצי מייתי: **יביא** אדם פסח על חבירו שכן אדם מביא קרבן על בניו כשהן קטנים וכו' אמר רבי זירא שה לבית לאו דאורייתא הוא. כלומר דקטנים אינם צריכים למנות דאם אוכלין מן הפסח לא הוי כנאכל שלא למנוייו דלא אסר רחמנא אלא להנהו דאיתנהו במנות תכוסו אבל אותם דלא שייך בהו לא איירי מידי דהוה אנשים דרשות הן שאע"פ שאין חייבות בפסח מותרות לאכול ממנו ואינו נקרא שלא למנויו וכן בקטנים: **על** בישרא קאי ומזכה להון. בתמיה כלומר לאחר שחיטה יכול להמנותם והא תנן (פסחים דף פט.) מושכין ידיהן עד שישחטו אבל לאחר שחיטה לא אלמא דהמנאת קטנים לאו דאורייתא ובניו דקטנים מיירי: **בקטנים** למה לי למימר להו. כיון דלא המנום. לזרזן:

ותורם

פי' הרא"ש

במחוסרי כפרה אבל ברייתא הוה סלקא דעתך דאיירי בכל חטאות ואשמות: **הכהנים שפגלו**. שחשבו באחת מארבע עבודות לאוכלו או להקריבו חוץ לזמנו או חוץ למקומו ותני עלה שוגגין פטורים אלא שפגולן פגול אלמא דהוי פיגול גמור מדאורייתא אבל ממתני' המ"ל דהוי פיגול דרבנן: **אי אמרת בשלמא שלוחי דשמיא נינהו היינו דקתני שפגולן פגול**. שהרי הפקיעה התורה קרבנו מרשות בעלים ונתנו לכהן מדלא בעינן דעת בעלים: **אמאי פגולן פגול**. הא אין אדם אוסר דבר שאינו שלו ואי משום דעשאו שליח לימא לתקוני שדרתיך כו': **שמקריב *) לו לא יחשב לו מ"מ**. ודרשינן בזבחים (דף כט:) קרוי ביה לא יחשב אלמא מחשבת המקריב הויא מחשבה לפסול אע"ג דלאו דידיה הוא: **אלא מעתה יביא אדם חטאת חלב על חבירו**. דכיון דילפת אפשר משאי אפשר א"כ בחטאת חלב נמי ליליף ויביא חטאת חלב על חבירו ומשני בעל אשתו שוטה נמי אי אפשר להביא חטאת דכיון דלאו בר דעת היא לאו לאיתויי חטאת היא דאף פיקח שהפריש קרבן ונשתטה נפסל הקרבן ואין הבעל מקריב עליה אלא כשהיא מחוסרת כפרה להתירה בקדשים: **שכן אדם מביא על בניו ובנותיו הקטנים**. אע"פ שכן צריכין פסח כדכתיב שה לבית אבות ואין להם דעת להמנות ופסח אינו נאכל אלא למנוייו אלא שהמנאת אביהם בלא דעתם הויא המנאה וה"ה ימנה חבירו על פסחו בלא דעתו: **שה לבית לאו דאורייתא**. הלכך לא ילפינן מהכא דגדול שהוא מחויב מן התורה שיוכל אחר למנותו בלא דעתו: **על בשרא קאי ומזכה להו**. הא תנן נמנין ומושכין את ידיהם עד שישחט דכתיב ואם ימעט הבית מהיות משה מהוית של שה יכולין להתמעט ולהתרבות עליו ולא אחר שנשחט: **בנות זריזות ובנים שפלים**. ולא קתני בנות זוכות ובנים אינן זוכין:

*) [נ"ל אותו]

כיון

כה א מיי' פ"ד מהל' תרומות הלכה ב סמג עשין קלד טור י"ד סימן שלא:

[ב"מ כב.]

כו ב מיי' פ"ו מהלכ' נדרים הלכה ו סמג לאוין רמב:

כז ג מיי' פ"ז מהלכות ערכין הלכה ד:

כח ד מיי' פ"א מהל' תמורה הלכה ד:

כט ה מיי' פ"ד מהל' תרומות הלכה ב:

תורה אור

אִיבַּעְיָא לְהוּ: הַתּוֹרֵם מִשֶּׁלּוֹ עַל שֶׁל חֲבֵירוֹ צָרִיךְ דַּעְתּוֹ אוֹ לֹא? מִי אָמְרִינַן: כֵּיוָן דִּזְכוּת הוּא לוֹ – [א]לֹא צָרִיךְ דַּעַת, אוֹ דִּלְמָא מִצְוָה דִּילֵיהּ הִיא, וְנִיחָא לֵיהּ לְמִיעַבְדֵיהּ? ת"ש: תּוֹרֵם אֶת תְּרוּמוֹתָיו וְאֶת מַעַשְׂרוֹתָיו לְדַעְתּוֹ. בְּמַאי עָסְקִינַן? אִילֵימָא (א) מִן בַּעַל הַכְּרִי עַל שֶׁל בַּעַל הַכְּרִי, וּלְדַעְתּוֹ דְּמַאן? אִילֵימָא לְדַעְתּוֹ דִּילֵיהּ – מַאן שַׁוְויֵהּ שָׁלִיחַ? אֶלָּא לְדַעְתּוֹ דְּבַעַל הַכְּרִי – הָא קָמְהַנֵּי לֵיהּ, דְּקָעָבֵיד שְׁלִיחוּתֵיהּ! אֶלָּא מִשֶּׁלּוֹ עַל שֶׁל (ב) הַכְּרִי. וּלְדַעְתּוֹ דְּמַאן? אִילֵימָא לְדַעְתּוֹ דְּבַעַל הַכְּרִי – הָא קָמְהַנֵּי לֵיהּ! אֶלָּא לָאו – לְדַעְתֵּיהּ דְּנַפְשֵׁיהּ, (ג) וּמִשֶּׁלּוֹ תּוֹרֵם עַל שֶׁל חֲבֵירוֹ. וא"א צָרִיךְ דַּעַת – הָא קָמְהַנֵּי לֵיהּ! אֶלָּא לָאו – אֵין צָרִיךְ דַּעַת. לְעוֹלָם מִשֶּׁל בַּעַל הַכְּרִי עַל בַּעַל הַכְּרִי. כִּדְאָמַר רָבָא: [ב]בְּאוֹמֵר "כָּל הָרוֹצֶה לִתְרוֹם יָבֹא וְיִתְרוֹם", הָכָא נַמִי בְּאוֹמֵר וכו'. בְּעָא מִינֵּיהּ רַבִּי יִרְמְיָה מר' זֵירָא: הַתּוֹרֵם מִשֶּׁלּוֹ עַל שֶׁל חֲבֵירוֹ, טוֹבַת הֲנָאָה שֶׁל מִי? מִי אָמְרִינַן: אִי לָאו פֵּירֵי דְּהָאֵיךְ – מִי מִתַּקְנָא כַּרְיָא דְּהַהוּא, אוֹ דִּלְמָא אִי לָאו כַּרְיָא דְּהַהוּא – לָא הָוְיָין פֵּירֵי דְּהָדֵין תְּרוּמָה? א"ל: אֲמַר קְרָא °"אֵת כָּל *תְּבוּאַת זַרְעֶךָ... וְנָתַתָּ". אֵיתִיבֵיהּ: תּוֹרֵם אֶת תְּרוּמוֹתָיו וְאֶת מַעַשְׂרוֹתָיו לְדַעְתּוֹ. וְאִי אָמְרַתְּ טוֹבַת הֲנָאָה דְּבַעַל הַכְּרִי הָא קָא מְהַנֵּי לֵיהּ! אֶלָּא ש"מ טוֹבַת הֲנָאָה דִּילֵיהּ. אָמְרִי: לָא, מִשֶּׁל בַּעַל הַכְּרִי עַל שֶׁל בַּעַל הַכְּרִי. וּלְדַעְתּוֹ דְּבַעַל הַכְּרִי, בְּאוֹמֵר "כָּל הָרוֹצֶה לִתְרוֹם יָבֹא וְיִתְרוֹם". ת"ש, *דְּאָמַר ר' אַבָּהוּ אָמַר ר' יוֹחָנָן: [ג]הַמַּקְדִּישׁ מוֹסִיף חוֹמֶשׁ, [ד]וּמִתְכַּפֵּר עוֹשֶׂה תְּמוּרָה, [ה]וְהַתּוֹרֵם מִשֶּׁלּוֹ עַל שֶׁאֵינוֹ שֶׁלּוֹ – טוֹבַת הֲנָאָה שֶׁלּוֹ.§ "מְלַמְּדוֹ מִדְרָשׁ הֲלָכוֹת וְאַגָּדוֹת אֲבָל לֹא יְלַמְּדֶנּוּ מִקְרָא".§ מִקְרָא מ"ט לֹא יְלַמְּדֶנּוּ – מִשּׁוּם דְּקָמְהַנֵּי לֵיהּ, מִדְרָשׁ נַמִי קָמְהַנֵּי לֵיהּ! אָמַר שְׁמוּאֵל: בְּמָקוֹם שֶׁנּוֹטְלִין שָׂכָר עַל הַמִּקְרָא וְאֵין נוֹטְלִין שָׂכָר עַל הַמִּדְרָשׁ. מַאי פָּסְקָא? הָא

דברים יד

רש"י

כֵּיוָן דִּזְכוּת הוּא לוֹ. שֶׁמַּרְוִיחַ, שֶׁתּוֹרֵם עָלָיו מִשֶּׁלּוֹ, וְלֹא צָרִיךְ לִיתֵּן לוֹ כְּלוּם. לֹא צָרִיךְ דַּעַת. שֶׁזָּכִין לְאָדָם שֶׁלֹּא בְּפָנָיו. אוֹ דִּלְמָא. כֵּיוָן דְּמִצְוָה דִּילֵיהּ הִיא. דְּבַעַל הַכְּרִי, נִיחָא לֵיהּ לְמִיעַבְדֵיהּ, שֶׁיְּקַיֵּים הוּא אֶת הַמִּצְוָה. לְפִיכָךְ צָרִיךְ שֶׁיּוֹדִיעוֹ. אִילֵימָא. מִשֶּׁל בַּעַל הַכְּרִי עַל בַּעַל הַכְּרִי. אִילֵימָא לְדַעְתֵּיהּ דִּילֵיהּ. לְדַעְתּוֹ שֶׁל תּוֹרֵם, שֶׁלֹּא הוֹדִיעוֹ לְבַעַל הַכְּרִי שֶׁהוּא תּוֹרֵם עָלָיו. מַאן שַׁוְויֵהּ שָׁלִיחַ. הָא קַיְימָא לָן: מָה אַתֶּם לְדַעְתְּכֶם – אַף שְׁלוּחֲכֶם לְדַעְתְּכֶם. הָא קָא מְהַנֵּי לֵיהּ דְּעָבֵד שְׁלִיחוּתֵיהּ. וְאִיהוּ הִדִּירוֹ. הָא קָא מְהַנֵּי לֵיהּ. הַאי שֶׁתּוֹרֵם עָלָיו. אֶלָּא לָאו לְדַעְתֵּיהּ דְּנַפְשֵׁיהּ. שֶׁלֹּא הוֹדִיעַ לְבַעַל הַכְּרִי שֶׁהוּא רוֹצֶה לִתְרוֹם עָלָיו. וְא"א צָרִיךְ דַּעַת הָא קָמְהַנֵּי לֵיהּ. כֵּיוָן שֶׁתּוֹרֵם עָלָיו בִּידִיעָתוֹ – הָא קָמְהַנֵּי לֵיהּ. אֶלָּא לָאו אֵין צָרִיךְ דַּעַת. וּלְהָכִי תּוֹרֵם עָלָיו, דְּכֵיוָן שֶׁתּוֹרֵם עָלָיו שֶׁלֹּא מִדַּעְתּוֹ – לָא מְהַנֵּי לֵיהּ כְּלָל. לְעוֹלָם מִשֶּׁל בַּעַל הַכְּרִי. מַיְירֵי, וּלְדַעְתּוֹ דְּבַעַל הַכְּרִי. וּדְקָאָמְרַתְּ: הָא קָמְהַנֵּי לֵיהּ, דְּעָבֵיד שְׁלִיחוּתֵיהּ וְתָרֵים. (ד)בְּאוֹמֵר כָּל הָרוֹצֶ' לִתְרוֹם יָבֹא וְיִתְרוֹם. דְּכֵיוָן דְּלָא שַׁוְויֵהּ שָׁלִיחַ מַמָּשׁ טְפֵי מֵאַחֲרִינֵי, וְאַחֲרִינֵי נַמִי יְכוֹלִין לִתְרוֹם כְּמוֹתוֹ – לָא מְהַנֵּי לֵיהּ כְּלָל, דְּאִי לָא תָּרֵים לֵיהּ הַאי – תָּרֵים לֵיהּ אִינִישׁ אַחֲרִינָא, וּמֵהָכָא לֵיכָּא לְמִשְׁמַע מִינֵּיהּ כְּלָל. טוֹבַת הֲנָאָה מִשֶּׁל מִי. אוֹתָהּ פְּרוּטָה שֶׁיָּכוֹל לְקַבֵּל מִיִּשְׂרָאֵל אַחֵר כְּדֵי לִיתְּנָהּ לְבֶן בִּתּוֹ כֹּהֵן, מִשֶּׁל מִי הִיא? אִי לָאו פֵּירֵי דְּהַאי. דְּתוֹרֵם, לָא מִתַּקַּן כַּרְיָא דְּהַהוּא, וְתֶיהֱוֵי אוֹתָהּ פְּרוּטָה דְּתוֹרֵם. אוֹ דִּלְמָא(ה) לָא וכו'. וּדְבַעַל הַכְּרִי הָוֵי טוֹבַת הֲנָאָה. אֵת כָּל תְּבוּאַת זַרְעֲךָ וְנָתַתָּ וגו'. שְׁמַע מִינָּהּ דְּבַעַל הַכְּרִי הִיא טוֹבַת הֲנָאָה, מִדִּכְתִיב "זַרְעֶךָ וְנָתַתָּ". תּוֹרֵם אֶת תְּרוּמוֹתָיו וּמַעַשְׂרוֹתָיו לְדַעְתּוֹ. שֶׁל תּוֹרֵם. וְקס"ד דְּמִשֶּׁלּוֹ עַל שֶׁל בַּעַל הַכְּרִי – הָא קָא מְהַנֵּי לֵיהּ, דְּשָׁקֵיל טוֹבַת הֲנָאָה. אֶלָּא. מִדְּתוֹרֵם לוֹ – שְׁמַע מִינָּהּ דְּטוֹבַת הֲנָאָה שֶׁל תּוֹרֵם הִיא. אָמְרִי. לְעוֹלָם מֵהָא לֵיכָּא לְמִשְׁמַע מִינֵּיהּ טוֹבַת הֲנָאָה שֶׁל מִי, דְּהָכָא לָא מַיְירֵי אֶלָּא בְּשֶׁל בַּעַל הַכְּרִי, וּלְדַעְתּוֹ דְּבַעַל הַכְּרִי. וּלְהָכִי טוֹבַת הֲנָאָה שֶׁלּוֹ, וַאֲפִילּוּ הָכִי לָא קָא מְהַנֵּי לֵיהּ. בְּאוֹמֵר כָּל הָרוֹצֶה כו'. כִּדְאוֹקִימְנָא לְעֵיל. הַמַּקְדִּישׁ. שֶׁפּוֹדֶה אֶת הֶקְדֵּשׁוֹ מוֹסִיף חוֹמֶשׁ, וְלֹא אָדָם אַחֵר, כְּדִכְתִיב "וְאִם הַמַּקְדִּישׁ יִגְאַל אֶת בֵּיתוֹ" (ויקרא כז). וּמִתְכַּפֵּר עוֹשֶׂה תְּמוּרָה. הַמַּפְרִישׁ קָרְבָּן לִפְטוֹר חוֹבָתוֹ שֶׁל חֲבֵירוֹ – הַמִּתְכַּפֵּר עוֹשֶׂה תְּמוּרָה בְּאוֹתוֹ קָרְבָּן, דְּהַשְׁתָּא הָוֵי דִּידֵיהּ וְלֹא הַמַּפְרִישׁוֹ. דְּמֵאַחַר שֶׁהִפְרִישׁ לְצוֹרְכּוֹ – קְנָאוֹ הַמִּתְכַּפֵּר. וְהַתּוֹרֵם וכו' טוֹבַת הֲנָאָה שֶׁלּוֹ. שֶׁל תּוֹרֵם. שֶׁנּוֹטְלִין שָׂכָר עַל לִימּוּד הַמִּקְרָא וכו'. וּלְהָכִי לֹא יְלַמְּדֶנּוּ מִקְרָא בְּחִנָּם לָזֶה, דְּקָמְהַנֵּי לֵיהּ הַשָּׂכָר שֶׁהָיָה לוֹ לִיתֵּן. אֲבָל מְלַמְּדוֹ הֲלָכוֹת בְּחִנָּם, דְּלָא קָא מְהַנֵּי לֵיהּ כְּלָל. מַאי פָּסְקָא. דִּבְמִנְהָגָא תַּלְיָא מִילְּתָא, וְלָאו אִיסּוּרָא אִיכָּא אֲפִי' לְמִשְׁקַל שָׂכָר שֶׁל הַמִּקְרָא. תְּרֵיץ, לָא וַדַּאי לָאו שַׁפִּיר עָבֵד דְּשָׁקֵל כְּלָל. וְהָא

ר"ן

איבעיא להו התורם משלו על של חבירו צריך דעתו או לא מי אמרינן כיון דזכות הוא לו לא צריך דעת. דזכין לאדם שלא בפניו, ומסתמא הוי ליה כשלוחיה. **אילימא** לדעתיה דיליה. דהאי תורם, מאן שוייה שליח? דהא דרשי':* מה אתם לדעתכם – אף שלוחכם לדעתכם. **אלא** לדעתו דבעל הכרי **הא** מהני ליה דעביד שליחותיה. וכל שעושה שליחותו – הרי מהנהו. **אלא** **אדעתא** דנפשיה. דתורם. ולא חשבינן ליה מהנה, כיון דמדעתיה עביד ולא יהיב ליה מידי למודר. ואתיא מתני' כחנן, דלרבנן אי אפשר דלא גרע מפורע חובו, דאסור לרבנן, הרשב"א ז"ל. ולי נראה: אפי' לרבנן שרי. דכיון דאסיק לקמן דתורם משלו על של חבירו טובת הנאה של תורם – איכא למימר דתורם לתת לאותו כהן שהוא רוצה מתכוין, ואדעתא דנפשיה קא עביד, ובעל הכרי בגרמא דמדיר בעלמא מתהני. **אלא לאו אין צריך** דעת. ומאי דכתוב במקצת נסחי: ואי אמרת צריך דעת הא קמהני ליה – לישנא יתירא הוא, דכבר אמרינן: אילימא לדעתו של בעל הכרי הא קמהני ליה. כדאמר רבא **באומר** כל הרוצה וכו' בבעיא דר' ירמיה בסמוך אמר הכי. **הכא** נמי **באומר** כל הרוצה לתרום יבא ויתרום. וכי האי גוונא מהני לגבי תרומה, דבגלוי דעת בלחוד ניחא ליה סגי. ולגבי מודר הנאה לא חשיב מהנה, כיון דלא משוי ליה אידך שליח בהדיא. ומיהו, דוקא באומר "כל הרוצה לתרום יבא ויתרום", אבל אי אמר "כל השומע קולי יתרום" – שליחות מעליא הוי, ואסור במודר הנאה. דהא אמרינן בפ' "המדיר" (כתובות דף ע:): "כל השומע קולי יזון" – שליחותיה קעביד, ומפקינן לה מדתנן בפ' "התקבל" (גיטין דף סו.) דגבי גט מהני אם אמר "כל השומע קולי יכתוב גט לאשתי". הלכך, דוקא באומר "כל הרוצה לתרום יבא ויתרום", דלאו שליחות גמור הוא. ומיהו, כי אמרינן דלתרומה מיהא מהני – דוקא דאמריה בהאי לישנא, דהא לישנא מליעתא הוה, ומש"ה נהי דלגבי מודר לא הוי שליחות – לתרומה מיהת מהני. אבל אי אמר "כל התורם אינו מפסיד" – אפשר דאפילו לגבי תרומה לא מהני, דלאו לישנא מעליא הוא כשיבא ויתרום. והכי נמי מוכח, דהא האומר "כל הזן אינו מפסיד" – והלך אחד וזן – אינו חייב לשלם, דלא שוייה שליח כלל. התורם משלו על של חבירו טובת הנאה של מי. כלומר, מי זכאי בנתינת תרומה זו, תורם או בעל הכרי, שתהא טובת הנאה שלו? טובת הנאה – שיתן לו ישראל דבר מועט שיתן אותה תרומה לבן בתו כהן. דאילו כהן אסור ליה למיתב מידי לישראל כדי שיתן לו תרומתו, דאפילו כהן המסייע בבית הגרנות (בכורות כו:) קרינן ביה "שחתם ברית הלוי". אי לאו פירי דהדין. של תורם. **תבואת** זרעך ונתת. תלה הנתינה בבעל הזרע, דהיינו בעל הכרי. **ואי** אמרת טובת הנאה לבעל הכרי הא קא מהני ליה. שמזכהו תורם לבעל הכרי ליתן אותה תרומה למי שירצה, ושקיל מיניה טובת הנאה, ונמצא מהנהו ממש. המקדיש מוסיף חומש. המקדיש בהמה לקרבנו של חבירו, והוממה ורוצה לפדותה – מקדיש קרוי בעלים לענין שצריך להוסיף חומש. שהבעלים בלבד מוסיפין חומש כשפודין את קדשיהם. המתכפר עושה תמורה. כלומר, אבל לענין תמורה הזוכה בה לצורך קרבנו קרוי בעלים, ומתפיס תמורה בה, אבל מקדיש לא. ובתמורה יליף לה מקראי [ע"ש בתמורה יוד. וצ"ע]. טובת הנאה שלו. של תורם. ולפי זה קרא דכתיב "עשר תעשר את כל תבואת זרעך ונתת" – א"עשר תעשר" קאי, וה"ק: עשר תעשר ונתת, דמעשר זכאי בנתינה. והכי מפרש לה במס' תמורה. מקרא מאי טעמא לא ילמדנו משום דקא מהני ליה. מדרש נמי קא מהני ליה. כשאינו נוטל ממנו שכר. מהאי טעמא גופיה.

הגהות הב"ח

(א) גמ' אילימא משל בעל הכרי על בעל הכרי ולדעתו כצ"ל ותיבת מן ותיבת של נמחק: (ב) שם אלא משלו על של בעל הכרי: (ג) שם אלא לאו לדעתיה דנפשיה ואי אמרת התורם משלו על של חבירו צריך דעת כצ"ל: (ד) רש"י ד"ה לעולם וד"ה באומר הכ"א: (ה) ד"ה או דלמא אי לאו וכו':

תוספות

ותורם תרומתו לדעתו בגמ' מפרש לדעת מאן: **מי** אמרינן כיון דזכות הוא לא צריך דעת. דזכין לאדם שלא בפניו וזכיה מטעם שליחות שפיר הוי שליחות והא דאמרינן בכל דוכתא דזכייה מטעם שליחות מהכא תניא ליה: **מאן** שוייה שליח. ואמאי תורם: **אלא** לדעתו דבעל הכרי הא קא מהני ליה דעביד שליחותיה. כיון דהוא ידע הוי כמו שמצוהו ואיכא איסורא ודאי אי לאו בדעתו לא הוה איסורא דמשום המצוה שרי אבל לדעתו דבעל [הכרי] מכי ידע ביה הוי כמו שמצוהו והוי שלוחו: **אלא** לאו אין צריך דעת. והא דאמרינן (בב"מ כב.) מה אתם לדעתכם אף שלוחכם לדעתכם י"ל דהיינו כשתורם משל בעל הכרי אבל בתורם משלו אז אין צריך דעת וא"ת מיהו קשה לרב דהסיא דשוקל שקלו אמאי צריך לאוקמא בהפריש ואבד אפי' בלא הפריש ואבד נמי דמצוה קעביד כי הכא צ"ע מיהו ק"ק מאי שנא גבי תורם דמצריך דעת לתרום אסור דשליחותיה קא עביד וגבי מחזיר אבידתו או ללמדו תורה אפי' [illegible] תלוי בשליחות דאין יכול [illegible] איכא פורתא למבין: **כל** [illegible] הכרי. תימה דהכא משמע [illegible] המדיר אשתו מליהנות לה [illegible] הזן אינו מפסיד ופריך וכי [illegible] קולו יכתוב גט לאשתו ומשמע [illegible] שליחותיה קעביד ויש לומר כ[illegible] יתרום ור"י אמר דודאי הכא [illegible] ומותר לה פרנסה דמצוה [illegible] ליכא דאי משום דתורם [illegible] דאמרינן לעולם משל בעל [illegible] אחר דינר כדי שיתן לבן [illegible] שיתן לו ישראל. הכא במאי [illegible]

[נ"ל תבואתך וכן איתא בפי' הרא"ש דהכא ודע דלדברי הר"ן בד"ה טובת הנאה עשר תעשר וכו' צ"ע טובה דבענין עשר תעשר לא כתיב ונתת כי אם באופן וכי ירבה ממך הדרך ונתתה בכסף וגו' ע"ש]

יומא נ: זבחים ו. תמורה [ב:] י:

פי' הרא"ש

כיון דזכות הוא לו. שהוא פוטר כריו בתבואתו לא צריך דעת דאין ספק דניחא ליה והוי כאילו עשאו שליח: **או דלמא מצוה דיליה הוא וניחא למעבדה.** ויותר הוא חפץ בחסרון ממונו ממה שיעשה אחר מצותו הלכך חוב הוא ולא הוי שלוחו: **מאן שוייה שליח.** הא אמרינן כה אתם לדעתכם אף שלוחכם לדעתכם: **אלא לאו אין צריך דעת.** דאע"ג דזכות הוא לו הוי כאילו שוייה שליח מ"מ כיון שבלא דעתו היה יכול לעשות לא מיקרי הנאה: **כל הרוצה לתרום יבא ויתרום.** דדעת איכא שליחות ליכא: **טובת הנאה של** [illegible] **ונתת.** מי שהתבואה שלו [illegible]רס משלו על של חבירו: [illegible]ומש דכתיב ואם המקדיש [illegible]בן להתכפר בו שממנו אם [illegible] מעשר תבואתך ונתת מי [illegible] ספרא וספרי שהוא כדרש [illegible]פסוקים: **לא ילמדנו מקרא.** [illegible]אב ללמד את בנו שמא היה [illegible] אמר דלא מיקרי הנאה: במקום [illegible] שפיר עביד וראיה כבר [illegible] של מי. שיתן לו ישראל [illegible] ליה בתרומה זו שוה דינר [illegible] חומש דחומש תלאו הכתוב

וְהָא קָא מַשְׁמַע לָן. מַתְנִי', דַּאֲפִי' בְּמָקוֹם שֶׁנּוֹטְלִין שָׂכָר וכו'. וּלְהָכִי לֹא יְלַמְּדֶנּוּ מִקְרָא, דְּהוֹאִיל וְשָׁרֵי לְמִשְׁקַל שָׂכָר, אִם מְלַמְּדוֹ בְּחִנָּם – מְהַנֵּי לֵיהּ מִן הַשָּׂכָר שֶׁהָיָה לוֹ לִיתֵּן. רַב אָמַר. מַאי טַעְמָא הִתִּירוּ לְמִשְׁקַל שָׂכָר מִן הַמִּקְרָא – מִפְּנֵי שֶׁאֵין נוֹטְלִין שָׂכָר אֶלָּא עַל שְׂכַר שִׁימּוּר שֶׁמְּשַׁמְּרִין הַתִּינוֹקוֹת, שֶׁאֵין מַנִּיחִין אוֹתָן לָצֵאת וְלַעֲסוֹק בִּדְבָרִים בְּטֵלִים, וְלֹא שְׂכַר לִימּוּד הַמִּקְרָא. וּקְטַנִּים דִּצְרִיכִין שִׁימּוּר לָמֵדִין מִקְרָא, וְלֹא גְּדוֹלִים. וּלְהָכִי לֹא יְלַמְּדֶנּוּ מִקְרָא לִקְטַנִּים בְּחִנָּם, דְּהוֹאִיל וְשָׁרֵי לְמִשְׁקַל עֲלַיְיהוּ שָׂכָר – קָמְהַנֵּי (ג) הַשָּׂכָר שֶׁהָיָה לוֹ לִיתֵּן. אֲבָל מְלַמְּדוֹ מִדְרָשׁ, דִּקְטַנִּים אֵין לוֹמְדִים מִדְרָשׁ, אֶלָּא לִגְדוֹלִים, וּגְדוֹלִים לֵית לְהוּ שְׂכַר שִׁימּוּר, וְלָא קָמְהַנֵּי לְהוּ כְּלָל, וּלְהָכִי שָׁרֵי. וְרַבִּי יוֹחָנָן אוֹמֵר שְׂכַר פִּיסּוּק טְעָמִים. שָׁקֵיל מִנַּיְיהוּ, שֶׁמְּלַמְּדָם נִיקּוּד וּטְעָמִים, וְהַהוּא שָׂכָר מָצֵי לְמִשְׁקַל. וּפִיסּוּק טְעָמִים אֵינוֹ אֶלָּא בְּמִקְרָא, וּלְהָכִי לֹא יְלַמְּדֶנּוּ מִקְרָא: (ד) בְּקָטָן. (מִשּׁוּם דְּקָא מְהַנֵּי לֵיהּ, שֶׁמַּנִּיחַ לוֹ אֶת הַשָּׂכָר) (ה), תָּרֵיץ מַתְנִי' דְּקָתָנֵי: לֹא יְלַמְּדֶנּוּ מִקְרָא – בְּקָטָן, מִשּׁוּם דְּקָא מְהַנֵּי לֵיהּ, שֶׁמַּנִּיחַ לוֹ אֶת הַשָּׂכָר שֶׁהָיָה לוֹ לִיתֵּן. וְהָכִי קָתָנֵי לֹא יְלַמְּדֶנּוּ מִקְרָא לְקָטָן. בְּחִנָּם, מִשּׁוּם דְּקָא מְהַנֵּי לֵיהּ שְׂכַר הַשִּׁימּוּר. אֲבָל אִם הָיָה גָּדוֹל – מְלַמְּדוֹ לוֹ וּלְבָנָיו מִקְרָא. גָּדוֹל – מִשּׁוּם דְּאִיהוּ לָא צָרִיךְ שִׁימּוּר, וְלָא קָמְהַנֵּי לֵיהּ. וּלְבָנָיו נַמִי, הוֹאִיל וַאֲבִיהֶן עִמָּהֶם – הוּא מְשַׁמְּרָם, וְלֵיכָּא שְׂכַר שִׁימּוּר. לֹא קוֹרִין בַּתְּחִילָּה בְּשַׁבָּת. אֵין מַתְחִילִין לְלַמְּדָם בַּתְּחִילָּה בְּשַׁבָּת בְּדָבָר שֶׁלֹּא לָמְדוּ מֵעוֹלָם. אֲבָל שׁוֹנִין בָּרִאשׁוֹן, כְּלוֹמַר, בְּדָבָר שֶׁלְּמָדוּהוּ כְּבָר פַּעַם רִאשׁוֹנָה לוֹמְדִים אוֹתָן פַּעַם שְׁנִיָּה בְּשַׁבָּת. וּלְהָכִי קָתָנֵי "בָּרִאשׁוֹן", דִּרְבוּתָא קמ"ל: אע"פ שֶׁלֹּא לְמָדוּהוּ הַתִּינוֹקוֹת אֶלָּא פַּעַם אַחַת – שׁוֹנִין. בִּשְׁלָמָא לְמַאן דְּאָמַר שְׂכַר פִּיסּוּק טְעָמִים. שָׁרֵי לְמִשְׁקַל. הַיְינוּ דְּאֵין קוֹרִין בַּתְּחִילָּה בְּשַׁבָּת. דְּהוֹאִיל וּמֵעוֹלָם לֹא לָמְדוּ דָּבָר זֶה אֶלָּא עַכְשָׁיו – אֵינוֹ מְלַמְּדוֹ אֶלָּא בְּשָׂכָר, וְאָתֵי לְמִשְׁקַל שָׂכָר בְּשַׁבָּת. אֲבָל שׁוֹנִין, דְּעָבֵיד לֵיהּ בְּלֹא שָׂכָר. אַמַּאי שׁוֹנִין בָּרִאשׁוֹן. אֲפִילּוּ שׁוֹנִין לֹא, דְּהָא אִיכָּא שְׂכַר שִׁימּוּר דְּשַׁבָּת, וְאָתֵי לְמִשְׁקַל שָׂכָר בְּשַׁבָּת! הַבְלָעָה הִיא. (ו) כִּדְקָתָנֵי וּמִישְׁרֵי שָׁרֵי. דְּתַנְיָא הַשּׂוֹכֵר אֶת הַפּוֹעֵל. שֶׁנּוֹתֵן לוֹ שְׂכָרוֹ שֶׁל כָּל יוֹם. לִשְׁמוֹר אֶת הַתִּינוֹק. מְטוּמְאָה. לִשְׁמוֹר אֶת הַזְּרָעִים. לְצוֹרֶךְ הָעוֹמֶר.
אִם

תורה אור

הָא קמ"ל דַּאֲפִילּוּ בְּמָקוֹם שֶׁנּוֹטְלִין שָׂכָר, אעַל הַמִּקְרָא – שָׁרֵי לְמִשְׁקַל, עַל הַמִּדְרָשׁ – לָא שָׁרֵי לְמִשְׁקַל. מַאי שְׁנָא מִדְרָשׁ דְּלָא – דִּכְתִיב °"וְאוֹתִי צִוָּה ה' בָּעֵת הַהִיא לְלַמֵּד אֶתְכֶם" (דברים ד) וּכְתִיב °"רְאֵה לִמַּדְתִּי אֶתְכֶם חֻקִּים וּמִשְׁפָּטִים כַּאֲשֶׁר צִוַּנִי ה'" (שם) (א) *מָה אֲנִי בְּחִנָּם – אַף אַתֶּם נַמִי בְּחִנָּם. מִקְרָא נַמִי בְּחִנָּם! רַב אָמַר: שְׂכַר שִׁימּוּר, וְרַבִּי יוֹחָנָן אָמַר: שְׂכַר פִּיסּוּק טְעָמִים. תְּנַן: לֹא יְלַמְּדֶנּוּ מִקְרָא. בִּשְׁלָמָא לְמַאן דְּאָמַר שְׂכַר פִּיסּוּק טְעָמִים – הַיְינוּ דְּלֹא יְלַמְּדֶנּוּ, אֶלָּא לְמַאן דְּאָמַר שְׂכַר שִׁימּוּר – גָּדוֹל בַּר שִׁימּוּר הוּא? בְּקָטָן קָתָנֵי. אִי בְּקָטָן – אֵימָא סֵיפָא: אֲבָל מְלַמֵּד אֶת בָּנָיו מִקְרָא, קָטָן בַּר בָּנִים הוּא?! חַסּוּרֵי מִחַסְּרָא וְהָכִי קָתָנֵי: לֹא יְלַמְּדֶנּוּ מִקְרָא – בְּקָטָן. אִם הָיָה גָּדוֹל – מְלַמְּדוֹ לוֹ וְלִבְנָיו מִקְרָא. מֵיתִיבֵי: בתִּינוֹקוֹת לֹא קוֹרִין בַּתְּחִילָּה בְּשַׁבָּת, (ב) אֶלָּא שׁוֹנִין בְּרִאשׁוֹן. בִּשְׁלָמָא לְמַאן דְּאָמַר שְׂכַר פִּיסּוּק טְעָמִים הַיְינוּ דְּאֵין קוֹרִין בַּתְּחִילָּה בְּשַׁבָּת. אֶלָּא לְמַאן דְּאָמַר שְׂכַר שִׁימּוּר – אַמַּאי אֵין קוֹרִין בַּתְּחִילָּה בְּשַׁבָּת וְאַמַּאי שׁוֹנִין בְּרִאשׁוֹן? הָא אִיכָּא שְׂכַר שִׁימּוּר דְּשַׁבָּת! וְלִיטַעֲמִיךְ, שְׂכַר פִּיסּוּק בְּשַׁבָּת מִי אָסוּר? הַבְלָעָה הִיא, וְהַבְלָעָה מִישְׁרָא שָׁרֵי. *גדְּתַנְיָא: הַשּׂוֹכֵר אֶת הַפּוֹעֵל לִשְׁמוֹר אֶת הַתִּינוֹק, לִשְׁמוֹר אֶת הַפָּרָה, לִשְׁמוֹר אֶת הַזְּרָעִים – אֵין נוֹתְנִין לוֹ שְׂכַר שַׁבָּת. לְפִיכָךְ
אִם

אמר שמואל במקום שנוטלין שכר על המקרא ואין נוטלין שכר על המדרש על המדרש לא שרי ליה למשקל. נראה בעיני דה"פ: מדינא מותר ליטול שכר על המקרא ולא על המדרש, כדמפרש ואזיל. מיהו, יש מקומות שמחמירין על עצמם שלא ליטול שכר אפי' על המקרא, כדי שלא יבא ליטול מן המדרש. ובאותן מקומות – אפילו מקרא יכול ללמדו, שהרי מכיון שהחמירו על עצמן למצוה – אינן רשאין ליטול שכר, והוה ליה מקרא כמדרש לכל המקומות. אלא דמתני' מתוקמא במקום שנוטלין שכר על המקרא, כלומר שלא החמירו על עצמן, ואפילו באותו מקום – על המקרא דוקא הוא דשרי למשקל. ומש"ה לא ילמדנו, דכיון שנוטלין עליה שכר, אם מלמדו בחנם – נמצא מהנהו. אבל על המדרש לא שרי למשקל, דמדינא אסור, כדמפרש ואזיל. הלכך, כי מלמדו מדרש בחנם – לא מהני ליה ולא מידי, דאגרא לא מחייב ביה, ולימוד גופיה נמי לאו הנאה הוא, דמצות לאו ליהנות נתנו. ולענין הלכה. קיימא לן הכי, דעל המדרש לא שרי למשקל. מיהו, ה"מ שכר לימוד, אבל אגר בטלה שרי. והכי איתא בירושלמי, דגרסינן התם: יכול אף על מקרא ותרגום כן – ת"ל "חוקים ומשפטים" חוקים ומשפטים אתם מלמדים בחנם, ואי אתם מלמדים בחנם מקרא ותרגום. וכן חמי מתניא נסבין אגריהון! אמר ר' יודן בר' ישמעאל: שכר בטלן הם נוטלין. **מאי שנא מדרש דלא דכתיב ואותי צוה ה' בעת ההיא.** האי קרא מייתי לאשמעינן דמשה נצטווה ללמוד תורה לישראל. **וכתיב ראה למדתי אתכם חוקים ומשפטים כאשר צוני ה'.** כלומר, שצוני ללמוד בחנם. דאי לא, "כאשר צוני" אמאי קאי דליכא למימר בשכר, דהיכי לימא "כאשר צוני", וכי צוהו בכך? לא סגיא דלא לישקול אגרא? וליכא למימר נמי ד"כאשר צוני" הכי קאמר: כאשר צוני, ולא מעצמי אני אומר. דודאי ישראל לא היו מפקפקין בכך דהא כתיב בך יאמינו לעולם אלא ודאי ה"ק כאשר צוני ללמד בחנם. **מקרא** נמי בחנם. מהאי קרא גופיה. רב **אמר** שכר שימור. דמסתמא לומדי מקרא קטנים, וצריכין שימור. ומש"ה, נהי דאגר לימוד אסור – שכר שימור שרי. ורבי יוחנן **אמר** שכר פיסוק טעמים. שמלמדין להם טעמים, דלאו מדאורייתא נינהו, הלכך לא הוו בכלל חוקים ומשפטים. ואיכא בין רב לרבי יוחנן ללמד מקרא לגדול, דלא בעי שימור, דלרב אסור, דס"ל דפיסוק טעמים דאורייתא, ולרבי יוחנן שרי משום שכר פיסוק טעמים. הלכך, לענין הלכה, כיון דקיי"ל דרב ור' יוחנן הלכה כר' יוחנן – נקטינן דאפי' מגדול שרי ליטול שכר על המקרא, וכך הם דברי הרמב"ם ז"ל בפ"ו מהלכות נדרים. תנן **לא** ילמדנו מקרא וכו' **אלא** למאן **דאמר** שכר שימור [גדול בר שימור] הוא. והא איהו נטר נפשיה. בקטן. דהוי האי מודר קטן. דאף על גב דקטן אוכל נבילות אין ב"ד מצווין להפרישו – אפילו הכי לא ספינן ליה בידים, וכשמלמדו – הרי הוא מהנהו. **ואם** היה גדול מלמד לו ולבניו מקרא. לו – דלא בעי שימור, לבניו נמי, אע"ג דבעו שימור – לא מתסר טפי מזן את בניו ואת בנותיו. מיתיבי תינוקות **לא** קורין בתחילה בשבת. מה שלא קראו מימיהם. אלא שונין בראשון – אם קראו פעם ראשונה לפני השבת – שונין אותו בשבת, אע"פ שהיא חזרה ראשונה. **בשלמא** למ"ד שכר **פיסוק** טעמים היינו **דאין** קורין בתחילה בשבת. לפי שעיקר השכר אינו אלא על קריאה ראשונה שטרחה מרובה, ומש"ה אין קורין בתחילה בשבת, דשכר שבת אסור. אבל שונין בראשון – משום דאחזרה לא שקלי אגרא. **אלא** למאן **דאמר** שכר שימור **אמאי** אין קורין וכו'. כלומר, מאי איכא בין פעם ראשונה לשניה? הרי השכר אינו אלא על השימור, וכי היכי דאיכא שימור בתחילה – הכי נמי איכא שימור כששונין. **הבלעה היא.** שמבליע שכר יום השבת בכלל שכר שאר הימים. לשמור **את** התינוק. שהיו מגדלין תינוקות בחצרות הבנויות על גבי הסלע מפני קבר התהום, כדי שימלאו מים מן המעיין לקדש אפר הפרה. לשמור הפרה. פרה אדומה. **את** הזרעים. לצורך עומר היו משמרין אותם קודם הבאת העומר. הכי מפרש לה רש"י ז"ל בפרק "הזהב" (ב"מ דף נח.). **לפיכך אם אבדו אינו חייב באחריותן.**
אם

תוספות

הא קמ"ל דאפילו במקום שנוטלין שכר על המקרא וכו'. מפרש ואזיל טעמא דמה אני בחנם דכתיב ראה למדתי אתכם ומסתמא משה לא נטל שכר מישראל שעשיר היה: **שכר** שימור. שמשמר מלמד תינוקות שלא ילכו אנה ואנה אבל מדרש אינו צריך ללמוד כ"א לגדול שאינו צריך שימור כבן עשר למשנה: **שכר** פיסוק טעמים. וסבר דפיסוק אינו צריך אלא מדרבנן ולא שייך לומר מה אני בחנם אף אתם בחנם: **גדול** בר שימור הוא. משמע ליה דמתניתין איירי אף בגדולים: **חסורי** מיחסרא והכי קתני. וה"פ לא ילמדנו מקרא ברגיל ללמוד מקרא דהיינו קטן אבל מלמד הוא בניו מקרא אם ראוי לבנים: **אין** קורין בתחלה בשבת. מפני עונג שבת: **אבל** שונין בראשון. פירוש יכולין לחזור חזרה ראשונה בשבת: **היינו** דאין קורין בתחילה. מפני שמשתכר בשבת ומחזי כמקח וממכר אבל שונין בראשון דכיון דלימדו זו מערב שבת יודעין אותו מערב שבת: **ואי** משום שכר שימור אמאי שונין בראשון. הא איכא שכר שימור: **הבלעה** היא. ששכר שבת נבלע ולא מיחזי כמקח וממכר שפוסק לו כך לחצי שנה: **לשמור** את התינוק. לצורך מי חטאת: **לשמור** הזרעים. לצורך עומר ושתי הלחם בשביעית אם שוכר ליומי אין נותנין לו שכר דמיחזי כמקח וממכר אם היה נוטל:
שכר

פי' הרא"ש

במקום שנוטלין שכר על המקרא. ואם היה מלמדו בחנם הרי הוא מוחל לו על השכר ומהנהו: **מאי פסקא.** שלעולם נוטלין שכר על המקרא ולא על המדרש ולא קתני איפכא: **מה אני בחנם.** צוה אותי ללמד אתכם בחנם כמו שהוא למדני בחנם: **שכר שימור.** נוטלין על נערים קטנים הלומדים מקרא לשמרם שלא ילכו ברחובות ובשוקין ויזיקו ויתנכו לדברים רעים: **שכר פיסוק טעמים.** לנגן המקראות כהלכתן ולאו דאורייתא הוא ושרי ליטול שכר עליו: **לא ילמדנו מקרא.** בקטן אם הדיר קטן הנאה ממנו: **אם היה גדול מלמד לו ולבניו מקרא.** לו משום דגדול הוא ולא בעי שימור ואין נוטלין עליה שכר ולבניו משום דמצוה קעביד (ולא) [גי' רש"א אפי'] בעי שימור ולא מהני ולא מידי: **היינו דאין קורין בתחילה.** משום דאסור ליטול שכר בשבת אבל שונין שכבר ידעו בפעם ראשונה פיסוק הטעמים ועל שאר הלימוד אינו נוטל שכר אלא למאן דאמר שכר שימור אמאי אין קורין בתחילה ואמאי שונין דמה לי פעם ראשונה ומה לי פעם שניה לעולם שימור איכא: **לשמור את התינוק.** חצרות היו בירושלים ומגדלין בהם תינוקות למלאות מים להזות על הכהן השורף את הפרה: **לשמור את הפרה.** פרה אדומה לשמרה שלא יעלה עליה עול: **לשמור את הזרעים.** שדה המבוכרת שומרין אותה לצורך העומר ושתי הלחם:

*)**דיפנון אכוסון דינוקא למלותא.** אם היו קורין בתחילה היה חמור להם והיו צריכים להאריך והאבות מצפין לסעוד עד שיבואו ומבטלין עונג שבת אבל מה שקראו מאתמול שונין בו היום כי אינן צריכין להאריך בו: **ויקיר לסון עלמא.** ואינם יכולים לסבול הטורח ללמוד דבר חמור: **שנוי וסת.** המשנה וסתו ומנהגו שהוא נהוג בו לסעוד בכל יום: **בנות מי בעיין שימור.** שאין דרכן לטייל ברחובות ומאי איצטריך לאשמועינן שמותר ללמוד בנותיו והא אין נוטלים עליהם שכר ואפילו לעצמן יכול ללמד בדבר שאין נוטלין עליו שכר ומתני' סתמא קתני ומלמד את בניו דמשמע אף בנות בכלל: **לדאורייתא הוא.** ואין נוטלין שכר:
מפורש

*) [שייך לע"ב]

עין משפט נר מצוה

ל א מיי' פ"ו מהל' ת"ת הל' ז ופ"ו מהלכות נדרים הלכ' ז סמג עשין יב וסמג לאוין רמב טוש"ע י"ד סי' רמו סעיף ב וסי' רמה סעיף ו:
לא ב מיי' פ"ב מהל' ת"ת הל' ב טוש"ע י"ד סי' רמה סעיף יד:
לב ג מיי' פ"ו מהל' שבת הלכ' יב סמג לאוין סה טוש"ע או"ח סימן שו סעיף ז:

מסורת הש"ס

בכורות כט.
ב"מ נח. [תוספתא דשבת פי"ח תוספתא ב"מ פ"ח]

הגהות הב"ח

(א) גמ' כאשר צוני ה' אלהי מה אני: (ב) שם בתחילה בשבת אבל שונין בראשון: (ג) רש"י ד"ה רב אמר וכו' קמהני ליה השכר: (ד) ד"ה ר' יוחנן וכו' ה"ה בקטן משום דקא מהני הד"א השכר הס"ד ותיבת בקטן נמחק: (ה) ד"ה תריך וכו' בקטן קתני משום: (ו) ד"ה הבלעה היא ומישרי שרי כצ"ל ותיבת כדקתני נמחק:

אם אָבְדוּ — אֵינוֹ חַיָּיב בְּאַחֲרָיוּתָן. וְאִם הָיָה שְׂכִיר שַׁבָּת, שְׂכִיר חֹדֶשׁ, שְׂכִיר שָׁנָה, שְׂכִיר שָׁבוּעַ — נוֹתֵן לוֹ שְׂכַר שַׁבָּת. לְפִיכָךְ, אִם אָבְדוּ — חַיָּיב בְּאַחֲרָיוּתָן. אֶלָּא גַּבֵּי שַׁבָּת הַיְינוּ טַעְמָא דְּאֵין קוֹרִאין בַּתְּחִילָּה — מִשּׁוּם דְּיִפְנוּ אֲבָהַתְהוֹן דְּיָנוּקֵי לְמִצְוָתָא דְּשַׁבְּתָא. וְאִיבָּעֵית אֵימָא: מִשּׁוּם דְּבְשַׁבְּתָא אָכְלִין וְשָׁתִין, וְיַקִּיר עֲלֵיהוֹן עָלְמָא. כִּדְאָמַר *שְׁמוּאֵל: שִׁינּוּי וֶסֶת תְּחִילַּת חוֹלִי מֵעַיִם. וּלְמַאן דְּאָמַר שְׂכַר פִּיסּוּק טְעָמִים, מ"ט לָא אֲמַר שְׂכַר שִׁימּוּר? קָסָבַר: בָּנוֹת מִי קָא בָּעֲיָין שִׁימּוּר? ולמ"ד שְׂכַר שִׁימּוּר, מ"ט לָא אֲמַר שְׂכַר פִּיסּוּק טְעָמִים? קָסָבַר: (שְׂכַר) פִּיסּוּק טְעָמִים דְּאוֹרַיְיתָא הוּא. *דא"ר אִיקָא בַּר אָבִין אָמַר רַב חֲנַנְאֵל אָמַר רַב: מ"ד °"וַיִּקְרְאוּ בַסֵּפֶר תּוֹרַת הָאֱלֹהִים מְפֹרָשׁ וְשׂוֹם שֶׂכֶל וַיָּבִינוּ בַּמִּקְרָא". "וַיִּקְרְאוּ בַסֵּפֶר תּוֹרַת הָאֱלֹהִים" — זֶה מִקְרָא, "מְפֹרָשׁ" זֶה תַּרְגּוּם, "וְשׂוֹם שֶׂכֶל" — אֵלּוּ הַפְּסוּקִים, "וַיָּבִינוּ בַּמִּקְרָא" זֶה פִּיסּוּק טְעָמִים, וְאָמְרִי לָהּ: אֵלּוּ הַמְּסוֹרוֹת. אָמַר רַבִּי יִצְחָק: מִקְרָא סוֹפְרִים, וְעִיטּוּר סוֹפְרִים, וְקַרְיָין וְלָא כְּתִיבָן, וּכְתִיבָן וְלָא קַרְיָין — הֲלָכָה לְמֹשֶׁה מִסִּינַי. מִקְרָא סוֹפְרִים (א) "אֶרֶץ" "שָׁמַיִם" "מִצְרָיִם". *עִיטּוּר סוֹפְרִים — °"אַחַר תַּעֲבֹרוּ" °"אַחַר תֵּלֵךְ" °"אַחַר תֵּאָסֵף" °"קִדְּמוּ שָׁרִים אַחַר נֹגְנִים" °"צִדְקָתְךָ כְּהַרְרֵי אֵל". *"קַרְיָין וְלָא כְּתִיבָן[א] °"פְּרָת" דִּ"בְלֶכְתּוֹ, °"אִישׁ" דִּ"כַאֲשֶׁר יִשְׁאַל אִישׁ בִּדְבַר הָאֱלֹהִים", °"בָּאִים" (ב) דִּ"נִבְנְתָה", °"לָהּ" דִּ"פְלֵיטָה",[ב] °"אֵת" דְּ"הֻגֵּד הֻגַּד", °"אֵלַי" דְּ"הַגֹּרֶן", °"אֵלַי" דְּ"הַשְּׂעֹרִים" — הָלֵין קַרְיָין וְלָא כְּתִבָן. וּכְתַבָן וְלָא קַרְיָין — °"נָא" דְּ"יִסְלַח".

זאת

(נחמיה ח; בראשית יח; בראשית כד; תהלים סח; תהלים לו; שמואל ב ח; שם טז; ירמיהו לח; רות ג; מלכים ב ה)

רש"י

אם אָבְדוּ. בַּשַּׁבָּת. אֵינוֹ חַיָּיב בְּאַחֲרָיוּתָן. הוֹאִיל וְאֵינוֹ שָׂכִיר בְּיוֹם שַׁבָּת. אם הָיָה שְׂכִיר שַׁבָּת. שֶׁנּוֹתְנִים לוֹ ז' פְּשִׁיטִים שְׂכָרוֹ לְשָׁבוּעַ, אע"פ שֶׁמַּגִּיעַ לְיוֹם שַׁבָּת פָּשׁוּט אֶחָד, כֵּיוָן דְּכָל יוֹם שַׁבָּת נִבְלָע עִם שְׂכִירוּת שְׁאָר הַשָּׁבוּעַ — זוֹ הִיא הַבְלָעָה, שֶׁשְּׂכַר שַׁבָּת מַבְלִיעַ בְּתוֹךְ יְמֵי הַשָּׁבוּעַ, נוֹתְנִין (ג) שְׂכַר שַׁבָּת — דְּהַבְלָעָה שָׁרֵי. אם אָבְדוּ. בְּשַׁבָּת, חַיָּיב בְּאַחֲרָיוּתָן, דְּהָא נוֹתְנִין לוֹ שְׂכַר הַשַּׁבָּת. אֶלָּא גַּבֵּי שַׁבָּת. (ד) דְּקָתָנֵי: לֹא קוֹרִין בַּתְּחִילָּה אֲבָל שׁוֹנִין, לָאו מִשּׁוּם שְׂכַר פִּיסּוּק וְלֹא מִשּׁוּם שְׂכַר שִׁימּוּר קָאָמַר, דְּהָא שָׁרֵי בְּהַבְלָעָה. דְּיִפְנוּ אֲבָהַתְהוֹן דְּיָנוּקָא לְמִצְוָותָא דִּלְהוֹן. שֶׁאִם הָיוּ עֲסוּקִין לְהַקְרוֹתָן בַּתְּחִילָּה בְּדָבָר חָדָשׁ — הָיוּ טְרוּדִין בָּהֶן, וְלֹא הָיוּ פְּנוּיִין לְמִצְוַת שַׁבָּת, לְהִתְעַנֵּג בּוֹ. אֲבָל שׁוֹנִין, הוֹאִיל וּכְבָר לְמָדוּהוּ — לָא מִטְרְדֵי בְּהוּ. דְּיִפְנוּ. כְּדֵי שֶׁיְּהוּ פְּנוּיִין. וְיַקִּיר לְהוּ עָלְמָא. שֶׁכָּבֵד עֲלֵיהֶם לִלְמוֹד מִפְּנֵי הַמַּאֲכָל, וּלְהָכִי אֵין קוֹרִין בַּתְּחִילָּה בְּשַׁבָּת, דְּמִצְטַעֵר לְהוּ. בָּנוֹת. שֶׁמְּלַמְּדִין אוֹתָן תּוֹרָה, מִי בָּעֲיָא שִׁימּוּר? אִינְהוּ לָאו אוֹרְחַיְיהוּ לְמֵיפַק אַבָּרָאֵי, דִּכְתִיב "כָּל כְּבוּדָּה בַת מֶלֶךְ פְּנִימָה" (תהלים מה), וְלֵיכָּא לְאוֹקְמָא בָּהּ שְׂכַר שִׁימּוּר. שְׂכַר פִּיסּוּק טְעָמִים דְּאוֹרַיְיתָא הוּא. וְלָא מָצֵי לְמִשְׁקַל עֲלַיְיהוּ אַגְרָא. אֵלּוּ הַפְּסוּקִים. עַד הֵיכָן מְסַיֵּים כָּל פָּסוּק וּפָסוּק. וּלְהָכִי קָרֵי לְהוּ "שׂוּם שֶׂכֶל" — שֶׁיָּכוֹל לְהַשְׂכִּיל בַּפָּסוּק, בֵּין כָּל פִּיסּוּק וּפִיסּוּק. מִקְרָא סוֹפְרִים (ה) אֶרֶץ אָרֶץ. כְּלוֹמַר, מַה שֶּׁקּוֹרִין אֶרֶץ אָרֶץ — דְּלָא כָּתְבִינַן הַהֲבָרָה, דְּלָא כָּתְבִינַן יו"ד בֵּין אָלֶ"ף לָרֵי"שׁ וּבֵין רֵי"שׁ לַצַּדִ"י, וְכֵן נַמִּי אָרֶץ — דְּלָא כָּתְבִינַן ב' אַלְפִי"ן אוֹ הֵ"א סָמוּךְ לָאָלֶ"ף, וְיוּ"ד בֵּין רֵי"שׁ לַצַּדִ"י. וְכֵן שָׁמַיִם — דְּלָא כָּתְבִינַן שָׁאמַיִם, אָלֶ"ף בֵּין שִׁי"ן לַמֵּ"ם וּבֵין מֵ"ם לַיּוּ"ד. וְכֵן מִצְרָיִם. הֲלָכָה לְמֹשֶׁה מִסִּינַי. דְּנִקְרָאִין הָכִי. עִיטּוּר סוֹפְרִים אַחַר תַּעֲבוֹרוּ. וְלָא כְּתִיב: תַּעֲבוֹרוּ אַחַר. וְהַיְינוּ עִיטּוּר, שֶׁמְּעַטְּרִין הַדִּיבּוּר, דְּהָכִי מַשְׁמַע יָפֶה. קִדְּמוּ שָׂרִים אַחַר נוֹגְנִים. וְלָא כְּתִיב: אַחַר נוֹגְנִים קִדְּמוּ שָׂרִים. צִדְקָתְךָ כְּהַרְרֵי אֵל. וְלָא כְּתִיב: כְּהַרְרֵי אֵל צִדְקָתְךָ, דְּהָכִי מִסְתַּבַּר טְפֵי, וּדְוּוּקָא מַשְׁמַע. אִישׁ דְּכַאֲשֶׁר יִשְׁאַל אִישׁ בִּדְבַר הָאֱלֹהִים. בַּאֲחִיתוֹפֶל כְּתִיב. בָּאִים דְּוְנִבְנְתָה. [קְרִי וְלָא] כְּתִיב. לָהּ דִּפְלֵיטָה. שְׁנֵיהֶן כְּתוּבִין בְּיִרְמְיָהוּ. אֵת דְּהֻגֵּד הוּגַּד אֵלַי (ו). דְּכוּלְּהוּ הָנֵי קַרְיָין וְלָא כְּתִיבָן. וּכְתִיבָן וְלָא קַרְיָין נָא דְּיִסְלַח. דְּנַעֲמָן.

זאת

ר"ן

אם נאבדו בשבת. דכיון דלא שקיל אגרא בשבתא – הוה ליה שומר חנם. אם היה שכיר שבת. שבוע אחת. שכיר שבוע. שמטה אחת. נותן לו שכר שבת. כיון שלא הזכירו בפירוש, אלא שהבליעו בכלל שאר הימים. לפיכך. כיון דהוי שומר שכר, אם אבדו בשבת – חייב באחריותן. דיפנו אבוהון דינוקא למצותא דשבתא. שאבות התינוקות פונין למצות שבת, ומשתעשעין עם התינוקות. ואם יקראו התינוקות לכתחילה – יחושו לבטולם. ויקיר עליהון עלמא. על התינוקות, שמתוך שאכלו יותר ממה שדרכן לאכול בחול אבריהם כבדין עליהן, ואין יכולין ללמוד בתחילה, שצריך עיון מרובה. גדול מי בעי שימור. בתמיה. כך היא הגירסא במקצת נסחאות. ואתי שפיר, דה"ק: סתמא דמתני' דקתני: ולא ילמדנו מקרא – בגדול היא, מדקתני סיפא: אבל מלמד את בניו. דמאי דמשנינן לעיל חסורי מחסרא – שינויא דחיקא היא. אלא ודאי בגדול מתוקמא, וגדול מי בעי שימור?! ואיכא נסחי דגרסי: בנות מי בעי שימור. והכי פריך: ודאי כל היכא דתנא תנא המודר הנאה מחבירו – בין איש בין אשה משמע, והיכי פסיק ותנא: לא ילמדנו מקרא? נהי דמוקמת לה בקטן, תינח בנים קטנים דבעו שימור, אבל בנות – אפי' קטנות לא בעו שימור, שאין דרכן לצאת לחוץ! קסבר פיסוק טעמים דאורייתא הוא. ואסור ליטול על לימודם שכר, דכיון דמדאורייי' נינהו הוו להו כחוקים ומשפטים. מפורש זה תרגום. דמפרש ליה לקרא. ושום שכל אלו הפסוקים. נקודות המפסיקות בין פסוק לפסוק. וקרי להו "שום שכל" – שעל ידיהן אדם מבין המקרא כפי תנועת הטעמים, כדאמר פרק קמא דחגיגה (דף ו:): נפקא מינה לפסוקי טעמי. המסורות. מה שנמסר במסרה. אמר רבי יצחק מקרא סופרים. הקריאה שמסרו לנו הראשונים שנקראו סופרים. ועטור סופרים. תיבות יתירות שנכתבו ליפות הלשון, ונקראות עטור לפי שהן מעטרין את הלשון. קריין ולא כתיבן. תיבות הנקראות ולא נכתבו. כתיבן ולא קריין. שנכתבות ואינן נקראות. הלכה למשה מסיני. כך קבל משה בסיני, ומסר לישראל. מקרא סופרים ארץ ארץ. שכשיש בו אתנחתא נקרא אָרץ בקמץ. שמים מצרים. שאע"פ שאין בהם אל"ף נקראים כאילו היתה בהם. עטור סופרים אחר תעבורו אחר תלכו אחר תאסף קדמו שרים אחר נוגנים. כל הני "אחר" מיותרין הן, ואינן אלא לתפארת הלשון. דהוה ליה למכתב "סעדו לבכם ותעבורו", "תסגר שבעת ימים ותאסף", "קדמו שרים נוגנים", אלא שנכתבו לתפארת הלשון. צדקתך כהררי אל. הוה ליה למכתב "צדקתך הררי אל", כדכתיב: משפטיך תהום רבה. לומר שההרים הרמים, כלומר המלאכים, צריכין לצדקת השם. אלא שכתב "כהררי אל" לתפארת הלשון. ובדברי מורי ראיתי דעטור סופרים – היינו שכותבין טעם מפסיק ב"אחר", כי היכי דלישתמע: אח"כ תלך, ואח"כ תעבורו, ואחר כן תאסף. קדמו שרים – ואח"כ נוגנים, "לדקתך כהררי" נפסק בטעם "כהררי" ממלת "אל", לומר שמלת "אל" הפוכה, כאילו היתה בתחלת הפסוק, ופירוש: אל, לדקתך נגלית כהרים, שהם גלויים. ואלמלא ההפסק היה במשמע: אחר שתלכו, אחר שתעבורו, אחר שתאסף, קדמו שרים אחר הנוגנים – שהנוגגים קדמו להם, לדקתך כהרים של אל. וקרי ליה עטור סופרים – משום דמעטרי לה למילתא בטעם הקריאה. קריין ולא כתיבן פרת דבלכתו. בשמואל הוא "להשיב ידו בנהר פרת", "פרת" קרי ולא כתיב. איש דכאשר ישאל. בשמואל נמי הוא גבי אחיתופל "כאשר ישאל איש בדבר האלהים", "איש" קרי ולא כתיב. באים דונבנתה. בירמיה הוא "הנה ימים באים נאם ה' [ונבנתה] העיר" וגו', "באים" קרי ולא כתיב. לה דפליטה. בסוף ירמיה בנבואת בבל "יהי לה לפליטה", "לה" קרי ולא כתיב. את דהגד הוגד. ברות "ויען בועז ויאמר לה הגד הוגד (את) [לי כל] אשר עשית את חמותך", האי "את" קרי ולא כתיבן. מיהו, בספרים שלנו קרי וכתיב. ואף במסרה לא מדכר ליה בהנך דקריין ולא כתיבן. אלי דהגורן. ברות נמי הוא "ותאמר אליה את כל אשר תאמרי אלי אעשה", והפסוק שאחריו "ותרד הגורן ותעש ככל אשר צותה חמותה". וקרי ליה "אלי" "דהגורן" אע"ג דבההוא קרא ליכא "הגורן", כיון דסמוך ליה בפסוק דלאחריו. אלי דהשעורים. ברות נמי הוא "ותאמר שש השעורים האלה נתן לי כי אמר אלי" "אלי" קרי ולא כתיב. כתיבן ולא קריין נא דיסלח. במלכים, ב"השתחויתי בית רימון יסלח נא ה' לעבדך"" כתיב "נא" ולא מקרי.

זאת

תוספות

שכר שבוע נותנין לו שכר שבת ואם אבדו חייב באחריותן. כדין שומר שכר דמחייב בגניבה ואבידה ואין להקשות תפלי שמים הוא דקבלת שכר לאו חפלי שמים: אלא היינו טעמא דאין קורין בראשון דיפנו אביהם של תינוקות ולאו משום שכר שבת כלל אלא אפי' כשאביהם של תינוקות מלמדין אותן בחנם שיהיה להם פנאי שיהא פנוים לסעודת שבת ואם יקראו בראשון ישהו שהייה מרובה וה"ה אם יש להם מלמד בשכר שאסור מהאי טעמא: אבל שונין בראשון. דתו ליכא שהייה כל כך כיון שמלמדים כבר: אוכלים טפי מבחול ויקיר עלייהו עלמא כלומר שכבדין הם מפני שינוי ווסת דאין יכולין לעסוק ולטרוח וללמוד בראשון: בנות מי בעיין שימור. ומתני' סתמא קתני בין בנים ובין בנות ובנות ליכא [illegible] ולא בעיא שימור א"כ לא שייך בהן שכר שימור: שכר פיסוק טעמים דאורייתא. ואסור ליטול שכר עליהם: אלו הפסוקים. מקום שהפסוק מסיים שם: ואמרי לה אלו המסורות. מאן דאית ליה פיסוק טעמים לאו דאורייתא מפרש אלו המסורות חסירות ויתירות: מקרא סופרים ארץ ארץ. [שמשתנין] באתנחתא וזקף קטן שמים מצרים: עיטור סופרים. דלכאורה משמע דאחר תעבורו וסבריה ואחר תעבורו וכן אחר תאסף ואחר מסתבר אחר נוגנים ואחר משמע: פרת דבלכתו. להשיב ידו בנהר פרת פרת איתו כתוב ונקרא: איש דכאשר ישאל. פי' כאשר ישאל איש בדבר האלהים איש קרי ולא כתיב:

פי' הרא"ש

מפורש זה תרגום. שמפרש המקרא: ושום שכל אלו הפסוקים. שבשבילם מפסיקין בין דבר לדבר: ויבינו במקרא זה פיסוק טעמים. שעל ידי הניגון מבינין לחבר המקרא למעלה או למטה: אלו המסורות. חסרות ויתרות: מקרא סופרים ארץ ארץ. שמשתנה באתנחתא וכן שמים מצרים שאין קורין שמים מצרים בחירק: עטור סופרים. כמו רק הכמות לא סרו דמתרגמינן לא עטרו שהוסרו מן התיבות אותיות הראויות להנתן בהם: אחר תעבורו. היה ראוי לכתוב בוי"ו דהוה משמע סעדו לבכם ואח"כ תעבורו אבל השתא דכתיב בלא וי"ו משמע סעדו לבכם אחר שתעבורו וכן כולם: משפטיך תהום רבה. היה ראוי לכתוב ומשפטיך בוי"ו: פרת דבלכתו. בלכתו להשיב ידו על נהר פרת פרת לא כתיב וקרי: איש דכאשר ישאל איש בדבר אלהים. דאחיתופל: באים דונבנתה. הנה ימים באים ונבנתה: את דהגד הוגד לי. את אשר עשית דרות: לי דהשעורים. (את) שש השעורים [האלה] נתן לי: נא דיסלח. בנעמן כתיב: *) ילכוד דסדוכך. שתי פעמים וחד לא קרי: חמש דפאת נגב. ביחזקאל: אם דיגאל. ברות: הלכה פסוקי. ויאמר ה' אל משה הנה אנכי בא אליך בעב הענן בעבור ישמע העם בדברי עמך וגו':

*) שייך לדף שאח"ז

הגהות הגר"א

[א] גמ' ולא כתיבן פרת כו'. נ"ב ובספרינו עוד ד' (וכ"ה במס' סופרים פ"ו ה"ח) בני דולא אבו (שופטים כ). כן לבן המלך (ש"ב יח). נבראות דקנאת ה' (מ"ב יט). בנוי של סנחריב (שם): [ב] שם (את דהגד הוגד) תא"מ:

[בערוך ערך עטר ב תמצא פי' הגאון מהד]

מסורת הש"ס

[כתובות קו. ב"ב קמו סנהדרין ק:]

מגילה ג.

במדבר לא

[מס' סופרים פ"ז ה"ח]

רות ג

הגהות הב"ח

(א) גמ' מקרא סופרים ארץ שמים מצרים וכו' אחר תלכו אחר: (ב) שם באים דונבנתה: (ג) רש"י ד"ה אם היה שכיר וכו' נותנין לו שכר שבת: (ד) ד"ה אלא גבי שבת הא דקתני לא קורין בתחילה לאו משום וכו' שרי בהבלעה אלא כדי דיפנו אבהתהון דינוקי למצותא דשבתא שאם היו וכו' ואם הוו כל"ל ותיבות אבל שונין נמחק: (ה) ד"ה מקרא סופרים ארץ ארץ כלומר וכו' וכן נמי ארץ דלא וכו' וכן שמים דלא וכו' מן מצרים: (ו) ד"ה את דהגד אלי דהגורן וכו' כולהו הני:

זאת [א] ד"הַמִּצְוָה", °"יִדְרֹךְ" ד"הַדּוֹרֵךְ", °"חֲמֵשׁ" ד"פְּאַת נֶגֶב", "אִם" °ד"כִּי גֹאֵל" — הָלֵין כְּתַבָן וְלָא קַרְיָין. *אָמַר רַב אַחָא בַּר אַדָּא: בְּמַעֲרָבָא פָּסְקִין לְהָדֵין פְּסוּקָא לִתְלָתָא פְּסוּקִין: °"וַיֹּאמֶר ה' אֶל מֹשֶׁה הִנֵּה אָנֹכִי בָּא אֵלֶיךָ בְּעַב הֶעָנָן". אָמַר רַבִּי חָמָא בר' חֲנִינָא: לֹא הֶעֱשִׁיר מֹשֶׁה אֶלָּא מִפְּסוֹלְתָּן שֶׁל לוּחוֹת, שֶׁנֶּאֱמַר °"פְּסָל לְךָ שְׁנֵי לֻחֹת אֲבָנִים כָּרִאשֹׁנִים" — פְּסוֹלְתָּן שֶׁלְּךָ יְהֵא. אָמַר רַבִּי יוֹסֵי בר' חֲנִינָא: לֹא נִיתְּנָה תּוֹרָה אֶלָּא לְמֹשֶׁה וּלְזַרְעוֹ, שֶׁנֶּאֱמַר °"כְּתָב לְךָ" "פְּסָל לְךָ", מַה פְּסוֹלְתָּן שֶׁלְּךָ — אַף כְּתָבָן שֶׁלְּךָ.(א) מֹשֶׁה נָהַג בָּהּ טוֹבַת עַיִן וּנְתָנָהּ לְיִשְׂרָאֵל, וְעָלָיו הַכָּתוּב אוֹמֵר °"טוֹב עַיִן הוּא יְבֹרָךְ" וגו'. מְתִיב רַב חִסְדָּא: °"וְאֹתִי צִוָּה ה' בָּעֵת הַהִיא לְלַמֵּד אֶתְכֶם"! וְאוֹתִי צִוָּה, וַאֲנִי לָכֶם. °"רְאֵה לִמַּדְתִּי אֶתְכֶם חֻקִּים וּמִשְׁפָּטִים כַּאֲשֶׁר צִוַּנִי ה' אֱלֹהָי"! אוֹתִי צִוָּה, וַאֲנִי לָכֶם. °"וְעַתָּה כִּתְבוּ לָכֶם אֶת הַשִּׁירָה הַזֹּאת"! הַשִּׁירָה לְחוּדָהּ. "לְמַעַן תִּהְיֶה לִּי הַשִּׁירָה הַזֹּאת לְעֵד בִּבְנֵי יִשְׂרָאֵל"! אֶלָּא פִּילְפּוּלָא בְּעָלְמָא. *אָמַר ר' יוֹחָנָן: אאֵין הקב"ה מַשְׁרֶה שְׁכִינָתוֹ אֶלָּא עַל גִּבּוֹר וְעָשִׁיר וְחָכָם וְעָנָיו, וְכוּלָּן מִמֹּשֶׁה. גִּבּוֹר — דִּכְתִיב °"וַיִּפְרֹשׂ אֶת הָאֹהֶל עַל הַמִּשְׁכָּן" וְאָמַר מָר: *מֹשֶׁה רַבֵּינוּ פְּרָסוֹ, וּכְתִיב °"עֶשֶׂר אַמּוֹת אֹרֶךְ הַקָּרֶשׁ" וגו'. אֵימָא דַּאֲרִיךְ וְקָטִין? אֶלָּא מִן הָדֵין קְרָא, דִּכְתִיב °"וָאֶתְפֹּשׂ בִּשְׁנֵי הַלֻּחֹת וָאַשְׁלִכֵם מֵעַל שְׁתֵּי יָדָי וָאֲשַׁבְּרֵם", וְתַנְיָא: *הַלּוּחוֹת אָרְכָּן שִׁשָּׁה וְרָחְבָּן שִׁשָּׁה וְעׇבְיָין שְׁלֹשָׁה. עָשִׁיר — "פְּסָל לְךָ", פְּסוֹלְתָּן שֶׁלְּךָ יְהֵא. חָכָם — רַב וּשְׁמוּאֵל *דְּאָמְרִי תַּרְוַיְיהוּ: חֲמִשִּׁים שַׁעֲרֵי בִינָה נִבְרְאוּ בָּעוֹלָם, וְכוּלָּם נִתְּנוּ לְמֹשֶׁה חָסֵר אַחַת, שֶׁנֶּאֱמַר °"וַתְּחַסְּרֵהוּ מְּעַט מֵאֱלֹהִים". עָנָיו — דִּכְתִיב °"וְהָאִישׁ מֹשֶׁה עָנָו מְאֹד". אָמַר ר' יוֹחָנָן: כׇּל הַנְּבִיאִים עֲשִׁירִים הָיוּ, מְנָלַן — מִמֹּשֶׁה וּמִשְּׁמוּאֵל מֵעָמוֹס וּמִיּוֹנָה. מֹשֶׁה — דִּכְתִיב °"לֹא חֲמוֹר אֶחָד מֵהֶם נָשָׂאתִי", אִי בְּלָא אַגְרָא — לְאַפּוֹקֵי מַאן דִּשְׁקַל בְּלָא אַגְרָא?! אֶלָּא דַּאֲפִי' בְּאַגְרָא. דִּילְמָא מִשּׁוּם דְּעָנִי הֲוָה. אֶלָּא מִן "פְּסָל לְךָ" — פְּסוֹלְתָּן יְהֵא שֶׁלְּךָ. שְׁמוּאֵל — דִּכְתִיב °"הִנְנִי עֲנוּ בִי נֶגֶד ה' וְנֶגֶד מְשִׁיחוֹ אֶת שׁוֹר מִי לָקַחְתִּי וַחֲמוֹר מִי לָקַחְתִּי", אִי בְּחִנָּם — לְאַפּוֹקֵי מַאן דִּשְׁקַל בְּחִנָּם?! אֶלָּא דַּאֲפִילּוּ בְּשָׂכָר. דִּלְמָא דְּעָנִי הֲוָה. אֶלָּא מֵהָכָא °"וּתְשֻׁבָתוֹ הָרָמָתָה כִּי שָׁם בֵּיתוֹ" *וְאָמַר רָבָא: כׇּל מָקוֹם שֶׁהָלַךְ — בֵּיתוֹ עִמּוֹ. אָמַר רָבָא: גָּדוֹל מַה שֶּׁנֶּאֱמַר בִּשְׁמוּאֵל יוֹתֵר מִשֶּׁנֶּאֱמַר בְּמֹשֶׁה, דְּאִילּוּ בְּמֹשֶׁה רַבֵּינוּ כְּתִיב "לֹא חֲמוֹר אֶחָד מֵהֶם נָשָׂאתִי" — דַּאֲפִי' בְּשָׂכָר, וְאִילּוּ גַּבֵּי שְׁמוּאֵל — אֲפִי' בִּרְצוֹן לֹא שְׂכָרוֹ, דִּכְתִיב °"וַיֹּאמְרוּ לֹא עֲשַׁקְתָּנוּ וְלֹא רַצּוֹתָנוּ" וגו'. עָמוֹס — דִּכְתִיב °"וַיַּעַן עָמוֹס וַיֹּאמֶר אֶל אֲמַצְיָה לֹא נָבִיא אָנֹכִי וְלֹא בֶן נָבִיא אָנֹכִי כִּי בוֹקֵר אָנֹכִי וּבוֹלֵס שִׁקְמִים" כִּדְמְתַרְגֵּם רַב יוֹסֵף: אֲרֵי מָרֵי גִיתֵי אֲנָא, וְשִׁקְמִין לִי בִּשְׁפֵלְתָּא וגו'. יוֹנָה — דִּכְתִיב °"וַיִּתֵּן שְׂכָרָהּ וַיֵּרֶד בָּהּ" וא"ר יוֹחָנָן: שֶׁנָּתַן שְׂכָרָהּ שֶׁל סְפִינָה כּוּלָּהּ. אָמַר ר' רוֹמָנוּס: שְׂכָרָהּ שֶׁל סְפִינָה הֲוָיָא ד' אַלְפִּים דִּינָרֵי דַּהֲבָא. וא"ר יוֹחָנָן: בַּתְּחִלָּה הָיָה מֹשֶׁה לָמֵד תּוֹרָה וּמְשַׁכְּחָהּ, עַד שֶׁנִּיתְּנָה לוֹ בְּמַתָּנָה, שֶׁנֶּאֱמַ' °"וַיִּתֵּן אֶל מֹשֶׁה כְּכַלֹּתוֹ לְדַבֵּר אִתּוֹ". §

מתני' בוְזָן אֶת אִשְׁתּוֹ וְאֶת בָּנָיו אע"פ שֶׁהוּא חַיָּיב בִּמְזוֹנוֹתָן. וְלֹא יָזוּן אֶת בְּהֶמְתּוֹ, בֵּין טְמֵאָה בֵּין טְהוֹרָה. ר' אֱלִיעֶזֶר אוֹמֵר: זָן אֶת הַטְּמֵאָה, וְאֵינוֹ זָן אֶת הַטְּהוֹרָה. אָמְרוּ לוֹ: מַה בֵּין טְמֵאָה לִטְהוֹרָה? אָמַר לְהוּ: שֶׁהַטְּהוֹרָה נַפְשָׁהּ לַשָּׁמַיִם וְגוּפָהּ שֶׁלּוֹ, וּטְמֵאָה נַפְשָׁהּ

רש"י

זאת (ב) הַמִּצְוָה. כְּתִיב בְּיִרְמְיָה א]. **יִדְרוֹךְ** דְּהַדּוֹרֵךְ. כְּתִיב, (ג) וּקְרָאֵי לָא גָּרַס לְהוּ יִדְרוֹךְ, דִּכְתַבָן וְלָא קַרְיָין. **דְּכִי גוֹאֵל** אָתָּה. בְּרוּת. **חֲמֵשׁ דִּפְאַת** נֶגֶב. וְטַעְמַיְיהוּ לָא מְפָרֵשׁ לֵיהּ. **לְלַמֵּד** אֶתְכֶם. אַלְמָא הקב"ה צִוָּה לִיתְּנָהּ לְיִשְׂרָאֵל. **כִּתְבוּ** לָכֶם. אַלְמָא שֶׁנִּיתְּנָה נַמִּי לָהֶן לְיִשְׂרָאֵל. **לְמַעַן** תִּהְיֶה לִי לְעֵד. שֶׁיִּלְמְדוּ כׇּל הַתּוֹרָה וְיִלְמְדוּ אוֹתָהּ. אַלְמָא לְיִשְׂרָאֵל נַמִּי נִיתְּנָה. **פִּלְפּוּלָא** בְּעָלְמָא. לְהָבִין דָּבָר מִתּוֹךְ דָּבָר הוּא דְּנִיתַּן לְמֹשֶׁה, וְנִיהֵג בָּהּ טוֹבַת עַיִן וּנְתָנָהּ לְיִשְׂרָאֵל. **פֵּירְסוֹ**. מִכְּלָל דְּגִבּוֹר (ד) הֲוָה וְגוּף גָּדוֹל. **וְאֵימָא** דַּאֲרִיךְ הָיָה וְקָטִין. שֶׁלֹּא הָיָה גּוּפָנִי, וְלֹא הָיָה בַּעַל כֹּחַ. **וְעוֹבְיָין** שָׁלֹשׁ. וַאֲפִי' הָכִי שִׁיבְּרָן. **וַתְּחַסְּרֵהוּ** מְעַט. וְזוֹ הִיא אַחַת, שֶׁאוֹתָהּ אַחַת הָיָה הקב"ה יְתֵירָה עָלָיו. **אִי בְּלָא אַגְרָא**. מַאי רְבוּתֵיהּ. **לְאַפּוֹקֵי** מִמַּאן דִּשְׁקַל בְּלָא אַגְרָא. כׇּל מִי שֶׁהוּא רוֹצֶה חֲמוֹרוֹ שֶׁל חֲבֵירוֹ בְּלֹא שָׂכָר, וּמַאי מַעַלְיוּתָא הִיא דְּלָא הֲוֵה גַּזְלָן? כ"ע נַמִּי (ה) לָא גּוֹזְלִין נִינְהוּ. **דִּלְמָא**. הַאי דְּלָא שָׁקֵיל אֲפִי' בְּאַגְרָא לָאו מִשּׁוּם עוֹשֶׁר. דִּלְמָא מִשּׁוּם דְּעָנִי הֲוָה, וְלָא הֲווּ לֵיהּ מַשּׂוּאוֹת, וּלְהָכִי לָא הֲוָה צָרִיךְ. **אֶלָּא מֵהָכָא**. שָׁמְעִינַן דְּעָשִׁיר הָיָה, מִ"פְּסָל לְךָ". **בֵּיתוֹ** עִמּוֹ. כְּלֵי תַּשְׁמִישׁוֹ, וְזֶה הָיָה מֵרוֹב עוֹשֶׁר. **לֹא חֲמוֹר אֶחָד מֵהֶם נָשָׂאתִי**. בְּעַל כׇּרְחוֹ, אֲפִי' בְּשָׂכָר, הָא בְּרָצוֹן בְּעָלִים — הָיָה שׂוֹכֵר. וְאִילּוּ גַּבֵּי שְׁמוּאֵל וכו' "לֹא עֲשַׁקְתָּנוּ וְלֹא רַצּוֹתָנוּ" — שֶׁלֹּא הָיָה שׂוֹכֵר, לֹא בְּאוֹנֶס וְלֹא בְּרָצוֹן. **מתני'** וְזָן אֶת אִשְׁתּוֹ וְאֶת בָּנָיו. שֶׁל מוּדָּר. **אע"פ**. שֶׁהַמּוּדָּר חַיָּיב בִּמְזוֹנוֹתָן, כֵּיוָן דְּלָאו לְפִטּוּמֵי עֲבִידָן, וְדַי לָהֶן בְּמַאי שֶׁהוּא מְפַרְנְסָן — לָאו הֲנָאָה מְרוּבָּה עָבֵיד לֵיהּ. **וְלֹא יָזוּן אֶת בְּהֶמְתּוֹ כו'**. הוֹאִיל וּלְפִטּוּמֵי עֲבִידָן — עָבֵיד לֵיהּ הֲנָאָה מְרוּבָּה. **נַפְשָׁהּ לַשָּׁמַיִם וְגוּפָהּ שֶׁלּוֹ**. לַאֲכִילָה, מִשּׁוּם הָכִי לֹא יָזוּן אוֹתָהּ לְפִטּוּמֵי, שֶׁמְּהַנֵּיהוּ הֲנָאָה מְרוּבָּה. נַפְשָׁהּ

ר"ן

זאת דהמצוה. בסדר ואתחנן. כך מצאתי כתוב, ולא נמצא בספרים שלנו. **ידרוך** דהדורך. בסוף ירמיה "ידרוך הדורך את קשתו" – "ידרוך" שני כתיב ולא קרי. **חמש** דפאת נגב. בסוף יחזקאל (והנה) "[ואלה] מדותיה וגו' חמש חמש מאות וארבעת אלפים" – "חמש" שני כתיב ולא קרי. **אם דכי גואל**. ברות "ועתה כי אמנם כי אם גואל אנכי" – האי "אם" כתיב ולא קרי. ובמסרה חשיב כל הני, וטפי עלייהו אחריני. מיהו לא חשיב *"את" דהמצוה אלא *"את" ד"הנפש" דכתיב בירמיהו *גבי לדקיה "חי ה' אשר עשה לנו את הנפש הזאת". **מתיב רב חסדא ואותי צוה ה' בעת ההיא**. אלמא דהשם צוהו ללמד את ישראל! ומפרקינן: ואני לכם. וקרא ה"ק: ואותי צוה ה' בעת ההיא, ואני נתתי את לבי ללמד חוקים ומשפטים. **למען תהיה** לי השירה הזאת לעד. ואי שירה לבדה קאמר – מאי סהדותא איכא?: **פלפולא בעלמא**. נתן לו למשה, והוא נהג בו טובת עין לישראל. **וכתיב עשר אמות ארך הקרש**. אלמא משה גבוה עשר אמות היה, וכיון שהיה גדול כל כך – מסתמא גבור היה. **אריך וקטין**. ארוך בקומה וקטין בכח. **חוץ מאחת**. ידיעת הש"י על אמיתתו, כדכתיב "ותחסרהו מעט מאלהים". **לאפוקי מאן דשקל בלא אגרא**. וכי משתבח היה שלא נטל בלא שכר?! **אלא אפילו באגרא**. שלא היה נהנה משל אחרים. **אפילו ברצון**. דזימנין מתרלו משום כסופא, ולא ניחא להו. **מתני' וזן את אשתו ואת בניו**. אפי' כרבנן* אתיא, דבתורת מלוה עסקינן ולא בתורת פרעון של בעל שחייב במזונותיהם. ואע"ג דהמודר מתהני, שאינו לריך לתת להם מזונות – ההיא הנאה דממילא היא. **ולא יזון את בהמתו בין טמאה בין טהורה**. דמהנהו הוא ממש, מפני שמעלה בדמים. **ר' אליעזר אומר זן את הטמאה**. כדמפרש ואזיל, שכיון שאין בה למודר הנאת אכילה – אינו נהנה במזונותיו של מדיר. **וגופה שלו**. לאכילה, הלכך אי

תוספות

זאת דהמצוה. פרשה ואתחנן ואינו כך בסוף חומש: **ידרוך** הדורך. בירמיה: **צדקתך** כהררי אל. ולא קרי כהררי אל לדקתך וי"א הוי"ו מולדקתך *)שאמר אנחנו ולדקתך: [**אותי** צוה]. הכי אמר משה לישראל אותי צוה ואני לכם: **למען** תהיה השירה הזאת לעד בבני ישראל. ואי בשירה לחוד מאי עדות איכא: **אלא** פלפולא בעלמא. שיטת חריפות והבינה נמסר למשה רבינו ונהג טובת עין ואמר משה כו': [**וכתיב** עשר אמות אורך הקרש]. אלמא ארוך היה וכיון דהיה ארוך גבור היה: **עביין** ג'. והולרך לחבטן בקרקע בכח גדול: **אי** בלא אגרא. מי הוא דשקיל בלא אגרא ומאי רבותא אלא אפילו באגרא לא שקיל דעשיר היה: **דלמא** משום דעני היה. ולא היה רוצה לשכור מהם: **ביתו** עמו. כלי תשמישו עמו ואינו נהנה משל אחרים: **דאילו** במשה כתיב לא חמור אחד מהם נשאתי. בעל כרחייהו מכלל דברצון שכרה ושמא לא היו רוצים ובושים לסרב מלהשכיר ואילו בשמואל כתיב רצותי משמע לא בקשתי לשכור ממנו ואפילו ברצוני: **וזן** את אשתו ובניו. אי אתיא כחנן ניחא דמבריח ארי בעלמא הוא וכי אתיא נמי כרבנן ניחא שפיר דמיירי הכא ממזונות יתירות ואין נפרע [מבעלה] דכי פליגי רבנן היינו במפרנס סתם אע"פ שלא פי' לשם הלואה מ"מ לשם מתנה לא יהיב והוי לרבנן כמו יורד לתוך שדה חבירו שלא ברשות דנוטל מה שהשביח וחנן מחלק בין השביח להיכא דלא הוה אלא מבריח ארי מנכסי חבירו א"כ אם נותן מתנה לאשה דין הוא שאין יכול לתבוע לבעל כלום והכא מיירי שנותן מתנה לאשה ממכירי הבעל: **לא** יזון את בהמתו בין טמאה בין טהורה. משום דלפטומא עבידא והוי הנאה גמורה שנהנה זו מגופה וזו מפירה: **אמר** להם כו'. שהטמאה נפשה וגופה לשמים שאינה יכולה ליהנות אלא בעוד נפשה בה הלכך לאו הנאה היא אבל טהורה נפשה לשמים כלומר אע"פ שנפשה לשמים גופה שלו לשחיטה

*) נ"א שאומרים

הרי

פי' הרא"ש

פסל לך שלך יהא. ושל סנפרינון היו: **טוב עין הוא יבורך**. זה משה דכתיב ביה כי טוב הוא כי נתן מלחמו לדל אין לחם אלא תורה דכתיב לכו לחמו בלחמי ואין דל אלא ישראל שנאמר וידל ישראל עד מאד: **למען תהיה לי השירה הזאת לעד**. ואם לא ניתן להם תורה אלא זו השירה על מה תעיד: **פלפולא בעלמא**. הבנה וחריפות והיינו כתבן שלך כי כל החכמה והשכל רמוזים בכתב התורה בעורות האותיות: **אין הקב"ה משרה שכינתו**. בקביעות: **לאריך וקטין**. אריך בקומה וקטין בכח תימה אמאי לא יליף מקרשים דכתיב ויפרש את המשכן [נ"ל קרשיו שמות מ]: **חמשים שערי בינה ונתנו לו למשה חוץ מאחד**. דכתיב מזוקק שבעתים: **משום דעניו הוא**. ומנהג חסידות היה שלא להטריח עליהם: **ולא רצותנו**. משמע אפילו מרצונו: **ויתן שכרה**. משמע של כל הספינה: **מתני' וזן את אשתו ואת בניו אע"פ שחייב במזונותיהן**. חייב אאשתו קאי אבל בניו מצוה הוא דאיכא ולא חיובא כדתניא בכתובות בפ' נערה (דף מט.) מצוה לזון את הבנות קל וחומר לבנים דברי רבי מאיר רבי יהודה אומר מצוה לזון את הבנים וכל שכן לבנות ובקטנים ליכא לאוקמי דתקנת אושא היא (שם מט:) שיהא אדם זן את בניו קטנים ולאו מתניתין היא ורבינו תם מוקי לה בגירש את אשתו ואהדרה ופסקה עמו לזון: **את בהמתו בין טמאה כו'**. דניחא ליה בפטומן וקא מהני ליה: *) **נפשה לשמים**. דלמלאכה קיימא ואינו חושש על פטומה: **שאם ירצה מוכרה לעובדי כוכבים**. לאכילה ונוטל דמיה בשביל פטומה:

*) שייך לע"ב

הרי

עין משפט נר מצוה

לג א מיי' פ"ז מהל' יסודי התורה הל' א:

לד ב מיי' פ"ו מהל' נדרים הל' ד סמג לאוין רמב טוש"ע י"ד סימן רכא סעיף ב:

מסורת הש"ס

קידושין ל.

שבת לב. [ע"ש ומלוה ליישב]

[בכורות מד.]

[ב"ב יד.]

ר"ה כא: ע"ש

ברכות י: ע"ש

[נ"ל זאת]

[נ"ל זאת]

[סי' לח פסוק טז ע"ש היטב]

[דלעיל לג: דפליגי על חנן]

הגהות הב"ח

(א) גמ' כתבן שלך ומשה: (ב) רש"י ד"ה זאת דהמלוה: (ג) ד"ה ידרוך כו' כתיב תרתי קראי ולא קרי' להו ידרוך שני דכתבן: (ד) ד"ה פירסו כו' דגבור היה: (ה) ד"ה לאפוקי וכו' כ"ע נמי לאו גזלנין נינהו:

הגהות הגר"א

[א] גמ' זאת דהמלוה. נמחק וכ"ב את דהנפש ובספרינו עוד ג' אם דאמנון (ש"ב י"ג). אם דבמקום (שם ט"ו). אם דכאשר (ירמיה ל"ט. וכ"ה במ"ם פ"ו ה"ט):

הגהות מהר"י לנדא

א] רש"י ד"ה זאת המלוה. כתיב בירמיה. נ"ל את דהנפש כתיב בירמיה (ל"ח ט"ז) ועי' בפי' הר"נ ד"ה אם דכי גואל:

לה א מיי' פ"ו מהל' נדרים הל' ה סמג לאוין רמב טוש"ע י"ד סימן רכא סעיף ג:
לו ב ג מיי' שם הל' יז סמג שם טוש"ע י"ד סימן רכג סעיף א:
לז ד ה ו מיי' שם הל' י סמג שם טוש"ע שם סימן רכא סעיף א:
לח ז מיי' שם הל' ח טוש"ע שם סעיף ד:

נַפְשָׁהּ וְגוּפָהּ לַשָּׁמַיִם. אָמְרוּ לוֹ: אַף הַטְּמֵאָה נַפְשָׁהּ לַשָּׁמַיִם וְגוּפָהּ שֶׁלּוֹ, שֶׁאִם יִרְצֶה — הֲרֵי הוּא מוֹכְרָהּ לְגוֹיִם אוֹ מַאֲכִילָהּ לִכְלָבִים.§

גמ' אָמַר רַב יִצְחָק בַּר חֲנַנְיָה אָמַר רַב הוּנָא: הַמּוּדָּר הֲנָאָה מֵחֲבֵירוֹ — מוּתָּר לְהַשִּׂיא לוֹ בִּתּוֹ. הָוֵי בָּהּ רַבִּי זֵירָא: בְּמַאי עָסְקִינַן? אִילֵימָא בְּשֶׁנִּכְסֵי אֲבִי כַלָּה אֲסוּרִין עַל הֶחָתָן — הֲרֵי מוֹסֵר לוֹ שִׁפְחָה לְשַׁמְּשׁוֹ! אֶלָּא (א) בְּנִכְסֵי חָתָן אֲסוּרִין עַל אֲבִי כַלָּה — גְּדוֹלָה מִזּוֹ אָמְרוּ: זָן אֶת אִשְׁתּוֹ וְאֶת בָּנָיו, וְאַע"פ שֶׁהוּא חַיָּיב בִּמְזוֹנוֹתָן. וְאַתְּ אָמְרַתְּ מוּתָּר לְהַשִּׂיא לוֹ בִּתּוֹ?! לְעוֹלָם בְּשֶׁנִּכְסֵי אֲבִי כַלָּה אֲסוּרִים עַל הֶחָתָן, וּבְבִתּוֹ בּוֹגֶרֶת, וּמִדַּעְתָּהּ. תַּנְיָא נַמִי הָכִי: אהַמּוּדָּר הֲנָאָה מֵחֲבֵירוֹ אָסוּר לְהַשִּׂיא לוֹ בִּתּוֹ, אֲבָל מַשִּׂיאוֹ בִּתּוֹ בּוֹגֶרֶת, וּמִדַּעְתָּהּ. אָמַר רַבִּי יַעֲקֹב: בהַמַּדִּיר בְּנוֹ לְתַלְמוּד תּוֹרָה — מוּתָּר לְמַלְּאוֹת לוֹ חָבִית שֶׁל מַיִם, וּלְהַדְלִיק לוֹ אֶת הַנֵּר. ר' יִצְחָק אָמַר: גלִצְלוֹת לוֹ דָּג קָטָן. אָמַר ר' יִרְמְיָה אָמַר רַבִּי יוֹחָנָן: הַמּוּדָּר הֲנָאָה מֵחֲבֵירוֹ — מוּתָּר לְהַשְׁקוֹתוֹ כּוֹס שֶׁל שָׁלוֹם. מַאי נִיהוּ? הָכָא תַּרְגִּימוּ: דכּוֹס שֶׁל בֵּית הָאֵבֶל, בְּמַעֲרָבָא אָמְרִי: הכּוֹס שֶׁל בֵּית הַמֶּרְחָץ.§ "וְלֹא יָזוּן אֶת בְּהֶמְתּוֹ בֵּין" כו'.§ תַּנְיָא, יְהוֹשֻׁעַ אִישׁ עוּזָּא אוֹמֵר: וזָן עֲבָדָיו וְשִׁפְחוֹתָיו הַכְּנַעֲנִים, וְלֹא יָזוּן אֶת בְּהֶמְתּוֹ, בֵּין טְמֵאָה בֵּין טְהוֹרָה. מַאי טַעְמָא? עֲבָדָיו וְשִׁפְחוֹתָיו הַכְּנַעֲנִים — לְמַנְחֲרוּתָא עֲבִידָן, בְּהֵמָה — לְפִטּוּמָא עֲבִידָא.§

מתני' זהַמּוּדָּר הֲנָאָה מֵחֲבֵירוֹ וְנִכְנָס לְבַקְּרוֹ — עוֹמֵד אֲבָל לֹא יוֹשֵׁב, וּמְרַפְּאוֹ רְפוּאַת נֶפֶשׁ אֲבָל לֹא רְפוּאַת מָמוֹן.§ **גמ'** בְּמַאי

רש"י

נַפְשָׁהּ וְגוּפָהּ לַשָּׁמַיִם. שֶׁאֵינָהּ רְאוּיָה לַאֲכִילָה, לְפִיכָךְ זָן אוֹתָהּ, דְּאֵינוֹ מְהַנֵּהוּ הֲנָאָה מְרוּבָּה. מוֹכְרָהּ לְגוֹיִם. וְנִיחָא לֵיהּ בְּפִיטּוּמָהּ. **גמ'** עַל הֶחָתָן. שֶׁהֶחָתָן הָוֵי מוּדָּר. הֲרֵי מוֹסֵר לוֹ שִׁפְחָה לְשַׁמְּשׁוֹ. וְאַמַּאי מוּתָּר. **אֶלָּא** בְּשֶׁנִּכְסֵי חָתָן אֲסוּרִין אֵצֶל אֲבִי כַלָּה. וְאַע"פ שֶׁהֶחָתָן מְהַנֵּהוּ, שֶׁזָּן אֶת בִּתּוֹ – אֲפִי' הָכִי מַשִּׂיא לוֹ אֶת בִּתּוֹ. וּמֵשִׁיב הַתַּלְמוּד: מִשּׁוּם הָא לָא צָרִיךְ לְמֵימַר דְּמוּתָּר לְהַשִּׂיא אֶת בִּתּוֹ. דִּגְדוֹלָה מִזּוֹ אָמְרוּ. בְּשֶׁנְּכָסָיו אֲסוּרִים עַל הַמּוּדָּר אָמַרְנוּ "וְזָן אֶת אִשְׁתּוֹ". **אע"פ** וכו' וְאַתְּ אָמַרְתְּ וכו'. פְּשִׁיטָא דְּמוּתָּר, דְּהָא לָא מְהַנֵּי כְּלָל. לְעוֹלָם בְּשֶׁנִּכְסֵי אֲבִי כַלָּה **אֲסוּרִין** עַל הֶחָתָן. וּדְקָאָמְרַתְּ הֲרֵי מוֹסֵר לוֹ שִׁפְחָה לְשַׁמְּשׁוֹ — תָּרֵיץ בְּבִתּוֹ בּוֹגֶרֶת עָסְקִינַן, שֶׁיָּכוֹל לְהַשִּׂיאוֹ, וּמִדַּעַת עַצְמָהּ. דְּהוֹאִיל וְאֵינוֹ מַשִּׂיאָהּ אֶלָּא מִדַּעַת עַצְמָהּ – לָאו הֲנָאָה דְּקָא מְהַנֵּי לֵיהּ אִיהוּ אֶלָּא הֲנָאָה מוּעֶטֶת. **תַּנְיָא** נַמִי הָכִי. דַּהֲנָאָה מוּעֶטֶת מוּתֶּרֶת. הַמַּדִּיר **אֶת** בְּנוֹ. מִנְּכָסָיו אִם לֹא יִלְמוֹד תּוֹרָה. מוּתָּר. הָאָב לְמַלְּאוֹת כו'. שֶׁהֲנָאָה מְרוּבָּה נָדַר הֵימֶנּוּ וְלֹא הֲנָאָה מוּעֶטֶת, וְזוֹ הֲנָאָה מוּעֶטֶת הִיא. כּוֹס שֶׁל בֵּית הַמֶּרְחָץ. הֲנָאָה מוּעֶטֶת הִיא. לְמַנְחֲרוּתָא **עֲבִידָן**. לְצוֹרֶךְ עֲבוֹדָה עֲשׂוּיִין וְלֹא לְהִתְפַּטֵּם. בְּמַאי

ר"ן

אי מפטם לה מהני ליה. והטמאה נפשה וגופה לשמים. שאין לו בה היתר אכילה, ונמלא שאינו נהנה בפטומה. שאם ירצה הרי זה מוכרה לנכרי. שאוכלין אותה, וכשהיא מפוטמת לוקחין אותה ביותר. או מאכילה לכלבים ונמלא נהנה בפטומה ורבוי בשרה. וי"ל דר"א לא שרי בטמאה אלא לזונה מזונות יתרים כדי לפטמה, משום דס"ל דכיון דאינה עומדת לאכילה אלא למלאכה – אינן נהנין בעלים בפטומה, דאדרבה מפנקא טפי ולא עבדא שפיר. אבל במזונות הלריכין לכדי חייה – לא שרי ר' אליעזר, דבכי האי גוונא ודאי מהנהו. ומשום דת"ק פסיק ותני ולא יזון את בהמתו בין טמאה בין טהורה, דמשמע דבכולהו גווני דמתסר בטהורה מתסר נמי בטמאה – מהדר ליה רבי אליעזר: לא כי, אלא איכא גוונא דזן את הטמאה אע"פ שאינו זן את הטהורה. ונהי דתנא מסתם לישניה, סמיך ליה אמאי דאמרו לו ודקמהדר להו ר"א, דמשקלא וטריא דידהו מוכח דר"א לא שרי בטמאה אלא במזונות יתרים כדי לפטמה, ולא בכדי חייה. וראיתי להרשב"א שכתב בהפך, ולא נתחוורו דבריו. **גמ'** הרי מוסר לו שפחה לשמשו. דקס"ד דבבתו נערה עסקינן. **אלא** בשנכסי חתן **אסורין על אבי** כלה. וקמ"ל, שאע"פ שנכסיו אסורין עליו – מותר להשיא לו בתו, אע"פ שיתחייב לזונה אחר כן, ונמלא מהנהו. גדולה מזו אמרו זן את **אשתו ואת בניו וכו' ואת אמרת מותר להשיא לו בתו**. כלומר, אם הוא יכול לזון את בתו בעודה ברשותו, שהוא חייב במזונותיה – כ"ש שיוכל לזון אותה אחר שנשאה, שנתחייב במזונות אשתו, ומאי קמ"ל רב הונא?: ובבתו בוגרת. דלא איהו קמסר לה, אלא היא עלמה. ומדעתה – טעמא קא יהיב למילתיה, כלומר, מש"ה שרי – דהא מדעתה היא, דכיון שבגרה שוב אין לאביה רשות בה. אי נמי, כי קאמר מדעתה – למעוטי דעתו דחתן, שאם עשאו שליח לדבר עמה על עסקי נשואין – אסור, דהא קא מהני ליה. המדיר **את** בנו לת"ת. האב הדירו שלא יהנה אביו ממנו, כדי שלא יתבטל מת"ת. מותר הבן למלאות לאביו חבית של מים ולהדליק לו **את** הנר. דמסתמא ממילי זוטרי כי הני, דליכא בהו בטול למוד תורה – לא אדריה. והכי מוכח האי פירושא בתוספתא דבכורות (פ"ו). דתניא: מעשה באחד שהרלה בנו לת"ת והדירו מלעשות מלאכה, והתיר לו יוסי ברבי למלאות לו חבית של מים ולהדליק לו את הנר. ירושלמי. במס' ביכורים, תני: המדיר את בנו לת"ת מותר למלאות לו חבית של מים ולהדליק לו את הנר. רבי יעקב בר אידי בשם רבי יוחנן: אף ליקח לו תפלים מן השוק. מה פליגין – כאן באיש, כאן באשה. אם היה אדם מסויים – עשו אותו כאשה. כלומר, דאשה ואדם מסויים אין דרכן ליקח תפלים מן השוק, ואנן סהדי דאדעתא דהכי לא אדריה. אבל איש שאינו מסויים, כיון שדרכו לילך בשוק – אפי' בהני אדריה. כלומר, מותר לשמשו בכוס של בית אבל, אי נמי של בית המרחץ, מפני דרכי שלום. שהיה דרכן בכך. ומיהו, דוקא האי כוס של מודר, דלשמשו בכגון זה בלבד התירו, דומיא דאידך דהמדיר את בנו לת"ת שהתירו לבן למלאות לאביו מים משל אב. **את עבדיו ואת שפחותיו הכנענים**. נ"ל דבמזונות יתרים קאמר, ואדר"א קאי. וה"ק: ההוא שריותא דשרי ר"א בבהמה טמאה, דהיינו מזונות יתרים, כמו שפירשתי במשנתנו – ליתיה, דאפי' בהמה טמאה לפטומא עבידא ולמוכרה לנכרי. אבל בעבדיו ושפחותיו הכנענים איתא איתיה, דאינהו למנקרותא עבידן. כלומר, לנקר הבית ולתשמיש בלבד. ואיכא דגרסי למנחרותא, כלומר שאין עומדין לאכילה אלא לנחירה בעלמא, שכשהן מתין מניחין אותן ואין אדם אוכלן. **מתני'** נכנס לבקרו עומד **אבל לא יושב**. מפרש בגמרא. **גמ'** אי

תוספות

הרי מוסר שפחה לשמשו. דס"ד דאיירי בקטנה שניסת על ידו ואת אמרת דמותר להשיא בתו הא פשיטא דאסור: **בבתו** בוגרת דמדעתה. וקמ"ל אף על גב שהוא מדבר עמה ומשיא עלה לה להנשא לו הנאת דבור לא מקרי הנאה:

הגהות הב"ח

(א) גמ' אלא כשנכסי חתן:

פי' הרא"ש

הרי מוסר לו שפחה לשמשו. קא סלקא דעתך בקטנה או בנערה איירי שבידו למוסרה וגם מעשה ידיה שלו: **גדולה מזו אמרו זן את אשתו ואת בניו**. ואע"פ שאינו נהנה מהם כל כך שמותר לזון את בתו אם ישיאנה לו: **בבתו בוגרת ומדעתה**. ואע"פ שנשיאה עלה ואינה עוברת על דעתו שרי: **המדיר את בנו לת"ת**. הדירו שלא יהנה ממלאכתו ומשימושו כדי שיהא פנוי לת"ת אלו מלאכות קטנות מותר לקבל ממנו כי אינן מבטלות אותו כ"כ מת"ת וי"ת שהדירו אביו שלא יהנה ממנו לפי שלא היה רוצה ללמוד מותר ליהנות מן האב בדברים קטנים הללו: **כוס של בית האבל**. שרגילין לשתות שם כדאמרינן (פסחים קי. כתובות ח:) עשרה כוסות בבית האבל ואם האבל מודר הימנו הנאה מותר להוליך שמה יין דמצוה קעביד ולא מטי ליה הנאה כל כך לאבל כי מרובים השותים: **כוס של בית המרחץ**. מים חמין כדאמר בפ' כירה (שבת מא.) רחץ ולא שתה מים חמין דומה לתנור שהסיקוהו מבחוץ ולא מבפנים והנאה מועטת היא: **עבדיו ושפחותיו למנחרותא עבידן**. למראית העין לכבוד לעמוד לפניו לשמשו ואינו חושש בפטומן: *) **אפי' יושב נמי**. דהנאת כבוד לא חשיבא הנאה לאוסרה על החולה דמצוה קא עביד ואין החולה נהנה מדריסת הרגל אף על פי שלא נכנס להנאתו אלא לצורך החולה ואין הנאת דריסה שלו אפ"ה דבר תימה הוא לאסור דריסה זו: **ובמקום שנוטלין שכר על הישיבה**. והוא עושה בחנם ורווח לו השכר ומהנהו: **על העמידה לא בעי למשקל**. דנראה כמבזה מלות ביקור ועל (ידי) הישיבה הוא דבעי למשקל כי נוטל שכר טרחו ובטול מלאכתו:

איבעית

*) [שייך לקמן מ"ג]

במאי עסקינן? אי בשנכסי מבקר אסורין על חולה — אפילו יושב נמי, אי בשנכסי חולה אסורין על המבקר — אפי' עומד נמי לא! אמר שמואל: [א]לעולם בשנכסי מבקר אסורין על החולה, ובמקום שנוטלין שכר על הישיבה, ואין נוטלין שכר על העמידה. מאי פסקא? הא קא משמע לן: דאף במקום שנוטלין שכר, על הישיבה — בעי למשקל, על העמידה — לא בעי למשקל. ואיבעית אימא (א) כדרבי שמעון בן אליקים: גזירה שמא ישהא בעמידה, הכא נמי: גזירה שמא ישהא בישיבה. עולא אמר: לעולם בשנכסי חולה אסורין על המבקר, וכגון דלא אדריה מן חיותיה. אי הכי, אפילו יושב נמי! הא אפשר בעמידה. מיתיבי: חלה הוא — נכנס לבקרו, חלה בנו — שואלו בשוק. בשלמא לעולא, דאמר בשנכסי חולה אסורין על המבקר, וכגון דלא אדריה מן חיותיה — שפיר. אלא לשמואל, דאמר בשנכסי מבקר אסורין על החולה, מאי שנא הוא ומאי שנא בנו? אמר לך: מתניתין בשנכסי מבקר אסורין על החולה, ברייתא — בשנכסי חולה אסורין על המבקר. מאי פסקא? אמר רבא (*אמר) שמואל: מתניתין

רש"י

במאי עסקינן. נכנס לבקרו. אפילו יושב נמי. יהא מותר, שהרי נכסי חולה אין אסורין על המבקר ומותר ליהנות משלו. אי בשנכסי כו'. ולהכי אינו יושב בישיבה — שלא יהנה משלו. אפי' עומד (ב) לא. דהנאה היא לו שנהנה. ובמקום שנוטלין שכר על הישיבה. שכר שהולך לבקר את החולה ויושב עמו לנוותא, ומשכירין אותו. ואין נוטלין (ג) על העמידה. ולהכי אינו יושב, שאם היה יושב שם המבקר בחנם, מוותר היה לו שכרו, ומהנהו אם לא יטול שכר. אבל עומד, הואיל ואין נוטלין שכר על העמידה — מותר. מאי פסקא. דעל זה נוטלין שכר ולא על זה. על העמידה לא בעי למשקל. דערא הוא, דכך הוא (ד) בכל מקום. ולהכי עומד אבל לא יושב, דכיון דליכא שכר [על העמידה] לא מהני ליה כלל. ואיבעית אימא. לעולם בשנכסי מבקר אסורין על החולה, ואפילו במקום שאין נוטלין שכר על הישיבה. ודקאמרת אפי' יושב נמי — כדקאמר רבי שמעון בן אליקים לקמן (דף מב:) לענין שביעי' (ה). גזירה שמא ישהא בעמידה הכא נמי שמא ישהא בישיבה. ושהייה דישיבה ודאי הנאה היא לחולה, ולהכי לא ישב עמו. ואי קשיא: אפילו עומד נמי לא, גזירה שמא ישהא בעמידה — הא לא קשיא. דהתם, כיון דאכל מפירי דשדה, איכא למימר דלמא אגב דאכיל שהייה תמן אע"ג דקאי. והכא דלא אכל, משום הכי קאי: (לא מצאתי יותר מזה הלשון וזהו אמר ליה): *למנהרותא. לעבודתו. והואיל וקי"ל יכול הרב לומר לעבד "עשה עמי ואיני זנך", אינה הנאה למודר אם זה מפרנס עבדיו. לפטומא עבידא. דטהורה לשחיטה וטמאה לעובד כוכבים. המודר הנאה מחבירו נכנס לבקרו עומד אבל לא יושב. כדמפרש לקמן. אפילו יושב נמי. להוי, דהא מבקר מותר בנכסי חולה. אפילו עומד (ו). דהא אסור בדריסת הרגל. לעולם בשנכסי מבקר אסורין על החולה. ומשום הכי עומד אבל לא יושב, כדמפרש בגמרא. במקום שנוטלין שכר על הישיבה. דהיושב לפני החולה משתכר פורתא משום דקעביד ליה נוותא בעלמא, והלכך בישיבה אסור, משום דקא מהני ליה ההוא אגרא דניתיב לאיניש אחרינא דיתיב קמיה. אבל בעמידה דמותר. משום דלא קמהני ליה ולא מידי, דהא לא עביד למיתב אגרא אעמידה: מאי פסקא הא קמ"ל אע"ג דאיכא דוכתא שנוטלין שכר — על הישיבה נוטלין, אבל לא על העמידה. (ז) והיינו טעמא דבעמידה מותר אבל לא בישיבה, כדאמר ר"ש בן אליקים בשילהי פירקין גבי שביעית: (חסר כאן) שהרי עומד ואוכל. גזירה שמא ישהא בישיבה מרובה, והוי הנאת חולה. וא"ת: נגזור בעמידה כי היכי דגזרינן התם בעמידה — הא לא קשיא, דאילו התם (ח) גזרי' בעמידה, אבל הכא דלא מטיא ליה הנאה בעמידה — ליכא למיגזר שמא ירבה בעמידה. אבל לא בישיבה, שנוח לו לזה לישב — גזירה שמא ישהא בישיבה. לעולם בשנכבסי חולה אסורין על המבקר. (ט) וכשאין נוטלין שכר על העמידה. ולהכי מותר בעמידה — דהא לאו מן חיותיה נדר, כדאמר לקמן: כל המבקר את החולה גורם לו שיחיה, ואהכי מותר. הא אפשר בעמידה. מבקרו בעמידה, דמהא לא אדריה. (י) אבל בישיבה אדריה. חלה הוא. המדיר, מותר לבקרו. חלה בנו (כ). מודר שואלו בשוק על עסקי בנו. היינו דשני בין הוא לבנו. דאילו בשחלה הוא מותר ליכנס לשם, דהא לא אדריה מן חיותיה. אבל כשחלה בנו אינו נכנס לבקרו, דהא ליכא חיותא דמדיר. אלא לשמואל דאמר כו' מאי שנא הוא. דמותר, ומ"ש בנו דאסור? הא בעמידה ליכא הנאה כלל! אלא ודאי בנכסי חולה אסורין על המבקר מיירי, וכדעולא, וקשיא לשמואל. אמר לך שמואל כו' וברייתא. מודינא דהכי הוא כדמוקי לה עולא, בהא פליגנא עליה, דאיהו מוקי לה בעומד אבל לא ביושב, דהא אפשר בעמידה. ואנא אמינא דברייתא אפי' יושב שפיר דמי, דאמר דלא אדריה מן חיותיה ל"ש עומד ול"ש יושב. ודיקא נמי מדקתני סתמא: חלה הוא נכנס לבקרו אפי' יושב. מאי פסקא. דמתני' בשנכסי מבקר אסורין על החולה קא מתני'

ר"ן

אי בשנכסי מבקר אסורין על החולה **אפילו יושב נמי**. דעומד מאי טעמא שרית ליה — משום דמבקר מצוה דנפשיה עביד, ונהי דחולה מתהני — ממילא שרי. וכיון שכן, אפילו יושב נמי אית לך למישרי מהאי טעמא. ואי בשנכסי חולה אסורין על המבקר **אפילו עומד לא**. שהרי נהנה בדריסת הרגל. ומשום מצוה לית ליה לאתהנויי מאיסורא. **דאפי' במקום שנוטלין שכר על הישיבה וכו'**. נ"ל דה"פ: דאיכא דוכתי שהחמירו על עצמן שלא ליטול שכר אפי' מישיבה אע"פ שהוא מותר, משום דמצות ביקור די לה בעמידה. ואפ"ה, כדי שלא יבאו ליטול שכר על העמידה, החמירו על עצמן שלא ליטול שכר אף על הישיבה. ובאותן מקומות בין עומד בין יושב שרי, דישיבה נמי לדידהו מצוה. אלא אפי' במקום שאין מחמירין על עצמן — אפ"ה על העמידה לא שרי להו למשקל. ומש"ה פסיק תנא ותני "נכנס לבקרו עומד" בכולהו דוכתי, דמצוה קעביד ואידך ממילא מתהני. אבל לא יושב בכולהו דוכתי, דמקום שאין מחמירין על עצמן בישיבה ליכא מצוה, ונמצא חולה חייב בשכרו, וכשאינו נוטל ממנו כלום נמצא מהנהו. **ואי בעית אימא כדאמר ר' שמעון בן אליקים**. לקמן בפרקין (דף מב:) וה"ק: דינא דמתניתין בכולהו דוכתי איתיה, ואפילו במקום שאין נוטלין שכר לא על העמידה ולא על הישיבה. ונהי דבההוא דוכתא מדינא בין עומד בין יושב שרי — אפי' הכי גזרינן שמא ישהא בישיבה יותר מכדי הצורך, וכי האי גוונא בכולהו דוכתי לית להו למעבד הכי בלא אגרא. אבל בעמידה לא גזרינן שמא ישהא; דכיון שאתה מצריכו לעמוד — אית ליה היכרא. משא"כ בההיא דר"ש בן אליקים, כמו שנפרש עלה דההיא בס"ד. **עולא אמר לעולם בשנכסי חולה אסורין על המבקר**. וכ"ת: א"כ אפי' עומד ליתסר משום דלא אדריה מן חיותיה! כלומר, דמסתמא חולה כי אדריה למבקר — לא אדריה במילתא דצריכא ליה כי הכא, שהחולה נהנה ממנו בביקורו. ואיכא נסחי דגרסי: וכגון דלא אדריה מן חיותיה. ולהך נסחא נמי לאו דבעי דאמר הכי בפירוש, אלא סתמא דמילתיה הכי איתא. והכי מוכחא הך מיתיבי דמייתי בסמוך. מיתיבי חלה הוא נכנס לבקרו כו'. היינו דשאני בין הוא לבנו; דחלה הוא נכנס לבקרו — משום דמסתמא מן חיותיה לא אדריה. וחלה בנו שואלו בשוק אבל אינו מותר ליכנס לביתו, דאפשר דאפילו מן חיותיה דבריה אדריה. והא מוכחא דכי אמרינן מן חיותיה לא אדריה — מסתמא הוא דאמר הכי, אף על גב דלא פריש. דאי בעינן דפריש, אכתי קשיא לעולא: מ"ש הוא ומ"ש בנו? אי פריש — בתרוייהו שרי, ואי לא פריש — בתרוייהו אסור! אלא ודאי בסתמא עסקינן, וסתם הוי כמפרש לגבי דידיה אבל לא לגבי דבריה. **אלא לשמואל דאמר בשנכסי מבקר אסורין על החולה מ"ש הוא ומ"ש בנו**. כלומר, דאדרבה, בבנו שרי טפי שאינו מודר ממנו! ואי מודר נמי מבנו — מ"ש הוא ומ"ש בנו? בתרוייהו אית לן למימר נכנס לבקרו עומד! **אמר לך**. שמואל: אין, ודאי דברייתא מתוקמא בשנכסי חולה אסורין על המבקר, דמודינא בטעמא דידך דמסתמא מחיותיה לא אדריה, ואמינא נמי טפי מינך, דאפילו מישיבה לא אדריה. ומשום הכי לא מצינא לאוקמי מתניתין כדמוקמית לה, דהיינו בנכסי חולה אסורין על המבקר, דא"ה אפי' יושב נמי שרי, דישיבה נמי דמבקר — חיותיה דחולה הוא, ולא אדריה. ולענין הלכה. קיימא לן כשמואל. דכיון דרבא מפרש מילתיה ואמר דמתני' דיקא ליה הכי — הלכתא כוותיה. הלכך, בשנכסי חולה אסורין על

עין משפט נר מצוה

לט א מיי' פ"ו מהל' נדרים הל' ח סמג לאוין רמב טוש"ע יו"ד סי' רכא סעיף ז:

הגהות הב"ח

תוספות

אפי' עומד. דקא מתהני מדריסת הרגל: **במקום** שנוטלין שכר על הישיבה. לכך אסור לבקר בחנם אבל בעמידה דאין נוטלין שכר עליה מותר בחנם דמצוה קעביד: **על** העמידה לא בעי למשקל. כיון דמצוה הוא ויש לו לעשות בחנם. על הישיבה דעומד ואע"ג דאדריה **אפשר** בעמידה. והלכך לאסור ליכנס בביתו [כיון לבקרו הוא ולבנו אסור הברייתא בענין דמתניתין: מתני'

פי' הרא"ש

מ א ב ג מיי' פי"ד מהל' אבל הל' ד סמג עשין מדברי סופרים ב טוש"ע י"ד סי' שלה סעיף ב:

מא ד מיי' פ"כ מהל' אישות הל' ד סמג לאוין פא טוש"ע אה"ע סימן קיג סעיף ז:

מתניתין קשיתיה; מאי איריא דתני עומד אבל לא יושב – שמע מינה דנכסי מבקר אסורין על החולה. אמר ריש לקיש: רמז לביקור חולין מן התורה מנין – שנאמר "אם כמות כל האדם ימתון אלה ופקדת כל אדם" וגו'. מאי משמע? אמר רבא: אם כמות כל האדם ימותון אלה שהן חולים ומוטלים בעריסתן, ובני אדם מבקרים אותן, מה הבריות אומרים – לא ה' שלחני לזה. *דרש רבא: "אם בריאה יברא ה'" אם בריאה גיהנם – מוטב תהיה, אם לאו – יברא ה'. איני? והא תניא: *שבעה דברים נבראו קודם שנברא העולם, אלו הן: תורה, ותשובה, גן עדן, וגיהנם, כסא הכבוד, ובית המקדש, ושמו של משיח. תורה – דכתיב "ה' קנני ראשית דרכו" וגו'. תשובה – דכתיב "בטרם הרים יולדו ותחולל" וגו' "תשב אנוש עד דכא" וגו'. גן עדן – דכתיב "ויטע ה' אלהים גן בעדן מקדם" וגו', גיהנם – דכתיב "כי ערוך מאתמול תפתה". *כסא כבוד – דכתיב "נכון כסאך מאז". בית המקדש – דכתיב "כסא כבוד מרום מראשון". שמו של משיח – דכתיב "יהי שמו לעולם" וגו'! אלא הכי קאמר: אי איברי ליה פומא – מוטב, ואם לא – יברא ה'. והכתיב: "אין כל חדש תחת השמש"! הכי קאמר: אי הכא לא מקרב פומא – להכא ליקרב. דרש רבא, ואמרי לה אמר ר' יצחק: *מאי דכתיב "שמש ירח עמד זבלה", שמש (א) וירח בזבול מאי בעיין? והא ברקיע קביעי! מלמד שעלו שמש וירח מרקיע לזבול, ואמרו לפניו: רבונו של עולם! אם אתה עושה דין לבן עמרם – אנו מאירים, ואם לאו – אין אנו מאירין. באותה שעה ירה בהן חיצים וחניתות, אמר להם: בכל יום ויום משתחוים לכם ואתם מאירים, בכבודי לא מחיתם – בכבוד בשר ודם מחיתם! ובכל יום ויום יורין בהן חיצין וחניתות ומאירים, שנא' "לאור חציך יהלכו" וגו'. תניא: ביקור חולים אין לה שיעור. מאי אין לה שיעור? סבר רב יוסף למימר: אין שיעור למתן שכרה. אמר ליה אביי: וכל מצות מי יש שיעור למתן שכרן? והא תנן: *הוי זהיר במצוה קלה כבחמורה, שאין אתה יודע מתן שכרן של מצות! אלא אמר אביי: [א]אפי' גדול אצל קטן. רבא אמר: [ב]אפי' מאה פעמים ביום. *אמר רבי אחא בר חנינא: *כל המבקר חולה נוטל אחד מששים *בצערו. *אמרי ליה: אם כן ליעלון שיתין ולוקמוה! אמר ליה: כעישורייתא דבי רבי, [ג]ובבן גילו. דתניא, *רבי אומר: בת הניזונית מנכסי אחין – נוטלת עישור נכסים. אמרו לו לרבי: לדבריך, מי שיש לו עשר בנות ובן, אין לו לבן במקום בנות כלום! אמר להן: [ד]ראשונה נוטלת עישור נכסים, שניה במה ששיירה, שלישית במה ששיירה, וחוזרות וחולקות בשוה. רב חלבו חלש, נפק (ג) אכריז רב כהנא:

רב

רש"י

מתניתין קשיתיה. מדוקיא קא משמע ליה. מאי איריא דתני עומד אבל לא יושב. והרי (ג) אין מבקר אסור בנכסי חולה! אלא שמע מינה וכו'. וא"ת: מאי טעמא דשמואל דמתרץ לה הכי? לוקמא כדעולא! הא לא קשיא, דשמואל לא מוקי לה כדעולא, דקסבר האי שינויא דחיקא היא. ופקודת כל אדם. שבני אדם מבקרין אותן. לא ה' שלחני לזה. לפי שהיו עדת קרח מלעיגין עליו, ואומרים שהיה משה אומר להם מדעתו, בלא ציווי של מקום. ואם לאו. שאין גיהנם נברא עדיין. איני. מי מספקא ליה למשה?! כי ערוך מאתמול תפתה. איזהו יום שיש לו אתמול ולא שלשום, כלומר שהיה לו לפניו ולא לפני פניו – הוי אומר זה יום שני, שבו נברא גיהנם. אלא ה"ק. אי הכא – אין לו פומא, ואי לא מקרב הכא – יקריבנו המקום. והא ברקיע קביעי. למטה מזבול, כדאמרי' במסכת חגיגה (דף יב:). אם אתה עושה דין לבן עמרם. מקרח ועדתו. ובכל יום ויום. מאותו יום ואילך אינן יוצאין, מפני שמשתחווין להם עובדי כוכבים, עד שמורים בהן חיצים וחניתות. ואפי' גדול אצל קטן. שלא יאמר: לא אבקר אלא גדול כמוני. אין לו שיעור. דמצוה בקטן כמו בגדול. ליעיילו שיתין ולוקמוה. יכנסו ששים בני אדם כאחת לבקרו, ויטול כל אחד ואחד מששים בצערו, ומיד מתרפא. כעישורייתא דבי רבי. דאמר: מי שיש לו עשר בנות ובן אחד, הראשונה נוטלת עישור נכסים, והשניה במה ששיירה, וכן לכולן. ומפרש בתלמוד ירושלמי: נמצאו בנות שנוטלות במנה תרי תילתי פחות ליבחר והאי תלתא ומוסיף ליבחר (ד). וגבי חולה נמי, מבקר הראשון נוטל אחד מששים בחליו, והשני א' מששים במה ששייר. ובבן גילו. בחור כמותו, או זקן לזקן. וחוזרות כולן וחולקות בשוה. מילתא אחריתי (ה), דהיכא דאזלו לינשא כאחת – כל אחת נוטלת עישורה במה ששיירה חבירתה, ואז חולקות בשוה. אבל כשבאו לינשא זו אחר זו – לא.

באים

ר"ן

על המבקר נכנס לבקרו אפי' יושב, דישיבה נמי חיותיה דחולה הוא ולא אדריה, דבהכי ניחא ליה. אבל חלה בנו – לא יכנס לביתו כלל, אלא שואלו בשוק. ומיהו, דוקא היכא דאדריה חולה למבקר, דאומדן דעתא הוא דמן חיותיה לא אדריה. אבל היכא שהמבקר אסר על עצמו נכסיו של חולה – לא יכנס לביתו כלל, דבכי האי גוונא ליכא אומדנא. הדין הוא דינא דנכסי חולה אסורין על המבקר. והיכא דנכסי מבקר אסורין על החולה – נכנס לבקרו עומד, משום דמחויב לעשות בחנם, ומצוה דיליה קעביד, ואידך ממילא קא מתהני. אבל לא יושב. ואפילו במקומות שמחמירין על עצמן שלא ליטול שכר אפי' על הישיבה משום גזירה שמא ישהא בישיבה. וכי אמרינן בנכסי מבקר אסורין על החולה דנכנס לבקרו עומד משום דמצוה דנפשיה קעביד, ואידך ממילא מתהני – הני מילי בכי האי גוונא דהנאה ממילא היא, אבל היכא דיהיב ליה מידי, כיון שהוא מהנהו ממש מיד ליד, ולא גרמא היא – אסור. והיינו דתנן לקמן בפרקין (דף מג.): המודר הנאה מחבירו ואין לו מה יאכל הולך אצל חנווני הרגיל אצלו, ויאמר לו וכו'. וכן היו מהלכים בדרך ואין לו מה יאכל נותן על גבי הסלע – דוקא בכה"ג שרי, אבל מידו לידו – לא, ואף על גב דמצוה קעביד. וטעמא דמילתא כדאמרינן, דדוקא הנאה דממילא שריא במקום מצוה, אבל הנאה דבידים – לא. ובני אדם מבקרין אותן. והיינו דכתיב "ופקודת כל אדם יפקד עליהם". שבעה דברים נבראו קודם שנברא העולם. כלומר, שעלו במחשבה להבראות קודם שנברא העולם, שא"א לעולם בלא הם, וכדאמרי' שמחשבתן של ישראל קדמה לכל. ועל כרחיך לא נברא העולם בלא גיהנם לצורך הרשעים. אי לא מקרב פומא להכא ליקרב. וקרינה בעלמא ליתא בכלל "אין כל חדש". והא ברקיע קביעי. כדכתיב "ויתן אותם אלהים ברקיע השמים", וזבול למעלה מן הרקיע הוא, כדאיתא בפ' "אין דורשין" (חגיגה יב:). אם אתה עושה דין לבן עמרם. ממחלוקתו של קרח. ומשמע להו דהאי קרא במחלוקתו של קרח מדריש, משום דביציאת מצרים ובקריעת ים סוף משתעי בספר חבקוק, וכתיב ביה "מחצת ראש מבית רשע" ומשמע להו דהיינו קרח, וכתיב בתריה "שמש ירח עמד זבולה". כעישורייתא דרבי. שכל אחת נוטלת עישורה מנכסים שנותרו אחר שנטלה אותה שלפניה עישור שלה. וכן נמי, כל אחד מן המבקרין נוטל אחד מששים מן החולי שנשאר לחולה אחר שבקרו אותו שלפניו. ובבן גילו. שנולד המבקר במזלו של חולה. וחוזרות כולם וחולקות בשוה. שכיון שבבת אחת באו ליטול – אינו בדין שיהא חלקן של ראשונות יותר מן האחרונות.

באים

הגהות הב"ח

(א) גמ' שמש ירח בזבול: (ב) שם רב חלבו חלש נפק רב כהנא אכריז רב חלבו: (ג) רש"י ד"ה מאי איריא וכו' והרי מבקר אסור בנכסי חולה אלא כצ"ל והד"א ותיבת אין נמחק: (ד) ד"ה כעשורייתא וכו' ומוסיף ליבחר לבן והכי נמי גבי חולה מבקר הראשון: (ה) ד"ה וחוזרות וכו' אחריתי היא דהיכא:

תוספות

מתניתין קשיתיה. והוזקק להעמידה בנכסי מבקר אסורים על החולה: **ופקודת** כל אדם. שב"א מבקרין אותם:

פי' הרא"ש

מתני' קשיתיה. אמאי תני עומד אבל לא יושב דתרווייהו חיותיה נינהו וטעמא דעולא דקאמר משום דאפשר בעמידה לית ליה לשמואל: **רמז לביקור**

חולים מן התורה. פי' רמז מפורש דהא דדרשינן ליה [ב"ק ק. ב"מ ל:] מילתא כה אינו מפורש: **ערוך מאתמול.** היינו קודם שנברא העולם: **תפתה.** היינו גיהנם שכל המפתה בילדו נופל שם. ובקרא דקמיה כתיב בטרם הרים יולדו ותחולל ארץ ותבל: **בת הניזונית מן האחים.** בתנאי כתובה שכן כתב לה בנין נוקבן דיהווין ליכי מינאי כו': **נוטלת עישור נכסים.** לפרנסת נשואיה. **ובבן גילו.** שנולד במזלו: רב

במדבר טז | שם | משלי ח | תהלים צ | שם | בראשית ב | ישעיהו ל | תהלים צג | ירמיהו יז | תהלים עב | קהלת א | חבקוק ג | שם | נ"א מחליו

סנהדרין קי. ע"ש | פסחים נד. | [שם כ"ש ובפרש"י] | [סנהדרין קי. ע"ש] | שם | אבות פ"ב משנה א | [ב"מ ל:] | [ל"ל א"ל אביי לרבא] | כתובות סח.

[ל"ל תנא בקור חולים אין לו שיעור אפילו גדול אצל קטן ואפילו מאה פעמים ביום אמר ר"א ב"ח וכו']

רש"י

באיש. חלה. ואית דגרסי: באש. כאילו שופך דמים. מפני שבני אדם שנכנסין לבקרו עושים לו לחולה כל צרכיו. לא שיחיה ולא שימות. שהרי אינו יודע בעניינו של חולה. דלא ליתרע מזליה. דדילמא מתגלגלא לאלתר. אי נמי, דלא לישתעי מילי עילויה. מכאן ואילך. חזי דלא מתרפא – אמר להו. פוקו ואכריזו. ריעים כנעמן. שריפאוהו מצרעתו, כגון אלישע דהוה נביא וזקן והשיאו עצה לנעמן. אם יאמרו לך נערים בנה. בית המקדש. וזקנים אומרים סתור. ואל תבנה. וסימן לדבר מרחבעם. דכתיב (מלכים א יב) "ויעזוב את עצת הזקנים" וגו', ונחרב בית המקדש על אותה עצה. והמורה לא פירש בבית המקדש, ואיכא ברייתא *דקתני בהדיא בבית המקדש. לא לסעוד. כמו (במדבר טז) "ופקודת כל האדם" מתרגמינן: וסעודא. תלת שעי קמייתא רווחא דעתיה. כדאמר בעלמא (ב"ב טז:): אידלי יומא אידלי קצירא, ודילמא אמר לא אצטריך למבעי רחמי עליה, דאינו כל כך חולה. יסעדנו. כמו "ולחם לבב אנוש יסעד" (תהלים קד). ומנין שהשכינה כו' שנאמר ה' יסעדנו. קרי ביה יסערנו. אי נמי יסעדנו ממש, שמסעד שכינה על ראשו, כדאמרן בהדיא שהשכינה שרויה למעלה ממיטתו. סהדא רבה פרת. כשנהר פרת גדול הוי עדות לגשמים שיורדין לא"י, דא"י גבוה מכל הארצות, ובאין גשמים ונופלין בפרת ומתגדל מהן. והאי דאמרי' דנהר מתגדל ממי הגשמים, הוי פלוגתא אדשמואל. נהרא מכיפיה מתבר'. שנובע מגדותיו ולא ממי גשמי'. אלא

גמרא

תורה אור

רב חלבו באיש. לא איכא דקא אתי. אמר להו: לא כך היה: מעשה בתלמיד אחד מתלמידי ר' עקיבא שחלה. לא נכנסו חכמים לבקרו, ונכנס ר' עקיבא לבקרו, ובשביל שכיבדו וריבצו לפניו חיה. א"ל: רבי, החייתני. יצא ר' עקיבא ודרש: אכל מי שאין מבקר חולים – כאילו שופך דמים. כי אתא רב דימי אמר: כל המבקר את החולה – גורם לו שיחיה, וכל שאינו מבקר את החולה – גורם לו שימות. מאי גרמא? אילימא כל המבקר את החולה מבקש עליו רחמים שיחיה, וכל שאין מבקר את החולה מבקש עליו רחמים שימות – שימות ס"ד? אלא: כל שאין מבקר חולה – אין מבקש עליו רחמים לא שיחיה ולא שימות. *רבא, יומא קדמאה דחליש אמר להון: לא תיגלו לאיניש, דלא לתרע מזליה. מכאן ואילך אמר להון: פוקו ואכריזו בשוקא. דכל דסני לי ליחדי לי, וכתיב °"בנפל אויבך אל תשמח" *וגו', ודרחים לי ליבעי עלי רחמי. אמר רב: כל המבקר את החולה ניצול מדינה של גיהנם, שנאמר °"אשרי משכיל אל דל ביום רעה ימלטהו ה'" אין דל אלא חולה, שנאמר °"מדלה יבצעני", אי נמי מן הדין קרא °"מדוע אתה ככה דל בן המלך בבקר בבקר" וגו'. *אין רעה אלא גיהנם, שנאמר °"כל פעל ה' למענהו וגם רשע ליום רעה". ואם ביקר מה שכרו? מה שכרו?! כדאמר: ניצול מדינה של גיהנם! אלא מה שכרו בעוה"ז? °"ה' ישמרהו ויחיהו ואשר בארץ ואל תתנהו בנפש איביו". "ה' ישמרהו" – מיצר הרע, "ויחיהו" מן היסורין, "ואשר בארץ" – שיהו הכל מתכבדין בו, "ואל תתנהו בנפש איביו" – שיזדמנו לו ריעים כנעמן שריפאו את צרעתו, ואל יזדמנו לו ריעים כרחבעם שחילקו את מלכותו. תניא, *ר"ש בן אלעזר אומר: אם יאמרו לך ילדים "בנה" וזקנים "סתור" – שמע לזקנים, ואל תשמע לילדים. שבנין ילדים סתירה, וסתירת זקנים בנין. וסימן לדבר °רחבעם בן שלמה. אמר רב שישא בריה דרב אידי: בלא ליסעוד איניש קצירא לא בתלת שעי קדמייתא ולא בתלת שעי בתרייתא דיומא, כי היכי דלא ליסח דעתיה מן רחמי. תלת שעי קדמייתא – רווחא דעתיה, בתרייתא – תקיף חולשיה. *אמר רבין אמר רב: מניין שהקב"ה זן את החולה – שנאמר °"ה' יסעדנו על ערש דוי" וגו'. ואמר רבין אמר רב: מניין שהשכינה שרויה למעלה ממטתו של חולה – שנאמר "ה' יסעדנו על ערש דוי". תניא נמי הכי: גהנכנס לבקר את החולה לא ישב לא על גבי מטה, ולא ע"ג ספסל, ולא על גבי כסא, אלא מתעטף ויושב ע"ג קרקע, מפני שהשכינה שרויה למעלה ממטתו של חולה, שנאמר "ה' יסעדנו על ערש דוי". ואמר רבין *אמר רב: מטרא במערבא – סהדא רבה פרת. ופליגא דשמואל, דאמר שמואל: נהרא מכיפיה מתבריך. ופליגא דשמואל אדשמואל, דאמר שמואל: אין המים מטהרין בזוחלין אלא

ר"ן

באיש. חלה. אין מבקש עליו רחמים לא שיחיה ולא שימות. נראה בעיני דה"ק: פעמים שצריך לבקש רחמים על החולה שימות, כגון שמצטער החולה בחליו הרבה ואי אפשר לו שיחיה. כדאמרינן בפרק "הנושא" (כתובות קד.) דכיון דחזאי אמתיה דרבי דעל כמה זימנין לבית הכסא ואנח תפילין וקא מצטער, אמרה: יהי רצון שיכופו העליונים את התחתונים, כלומר דלימות רבי. ומש"ה קאמר דהמבקר חולה מועילו בתפלתו אפי' לחיות, מפני שהיא תפלה יותר מועלת. ומי שאינו מבקרו אין צריך לומר שאינו מועילו לחיות, אלא אפי' היכא דאיכא ליה הנאה במיתה, אפי' אותה זוטרתי אינו מהנהו. לא ליסעוד איניש. לא יבקר. "ופקודת כל האדם" מתרגמינן: וסיעדא. קצירא בתלת שעי קמייתא רווחא דעתיה. וכסבור המבקר שנתרפא ואין צריך לבקש רחמים עליו. בתרייתא תקיף חולשיה. וכסבור שהוא באפס תקוה, ומתיאש מן הרחמים. לא ישב לא על גבי מטה ולא על גבי ספסל. איכא מאן דאמר דדוקא כשהחולה שוכב על גבי קרקע, שנמצא מבקר גבוה ממקום שכינה. אמר ר' אבין אמר רב מטרא במערבא סהדא רבה פרת. כשיורד מטר בא"י מעיד עליו פרת בבבל. שכל שהוא גדול – בידוע שאע"פ שלא ירדו גשמים כאן – ירדו גשמים בא"י. ונפקא מינה שאסור לטבול בו, לפי שאין מי גשמים הנוטפין מטהרין בזוחלין אלא באשבורן, כלומר דקוו וקיימי. כדתניא בספרי: אי מה מעיין מטהר בזוחלין אף מקוה מטהר בזוחלין – ת"ל "אך מעין ובור", מעיין מטהר בזוחלין ומקוה באשבורן. הילכך, כל היכא דאיכא למיחש שמא רבו נוטפין על הזוחלין – אסור. והיינו כשהנהר גדול הרבה, אבל אם היה הולך לאטו, או שלא נתרבה אלא מעט, דליכא לספוקי ברביית נוטפין – שרי, כדתניא בתוספתא: העיד ר' אלעזר בר צדוק על הזוחלין שרבו על הנוטפין שהם כשרים. ופליגא דשמואל דאמר שמואל נהרא מכיפיה מתבריך. מכיפיה – מסלעו, כלומר ממקורו הוא מתגדל. שאע"פ שאנו רואים שכשהגשמים יורדין נהרות מתרבים – עיקר רבויין ממקורן הוא, כדאמרי' בפרק "סדר תעניות" (דף כה:): אין לך כל טפח וטפח יורד מלמעלה שאין תהום עולה לקראתו טפחיים, ונמצא שלעולם זוחלין רבין על הנוטפין, דהא לטפח של גשמים איכא טפחיים דמעיין. הילכך לשמואל מותר לטבול בנהרות לעולם, אפי' כשראה לעין שנתרבו הרבה מחמת המטר. ופליגא דידיה אדידיה דאמר שמואל אין המים מטהרין בזוחלין. דאיכא למיחש לרבו הנוטפין. אלא

מסורת הש"ס

[תוספתא ע"ז פ"א] · ברכות נה: · נ"ל ובבשלו אל יגל לבך פן יראה ה' וגו' והשיב מעליו אפו · [לעיל כב.] · תהלים מא · [מגילה לא: תוספתא ע"ז פ"א] · מלכים א יב · שבת יב: · תהלים מא · שבת סה: בכורות נה:

עין משפט נר מצוה

מב א מיי' פי"ד מהל' אבל הל"ד:
מג ב מיי' שם הל"ה סמג עשין מד"ס ב טוש"ע יו"ד סי' שלה סעי' ד:
מד ג מיי' שם הל"ו טוש"ע שם סעי' ג:

גליון הש"ס

גמ' לא לסעוד איניש. עיין רש"י שבת דף יב ע"ב ד"ה סועד וצ"ל דגרסי' כאן לא ליסעוד:

תוספות

לסעוד אם יבקר לחולה. פוקד מתרגמינן וסעד: רווח נפשיה. החולה וסבור המבקר החולה שכבר לו חליו ונמנע מלבקש רחמים: בתלת בתרייתא תקיף חולשיה. ומסית מלבקש רחמים עליו: סהדא רבה פרת. שרבו מימיו מן הגשמים.

פי' הרא"ש

רב חלבו באיש. פי' חלה כדאמרי' בבמה מדליקין (דף ל.) מן קדם באישא בשבת:

שכבדו ורבצו לפניו. לפני החולה בצווי רבי עקיבא כי הנכנס לבקר את החולה מפקח כל צרכיו ומחיהו: אינו מבקש עליו רחמים לא שיחיה ולא שימות. וזו היא רעה גדולה שאם היה מבקרו היה מבקש עליו רחמים ואפשר שעת רצון הוא ותהיה תפלתו נשמעת ומניעות הביקור גורם שימות: דלא ליתרע מזליה. דנפל תורא חדדו סכיני (שבת לב.) ואולי בבקשה מועטת שיבקש שונאו רעתו יתוסף חליו: משכיל אל דל. אליו לבקרו ולפקח בצרכיו: שריפאהו מצרעתו. שהשיאוהו עצה לטבול בירדן: רחבעם בן שלמה. שהשיאוהו עצה לומר אבי יסר אתכם בשוטים ואני בעקרבים: לא ליסעוד. לא לפקוד: רווחא דעתיה. שנתרפא ולא יתפלל עליו: תקיף חולשיה. וכבר הוא מסוכן שאין תפלתו מועלת לו: סהדא רבה פרת. כי מרוב גשמים שירדו בארץ ישראל גדל הנהר ורבה ורואין בני בבל ושמחים בטובת אחיהם: נהרא מכיפיה. מסלעו ומקדקדו מימיו גדלים כי רוב גדול הנהר מן התהום כדאיתא בתענית בפרק סדר תעניות (דף כה:) שאין לך טפח יורדת מלמעלה שאין לך טפחיים עולין כנגדה הילכך לא יגדל הנהר ממי גשמים שנופלים אחד: אין המים מטהרין בזוחלין. דחיישינן שמא רבו עליו נוטפים שמי גשמים רבו על עיקר מי הנהר ונתבטלו ברוב ולא אמר קמא קמא בטיל שכל דבר שדרכו ליגדל וגם גדל בלי הפסק לא אמר קמא קמא כמו שנבאר לקמן בפרק הנודר מן הירק (דף נח:) וכיון דאינו בטל נהפכו כולם לנוטפים ותנן במסכת מקואות (פ"ה מ"ה) הנוטפין כמקוה ומקוה אינו מטהר בזוחלין [כו'] ת"ל אך חלק מעיין מטהר ומקוה באשבורן אבל מעיין לא אימעט מאשבורן דתניא בתוספתא (מקואות פ"ה) מעיין שמימיו מועטים וריבה עליו והרחיבו מטהר באשבורן ותנן נמי (שם פ"ד מ"ה) כל הימים כמקוה והימים ממעינות הם טעמא דלשון מקוה משמע אשבורן ולא זוחלין כדכתיב יקוו המים אל מקום אחד אבל מעין בין זוחל בין עומד במקום אחד נקרא מעין ומ"מ אי לאו אך חלק הוה מקשינן מקוה למעין לטהר בזחילה:

אלא

מה א מיי' פ"א מהל' מקוואות הל' יא ופ"ט שם הל' יג סמג עשין רמח טוש"ע יו"ד סי' קלא סעי' לג וסי' רא סע' ב:

אֶלָּא פְּרָת בְּיוֹמֵי תִשְׁרֵי בִּלְבַד. *[א]אֲבוּהּ דִּשְׁמוּאֵל עֲבַד לְהוֹן מִקְוָואוֹת לִבְנָתֵיהּ בְּיוֹמֵי נִיסָן, וּמַפְּצֵי בְּיוֹמֵי תִשְׁרֵי.§ *ר' אַמִי אָמַר רַב: מַאי דִּכְתִיב °"וְאַתָּה בֶן אָדָם עֲשֵׂה לְךָ כְּלֵי גוֹלָה" (יחזקאל יב) – זוֹ נֵר וּקְעָרָה וְשָׁטִיחַ

רש"י

אֶלָּא פְּרָת בְּיוֹמֵי תִשְׁרֵי בִּלְבַד. דְּכָל יְמוֹת הַשָּׁנָה רָבִין נוֹטְפִין עַל הַזּוֹחֲלִין מִן הַגְּשָׁמִים שֶׁיּוֹרְדִין לְתוֹכוֹ, וּמִן הַשְּׁלָגִים שֶׁמִּתְפַּשְּׁרִין כָּל יְמוֹת הַחַמָּה. אֲבָל בְּתִשְׁרֵי כְּבָר פָּסְקוּ הַשְּׁלָגִים וְנִתְפַּשְּׁרוּ כּוּלָּן וְהָלְכוּ לָהֶן – מְטַהֲרִין הַזּוֹחֲלִין, וְאֵין בַּנְּהָרוֹת אֶלָּא מֵימָיו שֶׁנּוֹבְעִין בִּלְבַד. **אֲבוּהּ דִּשְׁמוּאֵל.** סְבִירָא לֵיהּ כְּאִידָךְ דִּשְׁמוּאֵל. וַעֲבֵיד לְהוּ לִבְנָתֵיהּ מִקְוָואוֹת בְּיוֹמֵי נִיסָן. לְפִי שֶׁבְּיוֹמֵי נִיסָן רָבִין נוֹטְפִין עַל הַזּוֹחֲלִין מֵחֲמַת הַגְּשָׁמִים, שֶׁהֲרֵי כָּל הַשְּׁלָגִים וְהַקֶּרַח (א) שֶׁנִּתְפַּשְּׁרוּ בָּאִין הַמַּיִם דֶּרֶךְ צִינּוֹרוֹת, דְּהָווּ לְהוּ שְׁאוּבִין. אֲבָל לֹא בָּאִין דֶּרֶךְ צִינּוֹרוֹת אֶלָּא מֵאֲלֵיהֶן שׁוֹטְפִין וּבָאִין – טוֹבְלִין בָּהֶן, כִּדְאָמַר: זָבָה וְנִדָּה וְיוֹלֶדֶת טְבִילָתָן בְּמֵי מִקְוֶה שֶׁל מ' סְאָה, וַאֲפִי' מֵי גְשָׁמִים מְכוּנָּסִים, שֶׁלֹּא מָצִינוּ מַיִם חַיִּים אֶלָּא לְזָב בִּלְבַד, שֶׁנֶּאֱמַר בּוֹ "מַיִם חַיִּים". וְהַמְפָרֵשׁ לֹא פֵּירֵשׁ הָכִי. וְלָאו דַּוְקָא, דְּכָל נָשִׁים בַּזְּמַן הַזֶּה זָבוֹת נִינְהוּ. **מַפְּצֵי בְּיוֹמֵי תִשְׁרֵי.** שֶׁבְּתִשְׁרֵי מִתְמַעֲטִין הַנְּהָרוֹת מִן כָּל יְמוֹת הַשָּׁנָה וּמַעֲלִין טִיט, וְהָיָה נוֹתֵן הַמַּפָּץ בְּקַרְקָעִית הַנָּהָר, שֶׁלֹּא יִכָּנֵס הַטִּיט בְּרַגְלֵיהֶן וִיהֵא חֲצִיצָה. **וְשָׁטִיחַ**

ר"ן

אלא פרת ביומי תשרי בלבד. לפי שאינו עת גשמים ולא זמן הפשרת שלגים. ולא למיסר כל הנהרות חוץ מפרת אתא, ולא למיסר נמי פרת בכל השנה אלא ביומי תשרי אתא. דכיון דכולא חששא משום שמא ירבו נוטפים על הזוחלין היא, כל שאנו בקיאים בפרת ביומי תשרי כמה היא עלייתו, וכן בשאר נהרות, ויודעין אנו בהם שלעולם אינו מתמעט משיעור כך ואפי' בעת יובש גדול, כל שאין אנו רואים בו כי אם אותו שיעור – למה נחוש לו? הא ליכא למיחש לשמא ירבו נוטפין על הזוחלין. אלא שמואל תרתי קמשמע לן; חדא – דנהרות שהן מכזבין מימיהן אין טובלים בהן לעולם, דכיון שפעמים שמכזבים – לעולם חוששין בהם לגשמים או להפשרת שלגים, וכדתנן במס' פרה (פ"ח מ"ט): המים המכזבין פסולין. אלו הם המים המכזבין – המכזבין פעם אחת בשבוע. והמכזבין בפולמוסיאות ובשני בצורת כשרין. והכי פירושו: דכל שמכזבין בלא טענה, אע"פ שאין מכזבים אלא לעתים רחוקות, פעם אחת בשבוע – פסולין, דחיישינן שמא מי גשמים הן, ואין מטהרין בזוחלין אלא באשבורן. אבל המכזבין מחמת טענה, כגון בפולמוסיאות ובשני בצורת – כשרין. ומש"ה קאמר שמואל שאין המים מטהרין בזוחלין אלא פרת וכיוצא בו, שאינו מכזב לעולם. ולמעוטי מים המכזבין הוא דקאמר פרת, ופרת וכיוצא בו קאמר. וקאמר נמי דבפרת וכיוצא בו שאינו מכזב – אינו מותר לטבול בו מן הסתם בכל השנה כולה מי שאינו בקי בו, אלא ביומי תשרי בלבד, לפי שביומי תשרי אינו עת גשמים ולא זמן הפשרת שלגים, ולפיכך אפי' מי שאינו בקי בו – אין לו לחוש שמא רבו עליו נוטפין. אבל אין ה"נ, דמי שבקי בפרת וכיוצא בו כל השנה, כל שהוא רואה שלא נתרבה על מה שהוא זוחל בתשרי בכדי שיהא ראוי לחוש לרבוי נוטפין – טובל בו בכל השנה. וכן נמי אם רואה בתשרי שנתרבה כל כך עד שאפשר לו לחוש שמא רבו בו נוטפין – אפי' בתשרי אינו טובל בו. אלא שמואל סתמא קאמר, דמי שאינו מכיר אפי' בנהרות שאין מכזבין – יש לו לחוש כל השנה ברבייתן, וביומי תשרי אין לו לחוש. כן נ"ל. וראיתי מי שכתב בהפך, ולא נראו לי דבריו. **אבוה דשמואל עביד להו לבנתיה מקוואות ביומי ניסן.** שמפני שהיה חושש להפשרת שלגים לא היה מניחן לטבול בזוחלין. **ומפצי ביומי תשרי.** בנהר היה נותנן תחת כפות רגליהן משום טיט, דלא ליהוי חציצה. א"נ – לצניעותא בעלמא. והיה מניחן לטבול בנהר משום דביומי תשרי ליכא למיחש *לזוחלין [נ"ל לנוטפין]. ומאי דקאמר ביומי ניסן – מניסן ועד תשרי קאמר, וכ"ש בימות הגשמים. כך פירשו. ואין הלשון נוח לי, דהוה ליה למימר: עביד להו מקוואות לבנתיה כולה שתא, ומפצי ביומי תשרי. לפיכך נ"ל דבנתיה דאבוה דשמואל בסתוא לא היו טובלות בנהר משום צנה, אלא במקוואות שבבתיהן. וביומי ניסן דרויח עלמא היו מתחילות לטבול בנהרות, והיה מתקן להם אביהם שם בתחילת ניסן מקוואות שהיו טובלות בהן עד תשרי. וביומי תשרי לא היה מצריכן למקוואות, משום דליכא למיחש לנוטפין, ולפיכך היה מתקן להן מפצי. וכשעוברין ימי תשרי – כבר היו חוזרות לטבול בבתיהם משום צנה. ולענין הלכה. פסק ר"ת כשמואל, דאמר נהרא מכיפיה מבריך. דאע"ג דרב פליג עליה, ורב ושמואל הלכה כרב באיסורי (בכורות מט:), ועוד דאבוה דשמואל נמי ס"ל כרב, ואידך דשמואל נמי פליגא אדידיה – אפ"ה קיימא לן כשמואל דתניא בבכורות בפ' "מעשר בהמה" (דף נה:): יובל שמו, ולמה נקרא שמו פרת – שמימיו פרין ורבין, דברי ר' מאיר. וחכ"א: פרת שמו, שמימיו פרין ורבין. מסייע ליה לשמואל, דאמר שמואל: נהרא מכיפיה מבריך. כלומר, דנהי דשמואל אמר הכי בכל הנהרות דמכיפייהו מברכי, והכא לא אמרינן הכי אלא בפרת – אפ"ה מסייע ליה. משום דכיון דפרת מבריך מכיפיה – כולהו נהרות נמי מכיפיה דפרת הם מתברכים, שהרי כל הנהרות מפרת הם נמשכים, כדאמרי' התם בבכורות (דף נה.): הנודר ממי פרת – אסור בכל מימות שבעולם, דאפי' עינותא דמדליין – סולמי דפרת ניהו. הילכך, ההיא מתני' מסייעא ליה לשמואל בין מדר' מאיר בין מדרבנן. דרבנן נמי אמרי פרת שמו, שמימיו פרין ורבין. וכיון דר' מאיר ורבנן מסייעי ליה – כותיה נקטינן. ונמצא לפי דעת זה שלעולם טובלים בנהרות, ואפי' כשמתברכין הרבה מחמת גשמים, לפי שאין טפח יורד מלמעלה שאין תהום עולה לקראתו טפחיים, זהו דעת ר"ת ז"ל. ומ"מ נ"ל שאף הוא ז"ל לא אמרה אלא בנהרות שאין מכזבין, אבל מכזבין – ליכא למימר בהו דמברכי מכיפייהו. אבל ר"ח והרב אלפסי ז"ל פסקו כרב וכאבוה דשמואל, דאין המים מטהרין בזוחלין אלא פרת ביומי תשרי בלבד. וקא יהיב הרמב"ן ז"ל טעמא למילתייהו, דאע"ג דאמר שמואל נהרא מכיפיה מבריך – לא דחינן מימרא דאיסורא דהוו נהיגין בה הלכה למעשה, כאבוה דשמואל דעבד לבנתיה מקוואות, משום מימרא דאגדתא. ושמואל נמי לאו לענין מעשה אמרה, דכיון דאיהו נמי אמר אין המים מטהרין בזוחלין – משמע דה"ק: נהי דמדינא שרי, להלכה למעשה איכא למיחש. °וכדאמר בעלמא: השתא דאמר שמואל אסור, ותנא דבי שמואל מותר – שמואל הלכה למעשה אתא לאשמועי'. ואע"ג דאמר: ופליגא דשמואל אדשמואל – היינו לומר דתרוייהו מימרי דשמואל לא קושטא אינון, אלא חדא מינייהו, דאי איתא לחדא – ליתא לאידך. אבל איהו לא פליג דידיה אדידיה, אלא מיחש הוא דחייש הלכה למעשה. וה"נ משמע בפ' "תינוקת" (נדה סז.) דמייתינן מילתא דאבוה דשמואל ולא מסיימינן עלה פלוגתא דבריה, אלמא שמואל נמי למעשה חייש. וכ"ת: אמאי חייש? כיון דר' מאיר ורבנן אמרי בברייתא דבכורות (דף נה:) דפרת מימיו פרין ורבין, ורב ואבוה דשמואל נמי, אמאי סברי דלאו מכיפיה מבריך? איכא למימר דאינהו ידעי דאיכא תנאי בעלמא דלא סבירא להו הכי. ועוד, דאיכא נסחי דלא גרסי במילתא דרבנן "שמימיו פרין ורבין", אלא, וחכ"א: פרת שמו, ותו לא. ולפי זה סייעתא דמייתי התם לשמואל – מדרבי מאיר הויא, לא מדרבנן. ואפ"ה שפיר דייק מדרבי מאיר, כיון דרבנן לא פליגי עליה בהדיא, לומר שאינו פרה ורבה. ורב ואבוה דשמואל סברי דרבנן פליגי עליה, ושמואל נמי מיחש הוא דחייש. **נמצא עכשיו** לפי דרך זה, שהנהרות המכזבין – אין טובלין בהן כלל, שלעולם חוששין להן למי גשמים והפשרת שלגים. ונהרות גדולים שאין מכזבין, כל שהוא בקי בהן ויודע עיקר המשכתן בימי תשרי – טובל בהן כל השנה, כל שהוא רואה שאין לחוש שנתרבו נוטפין על עיקר המשכתן. אבל כל שהוא רואה מתוך רבייתן שיש לחוש לכך – אפי' ביומי תשרי אין טובל בהן. ומי שאינו בקי בהן בכל השנה כולה – צריך לחוש להן, חוץ מיומי תשרי בלבד, שבתשרי מן הסתם אין נוטפין רבין עליהן. מיהו, איכא מאן דאמר דכי חיישינן לרבו נוטפין על הזוחלין – דוקא לטבול במקום שלא היתה שם זחילתו של נהר קודם לכן, אבל במקום שהיתה זחילתו מתחילה, אע"פ שעכשיו רבו נוטפין על הזוחלין – מותר לטבול בו. ומוכח לה מדתנן בפ"ק דמקוואות (משנה ז): מעיין שמימיו מועטין שרבו עליו מים שאובין – שוה למקוה לטהר באשבורן, ולמעיין להטביל בכל שהוא. ומדקתני שוה למקוה לטהר באשבורן – אלמא מקום יש בו שאינו מטהר בזוחלין, שאין עליו דין מעיין, אלא הרי הוא כמקוה שצריך אשבורן. והדר קתני: ולמעיין להטביל בו בכל שהוא. ובודאי מדקתני דשוה למעיין להטביל בו בכל שהוא – ה"ה דמטהר בזוחלין, כיון דתורת מעיין עליו, וקשיא רישא אסיפא! אלא ודאי ה"ק: מעיין זה שרבו עליו מים שאובין – מקומות יש בו שתורת מקוה עליהן וצריך אשבורן, והיינו אותן מקומות שהוא זוחל בהן עכשיו מחמת רבוי הנוטפין, ולא היה זוחל בו בתחילה. ומקומות יש בו שלא נשתנה דינו מכמו שהיה, אלא הרי הוא כמעיין להטביל בו בכל שהוא – והיינו אותו מקום שאפי' מתחילה היה זוחל בו. והאי דלא קתני: ולמעיין להטביל בו בזוחלין, אי נמי דליתני ברישא: שוה למקוה שצריך שיעור – נ"ל דתנא הכי לאשמועי' תרי דיני במקוה ובמעיין, ובכל חד מכלל חבריה משמע. דמדקתני רישא שוה למקוה לטהר באשבורן – מכלל שאותו מקום ששוה בו למעיין דקתני סיפא – אינו צריך אשבורן. ומדקתני סיפא ולמעיין להטביל בו בכל שהוא – דאותו מקום ששוה למקוה דקתני רישא – צריך שיעורא. ומכל מקום למדנו מזו שיש מקום במעיין, שאע"פ שנתרבה מחמת נוטפין – תורת מעיין עליו, והיינו המקום שהיה מהלך בו מתחילתו. והכי איתא בתוספתא (דמקוואות פ"ה) דקתני התם: מעיין שמימיו מועטין ורבו עליו והרחיבו

מטהר

מסורת הש"ס

כ"ה סז. שבת סה. בכורות נה:

[בעין יעקב איתא רבין (אמר רב) ובכן יתכן דצ"ל ואמר רבין אמר רב]

הגהות הב"ח

(א) רש"י ד"ה ועביד להו וכו' והקרח נתפשרו ובאין המים לדרך וכו' אבל אם לא באין:

גליון הש"ס

בהר"ן ד"ה ולענין הלכה וכו' וכדאמר בעלמא וכו'. שבת דף נד ע"א ביצה דף כט ע"א:

פי' הרא"ש

אלא פרת ביומי תשרי שהוא נהר גדול ואינו גדל אלא במטר מרובה אבל ביומי ניסן גדל פרת מרוב מטר של ימות הגשמים וכל נהרות קטנים גדלים אפילו ביומי תשרי ע"י מעט מטר ואי נהרא מכיפיה מבריך לא מיפסל הנהר ממי גשמים כי רוב גידול ממקורו **מקוואות ביומי ניסן.** לפי שנהר גדל מרוב גשמי החורף ורב הנוטפים: **ומפצי ביומי תשרי.** היו טובלות בנהר והיו בושות מהלכלוך סביבו' לצניעות א"נ תחת כפות רגליהם מפני הטיט שלא יחוצו: **נאד לשתות בו מים.** איכא דגרסי נר לתת בו שמן להאיר:

וְשָׁטִיחַ. °"בְּחֹסֶר כֹּל" — א"ר אַמִּי אָמַר רַב: בְּלֹא נֵר וּבְלֹא שֻׁלְחָן, רַב חִסְדָּא אָמַר: בְּלֹא אִשָּׁה, רַב שֵׁשֶׁת אָמַר: בְּלֹא שַׁמָּשׁ, רַב נַחְמָן אָמַר: בְּלֹא דֵּעָה. תָּנָא: בְּלֹא מֶלַח וּבְלֹא רְבָב. אָמַר אַבַּיֵי: *נָקְטִינַן, אֵין עָנִי אֶלָּא בְּדֵעָה. בְּמַעְרְבָא אָמְרִי: דְּדָא בֵּיהּ — כּוֹלָּא בֵּיהּ, דְּלָא דָּא בֵּיהּ — מַה בֵּיהּ, דָּא קָנֵי — מַה חָסֵר, דָּא לָא קָנֵי — מַה קָּנֵי. אָמַר ר' אֲלֶכְּסַנְדְּרִי א"ר חִיָּיא בַּר אַבָּא: אֵין הַחוֹלֶה עוֹמֵד מֵחָלְיוֹ עַד שֶׁמּוֹחֲלִין לוֹ עַל כָּל עֲוֹנוֹתָיו, שֶׁנֶּאֱמַר °"הַסֹּלֵחַ לְכָל עֲוֹנֵכִי הָרֹפֵא לְכָל תַּחֲלוּאָיְכִי". רַב הַמְנוּנָא אָמַר: חוֹזֵר לִימֵי עֲלוּמָיו, שֶׁנֶּאֱמַר °"רֻטֲפַשׁ בְּשָׂרוֹ מִנֹּעַר יָשׁוּב לִימֵי עֲלוּמָיו". °"כָּל מִשְׁכָּבוֹ הָפַכְתָּ בְחָלְיוֹ" — אָמַר רַב יוֹסֵף: לוֹמַר דְּמִשְׁתַּכַּח לְמוּדוֹ. רַב יוֹסֵף חֲלַשׁ, אִיעֲקַר לֵיהּ תַּלְמוּדֵיהּ, אַהַדְרֵיהּ אַבַּיֵי קַמֵּיהּ. הַיְינוּ דִּבְכָל דּוּכְתָּא אָמְרִינַן: *אָמַר רַב יוֹסֵף: לָא שְׁמִיעַ לִי הָדָא שְׁמַעֲתָא, א"ל אַבַּיֵי: אַתְּ אֲמַרְתָּהּ נִיהֲלַן, וּמֵהָא מַתְנִיתָא אֲמַרְתָּהּ נִיהֲלַן. כִּי הֲוָה גָּמֵיר ר' תְּלָת עַשְׂרֵי אַפֵּי הִילְכְתָא — אַגְמְרֵיהּ לְרַבִּי חִיָּיא שִׁבְעָה מִנְּהוֹן. לְסוֹף חֲלַשׁ רַבִּי, אַהֲדַר ר' חִיָּיא קַמֵּיהּ הָנְהוּ שִׁבְעָה אַפֵּי דְּאַגְמְרֵי', שִׁיתָּא אָזְדוּ. הֲוָה הַהוּא קַצְרָא, הֲוָה שְׁמִיעַ לֵיהּ לְרַבִּי כְּדַהֲוָה גָּרֵים לְהוּ, אֲזַל ר' חִיָּיא וְגָמַר יַתְהוֹן קַמֵּי קַצְרָא, וַאֲתָא וְאַהֲדַר יַתְהוֹן קַמֵּי רַבִּי. כַּד הֲוָה חָזֵי לֵיהּ רַבִּי לְהַהוּא קַצְרָא א"ל רַבִּי: אַתָּה עָשִׂיתָ אוֹתִי וְאֶת חִיָּיא. א"ד, הָכִי קא"ל: אַתָּה עָשִׂיתָ אֶת חִיָּיא, וְחִיָּיא עָשָׂה אוֹתִי. וא"ר אֲלֶכְּסַנְדְּרִי א"ר חִיָּיא בַּר אַבָּא: גָּדוֹל נֵס שֶׁנַּעֲשָׂה לַחוֹלֶה יוֹתֵר מִן הַנֵּס שֶׁנַּעֲשָׂה לַחֲנַנְיָה מִישָׁאֵל וַעֲזַרְיָה. שֶׁל חֲנַנְיָה מִישָׁאֵל וַעֲזַרְיָה — אֵשׁ שֶׁל הֶדְיוֹט, וְהַכֹּל יְכוֹלִים לְכַבּוֹתָהּ. וְזוֹ שֶׁל חוֹלֶה — שֶׁל שָׁמַיִם הִיא, וּמִי יָכוֹל לְכַבּוֹתָהּ? וא"ר אֲלֶכְּסַנְדְּרִי א"ר חִיָּיא בַּר אַבָּא, וְאָמְרִי לָהּ אריב"ל: כֵּיוָן שֶׁהִגִּיעַ קִיצּוֹ שֶׁל אָדָם — הַכֹּל מוֹשְׁלִים בּוֹ, שֶׁנֶּא' °"וְהָיָה כָל מֹצְאִי יַהַרְגֵנִי". רַב אָמַר: מִן הָדֵין קְרָא °"לְמִשְׁפָּטֶיךָ עָמְדוּ הַיּוֹם כִּי הַכֹּל עֲבָדֶיךָ". רַבָּה בַּר שֵׁילָא אֲמַרוּ לֵיהּ: שְׁכֵיב גַּבְרָא. גָּבוֹהַּ הֲוָה רָכֵיב גִּירְדוֹנָא זוּטְרָא, מְטָא תִּיתּוֹרָא אִיסְתַּוִיט, שָׁדְיֵיהּ וְקָא שְׁכֵיב. קָרֵי עַל נַפְשֵׁיהּ: "לְמִשְׁפָּטֶיךָ עָמְדוּ הַיּוֹם". שְׁמוּאֵל חַזְיֵיהּ לְהַהוּא (*קְרוֹקִיתָא דְּעַקְרַבָּא) יְתִיבָא עַל אַקְרוֹקְתָא וְעָבְרָה נַהֲרָא, טַרְקָא גַּבְרָא וּמָיֵית. קָרֵי עֲלֵיהּ "לְמִשְׁפָּטֶיךָ עָמְדוּ הַיּוֹם". אָמַר שְׁמוּאֵל: אֵין מְבַקְּרִין אֶת הַחוֹלֶה אֶלָּא לְמִי שֶׁחֲלָצַתּוּ חַמָּה. לְאַפּוּקֵי מַאי? לְאַפּוּקֵי הָא דְּתַנְיָא, ר' יוֹסֵי בֶּן פְּרָטָא אוֹמֵר מִשּׁוּם ר' אֱלִיעֶזֶר: אאֵין מְבַקְּרִין לֹא חוֹלֵי מֵעַיִים, וְלֹא חוֹלֵי הָעַיִן, וְלֹא מֵחוּשֵׁי הָרֹאשׁ. בִּשְׁלָמָא חוֹלֵי מֵעַיִים — מִשּׁוּם כִּיסּוּפָא, אֶלָּא חוֹלֵי הָעַיִן, וּמֵחוּשֵׁי הָרֹאשׁ מ"ט? מִשּׁוּם דְּרַב יְהוּדָה. דַּאֲמַר רַב יְהוּדָה: דִּיבּוּרָא קַשְׁיָא לְעֵינָא [א] וּמַעֲלֵי לְאִישְׁתָּא. אֲמַר רָבָא: הַאי אִישְׁתָּא, אִי לָאו דְּפַרְוָונְקָא דְּמַלְאֲכָא דְּמוֹתָא — מַעֲלֵי כְּחִיזְרָא

רש"י

וְשָׁטִיחַ. עוֹר לֶאֱכוֹל עָלָיו. בְּלֹא מֶלַח וּבְלֹא רְבָב. דְּמְלַפֵּת בְּהוּ. רְבָב. שׁוּמָּן. דְּדָא בֵּיהּ כּוּלָּא בֵּיהּ. מִי שֶׁיֵּשׁ בּוֹ דַּעַת – כְּמִי שֶׁיֵּשׁ בּוֹ הַכֹּל, שֶׁאֵינוֹ נֶחְסָר כְּלוּם. דָּא קָנֵי מַה חָסֵר. מִי שֶׁקָּנָה דַּעַת אֵינוֹ חָסֵר כְּלוּם. חוֹזֵר לִימֵי עֲלוּמָיו. דְּנַעֲשֶׂה כְּתִינוֹק שֶׁלֹּא טָעַם טַעַם חֵטְא. שֶׁנֶּא' רוּטֲפַשׁ. כְּלוֹמַר, כְּשָׁעָה רָטוֹב וּפָשׁ – כְּמוֹ ["פְּרוּ וּרְבוּ" מְתַרְגְּמִינַן] פּוּשׁוּ וּסְגוּ. מִנּוֹעַר. מִן הַחוֹלִי יָשׁוּב כְּמוֹ שֶׁהָיָה בִּימֵי עֲלוּמָיו. כָּל מִשְׁכָּבוֹ הָפַכְתָּ בְחָלְיוֹ. כָּל סֵדֶר הַלָּעַת לִמּוּדוֹ הַמְסוּדָּר לוֹ נֶהְפַּךְ לוֹ בְּחָלְיוֹ, וּמְשַׁכְּחוֹ. תְּלֵיסַר אַפֵּי הִלְכְתָא. שֶׁהָיָה שׁוֹנֶה לְמוּדוֹ בְּי"ג פָּנִים. שִׁיתָּא אָזְלוּ לֵיהּ. שֶׁשְּׁכָחָם. קַצְרָא. כּוֹבֵס. אַתָּה עָשִׂיתָ אוֹתִי וְאֶת חִיָּיא. דְּגָמַר לְהוּ, דְּכָל הַמְלַמֵּד אֶת בֶּן חֲבֵרוֹ תּוֹרָה מַעֲלֶה עָלָיו הַכָּתוּב כְּאִילּוּ עֲשָׂאוֹ, שֶׁנֶּאֱמַר "וְאֶת הַנֶּפֶשׁ אֲשֶׁר עָשׂוּ בְחָרָן" *. הַכֹּל מוֹשְׁלִין בּוֹ. לַהֲמִיתוֹ, אֲפִי' זְבוּב אֲפִילּוּ יַתּוּשׁ. לְמִשְׁפָּטֶיךָ עָמְדוּ הַיּוֹם (א) כֹּל עֲבָדֶיךָ. דְּכֵיוָן שֶׁנִּשְׁפַּט בִּישִׁיבָה שֶׁל מַעְלָה – הַכֹּל נַעֲשׂוּ עֲבָדָיו שֶׁל הקב"ה לִיפָּרַע הֵימֶנּוּ. גַּבְרָא גָּבוֹהַּ הֲוֵי רָכֵיב גִּירְדָּנָא זוּטָא. פִּרְדָּה קְטַנָּה. תִּיתּוֹרָא. גֶּשֶׁר. וְאִסְתַּוִיט. נִתְפַּחֲדָה הַפִּרְדָּה וְשַׁדְיֵיהּ מִינָּהּ וּשְׁכִיב. וְאע"פ שֶׁהַפִּרְדָּה נְמוּכָה וְאִיהוּ הָיָה אָרוֹךְ כָּל כָּךְ, דְּלֹא נָפַל אֶלָּא מְעַט – מֵת. אַקְרוֹקְתָא. לְצַפַרְדֵּעַ. וְעַקְרָב אֵינוֹ יָכוֹל לָשׁוּט בַּנָּהָר, וּנְשָׂאוֹ צְפַרְדֵּעַ עָלָיו לְהַעֲבִירוֹ בַּנָּהָר לִנְשׁוֹךְ אֶת הָאִישׁ. כִּי

ר"ן

מטהר באשבורן, ואין מטהר בזוחלין אלא עד המקום שהיה יכול להלך מתחילתו. והיינו נמי דתנן בפרק *ראשון דמקואות: מעיין שהוא מושך כנדל, רבה עליו מים והמשיכו – הרי הוא כמות שהיה. היה עומד, ורבה עליו והמשיכו – שוה למקוה לטהר באשבורן, ולמעיין להטביל בו בכל שהוא. וה"פ: מעיין שהיה מושך מעט מעט, כנדל זה שהוא שרץ קטן מרובה הרגלים, והמשיכו עכשיו בשטף, אבל אינו נמשך אלא באותו מקום שהיה מהלך בו מתחילתו – הרי הוא כמות שהיה. וסיפא קתני דאם היה עומד, כלומר שלא היה נמשך כלל, ורבה עליו והמשיכו – שני דינין יש בו; דבמקום שלא היה מהלך מתחלתו – שוה למקוה שצריך אשבורן, וה"ה שאין מטבילין בו בכל שהוא. ובמקום שהיה עומד מתחלתו – שוה למעיין להטביל בו בכל שהוא, ומינה שהוא מטהר בזוחלין. נמצא לפי דעת זה, שאפי' בזמן גשמים שהנהרות רבים – אדם טובל בנהרות שאינן מכזבין באותן מקומות שהן נמשכין והולכין אפי' ביומי תשרי. אבל באותן מקומות שנמשכים ומתרחבים יותר מהגשמים, כל היכא דאיכא למיחש שרבו הנוטפין על הזוחלין – אין טובלין בהם, אבל היכא שרבו זוחלין על הנוטפין, אפי' באותן מקומות שלא היה הולך שם מתחלתו – טובלין בו. והיינו ההיא דר"א בר צדוק שהעיד על הזוחלין שרבו על הנוטפין שכשרי', ומטהרין בזוחלין. ובודאי אפי' במקום שנתרבה קאמר, דאי באותו מקום בלבד שהיה מהלך מתחלתו – מאי אסהדתי'? פשיטא, דהיכי תיסק אדעתין ששנים או שלשה טיפי מים יפסלו פרת מלטבול בו? אלא ודאי כדאמרן. וזהו דעת הראב"ד ז"ל. אבל דעת הרמב"ם ז"ל. דכי קתני בכל הני דאע"פ שרבו עליו נוטפין דינו כמעיין – דוקא כשרבו המים בגומת המעיין עצמו, ששם הוא חשיבות מימיו, ומבטלים כל המים הבאים עליהם. אבל רבה במקום משך הנהר למטה, כל שרבו נוטפין על הזוחלין – נפסל כולו. ולפי זה אתיא מימרא דשמואל כפשטה, דאין המים מטהרין בזוחלין אפילו באמצע הנהר, במקום שהיה מהלך בו בתחלה, אלא פרת ביומי תשרי בלבד, וכפי מה שפירש' למעלה. ולפי זה הא דמפליג בתוספתא בין נתרחב ללא נתרחב – נ"ל דאריבה בגומת המעיין קאי, דאפי' הכי כל שרבו נוטפין אינו מטהר אלא במקום שהיה מהלך מתחלתו, אבל במקום שנתרחב – אינו מטהר אלא באשבורן. ואע"ג דאיכא למימר איפכא, דאריבה בהמשך הנהר קאי, אבל ריבה בגומת המעיין אפי' בנתרחב כשר מינקט לחומרא עדיף. ועוד: דמשמע דתוספתא אגומא דמתני' קיימא. מיהו, סהדותא דרבי אלעזר בר צדוק אפי' לפי שיטה זו, ודאי משמע דאפי' אמקום שנתרחב הנהר קאי, דכל שרבו זוחלין כשר. דליכא למימר דאריבה במקום משך הנהר קאי, ואשמעינן רבותא שאע"פ שלא ריבה במקום גומת המעיין אלא במקום שנמשכו מימיו כשר – דהאכתי פשיטא, וכי ג' טיפי מים יפסלו פרת? תנן במס' מקואות (פ"ה מ"ה): הנוטפין שעשאן זוחלין. כלומר שהמשיכן, סומך אפי' מקל ואפי' קנה ואפי' זב ואפי' זבה. כלומר, גודר בפניהם באלו, והוו להו כאשבורן, ומטהרין. ר' יוסי אומר: אין מזחילין בדבר המקבל טומאה. כלומר, אין עושין בו גדר, וקי"ל כר' יוסי. ותנן נמי (שם מ"ד) שהימים מטהרין בזוחלין, ותנן נמי (פרה מ"ח מ"ט ומקואות פ"א מ"ח): המים המוכין פסולין למי חטאת וכשרין לטבילה ומטהרין בזוחלין, ואלו הם המים המוכים – המלוחין והפושרין. ושטיח. עור לאכול עליו. ובלא רבב. שמן. דלא קני דעה מה קנה. מה יועיל לו כל מה שיקנה. חוזר לימי עלומיו. אחר שחלה ונתרפא מתחזק טבעו להיות יותר בריא ממה שהיה קודם חליו. שנאמר רוטפש. נוטריקון רטוב ופש. לומר דמשכח למודו. ימי עלומיו קדרים, מענין העלמה. אייקר ליה לימודיה. הכביד עליו למודו, ששכחו. תלת עשרי אפי. בי"ג פנים. קצרא. כובס. למשפטיך עמדו היום כי הכל עבדיך. כיון שלמשפטיך עמדו, שהגיע קצם למות – הכל עבדיך לקיים את דבר המשפט. שכיב ההוא גברא גבוה. אדם שהיה גבוה, כלומר ארוך. רכיב גירדונא זוטרא. רוכב פרדה קטנה. תיתורא. גשר. איסתויט. אחזתה רוח שטות לאותה פרדה, והשליכתו בנהר. איסתויט מלשון שטיא, רוח של שגעון, וכדאמר בעלמא: שיוטא הוא דנקטיה. אקרוקתא. צפרדע. שחלצתו. שלבשתו חמה, כאדם המזדיין, שע"י כלי זיין שעליו נקרא חלוץ. לאפוקי הא דתניא. דסבירא ליה לשמואל כי הך ברייתא דאין מבקרין להנך דקא מני, ודשמואל נמי לאפוקי הני. משום כיסופא. דזימנין שצריך לנקביו ומכסיף. דפרוונקא. שליח שעל ידו ממית. *כחיזרא לדיקלא. הוצין שסביב הדקל, ששומרים אותו מבהמות וחיות. תרייקא. מרקחת מועיל, וקורין לו תרייקא. חושלא דשערי. שעורים קלופים. דריש נפיא. בתחלת הרקדת הנפה. בורדם. תיבה אחת כשתי תיבות: בור דם, והוא חולי שמקלח דם מלמטה. אין מבקרין אותו. משום דזימנין דצריך לנקביו, ומכסיף ליה. ואין מזכירין שמו. לומר: פלוני חולה חולי בורדם, דלאו לשון נקיה הוא. רפואה

[פירושו תמצא בפרש"י עירובין ה. ד"ה והאמר]
[סנהדרין נט:]
[עירובין י. מח. סו: עג. פסו: מכות ד. נדה לט. סג.]
[נ"ל עקרבא וכ"ה בע"י ובילקוט]
[לע"ב]

דברים כח; תהלים קג; איוב לג; תהלים מא; בראשית ד; תהלים קיט

[נ"ל חמישי מ"ג]

מו א מיי' פי"ד מהל' אבל הלכה ה סמג עשין מד"ם ב טוש"ע יו"ד סי' שלה סעי' ח:

תוספות

שטיח. עור מבושל שאוכלין עליו ונושאין אותו עוברי דרכים עמם: דדא ביה. שיש בו דעה: דלא קני. דעה מה קני: הסולח לכל עוניכי הרופא לכל תחלואיכי: חוזר לימי עלומיו. דבריא החולה כשנתרפא יותר מלפני שחלה: תליסר אפי הלכתא. י"ג פנים של הלכות משנה: אתה עשית את חייא. כלומר למדת לו: למשפטיך. כלומר כשעמדו בריותיך למשפטיך הכל עבדים להביא עליהם מה שלוית: גברא רבה. אדם גדול: גירדנא זוטרא. פרד קטן: איטיוטי. נבעת. כמו *) קמא טיוטא נקטיה בבא קמא (דף לז:): אקרוקתא. צפרדע: שחלצתו חמה. שהחזיק חמימותו ועדיין הוא חולה:

*) לפנינו שם שיוטא

פי' הרא"ש

שטית. עור לישן עליו: דלא קני. דעה: שמשכח למודו. עלומיו קא דרש שנעלם ממנו למודו: תליסר אפי הילכתא. בי"ג פנים היה שונה הלכות: אתה עשית לחייא. כל המלמד חברו תורה [סנהדרין נט:] כאילו עשאו דכתיב ואת הנפש אשר עשו בחרן: ההוא גברא גבוה. אדם גדול וגבוה: רכיב גינדרונא זוטא. פרד קטן: אסתויט. נבהל כמו [יומא כב] חזא שיוטא בחלמיה: אקרוקתא. צפרדע: שחלצתו חמה: דיבורא קשיא לעינא. וכן נמי למיחוש הראש שטבע אחד להם: פרוונקא. שליח:

הגהות הב"ח

(א) רש"י ד"ה למשפטיך עמדו היום כי הכל עבדיך:

הגהות הגר"א

[א] גמ' קשיא לעינא ולאשתא כנ"ל (ועי' בפירוש הרא"ש):

כְּחִיזְרָא לְדִיקְלֵי, חַד לִתְלָתִין יוֹמִין, וְכִי תִּירַיְיקִי לְגוּפָא. רַב נַחְמָן בַּר יִצְחָק אֲמַר: לָא הִיא וְלָא תִּירַיְיקָה. *אֲמַר רַבָּה בַּר יוֹנָתָן אָמַר רַב יְחִיאֵל: עַרְסָן יָפֶה לַחוֹלֶה לִרְפוּאָתוֹ. מַאי עַרְסָן? אֲמַר ר' יוֹנָתָן: חוּשְׁלָא דְשָׂעֲרֵי עַתִּיקָתָא דְּרֵישׁ נָפְיָא. אֲמַר אַבַּיֵי: בָּעְיָין בִּישּׁוּלָא כְּעֵין בִּישְׂרָא דְתוֹרָא. רַב יוֹסֵף אֲמַר: סְמִידֵי דְשָׂעֲרֵי עַתִּיקָתָא דְּרֵישׁ נָפְיָא. אֲמַר אַבַּיֵי: בָּעְיָין בִּישּׁוּלָא כְּבִשְׂרָא דְתוֹרָא. א"ר יוֹחָנָן: בּוּרְדָּם אֵין מְבַקְּרִים, וְאֵין מַזְכִּירִין שְׁמוֹ. מ"ט? א"ר אֶלְעָזָר: מִפְּנֵי שֶׁהוּא כְּמַעְיָן הַנּוֹבֵעַ. וא"ר אֶלְעָזָר: לָמָּה נִקְרָא שְׁמוֹ בּוּרְדָּם — שֶׁהוּא כְּמַעְיָן הַנּוֹבֵעַ.§ "וּמְרַפְּאֵהוּ רְפוּאַת הַנֶּפֶשׁ" כו'.§ הֵיכִי קָתָנֵי? אִילֵימָא *דִּרְפוּאַת נֶפֶשׁ — בְּחִנָּם, רְפוּאַת מָמוֹן — בְּשָׂכָר, לִיתְנֵי הָכִי: מְרַפְּאֵהוּ בְּחִנָּם אֲבָל לֹא בְּשָׂכָר! [א]אֶלָּא: רְפוּאַת נֶפֶשׁ — גּוּפוֹ, רְפוּאַת מָמוֹן — בְּהֶמְתּוֹ. א"ר זוּטְרָא בַּר טוֹבִיָּה אָמַר רַב: אֲבָל אוֹמֵר לוֹ "סַם פְּלוֹנִי יָפֶה לָהּ, סַם פְּלוֹנִי רַע לָהּ".§

מתני' [ב]וְרוֹחֵץ עִמּוֹ בְּאַמְבָּטִי גְּדוֹלָה, אֲבָל לֹא בִּקְטַנָּה, וְיָשֵׁן עִמּוֹ בְּמִטָּה. ר' יְהוּדָה אוֹמֵר: [ג]בִּימוֹת הַחַמָּה, אֲבָל לֹא בִּימוֹת הַגְּשָׁמִים, מִפְּנֵי שֶׁהוּא מְהַנֵּהוּ. וּמֵיסֵב עִמּוֹ עַל הַמִּטָּה, וְאוֹכֵל עִמּוֹ עַל הַשּׁוּלְחָן, אֲבָל לֹא מִן הַתַּמְחוּי. אֲבָל אוֹכֵל הוּא עִמּוֹ מִן הַתַּמְחוּי הַחוֹזֵר.§

גמ' תַּנְיָא: *לֹא יִרְחַץ עִמּוֹ בְּאַמְבָּטִי, וְלֹא יִשַׁן עִמּוֹ בְּמִטָּה, בֵּין גְּדוֹלָה בֵּין קְטַנָּה, דִּבְרֵי רַבִּי מֵאִיר. רַבִּי יְהוּדָה אוֹמֵר: [ד]גְּדוֹלָה בִּימוֹת הַגְּשָׁמִים, וּקְטַנָּה בִּימוֹת הַחַמָּה — מוּתָּר. רוֹחֵץ עִמּוֹ בְּאַמְבָּטִי גְּדוֹלָה, [ה]וּמֵזִיעַ עִמּוֹ בִּקְטַנָּה. אֲבָל מֵיסֵב עִמּוֹ עַל הַמִּטָּה, וְאוֹכֵל עִמּוֹ עַל הַשּׁוּלְחָן, אֲבָל לֹא מִן הַתַּמְחוּי. אֲבָל אוֹכֵל *הוּא מִן הַתַּמְחוּי (ר"ל עמו) הַחוֹזֵר. א"ר יוֹסֵי בַּר חֲנִינָא: מִן הַתַּמְחוּי הַחוֹזֵר לבעה"ב.§

מתני' [ו]לֹא יֹאכַל עִמּוֹ מִן הָאֵבוּס שֶׁלִּפְנֵי הַפּוֹעֲלִים, וְלֹא יַעֲשֶׂה עִמּוֹ בְּאוּמָן, דִּבְרֵי רַבִּי מֵאִיר. וחכ"א: עוֹשֶׂה וְהוּא בְּרָחוֹק מִמֶּנּוּ.§

גמ' בְּקָרוֹב — לָא פְּלִיגִי דַּאֲסִיר, (א) כִּי פְּלִיגִי — בְּרָחוֹק; ר"מ סָבַר: גָּזְרִינַן רָחוֹק מִשּׁוּם קָרוֹב, דְּקָא מְרַפֵּי לָהּ לְאַרְעָא קַמֵּיהּ. [ז]וְרַבָּנַן סָבְרִי: לָא גָּזְרִי'.§

מתני'

רש"י

כי חיזרא לדיקלא. כמו האטד שמקיף הדקל ומגין לפירות, שאין יכולים למשמש בו – כך מגינה על גופו של אדם. תורייקי. תירייק"א בלע"ז. חושלא דשערי. שעורים ישנים קלופים. דריש נפה. שמדוקקין בנפה ובכברה כשמרקדין בהן. בורדם. בסמ"ך, שילשול גדול שיוצא כל שעה, כמעיין הנובע שאין לו שוליים ויצאו ממנו כל המים. ואית דאמרי בורדס בסמ"ך – כמו בור שנובע דם. ואית דאמרי: מכה שקורין בו"ן מלנ"ט, שיוצא נמי הימנו דם. מפני שהוא כמעיין הנובע. שקופץ מזה לזה, ויש בו סכנה להזכירו. [היכי קתני]. מתני' ומרפאו רפואת נפש? בחנם. כלומר, שאין לו הנאה אלא שמחזיק לו טובה בנפשו. רפואת נפש [גופו]. שאם חלה המדיר מותר למודר לרפאותו, כדאמרינן לעיל דלא אדריה מן חיותיה. רפואת ממון בהמתו. שאם חלתה בהמתו אסור לרפאותה, משום דקמהני ליה. אבל אומר לו כו'. דאמירה ולא כלום היא. מתני' ורוחץ עמו. המודר עם המדיר. אבל לא בקטנה. משום דקא מפשי מיא מיניה, ומפיש נמי הבלא. אבל לא מן התמחוי. ביחד, מפני שמרבה בעל הבית בשבילו. אבל אוכל הוא מן התמחוי החוזר לבעל הבית. כדמפרש בגמרא, שדרכן לאכול מעט ומחזירו לבעל הבית, שיש להן מאכילין הרבה. וכיון דאין אוכל אלא מעט ומחזיר המותר – לא מיתהני מיניה כלום, אפי' אם אוכל חבירו פחות הימנו – לא מיתהני, דהא אינו אוכל אלא מעט והמותר מחזיר. ע"א: לא יאכל עמו מן התמחוי – דדרך בני הסעודה לאחר שאכלו כפי שובען מצניעין המותר ונושאים עמם לבתיהן. דהתם לא יאכל עמו, דשמא אחד מהן אוכל פחות מחבירו, ולכשיביאו מותרן לבתיהן חולקין בשוה, ונמצא זה משתכר במה שאכל חבירו פחות ממנו. אבל אם דרך בני הסעודה לאחר שאכלו מחזירין מותרן לבעל הבית, ושוב אין מוסיפין בקערות – מותר לאכול עמו. מתני' לא יאכל עמו מן האבוס שלפני הפועלים. כלי גדול שנותן בו בעל הבית ירקות שאוכלין בו הפועלים יחד, ומשום טעם דתמחוי. ולא יעשה עמו באומן. שלא יעמוד עמו במענה אחת מפרש בגמ'. גמ' דקא מרפי לה לארעא קמיה. ונוח לו לחרוש אחריו. בקרוב כ"ע לא פליגי דאסור. לעדור, (ב) דקא מרפיא כו'.

מתני'

ר"נ

רפואת נפש בחנם. ונפש דקתני – פירושו רצון, כדאמרינן "אם יש את נפשכם" (בראשית כג), כלומר שמרפאהו ברצון לבו ולא בשכר. ומתוקמא מתני' בנכסי חולה אסורין על הרופא. אלא רפואת נפש גופו. ומתוקמא בנכסי רופא אסורים על החולה, ומשום הכי לא ירפא בהמתו. וכשיש שם רופא אחר, דאי לא – שרי לרפאותה, °דהא תנן: מחזיר לו אבידתו, ואין לך השבה גדולה מזו. אלא ודאי כשיש רופא אחר עסקינן. ואפילו הכי מרפאהו רפואת נפש, דהיינו גופו, לפי שלא מן הכל אדם זוכה להתרפאות. והכי איתא בירושלמי. אבל אומר לו סם פלוני יפה לה סם פלוני רע לה. דכיון דאיהו לא יהיב ההוא סם עליה – שרי, דהנאה ממילא אתיא. ומינה, דברפואת גופו אפילו לשום הסם בידיו – שרי. ומיהו, דוקא שיהא משל מודר, אבל משל מדיר – לא, דאפילו היכא דאין לו למודר ממה שיתרפא, דמצוה קא עביד – אפי' הכי, כיון דיהיב ליה מדיליה מיד ליד – אסור. כי ההיא דמודר הנאה מחבירו* דבעי שיניח על גבי הסלע, אבל לא שיתן מידו לידו ממש, וכמו שכתבתי למעלה (דף לט:). ומיהו, היכא דחולה אסר על עצמו נכסיו של רופא – אפשר דאפילו הסם של רופא שרי, °דמן חיותיה לא אדריה. מתני' ורוחץ עמו באמבטי גדולה. שכיון שהיא גדולה אין המים עולין על זה בשביל חבירו. אבל לא באמבטי קטנה, שמתוך שהיא קטנה כשרוחץ עמו – מעלה המים עליו, ומהנהו. רבי יהודה אומר בימות החמה. מילתא דתנא קמא מפרש ואזיל, דכי קאמר וישן עמו במטה – דוקא בימות החמה, שאינו נהנה בחימומו, אבל לא בימות הגשמים, מפני שהוא מחממו ומהנהו, כדכתיב (קהלת ד) "אם ישכבו שנים וחם להם". ומיסב עמו על המטה. אפי' בימות הגשמים, דבכי האי גוונא ליכא חימום. ואוכל עמו על השולחן. ולא גזרינן דילמא אכיל ממנתיה דחבריה. אבל לא מן התמחוי. אם נותנים לשניהם קערה ביחד, שאם האחד אוכל מעט והשני הרבה – נמצא מהנהו משל חבירו. אבל אוכל עמו מן התמחוי החוזר. שחוזר לבעל הבית, שהתמחוי גדול כל כך שאין יכולין לאכול כל מה שבתוכו, ומותרה חוזר לבעל הבית. ובכי האי גוונא לא מתהני חד מחבריה. לא יאכל עמו מן האבוס של פועלים. קערה גדולה שנותנין לפני הפועלים, שמתוך שהם עמלים אוכלין הרבה ואוכסין אותן כבהמות, ומש"ה נקרא אבוס. ואם אחד מהם אוכל מעט – נמצא מהנה את חבירו. ולפי שאין הפועלין מחזירין מן האבוס שלהם לבעל הבית לא תנא שריותא באבוס החוזר. באומן. חורש הכרם. ומש"ה לא יעשה עמו, שכשהוא חופר לפניו את הקרקע – מהנהו, דקא מרפי לה לארעא. ואפילו רחוק ממנו אסר ר"מ, דגזר רחוק משום קרוב, כדאיתא בגמרא. וחכ"א עושה הוא רחוק ממנו. דלא גזרי רחוק אטו קרוב. גמ' תניא לא ירחץ עמו באמבטי ולא ישן עמו במטה בין גדולה בין קטנה. אתרוייהו קאי, דגזר רבי מאיר באמבטי גדולה אף על גב דלא מהני ליה – אטו קטנה דמהני ליה, וגזר נמי במטה בין גדולה בין קטנה ואפילו בימות החמה – אטו קטנה בימות הגשמים דמהני ליה. ור' יהודה פליג בתרוייהו, דגדולה אפילו בימות הגשמים שרי, דלא גזרינן אטו קטנה. וקטנה נמי, נהי דבימות הגשמים אסור – בימות החמה שרי, דלא גזרינן ימות החמה אטו ימות הגשמים. ומהא משמע דרבי יהודה דאמר במתניתין: בימות החמה אבל לא בימות הגשמים – פירושי קא מפרש מאי דקתני ברישא וישן עמו במטה, וכולה מתני' כר' יהודה אתיא, דאי לא תימא הכי – הא דקתני סתמא "וישן עמו במטה" מני? לא ר"מ ולא ר' יהודה. אלא ודאי כדאמרינן. אבל לא מן התמחוי. שאוכלין בקערה אחת, וחוששין שמא ימשוך ידו מלאכול לכבוד חבירו, ונמצא מהנהו. החוזר לבעל הבית. שיש בו כל כך שמותרו חוזר לבעל הבית. בקרוב כ"ע לא פליגי דאסור. דמהני ליה לחבריה, דמרפי ארעא קמיה כשחופר סמוך לו, ואין הלה צריך לחפור בכח גדול. כי פליגי ברחוק. דכיון שהוא רחוק ממנו – לא מרפי ליה לארעא.

מתני'

עין משפט נר מצוה

מז א מיי' פ"ו מהל' נדרים הל' ח ט טוש"ע יו"ד סי' רכא סעי' ז:

מח ב ג ד ה ו ז מיי' שם הלכה ט טוש"ע שם סעי' ה:

הגהות הב"ח

(א) גמ' בקרוב לא פליגי לאסיר דקא מרפי לה לארעא קמיה כי פליגי ברחוק ר"מ סבר גזרינן רחוק משום קרוב ורבנן סברי כצ"ל: (ב) רש"י ד"ה בקרוב כ"ע וכו' לעדור הס"ד ותיבות דקא מרפיא כו' נמחק ואח"כ נ"ל ד"ה דקא מרפיא:

[לקמן מג.]

גליון הש"ס

בהר"נ ד"ה אלא רפואת כו' דהא תנן וכו'. תמיהני הא שם אין הטעם דמשום מצוה רשאי ליהנות אלא משום דנותן לו את שלו ומונע רק לאחרים ליטלו והוי מבריח ארי ולא מקרי מהנהו וזה שייך באבידה דבהשבתו אינו מבריח להאבידה עצמה אלא דמונע אחרים ליטלו אבל הכא דבהמתו חולה והוא מרפא אותה ומבריח נכסיו ועדיף ממפטם בהמתו ואסור וצ"ע: בהר"נ ד"ה אבל אומר לו וכו'. למן חיותיה וכו'. כדלעיל דף לט ע"א:

תוספות

כי חיזרא לדקלא. שחריות שסביב לדקל מגין עליו כדקל בלע"ז טורק"א: דריש נפיא. סולת של שעורים: ואין מזכירין שמו. לפי שמתבייש החולה כשמזכיר: בור דם בור נובע דם מתחתונים: אילימא רפואת נפש בחנם. מיירי בנכסי חולה אסורין על הרופא לכך שכר אסור: אלא רפואת נפש גופו. ומיירי בנכסי רופא אסורים על החולה ורפואת גופו מותרת בנוטלין עליו שכר ומצוה קעביד: רפואת ממון בהמתו. דלא מצוה קעביד הא קמהני ליה אף כי אין נוטלין עליהן שכר ולא הוה כמו מחזיר אבידתו דמצוה להשיב לו אבידתו אבל אינו מצוה לרפא לו בהמתו: אבל אומר לו סם פלוני יפה לה. דדיבור שרי לאחווי ולהנאתו מדיבורו וי"א רפואת נפש גופו דמיירי שנכסי חולה אסורין על הרופא ושרי לכנוס בביתו דמן חיותו לא אדריה אבל לא רפואת בהמתו דמתהני מדריסת הרגל ואפי' גבי צורך בהמתו אדריה כדאמרי' לעיל אבל אומר לו לא בבית אלא בשוק ולפי' ראשון ניחא טפי דלפי' זה אמאי נקט אומר אפי' לרפואת בהמתו בידוע שלא בביתו שרי ותו דמאי לפלוגי בין גופו לרפואת בנו: תניא לא ירחץ בין בגדולה בין בקטנה. קאי אאמבטי: גדולה. אם בימות הגשמים וכ"ש בימות החמה וקטנה בימות החמה אבל לא בימות הגשמים: מזיע בקטנה. שמאחר שאינו אלא מזיע לא מיתהני מיניה: מן התמחוי החוזר לבעל הבית. פי' במתני': בקרוב כ"ע לא פליגי לאסור. דמרפה ליה ארעא קמיה וניחא לחפור בה יותר:

מסורת הש"ס

[יומא מז.]

[ע"ז כח.]

[תוספתא פ"ב ע"ש]

פי' הרא"ש

כי חיזרא לדיקלא. כיון הגדל סביב הדקל ומגין על הדקל: כתריייקי לגופא. טריאקה היא סם [illegible]: חושלא דשערי. שעורים קלופים: אין מזכירים שמו. שלא יתבייש החולה: רפואת נפש בחנם. שאדם עושה מנפשו ומרצונו בלא קבלת שכר [דמצוה] קא עביד ולא מהני ליה כיון דאין נוטל עליה שכר: רפואת נפש גופו. ובנכסי רופא אסורין על החולה דמצוה קא עביד ואף נוטלין עליה שכר: רפואת ממון בהמתו. דלא מצוה קא עביד וקא מהני ליה אף אם אין נוטלין עליה שכר ולא הוי כמחזיר אבידתו שהתורה לא צותה לרפאות בהמה של חבירו: מתני' רי"א באמבטי גדולה אבל לא באמבטי קטנה. ר"י בא לפרש דברי ת"ק אבל לא בקטנה אם אמבטי של מים המים מתרבין בשבילו ואם אמבטי של זיעה מרבין לו חום בשבילו: ומיסב עמו במטה. ולא חיישינן שמא יישן אצלו: ואוכל עמו על השולחן. ולא חיישי' שמא יאכל עמו דכיון שהדירו מסתמא שונאין זה את זה טפי משני אכסנאין על שולחן א' זה בשר וזה גבינה: מן התמחוי החוזר. מפרש בגמרא: אבוס של פועלין. כלי גדול כאבוס של בהמה אע"פ שיש בו מאכל הרבה לא יאכל עמו: לא יעשה עמו באומן. בשורת הכרמים לא יחפור עמו מפני שהוא מרפה את הקרקע ומהנהו: גמ' גדולה בימות הגשמים. מותר ש[illegible] ואין מחממו וקטנה בימות החמה מותר מפני שהוא מצטער מפני החום: ומזיע עמו בקטנה. דבזיעה בעלמא אין תוספת חום: התמחוי החוזר לבעל הבית. לאחר שאכלו מה שבקערה מחזירין אותה לבעה"ב וממלא אותה עד שיאכלו כל שבעם הלכך אפילו אוכל יותר מחבירו אינו נהנה משל חבירו דבלאו הכי נותנין להם כל שבעם:

מתני'

מתני' אהמודר הנאה מחבירו לפני שביעית אינו יורד לתוך שדהו, ואינו אוכל מן הנוטות. ובשביעית – אינו יורד לתוך שדהו, אבל אוכל הוא מן (א) הנטיעות הנוטות. בנדר הימנו מאכל לפני שביעית – יורד לתוך שדהו ואינו אוכל מן הפירות, ובשביעית – יורד ואוכל.§ **גמ'** רב ושמואל דאמרי תרווייהו: (ב) "נכסים אלו עליך" לפני שביעית – אין יורד לתוך שדהו, ואינו אוכל מן הנוטות, אע"פ שהגיע שביעית. ואם בשביעית נדר – אין יורד לתוך שדהו, אבל אוכל מן הנוטות. ור' יוחנן וריש לקיש דאמרי תרווייהו: "נכסי עליך" לפני שביעית אין יורד לתוך שדהו ואין אוכל מן הנוטות, הגיע שביעית – אינו יורד לתוך שדהו, אבל אוכל הוא את הנוטות. לימא בהא קמיפלגי, דרב ושמואל סברי: *אדם אוסר דבר שברשותו אפילו לכשיצא מרשותו, ורבי יוחנן ור"ל סברי: אין אדם אוסר דבר שברשותו לכשיצא מרשותו? ותסברא? מי איכא למ"ד אין אדם אוסר דבר שברשותו לכשיצא מרשותו? (ג)א"כ ניפלגי ב"נכסים אלו", וכ"ש ב"נכסי"! ותו: הא תנן דאדם אוסר דבר שברשותו לכשיצא מרשותו. דתנן: *גהאומר לבנו "קונם שאתה נהנה לי", מת – יירשנו, "בחייו ובמותו", אם

רש"י

מתני' המודר הנאה מחבירו לפני שביעית. שהדירו חבירו קודם שנכנסה שביעית. אין יורד לתוך שדהו. לאכול מפירות שביעית, דאסור בדריסת הרגל. ואין אוכל מן הנוטות. מאותן פירות הנוטין חוץ לשדה, שיכול ליקח מהן, ואינו צריך ליכנס בתוך השדה. ואע"ג דהן שביעית – לא יאכל מהן, כדאמרינן בגמרא: אדם אוסר דבר שברשותו אפילו לכשיצא מרשותו. והאי נמי, כיון דלפני שביעית הדירו חבירו, כי אתי נמי שביעי' – אסור בהן. ובשביעית. אבל אם הדירו בשביעית – לא יורד לתוך שדהו. אבל אוכל הוא מן הנוטות. הואיל ולא הוי ברשותו השתא כי מדיר ליה. ובגמרא מפרש אמאי אינו יורד, ואמאי אוכל, הא ארעא נמי דהפקר היא! נדר הימנו מאכל לפני שביעית. אבל לא נדר הימנו הנאה, לכי מטי שביעית – יורד ואינו אוכל, דהא לא הדירו אלא מן מאכל. אבל אינו אוכל, כדפרישית לעיל, דאדם אוסר דבר שברשותו אפי' לאחר שיצא מרשותו. ובשביעי'. הדירו בשביעי'. יורד ואוכל. דעכשיו יצא מרשותו. ואית דמפרש: המודר הנאה מחבירו לפני שביעית לא ירד לתוך שדהו לפני שביעית ולא יאכל מן הנוטות – כיון דהדירו. ובשביעית, כלומר אם הגיעה שביעית – לא ירד לתוך שדהו כו'. ולישנא קמא עיקר. **גמ'** דאמרי תרווייהו נכסי אלו עליך. כלומר, כל נכסי עליך בכל מקום שהן. ואין אוכל מן הנוטות. ואע"פ שהגיע שביעית, ושל הפקר הן. ואם בשביעית נדר. דהשתא לאו ברשותו הוא, ולא מצי מדיר ליה מינייהו – אוכל מן הנוטות. ר' יוחנן ור"ל דאמרי. הגיע שביעית אין יורד, אבל אוכל מן הנוטות. **אדם אוסר דבר שברשותו אפילו לכשיצא מרשותו.** דכיון דבשעה שאסר הוין ברשותיה, אפילו לכי הגיע שביעית נפקן מרשותיה – אפילו הכי אסורין עליו. ר' יוחנן ור"ל סברי אין אדם כו'. ומשום הכי, כי הגיע שביעית, דנפקא מרשותיה – אוכל הוא מן הנוטות. ותסברא. דבהאי טעמא פליגי. ומי איכא למ"ד אין אדם אוסר כו'. ור' יוחנן ור"ל הכי סבירא להו: (ד) אם כן. דמשום האי טעמא פליגי, ואמרי דאוכל הוא בשביעית. ליפלגי בנכסים אלו. אפי' היכא דאמר "נכסים אלו עליך", ולימרו ר' יוחנן ור"ל דאוכל בשביעית משום הטעם (ה) דאמר, אין אדם אוס' דבר שברשותו לכשיצא מרשותו, כ"ש היכא דאמ' "נכסי", דמשמע כל זמן שהן ברשותו! אלא מדלא פליגי ב"נכסים אלו" אלא ב"נכסי" – ש"מ דלית להו האי סברא. ועוד: היכי מצי אמר לעולם דאין אדם אוסר דבר שברשותו לכשיצא מרשותו? והתנן דאוסר! האומר לבנו קונם שאתה נהנה לי. כלומר, שאי אתה נהנה לי מכל נכסי. מת יירשנו. שלא אסר עליו אלא כל זמן שהנכסים שלו, לפיכך יירשנו אם

ר"נ

מתני' לא ירד לתוך שדהו. של מדיר, דמודר אסור אפי' בדריסת הרגל, כדתנן לעיל (דף לג:). ואינו אוכל מן הנוטות. מן הפירות הנוטות על הדרך סמוך לשדה. ובשביעית לא ירד לתוך שדהו. ואי בשביעית נדר – לא ירד וכו'. ובגמרא מפרש לה. **גמ'** ואף על גב שהגיע שביעית. דקסברי רב ושמואל דאע"ג דכולהו פירי דהפקרא אינון, אפילו הכי, כיון שבשעה שהדירו היו שלו – חייל איסורא אפי' בשביעית, שילאו מרשותו. ומתני' תרי דיני קתני; רישא אשמעינן דכיון שהדירו לפני שביעית – חייל נדריה אפילו כי מטא שביעית. וסיפא אשמעינן דאם בשביעית נדר, נהי דלא חייל נדריה לגבי פירי, דהפקרא נינהו – לגבי ארעא מיהא חייל, וכדמפרש בגמרא טעמא לקמן. ור' יוחנן ור"ל דאמרי תרוייהו וכו' **אבל אוכל מן הנוטות.** ולא מתסר בהו משום נדרא דמקמי שביעית. **לימא בהא קמיפלגי דרב ושמואל סברי אדם אוסר** וכו' **ור' יוחנן ור"ל סברי אין אדם אוסר** וכו'. נראה לי דהכי פירוש' דשמעתא: דקא סלקא דעתין השתא דרב ושמואל ורבי יוחנן ור"ל כולהו אפירושא דמתניתין קיימי. רב ושמואל מפרשי לה כדפרישית. ור' יוחנן ור"ל מפרשי לה דחדא קתני, וכולה כשהדירו לפני שביעית. וקאמר דנדר זה שני דינין יש לו; דלפני שביעית – חייל נדרא לגמרי, שאינו יורד ואינו אוכל. אבל כשהגיע שביעית – הותר מקצתו, דנהי דאינו יורד בתוך שדהו משום דארעא אכתי ברשותי' קיימא, כדפרישי' טעמא לקמן – אפ"ה פירי שרו, דהא בשביעית נפקי מרשותיה. ואע"פ שהדירו בשעה שהיה ברשותו, דהיינו לפני שביעית, סברי ר' יוחנן ור"ל דאין אדם אוסר דבר שברשותו לכשילא מרשותו. ונהי דרישא לא אשמעינן מידי, דפשיטא דלפני שביעית אינו יורד ואינו אוכל – סבירא להו דנקט רישא משום סיפא, לאשמעינן דאע"פ שהדירו לפני שביעית, שהיו פירות ברשותו – אין איסורו חל לאחר שילאו מרשותו, דהיינו בשביעית. ומש"ה הוה סליק אדעתיה דר' יוחנן ור"ל סברי דאין אדם אוסר דבר שברשותו לכשילא מרשותו, אפילו היכא דאמר "נכסים אלו". א"נ, אפילו היכא דאמר בהדיא שהוא אוסר אותם אפילו לאחר שילאו מרשותו. והוה סבירא לן הכי אע"ג דר' יוחנן ור"ל לא איירו אלא "בנכסי" משום דבשלמא אי אמרינן דרי יוחנן ור"ל אמרי הכי ב"נכסים אלו" – איכא למימר דתנא רישא משום סיפא, וכדפרישית. ואע"ג דאמרי ר' יוחנן ור"ל "נכסי" – לאו דוקא דאמר "נכסי" בלחוד, אלא א"נכסים אלו" דאמרי רב ושמואל קיימי, ד"נכסים אלו" דינו כ"נכסי", וכמו שנפרש לפנינו. דאם איתא דר' יוחנן ור"ל דוקא ב"נכסי" קא אמרי – א"כ מה אשמעינן תנא דמתניתין? רישא ודאי לא צריכא לאשמעינן דלפני שביעית חייל נדרא לגמרי, וכי תימא: משום סיפא נקט לה, לאשמעינן דכיון דמעיקרא אמר "נכסי" – כשהגיע שביעית הותר מקצתו של נדר זה, דהיינו לענין אכילה – הא נמי לא צריכא לאשמעי', דפשיטא דבלשון "נכסי" לא משמע אלא בעוד שהיו ברשותו, דגדולה מזו שנינו בפירקא דלקמן (דף מו.), ומייתינן לה בסמוך בשמעתין: האומר לחבירו "קונם לביתך שאני נכנס, שדך שאני לוקח", מת או שמכרו לאחר – מותר. וכיון דאפילו גבי נודר, דליכא לספוקי דמאי אוסר אנפשיה נכסי חבירו אפילו לאחר שילאו מרשותו, אמרינן דכי אמר "ביתך" לא משמע אלא בעוד שהוא שלו, כ"ש לגבי מדיר דאיכא לספוקי אי מאי אסיר לבתר שילאו מרשותו, דפשיטא מילתא דבלשון "נכסי" אינו אוסר אלא בעודן ברשותו. דודאי כי אמר נודר "ביתך" או "נכסיך" וכי אמר מדיר "ביתי" או "נכסי" – לשונות שוין הן. הלכך, אם איתא דר' יוחנן ור"ל דוקא ב"נכסי" אמרי דאין אדם אוסר, תנא דמתני' לא אשמועי' מידי לא ברישא ולא בסיפא. וכ"ת: כולה לאשמועינן דינא דשביעית אינו יורד לתוך שדהו נקט לה, דלא תימא דארעא נמי רחמנא אפקריה, וקמ"ל דליתא, משום טעמא דאמר לקמן – לא מצית אמרת הכין, דלמאי שנויה בנדרים? אי האי דינא בעי למתני, לעולא דאמר לקמן בעומדין אילנות על הגבולין – ה"ל למתנייה גבי דיני ממונות, א"נ בשביעית, ואפי' לר"ש בן אליקים דאמר גזרה שמא ישהה בעמידה – לא ניחא דכולה תני לה משום האי דינא, דליתני שביעית גרידא! אלא ודאי ר' יוחנן ור"ל אפילו ב"נכסים אלו" ס"ל דאין אדם אוסר, ואתיא להו השתא מתניתין שפיר. דתנא רישא משום סיפא, לאשמועינן דאפילו הדירו בלשון "נכסים אלו" – אין נדרו חל לאחר שילאו מרשותו. דלא תימא דכי היכי דאמר גבי נודר, דכי אמר "לבית זה שאני נכנס" מת או מכרו לאחר – אסור, דמתסר עליה אפילו לאחר שילא מרשותו, הכי נמי כי הדירו חבירו, וא"ל "נכסים אלו" דליחול איסורא אפי' לאחר שילאו נכסים מרשות מדיר – דליתא. דה"מ בנודר עצמו, דמצי אסר אנפשיה נכסי חבירו, אפילו לאחר שילאו מרשותו הוו להו נכסי חבירו. אבל מדיר – לא, דלאחר שילאו מרשותו הוו להו נכסי חבירו, ואין אדם אוסר נכסי חבירו על חבירו. ואתיא מתניתין שפיר. ומקשינן: דאי איתא דר' יוחנן ור"ל סברי דאין אדם אוסר – הוה להו לאיפלוגי בהדיא אפילו היכא דאמר "נכסים אלו". ועוד, תנן דהיכא דאמר בהדיא אדם אוסר. **אם מת יירשנו.** דלאו מדידיה מתהני, אלא מירושתיה דזכי ליה רחמנא. **אם מת לא יירשנו.** לאו דוקא לא יירשנו, דנכסי ודאי דידיה

תוספות

המודר הנאה מחבירו לפני שביעית לא ירד לתוך שדהו. דדריסת הרגל אסורה ואינו אוכל אפילו מן הנטועות חוץ לשדה דאינו צריך לירד ולאוכלם: **ובשביעית.** פי' אם הדיר בשביעית לא ירד לתוך שדהו ליקח מן הנטוע' (אבל) אם יצטרך לירד ולאכול אסור. ובגמ' פריך אמאי אסור לירד בו לצורך אכילה הא רחמנא אפקריה לשדה לכל דבר אכילה: **נדר** ממנו מאכל לפני שביעי' יורד לתוך שדהו. דאינו מודר אלא מדבר המביא לידי מאכל ואינו אוכל מן הפירות: **ובשביעית** יורד ואוכל. דהפקר הוא וקשה דלעיל (דף לג.) מיבעיא ליה אם מפסק ומיזיל בארעא אי הוי הנאה המביאה לידי מאכל וי"ל דבשביעית אף השדה הפקר לצורך אכילה דהכי מסיק בגמ' ולאידך נמי דמשני שמא ישהה בעמידה הכא לא שייך במודר מאכל דאי שהה אין בכך כלום: **רב** ושמואל אמרי נכסי אלו עליך לפני שביעית אינו אוכל מן הנטועות. ואף על פי שהגיע שביעית דכיון דאמר אלו אסורין עליו אפי' לאחר שנתנס או שהפקירם ולכך אסור בשביעית והשתא ס"ד דבלא אמר נכסיי אלו והגיע שביעית אסור לאכול מן הנטועות דאדם אוסר דבר שברשותו אף כשילא מרשותו ומתני' דקתני ובשביעי' אוכל בנטועות מיירי בהדירו בשביעית עצמה: **רבי** יוחנן ור"ש בן לקיש [אמרי] נכסי עליך אינו יורד לתוך שדהו כו' הגיע שביעית אוכל מן הנטועות. והפקר הן ולא אסרן אלא כי איתנהו לדידיה אבל אי יהבינהו [לא] דאין אדם אוסר בקונמות לכשילא מרשותיה וה"ה היכא דאמר נכסי אלו הגיע שביעית מותר בנטועות ופריך אם כן דלא אסר רבי יוחנן כלל לכשילא מרשותו אמאי לא אשמועינן למילתא באלו אלא אית להו אדם

הגהות הב"ח

(א) במשנה אבל אוכל הוא מן הנטועות כצ"ל ותיבת הנטיעות נמחק: (ב) גמ' רב ושמואל דאמרי תרוייהו נכסי עליך כצ"ל ואות מ"ס ותיבת אלו נמחק וכן ברש"י: (ג) שם דא"כ ניפלגי: (ד) רש"י ד"ה דא"כ דמשום: (ה) ד"ה ליפלגי וכו' דאמרינן אין אדם וכו' וכ"ש היכא וכו' היכי מצו אמרי דלעולם אין אדם:

פי' הרא"ש

מתני' ובשביעית. כשיגיע שביעית לא ירד בתוך שדהו אף על גב דרחמנא אפקרי' ובגמ' מפרש: **אבל אוכל מן הנטועות.** דהפקר הן: **גמ' לימא בהא קא מיפלגי.** רב ושמואל: **נכסי אלו.** לאו דוקא והה"נ אם אמר נכסי דבכל ענין אדם אוסר דבר שברשותו אפילו לכשילא מרשותו הלכך הא דקתני במתניתין ובשביעית אוכל מן הנטועות ע"כ איירי בנודר בשביעית והאי דנקט ר' יוחנן ור"ל נכסי לאו דוקא הה"נ נכסים אלו דבכל ענין אין אדם אוסר דבר שברשותו לכשילא מרשותו הלכך הא דקתני במתניתין ובשביעית אוכל (אף) מן הנטועות איירי אף בשהדירו לפני שביעית: **א"כ לפלגו בנכסים אלו.** דאמרי' אין אדם אוסר כו': **דתנן שאומר לבנו כו'.** משנה היא בהגוזל קמא: **בחייו ובמותו לא יירשנו.** אלמא אדם אוסר נכסיו לאחר מותו אע"פ שילא מרשותו: *) **דהכי קאמר ליה בחייו ובמותו.** אבל אי לא פריש אפילו אמר נכסי אלו אינו אוסר לכשילא מרשותו: **מ"מ קשיא.** ליפלגו בנכסים אלו: **שדך שאני לוקח.** היכא דאמר המודר שדך הוי כאומר המדיר נכסי לבית זה הוי כמו נכסי אלו: **ולא פליגי.** ורב ושמואל שאמרו נכסים אלו אמתניתין קאי וניחא להו לפרושי מתניתין דקתני ובשביעית אוכל מן הנטועות דהיינו נדר בשביעית ורבי יוחנן ור"ל ניחא להו לפרש הגיע שביעית: אוסר ועוד תנן לאדם אוסר לכשילא מרשותו: **מת** יירשנו. דכשיש כח ברשותו אוסרה ותו לא: **בחייו** ובמותו לא יירשנו. אלמא אוסר אחריו לאחר מותו שילאו מרשותו ומשני לה לעולם לא תפשוט מידי דהיכא דאמר נכסי אלו עליך שיאסרו לאחר שילאו מרשותו דשאני הכא שפי' בהדיא שיאסרו לאחר מותו:

מכל

*) שייך לע"ב

עין משפט נר מצוה

מט א מיי' פ"ו מהל' נדרים הלכה יג:
נ ב מיי' שם הלכה טו:
נא ג מיי' שם פ"ה הל' ו סמג לאוין רמב טוש"ע יו"ד סימן רטז סעיף ז וסימן רכג סעיף ב:

מסורת הש"ס

[לקמן מז.]

ב"ק קח: [לקמן מז.]

נב א ב מיי' פ"ו מהל' נדרים הלכה יג יד סמג לאוין רמב:
נג ג מיי' שם הל' יג:
נד ד מיי' שם הלכה טז סמג שם טוש"ע יו"ד סימן רכא סעיף ה:

אִם מֵת — לֹא יִירָשֶׁנּוּ! שָׁאנֵי הָכָא, דְּקָא א"ל "בְּחַיָּיו וּבְמוֹתוֹ". מִכָּל מָקוֹם קַשְׁיָא! אֶלָּא בִּ"נְכָסִים אֵלּוּ" — כ"ע לָא פְּלִיגֵי. כִּי פְּלִיגֵי בִּ"נְכָסַי" רַב וּשְׁמוּאֵל סָבְרִי: ל"ש "נְכָסִים אֵלּוּ" ל"ש "נְכָסַי" — אָדָם אוֹסֵר, ור' יוֹחָנָן ור"ל סָבְרִי: "נְכָסִים" (א) אָדָם אוֹסֵר, "נְכָסַי" — אֵין אָדָם אוֹסֵר. וּמִי אִיכָּא לְמ"ד ל"ש "נְכָסִים אֵלּוּ" ול"ש "נְכָסַי"? וְהָא תְּנַן: *הָאוֹמֵר לַחֲבֵירוֹ "קוֹנָם לְתוֹךְ בֵּיתְךָ שֶׁאֲנִי נִכְנָס, שָׂדְךָ שֶׁאֲנִי לוֹקֵחַ", מֵת אוֹ שֶׁמְּכָרוֹ לְאַחֵר — מוּתָּר. "לְבַיִת זֶה שֶׁאֲנִי נִכְנָס, שָׂדֶה זוֹ שֶׁאֲנִי לוֹקֵחַ" מֵת אוֹ שֶׁמְּכָרוֹ לְאַחֵר — אָסוּר! אֶלָּא, א כִּי אָמְרִי ר' יוֹחָנָן וְרֵישׁ לָקִישׁ — בִּ"נְכָסַי", וְרַב וּשְׁמוּאֵל — ב בִּ"נְכָסִים אֵלּוּ", וְלָא פְּלִיגֵי.§ "וּבַשְּׁבִיעִית אֵין יוֹרֵד לְתוֹךְ שָׂדֵהוּ" כו'.§ מַאי שְׁנָא דְּאוֹכֵל מִן הַנּוֹטוֹת — דְּפֵירֵי דְּהֶפְקֵירָא אִינּוּן, אַרְעָא נַמִּי אַפְקְרָהּ! אָמַר עוּלָּא: בְּעוֹמְדִין אִילָנוֹת עַל הַגְּבוּלִים. *ר' שִׁמְעוֹן בֶּן אֶלְיָקִים אָמַר: ג גְּזֵירָה שֶׁמָּא יִשְׁהֶא בַּעֲמִידָה.§ **מתני'** ד הַמּוּדָּר הֲנָאָה מֵחֲבֵירוֹ — לֹא יַשְׁאִילֶנּוּ וְלֹא יִשְׁאַל מִמֶּנּוּ, לֹא יַלְוֶנּוּ וְלֹא יִלְוֶה מִמֶּנּוּ, וְלֹא יִמְכּוֹר לוֹ וְלֹא יִקַּח מִמֶּנּוּ.§

גמ'

ר"ן

[דף מז.] דידיה הוו וכמו שנפרש בפירקין דלקמן* בס"ד. אלא משום דתנא רישא יירשנו, לומר שדינו כשאר היורשים, אפי' ליהנות מן הנכסים – תנא סיפא נמי לא יירשנו, לומר שאינו מותר ליהנו' מירושתו. ומ"מ שמעי' מהא דיכול אדם לאסור פירותיו על חבירו לאחר שיצאו מרשותו, ולא הוי כאוסר נכסי חבירו על חבירו. ומהדרינן: שאני הכא דקא"ל "בחייו ובמותו".* והשתא נקטינן דרגא ממאי דסבירא לן מעיקרא, דהוה סבירא לן עד השתא דלא מהני שום לישנא למיסר לאחר שיצאו מרשותו, משום דהוו כנכסי חבירו על חבירו, והשתא מודינן דכי מפרש לישניה – מצי אסר. מיהו, אי מהך קושיא בלחוד – הוה מצינן למימר, דנהי דכי מפרש לישניה מצי אסר, אפ"ה בלשון "נכסים אלו" – לא משמע אלא עודן ברשותו. דאע"ג דכי קאמר מדיר "נכסים אלו", וכי קאמר נודר "ביתך זה" – לשונות שוין הן, ותנן לקמן גבי נודר דכי קאמר "ביתך זה" – משמע אפי' לאחר שיצאו מרשותו. וה"נ הל"ל כי קאמר מדיר נכסים אלו", כיון דמדיר נמי, אי מפרש לישניה מצי אסר אפילו לאחר שיצאו מרשותו – אפ"ה לא דמי. משום דכי אמר נודר "בית זה" – משמע דגופיה של בית אסר אנפשיה, אי משום דלא מקבל עליה ההוא ביתא, אי משום דריע מזליה, או מטעמא אחרינא – הלכך שפיר משמע לישניה דלא תלי אסוריה בדאיתיה ממריה קמיה. אבל כי אסר ליה מדיר, נהי דא"ל "נכסים אלו", כל היכא דלא פריש בהדיא אפילו לאחר שיצאו מרשותו – לא משמע אלא כי איתנהו ברשותיה, דמאי איכפת ליה אי מיתהני אידך במה שאין לו חלק ונחלה כלל? הלכך, כל היכא דלא פריש בהדיא, אלא אמר "נכסים אלו" – לא משמע אלא בעודן ברשותו, ואתיא לן מתני' שפיר, דהך דינא אשמעי', והוי רבותא טפי, ותנא רישא משום סיפא. אלא דאכתי לא ניחא לן, דמ"מ קשה קושיא קמייתא, דאם איתא דס"ל הכי לרבי יוחנן ור"ל – הוו להו לאפלוגי א"נכסי' אלו" בהדיא! ומהדרינן: אלא ב"נכסים אלו" לא פליגי, דודאי אדם אוסר. כי פליגי ב"נכסי", דרב ושמואל סברי אפילו "נכסי" אדם אוסר, וכי אמרי "אלו" – לאו דוקא, דפשיטא להו דכל היכא דאמר "נכסי", אפילו כי אמר "אלו" – אין דינו אלא א"נכסי", ואפ"ה אדם אוסר, אי משום ד"נכסי" נמי לעולם משמע, ואלו שהן עכשיו נכסי קאמר. אי משום דכיון דחיילא עלייהו איסורא – תו לא פקע. ור' יוחנן ור"ל סברי דדוקא "נכסים אלו" אדם אוסר, אבל "נכסי" – אין אדם אוסר. והשתא אתיא מתני' שפיר לר' יוחנן ור"ל כדאיתא לרב ושמואל. דר' יוחנן ור"ל ב"נכסים אלו" מוקמי לה, ורישא רבותא קמ"ל דאע"פ שהגיע שביעית – אינו יורד ואינו אוכל, דאדם אוסר דבר שברשותו. לכשיצא מרשותו וסיפא רבותא קמ"ל, דאם בשביעית נדר – אין יורד לתוך שדהו. וכי קאמרי ר' יוחנן ור"ל "נכסי עליך" וכו' – לאו דמוקמי לה למתני' ב"נכסי", אלא לרב ושמואל קמהדרי, וה"ק להו: אי ב"נכסי" איירי תנא – לא הוה תני הכי, אלא הכי הוי דינא: דלפני שביעית אין יורד ואוכל, וכשהגיע שביעית – אוכל, ואי הכי לא אשמעינן מידי. אלא ודאי מתניתין באומר "נכסים אלו" ומש"ה נדרא חייל אפילו לאחר שהגיע שביעית. ומקשינן: דא"א דלימרו רב ושמואל דאפי' כי אמר "נכסי" ליתסרו נכסים אפילו לאחר שיצאו מרשותו, דהא אפילו גבי נודר תנן דכי קאמר "לביתך" – לא משמע אלא כל עוד שיהא שלו, אבל לא לאחר שמכרו. וכ"ש גבי מדיר, דלא משמע כי אמר "נכסי" אלא בעוד שיהו ברשותו! ומהדרינן: אלא כי אמרי ר' יוחנן ור"ל ב"נכסי", ורב ושמואל ב"נכסי אלו", ולא פליגי. כלומר, דרב ושמואל מוקמי לה למתני' באומר "נכסי אלו" דכיון דאמר "אלו" אע"ג דאמר "נכסי" – הרי כאילו אמר "נכסים אלו", ואסירי אפי' לאחר שהגיע שביעית. ורישא רבותא קמ"ל. ור' יוחנן ור"ל נמי הכי מוקמי למתני', וה"ק: לא תיסק אדעתין דמתני' דקתני דאפילו הגיע שביעית אינו יורד ואינו אוכל מתוקמא אפילו ב"נכסי", וטעמא משום דכיון דנחית בהו איסורא תו לא פקע – דליתא. אלא כל היכא דלא אמר אלא "נכסי" – לא מתסרי אלא כי איתנהו ברשותיה, אבל הגיע שביעית – אוכל מן הנוטות, דפקע להו איסורייהו. הלכך, ודאי מתני' לא מיתוקמא אלא ב"נכסי אלו". ואע"ג דהאי דינא מצית למיגמרי' ממתני' דהאומר לחבירו "קונם לביתך שאני נכנס" וכו' – א"ר יוחנן אמתני' לפרושה ולברורה, דלא ניטעי בה, משום דסתם מודר הנאה מחבירו ב"נכסי" משמע, כדתנן לקמן: המודר הנאה מחבירו וכו' נותן לאחר לשם מתנה, והלה מותר בה. ואי באומר "נכסים אלו" – אין הלה מותר בה. כנ"ל פירושא דהאי שמעתא. ולא ידענא אמאי נקט התלמוד במסקנא ר' יוחנן ור"ל מקמי רב ושמואל, דה"ל למינקט רב ושמואל ברישא, כדקמסדר להו למימרינהו מעיקרא מקמי ר' יוחנן ור"ל. ונראה בעיני: משום דכל שקלא וטריא דסוגיין נקטינן דר' יוחנן ור"ל קיימי אמילתייהו דרב ושמואל לאפלוגי עליה, מש"ה כי הדרי למימר דלא פליגי – מקדמינן לדר' יוחנן ור"ל מקמי רב ושמואל, לומר דלאו אמילתייהו קיימי כלל. ואית דגרסי הכא: ורב ושמואל ב"נכסים אלו". מיהו, אפילו להך גירסא ה"ה ב"נכסי אלו", דאדם אוסר, שהולכין אחר לשון אחרון דאמר "אלו". והכי איתא בירושלמי: "ביתך זה" משום מה אתה תופסו, משום "ביתך" או משום "זה"? ומסקנא משום "זה". **ארעא** נמי רחמנא **אפקריה**. כלומר ללקיטת הפירות, ולמה לא ירד לתוכה ללקוט פירותיה?: **אמר עולא בעומדין אילנות על הגבולין**. אין הכי נמי, דללקוט אילנות שבאמצע השדה מותר לירד לתוכה. אבל ללקוט אילנות שעומדין על הגבולין – לא, דרחמנא לא אפקרה לארעא אלא ללקוט פירותיה. הלכך, כיון שאילנות הללו יכול ללקט אותם – לא ירד. ר"ש **בן אליקים אומר** גזרה שמא **ישהא בעמידה**. ומש"ה אפי' ללקט אילנות שבאמצע השדה לא ירד לתוכה, דנהי דמדינא שרי, דארעא רחמנא אפקרה – משום גזרה אסור. ואע"ג דהכא גזרינן שמא ישהה בעמידה, ולעיל (דף לט.) גבי חולה לא גזר שמואל אלא שמא ישהה בישיבה, אבל בעמידה לא גזר, דא"כ ליתסר לבקרו אפי' עומד – התם היינו טעמא: משום דכיון דדרך מבקר לישב, ואתה מצריכו לעמוד – אית ליה היכרא, ולא ישהה בעמידה. אבל הכא – מאי היכרא אית ליה? הא אין דרך ללקוט את הפירות אלא בעמידה, ושייך למיגזר שמא ישהה. **מתני'** לא **ישאילנו**. מודר למדיר, ובגמרא מפרש טעמא. **ולא ישאל ממנו**. מודר ממדיר, דהא מתהני מיניה. שאלה שייכא במידי דהדר בעיניה כבהמה וכלים, הלואה שייכא במידי דלא הדר בעיניה, כהלואת מעות.

רש"י

אִם מֵת. וְאִם נָדַר בְּחַיָּיו וּבְמוֹתוֹ. כֵּיוָן דִּמְפָרֵשׁ בְּמוֹתוֹ – מֵת, לֹא יִירָשֶׁנּוּ. אַלְמָא דְּאָדָם אוֹסֵר דָּבָר שֶׁבִּרְשׁוּתוֹ לִכְשֶׁיֵּצֵא מֵרְשׁוּתוֹ, לְאַחַר מוֹתוֹ. **שָׁאנֵי הָכָא** (ב) דַּאֲמַר בְּחַיָּיו וּבְמוֹתוֹ. אֲבָל הֵיכָא דַּאֲמַר בִּסְתָם, אֵימָא לְעוֹלָם אֵין אָדָם אוֹסֵר וכו'. **מ"מ קַשְׁיָא**. כִּדְאָמְרִינַן, אִי בְּהַאי טַעְמָא פְּלִיגֵי – לִיפְלְגוּ בְּ"נְכָסִים אֵלּוּ". **אֶלָּא בִּנְכָסִים אֵלּוּ כ"ע לָא פְּלִיגֵי**. דְּמַשְׁמַע נְכָסִים אֵלּוּ לְעוֹלָם. **כִּי פְּלִיגֵי** דַּאֲמַר נְכָסַי. ר' יוֹחָנָן וְר"ל סָבְרֵי: הֵיכָא דַּאֲמַר "נְכָסַי" – אֵין אָדָם אוֹסֵר וכו', דְּ"נְכָסַי" מַשְׁמַע כָּל זְמַן שֶׁהֵן בִּרְשׁוּתִי. וְרַב וּשְׁמוּאֵל סָבְרֵי: אֲפִילּוּ אָמַר "נְכָסַי" (ג) (אָמַר) אָדָם אוֹסֵר דָּבָר וכו'. **קוֹנָם לְתוֹךְ בֵּיתְךָ שֶׁאֲנִי נִכְנָס**. כָּל זְמַן שֶׁהוּא בֵּיתְךָ, דְּהָוֵי (ד) דּוּמְיָא דְּ"נְכָסַי עָלֶיךָ", כֵּיוָן שֶׁמֵּת בעה"ב אוֹ שֶׁמְּכָרוֹ לְאוֹתוֹ בַּיִת לְאַחֵר – מוּתָּר לִיכָּנֵס בּוֹ, דְּהַשְׁתָּא אֵינוֹ שֶׁלּוֹ. אֲבָל אָמַר "לְבַיִת זֶה שֶׁאֲנִי נִכְנָס", דְּהָוֵי מַשְׁמַע "נְכָסִים אֵלּוּ", דְּקָא אָסַר הַבַּיִת עָלָיו לְעוֹלָם, אע"פ שֶׁמֵּת אוֹ מְכָרוֹ לְאַחֵר – אָסוּ' לִיכָּנֵס בּוֹ. אַלְמָא דְּשָׁאנֵי בֵּין "נְכָסַי" לִ"נְכָסִים", וְהֵיכִי קָאָמְרִי רַב וּשְׁמוּאֵל ל"ש "נְכָסַי" וְל"ש "נְכָסִים" דְּאָדָם אוֹסֵר? וכו': **אֶלָּא כִּי אָמְרִי רַב וּשְׁמוּאֵל. בְּעוֹמְדִים אִילָנוֹת עַל הַגְּבוּלִין**. לַחוּץ, שֶׁיָּכוֹל לִתְלוֹשׁ מִן הַפֵּירוֹת מִבַּחוּץ. מש"ה אֵינוֹ יוֹרֵד, דְּהָא דְּרַחֲמָנָא אַפְקְרֵיהּ לְאַרְעָא גַּבֵּי שְׁבִיעִית לְצוֹרֶךְ אֲכִילָה, וְעַכְשָׁיו לֹא הָיָה נִכְנָס לְצוֹרֶךְ אֲכִילָה. **ר"ש בֶּן אֶלְיָקִים אָמַר**. הָא דְּקָתָנֵי "אוֹכֵל מִן הַנּוֹטוֹת" – וַדַּאי כִּדְקָאָמְרַתְּ, כְּגוֹן דְּעוֹמְדִין עַל הַגְּבוּלִין, מִשּׁוּם שֶׁיָּכוֹל לְהוֹשִׁיט יָדוֹ וְלִיקַּח מִבַּחוּץ. אֲבָל אֵין עוֹמְדִין עַל הַגְּבוּלִין – אֵינוֹ יוֹרֵד לְתוֹךְ שָׂדֵהוּ, דְּאָסוּר לוֹ לֵירֵד לְשָׁם. **גְּזֵירָה שֶׁמָּא יִשְׁהֶא בַּעֲמִידָה**. דִּלְאַחַר שֶׁאָכַל עוֹמֵד לוֹ לְשָׁם, וְקָמִיתְהַנֵּי מִנְּכָסִים דְּמַדִּיר, וְאָסוּר. דְּהַאי דְּאַפְקְרֵיהּ רַחֲמָנָא – כָּל זְמַן שֶׁהוּא אוֹכֵל, אָז יָכוֹל לַעֲמוֹד לְשָׁם, דְּהֶפְקֵר הוּא. אֲבָל שֶׁלֹּא לְצוֹרֶךְ אֲכִילָה – לָא אַפְקְרֵיהּ. **מתני'** הַמּוּדָּר הֲנָאָה מֵחֲבֵירוֹ לֹא יַשְׁאִיל לוֹ. **שְׁאֵלָה** – בְּכֵלִים, **הַלְוָאָה** – בְּמָעוֹת.

גמ'

לקמן מו.

[לעיל כו.]

תוספות

מכל מקום [קשיא] אי ס"ל דאין אדם אוסר דבר שלא ברשותו לשמעינן מילתיה באלו: אלא בנכסי אלו לא פליגי דאדם אוסר כי פליגי בנכסי דרב ושמואל סברי ל"ש נכסי אלו לא שנא נכסי אוסר. וקשה אמאי נקט במילתיה נכסי אלו הוה מצי למיפרך מהך ברייתא דלעיל קונם שאתה נהנה מת יירשנו אלמא בנכסי אינו אוסר או מהאי דלעיל (דף לה.) גבי קורדוס מת או נתנו במתנה מותר מיהו ניחא ליה טפי לאתויי ממתניתין דלקמן דדמי טפי לנכסי אלו דקתני: **מי** איכא למ"ד דבנכסי אדם אוסר. והתנן בפ' השותפין. מותר דלא נאסר אלא בעודהו ברשותו: **אלא** כי אמרי רבי יוחנן וריש לקיש בנכסי רב ושמואל בנכסי אלו. ולא פליגי: **מאי** שנא דאוכל מן הנוטות דפירי דהפקירא אינון ארעא נמי הפקירא הוא ואפקרה רחמנא לצורך אכילה ואמאי לא ירד בה לאכול מאותן שאינן נוטות: **בעומדים** על הגבולין. דיכול לתולשן בלא ירידה בתוך השדה ולכך אמר דלא ירד לתוך השדה כיון דאפשר לאוכלם בלא ירידה אבל היכא דלאו עומדין על הגבולין לעולם יורד ואוכל דרחמנא אפקריה: **אלא** גזירה שמא ירבה בעמידה. לאחר אכילה ולצורך אכילה אפקריה רחמנא שלא לצורך אכילה לא ואינו מותר אלא בנוטות שנוטות מתוך לשדה ואינו נכנס לתוך השדה כלל: **המודר** הנאה מחבירו. שחבירו הדירו שלא יהנה משלו: לא ישאילנו חבירו דקא מהני ליה ולא ישאל מחבירו ובגמרא פריך הא לא מהני ליה למודר: **ולא** ילוונו חבירו. דקמהני ליה: **ולא** ילוה חבירו ממנו. ובגמרא פריך אמאי: **לא** ימכור לו חבירו. לאמרינן בשילהי פירקין לעיל (דף לג.) דמיתהני מוכר *)ולוקח ולכך אסור בין למוכר בין ללוקח:

*) צ"ל ולוקח

אמר

הגהות הב"ח

(א) גמ' וכו"י וריש לקיש סברי נכסים אלו אדם: (ב) רש"י ד"ה שאני הכא דמפרש דאמר בחייו: (ג) ד"ה כי פליגי וכו' אמרינן אדם: (ד) ד"ה קונם וכו' דהוי משמע דומיא דנכסים אלו וכו' רב ושמואל וכו' הס"ד ואח"כ מ"ה בעומדין אילנות על הגבולין והפירות נוטין לחוץ שיכול וכו' לצורך אכילה אפקריה ועכשיו:

פי' הרא"ש

ארעא נמי רחמנא אפקרי'. לילך בתוך השדה כדי ללקט הפירו': **בעומדין על הגבולין.** ואינו צריך ליכנס בתוך השדה ואפשר לכל אדם אין לו רשות ליכנס כיון שיכול ליקח הפירו' או שמא אע"ג דלאיניש אחרינא מותר למודר אסור אבל ליקח פירות העומדין בתוך השדה יכול לירד: **גזירה שמא ישהא בעמידה.** יותר מכדי צורך לקיטת פירות הלכך לא יכנס לתוך השדה כלל ללקט הפירות: **מתנ' לא ישאל ממנו.** מפרש בגמרא וכן לא ילוה ממנו: **לא ימכור לו ולא יקח ממנו.** בזבינא מציעא דאיכא הנאה לתרווייהו שוה בשוה אבל למכור לו ביותר וליקח ממנו בפחות מותר: *) **קונם שאני חורש בה לעולם** אותה שביקש שישאילנה לו אסרה עליו: **אם היה דרכו לחרוש הוא אסור וכל אדם מותרים.** כי לפי רגילותו כיון לידור אם הוא אדם שהוא בעצמו רגיל לחרוש שדהו הוא אסור וכל אדם מותרין לחרוש שדהו באותה הפרה ואם אין דרכו לחרוש הוא [מותר] וכל אדם אסורים לחרוש בה שדהו:

*) שייך לדף שאח"ז

אלא

נה א מיי' פ"ו מהלכות נדרים הלכה טז:
נו ב מיי' פ"ז מהלכות נדרים הל' יב טוש"ע י"ד סי' ריח סעיף ה:
נז ג מיי' פ"ו מהלכות נדרים הלכה יב סמג לאוין רמב טוש"ע י"ד סי' רכא סעיף ח:
נח ד מיי' שם הלכה יד טוש"ע שם סעיף ט:

[ע"ז ו:]

גמ' בִּשְׁלָמָא לֹא יַלְוֶנּוּ — דְּקָא מְהַנֵּי לֵיהּ. אֶלָּא לֹא יִלְוֶה הֵימֶנּוּ, מַאי קָא מְהַנֵּי לֵיהּ? וּבִשְׁלָמָא לֹא יִלְוֶה הֵימֶנּוּ וְלֹא יִקַּח הֵימֶנּוּ — דְּקָמִיתְהַנֵּי מִינֵּיהּ, אֶלָּא לֹא יִשְׁאַל הֵימֶנּוּ, מַאי קָא מִיתְהַנֵּי מִינֵּיהּ? א"ר יוֹסֵי בר' חֲנִינָא: כְּגוֹן שֶׁנָּדְרוּ הֲנָאָה זֶה מִזֶּה. אַבַּיֵּי אֲמַר: אגְּזֵירָה *לִשְׁאוֹל מִשּׁוּם לְהַשְׁאִיל, וְכֵן בְּכוּלְּהוּ גְּזֵירָה.§ **מתני'** באָמַר לוֹ: הַשְׁאִילֵנִי פָּרָתְךָ. אָמַר לוֹ: אֵינָהּ פְּנוּיָה. אָמַר: "קוֹנָם שָׂדִי שֶׁאֲנִי חוֹרֵשׁ בָּהּ לְעוֹלָם". אִם הָיָה דַּרְכּוֹ לַחֲרוֹשׁ — הוּא אָסוּר וְכָל אָדָם מוּתָּרִים, וְאִם אֵין דַּרְכּוֹ לַחֲרוֹשׁ — הוּא וְכָל אָדָם אֲסוּרִין. *גהַמּוּדָּר הֲנָאָה מֵחֲבֵירוֹ וְאֵין לוֹ מַה יֹּאכַל, הוֹלֵךְ אֵצֶל הַחֶנְוָנִי וְאוֹמֵר: אִישׁ פְּלוֹנִי (א) נוֹדֵר מִמֶּנִּי הֲנָאָה, וְאֵינִי יוֹדֵעַ מָה אֶעֱשֶׂה. וְהוּא נוֹתֵן לוֹ, וּבָא וְנוֹטֵל מִזֶּה. הָיָה בֵּיתוֹ לִבְנוֹת, גְּדֵרוֹ לִגְדּוֹר, שָׂדֵהוּ לִקְצוֹר — הוֹלֵךְ אֵצֶל הַפּוֹעֲלִים, וְאוֹמֵר: אִישׁ פְּלוֹנִי מוּדָּר מִמֶּנִּי הֲנָאָה וְאֵינִי יוֹדֵעַ מָה אֶעֱשֶׂה. וְהֵן עוֹשִׂין עִמּוֹ, וּבָאִין וְנוֹטְלִין שָׂכָר מִזֶּה. דהָיוּ מְהַלְּכִין בַּדֶּרֶךְ וְאֵין לוֹ מַה יֹּאכַל — *נוֹתֵן לְאֶחָד לְשׁוּם מַתָּנָה, וְהַלָּה מוּתָּר בָּהּ. אִם אֵין עִמָּהֶם אַחֵר מַנִּיחַ עַל הַסֶּלַע אוֹ עַל הַגָּדֵר, וְאוֹמֵר: הֲרֵי הֵן מוּפְקָרִים לְכָל מִי שֶׁיַּחְפּוֹץ, וְהַלָּה נוֹטֵל וְאוֹכֵל. ור' יוֹסֵי אוֹסֵר.§ **גמ'** אָמַר ר' יוֹחָנָן: מ"ט דר' יוֹסֵי קָסָבַר: הֶפְקֵר כְּמַתָּנָה, מַה מַּתָּנָה — עַד דְּאָתְיָא מֵרְשׁוּת נוֹתֵן לִרְשׁוּת מְקַבֵּל, אַף הֶפְקֵר עַד דְּאָתֵי לִרְשׁוּת זוֹכֶה. מְתִיב ר' אַבָּא: וְהַלָּה נוֹטֵל וְאוֹכֵל, וְרַבִּי יוֹסֵי אוֹסֵר. א"ר יוֹסֵי: אֵימָתַי — בִּזְמַן שֶׁנְּדָרוֹ קוֹדֶם לְהֶפְקֵירוֹ. אֲבָל

רש"י

גמ' בִּשְׁלָמָא לֹא יַלְוֶנּוּ. מַדִּיר לַמּוּדָּר, דְּוַדַּאי קָמְהַנֵּי לֵיהּ הֲנָאָה מְפוּרְסֶמֶת. **אֲבָל לֹא יִלְוֶה מִמֶּנּוּ.** הַמַּדִּיר מִן הַמּוּדָּר. **מַאי הֲנָאָה.** קָא מָטֵי לֵיהּ לַמּוּדָּר מִמַּאי דְּאוֹזִיף לַמַּדִּיר? **וּבִשְׁלָמָא לֹא יִלְוֶה מִמֶּנּוּ.** מָצֵי נַמִי לְמֵימַר דְּקָא מִיתְהַנֵּי בְּכה"ג, כְּגוֹן דְּאוֹזְפֵיהּ מָעוֹת הָרָעוֹת וְקָא מְשַׁלֵּם לֵיהּ הֵיאָךְ יָפוֹת. **וְלֹא יִקַּח** מִמֶּנּוּ מַשְׁכַּחַת לָהּ דְּקָא מִתְהַנֵּי — בִּזְבִינָא דְּרָמֵי עַל אַפֵּיהּ. **אֶלָּא לֹא יִשְׁאַל מִמֶּנּוּ.** מַאי הֲנָאָה מָטֵי לַמּוּדָּר כִּי מַשְׁאִיל לוֹ כֵּלָיו? הָא קָא מַפְחִית וַדַּאי לְהַהִיא כְּלִי, וְלָא מַעֲלֵי לָהּ, דִּסְתָם שְׁאֵלָה הָכִי הוּא. **כְּגוֹן שֶׁנָּדְרוּ זֶה מִזֶּה.** דִּשְׁנֵיהֶם אֲסוּרִים זֶה בָּזֶה. **גְּזֵירָה לִשְׁאוֹל כו'.** דְּאִי שָׁרֵית לֵיהּ לִשְׁאוֹל אָתֵי נַמִי לְהַשְׁאִיל. **מתני' אָמַר לוֹ הַשְׁאִילֵנִי פָּרָתְךָ.** לָאו בְּמוּדָּר וּמַדִּיר עָסְקִינַן. **אֵינָהּ פְּנוּיָה.** דִּמְלַאכְתּוֹ הָיָה עוֹשֶׂה. וְנִתְעַצֵּב הַשּׁוֹאֵל כְּנֶגֶד הַמַּשְׁאִיל, וְאוֹמֵר: הוֹאִיל וְסֵרַבְתָּ לְהַשְׁאִילָהּ לִי. **קוֹנָם שָׂדֶה שֶׁאֲנִי חוֹרֵשׁ.** (ב) שֶׁלֹּא אֶחֱרוֹשׁ שָׂדִי בְּפָרָתְךָ עוֹלָמִית. וְאַחַ"כ הִשְׁאִילָהּ לוֹ. רוֹאִין, אִם הוּא פְּרָזִי, וְדַרְכּוֹ לַחֲרוֹשׁ שָׂדֵהוּ — הוּא אָסוּר לַחֲרוֹשׁ שָׂדֵהוּ בְּאוֹתָהּ פָּרָה. **וְכָל אָדָם מוּתָּר.** דְּוַדַּאי כִּי נָדַר — אַדַּעְתֵּיהּ דְּנַפְשֵׁיהּ נָדַר, וְלָא אַדַּעְתָּא דְּעָלְמָא. וְכָל אָדָם מוּתָּרִים לַחֲרוֹשׁ לוֹ שָׂדֵהוּ בְּאוֹתָהּ פָּרָה. **וְאִם אֵין דַּרְכּוֹ לַחֲרוֹשׁ.** שֶׁיֵּשׁ לוֹ אֲרִיסִין הַחוֹרְשִׁין בִּשְׁבִילוֹ. **הוּא וְכָל אָדָם אֲסוּרִים.** דְּוַדַּאי כִּי נָדַר — אַדַּעְתָּא דְּכוּלֵּי עָלְמָא נָדַר. **הַמּוּדָּר הֲנָאָה מֵחֲבֵירוֹ וְאֵין לוֹ מַה יֹּאכַל הוֹלֵךְ** הַמַּדִּיר **אֵצֶל חֶנְוָנִי וכו' וּבָא חֶנְוָנִי** וְנוֹטֵל מְעוֹתָיו מִן הַמַּדִּיר. אֲבָל בְּפֵירוּשׁ אָסוּר לוֹמַר לוֹ, דְּאִם כֵּן הֲוָה לֵיהּ הַחֶנְוָנִי שָׁלִיחַ, וּשְׁלוּחוֹ שֶׁל אָדָם כְּמוֹתוֹ. **ור' יוֹסֵי אוֹסֵר.** (ג) בָּהּ, כְּמַנִּיחוֹ עַל הַסֶּלַע אוֹ עַל הַגָּדֵר. **גמ' א"ר יוֹחָנָן מַאי טַעְמָא דְּר' יוֹסֵי.** דְּלָא חָשֵׁיב לֵיהּ הֶפְקֵר, דְּקָא אָסַר לֵיהּ לִיטְּלוֹ, דְּכִי מִתְהַנֵּי מִינֵּיהּ מַמָּשׁ דָּמֵי, וְאָסוּר. **מַה מַּתָּנָה.** לָא זָכֵי בָּהּ מְקַבֵּל עַד דְּאָתְיָא (ד) לִידֵיהּ. **אַף הֶפְקֵר.** נַמִי לָא נָפֵיק מֵרְשׁוּת מַפְקִיר עַד דְּאָתֵי לִידֵי זוֹכֶה. הִילְכָּךְ, בַּהֲדֵי דְּשָׁקֵיל לֵיהּ הֵיאָךְ מֵעַל הַסֶּלַע — כְּמַאן דְּשָׁקֵיל לֵיהּ מִיָּדוֹ מַמָּשׁ דָּמֵי וְאָסוּר. **מְתִיב ר' אַבָּא.** בָּרַיְיתָא הִיא, דְּקָתָנֵי נַמִי "מַנִּיחַ עַל הַסֶּלַע וְהַלָּה נוֹטֵל וְאוֹכֵל" (ה). **א"ר יוֹסֵי אֵימָתַי.** אֲנִי אוֹסֵר — בִּזְמַן שֶׁנְּדָרוֹ קוֹדֶם לְהֶפְקֵרוֹ. דְּהַשְׁתָּא מִסְתַּבְּרָא טַעְמָא דְּאָסוּר, מִשּׁוּם דִּכְשֶׁהִדִּירוֹ — מִכָּל נְכָסָיו הִדִּירוֹ, וַאֲפִילּוּ כִּי הִפְקִירָן אָסוּר בָּהֶן.
אֲבָל

כתובות ע: ע"ש

[לקמן מח.]

ר"ן

גמ' בשלמא **לא** ילוה ממנו ולא יקח ממנו ולא **ישאל** ממנו כלומר מודר ממדיר דקא מתהני מיניה ומשום הכי אסור אלא לא ישאילנו ולא ילונו ולא ימכור לו מאי קא מיתהני מיניה. נ"ל דמשמע ליה דמתני' בזבינא חריפא, ומש"ה משמע ליה הכי, ולא מוקי ליה בזבינא דרמי על אפיה וליפרוך איפכא. א"נ בזבינא מליעתא ולא תקשי ליה מידי במכר. משום דסבירא דכי היכי דבהני דקתני מקמי הא, דהיינו לא ישאילנו ולא ילונו – לא מהני מידי, הכי נמי בלא ימכור לו – לא מתהני מידי, והיינו בזבינא חריפא, ומש"ה פריך הכי. **א"ר יוסי בר' חנינא כגון שנדרו הנאה** זה מזה. וכי תימא: אם כן מאי קמ"ל? נראה דסתם לן כר"א דאמר ויתור אסור במודר הנאה. ואע"ג דכבר סתם לן כוותיה בריש פירקין (דף לג:) – קמ"ל דכל הני נמי לא גריעי מויתור, ואסירי לר"א. **אביי אמר גזירה לשאול משום** להשאיל וכן בולהון גזירה. דמש"ה אסרינן נמי למכור לו אטו ליקח ממנו. ואע"ג דתנן לעיל בפרק "ד' נדרים" (דף לא.): "שאיני נהנה לישראל" – לוקח ביתר ומוכר בפחות, "שישראל נהנין לי" – לוקח בפחות ומוכר ביתר. ואמרינן עלה בסוגיין דלעיל דכל היכא דהוי זבינא חריפא – שרי מודר למכור למדיר, ולא גזרינן – כבר כתב *הרמב"ס ז"ל דהתם, כיון דמכלהו ישראל נדר – לא גזרינן עלה, דאי גזרינן עלה ומצריכנא ליה ליהנות לנכרים – טריחא ליה מילתא. אבל כאן, שאינו אסור אלא להנאת חבירו בלבד – מצי למיקם עלה דמילתא, וגזרינן. וא"ת: והא אפי' במודר הנאה מחבירו בלבד תנן לקמן בפרק "השותפין" (דף מז:): "הריני עליך חרם" – המודר אסור, ומשמע: אבל מדיר – לא, ואמאי? הוה ליה למיתני שניהם אסורין, ומשום גזירה! י"ל דלאו קושיא היא, דכי גזרי' הכא – ה"מ בהני בלחוד דתנינן במתני', דלא משמע להו לאינשי דליתסרו במודר הנאה, ואי עביד להו מודר למדיר אתי נמי למישקל להו ממדיר. אבל בהנאה גמורה כאכילת פירות וכיוצא בה – ליכא למיגזר, הלכך לא מצי תני שניהם אסורין. **מתני'** קונם שדה שאני חורש בה לעולם. שואל אמר כך לחבירו, מתוך שכעס עליו, שלא רצה להשאילה לו. **אם היה דרכו לחרוש הוא אסור וכל אדם מותרין.** שכיון הוא חורש – אין במשמעות לשונו אלא חרישתו בלבד. **ואם אין דרכו לחרוש הוא וכל אדם אסורין.** שלא נתכוין לחרישתו, כיון שאין דרכו לחרוש, אלא שלא יהנה בחרישתו אכוין. ומש"ה הוא וכל אדם אסורים לחרוש בשבילו, כדי שלא יהנה בחרישתה. הולך **אצל** חנוני הרגיל **אצלו**. רבותא קמ"ל, דאע"ג דרגיל אצלו ומקיפו תדיר – לא אמרי' שליחותיה קעביד. וכ"ש שאם לא אמר לאדם מיוחד, אלא דאמר "כל הזן אינו מפסיד" – שרי, כדאיתא בפרק "המדיר". **ובא** ונוטל מזה. אם רצה, קאמר. ולומר דאף על גב דלבסוף נוטל מזה, ודעתייהו בהכי – לאו שליחותיה קעביד, דלא הוי שליח אלא באומר "כל השומע קולי יזון", כדאיתא ב"המדיר" (כתובות דף ע:). אבל ליכא למימר דכי קתני "ובא ונוטל מזה" מדינא קאמר. דכי מחייב לשלומי – אלמא שליחותיה קעביד, ומהני ליה, ואסור. היה ביתו לבנות. לא זו אף זו קתני. ברישא אשמעינן דלצורך מזונות שרי, וסיפא קמ"ל דאפילו לצורך בנין ביתו התירו. נותן **לאחר** משום מתנה. דלבתר הכי לא מתהני מיניה, אלא ממקבל מתנה. **והוא** נוטל ואוכל. דלאו מדידיה מתהני, אלא מהפקרא. ור' יוסי אוסר. בגמ' מפרש טעמא. **גמ'** מה מתנה עד דאתי מרשות נותן לרשות מקבל. שאם אמר "הריני נותן מתנה זו לפלוני" – יכול לחזור בו עד שיגיע לידו של מקבל. **אף הפקר עד דאתי** לרשו' זוכה. שאינו [יוצא] מרשות בעלי' עד שיזכה בו אחר, ואי בעי למיהד' – מצי הדר. הלכך, כי זכי בה מודר – ממדיר קא מתהני. **שנדרו קודם להפקרו.** שאסרו ואח"כ הפקירו. *)מה לי הפקרו קודם לנדרו. דהא כל זמן שלא זכה בו דמפקיר הוי, ודינא הוא דליחול נדריה עליה, ואמאי קתני ה"ז מותר?:
כל

*) [שייך לע"ב]

נ"ל הרמב"ן. יעב"ץ

הגהות הב"ח

(א) במשנה אלא החנוני ואומר איש פלוני מודר ממני: (ב) רש"י ד"ה קונם שדה שאני חורש בה שלא: (ג) ד"ה ור' יוסי אוסר בכה דמניחו: (ד) ד"ה מה מתנה וכו' דלאתיה לידי מקבל אף הפקר כל"ל והס"ד: (ה) ד"ה מתיב וד"ה אמר רבי יוסי הד"א:

פי' הרא"ש

אלא לא ילוה ממנו מאי קמהני ליה. בשלמא לא ישאילנו דהא מהני ליה אלא לא ישאל ממנו מאי קמהני ליה בשלמא לא ילוה ממנו ולא יקח ממנו דקא מהני ליה אלא לא ישאל ממנו מאי קמהני ליה ואיכא לפרש בשלמא לא יקח ניחא דקמהני ליה וכן קושיין דלא ילוה איכא לשנויי בדוחק שמא יפרע זוזי טבי ותקילי יותר מאותן שהלוה לו ונמצא נהנה מודר אלא לא ישאל הימנו שמחזיר לו החפץ בעין מה הנאה קא מטי ליה: **גזירה לישאל אטו להשאיל וכן כולהו.** האי כולהו לאו דוקא דלא קאי אלא ילוה: **מתני'** **המודר הנאה מחבירו ואין לו מה יאכל.** אורחא דמילתא: **ובא ונוטל מזה.** אם ירצה לתת לו אבל משום הכי אינו חייב לתת לו שהרי לא אמר לו שיתן דאם היה חייב לשלם לו על פי הדברים שאמר לו משום דמוכחא מילתא כשאמר לו איש פלוני מודר הנאה ממני ואין לו מה יאכל ואיני יודע מה אעשה לו דלשם כך אמר לו שיתן לו וכיון שהוציא ממון מידו על פי דבורו חייב לשלם לו אם כן היה אסור החנוני ליתן לו בשליחות המדיר: **היה ביתו לבנות וגדרו לגדור.** לא זו אף זו קתני: **נותן לאחר לשום מתנה כו'.** ודוקא באין לו מה יאכל התירו זה: **ור' יוסי אוסר.** בגמרא מפרש טעמא: **גמ'** **מה מתנה עד דאתי מרשות נותן לרשות מקבל.** כדאמרינן בכריתות (דף כד.) דהנותן מתנה לחבירו ואמר הלה אי אפשי בה הדרה למרה דברשות נותן היא עד שתבא ליד המקבל: **אף הפקר כן.** הלכך כי זכי ביה מרשותיה קא זכי וכאילו נותנו לידו: *) **ומה לי הפקרו קודם לנדרו.** הא ברשותיה קאי עד דאתי ליד הזוכה:

*) [שייך לע"ב]

אין

תוספות

אמר לו השאילני פרתך אמר ליה אינה פנויה. [illegible] קונם שדי שאני חורש בה לעולם אם היה דרכו לחרוש הוא אסור. [illegible] וכל אדם מותרין לחרוש לו שלא נתכוון לאסור אלא על מי שדרכו לחרוש בה: *בשלמא לא ילונו [illegible] אלא לא ילוה הימנו מאי קמתהני מיניה המודר. ה"ג בשלמא לא יקח הימנו ולא ילוה הימנו אלא לא ישאל [illegible]

הדר פרע מדיר ליה זוזי טבין ותקולי ומהני ליה אלא לא ישאילנו כלי בעין מאי מהני ליה מדיר: אמר אביי גזירה לשאול משום להשאיל למודר וכן כלהו לא שמא ילוה לו אבל לא יקח אסור מן הדין אטו ליקח בפחות כדמפרש בזבינא מליעתא דלא יקח בפחות קאמר דהשתא נפסד המוכר אלא משום גזירה דגזרינן אטו יקח המודר ליה וקשה דהא תנן (לקמן מז:) האומר הריני עליך המודר אסור וכן סוף פ' ארבע [illegible] לישראל לוקח ביותר למודר מותר ליהנות ולא מדיר ולא גזרינן דלא יהנה פן יהנה דגזרינן לשאול אטו להשאיל ונראה להר"מ דרגילות הוא כשאדם משאיל לחבירו שחבירו משאל דברים: **המודר** הנאה מחבירו ואין לו מה יאכל ילך וכו'. אורחא דמילתא [illegible] לו ובא ונוטל מזה. אם ירצה דהא אין הפועלים יכולין לתבוע כלום: **ביתו** לבנות. [illegible] מזון כל כך: **נותן** לאחר במתנה והלה מותר. ולא התירו אלא כשאין לו מה יאכל [illegible]

אסורות בין ברבים בין ביחיד בנדרים שלא התירו אלא בשעת הדחק שאין לו מה יאכל. לשון הרב רבי אליעזר ממי"ץ: **הרי** הן מופקרין כו' ורבי יוסי אוסר. מפרש בגמ' מאי טעמא דרבי יוסי קסבר הפקר כמתנה מה מתנה יכול לחזור עד דאתי לרשות מקבל ולא הוי כלום עד דאתי לידו אף הפקר עד דאתי לרשות זוכה [illegible] בשעה שזוכה בו של מדיר הוא והפקר דוקא פליג רבי יוסי אבל נותן במתנה לא פליג:

אֲבָל אִם הָיָה הֶפְקֵירוֹ קוֹדֶם לְנִדְרוֹ – הֲרֵי זֶה מוּתָּר. וְאִי אָמְרַתְּ עַד דְּאָתֵי לִרְשׁוּת זוֹכֶה – מַה לִּי נִדְרוֹ קוֹדֶם לְהֶפְקֵירוֹ, מַה לִּי הֶפְקֵירוֹ קוֹדֶם לְנִדְרוֹ? הוּא מוֹתִיב לָהּ וְהוּא מְשַׁנֵּי לָהּ: •כָּל הַנּוֹדֵר – אֵין דַּעְתּוֹ עַל מַה שֶּׁהִפְקִיר. מְתִיב רָבָא: *"מִקְצָתָן לָרִאשׁוֹן וְכוּלָּן לַשֵּׁנִי" – רִאשׁוֹן קָנָה, שֵׁנִי לֹא קָנָה! אֶלָּא אֲמַר רָבָא, הַיְינוּ טַעְמָא דְּרַבִּי יוֹסֵי: גְּזֵירָה מִשּׁוּם *מַתְּנַת בֵּית חוֹרוֹן. תַּנְיָא: *אהַמַּפְקִיר אֶת שָׂדֵהוּ, כָּל שְׁלֹשָׁה יָמִים – יָכוֹל לַחֲזוֹר בּוֹ, מִכָּאן וְאֵילָךְ – אֵין יָכוֹל לַחֲזוֹר בּוֹ. אָמַר

רש"י

אֲבָל אִם הָיָה הֶפְקֵירוֹ קוֹדֶם לְנִדְרוֹ מוּתָּר. דְּמִסְתָּמָא, כִּי מַדִּיר אֱינָשׁ – עַל מַה דְּאִית לֵיהּ בִּרְשׁוּתֵיהּ הוּא דְּאַדְרֵיהּ, וְלָא עַל מַה שֶּׁכְּבָר הִפְקִיר, וְאַהָכִי מוּתָּר. וְאִי אָמְרַתְּ טַעְמָא דְּרַבִּי יוֹסֵי מִשּׁוּם דְּלָא הָוֵי הֶפְקֵר עַד דְּאָתְיָא לִרְשׁוּת זוֹכֶה – מַה לִּי נִדְרוֹ קוֹדֶם כו', הָא כִּי נָדַר הַאי אַכַּתִּי לָא זָכָה בֵּיהּ שׁוּם אָדָם, וְאַמַּאי מוּתָּר? הַיְינוּ טַעְמָא דְּשָׁרֵי דְּכָל הַמַּדִּיר אֵין דַּעְתּוֹ עַל מַה שֶּׁהִפְקִיר. אֶלָּא עַל מַה שֶּׁעֲדַיִין בִּרְשׁוּתוֹ, וְאַהָכִי מוּתָּר. מְתִיב רָבָא כו' מִקְצָתָן לָרִאשׁוֹן וְכוּלָּן לַשֵּׁנִי. שכ"מ שֶׁכָּתַב מִקְצָת נְכָסָיו לְאֶחָד, וְהַשְּׁאָר כּוּלָּן כָּתַב לַשֵּׁנִי. רִאשׁוֹן קָנָה שֵׁנִי לֹא קָנָה. וְאִם עָמַד – חוֹזֵר בַּשֵּׁנִי וְאֵינוֹ חוֹזֵר בָּרִאשׁוֹן. לְפִי שֶׁכְּשֶׁכָּתַב לָרִאשׁוֹן שִׁייֵּר לְעַצְמוֹ מַה שֶּׁנָּתַן אַחַר כָּךְ לַשֵּׁנִי. וּמִן הַשֵּׁנִי חוֹזֵר – דְּלָא שִׁייֵּר כְּלוּם, וּמִשּׁוּם הָכִי לָא קָנָה. וְאִי אָמְרַתְּ לָא הָוֵי מַתָּנָה עַד דְּמָטֵי לְיַד מְקַבֵּל, אַמַּאי קָנָה רִאשׁוֹן טְפֵי מִשֵּׁנִי? הָא כֵּיוָן דְּלָא אָתֵי לִידֵיהּ – לָא הָוֵי שֶׁלּוֹ. וְכִי הֵיכִי דְּשֶׁל שֵׁנִי הָוֵי שִׁיּוּר לָרִאשׁוֹן – אִיכָּא לְמֵימַר נַמִי דְּשֶׁל רִאשׁוֹן הָוֵי שִׁיּוּר לַשֵּׁנִי, הוֹאִיל וּבִרְשׁוּתוֹ שֶׁל נוֹתֵן הֵן אַכַּתִּי כָּל זְמַן דְּלָא אָתֵי לִידֵיהּ דְּהַאי! אֶלָּא, מִדְּקָנָה רִאשׁוֹן – ש"מ לֵיתָא לְהָא דְּר' יוֹחָנָן, דְּאָמַר לָא זָכֵי מְקַבֵּל עַד דְּאָתְיָא לִידֵיהּ. אֶלָּא אֲמַר רָבָא. לְעוֹלָם קָסָבַר רַבִּי יוֹסֵי דְּמִן הַתּוֹרָה הָוְיָא (א) מַתָּנָה לְאַלְתַּר, אַע"ג דְּלָא אָתֵי לִרְשׁוּת זוֹכֶה, וְהוֹאִיל וּמִשָּׁעָה שֶׁהִפְקִירוֹ הָוֵי הֶפְקֵר. וְאַמַּאי טַעְמָא דְּר' יוֹסֵי דְּאָסַר הָכָא בְּמַתְנִיתִין. הַיְינוּ טַעְמָא דְּרַבִּי יוֹסֵי. דְּלָא אָמַר דְּלֶיהֱוֵי הֶפְקֵר. מִשּׁוּם מַתְּנַת בֵּית חוֹרוֹן. כְּדִתְנַן בְּפִרְקִין לְקַמָּן (דף מח.), דְּמוֹכְחָא מִילְּתָא דְּלָא יְהָבָהּ לַחֲבֵרוֹ אֶלָּא בִּשְׁבִיל שֶׁיָּבֹא אָבִיו וְיֹאכַל. וְהָכָא נַמִי, אִי אָמְרִינַן הָוֵי הֶפְקֵר, כֵּיוָן דְּאֵין שָׁם אַחֵר – מֶיחֱזֵי דְּבִשְׁבִיל מוּדָּר מַמָּשׁ הִפְקִיר, וְהַיְינוּ דּוּמְיָא דְּבֵית חוֹרוֹן. הִלְכָּךְ (ב) אוֹקְמִינַן אַדְּרַבָּנַן, דְּלָא הָוֵי הֶפְקֵר עַד דְּאָתֵי לִרְשׁוּת זוֹכֶה. וְאִית דִּמְפָרְשֵׁי: אֶלָּא אֲמַר רָבָא: לְעוֹלָם לר' יוֹסֵי מִדְּאוֹרַיְיתָא לָא הָוֵי הֶפְקֵר עַד דְּאָתֵי לִרְשׁוּת זוֹכֶה, וְלָא דָּמֵי לְמַתָּנָה. וּמִדְּרַבָּנַן הוּא דְּהָוֵי הֶפְקֵר אַע"ג דְּלָא אָתֵי לִרְשׁוּת זוֹכֶה, כִּדְאָמְרִי' לְקַמָּן כְּדֵי שֶׁלֹּא תִּשְׁתַּכַּח תּוֹרַת הֶפְקֵר, וְהָכָא בְּמַתְנִי' כו'. הַמַּפְקִיר אֶת שָׂדֵהוּ כָּל ג' יָמִים הָרִאשׁוֹנִים יָכוֹל לַחֲזוֹר בּוֹ. בֵּין אָמַר "אֵין רְצוֹנִי שֶׁיְּהֵא הֶפְקֵר", דְּחָזַר בּוֹ, וּבֵין זָכָה בּוֹ אִיהוּ בְּתוֹךְ ג' יָמִים, וְשֵׁם הֶפְקֵר לָא חָיֵיל בֵּיהּ וְלָא פָּקַע לֵיהּ מִידֵי מַעֲשֵׂר. דְּהֶפְקֵר פָּטוּר מִן הַמַּעֲשֵׂר, כִּדְקָאָמְרִינַן (שבת דף סח.): וְנֶאֱמַר – פְּרָט לְהֶפְקֵר. מִכָּאן וְאֵילָךְ אֵינוֹ יָכוֹל לַחֲזוֹר בּוֹ. וּפָטוּר מִן הַמַּעֲשֵׂר כָּל מַאן דְּזָכֵי בֵּיהּ.

אָמַר

ר"ן

כל הנודר אין דעתו על מה שהפקיר. אין הכי נמי דמלי הדר ביה, דדיליה הוי, ואי הוה אסר ליה לאותו דבר שהפקיר בפירוש – חייל נדרו. אלא הכא היינו טעמא, משום דכל האוסר נכסיו סתם אין דעתו על מה שהפקיר. הכי גרסינן: מתיב רבא מקצתן לראשון וכולן לשני שני זכה להשתעבד בראשון. וברייתא היא בתוספתא דבבא בתרא,* והכי פירושו: מי שיש לו שני עבדים, ונתן מקצת נכסיו לראשון, ואח"כ נתן לשני – לא קנה ראשון. דדלמא בגופיה שייר, וכיון שעצמו לא קנה – נכסים נמי לא קנה, דעבדא דקני נכסי הוא. אבל שני זכה בעצמו ובנכסים, וזכה נמי להשתעבד בראשון, דלגביה ליכא שיורא. ואי אמרת דאין דעתו על מה שהפקיר – ה"נ אין דעתו על מה שנתן כבר! **אלא אמר רבא***. טעמא דר' יוסי משום מתנת בית חורון אמר. ומדינא ודאי אפילו לר' יוסי שרי, דמכי אפקריה נפקא ליה מרשותיה. אלא דכיון דאנן סהדי דלא אפקריה אלא כדי שיזכה מודר, אי שרינן ליה – אתי למישרי אפי' היכא דאמר בפירוש, וכמעשה דבית חורון דתנן בפרקין דלקמן: ואינן לפניך אלא כדי שיבא אבא ויאכל עמנו. ומש"ה דוקא בנדרו קודם להפקרו אסור, דאיכא למגזר. אבל הפקרו קודם לנדרו שרי. **תניא המפקיר את שדהו כל ג' ימים יכול לחזור בו.** ראיתי שמועה זו שלא נתבררה יפה בדברי הראשונים ז"ל לפי עניות דעתי. וכך נראה לי בפירושה: כל שלשה ימים יכול לחזור בו, מכאן ואילך – אין יכול לחזור בו. מדקא מפליג בסיפא דאם אמר תהא שדה זו מופקרת ליום אחד וכו' בין זכה ללא זכה, דקתני שעד שלא זכה יכול לחזור בו ומשזכה אין יכול לחזור בו, וברישא לא מפליג בהכי, אלא תולה חזרה בקודם ג' ולאחר ג' – ש"מ הכי קתני: כל ג' ימים יכול לחזור בו מהפקירו, ואפילו זכה אחר קודם חזרתו – לא קנה. ומפרש טעמא לקמן: דמפקרין והדרין בהון. דמשום דהפקר פטור מן המעשר היו הרמאין מפקירין שדותיהן כדי להפטר, והיה דעתן בשעת הפקירן שיחזרו בהן ויזכו בהן, ונמצא שלא היה הפקירן אלא להערמה בלבד, ולפיכך הוצרכו לומר שאם יזכו בהם – לא יהו כזוכים מן ההפקר. והוצרכו גם כן לומר שאפילו יזכה בו אחר – לא יקנה, ויהא מפקיר יכול לחזור בו תוך ג'. ואע"ג דלגבי אחר ליכא למיחש לרמאין, אפ"ה – אי לא הא לא קיימא הא, שאם יראו הרמאין שכשיזכה בו אחר קנה – לא ישמעו לדברי חכמים שהם לא יקנו, דלימרו: כי היכי דלאחר זכי מהפקרא – אנן נמי מהפקרא זכינן. ועוד: שכיון שנהגו הרמאין ברמאותן זה כל ג' ימים – אינו מתברר שיהא הפקר, דאיכא למיחש דלא מדעתייהו מפקרי אלא להערמה בלבד, ולא הוי הפקר. ולפיכך ראוי לומר דאפי' זכה בו אחר – יכול מפקיר לחזור בו, שעדיין לא נגמר הפקירו. מכאן ואילך – אין יכול לחזור בו, ואפי' לא זכה בו אדם – לא כל הימנו לחזור בו, משום דלאחר שלשה תו ליכא למיחש לרמאין, שכל שנעשה ההפקר ברמאות – אין הבעלים מאחרין לזכות בו יותר מג'.

ואי

אמר

עין משפט נר מצוה

נט א מיי' פ"ב מהלכות נדרים הלכה יז סמג לאוין רמב טוש"ע ח"מ סימן רעג סעיף ט:

[פ"ט ע"ק]

הגהות הב"ח

(א) רש"י ד"ה אלא אמר רבא וכו' דמן התורה הויא הפקר לאלתר כמתנה אע"ג דלא אתי לרשות זוכה ודקשיא והואיל ומשעה: (ב) ד"ה היינו טעמא וכו' הלכך אמרו רבנן:

גליון הש"ס

גמ' כל הנודר. עי' לקמן דף מו ע"ב בר"ן ד"ה ה"ד ועי' בב"ק דף קב ע"ב:

תוספות

ואי אמרת עד דאתי לרשות זוכה מה לי נדרו קודם להפקירו מה לי הפקירו קודם לנדרו. בכלהו ליתסר דהא ברשותיה קיימי: **אין** דעתו לאסור מה שהפקיר. הלכך הוי הפקירו קודם לנדרו שרי: **מתיב** רבא מקצתה לראשון וכולה לשני. פירוש המחלק נכסיו: **ראשון** קנה. דהוי מתנה במקצת של שכיב מרע דבעינן קנין ואם עמד אינו חוזר והשני לא קנה דהויא מתנה בכולה דחוזר כשעמד ומיירי הכא כשעמד ומשום הכי ראשון קנה דהוה מתנה במקצת וע"כ בנמלך מעיקרא כי יהיב לראשון לא היה בדעתו ליתן כלל לשני דהכי אמר בפרק מי שמת (דף קמח:) המחלק נכסיו אם כנמלך עמד אינו חוזר אלא באחרון ואם כמחלק שמתחלה כי יהיב לקמא מאז היה בדעתו לחלק אף לשני עמד חוזר אף בראשון אם כן ע"כ כולן לשני דקאמר אף מקצת שנתן לראשון יהא נתון לשני הלכך כי אמר מקצתו לראשון לא היה בדעתו לומר ומקצתו לשני ושוב כי אמר וכולן לשני הוי נמלך דאי כולן לשני דקאמר היה רוצה לתת השאר שלא נתתי לראשון יהא לשני אם כן ראשון אמאי קנה שמא מתחלתו כי אמר מקצתו לראשון היה דעתו ליתן השאר לשני ומנלן שהוא נמלך והיה לו להזכיר אם כנמלך והוי כמחלק וניחא דאם עמד חוזר אלא ע"כ ר"ל אף מה שנתן לראשון ונמלך הוי אלמא דעתו על מה שנתן ה"נ נימא דעתו על מה שהפקיר. כך פר"ת. ויש ספרים דגרסי מקצתו לראשון לא קנה ורבינו נתנאל אמר דברייתא היא בתוספתא גבי עבדים דכתב לראשון מקצת נכסיו ולשני כתב כל נכסיו [ראשון] לא יצא לחירות כיון דשייר מנכסיו ושני קנה עצמו דהא לא שייר לכך משתעבד אף בראשון אלמא דעתו ליתן לשני אף מה שנתן לראשון דאל"כ לא קנה עצמו דהא שייר והוא עצמו נתנו לראשון והשתא אין לו כלום אלא ע"כ דעתו אמה שנתן כבר ה"נ נימא הכי: **אלא** אמר רבא משום מעשה בית חורון. בשלהי השותפין לקמן (דף מח.) ואסרו מטעם שלא היתה מתנה גמורה שלא גמר בלבו לתתה הכא נמי אין נראה הפקר שדומה כאילו לא הפקירו אלא לדעת שיזכה בו המודר: **תניא** המפקיר שדהו כל ג' ימים יכול לחזור בו. וחייב במעשר האוכל ממנו אם אינו מתכוין לדבר דהפקירו אינו הפקר כלל אע"פ שלא חזר בו נמי לא הוי הפקר וטעמא משום דאיסור טבל ידוע לכל ויודעין כל העולם דזה איסור טבל עליו וזה הפקר אינו מפורסם ולפיכך כל ג' ימים יכול לחזור בו בין זכה בו הוא בין זכה בו אחר ומש"ה חייב במעשר כיון דיכול לחזור ולכך גזרו מפני הרמאים דמפקרי והדרי בהו כדמסיק ועד שלשה ימים יש לחוש שמא יאמרו העולם הוא אוכל פירותיו שאינן מתוקנים אבל לאחר שלשה לא גזרו דמכאן ואילך ידוע ההפקר ומועיל ההפקר אפילו לא זכה בו אדם ואין חייב במעשר אבל במתני' המודר מותר מיד כשהפקיר דהתם כמו שאינו ידוע ההפקר כן אינו ידוע שהדירו חבירו דכוותיה דהכא אנו מתירין משום דידוע ההפקר לאחר שלשה ימים כמו איסור הטבל חייב במעשר וליכא למימר דזה מן החיוב על הפטור דמעשר הוא מיניה וביה:

אמר

מסורת הש"ס

ב"ב קמח:

כתובות עט. [לקמן מח. ב"ב קלז.] [תוספתא מעשרות פ"ג]

פי' הרא"ש

אין דעתו על מה שהפקיר. ואף על גב דברשותו קאי בתר דעתא דנודר אזלינן ואין דעתו עליו: **מקצתן לראשון וכולן לשני ראשון קנה שני לא קנה.** שכיב מרע המחלק נכסיו ונותן מקצתן לראשון בקנין ואח"כ אמר וכולן לשני ראשון קנה ואם עמד אינו חוזר דמתנת שכיב מרע במקצת הרי היא כמתנת בריא אם לא צוה מחמת מיתה שני לא קנה דהוי מתנת שכיב מרע בכולה ואם עמד חוזר ומדקנה ראשון אלמא חשבינן ליה כנמלך דמעיקרא כשנתן לראשון לא היה דעתו ליתן לשני דאי חשבינן ליה כמחלק שמעיקרא היה בדעתו ליתן לשניהן אף ראשון נמי לא קנה דהא אמרי' בפרק מי שמת שכיב מרע שכתב כל נכסיו לאחרים רואין אם כמחלק מת קנו כולם עמד חוזר בכולם אם כנמלך מת קנו כולם עמד אינו חוזר אלא באחרון ומדחשבינן ליה כנמלך אם כן כולן לשני דקאמר קאי גם אמקצת שנתן לראשון כי היה בדעתו לחזור בו ממתנת הראשון אם היה יכול ומעיקרא כשאמר מקצתן לראשון לא היה בדעתו ליתן לשני ושוב נמלך לחזור בו מן הראשון וליתן הכל לשני דאי וכולן לשני דקאמר היינו מה ששייר מנכסיו שלא נתנם לראשון ראשון אמאי קנה אם עמד הרי חילק כל נכסיו והוי מתנת ש"מ בכולה אלא ודאי כשנתן לראשון ה"נ דעתו על מה שנתן לשני דעתו על מה שהפקיר וי"ס גורסין ומקצתן לראשון וכולן לשני זכה שני להשתעבד בראשון וברייתא היא שנויה בתוספתא בהכותב נכסיו לשני עבדיו בשני שטרות וכתב לראשון מקצת נכסיו ולשני כתב כל נכסיו ראשון לא יצא לחירות כיון דשייר ושני יצא לחירות וקנה כל הנכסים והראשון בכללם אלמא דעתו על מה שנתן כבר לראשון ונתן הכל לשני דאל"כ גם לשני הוי מתנה במקצת ולא קנה: **משום מתנת בית חורון.** לקמן בפרק השותפין ואסורים משום שלא היתה מתנה גמורה ה"נ אינו נראה הפקר גמור כי נראה שלא הפקירו אלא בשביל שיזכה בה המודר: **כל שלשה ימים יכול לחזור בו.** ולומר אני חוזר בי ממה שהפקרתי ושוב אין אדם יכול לזכות בו הלכך אפילו קודם שחזר בו אין שם הפקר עליו אם אכל ממנו אדם ולא כוון לזכות מן ההפקר חייב במעשר וכן אם הוא לקטן שלא לשם זכיה מן ההפקר אלא לשם חזרה חייב במעשר ומיהו אם זכה בהן הוא או אחר פטור מן המעשר ולא יוכל אחר כך לבטל ההפקר כיון שכבר בא ליד אדם בתורת זכיה מן ההפקר וכן מוכח בסיפא גבי הפקר לזמן דקתני זכה בה בין הוא בין אחר אין יכול לחזור בו וקאי נמי אהפקר ליום אחד אלמא אע"ג שלא עברו ג' ימים כיון שזכה בתורת הפקר אין בו חזרה ומיהו מצינן לפרש הא דקתני בסיפא מי שזכה בו לאחר שלשה קאמר כדפרי' ברישא ואשבת חדש ושנה קאי אי נמי בהפקר בלא זמן תקנו חכמים שלא יהא פטור מן המעשר אם זכה בו בתוך שלשה ימים מפני הרמאין ואם לא יזכה בו בתוך ג' ימים יהיה ההפקר קיים ואם זכה בו אחר כך פטור מן המעשר אבל בהפקר ליום אחד עקרו תקנת חשש רמאין כדי שלא לבטל ההפקר לגמרי: **מכאן ואילך אינו יכול לחזור בו.** דמיד כשהפקירו חל ההפקר ויצא מרשותו ואין לו כח לחזור בו ופטור מן המעשר והא דאמרינן ברישא דתוך שלשה ימים יכול לחזור בו מפני תקנת הרמאין שרגילין להפקיר פירותיהן ולחזור ולזכות בהם כדי לפטרן מן המעשר לכך תקנו חכמים דלא הוי הפקר עד אחר שלשה לפטרו מן המעשר אגב זה תקנו בכל הפקר שיוכל לחזור תוך שלשה כל זמן שלא זכה בו אחר ואע"ג דתקנת הרמאים מפרש לקמן אליבא דר' יוסי גם רבנן נמי אית להו הך תקנתא ואי תקשי לך לפי מה שפירשתי דאם זכה לאחר בתורת זכיה פטור מן המעשר מאי אהנו חכמים בתקנתן וי"ל שהוא רוא(?) שאם הוא ילקט מלך זה אחרים ילקטו בו מלך אחר אבל אם היה יכול לחזור בו מדבורו היה מפקירו וחוזר בו מיד:

אמר

ם א ב מיי' פ"ב מהל' נדרים הלכה יח סמג לאוין רמב טוש"ע ח"מ סי' רעג סעיף ז:

א אָמַר "תְּהֵא שָׂדֶה זוֹ מוּפְקֶרֶת לְיוֹם אֶחָד, לְשַׁבָּת אַחַת, לְחֹדֶשׁ אֶחָד, לְשָׁנָה אַחַת, לְשָׁבוּעַ (א) אַחַת" עַד שֶׁלֹּא זָכָה בָּהּ, בֵּין הוּא בֵּין אַחֵר – יָכוֹל לַחֲזוֹר בּוֹ. מִשֶּׁזָּכָה בָּהּ, בֵּין הוּא בֵּין אַחֵר – אֵין יָכוֹל לַחֲזוֹר בּוֹ. רֵישָׁא רַבָּנַן, סֵיפָא ר' יוֹסֵי! אֲמַר עוּלָּא: ב סֵיפָא נַמִי רַבָּנַן הִיא. אִי הָכִי, אַמַּאי עַד שֶׁלֹּא זָכָה בָּהּ בֵּין הוּא בֵּין אַחֵר, יָכוֹל לַחֲזוֹ' בּוֹ? שָׁאנֵי שָׁנָה וְשָׁבוּעַ דְּלָא שְׁכִיחִי. ר"ל אֲמַר: מִדְּסֵיפָא ר' יוֹסֵי – רֵישָׁא נַמִי ר' יוֹסֵי, וְרֵישָׁא הַיְינוּ טַעְמָא – דְּלָא לִישְׁתַּכַּח תּוֹרַת הֶפְקֵר. אִי הָכִי אֲפִילּוּ מִיּוֹם הָרִאשׁוֹן נַמִי לֶיהֱוֵי הֶפְקֵר! אֲמַר רַבָּה: מִפְּנֵי הָרַמָּאִין, דְּמַפְקִירִין וְהָדְרִין בְּהוֹן. אֲבָל דְּאוֹרַיְיתָא לָא הָוֵי הֶפְקֵר?

וְדִלְמָא

רש"י

אָמַר תְּהֵא שָׂדֶה. מוּפְקֶרֶת. **לְשָׁבוּעַ א'.** לִשְׁמִיטָּה אַחַת (ב) **עַד שֶׁלֹּא זָכָה בָּהּ בֵּין הוּא בֵּין אַחֵר יָכוֹל לַחֲזוֹר בּוֹ.** אֲפִילּוּ בְּסוֹף שַׁבָּת אוֹ בְּסוֹף חֹדֶשׁ. **מִשֶּׁזָּכָה בָּהּ בֵּין הוּא בֵּין אַחֵר.** אֲפִילּוּ תּוֹךְ שָׁעָה (ג) מִשֶּׁהִפְקִירוֹ זָכָה בָּהּ שׁוּם אָדָם, אוֹ הוּא בְּעַצְמוֹ לְשׁוּם הֶפְקֵר – הָוֵי הֶפְקֵר. דְּקָסָבַר דְּלָא הָוֵי הֶפְקֵר עַד דְּאָתֵי לִרְשׁוּת זוֹכֶה. וּזְכִיָּה דִּידֵיהּ אוֹ דְּאַחֵר לָא חֲשִׁיבָא מִידֵּי עַד דְּרָפַק בָּהּ פּוּרְתָּא, כְּדַאֲמַר בְּמַסֶּכֶת עֵירוּבִין בְּפֶרֶק "עוֹשִׂין פַּסִּין" (דף כה.), בְּהַהִיא אִיתְּתָא דַּעֲבַדָא מְחִיצָּה בְּנִכְסֵי הַגֵּר, אֲתָא הַהוּא גַּבְרָא רַפַק בָּהּ פּוּרְתָּא, וְאוֹקְמוּהָ רַבָּנַן בִּידֵיהּ דְּהַהוּא גַּבְרָא. **רֵישָׁא רַבָּנַן וְסֵיפָא** רַבִּי יוֹסֵי. רֵישָׁא דְּאָמַר: מִשְּׁלֹשָׁה יָמִים וְאֵילָךְ, אֲפִילּוּ לָא אֲתָא לִרְשׁוּת זוֹכֶה אֵין יָכוֹל לַחֲזוֹר בּוֹ, דְּהָוֵי הֶפְקֵר – רַבָּנַן הִיא, וְדִין הוּא דַּאֲפִילּוּ מִיּוֹם רִאשׁוֹן הָוֵי הֶפְקֵר, אֶלָּא מִפְּנֵי הָרַמָּאִים, כִּדְאָמַר רַבָּה לְקַמָּן, לְדִבְרֵי הַכֹּל. וְסֵיפָא רַבִּי יוֹסֵי, דְּאָמַר: עַד שֶׁלֹּא זָכָה בָּהּ – בֵּין הוּא בֵּין אַחֵר יָכוֹל לַחֲזוֹר בּוֹ, דְּאָמַר דְּלָא הָוֵי הֶפְקֵר מִדְּאוֹרַיְיתָא עַד דְּאָתֵי לִרְשׁוּת זוֹכֶה, וּמִשּׁוּם הָכִי קָתָנֵי יָכוֹל לַחֲזוֹר בּוֹ, כְּר"י. **אָמַר עוּלָּא סֵיפָא נַמִי רַבָּנַן היא.** דְּוַדַּאי מִדְּאוֹרַיְיתָא אע"ג דְּלָא אַתְיָא לִרְשׁוּת זוֹכֶה – הָוֵי הֶפְקֵר לְאַלְתַּר, וַאֲפִילּוּ מִיּוֹם רִאשׁוֹן. וְהַאי דְּאָמַר כָּל שְׁלֹשָׁה יָמִים יָכוֹל לַחֲזוֹר, דִּלְגַבֵּיהּ לָא חֲשִׁיבָא הֶפְקֵר – מִפְּנֵי הָרַמָּאִין. דִּלְכוּלֵּי עָלְמָא אִית לְהוּ דְּרַבָּה דְּאָמַר מִפְּנֵי הָרַמָּאִין דְּהָדְרֵי וּמַחְזְקִי בְּהוּ, (ד) וְאָמְרִינַן דְּלָא הָוֵי הֶפְקֵר עַד שְׁלֹשָׁה יָמִים. וְסֵיפָא דְּאָמַר עַד שֶׁלֹּא זָכָה בָּהּ לָא הָוֵי הֶפְקֵר, דְּמַשְׁמַע עַד דְּאָתֵי לִרְשׁוּת זוֹכֶה – הַיְינוּ טַעְמָא, דְּשָׁאנֵי חֹדֶשׁ וְשָׁנָה וְשָׁבוּעַ דְּלָא שְׁכִיחִין דְּאֵין דַּרְכָּן שֶׁל בְּנֵי אָדָם לְהַפְקִיר לִזְמַן, וְכֵיוָן דְּזֶה שִׁינָּה – לְכָךְ אָמְרוּ חֲכָמִים דְּלָא לֶיהֱוֵי הֶפְקֵר, לְאַפְקוּעֵי מִמַּעֲשֵׂר, כָּל זְמַן דְּלָא אָתֵי לִרְשׁוּת זוֹכֶה. **ר"ל אָמַר מִדְּסֵיפָא** ר"י. דְּמַשְׁמַע דְּלָא לֶיהֱוֵי הֶפְקֵר עַד דְּאָתֵי לִרְשׁוּת זוֹכֶה. **רֵישָׁא** נַמִי. בְּתוֹךְ ג' וּלְאַחַר ג' – רַבִּי יוֹסֵי הִיא. וְרֵישָׁא הַיְינוּ טַעַם דִּלְאַחַר ג' יָמִים אֵין יָכוֹל לַחֲזוֹר בּוֹ, דְּהָוֵי הֶפְקֵר אע"ג דְּלָא אָתֵי לִרְשׁוּת זוֹכֶה (ה). מִשּׁוּם דְּלָא לִישְׁתַּכַּח תּוֹרַת הֶפְקֵר. דְּמִדְּאוֹרַיְיתָא וַדַּאי לָא הָוֵי הֶפְקֵר עַד דְּאָתֵי לִרְשׁוּת זוֹכֶה, וּלְעוֹלָם כָּל זְמַן דְּלָא אֲתָא לִידֵי זוֹכֶה – לָא הָוֵי הֶפְקֵר גָּמוּר, וְחַיָּיב חִיּוּב דִּתְרוּמָה וּמַעֲשֵׂר. וְהַאי דְּאוֹקְמוּהָ רַבָּנַן אַתּוֹרַת הֶפְקֵר – לָאו מִשּׁוּם לְאַפְקוּעֵי מִתְּרוּמָה וּמַעֲשֵׂר, דְּכֵיוָן דְּמִדְּאוֹרַיְיתָא חַיָּיב, דְּלָאו הֶפְקֵר הוּא – לָא מַפְקְעֵי לֵיהּ רַבָּנַן מִתְּרוּמָה וּמַעֲשֵׂר, דְּלָאו כָּל כְּמִינֵּיהּ, אֶלָּא כְּדֵי שֶׁלֹּא תִּשְׁתַּכַּח תּוֹרַת הֶפְקֵר. וּמ"מ גַּבֵּי שָׁנָה וְשָׁבוּעַ, כֵּיוָן דְּלָא שְׁכִיחִי – אוֹקְמוּהָ אַדְּאוֹרַיְיתָא, דְּלָא הָוֵי הֶפְקֵר עַד דְּאָתֵי לִידֵי זוֹכֶה, דְּלָא גָּזְרוּ בֵּיהּ רַבָּנַן – מִשּׁוּם שֶׁלֹּא תִּשְׁתַּכַּח תּוֹרַת הֶפְקֵר. **אִי הָכִי אֲפִילּוּ מִיּוֹם רִאשׁוֹן** (ו) לֶיהֱוֵי הֶפְקֵר. כְּדֵי שֶׁלֹּא תִּשְׁתַּכַּח כו'. **אָמַר רַבָּה.** בְּדִין הוּא דְּלֶהֱוֵי הֶפְקֵר מִדְּרַבָּנַן, אֶלָּא מִפְּנֵי הָרַמָּאִין דְּבָעֵי לְאַפְקוּעֵי שְׂדוֹתָם מִתְּרוּמָה וּמַעֲשֵׂר וְאַפְקְרֵי לְהוּ, וְאִי אָמְרִינַן דִּלְאַלְתַּר הָוֵי הֶפְקֵר וּפָטוּר מִן הַמַּעֲשֵׂר – הָדְרֵי (ז) מַחְזְקִי בְּהוּ. וְאַדְּהָכִי, כָּל שְׁלֹשָׁה יָמִים לָא הָוֵי הֶפְקֵר לְגַבֵּי אִיהוּ, דְּסָבְרֵי מִתּוֹךְ כָּךְ אָתֵי וּמַחֲזִיק בֵּיהּ וְהָוֵי דִּילֵיהּ, וּמִימְנְעֵי וְלָא מַפְקְרֵי. וּלְעוֹלָם אֲפִילּוּ לְאַחַר שְׁלֹשָׁה יָמִים לָא הָוֵי הֶפְקֵר מִדְּאוֹרַיְיתָא, עַד דְּאָתֵי לִרְשׁוּת זוֹכֶה: וּפָרֵיךְ. **אֲבָל מִדְּאוֹרַיְיתָא לָא הָוֵי הֶפְקֵר**

וְדִלְמָא

ר"ן

ואי אמר. תהא שדה זו מופקרת ליום אחד לשבת אחת וכו' עד שלא זכה בה בין הוא בין אחר יכול לחזור בו. **רישא** רבנן **וסיפא** רבי יוסי. קס"ד השתא דטעמא דרבי יוסי דאסר במתני' – כדרבי יוחנן, דאמר לעיל דהפקר כמתנה, דעד דאתי לרשות זוכה לא נפיק מרשות מפקיר. ומש"ה קאמר רישא רבנן וסיפא רבי יוסי. ובהכי אתיא ליה כולה ברייתא שפיר, דרישא קתני כל שלשה ימים יכול לחזור – מפני הרמאין, וכדפרישית. מכאן ואילך אין יכול לחזור בו – מדינא, דס"ל לרבנן דהפקר מעידנא דאפקריה מפקיר נפק ליה מרשותיה. וסיפא קתני דאם אמר "תהא שדה זו מופקרת ליום אחד" – בכה"ג ליכא למיחש לרמאין, דאי דעתיה בעידנא דאפקריה דליהדר וליזכי ביה לאלתר – למה ליה להפקירו לזמן ידוע? לאפקריה לגמרי, דכיון דדעתיה למיהדר ולמזכי ביה – לא נפקא ליה מידי. אלא ודאי לאותו זמן שהפקירו – גמר והפקיר בלא הערמה כלל. ולפיכך, משזכה בין הוא בין אחר – אין יכול לחזור בו. והא אתיא שפיר אפילו לרבנן. מיהו, מאי דקתני: עד שלא זכה בה בין הוא בין אחר יכול לחזור בו – רבי יוסי היא, דס"ל דעד דאתי לרשות זוכה לא נפיק מרשות המפקיר. דלרבנן, כיון דאמרי דנפיק מרשותו – היאך יכול לחזור בו? ואין הכי נמי דכי קתני לרבי יוסי: עד שלא זכה בה בין הוא בין אחר יכול לחזור בו – לאו דוקא בהפקר שהוא לזמן, כגוונא דסיפא. דאפילו בהפקר עולמית, דהיינו רישא – דיכול לחזור בו עד שלא זכה בה. ומיהו, משום דבדינא דמשזכה בה אינו יכול לחזור בו לא שוו הפקר שהוא לזמן עם הפקר עולמית, וכדכתיבנא, ואצטריך למיתני ליום אחד לשבת אחת – תנא נמי כההוא גוונא עד שלא זכה בה. וכי תימא: משזכה בה הוא, דקתני דאינו יכול לחזור בו, כלומר והוי הפקר אפילו לרבי יוסי, ופטור מן המעשר – היכי אתיא ליה שפיר? דהא כיון דס"ל לרבי יוסי דהפקר עד דאתי לרשות זוכה לא נפיק מרשות מפקיר – נמצא דכי הדר זכי ביה – מדידיה קא זכי, ולא מהפקרא, דלעולם לא נפקא מרשותי'! אפשר לומר: דנהי דקסבר רבי יוסי דעד דאתי לרשות זוכה לא נפיק מרשות מפקיר, אפילו הכי, כי היכי דאי זכי בה אחר זכי מהפקרא ולא ממתנה, כיון שהיה אפשר לאחר ג"כ לזכות בו – הכי נמי כי הדר איהו גופיה וזכי ביה בפירוש מתורת הפקר, ולא בסתם, כי היכי דלא ניתלי בחזרה – אף הוא עצמו זוכה מן ההפקר מיקרי, כיון שעדיין לא חזר בו, והיה אחר יכול לזכות בו. דמה לי הוא מה לי אחר. הלכך, אי רישא רבנן וסיפא רבי יוסי – מתוקמא ליה שפיר. מיהו, מילתא דתמיהא הוא היכי נקט לה תנא אליבא דתרי תנאי. ומשום הכי מתרץ עולא ואמר דסיפא נמי רבנן היא, וטעמא דעד שלא זכה בה בין הוא בין אחר דיכול לחזור בו – משום דשאני שבוע ושבת דלא שכיחן. כלומר, דלא שכיח דמפקרי אינשי בכי האי גונא. וכיון ששִׁנָּה זה – אמדינן לדעתיה דכיון שלא רצה להפקירו הפקר עולם, ואכתי אגיד גביה, אפילו באותו זמן שהפקירו – לא ניחא ליה דליפוק מרשותיה עד דזכי ביה אידך. הילכך סבירא להו לרבנן בהפקר שהוא לזמן מאי דסבירא ליה לרבי יוסי בהפקר עולמית. ואתיא סיפא שפיר לרבנן כדמתוקמא לרבי יוסי, שהרי בהפקר שהוא לזמן לא נחלקו. ור"ל **אמר מדסיפא** רבי יוסי **רישא** נמי רבי יוסי. ודקא קשיא לך: אי הכי, לאחר שלשה אמאי אין יכול לחזור בו – היינו טעמא: דלא לישתכח תורת הפקר. כלומר, אין הכי נמי דמדינא לרבי יוסי אפילו לאחר שלשה יכול לחזור בו. אלא היינו טעמא,

דאי

הגהות הב"ח

(א) גמ' לשבוע אחד עד: (ב) רש"י ד"ה אמר וכו' אחת הס"ד: (ג) ד"ה משזכה וכו' שעה אחת משהפקירו וכו' וזכיה דידיה: (ד) ד"ה אמר עולא וכו' ומחזקי בהו להכי אמרינן: (ה) ד"ה רישא נמי וד"ה משום הד"א: (ו) ד"ה אי הכי וכו' ראשון נמי להוי: (ז) ד"ה אמר רבה וכו' הדרי ומחזקי וכו' מתוך כך אתי אחר ומחזיק בהו והוי:

תוספות

אמר שדה זו מופקרת ליום א' לשנה א' עד שלא זכה בו בין הוא בין אחר יכול לחזור בו. וחייב במעשר מדרבנן ובטל ההפקר ומעשר מיניה וביה ואתי נמי כר' יוסי דמחמרינן עליה וה"ה בלא זמן והאי דנקט זמן לרבותא נקטיה דאע"ג דלא שכיח גזר ביה משום מתנת בית חורון כך פי' הר"ר אליעזר ועוד נרא' דנקט הפקר לזמן משום סיפא דאי משזכה בין הוא בין אחר אין יכול לחזור ואפילו תוך ג' ימים ודוקא משום דהפקר לזמן הוא אבל בסתם לא כדפרישית אבל האי דלזמן מועט מסתמא דעתו להפקר גמור דלא שייך למיגזר ועוד דלדוקא זכה אחר אבל הוא לא ולהכי נקטיה ומשום דרישא נקט הוא הכא נמי נקטיה דכיון דאתי לרשות זוכה לא שייך למיגזר אבל אם הוא יהיה פטור שייך למיגזר: **רישא** רבנן וסיפא ר' יוסי. בתמיה: **אמר** עולא סיפא רבנן וכו' כיון דלא שכיח וגריעי מודו רבנן ואף על גב דלא מחמירין במודר הכא מחמירין טפי דאינו הפקר עד שיזכה בו אחר כדפרישית אבל כשזכה פטור מן המעשר אפילו תוך שלשה ואף ע"ג דברישא אמר חייב עד לאחר שלשה הכא הטעם

פי' הרא"ש

אמר תהא שדה זו מופקרת ליום א' לשבת אחת כו'. ואחר הזמן הזה אם לא יזכה בו אדם תהיה שלי כבתחילה: **עד שלא זכה בו בין הוא בין אחר יכול לחזור בו.** ולבטל ההפקר דלא יצאת מרשות המפקיר עד שיזכה בו אחר הלכך כיון שחזר בו פקע ההפקר וחייב במעשר: **רישא רבנן וסיפא ר' יוסי.** דלרבנן חל הפקר מיד ולר' יוסי עד דאתי לרשות הזוכה וכדמוקי ר' יוחנן פלוגתייהו בהכי הלכך רישא רבנן כדפרישית דלאחר ג' אין יכול לחזור בו ותוך ג' ימים יכול לחזור בו מפני הרמאין וסיפא ר' יוסי דלא הוי הפקר עד דאתי ליד הזוכה הלכך כל זמן שלא זכה בו אדם יכול לחזור בו: **עולא אמר סיפא רבנן היא.** פירוש כמו רישא: **ושאני הפקר לזמן דלא שכיח.** הלכך הוי הפקר גרוע כיון שלא הפקירו לעולם ומודו רבנן בהא שלא גמר בדעתו שיהיה הפקר עד שיזכה בו אדם כי הוא מצפה שמא לא יזכה בו אדם בתוך זמן זה ויחזור אליו: **מדסיפא רבי יוסי כו' רישא נמי ר' יוסי כו' דלא לישתכח תורת הפקר.** ומן הדין לעולם היה יכול לחזור בו וחייבת במעשר דלא הוי הפקר עד דאתי לרשות הזוכ' אלא שתקנו חכמים דלאחר שלשה ימים לא יוכל לחזור כדי שלא תשתכח תורת הפקר שלא יטעו לומר אין הפקר פוטר כלל מן המעשר אפי' זכה בו אחר קודם חזרתו הלכך עשאוה הפקר דרבנן לפטרו מן המעשר ומיהו מדאוריי' מיחייב במעשר ונפקא מינה שצריך לעשר מיניה וביה ולא ממקום אחר עליו דעשאוהו הפקר מדבריהם כדי שלא תשתכח תורת הפקר ולרבא דס"ל דלר' יוסי נמי הוי הפקר לאלתר ולא פליגי ר' יוסי ורבנן בהפקר דאורייתא אלא דר' יוסי גזר מדרבנן משום מתנת בית חורון לדידיה מוקי הך ברייתא בין רבנן ובין ר' יוסי ושאני שנה ושבוע דלא שכיחי: **אי הכי אפילו יום ראשון נמי.** ליתקנו רבנן שלא יוכל לחזור בו כדי שלא תשתכח תורת הפקר כי במה שתקנו דלאחר ג' ימים אין יכול לחזור בו אין זו הוכחה שלא לשתכח תורת הפקר כי מילתא דלא שכיחא היא שיעמוד הפקר בלא זכיה שלשה ימים כי הכל ממהרין לזכות בו ואם באו לתקן שלא תשתכח תורת הפקר לר' יוסי היה להם לתקן אפילו תוך שלשה ימים נמי בשלמא לרבנן ניחא דוקא לאחר שלשה ימים מפני הרמאין: **ומשני** רבה דלר' יוסי נמי נמנעו לתקן דמיום ראשון לא הוי הפקר מפני הרמאין וקשה דמה יכוליהו הרמאין במה שיפקירו אליבא דר' יוסי והלא מן התורה חייבין לעשר ואפשר לפרש אליבא דר' יוסי [illegible]

ודלמא

(תוספות, המשך) כדפי': **ריש** לקיש אמר אפי' רישא אתיא כר' יוסי. דמחמיר במדיר הכא נמי חייב דאפילו לאחר שלשה לא הוי הפקר עד דאתי לרשות זוכה משום רמאות אבל אמרו חכמים לאחר שלשה כדי שלא תשתכח תורת הפקר והוי פטור מן המעשר: **אי** הכי אפי' מיום ראשון. [illegible] דחיישינן לשלא תשתכח תורת הפקר ושביק שיטתו דלא חל עד דאתי לרשות זוכה היכי [illegible] בשלמא לעולא דמוקי לה כרבנן דאמרי כשיטתייהו דמודר שלא תשתכח מפני [illegible] לא הוי הפקר אלא נתנו הכתוב לחכמים ויש לנו לפרש הפקר דאורייתא במקום דלא [illegible] דעיקר הפקר לא מצינו אלא בשביעית והתם לא אתי לידי רמאות דאינו יכול להחליף [illegible] שנית ודומיא דשביעית דלא אתי לידי רמאות כגון אחר שלשה הוי הפקר אבל תוך [illegible] אוסר במתניתין מפני רמאין תוך שלשה יהנה המודר לא משום מתנת [illegible] משום דאורייתא לא הוה הפקר כל כמה דיכול ליתי לידי רמאות כך פירש האביעזר. [illegible] דף מג:) דהפקר אם היה קודם נדרו אז יכול ליהנות אבל לאחר לא יהנה לעולם אפילו [illegible]

ודלמא

[illegible]

סא א מיי' פ"ה מהל' מתנות עניים הל' כז:

וְדִלְמָא אָתֵי לְעַשּׂוּרֵי מִן הַחִיּוּב עַל הַפְּטוּר, וּמִן הַפְּטוּר עַל הַחִיּוּב! דְּאָמְרִי' לֵיהּ: כִּי מַעַשְׂרַתְּ עֲשַׂר מִינֵּיהּ וּבֵיהּ. מֵיתִיבֵי: *אהַמַּפְקִיר אֶת כַּרְמוֹ, וְלַשַּׁחַר עָמַד וּבְצָרוֹ — חַיָּיב בְּפֶרֶט וּבְעוֹלְלוֹת וּבְשִׁכְחָה וּבְפֵיאָה, וּפָטוּר מִן הַמַּעֲשֵׂר. בִּשְׁלָמָא לְעוּלָּא — דְּרַבָּנַן קָתָנֵי לָהּ, וּדְאוֹרַיְיתָא קָתָנֵי לָהּ. אֶלָּא לְרֵישׁ לָקִישׁ, אַמַּאי פָּטוּר מִן הַמַּעֲשֵׂר? אָמַר לָךְ: כִּי אֲמַרִי אֲנָא — לר' יוֹסֵי, הָא — רַבָּנַן הִיא.

אִיבָּעֵית

רש"י

וְדִילְמָא אָתֵי לְעַשּׂוּרֵי מִן הַפְּטוּר עַל הַחִיּוּב וּמִן הַחִיּוּב עַל הַפְּטוּר. דְּכֵיוָן דְּאָמְרַתְּ דְּכָל שְׁלֹשָׁה יָמִים לָא הָוֵי הֶפְקֵר לָא מִדְּאוֹרַיְיתָא וְלָא מִדְּרַבָּנַן, וְאָמְרִינַן לֵיהּ דְּלִיתְרוֹם הַאי דְּהִפְקִיר, סָבַר הַמַּפְקִיר: וַדַּאי מִדְּאוֹרַיְיתָא הָוֵי הֶפְקֵר, וְהֶפְקֵר פָּטוּר מִלְּאַפְרוּשֵׁי מִינֵּיהּ תְּרוּמָה וּמַעֲשֵׂר, אֶלָּא מִדְּרַבָּנַן הוּא דִּמְחַיְּיבֵי לְאַפְרוּשֵׁי, מִפְּנֵי הָרַמָּאִין. וְאָתוּ לְעַשּׂוּרֵי מִן הַחִיּוּב עַל הַפְּטוּר. דְּדִילְמָא אִית לֵיהּ עָלִין שֶׁאֵינוֹ נָקוּב דְּחַיָּיב לְעַשּׂוּרֵי מִדְּרַבָּנַן וְלָא מִדְּאוֹרַיְיתָא, דְּלָא קָרֵינָא בֵּיהּ "הַיּוֹצֵא הַשָּׂדֶה", וְאָמַר: הַאי מִדְּרַבָּנַן וְהַאי מִדְּרַבָּנַן, וּמַפְרִישׁ מֵהַאי דְּהֶפְקֵר אַהַאי עָלִין שֶׁאֵינוֹ נָקוּב, וְהַתּוֹרָה אָמְרָה "וַהֲרֵמוֹתֶם מִמֶּנּוּ" — מִן הַחִיּוּב עַל הַחִיּוּב, וְלֹא מִן הַפְּטוּר עַל הַחִיּוּב, (א) מִפְּנֵי שֶׁנִּרְאֶה כְּפוֹדֶה תְּרוּמָה, כְּאָדָם זֶה שֶׁפּוֹדֶה הֶקְדֵּשׁוֹ בְּמָעוֹת, וּתְרוּמָה וּמַעֲשֵׂר אֵין לָהֶם פִּדְיוֹן לְעוֹלָם. הִלְכָּךְ, אֲפִילּוּ מִן הַחִיּוּב לֹא אָמְרוּ לִתְרוֹם אֶלָּא מִן הַמּוּקָּף. ומ"מ, אִם תָּרַם מִזֶּה עַל זֶה שֶׁלֹּא מִן הַמּוּקָּף — תְּרוּמָה, הוֹאִיל שֶׁזֶּה וָזֶה חַיָּיב הוּא. ל"א: אִם אָמַרְתָּ דְּמִכָּאן וְאֵילָךְ אֵין יָכוֹל לַחֲזוֹר בּוֹ, דְּמִדְּרַבָּנַן הָוֵי הֶפְקֵר אֲבָל מִדְּאוֹרַיְיתָא לָא הָוֵי הֶפְקֵר — הָשְׁתָּא נַמִי אָתֵי מִינֵּיהּ חוּרְבָּא, דְּהַאי מַפְקִיר סָבַר: אֲפִילּוּ מִדְּאוֹרַיְיתָא הָוֵי הֶפְקֵר, וְהַאי דִּמְחַיֵּיב תְּרוּמָה וּמַעֲשֵׂר — מִדְּרַבָּנַן הוּא, וְאָתֵי לְאַפְרוּשֵׁי מִן הַפְּטוּר עַל הַחִיּוּב. ע"א: דִּילְמָא אָתֵי לְאַפְרוּשֵׁי מִן הַחִיּוּב עַל הַפְּטוּר, דְּאִם הָיוּ מֵאָה כּוֹרִין, נ' שֶׁל חִיּוּב וַחֲמִשִּׁים שֶׁל פְּטוּר, וְהִפְרִישׁ מִן הַחִיּוּב עַל הַפְּטוּר כּוֹר, דְּהָשְׁתָּא מַפְקַע לֵיהּ לְהַהוּא כּוֹר מִתּוֹרַת חַלָּה, וְאָתֵי מִינֵּיהּ חוּרְבָּא לְעוֹלָם: לָא אָתֵי לִידֵי תַּקָּלָה דְּאָמְרִי' לֵיהּ כִּי מַעַשְׂרַתְּ מֵהַאי הֶפְקֵר מִינֵּיהּ וּבֵיהּ. מֵיתִיבֵי הַמַּפְקִיר אֶת כַּרְמוֹ וְלַשַּׁחַר עָמַד וּבְצָרוֹ. וְזָכָה בֵּיהּ אִיהוּ עַצְמוֹ. חַיָּיב בְּפֶרֶט וְעוֹלֵלוֹת. כְּמוֹ מִשְּׁאָר כֶּרֶם. וּפָטוּר מִן הַמַּעֲשֵׂר. דְּחַשְׁבִינַן לֵיהּ הֶפְקֵר. וְהָנֵי מִיחַיֵּיב (ב) מֵהָנֵי טְפֵי מִמַּעֲשֵׂר — דִּכְתִיב בְּהוּ "תַּעֲזוֹב" יְתֵירָא, כִּדְאָמְרִינַן בְּב"ק בְּפֶרֶק "הַגּוֹזֵל" (דף צד.): שָׁאנֵי פֶּרֶט דִּכְתִיב בֵּיהּ "תַּעֲזוֹב" יְתֵירָה, חַד בְּפָרָשַׁת "אֱמוֹר אֶל הַכֹּהֲנִים", וְחַד בִּ"קְדוֹשִׁים תִּהְיוּ", דְּמַשְׁמַע אֲפִילּוּ דְּהֶפְקֵר חַיָּיב. אֲבָל בְּמַעֲשֵׂר, דְּלָא כְּתִיב בֵּיהּ "תַּעֲזוֹב" יְתֵירָא — פָּטוּר מִדְּאוֹרַיְיתָא, אֲבָל מִדְּרַבָּנַן חַיָּיב. בִּשְׁלָמָא לְעוּלָּא. דְּמוֹקֵים לְבָרַיְיתָא דִּלְעֵיל דְּקָתָנֵי: כָּל ג' יָמִים יָכוֹל לַחֲזוֹר בּוֹ — דְּמִדְּאוֹרַיְיתָא הָוֵי הֶפְקֵר, אע"ג דְּלָא אָתֵי לִרְשׁוּת זוֹכֶה, אֲבָל רַבָּנַן הוּא דַּאֲמוּר דְּלָא הָוֵי הֶפְקֵר עַד לְאַחַר שְׁלֹשָׁה יָמִים מִפְּנֵי הָרַמָּאִין, הָא נַמִי דְּתָנֵי הָכָא: פָּטוּר מִמַּעֲשֵׂר וְהָוֵי הֶפְקֵר — דְּאוֹרַיְיתָא קָאָמַר, אֲבָל מִדְּרַבָּנַן חַיָּיב מִפְּנֵי הָרַמָּאִין. **אֶלָּא** לְרֵישׁ לָקִישׁ. דְּאוֹקִים לָהּ לְבָרַיְיתָא דִּלְעֵיל אַלִּיבָּא דְּרַבִּי יוֹסֵי, דְּאָמַר: ג' יָמִים לָא הָוֵי הֶפְקֵר אֲפִילּוּ מִדְּאוֹרַיְיתָא, (ג) דִּלְאַחַר ג' יָמִים לָא הָוֵי הֶפְקֵר אֶלָּא מִדְּרַבָּנַן, דִּגְזָרוּ שֶׁלֹּא תִּשְׁתַּכַּח תּוֹרַת הֶפְקֵר — אַמַּאי אִם בְּצָרוֹ לְמָחָר פָּטוּר מִן הַמַּעֲשֵׂר? הָאָמַר ר' יוֹסֵי דַּאֲפִילּוּ מִדְּרַבָּנַן לָא הָוֵי הֶפְקֵר עַד לְאַחַר שְׁלֹשָׁה יָמִים! **אָמַר** לָךְ ר"ל **כִּי אֲמַרִי אֲנָא** לְרַבִּי יוֹסֵי. אֲבָל הָךְ דְּקָתָנֵי: וְלַשַּׁחַר הִשְׁכִּים וּבְצָרוֹ פָּטוּר מִן הַמַּעֲשֵׂר (ד). **רַבָּנַן הִיא**. דְּאָמְרִי בְּמַתְנִיתִין: לְאַלְתַּר הָוֵי הֶפְקֵר, אע"ג דְּלָא אָתֵי לִרְשׁוּת זוֹכֶה.

וְאִיבָּעֵית

ר"ן

דאי אמרינן הכי – אתו למימר דכי לא חזר בו נמי, וזכה בו אחר – לא מהפקרא קא זכי. דכיון דמקמי דליזכי ביה היה יכול מפקיר לחזור בו – אלמא ברשותיה הוה קאי, ונמצא שאין זה זוכה מן ההפקר אלא מקבל מתנה. וקא סברי דמחייב במעשר, ואתו לעשורי ממקום אחר עליו, והוה ליה מן החיוב על הפטור, וממנו על מקום אחר והוה ליה מן הפטור על החיוב. להכי תקון שלאחר שלשה ימים לא יהא יכול לחזור בו, כי היכי דמדרבנן להוי הפקר. **אי הכי אפי'** מיום ראשון להוי הפקר. כלומר, הוה לן לתקוני דאפי' מיום ראשון להוי הפקר מהאי טעמא גופיה, ומ"ט תוך ג' מאחר ג'? ומפרקינן, אמר רבא: מפני הרמאין דמפקרין והדרין בהון. כלומר, שאפילו מתחלתן אינן מפקירין אלא כדי שיחזרו בהן, ונמצא שאין הפקרן הפקר אלא הערמה בלבד. ולפיכך, כל ג' – העמידו דבריהם על דין תורה, אבל לאחר ג' – ליכא למיחש להכי, כדפרישית לעיל. ואין ה"נ, דהאי טעמא מפני הרמאין, כי מוקמינן נמי בריש שמעתין רישא רבנן – צריכין ליה, כדפרישית לעיל, אלא דכיון דהשתא דייקא טפי ברישא, כי היכי דאפשר דתיקום כרבי יוסי מפרש לה נמי להאי טעמא. ואין ה"נ, דכי היכי דצריכין ליה לרבי יוסי כדי להעמידו על דין תורה, צריכין ליה נמי לרבנן לאפוקי מדין תורה ולתקוני. ופרכי': **אבל דאורייתא לא הוי הפקר ודלמא אתי לעשורי מן החיוב על הפטור**. אמכאן ואילך אין יכול לחזור בו פריך, דקאמר דנהי דמדינא לרבי יוסי יכול לחזור בו ולא הוי הפקר, תקון רבנן דליהוי הפקר. ובודאי שחייבוהו במעשר, כיון דמדאורייתא לא הוי הפקר. דנהי שהיו יכולים לפטרו *משום דהפקר ב"ד היה הפקר, אפילו הכי לא באו חכמים להקל ולפטור מן המעשר מה שהוא חייב בו מן התורה. וכיון שכן, איכא למיחש דלמא אתי לעשורי מן החיוב על הפטור, דאמר זוכה זה: ודאי, כיון שזכוני חכמים במה שזכיתי – הפקר גמור היה, וחזרה דאידך מדינא לא כלום הוא, וזה שחייבוני במעשר – אינו אלא מדבריהם, מפני גזירת הרמאים ששמעו חזרתו וחשבו שהיתה חזרה. ואינה כלום, שאילו כן – היאך זכוני בהפקרו? ואתי לעשורי מדבר זה שהוא סבור שיהא פטור, על דבר אחר שהוא פטור מן הדין, כגון חטין שגדלו בעציץ שאינו נקוב, וסבור הוא דליהוו תרווייהו מדרבנן. וליתא, דמאי דזכי ביה זוכה – מדאורייתא מחייב, דכיון דחזרתו דמפקיר מהניא מדינא, נמצא שאין זה זוכה מן ההפקר, וכי מעשר מפירות הללו על אותן של עציץ שאינו נקוב – הוה ליה מעשר מן החיוב על הפטור. ובדין הוא דהוה מצי למיפרך: דילמא אתי לעשורי מן הפטור על החיוב, כלומר מפירות של עציץ שאינו נקוב על זה, וחדא מנייהו נקט. ובמאי דמפרקינן נמי מיפרקי כולהו פירכי, דאמרי': כי מעשרת – עשר מיניה וביה, כלומר, לא תעשר ממנו על מקום אחר ולא ממקום אחר עליו, אלא עשר מיניה. **מיתיבי המפקיר את כרמו ולשחר עמד ובצרו חייב בפרט ובעוללות ובשכחה ובפאה**. משום דאע"ג דהפקר פטור מכולהו, וכדאמרי' בעלמא (שבת דף סח.): נשמר – למעוטי הפקר, אפי' הכי משום דבכולהו הני כתיב "תעזוב" יתירא – מחייב בהו כל היכא שהחזיק בו הוא עצמו. והכי איתא בפ' "הגוזל" (ב"ק צד.). **ופטור מן המעשר**. דכיון דלא כתיב במעשר "תעזוב" יתירא, לא שנא הוא ולא שנא אחר – פטור. **בשלמא לעולא** דרבנן קתני לה **ודאורייתא קתני** לה. כלומר, דאע"ג דתקון רבנן דתוך שלשה יכול לחזור בו, וכיון שכן כי זכה בה הוא – מחייב במעשר מדרבנן, אפילו הכי, כי אתיא הך אליבייהו – שפיר, דפטור דקאמר מדאורייתא קתני, אבל מדרבנן אין הכי נמי דמחייב. **אלא לריש לקיש**. דמוקים לה לאידך כר' יוסי, הך היכי אפשר דתיתי אליביה? דהא לרבי יוסי כיון דאמר דמפקיר יכול לחזור בו מדינא עד דאתי לרשות זוכה, כשהשכים זה ובצרו אמאי פטור? דכיון דלא פריש שהוא זוכה בו מן ההפקר – נימא דמהדר קא הדר ביה, ונמצא שמשלו בצר ולא מן ההפקר! דנהי דסבירא ליה לרבי יוסי דאיהו נמי מצי זכי בתורת הפקר מהפקירא דנפשיה – הני מילי כשפירש, אבל כשבצר סתם, כיון שבידו לחזור בו – שלו הוא בוצר. **אמר לך כי אמרי אנא לרבי יוסי הא רבנן היא**. כלומר, דנהי דאידך ברייתא מוקים לה כולה כרבי יוסי – על כרחיך הא – רבנן היא ולא רבי יוסי.

ואיבעית

מסורת הש"ס

*[לעיל כט.]: תמורה ו. ב"ק כח. ועי'. נדה נח.

הגהות הב"ח

(א) רש"י ד"ה ודילמא וכו' ולא מן הפטור על החיוב ולא מן החיוב על הפטור מפני שנראה וכו' חורבא הס"ד ואח"כ מ"ה לעולם וכו' הפקר עשר מיניה וביה: (ב) ד"ה ופטור וכו' בהני טפי: (ג) ד"ה אלא וכו' ולאחר ג' ימים: (ד) ד"ה אמר לך וד"ה רבנן הס"ד:

גליון הש"ס

ר"ן ד"ה ופרכינן. משום דהפקר כו'. ועי' לעיין ממתני' דפאה רפ"ה:

תוספות

ודלמא אתי לעשורי מן החיוב על הפטור. ...

פי' הרא"ש

ודלמא אתי לעשורי מן החיוב על הפטור כו'. ...

אִיבָּעֵית אֵימָא: הָא — דְּאַפְקְרֵיהּ בְּאַנְפֵּי תְרֵין, וְהָא — דְּאַפְקְרֵיהּ בְּאַפֵּי תְלָתָא. דְּאָמַר ר' יוֹחָנָן מִשּׁוּם רַבִּי שִׁמְעוֹן בֶּן יְהוֹצָדָק: כָּל הַמַּפְקִיר בִּפְנֵי שְׁלֹשָׁה — הָוֵי הֶפְקֵר, בִּפְנֵי שְׁנַיִם — לֹא הָוֵי הֶפְקֵר. •ור' יְהוֹשֻׁעַ בֶּן לֵוִי אָמַר: אדְּבַר תּוֹרָה אֲפִילּוּ בְּאֶחָד הָוֵי הֶפְקֵר, וּמַה טַּעַם אָמְרוּ בִּשְׁלֹשָׁה — כְּדֵי שֶׁיְּהֵא אֶחָד זוֹכֶה וּשְׁנַיִם מְעִידִין.§

הדרן עלך אין בין המודר

רש"י

וְאִיבָּעֵית אֵימָא. כִּי פָּלֵיג ר' יוֹסֵי עֲלַיְיהוּ דְּרַבָּנַן, דְּאָמְרִי לָא הָוֵי הֶפְקֵר. (א) כְּגוֹן דְּלָא **אַפְקְרֵיהּ** אֶלָּא **בְּאַפֵּי** תְרֵי. וַאֲדְּהָכִי הָכִי קָתָנֵי ר' יוֹסֵי בְּמַתְנִיתִין דְּאָסוּר, דְּלָא הָוֵי הֶפְקֵר כָּל זְמַן דְּלָא אָתָא לְיַד זוֹכֶה. אֲבָל הֵיכָא דְּאַפְקְרֵיהּ בְּאַפֵּי בֵּי תְּלָתָא — הָוֵי הֶפְקֵר, וְאַע"ג דְּלָא אָתָא לְיַד זוֹכֶה. וְכִי קָתָנֵי דְּפָטוּר מִן הַמַּעֲשֵׂר — דְּאַפְקְרֵיהּ בְּאַפֵּי בֵּי תְּלָתָא. וְר' יְהוֹשֻׁעַ בֶּן לֵוִי אָמַר דְּבַר תּוֹרָה אֲפִי' בְּחַד הָוֵי הֶפְקֵר. דְּאַע"ג דְּלָא הִגִּיעַ לִרְשׁוּת זוֹכֶה — הָוֵי הֶפְקֵר לְאַלְתַּר. וּמַה טַּעַם אָמְרוּ כו' וּשְׁנַיִם מְעִידִין. דְּאִי לֵיכָּא אֶלָּא תְּרֵי, כִּי זָכֵי חַד — מַאן מֵעִיד עֲלֵיהּ דְּהַלָּה הִפְקִירוֹ? וּלְעוֹלָם לְאַלְתַּר הָוֵי הֶפְקֵר, וְהַיְינוּ כְּרַבָּנַן. דְּרַבִּי יְהוֹשֻׁעַ בֶּן לֵוִי סְבִירָא לֵיהּ כְּרַבָּנַן.

הדרן עלך אין בין המודר

ר"ן

ואיבעית אימא הא דאפקריה באפי תרי הא דאפקריה באפי תלתא. כלומר, הך מתניתא נמי דהמפקיר את כרמו – כר' יוסי אתיא, דעד כאן לא קאמר ר' יוסי דמפקיר יכול לחזור בו – אלא דאפקריה באפי תרי – כלומר שאין שם שלשה, דומיא דמתניתין, דקתני דאין עמהם אחר, ובהא בלחוד הוא דאסר ר' יוסי, דסבירא ליה דכל כי ה"ג הפקר כמתנה, דעד דאתי לרשות זוכה לא נפיק מרשות מפקיר. וטעמיה משום דאין עמהם אחר, א"נ, דליכא בהדיה אלא תרי – אדעתא דחד דמהנך בלחוד אפקריה, דכל בי תרי ליכא קלא. משום הכי דמי למתנה, דכי היכי דבמתנה לא מפיק ליה מרשותיה אלא אדעתא דאידך – ה"נ הכא, לא מפקיר אלא אדעתא דאידך או אדעתא דחד מתרוייהו. הילכך, כי היכי דבמתנה לא נפיק מרשותיה עד דאתי לרשות מקבל – ה"נ בהפקר כי האי, דהפקר זה למתנה דמי. ומתני' דהמפקיר את שדהו – בכי האי הפקר מתוקמא, ומשום הכי קתני דעד שלא זכה, בין הוא בין אחר – יכול לחזור בו. אבל הך מתניתא דהמפקיר את כרמו – מתוקמא דאפקריה באפי תלתא, וכל היכא דאיכא תלתא – אוושא מילתא, ואדעתא דכולי עלמא אפקריה, ולא דמי כלל למתנה. הלכך, אע"ג דבמתנה עד דאתי לרשות מקבל לא נפיק מרשות זוכה, בהפקר כי האי אפי' ר' יוסי מודה דלאלתר נפיק מרשותיה. **דאמר** ר' יוחנן כל המפקיר בפני שלשה הוי הפקר. משום דאדעתא דכולי עלמא אפקריה. **בפני שנים לא הוי הפקר.** דכיון דליכא קלא – אדעתא דידהו בלחוד אפקריה, ודמי למתנה. כן נראה לי פירושא דשמעתא כולה. ויש במה שכתבתי קצת דברים שלמדתי מדברי הראשונים זכרונם לברכה. והך **סוגיא** כולה למאי דסלקא דעתיה מעיקרא, דטעמא דרבי יוסי משום דקסבר הפקר כמתנה אתיא, ור' יוחנן דאמר הכי לעיל – הא איתותב. וכיון שכן, למסקנא דלעיל אדחיא לה כל הך סוגיא, ונקטינן לפירושא לברייתא דהמפקיר את שדהו אוקמתא דעולא דכולה רבנן היא, ור' יוסי נמי היא, דר' יוסי לא פליג עלייהו דרבנן בדינא דהפקר כלל. והיינו טעמא דסיפא דקתני דעד שלא זכה בה בין הוא בין אחר יכול לחזור בו, משום דכיון דשבוע ושנה לא שכיחן לא נפיק מרשות מפקיר עד דאתי לרשות זוכה, וכולה כדפרישית לעיל. ולענין הלכה. בפלוגתייהו דר' יוחנן ור' יהושע בן לוי – נקטינן כר' יהושע בן לוי דאמר דבר תורה אפי' באחד הוי הפקר ומה טעם אמרו בשלשה כדי שיהא אחד זוכה ושנים מעידים. הילכך מדברי סופרים אינו הפקר עד שיפקיר בפני שלשה. וכן כתב הרמב"ם ז"ל בפ"ב מהלכות נדרים (הלכה טז). **הדרן עלך אין בין המודר**

עין משפט נר מצוה

סב א מיי' פ"ב מהל' נדרים הלכה טז סמג לאוין רמב טוש"ע ח"מ סימן רעג סעיף ז:

הגהות הב"ח

(א) רש"י ד"ה ואיבעית אימא הד"א עם ד"ה כגון וכו' ואדהכי קתני כצ"ל ותיבת הכי נמחק:

גליון הש"ס

גמ' ור' יהושע ב"ל אמר: עיין שבת דף יח ע"ב תוד"ה דמפקרא. פסחים דף ד ע"ב תוד"ה מדאורייתא:

תוספות

הא כגון דאפקריה בפני שלשה ואינו יכול לחזור בו. ודמי כאילו אתי לרשות זוכה והא דאית ליה דאינו הפקר עד דאתי לרשות זוכה באפי תרי דיכול לחזור בו דאמר רבי יוחנן בפני שנים איכא למיחש לרמאי וגם סתם הפקר מועיל אפי' שלא בפני שלשה: **רבי** יהושע בן לוי אומר דבר תורה אפי' באחד הוי הפקר. פר"ת דר' יוחנן סבר לה כרבי יוסי ורבי יהושע בן לוי כרבנן ומן התורה הוי הפקר לאלתר וזו היא כפר"ת דלעיל דמדאוריי' אמר רבי יוסי דלא הוי הפקר אבל לפר"י דלעיל מאי סבר כר' יוסי דלא פליג אר' יוחנן מידי (אלא). מהכא שמעינן דדוקא [בקרקעות הוא דשייך] רמאות אבל במטלטלין הוי הפקר לאלתר אפי' בפני שנים ואפי' לפירוש ר"ת הלכתא כר' יהושע בן לוי דקיימי רבנן כוותיה ועוד ר' יהושע בן לוי ור' יוחנן הלכה כרבי יהושע בן לוי בכל מקום לשון הרב ר"א מדפסקינן בפ' תפלת השחר (ברכות כח:) דלית (ליה) הלכתא כוותיה אלא בתרי והתם מפרש להו אבל באחריני הלכתא כוותיה דרבי יהושע בן לוי דלא מצריך תלתא מדרבנן אלא גבי מעשר וכדפרישית טעמא שלא יפקיענו ממעשר אבל לא להפקיר כליו בשבת שלא יעבור על שביתת כלים וכן בהמתו לא בעי תלתא אלא כדפריש בינו לבין עצמו שפיר דמי כדאמר פ"ק דשבת (דף יח:) גבי כלים דמפקר אפקוריה וסתמא קאמר בכל ענינים:

הדרן עלך אין בין המודר

פי' הרא"ש

איבעית אימא הא דאפקריה באפי תרי כו'. ואתי שפיר כרבי יוסי הא דקאמ' במתני' דלא הוי הפקר עד דאתי ליד זוכה ה"מ באפי תרי אבל באפי תלתא כיון דהוי ההפקר הפקר מפורסם מודה רבי יוסי דיצא מרשותו והוי הפקר ופטור מן המעשר והשתא דאתית להכי ברייתא דלעיל מצי לאוקמי כרבי יוסי ודאפקריה באפי תלתא וריש' מפני הרמאין: **דאמר רבי יוחנן משום רבי שמעון בן יהוצדק כל המפקיר בפני שנים לא הוי הפקר.** לענין זה שלא יוכל לחזור בו ומיהו הפקר הוי דאם קדם אחר וזכה בו זכה וזהו דוחק דלישנא דלא הוי הפקר משמע שאינו הפקר כלל ואי הוה מצי לפרושי הא דאפקריה באפי תרי דאז לא הוי הפקר כלל אז הוה ניחא ועתה חזר בו מהך טעמא דפריש רבי יוחנן לעיל טעמיה דרבי יוסי משום דהוי ברשות מפקיר עד דאתי לרשות זוכה אלא סבר דר' יוסי אוסר משום דהפקר בפני שנים לא הוי הפקר כלל ומיהו קשיא דרבי יוחנן גופיה פריש טעמא דרבי יוסי לעיל ואיכא למימר הא דידיה הא דרביה ורבי יהושע בן לוי דאמר דבר תורה אפילו באחד הוי הפקר דסבירא ליה כרבנן דלאלתר יצא מרשות הפקר. **וה"ר אליעזר ממי"ץ** פירש שמועה זו אליבא דרבא המפקיר שדהו כל ג' ימים יכול לחזור בו וחייב במעשר מכאן ואילך אין יכול לחזור בו ופטור מן המעשר ואתיא כרבנן דאמרי במתני' דהוי הפקר קודם שזכה בו אחר ולא גזרינן להיות ברשותו לחייבו במעשר כי היכי דלא גזרינן במתני' להיות ברשותו לאסרו על המודר משום מתנת בית חורון ומיהו בתוך ג' סברי רבנן דחייב לעשר אם חזר בו משום שלא נתפרסם ההפקר ויאמרו העולם שהוא אוכל טבל ומיהו גבי נדרים לאלתר יצא מרשותו לפי שאינו ידוע לכל שהדירו ואע"פ שלא נתפרסם ההפקר גם הנדר אינו ידוע וליכא למיחש שמא יאמרו הוא נהנה מנכסי המדיר באיסור אבל איסור טבל ידוע לכל: **עד שלא זכה בו בין הוא בין אחר יכול לחזור בו וחייב במעשר.** דגזרינן שיהא ברשותו לחייבו במעשר עד שיבא ליד אחר כי היכי דגזרינן במודר משום מתנת בית חורון ור' יוסי היא והאי דנקט הפקר לזמן לרבותא נקטיה ואפי' בהפקר כי האי דלא שכיח גזר ר' יוסי כי היכי דגזרינן במתניתין משום מתנת בית חורון: **ומתמה רישא רבנן וסיפא ר' יוסי.** ומוקי לה עולא כולה כרבנן אי הכי אמאי עד שלא זכה כו' הא לא גזר במתניתין משום מתנת בית חורון **ומשני** שאני הפקר לזמן דלא שכיח ויטעו העולם לומר שאינו הפקר ואי פטרת ליה ממעשר יאמרו שטבל הוא אוכל לכך חייבוהו במעשר עד שיזכה בו אחר: **רישא נמי ר' יוסי.** והיינו טעמא דלא גזר להיות ברשותו ולחייבו במעשר עד שיזכה בו אחר כי היכי דגזר במודר משום דלא תשתכח תורת הפקר ואתי למימר הפקר חייב במעשר ולהכי אוקמא אחרי שלשה דאורייתא ופטור מן המעשר כדי שלא יבא לידי מכשול שיטעו לומר הפקר חייב במעשר ורבו חכמים שיותר יש לחוש שלא תשתכח תורת הפקר ממה שיש לחוש לגזרת מתנת בית חורון: **אי הכי מיום ראשון נמי.** הוה לן לאוקומיה אדאורייתא משום הך חששא גופא בשלמא אי מוקמת רישא רבנן ניחא דבענין שלשה ימים כדי שיתפרסם ההפקר כדפרישית לעיל אלא כיון דמוקמת לה כרבי יוסי ואחר שלשה ימים עקרוה רבנן לחשש גזירת מתנת בית חורון ואוקמוה אדאורייתא משום דלא תשתכח תורת הפקר ואתי לאפרושי מן החיוב על הפטור אפילו מיום ראשון נמי הוה לן למיחש להכי כי עיקר זכיית הפקר הוא תוך שלשה דלא שכיח שיעמוד ג' ימים בלא זכיה והיה צריך לתקן בדבר המצוי ושכיח: **אמר רבה מפני הרמאין כו'.** פי' מה שבתוך שלשה ימים לא הוי הפקר לאו משום גזרת מתנת בית חורון דלאו הואי טעמא משום גזירה היינו מפקיעין אותה גזירה משום חשש שלא תשתכח תורת הפקר כמו שאנו מפקיעין אותו לאחר ג' אלא בתוך ג' ימים לא הוי הפקר מדאורייתא מפני הרמאין שלא נמסר הדבר אלא לחכמים דעיקר הפקר ילפינן משביעית כדדריש בירושלמי והשביעית תשמטנה מה תלמוד לומר ונטשתה יש לך נטישה אחרת שהיא כזו ואיזו זו הפקר מה זו לעניים ולעשירים אף זו כו' ובשביעית דלית בה רמאות והיכא דאיכא למיחש לרמאות כגון בתוך שלשה לא הוי הפקר אבל מדאוריי' לא הוי הפקר סיום מילתיה דרבה היא וכיון דמדאוריי' חייב במעשר משום שלא תשתכח תורת הפקר לא מפקעינן ליה ורבי יוסי אוסר במתני' תוך ג' מן התורה ולאחר ג' משום גזירת מתנת בית חורון: **ודילמא אתי לעשורי מן החיוב על הפטור כו'.** כי מוקמת לה כרבנן ותוך ג' חייב לעשר מדרבנן שלא נתפרסם ההפקר כדפרישית לעיל וכי מוקמת לה כר' יוסי ועד שלא זכה בו אחר חייב לעשר משום גזירת מתנת בית חורון ניחוש דילמא אתי לעשורי כו': **לאמרי ליה כי מעשרת עשר מיניה וביה.** ויותר חשו חכמים לרבנן משום שלא נתפרסם ההפקר ואתו למימר קא אכל טבל ולר' יוסי משום גזירת מתנת בית חורון ממה שחשו דילמא אתי לאפרושי מן החיוב על הפטור: **בשלמא לעולא.** רבנן קתני לה ופטור מן המעשר מדאורייתא לאלתר אלא לר"ל דלר' יוסי לא הוי הפקר מן התורה תוך ג' ימים אמאי פטור מן המעשר: **איבעית אימא הא דאפקריה באפי תרי כו'.** לטעמא דר' יוסי דלא הוי הפקר תוך שלשה משום דליכא למיחש לרמאות וכיון דאפקריה באפי תלתא והדבר מפורסם לכל ליכא למיחש לרמאות והוי כמו הפקר לאחר ג' הלכך לאלתר הוי הפקר: **המפקיר בפני ב' לא הוי הפקר.** לאלתר: **דבר תורה אפילו באחד הוי הפקר.** לאלתר כרבנן: **ומה טעם אמרו בג' כדי שיהא אחד זוכה ושנים מעידין.** ומתוך זה ירא בעל הבית להפקיר כדי להפקיע ממעשר וקי"ל בכל מקום הילכתא כריב"ל לגביה דר' יוחנן הלכך הוי הפקר מן התורה אפילו באחד וה"ה אפילו בינו לבין עצמו הלכך בשבת יכול להפקיר כליו שלא יעבור על שביתת כליו וכן בהמתו אם השאילה לעובד כוכבים ולא החזירה לו קודם השבת אפילו בינו לבין עצמו:

הדרך עלך אין בין המודר

א א מיי' פ"ז מהלכות נדרים הלכה ד סמג לאוין רמב טוש"ע יו"ד סימן רכו סעיף א וטור שו"ע ח"מ סימן קפ:

השותפין שנדרו הנאה זה מזה אסורים ליכנס לחצר. דקסבר האי תנא: ויתור אסור במודר הנאה. **רבי אליעזר בן יעקב אומר זה נכנס** לתוך שלו וזה נכנס לתוך שלו. אוקימנא בגמרא בחצר שאין בה דין חלוקה, אבל בחצר שיש בה דין חלוקה – דברי הכל אסור. ובפרק "שור שנגח את הפרה" (ב"ק דף נא:) אוקימנא פלוגתייהו ביש ברירה או אין ברירה, דר"א סבר: יש ברירה, והאי לדנפשיה קא עייל והאי לדנפשיה קא עייל. ורבנן סברי: אין ברירה. ותמהני: נהי דקא סברי רבנן אין ברירה, אמאי אסורין ליכנס לחצר? דהא כיון דחצר שאין בה דין חלוקה היא, ואין שותף יכול לכוף את חבירו לחלוק, ולא לעכב עליו שלא ליכנס לחצר – היאך הוא יכול לאסרה עליו? הא אין אדם אוסר דבר שאינו שלו! ואפילו נדרו ג"כ הן עצמן – למה הן אסורים? הרי כשכל אחד נכנס לחצר – משלו הוא נהנה, ולא משל חבירו, כיון שאין הלה יכול לעכב עליו! וי"ל: דהיינו טעמייהו דרבנן, משום דכיון דאי אפשר לומר דכל חד קני לכוליה חצר קנין הגוף לעולם, דאי [דמר לאו דמר], וא"א לומר ג"כ דבשעה שמשתמש בו איגלי מילתא למפרע דבשעת קניה קנה לה להאי שעתא קנין הגוף – דאין ברירה. אלא כל חד מהנך שותפין יש לו לעולם בחצר זה קנין הגוף, דהיינו חלקו. וקנין שעבוד בחלקו של חבירו, שאין הלה יכול לעכב עליו מן הדין אע"ג דלא קני ליה גופא. הלכך קסברי רבנן דאותו קנין שעבוד שיש לו על חלקו של חבירו – קונמות מפקיעין אותו, ומש"ה אסור, דקונמות מפקיעין מידי שעבוד, כדאיתא בסוף מכילתין. ורבי אליעזר בן יעקב פליג עלייהו, משום דסבירא ליה דיש ברירה. ומש"ה אמרינן דכל שעה ושעה שנכנס לחצר – בדנפשיה קא עייל, וגוף החצר קנויה לו לגמרי לאותו תשמיש, שאינו משתמש בה מקנין שעבוד אלא מקנין הגוף. שכל שאי יכול לומר שיש לכל אחד קנין הגוף – אין ראוי לומר שיהא קנין שעבוד, שאין נקרא קנין שעבוד אלא מה שהוא עומד כן לעולם בעל כרחו של כל אחד מהם. ורבנן נמי לא דייני ליה כקנין שעבוד אלא מפני שאי אפשר להם לדונו כקנין הגוף, דאין ברירה. ובסמוך תראה עוד דעתי בברירה זו. ומכאן נראה לי ראיה ברורה דמשכיר יכול לאסור ביתו על השוכר, אע"פ שנחלקו בזה הראשונים, וכמו שנכתוב לפנינו בסייעתא דשמיא. אע"ג דמשכיר מדינא לא מצי לעכובי לאידך – אפי' הכי מצי אסר ליה בקונם, משום דקונמות מפקיעין מידי שעבוד, ומשכיר נמי בקונם מפקיע מידי שעבוד השוכר, אפי' היכא שהקדים השוכר דמי שכירותו למשכיר. אע"פ שיש שאין סוברין כן, כמו שנכתוב לפנינו בסייעתא דשמיא. דהא הכא אין שותף צריך ליתן דמים לחבירו – ואפילו הכי מצי אסר ליה אידך לרבנן, מטעמא דכתיבנא. דהא בהדירו זה את זה בעיא ולא איפשיטא היא בגמרא. כן נראה לי, ולפנינו נאריך בדין זה בסייעתא דשמיא. **ואיכא** דמקשו: כיון דפלוגתייהו דרבי אליעזר ורבנן ביש ברירה ואין ברירה היא, דהכי אוקמא רבינא בפרק "שור שנגח את הפרה" (שם דף נא:) היכי פסקינן בגמרא כר' אליעזר בן יעקב דסבירא ליה דיש ברירה? והא בפרק "משילין" (ביצה דף לח.) אסיקנא דכי לית ליה לרבי אושעיא ברירה – בדאורייתא, אבל בדרבנן אית ליה. ואפסיקא הלכתא כר' אושעיא. אלמא בדאורייתא אין ברירה, וקשיא הלכתא אהלכתא! תירץ ר"ת ז"ל: דהכא הלכה כר' אליעזר, ולא מטעמיה קאמרינן. דאיהו סבר דיש ברירה, וויתור אסור במודר הנאה. ואנן סבירא לן דאין ברירה, אבל ויתור סבירא לן דמותר במודר הנאה. הלכך לאו בחצר שאין בה דין חלוקה בלבד איירי, אלא אפי' יש בה דין חלוקה נמי שרי. ולפי פי' זה, אם נדרו הנאה בפירוש אפי' מדריסת הרגל – אסורין ליכנס לחצר. ורבינו יצחק ז"ל לא נראה לו דבריו, דלא מסתברא לדחות כמה סתמות שנסתמו במכילתין כמאן דאמר ויתור אסור במודר הנאה, וכולה פירקין דלעיל כוותיה אזיל. לפיכך תירץ הוא ז"ל: דודאי קי"ל כמאן דאמר אפי' בדאורייתא יש ברירה מהא דשמעתין. והא דאפסיקא הלכתא כר' אושעיא בפרק "משילין" – ממאי דאמר דבדרבנן יש ברירה בלחוד הוא דאפסיקא הלכתא, משום דאיהי היא עיקר פלוגתייהו התם. וראיה לדבר מדתנן בתמורה בפ' "כל *הפסולין" גבי מחיר כלב: וכן שני שותפין, אחד נטל עשרה טלאים ואחד נטל תשעה טלאים וכלב א', שעם הכלב – כולן מותרין, שכנגד הכלב – כולן אסורין. ואקשינן עלה בגמרא: ונשקול חד כנגד כלב ולשתרו אינך! אלמא אפי' בדאוריי' יש ברירה. ולא מחוור, דודאי בדאורייתא אין ברירה, דהא קי"ל כשמואל דאמר (ב"ק ע.): האחין שחלקו – לקוחות, הן ומחזירין [זה לזה ביובל], וכדפסק רב נחמן כוותיה בפרק השולח (גיטין מח.), וטעמא דשמואל משום דקסבר אין ברירה, וכדאיתא בהדיא בגיטין בריש פרק "כל הגט" (דף כה.). וההיא דתמורה לא קשיא, דלאו אליבא דהלכתא פריך, אלא אליבא דמאן דאמר בדאורייתא יש ברירה. ובדרך "אי אמרת בשלמא" קא נסיב לה, ודכוותיה בהש"ס טובא. וכי תימא: א"כ הדרא קושיא לדוכתה! כתב הרב רבינו משה ז"ל בהלכותיו: דלא דמיא הך ברירה דהכא לדעלמא, דהכא לאו מידי דלא מתברר האידנא ומתברר למחר הוא, דנימא אתברירא מילתא למפרע. אלא בדהשתא הוא, דחצר שאין בה דין חלוקה הוא, וכל חד משתמש בכולה, וכיון דשותפין נינהו – כי האי גוונא הוי תשמישתייהו, מהשתא אמרינן כמאן דעייל בדנפשיה הוא, ולא משתמש בדחבריה. שאם תאסור עליו – נמצא זה מוציא אותו מחצירו, ואין אדם אוסר נכסי חבירו על בעליהן. ובכי האי גוונא אתמר התם בגמרא. תדע, דהא מיבעיא בעיא לה הכא בהדירו דלמא אפילו רבנן מודו ליה לרבי אליעזר בן יעקב, משום דכאונסים דמו, ולאו כל כמיניה דאסר נכסי חבירו עליו, זה לשונו ז"ל. ואינו נוח לי, דאם איתא – מאי לישנא דאין ברירה ויש ברירה דאמרינן התם בפרק "הפרה"? הרי אין טעמו של רבי אליעזר בן יעקב משום יש ברירה כלל, אלא מפני שאתה אומר משעה ראשונה כל החצר קנוי לכל אחד מהם! לפיכך נראין לי דברים כפשטן, דברירה דהכא כברירה דעלמא. אלא משום דהך ברירה עדיפא פסקינן הכא כר"א בן יעקב. מיהו, הכא נמי אנו צריכין לברירה דאיגלי מילתא למפרע, כברירה דעלמא, משום דליכא למימר דהאי חצר כולה דמר וכולה דמר, דאי דמר – לאו דמר, ואי דמר – לאו דמר. אלא הכי קאמרינן: שהשותפין הללו בשעה שלקחו החצר – על דעת כן לקחוה, שבשעה שישתמש בה אחד מהם – תהא כולה שלו לתשמיש. ולפי שמשעה ראשונה אין אנו יודעין באי זה יום ובאיזו שעה ישתמש בו כל אחד מהם – אנו צריכין לברירה, לומר שעכשיו שאחד מהם משתמש בה – הוברר הדבר למפרע שמשעה ראשונה קנה אותה כולה לשעה זו. ובודאי יכול אדם להקנותה חדש אחד לראובן וחדש אחד לשמעון, ובזמן כל אחד ואחד קנוי הוא לו לגמרי, דהיינו "נכסי לך ואחריך לפלוני". אלא משום דהכא אין זמן כל אחד ואחד ידוע – לא מהני אלא למאן דאית ליה ברירה, דאמרינן דאיגלי מילתא דמשעה ראשונה קנו לזמנים הללו. וכי תימא: וכיון דברירה דהכא כברירה דעלמא, דאיגלי השתא מאי דלא הוה ידיע לן בשעת קניה, היכי פסקינן כרבי אליעזר בן יעקב, כיון דבעלמא סבירא לן דבדאורייתא אין ברירה? היינו טעמא, משום דברירה דהכא עדיפא מברירה דעלמא. דהיינו טעמא דאמרינן בעלמא דאין ברירה – לפי שאין ראוי שיחול דבר על הספק. ולפיכך האומר לסופר "כתוב גט לאשתי ולאיזה מהן שארצה אגרש" – פסול לגרש בו, לפי שיש ספק משעה ראשונה בעיקר הגט לשם מי חל. וכן נמי "אם בא חכם למזרח ערובי למזרח, למערב – ערובי למערב" – לא מהני, משום דבשעת קניית העירוב לא היה מתברר כלל איזה מהן יקנה, ולפיכך כיון דבכל חד מהנך עירובי איכא למימר שמא לא יקנה כלל, אע"פ שלאחר מכן יתברר הדבר – אין ברירה. וכן נמי גבי האחין שחלקו, כיון דמשעה ראשונה איכא לספוקי שמא לא יזכה בחלק זה כלל – נמצא שהוא ספק גמור משעה ראשונה, וכל כיוצא בזה אין ברירה. אבל הכא עקרו של דבר מתברר משעה ראשונה, ומיעוטו לאחר מכן. לפי שאף משעה ראשונה אין אנו מסופקין שלא יזכה כל אחד מהם בכל גוף חצר זה, ואין אנו מסופקים גם כן שמא אפילו ירצה לזכות פלוני לא יזכה בה – שהרי משעה ראשונה אנו יודעין שעתיד כל אחד לזכות בכל גוף חצר זה, ושיזכה בו כל שעה שירצה. הלכך, כיון שעקרו של דבר מתברר מתחלתו, ומה שהוא מתברר לאחר מכן שלא נתבררה מתחלה אינו אלא מיעוטא, דהיינו הזמן שרצה לזכות בגופה של חצר וזכה בה – כל כהאי גוונא יש ברירה, שאין

המיעוט

משנה

השותפין *שנדרו הנאה זה מזה – אסורין ליכנס לחצר. ר"א בן יעקב אומר: זה נכנס א לתוך שלו, וזה נכנס לתוך שלו. ושניהם

ביצה לח: ב"ק נא: ב"ב נז:

רש"י

השותפין שנדרו הנאה זה מזה. מפרש בגמ' אי בנדרו אי בהדירו מיירי. **אסורים** ליכנס לחצר. בחצר של שניהן, דכל חד אסור בדריסת הרגל של חבירו. וקא סבר: אין ברירה, דאימור: האי לחלק חבירו עייל, והאי לחלק חבירו עייל. **ר"א בן יעקב אומר** זה נכנס כו'. דקסבר: יש ברירה. ושניהם

[נ"ל הפסולין (דף ל.)]

תוספות

השותפין אסורין ליכנס בחצר. דאדריסה קפדי ובפרק חזקת הבתים (דף נז:) מוקמינן ליה כרבי אליעזר דאמר דויתור אסור במודר הנאה: **רבי** אליעזר ב"י אמר זה מהלך בתוך שלו. דסבר דיש ברירה והאי בדידיה קמהלך והאי בדידיה קמהלך והכי מפרש בפרק שור שנגח את הפרה ומיהו ודאי אסור ליה לשטות פירות בכל החצר אבל להלך בכולו מותר דאמר בכל דוכתא דקמהלך היינו חלקו:

ושניהן

מודר הנאה מחבירו לא יכנס לחצר. משום דבעי למתני כופין נקטיה דכופין את הנודר למכור חלקו לחבירו דחיישינן כיון שרואה את חבירו נכנס גם הוא ישכח נדרו ויכנס אבל ברישא שניהם אסורים לא חיישינן שמא יכנסו: **היה אחד מן השוק מודר כו'.** משום רבותא דרבי אליעזר בן יעקב נקטו ואף על פי שאין לו חלק בחצר מתירו ליכנס מטעם ברירה:

*) [שייך לדף שאח"ז]

פי' הרא"ש

השותפין אסורין ליכנס לחצר. דבחצר קפדי כולי עלמא אדריסת הרגל ואתיא אפילו כרבנן ובחזקת הבתים (דף נז:) אית דמוקי להך כר' אליעזר דאמר ויתור אסור במודר הנאה משום דשותפין לא קפדי אהדדי: **רבי** אליעזר אומר זה נכנס לתוך שלו כו'. דקסבר יש ברירה והאי מהלך בדידיה [והאי מהלך בדידיה]: *) **אסורים לסעמיד תנור ורחים כו'.** דבכל הני יכולין שותפין לעכב זה על זה כדאיתא בפרק חזקת הבתים הלכך לא דמי להלוך ולא שייך להתירו מטעם ברירה כיון דיכול לעכב עליו ואינו מעכב: **היה אחד מהם** שניהם אסורים לא חיישינן

אם

אוּשְׁנֵיהֶם אֲסוּרִים לְהַעֲמִיד רֵיחַיִם וְתַנּוּר וּלְגַדֵּל תַּרְנְגוֹלִים. הָיָה אֶחָד מֵהֶם מוּדָּר הֲנָאָה מֵחֲבֵירוֹ — לֹא יִכָּנֵס לֶחָצֵר. רַבִּי אֱלִיעֶזֶר בֶּן יַעֲקֹב אוֹמֵר: ביָכוֹל הוּא לוֹמַר לוֹ: לְתוֹךְ שֶׁלִּי אֲנִי נִכְנָס, וְאֵינִי נִכְנָס לְתוֹךְ שֶׁלְּךָ. וְכוֹפִין אֶת הַנּוֹדֵר לִמְכּוֹר אֶת חֶלְקוֹ. הָיָה אֶחָד מִן הַשּׁוּק מוּדָּר בְּאֶחָד מֵהֶם הֲנָאָה — לֹא יִכָּנֵס לֶחָצֵר. רַבִּי אֱלִיעֶזֶר בֶּן יַעֲקֹב אוֹמֵר: גיָכוֹל לוֹמַר לוֹ: לְתוֹךְ שֶׁל חֲבֵירְךָ אֲנִי נִכְנָס, וְאֵינִי נִכְנָס לְתוֹךְ שֶׁלְּךָ. דהַמּוּדָּר הֲנָאָה מֵחֲבֵירוֹ וְיֵשׁ לוֹ מֶרְחָץ וּבֵית הַבַּד מוּשְׂכָּרִין בָּעִיר, אִם יֵשׁ לוֹ בָּהֶן תְּפִיסַת יָד — אָסוּר, אֵין לוֹ בָּהֶן תְּפִיסַת יָד — מוּתָּר.* ההָאוֹמֵר לַחֲבֵירוֹ: "קוֹנָם לְבֵיתְךָ שֶׁאֲנִי נִכְנָס וְשָׂדְךָ שֶׁאֲנִי לוֹקֵחַ", מֵת אוֹ שֶׁמְּכָרוֹ לְאַחֵר — מוּתָּר. ו"קוֹנָם בַּיִת זֶה שֶׁאֲנִי נִכְנָס, שָׂדֶה זוֹ שֶׁאֲנִי לוֹקֵחַ", מֵת אוֹ שֶׁמְּכָרוֹ לְאַחֵר — אָסוּר.§ **גמ'** אִיבַּעְיָא לְהוּ: בְּנָדְרוּ פְּלִיגִי, הִדִּירוּ זֶה אֶת זֶה מַאי? מִי אָמְרִינַן: בְּנָדְרוּ הוּא דִּפְלִיגִי, אֲבָל בְּהִדִּירוּ זֶה אֶת זֶה — מוֹדוּ לֵיהּ רַבָּנַן לראב"י דִּכְאֲנוּסִין דָּמוּ. אוֹ דִּילְמָא: אֲפִילּוּ בְּהִדִּירוּ זֶה אֶת זֶה פְּלִיגִי רַבָּנַן? ת"ש: הָיָה אֶחָד מֵהֶן מוּדָּר הֲנָאָה מֵחֲבֵירוֹ, וּפְלִיגִי רַבָּנַן. תְּנֵי: נָדוּר מֵחֲבֵירוֹ הֲנָאָה. הָכִי נַמִי מִסְתַּבְּרָא, דְּקָתָנֵי סֵיפָא: וְכוֹפִין אֶת הַנּוֹדֵר לִמְכּוֹר אֶת חֶלְקוֹ. אִי אָמְרַתְּ בִּשְׁלָמָא דְּנָדַר הוּא — הַיְינוּ דְּקָתָנֵי כּוֹפִין, אֶלָּא אִי אָמְרַתְּ דְּאַדְּרֵיהּ — אַמַּאי כּוֹפִין אוֹתוֹ? הָא מֵינָס אָנֵיס! אָמַר רַבָּה אָמַר זְעֵירִי: מַחֲלוֹקֶת

רש"י

וּשְׁנֵיהֶם אֲסוּרִין (א) מִלְּהַעֲמִיד רֵיחַיִם וְתַנּוּר. לִקְבּוֹעַ רֵיחַיִם וּלְגַדֵּל תַּרְנְגוֹלִים בְּאוֹתָהּ חָצֵר: הָכִי גָּרְסִינַן. הָיָה אֶחָד מֵהֶם מוּדָּר הֲנָאָה עַל חֲבֵירוֹ כּוֹפִין אֶת הַנּוֹדֵר. שֶׁהִדִּיר אֶת חֲבֵירוֹ, לִמְכּוֹר אֶת חֶלְקוֹ. אַתָּאן לְרַבָּנַן, דְּאָמְרִי: אֲסוּרִים לִיכָּנֵס לֶחָצֵר. הָיָה אֶחָד מִן הַשּׁוּק מוּדָּר מִן א'. מִן הַשּׁוּתָּפִים, לֹא יִכָּנֵס. **גמ'** בְּנָדְרוּ הוּא דִּפְלִיגִי. הֵיכָא דְּנָדְרוּ שְׁנֵיהֶם זֶה מִזֶּה, דְּזֶה אָמַר לַחֲבֵירוֹ "קוֹנָם שֶׁאֲנִי נֶהֱנֶה לָךְ" וְזֶה אוֹמֵר "קוֹנָם שֶׁאֲנִי נֶהֱנֶה לָךְ", דְּעַכְשָׁיו נָדְרוּ זֶה מִזֶּה מַמָּשׁ. וְהָתָם הוּא דְּקָא אָסְרִי רַבָּנַן לִיכָּנֵס לֶחָצֵר, דְּאִיהוּ עַצְמוֹ קָאָסַר עֲלֵיהּ. אֲבָל הִדִּירוּ זֶה אֶת זֶה, דְּכָל אֶחָד הִדִּיר אֶת חֲבֵירוֹ וְאָמַר "קוֹנָם שֶׁאַתָּה נֶהֱנֶה לִי, קוֹנָם נְכָסַי עָלֶיךָ", דְּתַרְוַיְיהוּ אֲנוּסִים, דְּכָל אֶחָד אָסַר לֵיהּ חַבְרֵיהּ שֶׁלֹּא מִדַּעְתֵּיהּ — הָתָם מוֹדוּ לֵיהּ רַבָּנַן לְר' אֱלִיעֶזֶר דְּזֶה נִכְנָס לְתוֹךְ שֶׁלּוֹ וְזֶה נִכְנָס לְתוֹךְ שֶׁלּוֹ. אוֹ דִּילְמָא אֲפִילּוּ בְּהִדִּירוּ [זֶה אֶת זֶה] נַמִי פְּלִיגִי. דְּלָא שְׁנָא אֲנוּסִין וְל"ש רוֹצִין. ה"נ מִסְתַּבְּרָא. דִּבְנָדְרוּ מַיְירֵי, וּבְנָדְרוּ הוּא דִּפְלִיגִי, דְּקָתָנֵי: כּוֹפִין אֶת הַנּוֹדֵר. אִי אָמְרַתְּ בִּשְׁלָמָא דְּנָדְרוּ. שֶׁנָּדַר שֶׁלֹּא יֵהָנֶה מֵחֲבֵירוֹ, לְהָכִי כּוֹפִין, דְּאִיהוּ הוּא דַּאֲסַר אַנַּפְשֵׁיהּ. אֶלָּא אִי אָמְרַתְּ דְּהִדִּירוֹ חֲבֵירוֹ אַמַּאי כּוֹפִין אוֹתוֹ. הָא אִיהוּ לָא פָּשַׁע, דְּמֵינַס אָנִיס. אֶלָּא וַדַּאי בְּנָדְרוּ פְּלִיגִי: *בְּשֶׁיֵּשׁ בָּהּ כְּדֵי חֲלוּקָה. אַרְבַּע אַמּוֹת לָזֶה וְאַרְבַּע אַמּוֹת לָזֶה. וְטַעְמָא דְּמַאן דְּאָסַר — הוֹאִיל וְאֶפְשָׁר בַּחֲלוּקָה. אֲבָל אֵין בָּהּ כְּדֵי חֲלוּקָה דִּבְרֵי הַכֹּל מוּתָּר. דְּמַאי אֶפְשָׁר לֵיהּ לְמֶיעֱבַד. כְּדָבָר

ר"ן

הַמִּיעוּט הַמְסוּפָּק מִתְּחִלָּתוֹ וּמִתְבָּרֵר לְאַחַר מִכָּאן מְעַכֵּב אֶת הָרוֹב שֶׁהָיָה בָּרוּר מִתְּחִלָּתוֹ. וּמש"ה, נְהִי דִּבְעָלְמָא סְבִירָא לָן דִּבְדְאוֹרַיְיתָא אֵין בְּרֵירָה — פָּסְקִינַן הָכָא כְּר' אֱלִיעֶזֶר בֶּן יַעֲקֹב, דְּבְכִי הָא יֵשׁ בְּרֵירָה. וְרַבָּנַן פְּלִיגֵי עֲלֵיהּ, דְּכֵיוָן דְּמכ"מ אַתָּה צָרִיךְ לוֹמַר שֶׁהוּבְרַר הַדָּבָר עַכְשָׁיו שֶׁבְּשָׁעָה פְּלוֹנִית הָיְתָה קְנוּיָה לוֹ לְגַמְרֵי, שֶׁלֹּא הָיָה מִתְבָּרֵר זֶה מִתְּחִלָּה — אֲפִילּוּ בְּכִי הַאי גַּוְונָא אֵין בְּרֵירָה, וְנִמְצָא שֶׁאֵין לְכָל א' בְּחֶלְקוֹ שֶׁל חֲבֵירוֹ אֶלָּא קִנְיַן שִׁעְבּוּד, שֶׁקּוֹנָמוֹת מַפְקִיעִין אוֹתוֹ. כָּךְ נִרְאֶה לִי. **וּשְׁנֵיהֶם אֲסוּרִין** לְהַעֲמִיד רֵיחַיִם וְתַנּוּר וּלְגַדֵּל תַּרְנְגוֹלִין. דְּאַע"ג דְּאָמְרִי' בְּפֶרֶק "חֶזְקַת הַבָּתִּים" *דְּשׁוּתָּפִין אַהַעֲמָדָה כְּדֵי לָא קָפְדִי, מ"מ אִי קָפְדִי — יְכוֹלִין לְעַכֵּב זֶה עַל זֶה. וְאַע"פ שֶׁדַּרְכָּן לְוַתֵּר — וִיתּוּר אָסוּר בְּמוּדָּר הֲנָאָה. **הָיָה אֶחָד** מֵהֶן מוּדָּר הֲנָאָה מֵחֲבֵירוֹ וְכוּ'. הָךְ בָּבָא לָא אִצְטְרִיכָא לָא לְרַבָּנַן וְלָא לר"א בֶּן יַעֲקֹב, דְּדִין לְמָר וְדִין לְמָר מָה לִי נָדְרוּ שְׁנֵיהֶם מָה לִי נָדַר אֶחָד מֵהֶם. אֶלָּא מִשּׁוּם סֵיפָא נְקָטָהּ, דְּקָתָנֵי: וְכוֹפִין הַנּוֹדֵר לִמְכּוֹר אֶת חֶלְקוֹ. דְּדַוְקָא כְּשֶׁנָּדַר אֶחָד מֵהֶם, מִשּׁוּם דְּכֵיוָן דְּאִיהוּ אָסוּר וַחֲבֵירֵיהּ מוּתָּר — חָיְישִׁינַן שֶׁמָּא יִתְקַנֵּא בַּחֲבֵרוֹ וְיִשְׁתַּמֵּשׁ בָּהּ אַף הוּא, וּלְפִיכָךְ כְּדֵי שֶׁלֹּא יִכָּשֵׁל — כּוֹפִין אוֹתוֹ לִמְכּוֹר. אֲבָל כְּשֶׁנָּדְרוּ הֲנָאָה זֶה מִזֶּה, דִּשְׁנֵיהֶם אֲסוּרִין — לָא חָיְישִׁינַן, דְּכָל חַד וְחַד מִזְדַּהֵר בְּאִסּוּרֵיהּ. וְכֵן בְּאוֹסֵר נְכָסָיו עַל עַצְמוֹ, מֵהַךְ טַעְמָא גּוּפָא אֵין כּוֹפִין אוֹתוֹ לִמְכּוֹר — דְּדַוְקָא בְּשׁוּתָּפִין שֶׁנָּדַר אֶחָד מֵהֶם הוּא שֶׁכּוֹפִין. וַאֲפִילּוּ לְרַבִּי אֱלִיעֶזֶר בֶּן יַעֲקֹב נַמִי, דְּשָׁרֵי לִיכָּנֵס לֶחָצֵר — כּוֹפִין אוֹתוֹ לִמְכּוֹר, דִּלְדִידֵיהּ נַמִי אִיכָּא לְמֵיחַשׁ שֶׁמִּתּוֹךְ שֶׁרוֹאֶה אֶת חֲבֵרוֹ מַעֲמִיד רֵיחַיִם וְתַנּוּר וְהוּא אֵינוֹ רַשַּׁאי — יִתְקַנֵּא בּוֹ וְיָבֹא לַעֲשׂוֹת כֵּן. וכ"ת: בִּשְׁלָמָא לְרַבָּנַן דְּאָסְרֵי לֵיהּ אֲפִילּוּ בִּדְרִיסַת הָרֶגֶל אִיכָּא טַעְמָא דְּשֶׁמָּא יִתְקַנֵּא, לְפִי שֶׁהוּא אָסוּר בִּדְרִיסַת הָרֶגֶל וַחֲבֵירוֹ מוּתָּר, וְאֵין בְּיָדוֹ לִמְחוֹת. אֲבָל לְרַבִּי אֱלִיעֶזֶר בֶּן יַעֲקֹב, מַאי אִיכְפַּת לֵיהּ בִּדְרִיסַת הָרֶגֶל? אִיהוּ נַמִי שָׁרֵי! וְאִי מְקַנֵּא בַּחֲבֵרֵיהּ בְּהַעֲמָדַת רֵיחַיִם — לִיעַכֵּב עָלֵיהּ, דְּהָא כִּי הַאי גַּוְונָא שׁוּתָּפִין יְכוֹלִין לְעַכֵּב! אִיכָּא לְמֵימַר: דְּכֵיוָן דְּהַשּׁוּתָּפִין כִּי הַאי גַּוְונָא לָא קָפְדִי — זִילָא בֵּיהּ מִילְּתָא לְעַכּוֹבֵי. דְּהָא הָךְ סֵיפָא בְּנָדְרוּ זֶה מִזֶּה אוֹקִימְנָא לָהּ בַּגְּמָרָא, וְכֵיוָן שֶׁחֲבֵירוֹ לֹא גָּרַם לוֹ אִיסּוּר אֶלָּא הוּא עַצְמוֹ גָּרַם, שֶׁנָּדַר — לָמָּה יְעַכֵּב חֲבֵירוֹ מִדָּבָר שֶׁאֵין הַשּׁוּתָּפִין מַקְפִּידִין בּוֹ? הִילְכָּךְ לְעַכּוֹבֵי — כְּסִיפָא לֵיהּ מִילְּתָא, וּמִתּוֹךְ שֶׁחֲבֵירוֹ מַעֲמִיד רֵיחַיִם — יִתְקַנֵּא בּוֹ, לוֹמַר: אֶעֱשֶׂה כֵּן גַּם אֲנִי. **הָיָה אֶחָד** מִן הַשּׁוּק מוּדָּר מֵאֶחָד מֵהֶם הֲנָאָה הֲרֵי זֶה **לֹא** יִכָּנֵס לֶחָצֵר. הָךְ בָּבָא לָא תְּנָא לָהּ מִשּׁוּם תַּנָּא קַמָּא, דִּלְדִידֵיהּ פְּשִׁיטָא: אִם עַל חֲבֵירוֹ יָכוֹל לְעַכֵּב — עַל אֶחָד מִן הַשּׁוּק צְרִיכָא לְמֵימַר?! אֶלָּא לְאַשְׁמוּעִינַן רְבוּתָא דְּר' אֱלִיעֶזֶר בֶּן יַעֲקֹב תְּנָא לֵיהּ, דַּאֲפִילּוּ עַל אֶחָד מִן הַשּׁוּק אֵין שׁוּתָּף יָכוֹל לְעַכֵּב. וּלְפָנַיו נִרְאֶה דַּעְתִּי, דַּאֲפִילּוּ לִרְבוּתָא דְּרַבָּנַן תְּנָא לֵיהּ. מִיהוּ כָּתַב הרשב"א ז"ל דְּדַוְקָא כְּשֶׁהוּא נִכְנָס לְצוֹרֶךְ הַשּׁוּתָּף, בֵּין שֶׁהוּא צָרִיךְ לַשּׁוּתָּף אוֹ שֶׁהַשּׁוּתָּף צָרִיךְ לוֹ, לְפִי שֶׁהֶחָצֵר קָנוּי לְכָל אֶחָד מֵהֶם, וּלְכָל מִי שֶׁצָּרִיךְ לָהֶם. אֲבָל לִיכָּנֵס בְּתוֹכוֹ אֶחָד מִן הַשּׁוּק לְעַצְמוֹ, שֶׁלֹּא לְצוֹרֶךְ הַשּׁוּתָּף — אָסוּר, שֶׁאִם הִקְנוּ זֶה אֶת זֶה אֶת הֶחָצֵר לִדְרִיסַת רַגְלֵיהֶם וּלְכָל מִי שֶׁצָּרִיךְ לָהֶם — לֹא הִקְנוּ אוֹתוֹ לְכָל הָעוֹלָם. אֲבָל הרא"ה ז"ל כָּתַב דִּבְכָל עִנְיָן שָׁרֵי, וְלֹא נִרְאוּ לִי דְּבָרָיו א). **גמ'** מִי אָמְרִינַן בְּנָדְרוּ הוּא דִּפְלִיגִי רַבָּנַן **אֲבָל** בְּהִדִּירוּ מוֹדוּ לֵיהּ רַבָּנַן לְר' **אֱלִיעֶזֶר בֶּן יַעֲקֹב** דִּכְאֲנוּסִים דָּמוּ. כְּלוֹמַר, דִּילְמָא כּוּלְּהוּ סְבִירָא לְהוּ דְּיֵשׁ בְּרֵירָה, וּמִדִּינָא אֲפִילּוּ בְּנָדְרוּ שָׁרֵי, אֶלָּא דְּרַבָּנַן סָבְרֵי קָנְסִינַן לְהוּ, וְר' אֱלִיעֶזֶר בֶּן יַעֲקֹב סָבַר דְּלָא קָנְסִינַן. אֲבָל בְּהִדִּירוּ, דְּלָא שַׁיָּיךְ קְנָסָא — שָׁרֵי מִדִּינָא, דְּיֵשׁ בְּרֵירָה. וְאָתְיָא הָא דְּלָא כְּרַבִּינָא, דְּאוֹקֵי פְּלוּגְתַּיְיהוּ בְּפֶרֶק "שׁוֹר שֶׁנָּגַח אֶת הַפָּרָה" בְּיֵשׁ בְּרֵירָה וְאֵין בְּרֵירָה. אוֹ דִּילְמָא בְּהִדִּירוּ נַמִי פְּלִיגִי רַבָּנַן, וּכְסָבְרֵיהּ דְּרַבִּינָא הָתָם. ת"ש **הָיָה אֶחָד** מֵהֶן מוּדָּר הֲנָאָה מֵחֲבֵירוֹ וּפְלִיגִי רַבָּנַן. וְסָתָם מוּדָּר מֵחֲבֵירוֹ קָתָנֵי, אַלְמָא אֲפִילּוּ בְּהִדִּירוּ פְּלִיגִי. תְּנֵי נָדוּר מֵחֲבֵירוֹ. כְּלוֹמַר, דְּנוֹדֵר נַמִי "מוּדָּר" קָרֵי לֵיהּ, דְּמוּדָּר מַשְׁמַע בֵּין מִפִּי עַצְמוֹ בֵּין מִפִּי אֲחֵרִים. **אִי אָמְרַתְּ בִּשְׁלָמָא** דְּנָדַר הוּא הַיְינוּ דְּכוֹפִין. לְפִי שֶׁהוּא גָּרַם לְעַצְמוֹ. אֶלָּא אִי אָמְרַתְּ דְּלָא נָדַר הוּא — אַמַּאי כּוֹפִין? הָא מֵינַס אָנִיס! וְאִם תֹּאמַר: וְלֵימָא לֵיהּ לְעוֹלָם בְּהִדִּירוֹ חֲבֵירוֹ עָסְקִינַן, וְכִי קָתָנֵי כּוֹפִין אֶת הַנּוֹדֵר — אֶת הַמַּדִּיר קָאָמַר! יֵשׁ לוֹמַר: דְּלָא סְבִירָא לָן שֶׁיְּהֵא בַּדִּין לָכוֹף אָדָם לִמְכּוֹר אֶת שֶׁלּוֹ מִפְּנֵי שֶׁאָסַר נְכָסָיו עַל חֲבֵירוֹ. אֲבָל לְנוֹדֵר עַצְמוֹ רָאוּי לָכוֹף, דְּמַה הֲנָאָה יֵשׁ לוֹ לֶאֱסוֹר עַל עַצְמוֹ נְכָסָיו [שֶׁל חֲבֵירוֹ], וְאִיכָּא לְמֵיחַשׁ שֶׁמָּא יִכָּשֵׁל. וְיֵשׁ לִתְמוֹהַּ עַל הָרַב רַבֵּינוּ מֹשֶׁה בַּר מַיְימוֹן ז"ל שֶׁכָּתַב דְּלַמַּדִּיר הוּא שֶׁכּוֹפִין. שֶׁאַע"פ שֶׁזֶּה הוּא דֶּרֶךְ הַיְרוּשַׁלְמִי — אֵין זֶה דֶּרֶךְ הַגְּמָרָא שֶׁלָּנוּ, וּכְבָר הִשִּׂיג עָלָיו הראב"ד ז"ל. וּמִיהוּ, אִם הָיָה רָגִיל לְהַדִּיר — כּוֹפִין אוֹתוֹ לִמְכּוֹר. וְהָכִי תַּנְיָא בַּתּוֹסֶפְתָּא (פ"ג): הָיָה א' מֵהֶם רָגִיל לְהַדִּיר הֲנָאָה עַל חֶלְקוֹ — כּוֹפִין אֶת הָרָגִיל לִמְכּוֹר חֶלְקוֹ. וּמְפָרֵשׁ בִּירוּשַׁלְמִי דִּבְתְרֵי זִמְנִין מִיקְרֵי רָגִיל, דְּאָמְרִינַן הָתָם: עָבְרַת לָךְ קַמַּיְיתָא וְעָבְרוּ עֲלָךְ, תִּנְיָינָא וְעָבְרוּ עֲלָךְ, מִכָּאן וְאֵילָךְ — אוֹ מְכוֹר חֶלְקָךְ אוֹ שָׁרֵי נִדְרָךְ. וְלָא אִיפְּשִׁטָא בַּעְיָין אִי פְּלִיגִי רַבָּנַן אֲפִי' בְּהִדִּירוּ. וא"ת: וְלִיפְשׁוֹט לֵיהּ מִדִּתְנַן לְקַמָּן (דף מז:) "הֲרֵינִי עָלֶיךָ חֵרֶם וְאַתְּ עָלַי" — שְׁנֵיהֶם מוּתָּרִים בְּדָבָר שֶׁל עוֹלֵי בָּבֶל וַאֲסוּרִים בְּדָבָר שֶׁל אוֹתָהּ הָעִיר, וְאֵיזֶה דָּבָר שֶׁל אוֹתָהּ הָעִיר — הָרְחָבָה וְהַמֶּרְחָץ וּבֵית הַכְּנֶסֶת, אַלְמָא אֲפִילּוּ בְּהִדִּירוּ פְּלִיגִי! תֵּירֵץ הָרַב ר' יוֹנָה ז"ל: דְּהָתָם הַיְינוּ טַעְמָא מִשּׁוּם דְּאַע"ג דְּמוּדָּר אָנִיס, כֵּיוָן דְּנוֹדֵר לָא אָנִיס וְאָסוּר — שְׁנֵיהֶם אֲסוּרִים, דְּאִי שָׁרֵית מוּדָּר — לָא לַיְיתִ נוֹדֵר, וּמִשּׁוּם הָכִי לָא פְּלוּג רַבָּנַן. מחלוקת

א) עי' פי' הר"נ עד סוף המתני' לקמן בע"ב ובדף מז.

עין משפט נר מצוה

ב א מיי' פ"ז מהלכות נדרים הלכה ד סמג לאוין רמב טוש"ע י"ד סי' רכו סעיף ב:

ג ב ג מיי' שם הלכה ה ו טוש"ע שם סעיף א:

ד ד מיי' פ"ו מהלכות נדרים הלכה יב סמג לאוין רמב טוש"ע י"ד סי' רכא סעיף ו:

ה ה מיי' פ"ה שם הלכה ה ופרק ח הלכה יא סמג שם טוש"ע י"ד סי' רטז סעיף ד:

ו ו מיי' שם טוש"ע שם סעיף ה:

ב"ב נז:

לעיל מב:

שייך לע"ב

תוספות

ושניהן אסורין להעמיד שם ריחים ותנור ולהעמיד שם תרנגולין. דבכל הני יכולין למחות זה על זה בלא נדר כדאמר בפרק חזקת הבתים (ב"ב נז:) הלכך אסור לעשות עתה בחצר כשנדר דאם כן מהני ליה חבירו על שלא עיכב דדוקא דריסת הרגל אינו יכול לעכב כל כמה דלא חלקו וי"מ דכשהעמיד ריחים באיש רוב עם לשם וממלא חלקו וחלק חבירו וכן לגדל תרנגולין דמתפשטין בכל החצר: **היה** אחד מהם מודר הנאה מחבירו. משום דבעי למתני כופין כו' דלא שייך למתני בשניהם מודרין וכופין הנודר למכור חלקו דחיישינן פן יעבור אבל רישא דשניהם מודרין אין כופין משום דמנכר אבל הכא דאין אסור אלא האחד והשני מותר לחיישינן שמא יכנס המודר כשירצה חבירו נכנס ולכך כופין למודר *)ותנא שמא יכנס קתני לה ולרבי אליעזר כיון דשניהם מותרין למה כופין: **היה** אחד מן השוק. הך בבא לר"א איצטריך [דהוה אמינא] דלא קא שרי ר"א אלא כשהחצר שלו דקמפסיד בדבר אבל אחד מן השוק לא שרינן ולא סמכינן אברירה כיון שאינו מפסיד כלום קמ"ל: **אם** יש לו תפיסת יד למשכיר אסור. דעדיין הוא ברשותו ומדידיה קמיתהני כיון דגם אחר שהשכיר יש לו בה תפיסת יד אבל כשאין לו בה תפיסת יד יעלה כלום ואין לו בה כלום ואינו יכול ליאסר. ומכאן פסק ר"ת מי שהשכיר בית ואח"כ אסרו עליו דאין באיסורו כלום ומיהו יש לי לדחות דמיירי דאדריה סתמא דאין עליו תפיסת יד ואין דעתו לאסור מה שמשכיר אבל אם אסר בהדיא מני אסרה וכ"מ בערכין (דף כא.) (כל) המשכיר בית לחבירו והקדישו הדר בו מעל ומעלה שכר להקדש ועל ההיא נמי קשה מההיא דפרק אף על פי (דף נט:) שדה שמשכנתי לך לכשאפדנה מקדש דקודש שפלאה לא קדשה ויש לומר דודאי מה שהבית שוה יותר מן השכירות קדוש אבל כנגדו חולין והוי שותפים המשכיר והמקדיש לכך מעל והא דאע"פ ה"ק לכשאפדנה תיקדש כל השדה לגמרי דודאי בהקדש גמור לאסר לכ"ע דודאי מני מקדיש המשכיר ובשמעתין דקאמר מותר מיירי שאסר בקונם בעלמא ואלומי אלימי לשיעבודא דשוכר כדאמר גבי שיעבודא דבעל והא דאע"פ דאמר דלא קדשה עד שיפדנה מיירי שאסר בקונם בעלמא אבל אם הקדישה הקדש גמור חל ההקדש אם שוה השדה יותר על החוב ועוד יש לחלק דודאי הך דפרק אע"פ מיירי בב"ח כדתנן מוסיף עוד דינר ופודה כל הנכסים הללו אבל שוכר ומני מקדיש משום דסופו לחזור אליו אבל גבי חוב דלא תחזור לו לבסוף אם לא יפרע לו חובו לא מני מקדיש ובירושלמי מחלק בההיא דערכין בין הקדים לו שכרו ללא הקדים לו שכרו דודאי כשהקדים לו שכרו אינו של משכיר כלל: **[בנדרו** הוא דפליגי]. בנדר מעצמו לכל אחד ואחד אסר נפשו שאמר קונם שלא אהנה ממך הלכך יש להחמיר וקנסו רבנן אבל הדירו כל אחד חבירו ליהנות משלו מודו ליה רבנן לר' אליעזר דכאנוסין דמו ולא מיתסרו דאית להו ברירה [ובנדרו] קנסו אבל בהדירו לא קנסו. ונ"ע בהא דתנן האומר הריני עליך חרס ואת עלי שניהם אסורים בדברים של אותה העיר אלמא בהדירו נמי אסרו רבנן הרי אתה עלי חרס קנסינן ליה גם על חבירו קנסו רבנן. אי נמי **)לית להו ברירה ומייתא בפ' שור שנגח את הפרה דלרבנן לית להו ברירה וצריך למימר דלית להו הך סוגיא (אלא בת"ש היה אחד מהם מודר ופליגי): **ת"ש** היה אחד מהם מודר. משמע שחבירו הדירו ואסרי רבנן: **תני** נודר. שאסר עצמו מחבירו: **אי** אמרת בשלמא בנודר היינו דקתני כופין. דפושע שאסר עצמו מחבירו ויכול לבא לידי תקלה: **אלא** אי אמרת שהדירו אמאי אמר כופין. דכופין הנודר היינו המודר אמאי כופין המודר דמאי חטא:

מחלוקת

*) נ"ל ומ"ק קתני לה. **) נ"ל אית.

פי' הרא"ש

אם יש לו בהם תפיסת יד. בגמ' מפרש כמה: **אין לו בהן תפיסת יד מותר.** דברשות השוכר קיימא ואין המשכיר יכול לאסרה עליו: **מת או שמכרם לאחר מותר.** דכיון דאמר ביתך שלך לא אסרם עליו אלא בזמן שהם שלו אבל אם אמר לבית זה או שדה זו אסרם עליו לעולם: **גמ' בנדרו הוא דפליגי רבנן.** דכיון דמדעתם נדרו הנאה זה מזה קנסו אותם ולא סמכינן אברירה אבל בהדירו דאנוסין היו סמכינן אברירה או דילמא אפי' בהדירו פליגי רבנן דלית להו ברירה: **היה אחד מהם מודר כו'.** משמע שחבירו היה מדירו: **אלא אי אמרת דאדריה אמאי כופין.** מה פשע המודר שיכפוהו למכור חלקו שאם אתה אומר כן כל אחד ידור חבירו כדי שיכפוהו למכור חלקו:

הגהות הב"ח

(א) רש"י ד"ה ושניהם אסורין להעמיד וכו' רחיים ותנור ולגדל.

עין משפט נר מצוה

ז א מיי' פ"ז מהלכות נדרים הלכה ד סמג לאוין רמב טוש"ע י"ד סימן רכו סעיף א:

ח ב מיי' פ"ז מהלכות נדרים הלכה יב סמג לאוין רמב טוש"ע י"ד סי' רכא סעיף ו:

גמרא

מַחֲלוֹקֶת (א) שֶׁיֵּשׁ בָּהּ כְּדֵי חֲלוּקָה, אֲבָל אֵין בָּהּ כְּדֵי חֲלוּקָה — דִּבְרֵי הַכֹּל מוּתָּר. א"ל רַב יוֹסֵף: הֲרֵי בֵּית הַכְּנֶסֶת, דִּכְמִי שֶׁאֵין בּוֹ כְּדֵי חֲלוּקָה דָּמֵי, וּתְנַן: שְׁנֵיהֶן אֲסוּרִין בְּדָבָר שֶׁל אוֹתָהּ הָעִיר! אֶלָּא אָמַר רַב יוֹסֵף אָמַר זְעֵירֵי: [א]מַחֲלוֹקֶת שֶׁאֵין בָּהּ כְּדֵי חֲלוּקָה, אֲבָל יֵשׁ בָּהּ כְּדֵי חֲלוּקָה — דִּבְרֵי הַכֹּל אָסוּר. אָמַר רַב הוּנָא: הֲלָכָה כר"א בֶּן יַעֲקֹב, וְכֵן א"ר אֶלְעָזָר: הֲלָכָה כְּר' אֱלִיעֶזֶר בֶּן יַעֲקֹב.§ "הַמּוּדָּר הֲנָאָה מֵחֲבֵירוֹ וְיֵשׁ לוֹ שָׁם מֶרְחָץ" וכו'.§ וְכַמָּה תְּפִיסַת יָד? אָמַר רַב נַחְמָן: לְמֶחֱצָה לִשְׁלִישׁ וְלִרְבִיעַ, אֲבָל בִּבְצִיר — לָא. אַבַּיֵי אָמַר: [ב]אֲפִילּוּ בִּבְצִיר אָסוּר. הֵיכִי דָּמֵי דְּשָׁרֵי — דִּמְקַבֵּל בְּטַסְקָא.§ הָאוֹמֵר

רש"י

בְּדָבָר שֶׁל אוֹתָהּ הָעִיר. כִּדְמְפָרֵשׁ: בֵּית הַכְּנֶסֶת וְהַתֵּיבָה וכו'. שֶׁאֵין בָּהּ כְּדֵי חֲלוּקָה. וּמַאן דְּאָסַר – מִשּׁוּם דִּכְבֵית הַכְּנֶסֶת דָּמֵי, דְּקָתָנֵי דִּשְׁנֵיהֶם אֲסוּרִים. וּמַאן דְּשָׁרֵי – הוֹאִיל וְאִי אֶפְשָׁר בַּחֲלוּקָה. אֲבָל יֵשׁ בָּהּ כְּדֵי חֲלוּקָה דִּבְרֵי הַכֹּל אָסוּר. דְּסַגֵּי לֵיהּ בַּחֲלוּקָה. וְכַמָּה תְּפִיסַת יָד. יֵשׁ לוֹ לַמַּדִּיר בְּאוֹתוֹ מֶרְחָץ, דְּלִיתְּסַר בֵּיהּ הַאי. אֲבָל בִּבְצִיר. מֶרְדִּיעַ לָא חָשֵׁיב תְּפִיסַת יָד, וּמוּתָּר בּוֹ הַמּוּדָּר. וּסְפָרִים דִּכְתִיב בְּהוּ "בִּבְלָין" – מַשְׁמַע נַמִּי (ב) בִּבְלָיִם. וְאִית דְּגָרְסֵי "בְּבֵילִין", כְּמוֹ בֵּילִין שֶׁל יוֹצֵר, כִּדְאָמַר בְּב"מ (דף עד.) שֶׁהַיּוֹצֵר עוֹשֶׂה כְּמִין בֵּילִים שֶׁל חוֹמֶר וּמֵהֶם עוֹשֶׂה קְדֵרוֹת. וְהָכִי מַשְׁמַע לֵיהּ: דְּאִית לֵיהּ תַּשְׁמִישְׁתָּא כְּלוּם, אֲבָל כְּדֵי לְהַנִּיחַ בֵּילִים שֶׁל יוֹצֵר לְהָתָם לְיַיבְּשָׁם – אֵין זוֹ תְּפִיסַת יָד. אַבַּיֵי אָמַר אֲפִי' בִּבְצִיר. מֶרְדִּיעַ הָוֵי תְּפִיסַת יָד, וְאָסוּר בָּהֶם הַמּוּדָּר. וְהָכִי נַמִּי אִיכָּא לְפָרֵשׁ כָּל הָנֵי לִישָּׁנֵי. דִּמְקַבֵּל בְּטַסְקָא. שֶׁקִּיבְּלוֹ הַשּׂוֹכֵר לָתֵת מִמֶּנּוּ מַס בְּכָל שָׁנָה וְשָׁנָה, דְּהַאי לָא הָוֵי תְּפִיסַת יָד כְּלָל.

ה"ג

ר"נ

מחלוקת בשיש בה כדי חלוקה. דרבנן אסרי משום דסברי אין ברירה, ולא אמרי' הוברר הדבר כשמשתמש דגוף החצר קנוי לו לתשמישו. משום דכיון שיש בה דין חלוקה בשעת קנייתן – לא הוברר שיהא רשאי זה להשתמש בחלק זה, דשמא לא יצא לחלקו. ור"א סבר דאפי' בכי הא אמרינן ברירה, לפי שבתחלה כשקנו אותה – על דעת כן קנאוה, שכל עוד שלא יחלוקו אותה יהא כל גוף החצר קנוי לתשמיש כל אחד מהם. אבל אין בה דין חלוקה דברי הכל מותר. משום דכיון דאין בה דין חלוקה, והדבר ידוע שלעולם תעמוד בשותפות, ושיש רשות לכל אחד מהם להשתמש בה כל שעה שירצה – כ"ע מודו דיש ברירה, לפי שרוב קניה זו הוררה מתחילתה. ולא דמיא לשאר ברירות דעלמא, וכמו שפירשתי אני במשנתינו. אמר ליה רב יוסף והא בית הכנסת דכמי שאין בו כדי חלוקה דמי ותנן שניהם אסורים בדבר של אותה העיר. ומפרש ואזיל בהא מתניתין דפרקין (לקמן מח.) דדבר של אותה העיר, כגון בית הכנסת. ובשלמא אי אמרת דבחצר שאין בה דין חלוקה פליגי – הא מני רבנן היא. אלא אי אמרת דבחצר שאין בה דין חלוקה דברי הכל מותר – מתניתין אמאן תרמייה?. אלא אמר רב יוסף אמר זעירי מחלוקת שאין בה כדי חלוקה. דרבנן סברי דאפי' בכי הא אין ברירה, ור' אליעזר סבר דכיון שאי אפשר לאחד מן השותפין לעכב את חבירו מלהשתמש בו לעולם, ולא לכופו לחלוק – מתחלה ע"מ כן קנאוה, שתהא גופה קנויה לגמרי לכל אחד לתשמישו, בשעת תשמישו וכשמשתמש בה – אמרי' הוברר הדבר למפרע שמתחלה היתה קנויה לו לשעה זו. וס"ל לר' אליעזר דנהי דבעלמא אין ברירה, בכי הא יש ברירה, לפי שעיקר הקניה נתבררה משעה ראשונה. אבל יש בה דין חלוקה דברי הכל אסור. משום דכיון שחצר זו לחלוקה היא עומדת – אי אפשר לומר שמתחלה קנאוה כולה כל אחד לתשמישו, דשמא הא' יכוף את חבירו. הלכך, אפי' לר' אליעזר בן יעקב אסורין. וכתב הרשב"א ז"ל: דלא מיבעיא קודם חלוקה דאסורים, אלא אפילו לאחר חלוקה נמי אסורין. דליכא למימר כיון שחלקו הוברר הדבר למפרע שהוא חלקו המגיעו משעה ראשונה, והוא לא נאסר אלא בחלק חברו. דא"ה – הויא ליה הך ברירה כשאר ברירות דעלמא, וקי"ל בדאורייתא אין ברירה. וכ"ת: מ"מ, הא קי"ל כשמואל דאמר (ב"ק ט.): האחין שחלקו – לקוחות הן, והרי זה כאילו לקחה ממנו! ליתא, דאפילו לקחה ממנו אסורה, כדאמרי' לעיל (דף לד:) גבי "ככרי עליך" דאע"ג דיהבי' ניהליה במתנה, כל היכא דלא אפקיה אחר – אסור. ומכירה הרי היא כמתנה. וכדתנן "קונם ביתך שאני נכנס", "שדך שאני לוקח", מת או מכרו לאחר – מותר. הא מכרו לו, אפי' באומר "קונם ביתך שאני נכנס" – אסור, זהו דעת הרשב"א ז"ל. אבל הרמב"ם ז"ל כתב בפ"ז מהל' נדרים (ה"ד): היו שניהן שותפין בחצר, אם יש בה דין חלוקה – הרי אלו אסורים ליכנס בה עד שיחלוקו, ויכנס כל א' וא' לחלקו. אלמא ס"ל ז"ל דלאחר חלוקה שרי. ונ"ל בטעמו ז"ל, דאע"ג דקיי"ל דבדאורייתא אין ברירה – אפ"ה אנן סהדי שע"מ כן נשתתפו, שלא יוכל אחד מהן לאסרה על חברו בענין שתהא נאסרת עליו לאחר חלוקה. דא"ה – אסר עליה נכסי דידה, ואינו בדין. **מתני'** *המודר הנאה מחבירו ויש לו מרחץ ובית הבד, מושכרים בעיר. ויש לו למדיר מרחץ ובית הבד אלא שהשכירן לאחר. אם יש לו בהן תפיסת יד. למדיר, אסור מודר ליהנות מהם. דכיון דיש לו למדיר בהם תפיסת יד – הוו להו כדידיה. ובגמרא מפרש היכי דמי תפיסת יד. ואם אין לו בהם תפיסת יד מותר. דלאו מדידיה מהני אלא [מהשוכר]. וכתב הרשב"א ז"ל: דכי אמרי' דבשאין לו בהן תפיסת יד מותר – דוקא כשהיו מושכרין כבר, אבל השכירן לאחר מכן – לא. דאע"ג דתנן בסמוך: "לביתך שאני נכנס" מת או מכרו לאחר – מותר, דוקא במכירה הוא דשרי, אבל בשכירות – לא. דאם איתא דאפי' בשכירות שרי – ליתני השכירן, וכ"ש מכרן. אלא ודאי כל שקדם נדרו לשכירותו אין האיסור מסתלק ע"י שכירות. אבל מתני' בהשכירן כבר, ולפיכך כל שאין לו בהן תפיסת יד – אין האיסור חל עליהם. **גמ'** וכמה תפיסת יד אמר רב נחמן למחצה לשליש ולרביע. דכיון דבעל המרחץ משתכר כפי מה שהמרחץ מרויח – הוה ליה כדידיה. אבל בביצים מותר. דרכן היה שבעל המרחץ משתכר בבילים, שהבאים לרחוץ שם היו לוקחים אותם ממנו, ומש"ה קאמר שאם אין בעל המרחץ משתכר בריוח המרחץ כלל, אלא שייר לעצמו אותו ריוח של בילים – [מותר], לפי שאינו מגוף המרחץ. אביי אמר אפי' בביצים אסור. דאפי' כה"ג מקרי תפיסת יד. היכי דמי דשרי דמקבל בטסקא. שאינו נוטל חלק הידוע בריוח המרחץ, אלא שנותן לו שכר דבר קצוב לשנה, וכל כה"ג אסתלק ליה בעל המרחץ ממרחצו לגמרי. ואיכא למידק אשמעתין: ואפי' כה"ג היכי שרי? דהא מ"מ גוף המרחץ של משכיר הוא, ויכול לאסור אותו על השוכר עצמו, כדאמרינן בערכין בפ' "האומר משקלי עלי" (דף כא.): המשכיר בית לחבירו והקדישו, הדר בו מעלה שכר להקדש. ומוקמינן לה כשהקדישו משכיר, דשוכר מעלה שכר להקדש. ואקשינן התם: הדר בו מעלה שכר להקדש?! היכי דייר בו? במעילה קאי! אלמא יכול לאסרה על השוכר, כיון שהגוף הקרקע שלו, וכ"ש שיכול לאסרה על אחרים, וכי אין לו בהם תפיסת יד – אמאי שרי? תרצו בתוספות: דאין ה"נ, שאם אסר אותו המרחץ בפי' – חייל אסוריה, כיון שהגוף שלו, כי ההיא דפרק "משקלי עלי" שהקדיש הבית עצמו. אבל הכא במודר הנאה מנכסיו סתם איירי, ואין דעתו על מה שהשכיר. ואי קשיא לך: דהא לעיל בפרק "אין בין המודר" (דף מג:) הוה סלקא דעתך דאין דעתו על מה שהפקיר, ואדחיה ליה! איכא למימר דלא דמי, דודאי כשאדם אוסר נכסיו סתם – דעתו על כל מה שהוא ברשותו, ולפיכך כיון שאין ההפקר עדיין הפקר, ולא המתנה מתנה – אף הם בכלל האיסור. אבל מה שיצא מרשותו לשעתו בשכירות, כיון דהשתא מיהת לאו ברשותיה קאי – אין דעתו לאסרו. ור"ת ז"ל תירץ: דההיא דפרק "משקלי עלי" – דוקא גבי הקדש, ומשום דהקדש מפקיע מידי שעבוד. אבל הכא גבי קונמות, אע"ג דמפקיעין מידי שעבוד, כדאיתא בפ' "אע"פ" (כתובות נט:) ובפרק בתרא דמכילתין (דף פו:) ה"מ בקונם כללי כעין הקדש, אבל בקונם פרטי, כיון דלא דמי להקדש – אלמוה רבנן לשעבודיה דאידך דלא ליפקע ליה, כי היכי דאמר התם דאלמוה רבנן לשעבודיה דבעל. וכך הורה ר"ת ז"ל. ואחרים תירצו: דההיא דפרק "משקלי עלי" – בשלא הקדיש שכרו למשכיר. וכיון דלא סגיא שלא יתחייב השוכר לתת שכר להקדש – נמצא שיש להקדש יד וזכות בכל הבית כמו שהיה למשכיר, ולפיכך חל הקדש על הבית, וכי דייר ביה – במעילה קאי. אבל מתני' – כשהקדיש שוכר למשכיר שכרו, וכיון דאסתלק ליה משכיר לגמרי – לא מצי אסר. ובירושלמי נמי מפליג כה"ג בין הקדיש לו שכרו ללא הקדיש. ובודאי דההיא דפרק "משקלי עלי" לא קשיא, דהתם במשכיר בית סתם עסקינן. וראיה לדבר – דקתני התם: נפל – חייב להעמיד לו בית, ואי ב"בית זה", נפל – אזדא. אלא ודאי בבית סתם עסקינן, ומש"ה פרכינן: היכי מצי דייר ביה, במעילה קאי! דכיון דלא השכיר לו בית ידוע אלא בית סתם – ודאי מצי מקדיש ליה משכיר, ויהיב ליה לשוכר ביתא אחרינא. אבל ב"בית זה" – ודאי לא מצי משכיר מקדיש ליה, דהא אע"ג דהקדש מפקיע מידי שעבוד – ה"מ הקדש מזבח, אבל הקדש בדק הבית – לא, כדעת רש"י ז"ל, ושלא כדברי ר"ת ז"ל שהוא סובר שאפי' הקדש בדק הבית מפקיע מידי שעבוד. וראיה לדבר מדאמר בפרק "אע"פ" ובסוף מכילתין: הא לא דמיא אלא לאומר לחבירו "שדה זו שמשכנתי לך לעשר שנים לכשאפדנה ממך תקדוש" דקדשה. אלמא, דוקא לכשיפדנה. אבל קודם לכן – לא קדשה. הילכך, ההיא דפרק "משקלי עלי" לא קשיא כלל אמתניתין. ומיהו, אכתי מתניתין לא ניחא, דהא קונמות כקדושת הגוף דמיין, כדאיתא בפרק "אע"פ" (שם) ובסוף מכילתין, ואמאי לא מפקיעין מידי שעבוד? הילכך לא מפרקא מתני' אלא בחד מהנך פירוקא דכתיבנא. ואני כבר כתבתי במשנתינו דאפילו קונם פרטי, ואפי' הקדיש שכר שוכר – מצי משכיר לאסרו עליו, ואדחיאן להו תרי פירוקי בתראי. ואחרים תירצו עוד: דהאי מושכרים דהכא – לאו מושכרים כעין שכירות אחר

שייך למתני' ־לעיל בע"א

תוספות

מחלוקת בשיש בו כדי חלוקה. דאז מתהני בחלוקה שיכול לכוף את חבירו לחלוק לכך לא קנסוה רבנן אבל אין בה דין חלוקה שאין יכול לכוף את חבירו קנסו רבנן: **אמר** רב הונא הלכה כרבי אליעזר בן יעקב. וקשה דבפרק בתרא *) פסקינן כרבי אושעיא דאמר בדאורייתא אין ברירה בדרבנן יש ברירה והכא דאורייתא הוא ומפרש ר"ת דהא דפסקי' כרבי אליעזר בן יעקב לאו מטעם דיש ברירה אלא משום דויתור מותר במודר הנאה וכשהדירו זה את זה מדריסת הרגל לא נאסרו וא"כ לפי זה שאם אסרו עצמם בדריסה אסורין ליכנס לחצר ואדם מן השוק שאסר מותר ליכנס דויתור מותר ור"י פי' דפסקינן שפיר מטעמא דיש ברירה ובבילה (דף לח:) לא פסיק כר' אושעיא אלא ממאי דאמר בדרבנן יש ברירה הילכך שותפין שנדרו דריסת הרגל מותרין בחצר ואדם מן השוק מודר הנאה מחבירו אסור ליכנס דויתור אסור לאשכחן סתמא בפרקין לעיל דויתור אסור: **למחצה** לשליש ולרביע. שהמשכיר מקבל שליש הריוח ואין לשוכר כ"א ב' חלקים דברשותו הוא מקבל ואסור: **אבל** בבציר. פירוש בפחות מותר: **אביי** אמר אפילו בבציר אסור כך הגירסא ראשונה: **דמקבל** בטסקא. פירוש שמקבל השוכר מן המשכיר בכך וכך לשנה ואיתא ספרים דגרסי אפילו בבנין פירוש קרקע היוצר כמו על הבנין של יוצר (ב"מ דף עד.) ורגילין לייבשן במרחץ ואם רגילות להשכיר לייבש בנין של משכיר באותו מרחץ הוה תפיסת יד:

*) נ"ל בתרא דבילה

פי' הרא"ש

מחלוקת שיש בה כדי חלוקה. ד' אמות לכל א' כיון דאפשר בחלוקה לא סמכינן אברירה: **מחלוקת בשאין בה כדי חלוקה.** דכיון דאי אפשר לחלוק אית ליה לראב"י דסמכינן אברירה: **למחצה לשליש ולרביע.** שחולקים כך השכר ביניהן: **אבל בבציר לא.** אם יש למשכיר פחות משליש בשכר לא מקרי תפיסת יד ויש"ג אבל בבילים לא וה"פ אם שייר המשכיר לעצמו שיש לו כח לייבש בבית המרחץ בילים של יוצר כדאמרינן באיזהו נשך (ב"מ דף עד.) על הבילים של יוצר משיקשעם בכבשן וכנגד זה מלאכה קטנה בית הבד לא מיקרי בהם תפיסת יד: **דמקבל בעסקא.** שהשוכר נותן גם מס של המרחץ ובית הבד דהוי שכירות בריא' כדאמר בפרק הדר עם העובד כוכבים (עירובין דף סב.) היכי דמי שכירות בריאה במוהרקי ואבורגני פי' שנוה השוכר מס ואז נסתלק בעל הבית לגמרי ואית דגרסי בפסקא שנותן השוכר דבר קצוב למשכיר ואין לו בחלק שמרויח השוכר:

הגהות הב"ח

(א) גמ' מחלוקת כשיש בה: (ב) רש"י ד"ה אבל בבציר וכו' משמע נמי בבציר ואית וכו' והכי משמע ליה תפיסת יד דאית ליה:

"הָאוֹמֵר לַחֲבֵירוֹ" וכו'.§ בָּעֵי *אֲבִימִי: "קוֹנָם לְבַיִת זֶה שֶׁאַתָּה נִכְנָס", מֵת אוֹ שֶׁמְּכָרוֹ לְאַחֵר, מַהוּ? *אָדָם אוֹסֵר דָּבָר שֶׁבִּרְשׁוּתוֹ לִכְשֶׁיֵּצֵא מֵרְשׁוּתוֹ אוֹ לֹא? אֲמַר רָבָא, ת"ש: *הָאוֹמֵר לִבְנוֹ "קוֹנָם שֶׁאִי אַתָּה נֶהֱנֶה לִי" וּמֵת — יִירָשֶׁנּוּ. "בְּחַיָּיו וּבְמוֹתוֹ" וּמֵת — לֹא יִירָשֶׁנּוּ. אש"מ: אָדָם אוֹסֵר דָּבָר שֶׁבִּרְשׁוּתוֹ לִכְשֶׁיֵּצֵא מֵרְשׁוּתוֹ, שְׁמַע מִינָּהּ.§ *תְּנַן הָתָם: ב"קוֹנָם פֵּירוֹת הָאֵלּוּ עָלַי, קוֹנָם הֵן עַל פִּי, קוֹנָם הֵן לְפִי" — אָסוּר בְּחִילּוּפֵיהֶן וּבְגִידּוּלֵיהֶן. גבָּעֵי רָמִי בַּר חָמָא: אָמַר "קוֹנָם פֵּירוֹת הָאֵלּוּ עַל פְּלוֹנִי" מַהוּ בְּחִילּוּפֵיהֶן? מִי אָמְרִינַן: גַּבֵּי דִּילֵיהּ, הוֹאִיל וְאָדָם אוֹסֵר פֵּירוֹת חֲבֵירוֹ עַל עַצְמוֹ — אָדָם אוֹסֵר דָּבָר שֶׁלֹּא בָּא לָעוֹלָם עַל עַצְמוֹ, גַּבֵּי חֲבֵירוֹ, הוֹאִיל *וְאֵין אָדָם אוֹסֵר פֵּירוֹת חֲבֵירוֹ עַל חֲבֵירוֹ — אֵין אָדָם אוֹסֵר דָּבָר שֶׁלֹּא בָּא לָעוֹלָם עַל חֲבֵירוֹ. אוֹ

רש"י

ה"ג בָּעֵי אֲבִימִי קוֹנָם בַּיִת זֶה שֶׁאַתָּה נִכְנָס וּמֵת אוֹ שֶׁמְּכָרוֹ לְאַחֵר מַהוּ. אָדָם אוֹסֵר דָּבָר וכו'. וַאֲפִילּוּ לְאַחַר שֶׁמֵּת אוֹ שֶׁמְּכָרוֹ לְאַחֵר הָוֵי נַמִי אָסוּר, אוֹ לָא? תְּנַן הָתָם. לְקַמָּן בְּפֶרֶק "הַנּוֹדֵר מִן הַיָּרָק" (א). קוֹנָם פֵּירוֹת הָאֵלּוּ עָלַי אוֹ קוֹנָם הֵן לְפִי אוֹ קוֹנָם הֵן עַל פִּי אָסוּר בְּחִילּוּפֵיהֶן. אִם נִתְחַלְּפוּ בְּפֵירוֹת אֲחֵרוֹת, וְדָבָר שֶׁלֹּא בָּא לָעוֹלָם הוּא. גִּידּוּלֵיהֶן. שֶׁנְּטָעָן וְהִגְדִּילוּ. עַל פְּלוֹנִי. שֶׁאֲסָרָן עַל חֲבֵירוֹ. מַהוּ. (ב) אִי הָוֵי אָסוּר בְּחִילּוּפֵיהֶן כְּמוֹ שֶׁהוּא אָסוּר, אִי לָא? מִי אָמְרִינַן: גַּבֵּיהּ דִּילֵיהּ, כִּי אֲמַר "קוֹנָם הֵן לְפִי" אוֹ "עַל פִּי" — אָסוּר בְּחִילּוּפֵיהֶן, אַף עַל גַּב דְּהָוֵי דָּבָר שלב"ל, הוֹאִיל וְאַשְׁכַּחַן גַּבֵּי דִּילֵיהּ כִּי הַאי חוּמְרָא דְּאִיהוּ אוֹסֵ' פֵּירוֹת חֲבֵירוֹ עָלָיו, וְאַהָכִי מַחְמִירִי' לְגַבֵּיהּ דְּאוֹסֵר נַמִי עָלָיו דָּבָר שלב"ל. אֲבָל גַּבֵּי חֲבֵירוֹ, הוֹאִיל וְאֵינוֹ אוֹסֵר פֵּירוֹת חֲבֵירוֹ עַל חֲבֵירוֹ, דְּאִי אָמַר לַחֲבֵירוֹ "קוֹנָם פֵּירוֹת שֶׁל פְּלוֹנִי עָלֶיךָ" — לָא הָוֵי כְּלוּם, לָא אָמְרִינַן נַמִי דְּאִית בְּיָדוֹ לְמֵיסַר לֵיהּ בַּחֲלִיפִין, דְּהָוֵי דָּבָר שֶׁלֹּא בָּא לָעוֹלָם.

ר"ן

אחר דעלמא, דהא אמרינן בגמרא: היכי דמי דשרי — דמקבל בטסקא, ומקבל בטסקא לאו היינו שכירות, אלא הקרקע הרי הוא של מחזיק לעולם, ומורישו לבניו, אלא שנותן דבר ידוע בכל שנה לבעלים הראשונים. וכל כי האי גוונא — קנין הגוף מיקרי, ולא שעבוד בלבד שיפקיענו קונם. והאי דנקט מושכרין במתניתין — משום דטסקא זו כעין שכירות הוא, שאם אינו פורע המוטל עליו שנה שנה — הדרא ארעא למרא, וכדאמרינן בעלמא (ב"מ ד' עג:): ארעא לטסקא משתעבדא, ומלכא אמר: דיהיב טסקא — ליכול ארעא. ואפילו הכי, כיון דכל אימת דבעי למפרע לא מצי מסלק ליה אידך — קנין הגוף יש לו בקרקע, ומש"ה לא מצי אסר. אבל בשכירות דעלמא מצי אסר, כל זה פלפלו הראשונים ז"ל. ותמהני עליהם, לפי שאני אומר להלכה דאפי' בשכירות דעלמא, כל שאין לו למדיר תפיסת יד — שרי מודר לאתהניי ממרחץ ובית הבד שיש לו למדיר מושכרין בעיר. דאע"ג דמן דינא ודאי דמשכיר יכול לאסור על השוכר, ואפי' הקדיש השוכר למשכיר שכרו, וכדפרישנא לעיל במתניתין דריש פרקא. הני מילי — כשאוסר אותם לשוכר, או כשאוסר אותם על כל אדם, שהשוכר בכלל. משום דכיון דקונמות מפקעי מידי שעבוד — אסתלק ליה שעבודא דשוכר לגמרי. אבל לאסור אותו על אחר — לא כל הימנו, דכיון דאשתייר ליה שעבודא דשוכר, כשהמודר נהנה — לא ממדיר הוא נהנה אלא מן השוכר, כנ"ל, ודבר ברור הוא. ולפיכך אני אומר: דכי תנן לעיל: היה א' מן השוק מודר מא' מהם הנאה לא יכנס לחצר, ר"א בן יעקב אומר וכו' — לאו משום רבותא דרבי אליעזר בן יעקב בלחוד תנא ליה, אלא לרבותא דרבנן נמי נקטיה. דסד"א: נהי דקסברי רבנן דשותף מצי אסר אחבריה — ה"מ משום דמפקע מיניה קנין שעבוד, וכדכתיבנא לעיל, אבל לאחד מן השוק — לא מצי אסר הך חצר שאין בה דין חלוקה, דמצי א"ל: כיון דשעבוד חבירך עדיין נשאר אצלו — לתוך שלו אני נכנס, ולא לתוך שלך. קמ"ל, דכיון דהך מדיר מצי קני ליה בהא חצר קנין גוף ופירות — לא כל הימנו.

*מתני' האומר לחבירו קונם לביתך שאני נכנס. כלומר, למה שאני נכנס בו. שדך שאני לוקח. כלומר, אם אקחנו. מת או (ג) מכרן לאחר מותר. ד"ביתך" אמר, והשתא לאו ביתיה הוא. וה"ה דאי נתנן לאחר נמי שרי, אלא להכי נקט מכרן — לאשמועינן דדוקא מכרן לאחר, אבל אמר "ביתך שאני נכנס" ומכרו לו — אסור. קונם לבית זה שאני נכנס ושדה זה שאני לוקח מת או מכרו לאחר אסור. דכיון ד"בית זה" קאמר — שויה עילויה חתיכה דאסורא, הלכך אפילו מכרו לאחר — אסור. והוי יודע דכי היכי ד"בית זה" חמור מ"ביתך" לענין (ד) מכרן לאחר, הכי נמי "ביתך" חמור מ"בית זה" לענין נפילה. דאי אמר "ביתך שאני נכנס" ונפל ובנאו — אסור ליכנס בו, דכל שהוא ביתך משמע. ואי אמר "בית זה" ונפל, אף ע"פ שחזר ובנאו — מותר בו, דכיון דנפל אזדא. ואי אמר "ביתך זה" — משום "זה" אתה תופסו, בין לחומרא דמכירה בין לקולא דנפילה. והכי איתא בירושלמי: "ביתך זה" משום מה אתה תופסו — משום "ביתך זה", נפל ובני — הא לית הוא. ושמעינן מן הדא: האומר ליורשיו "תנו בית חתנות לבני או בית ארמלות לבתי" ונפל — היורשים חייבים לבנותו, "בית זה" ונפל — אין חייבין לבנותו. ומסתברא דכי אמרינן "בביתך שאני נכנס" דאי נפל ובני ליה אסור — לאו דוקא נפל ובני ליה במקומו, דה"ה אם בנהו במקום אחר אסור, דכל שהוא ביתך קאמר. והאי דנקט נפל ובני — לרבותא נקטיה, דבלומר "בית זה" אע"פ שחזר *)במקומו וכמדתו הראשונה — מותר. **גמ'** בעי אבימי קונם לבית זה שאתה נכנס מת או מכרו לאחר מהו. כלומר, דנהי דאמרי' במתניתין דבלומר "בית זה" מכרו לאחר אסור — ה"מ באוסר על עצמו, דמצי אסר אנפשיה בית זה, בין שיהא שלו או שימכרנו לאחר. אבל אחבריה, נהי ד"בית זה" לעולם משמע, וכדמוכחא מתניתין — מיהו לא כל הימנו לאסרו לכשילא מרשותו, דה"ל נכסי חבירו על חבירו. וה"ה דמבעיא ליה במפרש "בית זה שאתה נכנס אפילו לאחר שילא מרשותו" דאפשר דלא מהני, דאיהו לא מספקא בלישנא, דודאי פשיטא ליה ד"זה" לעולם משמע, וכדמוכחא מתניתין. אבל עיקר בעיא היא, אפילו כי בעי למיעבד הכי — אי מצי עביד, כיון דנכסיה השתא ברשותיה נינהו, או לאו, כיון דלאחר מכן נפקי מרשותיה — והוי להו כנכסי חבירו על חבירו. ומש"ה מייתי לה רב' ת"ש מדתנן "בחייו ובמותו" — מת לא יירשנו, דאלמא כי פריש מצי למיסר אפילו לאחר שיצאו מרשותו, כיון דהשתא ברשותו נינהו. וכיון דכי פריש חייל איסורא — פשיטא ליה ד"זה" כמפרש דמי, דמתני' נמי הכי מוכחא. ואע"ג דלעיל (דף מב:) דחינן: שאני התם דאמר "בחייו ובמותו", כלומר דאע"ג ד"זה" לגבי נודר עצמו לעולם משמע, לגבי מדיר לא משמע הכי, וכמו שפירשתי אני למעלה — הכא לא ניחא לן בההיא דחיא, ואמסקנא דלעיל סמכינן. והוי יודע, דכי תנן הכא אם מת לא יירשנו — לאו למימרא דכיון שנכסים אסורים לו בהנאה לא יזכה בהן, דהא קתני בסיפא דההיא מתניתין בפרק "הגוזל קמא" (דף קט.): ויתן לבניו או לאחיו, ואם אין לו — לוה, ובעלי חובין באין ונפרעין. ואם לא זכה בגוף הנכסים היאך נותנן לבניו או לאחיו, והיאך בעלי חובין באין ונפרעין? אלא ודאי נכסים *דידהו נינהו, אלא שאינו רשאי ליהנות מהן. ואיידי דתנא רישא יירשנו, לומר שמותר ליהנות מהן כשאר היורשין — תנא סיפא נמי לא יירשנו, ולאו דוקא. וכ"ת: היכי קתני נותנן לבניו או לאחיו? בשלמא לוה ובעלי חובין באין ונפרעין — שפיר, דבעלי חוב לאו מדעתיה קא מיפרעו דליהוי פורע חובו באיסורי הנאה, דכה"ג ודאי אסור, דנהי דאמרינן לעיל דמבריח ארי מנכסי חברו הוא — היינו כשאחר פורע שלא מדעתו, אבל מדעתו — ודאי אסור, דהוי מוליאן מרשות לרשות, ונמלא מועל. אלא בעל כרחו ב"ד מגבין להן, ואע"ג דאיהו ממילא מתהני — לא איכפת לן. אבל נותן לבניו או לאחיו היכי שרי? והא מתהני מטובת הנאה דידהו ואסור, כדאמרינן לעיל (דף לו:) גבי תורם משלו על חבירו! וי"ל: דלאו למימרא שיתנם להם ממש, אלא שמראה להם מקום, ואומר להם: נכסי אלו אסר עלי אבא, ואיני יודע מה אעשה בהם — טלו לעצמכם ועשו מהם מה שתרצו. וכה"ג לאו מתנה הוא, אלא גוונא דהפקר. וכן כתב הר"ם במז"ל בפ"ה מהל' נדרים (הל' ח) שצריך להודיעם: אלו נכסי אבי שאסר עלי אבא. עשאה הרמב"ם ז"ל כההיא דתנן לעיל מיניה: הגוזל את אביו ומת וכו' — לוה ובעלי חובין באין ונפרעין, ואמרינן עלה בגמרא: וצריך שיאמר: זה גזל אבא. תנן התם. לקמן בפ' "הנודר מן הירק" (דף נז.). קונם פירות האלו עלי קונם הם על פי קונם הם לפי אסור בחלופיהן ובגדוליהם. כלומר, כל שאמר א' מלשונות הללו — חלופיהן וגדוליהן בכלל. בעי רמי בר אבא קונם פירות האלו על פלוני מהו בחלופיהן. לאו בקונמות בלחוד קא מבעיא ליה, אלא בכולהו איסורי הנאה דעלמא נמי מספקא ליה. והיינו דמייתי לקמן ת"ש מהמקדש בערלה. ולאו להחליפן לכתחלה מיבעיא ליה, דודאי כל שהוא אסור בהנאה אסור למוכרו ולהחליפו. דאי לא תימא הכי — מאינו דמים לחמץ בפסח ולשור הנסקל, שיכול למוכרו לנכרים, ואמאי תנן שהגוזל פטור מן התשלומין? אלא ודאי פשיטא ליה דלכתחילה אסור. אלא בשעבר והחליפן מספקא ליה. ולאחר נמי לא מיבעיא ליה, דפשיטא ליה דמותרין, שאין לך תופס את דמיו אלא עבודה זרה ושביעית. והיינו דתנן, ומייתי לה בריש חולין (דף ד.): חמנן של עוברי עבירה אחר הפסח מותר מיד, מפני שהן מחליפין. אלא מספקא ליה אי מיתסרי למחליף מדרבנן בעלמא או לא. והכי הוי עיקר ספיקיה: מי אמרינן דכי תנן במתניתין אסור בחלופיהן ובגידוליהן — היינו משום שכוונת הנודר בכך. ואי משום כוונתו הוא — דוקא נודר אוסר עצמו בכך, דנהי דחילופיהן כדבר שלא בא לעולם דמו — לגבי דידיה מצי אסר, אבל לגבי חבירו לא מצי אסר. או דילמא דכי תנן במתניתין אסור בחילופיהן — לאו בתר דעתיה אזלינן, אלא דהכא הכי הוא, דכל אסורי הנאה חילופין אסורין מדרבנן למחליף עצמו, הלכך לא שנא הוא ולא שנא חבירו. ותמהני: אדבעי רמי במודר, ליבעי לה בנודר עצמו ובמתניתין גופה; אי טעמא דמתניתין משום כוונת הנודר — אפילו החליפן אחר חילופיהן אסורין לו, ואי משום דינא דאסורי הנאה — דוקא בשהחליפן הוא, אבל החליפן אחר — מותר בחלופיהן! וי"ל: דפשיטא ליה לרמי דנודר אפילו החליפן אחר אסור בחלופיהן. דכיון שפרט ואמר "אלו" — שוינהו עליו כהקדש, וכמו שנפרש בפ' "הנודר מן הירק" עלה דהא מתניתין, בס"ד. מיהו, הא מיבעיא ליה: מי אמרינן דאפילו בשהחליפן הוא צריך "אלו", דלא מיתסר בהו אלא משום שבכלל דבריו הוא, או דילמא להחליפן הוא לא צריך "אלו", דחלופיהן כגדוליהן דמי, הילכך, אפילו במודר אסור, וכי תנן "אלו" — להחליפן אחר איצטריך. מיהו, אין ה"נ דהוה מצי למבעי בנודר עצמו היכא דלא אמר "אלו" והחליפן הוא עצמו — מהו בחלופיהן, דהיינו דייניה דמודר. אלא דלישנא דמתניתין ב"אלו" עדיפא ליה, כנ"ל. ופשטינא לה מדתנן: האומר לאשתו "קונם שאני מהנה לך" ומיירי בשהדירה בעודה ארוסה, וכיון דהכתי לא משתעבד לה — חייל נדרא, ומסתברא אפילו לאחר שנשאה דמשועבד לה, והכי מוכח בכתובות בפרק "המדיר" (דף ע:).

*) נ"ל שחזר ובנאו במקומו. יעב"ץ

תוספות

מת או מכרו לאחר מותר. לפי שלא נתכוין לאסור אלא בעודו שלו: **שדה** זה שאני לוקח בית זו שאני נכנס והבית שלו מת או מכרו מהו. מי אמרי' כיון דדידיה הוא אינו יכול לאסור אלא בעודו שלו דנהי דתנן בית זה שאני נכנס ומכרו אסור ה"מ כשמדיר עצמו מבית חבירו דעתו לאוסרו עליו (שהרי אסרו עליו) כשאינו שלו ומיבעיא לאבימי כשאמר בהדיא בחייו ובמותו: ת"ש כו' הכא לא דחי שאני הכא דקאמר בחייו ובמותו כדאמר לעיל דהכא כי נמי אמר בחייו ובמותו מיבעיא ליה משום דאין אדם אוסר דבר שברשותו לכשילא מרשותו: **תנן** התם. לקמן בפרק הנודר מן הירק: **אסור** בחילופיהן. אם מכרם או החליפם אסורין [דמיהן וחלופיהן] דחשבינן להן כהקדש ותופס דמיו וגידולי הקדש הקדש: **אמר** קונם פירות אלו על פלוני מהו בחילופיהן וה"ה דמיבעיא ליה (בשאר איסורין) אם מכר מהו שיהנה המודר מן החילופין דשמא אסור כי ההוא דלעיל לאסור בחלופיהן וה"ה דמיבעיא ליה בשאר איסורי הנאה כגון ערלה וכלאי הכרם מדקמייתי למפשט בעיין ממתני' דמקדש בערלה וכלאי הכרם וליכא לפרושי דמיבעיא ליה באיסורי הנאה מהו בחילופיהן אם מותר למוכרם בתחילה דפשיט' דאסור כדמוכח פרק כל שעה (דף כח:) למ"ד לא תאכלו איסורי הנאה משמע מדאיצטרי' קרא למישרי נבילה למכרה לגוי אלמא דאסור למכור איסורי הנאה משום דבשעת מכירה הוא נהנה מגוף האיסור וה"ל כשרשיפא מעלי איסור וגם אם מכרם בדיעבד פשיטא ליה דמותרין מן התורה כדמפרש בשלהי פרק שני דקדושין (דף נח.) דאין לך דבר שתופס דמיו אלא עבודה זרה ושביעית וקאמר התם דהוו להו שני כתובים הבאים כאחד ואין מלמדין מהם שאר איסורין וכי קמיבעיא אם החליפן אסורין מדרבנן כדקאמר במתניתין קונם פירות אלו עלי אסור בחילופיהן דחילופיהן כגידוליהן או שמא גבי דידיה הואיל ואדם אוסר כו' אבל גבי חבירו דאין אדם אוסר פירות חבירו על חבירו וה"ה בכל איסורי הנאה שרי ונראה דלהכי לא קמיבעיא ליה בחליפין איסורי הנאה [לאסור לאותן] שלא החליפם דפשיטא דשרי כדאמר (חולין דף ד.) חמנן של עוברי עבירה אחר הפסח מותר מיד מפני שהם מחליפין ולא מיבעיא ליה אלא לאותו עצמו שהחליפן ומבעיא בהחלפתם אי קנסינן ליה ואסור ליהנות מדרבנן:

פי' הרא"ש

קונם לבית זה שאתה נכנס ומת או שמכרו לאחר כו'. ולא דמי לבית זה שאני נכנס דכיון למודר קאמר זה פשיטא דלעולם אסריה עילויה לאינה ברשותו ומה לי ברשות זה ליאסה מרשותו אבל הכא אע"ג דמדיר קאמר זה דילמא אין אדם אוסר דבר שברשותו לכשילא מרשותו אבל לעיל בפ' אין בין המודר כו' לא מפליג בין היכא דקאמר מודר שדך ובין היכא דקאמר בפרקין לבית זה שאתה נכנס שאני הכא דקאמר בחיי ובמותי מהם אסור דחשבינן ליה כהקדש: [illegible] היכא דקאמר מדיר נכסי משום דאין חילוק ביניהם בדבר התלוי בלשון ומיירי כגון דאמרינן [illegible] שאתה נכנס בחיי ובמותי ולהכי פשיטא ליה מהך מתניתין דהגוזל ולא דחי כדלעיל [illegible] בחיי ובמותי: **אסור בחלופיהן.** אם מכרן הדמים אסורין: **ובגידוליהן.** אם נטען הגדל [illegible] ליה כהקדש: **אוסר דבר שלא בא לעולם.** דכיון שלא הוחלפו עדיין וכמו שאינו אוסר פירות

עין משפט נר מצוה

ט א מיי' פ"ה מהלכות נדרים הל' ה טוש"ע י"ד סי' רכו סעיף ו:
י ב מיי' שם הלכה טו סמג לאוין רמב טוש"ע שם סעיף ח:
יא ג מיי' שם הלכה טז טוש"ע שם סעיף ב [וברא"ש בפסקיו לקמן פ"ח סי' ה]:

מסורת הש"ס

[גרסת הרא"ש בפסקיו אביי] [לעיל מב.] [ב"ק ק"ח לעיל מב.] לקמן נב: ונז. [נט.] [כתובות נט.] [שייך למתני' דלעיל מו.] נ"ל דידיה

הגהות הב"ח

(א) רש"י ד"ה תנן התם כו' הירק. נ"ב דף נז.: (ב) ד"ה על פלוני וכו' מהו מי הוי וכו' אסור בהן או לא וכו' בחלופיהן דהוי: (ג) בר"ן ד"ה האומר וכו' או מכרו לאחר וכו' דאי נתנו לאחר וכו' נקט מכרו וכו' דדוקא מכרו: (ד) ד"ה קונם לבית וכו' לענין מכרו לאחר וכו' מבית זה לענין וכו' משום מה אתה תופסו משום ביתך או משום זה נפל ובני לית הוא כשמעינה מן הדא וכו' נפל ובני ליה לרבותא:

גליון הש"ס

בהר"ן ד"ה בעי רמב"א בסה"ד ומסתברא נ"ל ומתסרא: **בא"ד** והכי מוכח וכו'. עם מסקי' לנשאת סברה וקבלה וצ"ע:

עין משפט נר מצוה

יב א מיי' פ"ה מהל' אישות הל' א ב סמג עשין מח טוש"ע אה"ע סי' כח סעיף כא כב:
יג ב מיי' פ"ה מהלכות נדרים ה"א סמג לאוין רמב טוש"ע י"ד סימן רכב סעיף א:

גמרא

או דילמא: משום דחילופין כגידולין דמי, לא שנא הוא ולא שנא חברו? אמר רב אחא בר מניומי, ת"ש: האומר לאשתו "קונם שאני נהנה ליך" לווה, ובעלי חובין באין ונפרעין. מ"ט בעלי חובין נפרעין – לאו משום דחילופין לאו כגידולין דמי? אמר רבא: דילמא לכתחילה הוא דלא, ואי עבד – עבד. אלא, ת"ש:* א המקדש בערלה – אינה מקודשת, *מכרן וקידש בדמיהן – הרי זו מקודשת. הכא נמי, לכתחילה הוא דלא, ואי עבד – עבד. § **מתני'** * ב "הריני עליך חרם" – המודר אסור, "הרי את עלי חרם" – הנודר אסור, "הריני עליך ואת עלי" – שניהם אסורין, ושניהם מותרין בדבר של עולי בבל, ואסורים

ר"נ

לווה. כלומר, האשה, ובעלי חוב באין ונפרעין. דנהי דמתסרי עלה נכסי בעלה, מיהו אכתי שיעבודה אנכסיה קאי. הילכך, בעלי חוב באין ונפרעין. דאפילו לחנן דאמר דהמפרנס אשתו של חבירו הניח מעותיו על קרן הצבי – ה"מ במעלה לה מזונותיה, אבל כשהיא לווה – חייבת היא במה שלוותה, ובעלי חוב נפרעין מן הבעל, דמוציאין מזה ונותנין לזה מדר' נתן. ובזה יצאתי ידי חובתי מכל מה שהאריך הרשב"א בזה. מאי טעמא בעלי חובין באין ונפרעין לאו משום דחלופיהן לאו כגדוליהן דמו. דקס"ד דכיון דבשעה שהיא לווה משעבדת נכסי הבעל – הרי היא כמחלפת נכסי הבעל בנכסי אחרים, כיון דלבסוף בע"ח באין ונפרעין. נהי דקא אמרינן מ"ט בע"ח באין ונפרעין – לאו היא גופה קשיא לן, דלדידהו ליכא איסורא כלל, אלא הכי קאמר: כיון דלבסוף בעלי חוב באין ונפרעין היכי שרית לה ללוות? כך פירשו רבותי. ולי נראה דה"ק: אם איתא דחלופיהן כגדוליהן דמו – היאך בעלי חובין באין ונפרעין? דנהי דמדינא מוציאין מזה ונותנים לזה מדרבי נתן, הכא אנן סהדי דאדעתא דידה נחית, ולאו אדעתא דבעל, כי היכי דלא לעביד היא איסורא על ידייהו! ונראה לי דלהכי פשיט לה מהך ברייתא, ולא פשיט מסיפא דמתני' דהאומר לבנו "קונם שאתה נהנה לי" וכו' דתנן בסיפא: לווה ובעלי חוב באין ונפרעין. משום דאיהו לא הוי כמחליף, דהא מלי קני נכסי. אבל אשה שאין לה קנין בלא בעלה – סליק אדעתין דהויא כמחלפת נכסי הבעל ממש. ומשני: ודילמא לכתחלה הוא דלא, ואי עבד – עבד. כלומר, כשהוא בא להחליף איסור בהיתר לכתחלה בידים – אסור, והחליפין אסורין. אבל זו, בשעה שלווה, אע"פ שהבעל מתחייב – אין כאן חליפי איסור ממש, הילכך יכולה היא ללוות ולאכול. ואע"פ שאח"כ נפרעין מן הבעל – דיעבד הוא שנעשו חליפין למה שאכלה. ת"ש המקדש בערלה **אינה** מקודשת מכרן וקידש בדמיהן הרי זו מקודשת. דקס"ד דכיון שאסור ליהנות מן החליפין, אפילו עבר ונהנה, שהחליפן באחר, דליהוי חליפי חליפין – אסורין. ומשום הכי קשיא ליה: כשעבר וקידש בדמיהן למה היא מקודשת גמורה, ואינה צריכה לקדש פעם אחרת? דאי אסירי חליפין מדרבנן – הוה לן לאצרוכה קדושי אחריני! ואמרינן: הכא נמי, לכתחלה הוא דלא, ואי עבד – עבד. כלומר, לכתחלה הוא שאסור ליהנות מן החליפין, אבל אם עבר ונהנה – נהנה, דחליפין מותרין. ולענין הלכה. לגבי נודר עצמו דאמר "אלו" – אפילו החליפן אחר, נודר אסור בהן, והיינו מתני'. אבל כשהדירו אחר, וכן נמי בנודר עצמו דלא אמר "אלו" – מסתברא דלקולא נקיטי'. דכיון דבכי האי גוונא גבי אסורי הנאה דעלמא ליכא למימר דחלופיהן כגדוליהן דמי, אלא מדרבנן בעלמא, וכדפרישית לעיל, הוה ליה ספיקא דרבנן ולקולא. ואפילו עבר והחליפן – חליפין מותרין. אבל הרב רבינו משה בר מיימון ז"ל כתב בפ' חמישי מהלכות נדרים (הלכה ט"ז): הרי גדוליהן וחלופיהן ספק, לפיכך חברו אסור בגידולי פירות אלו וחלופיהן. והרמב"ן ז"ל מסתם לה סתומי לקמן בפרק "הנודר מן הירק". **מתני'** הריני **עליך** חרם. שתהא הנאתו עליו כחרם של בדק הבית. ובגליל מיירי, דסתם חרמים לבדק הבית (לעיל דף יח:). הרי **את** עלי. שיהא הנאת חברו עליו כחרם. מותרין בדבר של עולי בבל. שהפקירום עולי בבל לכל ישראל. **ואסורין**

רש"י

או דילמא. הכי קאמר: דודאי אסור בחלופיהן, (א) דומיא דגידולין נינהו, וכי היכי דאסור בגידולין – הכי נמי אסור בחליפין. קונם שאני נהנה לך לווה ובעלי חובין באין ונפרעין. מבעלה, דרצון הבעל הוא שילוו לה. והא הכא (ב) דלוותה מאחרים, דחילופי ממונו של בעל הוי, ולא מיתסר. אלמא דאין אדם אוסר דבר שלב"ל על חבירו, דהא נפרעין מבעלה. לאו כגידולין דמי. ובגידולין אסור, אבל בחליפין מותר: אמר רבא: לעולם אימא לך דחליפין כגידולין דמו ומיתסרי, והכי לכתחילה – לא תלוה ותאכל. אבל בדיעבד – שפיר דמי. והא דאמרינן בהך פירקא דלעיל (דף מג.): המודר הנאה מחבירו ואין לו מה יאכל, נותן לזה, ובא הלה ונוטל מזה – לא דמיא להא. דהאי לא רמי עליה דהאי למיפרנסיה, והאי דקיהיב להאי – איסור לא משום מודר קא יהיב ליה, אלא מתנה בעלמא הוא דקא יהיב להאיך. אבל האי בעל דלמפרנסה קאי, אימא (ג) דליתסר ליה לפרוע לבעל חוב לכתחילה הוא דלא. **תא שמע.** דמותר אפי' לכתחילה. המקדש בערלה. שהוא איסור הנאה, אינה מקודשת. מכרן וקידש בדמיהן מקודשת. אלמא דחליפין לאו כגידולין דמו, דגידולין אסור ובחליפין משתרי. ה"נ. מיירי דלכתחילה לא ימכור, ואם קידש בדמיהם – מאי דעבד עבד. **מתני'** הריני עליך חרם. נכסי יהיו עליך חרם. המודר אסור. אבל המדיר – מותר. והבור

מסורת הש"ס

קדושין נז:
[גס ע"ז נב: סב.]
לעיל ה. [כילה לט.]

הגהות הב"ח

(א) רש"י ד"ה או דלמא וכו' דדומיא לגידולין: (ב) ד"ה קונם וכו' והא הכא דמאי דלוותה מאחרים חילופי ממונו: (ג) ד"ה אמר רבא וכו' אימא לך דליתסר וכו' דלכתחלה הוא:

גליון הש"ס

גמ' האומר לאשתו קונם. עי' ב"ק דף קט ע"א תד"ה בע"ח: **שם** אמר רבא דלמא לכתחלה. עי' לקמן דף פג ע"א בהר"ן ד"ה דלמא מיין:

תוספות

תא שמע האומר לאשתו קונם שאני נהנה לך ותלה הדבר בתשמיש שאמר הנאת תשמישך עלי אם תיהנה משלי דאל"כ כיון דמשועבד לה לא מצי מדיר לה אי נמי דאדרה כשהיא ארוסה (או) ונישאת: **לוה** ובעלי חובין נפרעין. כדאמר לותה ואכלה ועמדה ומיאנה אין לה מזונות הא לא מיאנה יש לה מזונות ואפילו לרבנן דתנן דאמרי הניח מעותיו על קרן הצבי ה"מ במפרנס אשת חבירו סתם אבל הלוה לה בתורת הלואה נפרע מן הבעל וא"ת ולרבנן דתנן היאך פורע חובה הרי אסור לפרוע למי שמודר הנאה ממנו וי"ל דהיינו בפורע חוב חבירו שהוא יכול לתובעו ולומר פרע לי מה שפרעתי בשבילך והוי כאילו הלוהו ממש אבל באשתו אינו חייב לפרוע לו כלל מה שפרע בשבילה: **מאי** טעמא בעלי חובות חוזרין ונפרעין לאו דחילופין לאו כגדולין דמו. ושרו ליהנות למודר דאי אסורין א"כ מעות שמוסרין לה המלוים הוו חליפי מעות הבעל ומההוא דתנן (לעיל דף מג.) המודר הנאה מחבירו הולך אצל חנוני הרגיל אצלו וכו' לא מצי למיפשט בעיין דסתם חנוני לית ליה למיתבע מידי מן המדיר הילכך מתנת חנם הוא דיהיב לחנוני ואם ירצה חנוני עדיין יוכל לתבוע מודר אבל הכא דבעלי חובות יש לו על הבעל שהבעל חייב במזונות אשתו א"כ מה שהם מלוים לה הוי ממש חליפי מעות הבעל: **דילמא** לכתחילה הוא דלא הא דיעבד עבד. כלומר לותה דוקא בדיעבד קאמר דאז בעלי חובין נפרעין אבל לכתחילה לא תלוה וכשלותה הרי זה דיעבד שאין זה חליפי איסור ממה שעדיין האיסור לא בא אבל מעיקרא סלקא דעתך דשרו רבנן ללוות בתחילה ולגרום דברים שיבא לידי איסור לכן פשיט מיניה דחליפי (טומאה) מותרין: **ת"ש** המקדש [בערלה] (בדמי ערלה פי' בדמים של ערלה) או כלאי הכרם אינה מקודשת משום דאיסורי הנאה אינון ולא הוי ממון. מכרם וקדש בדמיהן בערלה וכלאי הכרם מקודשת דאינן תופסין דמיהן אלמא שרי לאיתהנויי בחליפין דאי אסור ליהנות היה לנו לומר דאסור לשהות עמה באותם קידושין: **ה"נ** הא לכתחילה הא דיעבד. כלומר אכתי איבעיא ליה אי מותר לכתחילה הוא או דוקא דיעבד אבל לכתחילה לא ואע"ג דעל ידי הקידושין הוא נהנה ממנה לכתחילה דוקא בקידושין שלא תקנו חכמים להפקיע הקידושין דכיון שהיא אשתו הוא חייב ליהנות ממנה אבל משאר הנאות אם אסור למוכרם אם לקח מן המעות כלי אסור ליהנות ממנו לאסור בחלופיהן קרינן ביה. מפירו"ש רבינו שמעו"ן מקוצ"י: **הריני** עליך חרם המודר אסור. דהכי קאמר הרי ממוני אסור עליך הרי אתה עלי חרם הכי קאמר הרי ממונך עלי כחרם. וחרם הוי הקדש דסתם חרם לבדק הבית: **ומותרים** בדברים של עולי בבל כגון בור שבאמצע הדרך שעשאוהו עולי גולה. לפי שהפקירוהו לכל ישראל ולא נתנוהו להם להיות שותפין (כך) [בו] לענין שיוכל האחד לאסור חלק חבירו: **בדברים** של אותה העיר. שהם דרים בה שהן (מפני) שותפין וזה אסור מפני חלקו של זה:

רחבה

פי' הרא"ש

פירות חבירו על חבירו דאיכא תרתי שהפירות אינן ברשותו וגם חבירו אינו ברשותו לאסור דבר עליו גם אינו יכול לאסור דבר שלא בא לעולם כיון דאיכא תרתי: **או דילמא חליפין מיתסרי מידי דהוה אגידולים.** אף על גב דליתנהו בעולם וגדולים פשיטא כיון דיוצא מגוף האיסור אין חילוק בינו לבין חבירו: **לוה ובעלי חובין באין ונפרעין.** אפילו לחנן דאמר הניח מעותיו על קרן הצבי הני מילי במפרנס מעצמו אבל לותה חייב הבעל לשלם כדאמרינן בכתובות (דף קז:) גבי ממאנת דאין לה מזונות כגון לותה ואכלה ועמדה ומיאנה משמע הא אם לא מיאנה חייב הבעל לשלם מה שלותה ואין זה כמו פורע חובו דאסרינן אליבא דרבנן דמיירי הכא דבשעה שלותה אמרה שלא יפרעו אלא מבעלה: **לאו משום דחליפין לאו כגידולין דמו.** דאיחלפו אותן מעות שקבל מן הבעלים שאסורין עליה וכיון שחייב הבעל לפרוע למלוה הרי נעשו כבר המעות שנותן לאשה חליפי קונם ומהא דתנן לעיל בפרק אין בין המודר (דף מג.) שמותר המדיר לפרוע לחנוני ולפועלים אינו יכול להביא ראיה דשאני התם דאין המדיר חייב לפרוע להם הילכך מה שהם נותנים לו למודר לא הוי חליפי קונם דמתנה בעלמא יהבי למודר ומה שהמדיר נותן להם אינו אלא מתנה בעלמא דאי בעי לא יהיב ליה מידי: **דילמא לכתחילה הוא דלא הא דיעבד עבד.** הא דמיבעיא ליה אי חליפין אסורים היינו אם לכתחילה אסור להחליפן וליהנות מן הדמים אבל אם החליפן בדיעבד הדמים מותרים והכא בדיעבד קאמר אם לותה בעלי החובין באין ונפרעין ונראה לפרש דאפילו לכתחילה לוה כדמשמע לישנא דברייתא דקתני לוה ולא קתני לותה ותשיב ליה בדיעבד כיון שהמלוה נותן לה המעות קודם שקבל תמורתו מן הבעל לאיסורא דרבנן בעלמא הוא ולא אסרו אלא היכא שהוא מחליפן ממש: **אם מכרן וקידש בדמיהן מקודשת.** אלמא חלופי אסורי שרו דאי אסירי הא לא יהיב לה מידי ומשני הכא נמי כיון דמכרן בדיעבד שרו דמים: **מתני' הריני עליך חרם המודר אסור.** אבל לא הנודר אע"ג דלא אמר ואתה עליך לא: **שניהם אסורים.** הא לא אצטריך אלא אגב דבעי למתני שניהם מותרים בדבר של עולי בבל לאשמועינן דהפקר הוי ולא דשותפין: *) **והבאר שבאמצע הדרך.** שבין בבל לארץ ישראל ומצאוהו עולי גולה: **הרחבה והשווקים.** שבעיר: **והתיבה.** שנותנין בה ספרים: **והספרים.** שקנאום בני העיר ללמוד בהם: **והכותב חלקו לנשיא.** בגמרא מפרש: **אלא שהכותב לנשיא אין צריך לזכות.** מפני כבודו של נשיא תקנו שיקנה בלא קנין בדבר זה: **ואין לו מה יאכל.** לעיל (דף מג.) קתני היה מהלך בדרך והכא קא משמע לן דאפילו בעיר אם אין לו מה יאכל מותר: **כל מתנה.** שלא נגמרה שאם הקדישה אינה מקודשת אינה מתנה ויש ספרים גרסי שאם הקדישה מקודשת וה"פ שאינה מתנה לענין זה שאם הקדישה מקודשת אינה מתנה:

*) [שייך לדף שאח"ז]

גמרא

וַאֲסוּרִים בְּדָבָר שֶׁל אוֹתָהּ הָעִיר. וְאֵיזֶהוּ דָּבָר שֶׁל עוֹלֵי בָבֶל – אכְּגוֹן הַר הַבַּיִת, וְהָעֲזָרוֹת, וְהַבּוֹר שֶׁבְּאֶמְצַע הַדֶּרֶךְ. וְאֵיזֶהוּ דָּבָר שֶׁל אוֹתָהּ הָעִיר – בכְּגוֹן הָרְחָבָה, וְהַמֶּרְחָץ, וּבֵית הַכְּנֶסֶת, וְהַתֵּיבָה, וְהַסְּפָרִים. וְהַכּוֹתֵב חֶלְקוֹ לַנָּשִׂיא, ר' יְהוּדָה אוֹמֵר: אֶחָד כּוֹתֵב לַנָּשִׂיא וְאֶחָד כּוֹתֵב לְהֶדְיוֹט. (א) מַה בֵּין כּוֹתֵב לַנָּשִׂיא לְכוֹתֵב לְהֶדְיוֹט? שֶׁהַכּוֹתֵב לַנָּשִׂיא – אֵין צָרִיךְ לְזַכּוֹת, לְהֶדְיוֹט – צָרִיךְ לְזַכּוֹת. וַחֲכָמִים אוֹמְרִים: אֶחָד זֶה וְאֶחָד זֶה צְרִיכִין לְזַכּוֹת, לֹא דִּבְּרוּ בְּנָשִׂיא אֶלָּא בַּהוֹוֶה. רַבִּי יְהוּדָה אוֹמֵר: אֵין אַנְשֵׁי גָּלִיל צְרִיכִין לִכְתּוֹב, שֶׁכְּבָר כָּתְבוּ אֲבוֹתֵיהֶן עַל יְדֵיהֶן.§ **גמ'** אַמַּאי מִיתְסַר? אָמַר רַב שֵׁשֶׁת: הָכִי קָתָנֵי: וּמַה תַּקָּנָתָן – גיִכְתְּבוּ חֶלְקָן לַנָּשִׂיא. *(רַבִּי יְהוּדָה אוֹמֵר: אֶחָד כּוֹתֵב לַנָּשִׂיא וְאֶחָד כּוֹתֵב לְהֶדְיוֹט. וּמַה בֵּין כּוֹתֵב לַנָּשִׂיא לְכוֹתֵב לְהֶדְיוֹט? הַכּוֹתֵב לַנָּשִׂיא – אֵין צָרִיךְ לְזַכּוֹת, וְהַכּוֹתֵ' לְהֶדְיוֹט – צָרִיךְ לְזַכּוֹת. וַחֲכָמִים אוֹמְרִים: דאֶחָד זֶה וְאֶחָד זֶה צְרִיכִים לְזַכּוֹת, לֹא דִּבְּרוּ בְּנָשִׂיא אֶלָּא בַּהוֹוֶה.).§ "ר' יְהוּדָה אוֹמֵר: אֵין אַנְשֵׁי גָּלִיל צְרִיכִין לְזַכּוֹת, שֶׁכְּבָר כָּתְבוּ אֲבוֹתֵיהֶן עַל יְדֵיהֶן".§ תַּנְיָא, ר' יְהוּדָה אוֹמֵר: אַנְשֵׁי גָּלִיל *קַנְטְרָנִין הָיוּ, וְהָיוּ נוֹדְרִין הֲנָאָה זֶה מִזֶּה, עָמְדוּ אֲבוֹתֵיהֶם וְכָתְבוּ חֶלְקֵיהֶן לַנָּשִׂיא.§ **מתני'** ההַמּוּדָּר הֲנָאָה מֵחֲבֵירוֹ וְאֵין לוֹ מַה יֹּאכַל – *נוֹתְנוֹ לְאַחֵר לְשׁוּם מַתָּנָה, וְהַלָּה מוּתָּר בָּהּ. מַעֲשֶׂה *בְּאֶחָד בְּבֵית חוֹרוֹן שֶׁהָיָה אָבִיו (ב) נוֹדֵר הֵימֶנּוּ הֲנָאָה, וְהָיָה מַשִּׂיא אֶת בְּנוֹ, וְאָמַר לַחֲבֵרוֹ: חָצֵר וּסְעוּדָה נְתוּנִים *הֵינָן לְפָנֶיךָ, אֶלָּא כְּדֵי שֶׁיָּבֹא אַבָּא וְיֹאכַל עִמָּנוּ בַּסְּעוּדָה. אָמַר: אִם שֶׁלִּי הֵם – הֲרֵי הֵם מוּקְדָּשִׁין לַשָּׁמַיִם. א"ל: *נָתַתִּי לְךָ אֶת שֶׁלִּי שֶׁתַּקְדִּישֵׁם לַשָּׁמַיִם?! אָמַר לוֹ: *נָתַתָּ לִי אֶת שֶׁלְּךָ אֶלָּא שֶׁתְּהֵא אַתָּה וְאָבִיךָ אוֹכְלִין וְשׁוֹתִין וּמִתְרַצִּין זֶה לָזֶה, וִיהֵא עָוֹן תָּלוּי בְּרֹאשׁוֹ. (ג) *אָמְרוּ חֲכָמִים: וכָּל מַתָּנָה שֶׁאֵינָהּ שֶׁאִם הִקְדִּישָׁהּ תְּהֵא מְקוּדֶּשֶׁת – אֵינָהּ מַתָּנָה.§ **גמ'** מַעֲשֶׂה לִסְתּוֹר! חַסּוּרֵי מִיחַסְּרָא וְהָכִי קָתָנֵי: *וְאִם הוֹכִיחַ סוֹפוֹ עַל תְּחִילָּתוֹ – אָסוּר. וּמַעֲשֶׂה נַמִי בְּבֵית חוֹרוֹן בְּאֶחָד דַּהֲוָה סוֹפוֹ מוֹכִיחַ עַל תְּחִילָּתוֹ. אָמַר רָבָא: לֹא שָׁנוּ אֶלָּא דַּאֲמַר לֵיהּ (ד) "וְהִינָּן לְפָנֶיךָ אֶלָּא כְּדֵי שֶׁיָּבֹא אַבָּא". אֲבָל א"ל "שֶׁיְּהוּ לְפָנֶיךָ, שֶׁיָּבֹא אַבָּא" – מִדַּעְתָּךְ הוּא, דא"ל: לִישָּׁנָא אַחֲרִינָא אָמְרִין לָהּ, אָמַר רָבָא: לָא תֵּימָא טַעְמָא דא"ל "וְהִינָּן לְפָנֶיךָ" הוּא דְּאָסוּר, אֲבָל א"ל "הֵן לְפָנֶיךָ, שֶׁיָּבֹא אַבָּא וְיֹאכַל" – מוּתָּר. אֶלָּא אֲפִילּוּ אֲמַר לֵיהּ "הֵן לְפָנֶיךָ, יָבֹא אַבָּא וְיֹאכַל" – אָסוּר. מַאי טַעְמָא – סְעוּדָּתוֹ מוֹכַחַת עָלָיו.
הַהוּא

רש"י

וְהַבּוֹר שֶׁבְּאֶמְצַע (ה). כִּדְמְפָרֵשׁ בְּשִׁלְהֵי פֶּרֶק בַּתְרָא דְּעֵירוּבִין (דף קד.). בְּדָבָר שֶׁל אוֹתָהּ הָעִיר. דְּשֶׁל שְׁנֵיהֶן הֵן, שֶׁשְּׁנֵיהֶן נָתְנוּ בָּהֶן מָעוֹת עִם אַנְשֵׁי אוֹתָהּ הָעִיר. וְהַסְּפָרִים. סִפְרֵי תוֹרָה, בַּגְּמָרָא מְפָרֵשׁ לָהּ. שֶׁהַכּוֹתֵב לַנָּשִׂיא **א"צ** לְזַכּוֹת. ע"י אַחֵר. אֲבָל הַכּוֹתֵב לְהֶדְיוֹט – צָרִיךְ לְזַכּוֹת, וּבָזֶה כֹּחַ נָשִׂיא יָפֶה מִכֹּחַ הֶדְיוֹט. בַּהוֹוֶה. שֶׁכֵּן דֶּרֶךְ לַחֲלוֹק כָּבוֹד לַנָּשִׂיא: גמ' תַּנְיָא רַבִּי יְהוּדָה אוֹמֵר אַנְשֵׁי גָלִיל קַנְטְרָנִין הֵן. כַּעֲסָנִים הֵן. וְכָתְבוּ. מִדָּבָר שֶׁל אוֹתָהּ הָעִיר לַנָּשִׂיא, כְּדֵי שֶׁיְּהוּ אֵלּוּ וָאֵלּוּ מוּתָּרִין בָּהֶן. **מתני'** הַמּוּדָּר הֲנָאָה מֵחֲבֵירוֹ וְאֵין לוֹ מַה יֹּאכַל. הָךְ מַתְנִיתִין אַיְיתִי נַמִי לְעֵיל בְּאִידָךְ פִּירְקִין (ד' מג.), אֶלָּא דְּהָתָם לֹא נָקַט לָהּ אֶלָּא מִשּׁוּם דִּיּוּקָא, מִשּׁוּם דְּבָעֵי לְמִיתְנָא עֲלָהּ הֶפְקֵר, דִּפְלִיג בָּהּ רַבִּי יוֹסֵי. וִיהֵא הֶעָוֹן תָּלוּי בְּרֹאשׁוֹ. שֶׁיְּהֵא אָבִיו הַמּוּדָּר הֲנָאָה אוֹכֵל עַל יָדוֹ. אָמְרוּ חֲכָמִים כָּל מַתָּנָה שֶׁאֵינָהּ. כָּל כָּךְ בִּרְשׁוּת הַמְקַבֵּל, שֶׁאִם הִקְדִּישָׁהּ אֵינָהּ מְקוּדֶּשֶׁת – אֵינָהּ מַתָּנָה. **גמ'** מַעֲשֶׂה לִסְתּוֹר. דִּבְרֵישָׁא קָתָנֵי: הַמּוּדָּר הֲנָאָה וכו', וְקָתָנֵי תַּקַּנְתָּא, דְּמָצֵי לְמֶעֱבַד כה"ג, וַהֲדַר תָּנֵי מַעֲשֶׂה וכו' לִסְתּוֹר דְּבָרָיו הָרִאשׁוֹנִים. חַסּוּרֵי מִחַסְּרָא וְהָכִי קָתָנֵי. בְּמַתְנִיתִין: הַמּוּדָּר הֲנָאָה וכו'. וְאִם הוֹכִיחַ סוֹפוֹ עַל תְּחִלָּתוֹ. שֶׁלֹּא נָתַן לוֹ אֶלָּא עַל מְנָת שֶׁיִּתֵּן לָזֶה וְיֹאכַל – אָסוּר, וּמַעֲשֶׂה נַמִי וכו'. לֹא שָׁנוּ. דְּאֵינָהּ מַתָּנָה, אֶלָּא דַּאֲמַר לֵיהּ (ו) "וְהִינָּן לְפָנֶיךָ", דְּמַשְׁמַע דְּהָכִי א"ל: וְהִינָּן נְתוּנִין לְךָ אֶלָּא עַל מְנָת שֶׁיָּבֹא אַבָּא. **אֲבָל אָמַר לֵיהּ** וְהֵן לְפָנֶיךָ **שֶׁיָּבֹא אַבָּא וְיֹאכַל** מִדַּעְתֵּיהּ **הוּא** דְּקָא **אָמַר לֵיהּ**. דְּהָכִי מַשְׁמַע: וְהֵן נְתוּנִים לְךָ, וְהֵם בְּדַעְתְּךָ שֶׁיָּבֹא אַבָּא, הָוֵי דַּוְקָא לוֹ. ע"א: אָמַר רָבָא: לֹא תֵּידוּק וְתֵימָא דְּאִיכָּא חִילּוּק בֵּין "וְהִינָּן לְפָנֶיךָ" בֵּין "וְהֵן לְפָנֶיךָ", דְּוַדַּאי תַּרְוַיְיהוּ אֲסִירִי, דְּהָא סְעוּדָּתוֹ מוֹכַחַת עָלָיו שֶׁלֹּא נָתַן לוֹ אֶלָּא עַל מְנָת שֶׁיָּבוֹא אָבִיו וְיֹאכַל, דְּה"ל כְּמ"ד "וְהִינָּן לְפָנֶיךָ".
כֵּיפֵי

ר"ן

ואסורין בדבר של אותה העיר. שהם דריס בה, מפני שאין לאנשי עיר אחרת חלק בהן, שהם יכולין למכרן ז' טובי העיר במעמד אנשי העיר, והוו להו כשותפין שאוסרין זה על זה. והתיבה. שנותנין עליה ספר תורה לקרות, והספרים שקורין בהן. **והכותב חלקו לנשיא.** מפרש בגמרא דה"ק: מה תקנתן – יכתבו חלקן לנשיא. דבהכי שרי, כדתנן: נותן לאחר משום מתנה, והלה מותר בה. שהכותב **לנשיא אין צריך** לזכות. שמיד שכתב לו שטר מתנה – קנה, אע"פ שלא זכה אדם בשבילו, משום דיפה כח הנשיא. **ולא** דברו **בנשיא אלא** בהווה. שאין אדם סומך להקנות לאדם אחר, דמספקי שמא יאסרנו עליו. ולפיכך נהגו לכתוב לנשיא, שאין דרכו לאסור הנאתו על הבריות. וקשה לי: לרבנן דאמרי דאחד זה ואחד זה צריכין לזכות – אם כן מאי קמ"ל מתני'? הא תנן לה תרי זמני: נותן לאחר משום מתנה, והלה מותר בה. בשלמא לרבי יהודה – קא משמע לן דאינו צריך לזכות, אלא לרבנן מאי קמ"ל? ונראה בעיני: דקמ"ל דאע"ג דאין הלה מסתלק ממה שנתן, שעדיין משתמש בביהכ"נ כבתחילה – שרי. דלא תימא הערמה בעלמא היא, ואסור. ומתני' דקתני ואסורין בדבר של אותה העיר – רבנן היא ולא רבי אליעזר בן יעקב, כדאמר לעיל דבית הכנסת כחצר שאין בה דין חלוקה דמי. הילכך, כיון דאפסיקא הילכתא לעיל כר' אליעזר בן יעקב – ליתא למתני'. ויש לתמוה על הרמב"ם ז"ל שפסק בפ"ז מהלכות נדרים (הל' ד ה ו) כרבי אליעזר בן יעקב, ופסק נמי למתני'. וכבר השיגו הרמב"ן ז"ל בהלכותיו, היכי מזכי שטרא לבי תרי. המודר הנאה מחברו וכו'. הך מתני' תנן לה בפירקין דלעיל (דף מג.) ולא נשנית כאן אלא בשביל דבר שנתחדש בה, שאם הוכיח סופו על תחלתו – הערמה הוי, ואסור. **והיה משיא את בנו.** מדיר היה משיא את בנו. **כל מתנה שאינה שאם הקדישה אינה מקודשת אינה מתנה.** כלומר, דנהי דמתנה על מנת להחזיר שמה מתנה אע"ג דאם הקדישה אינה מקודשת, וכדאמרינן בפרק "יש נוחלין" (ב"ב קלז:) ד"על מנת שתחזירהו לי", הקדישו – אינו קדוש, דמידי דחזי ליה קאמר ליה, שאני התם דמ"מ לשעתה מתנה היא. אבל מתנה זו של בית חורון – אפי' לשעתה אינה, שלא נתכוון להקנותה לו כלל, אלא שתקרא על שמו כדי שיהא אביו מותר בה. והיינו לישנא דמתני', דקתני: כל מתנה שאינה שאם הקדישה אינה מקודשת וכו'. ולא קתני: כל מתנה שאם הקדישה אינה מקודשת וכו'. משום דתנא הכי קאמר: כל מתנה שאינה כלום, כזו שהיא בהערמה, שאם הקדישה אינה מקודשת – אינה מתנה. והכי איתא בירושלמי: רבי ירמיה בעי: וכי אין אדם נותן מתנה על מנת שלא יקדישנה? כיני מתניתא, כל מתנה שהיא בהערמה, שאינה שאם הקדישה תהא מקודשת – אינה מתנה. **גמ'** ומה תקנתן. שלא יהו אסורין. מעשה לסתור. לא לסתור ממש קאמר, דהכא שאני דאמר ליה "והינן לפניך". אלא הכי פריך: כיון דמעיקרא תנא שרי, היכי מייתי עובדא דאסור? דאורחיה דתנא למיתני מעשה לסיועיה למאי דתנא ברישא! **ואם הוכיח סופו** על תחלתו. שהוכיח סוף דבריו על תחלתן שאינן אלא הערמה, וכגון מתנת בית חורון, דאסיק למילתיה ואמר "והינן לפניך". אבל כל שלא אמר בפירוש, אע"פ שהענין מוכיח בעצמו דלא יהיב ליה אלא כי היכי דליתהני מודר – אפ"ה הויא מתנה. **לא שנו אלא דאמר** ליה *והינן לפניך. דהוי תנאי גמור. אבל א"ל "ויבא אבא" – מדעתך הוא דאמר ליה, דלאו תנאה הוא, ומתנה גמורה היא, אלא דאי בעי עביד הכי. וכדאמרינן בפ' "יו"ט" (ביצה כ.) בההוא דאמר "הבו ד' מאה זוזי לפלניא ולנסיב ברתאי", דאמר *רבא: ד' מאה זוזי שקיל, ברתיה – אי בעי נסיב, אי בעי לא נסיב. **ל"א אמרי לה אמר רבא לא תימא טעמא דא"ל** והינן לפניך **הוא דאסור אלא אפילו יבא אבא ויאכל אסור מ"ט** סעודתו מוכחת עליו. דנהי דבעלמא "ויבא" לאו תנאי הוא, הכא שאני משום דלאו סהדי שאין אדם מכין סעודה לנשואי בנו ונותנה לאחר. הלכך סעודתו מוכחת עליו, דמאי דאמר "ויבא אבא" – לתנאי גמור קאמר. מיהו, כתב הרשב"א ז"ל דדוקא כשאמר כן בשעת מתנה, אבל לאחר מכן – לא, כיון דבשעת מתנה לא אמר מידי. אבל הרב רבינו משה בר מיימון ז"ל כתב (בפ"ז מהל' נדרים הל' טו) דאפי' לאחר שעה אסור, ואינה מתנה.
ההוא

עין משפט נר מצוה

יד א ב ג ד מיי' פ"ז מהל' נדרים הל"ב וה"ג סמג לאוין רמב טוש"ע יו"ד סי' רכה:
טו ה ו מיי' שם הל' יד סמג שם טוש"ע יו"ד סי' רכא סעיף ט:

מסורת הש"ס

[מכאן עד אלא בהווה נראה מיותר]
[בערוך ערך קנטר איתא קנתרנין]
[לעיל מג.]
[כתובות עח. ב"ב קלד. לעיל מג:]
נ"א לך במתנה ואינן לפניך
נ"א לא נתתי
נ"א לא נתת
נ"א וכשבא הדבר לפני חכמים
[גיטין סו. זבחים ב: חולין לט:]
ס"א ואינן
[נ"ל רב פפא]

הגהות הב"ח

(א) במשנה ואחד כותב להדיוט שהכותב לנשיא אין צריך כצ"ל ותיבות מה בין כותב לנשיא לכותב להדיוט נמחק: (ב) שם במשנה שהיה אביו מודר הימנו וכו' וסעודה נתונים לך במתנה ואינן לפניך אלא וכו' אמר לו אם שלי וכו' א"ל לא נתתי את שלי וכו' אמר לו לא נתת לי את שלך: (ג) שם תלוי בראשו (אמרו חכמים וכו' אינה מתנה) תא"מ ונ"ב ס"א וכשבא הדבר לפני חכמים אמרו כל מתנה שאינה שאם הקדישה אינה מקודשת אינה מתנה: (ד) גמ' דאמר ליה ואינן לפניך וכו' שיבא אבא וכו' אבל א"ל וכו' שיבא אבא וכו' מדעתך וכו' דא"ל ואינן לפניך הוא דאסור: (ה) רש"י ד"ה והבור שבאמצע הדרך כדמפרש: (ו) ד"ה לא שנו וכו' דאמר ליה ואינן לפניך אלא וכו' דמשמע דהכי אמר ליה ואינן נתונין וכו' והם נתונים לך ואם בדעתך שיבא אבא הוי קורא לו ע"א אמר וכו' חילוק בין ואינן לפניך בין וכו' כמאן דאמר ואינן לפניך:

פי' הרא"ש

גמ' אמאי מיתסר. המודר כיון שהמדיר כתב חלקו לנשיא: **מעשה לסתור.** מעיקרא תנא דשרי והדר מייתי עובדא דאסור: **ואם הוכיח סופו על תחילתו.** שלא היתה מתנה גמורה אסור: **אבל אמר לו והן לפניך שיבא אבא מדעתו הוא דא"ל.** תלה הדבר בו אם הוא רוצה פייס לאבא שיאכל עמך כי הכל שלך:
דהוה

תוספות

רחבה ומרחץ ובית הכנסת. אתיא כרבנן דאסרו בחצר דאין ברירה: **אסור** ברחבה ובבית הכנסת. יש לדקדק לכאורה משמע דאתי' כרבנן דאמרי אין ברירה ולא אמר האי בדידיה קמהלך כמו בחצר לרבי אליעזר ובפרק בתרא דביצה (דף לט.) גבי בור דמתניתין דעולי בבל קבעי למימר דמתני' דהכא אית ליה ברירה ולכך מותר בבור משום דהאי בדידיה קממלא והאי בדידיה קממלא ואם כן אמאי אסור בבית הכנסת ובדברים של אותה העיר ויש לחלק [בממלא] מים מן הבור בהא סבר תנא דיש ברירה בהא שהוא מסלקו מחלק חבירו אבל להשתמש או להכנס בדבר שחבירו שותף ודאי לית להו ברירה וה"ה דהוי מצי למיתני דשניהן מותרין למלאות מבור שבעיר בפרק הדר (עירובין מה:) עוד נראה להר"ר שמואל מאוירא ז"ל דסוגיא דהתם סברה כסברא דריש פירקין דרבנן סברי שפיר דיש ברירה ולא אסרו אלא (בברירה) משום קנסא ודווקא בדברים של אותה העיר אבל בדברים של עולי בבל לא רצו לקנוס לפי שהוא לכל העולם: **והתיבה.** ארון שנותנין בו ס"ת: **והספרים.** היו רגילין לקנות ספרים משל צבור ללמוד בהם בני העיר: **והכותב** חלקו לנשיא. מפרש בגמרא דה"ק כיצד תקנתם יכתבו חלקם לנשיא והא דלעיל גבי חצר לא קאמר הך תקנתא דחצר שהיא מיוחדת ממש אין תקנה לתת אותה לנשיא אבל הכא דמעיקרא נמי אין כל הדברים הללו מיוחדים להם לא יפסידו אם יכתבו חלקם לנשיא שגם אחר כך יכולין לילך וליהנות שהנשיא לא יקפיד עליהן כיון שגם לו אינה מיוחדת שהרי היא לכל בני העיר ולנשיא לאו דווקא ה"ה אם לאחד מבני העיר אלא לרווחא דמילתא נקט כדמוכח לקמן לא דברו חכמים אלא בהווה והטעם לפי שחולקים כבוד לנשיא א"נ כיון שאנו מתחילים לעשות תקנה בחלק זה יש לנו לעשות התקנה הטובה שנוכל ואם נתקן שיתנוהו לאחד מבני העיר שגם הוא ידיר אחד מחבירו הנאה אבל הנשיא אינו רגיל להדיר ולהקפיד על ישראל: **אין** צריך לקנות. דאלים כחו ולכך תיקנו שיכתוב לנשיא דאין צריך לקנות שאם יתקנו לכתוב לאחר פעמים ישכחו לזכות ואתי לידי תקלה: **שכבר** כתבו אביהם. כלומר זכותם כתבו לנשיא מדורות הראשונים: **כל** מתנה שאם הקדישה אינה מקודשת אינה מתנה. כלומר שאם הקדישה בעודה בידו אינה מקודשת אינה מתנה גם לשאר מינים ואסור אביו ליכנס בחצר וא"ת והא אמר מתנה על מנת להחזיר שמה מתנה וי"ל דהתם כל כמה דלא החזיר הוי מתנה גמורה לכל מה שירצה אבל הכא אין בידו להקנותה לשום אדם דלא נתנה אלא כדי שיאכל אביו: **אמאי** מיתסר. בשביל שכתב חלקו לנשיא: **עמדו** אבותיהם. ראשי בית אבות שלהם והכריזום שיכתבו חלקיהם לנשיא: **מעשה** לסתור. דעד השתא לא חזינן מתנה גרועה: **ואם** הוכיח סופו על תחילתו. פירוש סוף דיבורו כגון שסיים ואינם לפניך אלא כדי שיאכל פלוני אבל אמר ליה והם לפניך שיבא אביו מדעתו קאמר ליה: **סעודתו** מוכיח עליו. שלא היה בדעתו ליתן כ"א שיבא אביו:
דהוה

טז א מיי' פ"ח מהל' נדרים הל' ז סמג לאוין רמב טוש"ע יו"ד סימן רכג סעיף ג:
יז ב טוש"ע חו"מ סימן קכה סעיף ה:

ר"ן

ההוא גברא דהוה ליה ברא דהוה שמיט כיפי דכתנא. שהיה גונב אגודות של פשתן. **אמרו ליה ואי הוי בר ברך צורבא מרבנן מאי.** מה תהא עליו, למה לא יקנה אותם? ואם תאמר: דהא אע"ג דאסרינהו עליה הוה קני להו בר בריה. דהא כתבינן לעיל דמאן דאסר נכסיה אבריה, אע"ג דאינו רשאי ליהנות מהן – אפי' הכי גוף הנכסים דידיה הוי, דמכל מקום תנן: נותן לבניו או לאחיו. וכיון שכן – בר בריה הוה ירית להו אי הוי צורבא מרבנן או ע"ה. ומהיים נמי, אי בעי למתנינהו לבריה – מצי עביד, כדתנן: נותן לבניו או לאחיו, וכדפירשנו לעיל (ד' מז.)! י"ל דהך עובדא הכי הוי; דלההוא גברא הוו ליה תרין בני, חד דמעלי, ואידך דהוי שמיט כיפי דכתנא. והכירו בו דהוה בעי למתבינהו לנכסיה להוא דמעלי, ומשום הכי אמרו ליה: אי הוי בר ברך צורבא מרבנן למה לא יזכה בנכסים? ואהדר להו: שפיר קאמריתו, ליקני הדין פלגא, ואי הוה בריה צורבא מרבנן – ליקניה בריה לההוא פלגא, ואי לא – ליהוו כולהו להך ברא דמעלי. **אמרי פומבדיתאי** קני על מנת להקנות הוא **ולא** קני. דאע"ג דמתנה על מנת להחזיר שמה מתנה – התם שאני, דמכל מקום הרי הוא זוכה בה לשעתו ומשתמש ממנה. אבל הכא, דלא אקני ליה לבריה כי היכי דליזכי בהו כלל, אלא כי היכי דליקנינהו לבריה כי הוי צורבא מרבנן – לא קנה. והך ברא דמעלי קני כולהו נכסי, דהא כל היכא דהאי לא קני – לאידך אקנינהו. **ורב נחמן אמר** קני על מנת להקנות קנה. אע"פ שלא נתן לזה כלל, אלא כדי שיקנה לפלוני. **דהא סודרא** קני על מנת להקנות הוא. דכי יהיב קונה סודריה למקנה – אינו מזכהו בו לשום דבר, אלא שיהא לו בו קנין, בכדי שיקנה לו קרקע שלו. ואפי' הכי חשבינן ליה קנין, שעל ידו קנה לוקח את השדה. אלמא: קנין כי האי קנה. **אמר ליה רב אשי מאן לימא לן דסודרא אי תפיס ליה לא מתפיס.** כלומר, מנא לך דאי בעי מקנה לעכוביה לגמרי לא מצי עביד? ועוד סודרא קני על מנת להקנות מן השתא הוא. כלומר, לכשתמצא לומר דסודרא "קני על מנת להקנות" הוא, מיהו איכא ביה חדא למעליותא – דהוי "קני על מנת להקנות" מן השתא, מקמי דמהדר סודרא מקנה לקונה. דסתם קנין מעכשיו הוא. אבל הכא, הלין נכסי לאימת קני – לכי הוי בריה צורבא מרבנן, דמסתמא כיון שלא הקנהו אלא להקנותם לבנו – ודאי לא היה דעתו שיקנס עד אותה שעה, דמאי לעביד בהו בנתיים? **וההוא שעתא הדר סודרא** למריה. כלומר, כלתה לה אותה הקנאה, בין שהקנהו בקנין בין שהקנהו בחזקה. ורב נחמן, דאמר "קני על מנת להקנות" קנה, נהי דמודה במקנה לאחר שלשים יום דלא קנה, דאיהו גופיה אמר בפרק "האשה שנפלו לה נכסים" (כתובות פב.) דהאומר לחבירו "משוך פרה זו ולא תקנה עד לאחר שלשים יום" – דלא קנה בעומדת באגם, הוה ס"ד דרב נחמן דהכא כיון דלא אמר בהדיא דלא ליקני עד דהוי צורבא מרבנן, ואמר סתמא – כמאן דאמר מעכשיו ולכי הוי דמי. ורב אשי דחי ליה, דכיון שלא רצה להקנות אלא כי היכי דלקנייה לבר בריה – מסתמא לא נתכוין שיקנה עד אותה שעה, וההיא שעתא כלתה לה קנייתו. ומיהו, כי אמרי' הכי – דוקא בקנין *)ומשיכה וחזקה שאינן מתקיימין, אבל בקנין שטר, שהשטר קיים ועומד, לכי הוי בר בריה צורבא מרבנן – קני. דהא המקדש את האשה בשטר ואמר לה "הרי את מקודשת לי לאחר ל' יום" – מקודשת אם לא נאבד השטר ולא נתקתו. וכן לענין הגט, וכדאיתא התם. הרשב"א ז"ל. ולי נראה דהכא אפי' בשטר לא מהני, דהאי גברא מלוה מחמת מיתה הוא, ואי בשעתיה לא קני – לאחר מיתה נמי לא קני, דאין שטר לאחר מיתה. *)והיכי דקא פליג רב אשי סתמא. **אמר ליה רבא** לרב נחמן **והא** מתנת בית חורון דקני ע"מ להקנות הוא **ולא** קני. דאי קני – ליהוי מודר מותר בו, דהא אפסקיה אחר. זמנין **א"ל** משום דסעודתו מוכיח עליו. שאין אדם עשוי ליתן לאחר סעודה שהכין לנשואי בנו, הילכך לא הוי אלא הערמה, ואסור. כך פי' רבותי. וקשה לי: נהי דמוכחת עליו, הא בהדיא אמר דלא יהיב מידי לבר בריה, אלא לאקנויי לבר בריה, ואפ"ה אקשינן דאם איתא דקני – במתנת בית חורון הוה למשרי, אע"ג דאמר ליה "והינן לפניך", דמ"מ כיון דקני – הא אפסקיה אחר. וכיון שכן – מאי שני ליה סעודתו מוכחת עליו? וכי מוכחת יותר ממאי דאמר בהדיא "והינן לפניך"! ונ"ל דה"ק: סעודתו מוכחת עליו דבעי מדיר דליתהני אבוה מסעודה דעביד איהו לבריה, דהכי הוא אורחא דמילתא. דלאיתהנויי אבוה מסעודה דאיניש אחרינא – מאי נפקא ליה מינה? הלכך סעודתו מוכחת עליו דאבוה מדידיה מתהני. אבל הכא, אדרבה, ניחא ליה להאי גברא דליתהני בר מאבוה, שכך סדר נחלות, ולא שתקפוץ נחלה ממנו לבן בנו. וזמנין **א"ל** ר' **אליעזר היא דאמר אפי' ויתור אסור במודר הנאה.** לאו דשייך הכא דין ויתור, אלא לדמיון בעלמא נקטיה. דכי היכי דמחמיר ר' אליעזר בנדרים טפי מבדיני ממונות, דאילו בדיני ממונות דריסת הרגל שריא ולית בה משום גזל, ואילו מודר הנאה מחבירו אסור ליכנס בחצרו – ה"נ, נהי ד"קני ע"מ להקנות" לענין דינא קני, משום חומרא דנדרים – אמרינן דלא קני. **מאי לאו לאתויי הא מילתא דכיפי.** דאפי' לענין דינא קני ע"מ להקנות לא קנה. **לא לאתויי לישנא בתרא דשמעתיה דרבא.** דאמר דאפי' "יבא אבא ויאכל" אסור, משום דסעודתו מוכחת עליו.

*) נ"ל משיכה   *) נ"ל והיינו

הַהוּא גַּבְרָא דַּהֲוָה לֵיהּ בְּרָא דַּהֲוָה שָׁמֵיט כֵּיפֵי דְּכִיתָנָא, אָסְרִינְהוּ לְנִכְסֵיהּ עֲלֵיהּ. אָמְרוּ לֵיהּ: וְאִי הֲוַאי בַּר בְּרָךְ צוּרְבָא מֵרַבָּנַן מַאי? אֲמַר לְהוֹן: (א) לִיקְנֵי הָדֵין, וְאִי הֲוַאי בַּר בְּרִי צוּרְבָא מֵרַבָּנַן – לִקְנְיֵיהּ. מַאי? אָמְרִי פּוּמְבְּדִיתָאֵי: "קְנֵי עַל מְנָת לְהַקְנוֹת" הוּא, וְכָל "קְנֵי עַל מְנָת לְהַקְנוֹת" – לָא קָנֵי. [א]וְרַב נַחְמָן אֲמַר: קָנֵי, דְּהָא סוּדָרָא קְנֵי עַל מְנָת לְהַקְנוֹת הוּא. אֲמַר רַב אַשִׁי: וּמַאן לֵימָא לָן דְּסוּדָרָא, אִי תָּפֵיס לֵיהּ לָא מִיתְפִּיס? [ב]וְעוֹד: סוּדָרָא "קְנֵי עַל מְנָת לְהַקְנוֹת וּקְנֵי מִן הַשְׁתָּא", הָלֵין נִיכְסִין דְּהָדֵין, לְאֵימָתַי קָנֵי – לְכִי הָוֵי בַּר בְּרֵיהּ צוּרְבָא מֵרַבָּנַן, לְכִי הָוֵה – הֲדַר סוּדָרָא לְמָרֵיהּ! אֲמַר לֵיהּ רָבָא לְרַב נַחְמָן: וְהָא מַתְּנַת בֵּית חוֹרוֹן, דְּ"קְנֵי עַל מְנָת לְהַקְנוֹת" הוּא, וְלָא קָא קָנֵי! °זִימְנִין אֲמַר לֵיהּ: מִשּׁוּם דִּסְעוּדָתוֹ מוֹכַחַת עָלָיו, וְזִימְנִין אֲמַר לֵיהּ: ר' אֱלִיעֶזֶר הִיא, דְּאָמַר: *אֲפִילּוּ וִיתּוּר אָסוּר בְּמוּדַּר הֲנָאָה. תְּנַן: אָמְרוּ חֲכָמִים, כָּל מַתָּנָה שֶׁאֵינָהּ שֶׁאִם הִקְדִּישָׁהּ תְּהֵא מְקוּדֶּשֶׁת – אֵינָהּ מַתָּנָה. "כָּל" לְאִיתוּיֵי מַאי, לָאו לְאַתּוּיֵי הָא מִילְּתָא *דְּשַׁדְיָא (ב) בְּבֵיפֵי? לָא, לְאַתּוּיֵי לִישָּׁנָא בַּתְרָאָה דִּשְׁמַעְתֵּיהּ דְּרָבָא.§

הדרן עלך השותפין

רש"י

כֵּיפֵי דְּכִיתָנָא. שֶׁהָיָה גּוֹזֵל אֲנִיצֵי פִשְׁתָּן. וְאִית דְּאָמְרִי: שֶׁהָיָה מְשַׁמֵּט עַצְמוֹ מִלִּלְמוֹד תּוֹרָה וְהָיָה עוֹסֵק בַּאֲנִיצֵי פִשְׁתָּן. **וְאִי הָוֵה בַּר בְּרָךְ צוּרְבָא מֵרַבָּנַן מַאי.** כְּלוֹמַר, מַה יְּהֵא, וּמִי יוֹרֵשׁ נְכָסֶיךָ? לִיקְנֵי הָדֵין דְּאִי הָוֵי בַּר בְּרֵיהּ **צוּרְבָא** מֵרַבָּנַן וכו'. מִשּׁוּם דַּחֲכַתִּי לָא הָוֵי בַּר בְּרֵיהּ בָּעוֹלָם, וְהָוֵה לֵיהּ מְזַכֶּה לְעוּבָּר, וְהַמְזַכֶּה לְעוּבָּר לֹא קָנָה. **קְנֵי עַל מְנָת לְהַקְנוֹת הוּא.** דְּבָרָא בְּנִכְסֵי אָבִיו לֹא צָרִיךְ קִנְיָן, הִלְכָּךְ, מַקְנֵי לֵיהּ לִבְרֵיהּ אַדַּעְתָּא לְאַקְנוּיֵי לְבַר בְּרֵיהּ הִיא (ג). **וְכָל דִּקְנֵי עַל מְנָת לְהַקְנוֹת.** לֹא הָוֵי קִנְיָן. **דְּהָא סוּדָרָא** קְנֵי עַל מְנָת לְהַקְנוֹת הוּא. דְּהָא לָא (ד) מַקְנֵי נוֹתֵן לַמַּקְנֶה כֵּלָיו שֶׁל קוֹנֶה, וְהָא מַקְנֵי לֵיהּ לְדִידֵיהּ, דְּקָא מַקְנֵי לֵיהּ לְהַהוּא חֵפֶץ לַקּוֹנֶה. הָכָא נַמִי, כִּי אֲמַר: עַל מְנָת לְהַקְנוֹת – קָנֵי. **אִי תָּפֵיס לֵיהּ לָא** מִתְפִּיס. בִּתְמִיָּה, דְּאִי בָּעֵי מַקְנֶה לְמִישְׁקַל בִּכְנָפָא דְּסוּדָרָא (ה) וּלְמִיקְנְיֵיהּ, לְמִישְׁקְלֵיהּ לְדִידֵיהּ – לֵיכָּא מַאן דְּמָחֵי לֵיהּ. **וְעוֹד סוּדָרָא.** לָא דָּמֵי לְהַהִיא כְּלָל. דְּאִילּוּ גַּבֵּי סוּדָרָא, כִּי תָּפֵיס לֵיהּ – מַשְׁמַע דְּהָכִי אָמַר לֵיהּ: קְנֵי הַשְׁתָּא (ו) בִּשְׁעַת קִנְיָן עַל מְנָת לְהַקְנוֹת. וּקְנֵי הַשְׁתָּא הַסּוּדָר, וּמַקְנֵי לֵיהּ בִּשְׁעַת קִנְיָן הַחֵפֶץ. אֲבָל קְנֵי נִכְסֵי דְּהָדֵין, לְאֵימַת קָא קָנֵי לְהוּ – לְכִי הָוֵי בַּר בְּרֵיהּ צוּרְבָא מֵרַבָּנַן, הִלְכָּךְ הַשְׁתָּא נַמִי לָא קָנֵי. וְאָסוּר לִקְנוֹת לָהֶן, וְגַן בְּנוֹ נַמִי לֹא קָנָה וְאִי בָּעֵי אָבִיו יָהֵיב לֵיהּ לְנִכְסֵיהּ וּלְכָל מַאן דְּבָעֵי. **וְהָא** מַתְּנַת בֵּית חוֹרוֹן דִּקְנֵי עַל מְנָת לְהַקְנוֹת הוּא **וְלָא** קָנֵי זִימְנִין **אֲמַר** לֵיהּ וכו'. דְּהָתָם הַיְינוּ טַעְמָא דְּלָא קָנֵי, דִּסְעוּדָּתוֹ מוֹכַחַת עָלָיו דְּוַדַּאי לָא יָהֵיב לֵיהּ אֶלָּא מִשּׁוּם סְעוּדָה, וְאָסוּר, (ז) הוֹאִיל וּמֶחֱזֵי דְּמִיתְהַנֵּי מִינֵּיהּ. הָכָא נַמִי, כֵּיוָן דְּקָא בָּעֵי דְּיֵאכַל אַבָּא – לֹא קָנָה אִידָךְ, מִשּׁוּם דְּקָא מִתְהַנֵּי אָבִיו מִינֵּיהּ, וְהָכִי אָסוּר. **לָאו לְאַתּוּיֵי הָא מִילְּתָא דְּשַׁדְיָא בִּבְפִילָה.** כְּלוֹמַר, הַאי מַעֲשֶׂה שֶׁמּוּטָּל בִּתְנַאי כָּפוּל, דְּכָפַל לְדִיבּוּרֵיהּ, (ח) דַּאֲמַר: לִיקְנֵי הָדֵין, וְאִי הָוֵי בַּר בְּרֵיהּ צוּרְבָא מֵרַבָּנַן – לִיקְנְיֵיהּ לִבְרֵיהּ, דְּוַדַּאי לֹא קָנָה. וְאִית דְּגָרְסִי: מַאי לָאו לְאַתּוּיֵי הָא מִילְּתָא דְּשָׁמִיט בֵּיפֵי. מִילְּתָא דְּבֵית חוֹרוֹן דְּדָמְיָא לְאוֹתוֹ מַעֲשֶׂה דְּכֵיפֵי דְּכִתָּנָא. **לָא לְאִיתוּיֵי לִישָּׁנָא בַּתְרָא** דִּשְׁמַעְתֵּיהּ **דְּרָבָא.** דַּאֲמַר לְעֵיל: אֲפִי' א"ל "וְהֵן לְפָנֶיךָ שֶׁיָּבֹא אַבָּא וְיֹאכַל" – דְּאָסוּר. אֲבָל הֵיכָא דְּא"ל "לִיקְנֵי הָדֵין דְּאִי (ט) הָוֵי בַּר בְּרֵיהּ צוּרְבָא מֵרַבָּנַן לִקְנְיֵיהּ" – קְנֵי עַל מְנָת לְהַקְנוֹת הוּא.

הדרן עלך השותפין

[לעיל לב: וש"נ]

[לפרש"י הרא"ש ל"ל דשדיא בבפילה לא לאתויי וכו']

תוספות

דהוה שמיט כיפי דכיתנא. אנילי פשתן היה שמיט ומקלקל אותם: **אסרינהו** לנכסיה. הדירו שלא יהנה מנכסיו בחייו ובמותו: **אמרו** לו. לאביו למה אסרת בנך אחר מותך: **אמר** ליה ליקני הדין דאי הוה ברי' צורבא מרבנן ליקני. כלומר יקנה נכסי' הללו שאם יהיה בנו צורבא מרבנן יקנה אותם לו: **קנה** על מנת להקנות הוא. שהבן קונה לעצמו כדי להקנות לבנו ולא הוי כשאר זוכים בשביל חביריהם ומועיל דכל עיקר הזכייה אינה בשביל עצמו כי אם בשביל חבירו המקבל המתנה אבל הכא אמר ליה קנה כדי שתקנה לבנך כשיהיה צורבא מרבנן וגם לעצמו לא נגמרה המתנה ולא הויא לה כמתנה על מנת להחזיר דמסיק בקידושין (דף ו:) דמקנה בה קרקע לנותן דהתם נגמר המכירה כשאמר ליה הריני נותן לך דבר זה על מנת להחזיר ובכסף זה תקנה לי שדי אבל הכא מפרש בהדיא שאינו מקנה לו אלא ע"מ להקנות: **ורב** נחמן אמר קני. (והכא קני) ואע"ג דהשתא אין הבן בעולם ולא מחלק בין בא לעולם ובין לא בא לעולם ובין שמקנה לבן עצמו כדי להקנות לבנו: **דהא** סודרא. שקונין בו חליפין: קנה על מנת להקנות הוא. כלומר ורגילות הוא שהוא מחזיר לו הסודר ויודע הוא שלא יתקיים בידו וקני ליה שהרי יודע שמקנה הוא לו ע"י הקנין החפץ שלו וכמו כן [הכא על מנת] להקנות הוא אע"פ שלא תתקיים מתנה בידו קנה שפיר ויקנה אותה לבן: **ומאן** לימא לן דהך סודרא אי תפיס ליה לא מתפיס. כלומר מאן לימא לן דאי בעי לא פסיק ליה דילמא ודאי אי בעי פסיק ליה ומתנה מעליא היא (אבל) [ועוד] קני ע"מ להקנות ליכא לדמויי לסודרא דבסודרא קני על מנת להקנות שמעינן מינה אם אמר להקנות הדרא סודרא למריה. ולאו גרוע הוא ולא גמר להקנות נתן לו שטר ואמר לו קנה זמן ולא דמי לסודר שקנה

להקנות מהשתא הוא דבשעה שמקנה לו הסודר אמר לו שיקנה לו בחליפין מיד ה"נ אלא ודאי מנהגא בעלמא הוא מה שנהגו להחזיר **מאן לימא לן דהאי סודרא דאי בעי לא תפיס ליה.** ... להקנות מיד בשעת הקנאה קני: **הלין** נכסים לאימת קני לכי הוי צורבא מרבנן כבר ... לא מצי לקנויי לבר בריה:

פי' הרא"ש

דהוה שמיט כיפי דכיתנא. גוזל תכשיטי שיש שעושין כיפי והם של פשתן כדאמרינן בשבת (דף נז:) כיפה של צמר **אסרינהו לנכסיה עלוה.** בחייו ובמותו והעביר נחלתו ממנו ונתנה לאביו: **ואי הוי בר ברך צורבא מרבנן מאי.** לא ירש חלק הראוי לאביו: **אמר להון לקני הדין כו'.** ע"מ שיקנה לבנו אי הוי צורבא מרבנן: **כל קני על מנת להקנות לא קני.** דכיון דהוא אינו קונה לעצמו לא חשיב להקנות לאחר זמן כיון שאינו זוכה לו עתה בקנין זה: **דהא סודרא קני על מנת להקנות הוא.** שהקונה מקנה סודרו למקנה שיתן לו חפץ אחר חליפי הסודר והוא אינו קונה הסודר אלא מחזירהו לקבה ומקנה לו החפץ וה"נ אע"פ שזה אינו קונה מה שנותנים לו יכול הוא להקנותו לאחר:

גליון הש"ס

גמ' זמנין אמר וכו'. כעין זה שבת דף ז' ע"ב:

הַנּוֹדֵר אמִן הַמְבוּשָּׁל – מוּתָּר בְּצָלִי וּבְשָׁלוּק. אָמַר "קוֹנָם תַּבְשִׁיל שֶׁאֵינִי טוֹעֵם" – אָסוּר בְּמַעֲשֵׂה קְדֵרָה רַךְ, וּמוּתָּר בְּעָבֶה, וּמוּתָּר בְּבֵיצָה טוּרְמוּטָא וּבִדְלַעַת הָרְמוּצָה. בהַנּוֹדֵר מִמַּעֲשֵׂה קְדֵרָה אֵין אָסוּר אֶלָּא מִמַּעֲשֵׂה רְתַחְתָּה. אָמַר "קוֹנָם הַיּוֹרֵד לַקְּדֵרָה שֶׁאֵינִי טוֹעֵם" – אָסוּר בְּכָל הַמִּתְבַּשְּׁלִין בִּקְדֵרָה.§

גמ' תַּנְיָא: ר' יֹאשִׁיָּה אוֹסֵר. וְאע"פ שֶׁאֵין רְאָיָה לַדָּבָר – זֵכֶר לַדָּבָר, שֶׁנֶּאֱמַר °"וַיְבַשְּׁלוּ (אֶת) הַפֶּסַח בָּאֵשׁ כַּמִּשְׁפָּט" לֵימָא בְּהָא קָמִיפַּלְגִי; דְּרַבִּי יֹאשִׁיָּה סָבַר: הַלֵּךְ אַחַר לְשׁוֹן תּוֹרָה, וְתַנָּא דִּידָן סָבַר: *בִּנְדָרִים הַלֵּךְ אַחַר לְשׁוֹן בְּנֵי אָדָם? לָא, דְּכוּלֵּי עָלְמָא גבִּנְדָרִים הַלֵּךְ אַחַר לְשׁוֹן בְּנֵי אָדָם, *מָר כִּי אַתְרֵיהּ וּמָר כִּי אַתְרֵיהּ; בְּאַתְרָא דְּתַנָּא דִּידָן – לְצָלִי קָרוּ לֵיהּ צָלִי, וְלִמְבוּשָּׁל קָרוּ לֵיהּ מְבוּשָּׁל. בְּאַתְרָא דר' יֹאשִׁיָּה – אֲפִילּוּ צָלִי קָרוּ מְבוּשָּׁל. וְהָא קְרָא נָסֵיב לַהּ! אַסְמַכְתָּא בְּעָלְמָא.§ "קוֹנָם תַּבְשִׁיל" כו'.§ וְהָא מִתַּבְשִׁיל נָדַר! אָמַר אַבָּיֵי: הַאי תַּנָּא, כָּל מִידֵּי דְּמִתְאַכְלָא בֵּיהּ רִיפְתָּא – תַּבְשִׁיל קָרוּ לֵיהּ. וְהָתַנְיָא: *הַנּוֹדֵר מִן הַתַּבְשִׁיל – אָסוּר בְּכָל מִינֵי תַּבְשִׁיל, וְאָסוּר בְּצָלִי וּבְשָׁלוּק וּבִמְבוּשָּׁל, וְאָסוּר בְּהִיטְרִיּוֹת רַכּוֹת שֶׁהַחוֹלִין אוֹכְלִין בָּהֶן פִּיתָּן. אִינִי?! וְהָא רַבִּי יִרְמְיָה חֲלַשׁ, עָל לְגַבֵּיהּ הַהוּא אָסְיָא לְאַסְוּוֹהּ. חֲזָא קְרָא דְּמַחַת בְּבֵיתֵיהּ – שְׁבַקֵיהּ וּנְפַק, אֲמַר: מַלְאַךְ מוֹתָא אִית לֵיהּ לְדֵין בְּבֵיתֵיהּ, וַאֲנָא אֵיעוּל לְאַסָּאָה יָתֵיהּ?! לָא קַשְׁיָא; הָא – בְּרַכִּיכֵי, הָא – בְּאַשּׁוּנֵי. רָבָא בַּר עוּלָּא אֲמַר: הָא – בְּקָרָא גּוּפֵיהּ, וְהָא – בְּגַוֵּויהּ דְּקָרָא. דְּאָמַר רַב יְהוּדָה: לוּלִיבָא דְּקָרָא בְּסִילְקָא, לוּלִיבָא דְּכִיתָנָא בְּכוּתְחָא. *)וְדָבָר זֶה אָסוּר לְאוֹמְרוֹ בִּפְנֵי עַם הָאָרֶץ. רָבָא אֲמַר: מַאן חוֹלִין – רַבָּנַן. רָבָא לְטַעְמֵיהּ, **)דְּאָמַר רָבָא: כְּמַאן

*) [מנחות לט:] **) ר"ה טז. ע"ש

רש"י

*הַנּוֹדֵר מִן הַמְבוּשָּׁל מוּתָּר בְּצָלִי וּבְשָׁלוּק. מְבוּשָּׁל. מְבוּשָּׁל כָּרָאוּי (א). שָׁלוּק. מְבוּשָּׁל יוֹתֵר מִדַּאי. קוֹנָם תַּבְשִׁיל שֶׁאֵינִי טוֹעֵם. כָּל תַּבְשִׁיל בְּמַשְׁמַע. מַעֲשֵׂה קְדֵרָה רַךְ. שֶׁיֵּשׁ בָּהּ רוֹטֶב. אֲבָל לֹא בְּעָבֶה. כְּגוֹן דַּיְיסָא. טוּרְמוּטָא הָרְמוּצָה. מְפָרֵשׁ בַּגְּמָ'. רְתַחְתָּה. דָּבָר הָרוֹתֵחַ, כְּגוֹן רוֹטֶב וְכָל דְּדָמֵי לֵיהּ. הַיּוֹרֵד לַקְּדֵרָה. דְּמַשְׁמַע בֵּין לוֹנֵן בֵּין רוֹתֵחַ. אָסוּר בְּכָל הַמִּתְבַּשְּׁלִין. בֵּין רַךְ בֵּין עָבֶה. **גמ'** ר' יֹאשִׁיָּה אוֹסֵר. בְּצָלִי וּבְשָׁלוּק, דְּמִתְקְרֵי נַמִי מְבוּשָּׁל. הַלֵּךְ אַחַר לְשׁוֹן בְּנֵי אָדָם. דְּאֵין דַּרְכָּם לִקְרוֹת לְצָלִי מְבוּשָּׁל. וְהָא מִתַּבְשִׁיל נָדַר. דְּמַשְׁמַע בֵּין רַךְ בֵּין עָבֶה. הַאי תַּנָּא. דְּמַתְנִיתִין, דְּלָא קָרֵי לְעָבֶה תַּבְשִׁיל. בְּכָל מִידֵּי דְּמִתְאַכְלָא בֵּיהּ רִיפְתָּא. דִּמְלַפְּתִין בּוֹ אֶת הַפַּת קָרֵי תַּבְשִׁיל. וְהָא תַּנְיָא. בְּנִיחוּתָא. בְּהִיטְרִיּוֹת רַכּוֹת. בְּדִילּוּעִין רַכּוֹת שֶׁהַחוֹלִין אוֹכְלִין בָּהֶן פִּיתָּן. אִינִי. מִי אוֹכְלִין הַחוֹלִין מֵהֶן?! חֲזָא קְרָא דְּמְחִיתָא. דְּלַעַת מוּנַּחַת שָׁם שֶׁהָיָה אוֹכֵל מִמֶּנָּה. לוּלִיבָא דְקָרָא בְּסִלְקָא. תּוֹכוֹ שֶׁל דְּלַעַת יָפֶה לֶאֱכוֹל עִם הַתְּרָדִין. לוּלִיבָא דְּכִיתָנָא. תּוֹכָן שֶׁל זֵרְעוֹנֵי פִּשְׁתָּן יָפִיס לְאָכְלָן בְּכוּתָּח. וְדָבָר זֶה אָסוּר לְאוֹמְרוֹ בִּפְנֵי עַם הָאָרֶץ. מִשּׁוּם דְּדָבָר מְעוּלֶּה הוּא לִרְפוּאָה, וְאָסוּר לוֹמַר לָהֶם שׁוּם דָּבָר שֶׁיֵּהָנוּ מִמֶּנּוּ. וְאִית דְּאָמְרִי: דְּלָא לֵיכְלוּ טוּבָא וְלִיפַּסְדוּ כִּיתָּנָא. חוֹלִין רַבָּנַן. שֶׁעוֹסְקִין בַּתּוֹרָה וְאֵינָם נֶהֱנִים מִן הָעוֹלָם, וּבָאִים לִידֵי חוֹלִי.

מְנַלַּיְינַן

ר"ן

ולענין הלכה. בסודר קיימא לן כרב נחמן דסודרא "קני על מנת להקנות" הוא, ולא מצי מקנה לעכובי. דאע"ג דרב אשי אמר ליה: מאן לימא לן דסודרא אי תפיס ליה לא מתפיס – דהויא בעלמא הוא דקאמר ליה, ולא סבר לה. דאיהו גופיה אמר בפ"ק דקידושין (ד' ו:) גבי האומר לאשה "הרי את מקודשת לי במנה זה על מנת שתחזירהו לי" דבכולהו קני לבר מאשה, גזרה שמא יאמרו אשה נקנית בחליפין. ואי סלקא דעתך °דאי תפיס מתפיס – מאי גזרה? דאי הכי נקנית היא בחליפין, ואין לך [קנין] גדול מזה! אלא ודאי רב אשי גופיה סביר' ליה דסודרא אי תפיס ליה מקנה לא מתפיס, והכא דחויא בעלמא הוא דדחי ליה לרב נחמן. מיהו, נהי דלענין סודרא קיימא לן כרב נחמן – לענין "קני על מנת להקנות" משמע דלא קי"ל כותיה, דבהא רב אשי פליג עליה לגמרי משום טעמא דסודרא "קני ע"מ להקנות מן השתא" הוא, אבל הכא הדר סודרא למרה. אבל הרמב"ם ז"ל פסק בשתיהן כרב נחמן. משמע דס"ל ז"ל דכיון דפרכא קמייתא דרב אשי דרך דחויא היא כדכתיבנא, כל מאי דקאמר ליה נמי לדחויי מכוין ולאו לאיפלוגי עליה. *והרמב"ם ז"ל בהלכותיו מסתם לה סתומי.

הדרן עלך השותפין שנדרו

הנודר מן המבושל מותר בצלי ובשלוק. שאינם בכלל לשון מבושל. שלוק – בשיל ולא בשיל. דנהי דשלוק נמי משמע מבושל יותר מדאי, כדאמרינן בפ' "כל הבשר" (חולין דף קי:): הכבד אוסרת ואינה נאסרת, שלוקה אוסרת ונאסרת, שלוק דהכא בשיל ולא בשיל הוא, דבנדרים הלך אחר לשון בני אדם, ותבשיל שנתבשל יותר מדאי בכלל מבושל הוא. **אמר** קונם תבשיל שאיני טועם **אסור** במעשה קדרה רך ומותר בעבה. מעשה קדרה כגון חלקא טרגים וטיסני. וקאמר דאם הוא רך – אסור, אבל עבה – מותר. דהאי תנא כל מידי דמתאכלא ביה ריפתא תבשיל קרי ליה, כדאי' בגמ', ומעשה קדרה עבה נאפי נפשיה אכלי ליה בלא פת. ואמרי' בגמ' דאסור בצלי ובשלוק דהא מתאכלא ביה ריפתא, וכי קתני "שאני טועם" – לאו דוקא דאמר הכי, אלא לרבותא נקטה, לומר דאפילו אמר "שאני טועם" – מותר בעבה. ומפורש בירושלמי דכי היכי דבקונם תבשיל מותר בעבה, הכי נמי נודר מן המבושל מותר בעבה. **ומותר בביצה טרמיטא.** מפרש בגמרא דשלקי לה במיא חמימי אלפא זימני, ואלפא זימני במיא קרירי עד דמתזוטרא כדבלע לה, ולא מתאכלא בה ריפתא. ומשמע דדוקא בה הוא דשרי, אבל כל שלא נתבשלה כל כך – אסורה, דהא מתאכלא ריפתא בהדה. והכי איתא בירושלמי בשם רב חסדא: אסור בבילה מגולגלת שכן דרך החולה לאכול בה פתו. דאלמא כל שלא נצטמקה כל כך, שהפת נאכלת עמה – בכלל תבשיל הוא. **גמ'** תניא ר' **יאשיה אוסר.** דנודר מן המבושל אסור בצלי. ואע"פ שאין ראיה לדבר. שהצלי יהא בכלל מבושל – זכר לדבר, דכתיב "ויבשלו (את) הפסח", ופסח אינו נאכל אלא צלי, וכתיב "ויבשלו". ומיהו, לאו ראיה גמורה היא, כדאמר במסקנא, דבנדרים הלך אחר לשון בני אדם. ירושלמי. אמר רבי יוחנן: הלכו בנדרים אחר לשון בני אדם, אמר ר' יאשיה: הלכו בנדרים אחר לשון תורה. מה נפיק ביניהון? אמר "קונם יין שאיני טועם בחג", על דעתיה דרבי יוחנן – אסור ביום טוב האחרון של חג, על דעתיה דר' יאשיה – מותר. אף ר' יאשיה מודה שהוא אסור, לא אמרה ר' יאשיה אלא לחומרין, ע"כ. ולפום גמרא דילן דאפי' ר' יאשיה מודה דאין הולכין בנדרים אלא אחר לשון בני אדם, שמעינן מינה דבין להקל בין להחמיר האומר "בחג" – יו"ט האחרון של חג בכלל. **והא מתבשיל נדר.** ואמאי מותר בעבה? דהא תבשיל הוא! **האי תנא כל מידי דמתאכלא ביה ריפתא תבשיל** קרי ליה. אבל מעשה קדרה עבה, דלא מתאכלא ריפתא בהדיה – לא מיקרי תבשיל. ואית דמפרשי דאסור במעשה קדרה רך קא קשיא ליה, דלאו תבשיל הוא, ושני דכיון דמתאכלא ביה ריפתא – תבשיל קרי ליה. **והתניא.** בניחותא. **ואסור בהיטריות רכות.** דלועין קטנים. **שהחולין אוכלין** בהן **פתן.** מדקא יהיב טעמא לאיסורא מפני שהחולין אוכלין בהן פתן – ש"מ דכל מידי דמתאכיל ביה ריפתא תבשיל מיקרי. **איני.** דדלועין יפין לחולה. ברכיכי. מעלו. **אשוני.** קשין. **בקרא** גופיה. קשה. גוויה דקרא. מה שבתוכו מעלי. **לוליבא דקרא.** מה שבתוכו. בסילקא. יבשלנו עם תרדין. לוליבא דכיתנא בכותחא. מה שבתוכו טוב לאכלו עם כותח. ודבר זה **אסור לאמרו בפני עם הארץ.** כדי שלא יעקרו הפשתן לכך. **מאן חולין** רבנן. אין הכי נמי דקרי בין רכיכי בין אשוני, קשין לחולי. וכי קתני שחולין אוכלין בהן פתן – לאו חולין ממש, אלא מאן חולין – רבנן, דאפילו בבריאותן הן תשושי כח, מפני שהתורה מתשת כחם.

כמאן

תוספות

הנודר מן המבושל מותר בצלי ובשלוק. שלוק שאין מבושל יותר: **קונם** תבשיל שאני טועם אסור במעשה קדירה רך. מפרש בגמרא כל מידי שנותנין בו פת לשרות קרוי תבשיל ומותר בעבה שאינו נאכל עם פת וצ"ע אמאי שני למיתני ענין אחר מרישא לפלוג בנודר מן התבשיל בלא שאומר שאני טועם ובשאר בבי כבוש ושלוק ומליח נקט דווקא שאני טועם להוסיף בו איסור וי"ל רבותא נקטי' דאפ"ה מותר בעבה וברישא מצי למיתני מבושל שאני טועם מותר בצלי ובשלוק אלא לא היה תופס חידוש [בהאי] דמבושל לא משמע בשום ייתור צלי ושלוק: [**טורמוטא** והרמוצה]. מפרש בגמ': **רבי** יאשיה אוסר בצלי ואע"פ שאין ראיה לדבר זכר לדבר. ולכך לא הוי ראיה דבנדרים הלך אחר לשון בני אדם: **והא** מן תבשיל נדר. ורך לא הוי תבשיל כיון שהוא רך כמים בעלמא: **בהיטריות.** פירוש קרייאתי: **[איני]** וכי קרי טובים לחולים וכו': **ברכיכי.** מועילים

פי' הרא"ש

[שייך לעמוד שלפניו] **סלין נכסין לאימת קנה.** אימת יקנה בר בריה **לכי סוי גורבא מרבנן** באותה שעה **בבר סדר סודר למריה.** כלומר בקנין סודר לא היה מועיל אם היה אומר קנה חפץ זה בחליפי סודר לאחר ל' יום אם לא א"ל מעכשיו ולאחר ל' יום הילכך ה"נ לא קני: **וסא מתנת בית חורון דקני על מנת לסקנות סוא.** שמקנה לו החצר והסעודה ולא שיהו שלו אלא שיוכל אביו לאכול בהיתר ולא קני זה על מנת לעשות מה שאמר זה כאילו קני ויאלו החצר והסעודה מרשות הבן ויוכל האב לאכול בהיתר אלא ודאי קני על מנת להקנות אינו קונה הלכך ה"נ לא יצאו החצר והסעודה מרשות הבן: **משום דסעודתו מוכחת עליו.** שלא היה קנין כי אם להערים ולא כוון לשם מתנה כלל: **סא מני רבי אליעזר סיא דאמר אפילו ויתור כו'.** הלכך ה"נ אע"ג דמדינא שרי דקנין על מנת להקנות קנה מחמיר הוא במודר הנאה: **לאתויי כך דקמיץ כיפי.** דלא הויא מתנה

ואיש גורסי לשנא בכפילה לשון המוטלך בכפל שכפל דבריו ואמר קני על מנת להקנות: לישנא בתרא לחולים: **באשוני.** פירוש קשות הם רעות לחולה שאינן מבושלות כלורך: **בקרא** גופה. פירוש [illegible]

הנודר מן המבושל. [illegible]

כמאן

עין משפט נר מצוה

א א מיי' פ"ט מהלכות נדרים הלכה א סמג לאוין רמב טור שו"ע יו"ד סי' ריז סעיף א:

ב ב מיי' שם הלכה ז טור ש"ע שם סעיף ב:

ג ג מיי' שם הלכה א טוש"ע שם סעיף א:

הגהות הב"ח

(א) רש"י ד"ה הנודר וד"ה שלוק הד"א:

גליון הש"ס

גמ' שנאמר ויבשלו (את) הפסח. קשה לי אמאי לא מייתי מקרא בתורה בפ' ראה גבי פסח ובשלת ואכלת וי"ל: **שם** ותנא דילן סבר בנדרים. לעיל דף ל ע"ב. ולקמן דף נא עב: **בהר"ן** ד"ה ולענין הלכה וכו' דאי תפיס. עיין בתוס' קידושין שם ובדף כו ע"ב ד"ה אלא מאי לדמי:

נ"ל והרמב"ן

מסורת הש"ס

[לעיל ל: וש"נ]

[פסחים ג. וש"נ]

[תוספתא פ"ג]

כמאן מצלינן אקצירי ואמריעי. בכל ימות השנה. כמאן כר' יוסי. דאמר בפ"ק דר"ה (ד' טז.): אדם נדון בכל יום. דאילו לרבנן דאית להו דנדון בר"ה, כיון שנגמר דינן – אין תפלה מועלת להן. קצירי קצירי ממש. חולין, ומיקרו קצירי לפי שנפסק קצרה מחמת חליים. **מתני'** דלא כבבלאי. מתני' דשרי עבה משום דלא מתאכלא בי' ריפתא. דלא כבבלאי. דאילו לבבלאי, כיון דאכלי בהדי ריפתא – תבשיל מיקרי, ואסור. נקרני. שאוכלי' בנקיות. לשון אחר: נקדני, שמדקדקים באכילתן. וכדאמרי' בפ' "שלשה שאכלו" (ברכות דף נ.): הנקדנים תופסין אותו בכך. **דייסא.** מאכל של חטים מבושלים. דחיטי **בלחמא** דחיטי. דרב חסדא מבני בבל היה, שהיו אוכלים פת בדייסא. בחסיסי. קמח של קליות. עד פרסה. לך פרסה כדי לאכול דייסא. לפתילה של **אבר.** שאינו מתעכל. **בהוצא.** בקליפת עץ. **מאכילני** רוקך. שאין דרך לקנח הסולא לאחר שנתנה לתוך פיו כשמחזירה בקערה. **מאכילני צואתך.** צואה שתחת הצפרנים. **בלוספיין.** מין תאנים, שקשין להתעכל. כ"ש שנסמוך עליהן למחר. שמתוך שאין מתעכלין מתעכבין במעים, וכל זמן שעומדין שם – זנין את הגוף. מורה ורוי. בעל הוראה ומשתכר?! שמתוך שראתה פניו צהובין היתה סבור' שנשתכר. כמגדלי חזירי'. שמתוך שמרויחין הרבה פניהם צהובין. **גולפא.** קנקן, והיה מביאו לבית המדרש כדי שישב עליו. שמכבדת את בעליה. שלא היה יושב ע"ג קרקע. דהוטבי. גלימא חשוב'. שעטני מעיל. שהיה חשוב בעיניו כמעיל.

דלי

תורה אור

כְּמַאן מְצַלֵּינַן עַל קְצִירֵי וְעַל מְרֵיעֵי – [כְּמַאן – כר' יוֹסֵי] מִדַּאֲמַר קְצִירֵי וּמְרֵיעֵי, שְׁמַע מִינָּהּ: קְצִירֵי – קְצִירֵי מַמָּשׁ, מְרֵיעֵי – רַבָּנַן. § "וּמוּתָּר בְּעָבֶה". § מַתְנִי' דְּלָא כְּבַבְלָאֵי. *דַּאֲמַר ר' זֵירָא: בַּבְלָאֵי טִפְּשָׁאֵי, דְּאָכְלִי לַחְמָא בְּלַחְמָא. א"ר חִסְדָּא: (א) דְּמַשְׁאִיל לְהוֹן לְהָלֵין נַקְדָּנֵי דְּהוּצַל: הָדֵין דַּיְסָא הֵיכִין מַעֲלֵי לְמֵיכְלָהּ? דְּחִיטֵּי – בְּלַחְמָא דְחִיטֵּי, וּדְשַׂעֲרֵי – בְּלַחְמָא דְשַׂעֲרֵי, אוֹ דִלְמָא: דְחִיטֵּי – בִּדְשַׂעֲרֵי, וּדְשַׂעֲרֵי – בִּדְחִיטֵּי? רָבָא אָכְלֵיהּ בְּחַסִּיסֵי. רַבָּה בַּר רַב הוּנָא אַשְׁכְּחֵי' לְרַב הוּנָא דְּקָאָכֵיל דַּיְסָא בְּאֶצְבְּעָתֵיהּ. אֲמַ' לֵיהּ: אַמַּאי קָאָכֵיל מָר בִּידֵיהּ? א"ל, הָכִי אֲמַר רַב: דַּיְסָא בְּאֶצְבְּעָתָא בְּסִים, וְכָל דְּכֵן בְּתַרְתֵּין, וְכָל דְּכֵן בִּתְלָת. אֲמַר לֵיהּ רַב לְחִיָּיא בְּרֵיהּ, וְכֵן א"ל רַב הוּנָא לְרַבָּה בְּרֵיהּ: מְזַמְּנִים לָךְ לְמֵיכַל דַּיְסָא – עַד פַּרְסָה, לְמֵיכַל בִּישְׂרָא דְתוֹרָא – עַד תְּלָתָא פַּרְסִין. אֲמַר לֵיהּ רַב לְחִיָּיא בְּרֵיהּ, וְכֵן א"ל רַב הוּנָא לְרַבָּה בְּרֵיהּ: *כָּל מִידַּעַם לָא תִּפְלוֹט קַמֵּיהּ רַבָּךְ, לְבַר מִן קָרָא וְדַיְסָא, שֶׁהֵן דּוֹמִין לִפְתִילְתָּא שֶׁל אֵבֶר, וַאֲפִילּוּ קַמֵּי שָׁבוּר מַלְכָּא פְּלוֹט. רַבִּי יוֹסֵי וְרַבִּי יְהוּדָה, חַד אָכֵיל דַּיְסָא בְּאֶצְבְּעָתֵיהּ וְחַד אָכֵיל בְּהוּצָא. א"ל דְּאָכֵיל בְּהוּצָא לִדְאָכֵיל בְּאֶצְבְּעָתֵיהּ: עַד מָתַי אַתָּה מַאֲכִילֵנִי צוֹאָתְךָ! אֲמַר לֵיהּ דְּאָכֵיל בְּאֶצְבְּעָתֵיהּ לִדְאָכֵיל בְּהוּצָא: עַד מָתַי אַתָּה מַאֲכִילֵנִי רוּקְךָ! רַבִּי יְהוּדָה וְרַבִּי שִׁמְעוֹן אַיְיתוּ לְקַמַּיְיהוּ *בְּלוֹסְפַּיִין, רַבִּי יְהוּדָה אֲכַל, ר' שִׁמְעוֹן לָא אֲכַל. א"ל רַבִּי יְהוּדָה: מַאי טַעְמָא לָא אָכֵיל מָר? אֲמַר לֵיהּ ר' שִׁמְעוֹן: אֵלּוּ אֵין יוֹצְאִין מִבְּנֵי מֵעַיִם כָּל עִיקָּר. אֲמַר לֵיהּ רַבִּי יְהוּדָה: כ"ש שֶׁנִּסְמוֹךְ עֲלֵיהֶן לְמָחָר. רַבִּי יְהוּדָה הֲוָה יָתֵיב קַמֵּיהּ דר' טַרְפוֹן. אֲמַר לֵיהּ רַבִּי טַרְפוֹן: הַיּוֹם פָּנֶיךָ צְהוּבִין. אֲמַר לֵיהּ: אֶמֶשׁ יָצְאוּ עֲבָדֶיךָ לַשָּׂדֶה, וְהֵבִיאוּ לָנוּ תְּרָדִין, וַאֲכַלְנוּם בְּלֹא מֶלַח. וְאִם אֲכַלְנוּם בְּמֶלַח – כָּל שֶׁכֵּן שֶׁהָיוּ פָּנֵינוּ צְהוּבִין. אָמְרָה הַהִיא מַטְרוֹנִיתָא לְרַבִּי יְהוּדָה: מוֹרֶה וְרָוֵי?! אֲמַר לָהּ: הֵימְנוּתָא בִּידָא דְּהַהִיא אִיתְּתָא, אִי טָעֵימְנָא אֶלָּא קִידּוּשָׁא וְאַבְדַּלְתָּא וְאַרְבָּעָה כָּסֵי דְּפִסְחָא, וְחוֹגְרַנִי צִידְעַי מִן הַפֶּסַח עַד הָעֲצֶרֶת. אֶלָּא: °"חָכְמַת אָדָם תָּאִיר פָּנָיו". *אֲמַר לֵי' הַהוּא מִינָא לְרַבִּי יְהוּדָה: פָּנֶיךָ דּוֹמִין אִי כְּמַלְוֵי רִבִּית אִי כִּמְגַדְּלֵי חֲזִירִין. א"ל: בִּיהוּדָאֵי תַּרְוַיְיהוּ אֲסִירָן, אֶלָּא עֶשְׂרִים וְאַרְבָּעָה בֵּית הַכִּסֵּא אִית לִי מִן בֵּיתָא עַד בֵּי מִדְרָשָׁא, וְכָל שָׁעָה וְשָׁעָה אֲנִי נִכְנָס לְכָל אֶחָד וְאֶחָד. ר' יְהוּדָה כַּד אָזֵיל לְבֵי מִדְרָשָׁא שָׁקֵיל גּוּלְפָּא עַל כַּתְפֵיהּ, אֲמַר: גְּדוֹלָה מְלָאכָה שֶׁמְּכַבֶּדֶת אֶת בְּעָלֶיהָ. רַבִּי שִׁמְעוֹן שָׁקֵיל צַנָּא עַל כַּתְפֵיהּ, אֲמַר: גְּדוֹלָה מְלָאכָה שֶׁמְּכַבֶּדֶת אֶת בְּעָלֶיהָ. דְּבֵיתְהוּ דְּרַבִּי יְהוּדָה נָפְקַת נָקְטַת עַמְרָא, עָבְדָה גְּלִימָא דְּהוּטְבֵי. כַּד נָפְקַת לְשׁוּקָא מִיכַּסְיָא בֵּיהּ, וְכַד נָפֵיק רַבִּי יְהוּדָה לְצַלּוֹיֵי הֲוָה מְכַסֵּי וּמְצַלֵּי. וְכַד מִיכַּסֵּי בֵּיהּ הֲוָה מְבָרֵךְ "בָּרוּךְ שֶׁעֲטָנִי מְעִיל". זִימְנָא חֲדָא גָּזַר רַבָּן שִׁמְעוֹן בֶּן גַּמְלִיאֵל תַּעֲנִיתָא, ר' יְהוּדָה לָא אֲתָא לְבֵי תַּעֲנִיתָא. אָמְרִין לֵיהּ: לָא אִית לֵיהּ כְּסוּיָא. שְׁדַר לֵיהּ גְּלִימָא וְלָא קַבֵּיל.

דלי

קהלת ח

מְצַלֵּינַן אַקְּצִירֵי. "רוֹפֵא חוֹלֵי עַמּוֹ יִשְׂרָאֵל". מְרֵיעֵי. "עַל פְּלֵיטַת סוֹפְרֵיהֶן". מַתְנִיתִין. דְּקָתָנֵי דְּעָבֶה לָא מִיתְאַכְלָא בְּרִיפְתָּא. דְּלָא כְּבַבְלָאֵי. דִּמְלַפְּתִי פִּיתָּן בְּדַיְיסָא, דְּהָוְיָא עָבָה. נַקְדָּנֵי. דַּיְיקָנִים בְּמַאֲכָל. [הֵיכִין מַעֲלֵי]. בְּאֵיזֶה דָּבָר מְעוּלָּה אֲכִילַת הַדַּיְיסָא. דְּחִיטֵּי. יָכוֹל לְאָכְלָהּ בְּלֶחֶם שֶׁל חִטִּים, וְדַיְיסָא דְּשַׂעֲרֵי יָכוֹל לְאָכְלָהּ בְּלֶחֶם שֶׁל שְׂעוֹרִים. אוֹ דִילְמָא. דַּיְיסָא שֶׁל חִטִּים יָפֶה לֶאֱכוֹל בְּשֶׁל שְׂעוֹרִים, וְשֶׁל שְׂעוֹרִים בְּשֶׁל חִטִּים. וְאִית דְּגָרְסִי "נַקְרָנֵי", מִלָּשׁוֹן "כִּי קָרַן עוֹר פָּנָיו" (שמות לד) – מְלֵאִים חָכְמָה וּמְאִירָה פְּנֵיהֶם, שֶׁנֶּאֱ' "חָכְמַת אָדָם תָּאִיר פָּנָיו". **אָכְלֵהּ בְּחַסִּיסֵי.** הָיָה מְלַפֵּת פִּיתּוֹ בְּחַסִּיסֵי. וּמְפָרֵשׁ לָהּ בְּמַסֶּכֶת פְּסָחִים (דף לט:): קִימְחָא דַּאֲבִישׁוּנָא – קֶמַח שֶׁל קְלָיוֹת שְׂעוֹרִים שֶׁלֹּא הֵבִיאוּ שְׁלִישׁ, וּמְיַיבְּשִׁין אוֹתָן בְּתַנּוּר, וְקִלּוּפֵיהֶן הֵן. מְזַמְּנֵי לָךְ לֶאֱכוֹל דַּיְסָא עַד פַּרְסָה. דַּע שֶׁאוֹתוֹ מַאֲכָל אֵינוֹ סוֹעֵד לִבְּךָ אֶלָּא עַד הִילּוּךְ פַּרְסָה. וּבְשַׂר הַשּׁוֹר עַד שָׁלֹשׁ פַּרְסָאוֹת: ע"א: אִי מְזַמְּנֵי לָךְ לֶאֱכוֹל דַּיְסָא עַד פַּרְסָה. לֵךְ אַחַר דַּיְסָא לֶאֱכוֹל, וּטְפֵי לָא. וְלֶאֱכוֹל בְּשַׂר שׁוֹר – לֵךְ עַד שָׁלֹשׁ פַּרְסָאוֹת. **כָּל מִידַּעַם לָא תִּפְלוֹט קַמֵּי רַבָּךְ.** לֹא תָּרוֹק רוֹק בִּפְנֵי רַבְּךָ, כִּדְאָמַר בְּמַסֶּ' עֵירוּבִין (דף נט.): הָרָק לִפְנֵי רַבּוֹ – חַיָּיב מִיתָה, שֶׁנֶּאֱמַר "וְכָל מְשַׂנְאַי אָהֲבוּ מָוֶת". אֲבָל אִם אָכַלְתָּ דְּלַעַת וְדַיְיסָא וְנִזְדַּמֵּן לָךְ הָרוֹק בְּפִיךָ – פְּלוֹט בִּפְנֵי רַבְּךָ וּזְרוֹק אוֹתוֹ לַחוּץ, שֶׁיֵּשׁ בּוֹ סַכָּנַת נְפָשׁוֹת, שֶׁהֵן קָשִׁין לְגוּפוֹ שֶׁל אָדָם כִּפְתִילָה שֶׁל אֵבֶר. וַאֲפִילּוּ לִפְנֵי שָׁבוּר מַלְכָּא **פְּלוֹט.** וְאַל תִּתְבַּיֵּישׁ. **עַד מָתַי אַתָּה מַאֲכִילֵנִי רוּקְךָ.** שֶׁהָיָה נוֹתֵן הַסּוֹלָא בְּפִיו וּמַדְבִּיק בּוֹ הָרוֹק שֶׁבְּפִיו, וּמַחֲזִירוֹ בַּקְּעָרָה. **צוֹאָתְךָ.** עַפְרוּרִית שֶׁבְּצִפָּרְנָיו. **בְּלוֹסְפַּיִין.** תְּאֵנִים שֶׁנִּתְבַּשְּׁלוּ יוֹתֵר מִדַּאי. בֵּיוָן שֶׁאֵין יוֹצְאִין מִבְּנֵי מֵעַיִם (ב). **כ"ש.** דְּמַעֲלוּ, שֶׁנִּסְמוֹךְ עֲלֵיהֶן, שֶׁאֵין אָנוּ צְרִיכִים לֶאֱכוֹל מַאֲכָל אַחֵר לְמָחָר. **מוֹרֶה וְרָוֵי.** אַתָּה תַּלְמִיד בַּעַל הוֹרָאָה, וְאַתָּה שִׁיכּוֹר?! מִפְּנֵי שֶׁהָיוּ פָּנָיו צְהוּבִּין כָּל שָׁעָה. **הֵימְנוּתָא בִּידָא דְּהַהִיא אִיתְּתָא.** אֱמוּנָתִי בְּיָדֵךְ שֶׁאֵינִי שׁוֹתֶה כָּל הַשָּׁנָה יַיִן אֶלָּא קִידּוּשָׁא וְאַבְדַּלְתָּא. **וְחוֹגֵר אֲנִי צְדָעַי.** וְקוֹשֵׁר אֲנִי לִצְדָעַי פַּדַּחְתִּי מִשּׁוּם מֵיחוּשׁ רֹאשִׁי, מִפְּנֵי ד' כּוֹסוֹת שֶׁשָּׁתִיתִי, שֶׁאֲנִי חוֹשֵׁשׁ מֵהֶן מִפֶּסַח עַד עֲצֶרֶת. **אִי כִּמְלְוֵי בְּרִבִּית כו'.** שֶׁהֵן מַרְוִיחִין בְּיוֹתֵר, וּפְנֵיהֶן צְהוּבִּין וְיָפִין. **תַּרְוַיְיהוּ.** לְגַדֵּל חֲזִירִין וּלְהַלְווֹת בְּרִבִּית אֲסִירֵי לִיהוּדָאֵי, וַדַּאי לָאו מִינַּיְיהוּ פְּנֵי צְהוּבִּין. **שָׁקֵיל גּוּלְפָּא.** הָיָה נוֹשֵׂא הַקַּנְקַן לְבֵית הַמִּדְרָשׁ לֵישֵׁב עָלֶיהָ. **מְלָאכָה שֶׁמְּכַבֶּדֶת כו'.** דְּעַכְשָׁיו יֵשֵׁב עָלֶיהָ בְּבֵית הַמִּדְרָשׁ. **נָפְקַת נָקְטַת עַמְרָא.** יָצְאת לַשּׁוּק וְקָנְתָה לַצֶּמֶר (ג) וְעָבְדָה גְּלִימָא. **דְּהוּטְבֵי.** וְעָשְׂתָה מִמֶּנּוּ סַרְבָּל טוֹב. **וְכַד נָפְקַת.** אִיהִי לְשׁוּקָא הֲוַת מִיכַּסֵּי בֵּיהּ. (ד) וְרַבִּי יְהוּדָה כַּד הֲוָה מְצַלֵּי הֲוָה נַמִי מְכַסֵּי בֵּיהּ. **שֶׁעֲטָנִי מְעִיל.** שֶׁהָיָה לָהֶן חָבִיב כָּל כָּךְ, שֶׁלֹּא הָיָה לָהֶן אַחֵר.

דלי

הגהות הב"ח

(א) גמ' אמר רב חסדא ליכא דמשאיל: (ב) רש"י ד"ה כיון שאין וד"ה כ"ש דמעלו הד"א: (ג) ד"ה נפקת וכו' לצמר הס"ד ואח"כ מ"ה ועבדה גלימא דהוטבי הד"א: (ד) ד"ה וכד נפקת וד"ה ר' יהודא הד"א:

תוספות

כמאן מצלינן האידנא על החולים כר' יוסי. דאמר אדם נדון בכל יום דאילו למאן דאמר דנדון בראש השנה הוי תפלת שוא: **מתני'** דלא כבבלאי דאכלי דייסא בנהמא. וא"כ גם תבשיל עבה אסור לדידהו: **איכא** דמשאיל להני נקרני. פירוש מי ימצא שישאל להני נקיי הדעת כמו נקיר שמיה (פסחים קיח:) וכן לנקר חצירו (ביצה ח:) ויש מפרשין נקדני כמו (ברכות נ.) הנקדנין תופסים אותו ע"כ וכל המדקד' בדברי' נקרא נקדן: **בחסיסי.** קמח של קליות וכן פר"י (פרק כל שעה ד' לט) ור"ח פירש קמח של עדשים ופירושו נראה יותר דלפרש"י היה לו לקרותו קימחא דאבישונא ועוד אמר פ' כל שעה ממחו ליה קדרה בחסיסי ואי קימחא דאבשונא הא אמר לעיל מנייה בהדיא פירקא דאסור: **לפלוט.** כלומר אם יצטרך לרוק ירוק ואל יניח בשביל כבוד רבו: **בלוספיין.** מין תאנים רעים: **כל** שכן דנסמוך עליהם למחר. שלא יתעכלו מהר וכל זמן שהמאכל בתוך הבני מעיים הלב נסעד: **וחוגרני** לצדעי. פירוש חוגר וקושר היה לצדעיו לפי שהיה חש בראשו על היין ששתה בפסח: **שקיל** גולפא. לישב בבית המדרש: **שמכבדת** בעליה. שלא אצטרך לישב על גבי קרקע: **שעטני** מעיל. חשוב היה לו כמעיל

דלי

פי' הרא"ש

כמאן מצלינן אמריעי ואקצירי כר' יוסי. דאמר אין אדם נדון בר"ה: **מריעי רבנן.** מרוב גרסתם חלשי: **מתני' דלא כבבלאי.** דלדידהו אפי' עבה מיקרי תבשיל: **נקרני דהולל.** נקיי הדעת כמו המנקר חצרו: **בחסיסי.** קמח של קליות: **באצבעתא בסים.** האוכל באצבע אחד הוא טוב וכ"ש שכן בשתי אצבעות או בשלש: **למיכל דייסא עד פרסה.** לך שמה: **כל מדעם לא תפלוט.** כל מאכל שאכלת פס אתה יושב לפני רבך ויש לך רוק בתוך פיך תבלענו ולא תפלוט אותו לפני רבך: **לבר מקרא ודייסא שדומין לפתילה של אבר.** הבולע רוקו אחר שאכלם: **מאכילני רוקך.** הנדבק בסולא אבל אצבעו היה מקנח מן הרוק: **מאכילני צואתך.** שבין צפורן לבשר: **בלוספיין.** מין תאנים: **מורה ורוי.** בעל הוראה כמותך ישתכר: **וחוגרני לצדעי.** מכאב הראש: **שקיל גולפא אכתפיה.** חבית לישב עליה בבית המדרש: **נקטת עמרא.** לקחה צמר: **שעטני מעיל.** שהיה חשוב עליו כמעיל:

דלי

ביצה טז. ע"ש

[תמיד כז:]

[נ"ל בלוספין וער' לקמן נ: היה עושה וכו']

ברכות נה. ע"ש

דְּלִי צִיפְתָּא, וַאֲמַר לֵיהּ לִשְׁלוּחָא: חֲזִי מַאי אִיכָּא. מִיהוּ, לָא נִיחָא לִי דְּאִיתְהַנֵּי בְּהָדֵין עָלְמָא. *ר' עֲקִיבָא אִיתְקַדְּשַׁתְּ לֵיהּ בְּרַתֵּיהּ (דְּבַר) דְּכַלְבָּא שָׂבוּעַ, שָׁמַע (בַּר) כַּלְבָּא שָׂבוּעַ אַדְּרַהּ הֲנָאָה מִכָּל נִכְסֵיהּ. אָזְלָא וְאִיתְנְסִיבָה לֵיהּ. בְּסִיתְוָא הֲוָה גָּנוּ בֵּי תִּיבְנָא, הֲוָה קָא מַנְקֵיט לַהּ תִּיבְנָא מִן מַזְיַיהּ. אֲמַר לָהּ: אִי הֲוַאי לִי — רָמֵינָא לִיךְ יְרוּשָׁלַיִם דְּדַהֲבָא. אֲתָא אֵלִיָּהוּ אִידַּמֵּי לְהוֹן כְּאֶינָשָׁא, וְקָא קָרֵי אַבָּבָא, אֲמַר לְהוּ: הֲבוּ לִי פּוּרְתָּא דְּתִיבְנָא, דִּילְדַת אִתְּתִי וְלֵית לִי מִידַּעַם לְאַגּוּנַהּ. אֲמַר לָהּ ר' עֲקִיבָא לְאִנְתְּתֵיהּ: חֲזִי גַּבְרָא דַּאֲפִילּוּ תִּיבְנָא לָא אִית לֵיהּ. אָמְרָה לֵיהּ: זִיל הֱוֵי בֵּי רַב. אֲזַל (א) תַּרְתֵּי סְרֵי שְׁנִין קַמֵּי דר' אֱלִיעֶזֶר ור' יְהוֹשֻׁעַ. לְמִישְׁלַם תַּרְתֵּי סְרֵי שְׁנִין, קָא אָתָא לְבֵיתֵיהּ, שָׁמַע מִן אֲחוֹרֵי בֵּיתֵיהּ דְּקָאָמַר לַהּ חַד רָשָׁע לִדְבֵיתְהוּ: שַׁפִּיר עָבֵיד לִיךְ אֲבוּךְ; חֲדָא — דְּלָא דָּמֵי לִיךְ, וְעוֹד (ב) [שְׁבַקִּךְ] אַרְמְלוּת חַיּוּת כּוּלְּהוֹן שְׁנִין. אָמְרָה לֵיהּ: אִי צָאֵית לְדִילִי — לֶיהֱוֵי תַּרְתֵּי סְרֵי שְׁנִין אַחֲרָנְיָיתָא. אֲמַר: הוֹאִיל וִיהַבַת לִי רְשׁוּתָא — אִיהֲדַר לַאֲחוֹרַי. הֲדַר אֲזַל הֲוָה תַּרְתֵּי סְרֵי שְׁנֵי אַחֲרָנְיָיתָא. אֲתָא בְּעֶשְׂרִין וְאַרְבָּעָה אַלְפִין *זוּגֵי תַּלְמִידֵי. נְפוּק כּוּלֵּי עָלְמָא לְאַפֵּיהּ, וְאַף הִיא קָמַת לְמֵיפַּק לְאַפֵּיהּ. אֲמַר לָהּ הַהוּא רְשִׁיעָא: וְאַתְּ לְהֵיכָא? אָמְרָה לֵיהּ: °"יוֹדֵעַ צַדִּיק נֶפֶשׁ בְּהֶמְתּוֹ". אֲתַת לְאִיתַחֲזוֹיֵי לֵיהּ, קָא מַדְחָן לַהּ רַבָּנַן. אֲמַר לְהוֹן: הַנִּיחוּ לָהּ, שֶׁלִּי וְשֶׁלָּכֶם שֶׁלָּהּ הוּא. שָׁמַע (בַּר) כַּלְבָּא שָׂבוּעַ, אֲתָא וְאִיתְשִׁיל עַל נִדְרֵיהּ *וְאִשְׁתְּרַיי וְאִשְׁתְּרִי. (ג) מִן שִׁית מִילֵּי אִיעֲתַר רַבִּי עֲקִיבָא: מִן כַּלְבָּא שָׂבוּעַ, מִן אֵילָא דִּסְפִינְתָּא — דְּכָל סְפִינְתָּא עָבְדִין לֵיהּ (ד) מִין עֵינָא, זִימְנָא חֲדָא אַנְשְׁיוּהּ עַל כֵּיף יַמָּא, אֲתָא הוּא אַשְׁכְּחֵיהּ. וּמִן גַּוְוזָא — דְּזִימְנָא חֲדָא יְהֵיב אַרְבָּעָה זוּזֵי לְסַפּוּנָאֵי, אֲמַר לְהוּ: אַיְיתֵי לִי מִדַּעַם, וְלָא אַשְׁכְּחוּ אֶלָּא גַּוְוזָא עַל כֵּיף יַמָּא. אַתְיוּהּ לֵיהּ, אָמְרוּ לֵיהּ: (ה) עָבֵיד מָרָנָא עֲלֵיהּ. אִישְׁתַּכַּח דַּהֲוָה מְלֵי דִּינָרֵי, דְּזִימְנָא חֲדָא טָבְעַת סְפִינְתָּא (ו) וְכוּלֵּי עִיסְקָא הֲוָה מָחֵית בְּהַהוּא גַּוְוזָא, וְאִישְׁתַּכַּח בְּהַהוּא זִימְנָא. דְּמִן *דִּסְרוּקִיתָא, וּמִן מַטְרוֹנִיתָא, וּמִן

משלי יב

רש"י

דְּלִי צִיפְתָּא. הִגְבִּיהַּ הַמַּחְצֶלֶת שֶׁהָיָה יוֹשֵׁב עָלֶיהָ. וַאֲמַר לֵיהּ לִשְׁלוּחָא. דַּאֲזַל לְבֵיתֵיהּ. חֲזִי מַאי אִיכָּא. רְאֵה כַּמָּה עוֹשֶׁר יֵשׁ לִי. שֶׁנַּעֲשָׂה לוֹ נֵס וְנִתְמַלֵּא כָּל אוֹתוֹ מָקוֹם זְהוּבִים. וְאִיתְנְסִיבַת לֵיהּ בְּסִיתְוָא. בִּימוֹת הַחוֹרֶף. הֲוָה גָּנוּ בֵּי תִּיבְנָא. הָיוּ יְשֵׁנִים בֵּין הַתֶּבֶן. שֶׁלֹּא הָיוּ לָהֶם כָּרִים וּכְסָתוֹת. קָא מַנְקֵיט לֵיהּ תורה אור תִּיבְנָא מִן מַזְיֵיהּ. הָיָה מְלַקֵּט הַתֶּבֶן מִשְּׂעָרוֹ. אִי הֲוֵי לִי רָמֵינָא לָךְ יְרוּשָׁלַיִם דְּדַהֲבָא. אִם יִהְיֶה לִי סִיפּוּק, שֶׁאֶתְעַשֵּׁר – אֶעֱשֶׂה לָךְ יְרוּשָׁלַיִם שֶׁל זָהָב. בָּתֵּי נֶפֶשׁ שֶׁמְּצוּיֶּרֶת בְּכָל עִנְיְינֵי יְרוּשָׁלַיִם. וְהַיְינוּ דְּאָמְרִינַן בְּמַסֶּכֶת שַׁבָּת (דף נט.): עִיר יְרוּשָׁלַיִם שֶׁל זָהָב, כְּדַעֲבַד לַיהּ רַבִּי עֲקִיבָא לִדְבֵיתְהוּ. אֲתָא אֵלִיָּהוּ קָרָא אַבָּבָא וכו'. עֲבַד הָכִי מִשּׁוּם קוֹרַת רוּחַ לָהֶן. דִּלְדִידֵיהּ לֹא הָיָה לוֹ אֲפִילּוּ תֶּבֶן כְּמוֹ לָהֶם. שַׁפִּיר עֲבֵיד לֵיךְ אֲבוּךְ. דְּמַדְּרֵיךְ מִנִּכְסֵיהּ. חֲדָא דְּלָא דָּמֵי לָךְ. שֶׁהוּא גָּרוּעַ מִמֵּךְ. וְעוֹד שֶׁמַּנִּיחֵךְ בְּאַלְמְנוּת חַיּוּת, שֶׁהֲרֵי הִנִּיחֵךְ כַּמָּה שָׁנִים (ז). יוֹדֵעַ צַדִּיק נֶפֶשׁ בְּהֶמְתּוֹ. אִית דְּאָמְרֵי דְּאִיהִי הֲוַת יָדְעָה דְּר' עֲקִיבָא הֲוָה, וְאָמְרָה לֵיהּ דְּלָא מִיתְגַּנְיָא בְּעֵינֵיהּ. וְאִית דְּאָמְרֵי דְּלָא הֲוַת יָדְעָה, אֶלָּא הָכִי קָא אָמְרָה: דְּצַדִּיק לֹא מְבַזֶּה לַאֲנָשָׁיו. שֶׁלִּי וְשֶׁלָּכֶם שֶׁלָּהּ הִיא. עַל יָדָהּ הוּא כָּל מַה שֶּׁלָּמַדְתִּי. מִן שִׁית מִילֵּי אִיעֲתַר רַבִּי עֲקִיבָא מִן כַּלְבָּא שָׂבוּעַ. דְּפָלֵיג לֵיהּ בְּנִכְסֵיהּ. וּמִן אֵילָא דִּסְפִינְתָּא דְּכָל סְפִינְתָּא עָבְדִין לֵיהּ מִן עֵינָא. עוֹשִׂין לָהֶן (ח) מִן אוֹתוֹ עִנְיָן שֶׁל אַיִל. וְאִית דְּגָרְסִי: מִין עַיְינָא. הָיוּ עוֹשִׂין כְּמִין צֹאן שֶׁל עֵץ, וְהָיוּ נוֹתְנִים בּוֹ כַּסְפָּם. אַנְשִׁיוּהּ עַל כֵּיף יַמָּא. שֶׁשָּׁכְחוּ לְאוֹתוֹ אַיִל עַל שְׂפַת הַיָּם, וּמְצָאוֹ רַבִּי עֲקִיבָא. וּמִן גַּוְוזָא. תֵּיבָה. אַרְבָּעָה זוּזֵי לְסַפּוּנָאֵי. לְיוֹרְדֵי הַיָּם לְרֵיוַח. אַיְיתוּ לִי מִדַּעַם. הָבִיאוּ לִי שׁוּם דָּבָר: (ט) מָרְנָא עֲלֵיהּ. יַמְתִּין אֲדוֹנֵינוּ עָלָיו עַד שֶׁנָּבִיא לָךְ יוֹתֵר. דְּזִימְנָא חֲדָא טָבְעָה סְפִינְתָּא. וְכָל מָמוֹנָא דַּהֲוָה בִּסְפִינְתָּא הֲוָה מוּנָּח בְּהַהוּא גַּוְוזָא. וּמִן מַטְרוֹנִיתָא. שֶׁפַּעַם אַחַת הוּצְרְכוּ חֲכָמִים מָמוֹן הַרְבֵּה לְבֵית הַמִּדְרָשׁ, וְשִׁיגְּרוּ אֶת ר' עֲקִיבָא אֵצֶל מַטְרוֹנִיתָא אַחַת, וְלָוָה מִמֶּנָּה מָמוֹן גָּדוֹל. וּכְשֶׁנָּתְנָה לוֹ אָמְרָה לוֹ: מִי יִהְיֶה לִי עָרֵב שֶׁתִּפְרַע לִי לִזְמַן קָבוּעַ? אָמַר לָהּ: מִי שֶׁתִּרְצֶה. אָמְרָה לוֹ: הקב"ה וְהַיָּם, שֶׁהָיָה בֵּיתָהּ עַל שְׂפַת הַיָּם. אָמַר לָהּ ר"ע: כֵּן יִהְיֶה. כְּשֶׁהִגִּיעַ הַזְּמַן חָלָה ר"ע וְלֹא הָיָה יָכוֹל לְהָבִיא הַמָּמוֹן, יָצְאת אוֹתָהּ מַטְרוֹנִיתָא עַל שְׂפַת הַיָּם, וְאָמְרָה: רבש"ע, גָּלוּי וְיָדוּעַ לְפָנֶיךָ כִּי לְךָ וְלַיָּם הַזֶּה הֶאֱמַנְתִּי מְעוֹתַי. הִכְנִיס הקב"ה רוּחַ שְׁטוּת בְּלִבּוֹ שֶׁל [בַּת] קֵיסָר, וְנִכְנַס' לְבֵית גְּנָזָיו וְנָטְלָה קַרְטָלִית וְזָרְקָה לַיָּם, וְהִשְׁלִיכָהּ הַיָּם לְפֶתַח בֵּיתָהּ שֶׁל אוֹתָהּ מַטְרוֹנִיתָא וּנְטָלַתָּהּ. וּלְאַחַר זְמַן הֵבִיא לָהּ ר' עֲקִיבָא הַמָּמוֹן, וְאָמַר לָהּ: אַל יֵחַר לֵיךְ שֶׁלֹּא הֵבֵאתִי לָךְ הַמָּמוֹן בִּזְּמַן שֶׁקָּבַעְנוּ, שֶׁחָלִיתִי. אָמְרָה לוֹ: יְהֵא הַכֹּל שֶׁלָּךְ, שֶׁמָּמוֹנִי בָּא לְיָדִי בִּזְמַנּוֹ. וְסִפְּרָה לוֹ כָּל הַמַּעֲשֶׂה, וְנָתְנָה לוֹ מַתָּנוֹת גְּדוֹלוֹת, וּפְטָרַתּוּ לְשָׁלוֹם. וּמִן

ר"ן

דלי ציפתא. מחללת. חזי מאי איכא. מעשה נסים הוה נקיט. מן מזייה. היה מלקט התבן משערותיה. רמינא לך ירושלים דדהבא. תכשיט של זהב שירושלים מצוייר בה. והכי עבד לה, כדאיתא בפרק "במה אשה" (שבת דף נט.). אתא אליהו אדמי להון כאנשא. כדי לנחם אותם, ולהראות להם שיש עניים יותר מהם. דלא דמי לך. שאינו דומה לך, ממשפחה חשובה כמותך. ואת להיכא. שלא היו לה בגדים ראויים. יודע צדיק נפש בהמתו. יודע הוא זה שנצטערתי בשבילו. שלי ושלכם שלה הוא. תורתי ותורתכם בשבילה. היא שנתנה לי עצה למיזל לבי רב. אילא דספינתא. בכל ספינה היו עושין דמות איל מעץ, לנחש ולסימן שתהא הספינה קלה בהליכתה כאיל, והיו ממלאין אותו דינרי זהב. ומן גוזא. תיבה העשויה להצניע בתוכה ממון הספינה, כדאמרינן (ר"ה ו.) בי גזא דרחמנא – לשון אוצר. ומן מטרוניתא. פעם אחת הוצרכו ר"ע ותלמידיו מעות, והלכו אצל מטרוניתא. אמרה לו לר"ע: הריני מלווה אותך, ותהיה אתה לווה והקב"ה והים ערבים בדבר. קבע לה זמן לפרעון. וכשהגיע זמנה הלכה אותה מטרוניתא על שפת הים, אמרה: רבש"ע, גלוי וידוע לפניך שר"ע חולה, ולא היה בידו לפרוע חובו – ראה שאתה ערב בדבר. מיד נשטטית בתו של קיסר ונטלה ארגז מלא אבנים טובות ודינרי זהב, וזרקה לתוך הים, והים הביאתו במקום שהיתה אותה מטרוניתא יושבת על שפת הים. מיד נטלה אותו ארגז והלכה לה. לימים נתרפא ר"ע ובא לו אצל ההיא מטרוניתא ומעותיו בידו לפרעון חובו. אמרה לו: חזרתי אצל הערב, והוא פרע כל החוב, והא לך מה שנתן לי יותר. ומאותו ממון שהחזירה לו נתעשר ר"ע. ומן

[בע"י ליתא]

תוספות

דלי ציפתא. פירוש הגביה המחצלת וסמך שימצא שם מעות הרבה בנס: גני בתיבנא. מחמת עוני: מנקיט ליה תיבנא. ממה שנאחז לו בשערו: רמינא ליך ירושלים דדהבא. וכן עשה כדאיתא בשבת (דף נט.): דלא דמי ליך. אינו ראוי והגון לך: אילא דספינתא. כל הספינות עושין להם איל של זהב: ומן מטרונית'. פעם אחת הוצרכו תלמידי רבי עקיבא למעות הלכו אצל מטרוניתא ללוות ממנה אמרה להם איני מאמנת אמר לה רבי עקיבא מי את חפצה שאתן ליך ערב אמרה לו מי שאמר והיה העולם וים הגדול וכשהגיע הזמן חלה רבי עקיבא ולא בא הלכה על שפת הים אמרה רבש"ע היום חלה רבי עקיבא עבדך והוא העמידך ערב לי מה עשה הקב"ה באותו היום נשטית בת קיסר ונטלה קופסא מליאה כסף וזהב והטילה לים וצפה ובאת לאותו מקום ונטלה אותו ומצאה בה ממון גדול וכשנתרפא רבי עקיבא בא אצלה ואמר גלוי וידוע לפני מי שאמר והיה העולם שחליתי באותו הזמן עכשיו הרי כל ממונך בידי וסיפרה לו כל המעשה והכניסתו בבית גנזיה ונתנה לו מתנות גדולות:

כתובות סב: [וע"ש כמה שינויים]

הגהות הב"ח

(א) גמ' אזל הוה תרתי סרי: (ב) שם ועוד שבקיך לארמלות חיות: (ג) שם מאשתרי מן נכסיה מן שית מילי: (ד) שם עבדין ליה חד מן עינא: (ה) שם אמרו ליה יעביד מרנא: (ו) שם טבעת ספינתא דמן לסרוקיתא וכוליה עיסקא וכו' בההוא זימנא יהון מטרוניתא כו"ל: (ז) רש"י ד"ה חדא דלא וכו' שנים הס"ד ואח"כ מ"ה ואת להיכא שלא היה לה בגדים ראויים הס"ד: (ח) ד"ה ומן אילא וכו' עושין להן אותו מין ענין של איל ואית דגרסי מין עינא היו עושין: (ט) ד"ה איתיו וכו' דבר הס"ד ואח"כ מ"ה יעביד מרנא:

[כתובות ליתא וכן משמע ביבמות סב: ע"ש]

[בערוך ערך סרק אורחת ישמעאלים תרגום ירושלמי סיען דסרקאי]

פי' הרא"ש

דלי ציפתא. הגביה המחצלת וסמך על הנס שיראה שם מעות. דכלבא שבוע. עשיר גדול היה כדאיתא בפרק הניזקין (גיטין דף נו.). רמינא לך ירושלים דדהבא. אם יהיה לי סיפוק אעשה ליך ירושלים של זהב עטרה הנקראת עיר של זהב על שם שהיו מצויירין לה ירושלים בה כדאיתא בפרק במה אשה (ד' נט.): אתא אליהו כו'. כדי לנחמם מצער הסרונם: מן ענא. עושין איל של זהב או עז אחד ממין הצאן: גוזא. תחיכת עץ גדול: מן מטרוניתא. פעם אחת הוצרכו ישראל ללות מעות ולוה אותם ר' עקיבא ממטרוניתא אחת אמרה לו מי שאמר והיה העולם והים הגדול יהיו ערבים שלי כשהגיע זמן הפרעון חלה ר"ע הלכה ועמדה על שפת הים ואמרה ידעתי שאלמלא שעכבו אונס את ר"ע היה פורע בזמנו מי שאמר והיה העולם והים ישלימו ערבותם מה עשה הקב"ה שלח רוח שטות בבתו של קיסר ונטלה קופסא מלאה זהב ומרגליות ושלחה על פני המים והרוח הביאתה לפני אותה מטרוניתא ונטלתה וכשעמד ר"ע מחליו נטל בידו הממון והביאו לה אמרה לו כבר פרעו לי ערביך לקחה

וּמִן אִשְׁתּוֹ שֶׁל טוּרְנוּסְרוּפוּס, וּמִן קְטִיעָא בַּר שָׁלוֹם.§ רַב גַּמְדָּא יָהֵיב ד' זוּזֵי לְסַפּוּנָאֵי לְאַתּוּיֵי בְּהוֹן מִידַּעַם, לָא אַשְׁכָּחוּ. אַתְיוּהּ לֵיהּ בְּהוֹן קוֹפָא. אִישְׁתַּמִּיט, עַל (א) לְחַרְתָּא, חָפְרוּ בָּתְרֵיהּ, אַשְׁכַּחוּהּ דִּרְבִיעַ עַל מַרְגָּלְיָיתָא, אַיְיתִינוּן לֵיהּ כּוּלְּהוֹן. *אָמְרָה לֵיהּ בַּת קֵיסָר לְרַבִּי יְהוֹשֻׁעַ בֶּן חֲנַנְיָה: *תּוֹרָה מְפוֹאָרָה בִּכְלִי מְכוֹעָר! א"ל: לְמְדִי מִבֵּית אָבוּךְ, בַּמֶּה מַנִּיחִין יַיִן? אָמְרָה לֵיהּ: בְּמָאנֵי דְּפַחְרָא. אֲמַר לָהּ: כּוּלֵּי עָלְמָא בְּפַחְרָא וְאַתּוּן בְּמָאנֵי דְּפַחְרָא?! אַתּוּן אַחִיתוּן בְּמָאנֵי דְּכַסְפָּא וְדַהֲבָא! אָזְלַתְּ וּרְמַתְּ חַמְרָא בְּמָאנֵי דְּכַסְפָּא וְדַהֲבָא, וּסְרִי. אֲמַר לָהּ: אַף אוֹרַיְיתָא כֵּן. (ב) וְהָאִיכָּא שַׁפִּירִין וּגְמִירִין! אֲמַר לָהּ: אִי הָווּ סְנוּ — הָווּ גְּמִירִין טְפֵי. הַהִיא דְּאָתְיָא לְקַמֵּיהּ דְּרַב יְהוּדָה מִנְּהַרְדְּעָא לְדִינָא, וְאִיתְחַיְּיבַתְּ מִן דִּינָא. אָמְרָה לֵיהּ: שְׁמוּאֵל רַבָּךְ הָכִי דָּנַן?! אֲמַר לָהּ: יָדַעַתְּ לֵיהּ? אָמְרָה לֵיהּ: אִין. גּוּצָא, וְרַבָּה כְּרֵיסֵיהּ, אוּכָּם וְרַבָּה שִׁינֵּיהּ. אֲמַר לָהּ: לְבַזּוּיֵיהּ קָאָתֵית? תֶּיהֱוֵי הַהִיא אִתְּתָא בְּשַׁמְתָּא! פָּקְעָה וּמֵתָה.§ "וּמוּתָּר בְּבֵיצָה טוּרְמִיטָא".§ מַאי בֵּיצָה טוּרְמִיטָא? אֲמַר שְׁמוּאֵל: עַבְדָּא דְּעָבֵיד לָהּ שָׁוֵי אַלְפָּא דִּינָרֵי, (ג) וּמְעַיֵּיל לָהּ אַלְפָּא זִימְנֵי בְּמַיָּא חֲמִימֵי, וְאַלְפָּא זִימְנֵי בְּמַיָּא קְרִירֵי, עַד דְּמִתְזוּטְרָא כִּי הֵיכִי דְּבָלְעִיתָהּ. וְאִם אִית (ד) כִּיבָא — סָרִיךְ עֲלָהּ, וְכַד נָפְקָא וְאָתְיָא — יָדַע אָסְיָא מַאי סַמָּא מִתְבָּעֵי לֵיהּ וּבְמַאי מִתַּסֵּי. שְׁמוּאֵל הֲוָה בָּדֵיק נַפְשֵׁיהּ *בְּקוּלְחָא עַד דְּמִסְתַּרִין אֱינָשֵׁי בֵּיתֵיהּ עֲלֵיהּ שַׂעֲרֵיהוֹן. תְּנַן הָתָם: *אהָיָה עוֹשֶׂה בִּכְלוּפְסִין — לֹא יֹאכַל בִּבְנוֹת שֶׁבַע, בִּבְנוֹת שֶׁבַע — לֹא יֹאכַל בִּכְלוּפְסִין. מַאי כְּלוּפְסִין? מִינָא דִּתְאֵינֵי דְּעָבְדִין מִנְּהוֹן לְפְדֵי. הַהוּא גַּבְרָא דִּיהַב עַבְדָּא לְחַבְרֵיהּ לְאַגְמוּרֵיהּ אַלְפָּא מִינֵי לִפְדֵי, אַגְמְרֵיהּ תַּמְנֵי מְאָה. אַזְמְנֵיהּ לְדִינָא לְקַמֵּיהּ דְּרַבִּי. אָמַר רַבִּי: אֲבוֹתֵינוּ אָמְרוּ "נָשִׁינוּ טוֹבָה", אָנוּ — אֲפִילּוּ בְּעֵינֵינוּ לֹא רָאִינוּ. רַבִּי עֲבַד לֵיהּ הִלּוּלָא לר"ש *בְּרַבִּי. כְּתַב עַל בֵּית גְּנָנָא: עֶשְׂרִין וְאַרְבְּעָה אַלְפִּין רִיבּוֹאִין דִּינָרִין נְפַקוּ עַל בֵּית גְּנָנָא דֵּין, וְלָא אַזְמְנֵיהּ לְבַר קַפָּרָא. •אֲמַר לֵיהּ: אִם לְעוֹבְרֵי רְצוֹנוֹ כָּךְ — לְעוֹשֵׂי רְצוֹנוֹ עַל אַחַת כַּמָּה וְכַמָּה. אַזְמְנֵיהּ, אֲמַר: לְעוֹשֵׂי רְצוֹנוֹ בָּעוֹלָם הַזֶּה כָּךְ — לעוה"ב עאכ"ו.§ יוֹמָא דְּמְחַיֵּיךְ בֵּיהּ רַבִּי, אָתְיָא פּוּרְעֲנוּתָא לְעָלְמָא. א"ל לְבַר קַפָּרָא: לָא תְּבַדְּחָן, וְיָהֵיבְנָא לָךְ אַרְבְּעִין גְּרִיוֵי חִיטֵּי. א"ל: לֶיחֱזֵי מָר

דְּכָל

ר"נ

ומן אשתו של טורנוסרופוס. שהיה ר"ע מקפחו בקראי בפני קיסר ומקנתרו בדברים. פעם אחת בא לביתו סר וזעף, אמרה לו אשתו: מפני מה פניך זועפים? אמר לה: מפני ר"ע שמקנטר אותי בכל יום בדברים. אמרה לו: אלהיהם של אלו שונא זמה הוא, תן לי רשות ואכשיל אותו בדבר עבירה. נתן לה רשות, ונתקשטה והלכה לה אצל ר"ע. כשראה ר"ע אותה, רק שחק ובכה. אמרה לו: מה אינון הנך תלת מילין? אמר לה: שנים אפרש, שלישי לא אפרש. רקקתי – על שבאת מטיפה סרוחה, בכיתי – על האי שופרא דבלי בארעא. והוא שחק – שצפה ברוח הקדש שעתידה להתגייר ולהנשא לו, ולא רצה להודיעה. אמרה לו: כלום יש תשובה? אמר לה: הן. הלכה ונתגיירה, ונשאת לו לר"ע, והכניסה לו ממון הרבה. האי דקטיעא בר שלום מפורש בע"ז (דף י:). *ודאמרן הכא דשמע אבוה ואתשיל על נדרה – מפרש בכתובות בפ' "אע"פ" (דף סג.) דפתח ליה: אילו הוית ידיע דההוא חתנך גורבא מרבנן מי אדרתיה? אמר לו: אפי' פרק אחד, אפילו הלכה אחת. איכא לאקשויי: היכי פתח ליה בהא פתחא? והא נולד הוא, ותנן לקמן בפ' "פותחין" (דף סד.) דאין פותחין בנולד, כילד? אמר "קונם שאני נהנה לאיש פלוני" ונעשה סופר, ואמר: אילו הייתי יודע שיעשה סופר – לא הייתי נודר! יש לומר: דשאני הכא, דר"ע על דעת שיעשה סופר נשאה, כדאיתא התם בפ' "אע"פ" בהדיא, וכיון שכן – לאו נולד הוא, דשכיח טובא שילמוד פרק אחד והלכה אחת. רב גמדא וכו' קופא. קוף. אשתמיט. ברח, ונכנס בתוך חור אחד. אייתינון ליה כולהון. ממדת חסידות, ולא מן הדין: וסרי. נתקלקל היין. אי הוו סנו. טפי הוו גמירין, שלא יהו נאים. כי היכי דבלע יתה. כשיעור שאדם יכול לבלעה כאחת בלא לעיסה. סריך עלה. הכאב היה נאחז ונסרך בבילה. וכד נפקא ואתיא. כשהיתה יוצאה מן הגוף. ידע אסיא מאי סמא מתבעי ליה. לפי מראה שבה היה מכיר הרופא באיזה סם יתרפא החולי. בקולחא. לא ידעתי מה הוא. ולפי שלא היה בקי שמואל בבילה טורמיטא היה בודק עצמו בקולחא. עד דמסתרין אינשי ביתיה עליה שעריהון. שכל כך היה אותו קולחא בודק אותו עד שהיה שמואל מתעלף, ואינשי ביתיה, מתוך צערן היו סותרות קליעת שער שלהן. היה עושה בכלופסין. מין תאנים. לא יאכל בבנות שבע. מין אחר של תאנים. ומש"ה לא יאכל – שאין לו לפועל לאכול אלא מאותו מין ממש שעושה בו. לפדי. שם תבשיל של תאנים. אבותינו אמרו נשינו טובה. כדכתיב (איכה ג) "נשיתי טובה". היה תמה על שהוא כל כך במיני תענוג. נפקו על בית גננא דין. להוצאת הנישואין:

דיקולא

רש"י

וּמִן אִשְׁתּוֹ שֶׁל טוּרְנוּסְרוּפוּס. אָדוֹן אֶחָד שֶׁשְּׁמוֹ רוּפוּס, וְהָיָה מְפַטְפֵּט בְּדִבְרֵי תּוֹרָה כְּנֶגֶד ר"ע, וְהָיָה ר"ע מְנַצְּחוֹ בְּכָל פַּעַם. וְהָיָה אוֹתוֹ אָדוֹן מִתְבַּיֵּשׁ, וּבָא וְסִיפֵּר לְאִשְׁתּוֹ. אָמְרָה לוֹ: אֲנִי אֲפַתֵּהוּ וְאַכְשִׁילֵהוּ, לְפִי שֶׁהָיְתָה יְפַת תּוֹאַר בְּיוֹתֵר. בָּאתָה אֶצְלוֹ וְגִילְּתָה שׁוֹקָהּ כְּנֶגְדוֹ, וְרָק ר"ע וְשָׂחַק וּבָכָה. אָמְרָה לוֹ: מַדּוּעַ עָשִׂיתָ כֵּן? אָמַר לָהּ: הַשְּׁנַיִם אוֹמַר לָךְ: מַה שֶּׁרָקַקְתִּי – בִּשְׁבִיל שֶׁמִּטִּיפָּה סְרוּחָה בָּאת; וּבָכִיתִי – בִּשְׁבִיל שֶׁיּוֹפְיֵךְ עָתִיד לִבְלוֹת בָּאָרֶץ. וּמַה שֶּׂשָּׂחַק – לֹא רָצָה לוֹמַר לָהּ. אעפ"כ הִפְצִירָה בּוֹ, עַד שֶׁאָמַר לָהּ שֶׁעֲתִידָה לְהִתְגַּיֵּיר וְתִנָּשֵׂא לוֹ. אָמְרָה לוֹ: וְכִי יֵשׁ תְּשׁוּבָה? אָמַר לָהּ: הֵן. וְנִתְגַּיְּירָה לְאַחַר שֶׁמֵּת בַּעְלָהּ, וְנִשֵּׂאת לוֹ, וְהֵבִיאָה לוֹ מָמוֹן גָּדוֹל. מִן קְטִיעָא בַּר שָׁלוֹם. מְפוֹרָשׁ בְּמַסֶּכֶת ע"ז בְּפ"ק (דף י:). קוֹפָא. קוֹף. עַל לְחַרְתָּא. נִכְנַס הַקּוֹף בְּחוֹר אֶחָד בַּקַּרְקַע. רְבִיעַ. רוֹבֵץ. הָכִי דָּנַן. כְּמוֹ שֶׁדַּנְתַּנִי אַתָּה? בִּתְמִיָּה. יָדַעַתְּ לֵיהּ. מַכֶּרֶת אוֹתוֹ? וְרַבָּה כְּרֵיסֵיהּ. בֶּטֶן גָּדוֹל יֵשׁ לוֹ. טוּרְמִיטָא עַבְדָּא דְּעָבֵיד לֵיהּ. לְהַהִיא בֵּיצָה טוּרְמִיטָא, שָׁוֵי אַלְפָּא זוּזֵי. עַד דְּמִתְזוּטְרָא. שֶׁמִּתְמַעֶטֶת, כְּדֵי שֶׁיָּכוֹל לְבוֹלְעָהּ שְׁלֵימָה. וְאִי אִית בֵּיהּ כִּיבָא. בְּמֵעָיו – סָרִיךְ עָלֶיהָ עַל הַהִיא בֵּיצָה, וְנִיכָּר בָּהּ. וְכִדְנָפְקָא מִמֵּעָיו. שְׁלֵימָה, יָדַע אָסְיָא כו'. הֲוָה בָּדֵיק נַפְשֵׁיהּ בְּקוּלְחָא. הַיְינוּ דּוּמְיָא דְּבֵיצָה טוּרְמִיטָא, וְהָיָה מְפַשְׁפֵּשׁ כָּל מֵעָיו אִם יֵשׁ בָּהֶן כְּאֵב. וְהָיָה מִתְחַלֵּשׁ וּמִתְעַלֵּף כָּל כָּךְ עַד שֶׁאִשְׁתּוֹ בּוֹכָה עָלָיו וְתוֹלֶשֶׁת שְׂעָרָהּ מֵחֲמַת דְּאָגָה. הָיָה עוֹשֶׂה. הַפּוֹעֵל שֶׁמְּלַקֵּט לוֹ בִּכְלוּפְסִין. לֹא יֹאכַל בִּבְנוֹת שֶׁבַע. שֶׁלֹּא הִרְשַׁתּוּ הַתּוֹרָה לֶאֱכוֹל אֶלָּא מֵאוֹתוֹ הַמִּין שֶׁהוּא מְלַקֵּט, דִּכְתִיב "כִּי תָבֹא בְּכֶרֶם רֵעֶךָ וְאָכַלְתָּ עֲנָבִים" וגו' (דברים כג). לִפְדֵי. מִינֵי מַאֲכָל. לְאַגְמוּרֵי אַלְפָּא מִינֵי לִפְדֵי. שֶׁיְּלַמְּדוֹ לַעֲשׂוֹת אֶלֶף מִינֵי מַאֲכָל. אַזְמְנֵיהּ לְדִינָא. עַל מָאתַיִם מִין שֶׁלֹּא לִימְּדוֹ. אֲבוֹתֵינוּ אָמְרוּ נָשִׁינוּ טוֹבָה. דִּכְתִיב "נָשִׁיתִי טוֹבָה" (איכה ג) שֶׁרָאוּהָ כְּבָר, אֶלָּא שֶׁעַכְשָׁיו שְׁכֵחוּהָ. אֲבָל אָנוּ לֹא רָאִינוּ טוֹבָה מֵעוֹלָם, שֶׁאֵין אָנוּ יוֹדְעִים כַּמָּה מִינֵי טַעַם יֵשׁ בַּפֵּירוֹת. כְּלוֹמַר, דָּבָר מוּפְלָא הוּא שֶׁכָּל כָּךְ לִימְּדוֹ. לָא אַזְמְנֵי' לְבַר קַפָּרָא. לְפִי שֶׁהָיָה אִישׁ בַּדְחָן, וּמִתְיָירֵא שֶׁמָּא יַעֲשֶׂה שׁוּם דָּבָר שֶׁיִּשְׂחוֹק. אֲמַר. בַּר קַפָּרָא לְרַבִּי: אִם לְעוֹבְרֵי רְצוֹנוֹ מַשְׁפִּיעַ לוֹ טוֹבָה כ"כ, לְעוֹשֵׂי רְצוֹנוֹ כו'. שֶׁהָיָה מְגַנֵּהוּ עַל שֶׁלֹּא זִימְּנוֹ. לְעוֹשֵׂי רְצוֹנוֹ. מַשְׁפִּיעַ לוֹ בָּעוה"ז טוֹבָה כ"כ. שֶׁהִתְחִיל לְסַפֵּר בְּשִׁבְחוֹ בִּשְׁבִיל שֶׁזִּימְּנוֹ.

דְּבָכָל

עין משפט נר מצוה

ד א מיי' פי"ב מהל' שכירות הל"י סמג עשין לא טוש"ע חו"מ סי' שלז סעי' ט:

תוספות

אשתו של טורנוסרופוס. שהיה ר"ע מקפח טורנוסרופו' לפני קיסר בקראי פעם אחת הלך לביתו זועף אמרה לו אשתו מפני מה פניך זועפים היום אמר לה מפני פלוני שמנצח אותי אמרה לו אלהיהם של אלו שונא זימה תן לי רשות ואכשיל אותו בדבר עבירה והלכה וקישטה עצמה ובאת לפני רבי עקיבא כשראה אותה רקק ושחק ובכה אמרה ליה פרש לי שלשה דברים הללו אמר לה שתים אפרש והשלישית לא אפרש מה שרקקתי שאת כותית ובאת מטיפה סרוחה ופסולה מה שבכיתי על האי שופרא דבלי בארעא ומה ששחק לה לא פירש לה והוא שחק לפי שראה ברוח הקודש שעתידה להתגייר ולהנשא לו אמרה לו יש לי תשובה אמר לה הן הלכה ונתגיירה והכניס' לו ממון הרבה ונשאה: **קטיעא** בר שלום. פ"ק דע"ז (דף י:) מפ': **קופא.** קוף: **לחרתא.** לחור: **דרביע.** רבוץ: **אייתינהו** נהליה. מדת חסידות עשו לו ולא מן הדין אלא אמרו אחרי אשר על ידי גלגולו בא נתנו לו: **אי** הוי סנו. פי' מכוערין: **טורמיטא.** אין בו משמשות: **דזוטרא.** ויכול לבולעה: סריך עלה. כלומר הכאב נדבק עליה: **בקולחא. היינו** בילת טורמיטא והיתה בודקת כל גופו עד שהיה מפיג לבו: **עד** דמסתרין אנשי ביתי' עליה. מסירין שערן מרוב צער: **עשה** בכלופסין לא יאכל בבנות שוח. פי' בפועל קאמר שאמרה תורה שאוכל ואמר התם שאינו אוכל אלא באותו המין וכלופסין אינו ממין בנות שוח ואע"ג שניהם תאנים שני מינים הם: **לפדי.** תבשיל

הגהות הב"ח

(א) גמ' על לחורתא חפרו: (ב) שם אף אורייתא כן א"ל והאיכא: (ג) שם אלפא דינרי דמעייל לה: (ד) שם ואם אית ביה כיבא:

גליון הש"ס

גמ' א"ל אם לעוברי רצונו כך. עיין בזה דבר נחמד בתשובת שבות יעקב ח"א סי' קפב:

מסורת הש"ס

תענית ז.

ע' פרש"י ע"ז טז: ד"ה אבני' אוכמתא]

בערוך ערך קלח מפרש קלר של כרוב בפיו וכלשו [מתבררת פ"ב מ"ח]

[נ"ל בריה ולא אזמניה לבר קפרא כתב וכ"ה בע"י

[מכור כד:]

פי' הרא"ש

לקחה כדי חובה והמותר נתנה לו: **ומן אשתו של טורנוסופוס.** שנתגיירה ונשאה ר' עקיבא: **ומן קטיעא בר שלום.** בפ"ק דע"ז (דף י:) שנתן כל ממונו לר"ע ותלמידיו: **על לחרתא** נכנס הקוף

לחור אחד מצאו רבוע על מרגליות ונתנו לו המרגליות לפניס מסורת הדין: **בכלי מכוער.** שהיה שחור: (פיסקא) **עד דמתזוטרא.** עד שקטנין שיוכל לבלעה: **בקולחא.** היינו בילת טורמיטא והיה נחלש עד שבני ביתו מורטין שער לראש עליו: **בכלופסין לא יאכל בבנות שוח.** פועל העושה מלאכה אלא בעל הבית אוכל במה שהוא עושה דכתיב כי תבא בכרם רעך וגו' ומוקמינן ליה בפועל ואמרינן בב"מ (ד' נח:) דאינו אוכל אלא מאותו המין שהוא עושה מלאכה וקמ"ל הכא דאע"ג דכלופסין ובנות שוח שניהם מין תאנים אפי' הכי חשיבי כשני מינין: **דעבדין מנהון לפדי.** מיני מאכלים: **אנו אפילו בעינינו לא ראינו.** שאין אנו יודעין לתקן כל כן מיני מאכלים:

דיקולא

תורה אור

דכל גריוא דבעינא שקילנא. שקל דיקולא רבה, חפייה כופרא וסחפיה על רישיה, ואזל ואמר ליה: ליכיל לי מר ארבעין גריוי חיטי דרשינא בך. אחוך רבי. א"ל: לאו אזהרתך דלא תבדחן! א"ל: חיטי דרשינא קא נסיבנא. א"ל בר קפרא לברתיה דרבי: למחר שתינא חמרא בריקודא דאבוך ובקירקני דאמך. בן אלעשה חתניה דרבי הוה, ועשיר גדול הוה, אזמניה לבי הילולא דרבי שמעון ברבי. א"ל: בר קפרא לרבי: מאי °"תועבה"? כל דא"ל רבי דהכין הוא "תועבה"? פרכה בר קפרא. א"ל: פרשיה את! א"ל: תיתי דביתכי תירמי לי נטלא. אתת רמיא ליה. א"ל לר': קום רקוד לי, דאימר לך. הכי אמר רחמנא: "תועבה"? תועה אתה בה. לכסא אחרינא א"ל מאי °"תבל"? א"ל: כי עניינא קדמאה. א"ל: עביד לי דאומר לך. עבד. אמר ליה: "תבל הוא" — תבלין יש בה? מי שניא הדא ביאה מן כולהון ביאות? אמר ליה: ומאי °"זימה". אמר ליה: עביד כי עניינא קדמאה. עבד, ואמר ליה: *זו מה היא. לא יכיל בן אלעשה למיסבל, קם ונפק הוא ואינתתיה מתמן. מאי בן אלעשה? דתניא: *לא לחנם פיזר בן אלעשה את מעותיו, אלא להראות בהן תספורת של כ"ג, דכתיב °"כסום יכסמו את ראשיהם". תנא: כעין לולינית. מאי לולינית? א"ר יהודה: תספרתא יחידתא. היכי דמי? אמר רבא: אראשו של זה בצד עיקרו של זה, והיינו תספורת של כהן גדול.§ "ובדלעת הרמוצה".§ מאי דלעת הרמוצה? אמר שמואל: קרא קרקוזאי. רב אשי אמר: דלעת הטמונה ברמץ. איתיביה רבינא לרב אשי: *רבי נחמיה אומר: דלעת ארמית היא דלעת המצרית, כלאים עם היונית, כלאים עם הרמוצה! תיובתא.§

מתני' *) בהנודר ממעשה קדרה — אין אסור אלא ממעשה רתחתא. אמר "קונם היורד לקדרה (א) שאני טועם" — אסור בכל הנעשה בקדרה.§ **גמ'** תניא: *הנודר מן היורד לקדרה אסור ביורד לאלפס, שכבר ירד לקדרה קודם שיורד לאלפס. מן היורד לאלפס — מותר ביורד לקדרה. מן הנעשה בקדרה — מותר בנעשה באלפס, מן הנעשה באלפס — מותר בנעשה בקדרה. גהנודר מן היורד לתנור אין אסור אלא בפת. ואם אמר "כל מעשה תנור עלי" אסור בכל הנעשים בתנור.§

מתני'

ויקרא כ | שם יח | שם | יחזקאל מד

[יבמות לז:]

סנהדרין כב:

נ"ל אפר יעב"ץ

כלאים פ"א מ"ה [במשנה דכלאים ליתא ועיין היטב בר"ש פ"א דכלאים מ"ב מה שהביא בשם ירושלמי ונוסחא כאן בסוגיא דהכא ר' נחמיה אומר דלעת מצרית כלאים עם הרמוצה תיובתא]

[תוספתא פ"ג ע"ש]

רש"י

דבכל גריוא דבעינא. באיזה מדה שארצה אקח. **חפייה כופרא.** זיפתו מבחוץ כדי שיחזיק החטים. **ליכיל לי.** ימוד לי. **דרשינא בך.** כלומר, שאתה חייב לי. **שתינא חמרא ברקודא דאבוך.** שאביך ירקד. **ובקירקני דאמך.** במזיגתה, שאמך תמזוג לי הכוס. **מאי תועבה.** עשו שניהם. **תרמי לי נטלא.** תמזוג לי הכוס, כמו אנטל. **תועה אתה בה.** כלומר: שמניח את אשתו של היתר, ותפס זו של זנות. **כי עניינא קמא.** תיתי דביתכי תירמי לי, ולדידיה א"ל: קום רקוד לי: [**מאי תבל.** דכתיב] "ואשה לא תעמוד לפני בהמה לרבעה תבל הוא" (ויקרא יח). **וכי תבלין יש בה.** כלומר, יש בביאה זו טעם מבאחרות, שמנחת בעלה ונרבעת לבהמה? **זו מאי היא.** ומפרש ביבמות (דף לז:) באיש הבא על נשים הרבה, וכן אשה שנבעלה לאנשים הרבה, ואינה יודעת מאיזה מהם נתעברה, והולידה בת. נמצא אב נושא את בתו, ואח נושא את אחותו — על זה נאמר "ומלאה הארץ זמה", כלומר: זו מה היא, שאין אדם יודע אותה אשה שהוא נושא, אם מותרת לו אם לאו. **לא יכיל בן אלעשה למיסבל.** אותו זילותא של רבי, לפי שהיה עשיר גדול ולא היה יכול לראות דבר של זילותא מחמיו. **מאי בן אלעשה.** כלומר, מנין דהוה עשיר? **תספורת יחידתא.** שאין כמותה. **פיזר מעותיו.** שהיה נותן ממון גדול לספר שהיה מספר לו כתגלחת של כ"ג. **הרמוצה קרא קרקוזאי.** דלועין של אותו מקום, שאינן מתבשלין לעולם יפה. **הטמונה ברמץ.** *עפר של גחלים, דלאו תבשיל הוא. **כלאים עם דלעת הרמוצה.** אלמא דהרמוצה לאו טמונה ברמץ, אלא שם מקום הוא, וממין זרעים הוא. **מתני' ממעשה רתחתא.** היינו דבר שנגמר בישולו בקדרה. ואינו אלא מחמשת המינין, לאפוקי דבר שאין גמר בישולו בקדירה עד שמבשלין אותו באילפס. **בכל הנעשה בקדרה.** אפילו מבושל באילפס אסור. **גמ' ביורד באילפס שכבר כו'.** הואיל וקודם שמניחו באילפס מבשלו בקדרה והדר מניחו באילפס. כן היה מנהגן. והוי יורד לקדרה, ולפיכך אסור. **מן היורד באילפס מותר ביורד לקדרה.** קודם שירד לאילפס. **מן הנעשה בקדירה.** לגמרי, כל בישולו, שאינו יורד לאילפס כלל. **מותר בנעשה באילפס.** אע"פ שהיה קודם לכן בקדרה. **מותר בנעשה בקדירה.** בנגמר בקדרה.

מתני'

ר"ן

דיקולא רבה. סל גדול. **חפייה בכופרא.** טח אותו בזפת, כדי שלא יצאו החטים מתוך נקבי הסל. **וסחפיה על רישיה.** הפכה על ראשה. **ליכיל לי מר.** ימדוד. **חטים דרשינא.** שהלויתיך. ולבדיחותא קאמר. **ברקודא דאבוך.** שירקד אביך לפני כשאשתה. **ובקירקני דאמך.** שתהא אמך מקרקרת ומזמרת. **מאי תועבה.** דכתיב גבי משכב זכור. **נטלא.** כלי קטן. **תועה אתה בה.** שמניח משכבי אשה והולך אצל זכר. **מאי תבל.** דכתיב גבי אשה הנרבעת לבהמה. **תבלין יש בה.** בתמיה. **מאי שניא הדא ביאה מכולהו ביאות.** כלומר, היאך מנחת בן מינה לילך אצל הבהמה. **זו מה היא.** לשון ספק, שאין ידוע ממי היא מתעברת. **תספורתא יחידתא.** תספורת נאה. **בצד עקרו של זה.** מגולח היה, שלא יעלה אחד מן השערות על חבירו. **קרקוזאי.** על שם מקומן. **דלעת ארמית היא דלעת המצרית.** כלומר, זו היא דלעת המצרית. **והיא כלאים עם הרמוצה.** אלמא לאו טמונה ברמץ קאמר, אלא מין דלעת היא שנקראת רמוצה. **מתני'** הנודר ממעשה קדרה **אינו אסור אלא במעשה רתחתא.** מפרש בירושלמי: איזהו מעשה רתחתא — כגון חילקא טרגין וטסני סלת ואורז זריד וערסן. והיינו דקאמר אינו אסור אלא ממעשה רתחתא. ונקראת רתחתא — על שם שצריך להרתיח ולבשל הרבה. **גמ'** שכבר ירד לקדרה קודם שירד לאילפס. כך היה דרכן במעשה אילפס שהיו מרתיחין אותו בקדרה רתיחה קלה. מן היורד לאילפס מותר ביורד לקדרה. קמ"ל דלא תימא: כל שהרתיחו אותו רתיחה קלה כמו שירד לאילפס "יורד לאילפס" מיקרי, מפני שהוא מוכן לכך, אע"פ שעדיין לא ירד — קמ"ל דלא. כך נראה בעיני. מן הנעשה בקדרה מותר בנעשה באילפס. משום דנעשה — גמר עשיה משמע, ומשום הכי מותר בנעשה באילפס אף על פי שכבר ירד לקדרה, משום דמ"מ גמר עשייתו לא היה בקדרה. מן הנעשה באילפס מותר בנעשה בקדרה. כלומר, אף על פי שאחר מכן הורידו באילפס — שרי, כיון דגמר עשייתו בקדרה היה. כך נראה בעיני. הנודר מן היורד לתנור **אינו אסור אלא בפת.** דסתם יורד לתנור משמע פת, ואם אמר "כל מעשה תנור עלי" — אסור בכל הנעשה בתנור.

מתני'

עין משפט נר מצוה

ה א מיי' פ"ה מהל' כלי המקדש הל"ו:

ו ב ג מיי' פ"ט מהל' נדרים הל"ז טוש"ע יו"ד סי' ריז סעי' ב:

תוספות

טחייה כופרא. **טחו** בכופרא: **דיקולא.** סל גדול: **דרשינא** בך. שהלויתיך ומילי דבדיחותא היה אומר: **ברקודא** לאבוך ובקורקני לאימך. כמו מרקדים טרפיי"ד: **תועה** אתה בה. שמניחין נשותיהן והולכין אצל משכב זכור: **תבלין** יש בביאה זו משניא הדא ביאה מכל ביאות: **קרי** קרקוזאי. דילועין של אותו מקום שאינו בכלל תבשיל: **דלעת** הטמונה ברמץ. אינו בכלל תבשיל: **כלאים.** מכלל דהרמוצה לא הוי טמונה ברמץ אלא על שם מקום הוא: **הנודר** ממעשה קדירה אינו אסור אלא במעשה רתחתא. דבר שנגמרה בקדירה ואין אסור [אלא] בדבר שנגמר בו: **באילפס.** אסור בכל המתבשל בקדירה ואפילו גמרו באילפס: **תנא** הנודר מן היורד בקדירה אסור ביורד לאילפס. אחר שירד לקדירה דיורד לקדירה משמע שירד תחלה לקדירה: **מן** היורד [לאילפס] מותר ביורד לקדירה. תחילה אע"פ שנגמר באילפס דיורד לעולם משמע על שם תחלת ירידתו ולא על שם סופו: **מן** הנעשה בקדירה. משמע הנגמר הלכך מותר היורד לקדירה תחלה ונגמר באילפס: **מן** היורד לתנור אינו אסור אלא בפת. דלא איקרי יורד בתנור אלא פת בלבד: **כל** מעשה תנור עלי אסור בכל הנעשה בתנור. נ"ע דמשמע דהחילוק בין יורד למעשה ואמאי תנא כל מעשה א"כ ברישא ליתני כל יורד:

הגהות הב"ח

(א) משנה שאיני טועם:

פי' הרא"ש

דיקולא רבה וחפייה כופרא. לקח סל גדול וחפהו בזפת: **ליכיל לי מר.** ימדוד: **בריקודא לאמך ובקרקני לאבוך.** שתהא אמך מרקדת לפני ואביך מכרכר: **תירמי לי נטלא.** תמזוג לי הכוס: **תועה אתה בה.** שמניחין נשותיהן והולכין אחר משכב זכור: **תבלין יש בה.** נעמה עליו ביאה מגונה של בהמה: **כסום יכסמו את ראשיהם.** כסוסמת הזה שראשו של זה בצד עיקרו של זה וככ"ג איירי מדכתיב בקרא ויין לא ישתו כל כהן מכלל דהך לאו בכל כהן איירי ועוד דברישא כתיב וראשם לא יגלחו והיינו בשאר כהנים: **קרא קרקוזאי.** לדועין של אותו מקום: **ובדלעת הרמוצה.** דלעת הטמונה ברמץ כל דלעת הטמונה ברמץ נקרא דלעת הרמוצה: **כלאים עם הרמוצה.** אלמא מין בפני עצמו הנקרא כן על שם שמאותן המינין רגילין לטמון ברמץ אבל שאר מיני דלועין אינם נקראים כך אפי' אם טומנין אותן ברמץ: (מתני') **שכבר ירד לקדרה קודם שירד לאילפס.** ש... אותו קצת תחילה קודם שמטגנין אותו באילפס: **מן היורד באילפס מותר ביורד לקדרה.** כי היורד לקדרה אין דרך לתתו באלפס ויש מפרש אפי' אם אחר כך נתנוהו באילפס כיון שירד תחלה לקדרה כי לאילפס משמע שתחילת ירידתו לאילפס: **מן הנעשה בקדרה מותר בנעשה באילפס.** אע"פ שירד לקדרה תחלה כי הנעשה בקדרה משמע שנגמר בקדרה: **מותר בנעשה בקדרה.** אפילו ירד לאילפס תחלה:

מתני'

*) [פליאה כי כלל המשנה הלזה כבר שנויה במשנה לעיל מט. ובעל כרחך טעות איתרמי במשנה לעיל והעיקר משנה מסודר הכא וכן נראה מתוך פירוש הר"ן או דמלת מתני' ומלת גמ' נדפס הכא בטעות אלא שכל דברים הללו הנודר ממעשה קדירה וכו' עד בכל הנעשה בקדירה פיסקא הוא כדס בשינויי פירושי רש"י במתני' לעיל מט. ומה שפרש"י הכא במכוון אחר צריך פנים]

עין משפט
נר מצוה

ז א מיי' פ"ט מהל' נדרים הל"ג טוש"ע יו"ד סי' ריז סעי' ג:
ח ב מיי' שם הל"ה טוש"ע שם סעי' יב:
ט ג ד ה מיי' שם טוש"ע שם סעי' יח:

מתני' א"מן הכבוש" — אין אסור אלא מן הכבוש של ירק, "כבוש (א) שאני טועם" — אסור בכל הכבושים. "מן השלוק" — אינו אסור אלא מן השלוק של בשר, "שלוק שאני טועם" — אסור בכל השלוקים.§ **גמ'** א"ל רב אחא בריה דרב אויא לרב אשי: אמר "דכביש" מאי, "דשליק" מאי, "דצלי" מאי, "דמליח" מאי, היכן משמע? תיבעי.§ **מתני'** "מן הצלי" — אין אסור אלא מן הצלי של בשר, דברי ר' יהודה. "צלי שאני טועם" אסור בכל הצלויים. "מן המליח" — אין אסור אלא מן המליח של דג, "מליח שאני טועם" — אסור בכל המלוחים. *"דג בדגים שאני טועם" — אסור בהן בין גדולים בין קטנים, בין מלוחים בין תפלים, בין חיים בין מבושלים, ומותר בטרית טרופה ובציר. (ב) הנודר מן הצחנה אסור בטרית טרופה ומותר בציר ובמוריים, הנודר מטרית טרופה — *אסור בציר ובמוריים.§ **גמ'** תניא,* רבי שמעון בן אלעזר אומר: "דג שאני טועם" — אסור בגדולים ומותר בקטנים, "דגה שאני טועם" — אסור בקטנים ומותר בגדולים, "דג דגה שאני טועם" — אסור בין בגדולים בין בקטנים. אמר ליה רב פפא לאביי: ממאי ד"דג שאני טועם" גדול הוא — דכתיב °"וימן י"י דג גדול לבלוע את יונה" (יונה ב). והכתיב °"ויתפלל יונה אל י"י אלהיו ממעי הדגה" (שם)! הא לא קשיא; דלמא פלטיה דג גדול ובלעיה דג קטן. אלא °"והדגה אשר ביאור מתה" (שמות ז) — קטנים מתו, גדולים לא מתו?! אלא: דגה משמע גדולים ומשמע קטנים, *ובנדרים הלך אחר לשון בני אדם.§ "הנודר מן הצחנה" כו'.§ אמר ליה רבינא לרב אשי: אמר "הרי עלי ציחין" מאי? תיבעי.§ **מתני'** גהנודר מן החלב מותר בקום, ור' יוסי אוסר. דמן הקום — מותר בחלב. אבא שאול אומר: ההנודר מן הגבינה — אסור בה בין מלוחה *וטפלה. הנודר מן הבשר — מותר

תורה אור

רש"י

מתני' אינו אסור אלא בכבוש של ירק. דסתם כבוש ירק הוא. אבל אמר "כבוש שאני טועם", הואיל ואמר כי האי לישנא – אסור בכל הכבושין. וה"ה בכל הנך, אם אמר בשלוק סתם – אינו אסור כו', דסתם שלוק שלהן אינו אלא בשר, ודעתיה לא הוי אלא בשר, דדרכו להתבשל ולהשלק. **גמ'** אמר קונם דכביש עלי או דשליק עלי מאי. מי אמרינן דכביש דמי כמ"ד "הכבוש", או דילמא דמי כמאן דאמר "כבוש שאני טועם", ואסור בכל הכבושין? תיבעי. כלומר, תיקו. **מתני'** דג דגים שאני טועם. דג משמע גדול, דגים משמע קטנים, וכיון דאמר שניהם – אסור בהן בין גדולים בין קטנים. ומותר בטרית טרופה. דג ששמו טרית ומוכרין אותו בחתיכות. שלא נדר אלא מדג הנמכר שלם. ובציר. שעושין מקרבי דגים, וכל שכן במוריים שאין עושין אותו אלא משומן של דגים. אסור בציר ובמוריים. דהני בכלל טרופין נינהו. **גמ'** הלך אחר לשון בני אדם. שקורין "דג" לגדול, ו"דגה" לקטנים. להכי כי אמר "דג" – מותר בקטנים, וכי אמר "דגה" – אסור בקטנים, וכי אמר "דג דגה" – אסור בשניהם. אמר הרי עלי ציחין. מי אמר דמדגים ממש קאמר ולא מדבר אחר, או דילמא דמי כמאן דאמר מן הצחנה. **מתני'** מן הקום. מסג"א, היינו נסיובי דחלבא, דקום אינו בכלל חלב. אוסר. (ג) דקא סבר יש בו לחלוח חלב, והוי בכלל חלב. מן הקום מותר בחלב. דברי הכל, דחלב אינו בכלל קום.

ר"ן

מתני' מן הכבוש אין אסור אלא מן הכבוש של ירק. משום דכיון דאמר "הכבוש" – משמע הידוע, וסתמא דירק הוא. כבוש שאני טועם אסור בכל הכבושין. דכיון שהזכירו בלא ה"א הידיעה – כל כבוש במשמע. ודקתני "שאני טועם" – לאו משום דאי לא אמר "שאני טועם" לא מיתסר בכל הכבושים, דודאי כיון דאמר "כבוש" – מיתסר בכולהו. אלא לרבותא נקטיה, דאפי' אמר "שאני טועם", אי אמר כבוש – אין, ואי לא – לא. וכולה מתני' בכי האי גונא מפרשא, ברישא "מן הצלי" – דמשמע הידוע, ובסיפא "צלוי" – דמשמע כל צלוי. ברישא "המליח" דמשמע הידוע, ובסיפא "מלוח" – דמשמע כל המלוחים. ואית דמפרשי: דלא הוי הפרשה דמתני' בין "הכבוש" ל"כבוש", אלא סיפא דקתני: בכל הכבושין – משום דקאמר "שאני טועם" הוא, ובכי האי גוונא נמי באינך כולהו. ירושלמי: הוון בעי מימר מלוח לעולם, הא לשעה – לא. אמר ר' יודן: מן מה דתנינן* הרי עלי כבשר מליח וכיין נסך, הדא אמרן: מלוח לשעה – מלוח הוא. **גמ'** דכבוש מאי דשלוק מאי וכו'. לפי פירוש הראשון שפירשתי במשנתינו, שעיקר החילוק הוא אם הזכירו בשם הידיעה אם לאו, הכא הכי מיבעיא ליה: כי אמר "דכבוש" "דשלוק" בדל"ת, אי משמע הידוע או לא. ולפי פירוש אחרון שפירשנו, דאיסורא דמתני' משום "שאני טועם" הוא, הכא מספקא ליה אי אמר "כבוש" בלא "שאני טועם" היכי משמע. וסלקא בעיין בתיקו, ולחומרא. **מתני'** דג דגים שאני טועם אסור בהם בין גדולים בין קטנים. משום דאמר תרי לישני "דג דגים", דדג משמע גדול, משום דנמכר בפני עצמו, ודגים משמע קטנים, לפי שאין נמכרים אלא ביחד. ומותר בטרית טרופה ובציר ובמוריים. טרית טרופה – דג גדול טרוף דק דק. ומשום הכי שרי, משום ד"דג" – דגים שלמים משמע ולא טרופים. וכל שכן שמותר בציר של דגים, שהוא שומן היוצא מהן וקרבי דגים מעורבים בו, וכל שכן שמותר במורייס שהוא שמנו של דג בלבד, ו"זו וא"צ לומר זו" קתני. הנודר מן הצחנה אסור בטרית טרופה. צחנה – דגים קטנים הרבה מלוחים. ויש מהם טרופין, אלא שרובן שלמים. וקתני דכיון שיש מהן טרופין – אסור בטרית טרופה. ומיהו, בציר ומורייס מותר, לפי שאין בהן חתיכות של דג אלא שמנו וקרביו. הנודר מן טרית טרופה מותר בציר ובמוריים. נ"ל דלא שייך למיתני הכא לא אסור בצחנה ולא מותר בה, משום דמקצתה מותר ומקצתה אסור. דכיון דבצחנה איכא שלמים וטרופים, בשלמים – שרי, בטרופים – אסור, ומשום הכי לא תני הכא צחנה כלל. ומותר בציר ובמורייס איצטריכא ליה למיתני, דס"ד אמינא כיון דנדר מטרית שהיא טרופה דק דק – יאסר אף בציר ומורייס, קמ"ל. **גמ'** דג שאני טועם אסור בגדולים. משום ד"דג" – גדול משמע, שנמכר בפני עצמו. ובירושלמי מפרש דכל דג שהוא פחות מליטרא – קטן מיקרי. ומיהו, בכגון זה הכל לפי המקומות. דג דגה שאני טועם אסור בין בגדולים בין בקטנים. דלא תימא: מהדר הוא דקא הדר ביה, דמעיקרא דבעי מיסר נפשיה בגדולים אמר "דג", ובסוף הדר ביה ואמר "דגה", קמ"ל דלא אמר הכי, אלא מכולהו אסר נפשיה. דילמא פלטיה דג גדול ובלעיה דג קטן. ואע"ג דההוא נמי דבלעיה בסוף גדול מליטרא היה, נקרא קטן בערך הראשון. אלא והדגה אשר ביאור מתה קטנים מתו גדולים לא מתו. בתמיה. והא כיון שהיאור נהפך לדם – ודאי מתו [להון] בין גדולים בין קטנים! אמר הרי עלי ציחין מאי. מי מיתסר בציר ובמורייס או לא דמשום הכי מיקרו דגים קטנים כבושין לצחנה – מפני שהציר היוצא מהן ריחו נודף, מלשון "ותעל צחנתו", ומיבעיא ליה אי אמר ציחין דמשמע רבויא, אי משתמע ביה נמי ציר ומורייס או לא. **מתני'** הנודר מן החלב מותר בקום. קום היינו מים היוצאין מן החלב, וקורין לו סיר"ו. ר' יוסי אוסר. בגמרא מפרש טעמא. מן הקום מותר בחלב. לפום לישנא דמתני' משמע דר' יוסי נמי מודה בהא, ומיהו *) בברייתא בגמרא פליג. הנודר מן הגבינה אסור בה בין מלוחה בין טפילה. דלא תימא: מפני שרוב הגבינות מלוחות הן, סתמא – מלוחה משמע, קא משמע לן.

*) [בברייתא שלפנינו לא נמצא ועיין בב"י סי' רי"ז ובתוס' י"ט]

תוספות

קונם מן הכבוש. שאמר קונם כבוש עלי אינו אסור אלא בכבוש של ירק דסתם כבוש משמע כבוש של ירק אבל לא כבוש שאני טועם כיון שאמר שאני טועם אסור בכל הכבושים: **מן** השלוק. סתמא הוי של ירק: **דכבוש** מאי. פירוש אם אמר קונם דכבוש עלי מאי כסתם כבוש דמי ואינו אסור אלא בכבוש ירק או דילמא כשאני טועם דמי ואסור בכל הכבושי': **מן** הצלי. סתמא הוי דבשר: **מן** המליח. סתם מליח הוי דג מליח: **דג** דגים שאני טועם. פירוש דג או דגים ורבי שמעון דאמר בגמרא דג גדולים משמע פליג אהא וי"א דג ודגים דאמר לתרוייהו: **בטרית** טרופה. מין דג גדול שחותכין וטורפין אותו ולא מיקרי לא דג ולא דגים אלא יש להם שם בפני עצמם: **טרית** טונינ"א בלע"ז וי"מ שלכך מותר בטרית שלא נתכוון אלא בדגים שלמים: **ומותר** בציר. אע"פ שדגים מעורבין בו וא"צ לומר מוריים שאין בו אלא שומן דגים: **הנודר** מן הצחנה.

*) שייך לדף נ"ב ע"א

פי' הרא"ש

מתני' אינו אסור אלא מן הכבוש של ירק. דסתם כבוש הוא של ירק: **כבוש שאני טועם כו'.** דכיון דאמר שאני טועם וכן שלוק צלי מלוח: **גמ' דכביש מאי דשליק מאי.** כאילו *) כבוש דמי או כאילו נמי שאני טועם ולאידך פירושא מי הוי ככבוש או הכבוש: **מתני' דג דגים שאני טועם.** או דג או דגים ופליגא

מסורת הש"ס

[לעיל יח:]

[תוספתא פ"ג ע"ש]

[לקמן נב:]

[במשנה שבמשניות איתא נ"א מותר וכן גירסת הר"ן בפירושו אבל גירסת רש"י והרא"ש אסור]

[לעיל ל: וש"נ]

הגהות הב"ח

(א) במשנה שאני טועם כל"ל וכן בכל העמוד: (ב) שם בטרית טרופה ובציר ובמורייס הנודר: (ג) רש"י ד"ה אוסר דקסבר יש בו:

י א מיי' פ"ה מהל' נדרים הלכה יא סמג לאוין רמב טוש"ע י"ד סימן רטז סעיף ט:

מותר ברוטב וקיפה. קיפה היינו דק דק של בשר, שיורד לשולי קדרה. **אמר רבי יהודה מעשה ואסר עלינו** כו'. לסייע לר' יוסי מייתי הך עובדא. **אמרו לו.** בעלי מחלוקתו של רבי יוסי. כן הדבר. כמו שאתה מעיד, אבל אין זו ראיה. שלא אסר רבי טרפון אלא בזמן שאמר "בשר זה עלי", דכיון דאמר "זה" – שויה אנפשיה חתיכה דאיסורא, ואסור ביוצא ממנו. שהנודר מן הדבר. כלומר "דבר זה". **ונתערב באחר אם יש בו בנותן טעם.** אם יש במין [האוסר] כדי ליתן טעם בשל היתר, וכגון דליכא ששים בשל היתר – ה"ז אסור. **וקשיא** להו לרבותא ז"ל: היכי אמרינן הכא דאם יש בו בנותן טעם אסור, דמשמע הא אין בו בנותן טעם – מותר, והא נדרים דבר שיש לו מתירין הוא, כדאמרינן לקמן בפרק "הנודר מן הירק" (דף נט.) משום דמצוה לאיתשולי עלייהו מדרבי נתן, וקיימא לן: דכל שיש לו מתירין – אפילו באלף לא בטיל! ויש לומר: דכי אמרינן אפילו באלף לא בטיל – הני מילי מין במינו, אבל הכא כי קתני ונתערב באחר – שאינו מינו, דומיא דביצים שנתבשלו עמו. וכל שאינו מינו, אפילו בדבר שיש לו מתירין – בנותן טעם. והיינו דתנן במסכת חלה (פ"ג מ"י): הנותן שאור מעיסת חטים לתוך עיסת האורז, אם יש בה טעם דגן – חייבת, ואם לאו – פטורה. א"כ למה אמרו הטבל אוסר בכל שהוא – במינו, ושלא במינו – בנותן טעם. וטבל דבר שיש לו מתירים הוא, ואפ"ה קתני דשלא במינו בנותן טעם. וה"נ איתא בהדיא בירושלמי [דפירקין], דגרסי' תמן: זה הכלל היה ר' שמעון אומר משום ר' יהושע: כל דבר שיש לו מתירין, כגון טבל ומעשר שני והקדש וחדש – לא נתנו בו חכמים שיעור, אלא מין במינו – במשהו, ושלא במינו – בנותן טעם. וכל שאין לו מתירין, כגון תרומה וכו' מין במינו ושלא במינו – בנותן טעם. הלין נדרי, מה את עביד לון, כדבר שיש לו מתירין או כדבר שאין לו מתירין? [מסתברא מעבדינן כדבר שיש לו מתירין], דתנינן תמן: שהזקן עוקר הנדר מעיקרו וכו'. והא מתניתא עבדא לון כדבר *[שיש] לו מתירין, דתנינן: שהנודר מן הדבר ונתערב באחר, אם יש בו בנותן טעם אסור! תפתר במין בשאינו מינו [בדבר *שיש לו מתירין]. והרי זה מפורש כמו שכתבנו, ולפיכך הקשו על הרב אלפס ז"ל שכתב בהלכותיו בפ' "גיד הנשה" בענין פת שאפאה עם הצלי בתנור, דמאי דאמרינן דאסור לאכלה בכותח, אף על גב דקי"ל דריחא לאו מילתא היא – היינו טעמא משום דהוי דבר שיש לו מתירין, דהא מצי למיכלה בהדי בישרא, ומשום הכי – אפילו באלף לא בטיל, אלו דבריו ז"ל. אלמא דסבירא ליה ז"ל דאפילו שלא במינו לא בטיל. ואי אפשר, כמו שכתבנו בראיות ברורות. ואמרו: שאפשר שסמך הרב ז"ל על אותה שאמרו בפ' "משילין" (ביצה לט.) גבי האשה ששאלה מים ומלח לעיסתה – הרי היא כרגלי שתיהן, ופרכינן: ואמאי? ליבטל מים ומלח לגבי עיסה! ופרקה רב אשי: משום דהוה ליה דבר שיש לו מתירין, ואפי' באלף לא בטיל. והא מים ומלח לגבי עיסה מין בשאינו מינו הוא, ואפי' הכי יהיב טעמא משום דהוה ליה דבר שיש לו מתירין. אלמא – אפי' שלא במינו לא בטיל. ואי מהא לא אריא, דשאני מים ומלח, כיון דעיסה לא מתעבדא אלא בהו – כמין במינו דמי. תדע, דאמרינן בריש שמעתא דהתם, כי מקשינן וליבטל מים ומלח לגבי עיסה, אמר להו ר' אבא: הרי שנתערב קב חטים שלו בעשרת קבין של חבירו יאכל הלה וחדי? ואחיכו עליה, ואמר רבי אושעיא דשפיר עבוד דאחיכו עליה, מאי שנא חטים בשעורים דלא קאמר להו דהוה ליה מין בשאינו מינו, ובטל. חטים בחטים נמי – לר' יהודה הוא דלא בטיל, לרבנן בטל. מדקאמר ר' אושעיא הכי, ולא קאמר: הא מים ומלח לגבי עיסה חטים ושעורים הוא – שמע מינה לחטים בחטים איכא לדמויי, לפי שאי אפשר לעיסה בלא מים ומלח. אלו דברי הראשונים ז"ל. ולי נראין דברי הרב אלפסי ז"ל, דכי תנן הכא דדבר שיש לו מתירין בשאינו מינו בטיל – הני מילי כל שאסור עכשיו ועתיד להיות ניתר אחר זמן, כנדרים. משום דקא מיבעיא: לי כיון דלרבנן בכולהו איסורי מין במינו בטיל כמו בשאינו מינו, מה ראו חכמים לחלק בדבר שיש לו מתירין בין מינו לשאינו מינו, ומאיזה טעם? וכך נראה לי בטעמו של דבר: דחזינא לרבנן ולר' יהודה דאיפלגו במין במינו אי בטיל או לא, ואמרינן בפ' "הקומץ רבה" (מנחות כב.) דשניהם מקרא א' דרשו, דכתיב "ולקח מדם הפר ומדם השעיר", שאע"פ שדמו של פר מרובה – קרי ליה דם השעיר, אלמא לא בטיל. וקסבר ר' יהודה: דהיינו טעמא, משום דמין במינו לא בטיל, לפי שכל דבר שהוא דומה לחבירו – אינו מחלישו ומבטלו, אלא מעמידו ומחזקו. ומשום הכי סבירא ליה לר' יהודה בכולהו איסורי דמין במינו לא בטיל. ורבנן לא משמע להו הכי, דמכל מקום מין במינו דאיסור והיתר אין דומין זה לזה, כיון דחד אסור וחד שרי, שאין ראוי לילך אחר דמיונן בעצם, אלא אחר חילוקן באיסור והיתר. אלא היינו טעמא דדם הפר אינו מבטל דם השעיר – משום דכיון דשניהן עולין, כלומר שכשרים לזריקה – אין מבטלין זה את זה. דכי היכי דר' יהודה אזיל אחר דמיון העצם, אזלו רבנן אחר דמיון ההיתר. ולפיכך, כל שחלוקין באיסור והיתר – אפי' מין במינו בטיל, דהוה ליה כמין בשאינו מינו. ומשום הכי אמרינן דבדבר שיש לו מתירין נטו רבנן משום חומרא לדרבי יהודה, דכיון שאין דבר זה חלוק מן ההיתר לגמרי באיסור והיתר, שהרי אף הוא סופו להיות ניתר כמוהו – אמרינן שאינו בטל במינו. דאי הכי – הוה דמו טובא; חדא שהן שוין במין, ועוד שאינן חלוקים לגמרי באיסור והיתר. ומשום הכי לא בטיל אלא בשאינו מינו – כדי שאותו חילוק שיש בין מינו לשאינו מינו ישלים אותו שווי שניתוסף כאן, משום דבר שיש לו מתירין, לפי שהחילוק שבין המינין סיבת הביטול, והשווי נותן שלא יהו בטלין. הלכך, כל שהוא אסור עכשיו, ואינו חסר מן איסורו, אלא שעתיד להיות ניתר לאחר זמן – אותו חסרון של איסור, כיון שהוא מועט – ראוי הוא שישלימנו אותו חילוק שיש בין מינו לשאינו מינו. אבל כשיש לו עכשיו היתר, כי ההיא דפ' "משילין" שאף מים ומלח מותרין עכשיו במקום שרגלי שתיהן שוין בה – הרי נתקרב הרבה היתר של עיסה למים ומלח, שאף עכשיו שניהן מותרין, וכיון שהיתרן קרוב – אי אפשר לחילוק שיש בין מינו לשאינו מינו שישלימנו. דהא התלמוד לרבנן חילוק דהיתר ואיסור עדיף להו מחילוק דמינו ושאינו מינו, דבה הוא דפליגי עליה דר' יהודה. הלכך דבר שהוא ניתר עכשיו, כמים ומלח – ראוי יותר שלא יתבטל לגבי עיסה, אע"ג דהוי מין בשאינו מינו, ממה שראוי שלא יתבטל דבר שהוא אסור עכשיו ועתיד להיות ניתר אחר זמן לגבי מין במינו. ומש"ה, נהי דמסקינן דדבר שיש לו מתירין בשאינו מינו בטל, מפני שהוא אסור עכשיו, אסיק רב אשי התם דמים ומלח שהן ניתרין עכשיו – אינן בטלין לגבי עיסה, אע"פ שהוא מין בשאינו מינו. [והא] דאמרינן התם בריש שמעתא (לח:): [מ"ש] מחטים בחטים וחטים בשעורים – הוייה בעלמא ניהו דלא סלקן, דהא אחיכו עליה, כדאיתא התם. ולמסקנא לא סמיך עלייהו רב אשי כלל, אלא אסקה *דכיון דהוי דבר שיש לו מתירין, שאף עכשיו יש לו שעת היתר – אפי' בשאינו מינו לא בטיל. ופת שאפאה עם הצלי בתנור – להא דמיא, שאף עכשיו יש לה היתר לאכלה שלא בכותח, הלכך בדין הוא דאפי' בשאינו מינו לא בטיל. ועוד: דאפי' לא בעית למידק כולי האי – זיל בתר טעמא; הרי אתה רואה שכל שהוא מוסיף היתר החמירו בבטולו, שמפני שעתיד להיות ניתר אמרו שלא יתבטל במינו, וכיון שכן, כל שהוא מוסיף עוד היתר – שאף עכשיו יש לו שעת הכושר, ראוי להחמיר בבטולו שלא יתבטל אפי' בשאינו מינו. ומש"ה לא קשיא מסקנא דהכא, דמסקינן דבר [שיש] לו מתירין בטל בשאינו מינו, אמסקנא דפרק "משילין", דאסיק רב אשי דאפי' בשאינו מינו לא בטיל, ולא צריכינן לתרוצי לדחוקי כלל. וההיא דפת שאפאה עם הצלי בתנור – לההיא דפרק "משילין" דמיא, ולא עוד אלא דעדיפא מינה, משום דאיכא למימר דכי מלינן לאחמורי אדבר שיש לו מתירין במינו – לא מחמרינן עליה בשאינו מינו, אבל בההיא דפת שאפאה עם הצלי בתנור, דליכא לאחמורי עליה במינו, דלא שייך כלל, אי לא מחמרינן עליה בשאינו מינו – נמצא שלא החמיר בו כלל. ועלו דברי הרב אלפסי ז"ל נכונים בטעמם. כן נראה לי. עוד ראיתי שהקשו עליו מדאמרינן בסוף פרק "הערל" (יבמות פא:) גבי חתיכה של חטאת שנתערבה במאה חתיכות של חולין – לא תעלה. וקא יהיב רב אשי טעמא התם: משום דהוה ליה דבר שיש לו מתירין, וכל דבר שיש לו מתירין – אפי' באלף לא בטיל. ואסיקנא התם: דהא דרב אשי בדותא היא, ולמאן? אי לכהן – מיסרא סרי, אי לישראל – לעולם אסור, אלא דהא דרב אשי בדותא היא. אלמא לא מיקרי דבר שיש לו מתירין אלא מאי דאסיר האידנא ולבתר זימנא שרי, אבל האי פיתא – בהדי בשרא לעולם שרי, ואי בכותחא – לעולם אסור, ולא מיקרי דבר שיש לו מתירין כמסקנא דהתם! ומיתחזי לי דהא דפרכינן עליה מיהא – ודאי בדותא היא, דהתם הכי קאמרינן: דכיון לישראל לעולם אסור למה נחמיר אבל ישראל מפני היתרו של כהן? אינו בדין. אבל פת שאפאה עם הצלי בתנור כיון שיש לו ולכל אדם היתר בה עכשיו – ראוי להחמיר בבטולה, ודבר פשוט הוא.

בסה"מ הגי' עלי

ס"א שאין

[נ"ל שאין]

[דף נט.]

מותר ברוטב. מרק. ובקיפה. מקפה עבה מתבלין, פונדליר"ש בלע"ז. שנתבשלו. בתוכו, בשביל רוטב שנכנס בביצה, ובשביל טעם בשר שהיה בבצים. כן הדבר. שאסור(ג) כשאמר "בשר זה עלי שיש בקדרה" לכשאמר כן – כל מה שיש בקדרה שיש בו טעם בשר – אסור. שהנודר מן הדבר. כגון שאמר "בשר זה עלי" ונתערב כו'. אבל כי לא אמר "בשר זה עלי", אלא "קונם בשר עלי", דמשמע בשר ממש – מותר ברוטב ובקיפה. [נ"ל שאמר]

מותר ברוטב ובקיפה, ור' יהודה אוסר. אמר רבי יהודה: מעשה ואסר *עלינו רבי טרפון (א) בביצים שנתבשלו עמו. אמרו לו: כן הדבר, *אימתי – בזמן *שיאמר "בשר זה עלי", שהנודר מן הדבר ונתערב באחר, אם יש בו בנותן טעם – אסור. הנודר מן היין – מותר בתבשיל שיש בו טעם יין. אמר "קונם יין זה (ב) שאני טועם" ונפל לתבשיל, אם יש בו בנותן טעם – הרי זה אסור.§

גמ'

פי' הרא"ש

מותר ברוטב ובקיפה. היינו דק דק בשר ורוטב הנקפה בשולי הקדרה דמשמע בשר דוקא מה שנקרא בשר: **ר' יהודה אוסר.** דכיון שיש בו טעם בשר אסור: **אימתי בזמן שאמר בשר זה עלי.** דכיון דאמר בשר זה שויה עליה חתיכה דאיסורא ואסור בטעמו ובהנאתו אבל כשאמר קונם בשר עלי לא אסר עצמו אלא בדבר הנקרא בשר: **מותר בתבשיל שיש בו טעם יין.** כרבנן דרבי יהודה:

הגהות הב"ח

(א) גמ' רבי טרפון ביצים כצ"ל ואות ב' נמחק: (ב) שם שאיני טועם: (ג) רש"י ד"ה כן הדבר שאסור הס"ד ואח"כ מ"ה שאמר בשר זה עלי לכשאמר כן כצ"ל ותיבות שיש בקדירה נמחק:

גליון הש"ס

בהר"ן ד"ה וקשיא להו כו' אלא אחר חילוקן באו"ה. עי' בהר"ן לקמן דף נט ע"ב ד"ה שאני גבי מעשר:

תוספות

אמר ר"י מעשה ואסר וכו'. פירוש דכי היכי דבשר שאני טועם אסור ברוטב ה"נ אם אמר שאני אוכל ובגמרא נמי הכי הוא כי קא מיבעי ליה בשאיני אוכל בשאיני טועם דוקא או לאו דוקא וכן לענין שלוק שאני טועם: **אמרו** לו כן הדבר. שאסורין אפילו ביצים שנתבשלו עם הבשר ואימתי בזמן שאמר בשר זה עלי דמשמע היא וטעמה שהנודר מן הדבר שאמר דבר זה עלי וכו': **הנודר** ביין מותר בתבשיל. כרבנן דלר"י אסור: **קונם** יין זה וכו' אסור אם יש בו בנ"ט. וא"ת כי נמי אין בו בנ"ט דקונמות הוי דבר שיש לו מתירין כדאמרינן בשילהי פירקין לקמן וי"ל דחומר דבר שיש לו מתירין אינו נוהג אלא במין במינו אבל במין בשאין מינו אפילו יש לו מתירין בטל בששים וכן משמע בשמעתין דבגל (לקמן דף נח.):

ורמינהו

עין משפט נר מצוה

יא א טוש"ע י"ד סי' ריז סעיף יח:

יב ב ג מיי' פ"ה מהל' נדרים הלכה יג ופ"ט הל' יד סמג לאוין רמב טוש"ע י"ד סימן רטז סעיף יב:

גמ' וּרְמִינְהוּ: *"מִן הָעֲדָשִׁים" — אָסוּר בַּאֲשִׁישִׁים, ור' יוֹסֵי מַתִּיר! לָא קַשְׁיָא; *מָר כִּי אַתְרֵיהּ וּמָר כִּי אַתְרֵיהּ. אבְּאַתְרָא דְּרַבָּנַן קָרוּ לַחֲלָבָא חֲלָבָא וְלְקוּמָא קוּמָא, בְּאַתְרֵיהּ דְּרַבִּי יוֹסֵי לְקוּמָא נַמִי קָרוּ לֵיהּ "קוּמָא דַחֲלָבָא". תַּנְיָא: הַנּוֹדֵר מִן הֶחָלָב — מוּתָּר בְּקוּם, מִן הַקּוּם — מוּתָּר בְּחָלָב. מִן הֶחָלָב — מוּתָּר בִּגְבִינָה, מִן הַגְּבִינָה — מוּתָּר בְּחָלָב. מִן הָרוֹטֶב — מוּתָּר בְּקִיפָה, מִן הַקִּיפָה — מוּתָּר בְּרוֹטֶב. אִם אָמַר "בָּשָׂר זֶה עָלַי" — אָסוּר בּוֹ וּבְרוֹטְבוֹ וּבְקִיפוֹ. הַנּוֹדֵר מִן הַיַּיִן — מוּתָּר בְּתַבְשִׁיל שֶׁיֵּשׁ בּוֹ טַעַם יַיִן. אָמַר "קוֹנָם יַיִן זֶה שֶׁאֵינִי טוֹעֵם" וְנָפַל לְתוֹךְ הַתַּבְשִׁיל, אִם יֵשׁ בּוֹ טַעַם יַיִן — הֲרֵי זֶה אָסוּר.§ **מתני'** בהַנּוֹדֵר מִן הָעֲנָבִים — מוּתָּר בְּיַיִן, מִן הַזֵּיתִים — מוּתָּר בְּשֶׁמֶן. אָמַר "קוֹנָם זֵיתִים וַעֲנָבִים אֵלּוּ שֶׁאֵינִי טוֹעֵם" — אָסוּר בָּהֶן וּבַיּוֹצֵא מֵהֶן.§ **גמ'** גבָּעֵי רָמִי בַּר חָמָא: "אֵלּוּ" דַּוְקָא, אוֹ "שֶׁאֵינִי טוֹעֵם" דַּוְקָא? אִי ס"ד "אֵלּוּ" דַּוְקָא, "שֶׁאֵינִי טוֹעֵם" למ"ל? הָא קמ"ל דאע"ג דְּאָמַר "שֶׁאֵינִי טוֹעֵם" אִי דְּאָמַר "אֵלּוּ" — מִיתְּסַר, וְאִי לָא — לָא. אֲמַר רָבָא, ת"ש *"קוֹנָם פֵּירוֹת הָאֵלּוּ עָלַי" "קוֹנָם הֵן לְפִי" — אָסוּר בְּחִילּוּפֵיהֶן וּבְגִידּוּלֵיהֶן. הָא בַּיּוֹצֵא מֵהֶן — מוּתָּר! ה"ה דאפי' בַּיּוֹצֵא מֵהֶן אָסוּר, וְהָא עֲדִיפָא לֵיהּ לְאַשְׁמוּעִינַן, דְּחִילּוּפֵיהֶן כְּגִידּוּלֵיהֶן דָּמֵי. ת"ש: "שֶׁאֵינִי אוֹכֵל" וְ"שֶׁאֵינִי טוֹעֵם" — מוּתָּר בְּחִילּוּפֵיהֶן וּבְגִידּוּלֵיהֶן. הָא הַיּוֹצֵא מֵהֶן — אָסוּר. אַיְּידֵי דְּלָא נָסֵיב בְּרֵישָׁא יוֹצֵא מֵהֶן, לָא נָסֵיב נַמִי בְּסֵיפָא יוֹצֵא מֵהֶן. ת"ש אָמַר ר' יְהוּדָה: מַעֲשֶׂה וְאָסַר רַבִּי טַרְפוֹן עָלַי בֵּיצִים שֶׁנִּתְבַּשְּׁלוּ עִמּוֹ. אָמְרוּ לוֹ: (א) אֵימָתַי — בִּזְמַן שֶׁאָמַר "בָּשָׂר זֶה עָלַי", שֶׁהַנּוֹדֵר מִן הַדָּבָר וְנִתְעָרֵב בְּאַחֵר, וְיֵשׁ בּוֹ בְּנוֹתֵן טַעַם — הֲרֵי זֶה אָסוּר. בְּ"אֵלּוּ" לָא קָא מִבָּעֲיָא לָן דְּדַוְקָא הוּא. כִּי מִבָּעֲיָא לָן בְּ"שֶׁאֵינִי טוֹעֵם", דַּוְקָא אוֹ לָאו דַּוְקָא? ת"ש: *"דָּג דָּגִים שֶׁאֵינִי טוֹעֵם" — אָסוּר בָּהֶן, בֵּין גְּדוֹלִים בֵּין קְטַנִּים, בֵּין חַיִּים בֵּין מְבוּשָּׁלִים, וּמוּתָּר בְּטָרִית טְרוּפָה וּבְצִיר. אָמַר רָבָא: וּכְבָר יָצָא מֵהֶן.§ מתני'

[פסחים ג. וש"נ]

[לעיל ע"א]

ר"ן

גמ' ורמינהו מן העדשים אסור באשישים ור' יוסי מתיר. אשישין אמרי בירושלמי דאינון טלפחי דמגבלן ומטגנן בדבש. ומדרבי יוסי קפריך, דאילו לרבנן לא קשיא. דאע"ג דגבי חלב שרו בקום היינו משום דקום לאו חלב הוא, אבל אשישים אע"ג דמטגנן בדבש – עדשים נינהו. אבל דרבי יוסי אדרבי יוסי קשיא; דאי הכא שרי משום דכיון דאית בהו דובשא אשישין מיקריין – כ"ש דלא ה"ל למיסר בקום שהוא ד"א לגמרי! ומפרקינן: דטעמא דרבי יוסי משום דבאתריה הוו קרו לקומא "קומא דחלבא", וכל שם אביו עליו – אסור. אבל אשישים, כיון שנשתנו ואין שם עדשים עליהן – שרו. ורבנן נמי משום הכי שרו בקום – משום דבאתרייהו לחלבא קרו ליה חלבא ולקומא קומא. וא"ת: לר' יוסי, תינח דנודר מן החלב אסור בקום, לפי שעדיין שם חלב עליו, ד"קומא דחלבא" קרו ליה. אלא נודר מן הקום אמאי אסור בחלב? הא לא קרו ליה "חלבא דקומא"! יש לומר: דכיון דקרו לקומא "קומא דחלבא" – הוו להו חלב וקום דבר אחד. ***מתני'** הנודר מן היין מותר בתבשיל שיש בו טעם יין. שאין במשמעות של נודר מן היין אלא כשהוא בעינו. קונם יין שאני טועם ונפל לתבשיל אם יש בו טעם יין הרי זה אסור. דכיון דאמר "שאני טועם" אסור אפי' ע"י תערובות, דכיון שיש בו טעם יין הרי הוא טועמו בו. אמר קונם זיתים וענבים אלו שאני טועם אסור בהן וביוצא מהן. בגמ' מפרש איסורא אי הוה משום "אלו" או משום "שאני טועם". **גמ'** בעי רמי בר חמא אלו דוקא או שאני טועם דוקא. ודאי פשיטא ליה לרמי בר חמא דבחד מינייהו סגי. אלא דמספקא ליה אי "אלו" דוקא ולא "שאני טועם" דלא מהניא מידי, או "שאני טועם" דוקא ו"אלו" לא מהני כלל. ואהדר ליה: אי ס"ד "אלו" דוקא, "שאני טועם" למה לי? ובדין הוא דהוה מצי למימר ליה נמי: אי "שאני טועם" דוקא "אלו" למה לי. אלא דקמייתא נקט וה"ה לאידך. ומתרלינן: הא קמ"ל דאע"ג דאמר "שאני טועם", אי אמר "אלו" מיתסר, ואי לא – לא. ומינה נמי דאי "שאיני טועם" דוקא, הא קמ"ל דאע"ג דאמר "אלו", אי אמר "שאיני טועם" מיתסר ואי לא – לא. ואיבא למידק: היכי מספקא ליה לרמי בר חמא דליהוי "שאני טועם" עדיף טפי מאלו? דהא אנן תנן איפכא: "קונם פירות אלו עלי" אסור בחילופיהן ובגידוליהן, "שאני אוכל" "שאני טועם" מותר בחילופיהן ובגידוליהן. אלמא טפי עדיף "אלו" מ"שאני טועם"! יש לומר: כי עדיף – ה"מ לגבי חילופיהן וגדוליהן דאיתנהו בכלל "אלו" כיון דיתדינהו שוינהו כהקדש, וכמו שנפרש לפנינו בסיעתא דשמיא, ומש"ה בדין הוא דליתסרו חלופיהן וגידוליהן כי היכי דאסירי בהקדש. אבל כי אמר "שאני אוכל" "שאני טועם" לא משמע דליתסרו חלופיהן וגדוליהן, דאדרבה הא אפקינהו, שהרי כשאוכל חילופיהן וגידוליהן אינו טועם מהם כלל. **אמר רבא ת"ש** קונם פירות האלו עלי וכו' **הא ביוצא** מהן מותר. דס"ד דאי יוצא מהן אסור – טפי הוי רבותא לישמעינן דיוצא מהן אסור, אע"פ שנשתנית צורת הפירות שאסר עליו, מחילופיהן וגדוליהן שעדיין היא קיימת. ומפיך ליה: דאדרבה, הא עדיפא ליה לאשמועינן דחילופיהן אע"פ שלא יצאו מגוף האיסור כגידוליהן דמו, וכל שכן יוצא מהן שיצא מגוף האיסור ממש. ובדין הוא דהוה מצי למיפשט בעיין ממתניתא דתניא לעיל בסמוך: ואם אמר "בשר זה עלי" אסור בו וברוטבו וקיפו, אלא דממתניתין בעי למיפשטה. **ת"ש שאיני אוכל** וכו' **הא ביוצא** מהן אסור. דאי יוצא מהן מותר – ודאי לגבי "שאיני אוכל" "שאיני טועם" הויא רבותא טפי שריותא דיוצא מהן משריותא דחילופיהן וגידוליהן כדכתיבנא לעיל. ומהדר ליה דאין ה"נ, אלא איידי דלא נסיב רישא יוצא מהן, משום דלאיסורא דחילופיהן הויא רבותא טפי – לא נסיב סיפא יוצא מהן. **תא שמע אמר רבי יהודה** וכו'. אלא ב"אלו" לא קמבעיא לן דדוקא הוא, דמתניתין היא. כי קמבעיא לן "שאיני אוכל" "שאיני טועם"; דוקא הוא, ומתני' או או קתני. או לאו דוקא הוא, והא קמ"ל דאע"ג דאמר "שאיני טועם" אי אמר "אלו" אין, ואי לא – לא. ואתינן למיפשטה מדקתני: ומותר בטרית טרופה ובציר, אלמא "שאיני טועם" לאו דוקא. **אמר רבא וכבר יצא** מהן. לעולם "שאיני טועם, נמי דווקא, ואי יצא לאחר מכן אין ה"נ דאסיר. וכי תנן דשריין – בשכבר יצא מהן קודם נדרו. ולענין הלכה. ב"אלו" פשיטא לן דדוקא הוא ואסור ביוצא מהן. ב"שאיני טועם" מספקא לן ולא איפשיטא בעיין, וכיון דלא איפשיטא משמע דנקטינן לחומרא. ואיכא מ"ד דהיינו טעמא דאסור ביוצא מהן, משום דכיון דנחית כולי

רש"י

גמ' מִן הָעֲדָשִׁים אָסוּר בַּאֲשִׁישִׁים. בְּלֶחֶם שֶׁמְּעוֹרָב בּוֹ קֶמַח שֶׁל עֲדָשִׁים, דְּקָסָבַר אֲשִׁישִׁים בִּכְלַל עֲדָשִׁים הֵם. וְרַבִּי יוֹסֵי מַתִּיר. דְּלָא הָוֵי בִּכְלַל עֲדָשִׁים. קַשְׁיָא דְּרַבִּי יוֹסֵי אַדְּר' יוֹסֵי, קַשְׁיָא דְּרַבָּנַן אַדְּרַבָּנַן. דְּרַבָּנַן אָסְרֵי הָכָא וְאָמְרֵי: אֲשִׁישִׁים בִּכְלַל עֲדָשִׁים, וּבְמַתְנִיתִין שָׁרוּ, דְּקָאָמְרֵי: קוּמָא לָאו בִּכְלַל חָלָב הוּא. וְהָכִי נַמִי קַשְׁיָא לְרַבִּי יוֹסֵי, דְּהָכָא מַתִּיר מִשּׁוּם דִּסְבִירָא לֵיהּ דַּאֲשִׁישִׁים לָאו בִּכְלַל עֲדָשִׁים, וּבְמַתְנִי' קָאָסַר דִּסְבִירָא לֵיהּ קוּמָא בִּכְלַל חָלָב הִיא קָיְימָא. קוּמָא **דַּחֲלָבָא.** וְהוֹאִיל וְהָוֵי בִּכְלַל חָלָב – לְהָכִי אָסוּר. וְהָכִי נַמִי מִתָּרְיְצָא לְבָרַיְיתָא: בְּאַתְרֵיהּ דְּתַנָּא קַמָּא קָרוּ לֵיהּ אֲשִׁישִׁים לְפַת שֶׁל עֲדָשִׁים, וּבְאַתְרֵיהּ דְּר' יוֹסֵי לָא קָרוּ אֲשִׁישִׁים, הִלְכָּךְ שָׁרֵי ר' יוֹסֵי. מוּתָּר בְּתַבְשִׁיל שֶׁיֵּשׁ בּוֹ טַעַם יַיִן. שֶׁהֲרֵי לֹא נָדַר מִטַּעֲמוֹ שֶׁל יַיִן. **מתני'** קוֹנָם זֵיתִים וַעֲנָבִים אֵלּוּ שֶׁאֵינִי טוֹעֵם. הוֹאִיל וְאָמַר (ב) "טוֹעֵם" – אָסוּר בָּהֶן. וּבַיּוֹצֵא מֵהֶן. בְּשֶׁמֶן וּבְיַיִן. **גמ'** אֵלּוּ דַּוְקָא. דְּמִשּׁוּם "אֵלּוּ" אָסוּר בָּהֶן וּבַיּוֹצֵא מֵהֶן. אוֹ דִּילְמָא "שֶׁאֵינִי טוֹעֵם" דַּוְקָא, דְּמִשּׁוּם דְּאָמַר "שֶׁאֵינִי טוֹעֵם" אָסוּר בָּהֶן וּבַיּוֹצֵא מֵהֶן. אִי ס"ד אֵלּוּ דַּוְקָא. וְ"שֶׁאֵינִי טוֹעֵם" לָאו לְהָכִי תָּנָא, "שֶׁאֵינִי טוֹעֵם" לָמָּה לִי? הָא קָא מַשְׁמַע לָן דאע"ג דַּאֲמַר שֶׁאֵינִי טוֹעֵם אִי אֲמַר אֵלּוּ מִיתְּסַר. בַּיּוֹצֵא מֵהֶן, אִי לָא – לָא. וְהָכִי נַמִי [אִי הֲוֵי] אָמְרִי': וְאִי אָמְרַתְּ "שֶׁאֵינִי טוֹעֵם" דַּוְקָא וְ"אֵלּוּ" לָאו דַּוְקָא, לְמַאי תָּנָא "אֵלּוּ", [וַהֲוָה מְתָרְצִינַן]: הָא קָמַשְׁמַע לָן, אע"ג דַּאֲמַר "אֵלּוּ", אִי אֲמַר "שֶׁאֵינִי טוֹעֵם" מִיתְּסַר בַּיּוֹצֵא מֵהֶן, אִי לָא – לָא, מַאי? פֵּירוֹת הָאֵלּוּ. כֵּיוָן דַּאֲמַר "אֵלּוּ" אָסוּר בְּחִילּוּפֵיהֶן וּבְגִידּוּלֵיהֶן, וְדָיְיקִינַן מִינֵּיהּ: הָא בַּיּוֹצֵא מֵהֶן, כְּגוֹן סַחַט מַשְׁקֶה – מוּתָּר. וּשְׁמַע מִינָּהּ דְּ"אֵלּוּ" לָאו דַּוְקָא. תְּרֵיץ: לָא תֵּימָא הָא בַּיּוֹצֵא מֵהֶן מוּתָּר, אֶלָּא הוּא הַדִּין דַּאֲפִי' יוֹצֵא מֵהֶן אָסוּר, דְּהָא "אֵלּוּ" קָאָמַר, וְ"אֵלּוּ" דַּוְקָא. וְהָא דְּלָא נָקַט בְּהֶדְיָא אָסוּר בַּיּוֹצֵא מֵהֶן. הָא עֲדִיפָא לְאַשְׁמוּעִינַן דְּחִילּוּפֵיהֶן. אע"ג דְּלָא הָווּ גּוּפַיְיהוּ – כְּגִידּוּלִין דָּמוּ. שֶׁאֵינִי אוֹכֵל וְשֶׁאֵינִי טוֹעֵם. כְּגוֹן דְּלָא אֲמַר (ג) "אֵלּוּ". טוֹעֵם מַשְׁמַע דְּמִדִּידְהוּ גּוּפַיְיהוּ קָאָמַר, לְפִיכָךְ מוּתָּר בְּגִידּוּלֵיהֶן וּבְחִילּוּפֵיהֶן. וְדָיְיקִינַן: הָא בַּיּוֹצֵא מֵהֶן אָסוּר, דְּהָא טוֹעֵם מִגּוּפַיְיהוּ קָאָמַר, אַלְמָא דְּ"שֶׁאֵינִי טוֹעֵם" דַּוְקָא. הוּא הַדִּין דַּאֲפִי' בַּיּוֹצֵא מֵהֶן מוּתָּר (ד) אַיְּידֵי דְּלָא תָּנָא בְּרֵישָׁא יוֹצֵא מֵהֶן מוּתָּר. דַּעֲדִיפָא לֵיהּ נָקַט, לָא קָתָנֵי בְּסֵיפָא "יוֹצֵא מֵהֶן". בִּזְמַן שֶׁאָמַר בָּשָׂר זֶה עָלַי. דַּהֲוֵי כְּמ"ד "אֵלּוּ עָלַי", וש"מ "אֵלּוּ" דַּוְקָא. וּמוּתָּר בְּצִיר. דְּהַיְינוּ צִיר הַיּוֹצֵא מֵהֶן, אַלְמָא דְּ"שֶׁאֵינִי טוֹעֵם" לָאו דַּוְקָא. אָמַר רָבָא. תְּרֵיץ הָא דְּקָתָנֵי מוּתָּר – בְּצִיר שֶׁכְּבָר יָצָא מֵהֶן קוֹדֶם שֶׁנָּדַר, וּלְהָכִי מוּתָּר. אֲבָל אִם לְאַחַר שֶׁנָּדַר יָצָא מֵהֶן, לְעוֹלָם אֵימָא לָךְ דְּאָסוּר, וְ"שֶׁאֵינִי טוֹעֵם" דַּוְקָא. מתני'

[לקמן נג:]

לעיל מז. [לקמן נז. נט.]

[לעיל נח:]

תוספות

ורמינהו אסור באשישין. דפסולת עדשים (אינם) בכלל עדשים ורבי יוסי מתיר קשיא דרבי יוסי אדרבי יוסי ודרבנן אדרבנן: **לא** קשיא דבנדרים הלך אחר לשון בני אדם [ובאתרי' דר"י לקומא] קרו ליה נמי קומא דחלבא: **מן** הרוטב מותר בקיפה. דקדוקי בשר אף כי איכא נתינת טעם מן הרוטב דלא אסור אלא הקרוי רוטב בלבד וכרבנן דפליגי ארבי יהודה במתני': **בשר** מותר ברוטב בשר זה אסור ברוטבו ובמקפה אי איכא נתינת טעם: **אלו** דוקא או שאני טועם דוקא. אמתני' בעי דקתני קונם זיתים אלו שאני טועם אסור בהם וביוצא מהם ומיבעי ליה מה שאנו אוסרין יוצא מהם איירי דאמר שאני טועם דוקא אבל אם לא אמר אלא קונם אלו עלי לא מיתסר אלא (ביוצא) מהם וא"ת היכי מצינו למימר דשאני טועם חמור מקונם אלו והא גבי חילופיהן וגדוליהן דמותר בהם [כשאמר שאני טועם] וכשאמר קונם פירות אלו אסור ויש לומר דשאני גבי חילופיהן שאינו תלוי באלו כלל אלא בהזכרה כשאמר שאני אוכל שאני טועם דלא נתכוון לאסור כ"א גופם לאכול ולא חילופיהן ובשלא הזכיר שאני אוכל ואמר קונם עלי פירות כי נמי לא אמר אלו שוינהו עליה איסור בין הם בין חילופיהן אבל לענין יוצא מהם יכול להיות דאלים טפי לישנא דשאני אוכל ושאני טועם מקונם אלו: **דאי** סלקא דעתך אלו דוקא שאני טועם ל"ל הא קמ"ל דאע"ג דאמר שאני טועם אי אמר אלו אין אי לא לא [הגה"ה ז"ו מנאת"י מבחו"ן]: **ת"ש** שאני אוכל ושאני טועם מותר בחילופיהן. נראה דקאי אקונם פירות אלו דאע"ג דאמר אלו כשאמר שאני אוכל מגרע ליה איסור הנאה דגלי אדעתיה שאינו אוסר אלא באכילה אע"ג דלענין יוצא מהם אהני שאני טועם להחמיר ורוצה לדבר דהא שאני אוכל קאי נמי אפירות אלו לאידך בבא האומר לאשתו קונם מעשה ידיך אסור בחילופיהן ואיירי כגון דאמר אלו או שמא משמעות הלשון כך כשאוסר מעשה ידיה כגון אם אמר פירות אלו וקתני עלה שאני אוכל שאני טועם מותר בחילופיהן ובגידוליהן ולפירוש זה ק' דדייק הא ביוצא מהם אסור [למאי] שאני הכא דקאמר אלו ושאני טועם ושמא מדלא נקט התנא בהדיא בסיפא קונם פירות אלו שאני טועם אלא נקט שאני טועם גרידא משמע דאפילו לא אמר אלו אשמעינן תנא "מותר בחילופיהן ואסור ביוצא מהם: **ע"ד** כא"ן הגה"ה מהר"ם וז"ה מנאת"י בפני"ם: **ת"ש** [קונם פירות האלו עלי וכו'] הא ביוצא מהם מותר. דאי אסור ליתני אסור ביוצא מהם וכ"ש בחילופיהן דמשמע ליה דמסתבר טפי להתיר יוצא מהם מחילופיהן [ומשני] דהה"נ דיוצא מהם אסור ולרבותא נקט יוצא מהם ואשמעינן חלופיהן כגידוליהן ואוסרין דאי תנא יוצא מהם אסור ה"א דחילופיהן דקרו הואיל ולא באו מגוף האיסור עצמו: **ת"ש** שאני אוכל שאני טועם ולא אמר אלו מותר בחילופיהן הא יוצא מהם אסור. אע"ג דלא אמר אלו דאי מותר לישמעינן יוצא מהם וכ"ש חילופיהם שאינם מגוף הפירות דהכי [משני] לעיל דחילופיהן עדיף לאשמועינן בריש לאיסורא מביוצא מהם וקשה לידחי כמאי דסלקא דעתך בת"ש דלעיל דאדרבה מסתבר טפי לאיסורא חילופיהן מיוצא מהם וזיל הכא קמדחי ליה [וזיל הכא קמדחי ליה] ומשני איידי דלא נסיב רישא יוצא מהם כו' דהא שניא דהא עדיף ליה למיתני חילופיהן כגידוליהן לא נקט נמי בסיפא יוצא מהם ואע"ג דה"ה ודאי שרו בחילופיהן: **בשר** זה עלי כו' אסור בנותן טעם. ומדמי יוצא מהם לנ"ט דכי היכי דאסר אדנפשיה כשאמר בשר זה עלי בנ"ט ה"נ אסור יוצא מהן וזה היינו כמו אלו אלמא דבאלו מיתסר יוצא מהן. **ת"ש** ומותר בטרית טרופה ובציר. וציר היינו יוצא מהן אלמא בשאני טועם גרידא מותר יוצא מהם: **אמר** רבא שכבר יצא. פי' האי ציר דקשרי היינו בציר שיצא מהם קודם נדרו ובההוא אינו נאסר אף כשאני טועם דוקא אבל ביוצא מהם אחר נדרו (אסור) אימא לך דלאסור דשאני טועם דוקא ולא איפשיטא לן אי שאני אוכל דוקא הלכך בשל תורה הלך לחומרא ובשאני טועם גרידא אסור יוצא מהם ועוד נשמעינן שאם אדם אוסר שלא יאכל בשר עד זמן פלוני שאסור ברוטב דהא בהא תליא דאי יוצא מהם אסור ה"נ נתינת טעם אסור דמדמה לה בדידי: הגו"ר

פי' הרא"ש

ורמינהו מן העדשים אסור באשישים ור' יוסי מתיר. וקשה לתרוייהו: ותשני **מר כי אתריה כו' באתריה דר' יוסי לקומא קרו נמי קומא דחלבא.** וכן בעדשים באתרא דרבנן קרו לאשישים אשישים דעדשים אי נמי לרבנן דפסולת נקרא על שם העיקר ולרבי יוסי לא: **אלו דקא או שאיני טועם דוקא.**

הגהות הב"ח

(א) גמ' אמרו לו כ הדבר אימתי בזמן: (ב) רש"י ד"ה קונם וכו' הואיל ואמר שאיני טועם: (ג) ד"ה שאיני אוכל ושאיני טועם כגון דלא אמר אלא שאיני טועם דמשמע למדידהו: (ד) ד"ה הוא הדין וכו' מותר אלא איידי דלא:

מתני' [א]הנודר מן התמרים — מותר בדבש תמרים, מסתוניות — מותר בחומץ סתוניות. רבי יהודה בן בתירא אומר: כל ששם תולדתו קרויה עליו, ונודר הימנו — אסור ביוצא הימנו, וחכמים מתירים.§ **גמ'** [חכמים] היינו ת"ק! [ב]איכא בינייהו הדא דתניא: כלל זה אר"ש בן אלעזר: כל שדרכו (א) לאכול, ודרך היוצא ממנו לאכול, כגון תמרים ודבש תמרים, נדר בו [א] אסור ביוצא ממנו, נודר מיוצא ממנו [ב] אסור בו. כל שאין דרכו לאכול, ודרך היוצא ממנו לאכול, נודר בו — אין אסור אלא ביוצא ממנו, שלא נתכוון זה אלא ליוצא ממנו.§ **מתני'** [ג]הנודר מן היין — מותר ביין תפוחים, [ד]מן השמן — מותר בשמן שומשמין, [ה]מן הדבש — מותר בדבש תמרים, מן החומץ — מותר בחומץ סתוניות, [ו]מן הכרישין — מותר בקפלוטות, מן הירק — מותר בירקות השדה, שהוא שם לווי.§ **גמ'** תניא: *[ז]הנודר מן השמן, בארץ ישראל — מותר בשמן שומשמין ואסור בשמן זית, ובבבל — אסור בשמן שומשמין ומותר בשמן זית, [ח]מקום שמסתפקין מזה ומזה — אסור בזה ובזה. פשיטא! לא צריכא, דרובא מן חד מסתפקין. מהו דתימא: איזיל בתר רובא, קא משמע לן: *[ט]ספק איסורא לחומרא. הנודר מן הירק בשאר שני שבוע — אסור בירקות הגינה ומותר בירקות השדה, ובשביעית — אסור בירקות השדה ומותר בירקות הגינה. אמר רבי אבהו משום רבי חנינא בן גמליאל:

לא

רש"י

מתני' מן הסתוניות. היינו ענבים קשים, שמניחן בכרם כל ימי הסתיו, ועושין מהן חומץ. כל ששם תולדתו קרויה עליו. כגון חומץ זה שיוצא ממנו — קרוי נמי על שם אמו, חומץ סתוניות, ולא חומץ סתם. נדר ממנו **אסור ביוצא** כו'. והכי נמי כי נדר בסתוניות — אסור נמי בחומץ היוצא ממנו. וחכמים מתירין. וקא פריך בגמרא: היינו תנא קמא, דקתני: מותר בחומץ סתוניות. **גמ'** נדר בו. בתמרים. **אסור ביוצא** ממנו. בדבש תמרים. כל שאין דרכו לאכול. כגון סתוניות, דדרך היוצא ממנו לאכול והן עצמן אין דרכן לאכול. תנא קמא דמתניתין, דאמר מותר בחומץ סתוניות — לית ליה דרבי שמעון בן אלעזר, אלא קסבר: נדר בו — אין אסור אלא בו, אע"ג שאין דרכו לאכול. וחכמים, תנא בתרא, אית להו דרבי שמעון בן אלעזר. ודקתני: וחכמים מתירים בו — בגופו, אבל ביוצא ממנו — לא, דאין אסור אלא ביוצא ממנו, והיינו כר' שמעון בן אלעזר, דאמר: לא נתכוון זה כו'. ורבי יהודה בן בתירא היה אוסר בו וביוצא הימנו. **מתני'** מן השמן. משמע שמן זית, להכי מותר בשמן שומשמין. כרישין.(ג) קטנית. מותר בירקות השדה. דהיינו שם לווי, ירק השדה ולא ירק סתם. **גמ'** מותר בשמן שומשמין. לפי שאין מלוי בא"י שמן שומשמין אלא שמן זית, ובאותו שמן נדר. מזה ומזה. משמן זית ומשמן שומשמין. **ספק איסורא לחומרא**. ומשמן שמסתפקין בו נדר, בין רב בין מעט. **אסור** בירקות הגינה. גרי"ס המור"ה במסכת"א ז"ו: ומותר בירקות השדה*. שעליהן סומכין בשביעית, שהפקירו הגנות לעניים, ואין מסתפקין אלא בירקות השדה.

לא

ר"ן

ככולי האי לדיוקא – משמע דדעתיה אכל מאי דנפיק מינייהו. וכי תימא: תינח ב"שאני טועם", כיון דלא צריך וקאמר – אפושי איסורא הוא. אבל "שאני אוכל" מאי איכא למימר? דהא כיון דלא סגי ליה אם אמר "קונם פירות האלו" דאי הכי – משמע בין באכילה בין בהנאה, ואיהו לא בעי למסרינהו אלא באכילה, הלכך כי אמר "שאני אוכל" – ליכא שום הוכחה למיסר אפילו ביוצא מהן! איכא למימר: דכיון דהוה מצי למימר "קונם פירות האלו באכילה עלי" וקאמר "שאני אוכל" – אף יוצא מהן משמע. ואמרו לפי זה, דבשבועה דלא מצי למימר "באכילה עלי", דלשון נדר הוא, ועל כרחיה אית ליה למימר "שאני אוכל" – לא מיתסר ביוצא מהן. ואחרים אומרים זה הוא דעת הרמב"ס ז"ל *דלא שנא נדר ולא שנא שבועה, דלאו משום יתורא דלישנא הוא, אלא שהלשון בעצמו מוכיח כן, דלשון "שאני אוכל ושאני טועם" – משמע שאוסר כל אכילה וטעימה הבאה מהם. **מתני'** הנודר מן התמרים וכו' מסתוניות מותר בחומץ סתוניות. סתוניות – ענבים שאינם מתבשלים, ועומדים בימי החורף. כל ששם תולדתו קרויה עליו. כגון דבש תמרים וחומץ סתוניות. וחכמים מתירים. בגמרא פריך: היינו ת"ק. ואיכא למידק: תנא קמא מני לא ר' יוסי ולא רבנן, דהא אמרינן לעיל בפלוגתא דקום וחלב דכל היכא דקרו ליה קומא דחלבא – אסור אפילו לרבנן, ודבש תמרים וחומץ סתוניות ליתסר מהאי טעמא! [י"ל]: דלא דמי, דאילו גבי קום דחלב – הקום לא נשתנה מצורה לצורה, דמעיקרא נמי כשהיה מעורב בחלב – באותה צורה עצמה היה, אבל הכא – הרי נשתנה הגוף, הרשב"א ז"ל. ועוד: דבקום כי קרי ליה קומא דחלבא – מפני שעדיין תורת חלב עליו קרו ליה, ולא להפריש בין זה לאחר, שאין נקרא קום אלא זה. אבל הכא, כי אמרו דבש תמרים וחומץ סתוניות – לא שיהא עדיין תורת תמרים וסתוניות עליהן, אלא להפריש בין דבש תמרים לדבש אחר, ובין חומץ סתוניות לחומץ אחר. **גמ'** חכמים היינו ת"ק **איכא בינייהו הא דתניא כלל אר"ש** [ב"א] **כל שדרכו לאכול ודרך היוצא** ממנו **לאכול** כגון תמרים ודבש תמרים, נדר בו – אסור ביוצא ממנו, [ביוצא ממנו] – אסור בו, וכל שאין דרכו לאכול ודרך היוצא ממנו לאכול, נדר בו – אסור ביוצא ממנו. כך גרסינן בהלכות הרמב"ן ז"ל. וה"פ: דבהא פליגי; ת"ק פליג אדרשב"א בתרוייהו, דסבירא ליה לתנא קמא דבין דרכו לאכול בין אין דרכו לאכול – אסור בו, ולא ביוצא ממנו. ורשב"א סבירא ליה דבשדרכו [לאכול] ודרך היוצא ממנו לאכול – אסור בשניהם, ובשאין דרכו לאכול ודרך היוצא ממנו לאכול – אסור ביוצא ממנו, ולא בו, ובהא מפיק ליה לת"ק לגמרי. ור' יהודה בן בתירא סבר לה כר"ש בדרכו [לאכול] ודרך היוצא ממנו לאכול – דאסור בשניהם, ופליג עליה בשאין דרכו לאכול ודרך היוצא ממנו לאכול, דרבי יהודה בן בתירא לא שני ליה, ומיתסר נמי בתרוייהו. ולרשב"א שני ליה, ולא מיתסר אלא ביוצא ממנו. ורבנן בתראי דמתני' – היינו ר' שמעון בן אלעזר, ושריותא דידהו קאי אאין דרכו לאכול דשרי הוא גופיה. ומשמע לי, דמשום הכי משמע ממלתייהו דלהאי גוונא, מדקתני סתמא וחכמים מתירים – דמשמע דאתרוייהו פליגי, ובמאי [דשוו] ת"ק ור' יהודה לאיסורא שרו אינהו. ומש"ה פשיטא דאסתוניות קאי, דאיכא טעמא להיתרא דמשום שאין דרכו לאכול – איכא למימר דלא נתכוון אלא ליוצא מהן. דאתמרים דשוו נמי תרווייהו לאיסורא – ליכא למימר דשרו רבנן בתראי מן התמרים, דלישרי בתמרים גופייהו ליכא טעמא להיתרא. ולענין הלכה קיימא לן כתנא קמא, דבין בתמרים בין בסתוניות אינו אסור אלא בהן אבל לא בדבש וחומץ שלהן. **מתני'** הנודר מן היין מותר ביין תפוחים. דכיון שיש לו שם לווי – לא מיקרי יין סתם. מותר בקפלוטות. דלא הוי בכלל כרישין. מותר בירקות השדה. דסתם ירק לא משמע אלא ירק גינה. *) **אספרגוס**. מין כרוב הוא. **אסור** מן המקפה. תבשיל עב של גריסין. ואסור משום דקרו ליה מקפה דגריסין. ר' יוסי מתיר. דאתריה קרו למקפה מקפה, ולגריסין גריסין. **אסור** בשום. משום דמקפה כולל כל דבר קפוי ועבה, ושום נמי קרוי מקפה על שם שממחין אותו במעט מים ונאכל בכך. מותר לכוס חיים. שהכוסס אינו כוסס אחת אחת בפני עצמה. אבל פת, כיון שהוא גוף אחד – חיטה מיקרי. והכי איתא בירושלמי, דגרסינן התם: חטה, ואת מר כן? בתמיה. אמר רבי יוסי: ארחא דבר נשא מחמי פיתא – נקטה ומימר "בריך דברא הדא חיטתא". **גמ'** מותר בשמן שומשמין. דבא"י אין מסתפקין כלל אלא בשמן זית. **ספק איסורא לחומרא**. וכיון דאיכא מיעוטא דמסתפקי מההוא מינא – איכא לספוקי דלמא אפי' לאלו נתכוין. **אסור** בירקות הגינה. דסתם ירק – של גינה משמע, ולא ירק שדה שיש לו שם לווי. מיהו אפ"ה הנודר מן היין אסור בחמרא מבשלא. וכן כתב הרמב"ן ז"ל. ולא דמי לירקות השדה, דהני מינא אחרינא נינהו. אבל חמרא וחמרא מבשלא – חד מינא נינהו, ומפני שנתבשל – לא הפסיד שמו. בשביעית **אסור** בירקות השדה. אם נדר בשביעית א"א לומר שנתכוון לירק גינה – דהא אין זורעין ולא נוטעין בשביעית, אלא ודאי לירק השדה שעולה מאליו נתכוון.

*) מכאן עד סוף המתני' שייך לע"ב

אבל

עין משפט נר מצוה

יג א מיי' פ"ט מהל' נדרים הלכה יד סמג לאוין רמב טוש"ע י"ד סימן ריז סעיף יג:
יד ב מיי' שם טוש"ע שם בהג"ה:
טו ג מיי' שם טוש"ע שם סעיף טו:
טז ד מיי' שם טוש"ע שם סעיף יז:
יז ה מיי' טוש"ע שם סעיף יד:
יח ו מיי' שם טוש"ע שם סעיף י:
[פ"ט מהל' נדרים הלכה יד]
יט ז ח ט מיי' שם הלכה ה טוש"ע שם סעיף יז:

מסורת הש"ס

[תוספתא פ"ג ע"ש]

[כתובות עג: וש"נ]

[נ"א ובשביעית אסור בירקות השדה שעליהן כו']

הגהות הב"ח

(א) גמ' שדרכו לאכול. וכן בכל העמוד: (ב) רש"י ד"ה כרישין קטניס קפלוטות גדולים הס"ד:

הגהות הגר"א

[א] גמ' נדר בו אסור. נ"ב גירסת הירושלמי מותר וכן עיקר: [ב] שם מיוצא ממנו אסור. נ"ב מותר ככ"ע (ועי' בהגר"א יו"ד סי' רי"ז ס"ק י"ח) וכפירוש ר"מ בתוס' וכ"ד הרמב"ם ופסק כחכמים:

תוספות

הנודר מן התמרים מותר בדבש. פירוש דאמר קונם תמרים עלי מותר בדבש היוצא מהם דדבש איקרי תמרים [לא איקרי] וקשה אמאי לא תנא הכא כדקתני בשאר בבי תמרים אלו שאני טועם אסור ביוצא מהם: **בסתוניות.** ענבים קשים ורעים לאכול מותר בחומץ היוצא מהן: **כל** ששם תולדתו עליו. פירוש שאינו מפסיד שמו הראשון כמו דבש תמרים ששם תמרים עליו נדר בתמרים אסור בדבש: **וחכמים** מתירין. בגמ' פריך היינו תנא קמא: **מותר** ביין תפוחים. דסתם יין דענבים קאמר: **מותר** בשמן שומשמין. דסתם שמן הוא שמן זית: **מותר** בדבש תמרים. דסתם דבש זהו דבש דבורים: **מותר** בחומץ סתוניות. דסתם חומץ מיין טוב שהחמיץ: **מן** הכרישין מותר בקפלוטות. אע"פ שממין כרישין הן באו שיש להן שם לווי: **מן** הירק סתם מותר בירק שדה. דסתם ירק של גינה: **חכמים** היינו ת"ק. דשרי בדבש תמרים איכא בינייהו דתניא כו' כל שדרכו לאכול כו' ומיירי שגם תולדתו עליו דאל"כ לית ליה [הנודר] בענבים מותר ביין וכל שאין דרכו לאכול כגון סתוניות שאין דרכן לאכול וחומץ שלהם דרכו לאכול: **נדר** בו אינו אסור אלא ביוצא ממנו. ת"ק לית ליה דרבי שמעון וחכמים אית ליה דרבי שמעון [ולאו לגמרי כר"ש סבירא להו] דודאי בדבש תמרים לא סברי כוותיה אלא בדינא דסתוניות וה"ק וחכמים מתירין בתמרים לאכול בדבש אבל בסתוניות לא שרינן בחומץ וקשה דהוה להו למיתני וחכמים אוסרין בסתוניות והר"ס פי' לפי מה שפירש דסתוניות אין דרכן ליאכל אלא היוצא מהם יש לפרש ת"ק ורבי יהודה בן בתירא לית להו דר"ש בן אלעזר דאסרו בסתוניות גופייהו ולא אסרי אלא ביוצא מהם וי"מ איכא בינייהו דת"ק נקט מן התמרים מותר בדבש משמע דדוקא בתמרים וסתוניות שהם ראויין אסור בהם ומותר ביוצא מהם הא נדר מדברים שאינם ראוים לאכול אסור בין בהם בין ביוצא מהם: **בשאר** שני שבוע אסור בירקות גינה ומותר בירקות שדה. דסתמא מירקות גינה נדר דירקות שדה יש להם שם של לואי בכל שאר שני שבוע ומרישא שמעינן לה דקתני מותר בירקות שדה אלמא אסור בירקות גינה אבל סיפא איצטריך ליה: **בשביעית.** פירוש שנדר בשביעית דירקות שדה מצויין בשביעית שבאות מאליהן אבל ירקות גינה אינם [illegible] ידי זריעה הלכך סתם ירקות בשביעית ירקות שדה היא: **בארץ** ישראל. דסתם שמן שלהן של זית: **מהו** דתימא זיל בתר רובא. ולא נתכוין לאסור עצמו אלא באותו מין שמסתפקין [illegible] המיעוט אסר עצמו: *)**לא** שנו דבשביעית מותר בירקות גינה משום דלא שכיחי שיאכלו ירקות גינה אלא במקום שאין מביאין כו' אבל במקום שמביאין שכיח הוא ירקי [illegible] **משום** גוש. דלכך הירק להיות גוש תלוי בו וגזרו על גוש ארץ העמים: **איספרגוס** מין כרוב הוא ובכלל כרוב הוא: **מן** האיספרגוס מותר בכרוב. דשאר כרוב אינו [illegible] אסור במקפה של גריסין. שנקראת גריסין אף כשהן בתבשיל אבל מן המקפה מותר בגריסין יבשין דלא תימא דכי נדר במקפה מן הראוי למקפה קאמר והיינו גריסין ולרבנן איצטריך [illegible] [מ]קפה הכא מודו: **מן** השום מותר במקפה. דלא נתכוון אלא לשום יבש: **מן** המקפה מותר בשום. אע"ג דלא נתכוון אלא לראוי למקפה ושום ראוי למקפה: **מן** האשישים. פי' [illegible] העדשים נקראין אשישין מן העדשים אסור באשישים שהם נקראים על שם העדשים ור"י מתיר לסבר לאינם בכלל עדשים: **חטה** חטין שאני טועם אסור בין בחטין [illegible] ומיהו בברייתא בגמ' גרסינן איפכא ושמא טוב לפרש הכא חטה או חטים גרים או גריסין אסור בין מבושלין בין חיין ורבי שמעון ורבי יהודה מחלקין בין גריסין כדמפרש גבי חטה חטין רבי יהודה אמר קונם גרים או חטה שאני טועם מותרין לכוס חיין דחטה וגרים משתמעי מבושלין:

פי' הרא"ש

הא דאמרינן במתניתין דאסור ביוצא מן הזיתים ומן הענבים כי אמר קונם זיתים וענבים אלו שאני טועם במאי תלי האיסור מי אמרינן דאלו הוי כמו בשר זה דאסור ברוטבו ובקיפו והוא הדין נמי ביוצא ממנו או דלמא כשמיחד דבר הנאסר זה מועיל לאסור נתינת טעם כדאמרינן במתני' הנודר מן הדבר ונתערב באחר אם יש בו בנותן טעם אסור אבל לא לאסור היוצא מן הזיתים ומן הענבים דמפקד פקיד בתוכן ודבר אחר הוא אבל כי אמר שאני טועם משמע כל מה שאני טועם מהם:

*) **שאני טועם למה לי.** הוא הדין נמי דמלי למיבעי אם שאני טועם דוקא אלו למה לי אלא בו פתח בראשון והוא הדין נמי דמלי למיבעי אם תרוייהו דוקא: **הא ביוצא מהם מותר.** דאי אסור ליתני יוצא מהן וכל שכן חילופיהן שבאו מכח האיסור עצמו אבל יוצא מהם דבר אחר הוא: **הא עדיפא ליה לאשמועינן לחילופיהן** כגדוליכן

*) [שייך לע"ב]

רבי

(גמ') לא שנו. דשביעית מותר בירקות הגינה, אלא במקום שאין מביאין ירק מח"ל דכיון שאין מביאין – ודאי לא נדר אלא מאותם שמסתפקים שם, היינו מירקות השדה, ולהכי מותר בשל גינה. **אבל במקום שמביאין כו' אסור.** אף בירקות הגינה, הואיל ורגילין לאכול שם בין ירקות השדה בין ירקות הגינה, דודאי אדעתא דהכי נדר. **כתנאי כו'.** לדעתא דמ"ד אין מביאין ירקות כו' – לדידיה מותר בירקות גינה ואסור בירקות שדה, דכיון דאין מביאין – לאו עליה נדר. ולמ"ד מביאין – אסור אף בירקות גינה. **משום גוש.** שמא יש מעפר חוצה לארץ בעיקרייהו, וטמא משום ספק מת.

לא שנו אלא במקום שאין מביאין ירק מחוצה לארץ לארץ, אבל במקום שמביאין ירק מחוצה לארץ לארץ — אסור. *כתנאי: אין מביאין ירק מן חוצה לארץ לארץ. רבי חנניה בן גמליאל אומר: מביאין ירק מחוצה לארץ. מ"ט דמאן דאמר אין מביאין? *אמר רבי ירמיה: משום גוש.§ **מתני'** [א]מן הכרוב — אסור[א] באיספרגוס, מן האיספרגוס — מותר בכרוב. [ב]מן הגריסין — אסור במקפה, ורבי יוסי מתיר. [ג]מן המקפה — מותר בגריסין, [ד]מן המקפה — אסור בשום, ור' יוסי מתיר. מן השום — מותר במקפה. *מן העדשים — אסור [ב] באשישים, ר' יוסי מתיר. מן האשישים — מותר בעדשים. [ה]"חטה חטין שאני טועם" — אסור בהן, בין קמח בין הפת. [ו]"גרים גריסין שאני טועם" — אסור בהן, בין חיין בין מבושלין. רבי יהודה אומר: "קונם גרים או חטה שאני טועם" — מותר לכוס חיים.§ **גמ'** תניא, ר' שמעון בן גמליאל אומר: [ז]"חטה שאני טועם" — אסור לאפות ומותר לכוס, "חטים שאני טועם" — אסור לכוס ומותר לאפות, "חטה חטין שאני טועם" — אסור בין לכוס בין לאפות. [ח]"גרים שאני טועם" — אסור לבשל ומותר לכוס, "גריסין שאני טועם" — אסור לכוס ומותר לבשל, "גרים גריסין שאני טועם" — אסור בין לבשל בין לכוס.§

הדרן עלך הנודר מן המבושל

ר"ן

אבל במקום שמביאין ירק מח"ל לארץ אסור. כלומר אסור בשניהם, דהוי ליה מקום שמסתפקין *זה מזה. **משום גוש.** חוששין להביאו משום חששא דגוש הנדבק בו. וגושא דארץ העמים טמא, כדאיתא בפ"ק דשבת (דף טו:). **חטה שאני טועם אסור לאפות.** דפת חטה מיקרי, דחד גופא נמי הוא. אבל חטים – משמע לכוס, מפני שאדם כוסס חטים חלוקין ביחד.

הדרן עלך הנודר מן המבושל

רש"י

מתני' אסור באיספרגוס. דהוי בכלל כרוב, דמין כרוב הוא. **מותר בכרוב.** דאין כרוב בכלל איספרגוס (א). **אסור בשום.** שנותנים ממנו בקדרה, דהיינו בכלל מקפה. **מותר במקפה.** דאין מקפה בכלל שום. **אסור במקפה.** של גריסין. **מותר בגריסין.** ד"ה, דאין גריסין בכלל מקפה. **מן המקפה.** של גריסין. **ר' יוסי מתיר.** דקסבר: אין מקפה בכלל גריסין. **אסור בשום.** של מקפה. **אסור באשישים.** כפת שמעורב בו קמח עדשים, דיש בכלל עדשים אשישים. **ומן אשישים כו'.** דברי הכל היא. **ר' יהודה אומר קונם גרים או חטה שאני טועם מותר לכוס.** חטה וגרים (ב) סתם, דלא אמר "חטה חטין" "גרים גריסין". דקסבר [ר"י: גרים או חטה] – מבושלים משמע, חיין לא משמע. ור' יהודה לא פליג עליה דתנא קמא. **גמ' אסור לאפות.** דאדעתא דהכי אמר חטה כדי לאפות, דחטה בגרגיר א' משמע, ומגרגיר לא קאמר. **חטין.** משמע חיין. **גרים.** משמע מבושל (ג). **גריסין.** משמע נמי חיין.

הדרן עלך הנודר מן המבושל

סנהדרין יב. ע"ש

[בס]

[לעיל נב: ע"ש בר"ן מירושו על מלת אשישים]

עין משפט נר מצוה

כ א ב ג ד מיי' פ"ט מהלכות נדרים הל' י טוש"ע י"ד סימן ריז סעיף י:

כא ה מיי' שם הלכה ט טוש"ע שם סעיף כ:

כב ו מיי' שם הלכה י טוש"ע שם סעיף כא:

נ"ל מזה ומזה

כג ז מיי' שם הלכה ט טוש"ע שם סעיף כ:

כד ח מיי' שם טוש"ע שם סעיף כא:

הגהות הגר"א

[א] משנה באספרגוס. נ"ב פירש רב האי גאון מין כרוב שעורין אותו ביין ובלשון יוני יין של בקר נקרא אספרגוס (ועי' רש"י ברכות נ"א ע"א ד"ה אספרגוס): [ב] שם באשישים. נ"ב בירושלמי מפרש טלופחין מקלין וטוחנין ומגבלן בדבש ומטוגנין:

תוספות

רבי יהודה אומר גרים או חטה שאני טועם מותר לכוס חיים. מדקאמר חטה וגרים סתם ולא אמר (חטה) חטין גריסין קסבר [חטה גרים] מבושלין משמע חיין לא משמע: **חטה** שאני טועם מותר לאפות. דחטה לא משמע אלא חיין חטין משמע לאפות ורבי שמעון ורבי יהודה לא פליגי לתרווייהו גרים חטה מבושלין משמע ולא חיין גריסין חטין משמע חיין אבל לא מבושלים: **הדרן עלך הנודר מן המבושל**

הנודר

פי' הרא"ש

[שייך לדף שלפניו] **כדוליהן.** דיותר הוא חדוש מה שחילופיהן אסור דאין לך דבר שתופס את דמיו אלא קודשו ומומרא שהחמירו חכמים באיסורי הנאה למי שהחליפן לכתחלה וא"ת אכתי ליתני חילופיהן ויוצא מהם לאשמועינן דחילופיהן כיוצא מהן וי"ל לחילופיהן וגדוליהן דמו להדדי דשניהם לא היו בשעה שאסרן עליו הלכך ניחא ליה למיתלי חילופיהן כגידוליהן: **תא שמע שאני אוכל שאני טועם כו' הא ביוצא מהם אסור** דאי מותר ליתני יוצא מהם וכ"ש חילופיהן לפי מאי דשני ליה דיוצא מהם עדיף מחילופיהן אפי' מגדוליהן עדיף בעי למימר השתא אלמא שאני טועם גורם לאסור היוצא מהם ואע"ג דמשמע פשטא דמתני' דקאי ארישא דאמר קונם פירות האלו והוסיף לומר שאני טועם וא"כ היכי דייק דשאני טועם גורם האיסור וי"ל דמ"מ דייק שפיר דאם איתא דשאני טועם אינו גורם האיסור אלא לשון היתר משמע דוקא מאלו איני טועם אבל מיוצא מהם אני טועם כמו בחילופיהן וגידוליהן אפי' כי אמר נמי האלו שאני טועם שרי: **איידי דלא נסיב רישא יוצא מהם.** משום דעדיף לאשמועינן איסורא חליפין: **ת"ש אמר רבי יהודה מעשה ואסר עלי כו'.** ופשיטא ליה השתא דאין חלוק בין נתינת טעם ליוצא מהם כשמברר הדבר הנאסר הכל אסור: **ומותר בטרית טרופה וכליל.** וליר היינו יוצא מהן. לאו דוקא: **אמר רבא וככר יצא מהן.** קודם הנדר: *) **מתני' סתוניות.** ענבים רעים ונשארים בגפנים עד ימות הסתיו ואינן ראויין ליין ועושין מהם חומץ ואית דגרסי ספוניות כמו סופי ענבים: **כל שהם תולדתו קרויה עליו.** אף כי נשתנה מתכונה על שם עיקרו כמו דבש תמרים חומץ סתוניות: **וחכמים מתירין.** בגמרא פריך היינו ת"ק: **גמ' כל שאין דרכו לאכול ודרך היוצא ממנו לאכול.** כגון סתוניות ת"ק פליג אדר"ש בין בדבש תמרים בין בחומץ סתוניות דרבנן שרו תרווייהו ואסרי סתוניות גופייהו ור"ש אוסר בדבש תמרים ובחומץ סתוניות ומתיר הסתוניות ורבנן בתרתי קיימי אהא דקאמר ת"ק מן הסתוניות מותר בחומץ סתוניות הא בסתוניות גופייהו אסור וחכמים מתירים סתוניות גופייהו: **מתני' מפני שהוא שם לווי.** אכולה קאי: **גמ' ירקות שדה.** אינן קרוין ירק סתם והרוצה לומר ירקות שדה צריך לא שדה לפיכך בלשון העולם סתם הואי ירקות שדה: **גמ' אבל במקום שמביאין ירק מחוצה לארץ אסור.** אף בירקות גינה דכיון דמצויין שם דעתם גם עלייהו: **משום גוש.** עפר הנדבק בירק וחכמים גזרו טומאה על גוש עפר הבא מארץ העמים בפ"ק דשבת (דף טו:): **מתני' אסור באיספרגוס.** הוא מין כרוב אבל אין כרוב נקרא על שמו: **מן הגריסין אסור במקפה.** ואפי' כי נתנן במקפה עדיין שם גריסין עליהן: **ור' יוסי מתיר.** דקסבר לא מיקרו גריסין אלא מקפה של גריסין והוא מן גריסין נדר: **מן המקפה מותר בגריסין.** דלא תימא כי היכי דנודר מן המקפה אסור בשום משום שדרך ליתן שום במקפה הוא הדין נמי כי נדר מן המקפה יהא אסור בגריסין משום שדרך לעשות הגריסין מקפה קא משמע לן דלא דמי לשום דשום רגילין ליתן בכל מיני מקפה כי נותן טעם והשום הוא המקפה אבל אין עושין מגריסין לבדן מקפה אלא מכמה מינין עושין מקפה: **אסור באשישים.** פסולת עדשים: **חטה שאני טועם כו'.** מייתור לשונו שהזכיר שתיהם נאסר בכל אי נמי כלמפרש רשב"ג בברייתא דחטה משמע לאפות וחטים משמע לכוס: **גריס חטה שאני טועם מותר לכוס חיין.** לא פליג אתנא קמא: **הדרן עלך הנודר מן המבושל**

*) ע"כ שייך לדף נ"ב: ומדבור זה עד ד"ה גמ' אבל וכו' שייך לעא"ה.

הנודר

הגהות הב"ח (א) רש"י ד"ה מותר בכרוב וכו' איספרגוס הס"ד ואח"כ נ"ל ד"ה אסור במקפה של גריסין הס"ד ואח"כ נ"ל ד"ה ר' יוסי מתיר דקסבר אין מקפה בכלל גריסין הס"ד ואח"כ נ"ל ד"ה מן המקפה של גריסין הס"ד ואח"כ נ"ל ד"ה מותר בגריסין דברי הכל דאין גריסין בכלל מקפה הס"ד ואח"כ נ"ל ד"ה אסור בשום של מקפה הס"ד ואח"כ נ"ל ד"ה אסור בשום שנותנין וכו' בכלל מקפה הס"ד ואח"כ מ"ה מותר במקפה וכו' בכלל שום הס"ד ואח"כ ד"ה אסור באשישים: (ב) ד"ה ר' יהודה וכו' לכוס חטה וגרים חיים כיון דלא אמר חטה חטין גרים גריסין קסבר חטה וגרים סתם מבושלים משמע חיין לא משמע כצ"ל: (ג) ד"ה גרים משמע מבושל גריסין משמע חיין גרים גריסין משמע נמי חיין וה"א:

*הַנּוֹדֵר מִן הַיָּרָק – מוּתָּר בִּדְלוּעִין, וְרַבִּי עֲקִיבָא [א]אוֹסֵר. אָמְרוּ לוֹ לְרַבִּי עֲקִיבָא: וַהֲלֹא אוֹמֵר אָדָם לִשְׁלוּחוֹ "קַח לִי יָרָק", וְהוּא אוֹמֵר "לֹא מָצָאתִי אֶלָּא דְלוּעִין"! אָמַר לָהֶם: כֵּן הַדָּבָר, אוֹ שֶׁמָּא אוֹמֵר הוּא (א) "לֹא מָצָאתִי אֶלָּא קִיטְנִית"? אֶלָּא שֶׁהַדְּלוּעִין בִּכְלַל יָרָק, וְקִיטְנִית אֵינוֹ בִּכְלַל יָרָק. [ב]וְאָסוּר בְּפוֹל הַמִּצְרִי לַח, וּמוּתָּר בְּיָבֵשׁ.§

גמ' "הַנּוֹדֵר מִן הַיָּרָק" כו'.§ וְהָא מִן יָרָק נָדַר! אָמַר עוּלָּא: בְּאוֹמֵר "יַרְקֵי קְדֵרָה עָלַי". וְדִילְמָא יָרָק הַנֶּאֱכָל בִּקְדֵרָה קָאָמַר? [ג]בְּאוֹמֵר "יָרָק הַמִּתְבַּשֵּׁל בִּקְדֵרָה עָלַי". בְּמַאי קָא מִיפַּלְגִי? רַבָּנַן סָבְרִי: כָּל מִילְּתָא דִּצְרִיךְ שְׁלִיחָא לְאִמְּלוּכֵי עֲלָהּ – לָאו מִינֵּיהּ הוּא, וְרַבִּי עֲקִיבָא סָבַר: [ד]כָּל מִילְּתָא דְּמִימְלִיךְ שְׁלִיחָא עֲלָהּ – מִינֵּיהּ הוּא. אָמַר אַבַּיֵי: מוֹדֶה רַבִּי עֲקִיבָא לְעִנְיַן מַלְקוֹת, שֶׁאֵינוֹ לוֹקֶה. *תְּנַן הָתָם: [ה]הַשָּׁלִיחַ שֶׁעָשָׂה שְׁלִיחוּתוֹ – בַּעַל הַבַּיִת מָעַל, לֹא עָשָׂה שְׁלִיחוּתוֹ – שָׁלִיחַ מָעַל. מַאן תַּנָּא? אָמַר רַב חִסְדָּא: מַתְנִיתִין דְּלָא כְּרַבִּי עֲקִיבָא. *דִּתְנַן: כֵּיצַד? [ו]אָמַר לוֹ "תֵּן בָּשָׂר לָאוֹרְחִים" וְנָתַן לָהֶם כָּבֵד, "תֵּן כָּבֵד" וְנָתַן לָהֶם בָּשָׂר – הַשָּׁלִיחַ מָעַל. וְאִי רַבִּי עֲקִיבָא – הָא א"ר עֲקִיבָא: כָּל מִילְּתָא דְּמִימְלִיךְ עֲלָהּ שָׁלִיחַ – מִינֵּיהּ הוּא, לִמְעוֹל בַּעַל הַבַּיִת וְלָא לִמְעוֹל שָׁלִיחַ! אָמַר אַבַּיֵי: אֲפִילּוּ תֵּימָא רַבִּי עֲקִיבָא,

מִי

רש"י

הַנּוֹדֵר מִן הַיָּרָק וכו' וְרַבִּי עֲקִיבָא אוֹסֵר. דְּקָסָבַר דִּילּוּעִין בִּכְלַל יָרָק. **אֶלָּא** דִּילּוּעִין. מִכְּלָל דְּלָאו מִינֵּיהּ הוּא. **לֹא מָצָאתִי אֶלָּא** קִיטְנִית. בִּתְמִיָּה. כְּלוֹמַר, לְהָכִי לָא קָאָמַר לֵיהּ אֶלָּא דִּילּוּעִין – מִכְּלַל דְּדִילּוּעִין מִינֵּיהּ הוּא, וְלָא מִין קִיטְנִית. **פּוֹל הַמִּצְרִי לַח.** הָוֵי מִין יָרָק. **וּמוּתָּר בְּיָבֵשׁ.** שֶׁהוּא מִין דָּגָן. **גמ' אַמַּאי אוֹסֵר** ר"ע **הָא** מִן יָרָק נָדַר. וְדִילּוּעִין לָא אִיקְרִי יָרָק. **יַרְקֵי** קְדֵרָה עָלַי. וְדִילּוּעִין בִּכְלַל יַרְקֵי קְדֵרָה הֵן, שֶׁהֲרֵי מִתְבַּשְּׁלִין בִּקְדֵרָה. **וְדִילְמָא.** הַאי דְּקָאָמַר "יַרְקֵי קְדֵרָה עָלַי" – "יָרָק הַנֶּאֱכָל בִּקְדֵרָה עָלַי" קָאָמַר, כְּגוֹן שׁוּמִים וּבְצָלִים שֶׁהֵן נֶאֱכָלִים בִּקְדֵרָה, שֶׁנּוֹתְנִין אוֹתָן בַּקְּדֵרָה כְּדֵי לִיתֵּן טַעַם בַּתַּבְשִׁיל. **בְּאוֹמֵר** יָרָק הַמִּתְבַּשֵּׁל בִּקְדֵרָה. דְּדִילּוּעִין נַמִּי הֵן מִתְבַּשְּׁלִין בִּקְדֵרָה, וְנוֹתְנִין אוֹתָן בִּשְׁבִיל תַּבְשִׁיל. אֲבָל שׁוּמִין אֵין נוֹתְנִין אוֹתָן אֶלָּא בִּשְׁבִיל טַעַם, וּלְהָכִי ר"ע אוֹסֵר. **דִּצְרִיךְ שְׁלוּחָא** לְאִימְּלוּכֵי עֲלֵיהּ. כְּגוֹן דִּילּוּעִין, כִּי אָמַר לִשְׁלוּחוֹ "קַח לִי יָרָק" – אֵינוֹ מֵבִיא לוֹ דִּילּוּעִין, אֶלָּא אוֹמֵר לוֹ "לֹא מָצָאתִי אֶלָּא דִּילּוּעִין", וּמִימְלִיךְ עֲלֵיהּ, וְקָאָמַר לֵיהּ: דְּרוֹצֶה אַתָּה שֶׁאָבִיא לְךָ דִּילּוּעִין? וְכִהַאי גַּוְונָא – לָאו מִינֵּיהּ, לְפִיכָךְ כִּי נָדַר בְּיָרָק – מוּתָּר בְּדִילּוּעִין. **וְרַבִּי עֲקִיבָא** סָבַר כו'. מִדְּקָאָמַר לֵיהּ "לֹא מָצָאתִי אֶלָּא דִּילּוּעִין", וְלָא אָמַר "לֹא מָצָאתִי אֶלָּא קִיטְנִית" – אַלְמָא דִּילּוּעִין מִין יָרָק הוּא. **מוֹדֶה רַבִּי עֲקִיבָא.** אע"ג דְּאוֹסֵר בְּדִילּוּעִין, אִם אָכַל דִּילּוּעִין – אֵינוֹ לוֹקֶה. דְּקָסָבַר: לֵיכָּא מַלְקוּת דְּ"לֹא יַחֵל דְּבָרוֹ", הוֹאִיל וְצָרִיךְ לְאִימְּלוּכֵי בֵּיהּ עֲלָהּ. **מַתְנִיתִין.** דִּמְעִילָה, דְּשָׁלִיחַ מָעַל – דְּלָא כְּר"ע, דְּקָתָנֵי סֵיפָא: לֹא עָשָׂה שְׁלִיחוּתוֹ – שָׁלִיחַ מָעַל. **אָמַר** לִשְׁלוּחוֹ תֵּן בָּשָׂר לָאוֹרְחִים וְנָתַן לָהֶם כָּבֵד שָׁלִיחַ מָעַל. דְּלֹא עָשָׂה שְׁלִיחוּתוֹ, דְּאֵין כָּבֵד בִּכְלַל בָּשָׂר. **וְאִי ר"ע.** הָא אָמַר כָּבֵד בִּכְלַל בָּשָׂר הָוֵי, דְּמִילְּתָא דְּמִימְלִיךְ עֲלָהּ שָׁלִיחַ מִינֵּיהּ הוּא. וְה"נ, אע"ג דְּלָא אִימְלִיךְ הַשְׁתָּא – אוֹרְחֵיהּ הוּא לְאִימְּלוּכֵי, דְּכִי אָמַר לוֹ "תֵּן בָּשָׂר לָאוֹרְחִין" וְלֹא הָיָה לוֹ בָּשָׂר אֶלָּא כָּבֵד – דַּרְכּוֹ לוֹמַר: אֵין לִי אֶלָּא כָּבֵד, וּכְמַאן דְּמִימְלִיךְ דָּמֵי. **לִמְעוֹל** בַּעַל הַבַּיִת. דְּהָא עָשָׂה שְׁלִיחוּתוֹ.

תְּרֵיץ

ר"נ

הנודר מן הירק מותר בדילועין כו'. דלא הוי ירק אלא פרי. ואית דמפרשי דסתם ירק נאכל כמות שהוא חי, ודלועין אינן כן. **והוא אומר לא מצאתי אלא דילועין.** אלמא: לא מיקרו ירק, דאי מיקרו ירק – יקחם. **אמר להם כן הדבר.** מזה אני מביא ראיה לאסור דלועין. **אסור בפול המצרי לח.** דכל שהוא לח – ירק הוי. **גמ' והא מן ירק נדר.** לרבי עקיבא פריך: היכי אסר בדילועין? דהא מן ירק נדר, ודילועין לאו ירק נינהו אלא פרי. דבשלמא פול המצרי א"ל דכיון שעושים ממנו דגן כשהוא יבש, ומקמי הכי לא – עד השתא שעתא ירק הוי, ולא פרי. אלא דלועין קשיא! ואף ע"ג דר"ע יהיב טעמא, דמימליך עליה שליח – לא סגי ליה ההוא טעמא, כיון דמן ירק נדר, ודלועין לאו ירק נינהו. **אמר עולא באומר ירקי קדרה עלי.** וכיון דמייתר לישניה – למיכלל דלועין אתי, כיון דמימלך שליחא עלייהו. **ודילמא ירק הנאכל בקדרה קאמר.** דכיון דדלועין ליתנהו בכלל ירק – לית לך לרבויינהו מייתורא דלישניה, אלא מאי דליכא לספוקי דמשתמע מיניה, כגון שומים ובצלים הבאים להטעים את הקדרה, אבל דלועין – לא משתמעי מיניה, ד"ירקי קדרה" – להטעים את הקדרה משמע. **באומר ירק המבושל בקדרה עלי.** וכל כה"ג סבירא ליה לרבי עקיבא, דכיון דדלועין ממליך שליחא עלייהו – אסור בהן. ורבנן סברי דכיון דצריך לאימלוכי עלייהו – לאו מיניה הוא. וקיי"ל כר' עקיבא, כמו שנפרש לפנינו בס"ד. הילכך, נודר מן הירק אינו אסור בפרי האדמה. אמר "ירק קדרה עלי" – אסור בפירות האדמה הבאים להכשיר המאכל, כשומים ובצלים, ומותר בדלועין. אמר "ירק המתבשל בקדרה עלי" – אסור בכל פירות האדמה דמימלך שליחא עלייהו כי אמר ליה משלח "ירק". ואית דמפרשי: והא מן ירק נדר – דסתם ירק נאכל כמות שהוא חי. ואמר עולא: באומר "ירקי קדרה עלי". דכיון דאמר הכי – אפילו ירק המתבשל בכלל. ודילמא ירק הנאכל בקדרה קאמר. דכיון דסתם ירק נאכל כמות שהוא חי, ואמר "ירקי קדרה" – לרבויי אתא ירק הנאכל חי ובקדרה, כגון שומים וחזרת. אבל דילועין, שאין נאכלין חיים כלל – לא. ופרקינן: "המתבשל בקדרה עלי". דכיון דאמר "המתבשל" – משמע הנך דבעו בשול טובא, ואין דרכן לאכלן חיים, כדלועין. ונמצא עכשיו לפי דרך זה: דנודר מן הירק – אסור בירק הנאכל כמות שהוא חי בלבד, ומותר בכל מה שמתבשל, אע"פ שלפעמים נאכל חי. אמר "ירקי קדרה עלי" – אסור אף באותן שנאכלין חיים ומבושלין, אבל לא באותן שאין נאכלין אלא מבושלין. אמר "ירק המתבשל בקדרה" – אסור אף באותן שאין נאכלין בלא בשול. **אמר אביי מודה ר"ע לענין מלקות שאינו לוקה.** דכיון [°]דדלועין לא משתמעי בהדיא, אלא מרבוייא דלישניה, אע"ג דממליך שליחא עליה – לא מתסרי בודאי אלא מספיקא, הילכך לא לקי. **תנן התם.** מתני' היא במסכת מעילה (ד' כ.). **השליח שעשה שליחותו בעל הבית מעל.** דאע"ג דקיי"ל אין שליח לדבר עבירה – שאני מעילה, דילפינן "חטא" "חטא" מתרומה, כדאיתא בפ"ב דקדושין (דף מג:). **לא עשה שליחותו שליח מעל.** דאדעתא דנפשיה קעביד. **מאן תנא אמר רב חסדא** מתניתין. כולה, דלא כר' עקיבא. כלומר, מאן תנא האי דמפרש ואזיל, דאמר לו "תן בשר לאורחים" ונתן להם כבד מיקרי לא עשה שליחותו – דלא כרבי עקיבא. דהא דתנן "תן בשר לאורחים" וכו' סיפא דההיא דהשליח שעשה שליחותו היא. ומסיפא קאמר דאתיא דלא כר"ע, דאילו רישא – ודאי דברי הכל היא. אבל סיפא, דהויא פירושא דרישא – דלא כרבי עקיבא, דאי רבי עקיבא – הא אמר דכל מילתא דמימליך שליח מיניה הוא, והא עביד דמימליך מבשר לכבד. הלכך עשה שליחותו מיקרי, ולמעול בעל הבית. דנהי דאמרינן לעיל דמודה רבי עקיבא לענין מלקות שאינו לוקה – הא פרישית דדוקא במידי דלא משתמע אלא מריבויא, כדלועין. אבל כבד – מכלל בשר בלא ריבויא. הילכך כי אמר ליה בעל הבית "תן להם בשר" ונתן להם כבד – למעול בעל הבית, ולא למעול שליח!:

מי

תוספות

הנודר מן הירק אסור בדילועין. והוא אומר לא מצאתי אלא דלועין. ואין לוקחם מיד אלמא לא קרי להו אינשי ירק: **אמר** להם כך הדבר. כלומר משם אני מביא ראיה: **אסור** בפול המצרי. דלכולי עלמא הוי בכלל ירק: **ומותר** ביבש. דלא מיקרי ירק: **והא** מן ירק נדר. ולמה אסור בדלועין שהם פירי באומר ירקי קדירה עלי. כשדרכם לבשלם והני דרכם לבשלם: **ודלמא** ירק הנאכל בקדירה קאמר. כגון שומין ובצלים שהוא נאכל בקדירה כגון ליתן טעם בתבשיל: **באומר** ירק המתבשל בקדירה. מפני שהוא קשה וקסבר ר"ע דלועין בכלל ירק המתבשלים בקדירה: **וצריך** לאימלוכי. דאין לוקח אותן בסתם (כיון) [עד] דאימליך עליה: **מודה** הוא לענין מלקות. בל יחל שאינו לוקה דמספקא ליה אי דלועין בכלל ירק ומספיקא [לא] אמר למילקיה: **תנן** התם. פרק בתרא דמעילה (דף כ.): **בעה"ב** מעל. דגמרינן חטא חטא מתרומה מה התם ע"י שליח אף הכא ע"י שליח אע"ג דבעלמא אין שליח לדבר עבירה: **ונתן** להם כבד. דכבד לאו מין בשר וכי אמר לשלוחו קח לי בשר ולא מצא אלא כבד לא מימליך עליה וכששולחו לבקש בשר אינו חוזר ואומר לא מצאתי אלא כבד אלא אומר לא מצאתי בשר כלל: **מיניה** הוא. ועשה שליחותו ולמעול בעה"ב וקשה דרבי עקיבא מודה דאין לוקה דמספקא ליה אי מידי דמימליך עליה מיניה הוא ונראה דלא קשה כלל דדוקא בדלועין דלאו ירק הוא אלא פירי מספקא ליה אבל במידי אחרינא פשיטא ליה דמימליך עליה ומיניה הוא וי"מ דהיינו הא דמשני מי לא מודה ר"ע דצריך לאימלוכי ביה ומן הדין הוא דלאו מינו ולהחמיר אר"ע [דמינו הוא] אבל לא למעול דהאמר לעיל שאינו לוקה ול"נ דא"כ שליח אמאי מעל כיון דמספקא ליה אם מינו [הוי או] אינו מינו א"כ עשה שליחותו ולכ"נ דודאי הפירוש כך הוא מי לא מודה ר"ע דצריך לימלוכי ביה דבסתם אין השליח לוקח אם אין שואל למשלח אם יחפוץ הילכך לא נמלך לא הוי עשה שליחותו ולכך מעל השליח כי נמי הוי מינו לגמרי וקושיא למעול בעה"ב נתרץ בעה"ה כמו שפירשתי והר"ס היה אומר דלמעול בעל הבית לאו דוקא אלא כלומר לא ימעול שליח וכדפרישית דשמא עשה שליחותו ומשני לא מודה דצריך לאימלוכי כדפרישית:

אסור

פי' הרא"ש

הנודר מן הירק. והוא אומר לא מצאתי אלא דלועין. ואם מין ירק הוא למה לא לקחו: **אמר להם כן הדבר.** ומשם אני מביא ראיה שמא אומר לא מצאתי אלא קיטנית אלא הוא אומר לא מצאתי ירק אבל על הדלועין הוא צריך לימלך אלמא מין ירק הוא: **ואסור בפול המצרי לח.** דכולי עלמא מין ירק הוא: **גמ' והא מן ירק נדר.** וסתם ירק בלשון בני אדם הוא ירק הנאכל חי: **באומר ירקי קדרה עלי: ודילמא ירק הנאכל בקדרה.** ע"י כבישת קדרה כדתנן האשה שהיתה כובשת ירק בקדרה ולשון בני אדם יותר נקרא ירק מירק המתבשל בקדרה: **ומשני** שאמר בפירוש ירק המתבשל בקדרה: **מודה ר"ע לענין מלקות שאינו לוקה.** דלחומרא אסר ליה כיון שהשליח נמלך עליו מ"מ כיון שאינו לוקחו בלא המלכה לא צריך לן שהוא מינו: **תנן התם.** במעילה: **השליח שעשה שליחותו בעל הבית מעל.** אע"ג דבכל התורה כולה אין שליח לדבר עבירה ילפינן לה במעילה חטא חטא מתרומה דמתחייב ע"י שליח: **מאן תנא.** דסבר דבשינוי כל דהו משנה השליח נתבטל השליחות: **ונתן להם כבד כו' השליח מעל.** והאומר לשלוחו קנה לי בשר ולא מצא אלא כבד נמלך אם יקנהו:

מי

במעילה כיון דשליח לא נמלך

עין משפט נר מצוה

א א ב ג מיי' פ"ט מהל' נדרים הל' י [וע' כ"מ] טוש"ע יו"ד סי' ריז סעי' ד ה:

ב ד מיי' שם הל"ו טוש"ע שם סעי' ד:

ג ה ו מיי' פ"ז מהל' מעילה הל"א סמג עשין רי:

מסורת הש"ס

חולין קז. [מעילה כ:]

מעילה כ. כתובות לח: קדושין מב: חגיגה י:

[מעילה כ.]

הגהות הב"ח

(א) במשנה שמא אומר הוא לו לא:

גליון הש"ס

בהר"ן ד"ה אמר אביי מודה וכו' דדלועין לא משתמעי. ע' חולין דף קד ע"א תד"ה הא עוף:

מי לא מודה רבי עקיבא דצריך אימלוכי? איתמר שמעתא קמיה דרבא. אמר להון: *שפיר אמר נחמני. מאן תנא דפליג עליה דרבי עקיבא — רבן שמעון בן גמליאל היא. דתניא: אהנודר מן הבשר — אסור בכל מיני בשר, ואסור בראש וברגלים ובקנה ובכבד ובלב ובעופות, ומותר בבשר דגים וחגבים. רשב"ג אומר: הנודר מן הבשר — אסור בכל מיני בשר, ומותר בראש וברגלים ובקנה ובכבד ובלב ובעופות, ואין צריך לומר בבשר דגים וחגבים. וכן היה רשב"ג אומר: קרביים לאו בשר, ואוכליהן לאו בר אינש. (א) אוכליהן — כבשר, לענין זביני — לאו בר אינש. מ"ש בשר עוף לתנא קמא דאסיר — דעביד שליחא דמימליך עליה. בשר דגים נמי עביד שליחא דאי לא משכח בישרא מימליך עליה, דאמר: אי לא משכחנא בישרא — אייתי דגים? וליתסרו! אמר *אביי: בכגון שהקיז דם, דלא אכיל דגים. אי הכי אפילו עופות נמי לא אכיל, דאמר שמואל: *דמסוכר ואכיל בישרא דצפרא — פרח לביה כצפרא. ותניא: אין מקיזין *לא על דגים ולא על עופות ולא על בשר מליח. *ותניא: הקיז דם — לא יאכל לא חלב, ולא גבינה, ולא ביצים, ולא שחליים, ולא עופות, ולא בשר מליח! שאני עופות דאפשר על ידי שליקה. (ב) *אביי אמר: כגון דכייבין ליה עיניה, דדגים קשין לעינים. אי הכי אכיל דגים, דהא אמר שמואל: נו"ן סמ"ך עי"ן — נונא סמא לעינים! ההוא סוף אוכלא.§

מתני'

מי לא מודה רבי עקיבא דצריך אימלוכי. הלכך, לענין מעילת שליח, ודאי כיון דצריך אימלוכי ולא ממליך — אדעתא דנפשיה קעביד. ובעל הבית נמי, סמיך דכל כמה דלא מימליך לא יתן להם כבד, הלכך לא עשה שליחותו. אבל לענין נדרים, כיון דבכלל לישניה הוא, דהא מימליך עליהם שליחא — נודר אמאי סמיך? אלא ודאי בכולהו אסר נפשיה. איתמר שמעתא קמיה דרבא. מאי דמתרץ אביי מתניתין דמעילה אליבא דר"ע, ואמר להון: שפיר אמר נחמני. היינו אביי, וקרי ליה הכי לפי שנתגדל בבית רבה בר נחמני. מאן תנא דפליג עליה דרבי עקיבא וכו' ומותר בראש וברגלים וכו'. דכיון דצריך שליח לאימלוכי עלייהו — ליתנהו בכלל בשר סתמא. כגון שהקיז דם. קודם נדרו, וכיון שכן — לא נתכוון לאסור בשר דגים, דהא בלאו הכי לא אכיל מינייהו, דהא קשו להקזה. אי הכי אפילו עופות נמי לא אכיל. וליסתרי בהו נמי, ואמאי קתני אסור בעופות?־ דסבר. הקזה של כתפים. דאפשר על ידי שליקה. כשהן שלוקים הרבה לא מזקי ליה. נו"ן סמ"ך עי"ן. סימן היה עושה מאותיות של אלפא ביתא. בסוף אוכלא. סוף החולי. ולענין הלכה. קיי"ל כרבי עקיבא, דכל מידי דממליך עליה שליחא — מיניה הוא. דהא סתם לן תנא בפרק "כל הבשר" (חולין דף קד.) כרבי עקיבא. אע"ג דלא ידעינן אי מחלוקת ואח"כ סתם או סתם ואח"כ מחלוקת, אפ"ה נקטינן כוותיה. חדא — דמחמיר. ועוד: דהא מפרש בגמ' דמאן דפליג עליה דר"ע — יחידאה הוא, דהיינו רשב"ג, וקיי"ל:* הלכה כר"ע מחבירו. הלכך, הנודר מן הבשר — אסור בכל מיני בשר ובעופות ובדגים, כל שלא הקיז דם ולא כאיבין ליה עיניה. מיהו, דוקא באתרא דמימליך שליחא עלייהו, אבל באתרא דלא מימליך עליה — מותר, דכל מידי דלא מימליך עליה — לאו מיניה הוא. וזה שלא כדברי הרמב"ם ז"ל, שכתב בפרק תשיעי מהל' נדרים דדגים לא מתסרי אלא באתרא דמימליך שליחא עלייהו, ועופות מיתסרי בכל דוכתא. והוא מן התימה, דבגמרא משוינן להו. הילכך, תרוייהו לא מיתסרי אלא באתרא דמימליך שליחא עלייהו, וכשלא הקיז דם ולא כיבין ליה עיניה. אבל הקיז דם וכיבין ליה עיניה, אע"פ שאסור בעופות — מותר בדגים. מיהו, כי אמרינן דמותר בדגים כשהקיז דם וכיבין ליה עיניה — לא שוו אהדדי. דכשהקיז דם — לא שרי בדגים אלא דוקא באוסר בשר על עצמו ליום ההקזה בלבד, דכי האי גוונא אין דגים בכלל, משום דבלאו הכי לא אכיל מינייהו ההוא יומא. אבל אי אסר עליה בשר שמנה ימים או יותר — דגים בכלל, דאע"ג דלא איצטריך למסרינהו לההוא יומא — משום איך יומי אסרינהו. ובדכיבין ליה עיניה אינו כן, דאפילו באוסר לשלשים יום או יותר — אין דגים בכלל. שאין לומר שמפני הימים האחרים נדר, שהרי אינו יודע מתי יתרפא שילטרך לאסור דגים עליו, הרשב"א ז"ל. ולי לא שרי בדגים אלא אי נדר יומי דמוכחי, לפום מאי דכיבין ליה עיניה, דבלאו נדרא לא אכיל מינייהו. ומסתברא דבשר מליח אפי' ביומא דהקזה אסור. דנהי דאין מקיזין על בשר מליח, כיון דבשר ממש הוא, ולא צריך שליחא לאמלוכי עליה כדגים — מיתסר. דיומא דהקזה לאו הוכחה מעליא הוא, הלכך לא מהני אלא למידי דצריך שליחא מיהא לאמלוכי עליה כדגים, אבל לגבי בשר מליח — לא הוי הוכחה. דאי לא תימא הכי, אדקתני מותר בבשר דגים — ליתני נמי ובבשר מליח, דהוי רבותא טפי. אלא ודאי כדאמרינן. ולענין חגבים בכל דוכתא שרו, דלא ממליך עלייהו שליח כלל, מדאמרינן דגים נמי עביד שליחא דממליך עלייהו, ולא אמר דגים וחגבים. וכן כתב הרמב"ם ז"ל בפרק הנזכר, שבכל מקום מותר בחגבים.

מתני'

תריץ מי לא מודה ר"ע דצריך אימלוכי. שליח כבעל הבית, ואע"ג דס"ל דמיניה הוא, במילתא דצריך לאימלוכי הכי איבעיא ליה למימר שליח לבעל הבית: רוצה אתה שאתן להם כבד? וכיון דלא מימליך — לא עשה שליחותו, ופשע. ושליח מעל, אע"ג דסבר דמין בשר הוי. לשמעתא. האי פירושא דקא מתרץ אביי. בכל מיני בשר. בין בהמה ובין חיה. אסור בראש וכו'. דכל הני מיני בשר נינהו, ואפילו כבד. רבן שמעון אומר מותר בראש וכו'. דקסבר: לאו מינא דבשר הם. אבל בקרביים — הכל מודו דמין בשר הוו, הואיל ואית בהו שומן טפי מכל הנך, מראש והכבד והלב. והיינו דפליג עליה דר"ע, דקא סבר כבד לאו מין בשר, ור"ע סבר מיניה הוא. וכן היה רבי שמעון אומר. שמעתא אחריתי: קרביים לאו בשר ואוכליהן לאו בר נש הוא. ואמרינן: למאי הלכתא קרביים לאו בשר הוו? הא אמרינן לעיל גבי נדרים אסור בכל מיני בשר, ולא הוציא קרביים! וקא מתרץ דהאי אוכליהן לאו בר נש — לענין זביני, שהקונה קרביים בדמי בשר, שיכול לקנות הבשר וקונה קרביים — לאו בר נש הוא, דבטלה דעתו אצל בני אדם. דעביד שליח דמימליך עליה. דכי לא משכח בישרא מימליך עליה דבעל הבית, ואמר: לא משכחנא בישרא אלא בשר עוף. ולהכי אסור, דמיניה הוא. דגים נמי כו' וליתסרי. ואמאי מותר בבשר דגים? כגון שהקיז דם. בשעת הנדר, דכיון דלא אכיל דגים בההיא שעתא — לא נדר אדעתא דדגים, ולא ממליך עליה כלל. אפי' (ג) דעופות נמי כו'. דלאו אדעתא דעופות נדר, ולא מימליך עליה הוא. וכיון דלא אכיל עופות השתא — ליתסרי. שאני עופות. שאפשר להו בתקנתא להקזה דאפשר לאכלן ע"י שליקה. אע"פ שהקיז דם. ומידי דמלי למיכל בשום ענין — נדר וממליך עליה, ואסור. כגון דכייבין ליה עיניה. בשעת הנדר. דדגים קשין לעינים. וכל מילי דלא הוה מלי למיכל — לא נדר, אלא אדעתא דמידי דמלי למיכל. ולהכי (ד) אדגים שרי, ומן העופות אסור. נו"ן סמ"ך עי"ן כו' בסוף אוכלא. בסוף החולי, שכבר עבר זמן מרובה שחשש בעיניו, דהתם סם טוב לכאב העינים. והאי דקא תני דגים קשים לעינים — בתחלת אוכלא, כשהתחיל לחשוש בעיניו. ובשעת הנדר הוה תחלת אוכלא.

מתני'

ד א מיי' פ"ט מהל' נדרים הל"ו סמג לאוין רמב טוש"ע יו"ד סי' ריז סעי' ח [וברב אלפס חולין פ"ח ד' רנז.]

הגהות הב"ח

(א) גמ' ואוכליהן לאו בר אינש למאי הילכתא אוכליהן כבשר: (ב) שם רבא אמר כגון דכייבין: (ג) רש"י ד"ה אפילו עופות נמי וכו' דכיון דלא: (ד) ד"ה דדגים וכו' ולהכי בדגים שרי:

[עירובין מו:]

תוספות

אסור בראש וברגלים. דסבר רבי עקיבא דכל מאי דמימליך הוי מיניה: **מותר** בראש. דסבר כתנא קמא דרבי עקיבא דמימליך לא הוי מינו: **לענין** זביני [לאו אינש הוא]. דשביק בשר וזבין קרביים: **שהקיז** דם. דקשיא לו הילכך מותר בדגים וחגבים: **עופות** נמי אין דרכם למיכל. ואמאי אסור בעופות: **שאני** עופות לאפשר ע"י שליקה. והא דאמר שמואל פרח לבו היינו ע"י צלי אבל דגים בין שלוק בין צלי קשה להקזה: **סוף** אוכלא. סוף החולי

[שבת עז.]

[בתעילה כ: איתא רב פפא]

[גי' הערוך בערך סכר ד' דמסובר וע' ע"ז כט. חלא לסבורי]

[ע' תוספות ע"ז כט. ד"ה שנ לדג]

ע"ז כט. ע"ש היטב

[במעילה שם איתא ר"פ וע"ש גם שאר שינויים]

פי' הרא"ש

מי לא מודה ר"ע דצריך אמלוכי. ומטעם זה חשיב ליה מינו שהרי על דבר שאינו מינו כלל אינו נמלך ומכל מקום לענין שליחותו לא חשיב עשה שליחותו שהרי שינה שהרי דרך השליח לימלך עליו ואין לו לעשות בלא דעת המשלחו: **מאן תנא דפליג עליה דרבי עקיבא.** מה שם התנא דפליג על ר"ע במתני' אבל במעילה כולהו מודו: **אסור בכל מיני בשר.** בקר ואף וחיה: **לאו בר איניש הוא** אלא הדיוט: **אוכליהן כבשר לענין זביני.** מי שמניח בשר וקונה אלו: **כגון שהקיז דם דלא אכיל דגים.** ומסתמא לא נדר אלא מדבר שדרכו לאכול ביום נדרו: **ע"י שליקה** דלא פרח לבו אלא כשאוכלהו צלי: **הסוא בסוף אוכלא.** בשפסק כאב החולי:

מתני'

מתני' הנודר מן הדגן אסור בפול המצרי יבש, דברי רבי מאיר. וחכ"א [א]אינו אסור אלא בחמשת המינין. רבי מאיר אומר: הנודר מן התבואה – [ב]אינו אסור אלא מחמשת המינין, אבל הנודר מן הדגן – אסור בכל, ומותר בפירות האילן ובירק.§ **גמ'** למימרא *דדגן כל דמידגן משמע. מתיב רב יוסף: °"וכפרוץ הדבר הרבו בני ישראל [ראשית] דגן תירוש ויצהר וכל תבואת שדה *לרב" וגו', ואי אמרת דגן כל דמידגן משמע – מאי *"כפרוץ הדבר הרבו"? אמר אביי: לאתויי פירות האילן וירק.§ "ר' מאיר אומר: הנודר מן התבואה" וכו'.§ אמר ר' יוחנן: הכל מודים בנודר מן התבואה שאין אסור אלא מחמשת המינין. תניא נמי הכי: (א) שוין בנודר מן התבואה שאין אסור אלא מה' המינין. פשיטא! מהו דתימא: תבואה – כל מילי משמע, קמשמע לן דלא משמע כל מילי. מתיב רב יוסף: "וכפרוץ הדבר הרבו בני ישראל" כו'! אמר רבא: תבואה לחוד, תבואת שדה לחוד. בר מר שמואל פקיד דליתנון תליסר אלפי זוזי לרבא מן עללתא דנהר פניא. שלחה רבא לקמיה דרב יוסף: עללתא היכי מיקריא? אמר רב יוסף, *[ג]מתניתין היא: ושוין בנודר מן התבואה שאין אסור אלא מחמשת המינין. א"ל אביי: מי דמי? תבואה לא משמע אלא מחמשת המינין, עללתא – כל מילי משמע. אהדרוהו לקמיה דרבא. אמר: הא לא קא מיבעיא לי דעללתא כל מילי משמע. הדא הוא דאיבעיא לי: שכר בתים ושכר ספינות מאי? מי אמרינן: כיון דפחתן – לאו עללתא היא, או דילמא: כיון דלא ידיע פחתייהו – עללתא היא. אמרוה רבנן קמיה דרב יוסף. אמר: וכי מאחר דלא צריך לן אמאי שלח לן? איקפד רב יוסף. שמע רבא *ואתא לקמיה במעלי יומא דכפורי. אשכחיה לשמעיה דהוה קא מזיג קמיה כסא דחמרא. אמר ליה: הב לי דאמזיג ליה אנא. יהב ליה וקא מזיג איהו כסא דחמרא. כי קא שתי, אמר: הדין מיזגא דמי למיזגא דרבא בריה דרב יוסף בר חמא. אמר ליה: הוא ניהו. אמר ליה: *לא תיתיב אכרעך עד דאמרת לי פירושא דהדין מילתא: מאי דכתיב °"וממדבר מתנה וממתנה נחליאל ומנחליאל במות". א"ל: כיון שעושה אדם את עצמו כמדבר, שהוא מופקר לכל – תורה ניתנה לו במתנה, שנאמר "וממדבר מתנה". וכיון שניתנה לו במתנה – נחלו אל, שנאמר "וממתנה נחליאל". וכיון שנחלו אל – עולה לגדולה, שנאמר "ומנחליאל במות". ואם הגביה עצמו – הקב"ה משפילו, שנאמר °"ומבמות הגיא", ולא עוד אלא *) ששוקעין אותו בקרקע, שנאמר °"ונשקפה על פני הישימון". ואם חוזר בו – הקב"ה מגביהו, שנאמר

*) [גירסת הערוך בערך שקף ב' ששוקפין וכ"ה בשאלתות פרשת נשא סימן קכח]

תורה אור: דה"ב לא; במדבר כא; שם; שם

רש"י

מתני' אלא מחמשת מינין. חטה ושעורה וכוסמין ושיפון ושבולת שועל. רבי מאיר אומר כו'. השתא ודאי מודינא לך שהנודר מן התבואה אינו אסור אלא מחמשת מינין. אבל הנודר מן הדגן – אסור בכל מין דמידגן, (ב) משמע דבר שעושין ממנו כרי, ופול המצרי יבש עושין ממנו כרי, ולהכי אסור. **גמ'** למימרא דדגן. דכתיב בקרא – כל מין דמידגן משמע, וחייב במעשר מן התורה, ואפי' משאר מינין, מדקתני: הנודר מן הדגן אסור בכל. וכפרוץ הדבר. כלומר, קיבלו עליהם תקנתא של חזקיהו לעשר הכל, כדכתיב "הרבו בני ישראל" וגו'. אי אמרת בשלמא דדגן לא משמע אלא מחמשת מינין – היינו דאתא קרא למימר הרבו בני ישראל, דאפי' דבר שלא נתחייב במעשר מן התורה, כגון שאר מיני דמידגני – היו מעשרים, כדי להחזיק בתקנה. אלא אי אמרת דגן כל מיני דמידגן משמע, מאי "וכפרוץ הדבר הרבו", כלומר: מה הוסיפו על מה שכתוב בתורה? אמר אביי. (ג) כל דמידגן משמע, ומאי "וכפרוץ הדבר הרבו" – לאיתויי פירות האילן וירק, דהרבו בו בני ישראל ליתן מהן מעשר. דמדאורייתא לא מחייב במעשר אלא מידי דמידגן, דלא משמע אלא מחמשת מינין. ותבואת השדה לרוב. אלמא דתבואה משמע כל מילי, דהא דכתיב "ותבואת השדה" – לאו מחמשת מינין (ד) דאיקרו תבואה. תבואה סתם לא משמע אלא מחמשת מינין, תבואת השדה – משמע כל מידי הגדל מן השדה. פקיד. צוה בצוואתו. היכי מיקריא. כלומר, ממה אגבה אותו ממון. אלא מחמשת מינין. ואינו גובה אלא מחמשת מינין. עללתא. משמע כל מילי שעולה ומשבח, ואפי' משאר פירות שמשבחין נוה לגבות מהן. אהדרוה לקמיה דרבא. לאותה תשובה. שכר בתים ושכר ספינות. גובה מהן או לא. מי אמרינן כיון דפחתן. שמתחסרין כל זמן שמתיישנין. לאו עללתא. מיקרו, שאין עולה ומשביח ולא גבי מינייהו. או דילמא כיון דלא ידיע פחתייהו. שעל יד על יד מתחסר, ואינו ניכר פחיתותו להדיא, והואיל ונוטל הימנו שכר – עולה ומשביח הוי, ויהבו ליה מההוא אגרא. אמרוה קמיה דרב יוסף. הא דאמר רבא, דהא לא מיבעיא ליה דעללתא כל מידי משמע. דמי למיזגא דרבא. שכשהיה רבא לומד לפניו היה מוזג לו בענין זה. לא תיתיב אכרעך כו'. לפי שהגיס לבו שאל לו מקרא זה, כדי להשפיל דעתו. כמדבר שהוא מופקר לכל. מלמד תורה בחנם לכל. נחליאל. (ה) נעשית לו התורה כמו נחלה. ששוקעין אותו בארץ. כמו (ו) המשקוף.

[כ"ק יג:] [ע' תוספות ר"ה יב. ד"ה תנא] [נ"ל ומעשר הכל לרוב וגו'] [בשאלתות פ' נשא סי' קכח איתא וכל תבואת שדה אמר אביי וכו' כזה תכין פי' הר"ן ד"ה הכהן] [נ"ל מתניתא] עירובין נד. [ע"ש כמה שינויים] [קדושין לו ושם נסמן וע' תוס' מיר כג: ד"ה אמר שמואל וכו' פירוש על זה]

ר"ן

מתני' הנודר מן הדגן אסור בפול המצרי יבש. דכיון דמידגן, שעושין ממנו דגן – סבירא ליה לר' מאיר דדגן מיקרי. **גמ'** וכפרוץ הדבר. מקרא הוא בד"ה. דבימי חזקיה לא היו זריזין להפריש תרומות ומעשרות, עמד חזקיה ותקן שיביאו אותם בית ה', וכתיב "וכפרוץ הדבר" שנתחזקה וגברה תקנתו של חזקיה. הרבו בני ישראל וגו' ואי אמרת דגן כל דמידגן משמע מאי וכל תבואת השדה. דהא כל דמידגן הוו בכלל דגן, ואם כן כל תבואת השדה בכלל. לאיתויי פירות האילן וירק. שאין עושין דגן מהן. הכל מודים בנודר מן התבואה וכו'. דאע"ג דתני לה במתניתין בלשון יחיד – דברי הכל היא. מהו דתימא תבואה כל מילי משמע. מדמתרגמינן עללתא, ועללתא משמע כל מילי, כדאמרינן לקמן. בר מר שמואל פקיד וכו' עללתא היכי מיקריא. שלא היה לו לרבא ליטול אלא מעללתא שייחד לו [בר] מר שמואל. אינו אסור אלא בחמשת המינין. והוה סבירא ליה לרב יוסף, דכיון דעללתא תרגום תבואה הוא – חמשת המינין בלחוד משמע. עללתא כל מילי משמע. דעללתא לשון ביאה והכנסה ושבח. הדין מזגא דמי למזגא דבריה דרב יוסף בר חמא. דמזיג על חד תלתא מיא. דרבא הוא דאמר:* כל חמרא דלא דרי על חד תלתא מיא, לאו חמרא הוא. מאי דכתיב וממדבר מתנה*. נתכוון רב יוסף להזהיר רבא שיהא שפל רוח ביותר.

כל

[שבת עז.]

עין משפט נר מצוה

ה א ב מיי' פ"ט מהל' נדרים הל"ט טוש"ע יו"ד סי' ריז סעי' יח:

הגהות הב"ח

(א) גמ' תניא נמי הכי ושוין: (ב) רש"י ד"ה ר' מאיר וכו' בכל מין דמידגן דלדגן משמע: (ג) ד"ה אמר אביי לעולם דגן כל דמידגן משמע הס"ד ואח"כ מ"ה מאי וכפרוץ וכו' מידי דמידגן הס"ד ואח"כ מ"ה דלא משמע כל מילי אלא: (ד) ד"ה ותבואת וכו' מחמשת מינין קאמר ואיקרו תבואה הס"ד: (ה) ד"ה נחליאל שנעשה לו: (ו) ד"ה ששוקעין כו' כמו השקוף. נ"ב ע"ל בפירושו סוף דף נו:

תוספות

מתניתין אסור בפול המצרי. דכל מידי דאידגן שמעמידין אותו בכרי נקרא דגן: **וכפרוץ** הדבר. פסוק הוא בדברי הימים שתיקן חזקיהו שיביאו המעשרות לאוצר לבית המקדש וכפרוץ תקנתו הרבו בני ישראל מעשר דגן תירוש ויצהר וכל תבואת שדה לרוב והשתא ס"ד דכל תבואת שדה כלומר כגון פול המצרי אסיפא דקרא סמיך דכתיב כל תבואת שדה לרוב ואי דגן כל מילי דאידגן משמע ל"ל למיכתב כל תבואת שדה ונהי דדגן דכתיב באורייתא מעשר דגנך לא משמע אלא ה' מינין מיהו ההוא דדברי הימים משמע כל מילי דאי בלשון ב"א משמע כל מידי דמדגן ההוא נמי משמע כל מילי: **הכל** מודים. אפילו רבנן שאין אסור אלא מה' מינין: **מתיב** רב יוסף. וה"ה לרבי מאיר דמתני' מותיב ואמר אביי לאיתויי פירות האילן וירק: **תבואת** שדה לחוד. דודאי משמע כל מילי: **עללתא**. כל מין דמידגן משמע: **הא** לא מיבעיא ליה. דכל פירות איקרי עללתא כל דבר אוכלין מקרי עללתא וכן שאר נכסים דעללתא מידי דהוא בעין משמע כי קמיבעיא ליה שכר בתים שכר ספינות מי אמרינן כיון דבתים וספינות פוחתים בכל יום ומשתנים לאו בכלל עללתא דעללתא משמע מידי דמשבח ולא מידי דפוחת: **או** דלמא כיון דלא ידיע פחתייהו. פי' שפוחתין מעט מעט ולזמן מרובה ה"ל [מידי] דמשבח ואיקרי שפיר עללתא: **שיהא** מופקר לכל. שיהיה מלמד תורה לכל: **ששוקפין**. לשון אסקופה הנדרסת:

פי' הרא"ש

מתני' אסור בפול המצרי כו'. דדגן כל מיני דמידגן משמע שעושין ממנו כרי והנודר מן הדגן אסור בכל מיני קטניות שעושין מהם כרי: **גמ'** וכפרוץ הדבר. מקרא הוא בדברי הימים על חזקיהו שתקן לעשר מפירות ירק וכאשר נתחזקה התקנה הרבו בני ישראל להביא מעשר מכל: **אי אמרת דגן כל דמידגן משמע**. בלשון בני אדם: **מאי וכפרוץ הדבר**. רישיה דקרא נקט ומסיפיה קא פריך והאי ראשית דגן דכתיב בקרא היינו מה שנקרא דגן בלשון בני אדם ואי כל דמידגן משמע מאי האי כל תבואת השדה דכתיב בסיפיה דקרא ומה בא להוסיף: **לאיתויי פירות האילן וירק**. דליתנהו בכלל דגן ומיקרו תבואת השדה: (פיסקא) **הכל מודים בנודר מן התבואה שאינו אסור אלא בחמשת המינין**. דלא תימא לרבנן אע"ג דדגן לא משמע להו אלא חמשת המינין תבואה כל מילי משמע כדקאמר בתר הכי ותהיה סברת רבנן ורבי מאיר הפוכה בתבואה ודגן: **דעללתא כל מילי משמע**. שם דעללתא משמע כל דבר מעולה ומשובח: **שכר בתים ושכר בסמות**. כיון דפחתי שלפעמים נשכרים בזול: **כיון דלא ידיע פחתייהו**. אין ניכר בהם פחיתות השכר: **דמי האי מזיגא כו'**. שהיה רגיל ליתן הרבה מים ביין כדאיתא בתחלת פרק המוציא יין (דף עז.) אמר רבא כל חמרא דלא דרי על חד תלתא מיא לאו חמרא הוא: **שהוא מופקר לכל**. ללמוד תורתו לכל:

חילקא

שנאמר

שֶׁנֶּאֱמַר "כָּל גֶּיא יִנָּשֵׂא". תַּנְיָא – הַנּוֹדֵר מִן הַדָּגָן – אָסוּר אַף בְּפוֹל הַמִּצְרִי יָבֵשׁ, וּמוּתָּר בְּלַח. וּמוּתָּר בְּאוֹרֶז, בְּחִילְקָא, בְּטַרְגִּים וּבְטִיסְנֵי. הַנּוֹדֵר מִן פֵּירוֹת הַשָּׁנָה – אָסוּר בְּכָל פֵּירוֹת הַשָּׁנָה, וּמוּתָּר בִּגְדָיִים וּבִטְלָאִים וּבְחָלָב וּבְבֵיצִים וּבְגוֹזָלוֹת, וְאִם אָמַר "גִּידוּלֵי שָׁנָה עָלַי" – אָסוּר בְּכוּלָּן. הַנּוֹדֵר מִן פֵּירוֹת הָאָרֶץ אָסוּר בְּכָל פֵּירוֹת הָאָרֶץ, וּמוּתָּר בִּכְמֵהִין וּפִטְרִיּוֹת. וְאִם אָמַר "גִּידוּלֵי קַרְקַע עָלַי" – אָסוּר בְּכוּלָּן. וּרְמִינְהִי: עַל דָּבָר שֶׁאֵין גִּידוּלוֹ מִן הָאָרֶץ אוֹמֵר "שֶׁהַכֹּל נִהְיָה בִּדְבָרוֹ", וְתַנְיָא: עַל הַמֶּלַח וְעַל הַזָּמִית וְעַל כְּמֵהִין וּפִטְרִיּוֹת אוֹמֵר "שֶׁהַכֹּל נִהְיָה בִּדְבָרוֹ"! אָמַר אַבָּיֵי: מִירְבָּא רָבוּ מֵאַרְעָא, מֵינַק – מֵאֲוִירָא יָנְקֵי, וְלָא מֵאַרְעָא. וְהָא קָתָנֵי "עַל דָּבָר שֶׁאֵין גִּידוּלוֹ מִן הָאָרֶץ"! תָּנֵי: עַל דָּבָר שֶׁאֵין יוֹנֵק מִן הָאָרֶץ.§ **מתני'** הַנּוֹדֵר מִן הַכְּסוּת – מוּתָּר בְּשַׂק וּבִירִיעָה וּבַחֲמִילָה. אָמַר "קוֹנָם צֶמֶר עוֹלֶה עָלַי" – מוּתָּר לְהִתְכַּסּוֹת בְּגִיזֵּי צֶמֶר. (א) "הַפִּשְׁתָּן עוֹלֶה עָלַי" – מוּתָּר לְהִתְכַּסּוֹת בַּאֲנִיצֵי פִשְׁתָּן. ר' יְהוּדָה אוֹמֵר: הַכֹּל לְפִי הַנּוֹדֵר; טָעַן וְהִזִּיעַ וְהָיָה רֵיחוֹ קָשֶׁה, אָמַר "קוֹנָם צֶמֶר וּפִשְׁתִּים עוֹלֶה עָלַי" – מוּתָּר לְהִתְכַּסּוֹת, וְאָסוּר לְהַפְשִׁיל לַאֲחוֹרָיו.§ **גמ'** תַּנְיָא: הַנּוֹדֵר מִן הַכְּסוּת – מוּתָּר בְּשַׂק וּבִירִיעָה וּבַחֲמִילָה, וְאָסוּר בְּפוּנְדָּא וּבִפְסִקְיָא וּבִסְקוּרְטְיָא וּבְקַטַּבְלִיָּא וְאַנְפַּלְיָא וּפְלִינְיָא וּמִכְנָסַיִם וְכוֹבַע. מַאי אִיסְקוּרְטֵי? אָמַר רַבָּה בַּר בַּר חָנָה: כִּיתּוּנָא דְצַלָּא. תַּנְיָא: יוֹצְאִין בְּשַׂק עָבֶה וּבְסָגוֹם עָבֶה וּבִירִיעָה וּבַחֲמִילָה מִפְּנֵי הַגְּשָׁמִים, אֲבָל לֹא בְּתֵיבָה וְלֹא בְּקוּפָּה וְלֹא בְּמַחְצֶלֶת מִפְּנֵי הַגְּשָׁמִים. הָרוֹעִים יוֹצְאִין בְּשַׂקִּים. וְלֹא רוֹעִים בִּלְבַד אָמְרוּ אֶלָּא כָּל אָדָם, אֶלָּא שֶׁדִּבְּרוּ חֲכָמִים בַּהוֹוֶה.§ ר' יְהוּדָה אוֹמֵר הַכֹּל לְפִי הַנּוֹדֵר" כו'.§ תַּנְיָא, כֵּיצַד א"ר יְהוּדָה הַכֹּל לְפִי הַנּוֹדֵר? הָיָה לָבוּשׁ צֶמֶר, וְהֵצַר, וְאָמַר "קוֹנָם צֶמֶר עוֹלֶה עָלַי" אָסוּר לִלְבּוֹשׁ וּמוּתָּר לִטְעוֹן. הָיָה טָעוּן פִּשְׁתָּן, וְהִזִּיעַ, וְאָמַר "קוֹנָם פִּשְׁתָּן עוֹלֶה עָלַי" – מוּתָּר לִלְבּוֹשׁ וְאָסוּר לִטְעוֹן.§

מתני'

ר"ן

כל גיא ינשא. אע"ג דלא כתיב גבי האי קרא "ומנחליאל במות", דהא איתו בתורה והאי בנביאים, אפי' הכי כיון דכתיב דהקב"ה משפילו כגיא – מייתי ראיה שהמשפיל עצמו סופו לעלות, כדכתיב "כל גיא ינשא". ולענין הלכה. בעיין דרבא לא איפשיטא. הילכך לא גבי משכר בתים ושכר ספינות, דיד בעל השטר על התחתונה. אבל לגבי נדרים – נקטינן לחומרא, וכולן בכלל. **תניא** הנודר מן הדגן **אסור אף** בפול המצרי יבש. כיון דמדגן, ור' מאיר קתני לה. חילקא. חטה נחלקת לב'. טרגים. אחד לג'. טיסני. אחד לד', הכי אמר בפ' "מי שהפך" (מו"ק דף יג:). **ואם אמר** גדולי שנה עלי **אסור** בכולן. מיהו, דוקא בשלא אסרן עליו אלא זמן שהוא יכול לעמוד בו. אבל לעולם – לא הוי נדרא כלל, שאי אפשר לו לקיימו.

זמית. שלמור"א בלע"ז.

ומותר בכמהין ופטריות. דלאו פירות הארץ נינהו. מיהו, בכלל גידולי קרקע איתנהו, כדמפרש ואזיל. ועל כמהין ופטריות **אומר** שהכל נהיה בדברו. אלמא לאו גידולי קרקע נינהו, דהא תני ברישא דברייתא: על דבר שאין גידולו מן הארץ אומר "שהכל נהיה בדברו". **מירבא** רבו **מארעא**. ולפיכך כי אמר "גידולי קרקע עלי" – אסור בכמהין ופטריות. מיהו, עיקר יניקתם מאוירא ינקי, ומש"ה מברך עלייהו "שהכל". **תוספתא** (פ"ד) הנודר מן התירוש – אסור בכל מיני מתיקה ומותר ביין. וגרסינן עלה בירושלמי: כמאן דאמר הלכו בנדרים אחר לשון בני אדם. כלומר, שדרכן לקרות תירוש לדברים המתוקים ולא ליין. ברם כמאן דאמר לא הלכו בנדרים אחר לשון בני אדם – התורה קראה אותו "תירוש", "תירושך" – זה יין. הילכך, אנן דמשתעינן בלשון לעז, אם נדר מן התירוש בלשון הקדש – אסור ביין ומותר בכל מיני מתיקה, דאנן לא קרינן תירוש אלא ליין, כלשון תורה. ותנן בפ' "בכל מערבין" (עירובין דף ל.): הנודר מן המזון מותר במים ומלח. והוינן בה: מים הוא דלא איקרו מזון – הא כל מידי איקרי מזון, לימא תיהוי תיובתיה דרב ושמואל, דרב ושמואל אמרי תרווייהו: אין מברכין "בורא מיני מזונות" אלא על ה' המינים בלבד! אמר רב יוסף: באומר "כל הזן עלי" דכה"ג אסור בכל דבר חוץ ממים ומלח, אבל הנודר מן המזון – אינו אסור אלא מה' מינין. **מתני'** מותר בשק ובירידה ובחמילה. דלא מיקרי כסות. מותר להתכסות בגיזי צמר. שאינו במשמע [אלא] לבישה. הכל לפי הנודר. לפי מה שהיה ענין הנודר בשעת הנדר, ועל איזה ענין נדר. **גמ'** פונדא. אזור חלול. סקרטיא קטבליא. כולם מיני מלבושים של עור. וכדמפרש: מאי סקרטיא – כיתונא דצלא, חלוק של עור שלובשים העבדנים על בגדיהם. יוצאין בשק **עבה**. בשבת, ולא אמרינן משוי הוא. ולא שק ממש, אלא כעין שק, דהא תני בסיפא: הרועים יוצאין בשקים. **תניא ביצד א"ר** יהודה וכו' והצר. שהמלבוש היה צר, ונצטער בו. ומסתברא לי דברייתא פליגא אמתני' בסברא דרבי יהודה. דתנא דמתניתין סבירא ליה דרבי יהודה מודה לת"ק דכל היכא דליכא הוכחה – לבישה משמע ולא טעינה. ורבי יהודה דברייתא משמע דסבירא ליה דלמשרי טעינה נמי בעי הוכחה, אבל כל היכא דליכא הוכחה – אסור אפילו בטעינה. ומסתברא דכמתניתין קיימא לן, הילכך סתמא לבישה משמע ולא טעינה. אבל היה טעון ומתוך כך נדר – אסור בטעינה ומותר בלבישה, זהו מה שנ"ל. ודברי הרמב"ם ז"ל אינם כן בפ"ח מהלכות נדרים (הלכה ח).

מתני'

רש"י

חילקא. חטה שנחלקת לשנים. טרגים. לשלשה. טיסני. לארבעה. ולהכי שרי, שכבר נשתנה החטה. אסור בכולן. דכולן גידולי שנה ניהו. מותר בכמהין ופטריות. שגדלין נמי על העצים. אסור בכולן. דכמהין ופטריות גידולי קרקע ניהו. זומית. שלמור"א בלע"ז. אומר שהכל נ"ב. מדקא חשיב בכלל שאין גידולו מן הארץ כמהין ופטריות – אלמא דלאו גידולי קרקע ניהו. מאוירא ינקי. שאין להם שרשים בארץ, לפיכך אין מברכין עליהם כדבר שגדל מן הארץ. והא קתני על דבר שאין גידולו מן הארץ. והיינו כמהין ופטריות, אלמא אפי' מירבא נמי לא רבו מארעא. שאין יונק. דהיינו כמהין ופטריות, דמאוירא ינקי. **מתני'** חמילה. כעין יריעה היא. קונם צמר עולה כו'. משמע מלבוש של צמר. באניצי פשתן. דדייק ולא נפיץ. טעון צמר ופשתן והזיע. מחמת המשוי: והיה ריחו קשה וכו'. ואסור להפשילן לאחוריו. לעשות משוי מאותן מינין. דבענין שנצטער נדר, דהיינו לטעון ולא לכסות, ולהכי מותר לכסות. **גמ'** פונדא. אזור חלול שחוגרין בו. פסקיא. פייסול"א. אסקורטיא. מפרש לקמן. קטבליא. מלבוש של עור קשה שלובש על האסקורטיא. אנפליא. הוס"ש בלע"ז של עור. פליניא. סינר. כיתונא דצלא. מלבוש של עור. (ב) סגום עבה. מין שק הוא, עבה טפי מיריעה. יוצאין בשבת. בכל אלו דברים. אבל לא בתיבה. שלא יכוף תיבה על ראשו ויצא, דמשוי הוי. ומותר לטעון. שלא נדר אלא ממלבוש, שהרי היה מצטער ממלבוש. והזיע. מכובד משוי. ואסור לטעון. שלא נדר אלא כפי שהצר לו המשוי, הילכך מותר ללבוש.

מתני'

תוספות

חילקא. חטין כתושין חלוקין לשנים: **טרגים.** חד לתלתא: **טיסני.** חד לארבעה: **אסור** בכולן. דכמיהין ופטריות בכלל גדולי קרקע הן: [**מירבא** רבו מארעא]. כמהין ופטריות ודאי מארעא רבו ושפיר מיקרו גידולי קרקע אבל היניקה שלהם אינה אלא מאויר קרקע ולא מברכין בורא פרי האדמה: **שק** יריעה וחמילה. אינן בגדים הם: **מותר** להתכסות בגיזי צמר. שלא נתכוון זה אלא לבגד ארוג: **הכל** לפי הנודר. פירוש לפי ענין שהיה בשעת הנדר: **היה** טעון. פירוש מופשל לאחוריו כדרך נושאי משאות: **מותר** להתכסות. שלא נתכוון לאסור אלא בענין שהיה מצטער: **רוחו** קצרה. שמלבושן צר לו אינו אסור לו אלא בלבישה: **פונדא.** אבנט חלול וככסות דמי: **פסקיא.** פייש"א: **אנפליא.** קלצו"ן: **כיתונא** דצלא. פירוש מלבוש עור ויוצאין בשבת להגין מן הגשמים: **אבל** לא בתיבה. קטנה שעל ראשו דמשוי הוא: **והזיע.** מחמת כובד משאו וה"ה דברישא מצי למיתני פשתן ובסיפא צמר:

פי' הרא"ש

שנאמר כל גיא ינשא וגו'. קרא אחרינא הוא ודריש ליה אהאי קרא שהושפל כגיא ינשא: **ומותר באורז.** דאין עושין ממנו כרי: **בחילקא בטרגי' ובטיסני.** חילקא חטה שנחלקת לשנים. **טרגים** לשלשה טיסני לארבעה. ואע"פ שקודם שנחלקו היה אסור בחטים עתה שנחלקו ליתנהו בכלל דגן ולא אסר עצמו אלא במה שנקראת חטה מיירי אי נמי הא דקאמר מותר שנחלקו קודם נדרו ואלאו כבר מכלל דגן: **בכל פירות הארץ.** פרי העץ ופרי האדמה: **ועל הזומית.** שלמור"א בלע"ז: **מירבא מארעא קא רבו.** מלחלוחית הארץ הם גדלים אע"פ שאינם נוטעים בקרקע: **מתני' שק ויריעה וחמילה.** מיני בגדים הם: **מותר לכסות בגיזי צמר.** שלא נתכוין אלא לבגדי צמר: **הכל לפי הנודר.** לפי שעת הנדר כיון שניכר שמחמת כובד משאו נדר מותר לכסות: **גמ' פונדא ופסקיא.** וכן כל אלו מיני מלבושים הם יש שהם של עור ויש שהם של בגד: **יוצאים בשקים.** בשבת ואין בהם משום משוי כי דרך לצאת בהם מפני הגשמים והוא הדין בלא גשמים נמי שרו: **אבל לא בקופה.** דלאו דרך מלבוש הוא אלא משוי: **היה לבוש צמר והצר כו'.** מחמת כובד המלבוש: **היה טעון פשתן והזיע.** והוא הדין נמי אם היה טעון צמר והזיע:

מתני'

עין משפט נר מצוה

ו א מיי' פ"ט מהל' נדרים הל' יב טוש"ע יו"ד סי' ריז סעי' כב:
ז ב מיי' שם הל' יא טוש"ע שם סעי' כג:
ח ג מיי' פ"ח מהל' ברכות הלכה א סמג עשין כז טוש"ע א"ח סי' רד סעי' א:
ט ד מיי' פ"ט מהל' נדרים הל' טו טוש"ע יו"ד סי' ריז סעי' כז:
י ה מיי' פ"ח מהל' נדרים הל' ח סמג לאוין רמב טוש"ע יו"ד סי' ריח סעי' ל:
יא ו מיי' פי"ט מהל' שבת הל' יז סמג לאוין סה:
יב ז מיי' פ"ח מהל' נדרים הלכה ח סמג לאוין רמב טוש"ע יו"ד סי' ריח סעי' ל:

הגהות הב"ח

(א) במשנה פשתן עולה: (ב) רש"י ד"ה סגום עבה כ"ב והוא נזכר בפ"ח דנגעים משנה י"א ושם משמע דהוא מין מרדעת.

מסורת הש"ס

[ישעיהו מ] [תוספתא פ"ד מ"ק יג:] [תוספתא ריש פ"ד] [ברכות מ:] שם שם ולו. [תוספתא שבת פ"ו] [שבת סב. תוספתא שם] [תוספתא פ"ד ע"ש]

תורה אור

מתני' הנודר מן הבית – מותר בעלייה, דברי רבי מאיר. וחכמים אומרים: [א]עלייה בכלל הבית. [ב]הנודר מן עלייה – מותר בבית.§ **גמ'** מאן תנא: °"בבית" לרבות את [א] היציע, "בבית" – לרבות את העלייה? אמר רב חסדא: רבי מאיר היא. דאי רבנן – האמרי רבנן עלייה בכלל הבית, למה לי קרא "בבית" לריבויא? אביי אמר: אפי' תימא רבנן, בעיא קרא, דסלקא דעתך אמינא; °"בבית ארץ אחוזתכם" כתיב, דמחבר בארעא – שמיה בית, עלייה – הא לא מחבר בארעא. כמאן אזלא הא *דאמר רב הונא בר חייא משמיה דעולא: [ג]"בית בביתי אני מוכר לך" – מראהו עלייה. טעמא דא"ל "בית שבביתי אני מוכר לך", אבל "בית" סתם – אינו מראהו עלייה, לימא רבי מאיר היא? אפילו תימא רבנן, מאי עלייה – *מעולה *שבבתים.§ **מתני'** הנודר מן המטה – מותר בדרגש, דברי רבי מאיר. וחכ"א: [ד]דרגש בכלל מטה. הנודר מן הדרגש – מותר במטה.§ **גמ'** מאי דרגש? אמר עולא: ערסא דגדא. אמרו ליה רבנן לעולא: הא *דתנן: [ה]כשהן מברין אותו, כל העם מסובין על הארץ והוא מיסב על הדרגש. כולה שתא לא יתיב עלה, ההוא יומא יתיב עלה? מתקיף לה רבינא: מידי דהוה אבשר ויין, דכולה שתא אי בעי – אכיל, ואי בעי – לא אכיל, ההוא יומא – אנן יהבינן ליה! אלא הא קשיא; דתניא: דרגש לא היה כופהו אלא זוקפו. ואי אמרת ערסא דגדא הוא, והתניא: *[ו]הכופה את מטתו לא מטתו בלבד הוא [המיוחדת] כופה, אלא כל מטות שיש לו בתוך הבית הוא כופה! הא לא קשיא, מידי

[ויקרא יד] [שם]

רש"י

מתני' מותר בעלייה. שאין עלייה בכלל בית: דברי הכל אין בית בכלל עלייה. **גמ'** לאו בכלל בית היא. דאי וכו' (א). בבית ארץ משמע דמחובר בארעא הוי בית. עלייה דלא מיחבר בארעא לא הוי בכלל בית ארץ, ולהכי בעי קרא לרבויי, דהואיל דסמיכא אקירות הבית – מטמאה. האומר לחבירו בית שבביתי אני מוכר לך מראהו עלייה. משום דאמר "בית בביתי", משמע: עלייה בתוך ביתי. טעמא דאמר בית בביתי הא אם אמר בית סתם אין יכול להראות לו עלייה. דאין עלייה בכלל בית. לימא ר"מ היא. דאמר אין [עלייה] בכלל [בית]. אפי' תימא רבנן. לא תימא עלייה ממש, (ב) מאי עלייה דקתני. מעולה שבנכסיו. הבית המשובח שבבתיו צריך ליתן לו היכא דקאמר "בית בביתי". אבל אי הוה אמר "בית" סתם – היה יכול להראות לו עלייה ממש, דעלייה בכלל בית. **מתני'** מותר בדרגש. דאין דרגש בכלל מיטה. דרגש בכלל מיטה. ואסור. אבל הנודר מן הדרגש – דברי הכל אין המיטה בכלל דרגש. **גמ'** ערסא דגדא. מיטה שעורכין אותה למזל, ואין שום אדם ישן עליה. כשהן מברין אותו. *לכ"ג כשהוא (ג) אבל. כל העם כו' יתיב עליה. בתמיה, מכלל דדרגש לאו ערסא דגדא הוא. אנן יהבינן ליה. משום דכתיב "ויין למרי נפש". ה"נ, אף על גב דכולה שתא לא יתיב עליה – השתא יתיב. לא היה כופהו. ממש, הכרעים מלמעלה. אלא זוקפו. שמעמידו על שני כרעיו ודיו. ואי אמרת ערסא דגדא. דמיטה חשובה היא כ"כ, אמאי אין צריך לכפותה. והתניא וכו'. וזו נמי, הואיל ומיטה חשובה היא – צריך לכפותה. אלא שמע מינה דרגש לאו ערסא דגדא הוא.

[מנחות קח:] [ברכות י:] [נ"א שבנכסים] [נ"ל למלך] [סנהדרין כ. מ"ק כז.] [שם ושם תענית ל:]

ר"ן

מתני' מן הבית מותר בעלייה. דלרבי מאיר עלייה ליתא בכלל בית. ורבנן פליגי עליה, דסבירא להו דעלייה בכלל בית. מיהו, מודו דהנודר מן העלייה מותר בבית. דרגש. מפרש בגמ'. *מותר ליכנס לתחומה. תוך אלפים אמה הסמוכים לעיר. לעיבורה. תוך שבעים אמה ושיריים סמוך לעיר. מן האגף ולפנים. מסתימת הדלת ולפנים, אבל מה שעומד לחוץ כשהדלת נועלת – מותר בו. **גמ'** בבית דכתיב בנגעי בתים, דהיינו "בבית ארץ אחוזתכם" – לרבות את היציע. כך היא הגירסא בנסחאות. ואמרו בתוספות דלא גרסי' ליה, דהא בת"כ תניא איפכא: "בקירות הבית" – ולא בקירות היציע. ולפיכך כתב הרב ר' משה בר שניאור ז"ל דלא גרסינן הכא יציע, אלא נבוע. כלומר, בית נבוע במיני נבעונים. ואצטריך לרבוי, דסד"א נילף מנגעי בגדים שהנבועים אינן מטמאין בבגדים,* דכתיב "צמר ופשתים". מה פשתים שלא נשתנו – אף צמר שלא נשתנה, קמ"ל רבויא. בבית ארץ כתיב. כלומר, בית המחובר לארץ. מראהו עלייה. אם רצה מוכר אומר לו ללוקח: עלייה מכרתי לך, אע"ג דגריעא. דיד לוקח על התחתונה. לימא ר"מ היא ולא רבנן. דלרבנן, אע"ג דלא אמר "בית בביתי" אלא "בית אני מוכר לך" – מראהו עלייה, דהא לדידהו עלייה בכלל בית. מאי עלייה מעולה שבבתים. וה"ק: מראהו עלייה ע"כ של מוכר, דכיון דאמר ליה "בית בביתי" – צריך לברור לו המעולה. ודוקא דאמר "בית בביתי", הא אמר בית סתם – לא, אלא מראהו גרוע. והך מסקנא דהכא מחלפא אמסקנא דפ"ב דמנחות (דף קח:), דאמר התם: "שור בשורי הקדש" – הגדול הקדיש, תור בתורי קאמר. ואקשינן עליה מהא דאמר רב הונא בר חייא משמי' דעולא: "בית בביתי אני מוכר לך" – מראהו עלייה. מאי לאו עלייה ממש? ופרקי': לא, מאי עלייה – מעולה שבנכסיו. מיתיבי: "בית בביתי אני מוכר לך", נפל – מראהו נפול. "עבד בעבדי אני מוכר לך", מת – מראהו מת. ואם איתא – ליחזי הי נפל והי מת? אמר ליה: לוקח קאמרת? שאני לוקח, דיד בעל השטר על התחתונה. השתא דאתית להכי – עלייה נמי דגריעא, יד בעל השטר על התחתונה. ולפום הך מסקנא דאמרי' דעלייה ממש קאמר, דגריעא – משמע דליכא לאוקמה לדרב הונא כרבנן, דאם כן למה לי "בביתי" דקאמר? אפי' "בית" נמי, עלייה בכלל בית הוא. ואי הכי – אפשר דקיימא לן כר' מאיר. מיהו, כתב הרמב"ן דאפי' למסקנא דהתם, הא דרב הונא כרבנן אתיא, דאיכא למימר דהאי דנקט "בית בביתי" ולא נקט "בית" סתם – לא מיבעיא קאמר; לא מיבעיא בית סתם דמראהו עלייה דגריעא, אלא אפי' כי אמר "בית בביתי" דבכי האי גוונא למעליותא משמע, כדאמרי' התם הגדול הקדיש – אפי' הכי גבי לוקח מראהו עלייה, דגריעא. הילכך, כיון דלפום מסקנא דהתם איכא למימר דמימריה דרב הונא כרבנן אתיא – נקיטינן כוותייהו דעלייה בכלל בית, וכן פסק הרמב"ם ז"ל [פ"ט מהלכות נדרים הלכה ט"ו]. **ערסא דגדא.** נוהגין היו להניע מטה למזל הבית. גדא – מזל, ודומה לו בסוף פרק "במה אשה יוצאה" (שבת דף סז.): גד גדי וסנוק לא. לכהן גדול [נ"ל: למלך] שאירע לו אבל. ומתני' היא בפרק "כהן גדול". **כשהיו מברין אותו.** כולה שתא **לא יתיב עלה.** עד עכשיו לא ישב על אותו מטה, שהרי מונחת היא לשר הבית, והשתא דאבל הוא יתיב עלה?! מהיכא תיפוק לן. נוטל קרביטיו. מתיר

עין משפט נר מצוה

יג א ב מיי' פ"ט מהל' נדרים הל' טו טוש"ע י"ד סימן ריז סעיף כח:

מתני' לקמן בע"ב

יד ג מיי' פכ"א מהל' מכירה הל' יט טוש"ע ח"מ סימן ריד סעיף יב בהג"ה:

טו ד מיי' פ"ט מהל' נדרים הלכה טו:

טז ה מיי' פ"ז מהל' אבל הל' ח ופ"ב מהל' מלכים הלכה ד:

יז ו מיי' פ"ה מהל' אבל הל' יח סמג עשין דרבנן ב טוש"ע י"ד סימן שפז סעי' א:

[נגעים פי"א מ"ג]

הגהות הגר"א

[א] גמ' היציע. נ"ל הנבוע (ועי' ר"ן):

הגהות הב"ח

(א) רש"י ד"ה ר' מאיר וכו' דאי וכו' הס"ד ואח"כ מ"ה בבית ארץ וכו' הוי בית עלייה דלא הד"א: (ב) ד"ה אפילו תימא וכו' ממש אלא מאי עלייה דקתני מעולה הד"א: (ג) ד"ה כהן וכו' אבל כל העם וכו' הס"ד:

תוספות

הנודר מן הבית מותר בעלייה. דעלייה אינה בכלל בית: **בבית** לרבות היציע בבית לרבות העלייה. הק' ה"ר יצחק הא דרשינן בקירות הבית ולא בקיר היציע ואמר הר"ס דהכך ברייתא' איתא בת"כ וגרסינן לה הכי כנגע נראה לי ולא לאורי מכאן אמרו בית אפל אין פותחין לו חלונות לראות נגעו בבית להביא חצר הנבוע בבית להביא העלייה ולכך אילטריך לרבות נבוע לפי שמצינו בנגעים בבגד צמר או בבגד פשתים מה פשתן כברייתו אף צמר כברייתו והוציא את הנבוע לפי שהוקשו נגעי בתים ונגעי בגדים והייתי סבור למעט כותל נבוע אילטריך לרבויי ושמא ה"נ גרסינן בבית לרבות הנבוע. הא דאמר רב הונא פרק בתרא דמנחות (דף קח:) בית בביתי אני מוכר לך מראהו עלייה ואמר עלייה זו מכרתי לך טעמא דא"ל בית בביתי ולא בית סתם דמשמע בית חשוב אבל אם אמר בית סתם בית מכר לו וקשה דלשם קאמר דעלייה דגריעה קאמר ויד בעל השטר על התחתונה א"כ מאי איריא בית בביתי אפילו בית סתמא נמי כיון דהטעם תלוי ביד בעל השטר על התחתונה וי"ל דלשם נמי צריך לפרושי כיון דיד בעל השטר על התחתונה כבית סתם דמי ומראהו עלייה דגריע והכי נקט לאף כי אמר בית בביתי מראהו גרוע וא"כ בשמעתא ניחא כי [נמי] מראהו עלייה דגריעה אתיא כרבנן וה"ה בבית סתם מראהו עלייה דעלייה בכלל בית ונקיט בית בביתי לרבותא דאפי' הכי מראהו גרוע והכא לא חש הש"ס לתרץ כמסקנא דהתם ותירץ כס"ד התם וה"ה נמי דלמסקנא דהתם נמי מפרשינן שפיר. הר"ס: **מותר** בדרגש. מפרש בגמרא ערסא דגדא ואינו בכלל מיטה סתם: **ערסא** דגדא. מיטה העשויה לכבוד ולמזל ואין יושבין עליה: **אנן** יהבינן. מי שמברין אותו: **ואי** אמרת ערסא דגדא אמאי לא היה כופהו. דבשלמא אי ערסא דגדא ניחא דלא בעי כפייה דדרגש העור תלוי בלולאות ודיו שיזקוף ויקשרנו למעלה מארכובותיו ולא יוכלו לישב עליו: **כל** מטות שיש לו בבית. מפני כבודו:

דרגש

פי' הרא"ש

מתני' הנודר מן הבית. שלא יכנס לבית: **מותר ליכנס לעלייה.** דלאו בכלל בית הוא: **וחכמים אומרים עלייה בכלל בית.** נראה דחכמים מודים בחדר ויציע דלא הוו בכלל בית דהמוכר את הבית לא מכר את החדר ואת היציע [ב"ב סא.] אלמא בלשון בני אדם לא הוו בכלל בית: **גמ' לרבות את היציע.** לגבי נגעים מיתניא: **ר"מ היא.** ולהכי אילטריך קרא לרבויי דבלשון בני אדם לא הוו בכלל בית: **לימא ר"מ היא.** דמשמע משום שאמר בית בביתי דמשמע בית כל דהו הא אמר בית סתם אינו יכול ליתן לו עלייה והיינו כר"מ דאמר עלייה ליתא בכלל בית דאי רבנן אפילו אמר לו בית סתם נמי: **מאי עלייה מעולה שבבתים.** ודאי אם א"ל בית סתם מראהו עלייה אבל השתא דאמר ליה בית בביתי האי לישנא משמע לאפוקי עלייה דגריעא משום עלייה וירידה וצריך ליתן לו המעולה שבין שני בתים דהיינו בית ועלייה מיהו בית הגרוע שיש לו יכול ליתן לו והכי מסיק בשלהי מנחות דיד בעל השטר על התחתונה: **ערסא דגדא.** מטה העשויה למזל הבית כדאיתא *) בפסחים גד גדי וסינוק לא כי קרא דעתירותא נקיר שמיה ומצוי בבית השומרים אותו בנקיות לכך מכינים תמיד מטה מוצעת לנקיות: **כשהיו מברין אותו.** גבי כהן גדול [נ"ל מלך] מיתניא כשהוא אבל ומאכילים אותו סעודה ראשונה: **כל העם.** המברין אותו: **ההוא יומא.** שיש לו להתנהג בהכנעה ובנזיפות יתיב עליה: **דרגש לא היה כופהו אלא זוקפו.** כלומר מניחו כמו שהוא זקוף ואין לפרש זוקפו על צדו דא"כ הוה ליה למימר זוקפו ודיו כדקאמרינן לקמן גבי מטה שנקליטיה יוצאין ועוד לקמן ניחא שמן הדין היתה צריכה כפיה אלא שאינו יכול מפני הנקליטין הקבועין בה אבל הכא יכפה אם היא טעונה כפיה ואם אינה טעונה למה צריך לזוקפה: מידי

*) הך תיבת בפסחים שייך אחר תיבת נקיר שמיה ע"ש קיח: וכאן נ"ל שבת סז.

מִידֵי דַּהֲוָה אַמִּטָּה הַמְיוּחֶדֶת לְכֵלִים, דְּתַנְיָא: אאִם הָיְתָה מִטָּה הַמְיוּחֶדֶת לְכֵלִים אֵין צָרִיךְ לִכְפוֹתָהּ. אֶלָּא אִי קַשְׁיָא הָא קַשְׁיָא, דְּתַנְיָא, רשב"ג אוֹמֵר: בדַּרְגָּשׁ מַתִּיר קַרְבִיטָיו וְהוּא נוֹפֵל מֵאֵלָיו. וְאִי דַּרְגָּשׁ עַרְסָא דְּגַדָּא הוּא — קַרְבִיטִין מִי אִית לֵיהּ? כִּי אֲתָא רָבִין אֲמַר: שְׁאִילְתֵּיהּ לְהַהוּא מֵרַבָּנַן, וְרַב תַּחֲלִיפָא בַּר מַעַרְבָא שְׁמֵיהּ, דַּהֲוָה שְׁכִיחַ בְּשׁוּקָא דְּצַלָּעֵי, וַאֲמַר לִי: מַאי דַּרְגָּשׁ — עַרְסָא דְּצַלָּא. אִיתְּמַר, אֵיזֶהוּ מִטָּה וְאֵיזֶהוּ דַּרְגָּשׁ? אָמַר רַבִּי יִרְמְיָה: מִטָּה — מְסָרְגִין אוֹתָהּ עַל גַּבָּהּ, דַּרְגָּשׁ — מְסָרְגִין אוֹתוֹ מִגּוּפוֹ. מֵיתִיבֵי: *כְּלֵי עֵץ מֵאֵימָתַי מְקַבְּלִין טוּמְאָה? גהַמִּטָּה וְהָעֲרִיסָה — *מִשֶּׁיְּשׁוּפֵם בְּעוֹר הַדָּג. וְאִי מִטָּה מִסְתָּרֶגֶת עַל גַּבָּהּ — לָמָּה לִי שִׁיפַת עוֹר הַדָּג? אֶלָּא, הָא וְהָא מִגּוּפָן; מִטָּה — אַעוּלֵי וְאַפּוּקֵי בִּבְזִינֵי, דַּרְגָּשׁ — אַעוּלֵי וְאַפּוּקֵי בְּאַבְקָתָא.* א"ר יַעֲקֹב בַּר אַחָא אָמַר רַבִּי: דמִטָּה שֶׁנַּקְלִיטֶיהָ יוֹצְאִין — זוֹקְפָהּ, וְדַיּוֹ. א"ר יַעֲקֹב בַּר אִידִי אָמַר ר' יְהוֹשֻׁעַ בֶּן לֵוִי: הֲלָכָה כרשב"ג.§

מתני' ההַנּוֹדֵר מִן הָעִיר — מוּתָּר לִיכָּנֵס לִתְחוּמָהּ שֶׁל עִיר, וְאָסוּר לִיכָּנֵס לְעִיבּוּרָהּ. ואֲבָל הַנּוֹדֵר מִן הַבַּיִת — אָסוּר מִן הָאֲגַף וְלִפְנִים.§ **גמ'** מְנָלַן דְּעִיבּוּרָא דְּמָתָא כְּמָתָא דָּמֵי? א"ר יוֹחָנָן: דְּאָמַר קְרָא °"וַיְהִי בִּהְיוֹת יְהוֹשֻׁעַ בִּירִיחוֹ" וגו'. (יהושע ה) מַאי "בִּירִיחוֹ"? אִילֵימָא בִּירִיחוֹ מַמָּשׁ — וְהָכְתִיב °"וִירִיחוֹ (שם ו) סֹגֶרֶת וּמְסֻגֶּרֶת"! אֶלָּא ש"מ בְּעִיבּוּרָהּ. אֵימָא אֲפִי' בִּתְחוּמָהּ! הָא כְּתִיב בִּתְחוּמָהּ °"וּמַדֹּתֶם (במדבר לה) מִחוּץ לָעִיר".§ "הַנּוֹדֵר מִן הַבַּיִת אֵינוֹ אָסוּר אֶלָּא מִן הָאֲגַף וְלִפְנִים".§ אֲבָל מִן הָאֲגַף וְלַחוּץ — לֹא. מְתִיב רַב מָרִי: °"וְיָצָא הַכֹּהֵן מִן הַבַּיִת" (ויקרא יד) *זיָכוֹל יֵלֵךְ לְבֵיתוֹ וְיַסְגִּיר — ת"ל °"אֶל פֶּתַח הַבָּיִת". (שם) אִי אֶל פֶּתַח הַבַּיִת, יָכוֹל יַעֲמוֹד תַּחַת הַמַּשְׁקוֹף וְיַסְגִּיר — תַּלְמוּד לוֹמַר "מִן הַבַּיִת", עַד שֶׁיֵּצֵא מִן הַבַּיִת כּוּלּוֹ. הָא כֵּיצַד — עוֹמֵד בְּצַד הַמַּשְׁקוֹף וְיַסְגִּיר. וּמִנַּיִן שֶׁאִם הָלַךְ לְבֵיתוֹ וְהִסְגִּיר, אוֹ שֶׁעָמַד תַּחַת הַשָּׁקוֹף וְהִסְגִּיר, שֶׁהֶסְגֵּירוֹ מוּסְגָּר — ת"ל °"וְהִסְגִּיר (שם) אֶת הַבַּיִת", מִכָּל מָקוֹם! שָׁאנֵי גַּבֵּי בַּיִת דִּכְתִיב "מִן הַבַּיִת" — עַד שֶׁיֵּצֵא מִן הַבַּיִת כּוּלּוֹ.§

מתני'

רש"י

הַמְיוּחֶדֶת. לִיתֵּן עָלֶיהָ כֵּלִים, וְהוֹאִיל וְאֵין יְשֵׁנִים עָלֶיהָ — אֵין צָרִיךְ (א) לִכְפוֹתָהּ. קַרְבִיטִין. לוּלָאוֹת שֶׁבּוֹ. קַרְבִיטִין מִי אִית לֵיהּ. הָכִי קִים לְהוּ דְּלָא הֲווּ לְהוּ קַרְבִיטִין, שֶׁאֵינָהּ עֲשׂוּיָה לְהִתְפָּרֵק אֶלָּא עוֹמֶדֶת מוּפַעַת לְעוֹלָם. רַבָּן שִׁמְעוֹן אוֹמֵר אֵין צָרִיךְ לְזוֹקְפָהּ. אֶלָּא הוּא, הָאָבֵל, נוֹטֵל קַרְבִיטִין וְהִיא נוֹפֶלֶת. דְּצַלָּעֵי. מוֹכְרֵי עוֹרוֹת. עַרְסָא דְּצַלָּא. שֶׁל עוֹר, שֶׁיָּשֵׁן עָלֶיהָ, אֲבָל אֵינָהּ חֲשׁוּבָה כָּל כָּךְ. וּלְהָכִי, הוֹאִיל וְאֵינָהּ חֲשׁוּבָה — לֹא הָיָה כּוֹפָהּ, אֶלָּא זוֹקְפָהּ וְדַיּוֹ. וְהִלְכָּךְ אָמְרִי' בְּמַתְנִי' דְּמוּתָּר בְּדַרְגָּשׁ, שֶׁאֵינָהּ מִטָּה חֲשׁוּבָה. וְעַרְסָא דְּצַלָּא אִית לָהּ קַרְבִיטִין. וּפָלֵיג רשב"ג בַּגְּמָרָא, וְאָמַר דְּבָעֵי כְּפִיָּה כָּל כָּךְ שֶׁמַּתִּיר קַרְבִיטִין וְהָעוֹר נוֹפֵל מֵאֵלָיו. לְפִי שֶׁיֵּשׁ רְצוּעוֹת סָבִיב לָעוֹר וּמוֹתְחִין אוֹתוֹ בֵּין אֲרוּכוֹת הַמִּטָּה, וְקוֹשְׁרִין הָרְצוּעוֹת בָּאֲרוּכוֹת וְשׁוֹכְבִין עָלָיו, וּכְשֶׁמַּתִּירִין הָרְצוּעוֹת וְהָעוֹר נוֹפֵל — אֵין לְךָ כְּפִיָּה גְּדוֹלָה מִזּוֹ. מִטָּה מְסָרְגִין אוֹתָהּ עַל גַּבָּהּ. שֶׁכּוֹרְכִין הַבֶּגֶד אוֹ הָעוֹר שֶׁיְּשֵׁנִים עָלָיו סָבִיב אוֹתָם עֵצִים שֶׁעוֹמְדִים מְרַאֲשׁוֹתָיו, (ב) וּמַרְגְּלוֹתָיו נְקוּבִים, וּמַכְנִיסִין הַמְּשִׁיחוֹת שֶׁבַּבֶּגֶד אוֹ שֶׁבָּעוֹר לְתוֹךְ אוֹתָן נְקָבִים. מִשֶּׁיְּשׁוּפֵם בְּעוֹר הַדָּג. שֶׁמְּשַׁפְשֵׁף הָעֵצִים שֶׁל מִטָּה, הָאֲרוּכוֹת וְהַקְּצָרוֹת, בְּעוֹר הַדָּג, כְּדֵי לַעֲשׂוֹתָן נוֹחִין וַחֲלָקִים. לָמָּה לִי שִׁיפַת עוֹר הַדָּג. וַהֲלֹא הָעוֹר מְכוּסֶּה מִן הַחֲבָלִים אוֹ מִן הַבֶּגֶד אוֹ מִן הָעוֹר! הָא וְהָא. מִסְתָּרְגִין (ג) מִגּוּפָן. לְעַיּוּלֵי וּלְאַפּוּקֵי אַבְזִיוֹנֵי. שֶׁמַּכְנִיסִין רָאשֵׁי הַמְּשִׁיחוֹת שֶׁבַּבֶּגֶד דֶּרֶךְ הַנְּקָבִים, וְקוֹשְׁרִים זֶה בָּזֶה. אַעוּלֵי וְאַפּוּקֵי בְּאַבְקָתָא. שֶׁקּוֹשְׁרִין לוֹ לָאוֹת בַּעֲצֵי הַמִּטָּה מְרַאֲשׁוֹתָיו וּמִמַּרְגְּלוֹתָיו, וּמַכְנִיסִין רָאשֵׁי מְשִׁיחוֹת בַּנְּקָבִים וְקוֹשְׁרִין בְּלוּלָאוֹת. וְהַיְינוּ קַרְבִיטִין. שֶׁנַּקְלִיטֶיהָ יוֹצְאִין. כִּדְאָמְרִי' הָתָם: נַקְלִיטִין שְׁנַיִם, וְאוֹתָהּ מִטָּה אֵין אָדָם יָכוֹל לִכְפוֹתָהּ מִפְּנֵי נַקְלִיטֶיהָ, אֶלָּא זוֹקְפָהּ עַל ב' מַרְגְּלוֹתֶיהָ וּמַנִּיחָהּ, וְדַיּוֹ. הֲלָכָה כְּרַבָּן שִׁמְעוֹן (ד). דְּאָמַר: מַתִּיר קַרְבִיטִין: **מתני'** לִתְחוּמָהּ. בְּתוֹךְ אַלְפַּיִם אַמָּה. לְעִיבּוּרָהּ. הַיְינוּ פָּגוּם נִכְנָס פָּגוּם יוֹצֵא שֶׁל חוֹמַת הָעִיר. **גמ'** אֶלָּא שְׁמַע מִינָּהּ בְּעִיבּוּרָהּ הֲוָה קָאֵי. וְקָרֵי לֵיהּ "בִּירִיחוֹ". אֵימָא וַאֲפִילּוּ בִּתְחוּמָהּ. הָוֵי בְּתוֹךְ הָעִיר, וְהַאי דִּכְתִיב "וַיְהִי בִּהְיוֹת יְהוֹשֻׁעַ בִּירִיחוֹ" — בִּתְחוּמָהּ הֲוָה קָאֵי. תְּחוּמָהּ אִקְרֵי חוּץ לָעִיר, דִּכְתִיב "וּמַדּוֹתֶם מִחוּץ לָעִיר". מִן הָאֲגַף וְלִפְנִים. מִן סְגִירַת הַפֶּתַח וְלִפְנִים. אֲגַף כְּמוֹ (יומא יח.) הֲגָפַת דְּלָתוֹת. אֲבָל מִן הָאֲגַף וְלַחוּץ עַל עוֹבִי הַמִּפְתָּן — אֵינוֹ אָסוּר. יָכוֹל יֵלֵךְ לְבֵיתוֹ וְיַסְגִּיר. ע"י שְׁלוּחוֹ. ת"ל אֶל פֶּתַח הַבַּיִת. שֶׁל מְנוּגָּע צָרִיךְ לַעֲמוֹד. הָכִי גָּרְסִינַן. עַל הַשָּׁקוֹף. עַל עוֹבִי הַמִּפְתָּן. עַד שֶׁיֵּצֵא מִן הַשָּׁקוֹף. דְּעַל הַשָּׁקוֹף אִיקְרֵי בַּיִת. בְּצַד הַשָּׁקוֹף. מִבַּחוּץ. מִדְּקָאָמַר "עַד שֶׁיֵּצֵא מִן הַבַּיִת כּוּלּוֹ" — אַלְמָא דְּשָׁקוֹף נַמִי הָוֵי בַּיִת, וְאַמַּאי הַנּוֹדֵר מוּתָּר מִן הָאֲגַף וְלַחוּץ? שָׁאנֵי גַּבֵּי בַּיִת וכו'. אֲבָל גַּבֵּי נְדָרִים מוּתָּר מִן הָאֲגַף וְלַחוּץ. שָׁקוֹף — הַיְינוּ אִסְקוּפָּה, מַשְׁקוֹף — מַה שֶּׁעַל הַפֶּתַח.

מתני'

ר"ן

מתיר קרביטיו, דהיינו לולאותיו, דימי אבלו. **קרביטין מי אית ליה.** הרי כשאר מטות הוא עשוי! **בשוקא דצלעי.** מעבדי עורות. **ערסא דצלא.** מטה של עור, ותולין רצועות בשפת העור סביב, וכשרוצים לנטותו – עונבין הרצועות באורוכות המטה, וכשמתירין אותן – נופל מאליו, והן הן קרביטיו. וכדי שלא יתקלקל העור בלחלוח הקרקע, שלא היו ראשי כרעיו גבוהין מסרוגו למעלה, אמר תנא קמא דאינו כופהו. וקאמר *ר"ג דמתיר קרביטיו והוא נופל. **מטה*** **מסרגין אותה על גבה.** החבלים מרכיבים על אורוכות המטה. **דרגש מסרגים אותו מגופו.** שיש נקבים באורוכותיו, ותוחבים בהן ראשי רצועות התלויות בעור ועונבין, ואין מרכיבין הרצועות ע"ג אורוכות המטה. **והעריסה.** עריסת תינוקות. **משישופם בעור הדג.** כדי להחליק האורוכות ליפותן. **למה לי שיפת עור דג.** והרי מכוסות הן תמיד בראשי החבלים המסורגין על גבי המטה! **אעולי ואפוקי בבזעים.** בנקבים של אורוכות מכניס ומוציא ראש החבל. **באבקתא.** לולאות תלוין בנקבי אורוכותיו, ובהן מכניסין ראשי רצועות התלויות בשפת העור. **שנקליטיה יוצאין.** נקליטין – ב' עצים ארוכין שמעמידין אותם במטה, אחד במראשותיה ואחד במרגלותיה, ומופללין הן בראשיהן, ומניחין קנה מזה ומזה, ועליו פורסין הכילה. ויש שמחברין אותן נקליטין למטה, והיינו [יוצאים] – שמחוברין ויוצאין מן המטה עצמה. ואין יכול לכפותה מפני נקליטיה, ומשום הכי זוקפה ודיו. **מנלן דעיבורא דמתא כמתא דמי וכו'.** אלא ש"מ בעיבורה, תוך ע' אמה ושיריים, של יריחו היה יושב. **הא כתיב בתחומה ומדותם מחוץ לעיר.** אלמא, תחום העיר – חוץ לעיר מיקרי, ואינו מן העיר. **ילך לביתו ויסגיר.** על ידי חבל ארוך. **ת"ל אל פתח הבית.** דמשמע שצריך לעמוד על הפתח בשעת הסגר. **אי אל פתח הבית.** כלומר, אי כתביה לחודיה, ולא כתב "מן הבית" ה"א שיעמוד על האסקופה תחת המשקוף ויסגיר, להכי איצטרי' "מן הבית" – ללמד שצריך לצאת חוץ לאסקופה שתחת המשקוף. ומדאצרכיה הכי, אלמא כל שתחת המשקוף, אע"פ שהוא מן האגף ולחוץ – הוי בכלל בית. **שאני גבי בית.** דכתיב קרא "מן הבית" – עד שיצא מן הבית כולו. דכיון דכתב רחמנא "מן הבית" יתירא – לרבויי יציאה אחרת אתא, והיינו שיצא מכל מה שתחת המשקוף. דהא אי לא כתיב "מן הבית" אלא "ויצא הכהן אל פתח הבית" – הוה אמינא דעומד תחת המשקוף ומסגיר, אע"ג דכתיב "ויצא", דמן האגף ולחוץ כלחוץ. ומכאן לאותן שנשבעין לעמוד בבית אחד, דמן האגף ולפנים – מותרים, מן האגף ולחוץ – אסורין.

מתני'

עין משפט נר מצוה

יח א ב מיי' פ"ה מהל' אבל הל' יח:

יט ג מיי' פ"ה מהלכות כלים הלכה א:

כ ד מיי' פ"ה מהל' אבל הלכה יח:

כא ה מיי' פ"ט מהל' נדרים הלכה טז טוש"ע י"ד סימן רז סעיף כט:

נ"ל רשב"ג

כב ו מיי' שם טוש"ע שם סעיף ל:

כג ז מיי' פי"ד מהלכות טומאת צרעת הל' ה:

מסורת הש"ס

סנהדרין כ: כלים פט"ז מ"א [עי' תוס' חולין כה. ד"ה להטיח]

סנהדרין כ: [ע"ש] מ"ק כז. [ע"ש]

נגעים פי"ב מ"ו ת"כ פרשה מצורע תולין י:

הגהות הב"ח

(א) רש"י ד"ה המיוחדת וכו' לכפותה הס"ד ואח"כ נ"ל ד"ה רבן שמעון ב"ג אומר דרגש אין צריך וכו' נוטל קרביטיו והיא נופלת הס"ד ואח"כ נ"ל ד"ה קרביטין לולאות שבו ואח"כ ד"ה קרביטין מי אית ליה וכו' לעולם הס"ד ואח"כ מ"ה דצלעי: (ב) ד"ה מטה מסרגין וכו' ומרגלותיו הס"ד ואח"כ מ"ה מגופו שאותם עצים נקובים ומכניסים: (ג) ד"ה הא וכו' מגופן הס"ד ואח"כ מ"ה עיולי ואפוקי בבזיוני שמכניסין כצ"ל: (ד) ד"ה הלכה כר' שמעון ב"ג דאמר:

תוספות

דרגש מתיר קרביטיו והעור נופל. קרביטיו לולאות שמחוברין במטה וקושרין בעור: **ערסא** דצלא. מטה של עור ותולין רצועות בשפת העור סביב וכשרוצין לנטותו עונבים הרצועות באורוכות המטה וכשמתירין אותם הוא נופל והם קרביטיו: **מטה** מסרגין הסירוגין על גבה על האורוכות הלכך כשכופין אותו הסירוגין גבוהים ואין יכולין לישב עליו: **דרגש** סירוגין מבפני'. תחת האורוכות הלכך כי נמי כופהו הוא נמוך לישב עליו כאילו אינו כפוי לכך אמר דאינו צריך לכפותו ואית דגרסי איתמר נמי דדרגש אינו בר כפייה: **ל"ל** שיפת עור הדג. והלא אין יופיו נראה שהרי הן מכוסות בחבלים המסורגין על גבה: **בבזייני.** בנקבים שבאורוכות מקצת אורוכות מגולות וצריכה שיפה: **באבקתא.** לולאות שיש לולאות תלוין בנקבי אורוכותיו ובהם מכניסין ראשי הרצועות התלויות בשפת העור: **שנקליטיה** יוצאין. שנקליטיה קבועים בכרעי המטה כדרכה: **זוקפה.** פורס בגד באותן נקליטין [illegible] מקום הגפת הדלת: **אלא** שמע מינה בעיבורה קאי. וקרי ליה יריחו. ומדותם מחוץ לעיר אלפים באמה. אלמא תחום איקרי חוץ לעיר: **יכול** ילך לביתו ויסגיר. ע"י שליח או ע"י חבל ארוך תלמוד לומר אל פתח הבית אי אל פתח הבית יכול יעמוד תחת המשקוף ויסגיר [illegible] שהרי צריך הוא לצאת מן הבית: קונט'

פי' הרא"ש

מידי דהוה אמטה מיוחדת לכלים. והא דאמרינן שכופין כל המטות היינו מטות המיוחדות לשכיבה ולישיבה: **דרגש מתיר קרביטיו.** לולאות שקושר בה: **בשוקא** [ס"א דגלדאי] **דצלעי.** רצענים הבקיאים במלאכת עור: **ערסא דצלא.** מטה של עור ולפי שהעור מתקלקל בגנגו [illegible] בארץ פטרוהו מכפיה: **מסרגין אותה על גבה.** על גב האורוכות: **מסרגין אותו מתוכו.** מתחבר לאורוכות המטה: **משישופם בעור הדג.** להחליקם ואז נגמרה מלאכתם לקבל טומאה: **למה לי שיפת עור הדג.** והלא האורוכות מכוסות בסריגי המטה אעולי ואפוקי בבזיוני. בנקבי האורוכות: **באבקתא.** לולאות התלויות באורוכה: **שנקליטיה יוצאין.** עץ יוצא מאמצע המטה א' במראשותיה ואחד במרגלותיה והן גבוהין ונותנין עץ ארוך על שניהם ופורסין עליו סדין לאהל על המטה ואינם קבועין במטה ואם יש מטה שנקליטיה יוצאין מגופה וקבועין בה ואין יכול לכפותה מפני אותן נקליטין זוקפה על צדה ודיו: **מתני' ואסור ליכנס לעיבורה.** [illegible] **מן האגף ולפנים.** [illegible] **יכול ילך לביתו ויסגיר.** על ידי חבל ארוך או על ידי שליח: **ת"ל אל פתח הבית.** אי אל פתח הבית יכול **יעמוד תחת המשקוף ויסגיר.** דהיינו מן האגף ולחוץ אלמא קרינן ביה פתח הבית:

מתני'

כד א מיי' פ"ה מהל' נדרים הל' יג טוש"ע י"ד סימן רטז סעיף א:
כה ב מיי' שם הל' יד טוש"ע שם סעי' ב:
כו ג מיי' שם הל' טו טוש"ע שם סעי' ג:
כז ד (מיי' פ"י מהל' נדרים הל' יב) טוש"ע י"ד סימן רכ סעיף כא:
כח ה מיי' שם הל' יב טוש"ע שם סעיף כב:

מתני' *א"קוֹנָם פֵּירוֹת הָאֵלּוּ עָלַי" "קוֹנָם הֵן עַל פִּי" "קוֹנָם הֵן לְפִי" — אָסוּר בְּחִילּוּפֵיהֶן וּבְגִידּוּלֵיהֶן. (א) ב"שֶׁאֲנִי אוֹכֵל" וְ"שֶׁאֲנִי טוֹעֵם" — מוּתָּר בְּחִילּוּפֵיהֶן וּבְגִידּוּלֵיהֶן בְּדָבָר שֶׁזַּרְעוֹ כָּלֶה, אֲבָל בְּדָבָר שֶׁאֵין זַרְעוֹ כָּלֶה — אֲפִילּוּ גִּידּוּלֵי גִידּוּלִין אֲסוּרִין. ג"הָאוֹמֵר לְאִשְׁתּוֹ "קוֹנָם מַעֲשֵׂה יָדַיִךְ עָלַי" "קוֹנָם הֵן עַל פִּי" "קוֹנָם הֵן לְפִי" — אָסוּר בְּחִילּוּפֵיהֶן וּבְגִידּוּלֵיהֶן. "שֶׁאֲנִי אוֹכֵל" "שֶׁאֲנִי טוֹעֵם" — מוּתָּר בְּחִילּוּפֵיהֶן וּבְגִידּוּלֵיהֶן בְּדָבָר שֶׁזַּרְעוֹ כָּלֶה, אֲבָל דָּבָר שֶׁאֵין זַרְעוֹ כָּלֶה — אֲפִילּוּ גִּידּוּלֵי גִידּוּלִין אֲסוּרִין. ד"שֶׁאַתְּ עוֹשָׂה אֵינִי אוֹכֵל עַד הַפֶּסַח" "שֶׁאַתְּ עוֹשָׂה אֵינִי מִתְכַּסֶּה עַד הַפֶּסַח", עָשְׂתָה לִפְנֵי הַפֶּסַח — מוּתָּר לֶאֱכוֹל וּלְהִתְכַּסּוֹת אַחַר הַפֶּסַח. "שֶׁאַתְּ עוֹשָׂה עַד הַפֶּסַח אֵינִי אוֹכֵל" וְ"שֶׁאַתְּ עוֹשָׂה עַד הַפֶּסַח אֵינִי מִתְכַּסֶּה", עָשְׂתָה לִפְנֵי הַפֶּסַח — אָסוּר לֶאֱכוֹל וּלְהִתְכַּסּוֹת אַחַר הַפֶּסַח. *ה"שֶׁאַתְּ נֶהֱנֵית לִי עַד הַפֶּסַח אִם הוֹלֶכֶת אַתְּ לְבֵית אָבִיךְ עַד הֶחָג", הָלְכָה לִפְנֵי הַפֶּסַח — אֲסוּרָה בַּהֲנָאָתוֹ עַד הַפֶּסַח,

לְאַחַר

לעיל טו.

רש"י

מתני' בְּדָבָר שֶׁזַּרְעוֹ כָּלֶה. בַּקַּרְקַע, וְגָדֵל. כְּגוֹן חִטָּה וְכַיּוֹצֵא בָּהּ, דְּהַיְינוּ גִּידּוּלִין גְּמוּרִין. אֲבָל בְּדָבָר שֶׁאֵין זַרְעוֹ כָּלֶה. כְּגוֹן הַשּׁוּמִים וְהַבְּצָלִים, שֶׁאֵינוֹ כָּלֶה בַּקַּרְקַע, אֶלָּא שֶׁרָבֶה וְגָדֵל בְּגוּפוֹ. אֲפִילּוּ גִּידּוּלֵי גִידּוּלִין אֲסוּרִין. דִּכְגוּפַיְיהוּ דָּמוּ. מַעֲשֵׂה יָדַיִךְ עָלַי. וְנָתְנוּ לָהּ פֵּירוֹת בִּשְׂכַר מַעֲשֵׂה יָדֶיהָ. הוֹאִיל וְאָמַר "עָלַי" — אָסוּר בְּחִילּוּפֵיהֶן וכו'. אֲבָל כִּי אָמַר "שֶׁאֵינִי טוֹעֵם", מַשְׁמַע: מֵהֶן גּוּפָן אֵינִי טוֹעֵם, הִלְכָּךְ מוּתָּר בְּחִילּוּפֵיהֶן וּבְגִידּוּלֵיהֶן אִם זְרָעוֹ וְצָמְחוּ. שֶׁאַתְּ עוֹשָׂה אֵינִי אוֹכֵל עַד הַפֶּסַח. דְּאָמַר הָכִי "קוֹנָם עָלַי מַה שֶּׁאַתְּ עוֹשָׂה שֶׁאֵינִי אוֹכֵל מִמַּעֲשֵׂה יָדַיִךְ עַד הַפֶּסַח", אוֹ שֶׁאָמַר "קוֹנָם שֶׁאַתְּ עוֹשָׂה שֶׁאֵינִי מִתְכַּסֶּה מִכָּל מְלַאכְתֵּךְ עַד הַפֶּסַח". מוּתָּר לְאַחַר הַפֶּסַח. שֶׁהֲרֵי לֹא נָדַר מִכָּל מַה שֶּׁתַּעֲשֶׂה אֶלָּא עַד הַפֶּסַח (ב). אֲפִי' אַחַר הַפֶּסַח אָסוּר. לֶאֱכוֹל וּלְהִתְכַּסּוֹת מִכָּל שֶׁעוֹשָׂה לְעוֹלָם, שֶׁהֲרֵי לֹא קָבַע בּוֹ זְמַן: הָיָה עוֹמֵד בַּאֲדָר וְאָמַר "קוֹנָם שֶׁאַתְּ נֶהֱנֵית לִי עַד הַפֶּסַח אִם תֵּלְכִי לְבֵית אָבִיךְ מֵעַכְשָׁיו עַד הֶחָג" — הָלְכָה לִפְנֵי הַפֶּסַח, אֲסוּרָה בַּהֲנָאָתוֹ עַד הַפֶּסַח.

הָלְכָה

לעיל מז. נב: לקמן נט.

תורה אור

ר"ן

מתני' קונם פירות האלו עלי קונם הן על פי קונם הן לפי אסור בחילופיהן ובגידוליהן. משום דכיון שפרט הדברים הנאסרים עליו – שוינהו עליה כהקדש. ומש"ה מתסר בחילופיהן ובגידוליהן. כי היכי דחלופי הקדש וגדוליו אסירי. דלא דמי לנודר סתם מן התאנים ומן הענבים, שכיון שלא פרט, ואסר עליו כל המין – לא עשאם עליו הקדש, שלא נתכוון אלא מאכילת אותו מין. ומש"ה לא מתסר בחילופיהן ובגידוליהן אלא בפורט כי הכא דאמר "פירות האלו", והוא הדין נמי דאם אמר "פירות מקום פלוני" או "פירותיו של פלוני", דכיון שיחד – הרי הוא כפורט, ואסור בחילופיהן ובגידוליהן, וכמו שנפרש במשנה שלפנינו בס"ד. וכי תימא: היכי אמרינן דמאי דמתסר בחילופיהן ובגידוליהן משום פורט הוא, והא בעי רמי בר חמא לעיל בפ' "השותפין" (דף מז.): "קונם פירות האלו על פלוני" מהו בחילופיהן? וספיקיה דרמי בר חמא הוא אי טעמא דמתניתין משום כוונת הנדר הואי, הלכך דוקא נודר אסור – אבל מודר לא, או דלמא דלאו משום כוונת הנודר הוא, אלא משום דחילופיהן כגידוליהן דמו, והוא הדין בכל איסורי הנאה שחילופיהם אסורים למחליף עצמו, וכמו שכתבתי למעלה. ובודאי, אי טעמא דחילופיהן כגידוליהן דמו – לאו דוקא באומר "אלו", דבכל איסורי הנאה נמי אסירי חילופיהן. וכיון (להאי או דלמא) ד"אלו" לאו דוקא, כי נימא נמי דמשום כוונת הנודר הוא – משמע ד"אלו" לאו דוקא, דהוא הדין באוסר בכלל. דהא רמי בר חמא לא אסתפק ב"אלו" אי דוקא אי לאו דוקא! יש לי לומר: דלעולם "אלו" דוקא, ואפילו נימא דטעמא משום דחילופיהן כגידוליהן דמו – משום דההוא טעמא לא סגי אלא לאסרן על המחליף עצמו, אבל לאסרן לאחר – לא. ומתני' פסיק ותני אסור בחילופיהן ובגידוליהן, אפילו החליפן אחר. והאי איסורא על כרחיך משום "אלו" הוא, דהא חלופי איסורי הנאה כשהחליפן אחר לא אסירי. ורמי בר חמא לעיל הכי קאמר: פשיטא לי דכשהחליפן אחר – משום "אלו" מתסר, הלכך דוקא נודר אסור, אבל מודר לא. מיהו, הא מיבעיא לי: החליפן הוא, אי מתסרי חליפין דוקא משום "אלו", דנימא דדוקא גבי נודר, אבל מודר לא, כי היכי דאמר כשהחליפן אחר. או דלמא: נהי דבשהחליפן אחר אסירי – דוקא משום "אלו", כשהחליפן הוא – לא נריך "אלו", דטעמא משום דחילופיהן כגידוליהן דמו, לא שנא נודר ול"ש מודר. ודקתני תנא "אלו" – משום החליפן אחר נקט ליה, דבלאו "אלו" לא מתסר בחילופיהן. כך נראה לי, וכבר כתבתי מזה למעלה. **שאני אוכל שאני טועם מותר בחילופיהן ובגידוליהן.** דנהי ד"שאני אוכל" "שאני טועם" מפיק איסורא, אפי' הכי לא מיתסר בחילופיהן ובגידוליהן. דהא כי אכיל חליפין וגידולין – לא טעים הנהו פירות דאסר עליה. **בדבר שזרעו כלה אבל דבר שאין זרעו כלה אפי' גידולי גידולין אסורין.** אכולה מתני' קאי, וה"ק: מאי דאמרי' ברישא אסור בגידוליהן, דמשמע דוקא בגידוליהן מתסר, אבל בגידולי גדולין שרי – הני מילי בדבר שזרעו כלה. דבכי האי גוונא נהי דבגידולין ראשונים מיתסר דאע"ג דליכא מידי ממאי דאסר בגידולין, דהא זרעו כלה – אפי' הכי לא גרעי גידולין מחליפין, דחליפין נמי, אע"ג דלית בהו מידי ממאי דאסר עליה – אפי' הכי אסירי. מיהו, בגידולי גידולין שרי. דכיון דגידולין בדבר שזרעו כלה כחליפין דמו, כי היכי דחליפי חליפין מותרין, כדמוכח לעיל ב"השותפין" גבי מכרן וקדש בדמיהן מקודשת – ה"נ גידולי גידולין שרי. ומש"ה קתני ובגידוליהן, דמשמע: אבל גידולי גידולין לא, משום דמיירי בדבר שזרעו כלה. וכן נמי סיפא ד"שאני אוכל" "שאני טועם" מותר בחילופיהן ובגידוליהן – דוקא בדבר שזרעו כלה, אבל דבר שאין זרעו כלה – בין ברישא בין בסיפא, אפילו גידולי גידולין אסורים. משום דכיון דאין זרעו כלה – הרי בגידולי גידולין הללו מעורב בהן מן האיסור הראשון, ונדרים הוה להו דבר שיש לו מתירין, כדאמרי' בגמרא וכל דבר שיש לו מתירין – אפילו באלף לא בטיל. **האומר לאשתו קונם מעשה ידיך עלי וכו' אסור בחילופיהן ובגידוליהן.** אשמועינן רבותא, דמיחד פירותיו של פלוני, כי הכא דיחד מעשה ידי אשתו – כאומר "אלו" דמי, ומתסר בחילופיהן ובגידוליהן. ולא תקשי לך: מעשה ידיה דבר שאין בו ממש הוא, דהיכא לאוקמה באומר "קונם ידיך למעשיהם"? אי נמי: מעשה ידי אשתו – לאחר שתעשה, דבר שיש בו ממש הוא. מיהו, כתב הרב רבי יונה ז"ל: דלא מתסר אלא בכנגד מעשה ידיה, שאם אשתו טחנה ואפתה ומכרה לחם, להיות מעות שכנגד טחינה ואפיה – שלה, ודכנגד חטים – שלו. **שאני אוכל שאני טועם מותר בחילופיהן ובגידוליהן.** בהך סיפא נמי אשמועינן רבותא טפי ממתניתין קמייתא, דאע"ג דאמר "אלו", כיון דאסיק דבוריה ב"שאני אוכל" "שאני טועם" – מותר בחילופיהן ובגידוליהן. דהא מעשה ידי אשתו כ"אלו" דמי, וכדכתיבנא, ואפילו הכי קתני עלה: "שאני אוכל" "שאני טועם" מותר בחילופיהן ובגידוליהן. ד"שאני אוכל" "שאני טועם" לא מסתייה דלא מפיש איסורא לגבי חליפין וגידולין כי לא אמר "אלו", לאדרבה שרי בהו כי אמר "אלו" – משום דבחליפין וגידולין ליכא טעמא דאיסורא. הלכך, כי אסיק דבוריה "שאני אוכל" "שאני טועם" – למשרינהו אתא. והיינו רבותא דהאי "שאני אוכל" דהך מתני' טפי מ"שאני אוכל" דמתני' קמייתא – ד"שאני אוכל" דרישא לא קאי א"אלו". ורא"י לדבר בפרק "הנודר מן המבושל" (לעיל דף נג:) בעי למפשט בעיין ד"שאני אוכל" דוקא מדקתני מותר בחילופיהן ובגידוליהן – דמשמע: הא ביולא מהן אסור. ואם איתא ד"שאני אוכל" דרישא קאי א"אלו" – היכי פשטינן מינה? שאני הכא דאמר "אלו". אלא ודאי כדאמרן. **שאת עושה איני אוכל עד הפסח וכו' מותר לאכול ולהתכסות לאחר הפסח.** דלא מספקינן דלמא "עד הפסח" קאי על "שאת עושה", ו"איני אוכל" לעולם קאמר, דאי הכי הוה ליה למימר: שאת עושה עד הפסח איני אוכל, כדקתני סיפא. ומדלא קאמר הכי משמע ד"עד הפסח" אאכילה קאי (נמי*). **שאת נהנית לי עד הפסח וכו'.** הך מתני' פרישנא לה לעיל בפרק "ואלו מותרין" (דף טו.) לרב יהודה כדאית ליה ולרב נחמן כדאית ליה.

*) רש"א מ"ז

גמ'

הגהות הב"ח

(א) במשנה שאני אוכל כל"ל וכן בכל העמוד: (ב) רש"י ד"ה מותר וכו' עד הפסח הס"ד ואח"כ מ"ה אסור לאכול ולהתכסות אחר הפסח אפילו אחר הפסח וכו' מה שעושה:

פי' הרא"ש

מתני' קונם פירות האלו עלי כו' אסור בחילופיהן ובגידוליהן. אם החליפן לכתחלה אסור המחליף בדמיהן מדרבנן אסרו דמי כל אסורי הנאה וגדולי קונם אסורים כגדולי הקדש והוא הדין אפי' לא אמר אלו דכיון דאמר קונם ולא הזכיר אכילה אסר עצמו בחלופין וגדולין והא דקאמר אלו משום דבעי למימר ובגידוליהן דאי אסר עצמו בכל הפירות מאי נפקא מיניה בגידולין של אלו בלאו הכי אסר עצמו בכל הפירות שבעולם אי לאו דאמרי בגדולין קודם שהגיעו לכלל פירות: **שאני אוכל שאני טועם כו'.** דלא אסר עליו אלא אכילה וטעימה מהם: **אבל בדבר שאין זרעו כלה.** כגון בצלים וכיוצא בהם אפילו גדולי גדולין הוו כמו גוף האסור כיון שאין הזרע כלה: **קונם מעשה ידיך עלי.** אסר כל מה שהיא עושה ומכינה לו לאכול ואם נטעה אילן הגידולין אסורין: **שאת עושה איני אוכל עד הפסח כו' מותר לאכול ולהתכסות אחר הפסח.** שלא אסר על עצמו מעשה ידיה כי אם עד הפסח ולא אמרינן עד הפסח לא קאי כי אם על שאת עושה אבל איסור אכילה וכיסוי הוא לעולם: **שאת נהנית לי עד הפסח אם הולכת את לבית אביך עד החג.** היה עומד אחר החג ואסר עליה הנאתו עד הפסח אם תלך לבית אביה עד החג:

לאחר

תוספות

קונם פירות האלו עלי ולא גרסי' פירות אלו: **אסור** בחילופיהן ובגידוליהן. דכיון דהזכיר קונם סתם ולא הזכיר אכילה אסר עצמו בין בחילופיהן בין בגידוליהן: **שאני** אוכל שאני טועם. לא אסר עצמו אלא בגוף הפירות: **בדבר** שזרעו כלה. הגידולין הוו כגוף אחר: **אבל** בדבר שאין זרעו כלה אפילו גידולי גידולין אסורין. כגון בצלים שאין הבצל כלה אלא מוסיף אחרים עליו הלכך גידולין כגופן: **האומר** לאשתו קונם מעשה ידיך. פי' אם תעשה לי מאכל אסור בחלופיהן אם הכינה לו מאכל והחליפן בפירות. בגידולין פי' בגידולי פירות שלקח מן החליפין: **שאני** טועם מותר בחליפין. שלא אסר עצמו אלא מהם אבל בדבר שאין זרעו כלה אסור בגידולי גידוליהן ומשכחת לה כגון שנטע אילן או זרע דבר שאין זרעו כלה ונמצא שהגידולין אסורין עליהן דהיינו כמו מעשה ידיה והלכך גידולי גידולין אסורין בדבר שאין זרעו כלה אבל בדבר שזרעו כלה הגידולין אסורין וגידולי גידולין מותרין: **קונם** שאת עושה איני אוכל עד הפסח. ממה שאת עושה ואשמועינן דלא תימא דה"ק איני אוכל מכל מה שתעשה עד הפסח לעולם וכן כולם אשמועינן

לאחר

הכי: **שאת** נהנית לי עד הפסח אם תלכי לבית אביך עד החג. עומד בחודש אחד לפני הפסח ואמר קונם שלא תהא נהנית לי עד הפסח אם תלכי לבית אביך מעכשיו ועד החג והלכה לפני הפסח אסורה עד הפסח כלומר אם הלכה לבית אביה:

עין משפט נר מצוה

כט א מיי' פ"י מהל' נדרים הל' יג טוש"ע י"ד סימן רכ סעי' כג:
ל ב מיי' פ"ד מהל' שמיטה הל' כא:
לא ג מיי' פי"א מהל' תרומות הלכה כב:
לב ד מיי' פ"י מהלכות נטע רבעי הל' טז סמג עשין קלה טוש"ע י"ד סי' רלד סעיף כב:
לג ה מיי' פ"ה מהל' כלאים הל' כד טוש"ע שם סי' רצו סעיף יח:
לד ו מיי' פ"ו מהל' מעשר הלכה ד:

משנה

(א)לְאַחַר הַפֶּסַח – בְּ"בַל יַחֵל". א"שֶׁאַתְּ נֶהֱנֵית לִי עַד הֶחָג אִם הוֹלֶכֶת אַתְּ לְבֵית אָבִיךְ עַד הַפֶּסַח", הָלְכָה לִפְנֵי הַפֶּסַח – אֲסוּרָה בַּהֲנָאָתוֹ עַד הֶחָג, וּמוּתֶּרֶת לֵילֵךְ אַחַר הַפֶּסַח.§ **גמ'** הָאוֹמֵר לְאִשְׁתּוֹ "קוֹנָם מַעֲשֵׂה יָדַיִךְ עָלַי" "קוֹנָם הֵן עַל פִּי" "קוֹנָם הֵן לְפִי" וכו'.§ יִשְׁמָעֵאל אִישׁ כְּפַר יַמָּא, וְאָמְרִי לָהּ אִישׁ כְּפַר דִּימָא, הֶעֱלָה בְּיָדוֹ: בָּצָל שֶׁעֲקָרוֹ בַּשְּׁבִיעִית וּנְטָעוֹ בַּשְּׁמִינִית, וְרַבּוּ גִּידּוּלָיו עַל עִיקָּרוֹ. וְהָכִי קָא מִבַּעְיָא לֵיהּ: גִּידּוּלָיו הֶיתֵּר וְעִיקָּרוֹ אָסוּר, (ב) כֵּיוָן דְּרַבּוּ גִּידּוּלָיו מֵעִיקָּרוֹ – אוֹתָן גִּידּוּלֵי הֶיתֵּר מַעֲלִין אֶת הָאִיסּוּר, אוֹ לֹא? אֲתָא לְקַמֵּיהּ דְּרַבִּי אַמִי – לָא הֲוָה בִּידֵיהּ. אֲתָא לְקַמֵּיהּ דְּרַבִּי יִצְחָק נַפָּחָא – בפְּשַׁט לֵיהּ מִן הָדָא דְּאָמַר רַבִּי חֲנִינָא תְּרִיתָאָה אָמַר רַבִּי יַנַּאי: גבָּצָל שֶׁל תְּרוּמָה שֶׁנְּטָעוֹ, וְרַבּוּ גִּידּוּלָיו עַל עִיקָּרוֹ – מוּתָּר. א"ל ר' יִרְמְיָה, וְאִיתֵּימָא רַבִּי זְרִיקָא: *שָׁבֵיק מָר תְּרֵין וְעָבֵיד כְּחַד?! מַאן נִינְהוּ תְּרֵין? *דא"ר אֲבָהוּ א"ר יוֹחָנָן: דיַלְדָּה שֶׁסִּיבְּכָה בִּזְקֵינָה וּבָהּ פֵּירוֹת, אע"פ שֶׁהוֹסִיפָה מָאתַיִם – אָסוּר. *וא"ר שְׁמוּאֵל בַּר רַבִּי נַחְמָנִי א"ר יוֹנָתָן: הבָּצָל שֶׁנְּטָעוֹ בְּכֶרֶם, וְנֶעֱקַר הַכֶּרֶם – אָסוּר. הֲדַר אֲתָא לְקַמֵּיהּ דר' אַמִי, וּפָשֵׁיט לֵיהּ מִן הָדָא דְּאָמַר *ר' יִצְחָק אָמַר ר' יוֹחָנָן: וליטְרָא בְּצָלִים שֶׁתִּיקְּנָהּ וּזְרָעָהּ – מִתְעַשֶּׂרֶת לְפִי כּוּלָּהּ. אַלְמָא: אוֹתָן גִּידּוּלִין מְבַטְּלִין עִיקָּר. דִּלְמָא לְחוּמְרָא שָׁאנֵי! אֶלָּא מִן הָדָא: דְּתַנְיָא, רַבִּי שִׁמְעוֹן אוֹמֵר:

כָּל

רש"י

הָלְכָה אַחַר הַפֶּסַח. וַהֲרֵי הִיא נֶהֱנֵית מִמֶּנּוּ קוֹדֶם הַפֶּסַח – נִמְצָא עוֹבֵר בְּ"לֹא יַחֵל דְּבָרוֹ" בְּמַה שֶּׁנֶּהֱנֵית מִמֶּנּוּ קוֹדֶם הַפֶּסַח, שֶׁהֲרֵי הוּא הִדִּירָהּ עַד הַפֶּסַח. וּמוּתֶּרֶת לֵילֵךְ אַחַר הַפֶּסַח. שֶׁהֲרֵי לֹא הִדִּירָהּ אֶלָּא עַד הַפֶּסַח. **גמ'** הֶעֱלָה בְּיָדוֹ בָּצָל. בָּרַיְיתָא הִיא, אִיבַּעְיָ' הִיא דְּאִיבַּעְיָא בְּבֵי מִדְרָשָׁא. שֶׁעֲקָרוֹ בַּשְּׁבִיעִית וּנְטָעוֹ בַּשְּׁמִינִית. אִיכָּא דְּאָמְרִי: שֶׁעִיקָּרוֹ גָּדַל בַּשְּׁבִיעִית, וְנִתְגַּדֵּל (ג) עַד שֶׁרָבוּ גִּידּוּלָיו עַל עִיקָּרוֹ. וְקָא מִיבַּעְיָא לֵיהּ הָכִי. גִּידּוּלֵיהֶן אִיתִינְהוּ הֶיתֵּר, שֶׁגָּדְלוּ בַּשְּׁמִינִית. וְעִיקָּרוֹ אָסוּר בַּהֲנָאָה, שֶׁהֲרֵי גָּדַל בַּשְּׁבִיעִית, וְחַיָּיבִין בְּבִיעוּר. (ד) וְכֵיוָן דְּרָבוּ גִּידּוּלָיו עַל עִיקָּרוֹ, שֶׁהָיוּ יוֹתֵר מִן הָעִיקָּר – אוֹתָן גִּידּוּלֵי הֶיתֵּר מַעֲלִין אֶת הָאִיסּוּר, שֶׁמְּבַטְּלִין אֶת הָאִיסּוּר כּוּלּוֹ, אוֹ לֹא? מוּתָּר. דְּגִידּוּלֵי הֶיתֵּר מְבַטְּלִין אֶת הָאִיסּוּר, וְהָכָא נַמִי לָא שְׁנָא. יַלְדָּה. שֶׁל עָרְלָה. שֶׁסִּיבְּכָהּ. שֶׁהִרְכִּיבָהּ בְּתוֹךְ אִילָן זָקֵן שֶׁל הֶיתֵּר, וְהָיוּ בָּהּ פֵּירוֹת הָעָרְלָה. וְאע"פ שֶׁהוֹסִיפָה. פֵּירוֹת לְאַחַר שֶׁהִרְכִּיבָהּ, מָאתַיִם חֲלָקִים יוֹתֵר מִמַּה שֶּׁהָיְתָה בִּשְׁעַת הַרְכָּבָה, אע"ג דִּשְׁאָר עָרְלָה בְּטֵלָה בְּמָאתַיִם (ה). אָסוּר. אַלְמָא דְּלָא אָתוּ גִּידּוּלִין דְּהֶיתֵּר וּמַעֲלִין אֶת הָאִיסּוּר. וּפָשֵׁט לֵיהּ מִן הָדָא. דְּמוּתָּר, דְּהָוְיָן נַמִי תְּרֵין. לִיטְרָא. מַמָּשׁ, שֶׁל בְּצָלִים. שֶׁתִּיקְּנָהּ. שֶׁעִישְּׂרָהּ כְּהִלְכָתָהּ, וּזְרָעָהּ וְגָדְלָה. מִתְעַשֶּׂרֶת לְפִי כּוּלָּהּ. אע"פ שֶׁכְּבָר עִישֵּׂר מִן הָעִיקָּר, וְהָעִיקָּר קַיָּים וְאֵינוֹ כָּלֶה – צָרִיךְ לְהַפְרִישׁ מִן הַגִּידּוּלִים וּמִן הָעִיקָּר, לְפִי שֶׁבִּטְּלוּ גִּידּוּלִים אֶת הָעִיקָּר. (ו) הָכָא נַמִי, הַהוּא בָּצָל שֶׁהֶעֱלָה יִשְׁמָעֵאל – גִּידּוּלִין מְבַטְּלִין אֶת הָעִיקָּר. דִּלְמָא לְחוּמְרָא שָׁאנֵי. כְּגוֹן הָכָא גַּבֵּי לִיטְרָא בְּצָלִים, דִּלְחוּמְרָא קָאָמַר דְּצָרִיךְ לְעַשֵּׂר מִשּׁוּם דְּגִידּוּלִין מְבַטְּלִין אֶת הָעִיקָּר, אֲבָל לְקוּלָּא, כְּגוֹן בַּעְיָא דְּיִשְׁמָעֵאל דַּהֲוֵי לְהַתִּיר – לָא אָמַר.

כְּגוֹן

ר"ן

גמ' איש כפר ימא. שהיה דר בכפר שהיה עומד על שפת הים. העלה בידו. העלה שאלה זו בפיו, כדמתרגמינן "ובידו רצפה" – ובפומיה ממלל (ישעיהו ו). ורבו גדוליו על עיקרו. לאו רבייה בלחוד קאמר, אלא רבייה שכיולא בה במידי דאתי מעלמא היה בה כדי לבטל את האסור. מיהו, בגדולין מספקא ליה אי גדולי היתר מעלין את האיסור או לא. וצ"ל דעיקר ספיקיה אי אמרינן דגידולין, כיון שנמשכין ויוצאין מן העיקר שאינו כלה, אי הוו להו כעיקר ואסירי, אי הוו להו כהיתר ומעלין את האסור. ובדין הוא דהוה ליה למיבעי גידולין עצמן שרו או אסירי, מיהו הא בהא תליא; דאי גידולי היתר מעלין את האיסור – פשיטא דשרו, ואי אין מעלין – פשיטא דאסירי, דאי שרו היו מעלין. כך נראה בעיני, ובסמוך תראה מה שהזקיקני לפרש כך. בצל של תרומה שנטעו ורבו גידוליו על עיקרו מותר. כלומר, דלא הוי תרומה, דאתו גידולין ומבטלין עיקר. מיהו טבל הוי, דהא בטלו גדוליו את העיקר. ודקאמרינן מותר – לומר דפקע שם תרומה מיניה, ושרי באכילת ערלאי. שביק מר תרין. רבי יוחנן ורבי יונתן, דסבירא להו דלא אתו גידולין ומבטלין עיקר. ילדה שסבכה בזקנה. ילדה שלא עברו עליה ג' שנים, וקללה והרכיבה בנטיעה זקנה שעברו עליה ג' שנים, ובה פירות. שאילו לא היו בה פירות – אמרינן בפרק "משוח מלחמה" (סוטה מג:) דילדה שסבכה בזקנה בטלה. **אע"פ שהוסיף מאתים אסור.** אע"פ שהוסיפו אותן פירות בגידולין מאתי' על מה שהיו קודם שסבכה – אסור. אע"ג דגידולין של היתר מזקנה קאתו וקיימא לן ילדה שסבכה בזקנה בטלה, אפילו הכי כיון שפירות הללו כבר היו בה קודם שסבכה אין גידולין שבהם מבטלין עיקר. **אף על פי** שנעקר הכרם. וגדל אח"כ בהיתר – אסור. אלמא, גידולין כיון שמן העיקר הם יוצאין – הרי הם כמוהו, וגבי שביעית נמי, לא שנא. שתקנה. שהפריש תרומתה ומעשרותיה. וזרעה. לפי שיש באותה ליטרא כמה בצלים, והוא נוטע אילך ואילך, ושייך בה לשון זריעה. **מתעשרת לפי כולה.** לפי הגידולין והעיקר. אלמא, אתו גידולין המחויבין ומבטלין את העיקר הפטור. ואף על גב דלעיל בסמוך אמר רבי אבהו משמיה דרבי יוחנן דילדה שסבכה בזקנה ובה פירות, אע"פ שהוסיפה מאתים אסור, דאלמא לא אתו גידולין ומבטלין עיקר – אמוראי נינהו, ואליבא דר' יוחנן. **דלמא** לחומרא שאני. לעולם אימא לך דמדינא לא אתו גידולין ומבטלין עיקר, דאדרבה הרי הם כמוהו. אלא דהכא משום חומרא בעלמא אמרינן דמבטלין. ובמה שפרשתי לא קשיא לן הא דמקשו הכא: הא חומרא דאתי לידי קולא הוא, דאי מעשר מינה ובה – דלמא מעשר מן העיקר על הגידולין, והוי מן הפטור על החיוב, ואי מעשר עליה ממקום אחר – הוה ליה מרבה מעשרותיו. דלא קשיא כלל, דהואיל דאין גידולין מעלין את העיקר – הוו להו גידולין כעיקר, כיון דמיניה רבו, והך ליטרא עיקרה וגידולה פטירי מדינא, וכי מעשר מינה ובה – ליכא למיחש כלל.

כל

תוספות

לאחר הפסח. אם נהנית לפני הפסח משלו הרי היא בבל יחל שהרי תלה שלא תלך: **שאת** נהנית לי עד החג אם את הולכת עד הפסח. והיא עומדת בחלק אחד לפני הפסח: **הלכה** לפני הפסח אסורה להנות משלו עד החג ומותרת לילך לאחר הפסח. דבשלא הלכה לפני הפסח לא חל הנדר כלל: **כפר** ימא. יושב על שפת הים: **כפר** דימא. שם הכפר: **העלה** בידו בצל. שגדל בשביעית ועקרו בשביעית ויש לו דין פירות שביעית לענין ביעור ושאר דינין: **ונטעו** בשמינית. שכן דרך נוטעי בצלים שנוטע אחד והרבה גדלים ממנו והוא אינו כלה: **והכי** קמיבעיא לי' גידולי היתר הם דלא גזרו על גידולי שביעית להיות שביעית כמו שגזרו על גידולי תרומ' שבתרומה החמירו משום גזל השבט ועיקר אסור בפירות שביעית מי [אתו] גידולי היתר ומעלים את האיסור או לא דנהי למדאורייתא בטל ברוב שמא חכמים החמירו כיון דעיקר חשוב ולא בטל ומדרבנן הוא דמיבעיא ליה והקשה הרב ר' אליעזר ממיץ אמאי לא הוי זה וזה גורם ומותר שהקרקע שהיא היתר והעיקר שהוא איסור גורמין לגידולין ותירץ דסבר זה וזה גורם (מותר) [אסור] וקשיא להר"ס דהכא חד גורם הוא דקרקע לא חשבינן לה לגורם דהיתר כדאמר פרק אלו טריפות (דף נח.) [ומודו] בביצה טריפה שהיא אסורה בדספקא מארעא דחד גורם הוא והטעם משום דגורם דקרקע אינו מינו ואינו דומה לגורם דתרנגולת ולכך לא חשיב זה וזה גורם דדוקא גבי שאור של חולין ושל תרומה וכן גבי זבל של עבודה זרה דדמי אהדדי ולכן מפרש הר"ס דלא שייך זה וזה גורם [אלא] היכא דגורם דאיסור דהיינו עיקר מתבטל הוא בגידולים ואינו בעין שאינו ניכר לא שייך זה וזה גורם וכן בשאור של תרומה מיירי שהוא בעין: **בצל** של תרומה שנטעו. ולקמן מוקי לה בבצל דגידולי תרומה דגידולי גידולין מותרין: **ורבו** גידולים על עיקרו מותר. אלמא גידולי היתר מעלין עיקר לאיסור ואע"פ שאין זרעו כלה כמו בצל: **ילדה** שסיבכה בזקנה ובה פירות. שהם ערלה אפי' הוסיף במאתים דהיתר אסורים הפירות דעיקר חשוב ואינו בטל בתוספת היתר דכל התוספת למסיבוך ואילך מותרים דבטל בזקנה גם אילו לא היה בה פירות וסיבכה תהיה מותרת שמתבטלה בזקנה (אחר) [אלמא] גידולי היתר אין מבטלין עיקר של איסור: **בצל** שנטעו בכרם. ונאסר כדין כלאי הכרם ונעקר הכרם להשתא מותרין כל הגידולין: **אסור.** אפילו הוסיפו מאתים על העיקר אלמא דעיקר האסור אינו בטל ה"נ בבצל דשביעית אינו בטל אלמא (אי) איכא [תרין] דאמרי דגידולי היתר אין מבטלין לעיקר דאיסור: **ליטרא** בצל שתיקנה. פירוש שעישרה מתרומות ומעשרות וזרעה: **מתעשרת** לפי כולה. ולא אמרי' דליטרא א' שעם הגדולין היה מן העיקר שהרי אין זרעו כלה וככר היא מתוקנת משום דגידולי איסור מבטלין העיקר ה"נ נימא דגידולי שמינית מבטלין עיקר של שביעית: **דלמא** התם לחומרא. דגידולי איסור מבטלין היתר אבל של היתר שמא לא יבטלו איסור:

כל

מסורת הש"ס

[בכורות מב:]

סוטה מג: ע"ש מנחות סט:

מנחות סט:

שם ע.

הגהות הב"ח

(א) במשנה אחר הפסח בלא יחל דברו שלא נהנית כצ"ל: (ב) גמ' וכיון דרבו גידוליו על עיקרו: (ג) רש"י ד"ה שעיקרו וכו' ונתגדל בח' עד שרבו: (ד) ד"ה וקא מיבעי' וכו' וחייבין בביעור הס"ד ואח"כ מ"ה וכיון וכו האיסור כולו או לא הס"ד: (ה) ד"ה ואע"פ וד"ה אסור הד"א: (ו) ד"ה מתעשרת וכו' את העיקר והכי נמי:

פי' הרא"ש

לאחר הפסח בלא יחל דברו. אם הלכה לאחר הפסח עוברת בבל יחל למפרע על מה שנהנית ממנו קודם הפסח: **גמ' איש כפר ימא.** היה בכפר שעל שפת הים: כפר דימא כך שם העיר: **העלה בידו בצל.** הלכה זו כדאמרי' בגיטין (דף סו:) זו הלכה העלה חנניה איש כפר אונו: **גידוליו היתר ועיקרו אסור.** פשיטא לי דגידולין מותרין אפי' לא רבו כי העיקר אינו יכול לבטל הגידולין כדדרשינן בחולין כתיב המלאה וכתיב הזרע הא כילד זרוע מעיקרו בהשרשה זרוע ובא הוסיף אין לא הוסיף לא אלמא אע"ג שגדל האיסור מעט מעט לא אמרינן קמא קמא בטיל וה"ה נמי גידולי היתר בעיקר האיסור לא בטלי כי קא מבעיא לי אם רבו גידולי היתר על העיקר אם מבטלין אותו ברוב ואע"ג דעיקר לא מבטל גידולין היינו משום שגידולין חשיבי שתמיד גדלין והולכין או דילמא כי היכי דלא מבטל עיקר לגידולין הכי נמי לא מבטלין גידולין לעיקר ולא דמי לשאר איסורין שמבטלין ברוב משום דהנך לא מתערבי לגמרי יחד אלא נתוספו גידולין על העיקר: **בצל של תרומה.** אף על פי שהוא דבר שאין זרעו כלה אם נטעו ורבו גידוליו על עיקרו שהבצל יכול לעלות [באחד ומאה] של הגידולין מותר אלמא גידולין מבטלי לעיקר: **ילדה שסבכה בזקנה.** ייחור של ערלה שהרכיבה בענף זקנה: **ובה פירות.** של ערלה: **אף על פי שהוסיף מאתים של היתר אסור.** וגידולי היתר לא מבטלי לאיסור: **בצל שנטעו בכרם.** ונאסר בהשתלה: **ונעקר הכרם.** אע"פ שהוסיף מאתים של היתר אסורה: **ליטרא בצלים שתקנה.** שהפריש ממנה תרומה ומעשרות והאי דנקט ליטרא שהמשקל גורם לידע מה ניתוסף בהם: **וזרעה מתעשרת לפי כולה.** כי העיקר בטל בגידולין וחזר כולו להיות טבל: **דלמא לחומרא.** לחייבו במעשר מדרבנן ויעשר עליו מעציץ שאינו נקוב וכן התוספת הוי כטבל שנתערב בחולין וצריך לעשר עליו ממקום אחר מלקוח מן העובדי כוכבים למאן דאמר יש קנין או מעציץ שאינו נקוב כדאיתא בהקומץ רבה [מנחות לא.] אבל לא מן הדמאי כי נתרמה ממנו תרומה גדולה ומיהו לא דמי להך דסתם טבל שנתערב בחולין הוי רובא חולין ומדאורייתא בטלי אבל הכא דאיכא רובא תוספת מחייב מדאורייתא ונראה דאפילו למאן דאמר אין בילה בדבר היבש הכא מודה דיש בילה כי היניקה ולחלוחית הקרקע מבלבל ומערב יחד ותורם ומעשר מן החיוב שבו על החיוב שבו ומן הפטור שבו על הפטור שבו:

כל

אכָּל דָּבָר שֶׁיֵּשׁ לוֹ מַתִּירִין, כְּגוֹן טֶבֶל, וּמַעֲשֵׂר שֵׁנִי, וְהֶקְדֵּשׁ, וְחָדָשׁ — לֹא נָתְנוּ בָּהֶן חֲכָמִים שִׁיעוּר. וְכָל דָּבָר שֶׁאֵין לוֹ מַתִּירִין, בכְּגוֹן תְּרוּמָה, וּתְרוּמַת מַעֲשֵׂר, וְחַלָּה, וְעָרְלָה, וְכִלְאֵי הַכֶּרֶם — נָתְנוּ בָּהֶם חֲכָמִים שִׁיעוּר. אָמְרוּ לוֹ: °וַהֲלֹא שְׁבִיעִית אֵין לָהּ מַתִּירִין, וְלֹא נָתְנוּ בָּהּ חֲכָמִים שִׁיעוּר. דִּתְנַן: *גהַשְּׁבִיעִית אוֹסֶרֶת כָּל שֶׁהוּא בְּמִינָהּ! אָמַר לָהֶן: [א] אַף אֲנִי לֹא אָמַרְתִּי אֶלָּא לְבִיעוּר, אֲבָל לַאֲכִילָה בְּנוֹתֵן טַעַם. וְדִלְמָא הָא נַמִּי לְחוּמְרָא שָׁאנֵי! אֶלָּא מִן הָדָא פְּשַׁטָה, דִּתְנַן: *דבְּצָלִים שֶׁיָּרְדוּ עֲלֵיהֶם גְּשָׁמִים וְצָמְחוּ, אִם הָיוּ עָלִין שֶׁלָּהֶן שְׁחוֹרִין — אֲסוּרִין, הוֹרִיקוּ — מוּתָּרִין. ר' חֲנַנְיָא בֶּן אַנְטִיגְנוֹס אוֹמֵר: אִם יְכוֹלִין לִיתָּלֵשׁ בֶּעָלִין שֶׁלָּהֶן — אֲסוּרִין. וּכְנֶגְדָּן לְמוֹצָאֵי שְׁבִיעִית מוּתָּרִין. לְמֵימְרָא דְּגִידּוּלֵי הֶיתֵּר מַעֲלִין אֶת הָאִיסּוּר. וְדִלְמָא בִּמְדוּכָנִין! אֶלָּא מִן הָדָא, דְּתַנְיָא:

הַמְנַכֵּשׁ

רש"י

כְּגוֹן טֶבֶל. שֶׁיֵּשׁ לוֹ מַתִּירִין, שֶׁמְּתַקְּנוֹ וְנִיתָּר. וּמַעֲשֵׂר (א) וְהֶקְדֵּשׁ יֵשׁ לוֹ מַתִּירִין עַל יְדֵי פְּדִיָּיה, וְחָדָשׁ – עוֹמֶר מַתִּירוֹ. לְהָכִי אֲפִילּוּ בְּאֶלֶף לָא בָּטְלִי, דְּהָא אֶפְשָׁר לְהוּ בְּתַקַּנְתָּא. נָתְנוּ בָּהֶם חֲכָמִים שִׁיעוּר. דִּתְרוּמָה בְּטֵלָה בְּמֵאָה, וְעָרְלָה בְּמָאתַיִם. הַשְּׁבִיעִית אוֹסֶרֶת כָּל שֶׁהוּא בְּמִינָהּ. שֶׁאִם נִתְעָרְבָה סְאָה שֶׁל חִטִּין שֶׁל שְׁבִיעִית בְּאֶלֶף שֶׁל הֶיתֵּר – אֵינָהּ בְּטֵלָה. אָמַר לָהֶם אַף אֲנִי לֹא אָמַרְתִּי. שֶׁיְּהֵא שְׁבִיעִית אוֹסֶרֶת בְּמִינָהּ כָּל שֶׁהוּא. אֶלָּא לְבִיעוּר. שֶׁאִם נָטַל בָּצָל שֶׁל שִׁשִּׁית וּנְטָעוֹ בַּשְּׁבִיעִית, וְהוֹסִיפָה כָּל שֶׁהוּא – אוֹתוֹ כָּל שֶׁהוּא מְבַטֵּל אֶת הָעִיקָּר, וּמְחַיֵּיב כּוּלּוֹ בְּבִיעוּר (ב) דְּמוֹצָאֵי שְׁבִיעִית. אֲבָל לַאֲכִילָה. שֶׁאִם נִתְעָרְבוּ פֵּירוֹת שְׁבִיעִית בְּפֵירוֹת שְׁמִינִית לְאַחַר שֶׁנִּתְחַיְּיבוּ בְּבִיעוּר וְלֹא בִּיעֲרָן, דְּהַשְׁתָּא קָיְימִי בְּאִיסּוּר אֲכִילָה – אֵינָהּ אוֹסֶרֶת אֶלָּא בְּנוֹתֵן טַעַם. וְאִם אֵין בָּהּ בְּנוֹתֵן טַעַם – מִתְבַּטֵּל. וּמִדְּקָתָנֵי: לֹא אָמַרְתִּי אֶלָּא לְבִיעוּר, דְּגִידּוּלִין מְבַטְּלִין אֶת הָעִיקָּר – הָתָם נַמִּי בְּבַעְיָא שֶׁל יִשְׁמָעֵאל גִּידּוּלָיו מְבַטְּלִין אֶת הָעִיקָּר. הָא נַמִּי לְחוּמְרָא. דְּהָא דְּאָמַר לְעִנְיַן בִּיעוּר דְּגִידּוּלִין מְבַטְּלִין אֶת הָעִיקָּר – הַיְינוּ נַמִּי לְחוּמְרָא, שֶׁכּוּלָּן חַיָּיבִין בְּבִיעוּר, הָעִיקָּר וְהַתּוֹסֶפֶת. אֲבָל בַּעְיָא דְּיִשְׁמָעֵאל לְהֶיתֵּר הִיא. בְּצָלִים. שֶׁל שִׁשִּׁית, שֶׁיָּרְדוּ עֲלֵיהֶם גְּשָׁמִים בַּשְּׁבִיעִית, וְצָמְחוּ מֵאֲלֵיהֶן בְּלֹא נְטִיעָה. אִם הָיוּ עָלִין שֶׁלָּהֶן שְׁחוֹרִין. שֶׁמֵּחֲמַת שֶׁצָּמְחוּ (ג) יֵשׁ לָהֶן כֹּחַ עוֹד לִיגְדַּל – אֲסוּרִין, דְּוַדַּאי גָּדְלֵי מִמֵּי שְׁבִיעִית, וְגִידּוּלָיו מְבַטְּלִין אֶת הָעִיקָּר. הוֹרִיקוּ. שֶׁהֵן כְּמוֹ כְּמוּשִׁין, יְרוּקִין וְהִכְסִיפוּ פְּנֵיהֶם – מוּתָּרִין, שֶׁלֹּא גָּדְלוּ כְּלוּם בַּשְּׁבִיעִית. אִם יְכוֹלִין לִיתָּלֵשׁ. מִן הַקַּרְקַע בֶּעָלִין שֶׁלָּהֶן, שֶׁכָּל כָּךְ יֵשׁ לָהֶן כֹּחַ בֶּעָלִין שֶׁלָּהֶן, שֶׁכְּשֶׁאוֹחֵז בְּעָלֵיהֶן שׁוֹמֵט עִיקָּרוֹ עִמּוֹ מִן הַקַּרְקַע – אֲסוּרִין, דַּחֲשִׁיבִי גִּידּוּלֵי שְׁבִיעִית. כְּנֶגְדָּן לְמוֹצָאֵי שְׁבִיעִית מוּתָּרִין. שֶׁאִם (ד) שֶׁל שְׁבִיעִית וְצָמְחוּ בַּשְּׁמִינִית, וְיֵשׁ לָהֶן כֹּחַ בֶּעָלִין – מוּתָּרִין, דְּגִידּוּלֵי הֶיתֵּר מְבַטְּלִין הָעִיקָּר שֶׁל אִיסּוּר. וְהַיְינוּ לְהֶיתֵּר, כְּגוֹן הָךְ בַּעְיָא דְּיִשְׁמָעֵאל, וּמֵהָא פְּשַׁטְתָּהּ. וְדִלְמָא. לְעוֹלָם אֵין גִּידּוּלֵי הֶיתֵּר מְבַטְּלִין אֶת הָאִיסּוּר, וְהָכָא הֵיכִי דָּמֵי – בִּמְדוּכָנִין. כְּלוֹמַר, הַאי דְּקָתָנֵי "וּכְנֶגְדָּן לְמוֹצָאֵי שְׁבִיעִית מוּתָּרִין" – כְּגוֹן שֶׁהוּדְכוּ, שֶׁכְּתָשָׁן בִּמְדוֹכָה, דְּלֵיתְנְהוּ לְעִיקָּרָן בְּעֵינַיְיהוּ. אֲבָל בְּבַעְיָא דְּיִשְׁמָעֵאל, דְּאִיתֵיהּ לְעִיקָּר בָּעַיִן – אִיכָּא לְמֵימַר דְּלָא בָּטְלִי.

בַּחֲסָיוֹת

ר"ן

כל דבר שיש לו מתירין כגון טבל. שנתערב בחולין, ויש לו מתירין – שיכול להפריש ממקום אחר. ומעשר שני והקדש – יש להם היתר בפדייה. וחדש. שהעומר מתירו. **לא** נתנו בהם חכמים שיעור. שאוסרים בכל שהוא במינן. מיהו, שלא במינן בנותן טעם, כיון דהשתא אסירי, כמו שכתבתי למעלה.* ובפרק בתרא דמס' ע"ז* יהיב טעמא אחרינא לטבל דלא בטיל – משום דכהתירו כך איסורו. וכל דבר **שאין** לו מתירין כגון תרומה ותרומת מעשר וחלה. דאע"ג דמצי לאתשולי עלייהו, כיון דליכא מצוה למיעבד הכי – לא מיקרו דבר שיש לו מתירים, כדאמרינן לקמן. נתנו בהם חכמים שיעור. שאפי' נתערבו במינן בטלין; תרומה ותרומת מעשר וחלה – במאה, ערלה וכלאי הכרם – במאתים, ובשאינן מינן – כולן בששים. **השביעית אוסרת בכל שהוא במינה.** בין בתערובת פירות היתר בשל שביעית, בין בגידולין, כגון בצל ששית שנטעו בשביעית. **אמר להם אף הם לא אמרו אלא** לביעור. אף הם לא אמרו שהשביעית אוסרת בכל שהוא במינה אלא לענין שצריך לאכול התערובת קודם הביעור, דכיון שאפשר לאכלו – ה"ל כדבר שיש לו מתירין. **אבל לאכילה.** כלומר, אם נתערבו לאחר הביעור, שאם יהו אוסרים תערובתן לא שרו באכילה – בין במינן בין שלא במינן בנותן טעם אלמא, גדולין אינן נמשכין אחר העיקר להיות כמוהו. דא"ה – היאך תאסור שביעית בגידוליה? אלא ודאי אין גידולין כעיקר, הלכך מעלין. והרי אתה רואה דסבירא לן דאי אין מעלין – על כרחיך גידולין כעיקר, דאי לא – היכי פשיט דמדגדולין אסורין מעלין? אלא ודאי כדפרשינן לעיל. ודחי ליה: דלמא הא נמי לחומרא, אבל מדינא לעולם אימא לך שהגידולין הרי הן כעיקר, הלכך אין מעלין אותו להתירו. ונראה בעיני, דאף על גב דלעיל דחינן דלמא לחומרא, בעינן למפשטה מהא, דסליק אדעתין דליכא למידחי כי האי גוונא. משום דבשלמא לעיל – ליכא אלא חדא חומרא דמחמרינן, דגידולין כמאן דאתו מעלמא דמי. אבל הכא אי אמרינן לחומרא שאני – מחמרינן תרי חומרי; חדא, דלביעור, כיון דכיש לו מתירין דמי – אוסרת בכל שהוא, והא חומרא בעלמא הוא. ועוד, דגידולין שאינן דינן לאסור אפילו בכמה – יאסרו בכל שהוא. ואפילו הכי דחייה: ודלמא הא נמי לחומרא שאני, דתרי חומרי מחמרינן בה. ואיכא נוסחי דגרסי: "אף אני לא אמרתי אלא לביעור". והיינו הך, דהכי קאמר להו רבי שמעון: לא תותביתו לי מהך מתניתין דשביעית, דהרי היא כאילו אומרת בפירוש: אף אני לא אמרתי אלא לביעור. **אלא** מן הדא **פשטה דתניא בצלים** שירדו **עליהם** גשמים. בשביעית, ולמחו. אם היו עלין שלהן שחורין אסורין. לאו שחורין ממש, אלא נוטים לשחרות, שזה מוכיח שגדולן יפה, ומקרקע שביעית נתגדלו, ולפיכך אסורין. הוריקו מותרין. שכיון שהם ירוקים – לאו מחמת יניקת הקרקע נתגדלו, אלא מחמת הבצל עצמו. **אם** יכולין ליתלש בעלין שלהם **אסורין**. דכי האי גוונא מוכחא מילתא שיניקתם יפה. **וכנגדן למוצאי שביעית** מותרין. משום דבעלין הללו ודאי רבו גידולין על עיקר הבצל המעורב בהן, כך נראה בעיני. אלמא: אין גידולין נמשכין אחר העיקר, דאדרבה, מעלין אותו. **ודלמא** במדוכנין. שדך ושחק הבצלים. וכיון דמדוכנין ניהו – גריעי, ולא ממשכי גידולין בתרייהו.

המנכש

הגהות הב"ח

(א) רש"י ד"ה כגון וכו' ומעשר שני והקדש וכו' ולהכי אפילו: (ב) ד"ה אלא וכו' למוצאי שביעית: (ג) ד"ה אם היו עלין וכו' שצמחו מן הקרקע יש להן כח: (ד) ד"ה כנגדן למוצאי וכו' שאם היו של שביעית:

שביעית פ"ז מ"ז

[שם פ"ו מ"ג] לקמן נט.

הגהות הגר"א

[א] גמ' (אף אני) תא"מ:

עין משפט נר מצוה

לה א מיי' פט"ו מהל' מאכלות אסורות הל' ט ופ"א מהל' יו"ט הל' כ סמג לאוין קמא טוש"ע א"ח סי' תקיג סעיף א וטוש"ע י"ד סי' קב סע"א:

[נב. ד"ה וקשיא]

[דף עג: ע"ש בתוספות ד"ה טבל]

לו ב מיי' פט"ו מהלכות מאכלות אסורות הלכה יג:

לז ג מיי' שם הלכה ח ופ"ז מהלכות שמיטה הלכה כב:

לח ד מיי' פ"ד מהל' שמיטה ויובל הל' כ:

גליון הש"ס

גמ' והלא שביעית אין לה מתירין. קשה לי עדיין יקשה הא יין נסך דאין לו מתירין ואסור במינו במשהו. ומשום חמץ ליכא קושיא כל כך דיש לומר דמה דגם בשאינו מינו במשהו לא חשיב אבל מיין נסך קשה וצ"ע:

פי' הרא"ש

כל דבר שיש לו מתירין. דכיון שיכול להתיר את האיסור שבו אמרו חכמי' דלא בטיל ודוקא במינו כגון טבל אם נתערב בחולין יש לו היתר לעשר עליו מעציץ שאינו נקוב ומעשר שני להעלותו לירושלים או בפדיה: **וכן הקדש.** בפדיה: **וחדש.** שהאיר המזרח מתיר: **שביעית אין לה מתירין.** כל מה שגדל בשביעית צריך לבער: **דתנן השביעית אוסרת.** אין זה מלשון הברייתא אלא הש"ס קבעה בברייתא' ובמשנה היא בסוף כלל גדול בשביעית והוא סיום דברי ר"ש: **אף אני לא אמרתי אלא לביעור.** כלומר שעומדין בקרקע ולא הגיעו לכלל אכילה כגון פירות ששית שנכנסו לשביעית וגדלו מעט חייבין בביעור כפירות שביעית דגידולי איסור חשיבי ומבטלין את העיקר: **אבל לאכילה.** שהביאה לבית לאכול ונתערבו פירות שביעית עם פירות שמינית בנותן טעם אלמא גידולי איסור אוסרים את העיקר בתוספת כל שהוא הכא נמי גדולי היתר מתירין את העיקר ברוב: **ודלמא הכא נמי לחומרא.** לאסור את העיקר בכל שהוא אבל גידולי היתר אינן מתירין את העיקר אפילו ברוב: **בצלים שירדו עליהם גשמים.** בצלים של ששית שנכנסו לשביעית וצמחו: **אם היו עליהן שחורין אסורין.** כשהבצלים גדולין עלין שלהן משחירין ונפסטין הלכך אם השחירו בידוע שגדלו מעט וגידולי [illegible] העיקר בתוספת כל שהוא: **הוריקו מותרין.** עמדו במקומם ולא השחירו: **אם יכולין** [illegible] אע"פ שלא השחירו אם העלין שלהן חזקין שאוחזין בעלין ותולשין אותן מן הקרקע [illegible] מן הגשמים ונתחזקו שאלמלא כן היו העלין נפרכים: **וכנגדן למוצאי שביעית** [illegible] לאו בשוה להם ממש דאילו גידולי איסור אוסרין בכל שהן וגדולי היתר אינן מתירין [illegible] הכי קאמר וכנגדן למוצאי שביעית היתר מבטל האיסור האי כדיניה והאי כדיניה [illegible] פירש בפירוש המשנה דסיפא קאי ארישא בצלים של ששית שנכנסו לשביעית והשחירו [illegible] ועקרן וחזר ושתלן בשמינית והשחירו עלין שלהן חזרו להיתרן הראשון דעיקרו היתר [illegible] שהוא הותר נמי בתוספת כל שהוא להצטרף עם העיקר לעוקרו מאיסורו ולחזור [illegible] **ודלמא במדוכנין.** הא דאמר כנגדן למוצאי שביעית מותרין כגון שדרכן ועירבן [illegible] קר ובטלים בששים כשאר איסורין שבתורה אבל בלא דיכה לא חשבינן להו מעורבין לפי שכל אחד עומד לבדו ואינן מתערבין יחד:

המנכש

תוספות

כל דבר שיש לו מתירין כגון טבל. שנתערב בחולין דמצי מעשר עליו מדמאי או מעציץ שאינו נקוב: **ומעשר** שני. דאפשר להעלותו ולאוכלו או לפדותו: **וחדש.** דהאיר המזרח מתיר: **והקדש.** דאי בעי פריק ליה: **לא** נתנו חכמים שיעור. ואסורין בכל שהוא ואין להקשות דבפ' בתרא דע"ז (דף עג:) אמר דבטבל שלא במינו בנ"ט י"ל דהא נמי לאמר שלא נתנו בו שיעור משום דיש לו מתירין היינו דווקא במינו אבל שלא במינו בטל וכן משמע לעיל גבי יין שהוא בנ"ט ואע"ג דהוי דבר שיש לו מתירין וא"ת פרק בתרא דמסכת ע"ז (שם) דקאמר חוץ מטבל ויין נסך דבמינו במשהו ופריך בשלמא עבודה זרה משום חומרא דע"ז אלא טבל מאי טעמא ומסיק כהיתרו כך איסורו פירוש דחיטה אחת פוטרת את הכרי ולימא טעמא משום דיש לו מתירין וי"ל דהתם בטבל שהלכו בעליו למדינת הים דאין לו מי יתירו אבל קשה למה לי טעם דיש לו מתירין תיפוק ליה משום דכהיתרו כך איסורו: **וכל** שאין לו מתירין כגון תרומה. ולקמן מפרש אמאי הוי אין מתירין: **וערלה** וכלאי הכרם נתנו בו חכמים שיעור. תרומה בק' ערלה וכלאים במאתים ומיירי במין במינו דבשאינו מינו אמרי' פ' גיד הנשה (חולין דף צז.) דבתרומה בנ"ט: **דתנן** השביעית אוסרת בכל שהוא. והא דאיבעי' ליה לעיל אי גידולי דהיתר מבטלין לעיקר דשביעית י"ל דהכא מיירי בדבר לח אבל ביבש לא א"נ שמא גידולי חשיבי טפי ומבטלי עיקר: **אמר** להם שביעית אינה אוסרת בכל שהוא אלא לביעור פירות. פירש הרב רבי אליעזר כגון פירות ששית שנכנסו בשביעית וגדלו משהו וצריכין ביעור כפירות שביעית דגידולי איסור חשיבי ומבטלי לעיקר דהיתר אבל לאכילה כגון לאחר ביעור בפירות שביעית שנתערבו בפירות דהיתר אינו אוסר במשהו אלא בנותן טעם כשאר איסורין אלמא דגידולי שביעית מבטלין לעיקר דהיתר ה"נ נימא בבעיין דבצל דגידולי היתר מבטלי לעיקר דאיסור ודחי הא נמי לחומרא אזלינן דגידולי שביעית מבטלין העיקר אבל להקל לא מבטלי גידולי דהיתר לעיקר דאיסור ומה שפירש אלא לביעור לענין פירות ששית שנכנסין בשביעית ק' להר"מ דתניא כל הספיחין מותרין חוץ מספיחי כרוב ומפרשינן דמיירי בספיחי ששית הנכנסים בשביעית אלמא דגידולי שביעית אין אוסרין במשהו ונראה דשמא התם מיירי שגמרו בששית ולא גדלו כלל בשביעית וספיחי כרוב אסורין כדמפרש שמא יקח מן העלין ויאמר מן האמהות לקחתי ועוד קשה להר"ס מהך דמעביר עציץ נקוב בכרם אם הוסיף מאתים אסור לא הוסיף מאתים מותר אלמא דגידולי איסור אינם אוסרים במשהו וכן מצינו בהך דבצלים שירדו עליהם גשמים ולמחו הוריקו מותרין אלמא דגידולי שביעית אינם אוסרים במשהו לכך מפרש הר"ס דהכא מיירי בבצל שנעקר בששית ונטעה בשביעית ומכיון שהוסיף משהו נאסר כולו כמו כלאי הכרם דעיקרם נאסר [illegible] רעו מעיקרו בהשרשה כלומר כשתחלת זריעתו באיסור זרוע ובא הוסיף אין לא הוסיף לא והכי נמי תחלת זריעתו באיסור היתה מיהו *)יש לייסב דלביעור קשה דהיה לו לומר לגידולין אין לו ביעור: **בצלים.** של ערב שביעית: **וירדו** עליהם גשמים. בשביעית ולמחו: **אם** עלין שלהם שחורין. דדרכם להשחיר כשיורדין עליהם גשמים: אסורין. דבידוע שגדלו רובם בשביעית: **הוריקו.** לא גדלו רובם [illegible] רבי חנינא בן אנטיגנוס אומר. אף בשלא הושחרו אם יכולין וכו' שגדלו כל כך אסורין דבידוע שגדלו רובם בשביעית: **וכנגדם** למוצאי שביעית מותרין. כלומר בצלים שבאים משביעית לשמינית אלמא דגידולי היתר מבטלין לאיסור: **ודלמא** במדוכנים. שדכו אותם במדוכה בשביעית ולא חשיבי ובטלים בגידולין אבל היכא דלא דכו מיבעיא לן אי בטלו אי לא בטלו:

אלא

*) [נ"ל לשון דלביעור קשה. יעב"ץ]

*הַמְנַכֵּשׁ עִם הַכּוּתִי בְּחָסָיוֹת – אוֹכֵל מֵהֶן אֲכִילַת עֲרַאי, וּמְעַשְּׂרָן וַדַּאי. רַבִּי שִׁמְעוֹן בֶּן אֶלְעָזָר אוֹמֵר: אִם יִשְׂרָאֵל חָשׁוּד עַל הַשְּׁבִיעִית – לְמוֹצָאֵי שְׁבִיעִית מוּתָּר. לְמֵימְרָא דְּגִידּוּלֵי הֶיתֵּר מַעֲלִין אֶת הָאִיסּוּר. וְדִלְמָא בְּדָבָר שֶׁזַּרְעוֹ כָּלֶה! הָא תַּנְיָא: אֵלּוּ הֵן חָסָיוֹת – כְּגוֹן הַלּוּף הַשּׁוּם וְהַבְּצָלִים. וְדִלְמָא בִּמְדוּכָנִין? חָשׁוּד עַל הַשְּׁבִיעִית קָתָנֵי. וְדִלְמָא בְּתַעֲרוֹבֶת? הַמְנַכֵּשׁ קָתָנֵי. לֵימָא תֶּיהֱוֵי תְּיוּבְתֵּיהּ דְּרַבִּי יוֹחָנָן וּדְרַבִּי יוֹנָתָן? אָמַר רַבִּי יִצְחָק: שָׁאנֵי שְׁבִיעִית, הוֹאִיל וְאִיסּוּרָהּ ע"י קַרְקַע בְּטֵילָתָהּ נַמִּי ע"י קַרְקַע. הֲרֵי מַעֲשֵׂר, דְּאִיסּוּרוֹ ע"י קַרְקַע וְאֵין בְּטֵילָתוֹ עַל יְדֵי קַרְקַע. דְּתַנְיָא: א לִיטְרָא מַעֲשֵׂר טֶבֶל שֶׁזְּרָעָהּ בַּקַּרְקַע וְהִשְׁבִּיחָה, וַהֲרֵי הִיא כְּעֶשֶׂר לִיטְרִין – חַיֶּיבֶת בְּמַעֲשֵׂר וּבַשְּׁבִיעִית, וְאוֹתָהּ לִיטְרָא מְעַשֵּׂר עָלֶיהָ מִמָּקוֹם אַחֵר לְפִי חֶשְׁבּוֹן!

אָמְרִי

רש"י

בחסיות. מפרש לקמן. אוכל מהן עראי. כמו שאר טבל גמור. ומעשרן ודאי. ולא דמאי, דודאי כותי לא הפריש מעשר מהן כלל. רשב"א אומר כו'. טעמיה דנפשיה קאמר. אם ישראל חשוד על השביעית. שחשוד שנוטע חסיות שביעית בשמינית, (א) ישראל המנכש עמו בשמינית – מותר לו לאכול מהן, משום דגידולי היתר שגדלו בשמינית מעלין את האיסור. ודלמא. הא דרבי שמעון בן אלעזר דגידולי היתר מעלין את האיסור – בדבר שזרעו כלה. וקא פריך: ומי מצית אמרת דבדבר שזרעו כלה מיירי? והתניא: ואלו הן חסיות: הלוף = לופינ"א, מכלל דבדבר שאין זרעו כלה מיירי, ואפ"ה מותר. ושמע מינה גידולי היתר מעלין את האיסור, ולעולם מהא פשטה. וקא פריך עלה: דלמא מהא לא תפשוט, דבמדוכנין קא מיירי, ושמא כלו כשהן נידוכין, דליתא לעיקר בעין, שהוא מתכוין לכותשן כדי שיהו בטלין. תרין. הא לא מצית אמרת דחשוד על השביעית קתני. וכיון דחשוד הוא לא משגח ליה להאכילן נידוכים, ושלימים מאכילן, ולעולם תפשוט מינה דגידולי היתר מעלין את האיסור. ודלמא בתערובת. שמעורבין אותן חסיות בין שאר ירקות של היתר, ואוכלן על ידי תערובת – משום הכי שרי, הואיל דליתיה לעיקר בעין. אבל אי איתיה, (ב) כגון בעיא דישמעאל – אמרי' דאין גידולי היתר מעלין את האיסור. לא סלקא דעתך המנכש קתני. דאותו מין שמנכש עמו – אוכל, ולעולם פשטינא מהא דגידולי היתר מעלין את האיסור. והואיל דאוקימנא דגידולי היתר מעלין את האיסור – לימא תיהוי תיובתא דרבי יוחנן ורבי יונתן דאמרו אין מעלין? הואיל ואיסורו על ידי קרקע. דכתיב "ושבתה הארץ" (ויקרא כה). בטילתו נמי על ידי קרקע. כי רבו גידוליו על עיקרו. אבל ערלה דמיירי בה רבי יוחנן שאין איסורו אלא בשנים, וכלאי הכרם אינה אוסרת מחמת קרקע, אלא מיני תערובת זרעונין אוסרין – מש"ה אין בטילתן ע"י קרקע. הרי מעשר וכו' ליטרא מעשר טבל. ליטרא של טבל שהורם ממנו תרומה ומעשר ראשון, אבל גבי לוי הוי טבל, דאכתי לא תרם ממנו מעשר מן המעשר, דהיינו תרומת מעשר, וזרעה בקרקע כשאינה מעושרת. והרי היא כעשרה ליטרין. עם התוספת והעיקר, שרבו גידוליו כ"כ. חייבת במעשר. (ג) כל עשר ליטרין. ובשביעית. נמי, ששביעית נוהגת בהן. שהרי הוא כדגן מעושר בעלמא, שזרעו חייב בכל. ואותה ליטרא. שזרע בן לוי כשאינה מעושרת, אע"פ שעישרה עכשיו – צריך לעשרה פעם שניה תרומת מעשר שהניח הלוי אשתקד שלא הפריש ממנה. שבדין הוא שלא ישתכר בכך שזרעה כשאינה מעושרת. ומעשר עליה ממקום אחר. מפירות של אשתקד, וזהו "ממקום אחר". ולא מפירות של שנה זו, שאין מעשרין מן החדש על הישן. לישנא *)אחרינא: ממ"א לא ידעינן. מ"ר. לפי חשבון. יעשר הליטרא שהניח אשתקד. אלמא דאין בטילת' ע"י קרקע, דאע"ג שנזרעה – חייב בתרומת מעשר. וק' לר' אמי דפשיטא ליה דגידולי היתר מעלין את האיסור, דהא חזינן הכא דחייב להפריש מעשר של אותה ליטרא לפי חשבון.

תרין

*) [מלת אחרינא נדפס בטעות]

ר"ן

המנכש. מלקט עלין יתרים. בחסיות. מפרש לקמן דחסיות – דבר שאין זרעו כלה, כגון הלוף והשום והבצלים. אוכל מהם עראי. ולא חיישינן שמא קודם שזרעם הוטבלו למעשר, דכיון דמעשר דידהו מדרבנן בעלמא הוא – לא חיישינן להכי. ועוד: דכיון דקים לן בהאי כותי שלא עישר, כדקתני ומעשרן ודאי – מסתמא לא באו לידי גורן מחסיות אלא בשביל מעשר. כך נראה בעיני. ומעשרן ודאי. דקים לן ביה שלא עישר. למוצאי שביעית מותר. לאכול אותן עלין שגדלו בשמינית, דודאי גידוליהן רבין על עיקר איסור המעורב בהן. ואחרים פרשו: בדקים לן דהכי הוא, ואין צורך. ודלמא בתערובת. כלומר, שנתערבו מאיליהן אחר כך בחסיות אחרות. המנבש קתני. ובעוד שהוא מנכש – משמע שתולש ואוכל, אף על פי שאין כאן תערובת. ודלמא במדוכנין. שטוחן חסיות הללו קודם שנטען. חשוד קתני. ולא טרח בהכי. הלכך אפשיטא לה בעיין, דאתו גדולין של שמינית ומבטלין עיקר של שביעית. לימא תיהוי תיובתיה דרבי יוחנן ורבי יונתן. דרבי יוחנן דאמר לעיל: ילדה שסבכה בזקנה וכו' אסור, ולרבי יונתן דאמר לעיל: בצל שנטעו בכרם אע"פ שנעקר הכרם – אסור, אלמא סבירא להו דאין גדולין מעלין את העיקר. שניא שביעית הואיל ואיסורה על ידי קרקע. כדכתיב "ושבתה הארץ" – בטילתה על ידי קרקע. מה שאין כן ערלה, דחסרון זמן גרם לה איסורא. וכלאים נמי, תערובת הוא דקא גריס. חייבת במעשר. היינו מעשר מן המעשר שהיתה חייבת בו קודם שזרעה, ולא בטלה דפטירי בשביעית משום דהפקרא נינהו. ובשביעית. שצריך לבער את הכל קודם זמן הביעור. ואותה ליטרא מעשר עליה ממקום אחר. מעשר מן המעשר. אבל מיניה וביה – לא, דכיון דליטרין דתוספת פטירי – הוה ליה מן הפטור על החיוב.

מעשר

תוספות

אלא מן הדין המנכש עם הכותי. דבסתמא אם אינו עושה עמו במלאכה אינו אוכל דישראל מובדלים מהם: בחסיות. מפרש לקמן הלוף והשום והבצל. מנכש תולש אחד בינתים כדי שיגדלו יותר: אוכל מהם עראי. [ולא חיישינן] דלמא אותו שזרע הכותי נתחייבו והוקבעו למעשר והוו טבל וגידוליו טבל דמסתמא יש לנו לומר שאותם שזרע לא ראו פני הבית והיה מותר לאכול מהם עראי: ומעשרן. אם לוקח מהן מן הכותי דכותים אינם מעשרים אפילו תרומה גדולה: אם ישראל חשוד על השביעית. ומנכש עמו במוצאי שביעית: מותר. אם אותם חסיות שעושה גדלו מקצתם בשביעית ונכנסו בשמינית מותר לאכול מהם דאף כי הוא חשוד ושמא נטעם בשביעית אתו גידולי דשמינית ומבטלין לאיסור: בדבר שזרעו כלה. כגון תבואה אבל בדבר שאין זרעו כלה מיבעיא ליה: והתניא וכו' השום. ושום אין זרעו כלה: ודלמא במדוכנין. שדכן בשביעית: הא חשוד קתני. ולא טרח להתירו כולי האי ואין לנו לומר שדכן: ודלמא בתערובת. האדקתני למוצאי שביעית מותר לאכול עמו היינו בביתו פירות תלושין דאיכא למימר דאיכא רובא דפרי שגדלו כולם בשביעית ולא איירי כלל מפירות שנכנסו משביעית לשמינית: המנכש קתני. ואוכל מאותם המחוברות שגדלו בשביעית ואם כן על כרחך ההיתר משום *)שלותיו לגידולין: לימא תיהוי תיובתא דרבי יוחנן ורבי יונתן. דאמרי לעיל גבי ילדה שסיבכה בזקנה וגבי בצל שנטעו בכרם דגידולי היתר אינם מעלין האיסור: אמר רבי יצחק שאני שביעית הואיל ואיסור על ידי קרקע בטלה נמי על ידי קרקע. כלומר שביעית היתרו ואיסורו תלוי על ידי קרקע ואין התרת גידולין תלוי במעשה האדם דכי אתיא שמינית הם היתר אבל לעיל בכך דילדה שסיבכה בזקנה ההיתר תלוי במעשה האדם שסבכה ודמי למבטל איסור בתחלה אבל שביעית ממילא משתרין גידולין למוצאי שביעית וכן בהך דרבי יונתן דבצל שנטעו בכרם ונעקר הכרם ההיתר בא על ידי שנעקר הכרם ולכך לא מבטלת היתר לאיסור: והרי מעשר שאיסורו על ידי קרקע ואין התירו על ידי קרקע דתניא ליטרא מעשר טבל שנטעה והרי היא כעשר ליטרין חייבת במעשר ובשביעית ואותה ליטרא מעשר עליה לפי חשבון היתה טבולה לתרומת מעשר כלומר שהיא של מעשר ראשון והרי היא טבולה לתרומת מעשר וגידולין טבל גמור:

*) [נ"ל טעמות לגידולין. יעב"ץ]

מתיב

פי' הרא"ש

המנכש עם הכותי בחסיות. ברייתא היא בתרומות בפ' [הזורע תרומה]. הזורע פשתן עוקר ותולש מהם להרחיב לנותרים כדי שיגדלו היטב: אוכל מהן אכילת עראי. כדין פועל שאוכל במלאכתו שהוא עושה ומותר לאכול עראי מדבר שלא נגמרה מלאכתו למעשר ולא חיישינן שמא כותי זרע טבל גמור וקיימא לן דגידולי טבל טבל ואסור אף באכילת עראי: ומעשרן ודאי. אם בא לאכול מהם קבע או אם לקח מן הכותי דאינו מעשר מה שהוא מוכר: אם היה ישראל חשוד על השביעית. ויש לחוש שמא פירות אלו גדלו בשביעית: למוצאי שביעית מותרין. כי נתבטלו ברוב גדולי היתר ולאו דוקא חשוד והוא הדין נמי אם היו פירות שביעית ודאי אלא אורחא דמילתא נקט שביל חשודים נמצאים פירות שביעית דאי הוה אסרינן בודאי לא הוה מקילינן בחשוד: כי קאמר ר"ש בדבר שזרעו כלה. כגון תבואה אבל בצל דישמעאל דאין זרעו כלה לא מבטלין גדולין את העיקר: סלוף. מין קטנית הוא ואין זרעו כלה: ודלמא במדוכנין. שדרכן וערבן עם פירותיו ובטלין בנותן טעם: חשוד קתני. ואין דרכו לטרוח ולבטל האיסור על ידי דיכה: ודלמא בתערובת. הא דקתני במוצאי שביעית מותרין היינו לאכול עמו בביתו פירותיו תלושין ועירב כל פירותיו יחד דהיינו דבר שאין בו טורח ורוב פירותיו של היתר הם: המנכש קתני. דמשמע שאוכל בשעת ניכוש והכי נמי הוה מצי לשנויי אקושיא דמדוכנין: לימא תיהוי תיובתיה דרבי יוחנן ודרבי יונתן. דאמרי לעיל גבי ערלה וכלאי הכרם דאין גידולי היתר מעלין את האיסור: שניא שביעית הואיל ואיסורה על ידי קרקע בטילתה נמי על ידי קרקע. כלומר בעודו מחובר לקרקע יוצא מהיתר לאיסור שיוצא מששית לשביעית וכן מאיסור להיתר משביעית לשמינית והואיל ואיסור והיתר מתערבין מעצמן חשבינן להו מעורבין וגדולי היתר מעלין את האיסור אבל ערלה וכלאי הכרם שאי אפשר להתערב יחד איסור והיתר מעצמו במחובר בלא מעשה ידי אדם כגון בערלה על ידי שסבכה בזקנה ובכלאים על ידי עקירת הכרם לא חשבינן להו מעורבין ודמי למבטל איסור בידים הלכך אין גידולין מעלין את העיקר: והרי מעשר דאיסורו על ידי קרקע הוא. דהזורע סאה תבואה מתוקנת חזרה להיות טבל: ואין בטילתה על ידי קרקע. כשמתערבין ממילא גדילין מן העיקר: ליטרא מעשר טבל. מעשר ראשון שלא הופרש ממנה תרומת מעשר: חייבת. אותה ליטרא במעשר בשני המעשר ובשביעית אם זרעה בשביעית אבל הזורע בשביעית פטור מן המעשר ואף על פי שאותה ליטרא הופרש ממנה תרומה גדולה ומעשר הדרה לטבלה וצריך לתקן אותה כבתחלה לפי שנתבטלה בגידולין: ואותה ליטרא מעשר עליה לפי חשבון. כלומר מפריש עליה עשירי מליטרא ממעשר הטבול לתרומת מעשר ואף על פי שחייבנוה כדין טבל להפריש עליה תרומה ומעשר היינו מדרבנן בעלמא לחומרא דגדולין לא מבטלין לעיקר מדאורייתא הלכך עומד בטבלו וצריך להפריש עליו תרומת מעשר אלמא לא מבטלי גדולין לעיקר אף על גב דמתערבין ממילא:

אמרי

עין משפט נר מצוה

לט א מיי' פ"ו מהל' מעשר הלכה ז:

מסורת הש"ס

תוספתא תרומה פ"ח ע"ש

הגהות הב"ח

(א) רש"י ד"ה אם ישראל וכו' וישראל מנכש כמו בשמינית: (ב) ד"ה ודלמא וכו' אי איתיה בעין כגון בעיא: (ג) ד"ה חייבת במעשר כל העשרה ליטרין וכו' וחייב בכל:

אמרי: מעשר – דיגון הוא דקא גרים ליה. מתיב רמי בר חמא: *"קונם פירות האלו עלי" "קונם הן על פי" "קונם הן לפי" – אסור בחילופיהן ובגידוליהן. (א) "שאני אוכל" ו"שאני טועם" – מותר בחילופיהן ובגידוליהן בדבר שזרעו כלה, אבל בדבר שאין זרעו כלה – אפילו גידולי גידולין אסורין! אמר רבי אבא: שאני קונמות, הואיל ואי בעי מתשיל עלייהו הוו להו כדבר שיש לו מתירין, ואין בטיל ברוב. והרי תרומה, אדאי בעי מיתשיל עלה, ובטלי [א] ברוב. *דתנן: בסאה תרומה טמאה שנפלה לפחות ממאה חולין – תרקב, הא למאה – תעלה! אמרי: בתרומה ביד כהן עסקינן, דלא מצי מיתשיל עלה. אי הכי אימא סיפא: אם היתה טהורה – תמכר לכהן! אלא בישראל שנפלו לו מבית אבי אמו כהן עסקינן. [והא] קתני סיפא: תימכר לכהן חוץ מדמי אותה סאה! אלא אימא: בשלמא קונמות – מצוה לאיתשולי עליהן, משום דרבי נתן. *דאמר רבי נתן: כל הנודר – כאילו בנה במה, והמקיימו כאילו מקטיר עליה. (ב) °תרומה מאי מצוה לאיתשולי עלה? גופא, אמר רבי יוחנן: ליטרא בצלים שתיקנה וזרעה – מתעשרת לפי כולה. יתיב *רבה וקאמר להא שמעתא. אמר ליה רב חסדא: *מאן צאית לך ולר' יוחנן רבך! °היתר שבהן להיכן הלך? אמר ליה: מי לא תנן דכוותה: *בצלים שירדו עליהם גשמים וצימחו,

אם

רש"י

תריץ מעשר. תרומת מעשר – דיגון הוא [דקא גריס] ליה, דלא מחייב בתרומת מעשר עד דמידגן. והאי מאשתקד נידגנה, הלכך מעשר עליה משל אשתקד. ולא הוי איסורו על ידי קרקע, הלכך לא הוי בטילתו ע"י קרקע. אפילו גידולי גידולין אסורין. אלמא דאין גידולי היתר מעלין את האיסור, וקשיא לרבי אמי. ואין בטיל ברוב. כלומר ברוב מדתו, בגידוליו רבים. הרי תרומה דאי בעי מיתשיל עלה. שאם היה בדעתו להפריש תרומה ומעשר על פירותיו מפירות קופה זו, וטעה ונתן מקופה אחרת – יכול לשאל עליה לפני חכם, ולומר לו: לא היה בדעתי ליתן מקופה זו אלא מזו, ולא הויא תרומה. ואפילו הכי בטלה ברובא, דתנן וכו'. תירקב. הכל, שאין לה תקנה לא לכהן ולא לישראל. הא אם נפל למאה. תעלה סאה אחת, ושאר מותר. אלמא דבטלה ברוב דידיה כמו האי, דהיינו במאה. ואכתי קשיא לרבי אמי מתני' דנדרים: (ג) [ומשני:] הא תרומה בתרומה ביד כהן עסקינן. דמאחר שזכה בה כהן – לא מצי מיתשיל עלה איניש, ולא דמי לקונמות. תימכר לכהן. הרי ביד כהן היא, ואין צריך לו למוכרה! אלא ביד ישראל עסקינן שנפלו וכו'. דלא מצי איהו מיתשיל עלה, שכבר זכה בה כהן (ד). והא קתני סיפא אם היתה טהורה תימכר לכהן. שהרי ביד ישראל היא, חוץ מדמי אותה סאה. אם נפלה לו מבית אבי אמו כהן, אמאי קאמר "חוץ מדמי אותה סאה"? אפילו אותה סאה נמי תימכר, הואיל ובאתה לו בירושה! אלא. לעולם בתרומה ביד ישראל עסקינן, ומצי מתשיל [עליה], ואפילו הכי בטלה ברובא, (ה) והדרא קושיא לדוכתיה. תריץ, הכי גרסינן: אלא גבי קונמות מצוה לאיתשולי עלייהו, וכמאן דאיתשיל עלייהו דמי, והוה ליה דבר שיש לו מתירין, ואין בטל ברוב. אבל תרומה מאי מצוה איכא לאיתשולי עלה. וכיון דלאו מצוה היא – לא אתי לאיתשולי עלה, וכדבר שאין לו מתירין דמי. להכי בטיל ברובא. וזרעה מתעשרת לפי כולה. אפילו מן הליטרא של עיקר. היתר שבהן. אותה ליטרא של עיקר, שהיתה מתוקנת. היכן הלך. הואיל ואיתיה בעין – אין צריך (ו) לעשרם. בצלים. של שביעית וכו'. לימא: היתר שבהן, העיקר, שגדלו בשביעית, להיכן הלך? ותשתרי העיקר.

אתוספת

ר"ן

מעשר דיגון הוא דקא גרים ליה. שעל ידי דיגון מתחייב במעשר, ולא ע"י קרקע. מתיב רמי בר חמא קונם פירות האלו עלי וכו'. לר' ינאי פריך, דאמר לעיל: בצלים של תרומה שרבו גידוליו על עיקרו – מותר. דאלמא סבירא ליה דכולהו גידולין, אע"פ שאין איסורן ע"י קרקע – מעלין את העיקר. ומשום הכי פריך ליה מקונמות דאין מעלין. והא דלא פריך לי' מברייתא דליטרא מעשר טבל, דתניא לעיל בסמוך – משום דממתני' אלימא ליה לאקשויי. ועוד: דמעשר פשיטא ליה דדבר שיש לו מתירין הוא. והרי תרומה דאי בעי מתשיל עלה. על ידי פתח או חרטה כשאר נדרים. והא דלא פריך ליה: אי הכי, בצלים של תרומה נמי אמאי א"ר ינאי דגידולין מעלין אותו? אי בעי מתשיל עליה, והוי דבר שיש לו מתירין! משום דמצי למדחייה דבישראל שנפלה לו מבית אבי אמו כהן עסקינן. ומשום הכי פריך לי' מהך מתניתין, דליכא למדחייה בהכי. כך נראה בעיני. סאה תרומה טמאה. נקט תרומה טמאה לאשמועינן רבותא דדיוקא, דהא למאה אע"ג דטמאה היא – תעלה. תירקב. דכיון דטמאה היא – לא חזיא לכהן לאכילה, ובהיסק נמי לא שריא, דחיישינן לתקלה, כדאיתא פרק קמא דפסחים (דף כ:). בתרומה ביד כהן. דכיון דזכה בה כהן – שוב אינו יכול לישאל עליה. והא קתני סיפא תמכר לכהן חוץ מדמי אותה סאה. ואי דנפלו לו מבית אבי אמו כהן אמאי אינו מוכר אפילו אותה סאה?: אלא קונמות מצוה לאתשולי עלייהו. וכיון שכן – כאילו אתשיל עלייהו דמי. כל הנודר כאילו בנה במה. פירשתיו בפ' "ד' נדרים" (לעיל דף כב.). תרומה מאי מצוה לאתשולי עלה איכא. הלכך, כיון שאין ההיתר בא מעצמו, וליכא מצוה למעבד הכי – לא מיקרי דבר שיש לו מתירין. והקדש דקא מני לעיל בדבר שיש לו מתירין – בהקדש בדק הבית עסקינן, דעל כרחין לפדייה קאי. גופא ליטרא בצלים שתקנה וזרעה. כלומר, שהפריש כל מעשרותיה – מתעשרת לפי כולה ולא לפי גידולין בלבד, דאתו גידולים ומבטלי עיקר לגמרי. וכי היתר שבהן להיכן הלך. נראה בעיני דהכי מקשה: אפילו תימא דגידולין של היתר מבטלים עיקר של איסור, התם היינו טעמא – משום דכיון שרבו גידוליו על עיקרו נמצא שכשאוכל אינו טועם טעם האיסור כלל, הלכך אף על פי שאיסור שבו מעורב בתוכו, ולא אזל ליה לעלמא – שרי. אבל גבי מעשר, כיון דלפי חשבון הטבל חייביה רחמנא לעשורי, הכא אמאי מתעשרת לפי כולה? וכי היתר שבהן להיכן הלך?:

אם

עין משפט נר מצוה

מ א מיי' פ"ד מהלכות תרומות הלכה יז טוש"ע י"ד סימן שלא סעיף מח:

מא ב מיי' פי"ד מהל' תרומות הלכה יח:

הגהות הגר"א

[א] גמ' ברוב נמחק (דהא בעינן ק' ומ"ש בשיטה מקובלת לחוק דהא הכל מדרבנן קמיירי למדאורייתא אף דבר שיש לו מתירין בטל כמ"ש בב"מ נג.):

תוספות

מתיב רמי בר חמא קונם פירות הללו עלי קונם כו'. דכיון דאמר קונם סתמא אסרם עליו בהנאה בין בחליפין בין בגידולין: קונם שאני אוכל. לא אסר עצמו אלא בגופם והלכך בדבר שזרעו כלה הגידולין מותרין אבל בדבר שאין זרעו כלה אפילו גידולי גידולין אסורין אלמא גידולי היתר אינם מעלים את האיסור דאי מעלים גידולין אמאי אסורין הרי לא אסר עצמו אלא בגוף הפירות ולא אסר בגידולין וליתו גידולי היתר וליבטלו לעיקר אלא שמע מינה דגידולין לא מבטלין לעיקר הלכך העיקר מתפשט בגידולין ואסורין מטעם עיקר ועיקר חשוב ואינו בטל ונהי דודאי אינו מתיר ע"י קרקע כמו שביעית מכל מקום דמי לעל ידי קרקע התירו ולא שייך לשנויי דיגון הוא דקא גריס ליה: א"ר [אבא] שאני קונמות הואיל ואי בעי מיתשל עלייהו והוי כדבר שיש לו מתירין ולא בטיל. ולכך לא מבטלי גידולי לעיקר והא דתנן לעיל (דף נב.) קונם יין ונפל לתבשיל אם יש בו טעם יין אסור ואם אין בו טעם יין מותר דבטל היינו משום דהוי מין בשאינו מינו דהאי דדבר שיש לו מתירין לא בטיל היינו מין במינו והא דמסיק רב אשי פרק בתרא דביצה (דף לט.) דמים ומלח לא בטילי בעיסה משום דהוי דבר שיש לו מתירין ואע"ג דלא הוי מין במינו יש לומר דהתם משום דליכא נתינת טעם ולא בטלי: והרי תרומה כו' דתנן. ה"ה דהוי מצי למיפרך למאן דאמר תרומה אין לה מתירין: סאה של תרומה שנפלה לפחות ממאה תרקב. דאינה בטלה בפחות מק' ואסמכוה רבנן [אקרא דכתיב] תרימו ממנו מה שאתה מריס ממנו שנפל לתוכו מקדשו: א"ה. דמוקי להו ביד כהן אם כן איירי שהדימוע אירע בבית הכהן [אימא סיפא אם היתה טהורה] תמכר לכהן והא דידיה הוא אלא מיירי שהיא ביד ישראל וא"ה בישראל שנפלו לו תרומה מבית אבי אמו כהן דהשתא הוי דידיה: תמכר לכהן חוץ מדמי סאה. והא דידיה הוא אי מיירי שהן ביד הישראל ושפיר מצי מזכין לה אלא שמע מינה דמיירי בתרומה שהפריש ישראל ליתן לכהן: הכי גרסינן אלא בשלמא קונמות מצוה לאיתשולי עלייהו והוי דבר שיש לו מתירין: גופא כו' היתר שבהם להיכן הלכה. כלומר היתר שהיה בליטרא שעישר היכן הלך דסבירא להו דלא קאמר גידולי היתר מעלין את האיסור מני לאוכוחי דגידולי היתר מעלין את האיסור מההיא דמנכש דלעיל:

אם

מסורת הש"ס

לעיל מז. נב: נז.

תרומות פ"ה מ"א

יבמות קט: גיטין מו: לעיל כב. ע"ש [לקמן ס:]

נ"א רבא

[פסחים לג: שביעית י: מעילה יב.]

שביעית פ"ו מ"ג לעיל נח.

גליון הש"ס

גמ' תרומה מאי מצוה. עי' ב"מ נג ע"א תוס' ד"ה הו"ל ולע"ק: שם היתר שבהן להיכן הלך. עי' בר"נ ע"ז דף סו ע"א:

פי' הרא"ש

אמרי מעשר דיגון קא גריס לה. הא דאמרת דמעשר איסורו על ידי קרקע הא ליתא דתבואה הזרועה אינה חוזרת לטיבלה עד שתמרח בכרי הלכך אין איסורו על ידי קרקע ואינו בטל נמי על ידי קרקע דהעיקר והגידולין שלו חייבן בשעת המירוח והיינו על ידי אדם: קונם פירות האלו. מפורש למעלה: אבל בדבר שאין זרעו כלה אפילו גידולי גידולין אסורין. אלמא אין גידולי היתר מעלין את האיסור דאי מעלין אמאי אסור בגדולין הרי לא אסר עצמו אלא בגוף הפרי ולא בגדולים וניתו גידוליו [ויבטלו] העיקר אלא שמע מינה דלא מבטלי גידולין לעיקר הלכך טעם העיקר מתפשט בגידולין והכל אסור ונהי דלא דמי לשביעית לגמרי דלאיסורייהו תלוי בקרקע מכל מקום תערובתו היא ממילא דעל ידי גידוליו מתערבין יחד מעצמן ולא דמי למעשר דאין איסורו כלל כשמחובר לקרקע אלא עד שעת דיגון: הוה ליה כדבר שיש לו מתירין ואינו בטל ברוב. דאפילו באלף לא בטיל: והרי תרומה דלא בעי מתשיל עלה. אף על גב דאי מתשיל עלה הדרא לטבלה מכל מקום מכלל תרומה יצאה ע"י שאלה: ובטלה ברובא דתנן סאה תרומה. מברייתא דלעיל הוה מצי לאתויי דקרי בהדיא לתרומה אין לה מתירין אלא דניחא ליה לאיתויי ממתני': שנפלה לפחות ממאה חולין תרקב. אין זה לשון המשנה ודרך הש"ס לקצר לשון המשנה ומביא מה שהוא צריך ממנה והא דלא אמרינן תשרף בירושלמי פריך לה אליבא דרבי יוחנן דאמר בפרק כל שעה דמדליקין בחטין של תרומה טמאה דלא חיישינן לתקלה ומשני דדמוע קיל להו לאינשי והכא חייש לתקלה דלמא אתי למיכל מיניה: סאה למאה תעלה. דאפילו תרומה טהורה עולה באחד ומאה כדליף לה בספרי מקל וחומר הא דמהדר לאקשויי ולא מקשי מכמה [משניות] ששנו בהם בפירוש שתרומה עולה באחד ומאה [illegible] ביד כהן הוא: בתרומה ביד כהן דלא מצי לאיתשולי עלה. [illegible]

מי

הגהות הב"ח

(א) גמ' שאני אוכל ושאני: (ב) שם מקטיר עליה אבל תרומה מאי: (ג) רש"י ד"ה הא אם וכו' לנדרים הס"ד ואח"כ מ"ה אמרי הא: (ד) ד"ה אלא ביד ישראל וכו' בה כהן והיינו דקתני סיפא וכו' ישראל היא הס"ד ואח"כ מ"ה חוץ וכו' ואם נפלה: (ה) ד"ה אלא לעולם וכו' בטלה ברובה ולא הדרא קושיא: (ו) ד"ה היכן וכו' לעשרה הס"ד:

אם הָיוּ עָלִין שֶׁלָּהֶן שְׁחוֹרִין — אֲסוּרִין, הוֹרִיקוּ מוּתָּרִין. וְכִי שְׁחוֹרִין אַמַּאי אֲסוּרִין? לֵימָא: הֶיתֵּר שֶׁבָּהֶן לְהֵיכָן הָלַךְ? א"ל: מִי סָבְרַתְּ עַל עִיקָּר קָתָנֵי? אַתּוֹסֶפֶת קָתָנֵי אֲסוּרִין. אִי הָכִי מַאי אֲתָא רשב"ג לְמֵימַר? דְּתַנְיָא, רשב"ג אוֹמֵר: הַגָּדֵל בְּחִיּוּב — חַיָּיב, הַגָּדֵל בִּפְטוּר — פָּטוּר. תַּנָּא קַמָּא נַמִי הָכִי אָמַר! כּוּלָּהּ מַתְנִי' רַבָּן שִׁמְעוֹן בֶּן גַּמְלִיאֵל קָתָנֵי לָהּ. וְעַד כָּאן לָא שָׁמַעְתְּ לֵיהּ לְרַבָּן שִׁמְעוֹן בֶּן גַּמְלִיאֵל — דְּלָא קָא טָרַח, אֲבָל הֵיכָא דְּקָא טָרַח — בָּטֵיל בְּרוּבָּא. וְכָל הֵיכָא דְּקָא טָרַח בָּטֵיל בְּרוּבָּא? וַהֲרֵי לִיטְרָא מַעֲשֵׂר טֶבֶל, דְּקָטָרַח, וְקָתָנֵי: וְאוֹתָהּ לִיטְרָא מְעַשֵּׂר (א) עָלָיו מִמָּקוֹם אַחֵר לְפִי חֶשְׁבּוֹן! שָׁאנֵי גַּבֵּי מַעֲשֵׂר דְּאָמַר קְרָא °"עַשֵּׂר תְּעַשֵּׂר" וְגוֹ', (ב) וְהֶיתֵּירָא — זָרְעֵי אֱינָשֵׁי, אִיסּוּרָא — לָא זָרְעֵי אֱינָשֵׁי. גּוּפָא, א"ר חֲנִינָא תִּירְתָּאָה א"ר יַנַּאי: בָּצָל שֶׁל תְּרוּמָה שֶׁנְּטָעוֹ, וְרַבּוּ גִּידּוּלָיו עַל עִיקָּרוֹ — מוּתָּר. לְמֵימְרָא דְּגִידּוּלֵי הֶיתֵּר

דברים יד

רש"י

אַתּוֹסֶפֶת קָתָנֵי. דַּאֲסוּרִין לְאָכְלָן בַּשְּׁמִינִית, דְּחַיָּיב לְבַעֲרָן. אֲבָל הָעִיקָּר שָׁרֵי, דְּאָמְרִינַן: הֶיתֵּר שֶׁבָּהֶן לְהֵיכָן הָלַךְ. הַגָּדֵל בְּחִיּוּב. בַּשְּׁבִיעִית, חַיָּיב בְּבִיעוּר. וְהַגָּדֵל בִּפְטוּר. דְּזֶהוּ הָעִיקָּר הַגָּדֵל בַּשִּׁשִּׁית — פָּטוּר. הָכִי נַמִי קָאָמַר תַּנָּא קַמָּא כו': תְּרֵין. כּוּלָּהּ מַתְנִיתִין ר' שִׁמְעוֹן בֶּן גַּמְלִיאֵל קָתָנֵי לָהּ וְהָכִי קָתָנֵי שֶׁרשב"ג אוֹמֵר הַגָּדֵל כו'. וּלְעוֹלָם אָמְרִי' הֶיתֵּר שֶׁבָּהֶם לְהֵיכָן הָלַךְ. וְקָא מְהַדַּר גְּמָרָא: (ג) לְעוֹלָ' וַאֲפִי' לְר"ש לָא אָמְרִי' הֶיתֵּר שֶׁבָּהֶן לְהֵיכָן הָלַךְ. וְעַד כָּאן לָא אָמַר רשב"ג הַגָּדֵל בִּפְטוּר פָּטוּר, דְּאָמְרִינַן הֶיתֵּר שֶׁבָּהֶן לְהֵיכָן הָלַךְ — דְּלָא קָא בָּטֵיל הֶיתֵּר הֵיכָא דְּלָא קָא טָרַח, כְּגוֹן הָתָם שֶׁיָּרְדוּ עֲלֵיהֶן גְּשָׁמִים וְצָמְחוּ מֵאֵלֵיהֶן. אֲבָל הֵיכָא דְּקָא טָרַח, כְּגוֹן הָכָא דִּנְטַעַן, כִּדְקָתָנֵי שֶׁתִּיקְּנָהּ וּזְרָעָהּ, הוֹאִיל וְעָבַד בָּהּ מַעֲשֶׂה — גִּידּוּלִין שֶׁל אִיסּוּר מְבַטְּלִין אֶת הַהֶיתֵּר, וַהֲוֵי הַכֹּל אָסוּר, לְהָכִי מִתְעַשֵּׂר לְפִי כּוּלָּהּ. מְעַשֵּׂר עָלֶיהָ לְפִי חֶשְׁבּוֹן. וְאַף עַל גַּב דְּקָא טָרַח לְגַבֵּי שְׁאָר גִּידּוּלִין. הֶיתֵּירָא זָרְעֵי אֱינָשֵׁי. דָּבָר שֶׁהוּא מְתוּקָּן רְגִילִים בְּנֵי אָדָם לִזְרוֹעַ, וְסַגִּי לֵיהּ בִּשְׁנֵי מַעַשְׂרוֹת, בְּמַעֲשֵׂר רִאשׁוֹן וּמַעֲשֵׂר שֵׁנִי. אֲבָל דָּבָר שֶׁל אִיסּוּר — אֵין רְגִילִין בְּנֵי אָדָם לִזְרוֹעַ. וְהוֹאִיל וְאִיהוּ קָא זָרַע בְּאִיסּוּרָא, שֶׁזְּרָעָהּ בְּלֹא תְּרוּמָה וּמַעֲשֵׂר — קָנְסִינַן לֵיהּ הַשְׁתָּא שֶׁמְּעַשֵּׂר אוֹתוֹ עִישּׂוּר שֶׁהָיָה לוֹ לִיתֵּן אֶתְפְּקַד, שֶׁלֹּא יִתְחַסֵּר בְּכָךְ.

תְּרוּמָה

ר"נ

אם היו עלין שלהם שחורים וכו'. ומדקתני סתמא אסורין משמע שאסורין לפי כולן, כפירות שביעית עצמן. ואם איתא דאמרי' "וכי היתר שבהן להיכן הלך" – לא הוי ליה למפסק ולמתני אסורין, דהא אין תופסין דמיהן כשביעית עצמה, שהרי אם החליף כנגד היתר שבהן – אינו תופס דמיו. אלא ודאי גידולין מבטלי ליה לעיקר לגמרי, כאילו לא היה, לפי שאף העיקר עצמו משתנה דרך גדילתו. **ועד כאן לא שמעת לרבן שמעון בן גמליאל אלא היכא דלא טרח.** כלומר, אע"ג דלא מלינא למייתי סייעתא מהך – מכל מקום לא קשיא לי. דנהי דהכא אמרינן דגידולין לא מבטלי עיקר לגמרי – הני מילי היכא דלא טרח לבטולי, אבל היכא דקא טרח כי הכא, דליטרא בצלים שזרעה בקרקע – אתו גידולין ומבטלין עיקר לגמרי. ולא תקשי לי אמאי דכתיבנא לעיל בריש שמעתין, דסבירא לן דאי אין גידולין כעיקר פשיטא דמבטלין אותו, והכא אמרינן דגדל בחיוב חייב, אלמא אין גידולין כעיקר, ואפילו הכי קתני גדל בפטור פטור, אלמא אף על פי שאין גידולים כעיקר – אין מבטלין אותו! דהכא היינו טעמא משום דהיתרא לא בטיל, שהאיסור דרכו להתבטל, ולא ההיתר. ועוד, דלא טרח לבטולי עיקר, אלא גידולין מאליהן באו. ובדין הוא דלעיל נמי, כי בעי למפסט בעיין דבצל שעקרו בשביעית מבצל שנטעו בכרס ונעקר הכרס, דמצי לדחויי: שאני בצל שנטעו בכרס דלא טרח. אלא דכיון דהך דיחויא לא סגי לגבי ילדה שסבכה בזקנה – גבי בצל שנטעו בכרס נמי לא דחי ליה. כן נ"ל. הרי ליטרא מעשר דקטרח. דהא טרח לבטולי עיקר בזריעה, ואפילו הכי קתני: אותה ליטרא מעשר עליה ממקום אחר לפי חשבון. אלמא אע"ג דקא טרח – היתר שבה לא בטיל, דאי בטיל אמאי קתני מעשר עליה? תבטל ההיא ליטרא לגבי גידולי שביעית. **שאני גבי מעשר דאמר קרא עשר תעשר את כל תבואת זרעך דהיתרא זרעי אינשי דאיסורא לא זרעי אינשי.** כלו', רחמנא אמר דאף זרעך שזרעת, שהוא מתוקן כבר – תחזור ותעשר, דבטיל ליה עיקר לגבי גידולין. ומדכתיב "זרעך" – משמע דוקא דהיתירא, דהכי ארחייהו דאנשי. ובהיתרא קאמר דגידולין מבטלין עיקר, אבל איסורא לאו "זרעך" מיקרי, דלא זרעי ליה אינשי, הלכך מ"זרעך" משמע דבאיסורא לא אתו גידולין ומבטלין עיקר. וקשה בעיני: דהא כל הך שקלא וטריא בדבר שאין זרעו כלה היא, ומדאורייתא ליכא מידי שאין זרעו כלה דליחייב במעשר. וכיון שכן, היכי דייק מ"זרעך" דגידולין שאין זרעו כלה אין מעלין את העיקר? דבדאורייתא לענין מעשר לא משכחת לה! ונראה בעיני דקרא אסמכתא בעלמא הוא, וטעמא הוא דקיהיב למילתיה; דבדין הוא דלבטיל היתר דזרעי אינשי לגבי גידולין דאיסורא, משום דהוה ליה תערובת היתר באיסור, ודברים שאינם שוין מבטלין הן זה את זה. אבל איסורא באיסורא, כליטרא מעשר טבל בגידולים, דהוו איסורא, אי בשביעית – משום איסור שביעית, אי בשאר שני שבוע – משום טבל, אינו בדין שתהא לה בטלה. אע"פ שאין האיסורין שוין – מ"מ איסור באיסור הוא, ודברים שהן שוין זה לזה לגמרי אין אחד מהם מבטל את חבירו, וכמו שכתבתי בפ' "הנודר מן המבושל" (לעיל דף נב. ד"ה וקשיא). כן נ"ל, ועדיין אין דעתי נוחה, וצריך אני לעשות לי רב בזה. **גופא אמר רבי חנינא תירתאה אמר רבי ינאי בצל של תרומה** וכו' **והא אנן תנן גידולי תרומה** תרומה. אלמא, גידולין נמשכין אחר העיקר והרי הן כמותו, והיאך מעלין?: *)בגידולי גידולין קאמרינן. כי א"ר ינאי בצל של תרומה – לא שהיה הוא עצמו, אלא מגידולי בצל של תרומה. ומשום הכי גידוליו, דהוו גידולי גידולין, שרו ומעלין. **הא** נמי **תנינא** גידולי גידולין חולין. כלומר דלא הוו תרומה, מיהו טבל הוו. טבל גידוליו מותרין בדבר שזרעו כלה. טבל שהוקבע למעשר, כגון שנתמרח בכרי – אסור לאכול ממנו עראי, אם זרעו גידוליו מותרין לאכול ממנו עראי כל זמן שלא הוקבעו למעשר. **אבל דבר שאין זרעו כלה גידולי גידולין אסורין.** לאכול מהן עראי אפילו קודם אותו מירוח, מפני אותו טבל שנתמרח כבר, המעורב בהן. וכל שכן גידולי גידולין של תרומה בדבר שאין זרעו כלה, שאסורין. ה"ג: התם דלא רבו גידולין על עיקרו **הכא** דרבו גידולין על עיקרו. כלומר, כי אמרינן גבי טבל דגידולי גידולין אסורין – מיירי בשלא רבו גידולי גידולין על העיקר, דהיינו גידולין. אבל הכא, גבי בצל של תרומה, מיירי כגון שרבו גידולי גידולין על הגידולין. והקשה הרשב"א ז"ל: מעיקרא כי אקשי ליה "תנינא גדולי גידולין חולין" הוה ליה לאקשויי אדרבה: היכי שרי, דהא בצל אין זרעו כלה, ותנן דבדבר שאין זרעו כלה גידולי גדולין אסורין! ותירץ, דהכי קאמר: אי אמרת דבצל נקט רבי ינאי לאו דוקא, ולדמיון בעלמא נקטיה, וכי קאמר מותר – בדבר שזרעו כלה – תנינא. ומשום הכי, כי אמר ליה דבדוקא נקטיה לאשמועינן אפילו דבר שאין זרעו כלה – פריך ליה דלאו קושטא הוא, דהא בדבר שאין זרעו כלה גידולי גידולין אסורין. ושני ליה דברבו גידולי גידולין על הגידולין קאמר, דמותר.

*) שייך לדף ס

הדרן עלך הנודר מן הירק

תוספות

אם היו עלין [שלהן] שחורין אסורין. אף מה שגדלו בששית אלמא היתר דידהו פקע: **אמר** ליה רב חסדא מי סברת על עיקר קתני אסורין על תוספת קתני. אבל על עיקר מותר אם ניכר מן הגידולין: **א"ה.** דלת"ק אין איסור אלא בגידולין לבד מאי אתא למימר דתני ר"ג הגדל בחיוב חייב הגדל בפטור פטור רבן גמליאל [קאמר] אפי' עליהן שרי ואינם אסורין אלא הגדל בחיוב כלומר באיסור שביעית אבל הגדל בפטור כלומר בהיתר קודס שביעית ונהי דאין העיקר ניכר וכולו אסור מכל מקום נפקא מינה במה שהעיקר מותר שאינו צריך ששים רק מן הגידולין: **ת"ק** נמי הכי קאמר. בתמיה דלדידך דאמרת דלת"ק אינו אוסר אלא הגידולין: **ה"ג** כולה מתניתין ר"ג [קתני לה] (דלת"ק אינו אסור אלא גידולין) ועד כאן לא שמיע ליה לר"ג דלא טרח אבל טרח בטל ברוב כך השיב לו רבה דסבירא ליה דהתר פקע וקאמר דר"ג נמי לאמר גדלו בפטור פטור מודה הכא בליטרא בצל שתיקנה וזרעה שהיתר שבו פקע דהתם במילתי' דר"ג לא טרח בגידולין ומאיליהם הם באים הלכך לא חשיבי לבטל העיקר אבל בבצל דטרח בגידולין והחשיבם מבטלין את העיקר ואמר הר"ם דהאי טעמא דטרח ולא טרח היינו כדאמר במנחות פרק רבי ישמעאל (דף ע.) גבי הך דבצל שתיקנה דהכא דטרח בנטיעתו אבל התם בגידולין דשביעית לאו היינו נטיעתו כלו' אין הנטיעה באיסור שבערב שביעית נטועי' ובאים משביעית אבל הכא תחלת נטיעתה [באה בשביעית] לכך מבטלין גידולין לעיקר ודבר זה מגומגם דליתא להך מילתא דר"ג גבי הך ברייתא ואם היו שחורים עליהן: **והרי** ליטרא מעשר טבל. פי' לעיל אלמא אף על גב דלא קא טרח לא קמבטלי: **שאני** התם. בהך דקאמר דמתעשר לפי כולה לאמר דטרח לזרעה לא בטילא מדאורייתא: **עשר תעשר את כל תבואת זרעך וגו'.** שצריך לעשר את כל מה קרא עשר תעשר את תבואת זרעך אלמא תבואה זרועה בעי לעשורי כל המעשרות והך נמי שתיקנה שגדל בשדה ולא ינכה מן חשבון התבואה שזרע שהיתה כבר מתוקנת דהדרא לטבלה ודוקא מתוקנת הוי סתם זריעה דהיתירא זרעי אבל איסור לא זרעי שאין דרך לזרוע מעשר עצמו כשאינו מתוקן שדרך אדם לזרוע אבל איסורא דלא זרעי אינשי לא הדרא לטבלה: לתרומת מעשר ומינה לא איירי קרא הלכך לא בטל ולא בעי לעשורי כבתחלה כיון דטרח בטלה אבל בהך ליטרא שתיקנה דהיינו כלדך שבני אדם מוציאין לזריעה יש לנו להעמיד בזה קרא דעשר תעשר שצריך לחזור ולעשר כבתחלה: **גופא** אמר רבי חנינא טירטאה בצל של תרומה כו' מותר. דהוי חולין ומותר לזרים:

והתנן

פי' הרא"ש

מי סברת על עיקר קתני על תוספת קתני. ואם היה ניכר העיקר בין התוספת היה מותר ואם נתערבו באחרים אין צריך לבטל אלא התוספת והוה מצי לאקשויי מההיא דהמנכש לחזין דגידולי היתר מעלין את האיסור והכל מותר: **אי הכי מאי אתא רשב"ג למימר.** דתניא רשב"ג אומר הגדל בחיוב חייב והגדל בפטור פטור לא מלינו רשב"ג חולק על משנה דבצלים וגם לשון חיוב ופטור לא שייך למימר בשביעית אלא איסור והיתר וצריך לפרשו בדוחק דהכי פריך אי הכי למפרשת דאיסור אתוספת קאי וסבר האי תנא דבנטע אחד יש איסור והיתר הא דקאמר רשב"ג גבי אילן שמקצתו עומד בארץ ומקצתו עומד חוצה לארץ דהגדל בחיוב חייב ובפטור פטור ואשמועינן דבאילן אחד יש איסור והיתר הא האי תנא נמי הכי אית ליה ומדקאמר התם רשב"ג אומר משמע דאיהו לחודיה ס"ל הכי: **ת"ק נמי ס"ק.** הא דקאמר ת"ק לאו דוקא אלא דהוזכר תחלה בהך שמעתין קרי ליה קמא: **כולה מתניתא רשב"ג קתני לה.** ודאי רשב"ג לחודיה הוא דאית ליה הך סברא וכל משנה שתמנא שנוי בה שאיסור והיתר גדילין במקום אחד רשב"ג קתני לה: **ועד כאן לא שמעת ליה לרשב"ג כו'.** שנויא אחרינא קא משני וה"פ הא דקשיא לך דהאי תנא דבצלים ורשב"ג אית להו חדא סברא ומדקתני רשב"ג אומר משמע דאיהו לחודיה אית ליה הך סברא ודאי רשב"ג לא סבר דהך תנא דבצלים דעד כאן לא שמעת ליה לרשב"ג דישנן לאיסור והיתר במקום אחד ולא מבטלי להדדי אלא היכא דלא טרח כגון באילן דאיירי ביה אבל בצלים דטרח לזרען תנו חכמים על טרחו וסבירא ליה הך סברא: ופריך **מליטרא מעשר טבל.** דאע"ג

בגידולי

הגהות הב"ח

(א) גמ' מעשר עליה: (ב) שם היתירא זרעי: (ג) רש"י ד"ה וקא מהדר גמרא וקאמר לעולם אפילו לר"ש כו' פטור ואמרינן היתר כו' בטל היתר אלא היכא דלא כו' מאיליהן הס"ד:

רש"י

תְּרוּמָה. דְּאֵין גִּידּוּלֵי הֶיתֵּר מַעֲלִין אֶת הָאִיסּוּר. **בְּגִידּוּלֵי גִידּוּלִין קָאָמַר.** דְּהָכִי קָאָמַר: גִּידּוּלֵי בָּצָל שֶׁל תְּרוּמָה שֶׁנְּטָעָהּ, וְרַבּוּ גִּידּוּלָיו עַל עִיקָּרוֹ, דְּהָווּ לְהוּ גִּידּוּלֵי גִידּוּלִין. **תַּנְיָא** וכו'. דְּגִידּוּלֵי גִידּוּלִין שֶׁל תְּרוּמָה – חוּלִּין. **אֲפִי' בְּדָבָר שֶׁאֵין זַרְעוֹ כָּלֶה.** כְּגוֹן בָּצָל – גִּידּוּלֵי גִידּוּלִין מוּתָּר. **בְּדָבָר שֶׁזַּרְעוֹ כָּלֶה.** כְּגוֹן חִיטִּים. גִּידּוּלֵי גִידּוּלִין דְּהַיְינוּ הַשֵּׁנִי. **תְּרֵיץ: רִבּוּיָא** שֶׁל גִּידּוּלֵי גִידּוּלִין, דְּרַבּוּ גִּידּוּלָיו עַל עִיקָּרוֹ מוּתָּר **קָא מַשְׁמַע לָן.** כְּלוֹמַר, הָא אָתָא לְאַשְׁמוּעִינַן גִּידּוּלֵי גִידּוּלִין שֶׁל בָּצָל שֶׁל תְּרוּמָה, וְרַבּוּ אוֹתָן גִּידּוּלִין עַל עִיקָּרוֹ – מוּתָּר דְּהַיְינוּ הַשְּׁלִישִׁי.

הדרן עלך הנודר מן הירק

קוֹנָם יַיִן שֶׁאֲנִי טוֹעֵם הַיּוֹם. דְּמַשְׁמַע: כָּל זְמַן שֶׁהוּא יוֹם, וְתוּ לָא. **שַׁבָּת זוֹ.** וְהָיָה עוֹמֵד בְּשַׁבָּת – אָסוּר בְּכָל הַשַּׁבָּת, בְּשֵׁשֶׁת יְמֵי הַשָּׁבוּעַ. **וְהַשַּׁבָּת שֶׁעָבְרָה.** כְּלוֹמַר, (ב) בַּשַּׁבָּת שֶׁהוּא עוֹמֵד בָּהּ. וְלְהָכִי קָרֵי לֵיהּ שֶׁעָבְרָה, לְפִי שֶׁהַשַּׁבָּת זֶה אֵינוֹ מִתְחַשֵּׁב אַחַר יָמִים הַבָּאִים, אֶלָּא אַחַר שֵׁשֶׁת יָמִים שֶׁעָבְרוּ. **חֹדֶשׁ זֶה.** אָמַר "קוֹנָם יַיִן שֶׁאֵינִי שׁוֹתֶה בְּזֶה הַחֹדֶשׁ" וְהָיָה עוֹמֵד בְּאוֹתוֹ יוֹם שֶׁל ר"ח. **אָסוּר בְּכָל הַחֹדֶשׁ.** בְּכָל שְׁלֹשִׁים יוֹם הַבָּאִים. **וְרֹאשׁ חֹדֶשׁ לְהַבָּא.** כְּלוֹמַר (ג) ר"ח זֶה שֶׁהוּא עוֹמֵד לְתוֹכוֹ – הוּא נִמְנֶה עִם יָמִים הַבָּאִים, שֶׁהוּא רִאשׁוֹן שֶׁלָּהֶם. וְכֵן אִם הָיָה עוֹמֵד בְּרֹאשׁ הַשָּׁנָה וְאָמַר קוֹנָם יַיִן שֶׁאֵינִי טוֹעֵם שָׁנָה זוֹ. אָסוּר בְּכָל הַשָּׁנָה, וְאוֹתוֹ הַיּוֹם שֶׁל רֹאשׁ הַשָּׁנָה שֶׁהוּא עוֹמֵד בּוֹ. וּלְהָכִי קָרֵי לֶעָתִיד לָבֹא, לְפִי שֶׁהוּא נִמְנֶה לַיָּמִים וְלֶחֳדָשִׁים הַנִּכְנָסִים, שֶׁהוּא אַחַר זְמַן. וּלְהָכִי קָאָמַר "לֶעָתִיד", וְלָא קָאָמַר "לְהַבָּא". וְאִם הָיָה עוֹמֵד בִּשְׁנַת הַשְּׁמִיטָּה וְאָמַר קוֹנָם יַיִן שֶׁאֵינִי טוֹעֵם בְּשָׁבוּעַ זוֹ אָסוּר בְּכָל הַשָּׁבוּעַ הַבָּא. (ד) וְאוֹתָהּ שָׁנָה שְׁבִיעִית שֶׁהוּא עוֹמֵד בָּהּ נִמְנֵית לַשָּׁבוּעַ שֶׁעָבְרָה, לְהָכִי קָרֵי לֵיהּ שֶׁעָבְרָה. **וְאִם אָמַר.** "שֶׁאֵינִי טוֹעֵם יוֹם אֶחָד" (ה) – מֵעֵת לְעֵת. שֶׁאִם הָיָה עוֹמֵד בִּשְׁעַת הַנֶּדֶר בַּחֲצִי הַיּוֹם – אָסוּר לְמָחָר עַד חֲצִי הַיּוֹם. וְכֵן אִם אָמַר שַׁבָּת אֶחָד – בְּאֵיזֶה יוֹם שֶׁעוֹמֵד בַּשָּׁבוּעַ, אָסוּר עַד יוֹם שְׁמִינִי לְאוֹתוֹ יוֹם שֶׁנָּדַר. וְכֵן בְּשָׁנָה אַחַת, וְכֵן בְּשָׁבוּעַ אַחַת – אָסוּר שָׁנָה שְׁלֵימָה וְשָׁבוּעַ שָׁלֵם מִיּוֹם לְיוֹם. **גמ' לִכְשֶׁתֶּחְשַׁךְ.** אַף עַל פִּי שֶׁעָבַר הַיּוֹם. **צָרִיךְ שְׁאֵלָה לְחָכָם.** לְהַתִּיר לוֹ נִדְרוֹ, מִשּׁוּם הֶיכֵּרָא. **גְּזֵירָה הַיּוֹם אַטּוּ יוֹם אֶחָד.** דְּאִי אָמְרַתְּ לִכְשֶׁתֶּחְשַׁךְ, (ו) אַף עַל פִּי שֶׁעָבַר הַיּוֹם הָוֵי מוּתָּר, אָתוּ לְמֵימַר נַמִּי כִּי נָדַר "יוֹם אֶחָד" וְעוֹמֵד בַּחֲצִי הַיּוֹם – מוּתָּר לִכְשֶׁתֶּחְשַׁךְ, וְאִיהוּ לָא הָוֵי מוּתָּר עַד מֵעֵת לְעֵת. הִילְכָּךְ צָרִיךְ שְׁאֵלָה לְחָכָם, וְכֵיוָן דְּבָעֵי שְׁאֵלָה לְחָכָם – חָכָם חוֹקֵר בְּיַלְדֵי נֶדֶר, וְלָא יָבֹא לִידֵי חִילּוּל נֶדֶר. אִי

גמרא

הֶיתֵּר מַעֲלִין אֶת הָאִיסּוּר? *וְהָתְנַן [א]גִּידּוּלֵי תְרוּמָה – תְּרוּמָה! בְּגִידּוּלֵי גִידּוּלִין קָאָמְרִינַן. הָא נַמִּי תָּנֵינָא: [ב]גִּידּוּלֵי גִידּוּלִין – חוּלִּין! הָא קמ"ל אֲפִילּוּ בְּדָבָר שֶׁאֵין זַרְעוֹ כָּלֶה. וְהָתְנַן: *[ג]הַטֶּבֶל גִּידּוּלָיו מוּתָּרִין, בְּדָבָר שֶׁזַּרְעוֹ כָּלֶה. אֲבָל דָּבָר שֶׁאֵין זַרְעוֹ כָּלֶה – גִּידּוּלֵי גִידּוּלִין אֲסוּרִין! [ד]רִבּוּיָא דְּרַבּוּ גִּידּוּלִין עַל עִיקָּרוֹ מוּתָּר, קָא מַשְׁמַע לָן.§

הדרן עלך הנודר מן הירק

"**קוֹנָם** [ה]יַיִן שֶׁאֲנִי טוֹעֵם הַיּוֹם" – אֵינוֹ אָסוּר אֶלָּא עַד שֶׁתֶּחְשַׁךְ. [ו]"שַׁבָּת זוֹ" – אָסוּר בְּכָל הַשַּׁבָּת, וְשַׁבָּת (א) שֶׁעָבְרָה. [ז]"חֹדֶשׁ זֶה" – אָסוּר בְּכָל הַחֹדֶשׁ, ור"ח לְהַבָּא. [ח]"שָׁנָה זוֹ" – אָסוּר בְּכָל הַשָּׁנָה, וְרֹאשׁ הַשָּׁנָה לֶעָתִיד לָבֹא. [ט]"שָׁבוּעַ זֶה" – אָסוּר בְּכָל הַשָּׁבוּעַ, וּשְׁבִיעִית שֶׁעָבְרָה. וְאִם אָמַר [י]"יוֹם אֶחָד" [כ]"שַׁבָּת אַחַת" [ל]"חֹדֶשׁ אֶחָד" [מ]"שָׁנָה אַחַת" [נ]"שָׁבוּעַ אֶחָד" – אָסוּר מִיּוֹם לְיוֹם. * [ס]"עַד הַפֶּסַח" – אָסוּר עַד שֶׁיַּגִּיעַ, "עַד שֶׁיְּהֵא" – אָסוּר עַד שֶׁיֵּצֵא. "עַד *לִפְנֵי הַפֶּסַח"; רַבִּי מֵאִיר אוֹמֵר: [ע]אָסוּר עַד שֶׁיַּגִּיעַ, רַבִּי יוֹסֵי אוֹמֵר: אָסוּר עַד שֶׁיֵּצֵא.§ **גמ'** "קוֹנָם יַיִן שֶׁאֲנִי טוֹעֵם" כו'. אָמַר רַבִּי *יִרְמְיָה: [פ]לִכְשֶׁתֶּחְשַׁךְ צָרִיךְ שְׁאֵלָה לְחָכָם. מַאי טַעְמָא? אָמַר רַב יוֹסֵף: [צ]גְּזֵירָה "הַיּוֹם" מִשּׁוּם "יוֹם אֶחָד". א"ל

ר"ן

קונם יין שאני טועם היום אינו אסור אלא עד שתחשך. דכיון דאמר "היום" – לא משמע אלא עד שיגמור אותו יום, דהיינו עד שתחשך. **שבת זו.** אם נדר באחד מימי השבוע – אסור בכל ימי השבוע. ויום שבת עצמו בכלל איסור של שבוע שעבר, דכי אמרי אינשי "שבת זו" – דעתייהו על ימי החול הבאים, ועל יום השבת. **חדש זה.** אם נדר באחד מימי החדש – אסור בכל החדש. וראש חדש להבא – שאין ראש חדש שאחר ימי החדש מכלל האיסור, אלא להבא הוא נמנה ונותר. **שנה זו אסור בכל השנה.** דהיינו עד ראש חדש תשרי, אבל ראש חדש תשרי – לעתיד לבא, ואינו מכלל האיסור. **שבוע זה.** שני שמיטה זו, אסור עד שישלמו ששה שנים של שמיטה, ואסור גם כן בשנה השביעית, שדינה כלשעבר. זהו פירוש משנתינו. ואחרים פירשו: "שבת זו" אסור בכל השבת – כגון שעומד ביום השבת, ונדר ואמר "שבת זו". וקתני דאסור בכל השבת הבאה ויום שבת זה שעומד בה עכשיו, אע"פ שהוא מכלל שבוע שעברה, והיינו דקתני "והשבת לשעבר". "חדש זה" אסור בכל החדש וראש חדש להבא – כגון דקאי בראש חדש. וקתני דאסור בכל החדש הבא וביום ראש החדש עצמו שנדר. והא פרכינן בגמרא: פשיטא. "שנה זו" – כגון שנדר בראש השנה, אסור בשנה הבאה וביום ראש השנה עצמו, שדינו כלהבא. "שבוע זה" – אסור בכל השבוע ושביעית לשעבר. כלומר, דקאי בשנה השביעית ואמר "שבוע זה", וקתני דאסור כל שני שמיטה הבאים ובשנה השביעית עצמה שעומד בה, אע"פ שנימנית מכלל שבוע שעברה. ולפי האי פירושא נראה לי דמאי דקתני גבי שבת ושביעית לשעבר, וגבי חדש ושנה להבא, ולא קתני כולהו בלהבא – לאשמועינן דינא דנודר באמצע זמנים הללו, דבאמצע שבת ואמצע שביעית אסור בשבת ושביעית הבאים, מה שאין כן בנודר באמצע החודש ואמצע שנה – שמותר בראש חדש וראש השנה הבאים. מיהו, האי פירושא ליתיה. דכיון ד"שבת זו" או "שבוע זה" קאמר, למה יאסר בשבת ושבוע הבאים? הוה לן למימר שלא יאסר אלא ביום שבת ושנה שביעית שעומד בהן, וכדאמרינן בפ"ק דראש השנה דהמודר הנאה מחבירו לשנה, אפילו לא עמד אלא בכ"ט באלול, כיון שהגיע אחד בתשרי – עלתה לו שנה! אלא פירושא קמא עיקר. **ואם אמר יום אחד שבת אחת וכו' אסור מיום ליום.** כלומר: היקף אחד, וביום אחד אסור מעת לעת. **גמ' לכשתחשך צריך שאלה לחכם.** אע"ג דמדינא כי אמר "היום" מותר לכשתחשך, כדאמרינן במתניתין – אפילו הכי, מדרבנן צריך שאלה. **אמר רב יוסף גזירה היום משום** יום

פי' הרא"ש

והתנן גידולי תרומה [תרומה]. משנה היא בפ"ט דתרומות (מ"ד) ומפרש טעמא בפ"ק דשבת (דף יז:) דילמא משהי ליה ואתי לידי תקלה: **הא נמי תנינא.** אי איירי נמי בגידולי גידולין אכתי איכא לאקשויי מאי קמ"ל משנה שלימה שנינו גידולי גידולין מותרין סיפא דהך מתני' דגידולי תרומה תרומה היא: **והא תנן הטבל גידוליו תרומה כו'.** וכיון דאפילו גידולי גידולין של טבל אסורים בדבר שאין זרעו כלה כל שכן של תרומה דהא בדבר שזרעו כלה גידולי תרומה וגידולי טבל חולין: **רבויא דרבו גידוליו על עיקרו דמותר קמ"ל.** דהא דאסור גידולי גידולין בלא רבו אבל רבו אפי' גידולין מותרין דגידולי היתר מעלין את האיסור:

הדרן עלך הנודר מן הירק

עד שתחשך. שכן דרך בני אדם כשאומרים היום רוצים לומר עד השלמת היום: **שבת זו.** עומד באמצע השבת ואמר שבת זו אסור בכל השבוע: **והשבת שעבר.** ואסור נמי ביום השבת כי הוא בכלל שעבר: **חדש זה אסור בכל החדש.** אם עומד באמצע החדש ואמר חדש זה אסור עד תשלום החדש ור"ח להבא ומותר בר"ח כי הוא נמנה עם החדש הבא וכן פי' שנה זו שאם נדר באמצע השנה אסור עד תשלום השנה ומותר בר"ה כי הוא נמנה עם העתיד לבא ולמון העולם לומר חדש הבא ושנה העתידה לבא: **שבוע זו.** היה עומד באמצע השמיטה ואמר שבוע זו אסור עד תשלום השמיטה והשביעית בכלל שמיטה שעברה ...

קונם יין כו' שאני טועם היום אינו אסור אלא עד שתחשך. ולא אמר לאסור עד מעת לעת כמו בסיפא דאמר יום אחד: **שבת** זו. ועומד באמצע ביום ג' או ביום ד' אסור בכל ימי אותה השבוע עד סופה ושבת שעברה כלומר ושבת הבא עליו סוף השבוע אסור כמו כן דלאף השבת משבוע שעבר ובגמ' פריך פשיטא: **חדש** זה. ועומד בעו"ן ימים בעבת אסור בכל החדש עד סופו: ור"ח להבא. ...

תוספות

בגידולי גידולין. כהך דבלל גופיה הוי גידולין של תרומה: **קמשמע** לן רבי חנינא דאפילו דבר שאין זרעו כלה גידולי גידולין חולין: **והתנן** הטבל גידוליו מותרין לאכול אכילת ארעי בלא מעשר בדבר שזרעו כלה. כגון חיטין אבל דבר שאין זרעו כלה גידולי גידולין תרומה כמו טבל: ה"ג **התם** דלא רבו הכא דרבו. פירוש הא דאמר גידולי גידולין אסורין גבי טבל היינו כל כמה דלא רבו גידולי גידולין על העיקר אבל הכא ברבו הלכך מבטלי גידולין לעיקר ובספרים כתוב ריבויא דרבו גידולין על עיקרו מותר קמ"ל ויש לפרש כדפרישית דמלתא דרבי חנינא מיירי דרבו גידולין על עיקרו:

הדרן עלך הנודר מן הירק

גליון הש"ס גמ' הטבל גידוליו מותרין. קשה לי הא בטבל ל"ש דגדוליו יבטלו דהא טבל בכ"ש והוי כמו נדרים דגדולי גידולין אסורין דאין לו ביטול דהוי דשיל"מ ...